The Writer's Yellow Pages

Edited by Steve Davis

Address changes or corrections for future editions, as well as inquiries regarding discounts for bulk purchases, should be addressed to:

Steve Davis Publishing
P.O. Box 190831
Dallas, Texas 75219

First Edition

ISBN 0-911061-16-9

Library of Congress Catalog Card No. 86-90146

CONTENTS

Acknowledgement

Thanks to contributing editors
James C Mitchell
and
Candy Travis

INTRODUCTION

How to Use This Book

The purpose of this book is to save you, the working writer, time. All the publishers, producers and support services you are likely to need to contact are listed here. However, this book is not intended to be strictly a market guide. **A listing in this book should not be interpreted as an indication that a firm accepts free-lance material. Not all publishers, producers or agents listed here accept unsolicited material from writers.**

For those who are new to the business of writing, here are a few suggestions. If you are searching for a publisher or producer for your work, before submitting your material, be sure to investigate the type of material that company has published or produced in the past. Do not send unsolicited manuscripts inappropriately. If you find a firm that might be interested in your work, send a query letter. **Always enclose a self-addressed stamped envelope with queries and submissions.**

Questionnaires were mailed to nearly 40,000 firms in the process of compiling and verifying information for this book. If a firm is not listed, it may be because they requested deletion, a phone number was not available, or their questionnaire was returned by the post office with no forwarding address. If you are aware of changes of address or phone number in any of the listings, you can help us keep future editions up-to-date by sending this information to the address below. Likewise, if you wish to be listed, or if you know of other firms that should be included in future editions, send the name, address, phone number and appropriate classification information to: *The Writer's Yellow Pages*, Steve Davis Publishing, PO Box 190831, Dallas, Texas 75219. Listings are free, and advertising is not accepted. Also send your name and address if you wish to be notified of future editions.

AGENTS

This section lists author's agents. An asterisk (*) indicates an agent handling motion picture and television scripts. A plus (+) denotes a dramatic agent.

Carole Abel Literary Agent, 160 W 87th St, New York NY 10024..............212-724-1168
Dominick Abel Agency, 498 West End Ave, New York NY 10024..............212-877-0710
About Books Inc, PO Box 538, Saguache CO 81149.....................................303-589-8223
Edward J Acton Inc+, 928 Broadway Ste 301, New York NY 10010.........212-675-5400
Bret Adams Ltd+, 36 E 61st St, New York NY 10021.....................................212-752-7864
Adams Ray & Rosenberg, 9200 Sunset Blvd, Los Angeles CA 90069.........213-278-3000
Bill Adler Books, 551 5th Ave Ste 923, New York NY 10017......................212-972-1445
Agency for Artists, 9200 Sunset Blvd Ste 531, Los Angeles CA 90069.......213-278-6243
Agency for Performing Arts*, 9000 Sunset Blvd, Los Angeles CA 90069..818-994-9354
The Agency*, 10351 Santa Monica Blvd Ste 211, Los Angeles CA 90069...213-551-3000
Albert Literary Agency, 119 Richard Ct, Aptos CA 95003...........................408-688-7535
Maxwell Aley Assoc, 145 E 35th St, New York NY 10016.............................212-679-5377
All Talent Agency*, 2437 Washington Blvd, Pasadena CA 91104................818-797-2422
Lee Allan Agency*, PO Box 18617, Milwaukee WI 53218............................414-463-7441
Allen & Yanow Literary Agency, PO Box 5158, Santa Cruz CA 95063.......408-427-1293
Allen Writers' Agency, 29308 Eddy, Wickliffe OH 44092............................216-943-0632
Buddy Altoni Talent Agency*, 3355 Via Lido, Newport Bch CA 92663.....213-467-4939
Carlos Alvarado Agency*, 977 Wilshire Blvd, Beverly Hills CA 90211........213-652-0272
Am-Rus Literary Agency, 225 W 34th St, New York NY 10122.................212-564-5485
Amer Play Co Inc, 19 W 44th St, New York NY 10036.................................212-921-0545
Fed Amsel & Assoc*, 291 S La Cienega, Beverly Hills CA 90211................213-855-1200
Marcia Amsterdam Agency, 41 W 82nd St, New York NY 10024................212-873-4945
Animal Crackers Agency*, 204 Riverside, Newport Bch CA 92663............800-821-3191
Arizona Literary Agency, 1540 W. Campbell Ave, Phoenix AZ 85015.......602-277-9019
The Artists Agency*, 10000 Santa Monica Blvd, Los Angeles CA 90067...213-277-7779
Artists Career Management*, 8295 Sunset Blvd, Los Angeles CA 90046.213-654-6650
Artists Entertainment*, 10100 Santa Monica, Los Angeles CA 90067......213-557-2507
Artists Group Ltd*, 1930 Century Park W, Los Angeles CA 90067...........213-552-1100
Artists' Repertory Literary Agency, 881 10th Ave, New York NY 10019...212-581-0377
Associated Talent Intl*, 9744 Wilshire Blvd, Beverly Hills CA 90211........213-271-4662
Author Aid Assoc+, 340 E 52nd St, New York NY 10022.........................212-758-4213
Authors & Artists+, 14 E 60th St, New York NY 10022..............................212-754-9393
Authors & Writers Services, PO Box 911, Albuquerque NM 87103..........505-344-4781
The Authors Resource Ctr, 4001 E Ft Lowell Rd, Tucson AZ 85712........602-325-4733
The Axelrod Agency, 350 5th Ave Rm 5805, New York NY 10118.............212-629-5620
Julian Bach Literary Agency, 747 3rd Ave, New York NY 10017.............212-753-2605
Irving Baker, 790 Washington, Denver CO 80203....................................303-837-1226
The Bal Co, 299 Madison Ave, New York NY 10017...................................212-687-8266
The Balkin Agency, 850 W 176th St, New York NY 10033...........................212-781-4198
Mark Ballard Talent Agency*, 1915 W Glenoaks, Glendale CA 91201.....818-841-8305
Virginia Barber Literary Agency, 353 W 21st St, New York NY 10011.....212-255-6515
The Barskin Agency*, 11240 Magnolia Blvd, N Hollywood CA 91601.......818-985-2992
Scott Bartlett Assoc, 3 E 65th St, New York NY 10021.............................212-628-4651
Peter Basch, 322 W 72nd St, New York NY 10023......................................212-873-6666
Martin Bauer Agency*, 9255 Sunset Blvd #710, Los Angeles CA 90069...213-275-2421

Beakel & Jennings Agency*, 427 N Canon Dr, Beverly Hills CA 90210 213-274-5418
Maximilian Becker+, 115 E 82nd St, New York NY 10028........................212-988-3887
The Bennett Agency*, 150 S Barrington Ste 1, Los Angeles CA 90049.......213-471-2251
Bill Berger Assoc, 444 E 58th St, New York NY 10022.............................212-486-9588
Berkeley Square Agency*, PO Box 25324, Los Angeles CA 90025.............213-478-5745
Lois Berman+, 240 W 44th St, New York NY 10036 212-575-5114
Meredith Bernstein Agency, 470 West End Ave, New York NY 10024 212-799-1007
Bethel Agency+, 513 W 54th St, New York NY 10019...........................212-664-0455
Big Red Talent Enterprises*, 8330 3rd St, Los Angeles CA 90048.............213-463-4982
The Blake Group+, 1 Turtle Creek Vlg Ste 600, Dallas TX 75219.............214-828-2160
Blassingame McCauley & Wood, 432 Park Ave S, New York NY 10016 ..212-695-3241
Bleecker Street Assoc, 88 Bleecker St, New York NY 10012.....................212-677-4492
Harry Bloom Agency*, 8833 Sunset Blvd, Los Angeles CA 90069 213-659-5985
J Michael Bloom*, 9200 Sunset Blvd #1210, Los Angeles CA 90069.........213-275-6800
Ruth Blumenthal Agency*, 435 S La Cienega, Los Angeles CA 90048......213-657-1020
Richard Boehm Literary Agency, 737 Park Ave, New York NY 10021......212-734-7557
The Book Peddler, 18326 Minnetonka Blvd, Deephaven MN 55391 612-475-3527
George Borchardt Inc, 136 E 57th St, New York NY 10022.....................212-753-5785
Boston Literary Agency, 333 W 57th St #404, New York NY 10019..........212-765-3663
John Boswell Assoc, 123 E 54th St Ste 8D, New York NY 10022 212-753-9393
Barbara Bova Agency, 207 Sedgwick Rd, W Hartford CT 06107................203-521-5915
Bradley-Goldstein Agency, 7 Lexington Ave, New York NY 10010............718-672-7924
Paul Brandon & Assoc*, 9046 Sunset Blvd, Los Angeles CA 90069...........213-273-6173
Brandt & Brandt Lit Agents, 1501 Broadway, New York NY 10036 212-840-5760
The Helen Brann Agency, 157 W 57th St, New York NY 10019.................212-247-3511
Alex Brewis Agency*, 4721 Laurel Canyon, N Hollywood CA 91607.........818-509-0831
John Brockman Assoc Inc, 2307 Broadway, New York NY 10024.............212-874-0500
Ruth Hagy Brod Literary Agency, 15 Park Ave, New York NY 10016 212-689-2261
Broder/Kurland/Webb*, 9046 Sunset Blvd, Los Angeles CA 90069 213-274-8921
J Brown Agency*, 8733 Sunset Blvd Ste 102, Los Angeles CA 90069 213-550-0296
Ned Brown Inc*, PO Box 5020, Beverly Hills CA 90210 213-276-1131
Curtis Brown Ltd+, 10 Astor Pl, New York NY 10003.............................212-473-5400
Pema Browne Ltd, 185 E 85th St, New York NY 10028 212-369-1925
Jane Jordan Browne, 410 S Michigan Ave Rm 724, Chicago IL 60605......312-922-3063
Howard Buck Agency+, 80 8th Ave, New York NY 10011 212-807-7855
Knox Burger Assoc, 39 Washington Sq S, New York NY 10012................212-533-2360
Shirley Burke Literary Agent, 370 E 76th St B704, New York NY 10021..212-861-2309
Ruth Butler Talent Agent*, 8622 Reseda Blvd, Northridge CA 91324.......818-886-8440
Jane Butler+, 538 E Harford St PO Box 278, Milford PA 18337 717-296-7266
The Calder Agency*, 4150 Riverside Dr Ste 204, Burbank CA 91505 818-845-7434
Ruth Cantor, 156 5th Ave #133, New York NY 10010 212-243-3246
Cantrell-Colas Literary Agency, 229 E 79th St, New York NY 10021........212-737-8503
William Carroll Agency*, 1900 W Olive Ave 1st fl, Burbank CA 91506....818-848-9948
Martha Casselman, 1263 12th Ave, San Francisco CA 94122....................415-665-3235
Cavaleri & Assoc*, 6605 Hollywood Blvd, Hollywood CA 90028 213-461-2940
Ceppos Consultant, 50 E 10th St, New York NY 10003.............................212-674-7046
Charter Management*, 9000 Sunset Blvd, Los Angeles CA 90069.............213-278-1690
Chasman & Strick Assoc*, 6725 Sunset Blvd, Hollywood CA 90028.........213-463-1115
Terry Chiz Agency*, 5761 Whitnall Hwy Ste E, N Hollywood CA 91601...818-506-0994
Cinema Talent Agency*, 7906 Santa Monica, Los Angeles CA 90046........213-656-1937
Connie Clausen Assoc, 250 E 87th St, New York NY 10028 212-427-6135
The Clients' Agency*, 8600 Melrose Ave, Los Angeles CA 90069.............213-659-9999
CNA & Assoc*, 8721 Sunset Blvd Ste 202, Los Angeles CA 90069 213-657-2063

Ruth Cohen Literary Agency+, PO Box 7626, Menlo Park CA 94025.......415-854-2054
Hy Cohen Literary Agency Ltd, 111 W 57th St, New York NY 10019........212-757-5237
Joyce K Cole Literary Agency, 797 San Diego Rd, Berkeley CA 94707.....415-526-5165
Collier Assoc, 875 Ave of the Americas, New York NY 10001....................212-563-4065
Kingsley Colton & Assoc*, 16661 Ventura Blvd, Encino CA 91436...........818-788-6043
Columbia Literary Assoc, 7902 Nottingham, Ellicott City MD 21043........301-465-1595
Compass Management*, 211 S Beverly Dr, Beverly Hills CA 90210..........818-985-6266
Don Congdon Assoc Inc, 111 5th Ave, New York NY 10003....................212-473-3351
Connor Literary Agency, 640 W 153rd St, New York NY 10031.................212-491-5233
Contemporary-Korman Artists*, 132 Lasky, Beverly Hills CA 90212.......213-278-8250
Ben Conway & Assoc*, 999 N Doheny Dr, Los Angeles CA 90069...........213-271-8133
Molly M Cook Literary Agency, Box 338, Provincetown MA 02657...........617-487-4116
The Cooper Agency*, 1900 Ave of Stars, Los Angeles CA 90067................213-277-8422
Bill Cooper Assoc Agency+, 224 W 49th St #411, New York NY 10019...212-307-1100
The Coppage Co*, 12023 Ventura Blvd Ste 1, Studio City CA 91604........818-980-1106
Robert Cornfield Literary Agency, 5 W 73rd St, New York NY 10023......212-874-2465
Creative Artists Agency*, 1888 Century Park E, Los Angeles CA 90067...213-277-4545
Bonnie R Crown Agency, 50 E 10th St, New York NY 10003.....................212-475-1999
Lil Cumber Attractions*, 6515 Sunset Blvd, Los Angeles CA 90028.........213-469-1919
Richard Curtis Assoc+, 164 E 64th St Ste 1, New York NY 10021............212-371-9481
CWA/Chateau of Talent*, 1633 Vista Del Mar, Hollywood CA 90028.....213-461-2727
Dade/Rosen/Lichtman*, 12345 Ventura Blvd, Studio City CA 91604........818-761-0640
Daimler Artists Agency*, 2007 Wilshire Blvd, Los Angeles CA 90057.......213-483-9783
Liz Darhansoff, 1220 Park Ave, New York NY 10128.............................212-534-2479
Donna Lee Davies Agency*, 3518 Cahuenga W, Hollywood CA 90068......213-850-1205
Davis-Cohen Assoc, 182 Sullivan St, New York NY 10012.....................212-254-5764
Lois De La Haba Assoc+, 142 Bank St, New York NY 10014 212-929-4838
Dellwood Enterprises*, 409 N Camden Dr, Beverly Hills CA 90210..........213-271-7847
Anita Diamant, 310 Madison Ave, New York NY 10017 212-687-1122
Paula Diamond Agency, 60 Gramercy Pk N 4A, New York NY 10010......212-475-0549
Diamond Artists*, 9200 Sunset Blvd #909, Los Angeles CA 90069...........213-278-8146
Sandra Dijkstra Agency, 1237 Camino del Mar, Del Mar CA 92014.........619-755-3115
DJ Enterprises*, 339 S Franklin St, Allentown PA 18102........................215-437-0723
The Jonathan Dolger Agency, 49 E 96th St 9B, New York NY 10128........212-427-1853
The Dorese Agency, 41 W 82nd St, New York NY 10024 212-580-2855
Dorothy Albert, 162 W 54th St, New York NY 10019 212-586-4790
Dupree/Miller & Assoc Inc, 5518 Dyer St Ste 3, Dallas TX 75206............214-692-1388
The Gwen Edelman Agency, 352 W 21st St, New York NY 10011 212-807-8882
Educational Design Services, PO Box 253, Wantagh NY 11793 516-221-0995
Joseph Elder Agency, 150 W 87th St Apt 6D, New York NY 10024.........212-787-5722
Elek Intl Rights Agents, PO Box 223, New York NY 10013....................212-431-9368
Ann Elmo Agency+, 60 E 42nd St, New York NY 10165 212-661-2880
R J Erdmann, 26 Quarterhorse, Rolling Hls Est CA 90274......................213-544-5071
Erikson Literary Agency, 815 De La Vina, Santa Barbara CA 93101 805-963-8373
Exclusive Artists Agency*, 2501 W Burbank Blvd, Burbank CA 91505 818-846-0262
John Farquharson Ltd, 250 W 57th St, New York NY 10107 212-245-1993
Farwestern Consultants Inc, PO Box 47786, Phoenix AZ 85068................602-861-3546
Florence Feiler Agency, 1524 Sunset Plaza, Los Angeles CA 90069 213-652-6920
Robt L Fenton, 31800 Northwestern Hwy, Farmington Hills MI 48018.....313-855-8780
Carol Ferrell Agency*, Box 69A105, Los Angeles CA 90069....................213-708-7773
Film Artists Assoc*, 470 S San Vicente Blvd, Los Angeles CA 90048 213-651-1700
Film Artists Mgmt Ent*, 8278 Sunset Blvd, Los Angeles CA 90046..........213-656-9334
Sy Fischer Co*, 10960 Wilshire Blvd 10th fl, Los Angeles CA 90024.........213-557-0388

Frieda Fishbein Ltd+, 2556 Hubbard St, Brooklyn NY 11235......................212-247-4398
Joyce A Flaherty Literary Agent, 816 Lynda Ct, St Louis MO 63122..........314-966-3057
Flaming Star Literary Ent, 320 Riverside 12D, New York NY 10025........212-222-0083
Peter Fleming Agency, PO Box 458, Pacific Palisade CA 90272.....................213-454-1373
The Foley Agency, 34 E 38th St, New York NY 10016.................................212-686-6930
Joan Follendore, 13376 Washington Blvd, W Los Angeles CA 90066..........213-306-3986
Franklin/Nathan Agency, 386 Park Ave S, New York NY 10016.................212-689-1842
Robt Freedman Agency+, 1501 Broadway, New York NY 10036.................212-840-5760
Samuel French Inc+, 45 W 25th St, New York NY 10010.............................212-206-8990
Erik J Friis, 19 Shadow Lane, Montvale NJ 07645.......................................201-391-8970
Kurt Frings Agency*, 415 N Crescent Ste 320, Beverly Hills CA 90210....213-274-8881
Frommer Price Literary Agency, 185 E 85th St, New York NY 10028.......212-289-0589
G M A Talent Agency*, 1714 N Ivar Ste 221, Los Angeles CA 90028.......213-466-7161
Marlene Gabriel Agency, 333 W 56th St 8A, New York NY 10019..............212-397-8322
Gage Group Inc*, 9229 Sunset Blvd Ste 306, Los Angeles CA 90069.........213-859-8777
Mauri Garashin Agency*, 8170 Beverly Blvd, Los Angeles CA 90048.......213-651-1828
Jay Garon-Brooke, 415 Central Park W 17E, New York NY 10025.............212-866-3654
Dale Garrick Intl Agency*, 8831 Sunset Blvd, Los Angeles CA 90069.......213-657-2661
Max Gartenberg Literary Agent, 15 W 44th St, New York NY 10036.......212-860-8451
Geddes Agency*, 1509 N Crescent Hts, Los Angeles CA 90046................213-650-4011
Gelles-Cole Literary Enterprises, 424 E 52nd St, New York NY 10022....212-758-1396
Gerritsen Intl*, 8721 Sunset Blvd Ste 203, Los Angeles CA 90069.............213-659-8414
The Gersh Agency Inc*, 222 N Canon Dr, Beverly Hills CA 90210.............213-274-6611
J Carter Gibson*, 9000 Sunset Blvd Ste 811, Los Angeles CA 90069.........213-274-8813
Harry Gold & Assoc*, 12725 Ventura Blvd Ste E, Studio City CA 91604..818-769-5003
Lucianne Goldberg Agents+, 255 W 84th St, New York NY 10024...........212-799-1260
Allen Goldstein & Assoc*, 15012 Ventura, Sherman Oaks CA 91403........818-905-7771
Larney Goodkind+, 180 E 79th St, New York NY 10021.........................212-249-3185
Goodman Assoc, 500 West End Ave, New York NY 10024.........................212-873-4806
Irene Goodman Agency, 521 5th Ave 17th fl, New York NY 10017...........212-688-4286
Graham Agency+, 311 W 43rd St, New York NY 10036.............................212-489-7730
Stephan Gray Artists Agency*, 9025 Wilshire, Beverly Hills CA 90211.....213-550-7000
Ivan Green Agency*, 9911 W Pico Blvd #1490, Los Angeles CA 90035....213-277-1541
Sanford J Greenburger Assoc, 55 5th Ave, New York NY 10003...............212-206-5600
Harold R Greene Inc*, 760 N La Cienega Blvd, Los Angeles CA 90069...213-855-0824
Maia Gregory Assoc, 311 E 72nd St, New York NY 10021.........................212-288-0310
Blanche C Gregory Inc, 2 Tudor City Place, New York NY 10017.............212-697-0828
Maxine Groffsky Literary Agency, 2 5th Ave, New York NY 10011..........212-473-0004
Larry Grossman & Assoc*, 211 S Beverly Dr, Beverly Hills CA 90212.....213-550-8127
Reece Halsey Agency*, 8733 Sunset Blvd, Los Angeles CA 90069..............213-652-2409
Mitchell J Hamilburg*, 292 S La Cienega, Beverly Hills CA 90211............213-657-1501
Hannaway-We-Go*, 1276 N Hayworth Ave, Los Angeles CA 90046..........213-854-3999
Thos S Hart Literary Ent, 20 Kenwood St, Boston MA 02124.....................617-288-8512
Alexandria Hatcher Agency, 150 W 55th St, New York NY 10019..............212-757-8596
Heacock Literary Agency*, 1523 6th St Ste 14, Santa Monica CA 90401...213-393-6227
Shirley Hector Agency, 29 W 46th St, New York NY 10036.........................212-719-2482
Heinle & Heinle Enterprises, 29 Lexington Rd, Concord MA 01742..........617-369-4858
Susan Herner Rights Agency, 666 3rd Ave 10th fl, New York NY 10017..212-983-5232
HHM Literary Agency, PO Box 1153, Rahway NJ 07065..............................201-388-8167
Frederick Hill Assoc, 2237 Union St, San Francisco CA 94123....................415-921-2910
Alice Hilton Agency*, 13131 Welby Way, N Hollywood CA 91606.............818-982-5423
Hintz & Fitzgerald, 207 E Buffalo Ste 211, Milwaukere WI 53202............414-273-0300
Ronald Hobbs Literary Agency, 516 5th Ave, New York NY 10036............212-354-0140

John L Hochmann Book, 320 E 58th St, New York NY 10022....................212-319-0505
Berenice Hoffman Lit Agency, 215 W 75th St, New York NY 10023...........212-580-0951
Holub Assoc, 24 Old Colony Rd, N Stonington CT 06359............................203-535-0689
Scott Hudson Talent Rep+, 215 E 76th St, New York NY 10021................212-570-9645
Ansley Q Hyman Agency*, 3123 Cahuenga W, Los Angeles CA 90068......213-851-9199
Independent Literary Agents Assn, 55 5th Ave, New York NY 10003.......212-206-5600
Independent Publishers Services, PO Box 135, Volcano CA 95689...........209-296-7989
Information Research, 10367 Paw Paw Lake Dr, Mattawan MI 49071......616-668-2049
Intl Creative Management+, 40 W 57th St, New York NY 10019................212-556-5600
Intl Creative Management*, 8899 Beverly Blvd, Los Angeles CA 90048...213-550-4000
Intl Publisher Assoc, 746 West Shore, Sparta NJ 07871.............................201-729-9321
ISD Literary Agency, PO Box 1310, Miami FL 33153.................................305-756-8313
J & S Literary Services, 128 2nd Place, Brooklyn NY 11231.......................718-237-2339
J de S Assoc Inc, Shagbark Rd Wilson Point, S Norwalk CT 06854...........203-838-7571
Melanie Jackson Agency+, 250 W 57th St #1119, New York NY 10107...212-582-8585
Morton Janklow Assoc, 598 Madison Ave, New York NY 10022................212-421-1700
Janus Literary Agency, PO Box 107, Nahant MA 01908.............................617-593-0576
Sharon Jarvis & Co, 260 Willard Ave, Staten Island NY 10314.................718-273-1066
Asher D Jason Enterprises+, 111 Barrow St, New York NY 10014...........212-929-2129
JCA Literary Agency Inc, 242 W 27th St, New York NY 10001..................212-807-0888
JET Literary Assoc Inc, 124 E 84th St, New York NY 10028......................212-879-2578
Joseph/Knight Agency*, 6331 Hollywood Blvd, Los Angeles CA 90028 ...213-465-5474
The Robin Kaigh Literary Agency, 300 E 54th St, New York NY 10022 ...212-832-3051
Alex Kamaroff Assoc+, 200 Park Ave Ste 303 E, New York NY 10028 212-879-2578
Merrily Kane Agency*, 9171 Wilshire Blvd, Beverly Hills CA 90210.........213-550-8874
Kaplan-Stahler Agency*, 8383 Wilshire Blvd, Beverly Hills CA 90210......213-274-8889
Patricia Karlin Agency*, 12345 Ventura Blvd, Studio City CA 91604........818-506-5666
William Kerwin Agency*, 1605 N Cahuenga, Los Angeles CA 90028........213-469-5155
Keynan-Goff Assoc*, 2049 Century Park E, Los Angeles CA 90067..........213-556-0339
Virginia Kidd+, 538 E Harford St PO Box 278, Milford PA 18337...........717-296-7266
Kidde Hoyt & Picard+, 335 E 51st St, New York NY 10022.....................212-755-9461
Kimberly Agency*, 3950 W 6th St Ste 203, Los Angeles CA 90020...........213-738-6087
Daniel P King Lit Agent, 5125 N Cumberland, Whitefish Bay WI 53217...414-964-2903
Bertha Klausner Intl Lit Agency+, 71 Park Ave, New York NY 10016....212-685-2642
Harvey Klinger Inc+, 301 W 53rd St, New York NY 10019 212-581-7068
Joseph Knight*, 6331 Hollywood Blvd Ste 924, Hollywood CA 90028.......213-465-5474
Paul Kohner Agency*, 9169 Sunset Blvd, Los Angeles CA 90069...............213-550-1060
The Kopaloff Company*, 1930 Century Park W, Los Angeles CA 90067..213-203-8340
Barbara S Kouts, 788 9th Ave, New York NY 10019 212-265-6003
Sidney B Kramer, 20 Bluewater Hill, Westport CT 06880.........................203-227-1836
Kratz & Kompany*, 210 5th Ave, New York NY 10010.............................212-683-9222
Lucy Kroll Agency+, 390 West End Ave, New York NY 10024.................212-877-0627
Edite Kroll, 31 E 31st St Apt 2E, New York NY 10016.............................212-684-6278
Bill Kruger Literary Services, PO Box 40887, St Petersburg FL 33743.....813-381-5348
Lake & Douroux*, 445 S Beverly Sr Ste 310, Beverly Hills CA 90212........213-557-0700
Peter Lampack Agency+, 551 5th Ave Ste 2015, New York NY 10017......212-687-9106
The Lantz Office+, 888 7th Ave, New York NY 10106 212-586-0200
The Lantz Office*, 9255 Sunset Blvd Ste 505, Los Angeles CA 90069........213-858-1144
Paul Lapolla Publishing Properties, 3719 6th Ave, San Diego CA 92103.619-291-9126
Larsen/Pomada, 1029 Jones St, San Francisco CA 94109 415-673-0939
The Maureen Lasher Agency+, PO Box 888, Pacific Palisade CA 90272..213-459-8415
Fred Lawrence & Assoc*, 9044 Melrose Ave, Los Angeles CA 90069.......213-273-5255
Elizabeth Lay Literary Agent, 484 Lake Park Ave, Oakland CA 94610.....415-839-2480

Irving Paul Lazar Agency*, 211 S Beverly Dr, Beverly Hills CA 90212.....213-275-6153
Leading Artists Inc*, 445 N Bedford Dr, Beverly Hills CA 90210.............213-858-1999
Harry L Lee Literary Agency*, PO Box 203, Rocky Point NY 22778........516-744-1188
Jack Lenny Assoc*, 9701 Wilshire Blvd Ste 800, Beverly Hills CA 90212..213-271-2174
The Adele Leone Agency, 26 Nantucket Pl, Scarsdale NY 10583.................914-961-2965
Lescher & Lescher Ltd, 155 E 71st St, New York NY 10021....................212-249-7600
Ellen Levine Literary Agency, 432 Park Ave S, New York NY 10016 212-889-0620
Robert Lewis, 65 E 96th St, New York NY 10128 212-369-6132
The Light Company*, 113 N Robertson Blvd, Los Angeles CA 90048.......213-273-9602
Wendy Lipkind Agency, 225 E 57th St, New York NY 10022 212-935-1406
Literistic Ltd, 264 5th Ave, New York NY 10001....................................212-696-4770
London Star Promotions*, 7131 Owensworth, Canoga Park CA 91303....818-709-0447
The Sterling Lord Agency, 660 Madison Ave, New York NY 10021 212-751-2533
Los Angeles Literary Agency, 6525 Sunset Blvd, Los Angeles CA 90028...213-464-6444
Barbara Lowenstein Assoc+, 250 W 57th St, New York NY 10107 212-586-3825
Thomas Lowry Assoc, 156 W 86th St, New York NY 10024....................212-787-8788
Lund Agency*, 6515 Sunset Blvd Ste 204, Los Angeles CA 90028 213-466-8280
Lynne & Reilly Agency*, 6290 Sunset Blvd, Los Angeles CA 90028 213-461-2828
Grace Lyons Management*, 204 S Beverly Dr, Beverly Hills CA 90212....213-652-5290
Donald MacCampbell Inc, 12 E 41st St, New York NY 10017..................212-683-5580
Gina Maccoby Literary Agency, 19 W 21st St, New York NY 10010........212-627-9210
Major Talent Agency*, 11812 San Vicente Blvd, Los Angeles CA 90049 ..213-820-5841
Malsam Marketing, 3323 W 55th Ave, Denver CO 80221 303-433-9192
Management One Agency*, 6464 Sunset Blvd, Hollywood CA 90028.........213-461-7515
Carol Mann Agency, 55 5th Ave, New York NY 10003 212-206-5635
Sheri Mann Agency*, 8480 Beverly Blvd Ste 117, Los Angeles CA 90048.213-476-0177
Janet Manus Agency+, 370 Lexington Ave, New York NY 10017 212-685-9558
March Tenth Inc, 4 Myrtle St, Haworth NJ 07641..................................201-387-6551
Denise Marcil Literary Agency, 316 W 82nd St 5F, New York NY 10024.212-580-1071
Maria Carvainis Agency, 235 West End Ave, New York NY 10023...........212-580-1559
Betty Marks, 176 E 77th St Apt 9F, New York NY 10021 212-535-8388
Elaine Markson Agency, 44 Greenwich Ave, New York NY 10011...........212-243-8480
The Marshall Agency*, 2330 Westwood Blvd, Los Angeles CA 90064.......213-272-1290
Elisabeth Marton, 96 5th Ave, New York NY 10011................................212-255-1908
Harold Matson Co Inc+, 276 5th Ave, New York NY 10001....................212-679-4490
Margaret McBride Literary Agency, Box 8730, La Jolla CA 92038............619-459-0559
Renate B McCarter, 823 Park Ave, New York NY 10021 212-288-8505
McCartt Oreck Barrett*, 9200 Sunset Blvd, Los Angeles CA 90069..........213-278-6243
Gerard McCauley Agency, 141 E 44th St Apt 208, New York NY 10017...914-232-5700
Kirby McCauley Ltd, 425 Park Ave S, New York NY 10016......................212-683-7561
Helen McGrath & Assoc, 1406 Idaho Ct, Concord CA 94521 415-672-6211
McIntosh & Otis Inc, 475 5th Ave, New York NY 10017 212-689-1050
Toni Mendez Inc, 141 E 56th St, New York NY 10022.............................212-838-6740
Claudia Menza, 237 W 11th St, New York NY 10014...............................212-889-6850
Scott Meredith Literary Agency, 845 3rd Ave, New York NY 10022 212-245-5500
The Merit Agency*, 12926 Riverside Dr #C, Sherman Oaks CA 91423 818-986-3017
Helen Merrill Ltd+, 435 W 23rd St #1A, New York NY 10011................212-691-5326
Fred Messenger Agency*, 8235 Sunset Blvd, Los Angeles CA 90046.........213-654-3800
George Michaud Agency*, 10113 Riverside Dr, Toluca Lake CA 91602....818-508-8314
Midwest Literary Agency, 3660 Alsace Dr, Indianapolis IN 46226 317-897-4395
Martha Millard Literary Agency, 357 W 19th St, New York NY 10011....212-924-2087
Peter Miller Agency Inc+, PO Box 764, New York NY 10018....................212-221-8329
Lee Miller Talent Agency*, 1680 N Vine St, Hollywood CA 90028 213-468-0077

Howard Morhaim Agency, 175 5th Ave #709, New York NY 10010..........212-529-4433
William Morris Agency*, 151 El Camino Dr, Beverly Hills CA 90212......213-274-7451
William Morris Agency+, 1350 Ave of Americas, New York NY 10019...212-586-5100
Morton Agency Inc*, 1105 Glendon Ave, Los Angeles CA 90024............213-824-4089
Moulter Assoc, 20 Ashburton Pl 5th fl, Boston MA 02108.....................617-367-0660
Jean V Naggar Literary Agency, 336 E 73rd St, New York NY 10021.......212-794-1082
Charles Neighbors, 7600 Blanco Rd Ste 3607, San Antonio TX 78216......512-342-5324
B K Nelson Literary Agency+, 149 Madison Ave, New York NY 10016...212-779-0899
New Age World Service, 62091 Valley View Cir, Joshua Tree CA 92252...619-366-2833
New England Publishing Assn, Box 5, Chester CT 06412....................203-345-4976
New World Artists*, 1022 N Palm #2, Los Angeles CA 90069.................213-659-9737
Betsy Nolan Literary Agency, 50 W 29th St 9W, New York NY 10001......212-420-6000
The Norma-Lewis Agency, 521 5th Ave 17th fl, New York NY 10175.......212-751-4955
Northeast Literary Agency, 69 Broadway, Concord NH 03301................603-225-9162
Nugent & Assoc, 170 10th St N, Naples FL 33940.............................813-262-7562
Harold Ober Assoc Inc, 40 E 49th St, New York NY 10017....................212-759-8600
Evelyn Oppenheimer, 7929 Meadow Park Dr Apt 201, Dallas TX 75230..214-369-0904
Fifi Oscard Assoc+, 19 W 44th St, New York NY 10036.......................212-764-1100
The Otte Co, 9 Goden St, Belmont MA 02178.................................617-484-8505
John K Payne Literary Agency, 175 5th Ave, New York NY 10010............212-475-6447
Ray Peekner Literary Agency, 3210 S 7th St, Milwaukee WI 53215............414-482-0629
Rodney Pelter, 129 E 61st St, New York NY 10021............................212-838-3432
Pickering Assoc, 225 W 34th St #1500, New York NY 10001..................212-967-5588
Arthur Pine Assoc Inc, 1780 Broadway, New York NY 10019.................212-265-7330
Walter Pitkin Agency Inc, 11 Oakwood Dr, Weston CT 06883................203-227-3684
Lynn Pleshette Agency*, 2700 Beachwood Dr, Los Angeles CA 90068......213-465-0428
Sidney E Porcelain, PO Box 1229, Milford PA 18337.........................717-296-6420
Julian Portman Agency, 6677 Lincoln Ave, Chicago IL 60645................312-676-9815
Jim Preminger Agency*, 1650 Westwood Blvd, Los Angeles CA 90024....213-475-9491
Aaron M Priest Literary Agency+, 122 E 42nd St, New York NY 10168..212-818-0344
Progressive Artists Agency*, 400 S Beverly, Beverly Hills CA 90212.........213-553-8561
Susan Ann Protter Literary Agent, 110 W 40th St, New York NY 10018..212-840-0480
Publishers Media, 5507 Morella Ave, North Hollywood CA 91607...........818-980-2666
R L M Enterprises*, 5816 Lankershim #3, N Hollywood CA 91601.........818-506-1124
Raines & Raines, 71 Park Ave, New York NY 10016...........................212-684-5160
Raper Enterprises Agency*, 9441 Wilshire, Beverly Hills CA 90212..........213-273-7704
Ray Rappa Agency*, 7471 Melrose Ave Ste 11, Los Angeles CA 90046....213-653-7000
Ray Lincoln Literary Agency, 4 Surrey Rd, Melrose Park PA 19126.........215-782-8882
Helen Rees Literary Agency+, 308 Commonwealth, Boston MA 02116....617-262-2401
Paul R Reynolds Inc, 71 W 23rd St Ste 1600, New York NY 10010...........212-807-7040
Rhodes Literary Agency+, 140 West End Ave, New York NY 10023........212-580-1300
The Richland Agency*, 9046 Sunset Blvd, Los Angeles CA 90069............213-273-9661
Rights Unlimited, 156 5th Ave Ste 408, New York NY 10010.................212-741-0404
John R Riina, 5905 Meadowood Rd, Baltimore MD 21212...................301-433-2305
Susan Shapiro Ripps, 1016 5th Ave, New York NY 10028....................212-570-2430
RLR Assoc Ltd, 7 W 51st St, New York NY 10019...........................212-541-8641
Robbins & Covey Assoc, 866 2nd Ave, New York NY 10017..................212-223-0720
The Roberts Company*, 427 N Canon Dr, Beverly Hills CA 90210...........213-275-9384
Flora Roberts Inc, 157 W 57th St Penthouse A, New York NY 10019.......212-355-4165
Roday Literary Agency, 521 5th Ave, New York NY 10175...................212-752-7510
Rodell/Collin Literary Agency, 110 W 40th St, New York NY 10018........212-840-8664
Richard Roffman Assoc, 697 West End Ave 6A, New York NY 10025.....212-749-3647
Stephanie Rogers & Assoc*, 3855 Lankershim, N Hollywood CA 91604..818-509-1010

Eleanor Roszel Rogers, 1487 Generals Hwy, Crownsville MD 21032 301-987-8166
Irene Rogers, 9701 Wilshire Blvd, Beverly Hills CA 90212 213-837-3511
The Roistacher Literary Agency, 545 W 111th St, New York NY 10025....212-222-1405
Jack Rose Agency*, 6430 Sunset Blvd Ste 1203, Los Angeles CA 90028 213-463-7300
Rosenstone/Wender, 3 E 48th St, New York NY 10017.............................212-832-8330
James K Ross, 284 5th Ave, New York NY 10001 212-244-7328
Mary Jane Ross, 85 Sunset Lane, Tenafly NJ 07670 201-568-8739
Howard Rothberg Ltd*, 113 N Robertson Blvd, Los Angeles CA 90048...213-858-3000
Jane Rotrosen Agency, 318 E 51st St, New York NY 10022 212-593-4330
Rotzinger Enterprises*, 2000 11th St, Rock Island IL 61201.....................309-786-5370
Russell & Volkening, 50 W 29th St, New York NY 10001...........................212-684-6050
The Sackheim Agency*, 9301 Wilshire Blvd, Beverly Hills CA 90210 213-858-0606
Raphael Sagalyn Agency+, 2813 Bellevue Ter NW, Wash DC 20007........202-337-9660
Sanford-Beckett & Assoc*, 1015 Gayley Ave, Los Angeles CA 90024 213-208-2100
SBC Enterprise Inc*, 11 Mabro Dr, Denville NJ 07834............................201-366-3622
Jack Scagnetti Agency*, 5330 Lankershim, N Hollywood CA 91601.........818-762-3871
John Schaffner Assoc, 114 E 28th St, New York NY 10016......................212-689-6888
Irv Schechter Co*, 9300 Wilshire Blvd Ste 410, Beverly Hills CA 90212 213-278-8070
Schlessinger-Van Dyke Agency, 12 S 12th St, Philadelphia PA 19107 215-627-4665
Harold Schmidt Agency, 347 E 53rd St LC, New York NY 10022..............212-752-7037
Susan Schulman Literary Agency, 454 W 44th St, New York NY 10036....212-713-1633
Frances Schwartz Agency, 60 E 42nd St Ste 413, New York NY 10017 212-661-2881
Arthur P Schwartz Lit Agent, 435 Riverside Dr, New York NY 10025......212-864-3182
Rita Scott & Marje Fields, 165 W 46th St, New York NY 10036................212-764-5740
James Seligmann Agency, 175 5th Ave Ste 1101, New York NY 10010 212-477-5186
Edythea Ginis Selman, 14 Washington Pl, New York NY 10003................212-473-1874
David Shapira & Assoc*, 15301 Ventura, Sherman Oaks CA 91403.........818-906-0322
Shapiro-Lichtman*, 1800 Ave of Stars Ste 433, Los Angeles CA 90067....213-557-2244
Glenn Shaw Agency*, 3330 Barham Blvd #103, Los Angeles CA 90068....213-851-6262
Charlotte Sheedy Literary Agency, 145 W 86th St, New York NY 10024..212-873-4768
Lew Sherrell Agency*, 7060 Hollywood Blvd, Los Angeles CA 90028........213-461-9955
Shorr Stille & Assoc*, 800 S Robertson Blvd, Los Angeles CA 90035.......213-659-6160
The Shukat Co Ltd, 340 W 55th St Ste 1A, New York NY 10019...............212-582-7614
Shumaker Artists Agency*, 6533 Hollywood, Hollywood CA 90028..........213-464-0745
Jerome Siegel Assoc*, 8733 Sunset Blvd, Los Angeles CA 90069 213-652-6033
Rosalie Siegel Authors Agent, 111 Murphy Dr, Pennington NJ 08534.......609-737-1007
Bobbe Siegel Rights Representative, 41 W 83rd St, New York NY 10024.212-877-4985
Evelyn Singer Literary Agency, PO Box 594, White Plains NY 10602........914-949-1147
Singer Media Corp, 3164 Tyler Ave, Anaheim CA 92801............................714-550-3164
Freedman Smith & Assoc*, 123 N San Vicente, Beverly Hills CA 90211..213-852-4777
Gerald K Smith Assoc*, Box 7430, Burbank CA 91510..............................213-849-5388
Valerie Smith Literary Agent, PO Box 398, Milford PA 18337 717-828-7692
Michael Snell Literary Agency, Box 655, Truro MA 02666.......................617-349-3718
Nat Sobel Assoc Inc, 146 E 19th St, New York NY 10003 212-420-8585
Soc of Author's Representatives, PO Box 650, New York NY 10113.........212-228-9740
Sodsisky & Sons, 5914 Greentree Rd, Bethesda MD 20817........................301-897-8444
Elyse Sommer Inc, PO Box 1133, Forest Hills NY 11075 716-263-2668
Southern Writers, 333 St Charles Ave Ste 1111, New Orleans LA 70130..504-525-6390
Spectrum Literary Agency, 432 Park Ave S, New York NY 10016.............212-532-7377
F Joseph Spieler, 410 W 24th St, New York NY 10011 212-242-7152
Philip G Spitzer Literary Agency, 788 9th Ave, New York NY 10019........212-265-6003
Lyle Steel & Co, 511 E 73rd St Ste 7, New York NY 10021 212-288-2981
Ellen Lively Steele & Assoc, PO Drawer 447, Organ NM 88052.................505-382-5449

Michael Steinberg Literary Agent, PO Box 274, Glencoe IL 60022 312-835-8881
Stepping Stone Literary Agency, 59 W 71st St, New York NY 10023 212-362-9277
Gloria Stern Agency, 1230 Park Ave, New York NY 10128......................212-289-7698
Charles M Stern Assoc, 319 Coronet, San Antonio TX 78216 512-349-6141
Gloria Stern*, 12535 Chandler Blvd, N Hollywood CA 91607 818-508-6296
Larry Sternig Literary Agency, 742 Robertson St, Milwaukee WI 53213..414-771-7677
Jo Stewart, 201 E 66th St Ste 18G, New York NY 10021 212-879-1301
Stone-Masser Agency*, 1052 Carol Dr, Los Angeles CA 90069...................213-275-9599
Robin Straus Agency Inc, 229 E 79th St, New York NY 10021...................212-472-3282
Marianne Strong Literary Agency, 65 E 96th St, New York NY 10128.....212-249-1000
Gunther Stuhlmann Authors Rep, Box 276, Becket MA 01223...................413-623-5170
H N Swanson Inc*, 8523 Sunset Blvd, Los Angeles CA 90069 213-652-5385
Roslyn Targ Literary Agency, 105 W 13th St 15E, New York NY 10011...212-206-9390
Charles D Taylor, 23 Elm St, Manchester-Sea MA 01944 617-526-7936
Patricia Teal Literary Agency, 2036 Vista del Rosa, Fullerton CA 92631 .714-738-8333
Tenth Avenue Editions Inc, 885 10th Ave, New York NY 10019 212-307-6780
Thompson & Chris Agency, 3926 Sacramento, San Francisco CA 94118..415-386-2443
Willie R Thompson Agency*, 6381 Hollywood, Los Angeles CA 90028.....213-461-6594
Total Acting Experience*, 6736 Laurel Canyon, N Hollywood CA 91606..818-765-7244
Triad Artists*, 10100 Santa Monica Blvd, Los Angeles CA 90067 213-556-2727
20th Century Artists*, 3518 Cahuenge Blvd W, Los Angeles CA 90068....213-850-5516
2M Communications Ltd, 310 E 9th St, New York NY 10003....................212-460-5172
Universal Artist Agency*, 9465 Wilshire Blvd, Beverly Hills CA 90212.....213-278-2425
Susan P Urstadt Inc, 125 E 84th St, New York NY 10028..........................212-744-6605
Ione Vannerson Agency*, 10810 Bloomfield, Studio City CA 91602...........818-985-8725
Ralph M Vicinanza, 432 Park Ave S #1205, New York NY 10016...............212-725-5133
Victoria Management Co, 222 1st Ave 5C, New York NY 10009 212-529-4750
Carlson Wade, 49 Bokee Ct Rm 4K, Brooklyn NY 11223 718-743-6983
Austin Wahl Agency Ltd*, 53 W Jackson Blvd #342, Chicago IL 60604....312-922-3331
Erika Wain Agency*, 1418 N Highland, Los Angeles CA 90028...................213-460-4224
Mary Jack Wald Assoc, 799 Broadway Ste 325, New York NY 10003 212-254-7842
Wallace & Sheil Agency Inc, 177 E 70th St, New York NY 10021 212-570-9090
Bess Wallace Assoc, 1502 N Mitchell, Payson AZ 85541...........................602-474-2983
John A Ware Agency, 392 Central Park W, New York NY 10025..................212-866-4733
James Warren Agency, 13131 Welby Way, N Hollywood CA 91606...........818-982-5423
Harriet Wasserman Lit Agency, 137 E 36th St, New York NY 10016........212-689-3257
Waterside Productions Inc, 125 Via de la Valle, Del Mar CA 92014 619-481-8335
Watkins Loomis Agency Inc, 150 E 35th St, New York NY 10016 212-532-0080
Elliot Wax & Assoc*, 9255 Sunset Blvd Ste 612, Los Angeles CA 90069 ...213-273-8217
Wecksler Incomco, 170 West End Ave, New York NY 10023 212-787-2239
Cherry Weiner Literary Agency, 28 Kipling Way, Manalapan NJ 07726....201-446-2096
Rhoda Weyr Agency, 216 Vance St, Chapel Hill NC 27514...........................919-942-0770
Wieser & Wieser Inc, 118 E 25th St, New York NY 10010 212-260-0860
William-Jeffreys Agency*, 8455 Beverly Blvd, Los Angeles CA 90069......213-651-3193
Wingate Management*, 8383 Wilshire Blvd, Beverly Hills CA 90211 213-659-3207
Wingra Woods Press, 33 Witherspoon St, Princeton NJ 08542....................609-683-1218
Ted Witzer Agency*, 1900 Ave of Stars #1633, Los Angeles CA 90067.....213-552-9521
Audrey Adler Wolf, 1000 Potomac St NW Ste 105, Wash DC 20007 202-333-2702
Sylvia Wosk Agency*, 439 S La Cienega Blvd, Los Angeles CA 90048 213-274-8063
Ruth Wreschner, 10 W 74th St, New York NY 10023 212-877-2605
Ann Wright Representatives*, 136 E 57th St, New York NY 10022...........212-832-0110
Writer's Consulting Group, PO Box 492, Burbank CA 91503......................818-841-9294
Writer's Productions, PO Box 630, Westport CT 06881...............................203-227-8199

Writers & Artists Agency, 70 W 36th St Ste 501, New York NY 10018 212-947-8765
Writers & Artists Agency*, 11726 San Vicente, Los Angeles CA 90049 213-820-2240
Writers House Inc, 21 W 26th St, New York NY 10010 212-685-2400
Writers Readers, PO Box 14863, Austin TX 78761 512-926-6400
Writers' World Forum, PO Box 20383, New York NY 10129 201-664-0263
Wunsch Agency*, 9200 Sunset Blvd Ste 808, Los Angeles CA 90068 213-278-1955
Wycoff & Assoc*, 6331 Hollywood Blvd #1120, Los Angeles CA 90028 213-464-4866
Andrew Wylie Agency, 48 W 75th St, New York NY 10023 212-874-4754
Barbara W Yedlin, Pump St, Newcastle ME 04553 207-563-8335
Herb Yobias & Assoc*, 1901 Ave of Stars #840, Los Angeles CA 90067 ..213-277-6211
Mary Yost Assoc Inc, 59 E 54th St, New York NY 10022 212-980-4988
Susan Zeckendorf Assoc Inc, 171 W 57th St 11B, New York NY 10019 212-245-2928
Tom Zelasky Agency, 3138 Parkridge Crescent, Chamblee GA 30341 404-458-0391
George Ziegler Literary Agency, 160 E 97th St, New York NY 10029 212-348-3637

ASSOCIATIONS

This section includes writer's clubs and organizations related to publishing and the book trade.

Acad of Amer Poets, 177 E 8th St, New York NY 10128 212-427-5665
Acad of Motion Pict Arts & Sci, 8949 Wilshire, Beverly Hls CA 90211 213-278-8990
Acad of Television Arts & Sciences, 3500 W Olive, Burbank CA 91505 818-953-7575
Alaska Assn of Small Presses, PO Box 821, Cordova AK 99574 907-424-3116
Alaska Press Women, PO Box 104056, Anchorage AK 99510 907-248-4495
Amer Acad Inst Arts & Letters, 633 W 155th St, New York NY 10032 212-368-5900
Amer Auto Racing Writers, 922 N Pass Ave, Burbank CA 91505 818-842-7005
Amer Book Producers Assn, 319 E 52nd St, New York NY 10022 212-982-8934
Amer Bookdealers Exchange, PO Box 2525, La Mesa CA 92041 619-462-3297
Amer Booksellers Assn, 137 W 25th St, New York NY 10001 212-463-8450
Amer Business Communications Assn, Univ of IL, Urbana IL 61801 217-333-1007
Amer Business Press, 205 E 42nd St, New York NY 10017 212-661-6360
Amer Civil Liberties Union, 132 W 43rd St, New York NY 10036 212-944-9800
Amer Film Inst, Kennedy Ctr for Perf Arts, Washington DC 20566 202-828-4000
Amer Library Assn, 50 E Huron St, Chicago IL 60611 312-944-6780
Amer Literary Translators, PO Box 830688, Richardson TX 75083 214-690-2093
Amer Medical Writers Assn, 5272 River Rd #410, Bethesda MD 20816 ..301-986-9119
Amer Newspaper Publ Assn, 11600 Sunrise Vly, Reston VA 22091 703-620-9500
Amer Soc Business Press Editors, 4196 Porter, N Olmsted OH 44070 216-734-9522
Amer Soc of Indexers (ASI), 1700 18th St NW, Washington DC 20009 203-323-2826
Amer Soc of Jour & Authors, 1501 Broadway, New York NY 10036 212-997-0947
Amer Soc of Jour & Authors, PO Box 35282, Los Angeles CA 90035 213-931-3177
ASJA Midwest, 2428 W Coyle, Chicago IL 60645 312-943-7363
Amer Soc of Magazine Editors, 575 Lexington, New York NY 10022 212-752-0055
Amer Soc of Mag Photographers, 205 Lexington, New York NY 10016 ...212-889-9144
Amer Translators Assn, 109 Croton Ave, Ossining NY 10562 914-941-1500
Amer Women in Radio & TV, 1101 Connecticut Ave, Wash DC 20036 202-296-0008
Amer-Scandinavian Foundation, 127 E 73rd St, New York NY 10021 212-879-9779
Arizona Authors Assn, PO Box 10492, Phoenix AZ 85064 602-948-2354
Assn for Authors, 4189 Bellaire Blvd Ste 260, Houston TX 77025 713-666-9711
Assn of Amer Publishers, 220 E 23rd St, New York NY 10011 212-689-8920

Assn of Amer University Presses, 1 Park Ave, New York NY 10016 212-889-6040
Assn of Book Travelers, Box 308, Brightwaters NY 11718............................516-666-0177
Assn of Prof Translators, 3 Mellon Bank Ctr, Pittsburgh PA 15259..........412-234-5751
Assoc Business Writers, 1450 S Havana #620, Aurora CO 80012 303-751-7844
Associated Writing Programs, Old Dominion Univ, Norfolk VA 23508...804-440-3839
Austin Writers' League, 1501 W 5th St #108, Austin TX 78703 512-499-8914
Authors Guild, 234 W 44th St, New York NY 10036.....................................212-398-0838
Authors League Fund, 234 W 44th St, New York NY 10036.....................212-391-3966
Authors League of Amer Inc, 234 W 44th St, New York NY 10036...........212-391-9198
Authors Resource Ctr, 4001 E Ft Lowell Rd, Tucson AZ 85712.................602-325-4733
Aviation Space Writers, 17 S High St #1200, Columbus OH 43215...........614-221-1900
Baltimore Publishers Assn, PO Box 5584, Baltimore MD 21285 301-363-6400
Before Columbus Foundation, 1446 6th St Ste D, Berkeley CA 94710 415-527-1586
Bilingual Educational Svcs, 2514 S Grand Ave, Los Angeles CA 90007 ...213-749-6213
Bensalem Assn of Women Writers, Box 236, Croydon PA 19020 215-244-0525
Bibliographical Soc of Amer, PO Box 397, New York NY 10163................718-638-7957
BMI Musical Theatre Dept, 320 W 57th St, New York NY 10019................212-586-2000
Boating Writers Intl, 56 Hickory Hill Rd, Wilton CT 06897 203-762-2711
Book Industry Study Group, 160 5th Ave, New York NY 10010................212-929-1393
Book Manufacturers Inst, 111 Prospect, Stamford CT 06901......................203-324-9670
Book Publicists of S Calif, 6430 Sunset #503, Hollywood CA 90028.........213-461-3921
Brooklyn Writers Club, PO Box 184, Brooklyn NY 11214............................718-837-3484
Business Comm for Arts, 1501 Broadway #2600, New York NY 10036 ...212-921-0700
Byliners, The, PO Box 6015, Corpus Christi TX 78411..................................512-991-7404
Calif Writers Club, 2214 Derby, Berkeley CA 94705.....................................415-841-1217
Calif Writers Roundtable, 11684 Ventura #807, Los Angeles CA 91604..818-789-9175
Lewis Carroll Soc NA, 617 Rockford Rd, Silver Spring MD 20902 301-593-7077
Center for Book Arts, 626 Broadway, New York NY 10012 212-460-9768
Center for Book Research, Univ of Scranton, Scranton PA 18510 717-961-7764
Center for the Book, Library of Congress, Washington DC 20540 202-287-5221
Central Penn Writers Organization, Box 214, Bainbridge PA 17502.........717-426-3240
Chicago Publishers Assn, 1000 W Washington Blvd, Chicago IL 60607....312-666-4300
Chicago Women in Publishing, 230 N Michigan, Chicago IL 60611...........312-641-6311
Children's Book Council, 67 Irving Pl, New York NY 10003.......................212-254-2666
Christian Booksellers Assn, Box 200, Colo Spgs CO 80901 303-576-7880
Christian Writers Guild, 260 Fern Lane, Hume CA 93628............................209-335-2333
Coalition for Literacy, 50 E Huron St, Chicago IL 60611 312-944-6780
Columbia Scholastic Press Assn, Columbia Univ, New York NY 10027..212-280-3311
Comics Magazine Assn of Amer, 60 E 42nd St, New York NY 10165 212-682-8144
Computer Press Assn, 87 Edgecroft Rd, Kensington CA 94707...................415-527-8486
Connecticut Writers League, 9 Hiram Ln, Bloomfield CT 06002................203-242-9942
Coord Council of Literary Mag, 666 Broadway, New York NY 10012......212-614-6554
Copyright Clearance Ctr, 27 Congress St, Salem MA 01970......................617-744-3350
Copyright Soc of USA, 40 Washington Sq S, New York NY 10012 212-598-2280
Copywriters Council of Amer, 7 Putter Bldg, Middle Island NY 11953.....516-924-8555
Corp for Public Broadcasting, 1111 16th St NW, Wash DC 20036 202-293-6160
COSMEP, PO Box 703, San Francisco CA 94101 415-922-9490
Council of Writers Org, 160 West End Ave 12H, New York NY 10023....212-496-8833
Dance Critics of Amer, 606 W 116th St #61, New York NY 10027............718-499-4976
Deadline Club, PO Box 2503, New York NY 10017.......................................212-705-7317
Dixie Council Authors & Jour, 2826 Evansdale Cir, Atlanta GA 30340....404-939-1924
Dog Writers Assn of Amer, 9800 Flint Rock Rd, Manassas VA 22111.......703-369-2384
Dramatists Guild, 234 W 44th St, New York NY 10036 212-398-9366

Dramatists Guild, 2265 Westwood #462, Los Angeles CA 90064................213-470-3683
East Texas Writers Assn, 1607 Woodway Ln, Gilmer TX 75644....................214-843-3672
Editorial Freelancers Assn, PO Box 2050, New York NY 10159..................212-677-3357
Education Writers Assn, 1001 Connecticut Ave NW, Wash DC 20036.....202-429-9680
Feminist Writers Guild, PO Box 9396, Berkely CA 94709 415-524-3692
Florida Freelance Writers Assn, PO Box 9844, Ft Lauderdale FL 33310..305-485-0795
Football Writers Assn of Amer, Box 1022, Edmond OK 73083 405-341-4731
Foreign Press Assn, 18 E 50th St, New York NY 10022.............................212-826-4724
Garden Writers Assn, Box 433, Mt Dora FL 32757....................................904-343-0618
Georgia State Poetry Soc, 1399 Vista Leaf Dr, Decatur GA 30033............404-636-1316
John Gile Communications, 1710 N Main St, Rockford IL 61103...............815-968-6601
Give the Gift of Literacy, 7505 Metro Blvd, Minneapolis MN 55435..........612-893-7202
Golden Triangle Writers Guild, 4245 Calder, Beaumont TX 77076...........409-892-3078
Golf Writers Assoc of Amer, PO Box 37324, Cincinnati OH 45222............513-631-4400
Greater Dallas Writer's Assn, 4201 Nightfall, Plano TX 75075...................214-596-5335
Greater LA Press Club, 600 N Vermont, Los Angeles CA 90004................213-665-1141
Hawaii Literary Arts Council, PO Box 11213, Honolulu HI 96828............808-942-3907
Houston Area Booksellers Assn, PO Box 2608, Houston TX 77001 713-464-4050
Idaho Writers League, 423 N 11th St, Pocatello ID 83201.......................208-232-3038
Illinois Writers, Box 1087, Champaign IL 61820.....................................217-398-8526
Independent Literary Agents Assn, 55 5th Ave, New York NY 10003.......212-206-5600
Independent Publishers League, Drawer 5007, Bend OR 97708 503-382-6978
Independent Writers of Chicago, 645 N Michigan, Chicago IL 60611 312-951-9114
Independent Writers of S Calif, PO Box 19745, Los Angeles CA 90019 ...213-731-2652
Inter Amer Press Assn, 2911 NW 39th St, Miami FL 33142.....................305-634-2465
Intermtn Booksellers Assn, Univ of Utah, Salt Lake City UT 84112..........801-581-6325
Intl Assn Business Comm, 870 Market #940, San Francisco CA 94102....415-433-3400
Intl Assn of Scholarly Publishers, PO Box C50096, Seattle WA 98145.....206-543-8870
Intl Black Writers, PO Box 1030, Chicago IL 60690................................312-995-5195
Intl Black Writers & Artists, PO Box 43576, Oakland CA 94601...............415-532-6179
Intl Copyright Info Ctr, 2005 Massachusetts Ave NW, Wash DC 20036...202-232-3335
Intl Motor Press Assn, 555 W 57th St, New York NY 10019 212-399-5658
Intl Reading Assn, PO Box 8139, Newark DE 19714................................302-731-1600
Intl Soc of Dramatists, PO Box 1310, Miami FL 33153 305-756-8313
Intl Women's Writing Guild, PO Box 810, New York NY 10028................212-737-7536
Investigative Reporters & Editors, Box 838, Columbia MO 65205 314-882-2042
ISBN Agency, 245 W 17th St, New York NY 10011 212-645-9700
James Joyce Society, 41 W 47th St, New York NY 10036 212-719-4448
JForum, c/o Jim Cameron 117 Prospect Park W, Brooklyn NY 11215 718-788-8528
Katy Night Writers, PO Box 495, Katy TX 77492 713-391-9239
Linguistic Soc of Amer, 1325 18th St NW #211, Washington DC 20036...202-835-1714
The Loft, 2301 E Franklin Ave, Minneapolis MN 55406 612-827-3756
Magazine Publishers Assn, 575 Lexington, New York NY 10022...............212-752-0055
Marin Self-Publishers Assn, PO Box 1346, Ross CA 94957......................415-454-1771
Media Alliance, Ft Mason Ctr, San Francisco CA 94123 415-441-2557
Mercantile Library Assn of NY, 17 E 47th St, New York NY 10017.........212-755-6710
Miami Earth, PO Box 680-536, Miami FL 33168 305-688-8558
Michigan Mystery Writers, 21315 Pembroke, Detroit MI 48219...............313-532-3882
Mid-Amer Publishers Assn, PO Box 183, Oak Park IL 60303 312-386-3507
Mid-Atlantic Booksellers Assn, 1837 Chestnut, Philadelphia PA 19103....215-735-9599
Mid-South Booksellers Assn, 5823 Kavanaugh, Little Rock AR 72207 501-663-9198
Midwest Travel Writers, 111 N Canal St 11th fl, Chicago IL 60606 312-902-1640
Missouri Writers Guild, 2631 Sue Dr, Jefferson City MO 65101 314-893-5834

Modern Language Assn (MLA), 10 Astor Pl, New York NY 10003...........212-614-6314
Mystery Writers of Amer (MWA), 236 W 27th St, New York NY 10001...212-255-7005
MWA Midwest, 11351 S Lowe Ave, Chicago IL 60628 312-588-4833
MWA New England, 121 Follen Rd, Lexington MA 02173 617-861-2175
MWA New York, 6252 82nd St, Queens NY 11379.......................................212-642-4599
MWA Northern Calif, 48 Valley Rd, San Anselmo CA 94960....................415-457-5179
MWA Northwest, 1449 Olympic View Dr, Edmonds WA 98020.................206-356-3033
MWA Rocky Mtn, 520 University Blvd, Denver CO 80206 303-333-5924
MWA Southern Calif, 14600 Saticoy St #204, Van Nuys CA 91405...........818-780-6363
MWA Southwest, 1108 Danbury Rd, Houston TX 77055.............................713-686-5387
Natl Assn of Black Journalists, 1 Herald Plz, Miami FL 33101.................305-376-3934
Natl Assn of College Stores, 528 E Lorain, Oberlin OH 44074...................216-775-7777
Natl Assn of Desktop Publishers, PO Box 508, Boston MA 02215 617-437-6472
Natl Assn of Independent Publishers, Box 850, Moore Haven FL 33471..813-946-0293
Natl Assn of Science Writers, PO Box 294, Greenlawn NY 11740 516-757-5664
Natl Book Critics Circle, 756 S 10th St, Philadelphia PA 19147 215-925-8406
Natl Cartoonists Soc, 9 Ebony Ct, Brooklyn NY 11229 718-743-6510
Natl Coalition Against Censorship, 132 W 43 St, New York NY 10036....212-944-9899
Natl Conf of Editorial Writers, 6223 Executive, Rockville MD 20854.......301-984-3015
Natl Entertainment Journalists, PO Box 24021, Nashville TN 37202........615-327-9419
Natl Federation of Press Women, Box 99, Blue Springs MO 64015 816-229-1666
Natl Organization for Women, 1401 New York Ave, Wash DC 20005......202-347-2279
Natl Press Club, 529 14th St NW, Washington DC 20045............................202-662-7500
Natl Soc of Newspaper Columnists, PO Box 6955, Louisville KY 40206...502-426-3943
Natl Writers Club (NWC), 1450 S Havana Ste 620, Aurora CO 80012......303-751-7844
NWC Honolulu Chap, PO Box 123, Honolulu HI 96810................................808-536-7901
NWC Seattle Chap, PO Box 55522, Seattle WA 98155.................................206-367-5413
NWC Texoma Chap, 929 S Crockett, Sherman TX 75090.............................214-892-4966
Natl Writers Union, 13 Astor Place, New York NY 10003 212-254-0279
Nebraska Writers Guild, 4111 Gertie, Lincoln NE 68516............................402-488-9263
Network of Ind Publishers, 86-07 144th St, Briarwood NY 11435 718-297-5053
New England Booksellers Assn, PO Box 486, Brookline Vlg MA 02147...617-734-6322
New Mexico Book League, 8632 Horacio Pl, Albuquerque NM 87111.......505-299-8940
New Orleans Writers Netwk, 2115 S Carrollton F, New Orlns LA 70118..504-866-8243
NY Regional Booksellers Assn, 3721 Riverdäle, Bronx NY 10463.............212-796-3119
NY Rights & Permissions Group, 750 3rd Ave, New York NY 10017.......212-850-7048
Newsletter Assn, 1341 G St NW #700, Washington DC 20005 202-347-5220
Newswomen's Club of NY, 15 Gramercy Park S, New York NY 10003......212-777-1610
North Texas Romance Writers, 1203 Pebble Creek, Euless TX 76040......817-268-1203
N Calif Book Publicists Assn, 1 Hallidie Plz, San Francisco CA 94102.....415-777-7240
N Calif Booksellers Assn, 2454 Telegraph Ave, Berkeley CA 94704..........415-845-9033
Okla Ind Booksellers Assn, 12100 N May, Okla City OK 73120.................405-755-0020
Oklahoma Writers Federation, PO Box 96054, Weatherford OK 73096...405-772-2878
Oregon Assn of Christian Writers, 2495 Maple NE, Salem OR 97303 503-364-9574
Oregon State Poetry Assn, 608 Lake Bay Ct, Lake Oswego OR 97034......503-636-1816
Outdoor Writers Assn, 2017 Cato #101, State College PA 16801..............814-234-1011
Overseas Press Club, 52 E 41st St, New York NY 10017.............................212-679-9650
Ozark Writers & Artists Guild, Crowder College, Neosho MO 64850 417-451-3226
Pacific Arts & Letters, PO Box 640394, San Francisco CA 94164 415-771-3431
Pacific NW Booksellers Assn, Box 1931, Mt Vernon WA 98273 206-336-3345
PEN American Center, 568 Broadway, New York NY 10012......................212-334-1660
PEN Los Angeles Center, 1227 4th St, Santa Monica CA 90401 213-395-0977
Philadelphia Publishers Group, PO Box 42681, Phila PA 19101...............215-732-1863

Philadelphia Writers' Organization, 3618 Hamilton St, Phila PA 19104...215-387-4950
Phoenix Writer's Service, 57 Main St, Littlefork MN 56653 218-278-6626
Poetry Soc of Amer, 15 Gramercy Park, New York NY 10003....................212-254-9628
Poets & Writers Inc, 201 W 54th St, New York NY 10019 212-757-1766
Press Club of Dallas, 400 S Houston, Dallas TX 75202 214-748-3329
Professional Writers League, 473 E 55th St #3, Long Beach CA 90805 ...213-423-0042
Public Relations Soc of Amer, 845 3rd Ave, New York NY 10022 212-826-1757
Publication Services Guild, 325 Brooks Ave NE, Atlanta GA 30307.........404-378-0888
Publishers Assn of the South, PO Box 22433, Nashville TN 37202 615-352-4473
Publ Mktg Assn, 2401 Pac Coast Hwy #206, Hermosa Bch CA 90254......213-372-2732
Publishers Publicity Assn, 125 E 23rd St, New York NY 10010 212-777-1187
Religion Newswriters Assn, 801 Texas Ave, Houston TX 77002..................713-220-7171
Rocky Mtn Book Publ Assn, Univ of NM Press, Albuq NM 87131 505-277-2346
Romance Writers of Amer (RWA), 5206 FM 1960, Houston TX 77069.....713-440-6885
RWA Alabama, 116 Louise Ave, Gadsen AL 35903 205-442-1924
RWA Alaska, 1065 Cherry, Anchorage AK 99504.......................................907-333-1235
RWA Arkansas, 4306 Atchison, Springdale AR 72764 501-751-6234
RWA Austin, 2311 Indian Tr, Austin TX 78703...512-474-4508
RWA Bakersfield, Star Rt 1 Box 2330B, Tehachapi CA 93561....................805-822-3146
RWA Central Florida, 7 Quail Dr Rt 2 Box 475, Lake Lake FL 32659......317-753-4613
RWA Central Michigan, 215 Elm Ave, Caledonia MI 49316.....................616-891-1113
RWA Central Valley, 1178 E Sierra, Fresno CA 93710................................209-439-3008
RWA Chicago North, 429 S Clifton, Park Ridge IL 60068 312-696-4479
RWA Colorado, 10997 N Ash Way, Thornton CO 80233............................303-457-2296
RWA Columbus, 6800 State Rt 323, Mt Sterling OH 43143 614-869-2477
RWA Connecticut, 184 D Oak Grove St, Manchester CT 06040.................203-646-0155
RWA Cumberland Valley, 70 Beecherstown, Biglerville PA 17307.............717-677-9655
RWA Delaware, Rt 2 Box 796, Felton DE 19943 302-284-3341
RWA Detroit, 46604 Jonathan Cir, Utica MI 48087 313-254-4755
RWA East Texas, 1403 N Jackson, Palestine TX 75801...............................214-729-2665
RWA Georgia, 2098 Mulkey Rd, Marietta GA 30060 404-941-9568
RWA Heart & Scroll, 510 E Mulberry, Bloomington IL 61701 309-828-0946
RWA Houston Bay, 15703 Cavendish, Houston TX 77059...........................713-486-7568
RWA Hudson Valley, 36 Idlewild Ave, Cornwall-Hudson NY 12520 914-534-2231
RWA Indiana, 278 E 350 S, Danville IN 46122 317-696-4479
RWA Inland Empire, E 2221 Diamond, Spokane WA 99207......................509-489-7176
RWA Inland Valley, 11079 Mars Pl, Mira Loma CA 91752 714-681-5392
RWA Kansas City, 4128 Walnut #3S, Kansas City MO 64111.....................913-756-0958
RWA Little Rock, 331 Charles St, Little Rock AR 72205 501-663-0464
RWA Los Angeles, 970 N Palm Ave #305, West Hollywood CA 90069.....213-659-2778
RWA Maryland, 3342 Chesterfield, Baltimore MD 21213 301-483-9429
RWA Mass-NH, 16 Edwards Rd, Foxboro MA 02035 617-543-6565
RWA Miami, 12725 SW 94th Ct, Miami FL 33176 305-255-4415
RWA Mississippi, 206 Ford Ave, Hattiesburg MS 39401............................601-264-8277
RWA Missouri, 1107 Drayton Ave, Webster Groves MO 63119....................314-961-8813
RWA Montana, PO Box 212, Dillon MT 59725 405-683-4539
RWA Nebraska, 517 S 51st Ave, Omaha NE 68106 402-556-2405
RWA New Jersey, 208 Dogwood, Edgewater Park NJ 08010 609-387-1975
RWA New Orleans, 5835 Paris Ave, New Orleans LA 70122.......................504-283-7766
RWA New York City, 88-28 75th Ave, Glendale NY 11385........................718-897-9129
RWA North Canton, 7384 Rolling Ridge NE, N Canton OH 44721...........216-492-7332
RWA North Carolina, 601 Burton Ln, Denver NC 28037 704-483-5191
RWA North Central, 4216 Powderhorn Cir, Minnetonka MN 55345.........612-474-3615

RWA North Texas, 3817 Yellowstone, Irving TX 75063 214-255-0316
RWA Northern Louisiana, PO Box 688, Benton LA 71006 318-965-2605
RWA NW Florida, 5801 Thomas Dr #1411, Panama City Bch FL 32407..904-235-7820
RWA NW Houston, 17003 N Ivy Cir, Houston TX 77084............................713-463-4821
RWA Ohio, 2502 Noble Rd #1, Cleveland Hts OH 44121 216-381-7355
RWA Orange County, PO Box 395, Yorba Linda CA 92686 213-439-5463
RWA Panhandle, 2803 Ridgemere, Amarillo TX 79107............................806-376-4370
RWA Peninsula, 880 NW Hogan Ln, Bremerton WA 98310 206-692-9676
RWA Phoenix, 1109 E Carmen, Tempe AZ 85283 602-838-3659
RWA Portland-Vancouver, 2427 NE Saratoga, Portland OR 97211...........503-282-5101
RWA Quad Cities, 109 14th Ave, Moline IL 61265 309-762-1484
RWA Rhode Island, 44 4th St, Attleboro MA 02703...................................617-222-6002
RWA Richmond Virginia, Rt 3 Box 343-A, Emporia VA 23847 804-634-6418
RWA Sacramento, 1433 Elsdon Cir, Carmichael CA 95608 916-482-6660
RWA Salt Lake, 416 E 3075 N, Ogden UT 84404......................................801-782-8336
RWA San Antonio, 6061 Kinman, San Antonio TX 78238 512-684-4126
RWA San Diego, 6760 Bonnie View Dr, San Diego CA 92119....................619-466-9646
RWA San Francisco, 293 Casper Pl, San Ramon CA 94583......................415-828-3252
RWA San Luis Obispo, 129 Baker Ave, Shell Beach CA 93449..................805-656-2323
RWA Seattle, 16505 190th St NE, Woodinville WA 98072 206-788-2771
RWA South Carolina, 2129 Lyndale Dr S, Hartsville SC 29550................803-383-5406
RWA South Chicago, 1507 Burnham, Calumet City IL 60409 312-646-2530
RWA Southern Idaho, 886 Capri Dr, Twin Falls ID 83301......................208-733-2522
RWA Southwest Ohio, 1028 Arrowhead Dr, Oxford OH 45056................513-523-8268
RWA Springfield, 1438 E Cairo, Springfield MO 65802............................417-866-1923
RWA Tacoma, 2123 Mountain View W, Tacoma WA 98466......................206-564-1607
RWA Tennessee, 802 Ashwood, Cattanooga TN 37415 615-875-9450
RWA Triangle, 2517 Howard Rd, Raleigh NC 27612 919-846-7250
RWA Tucson, 4547 N Placita de las Chacres, Tucson AZ 86718................602-299-9140
RWA Washington, 1325 8th St NW #310, Washington DC 20036..............202-662-7259
RWA West Houston, 212 Benbrook Dr, Houston TX 77079 713-694-2523
RWA Western Carolina, 102 Shady Oaks Dr, Asheville NC 28803............704-274-3988
RWA Western Pennsylvania, RD 1 Box 1750, Leechburg PA 15656..........412-845-2969
RWA Willamette Valley, 5911 NW Pinewood Pl, Corvallis OR 97330........503-753-0349
RWA Wisconsin, 210 Wilson St, Mt Horeb WI 53572 608-437-4353
San Diego Booksellers Assn, PO Box 1908, San Diego CA 92112............619-454-4443
San Diego Writers Workshop, 8431 Beaver Lake, San Diego CA 92119...609-462-5847
San Diego Writers/Editors Guild, PO Box 22735, San Diego CA 92122..619-449-0968
San Francisco Press Club, 555 Post St, San Francisco CA 94102............415-775-7800
Science Fiction Research Assn, Kent State Univ, Kent OH 44242 216-673-9164
Science Fiction Writers of Amer, Box 27, Hatfield MA 01038 413-247-5016
Geo Bernard Shaw Soc, PO Box 1373, New York NY 10163 212-989-7833
Sigma Delta Chi, 53 W Jackson, Chicago IL 60604...................................312-922-7424
Soc for Scholarly Publishing, 2000 Florida Ave NW, Wash DC 20009......202-328-3555
Soc for Technical Communication, 815 15th St NW, Wash DC 20005 202-737-0035
Soc of Amer Bus Editors, Univ of Missouri, Columbia MO 65211 314-882-7862
Soc of Amer Travel Writers, 1120 Conn Ave NW, Wash DC 20036...........202-785-5567
Soc of Author's Representatives, PO Box 650, New York NY 10113.........212-228-9740
Soc of Children's Book Writers, PO Box 296, Los Angeles CA 90066.......818-347-2849
SCBW Rocky Mtn Chapter, 178 Emerald St, Broomfield CO 80020.........303-466-1678
Soc of Illustrators, 128 E 63rd St, New York NY 10021 212-838-2560
Soc of Midland Authors, 333 N Michigan, Chicago IL 60601......................312-332-3984
Soc of Professional Journalists, 53 W Jackson, Chicago IL 60604............312-922-7424

Soc of Southwestern Authors, PO Box 41897, Tucson AZ 85717 602-325-0529
Software Publishers Assn, 1111 19th St #1200, Washington DC 20036 202-364-0523
Southeast Booksellers Assn, 1315 E Northside Dr, Jackson MS 39211 601-362-4018
Southeastern Writers Assn, 4021 Gladesworth Ln, Decatur GA 30035 404-288-2064
Southwest Booksellers Assn, 6531 Ridgeview Cir, Dallas TX 75240 214-239-5761
Southwest Christian Writers' Assn, Box 2635, Farmington NM 87401 505-325-3240
Special Libraries Assn, 1700 18th St NW, Washington DC 20009..............202-234-4700
St Louis Writers Guild, PO Box 7245, St Louis MO 63177 314-997-3057
Teachers & Writers Collab, 5 Union Sq W, New York NY 10003 212-691-6590
Texas Assn Creative Writing Teachers, MSU, Wichita Falls TX 76309 817-692-6611
Texas Publishers Assn, 2315 Briarwood, San Antonio TX 78209 512-828-1605
Toledo Poets Center, UH 5070C Univ of Toledo, Toledo OH 43606.........419-537-2983
Translation Center, Columbia Univ Math Bldg, New York NY 10027......212-280-2305
Ukrainian Writers In Exile, 2 E 79th St, New York NY 10021 215-924-9147
Upper Midwest Booksellers Assn, PO Box 40034, St Paul MN 55104 612-333-0098
US Ski Writers Assn, 7 Kensington, Glen Falls NY 12801 518-793-1201
Wash Independent Writers, 733 15th St NW #220, Wash DC 20005 202-347-4973
Western Writers of Amer, 1753 Victoria, Sheridan WY 82801.................307-672-2079
Women In Communications, PO Box 9561, Austin TX 78766 512-346-9875
Women In Scholarly Publ, Indiana Univ Press, Bloomington IN 47405....812-335-5429
Women Writers West, PO Box 1637, Santa Monica CA 90406 213-398-1620
Women's Natl Book Assn, 160 5th Ave, New York NY 10010..................212-675-7804
Writer's Guild of Amer E, 555 W 57th St #1230, New York NY 10019....212-245-6180
Writer's Guild of Amer W, 8955 Beverly Blvd, Los Angeles CA 90048......213-550-1000
Writers Alliance, Box 2014, Setauket NY 11733................................516-751-7080
Writers: Free-Lance Inc, 12 Cavalier Dr, Ambler PA 19002 215-646-7550

BIBLIOGRAPHERS

Alternative Research, PO Box 432, New York NY 10015 212-683-3478
The Author's Friend, 160 W 71st St Apt 11E, New York NY 10023............212-877-1510
Bibliographical Soc of Amer, PO Box 397, New York NY 10163 718-638-7957
The Bookmill, 3610 Moore St, Los Angeles CA 90066 213-398-4645
The Bookworks Inc, PO Box 1189, Chicago IL 60690................................312-236-8472
Richard Carlin, 25 Oleander Ct, Lawrenceville NJ 08648 609-896-4465
Catologing Distribution Service, Library of Congress, Wash DC 20541 ...202-287-6100
E R Cole, PO Box 91277, Cleveland OH 44101.......................................216-234-1775
Nancy L Daniels, Box 68, Lemont PA 16851..814-237-7711
Data Research, 9 Prairie Ave, Suffern NY 10901 914-357-8215
Valerie Eads Et Al, Box 1459 Grand Central Sta, New York NY 10016....212-228-0900
Editing & Publishing Services, Pleasant Point Rd, Cushing ME 04563.....207-354-2467
Editorial & Graphic Services, Martinsville NJ 08836................................201-469-2195
Editorial Consultants Inc, 1605 12th Ave Ste #7, Seattle WA 98122........206-323-6475
Editorial Consultation Services, 2427 29th St, Lubbock TX 79411 806-793-0881
Janice J Feldstein Editorial Svcs, 860 N Lake Shore, Chicago IL 60611...312-951-6215
Norman Frankel, 5116 Wright Ter, Skokie IL 60077................................312-674-8417
Free Lance Exchange Inc, 111 E 85th St, New York NY 10028 212-722-5816
Harkavy Publishing Service, 33 W 17th St, New York NY 10011...............212-929-1339
Hendershot Individ Instruct, 4114 Ridgewood, Bay City MI 48706...........517-684-3148
Daniel W Hill, 3023 Honeysuckle Way N E, Salem OR 97303 503-364-9210
Information on Demand Inc, PO Box 9550, Berkeley CA 94709 415-644-4500

Frances Kianka, 2352 Generation Dr, Reston VA 22091 703-860-5115
L/A House Editorial, 5822 Uplander Way, Culver City CA 90230.............213-216-5812
Lazy Brown Assoc, 2800 Quebec St NW Ste 618, Washington DC 20008..202-686-0975
Lombardi Indexing & Info Svcs, 2900 Sandy Ln, Santa Cruz CA 95062....408-476-1131
Mount Ida Press, Box 87, Troy NY 12181...518-272-4597
Natl Evaluation Systems, 30 Gatehouse Rd, Amherst MA 01004...............413-256-0444
Lois Newman, 6545 Hollywood Blvd #201, Hollywood CA 90028................213-464-8382
Professional Editing & Typing, 410 E 20th St 3A, New York NY 10009...212-477-0615
Generosa Gina Protano, 16 N Chatsworth #104, Larchmont NY 10538...914-834-8896
Publishers Editorial Services, 23 McQueen St, Katonah NY 10536 914-232-7816
Publishers Workshop Inc, 63 Montague St, Brooklyn Hts NY 11201........718-855-1525
Reitt Editing Services, 3505 Hampton Hall Way, Atlanta GA 30319.........404-255-5790
Carol Z Rothkopf, 16 Rotary Ln, Summit NJ 07901 201-273-1255
C J Scheiner Books, 275 Linden Blvd Apt B2, Brooklyn NY 11226 718-469-1089
Sherwin Assoc, 2616 N Dayton, Chicago IL 60614 312-935-1581
Jean M Shirhall, 2700 N Norwood St, Arlington VA 22207 703-528-2617
SSR Incorporated, 116 4th St SE, Washington DC 20003............................202-543-1800
Elizabeth Peirce Swift, Pleasant Point Rd, Cushing ME 04563.................207-354-2467
M A Timmons Comm Svcs, 555 Evening St, Worthington OH 43085........614-846-2887
Vance Bibliographies, 112 N Charter PO Box 229, Monticello IL 61856...217-762-3831
Walking Bird Publication Services, PO Box 19499, Seattle WA 98109 206-285-1575
Western Reserve Publ Services, 1640 Franklin Ave, Kent OH 44240........216-673-2577
Eleanor B Widdoes, 417 W 120th St, New York NY 10027 212-686-1100
Wizards Bookshelf, PO Box 6600, San Diego CA 92106................................619-235-0340
Wordsworth Assoc, 9 Tappan Rd, Wellesley MA 02181 617-237-4761
Wordsworth Communication, PO Box 9781, Alexandria VA 22304 703-642-8775
The Writing Service, 315 W 102nd St Ste 7B, New York NY 10025...........212-866-5930

BOOK CLUBS

Advertising Mktg & Sales Club, Middle Island NY 11953 516-924-8555
AIMS Intl Books, 3216 Montana Ave, Cincinnati OH 45211 513-661-9200
Amer Life Foundation, PO Box 349, Watkins Glen NY 14891....................607-535-4737
The America Press, 106 W 56th St, New York NY 10019 212-581-4640
Jason Aronson Book Clubs, 230 Lexington, Northvale NJ 07647 201-767-4093
Arrow Book Club, 730 Broadway, New York NY 10003................................212-505-3000
ASI Book Clubs, 63 W 38th St #505, New York NY 10018...........................212-719-2919
Augsburg Reading Club, 426 S 5th St, Minneapolis MN 55440...................612-330-3319
Automobile Quarterly Publications, Box 348, Kutztown PA 19530...........215-683-8352
Better Homes & Gardens, 750 3rd Ave, New York NY 10017 212-557-6600
Birding Book Society, 382 Main St, Salem NH 03079.................................603-898-1200
Book Club for Poetry, Avery Rd, Francestown NH 03043 603-547-6622
Book Club Northwest, Box 66344, Seattle WA 98166 206-824-5996
Book of the Month Club, 485 Lexington Ave, New York NY 10017 212-867-4300
Books of Light, 4082 Clotts Rd, Columbus OH 43230.................................614-471-1163
Catholic Digest Book Club, 815 2nd Ave, New York NY 10017 212-867-9766
Century Book Club, 1560 N La Brea Ave, Los Angeles CA 90028..............213-466-8989
Christian Herald Assn, 40 Overlook Dr, Chappaqua NY 10514 914-769-9000
Cinema Book Society, 8344 Melrose Ave, Hollywood CA 90069 213-933-3345
Classics Club, Flower Hill, Roslyn NY 11576..516-627-4920
Conservative Book Club, 15 Oakland Ave, Harrison NY 10528 914-835-0900

Cookery Book Club, PO Box 768, Port Washington NY 11050 516-883-2227
Crittenden Books, Box 1150, Novato CA 94948 415-883-8771
Crown Publ Book Clubs, 225 Park Ave S, New York NY 10003................212-254-1600
Dance Book Club, PO Box 109, Princeton NJ 08540....................................609-737-8178
Designers Book Club, 475 Park Ave S, New York NY 10016.....................212-636-0555
Doubleday Book Clubs, 245 Park Ave, New York NY 10167.......................212-984-7561
ECA Assoc, PO Box 15004, Chesapeake VA 23320.....................................804-547-5542
Ecological Book Club, 6 N Water St, Greenwich CT 06830.......................203-531-7755
Episcopal Book Club, Box 153, Shrewsbury NJ 07701................................212-355-6100
Erotic Art Book Society, 251 W 57th St, New York NY 10019.....................212-581-2000
Far East Book Society, 168 State St, Teaneck NJ 07666................................212-564-4099
Fraggle Rock Book Club, 245 Long Hill Rd, Middletown CT 06457..........203-638-2400
Garden Book Club, 250 W 57th St, New York NY 10107 212-757-8070
Grolier Book Clubs Inc, 380 Madison Ave, New York NY 10017...............212-687-3000
Guideposts Books, 757 3rd Ave, New York NY 10017..................................212-371-6060
Harcourt Brace Jovanovich, 40 Guernsey St, Stamford CT 06904 203-359-4250
Herald Book Club, 1434 W 51st St, Chicago IL 60609................................312-254-4462
Irish-American Book Society, Box A, Old Greenwich CT 06870.................203-531-7755
Jewelers Book Club, Chilton Way, Radnor PA 19089.................................215-964-4480
Judaica Book Club, 68-22 Eliot Ave, Middle Village NY 11379 718-456-8611
Karate & Self Defense Book Club, Middle Island NY 11953.......................516-924-8555
Le Cercle du Livre, 8000 Cooper Ave #29, Glendale NY 11385................718-326-0577
Library of Human Behavior Ltd, 59 Boston Post, Madison CT 06443 203-245-4000
Libro Club, PO Box 21231, Concord CA 94521..415-827-3609
Limited Editions Club, 551 5th Ave, New York NY 10017..........................212-682-7115
Macmillan Book Clubs Inc, 866 3rd Ave, New York NY 10022 212-702-2000
McGraw-Hill Book Co, 1221 Ave of Americas, New York NY 10020........212-512-2000
Media Books, Perrin Rd, Woodstock CT 06281..203-974-1050
Minister's Book Club, 4800 W Waco Dr, Waco TX 76796 817-772-7650
The Moretus Press Inc, 274 Madison Ave, New York NY 10016 212-685-2250
Mott Media Inc, 1000 E Huron St, Milford MI 48042.................................313-685-8773
Movie Book Club, 15 Oakland Ave, Harrison NY 10528 914-835-0900
Mystic Arts Book Society, 120 Enterprise Ave, Secaucus NJ 07094 201-866-0490
New Professional Chef Book Guild, 115 5th Ave, New York NY 10003 212-254-3232
North Amer Book Clubs Inc, 51 Washington St, Dover NH 03820 603-742-4662
North Light Book Club, 9933 Alliance Rd, Cincinnati OH 45242...............513-984-0717
Pathway Book Clubs, 382 Main St, Salem NH 03079...................................603-898-1200
Performing Arts Book Club, 27 Union Sq W, New York NY 10003 212-924-6666
Prentice-Hall Book Clubs, Englewood NJ 07631 201-592-2477
Religious Book Club, 5 S Buckhout St, Irvington NY 10533.......................914-591-6505
Rodale Press Book Clubs, 33 E Minor St, Emmaus PA 18049 215-967-5171
Scholastic Book Clubs, 730 Broadway, New York NY 10003......................212-505-3000
Semantodontics Inc, PO Box 15668, Phoenix AZ 85060 602-955-5662
TAB Books Inc, Blue Ridge Summit, PA 17214..217-794-2191
Thomas Moore Book Club, 223 W Erie St, Chicago IL 60610 312-951-2108
Times Mirror Book Clubs, 380 Madison Ave, New York NY 10017 212-687-3000
Troll Book Club, 320 Rt 17, Mahwah NY 07430 201-529-4000
Watson-Guptill Book Clubs, 1515 Broadway, New York NY 10036 212-764-7300
Weekly Reader Book Club, 245 Long Hill Rd, Middletown CT 06457.......203-638-2400
Writer's Digest Book Club, 9933 Alliance Rd, Cincinati OH 45242 513-984-0717

BOOK PRODUCERS

About Books Inc, PO Box 538, Saguache CO 81149 303-589-8223
Abrams Editorial/Design, 129 Sanford Ave, Emerson NJ 07630 201-262-4709
Acorn Graphics Publishers, Box 3192, Palmer PA 18043...........................215-253-8263
Amer Baby Books, 167 Old Post Rd, Southport CT 06490............................203-259-4700
Amer Book Producers Assn, 319 E 52nd St, New York NY 10022...............212-982-8934
Amer Library Publishing Co, PO Box 203, New York NY 10024.................212-362-1442
Antietam Press, Box 62, Boonsboro MD 21713...301-432-6906
ARCsoft Publishers, Box 132, Woodsboro MD 21798...................................301-845-8856
Arrow Connection, PO Box 899, Pollock Pines CA 95726..........................916-644-2341
Associated Features Inc, PO Box 1762, New York NY 10156.....................212-889-4808
Avalon Communications Inc, 1705 Broadway, Hewlett NY 11557..............516-599-4555
Barnes Publishing, 1-1434 Nebo Pl, Ft Ann NY 12827 518-793-4791
Bascom Communications Co, 399 E 72nd St 8A, New York NY 10021 212-988-4212
Benjamin Co Inc, 1 Westchester Plaza, Elmsford NY 10523........................914-592-8088
Suzanne Bennett & Assoc, 251 5th Ave, New York NY 10016.....................212-686-6452
Bleecker St Assoc Inc, 88 Bleecker St, New York NY 10012........................212-677-4492
Book Creations Inc, Schillings Crossing Rd, Canaan NY 12029.................518-781-4171
Book Developers, 930 Forest Ave, Palo Alto CA 94301.................................415-325-2275
Bookmakers Inc, 298 E South St, Wilkers-Barre PA 18702..........................717-823-9183
Books from Magazines Inc, 44 Rt 25A Apt 415, Smithtown NY 11787.....516-979-0219
Boultinghouse & Boultinghouse, 153 E 30th St, New York NY 10016 212-679-7950
BSP Publishing, 111 Marshall St Box 1968, Mankato MN 56001................507-387-6640
Calderon Press Inc, 223 E 48th St, New York NY 10017.............................212-753-3800
Carlisle Graphics, Box 285, Galena IL 61036 319-557-1500
Carnival Enterprises, 2437 Park Ave S, Minneapolis MN 55404................612-870-0169
Carpenter's Book Dev, 175 Delaware Plz #4602, Chicago IL 60611 312-787-3569
Chanticleer Press Inc, 424 Madison Ave, New York NY 10017 212-486-3900
James Charlton Associates, 680 Washington St, New York NY 10014......212-691-4951
Chernow Editorial Services Inc, 39 W 14th St, New York NY 10011 212-242-0178
Chestnut House Group Inc, 540 N Lake Shore Dr, Chicago IL 60611........312-222-9090
Lawrence Chilnick Assoc, 399 E 72nd St 12E, New York NY 10021..........212-737-9655
Dean Clark Publishers, Box 3192, Palmer PA 18043....................................215-253-8263
Cloverdale Press Inc, 133 5th Ave, New York NY 10003..............................212-420-1555
Columbia Publishing Co Inc, 234 E 25th St, Baltimore MD 21218.............301-366-7070
CompuThink Inc, 10394 Cheviot Dr, Los Angeles CA 90064.......................213-838-1760
Thomas Congdon Books Inc, 120 W 87th St, New York NY 10024 212-580-1032
Connexions, 14011 Brookgreen Dr, Dallas TX 75240..................................214-234-4519
Cracom Corp, 933 Gardenview Office Pkwy, St Louis MO 63141...............314-997-1079
Create-A-Craft, PO Box 330008, Fort Worth TX 76163................................817-292-1855
Critique, PO Box 11368, Santa Rosa CA 95406..707-525-9401
Custom Editorial Productions, 3220 Jefferson, Cincinnati OH 45220........513-281-2374
Steve Davis Publishing, PO Box 190831, Dallas TX 75219.........................214-823-8660
Donovan Gosney, 3659 Nassau Dr, San Diego CA 92115............................619-287-7816
East Chelsea Press, 43 W 16th St Ste 5D, New York NY 10011..................212-989-1775
Editing Design & Prod Inc, 400 Market St, Philadelphia PA 19106...........215-592-1133
The Editorial Guild Inc, Box 594, Katonah NY 10536 914-232-7816
Effective Learning Inc, 7 N MacQuesten Pkwy, Mt Vernon NY 10550.....914-664-7944
Peter Elek Assoc, PO Box 223 Canal St Sta, New York NY 10013.............212-431-9368

ETC Associates, 507 Rider Rd, Clayville NY 13322......................................813-288-4821
First Editions, PO Box 1158, Sedona AZ 86336...602-282-1989
Footnote Productins Ltd, 20 W 20th St, New York NY 10011 212-929-5400
The Four Corners Press, 2056 College SE, Grand Rapids MI 49507.........616-243-2015
Eleanor Friede Books Inc, 45 W 12th St, New York NY 10011 212-741-2900
Michael Friedman Publ Group, 15 W 26th St, New York NY 10010.........212-685-6610
Helena Frost Assoc, 301 E 21st St, New York NY 10010 212-475-6642
Futura Media Services Inc, Box 30, Mount Kisco NY 10549 914-666-3505
G&H/Soho Ltd, 39 W 14th St, New York NY 10011..................................212-685-5444
Gabriel House Inc, 5045 W Oakton St Ste 7, Skokie IL 60077 312-675-1146
Gains & Harris Inc, 260 5th Ave, New York NY 10001.............................212-758-1396
Gelles-Cole Literary Ent, 424 E 52nd St 7B, New York NY 10022............212-758-1396
General Communications Co, 720 W 8th St, Los Angeles CA 90017.........213-689-2146
The K S Giniger Co Inc, 235 Park Ave S, New York NY 10003..................212-533-5080
Walter Glanze Word Books, 280 Riverside Dr, New York NY 10025.........212-666-6993
The Glusker Group Inc, 154 W 57th St, New York NY 10019 212-757-4438
Gousha/Chek-Chart, 2001 The Alameda, San Jose CA 95150 408-296-1060
Graphic Design Studio, 108 John St, N Massapequa NY 11758 516-293-0735
Gravity Publishing, 6324 Heather Ridge Way, Oakland CA 94611...........415-339-3774
Green Spring Inc, Box 999, Sharon CT 06069...203-364-0681
Grunwald & Radcliff Publ, 5049 Adm Wright #344, Va Bch VA 23462...804-490-1132
Guinness Productions, 655 Redwood #200, Corte Madera CA 99941......415-381-1111
Henson Assoc Inc, 117 E 69th St, New York NY 10021 212-794-2400
Heritage Books, 1445 E 2nd St, Plainfield NJ 07061 201-753-4000
Hopkinson & Blake Publ, 1001 Ave of Americas, New York NY 10018 ...212-354-8877
The Hudson Group Inc, 74 Memorial Plaza, Pleasantville NY 10570........914-769-8030
Hyst'ry Myst'ry House, 1 Brush Ct, Garnerville NY 10923 914-947-3141
Imago Imprint Inc, 150 5th Ave, New York NY 10011...............................212-620-3140
Inprint Designs, 10041 Conway Rd, St Louis MO 63124 314-993-4843
Intentional Eductions, 341 Mt Auburn St, Watertown MA 02172..............617-923-7707
Intervisual Comm, 6151 W Century Blvd #400, Los Angeles CA 90045...213-649-0333
Keim Publishing Associates, 26 W 17th St 8th Fl, New York NY 10011...212-206-1442
Kirchoff Wohlberg Inc, 866 U N Plz #525, New York NY 10017 212-644-2020
Arvid Knudsen & Associates, 592 A Main St, Hackensack NJ 07601 201-488-7857
Ellen R Komisarow, 19 Curley St, Long Beach NY 11561 516-432-5517
George Kurian Reference Books, Box 519, Baldwin Place NY 10505 914-962-3287
Layla Productions, 310 E 44th St, New York NY 10017...............................212-697-6285
Sarah Lazin Books, 302 W 12th St 11B, New York NY 10014.....................212-675-0597
The Philip Lief Group Inc, 319 E 52nd St, New York NY 10022..................212-355-5958
Lucas/Evans Books, 1123 Broadway, New York NY 10010.........................212-929-2583
Manuscripts Intl, 408 E Main St, Dayton WA 99328.................................509-382-2436
MassMarket Books, 872 Mass Ave #1011, Cambridge MA 02139 617-864-2126
Maverick Publications, Drawer 5007, Bend OR 97708 503-382-6978
Media Projects Inc, 305 2nd Ave Ste 340, New York NY 10003.................212-777-4510
Mega-Books of New York Inc, 116 E 19th St, New York NY 10003..........212-589-0909
Microtrend Slawson Comm Inc, 3719 6th Ave, San Diego CA 92103........619-291-9126
Kenneth Milford, 50 E 86th St, New York NY 10028.................................212-410-1455
The Miller Press Inc, 54 W 39th St, New York NY 10018 212-354-0264
Hughes Miller Publ Projects, 115 5th Ave, New York NY 10003..............212-254-9269
Morningside Editorial Assoc, 74 Memorial Plz, Pleasantville NY 10570 ..914-769-8030
Lowell Moss Publ Svcs, 760 Market St #1036, San Francisco CA 94102 ..415-956-5966
Mount Ida Press, Box 87, Troy NY 12181...518-272-4597
Mountain Lion Inc, Box 257 Rt 206, Rocky Hill NJ 08553 609-924-8369

Nash & Zullo Productions Inc, Box 6218, W Palm Beach FL 33405..........305-833-8174
Ruth Nathan, 386 Park Ave S, New York NY 10016 212-685-0808
Nautilus Communicatons, 375 5th Ave, New York NY 10016 212-685-7007
Charles Neighbors, 7600 Blanco Rd Ste 3607, San Antonio TX 78216......512-342-5324
New England Publishing Assn, Box 5, Chester CT 06412........................203-345-4976
Newmarket Book Properties, 3 E 48th St, New York NY 10017...................212-832-3575
October Press Inc, 200 Park Ave S, Ste 1320, New York NY 10003...........212-477-1251
Omni Books, 1965 Broadway, New York NY 10023 212-496-6100
Ondine Press, Box 3355, Van Nuys CA 91407 818-781-4360
Optic Graphics Inc, 101 Dover Rd, Glen Burnie MD 21061....................301-768-3000
Orion Book Services, South St RFD 2 Box 11, W Brattleboro VT 05301..802-254-2340
Oswego Art Guild-Artifacts Press, Box 315, Oswego NY 13126..............315-342-3579
Ottenheimer Publishers, 300 Reisterstown Rd, Baltimore MD 21208......301-484-2100
OZ Editions Inc, 19992 NE 5th Ct, Miami Beach FL 33179.....................305-654-7484
Parachute Press Inc, 200 5th Ave Rm 461, New York NY 10010...............212-691-1421
Cynthia Parzych Publishing Inc, 648 Broadway, New York NY 10012.....212-529-1133
James Peter Associates Inc, Box 772, Tenafly NJ 07670 201-568-0760
Photo Editors Inc, 60 E 56th St, New York NY 10022..........................212-758-3420
Police Bookshelf, PO Box 122, Concord NH 03301...............................603-224-6814
Byron Preiss Visual Publ, 24 W 25th St, New York NY 10010 212-654-9870
Professional Media Services, 10 Victoria Vale, Monterey CA 93940.........408-375-5584
Promised Land Productions Inc, 20 E 31st St, New York NY 10016.........212-684-3905
Publication Services, 615 Kirby St, Champaign IL 61821........................217-398-2060
The Publisher's Resource, Box 164, Brookfield Ctr CT 06805 203-775-4219
Publishers Services, 6318 Vesper Ave, Van Nuys CA 91411....................818-785-8039
Publishing Resources Inc, Box 41307, San Juan PR 00940......................809-724-0318
Quinlan Press, 131 Beverly St, Boston MA 02114..................................617-227-4870
Ramsey & Associates, 208 N 8th St, Marshalltown IA 50158 515-754-2303
Redtree Assoc Inc, 1200 18th St NW #206, Washington DC 20036.........202-628-2900
Resource Publications Inc, 160 E Virginia St #290, San Jose CA 95112...408-286-8505
Roundtable Press Inc, 80 E 11st St, New York NY 10003.......................212-777-7940
Roxbury Publishing Co, PO Box 491044, Los Angeles CA 90049..............213-458-3493
Rutledge Books, 122 E 25th St, New York NY 10010 212-598-6976
Regina Ryan Publ Ent, 251 Central Park W, New York NY 10024............212-787-5589
Sachem Publishing Assoc, 2 Graves Ave, Guilford CT 06437..................203-453-4328
Sang Froid Press, PO Box 272, Excelsior MN 55331..............................612-553-1400
Science Tech Inc, 701 Ridge St, Madison WI 53705...............................608-238-8664
Settel Associates Inc, 11 Wimbledon Ct, Jericho NY 11753 516-681-1505
Smallwood & Stewart, 156 5th Ave Rm 1118, New York NY 10010 212-620-8144
Lynn Sonberg Book Services, 166 E 56th St, New York NY 10022...........212-758-9604
Spec Graph Corp, 637 Manchester Rd, Norristown PA 19403....................215-539-4530
Steam Press, 56 Commonwealth, Watertown MA 02172 617-923-1046
Stearn Publishers Ltd, 500 E 77th St Ste 1204, New York NY 10162.......212-737-9304
Isadore Stephanus Sons Publ, PO Box 6772, Ithaca NY 14851 607-272-0056
The Stonesong Press Inc, 200 Haines Rd, Bedford Hills NY 10507............212-750-1090
Strawtown Associates Inc, 9905 Doubletress Ct, Potomac MD 20854.......301-279-2027
Sun Words Books, Box A, Hurley NY 12443..914-331-0748
Taly Design Group Inc, 430 Oak Grove #408, Minneapolis MN 55403 612-871-8336
TFH Publications, 211 W Sylvania Ave, Neptune City NJ 07753 201-988-8400
Thompson & Co Inc, 1313 5th St SE Ste 301, Minneapolis MN 55414......612-722-4235
Tilden Press, 1737 De Sales St NW Ste 300, Washington DC 20036..........202-638-5855
Tompson & Rutter, Box 297 Dunbar Hill Rd, Grantham NH 03753 603-863-4392
Trafalgar House Publ, 663 5th Ave 6th fl, New York NY 10022................212-319-8899

Tree Communications Inc, 209 Oakridge Commons, S Salem NY 10590 .914-533-6181
2M Communications Ltd, 310 E 9th St, New York NY 10003 212-460-5172
Ultralight Publications Inc, PO Box 234, Hummelstown PA 17036..........717-566-0468
Laurence Urdang Inc, Box 668, Essex CT 06426.....................................203-767-8248
Wecksler Incomco, 170 West End Ave, New York NY 10023 212-787-2239
Fred Weidner & Son Printers Inc, 111 8th Ave, New York NY 10011 212-989-1070
Weidner Associates Inc, Box C-50, Cinnaminson NJ 08077.......................609-486-1755
Wieser & Wieser Inc, 118 E 25th St, New York NY 10010 212-260-0860
Wingra Woods Press, 33 Witherspoon St, Princeton NJ 08542....................609-683-1218
Wordsworth Assoc, 9 Tappan Rd, Wellesley MA 02181 617-237-4761
Betty Wright & Assoc, PO Box 1069, Moore Haven FL 33471....................813-946-0293
Writers' Service, Box 536, Summerland CA 93067.....................................805-969-6092

BOOK PUBLISHERS

An asterisk (*) indicates a firm publishing 6 or more titles per year.

101 Productions*, 834 Mission St, San Francisco CA 94103.......................415-495-6040
2 AM Publications, PO Box 50444, Chicago IL 60605 312-652-0013
7 C's Press Inc, Box 57, Riverside CT 06878...203-637-9625
A-R Editions Inc*, 315 W Gorham St, Madison WI 53703 608-251-2114
Aames-Allen Publishing, 1106 Main St, Huntington Beach CA 92648.......714-536-4926
AASLH Press, 172 2nd Ave N, Nashville TN 37201 615-225-2971
Aatec Publications, PO Box 7119, Ann Arbor MI 48107...........................313-995-1470
Abaris Books Inc*, 24 W 40th St, New York NY 10018.............................212-354-1313
Abattoir Editions, Univ of Nebraska Annex 22, Omaha NE 68182...........401-554-2787
Abbetira Publications, PO Box 32272, Tuscon AZ 85751 714-381-3837
Abbeville Press*, 488 Madison Ave, New York NY 10022.........................212-888-1969
Abbey Press*, St Meinrad IN 47577..812-357-8011
Abbott Langer & Assoc*, 548 1st St, Crete IL 60417 312-672-4200
Abbott Press, PO Box 433, Ridgefield NJ 07657.....................................201-943-4867
ABC CLIO*, 2040 Alameda Padre Serra, Santa Barbara CA 93140..........805-963-4221
Abingdon Press*, 201 8th Ave S, Nashville TN 37203.............................615-749-6403
Ablex Publishing Corp*, 355 Chestnut St, Norwood NJ 07648 201-767-8450
Abrahamson Publishing Co, 10164 Norell Ave, Stillwater MN 55082 612-439-2680
Harry N Abrams Inc*, 100 5th Ave, New York NY 10011.........................212-206-7715
Abraxas Publishing, 10245 Main St Ste 1, Bellevue WA 98004..................206-455-8608
Abt Books*, 55 Wheeler St, Cambridge MA 02138..................................617-492-7100
ACA Books, 570 7th Ave, New York NY 10018 212-354-6655
Acacia Books, PO Box 3650, Berkeley CA 94703 415-451-9559
Academic Press Inc*, 6277 Sea Harbor Dr, Orlando FL 32821 305-345-2000
Academic Therapy Publ, 20 Commercial Blvd, Novato CA 94947.............415-883-3314
Academy Chicago Publishers*, 425 N Michigan Ave, Chicago IL 60611...312-644-1723
Acadia Publishing Co, PO Box 170, Bar Harbor ME 04609.......................207-228-9025
Accelerated Development Inc*, 3400 Kilgore, Muncie IN 47304................317-284-7511
Accent Books*, 12100 W 6th Ave PO Box 15337, Denver CO 80215..........303-988-5300
Accent On Living, PO Box 700, Bloomington IL 61702.............................309-378-2961
Ace Science Fiction*, 200 Madison Ave, New York NY 10016...................212-686-9820
Aceto Bookmen, 5721 Antietam Dr, Sarasota FL 33581 813-924-9170
Acheron Press, Bear Creek at Kettle, Friendsville MD 21531....................301-746-5885
Achievement Press, Box 608, Sheridan WY 82801 307-672-8475

Acoma Books, Box 4, Ramona CA 92065 619-789-1288
Acropolis Books*, 2400 17th St NW, Washington DC 20009......................202-387-6805
ACS Publications Inc*, PO Box 16430, San Diego CA 92116 619-297-9203
Active Learning Corp, PO Box 254, New Paltz NY 12561 914-255-0844
ACU Press, 1634 Campus Ct, Abilene TX 79601.......................................915-674-2720
Ad-Lib Publications, 51 N 5th St, Fairfield IA 52556................................515-472-6617
Adama Books*, 306 W 38th St, New York NY 10018.................................212-594-5770
Adams Houmes & Ward*, 660 W Fairbanks, Winter Park FL 32789.........305-740-7359
Bob Adams Inc*, 840 Summer St, Boston MA 02127 617-268-9570
Adasta Press, 101 Strong St, Easthampton MA 01027 413-527-3324
Addison-Wesley Publishing Co*, 1 Jacob Way, Reading MA 01867 617-944-3700
Adirondack Mountain Club Inc, 174 Glen St, Glens Falls NY 12801 518-793-7737
Adler & Adler Publ*, 4550 Montgomery Ave, Bethesda MD 20814...........301-654-4271
Adler Publishing Co, PO Box 9342, Rochester NY 14604 716-377-5804
Admont Corp, PO Box 3148, Staunton VA 24401.......................................703-886-4777
Adonis Studio, PO Box 6626, Cleveland OH 44101 216-226-1058
Adventures Unlimited, Box 22, Stelle IL 60919 815-253-6390
Advocate Publishing Group*, PO Box 351, Reynoldsburg OH 43068........614-861-7738
Aegina Press*, 4937 Humphrey Rd, Huntington WV 25704.........................304-429-7204
Aero Publishers Inc*, 329 W Aviation Rd, Fallbrook CA 92028..................619-728-8456
Aesculapius Publishers Inc*, 10 W 66th St 6D, New York NY 10023 212-595-0558
Afcom Publishing, PO Box H, Harbor City CA 90710 213-326-7589
Affirmation Books, 22 The Fenway, Boston MA 02215................................617-266-8792
AFIPS Press, 1899 Preston White Dr, Reston VA 22091.............................703-620-8918
Africa Research & Publications, PO Box 1892, Trenton NJ 08608 609-695-3766
African Studies Assn*, 405 Hilgard Ave, Los Angeles CA 90024................213-206-8011
Africana Publishing Co*, 30 Irving Pl IUB Bldg, New York NY 10003 212-254-4100
AGT Publishing Inc*, 230 Park Ave, New York NY 10169 212-687-8155
Ahsahta Press, Boise State Univ English Dept, Boise ID 83725..................208-385-1246
AIAS Ltd, 600 N McClurg Ct Ste 2502A, Chicago IL 60611 312-337-5066
AIGA Publications, Box 148, Laie HI 96762 808-293-5277
Akiba Press, PO Box 13086, Oakland CA 94611 415-339-1283
Alamitos Health Publ, 3801 Katella Ave, Los Alamitos CA 90720.............213-598-9428
The Alaska Adventure Book, 200 W 34th Ave, Anchorage AK 99503........907-243-1286
Alaska Angler Publications, 520 5th Ave Ste 412, Fairbanks AK 99701 907-456-8212
Alaska Northwest Publishing Co*, 130 2nd Ave S, Edmonds WA 98020..206-774-4111
Alba House*, 2187 Victory Blvd, Staten Island NY 10314............................718-761-0047
The Alban Inst, 4125 Nebraska Ave NW, Washington DC 20016................202-244-7320
Alchemy Books*, 717 Market St Ste 514, San Francisco CA 94103.............415-777-2197
Alchemy II Inc*, 9207 Eton Ave, Chatsworth CA 91311 818-700-8300
Aldine Publishing Co*, 200 Saw Mill River Rd, Hawthorne NY 10532.....914-747-0110
Alegra House Publshersoks, PO Box 1443, Warren OH 44482 216-372-2951
Alert Publishers, PO Box 1208, Rancho Cucamonga CA 91730 714-980-4992
Alfred Publishing Co*, 15335 Morrison St, Sherman Oaks CA 91413 818-995-8811
Algonquin Books of Chapel Hill*, PO Box 2225, Chapel Hill NC 27515...919-933-2113
Alice James Books, 138 Mt Auburn St, Cambridge MA 02138 617-354-1408
Alive Publications Ltd, 11 Park Place, New York NY 10007........................212-962-0316
Allegheny Press, Box 220, Elgin PA 16413 814-664-8504
Alleluia Press, 672 Franklin Turnpike Box 103, Allendale NJ 07401..........201-327-3513
Allen & Unwin Inc*, 8 Winchester Pl, Winchester MA 01890.....................617-729-0830
Allyn & Bacon Inc*, 7 Wells Ave, Newton MA 02159 617-964-5530
Almar Press*, 4105 Marietta Dr, Binghamton NY 13903 607-722-6251
Alpenglow Press, Box 1841, Santa Maria CA 93456....................................805-928-4904

Alpha Publishing Co, 3497 E Livingston Ave, Columbus OH 43227..........614-231-4088
Alphabet Press*, 60 N Main St Box 645, Natick MA 01760..........................617-655-9696
Alpine Fine Arts Collection*, 164 Madison Ave, New York NY 10016 212-213-9393
Alpine Guild, PO Box 183, Oak Park IL 60303...312-386-3507
Alpine Publications*, 214 19th St SE, Loveland CO 80537.............................303-667-2017
Alta Napa Press, 1969 Mora Ave, Calistoga CA 94515 707-942-4444
Alyson Publications*, 40 Plympton St, Boston MA 02118 617-542-5679
AMACOM Book Division*, 135 W 50th St, New York NY 10020 212-586-8100
Amana Books, 58 Elliot St, Battleboro VT 05301...802-257-0872
Ambleside Publishers Inc, 2122 E Concorda, Tempe AZ 85282 602-967-3457
Amdulaine Publications, 5800 1 Perkins Pl Dr, Baton Rouge LA 70808...504-769-5599
Ameco Publishing Corp, 220 E Jericho Tpke, Mineola NY 11501 516-741-5030
Amen Publishing Co, PO Box 3612, Arcadia CA 91006 818-355-9336
American Alliance Publ*, 1900 Association Dr, Reston VA 22091 703-476-3400
The American Alpine Club, 113 E 90th St, New York NY 10128.................212-722-1628
American Artist Publishing, PO Box 12, Dixon KY 42409 502-249-3685
American Assn Parapsychology, PO Box 225, Canoga Park CA 91305 818-710-6925
Amer Assn State-Local History*, 172 2nd Ave N, Nashville TN 37201......615-383-5991
American Astronautical Society, PO Box 28130, San Diego CA 92128 619-746-4005
American Atheist Press*, PO Box 2117, Austin TX 78768 512-458-1244
American Baby Books*, 167 Old Post Rd, Southport CT 06490 203-259-4700
American Bar Foundation, 750 N Lake Shore Dr, Chicago IL 60611........312-988-5000
American Bible Society*, 1865 Broadway, New York NY 10023.................212-581-7400
Amer Business Consultants, 1540 Nuthatch Ln, Sunnyvale CA 94087 408-738-3011
American Canadian Publishers Inc, PO Box 4595, Santa Fe NM 87502...505-471-7863
American Chemical Society*, 1155 16th St NW, Washington DC 20036 ...202-872-4600
American Cooking Guild, 2915 Fenimore Rd, Silver Spring MD 20902....301-949-6787
Amer Council for Arts, 1285 Ave of Americas, New York NY 10018........212-245-4510
American Enterprise Inst*, 1150 17th St NW, Washington DC 20036 202-862-5800
American Federation of Arts, 41 E 65th St, New York NY 10021..............212-988-7700
American Gothic Press, 1223 Rosell Ave, Oak Park IL 60302 312-386-1366
American Heritage Publishing*, 60 5th Ave, New York NY 10011............212-206-5500
American Hospital Publishing*, 211 E Chicago Ave, Chicago IL 60611...312-440-6800
Amer Indian Studies*, Campbell Hall UCLA, Los Angeles CA 90024.....213-825-4777
American Inst of Aeronautics*, 1633 Broadway, New York NY 10019 212-581-4300
Amer Inst of Architects*, 1735 New York Ave NW, Wash DC 20006 202-626-7575
Amer Inst of Chemical Engineers*, 345 E 47th St, New York NY 10017..212-705-7338
Amer Inst of CPAs*, 1211 Ave of Americas, New York NY 10036 212-575-6200
American Inst of Physics*, 335 E 45th St, New York NY 10017..................212-661-9404
Amer Judicature Soc, 25 E Washington #1600, Chicago IL 60602 312-558-6900
American Law Institute*, 4025 Chestnut St, Philadelphia PA 19104..........215-243-1600
American Library Association*, 50 E Huron St, Chicago IL 60611 312-944-6780
American Library Publishing Co, PO Box 203, New York NY 10024.......212-362-1442
American Life Books, Box 349, Watkins Glen NY 14891.............................607-535-4737
Amer Machinist & Automated Mfg, 11 W 19th St, New York NY 10011..212-337-7942
American Malacologists, PO Box 2255, Melbourne FL 32902....................305-725-2260
American Map Corp*, 46-35 54 Rd, Maspeth NY 11378 718-784-0055
American Mathematical Society*, PO Box 6248, Providence RI 02940.....401-272-9500
Amer Mutuality Foundation, 9428 S Western, Los Angeles CA 91004 213-754-7761
American Philosophical Society*, 104 S 5th St, Philadelphia PA 19106 215-627-0706
American Poetry Assn*, PO Box 1803, Santa Cruz CA 95061....................408-429-1122
American Press*, 520 Commonwealth Ave, Boston MA 02215 617-247-0022
Amer Printing House for Blind*, PO Box 6085, Louisville KY 40206........502-895-2405

American Psychiatric Press, 1400 K St NW, Washington DC 20005.........202-682-6268
American References Inc, 919 N Michigan, Chicago IL 60611......................312-951-6200
American Reprints Co, PO Box 370, Modesto CA 95353.............................209-524-9789
Amer School of Classical Studies, Princeton NJ 08543................................609-734-8386
American Showcase Inc, 724 5th Ave, New York NY 10019......................212-245-0981
Amer Soc Training & Dev*, 1630 Duke St, Alexandria VA 22313..............703-683-8100
Amer Soc Clinical Pathologists*, 2100 W Harrison, Chicago IL 60612.....312-738-1336
Amer Soc Hosp Pharmacists*, 4630 Montgomery, Bethesda MD 20814..301-657-3000
Amer Soc Mechanical Engineers*, 345 E 47th St, New York NY 10017...212-705-7722
Amer Soc of Civil Engineers*, 345 E 47th St, New York NY 10017...........212-705-7510
American Solar Energy Society Inc, 2030 17th St, Boulder CO 80302.......303-443-3130
American Studies Press Inc, 13511 Palmwood Ln, Tampa FL 33624.........813-961-7200
American Technical Publishers, 12235 S Laramie Ave, Alsip IL 60658.....312-371-9500
Amima Publications, 1053 Wilson Ave, Chambersburg PA 17201............717-263-8303
Ampersand Press, Roger Williams College, Bristol RI 02809.....................401-253-1040
Amphoto*, 1515 Broadway, New York NY 10036.....................................212-764-7441
AMS Press Inc*, 56 E 13th St, New York NY 10003......................................212-777-4700
Amsco School Publishing Inc*, 315 Hudson St, New York NY 10013.......212-675-7000
Anaheim Publishing Co Inc*, 2632 Saturn St Box 9600, Brea CA 92622...714-993-3700
The Analytic Press*, 365 Broadway Ste 102, Hillsdale NJ 07642.................201-666-4110
Ancestry Inc*, PO Box 476, Salt Lake City UT 84110.................................801-531-1790
Anchorage Press Inc*, PO Box 8067, New Orleans LA 70182.....................504-283-8868
Ancient City Press, PO Box 5401, Santa Fe NM 87502...............................505-982-8195
And Books, 702 S Michigan, South Bend IN 46618....................................219-232-3134
And/Or Press Inc, PO Box 522, Berkeley CA 94701...................................415-548-2124
Anderson Publishing Co*, 602 Main St, Cincinnati OH 45201 513-421-4393
Andrews & McMeel*, 4900 Main St, Kansas City MO 64112....................816-932-6700
Androgyne Books, 930 Shields, San Francisco CA 93132...........................415-586-2697
Andujar Communication Technologies, Box 2622, La Jolla CA 92038......714-459-2673
Angelstone Press, 316 Woodland Dr, Birmingham AL 35209....................205-870-7281
Annual Reviews Inc*, 4139 El Camino Way, Palo Alto CA 94306............415-493-4400
ANR Publications, Univ of CA 6701 San Pablo Ave, Oakland CA 94608..415-642-2431
Answers Period Inc, PO Box 72666, Corpus Christi TX 78472.....................512-852-8927
Anthony Press, PO Box 3722, Alhambra CA 91803.....................................213-948-8620
Anthroposophic Press*, 258 Hungry Hollow, Spring Valley NY 10977.....914-352-2295
Antler Books, 650 Market St, San Francisco CA 94104................................415-392-7378
Aperture*, 20 E 23rd St, New York NY 10010...212-505-5555
Appalachian Consortium Press*, Appalachian Univ, Boone NC 28608....704-262-2064
Appalachian Mountain Club Books, 5 Joy St, Boston MA 02108..............617-523-0636
Appalachian Trail Conference, PO Box 807, Harpers Ferry WV 25425....304-535-6331
Apple Island Books, Box 276, Shapleigh ME 04076....................................207-324-9453
Apple Press, 5536 SE Harlow, Milwaukie OR 97222..................................503-653-0895
Appleton & Lange*, 25 Van Zant St, E Norwalk CT 06855.......................203-838-4400
Applezaba Press, PO Box 4134, Long Beach CA 90804.............................213-591-0015
Applied Computer Science, 7350 W College Dr, Palos Hts IL 60463.........312-448-0837
Applied Publishing, 3402 Columbus Ave S, Minneapolis MN 55407 612-822-1998
April Publications Inc*, PO Box 1000, Staten Island NY 10314 212-713-5322
Aquamaps Inc, PO Box 417, Denver CO 80201..303-629-6111
Arbor House*, 105 Madison Ave, New York NY 10016...............................212-481-0350
Architectural Book Publishing*, 268 Dogwood Ln, Stamford CT 06903...203-322-1460
Architectural History Found, 350 Madison Ave, New York NY 10017.....212-557-8441
Arcline Publications, PO Box 1550, Pomona CA 91769...............................415-644-3229
Arco Publishing Inc*, 215 Park Ave S, New York NY 10003......................212-777-6300

ARCsoft Publishers*, Box 132, Woodsboro MD 21798.............................301-845-8856
Arcturus Publishing Inc, Cherry Hill NJ 08034......................................609-428-3863
Ardis Publishers*, 2901 Heatherway, Ann Arbor MI 48104 313-971-2367
Arena Lettres*, 8 Lincoln Pl Box 219, Waldwick NJ 07463.....................201-445-7154
Ares Publishers Inc*, 7020 N Western Ave, Chicago IL 60645.................312-743-1405
Argus Communications, 1 DLM Park, Allen TX 75002.............................214-248-6300
Ariel Press*, 3391 Edenbrook Ct, Columbus OH 43220 614-876-0211
The Aries Press Inc, PO Box 30081, Chicago IL 60630 312-725-8300
The Arion Press, 460 Bryant St, San Francisco CA 94107.........................415-777-9651
Aris Books, 1621 5th St, Berkeley CA 94710 415-527-5171
Arista Corp*, 2 Park Ave, New York NY 10016 212-686-6540
Arkham House Publishers Inc, Box 546, Sauk City WI 53583 608-643-4500
M Arman Publishing Inc, PO Box 785, Ormond Beach FL 32074 904-673-5576
Armenian Numismatic Soc*, 8511 Beverly Pk, Pico Rivera CA 90660 213-695-0390
Jason Aronson Inc*, 230 Livingston St, Northvale NJ 07647....................201-767-4093
Arriaga Publications, PO Box 652, Booneville AR 72927...........................501-675-3478
Arrowhead Press, 3005 Fulton, Berkeley CA 94705..................................415-540-7010
Arrowstar Publishing, 10134 University Park Sta, Denver CO 80210........303-692-6579
Art & Communications, 812 N Edwards, Carlsbad NM 88220 505-885-3295
Art Books Intl Ltd*, 9 E 32nd St 9C, New York NY 10016.....................212-213-9393
Art Direction Book Co*, 10 E 39th St 6th fl, New York NY 10016............212-889-6500
Art Inst of Chicago*, Michigan Ave at Adams St, Chicago IL 60603........312-443-3600
Art Museum Assn of Amer, 270 Sutter St, San Francisco CA 94108.........415-392-9222
Art Research Center, 820 E 48th St, Kansas City MO 64110.....................816-561-2006
Artacts Publishing, 1676 Bracken Road, Bloomfield Hills MI 48013.........313-626-4398
Arte Publico Press*, U of H 4800 Calhoun, Houston TX 77004................713-749-4768
Artech House Inc*, 888 Washington St, Dedham MA 02026.....................617-326-8220
Artex Press*, 1917 Center St, Stevens Point WI 54481 715-341-6959
Asher-Gallant Press*, 60 Shames Dr, Westbury NY 11590.......................516-333-7440
Ashlee Publishing Co Inc, 310 Madison Ave, New York NY 10017 212-682-7681
Ashley Books Inc*, 30 Main St, Port Washington NY 11050.....................516-883-2221
Ashod Press, Box 1147 Madison Sq Sta, New York NY 10159....................212-475-0711
ASI Publishers, 63 W 38th St, New York NY 10018..................................212-719-2919
Askon Publishing Co, PO Box 3156, Abilene TX 79604.............................915-672-3640
Aslan Publishing, PO Box 496, New York NY 10032.................................212-927-5038
Aspen Systems Corp*, 1600 Research Blvd, Rockville MD 20850..............301-251-5000
Associated Faculty Press Inc*, Rt 100, Millwood NY 10546 914-762-2200
Associated Features*, PO Box 1762, New York NY 10156..........................212-889-4808
The Association*, 1100 Wayne Ave, Silver Spring MD 20910 301-587-8202
Association Research*, 67th St & Atlantic, Virginia Beach VA 23151 804-428-3588
Dean Aster Publishing Co, PO Box 10752, Merrillville IN 46411 219-980-6554
ASTM*, 1916 Race St, Philadelphia PA 19103..215-299-5400
Astonisher Press, PO Box 80635, Lincoln NE 68501 402-477-2800
Astronomical Workshop, Furman Univ, Greenville SC 29613....................803-294-2208
Atcom Inc Publishers, 2315 Broadway, New York NY 10024 212-873-5900
Atheneum Publishers*, 866 3rd Ave, New York NY 10022.......................212-702-7894
Athletic Press, PO Box 80250, Pasadena CA 91108 818-283-3446
Atlantic Monthly Press*, 420 Lexington Ave, New York NY 10170 212-557-6030
Atlantis Publishing Co, 5432 Hallandale Beach, Hollywood FL 33023......305-981-1009
ATMA Books, PO Box 432, Fallasburg NY 12733....................................914-434-6707
Atticus Press, 720 Heber Ave, Calexico CA 92231...................................619-357-3721
Auburn House Publishing Co*, 14 Dedham St, Dover MA 02030 617-785-2220
Auction Press, 96 S Clermont St, Denver CO 80222.................................303-399-0049

Theodore Audel & Co*, 866 3rd Ave, New York NY 10022 212-702-3460
Auerbach Publishers Inc*, 6560 N Park Dr, Pennsauken NJ 08109...........609-662-2070
Augsburg Publishing House*, 426 S 5th St, Minneapolis MN 55440.........612-330-3300
J J Augustin Inc Publisher, Locust Valley NY 11560................................516-676-1510
Aum Publications*, PO Box 32433, Jamaica NY 11431 718-523-3471
Auromere Books and Imports, 1291 Weber St, Pomona CA 91768...........714-629-8255
Aurora Press, 205 3rd Ave Ste 2A, New York NY 10003............................212-673-1831
Author Aid Research, 340 E 52nd St, New York NY 10022.........................212-758-4213
Auto Book Press, PO Bin 711, San Marcos CA 92069 619-744-3582
Automedia Inc, PO Box 568, Brooklyn NY 11211 718-387-6471
Avalon Books, 401 Lafayette St, New York NY 10003...............................212-598-0222
Avalon Communications Inc, 1705 Broadway, Hewlett NY 11557.............516-599-4555
Avant Books, 3719 6th Ave, San Diego CA 92103 619-295-0473
Avcom International, PO Box 2398, Wichita KS 67201 316-262-1493
Ave Maria Press*, Notre Dame IN 46556 219-287-2831
Avenue Publishing Co, 9417 Conant Ave Ste 2, Hamtramck MI 48212 313-875-6635
Avery Color Studios, Box 275 Forest Lake Rd, Au Train MI 49806...........906-892-8251
Avery Publishing Group Inc*, 89 Baldwin Ter, Wayne NJ 07470.............201-696-3359
AVI Publishing*, 250 Post Rd E Box 831, Westport CT 06881 203-226-0738
Aviation Book Co, 1640 Victory Blvd, Glendale CA 91201 818-240-1771
Avon Books*, 105 Madison Ave, New York NY 10016.............................212-481-5609
Awani Press Inc, PO Box 881, Fredericksburg TX 78624...........................512-997-5514
Aztex Corp*, 1126 N 6th Ave PO Box 50046, Tucson AZ 85703................602-882-4656
Azure Coast Publishing Co, 7480 La Jolla Blvd, La Jolla CA 92037 619-459-0122
B & B Publishing, PO Box 165, Saugus CA 91350 805-255-3422
B of A Communications*, PO Box 22252 LSU, Baton Rouge LA 70893...504-272-6600
B Rugged, 11 S Adelaide Ave, Highland Park NJ 08904.............................201-828-6098
Backcountry Publications Inc*, Box 175, Woodstock VT 05091...............802-457-1049
Backwater Corp, 7438 SE 40th St, Mercer Island WA 98040 206-232-2171
Badlands Natural History Association, PO Box 6, Interior SD 57750.......605-433-5361
Baen Publishing Ent*, 260 5th Ave, New York NY 10001.........................212-532-4111
Baha'i Publishing Trust*, 415 Linden Ave, Wilmette IL 60091 312-251-1854
Baja Bush Pilots, PO Drawer 27310, Escondido CA 92027........................619-489-0590
Baker Book House*, PO Box 6287, Grand Rapids MI 49516 616-676-9185
Baker Publishing, 16245 Armstead St, Granada Hills CA 91344................818-360-1740
Balcom Books, 320 Bawden St, Ketchikan AK 99901 907-225-2496
Ball Stick Bird Publications Inc*, Box 592, Stony Brook NY 11790.........516-331-9164
Ballantine/Del Rey/Fawcett*, 201 E 50th St, New York NY 10022...........212-572-2620
Ballinger Publishing Co*, 54 Church St, Cambridge MA 02138................617-492-0670
Balsam Press Inc, 122 E 25th St, New York NY 10010................................212-598-6976
Bamboo Ridge Press, PO Box 61781, Honolulu HI 96822..........................808-395-7098
Bambook Publishing, PO Box 1403, Weatherford TX 76086 817-594-8202
Bandanna Books, 209 W De la Guerra, Santa Barbara CA 93101 805-962-9996
Bank Street Press, 24 Bank St, New York NY 10014 212-255-0692
Bankers Publishing Co, 210 South St, Boston MA 02111...........................617-426-4495
Banks Baldwin Law Publ, PO Box 1974, Cleveland OH 44106 216-721-7373
Bannister Publications, PO Box 63, Port Henry NY 12974.........................518-546-7539
Bantam Books Inc*, 666 5th Ave, New York NY 10103.............................212-765-6500
Banyan Books Inc, 7575 SW 62nd Ave, Miami FL 33143............................305-665-6011
Baptist Spanish Publishing*, 7000 Alabama, El Paso TX 79914................915-566-9656
Lilian Barber Press Inc*, PO Box 232, New York NY 10163 212-874-2678
D L Barber Ventures, PO Box 2248, Garden Grove CA 92642.....................213-425-3460
A S Barnes & Co Inc, 9601 Aero Dr, San Diego CA 92123..........................619-560-5163

Barnes & Noble Books*, 10 E 53rd St, New York NY 10022 212-207-7000
Barnes & Noble Imports/Reprints*, 81 Adams Dr, Totowa NJ 07512 201-256-8600
Barnwood, Box 11C, Daleville IN 47334 317-378-0921
Richard W Baron Publishing Co Inc, 20 5th Ave, New York NY 10011...212-260-2400
Barret & Co, PO Box 6700, Jackson MS 39212..601-373-4400
Barrington Press, 4102 E 27th St, Tucson AZ 85711.................................602-745-0070
Barron's Educational Series*, 113 Crossways Pk, Woodbury NY 11797...516-921-8750
Robert L Barth, 14 Lucas St, Florence KY 41042 606-283-1479
Bartholomew Books, Box 634, Iverness CA 94937 415-669-1664
Basic Books Inc Publishers*, 10 E 53rd St, New York NY 10022 212-207-7057
Basic English Revisited, Box J, Burlington WI 53105................................414-763-8258
Basil Blackwell Inc*, 432 Park Ave S Ste 1503, New York NY 10016........212-684-2890
Battery Press Inc*, PO Box 3107 Uptown Sta, Nashville TN 37219 615-298-1401
Wm L Bauhan Publisher*, Box 158 Old County Rd, Dublin NH 03444....603-563-8020
Baylor University Press, CSB 547 Baylor Univ, Waco TX 76798 817-755-3164
Bayshore Books, Box 848, Nokomis FL 33555 813-485-2564
Baywood Publishing*, 120 Marine St Box D, Farmingdale NY 11735 516-249-2464
Beacon Hill Press*, PO Box 419527, Kansas City MO 64141 816-931-1900
Beacon Press*, 25 Beacon St, Boston MA 02108....................................617-742-2110
Beanie Enterprises, 7443 Stanford, St Louis MO 63130...........................314-725-5012
Bear & Co Inc*, PO Drawer 2860, Santa Fe NM 87504...........................505-983-9868
Bear Creek Publishing, PO Box 254, Quray CO 81427............................303-325-4700
Bear Flag Books*, PO Box 1275, San Luis Obispo CA 93406 805-543-5404
Bear Tribe Publishing, PO Box 9167, Spokane WA 99209 509-326-6561
Bearly Limited*, 149 York St, Buffalo NY 14213.....................................716-883-4571
Beaufort Books Inc*, 9 E 40th St, New York NY 10016 212-685-8588
Beautiful America Publ*, 9725 SW Commerce, Wilsonville OR 97070 503-682-0173
Beaux-Arts Press, 808 Post St Ste 1106, San Francisco CA 94109 415-929-0910
The Beavers, HCR 70 Box 537, Laporte MN 56461 218-224-2182
Beech Tree Books*, 105 Madison Ave, New York NY 10016 212-889-3050
Beechcliff Books, 100 Severn Ave, Annapolis MD 20817.........................301-263-3580
Beekman Publishers Inc*, Box 888, Woodstock NY 12498 914-679-2300
Beginner Books, 201 E 50th St, New York NY 10022................................212-751-2600
Behrman House Inc*, 1261 Broadway, New York NY 10001......................212-689-2020
Bell Assn for the Deaf, 3417 Volta Pl NW, Washington DC 20007.............202-337-5220
Bell Publishing, 15 Surrey Lane, E Brunswick NJ 08816..........................201-257-7793
Bellerophon Books*, 36 Anacapa St, Santa Barbara CA 93101.................805-965-7034
Bench Press, 332 N 4th St, Seward NE 68434..402-643-4305
Matthew Bender & Co*, 2101 Webster St Ste 6108, Oakland CA 94612 ...415-446-7100
Benjamin Co Inc*, 1 Westchester Plaza, Elmsford NY 10523....................914-592-8088
Benjamin-Cummings Publ*, 2727 Sand Hill Rd, Menlo Park CA 94025...415-854-0300
Bennett & McKnight Publ*, 809 W Detweiller Dr, Peoria IL 61615..........309-691-4454
Robert Bentley Inc*, 1000 Massachusetts Ave, Cambridge MA 02138 617-547-4170
Bergin & Garvey Publishers*, 670 Amherst Rd, S Hadley MA 01075.......413-467-3113
Berkley Publishing Group*, 200 Madison Ave, New York NY 10016........212-686-9820
Berlitz Publications, 866 3rd Ave, New York NY 10022............................212-702-7985
Bern Porter Books*, 22 Salmond Rd, Belfast ME 04915 207-338-3763
The Berot Book Inc, 220 E Hillsdale St, Lansing MI 48933 517-482-6633
Berry Books, 1114 SE 22nd Ter, Cape Coral FL 33904 301-946-8905
Bess Press*, PO Box 22388, Honolulu HI 96822.....................................808-734-7159
Bethany College Press, 421 N 1st St, Lindsborg KS 67456 913-227-3314
Bethany House Publ*, 6820 Auto Club Rd, Minneapolis MN 55438..........612-944-2121
Bethel Historical Society, 15 Broad St, Bethel ME 04217..........................207-824-2908

Better Homes & Gardens Books*, 1716 Locust, Des Moines IA 50336.....515-284-3000
Betterway Publications Inc*, General Delivery, White Hall VA 22987.....804-823-5661
Beulah Publishing Co, Rt 1, Crossville IL 62827...618-966-3425
Bible Temple Publications, 7545 NE Glisan St, Portland OR 97213..........503-253-9020
Bibli O'Phile Publishing Co*, 156 E 61st St, New York NY 10021.............212-888-1008
Biblical Research Assn, The College of Wooster, Wooster OH 44691......216-263-2000
Biblio Press, PO Box 22, Fresh Meadows NY 11365.................................718-361-3141
Bicentennial Era Enterprises, PO Box 1148, Scappoose OR 97056...........503-684-0531
Bicycle Books Inc, PO Box 2038, Mill Valley CA 94941............................415-381-0172
The Bieler Press, 212 2nd St N, Minneapolis MN 55401.............................612-339-1978
Bilingual Books Inc*, 5903 Seaview NW, Seattle WA 98107......................206-789-7544
Bilingual Educ Svcs*, 2514 S Grand Ave, Los Angeles CA 90007.............213-749-6213
Bilingual Review/Press*, Ariz State Univ, Tempe AZ 85287.....................602-965-3867
Binford & Mort*, 1202 N 17th Ave, Portland OR 97209..............................503-221-0866
Joseph J Binns Publisher*, 6919 Radnor Rd, Bethesda MD 20817...........301-320-3327
Bioenergetics Press, 1129 Drake St, Madison WI 53715.............................608-255-4028
Biofeedback Inst, 3428 Sacramento St, San Francisco CA 94118................415-921-6500
Birch Tree Group*, 180 Alexander St Box 2072, Princeton NJ 08540........609-683-0090
Birkhauser Boston Inc*, 380 Green St, Cambridge MA 02139.....................617-876-2333
Birth Day Publishing Co, PO Box 7722, San Diego CA 92107....................619-296-3194
Bishop Graphics, 5388 Sterling Center Dr, Westlake Vlg CA 91359..........818-991-2600
Bison Books Corp*, 15 Sherwood Pl, Greenwich CT 06830........................203-661-9551
Bits Press, Case Western Reserve Univ, Cleveland OH 44106....................216-795-2810
BiWorld Publishers*, 671 N State PO Box 1144, Orem UT 84057...............801-224-5803
BkMk Press, 5216 Rockhill, Kansas City MO 64110..................................816-276-2258
Black & White & Read All Over, Box 452, Lake Bluff IL 60044 312-295-1077
Walter J Black Inc*, Flower Hill, Roslyn NY 11576....................................516-627-4920
Black Light Fellowship, PO Box 5369, Chicago IL 60680..........................312-722-1441
Rabbi Tzui Black Publications, 125 Carey St, Lakewood NJ 08701............201-363-2127
Black Resource Guide Inc, 501 Oneida Pl NW, Washington DC 20011....202-291-4373
The Black Scholar Press, PO Box 2869, Oakland CA 94609 415-547-6633
Black Swan Books Ltd, Box 327, Redding Ridge CT 06876........................203-938-9548
Black Willow Press, 401 Independence Dr, Harleysville PA 19438.............215-368-0163
Blackberry, Chimney Farm RR1 Box 228, Nobleboro ME 04555................207-563-8531
Blackwell Scientific Publications*, 52 Beacon St, Boston MA 02108.........617-720-0761
Blair of Columbus Inc, PO Box 7852, Columbus GA 31908........................404-563-8787
John F Blair Publisher, 1406 Plaza Dr, Winston-Salem NC 27103 919-768-1374
Blake Publishing, 2222 Beebee St, San Luis Obispo CA 93401..................805-543-6843
Blitz Publishing Co, 1600 Verona St, Middleton WI 53562........................608-836-7550
Bloch Publishing Co Inc*, 19 W 21st St, New York NY 10010 212-989-9104
Blue Bird Publishing, 1713 E Broadway #306, Tempe AZ 85282..............602-968-4088
The Blue Boar Press, 10407 Pinehurst Dr, Austin TX 78747......................512-282-3493
Blue Heron Press, PO Box 5182, Bellingham WA 98227 206-671-1155
Blue Mountain Arts Inc*, PO Box 4549, Boulder CO 80306......................303-449-0536
Blue Oak Press, Box 27, Sattley CA 96124 916-994-3397
Blue Sea Press, PO Box 9426, Arlington VA 22209 703-522-8826
Blue Sky Marketing Inc, PO Box 17003, St Paul MN 55117......................612-774-2920
Blue Tulip Press, 110 S El Camino Real #113, San Mateo CA 94402........415-348-4356
Blue Wind Press, PO Box 7175, Berkeley CA 94707 415-525-2098
Bluejay Books Inc*, 1123 Broadway Ste 306, New York NY 10010...........212-206-1538
BNA Books*, 2550 M St NW Ste 699, Washington DC 20037 202-452-4276
Boa Editions Ltd, 92 Park Ave, Brockport NY 14420 716-637-3844
Boardroom Books, 330 W 42nd St, New York NY 10036 212-239-9000

Bob Jones Univ Press*, 1700 Wade Hampton, Greenville SC 29614 803-242-5100
Bobley Publishing*, 311 Crossways Park Dr, Woodbury NY 11797 516-364-1800
Boise State Univ, 1910 University Dr English Dept, Boise ID 83725 208-385-1246
Bonus Books*, 160 E Illinois St, Chicago IL 60611 312-467-0580
Book of Revelation Explained, 339 E Laguna Dr, Tempe AZ 85282 602-967-3066
Book-Lab*, 500 74th St, N Bergen NJ 07047...201-861-6763
Bookcraft Inc*, 1848 W 2300 S, Salt Lake City UT 84119...........................801-972-6180
The Bookery Publishing Co, 8193 Riata Dr, Redding CA 96002 916-365-8068
Bookmakers Guild*, 1430 Florida Ave #202, Longmont CO 80501 303-442-5774
Bookman Publishing*, PO Box 13492, Baltimore MD 21203......................301-625-0067
Bookmates International, PO Box 9883, Fresno CA 92041..........................619-463-3441
Books Americana Inc*, PO Box 2326, Florence AL 35630 205-757-9966
Books For All Times Inc, PO Box 2, Alexandria VA 22313..........................703-548-0457
Books for Business Inc*, Box 1608, Tarpon Springs FL 34286 813-938-4040
BookWrights*, 220 Main St Box 49, Neshkoro WI 54960 414-293-8355
Boomerang Publishers, 616 W 83rd Way, Arvada CO 80003.......................303-423-5706
Borderland Sciences Research Found, Box 549, Vista CA 92083...............714-724-2043
The Borgo Press*, PO Box 2845, San Bernardino CA 92406.......................714-884-5813
Don Bosco Publications*, 475 North Ave, New Rochelle NY 10802..........914-576-0122
Boston Publishing Co Inc*, 314 Dartmouth St, Boston MA 02116 617-267-8800
Bottom Dog Press, Firelands College of BGSU, Huron OH 44839............419-433-5560
Thomas Bouregy & Co Inc*, 401 Lafayette St, New York NY 10003.........212-598-0222
F A Bowen Reports Inc, PO Box 213, Janesville WI 53547 608-752-6333
R R Bowker Co*, 245 W 17th St, New York NY 10011 212-645-9700
The Boxwood Press, 183 Ocean View Blvd, Pacific Grove CA 93950.........408-375-9110
Boyd & Fraser Publ*, 3627 Sacramento St, San Francisco CA 94118........415-346-0686
Betty Boyink Publishing, 818 Sheldon Rd, Grand Haven MI 49417..........616-842-3304
Boynton/Cook Publ*, 52 Upper Montclair, Upper Montclair NJ 07043 ...201-783-3310
Bradbury Press*, 866 3rd Ave, New York NY 10022 212-702-9809
Bradfords Directory, PO Box 276, Fairfax VA 22030..................................703-830-4646
Bradson Press, 120 Longfellow St, Thousand Oaks CA 91360....................818-707-0471
Braemar Books, PO Box 25296, Portland OR 97225 503-292-4226
Bragdon Books, 1322 Bragdon, Pueblo CO 81004 303-542-2231
Allen D Bragdon Publishers Inc*, 153 W 82nd St, New York NY 10024..212-787-6886
Braille Inc*, 157 Locust St, Falmouth MA 02540 617-540-0800
Braille Institute Press*, 741 N Vermont Ave, Los Angeles CA 90029 213-663-1111
Branden Publishing Co, 17 Station St, Brookline Vlg MA 02147 617-734-2045
Brandt Enterprises Inc, 95 Harvey St, Cambridge MA 02140 617-492-8776
Charles T Branford Co*, Box 41, Newton Centre MA 02159 617-964-2441
Brason-Sargar Publications, PO Box 872, Reseda CA 91335......................818-700-1109
George Braziller Inc*, 60 Madison Ave, New York NY 10010.....................212-889-0909
Bread & Butter Press, 2582 S Clayton, Denver CO 80210.........................303-753-0912
Breezewood Publishing Co, PO Box 5421, Greenville SC 29606 803-834-9836
Brethren Press*, 1451 Dundee Ave, Elgin IL 60120 312-742-5100
Brick House Publishing*, 3 Main St, Andover MA 01810 617-475-9568
Bridge Publications Inc*, 1414 N Catalina St, Los Angeles CA 90027 213-382-0382
Bridge Publishing Inc*, 2500 Hamilton Blvd, S Plainfield NJ 07080..........201-754-0745
Robert Briggs Assoc*, PO Box 9, Mill Valley CA 94942..............................415-472-4486
Bright Ring Publishing, 1900 North Shore Dr, Bellingham WA 98227 206-734-1601
Brighton Publications Inc, PO Box 12706, New Brighton MN 55112........612-636-2220
Brighton Publishing Co, 2950 N High St, Columbus OH 43202 614-261-6565
Brightwaters Press, 235 Park Ave S, New York NY 10003..........................212-777-1711
E J Brill*, 4300 NW 23rd Ave Ste 100, Gainesville FL 32606.....................904-371-9858

BRK Enterprises, 336 S Donald Ave, Arlington Heights IL 60004..............312-259-8376
Broadman Press*, 127 9th Ave N, Nashville TN 37234................................615-251-2533
Broadway Book Co, PO Box 445, Rutherford NJ 07070...............................201-933-3621
Broadway Press, 120 Duane St Ste 407, New York NY 10007......................212-693-0570
The Brolet Press, 33 Gold St Ste 702, New York NY 10038.........................212-233-6066
Bromfield St Educational Found, 167 Tremont St, Boston MA 02111......617-426-4469
Bronwen Press, 3909 E James, Seattle WA 98122..206-329-8157
Brook House Press, Box 709, Holbrook NY 11741.......................................516-542-4344
Paul H Brookes Publishing Co, PO Box 10624, Baltimore MD 21285 301-377-0883
Brookings Inst*, 1775 Massachusetts Ave NW, Washington DC 20036 202-797-6000
Brooklyn Publishing, PO Box 340328 Ryder St Sta, Brooklyn NY 11234..718-251-3690
Brooks/Cole Publishing Co*, 555 Abrego, Monterey CA 93940................408-373-0728
Brooktree & Co Inc, PO Box 795, Birmingham MI 48012 313-258-8947
E Arthur Brown Co, 3404 Pawnee Dr, Alexandria MN 56308.....................612-762-8847
Brown Mouse Publishing Co, PO Box 20082, Houston TX 77225...............713-699-1277
Bruccoli Clark Layman Inc, 2006 Sumter St, Columbia SC 29201.............803-771-4642
Brun Press Inc, 701 NE 67th St, Miami FL 33138.......................................305-756-6249
Dick Bruna Books Inc*, 300 Reisterstown Rd, Baltimore MD 21208........301-484-2100
Brunner/Mazel Inc, 1889 Palmer Ave, Larchmont NY 10538 914-834-3920
James A Bryans Books Inc*, 70 Fairfield Beach Rd, Fairfield CT 06430..203-259-0162
BSP Publishing*, 111 Marshall St Box 1968, Mankato MN 56001..............507-387-6640
Bucknell Univ Press*, Lewisburg PA 17837..717-524-3674
Buddhist Text Translation Society, Box 217, Talmage CA 95481 707-462-0939
Bull Publishing Co, PO Box 208, Palo Alto CA 94302................................415-322-2855
Bunkhouse Publishers Inc, 123 N Sultana Ave, Ontario CA 91764............714-984-6694
Burgess International Group Inc*, 7110 Ohms Ln, Edina MN 55435.......612-831-1344
The Burnell Co Publishers Inc, PO Box 304, Mankato MN 56002............507-625-4302
Burr Publications Ltd*, RD 1 Rt 33 Box 429, Hightstown NJ 08520.........609-448-2218
Business & Legal Reports*, 64 Wall St, Madison CT 06443 203-245-7448
Business & Professional Books, PO Box 9671, Westgate Sta CA 95157 ...408-294-3960
Business Publications Inc*, 1700 Alma Ste 390, Plano TX 75075 214-422-4389
Spencer Butte Press, 84889 Harry Taylor Rd, Eugene OR 97405 503-345-3692
Butterworth Legal Publishers*, 11004 Metric Blvd, Austin TX 78758.......512-835-7921
Butterworth Publishers*, 80 Montvale Ave Park, Stoneham MA 02180...617-438-8464
By George Publications, PO Box 172, Mt Horeb WI 53572.........................608-437-5607
Richard E Bye, 10956 Caminito Alvarez, San Diego CA 92104...................619-481-7659
BYLS Press, 6247 N Francisco Ave, Chicago IL 60659................................312-262-8959
C&T Publishing, PO Box 1456, Lafayette CA 94549 415-937-0605
Cactus Max Press, PO Box 12477, El Paso TX 79913................................915-584-7649
Caddylak Publishing*, 201 Montrose Rd, Westbury NY 11590..................516-333-7440
Cadmus Editions, PO Box 687, Tiburon CA 94920....................................707-894-3048
Cadmus Press, 25 Waterview Dr, Port Jefferson NY 11777........................516-928-9896
Caledonia Press*, PO Box 245, Racine WI 53401......................................414-637-6200
Calibre Press Inc, 666 Dundee Rd #1607, Northbrook IL 60062................312-498-5680
Calif College Health Sciences, 1810 State St, San Diego CA 92101...........619-232-3784
California Inst for Public Affairs*, PO Box 10, Claremont CA 91711 714-624-5212
California Street, 723 Dwight Way, Berkeley CA 94710 415-549-2461
Cam Tri Publications, 1845 Tigertrail Rd, Eugene OR 97405.....................503-344-0118
Camaro Publishing Co*, 90430 World Way Ctr, Los Angeles CA 90009..213-837-7500
Cambridge Adult Education Co*, 888 7th Ave, New York NY 10106.......212-957-5300
Cambridge Univ Press*, 32 E 57th St, New York NY 10022.......................212-688-8885
Camden House Inc*, Drawer 2025, Columbia SC 29202.............................301-338-8779
Camel Press, HC 80 Box 160, Big Cove Tannery PA 17212 717-294-3033

Cameron & Co Inc, 543 Howard St, San Francisco CA 94105 415-777-5582
Sandy Campbell, 230 Central Park S, New York NY 10019 212-582-6286
Candle Publishing, 101 Southwestern Blvd, Sugar Land TX 77478............713-242-6151
Canterbury Press, PO Box 2151, Berkeley CA 94702.................................415-843-1860
Aristide D Caratzas Publisher, 30 Church St, New Rochelle NY 10801 ...914-632-8487
Caravan Publishing Group, 303 5th Ave Ste 208, New York NY 10016....212-685-0543
Carcanet Press*, 108 E 31st St, New York NY 10016 212-686-1033
Cardinal Press, 76 N Yorktown, Tulsa OK 74110.....................................918-583-3651
Care Communications Inc, 200 E Ontario Ste 708, Chicago IL 60611.......312-943-0463
Career Management Press, 8301 State Line, Kansas City MO 64114 816-363-1500
Career Publishing Inc, PO Box 5486, Orange CA 92613 714-771-5155
Careers Unlimited, PO Box 470886, Tulsa OK 74147................................918-622-2811
Wm Carey Library*, 1705 N Sierra Bonita Ave, Pasadena CA 91104........818-798-4067
Caribbean Books, 801 4th Ave, Parkersburg IA 50665...............................319-346-2048
The Carnation Press, PO Box 101, Stata College PA 16804........................814-238-3577
Carolina Academic Press*, PO Box 8795, Durham NC 27707.....................919-489-7486
Carolina Biological Supply*, 2700 York Rd, Burlington NC 27215 919-584-0381
The Carolina Wren Press, 300 Carclay Rd, Chapel Hill NC 27514 919-967-8666
Carolrhoda Books Inc, 241 1st Ave N, Minneapolis MN 55401..................612-332-3344
Merlin R Carothers*, PO Box 2518, Escondido CA 92025.........................619-741-2755
Carousel Press, PO Box 6061, Albany CA 94706 415-527-5849
Carroll & Graf Publishers Inc*, 260 5th Ave, New York NY 10001..........212-889-8772
The Carroll Press, 43 Squantum St, Cranston RI 02920 401-942-1587
H G Carson Enterprises*, Star Rt 1 Box 157 B, Deming NM 88031 505-546-6100
Carstens Publications, PO Box 700, Newton NJ 07860...............................201-383-3355
Casino Publishing, PO Box 54081, San Jose CA 95154..............................408-365-1538
Cassandra Press, PO Box 2044, Boulder CO 80306 303-442-0139
Cassell Communications Inc, PO Box 9844, Ft Lauderdale FL 33310 305-485-0795
Castalia Publishing Co, PO Box 1587, Eugene OR 97440...........................503-343-4433
Castle Books Inc*, 110 Enterprise Ave, Secaucus NJ 07094.......................201-864-6341
Catalyst Publications, 143 Dolores St, San Francisco CA 94103 415-552-5045
Catholic Book Publishing Co*, 257 W 17th St, New York NY 10011 212-243-4515
The Catholic Health Assn*, 4455 Woodson Rd, St Louis MO 63134.........314-427-2500
Catholic Univ of Amer*, 620 Michigan Ave NE, Washington DC 20064...202-635-5052
Cave Books, 756 Harvard Ave, St Louis MO 63130 314-862-7646
The Caxton Printers Ltd, 312 Main St Box 700, Caldwell ID 83605...........208-459-7421
Cay-Bel Publishing Co*, 45 Center St, Brewer ME 04412..........................207-989-3820
CAYC Learning Tree, 9998 Ferguson Rd, Dallas TX 75228 214-321-6484
Cayuse Press, PO Box 9086, Berkeley CA 94709 415-525-8515
CB Publications, 329 Harvey Dr, Glendale CA 91206................................818-247-1721
CBI Books*, 115 5th Ave, New York NY 10003 212-265-8700
CBP Press, PO Box 179, St Louis MO 63166 314-231-8500
CBS Educ & Prof Publ*, 383 Madison Ave, New York NY 10017 212-872-2000
CCC Publications*, 20306 Tau Pl, Chatsworth CA 91311..........................818-407-1661
Cedarshouse Press, 406 W 28th St, Bryan TX 77803.................................713-822-5615
Cedarwood Press, 1115 E Wylie St, Bloomington IN 47401 812-332-3017
Celestial Arts*, PO Box 7327, Berkeley CA 94707....................................415-524-1801
Celestial Gems, Marigold Manor 404 State Blvd, Centralia WA 98531 206-736-5083
Celo Press, 1901 Hannah Branch Rd, Burnsville NC 28714........................704-675-4925
Ctr for Applied Linguistics, 1118 22nd St NW, Wash DC 20037................202-429-9292
Ctr for Asian Studies, Arizona State Univ, Tempe AZ 85287 602-965-7184
Ctr for Holocaust Studies, 1609 Ave J, Brooklyn NY 11230 718-338-6494
Ctr for Latin Amer Studies*, Arizona State Univ, Tempe AZ 85287........602-965-5127

Ctr for Migration Studies, 209 Flagg Pl, Staten Island NY 10304 718-351-8800
Ctr for Study of Multiple Births, 333 E Superior, Chicago IL 60611.........312-266-9093
Ctr for Sutton Movement Writing, Box 7344, Newport Bch CA 92658 714-644-8342
Ctr for Thanatology Res & Educ, 391 Atlantic, Brooklyn NY 11217 718-858-3026
Ctr for The Study of Elephants, PO Box 4444, Carson CA 90749...............714-897-8990
Ctr for Urban Policy, 820 N Michigan Ave, Chicago IL 60611.....................312-670-3112
Ctr for Urban Policy Res*, Rutgers Univ, New Brunswick NJ 08901 201-932-3133
Century House Publ, Amer Life Foundation, Watkins Glen NY 14891.....607-535-4004
CES Inc, 112 S Grant, Hinsdale IL 60521..312-654-2596
Chadwyck-Healey Inc*, 1021 Prince St, Alexandria VA 22314....................203-683-4890
Chain Store Guide*, 425 Park Ave, New York NY 10022 212-371-9400
Chalfant Press Inc, Box 787, Bishop CA 93514..619-873-3535
Irena Chalmers Cookbooks Inc*, 23 E 92nd St, New York NY 10128 212-348-3240
Chandler & Sharpe Publ, 11A Commercial Blvd, Novato CA 94949.........415-883-2353
Channel Island Publ, 1318 De La Vina St, Santa Barbara CA 93101 805-484-4399
Chanticleer Press Inc*, 424 Madison Ave, New York NY 10017 212-486-3900
Chantry Press, PO Box 144, Midland Park NJ 07432..................................201-423-5882
Chariton Review Press, Missouri State Univ, Kirksville MO 63501 816-785-4499
Charleston Junior League Publ, PO Box 1924, Charleston WV 25327.....304-346-5856
Charlton House Publishing, PO Box 2474, Newport Beach CA 92663......714-760-8528
Charter Oak Press*, PO Box 7783, Lancaster PA 17604 717-898-7711
Chartwell Books Inc*, 110 Enterprise Ave, Secaucus NJ 07094..................201-864-6341
Chatham House Publishers Inc*, Box 1, Chatham NJ 07928.....................201-635-2059
The Chatham Press*, Box A, Old Greenwich CT 06870..............................203-531-7880
The Chauncey Press, Turtle Pond Rd, Saranac Lake NY 12983 518-891-1650
Cheetah Publishing Co, 275 N Forest Lake, Altamonte Spgs FL 32714 305-862-2726
Chelsea Green Publishing Co, 1 Court St Box 283, Chelsea VT 05038......802-685-3108
Chelsea House, Box 419, Edgemont PA 19028 215-353-6625
Chelsea House Publ*, 95 Madison Ave 5th fl, New York NY 10016 212-683-4400
Chemical Publishing Co Inc*, 80 8th Ave, New York NY 10011.................212-255-1950
Cherry Lane Books*, Box 430, Port Chester NY 10573 914-937-8601
Cherryable Brothers*, 130 Seventy St Ste 448, Garden City NY 11530 516-486-5090
Chess Enterprises Inc*, 107 Crosstree Rd, Coraopolis PA 15108...............412-262-2138
Chicago New Art Association, 230 E Ohio Rm 207, Chicago IL 60611......312-642-6236
Chicago Review Press Inc*, 814 N Franklin, Chicago IL 60610 312-337-0747
Child Welfare League of Amer*, 67 Irving Pl, New York NY 10003 212-254-7410
Childbirth Graphics Ltd, 1201 Culver Rd, Rochester NY 14609 716-482-7940
Children's Book Press, 1461 9th Ave, San Francisco CA 94122....................415-664-8500
Children's Center Publications, Box 885, Bonita CA 92002.......................619-479-0602
Childrens Press*, 1224 W Van Buren St, Chicago IL 60607 312-666-4200
Chilton Book Co*, Chilton Way, Radnor PA 19089.....................................215-964-4000
China Books & Periodicals Inc*, 2929 24th St, San Francisco CA 94110..415-282-2994
Chisbro Press, PO Box 1326, Morgan Hill CA 95037...................................408-779-5930
Chockstone Press, 526 Franklin St, Denver CO 80218................................303-377-1970
Chosen Books*, 1415 Lake Dr SE, Grand Rapids MI 49506.......................616-698-6900
Christian Classics*, 73 W Main St PO Box 30, Westminster MD 21157..301-848-3065
Christian Ministries Publ, 173 Woodland Ave, Lexington KY 40502.........606-231-0000
Christian Record Braille Found*, 4444 S 52nd St, Lincoln NE 68516.......402-488-0981
Christian Schools Intl*, 3350 E Paris Ave SE, Grand Rapids MI 49508...616-957-1070
Christopher Publ House*, 106 Longwater Dr, Norwell MA 02061 617-878-9336
Chronicle Books*, 1 Hallidie Plaza Ste 806, San Francisco CA 94102.......415-777-7240
Chronicle Guidance Publications*, PO Box 1190, Moravia NY 13118......315-497-0330
Church & Synagogue Library Assn, Box 1130, Bryn Mawr PA 19010.......215-853-2870

Churches Alive, PO Box 3800, San Bernardino CA 92413 714-886-5361
Churchilliana Co, 4629 Sunset Dr, Sacramento CA 95822 916-448-7053
CIL Inc Books, PO Box 283855, Baca Raton FL 33427 305-342-3936
Cincinnati Art Museum, Eden Park Dr, Cincinnati OH 45202 513-721-5204
Cinco Puntos Press, 2709 Louisville, El Paso TX 79930 915-566-9072
Cistercian Publications Inc*, WMU Sta, Kalamazoo MI 49008 616-383-4985
Citadel Press, 120 Enterprise Ave, Secaucus NJ 07094 201-736-0007
City Lights Books*, 261 Columbus Ave, San Francisco CA 94113 415-362-8139
Clarion Books*, 52 Vanderbilt Ave, New York NY 10017 212-972-1190
Clarity Press, 3277 Rosewell Rd NE Ste 469, Atlanta GA 30305 404-662-6806
Clark Boardman Co Ltd*, 435 Hudson St, New York NY 10014 212-929-7500
The Arthur H Clark Co, PO Box 230, Glendale CA 91209 818-245-9119
Clarke Historical Library, Central Mich Univ, Mt Pleasant MI 48859 517-774-3352
Claycomb Press Inc, PO Box 70822, Chevy Chase MD 20813 301-656-1057
Cleaning Consultant Services, 1512 Western Ave, Seattle WA 98101 206-682-9748
Clearwater Publishing Co Inc*, 1995 Broadway, New York NY 10023 212-873-2100
Cleis Press, PO Box 14684, San Francisco CA 94114 415-864-3385
Cleveland State Univ Poetry Ctr, English Dept, Cleveland OH 44115 216-687-3986
Cliffhanger Press, PO Box 29527, Oakland CA 94604 415-763-3510
Cliffs Notes Inc*, Box 80728, Lincoln NE 68501 402-477-6971
Clothespin Fever Press, 5529 N Figueroa, Los Angeles CA 90042 213-254-1343
Clovernook Printing for Blind*, 7000 Hamilton, Cincinnati OH 45231 ...513-522-3860
Clymer Publications*, 12860 Muscatine St Box 4520, Arleta CA 91333 818-767-7660
CMI Press, 3301 Clinton Pkwy Ct Ste #1, Lawrence KS 66046 913-843-0697
Coach House Press Inc*, Box 458, Morton Grove IL 60053 312-967-1777
Coastline Publishing Co, PO Box 223062, Carmel CA 93922 408-625-9388
Cobbers, PO Box 261, Williamsburg VA 23185 804-220-2828
Cobblesmith, Box 191 RFD 1, Freeport ME 04032 207-865-6495
George R Cockle & Assoc, PO Box 1224, Omaha NE 68132 402-553-4744
Coelacanth Publications, 55 Bluecoat, Irvine CA 92714 714-544-0914
Coffee House Press*, PO Box 10870, Minneapolis MN 55440 612-338-0125
Coker Publishing House, 135 Gran-de Court, Fayetteville GA 30214 404-461-3386
Cold Spring Harbor Laboratory*, Box 100, Cold Spg Hrbr NY 11724 516-367-8351
Earl M Coleman Enterprises, Box T, Crugers NY 10521 914-271-5124
Coleman Publishing*, 99 Milbar Blvd, Farmingdale NY 11735 516-293-0383
Collage Books*, 1200 S Willie Ave, Wheeling IL 60090 312-541-9290
The Collamore Press*, 125 Spring St, Lexington MA 02173 617-862-6650
Collector Books*, 5801 Kentucky Dam Rd, Paducah KY 42001 502-898-6211
College Entrance Exam Brd*, 45 Columbus Ave, New York NY 10023 212-582-6210
College Hill Press Inc*, 4284 41st St, San Diego CA 92105 619-563-8899
College Press Publishing Co*, 205 N Main, Joplin MO 64801 417-623-6280
Collegiate Publishing Inc, PO Box 181947, Coronado CA 92118 619-571-1064
Colonial Williamsburg Found*, Drawer C, Williamsburg VA 23187 804-229-1000
Colophon Communications, 30 Milrace Dr, E Rochester NY 14445 716-586-5789
Colorado Associated Univ Press*, 1344 Grandview, Boulder CO 80309 303-492-7191
Colorado School of Mines Press, Publications Dept, Golden CO 80401 ...303-273-3607
Columbia Publishing Co Inc*, 234 E 25th St, Baltimore MD 21218 301-366-7070
Columbia University Press*, 562 W 113th St, New York NY 10025 212-316-7100
Commerce Clearing House*, 4025 W Peterson Ave, Chicago IL 60646 ...312-583-8500
Commonwealth Press Inc*, 415 1st St, Radford VA 24141 703-639-2475
Communication Creativity, Box 213, Saguache CO 81149 303-589-8223
Communication Skill Builders Inc, PO Box 42050, Tucson AZ 85733 ...602-323-7500
Communication Unlimited, PO Box 1001, Carpinteria CA 93013 805-684-2469

Communications Press*, 1346 Connecticut Ave NW, Wash DC 20036.....202-785-0865
Communicom Publishing Co, 548 NE 43rd Ave, Portland OR 97213........503-239-5141
Community Service Inc, Box 243, Yellow Springs OH 45387.....................513-767-2161
Compact Books Inc, 2131 Hollywood Blvd, Hollywood FL 33020..............305-925-5242
Compass Publications Inc, 1117 N 19th St, Arlington VA 22209 703-524-3136
CompCare Publications*, 2415 Annapolis Ln, Minneapolis MN 55441 612-559-4800
F E Compton Co, 310 S Michigan Ave, Chicago IL 60604 312-347-7000
Compton's Learning Co, 310 S Michigan Ave, Chicago IL 60604................312-347-7000
CompuBibs*, 358 Willis Ave, Mineola NY 11501 718-767-2776
CompuSoft Publishing, 535 Broadway, El Cajon CA 92021 619-588-0996
Compute! Publications*, 324 W Wendover, Greensboro NC 27408 919-275-9809
Computer Industry Almanac Inc, 8111 LBJ Fwy, Dallas TX 75251............214-231-8735
Computer Science Press*, 1803 Research Blvd, Rockville MD 20850 301-251-9050
Comstock Editions Inc, 3030 Bridgeway, Sausalito CA 94965 415-332-3216
Conch Magazine Ltd Publishers, 102 Normal Ave, Buffalo NY 14213 716-885-3686
Concordia Publishing House*, 3558 S Jefferson, St Louis MO 63118 314-664-7000
Condo Management Maintenance, PO Box 5465, Clinton NJ 08809 201-735-4438
The Conference Board Inc*, 845 3rd Ave, New York NY 10022 212-759-0900
Congressional Quarterly*, 1414 22nd St NW, Washington DC 20037.......212-887-8642
Conservation Foundation, 1250 24th St NW, Washington DC 20037 202-293-4800
Conservatory of Amer Letters*, PO Box 123, S Thomaston ME 04858.....207-354-6550
Construction Industry Press, 58 Paul Dr, San Rafael CA 94903................415-499-7674
The Consultant's Library, Box 309, Glenelg MD 21737.............................301-531-3560
Consultants News*, Templeton Rd, Fitzwilliam NH 03447........................603-585-2200
Consumer Guide Books*, 3841 W Oakton St, Skokie IL 60076 312-676-3470
Consumer Reports Books*, 110 E 42nd St, New York NY 10017 212-682-9280
Consumertronics Co*, 2011 Crescent Dr, Alamogordo NM 88310............505-434-0234
Contemporary Books Inc*, 180 N Michigan Ave, Chicago IL 60601..........312-782-9181
Contemp Learning Materials*, 425 E Crawford, Peotone IL 60468..........312-258-6125
Context Publications, 4482 Health Cir, Rohnert Park CA 94928 707-584-4122
Continental Heritage Press Inc*, 6 E 5th St, Tulsa OK 74103 918-582-5100
Continuum Publ Corp*, 370 Lexington Ave, New York NY 10017.............212-532-3650
David C Cook Publishing Co*, 850 N Grove Ave, Elgin IL 60120 312-741-2400
Cooperative Children's Book Center, PO Box 5288, Madison WI 53705...608-262-3930
Copley Books, PO Box 957, La Jolla CA 92038 619-454-1842
Copper Beech Press, Box 1852 Brown Univ, Providence RI 02912 401-863-2393
Copper Canyon Press*, Box 271, Port Townsend WA 98368......................206-385-4925
Copperfield Press, PO Box 15025, Austin TX 78761 512-837-2931
Copyright Information Services, Box 1460, Friday Harbor WA 98250......206-378-5128
Corbett Press, PO Box 403, Newport KY 41072..606-431-6054
Cordillera Press Inc*, PO Box 3699, Evergreen CO 80439 303-670-3010
Corinthian Press, 3592 Lee Rd, Shaker Heights OH 44120 216-751-7300
Cornell Maritime Press Inc*, Box 456, Centreville MD 21617 301-758-1075
Cornell Modern Indonesia Project, 102 West Ave, Ithaca NY 14850........607-255-4359
Cornell Univ Press*, 124 Roberts Pl Box 250, Ithaca NY 14851...............607-257-7000
Cornerstone Press, PO Box 28048, St Louis MO 63119 314-296-9662
Cornwall Books*, 440 Forsgate Dr, Cranbury NJ 08512 609-655-4770
Coronado Press Inc, PO Box 3232, Lawrence KS 66046...........................913-843-5988
Coronado Publishers Inc*, 1250 6th Ave, San Diego CA 92101................619-231-6616
Correlan Publications, PO Box 337, Watsonville CA 95706.......................408-728-1766
Cortina Learning Intl Inc*, 17 Riverside Ave, Westport CT 06880 203-227-8471
Cottontail Publications, R1 Box 198, Bennington IN 47011.....................812-427-3914
Cottonwood Publications, PO Box 264, Worthington OH 43085................614-883-8132

Cougar Books, PO Box 22879, Sacramento CA 95822 916-428-3271
Council for Indian Education, 517 Rimrock Rd, Billings MT 59102 406-252-7451
Council Oak Books, 8424 St Louis, Tulsa OK 74120 918-587-6454
Council of Planning Librarians*, 1313 E 60th St, Chicago IL 60637 312-947-2007
Council on Foreign Relations Inc*, 58 E 68th St, New York NY 10021....212-734-0400
Council On Interracial Books, 1841 Broadway, New York NY 10023.......212-757-5339
Country Bazaar Publ*, Honey Inc Bldg Rt 2, Berryville AR 72616 501-423-3131
The Country House, 15 Thomas Ave, Topsham ME 04086..........................207-729-8941
Country Music Foundation Press, 4 Music Sq E, Nashville TN 37203......615-256-1639
The Countryman Press Inc*, Box 175, Woodstock VT 05091.....................802-457-1049
The Countryside Press, PO Box 1275, San Luis Obispo CA 93406 805-543-5404
Cowley Publications*, 980 Memorial Dr, Cambridge MA 02138................617-876-3507
Harold E Cox, 80 Virginia Terrace, Forty Fort PA 18704............................717-287-7647
CPI Publishing Inc*, 223 E 48th St, New York NY 10017.............................212-753-3800
Crab Cove Books, PO Box 214, Alameda CA 94501....................................415-523-1857
Crabtree Publishing*, PO Box 3451, Federal Way WA 98063 206-927-3777
Craftsman Book Co, 6058 Corte Del Cedro, Carlsbad CA 92008...............619-438-7828
Crain Books*, 4255 W Touhy Ave, Lincolnwood IL 60646...........................312-679-5500
George F Cram Co, 301 S La Salle St, Indianapolis IN 46206 317-635-5564
Crambruck Press, 381 Park Ave S, New York NY 10016.............................212-532-0871
Cranbrook Inst of Science, PO Box 801, Bloomfield Hills MI 48013...........313-645-3255
Crane Publishing*, 1301 Hamilton Ave, Trenton NJ 08629 609-586-6400
CRC Press Inc*, 2000 Corporate Blvd NW, Boca Raton FL 33431............305-994-0555
CRCS Publications*, PO Box 20850, Reno NV 89515 702-358-2850
Creative Book Co*, 8210 Varna Ave, Van Nuys CA 91402...........................818-988-2334
Creative Education Inc*, 123 S Broad St Box 227, Mankato MN 56001....507-388-6273
Creative Homeowner Press, 24 Park Wy, Upr Saddle Rvr NJ 07458..........201-934-7100
Creative Learning Press Inc, Box 320, Mansfield Center CT 06250 203-423-8120
Creative Publications*, 1101 San Antonio Rd, Mtn View CA 94043 415-968-1101
Creative Publishing Co*, PO Box 9292, College Station TX 77840............409-696-7907
Creative Roots Inc, PO Box 401 Planetarium Sta, New York NY 10024...212-799-2294
Creative With Words Publications, PO Box 223226, Carmel CA 93922....408-625-3542
Creativity Unlimited, 30819 Casilina, Rancho Palos Verdes CA 90274.....213-377-7908
Creatures At Large Publishing, PO Box 687, Pacifica CA 94044 415-359-4341
Crestwood House Inc*, PO Box 3427, Mankato MN 56002.........................507-388-1616
Crisp Publications Inc, 95 1st Ave, Los Altos CA 94002 415-948-5810
Critic's Choice/Lorevan*, 31 E 28th St, New York NY 10016 212-685-1550
Critique, PO Box 11368, Santa Rosa CA 95406..707-525-9401
Crittenden Books, PO Box 1150, Novato CA 94948.....................................415-883-8771
Croissant & Co, PO Box 282, Athens OH 45701 614-593-3008
Cross-Cultural Communications*, 239 Wynsum, Merrick NY 11566 516-868-5635
The Crossing Press*, 22 D Roache Rd Box 207, Freedom CA 95019........408-722-0711
Crossroad Publishing Co*, 370 Lexington Ave, New York NY 10017.......212-532-3650
Crossroads Communications, PO Box 7, Carpentersville IL 60110...........312-888-7736
Crossroads Press*, 255 Kinsey Hall UCLA, Los Angeles CA 90024........213-206-8011
Crown Publishers Inc*, 225 Park Ave S, New York NY 10003....................212-254-1600
CSS Publications, PO Box 23, Iowa Falls IA 50126....................................515-648-2716
Cube Publications Inc, 1 Buena Vista Rd, Port Jefferson NY 11777 516-331-4990
Anges Cupar Publishers, 117 Hunt Dr, Princeton NJ 08540......................609-924-3358
Curbstone Press*, 321 Jackson St, Willimantic CT 06226..........................203-423-9190
John Curley & Assoc Inc*, Box 37, S Harmouth MA 02664.........................617-394-1282
Current Co, PO Box 46, Bristol RI 02809...401-253-7824
Curtin & London Inc, PO Box 363, Marblehead MA 01945 617-631-0762

Custom Publishing Co*, 11 Starglow Cir, Sacramento CA 95831 916-424-4726
Custombook Inc*, 77 Main St, Tappan NY 10983 914-365-0414
Cynthia Publishing, 4455 Los Feliz Blvd, Los Angeles CA 90027 213-664-3165
Cypress Publishing Group*, 1763 Gardena Ave, Glendale CA 91204.......818-244-8651
Da Capo Press Inc*, 233 Spring St, New York NY 10013....................212-620-8000
Daisy Publishing Inc, Box 67 A, Mukilteo WA 98275 206-347-1414
Dakota Press*, Univ of South Dakota, Vermillion SD 57069.....................605-677-5281
Dale Books Inc, 901 H St Ste 307, Sacramento CA 95814....................916-441-2452
Dance Horizons, PO Box 109, Princeton NJ 08542.............................609-737-8177
John Daniel Publisher*, PO Box 21922, Santa Barbara CA 93121.............805-962-1780
Dante Univ of Amer Press*, 17 Station St, Brookline Village MA 02147..617-734-2045
Daring Publishing Group*, PO Box 526, Canton OH 44701....................216-454-7519
William C Darrah, 2235 Baltimore Pike, Gettysburg PA 17325...............717-334-2272
The Dartnell Corp, 4660 Ravenswood Ave, Chicago IL 60640................312-561-4000
The Darwin Press Inc*, Box 2202, Princeton NJ 08543 609-737-1349
DATA Inc*, 9889 Willow Creek Rd, San Diego CA 92131....................619-578-7600
Datarule Publishing Co Inc, PO Box 488, New Canaan CT 06840...........914-533-2263
Daughter Culture Publ, 3109 Scotts Vly Dr, Scotts Vly CA 95066 408-438-7411
Daughters of St Paul*, 50 St Paul's Ave, Boston MA 02130.................617-522-8911
Byron Davenport Publishers, PO Box 34165, Bethesda MD 20817............301-983-0742
May Davenport Publ, 26313 Purissima, Los Altos Hills CA 94022.........415-948-6499
F A David Co*, 1915 Arch St, Philadelphia PA 19103 215-568-2270
Harlan Davidson*, 3110 N Arlington Hts Rd, Arlington Hts IL 60004 312-253-9720
L Davis Press Inc, 1125 Oxford Pl, Schenectady NY 12308...................518-372-8203
Davis Publications Inc*, 50 Portland St, Worcester MA 01608 617-754-7201
Davis Publications Inc*, 380 Lexington Ave, New York NY 10168 212-557-9100
Steve Davis Publishing*, PO Box 190831, Dallas TX 75219 214-823-8660
Steve Davis Publishing*, 2626 Cole Ave, Dallas TX 75219 214-954-4469
DAW Books Inc*, 1633 Broadway, New York NY 10019 212-397-8017
The Dawn Horse Press*, 750 Adrian Way, San Rafael CA 94903............415-492-0922
Dawn Publications, 14618 Tyler Foote Rd, Nevada City CA 95959...........916-292-3482
Dawnwood Press, 2 Park Ave Ste 2650, New York NY 10016................212-532-7160
Daye Press, PO Box 8021, Athens GA 30603 404-542-4244
DBI Books Inc*, 4092 Commercial Ave, Northbrook IL 60062................312-272-6310
Walter De Gruyter Inc*, 200 Saw Mill River Rd, Hawthorne NY 10532...914-747-0110
Juan De La Cuesta-Hispan, 270 Indian Rd, Newark DE 19711...............302-453-8699
De Vorss & Co*, Box 550, Marina del Rey CA 90294..........................213-870-7478
Decker Press Inc*, 2721 H Rd, Grand Junction CO 81506...................303-241-6193
Marcel Dekker Inc*, 270 Madison Ave, New York NY 10016 212-696-9000
Del Rey Books*, 201 E 50th St, New York NY 10022 212-572-2677
Delacorte Press*, 245 E 47th St, New York NY 10017.........................212-605-3000
Delapeake Publishing Co, Box 1148, Wilmington DE 19899...................302-652-0888
Dell Publishing Co*, 1 Dag Hammarskjold Plz, New York NY 10017 212-605-3000
Dellen Publishing Co, 400 Pacific Ave 3rd fl, San Francisco CA 94133 415-433-9900
Delmar Publishers*, 2 Computer Dr W, Albany NY 12212 518-459-1150
DeLong & Assoc Poetry Review, PO Box 1732, Annapolis MD 21404 301-263-5592
Delphinium Press, Sarah Lawrence College, Bronxville NY 10708............914-337-0700
Dembner Books*, 80 8th Ave Ste 1803, New York NY 10011 212-924-2525
DeMortmain Books/E S Matz, PO Box 1280, Pine Grove CA 95665........209-295-4644
The Denali Press, Box 1535, Juneau AK 99802....................................907-586-6014
T S Denison & Co Inc*, 9601 Newton Ave S, Minneapolis MN 55431.......612-888-1460
Denlingers Publishers Ltd*, PO Box 76, Fairfax VA 22030 703-830-4646
Depot Press, PO Box 60072, Nashville TN 37206 615-226-1890

Deseret Book Co*, PO Box 30178, Salt Lake City UT 84130......................801-534-1515
Design Enterprises of SF, PO Box 14695, San Francisco CA 94114...........415-282-8813
Designs III Publ, 515 W Commonwealth #105, Fullerton CA 92632.........714-871-9100
Devin-Adair Publishers Inc*, 6 N Water St, Greenwich CT 06830 203-531-7755
Devon Publishing Co, 2700 Virginia Ave NW, Washington DC 20037 202-337-5197
Devonshire Publishing, PO Box 7066, Chicago IL 60680 312-242-3846
Devyn Press, 151 Thierman Lane, Louisville KY 40207 502-895-1354
Dharma Publishing*, 2425 Hillside Ave, Berkeley CA 94704 415-548-5407
Diablo Press Inc, PO Box 7042, Berkeley CA 94707................................415-524-9623
Dial Books for Young Readers*, 2 Park Ave, New York NY 10016...........212-725-1818
Diamond Communications Inc*, PO Box 88, South Bend IN 46624.........219-287-5008
Diane Publishing Co*, 600 Upland Ave, Upland PA 19015.......................215-499-7415
Dicmar Publishing, PO Box 3533, Washington DC 20007...........................301-585-4320
Dicul Publishing, PO Box 091111, Columbus OH 43209 614-231-4670
Digital Press*, 12A Esquire Rd, Billenca MA 01862....................................617-663-4138
Dillon Press Inc*, 500 S 3rd St, Minneapolis MN 55415 612-333-2691
Dimension Books Inc*, Box 811, Denville NJ 07834...................................201-627-4334
Dimi Press, 3820 Oak Hollow Lane SE, Salem OR 97302............................503-364-7698
DIN Publications, PO Box 21126, Phoenix AZ 85036..................................602-257-0797
Direct Market Designs, PO Box 142, Island Lake IL 60042.........................312-526-5141
Direct Marketing Association Inc*, 6 E 43rd St, New York NY 10017 212-689-4977
Directed Media Inc, PO Box 3005, Wenatchee WA 98801 509-662-7693
The Distributors*, 702 S Michigan, South Bend IN 46618...........................219-232-8500
D C Divry Inc, 148 W 24th St, New York NY 10011......................................212-255-2153
Do It Yourself Legal Publishers, 150 5th Ave, New York NY 10011 212-242-2840
Doctor Jazz Press, 617 Valley View Dr, Pelham AL 35124 205-663-3403
Documan Press, 3201 Lorraine Ave, Kalamazoo MI 49008..........................616-344-0805
Dodd Mead & Co*, 71 5th Ave, New York NY 10003 212-627-8444
The Dog Ear Press, PO Box 143, S Harpswell ME 04079 207-729-7791
Dog Eared Publications, PO Box 814, Corvallis OR 97339 503-753-4274
DOK Publishers Inc*, 525 W Falls Rd, West Falls NY 14170.....................716-652-9131
Dome Press, PO Box 400, Beavertown PA 17813..717-658-3870
The Dominion Press, PO Box 37, San Marcos CA 92069.............................619-746-9430
Donning Co Publishers*, 5659 Virginia Beach Blvd, Norfolk VA 23502...804-461-8090
The Doodly-Squat Press, PO Box 480740, Los Angeles CA 90048 213-856-4867
Dorison House Publishers, 824 Park Square Bldg, Boston MA 02116 617-426-1715
Dormac Inc*, PO Box 1699, Beaverton OR 97075.......................................503-641-3128
Dorset House Publishing Co Inc, 353 W 12th St, New York NY 10014 212-620-4053
The Dorsey Press*, 224 S Michigan Ave Ste 440, Chicago IL 60604..........312-322-8400
Double M Press, 16455 Tuba St, Sepulveda CA 91343 818-360-3166
Doubleday & Co Inc*, 245 Park Ave, New York NY 10167.........................212-953-4561
Dover Publications Inc*, 31 E 2nd St, Mineola NY 11501...........................516-294-7000
Dow Jones-Irwin*, 1818 Ridge Rd, Homewood IL 60430 312-798-6000
Down East Books*, Box 679, Camden ME 04843..207-594-9544
Downey Place Publishing House, PO Box 1352, El Cerrito CA 94530.......415-529-1012
Downtown Communications, 496 LaGuardia Pl, New York NY 10012 212-969-0132
Dracula Press, 29 Washington Sq W, New York NY 10011 212-533-5018
Dragon's Teeth Press, El Dorado Natl Forest, Georgetown CA 95634 916-333-4224
The Dragonsbreath Press, 10905 Bay Shore Dr, Sister Bay WI 54234.......414-854-2742
Drama Book Publ*, PO Box 816 Gracie Sta, New York NY 10028............212-517-4455
Dramaline Publications, 10470 Riverside Dr, Toluca Lake CA 91602.......818-985-9148
Dramatic Publishing Co*, 311 Washington St, Woodstock IL 60098.........815-338-7170
Dramatists Play Service Inc*, 440 Park Ave S, New York NY 10016........212-683-8960

Dropzone Press, PO Box 882222, San Francisco CA 94188 415-776-7164
Chris Drumm Books, Box 445, Polk City IA 50226..................................515-984-6749
Dryad Press, 15 Sherman Ave, Takoma Park MD 20912...........................301-891-3729
The Dryden Press*, 1 Salt Creek Lane, Hinsdale IL 60521.......................312-920-2450
The Duck Book Digest, PO Box 1047, Fallon NV 89406 702-423-6643
Duke Publishing Co, PO Box 210368, San Francisco CA 94121..................415-759-0118
Duke University Press*, PO Box 6697 College Sta, Durham NC 27708 919-684-2173
Duquesne University Press*, 600 Forbes Ave, Pittsburgh PA 15282..........412-434-6610
Sanford J Durst*, 29-28 41st Ave, Long Island City NY 11101.................718-706-0303
The Dushkin Publishing Group Inc*, Sluice Dock, Guilford CT 06437....203-453-4351
Dustbooks, Box 100, Paradise CA 95969 916-877-6110
E P Dutton*, 2 Park Ave, New York NY 10016..212-725-1818
Dyad Services, Box C34069 Dept 284, Seattle WA 98124.........................604-734-0255
Dynamic Information Publ, 8311 Greeley Blvd, Springfield VA 22152 202-676-3869
Dynamo Inc*, PO Box 173, Wheaton IL 60189..312-665-0060
E-Heart Press Inc, 3700 Mockingbird Ln, Dallas TX 75205....................214-741-6915
Eagles View Publishing, 706 W Riverdale Rd, Ogden UT 84405...............801-393-3991
Eakin Publications*, PO Box 23066, Austin TX 78735 512-288-1771
Earth-Song Press, 202 Hartwell Place, Sacramento CA 95825 916-927-6863
Earthview Press, PO Box 11036, Boulder CO 80301 303-666-8130
Earthwise Publications, PO Box 680-536, Miami FL 33168 305-688-8558
Easi Bild Directions*, 529 N State St, Briarcliff Manor NY 10510............914-941-6600
East Eagle Press, Box 812, Huron SD 57350 605-352-5875
East Rock Press Inc, PO Box 2939, New Haven CT 06515........................207-354-2467
The East Woods Press*, 429 East Blvd, Charlotte NC 28203.....................704-334-0897
Eastman Kodak Co*, 343 State St, Rochester NY 14650...........................716-724-4377
Eastview Editions*, Box 783, Westfield NJ 07091 201-964-9485
ECA Assoc, PO Box 15004, Chesapeake VA 23320...................................804-547-5542
The Ecco Press*, 18 W 30th St, New York NY 10001................................212-685-8240
Echo Publications Inc, PO Box 6548, New Orleans LA 70174 504-368-4050
The Economy Co*, PO Box 25308, Oklahoma City OK 73125 405-840-1444
Ed-Venture Films/Books, PO Box 23214, Los Angeles CA 90023 213-261-1885
EDC Publishing*, 8141 E 44th St, Tulsa OK 74145 918-622-4522
The Edelweiss Press, 405 E 63rd #1B, New York NY 10021 212-355-4925
Edgewood Press, 2865 E Rock Rd, Clare MI 48617..................................517-386-7178
Ediciones del Norte*, Box A130, Hanover NH 03755...............................603-795-2433
Ediciones Huracan Inc, Gonzalez 1002, Rio Piedras PR 00925.................809-763-7407
Ediciones Universal*, 3090 SW 8th St, Miami FL 33135..........................305-642-3355
Editorial Caribe, 3934 SW 8th St Ste 303, Miami FL 33134 305-445-0564
Editorial Experts, 85 S Bragg St Ste 400, Alexandria VA 22312...............703-642-3040
Editorial Research Services, PO Box 1832, Kansas City MO 64141...........913-829-0609
Educational Insights Inc*, 150 W Carob, Compton CA 90220..................213-637-2131
Educational Publications, PO Box 41870, Tucson AZ 85717.....................602-791-9690
Educational Service Inc*, 5060 St Joe Rd, Stevensville MI 49127 616-429-1451
Educational Technology Publ*, 720 Palisade, Englwd Cliffs NJ 07632......201-871-4007
Educational Testing Service*, Rosedale Rd, Princeton NJ 08541 609-921-9000
Educators Progress Service Inc*, 214 Center St, Randolph WI 53956......414-326-3126
Educators Publishing Service*, 75 Moulton St, Cambridge MA 02238.....617-547-6706
Edward William Publishing Co, PO Box 3280 #231, Austin TX 78764.....512-288-5884
The Edwin Mellen Press, Box 450, Lewiston NY 14092 716-754-2266
Wm B Eerdmans Publ*, 255 Jefferson Ave, Grand Rapids MI 49503 616-459-4591
Effective Learning*, 7 N Macuesten Pkwy, Mt Vernon NY 10550 914-664-7944
Eileens Beautique, 16901 S Jonesville Rd, Columbus IN 47201 812-522-4079

El Camino Publishers, 4010 Calle Real Ste 4, Santa Barbara CA 93110...805-682-9340
Eldridge Publishing Co*, PO Box 216, Franklin OH 45005 513-746-6531
Electric Bank, 4225 University Ave, Des Moines IA 50311 515-283-4152
Electronic Publ & Bookselling, 2214 N Central, Phoenix AZ 85004 602-254-6156
Ell Ell Diversified Inc, PO Box 1702, Santa Rosa CA 95402.....................707-542-8663
The Ellis Press, PO Box 1443, Peoria IL 61655 309-676-7611
Elsevier Science Publishing*, 52 Vanderbilt Ave, New York NY 10017....212-370-5520
Elysium Growth Press, 5436 Fernwood Ave, Los Angeles CA 90027 213-455-1000
Embee Press Publications, 82 Pine Grove Ave, Kingston NY 12401.........914-338-2226
EMC Corp*, 300 York Ave, St Paul MN 55101....................................612-771-1555
Emergency Response Institute*, 1918 Mark St NE, Olympia WA 98506..206-491-7785
Emerson Books Inc, 121 Northhampton Dr, White Plains NY 10603........914-739-3506
Empey Enterprises, 810 Alexander, Greenville MI 48838.........................616-754-7036
Emporia State Univ, 1200 Commercial St, Emporia KS 66801 316-343-1200
Encyclopaedia Britannica Inc*, 310 S Michigan Ave, Chicago IL 60604...312-347-7000
Encyclopedia Cookbook, 5800 1 Perkins Pl Dr, Baton Rouge LA 70808...504-769-5599
Endeavor Publishing, 30064 Annapolis Cir, Inkster MI 48141...................313-729-7836
Energize Books, 5450 Wissahickon Ave, Philadelphia PA 19144 215-438-8342
ENRICH*, 2325 Paragon Dr, San Jose CA 95131 408-263-7111
Enslow Publishers*, Bloy St & Ramsey Ave Box 777, Hillside NJ 07205..201-964-4116
Ensminger Publishing Co, PO Box 429, Clovis CA 93612 209-299-2263
Entelek, PO Box 1303, Portsmouth NH 03801.....................................603-436-0439
Enterpress Partners, PO Box 7097, Redlands CA 92374..........................714-792-5188
Enterprise Publishing, 725 Market St, Wilmington DE 19801...................302-654-0110
Entrepreneurial Workshops, 4000 Aurora Bldg, Seattle WA 98103 206-633-5350
Environmental Law Inst*, 1616 P St NW #200, Wash DC 20036 202-328-5150
Epimetheus Press Inc*, PO Box 565 Gracie Sta, New York NY 10028.....212-879-0553
Epistemics Institute Press, PO Box 18672, Los Angeles CA 90007 213-659-4541
EPM Publications Inc*, 1003 Turkey Run Rd, McLean VA 22101............703-442-7810
Equality Press, 420 CSUC, Chico CA 95929.......................................916-895-6482
ERA CCR Corp/The Write Track, 4 Terrace Dr, Nyack NY 10960..........914-358-6806
Erasia Press Inc*, 302 5th Ave, New York NY 10001 212-564-4099
R J Erdmann Publ*, 26 Quarterhorse Ln, Rolling Hills Est CA 90274.....213-544-5071
Erie St Press, 221 S Clinton, Oak Park IL 60302..................................312-848-5716
Paul S Eriksson Publisher*, 208 Battell Bldg, Middlebury VT 05753 802-388-7303
Erin Hills Publisher, 1390 Fairway Dr, San Luis Obispo CA 93401..........805-543-3050
Lawrence Erlbaum Assoc*, 365 Broadway #102, Hillsdale NJ 07642........201-666-4110
Eros Publishing Co, PO Box 355 Parkchester Station, Bronx NY 10462...212-328-5569
Escortguide, 535 Cordova Rd Ste 125, Santa Fe NM 87501.....................505-988-7099
ESPress Inc, Box 55482, Washington DC 20011....................................202-723-4578
Essays in Literature, Western Illinois Univ, Macomb IL 61455 309-298-2212
ETC Publications, Drawer ETC, Palm Springs CA 92263........................619-325-5352
Blaine Ethridge Books, 15 E Kirby, Detroit MI 48202 313-838-3363
Eureka Publications, PO Box 372, Mantua NJ 08051.............................609-468-4145
Europe Through the Back Door, 120 4th Ave N, Edmonds WA 98020 206-771-8303
Evangel Press, 301 N Elm, Nappanee IN 46550 219-773-3164
M Evans & Co Inc*, 216 E 49th St, New York NY 10017.......................212-688-2810
Evans Publications Inc, PO Box 520, Perkins OK 74059 405-547-2144
Everett Press, 610 C Bicycle Path N, Port Jefferson NY 11776................516-928-4958
Evergreen Editors, Box 763, Laurel MD 20707 301-953-1861
Evergreen Paddleways, 1416 21st St, Two Rivers WI 54241....................414-794-8485
Evergreen Press, Box 4971, Walnut Creek CA 94596.............................415-933-9700
Executive Enterprises Publ*, 22 W 21st St 10th fl, New York NY 10010 ..212-645-7880

The Exhorters Inc, PO Box 492, Vienna VA 22180 703-698-6880
Exile Press, 765 Sunset Pkwy, Novato CA 94947 415-883-2132
Expedition Press, 311 W Vine, Kalamazoo MI 49001 616-381-5222
F & S Press*, 106 Fulton St, New York NY 10038................................212-233-1080
Faber & Faber Inc*, 50 Cross St, Winchester MA 01890.........................617-721-1427
Facts On File Inc*, 460 Park Ave S, New York NY 10016.........................212-683-2244
Fainshaw Press, Box 961, Westmoreland NH 03467 603-585-6654
Fairchild Books & Visuals, 7 E 12th St, New York NY 10003.....................212-741-5814
Fairleigh Dickinson Univ Press*, 285 Madison Ave, Madison NJ 07940 ..201-593-8564
The Fairmont Press Inc*, 700 Indian Trail, Lilburn GA 30247....................404-925-9388
Fairway House, PO Box 6344, Bakersfield CA 93386 805-322-6414
Falcon Press, 3660 N 3rd St, Phoenix AZ 85012.....................................602-246-3546
Falcon Press*, 2210 Wilshire Blvd, Santa Monica CA 90403....................213-821-3540
Falcon Press Publishing Co*, PO Box 729, Billings MT 59103...................406-245-0550
Falcon Publishing, PO Box 688, Ben Lomond CA 95005 408-336-2906
Fallen Leaf Press, PO Box 10034, Berkeley CA 94709 415-848-7805
The Family Album, RD 1 Box 42, Glen Rock PA 17327 717-235-2134
Family Service America, 44 E 23rd St, New York NY 10010.......................212-674-6100
Fan Publishing Co, PO Box 20306, Raleigh NC 27609.............................919-846-0607
Fandata Publcations, 7761 Asterella Ct, Springfield VA 22152...................703-644-7354
Fantagraphics Books, 1800 Bridgegate #101, Westlake Vlg CA 91361.....805-379-1881
Fantasy Workshop, 1400 W Cross St, Lakewood NJ 08701.......................201-363-3988
Farley Court of Pub*, 2623 Kaneville Rd PO Box 387, Geneva IL 60134..312-232-2711
Farrar Straus & Giroux Inc*, 19 Union Sq W, New York NY 10003........212-741-6900
Fathom Eight*, PO Box 80505, San Marino CA 91108 818-289-5088
Fathom Publishing Co, Box 1690, Cordova AK 99574...............................907-424-3116
The Faxon Co Inc, 15 Southwest Park, Westwood MA 02090 617-329-3350
Federal Research Press, 65 Franklin St, Boston MA 02110.........................617-423-0978
Philipp Feldheim*, 200 Airport Exec Park, Spring Valley NY 10977.........914-356-2282
Frederick Fell Publishers*, 2131 Hollywood Blvd, Hollywood FL 33020..305-925-5242
Feminist Press at CUNY, 311 E 94th St, New York NY 10128.....................212-360-5790
Ferguson Communications Publ, 1540 E Moore, Hillsdale MI 49242.......517-437-7205
J G Ferguson Publishing Co, 111 E Wacker Dr, Chicago IL 60601 312-861-0666
Howard Fertig Inc Purlisher*, 80 E 11th St, New York NY 10003 212-982-7922
FES Ltd Publishing, PO Box 70, Bayside NY 11361.................................718-423-6662
Festival Publications, PO Box 10180, Glendale CA 91209 818-718-8494
Fiction Collective, Brooklyn College English Dept, Brooklyn NY 11210...718-780-5547
Fiction Collective, Univ of Colo English Dept, Boulder CO 80302 303-492-0111
The Fideler Co, 203 Logan St SW, Grand Rapids MI 49503........................616-456-8577
Field Publications*, 245 Long Hill Rd, Middletown CT 06457 203-638-2400
Fiesta City Publishers, PO Box 5861, Santa Barbara CA 93150 805-969-2891
Fiesta Publishing Corp*, 6360 NE 4th Ct, Miami FL 33138 305-751-1181
Filter Press*, Box 5, Palmer Lake CO 80133...303-481-2523
Financial Publishing Co*, 82 Brookline Ave, Boston MA 02215................617-262-4040
Fine Arts Press, 1311A N Broadway PO Box 3491, Knoxville TN 37927...615-637-9243
Donald I Fine Inc*, 128 E 36th St, New York NY 10016 212-696-1838
Finesse Publishing, 2068 Via Las Cumbres Ste 7, San Diego CA 92111 ...619-569-7728
Finney Co Inc, 3350 Gorham Ave, Minneapolis MN 55426........................612-929-6165
Finnish Amer Literary Foundation*, PO Box 1838, Portland OR 97207..503-229-3064
Firebrand Books, 141 The Commons, Ithaca NY 14850 607-272-0000
Firehole Press, PO Box 255, Davenport CA 95017 408-426-8205
Fireside Books*, 1230 Ave of the Americas, New York NY 10020.............212-245-6400
Fireside Books*, 8356 Olive Blvd, St Louis MO 63132.............................314-991-1335

Fireweed Press, PO Box 83970, Fairbanks AK 99708 907-479-2398
First East Coast Theatre, PO Box A244, New York NY 10014 718-296-1979
Fischer Publishing Corp, PO Box 368, Canfield OH 44406 216-533-1232
The Fisher Institute, 6380 LBJ Fwy Ste 183, Dallas TX 75240.....................214-233-1041
Fjord Press, PO Box 16501, Seattle WA 98116...206-625-9363
Fleet Press Corp*, 160 5th Ave, New York NY 10010....................................212-243-6100
Flora & Fauna Publ*, 4300 NW 23rd Ave, Gainesville FL 32606...............904-371-9858
J Flores Publications, Box 14, Rosemead CA 91770 818-287-2195
Floricanto Press, 604 William St, Oakland CA 94612 415-893-3149
Florida Classics Library, PO Box 1657, Port Salerno FL 33492...................305-546-9380
Florida Trend Book Div, PO Box 611, St Petersburg FL 33731 813-821-5800
Flower Press, 10322 Shaver Rd, Kalamazoo MI 49002...................................616-327-0108
FM Atlas Publishing Co, Box 24, Adolph MN 55701 218-879-7676
Focal Point Press, 321 City Island Ave, New York NY 10464 212-885-1403
Focal Press*, 80 Montvale Ave, Stoneham MA 02180....................................617-438-8464
Fodor's Travel Publications Inc*, 201 E 50th St, New York NY 10022.....212-751-2600
Foghorn Press*, 2687 45th Ave, San Francisco CA 94116 415-564-4918
Folcroft Library Editions/Norwood*, 842 Main St, Darby PA 19023.........215-583-4550
Folder Editions, 103 26 68th Rd, Forest Hills NY 11375 718-275-3839
Folger Books*, 440 Forsgate Dr, Cranbury NJ 08512....................................609-655-4770
Folk Art Studios, 608 E 1st, Tustin CA 92680 714-731-3355
Food & Nutrition Press Inc, 155 Post Rd E Ste 6, Westport CT 06881.....203-227-6596
Food First Books, 1885 Mission St, San Francisco CA 94103......................415-864-8555
The Fool Court Press, Box 25824, Charlotte NC 28212.................................704-537-7375
Footprint Publishing Co, PO Box 1542, Loma Linda CA 92354...................714-883-4114
Fordham Univ Press*, Univ Box L, Bronx NY 10458 212-579-2320
Foreign Policy Association*, 205 Lexington Ave, New York NY 10016 212-481-8450
Forest Press, 85 Watervliet Ave, Albany NY 12206 518-489-8549
Foreworks, PO Box 9747, N Hollywood CA 91609 818-982-0467
Foris Publications, Box C 50, Cinnaminson NJ 08077.................................609-829-6830
Forman Publishing, 11661 San Vicente Blvd, Los Angeles CA 90049 213-820-8672
Formur Int, 4200 Laclede Ave, St Louis MO 63108......................................314-533-9600
Forrest Productions, PO Box 1245, Beverly Hills CA 90213........................213-557-2615
Fortress Press*, 2900 Queen Ln, Philadelphia PA 19129 215-848-6800
Fred Foster Publications, 5200 Stockton Blvd, Sacramento CA 95820.....916-383-8579
Fotofolio Inc, 75 Spring St, New York NY 10012 212-226-0923
The Foundation Center*, 79 5th Ave, New York NY 10003...........................212-620-4230
The Foundation Press Inc*, 170 Old Country Rd, Mineola NY 11501......516-248-5580
Fred Fox Publisher, 2407 Meadow Valley Ter, Los Angeles CA 90039.....213-666-8230
Foxfire Press, Box B, Rabun Gap GA 30568 404-746-5318
Franciscan Herald Press*, 1434 W 51st St, Chicago IL 60609 312-254-4462
Burt Franklin & Co Inc*, 235 E 44th St, New York NY 10017.....................212-687-5250
The Franklin Inst Press*, PO Box 2266, Philadelphia PA 19103.................215-844-6751
The Franklin Library*, 800 3rd Ave, New York NY 10022............................212-758-7400
The Chas Franklin Press, 7821 175th St SW, Edmonds WA 98020 206-774-6979
Fraser Publishing, PO Box 494, Burlington VT 05402................................802-658-0322
Free Press*, 866 3rd Ave, New York NY 10022...212-702-2000
Freelance Communications, PO Box 717, Arcata CA 95521 707-826-0102
W H Freeman & Co Publ*, 41 Madison Ave, New York NY 10010...........212-532-7660
Freeman Cooper & Co, 1736 Stockton St, San Francisco CA 94133...........415-362-6171
Freline Inc*, PO Box 889, Hagerstown MD 21741..301-797-9689
French Forum Publishers*, Box 5108 Cantrill Dr, Lexington KY 40505...606-299-9530
Samuel French Inc*, 45 W 25th St, New York NY 10010 212-206-8990

Freundlich Books*, 212 5th Ave Ste 1305, New York NY 10010 212-532-9666
Eleanor Friede Books Inc, 45 W 12th St, New York NY 10011 212-741-2900
Friendly Press, 401 Park Ave S, New York NY 10016.................................212-684-4255
The Friends of Photography, Box 500, Carmel CA 93921 408-624-6330
Friends United Press, 101 Quaker Hill Dr, Richmond IN 47374...............317-962-7573
Friendship Press*, 475 Riverside Dr, New York NY 10115 212-870-2495
The Frog In The Well, 25A Buena Vista Ter, San Francisco CA 94117.....415-431-2113
C J Frompovich Publ, RD 1 Chestnut Rd, Coopersburg PA 18036 215-346-8461
The Frontier Press Co, PO Box 1098, Columbus OH 43216 614-864-3737
Frontier Printing & Publishing*, 529 Dayton St, Edmonds WA 98020.....206-775-5877
Frozen Waffles Press, PO Box 1941, Bloomington IN 47402.....................812-334-0381
Fruition Publications Inc, Box 103, Blawenburg NJ 08504.......................609-466-3196
Fulcrum Inc*, 350 Indiana St, Golden CO 80401.....................................303-277-1623
Funk & Wagnalls Inc*, 53 E 77th St, New York NY 10021......................212-570-4500
Furuta Assoc, PO Box 399, Fallbrook CA 92028..619-723-8678
Futura Publishing Co Inc*, 295 Main St Box 330, Mt Kisco NY 10549.....914-666-3505
Future Science Research Publ Co, PO Box 06392, Portland OR 97206.....503-235-1971
Futures Unlimited Inc, 5200 W 73rd St, Minneapolis MN 55437 612-835-7729
Gain Publications, PO Box 2204, Van Nuys CA 91404 818-785-1895
The P Gaines Co Publishers, PO Box 2253, Oak Park IL 60303................312-524-1073
Gale Research Co*, Book Tower, Detroit MI 48226....................................313-961-2242
The Galileo Press, 15201 Wheeler Ln, Sparks MD 21152 301-771-4544
Gallaudet Univ Press*, 800 Florida Ave NE, Washington DC 20002 202-651-5488
Galley Press, PO Box 892, Portland OR 97207...206-693-1397
Gambit Inc Publishers, 535 Albany St, Boston MA 02118.........................617-423-5803
Gambling Times Inc*, 1018 N Cole Ave, Hollywood CA 90038 213-463-4833
W Paul Ganley Publisher, PO Box 149, Buffalo NY 14226.......................716-839-2415
Gannett Books*, PO Box 1460B, Portland ME 04104 207-775-5811
Willliam Gannon Publisher, 205 E Palace Ave, Santa Fe NM 87501.........505-982-1579
Garber Communications Inc*, 5 Garber Hill Rd, Blauvelt NY 10913.......914-359-9292
Garden Way Publishing*, Schoolhouse Rd, Pownal VT 05261....................802-823-5811
Gardner Press Inc*, 10 Union Sq W, New York NY 10003 212-924-8293
Garland Publishing Inc*, 136 Madison Ave, New York NY 10016.............212-686-7492
Gaslight Publications, 112 E 2nd, Bloomington IN 47401 812-332-5169
Gateway Books, 66 Cleary Ct #1405, San Francisco CA 94109...................415-821-3440
Gateways Books & Tapes, PO Box 370, Nevada City CA 95959 916-477-1116
Wm W Gaunt & Sons Inc, 3011 Gulf Dr, Holmes Beach FL 33510 813-778-5211
Gavea Brown Publications, Box O Brown Univ, Providence RI 02912......401-863-3042
Gay Sunshine Press*, PO Box 40397, San Francisco CA 94140...................415-824-3184
Gayellow Pages, PO Box 292 Village Sta, New York NY 10014...................212-674-0120
Gaz, 277 23rd Ave, San Francisco CA 94121...415-751-6852
Gazelle Publications, 5580 Stanley Dr, Auburn CA 95603...........................916-878-1223
GDE Publ Div of Glen Eley Ent, PO Box 340, Lima OH 45802 419-634-8221
Gem City College Press, 700 State St PO Box 179, Quiny IL 62306 217-222-0391
Gem Guides Book Co, 3677 San Gabriel Pkwy, Pico Rivera CA 90660 213-692-5492
Genealogical Publishing Co*, 1001 N Calvert St, Baltimore MD 21202....301-837-8271
Genera Historical Society, 543 S Main St, Geneva NY 14456 315-789-5151
General Hall Inc, 5 Talon Way, Dix Hills NY 11746 516-243-0155
General Synthetics, PO Box 1118, Poway CA 92064...................................619-679-1068
Genium Publishing Corp*, 1145 Catalyn St, Schenectady NY 12303 518-377-8855
Geological Society of America*, 3300 Penrose Pl, Boulder CO 80301 303-447-2020
Georgetown Univ Press*, Intercultural Ctr, Washington DC 20057 202-625-3385
Georgia State Univ*, College of Business Admin, Atlanta GA 30303........404-658-4253

Gessler Publishing Co Inc*, 900 Broadway, New York NY 10003 212-673-3113
Gibbes Art Gallery, 135 Meeting St, Charleston SC 29401 803-722-2706
The C R Gibson Co*, 32 Knight St, Norwalk CT 06851................................203-847-4543
Dot Gibson Publications, PO Box 117, Waycross GA 31502.....................912-285-2848
Gifted Education Press*, 10201 Yuma Ct, Manassas VA 22110.................703-369-5017
Gilgal Publications, Box 3386, Sunriver OR 97707 503-593-8639
The K S Giniger Co Inc*, 235 Park Ave S, New York NY 10003................212-533-5080
Ginn & Co*, 1250 Fairwood Ave Box 2649, Columbus OH 43216....617-861-1670
Ginseng Press, 74 Poplar Grove Rd, Franklin NC 28734 704-369-9735
Steve Ginter Naval Fighters, 1754 Warfield Cir, Simi Valley CA 93063....805-584-9732
Gladbrook Publishing Co, 92 Valley Rd, New Canaan CT 06840 203-966-4484
Glanville Publishers Inc*, 75 Main St, Dobbs Ferry NY 10522...............914-693-1320
Glastonbury Press, 12816 E Rose Dr, Whittier CA 90601...........................213-698-4243
Michael Glazier Inc*, 1723 Delaware Ave, Wilmington DE 19806..........302-654-1635
Glenbridge Publishing, 1303 W Adams, Macomb IL 61455 309-833-5704
Glencoe Publishing Co*, Front & Brown Sts, Riverside NJ 08075 818-990-3083
Glenmark Publishing*, 5041 Byrne Rd, Oregon WI 53575 608-255-1812
Peter Glenn Publications Ltd*, 17 E 48th St, New York NY 10017...........212-688-7940
Global Publishing Co, PO Box 35357, Los Angeles CA 90035..................213-937-4356
Globe Book Co Inc*, 50 W 23rd St, New York NY 10010.............................212-741-0505
The Globe Pequot Press, Old Chester Rd, Chester CT 06412...................203-526-9571
Globe Press Books*, PO Box 2045, New York NY 10159.............................212-362-3720
Glover Publications, PO Box 21745, Seattle WA 98111 206-932-2607
GMG Publishing Corp*, 25 W 43rd St, New York NY 10036......................212-354-8840
Gnomon Press, PO Box 106, Frankfort KY 40602 502-223-1858
David R Godine Publisher Inc*, 306 Dartmouth St, Boston MA 02116....617-536-0761
Goehringer & Sons Assoc, PO Box 9626, Pittsburgh PA 15226 412-531-9549
Gold Crest Publishing, 5644 Londonderry Rd, Charlotte NC 28210..........704-552-6255
Golden Books*, 850 3rd Ave, New York NY 10022......................................212-753-8500
The Golden Quill Press*, Avery Rd, Francestown NH 03043 603-547-6622
Golden West Books, PO Box 80250, San Marino CA 91108 213-283-3446
Golden West Publishers, 4113 N Longview, Phoenix AZ 85014 602-265-4392
Golf Sports Publishing, PO Box 3687, Lacey WA 98503 206-491-8067
Good News Publishers*, 9825 W Roosevelt Rd, Westchester IL 60153.....312-345-7474
Goodfellow Catalog Press, PO Box 4520, Berkeley CA 94704 415-845-2062
Goodheart-Willcox Co*, 123 W Taft Dr, S Holland IL 60473 312-333-7200
Gordian Press Inc*, 85 Tompkins St Box 304, Staten Island NY 10304.....718-273-4700
Gordon & Breach Science Publ*, 50 W 23rd St, New York NY 10010......212-206-8900
Gorsuch Scarisbrick*, 8233 Via Paseo del Norte, Scottsdale AZ 85258 ...602-991-7881
Gospel Publishing House*, 1445 Boonville Ave, Springfield MO 65802....417-862-2781
Gothic Bookshop, Box LM Duke Univ, Durham NC 27706.....................919-684-3986
Gothic Press, 4998 Perkins Rd, Baton Rouge LA 70808 504-766-2906
Gould Publications*, 199-300 State St, Binghamton NY 13901 607-724-3000
Bruce Gould Publications, Box 16, Seattle WA 98111................................206-284-6144
Government Institutes*, 966 Hungerford Dr #24, Rockville MD 20850...301-251-9250
Gower Medical Publishing Ltd*, 101 5th Ave, New York NY 10003.........212-929-6290
Graham-Conley Press, PO Box 2968, New Haven CT 06515 203-389-0183
Granger Book Co Inc*, PO Box 406, Great Neck NY 11022......................516-466-3676
Granville Publ, 10960 Wilshire Blvd #826, Los Angeles CA 90024...........213-477-3920
Grapevine Publications Inc, PO Box 118, Corvallis OR 97339 503-754-0583
Graphic Arts Ctr Publishing, 3019 NW Yeon Ave, Portland OR 97210...503-226-2402
Graphic Dimensions, 8 Frederick Rd, Pittsford NY 14834.......................716-381-3428
Graphics Plus, 3710 Robertson Blvd, Culver City CA 90232......................213-559-3732

Gravity Publishing, 6324 Heather Ridge Way, Oakland CA 94611.............415-339-3774
Graywolf Press*, 213 E 4th St, St Paul MN 55101................................612-221-9035
Great Eastern Book Co, PO Box 308, Boston MA 02117........................617-424-0030
Great Elm Press, RD2 Box 37, Rexville NY 14877................................607-225-4592
Great Northwest Publishing, PO Box 10-3902, Anchorage AK 99510.......907-373-0121
Great Ocean Publishers, 1823 N Lincoln St, Arlington VA 22207................703-525-0909
Great West Books, PO Box 1028, Lafayette CA 94549............................415-283-3184
Greater Phila Womens Yellow Pages, PO Box 42397, Phila PA 19101......215-235-4042
Green Acres School, 11701 Danville Dr, Rockville MD 20852....................301-881-4100
Green Hill Publishers*, 722 Columbus St, Ottawa IL 61350.....................815-434-7905
Warren H Green Inc*, 8356 Olive Blvd, St Louis MO 63132....................314-991-1335
Green Key Press, PO Box 3801, Seminole FL 33542..............................813-596-0215
Green Leaf Press, PO Box 6880, Alhambra CA 91802............................818-281-6809
The Green Street Press, PO Box 1957, Cambridge MA 02238....................617-547-6347
The Green Tiger Press, 1061 India St, San Diego CA 92101.....................619-238-1001
Greenberg Publishing Co*, 7543 Main St, Sykesville MD 21784................301-795-7447
Greencrest Press Inc, PO Box 7745, Winston Salem NC 27109.................919-722-6463
The Stephen Greene Press, 15 Muzzey St, Lexington MA 02173................802-257-7757
Greenfield Publications, 8720 E Forrest Dr, Scottsdale AZ 85257..............602-994-1452
Greenfield Review, RD 1 Box 80, Greenfield Ctr NY 12833......................518-584-1728
Greenhaven Press Inc*, 577 Shoreview Park Rd, St Paul MN 55126.........612-482-1582
Greenhouse Review Press, 3965 Bonny Doon Rd, Santa Cruz CA 95060..408-426-4355
Greenleaf Classics Inc*, PO Box 20194, San Diego CA 92120..................619-560-5711
Greenwillow Books*, 105 Madison Ave, New York NY 10016....................212-889-3050
Greenwood Press*, 88 Post Rd W Box 5007, Westport CT 06881..............203-226-3571
Howard Gregory Assoc, 640 The Village, Redondo Beach CA 92077.......213-379-7190
Grey Fox Press*, PO Box 31190, San Francisco CA 94131.......................415-824-5774
Grey House Publishing Inc*, Colonial Bank Bldg, Sharon CT 06069.........203-364-0533
Grid Publishing Co, PO Box 14466, Columbus OH 43214.......................614-261-6565
Griffin Books, 50 Penn Place Ste 380, Oklahoma City OK 73118.............405-842-0398
Griffon House Publications, PO Box 81, Whitestone NY 11357.................718-767-8380
Grolier Inc*, Sherman Tpke, Danbury CT 06816...................................203-797-3500
Grossman Stamp Co Inc, 5 E 17th St, New York NY 10003.....................212-807-7935
Groupwork Today Inc, PO Box 258, S Plainfield NJ 07080......................201-755-4803
Grove Press Inc*, 920 Broadway, New York NY 10010...........................212-529-3600
Grove's Dictionaries of Music, 15 E 26th St, New York NY 10010............212-481-1332
Growth Unlimited Inc, 31 E Ave S, Battle Creek MI 49015......................616-965-2229
Grune & Stratton Inc*, 6277 Sea Harbor Dr, Orlando FL 32887...............305-345-2000
Gryphon Editions Ltd*, PO Box 76108, Birmingham AL 35253.................205-879-8380
Gryphon House, 3706 Otis St Box 275, Mt Rainier MD 20712...................301-779-6200
Guild Press*, PO Box 22583, Robbinsdale MN 55422..............................612-566-1842
The Guilford Press*, 200 Park Ave S, New York NY 10003.....................212-674-1900
Gulf Publishing Co Book Division*, PO Box 2608, Houston TX 77252....713-529-4301
The Gun Room Press, 127 Raritan Ave, Highland Park NJ 08904.............201-545-4344
Hacker Art Books Inc*, 54 W 57th St, New York NY 10019.....................212-757-1450
Hackett Publishing Co Inc*, PO Box 44937, Indianapolis IN 46244.........317-635-9250
Hadronic Press Inc*, Nonantum MA 02195...617-864-9859
Haimowoods Press, 1101 Forest, Evanston IL 60202.............................312-864-7209
Halcyon Publishing, 8637 Navajo Rd, San Diego CA 92119....................619-465-7400
G K Hall & Co*, 70 Lincoln St, Boston MA 02111 617-423-3990
Halsted Press*, 605 3rd Ave, New York NY 10158 212-850-6000
Alexander Hamilton Inst*, 1633 Broadway, New York NY 10019.............212-397-3580
Hammond Inc*, 515 Valley St, Maplewood NJ 07040..............................201-763-6000

Hammond Publishing, 1220 3rd St, Spearfish SD 57783 605-642-7225
Hampton Court Publishers, Box 655, Lake Mahopac NY 10541................914-628-6155
Robin & Russ Handweavers, 533 N Adams St, McMinnville OR 97128....503-472-5760
Haney Books, PO Box 552, Salem IL 62881 618-548-1276
Hanging Loose Press*, 231 Wyckoff St, Brooklyn NY 11217 718-643-9559
Hanley & Belfus*, 210 S 13th St, Philadelphia PA 19107 215-546-4995
Hansa Publishing, 2334 Stuart St, Berkeley CA 94705.............................415-848-2641
The Hapi Press, 512 SW Maplecrest Dr, Portland OR 97219 503-246-9632
Harben Publishing Co, PO Box 1055, Safety Harbor FL 33572.................813-726-4235
Harbor House*, 221 Water St, Boyne City MI 49712 616-582-2814
Harbor Press, 1602 Lucille Pkwy NW, Gig Harbor WA 98335 206-851-9598
Harcourt Brace Jovanovich Inc*, 1250 6th Ave, San Diego CA 92101 619-231-6616
Hardin Publishing Co, Box 269, Avera GA 30803 404-598-2312
Max Hardy Publisher, PO Box 28219, Las Vegas NV 89126.....................702-368-0379
Harian Creative Press-Books, 47 Hyde Blvd, Ballston Spa NY 12020.......518-885-7397
Harmony Books*, 225 Park Ave S, New York NY 10003.........................212-532-9200
Harmony House Publishers*, 1008 Kent Rd, Goshen KY 40026................502-228-4446
Harmony Institute Press, Box 210, Tollhouse CA 93667 209-855-3643
Harper & Row Publishers Inc*, 10 E 53rd St, New York NY 10022..........212-207-7000
Harper Jr Books*, PO Box 6549, San Pedro CA 90734 213-547-4292
The Harrington Park Press Inc*, 28 E 22nd St, New York NY 10010.......212-228-2800
Harrison House Publishers*, PO Box 35035, Tulsa OK 74153...................918-582-2126
Harrow & Heston, PO Box 3934, Albany NY 12203 518-442-5223
Harrowood Books, 3943 N Providence Dr, Newtown Sqaure PA 19073....215-353-5585
Hartley & Marks Inc, Box 147, Point Roberts WA 98281 206-587-6251
Harvard Business School Press*, Gallatin E 118, Boston MA 02163........617-495-6700
The Harvard Common Press, 535 Albany St, Boston MA 02118................617-423-5803
Harvard Univ Press*, 79 Garden St, Cambridge MA 02138 617-495-2600
Harvest House Publishers Inc*, 1075 Arrowsmith, Eugene OR 97402 503-343-0123
Haskell House Publishers*, PO Box 420, Brooklyn NY 11219 718-435-0500
Hastings House Publishers Inc*, 10 E 40th St, New York NY 10016........212-689-5400
Hauser Productions, 475 N Ferndale Rd, Wayzata MN 55391 612-473-1173
Haven Publications*, PO Box 2046, New York NY 10001.........................212-219-0672
Havestman Assoc, PO Box 271, Menlo Park CA 94026 916-771-0353
Hawkes Publishing Inc*, 3775 S 5th W, Salt Lake City UT 84115............801-262-5555
The Haworth Press*, 28 E 22nd St, New York NY 10010..........................212-228-2800
J V Hays Inc, 531 W Pennsylvania Ave, DeLand FL 32720.......................904-734-8944
Hazelden Educational Materials*, Box 176, Center City MN 55012..........612-257-4485
Hazelden Foundation*, PO Box 176, Center City MN 55012.....................612-257-4010
HCP Research, 20655 Sunrise Dr, Cupertino CA 95014 415-493-1221
HCS Publishing, 5600 Duryea St, Frederick MD 21701............................301-694-5392
Health Administration Press*, 1021 E Huron St, Ann Arbor MI 48109 ...313-764-1380
Health Alert Press, PO Box 2060, Cambridge MA 02238 617-497-4190
Health Plus Publ, 14425 N Scottsdale Rd #700, Scottsdale AZ 85260.......602-992-0589
Health Science, PO Box 7, Santa Barbara CA 93102...............................805-968-1028
Healthmere Press Inc, PO Box 986, Evanston IL 60204............................312-251-5950
HealthProInk, 26941 Pebblestone Rd, Southfield MI 48034......................313-355-3686
HearSay Press, PO Box 42265, Portland OR 97242..................................503-233-2637
Hearst Books*, 105 Madison Ave, New York NY 10016............................212-889-3050
Heart of the Lakes Publishing*, 2989 Lodi Rd, Interlaken NY 14847 607-532-4997
D C Heath & Co*, 125 Spring St, Lexington MA 02173 617-862-6650
The Heather Foundation, PO Box 48, San Pedro CA 90733 213-831-6269
HeBo Inc, 4741 Guerley Rd, Cincinnati OH 45238 513-471-0825

Hebrew Publishing Co*, 100 Water St Box 875, Brooklyn NY 11202.........718-858-6928
Hebrew Union College Press, Clifton Ave, Cincinnati OH 45220...............513-221-1875
The Hegeler Institute, PO Box 600, La Salle IL 61301 815-223-1231
Heian International Inc*, PO Box 1013, S San Francisco CA 94083.........415-471-8440
Heidelberg Graphics, 1116 Wendy Way, Chico CA 95926.....................916-342-6582
Heinemann Educational Books*, 70 Court St, Portsmouth NH 03801......603-431-7894
Heinle & Heinle Publishers Inc*, 20 Park Plaza, Boston MA 02216.........617-451-1940
Helaine Victoria Press Inc, 411 E 4th St, Bloomington IN 47401...............812-331-0444
Helix Press, 4410 Hickey, Corpus Christi TX 78413 512-852-8834
Helm Publishing, PO Box 1275, San Luis Obispo CA 93406.....................805-543-5404
Hemingway Western Studies Ctr, 1910 University, Boise ID 83725...........208-385-1999
Hemisphere Publishing*, 79 Madison Ave #1110, New York NY 10016..212-725-1999
Hendershot Indiv Instruction, 4114 Ridgewood, Bay City MI 48706.........517-684-3148
Herald Press*, 616 Walnut Ave, Scottdale PA 15683 412-887-8500
Herald Publ House*, 3225 S Noland Rd, Independence MO 64055...........816-252-5010
Here's Life Publishers*, PO Box 1576, San Bernardino CA 92404.............714-886-7981
Heresy Press, 713 Paul St, Newport News VA 23605.....................804-380-6595
Heritage Books Inc*, 1540-E Pointer Ridge Pl, Bowie MD 20716 301-390-7709
Hermagoras Press, PO Box 1555, Davis CA 95617.....................916-756-5415
Hermes House Press*, 39 Adare Pl, Northampton MA 01060.....................413-584-8402
Hermetician Press, PO Box 61138, N Miami FL 33261.....................305-949-6148
Hermitage*, PO Box 410, Tenafly NJ 07670.....................201-894-8247
Hero Books*, 8316 Arlington Blvd Ste 400, Fairfax VA 22031 703-560-6427
Heroica Books, 4286 Redwood Hwy, San Rafael CA 94903 415-897-6067
Herzl Press*, 515 Park Ave, New York NY 10022 212-752-0600
Heyday Books*, PO Box 9145, Berkeley CA 94709.....................415-549-3564
Hickman Systems, 4 Woodland Lane, Kirksville MO 63501.....................816-665-1836
High Meadow Press, Rt 140, Middletown Spgs VT 05757 413-734-5963
High Plains Press, Box 123, Glendo WY 82213 307-735-4370
Highmark Publishing*, 21 Elm St, Camden ME 04843 207-236-4342
Hilary House Publishers, 1033 Channel Dr, Hewlett Harbor NY 11557...516-295-2376
Lawrence Hill & Co*, 520 Riverside Ave, Westport CT 06880.....................203-226-9392
Hill & Wang*, 19 Union Sq W, New York NY 10003.....................212-741-6955
Buck Hill Assoc, Box 28A Out Church St, Saratoga Springs NY 12866.....518-583-1166
Hillside Publications, Corporate Plaza PO Box 385, Keasbey NJ 08832...201-686-9410
Himalayan Publishers, RR 1 Box 400, Honesdale PA 18431 717-253-5551
Hippocrene Books Inc*, 171 Madison Ave, New York NY 10016 212-685-4371
Historic Baltimore Soc, 4 Willow Brook Ct, Randallstown MD 21133......301-922-3649
Historic Cherry Hill, 523 1/2 S Pearl St, Albany NY 12203 518-434-4806
Historic Fla Keys Preservation, 500 Whitehead St, Key West FL 33040...305-292-6718
Hive Publishing Co*, Box 1004 Alpha Bldg, Easton PA 18042 215-258-6663
Hobby House Press, 900 Frederick St, Cumberland MD 21502.....................301-759-3770
Robert Hoehler Publishing, PO Box 240, Conifer CO 80433 303-838-4046
Holden Day Inc*, 4432 Telegraph Ave, Oakland CA 94609.....................415-428-9400
Holderby & Bierce Publishers, 1332 42nd Ave, Rock Island IL 61201.......309-788-8200
Holiday House Inc*, 18 E 53rd St, New York NY 10022 212-688-0085
Holloway House Publ*, 8060 Melrose Ave, Los Angeles CA 90046...........213-653-8060
Hollywood Film Archive, 8344 Melrose Ave, Hollywood CA 90069...........213-933-3345
Holman Bible Publishers*, 127 9th Ave N, Nashville TN 37234.....................615-251-2520
Holmes & Meier Publishers*, 30 Irving Pl, New York NY 10003.............212-254-4100
Holocaust Library*, 216 W 18th St, New York NY 10011 212-691-9220
Holt Rinehart & Winston*, 521 5th Ave 6th fl, New York NY 10175 212-599-7600
Holy Trinity Monastery*, PO Box 36, Jordanville NY 13361 315-858-0940

Home Business News, 12221 Beaver Pike, Jackson OH 45640 614-988-2331
Home Planners Inc, 23761 Research Dr, Farmington Hills MI 48024 313-477-1850
Homestead Publishing*, Box 193, Moose WY 83012 406-538-8960
Homeward Press, PO Box 2307, Berkeley CA 94702.................................415-526-3254
Alan C Hood Book Services, PO Box 1, Putney VT 05346.........................802-387-4309
Hoover Institution Press*, Stanford Univ, Stanford CA 94305..................415-497-3373
Hope Farm Press, Strong Rd, Cornwallville NY 12418...............................518-239-4745
Hope Publishing House, PO Box 60008, Pasadena CA 91106....................818-792-2121
Horizon Books, 224 E Front St, Traverse City MI 49684 616-946-7203
Horizon Press*, PO Box 402, New York NY 10100....................................212-757-4420
Horizon Publishers*, 50 S 500 W PO Box 490, Bountiful UT 84010..........801-295-9451
Sylvia Horstein Publ, 21530 Califa St #209, Woodland Hills CA 91367....805-482-3068
Hot Off The Press Inc*, 7212 S Seven Oaks Ln, Canby OR 97013 503-266-8306
Houghton Mifflin Co*, 2 Park St, Boston MA 02108..................................617-725-5000
House of Collectibles Inc*, 1904 Premier Row, Orlando FL 32809...........305-857-9095
Leslie Howard Publ, 140 Duboce Ave #204, San Francisco CA 94103......415-863-1238
Howard Univ Press*, 2900 Van Ness St NW, Washington DC 20008 202-686-6696
Howe Brothers*, PO Box 6394, Salt Lake City UT 84106 801-485-7409
Howell Book House Inc*, 230 Park Ave, New York NY 10169 212-986-4488
Howell North Books, 850 N Hollywood Way, Burbank CA 91505 818-848-0944
HP Books*, PO Box 5367, Tucson AZ 85703..602-888-2150
HTC Publishing Co, 10636 Main St Ste 284, Bellevue WA 98004.............206-453-5569
Hudson Hills Press Inc*, 220 5th Ave, New York NY 10001 212-889-3090
Human Kinetics Publishers*, 1607 N Market St, Champaign IL 61820 217-351-5076
Human Resource Dev Press*, 22 Amherst, Amherst MA 01002 413-253-3488
Human Sciences Press*, 72 5th Ave, New York NY 10011 212-243-6000
Humana Press*, PO Box 2148, Clifton NJ 07015 201-773-4389
Humane Horizons Publ, 1546 28th St Box 602, Boulder CO 80302...........303-447-2629
Humanics Ltd*, 1389 Peachtree St NE Ste 370, Atlanta GA 30309 404-874-2176
Humanities Press Intl Inc*, 171 1st Ave, Atlantic Highlands NJ 07716.....201-872-1441
Carl Hungness Publishing, PO Box 24308, Speedway IN 46224................317-244-4792
Hunter House Inc Publishers*, PO Box 1302, Claremont CA 91711.........714-624-2277
Hunter Publishing*, 155 Riverside Dr, New York NY 10024 212-595-8933
Huntington House*, PO Box 78312, Shreveport LA 71137........................318-221-2767
Huntington Library & Gallery, 1151 Oxford Rd, San Marino CA 91108 ..818-405-2108
Hyperion Press Inc*, 47 Riverside Ave, Westport CT 06880.....................203-226-1091
Hyst'ry Myst'ry House, 1 Bush Ct, Garnerville NY 10923.........................914-947-3141
IBMS, PO Box 440, Hillsdale NJ 07642 201-343-6855
Icarus Press Inc*, 120 W La Salle Ste 906, South Bend IN 46601 219-233-6020
The ICC Publishing Corp*, 156 5th Ave Ste 820, New York NY 10010....212-206-1150
ICS Press*, 785 Market St Ste 750, San Francisco CA 94103....................415-543-6213
Ide House Inc*, 4631 Harvey Dr, Mesquite TX 75150...............................214-681-2552
IEEE Press*, 345 E 47th St, New York NY 10017 212-705-7557
Igaku Shoin Med Publ*, 1140 Ave of Americas, New York NY 10036......212-944-7540
Ignatius Press*, PO Box 18990, San Francisco CA 94118..........................415-387-2324
Ike & Dudatt Publ*, 9361 La Jolla Cir, Huntington Beach CA 92646........714-962-6443
Illuminations Press, 2110-B 9th St, Berkeley CA 94710 415-849-2102
Ilma Printing & Publishing*, PO Box 251, Tarzana CA 91356.................818-344-3375
ILR Press*, Cornell Univ NYSSILR, Ithaca NY 14851..............................607-255-3061
Image Makers of Pittsford, 6 Wood Gate, Pittsford NY 14534 716-385-4567
Image Press, PO Box 756, Sebastopol CA 95472..707-823-4351
Image Studio, Main St, Stockbridge MA 01262..413-298-5500
Images Unlimited, PO Box 305, Maryville MO 64468 816-582-4279

Imagine Inc, PO Box 9674, Pittsburgh PA 15226....................412-571-1430
Impact Publishers Inc, PO Box 1094, San Luis Obispo CA 93406 805-543-5911
IMS Press*, 426 Pennsylvania Ave, Ft Washington PA 19034....................215-628-4920
In The Right Direction Publications, PO Box C, Drain OR 97435 503-836-7056
Incentive Publications Inc*, 3835 Cleghorn Ave, Nashville TN 37215.......615-385-2934
Incremental Motion Control, PO Box 2772, Champaign IL 61820..............217-356-1523
Independent Community Consultants, Box 141, Hampton AR 71744.......501-798-4510
Independent School Press Inc*, 51 River St, Wellesley Hills MA 02181...617-237-2591
Index House, 7206 Farmington Way, Madison WI 53717....................608-833-1617
Indian University Press, Bacone College, Muskogee OK 74401..................918-683-4581
Indiana Univ Press*, 10th & Morton Sts, Bloomington IN 47405.............812-335-4203
Indira Publishing House*, PO Box 37256, Oak Park MI 48237..................313-661-2529
Industrial Press Inc, 200 Madison Ave, New York NY 10016 212-889-6630
Info Digest Publishers, PO Box 165, Morton Grove IL 60053 312-965-1456
INFORM, 381 Park Ave S, New York NY 10016 212-689-4040
Information Coordinators Inc, 1435-37 Randolph St, Detroit MI 48226 ..313-962-9720
Information Resources Press, 1700 N Moore St, Arlington VA 22209......703-558-8270
Information Sources Inc, 1807 Glenview Rd, Glenview IL 60025 312-724-9285
Information USA Inc*, PO Box 15700, Chevy Chase MD 20815.................301-657-1200
Infosources Publishing, 118 W 79th St, New York NY 10024....................212-595-3161
Inkblot Publications, 439 49th St #11, Oakland CA 94609....................415-652-7127
Inkstone Books, PO Box 22172, Carmel CA 93950....................408-375-3296
Inner Traditions Intl Ltd*, 377 Park Ave S, New York NY 10016.............212-889-8350
Inner Vision Publishing*, PO Box 1117, Virginia Beach VA 23451...........804-425-2245
Inquiry Press, 4925 Jefferson Ave, Midland MI 48640....................517-631-3350
Insight Press, 535 Cordova Ste 228, Santa Fe NM 87501....................505-471-7511
Insight Press, 614 Vermont St, San Francisco CA 94107....................415-826-3488
Inst for Contemporary Studies*, 243 Kearny, San Francisco CA 94108....415-981-5353
Institute for Policy Studies, 1901 Q St NW, Washington DC 20009 202-234-9382
Inst for Polynesian Studies, BYU Hawaii, Laie HI 96762....................808-293-3667
Inst for Studies in Amer Music, CUNY, Brooklyn NY 11210 718-780-5655
Inst for Study of Human Issues*, 210 13th St, Philadelphia PA 19107......215-732-9729
Inst for Study Trad Amer Indian Arts, Box 66124, Portland OR 97266....503-233-8131
Institute of Archaeology, 405 Hilgard Ave, Los Angeles CA 90024.............213-825-7411
Inst Early Amer History & Culture, Box 220, Williamsburg VA 23187.....804-229-2771
Inst of Intl Education*, 809 United Nations Plz, New York NY 10017.....212-883-8200
Institute of Logotherapy Press, 2000 Dwight Way, Berkeley CA 94704....415-845-2522
Institute of Mediaeval Music Ltd, Box 295, Henryville PA 18332..............717-629-1278
Inst of Modern Languages*, 4255 W Touhy, Lincolnwood IL 60646.........312-679-5500
Inst of Real Estate Management, 430 N Michigan, Chicago IL 60611.......312-661-1930
Institute of Universal Faith, Box 3732 RD 3, Grove City PA 16127 814-786-9085
Instrument Soc of Amer*, 67 Alexander, Research Triangle NC 27709 919-549-8411
Integrated Energy Systems, Rt 2 Box 61A1, Monroe GA 30655.................404-267-3534
Integrated Press, 526 Comstock Dr, Tiburon CA 94920 415-435-2446
Intelligent Choice Information, 4771 La Cresta, San Jose CA 95129.........408-249-4747
Inter Crescent Publishing, PO Box 31413, Dallas TX 75231....................214-341-4792
Inter Ski Services, PO Box 9595 Friendship Sta, Washington DC 20016...202-342-0886
Inter Varsity Press*, PO Box 1400, Downers Grove IL 60515 312-964-5700
Interchange Inc, PO Box 16012, St Louis Park MN 55416....................612-929-6669
Intercultural Press Inc, Box 768, Yarmouth ME 04096....................207-846-5168
Intl Council of Shopping Centers*, 665 5th Ave, New York NY 10022.....212-421-8181
Intl Culinary, Box 2002 Elberon Sta, Elberon NJ 07740 201-229-0008
Intl Dialogue Press, PO Box 1257, Davis CA 95617 916-758-6500

Intl Found of Employee Benefit Plans*, Box 69, Brookfield WI 53008......414-786-6700
Intl Human Resources Development*, 137 Newburt, Boston MA 02174 ..617-536-0202
Intl Ideas Inc*, 1627 Spruce St, Philadelphia PA 19103 215-546-0392
Intl Inst Prev Psychiatry, 11445 Dona Dolores, Studio City CA 91604 213-656-1545
Intl Library Book Publisher, 3865 Wilson Blvd, Arlington VA 22203 703-522-8624
Intl Marine Publishing Co*, 21 Elm St, Camden ME 04843......................207-236-4342
Intl Monetary Fund*, 700 19th St NW, Washington DC 20431 202-473-7430
Intl Publishers Co Inc*, 381 Park Ave S, New York NY 10016...................212-685-2864
Intl Resources, PO Box 1275, San Luis Obispo CA 93406............................805-543-5404
Intl Sport Fishing Publ, 11000 Metro Pkwy, Ft Myers FL 33912.................813-275-5567
Intl Universities Press Inc*, 315 5th Ave, New York NY 10016..................212-684-7900
Intl University Press, 1301 S Norland Rd, Independence MO 64055.........816-461-3633
Intl Wealth Success*, PO Box 186, Merrick NY 11566 516-766-5850
Interspace Books*, 4500 Chesapeake St NW, Washington DC 20016........202-363-9082
Interstate Printers & Publ Inc*, 19 N Jackson St, Danville IL 61832 217-446-0500
Interurban Press*, PO Box 6444, Glendale CA 91205 818-240-9130
Inverted-A Inc, 401 Forrest Hill, Grand Prairie TX 75051............................214-264-0066
Investigations Institute, 53 W Jackson Blvd, Chicago IL 60604...................312-939-6050
Investment Evaluations Corp, 2000 Goldenview Dr, Golden CO 80401 ...303-278-3464
Investment Information Services, 205 W Wacker Dr, Chicago IL 60606..312-750-9300
Investors Publications, 219 Parkade, Cedar Falls IA 50613 319-277-6341
Ion Books*, 3387 Poplar Ave Ste 205, Memphis TN 38111............................901-323-8858
The Iona Press, Box C 3183 College of Wooster, Wooster OH 44691.......216-262-8361
Iowa State University Press*, 2121 S State Ave, Ames IA 50010.................515-294-7194
IRD Productions, PO Box 366 Canal St Sta, New York NY 10013 212-420-9043
Iris I O Publishing*, 316 California Ave Ste 428, Reno NV 89509...............702-747-1638
Iron Crown Enterprises Inc*, PO Box 1605, Charlottesville VA 22901.....804-295-3918
Irvington Publishers Inc*, 740 Broadway, New York NY 10003 212-777-4100
Richard D Irwin Inc*, 1818 Ridge Rd, Homewood IL 60430.......................312-798-6000
ISC Press, Box 779, Fortuna CA 95540..707-768-3284
Ishi Press Intl, 1101 San Antonio Rd #302, Mtn View CA 94043..............415-964-7294
Ishiyaku EuroAmerica Inc*, 11559 Rock Island Ct, St Louis MO 63043 ..314-432-1933
ISI Press*, 3501 Market St, Philadelphia PA 19104.......................................215-386-0100
Island Press, 1718 Connecticut Ave NW #300, Washington DC 20009 202-232-7933
Island Press Publishing, 175 Bahia Via, Ft Meyers Beach FL 33931.........813-463-9482
ISS Publications, 160 Washington SE Ste 64, Albuquerque NM 87108.....505-255-2872
Italica Press Inc*, 625 Main St #641, New York NY 10044............................212-935-4230
Ithaca House, PO Box 6484, Ithaca NY 14851..607-272-4968
Ivory Tower Publishing Co Inc*, 125 Walnut St, Watertown MA 02712...617-923-1111
IWP Publishing Inc*, PO Box 2449, Menlo Park CA 94026..........................415-321-3100
J & B Books, 26 Marwood St, Albany NY 12209..518-489-4009
J & R Enterprises, PO Box 140264, Anchorage AK 99514 907-333-4442
J Rad Publications, PO Box 214741, Sacramento CA 95821 916-486-3857
Jacar Press, Box 4, Wendell NC 27591 919-365-4188
Jackson Mountain Press, Box 2652, Renton WA 98056 206-255-6635
JAI Press Inc*, 36 Sherwood Pl PO Box 1678, Greenwich CT 06836.........203-661-7602
Jaison Station Press, 7115 Pembroke Dr, Reno NV 89502.........................702-359-2178
Jakubowsky, 1565 Madison St, Oakland CA 94612......................................415-763-4304
Jalmar Press Inc, 45 Hitching Post Dr Bldg 2, Rolling Hills CA 90274.....213-547-1240
Jameson Books*, Box 738, Ottawa IL 61350...815-434-7905
Jamestown Publishers*, PO Box 9168, Providence RI 02940......................401-351-1915
JAMV, PO Box 1748, Novato CA 94948...415-883-4958
Jane's Publishing Inc*, 115 5th Ave, New York NY 10003...........................212-254-9097

January Productions*, 249 Goffle Rd PO Box 66, Hawthorne NJ 07507..201-423-4666
Janus Book Publishers*, 2501 Industrial Pkwy W, Hayward CA 94545 415-887-7070
The Jargon Society, 22 Hemingway Ave, E Haven CT 06512.....................203-467-4257
Jayell Enterprises Inc, PO Box 2616, Dearborn MI 48123 313-565-9687
Jeanies Classics Publishing, PO Box 4303, Rockford IL 61110..................815-968-4544
Jelm Mountain Publications, El Rancho Pequeno, Jelm WY 82063 307-745-9567
Jewish Braille Inst of Amer*, 110 E 30th St, New York NY 10016 212-889-2525
Jewish Cenealogical Society, 1025 Antique Ln, Northbrook IL 60062 312-564-1025
Jewish Combatants Publ House, PO Box 323, Brooklyn NY 11236...........718-763-7551
Jewish Publication Soc*, 1930 Chestnut St, Philadelphia PA 19103...........215-564-5925
JH Press, PO Box 294 Village Sta, New York NY 10014 212-255-4713
JMT Publications, PO Box 603, Camp Hill PA 17011........................717-761-6513
The Johns Hopkins University Press*, Baltimore MD 21211.....................301-338-6975
Johnson Books*, 1880 S 57th Ct, Boulder CO 80301...........................303-443-1576
Joint Comm on Accredit of Hosp*, 875 N Michigan, Chicago IL 60611....312-642-6061
Jonathan David Publ*, 68-22 Eliot Ave, Middle Village NY 11379 718-456-8611
Jones & Bartlett Publishers Inc*, 20 Park Plz, Boston MA 02116 617-426-5246
Jones Medical Publications, 355 Los Cerros Dr, Greenbrae CA 94904....415-461-3749
Jordan Valley Heritage House Inc, 43592 Hwy 226, Stayton OR 97383.....503-859-3144
Joshua Town Publishing Assoc*, Joshuatown Rd, Lyme CT 06371...........203-526-2486
Jossey-Bass Inc Publ*, 433 California St, San Francisco CA 94104...........415-433-1740
Jotarian Productions, PO Box 75683, Washington DC 20013.....................202-287-8321
JP Publications, 2952 Grinnel, Davis CA 95616 916-758-9727
Judaica Press Inc, 521 5th Ave, New York NY 10175.............................212-260-0520
Judson Press*, PO Box 851, Valley Forge PA 19482...........................215-768-2122
Junior League of Odessa Publications, PO Box 7273, Odessa TX 79760..915-367-5240
Jupiter Press, 360 MacLaren Ln, Lake Bluff IL 60044............................312-234-3997
Kajfez Consulting, PO Box 757, University MS 38677 601-234-4287
Kaleidoscopix Inc, PO Box 389, Franklin MA 02038............................617-528-6211
Kalimat Press*, 10889 Wilshire Blvd Ste 700, Los Angeles CA 90024.......213-208-8559
Kalmbach Publishing Co, 1027 N 7th St, Milwaukee WI 53233..................414-272-2060
Kane/Miller Book Publishers, PO Box 529, Brooklyn NY 11231 718-624-5120
James Kanegis, 3907 Madison, Hyattsville MD 20781............................301-699-5064
Kar-Ben Copies Inc*, 6800 Tildenwood Ln, Rockville MD 20852.............301-984-8733
Karoma*, 3400 Daleview, Ann Arbor MI 48105.................................313-665-3337
Karoma Publishers Inc*, 3400 Daleview Dr, Ann Arbor MI 48105...........313-665-3331
Karz-Cohl Publishing*, 77 Bleecker St PH 24, New York NY 10012........212-663-9059
William Kaufmann Inc, 95 1st St, Los Altos CA 94022...........................415-948-5810
Christopher Kaylor Co, PO Box 737, Huntsville AL 35804.....................205-534-6156
Kazi Publications*, 3023 27 W Belmont Ave, Chicago IL 60618 312-327-7598
KC Publications*, PO Box 14883, Las Vegas NV 89114............................702-731-3123
Keats Publishing Inc*, PO Box 876, New Canaan CT 06840 203-966-8721
Augustus M Kelley Publishers*, 300 Fairfield Rd, Fairfield NJ 07006 212-685-7202
Kelsey St Press, PO Box 9235, Berkeley CA 94709................................415-845-2260
Kelso Mfg Co, Rt 2 Box 499, Greenville MS 38701................................601-332-7926
Kendall Hunt Publishing Co*, 2460 Kerper Blvd, Dubuque IA 52001 319-588-1451
Kennebec River Press Inc, Box 164 RR1, Woolwich ME 04579 207-442-7632
Kent Publications Inc, 18301 Halsted St, Northridge CA 91325.................818-349-2080
Kent Publishing Co*, 20 Park Plaza, Boston MA 02116 617-542-1629
Kent State Univ Press*, Kent OH 44242...216-672-7913
Kenyon Publications, 361 Pin Oak Ln, Westbury NY 11590 516-333-3236
Kern Intl Inc*, 100 Weymouth St Ste G1, Rockland MA 02370 617-871-4982
Charles H Kerr Publishing*, 1740 W Greenleaf Ave, Chicago IL 60626 ..312-465-7774

Michael Kesend Publishing, 1025 5th Ave, New York NY 10028..............212-249-5150
Key Books Press, 1111 S Arroyo Pkwy, Pasadena CA 91109.......................818-793-2645
Key Curriculum Press, PO Box 2304, Berkeley CA 94702.....................415-548-2304
Keystone Publications*, 250 W 57th St Ste 823, New York NY 10107.......212-582-2254
KG Books Co, 5912 Schaefer Rd, Edina MN 55436.............................612-925-5134
Kid-Love Unlimited, 2036 Galaxy Dr, Newport Beach CA 92660..............714-642-1179
Kindred Joy Publications, 554 W 4th, Coquille OR 97423.....................503-396-4154
King Library Press, Univ of Kentucky, Lexington KY 40506.....................606-257-8611
The Kingston Press Inc*, PO Box 1456, Princeton NJ 08542.....................609-921-0609
Kinseeker Publications, Box 184, Grawn MI 49637.................................616-276-6745
Kitchen Sink Press Inc, 2 Swamp Rd, Princeton WI 54968......................414-295-6922
B Klein Publications, PO Box 8503, Coral Springs FL 33075....................305-752-1708
Klutz, 2170 Staunton Ct, Stanford CA 94306 415-857-0888
Kluwer Academic Publishers*, 190 Old Derby St, Hingham MA 02043....617-749-5262
Kluwer Nijhoff Publishing*, 190 Old Derby St, Hingham MA 02043........617-749-3282
The Knapp Press*, 5900 Wilshire Blvd, Los Angeles CA 90036...................213-937-3454
Knights Press*, Box 454, Pound Ridge NY 10576 203-322-7381
Knoll Publishing Co Inc, 831 W Washington Blvd, Ft Wayne IN 46802....219-422-1926
Alfred A Knopf Inc*, 201 E 50th St, New York NY 10022.......................212-751-2600
Knowledge Industry Publ*, 701 Westchester, White Plains NY 10604 914-328-9157
John Knox Press*, 341 Ponce de Leon Ave NE, Atlanta GA 30365 404-873-1549
Kodansha International USA Ltd*, 10 E 53rd St, New York NY 10022...212-207-7050
Krank Press, PO Box 16271, St Louis MO 63105.................................314-997-5907
The Krantz Co Publishers Inc, 2210 N Burling St, Chicago IL 60614........312-472-4900
Kraus Intl Publications*, 1 Water St, White Plains NY 10601 914-761-9600
Kregel Publications*, PO Box 2607, Grand Rapids MI 49501 616-451-4775
Robt E Krieger Publishing Co*, PO Box 9542, Melbourne FL 32902........305-724-9542
Ktav Publishing House*, 900 Jefferson St, Hoboken NJ 07030 201-963-9524
Kumarian Press Inc*, 630 Oakwood Ave #119, W Hartford CT 06110....203-524-0214
L'Avant Studios, PO Box 1711, Tallahassee FL 32302.............................904-576-1327
L'Epervier Press, 4522 Sunnyside N, Seattle WA 98103..........................206-574-8306
La Costa Music Business Consultants, PO Box 147, Cardiff CA 92007 ...619-436-7219
La Fray Young Publishing Co, 1720 SW 120th Ter, Davie FL 33329.........813-821-3233
The Labyrinth Press, 2814 Chapel Hill Rd, Durham NC 27707 919-493-5051
Laidlaw Brothers*, Thatcher & Madison Sts, River Forest IL 60305 312-366-5320
David S Lake Publishers*, 19 Davis Dr, Belmont CA 94002 415-592-7810
Lake View Press, PO Box 578279, Chicago IL 60657 312-935-2694
Lakewood Books Inc*, 1062 Cephas Rd, Clearwater FL 33575.................813-461-1585
Lal Publishing Co, PO Box 1225, Denison TX 75020............................214-465-7311
Lambert Publications Inc, 2433 18th St NW, Washington DC 20009 202-332-0973
Lamplight Publications, 340 Commercial St, Manchester NH 03105.........603-627-7827
Lampus Press, PO Box 541, Cape May NJ 08204 609-884-4906
Burton R Landes, 11 College Ave, Trappe PA 19426............................215-489-2908
Lane Publishing Co*, 85 Willow Rd, Menlo Park CA 94025....................415-321-3600
Peter Lang Publishing*, 62 W 45th St, New York NY 10036...................212-302-6740
Lange Medical Publications*, Drawer L, Los Altos CA 94023..................415-948-4526
Langenscheidt Publishers Inc*, 46-35 54 Rd, Maspeth NY 11378 718-784-0055
Language International, PO Box 26, Woodland Hills CA 91365................818-716-8222
The Lapis Press, Box 5408, Larkspur Landing CA 94939 415-461-5275
Lark Books, 50 College St, Ashville NC 28801 704-253-0468
Larksdale*, 1706 Seamist #575, Houston TX 77008.............................713-869-9092
Larlin Corp*, PO Box 1523, Marietta GA 30061 404-424-6210
Larousse & Co Inc*, 572 5th Ave, New York NY 10036..........................212-575-9515

Latin Amer Lit Rev, 1309 Cathedral Of Learning, Pittsburgh PA 15260 ...412-351-1477
The Latona Press, RFD 2 Box 154, Ellsworth ME 04605 207-667-5598
Laughing Bear Press, PO Box 36159, Denver CO 80236 303-989-5614
Laughing Dog Press, PO Box 1622, Vashon WA 98070 206-463-3153
Launch Press, PO Box 31491, Walnut Creek CA 94598..........................415-943-7603
Laura Books*, Box 918, Davenport FL 33837..813-422-9135
Lavin Assoc, 12 Promontory Dr, Cheshire CT 06410 203-272-9121
Law Journal Seminars Press*, 111 8th Ave, New York NY 10011 212-741-8300
Law of the Sea Institute, 2515 Dole St Rm 208, Honolulu HI 96822.........808-948-6750
Lawrence Hill & Co Publishers, 520 Riverside Ave, Westport CT 06880..203-226-9392
Merloyd Lawrence Inc*, 102 Chestnut St, Boston MA 02108....................617-523-5895
Lawyers & Judges Publ, 1105 Camino Del Mar, Del Mar CA 92014........619-481-5944
Lawyers Co-Operative Publ*, Aqueduct Bldg, Rochester NY 14694 716-546-5530
LDA Publishers, 42-36 209th St, Bayside NY 11361.................................212-224-0485
Le Jacq Publishing Inc*, 53 Park Pl, New York NY 10007 212-766-4300
Lea & Febiger*, 600 Washington Sq, Philadelphia PA 19106 215-922-1330
Leadership Dynamics Inc, 3775 Iris Ave Ste 3B, Boulder CO 80301 303-440-0909
Leadership Publishers, 407 Cherry St Box 51, New Sharon IA 50207 515-637-4563
Leading Edge Publ, 477 E Butterfield Rd Ste 310, Lombard IL 60148 312-963-7788
League Books, PO Box 91801, Cleveland OH 44101.................................216-348-4544
Learning Center Books*, 9 Liberty St, Newburyport MA 01950.................617-462-2292
The Learning Line, PO Box 1200, Palo Alto CA 94302.............................415-854-4400
Learning Publications Inc*, 5351 Gulf Dr, Holmes Beach FL 33510 813-778-5524
Learning Resources Intl Studies, 777 U N Plaza, New York NY 10017....212-972-9877
Learning Resources Network, PO Box 1425, Manhattan KS 66502.............913-539-5376
Lebanese Cuisine, PO Box 663958, Portland OR 97266............................503-236-1796
Lebhar-Friedman Books*, 425 Park Ave, New York NY 10022 212-371-9400
Lee Books, PO Box 906, Novato CA 94948...415-987-3550
Edward J Lefkowicz Inc, PO Box 630, Fairhaven MA 02719....................617-997-6839
Legacy Books, PO Box 494, Hatboro PA 19040..215-675-6762
Legacy Publishing, 1442A Walnut St #295, Berkeley CA 94709................415-549-3517
Legal Publication Inc, PO Box 3723, Van Nuys CA 91407 818-902-1671
Leisure Books*, 6 E 39th St, New York NY 10016 212-725-8811
Leisure Press*, PO Box 5076, Champaign IL 61820 217-351-5076
Hal Leonard Books*, 8112 W Bluemound Rd, Milwaukee WI 53213........414-774-3630
Lerner Publications Co*, 241 1st Ave N, Minneapolis MN 55401..............612-332-3344
Lewis Sloan Publishing Co, 2546 Etiwan Ave, Charleston SC 29407.........803-766-4735
Lexigrow Intl, 9202 N Meridian St, Indianapolis IN 46206......................317-844-5691
Lexikos, 4079 19th Ave, San Francisco CA 94132.....................................415-584-1085
Lexington Books*, 125 Spring St, Lexington MA 02173 617-862-6650
Liberty Fund Inc, 7440 Shadeland, Indianapolis IN 46256.......................317-842-0880
Liberty Publishing Co Inc*, 50 Scott Adam Rd, Cockeysville MD 21030..301-667-6680
Libra Publications, 5179 Perry Rd, Mt Airy MD 21771.............................301-875-2824
Libra Publishers Inc*, 3089C Clairemont Dr, San Diego CA 92117..........619-581-9449
Libraries Unlimited Inc*, PO Box 263, Littleton CO 80160......................303-770-1220
The Library of America*, 14 E 60th St, New York NY 10022......................212-308-3360
Library of Social Science*, 475 Amsterdam Ave, New York NY 10024 212-749-3567
Lidiraven Books, PO Box 5567, Sherman Oaks CA 91413 818-892-9433
Life Cycle Books, Box 792, Lewiston NY 14092..416-690-5860
Lifetime Press, 137 Campbell Ave, Roanoke VA 24011.............................703-982-1444
The Lighthouse Press, 1308 Lewis, La Junta CO 81050 303-384-2109
The Lightning Tree, PO Box 1837, Santa Fe NM 87504.............................505-983-7434
Liguori Publications*, 1 Liguori Dr, Liguori MO 63057.............................314-464-2500

Limelight Editions, 118 E 30th St, New York NY 10016..............................212-532-5525
Linch Publishing Inc, 1950 Lee Rd Ste 205, Winter Park FL 32789...........305-647-3025
Linden Press*, 1230 Ave of the Americas, New York NY 10020.................212-245-6400
Linden Publishers*, 1750 N Sycamore, Hollywood CA 90028 213-876-5190
The Lindisfarne Press, Box 778, Great Barrington MA 01230......................413-528-5245
Lingual House Publishing, PO Box 3557, Tucson AZ 85722.........................602-622-2366
Lintel, PO Box 8609, Roanoke VA 24014..703-982-2265
Linwood Publishers, PO Box 70152, N Charleston SC 29415.......................803-873-2719
Lion Publishers, PO Box 92541, Rochester NY 14692.................................716-385-1269
Lions Head Press, PO Box 5202, Klamath Falls OR 97601 503-883-2101
J B Lippincott Co*, E Washington Sq, Philadelphia PA 19105.....................215-238-4200
Alan R Liss Inc*, 41 E 11th St, New York NY 10003 212-475-7700
The Little Brick House, 621 St Clair St, Vandalia IL 62471..........................618-283-0024
Little Brown & Co Inc*, 34 Beacon St, Boston MA 02108.............................617-227-0730
Little River Press, 10 Lowell Ave, Westfield MA 01085................................413-568-5598
Littlefield Adams & Co*, 81 Adams Dr, Totowa NJ 07512 201-256-8600
The Liturgical Press*, St Johns Abbey, Collegeville MN 56321......................612-363-2213
Liturgy Training Publ*, 1800 N Hermitage Ave, Chicago IL 60622...........312-486-8970
Living Flame Press, Box 74 Birch Hill Rd, Locust Valley NY 11560 516-676-4210
Llewellyn Publications*, PO Box 64383, St Paul MN 55164 612-291-1970
LMA Enterprises Inc, PO Box 10608, St Petersburg FL 33733....................813-526-1405
Log Cabin Publishers, PO Box 1536, Allentown PA 18105 215-434-2448
Theotes Logos Research Inc, 4318 York Ave S, Minneapolis MN 55410 ..612-922-3202
Loiry Publishing House, 226 W Pensacola #301, Tallahassee FL 32301...904-681-0019
Loizeaux Brothers Inc*, Box 277, Neptune NJ 07754..................................201-774-8144
Mele Loke Publishing Co, PO Box 7142, Honolulu HI 96821 808-734-8611
Lollipop Power, PO Box 277, Carrboro NC 27510 919-933-9679
Lomond Systems Inc, PO Box 88, Mt Airy MD 21771................................301-829-1633
Lone Eagle Publ, 9903 Santa Monica Blvd, Beverly Hills CA 90212...........213-471-8066
Lone Star Press, Box 165, Laconner WA 98257...206-466-3377
Lonely Planet Publications, 1555D Park Ave, Emeryville CA 94608 415-428-2211
Long Beach Publications, PO Box 14807, Long Beach CA 90803 213-439-8962
Longman Financial Services*, 520 N Dearborn, Chicago IL 60610 312-836-0466
Longman Inc*, 95 Church St, White Plains NY 10601.................................914-993-5000
Longshanks Book, 30 Church St, Mystic CT 06355.....................................203-536-8656
Longwood Publishing Group Inc*, 51 Washington St, Dover NH 03820...603-749-5038
Looseleaf Law Publications Inc, 41-23 150th St, Flushing NY 11355 718-359-5559
Lord John Press*, 10973 Los Alimos St, Northridge CA 91326....................818-363-6621
Lost In Canada?, 1020 Central Ave, Sparta WI 54656 608-269-6361
Lost Music Network, PO Box 2391, Olympia WA 98507 206-352-9735
Lothrop Lee & Shepard*, 105 Madison Ave, New York NY 10016 212-889-3050
Lotus Press Inc, PO Box 21607, Detroit MI 48221 313-861-1280
Louisiana State University Press*, Baton Rouge LA 70893 504-388-6294
Love Publishing Co*, 1777 S Bellaire St, Denver CO 80222.........................303-757-2579
Lowen Publishing, PO Box 6870-12, Torrance CA 90504 213-326-7788
Loyola Univ Press*, 3441 N Ashland Ave, Chicago IL 60657......................312-281-1818
LSI Systems Inc, 11A Village Green, Crofton MD 21114.............................301-261-6363
Lucky Literature, PO Box 21043, Woodhaven NY 11421 718-296-5252
Lucy Mary Books, PO Box 2381, Grand Junction CO 81502.......................303-243-3231
Lumen Books Inc, 446 W 20th St, New York NY 10011 212-989-7944
Luna Bisonte Prods, 137 Leland Ave, Columbus OH 43214.......................614-846-4126
Luramedia, 10227 Autumnview Ln, San Diego CA 92126 619-578-1948
Lutheran Braille Evangelism*, 660 E Montana, St Paul MN 55106............612-776-8430

Nick Lyons Books Inc*, 31 W 21st St, New York NY 10010......................212-620-9580
M & T Publishing, 2464 Embarcadero Way, Palo Alto CA 94303..............415-424-0600
MA/AH Publishing*, Kansas State Univ, Manhattan KS 66506 913-532-6733
Press of MacDonald & Reinecke, Box 1275, San Luis Obispo CA 93406 ..805-543-5404
Macmillan Publishing Co*, 866 3rd Ave, New York NY 10022..................212-702-2000
Macoy Publishing*, 3011 Dumbarton Rd, Richmond VA 23228.................804-262-6551
Mad River Press Inc, 141 Carter Ln, Eureka CA 95501 707-443-2947
Madison Books*, 4720 Boston Way, Lanham MD 20706............................301-459-5308
Madison Square Press, 10 E 23rd St, New York NY 10010 212-505-0950
Madrona Publishers, 113 Madrona Pl E, Seattle WA 98112......................206-325-3973
Mafex Assoc Inc*, 90 Cherry St, Johnstown PA 15902.............................814-535-3597
Magpie Press, 16 Main Ave, Wallington NJ 07057......................................201-778-7503
Main St Press*, Wm Case House, Pittstown NJ 08867 201-735-9424
Maledicta Press, 331 S Greenfield Ave, Waukesha WI 53186....................414-542-5853
Mamre Press Inc, 315 Riverside Pl, Indialantic FL 32903..........................305-729-9059
Management & Systems Consultants, Box 40457, Tucson AZ 85717........602-299-9615
Management Info Sources*, 1107 NW 14th Ave, Portland OR 97209 503-222-2399
Management Resources Inc*, 155 E 56th St, New York NY 10022...........212-935-4800
Manion Outdoors Publishing Co, PO Box 188, Delafield WI 53018..........414-646-4196
Maplegrove Montgrove Press, 4055 N Keystone Ave, Chicago IL 60641 ..312-286-2655
Mar Vista Publishing, 11917 Westminster Pl, Los Angeles CA 90066.......213-391-1721
Marcor Publishing, PO Box 1072, Port Hueneme CA 93041......................805-985-7845
Mariner Publishing Co Inc, 4835 W Cypress St, Tampa FL 33607 813-877-3133
Market Data Retrieval Inc*, Ketchum Pl, Westport CT 06880....................203-226-8941
Marlance Inc, 1070 Barry Ln, Cincinnati OH 45229..................................513-280-0530
The Marlboro Press*, Box 157, Marlboro VT 05344...................................802-257-0781
Marlor Press, 4304 Brigadoon Dr, St Paul MN 55126................................612-483-1588
Marquis Who's Who*, 3002 Glenview Rd, Wilmette IL 60091....................312-441-2387
Marshall Cavendish Corp, Box 410 Merrick Rd, Freeport NY 11520.......516-546-4200
Maryland Historical Press, 9205 Tuckerman St, Lanham MD 20706........301-577-2436
Master Book Publisher*, PO Box 15908, San Diego CA 92115.................619-442-6671
The Master Teacher*, PO Box 1207, Manhattan KS 66502........................913-539-0555
Masterworks Inc, Box 901, Friday Harbor WA 98250................................206-378-4816
Mastery Education*, 85 Main St, Watertown MA 02172............................800-225-3214
Mathematical Assn of Amer*, 1529 18th St NW, Washington DC 20036 ..202-387-5200
Mathom Press Enterprises, PO Box 362, Oswego NY 13126 315-343-4851
Matrix Publishers Inc*, 8437 Mayfield Rd, Chesterland OH 44026 216-729-2808
Maverick Publications*, Drawer 5007, Bend OR 97708............................503-382-6978
Maxwell Music Evaluation Books, 1245 Kalmia, Boulder CO 80302........303-443-1603
May Day Press, PO Box 1351, Bellflower CA 90706..................................213-439-8423
Michael May Enterprises, PO Box 127, Billings MT 59103.......................406-248-4888
Mayfield Publishing Co*, 285 Hamilton Ave, Palo Alto CA 94301...........415-326-1640
Maynard-Thomas Publishing, PO Box 14753, Orlando FL 32857............305-658-1539
Mazda Publishers, PO Box 2603, Costa Mesa CA 92626..........................714-751-5252
McAllister Books, 410 Lake Ct, Waukegan IL 60085.................................312-662-1929
McBooks Press, 106 N Aurora St, Ithaca NY 14850 607-272-6602
McCaffery Enterprises, 15 Oakland Ave, Harrison NY 10528....................914-835-0900
McCutchan Publishing Corp*, PO Box 774, Berkeley CA 94701..............415-841-8616
McDougal Littel & Co*, Box 1667, Evanston IL 60204 312-967-0900
McFarland & Co Inc Publishers*, PO Box 611, Jefferson NC 28640........919-246-4460
McGraw-Hill Book Co*, 1221 Ave of Americas, New York NY 10020......212-512-2000
David McKay Co Inc*, 201 E 50th St, New York NY 10022........................212-751-2600
McMillan Publ Railroad Books, 3208 Halsey Dr, Woodridge IL 60517....312-968-3933

MCN Press, PO Box 702073, Tulsa OK 74170.....................................918-743-6048
McNally & Loftin Publishers*, PO Box 1316, Santa Barbara CA 93102...805-964-5117
McPherson & Co*, PO Box 638, New Paltz NY 12561.............................914-331-5807
MCS Publications, PO Box 486, Murray KY 42071...............................502-753-7750
Meadowbrook Press*, 18318 Minnetonka Blvd, Deephaven MN 55391....612-473-5400
Meadowlark Press*, Box 8172, Prairie Village KS 66208.....................913-341-9031
R S Means Co Inc*, 100 Construction Plz, Kingston MA 02364................617-747-1270
Meckler Publishing*, 11 Ferry Ln W, Westport CT 06880 203-226-6967
Media Distribution Co-op, 1745 Louisiana St, Lawrence KS 66044...........913-842-3176
Media Forum Intl, RFD 1 Box 107, W Danville VT 05873......................802-592-3444
The Media Institute, 3017 M St NW, Washington DC 20007....................202-298-7512
Media Productions & Marketing*, 2440 O St, Lincoln NE 68510..............402-474-2676
Media Projects Inc*, 305 2nd Ave Ste 340, New York NY 10003..............212-777-4510
MediaHealth Publications, PO Box 399, St Helena CA 94574..................707-963-1493
Medic Publishing Co, PO Box 89, Redmond WA 98073..........................206-881-2883
Medical Economics Books*, 680 Kinderkamack Rd, Oradell NJ 07649....201-262-3030
Medical Education Consultants, PO Box 67159, Los Angeles CA 90067..213-475-5141
Medical Sports Inc, PO Box 7187, Arlington VA 22207 703-525-8600
Medina Press, 2222 Silk Tree Dr, Tustin CA 92680.........................714-730-4046
Mee Enterprise Publishing Co, PO Box 6992, Beverly Hills CA 90212.....213-397-7176
Melbourne House Software*, 233 S Beverly Dr, Beverly Hills CA 90212..213-278-5850
Melius & Peterson Publishing, PO Box 925, Aberdeen SD 57401 605-226-0488
The Edwin Mellen Press*, 450 Ridge St Box 450, Lewiston NY 14092......716-754-8566
Memphis State University Press, Memphis TN 38152.........................901-454-2752
Menasha Ridge Press*, PO Box 59257, Birmingham AL 35259 205-991-0373
Mercer Univ Press*, Macon GA 31207.......................................912-744-2880
Mercury Books, PO Box 442, Yardley PA 19067..............................215-295-1870
Mercury House, 300 Montomery St Ste 700, San Francisco CA 94104 415-433-7042
Meredith Corp*, 1716 Locust St, Des Moines IA 50336 515-284-3000
Merging Media, 516 Gallows Hill Rd Ste 2, Cranford NJ 07016..............201-232-7224
Meriwether Publishing*, 885 Elkton Dr, Colorado Springs CO 80907......303-594-4422
Merl Miller & Assoc, Box 367, Lake Oswego OR 97034.......................503-636-2023
Mermaid Books, 5600 Greenwood Plaza, Englewood CO 80111................303-220-9329
Merriam Webster Inc*, 47 Federal St, Springfield MA 01105................413-734-3134
Merrill Publishing Co*, 1300 Alum Creek Dr, Columbus OH 43216.........614-890-1111
Frank Merriwell Inc*, 212 Michael Dr, Syosset NY 11791...................516-921-8888
Merry Thoughts Inc*, Bedford Hills NY 10507..............................914-241-0447
Merton House Travel Publ, 2100 Manchester Rd, Wheaton IL 60187........312-668-7410
Mesorah Publications*, 1969 Coney Island Ave, Brooklyn NY 11223.......718-339-1700
Metacom Press, 1 Tahanto Rd, Worcester MA 01602..........................617-757-1683
Metamorphous Press*, 3249 NW 29th Ave, Portland OR 92710...............503-228-4972
Methuen Inc*, 29 W 35th St, New York NY 10001............................212-244-3336
Metro Lifestyles, PO Box 532, Balboa CA 92661 714-675-5898
Metropolitan Museum of Art*, 5th Ave at 82nd, New York NY 10028.....212-879-5500
Meyerbooks Publisher, 235 W Main St, Glenwood IL 60425 312-757-4950
MGI Management Inst*, 378 Halstead Ave, Harrison NY 10528...............914-835-5790
Micah Publications, 255 Humphrey St, Marblehead MA 01945................617-631-7601
The Michie Co Law Publ*, PO Box 7587, Charlottesville VA 22906.........804-295-6171
Michigan State Univ Press*, 1405 S Harrison Rd, E Lansing MI 48824...517-355-9543
Michilander Industries, 1100 State St, St Joseph MI 49085 616-983-4972
Micro Pro Litera Press, PO Box 14045, San Francisco CA 94114............415-863-3037
Micro Publishing Press, 21150 Hawthorne #104, Torrance CA 90503.....213-371-5787
Microsignal Press, Box 388, Goleta CA 93116..............................805-964-2227

Microsoft Press*, 16011 NE 36th Way Box 97017, Redmond WA 98073..206-882-8080
Middle Atlantic Press*, PO Box 945, Wilmington DE 19899........................302-654-9922
Middle Coast Publishing*, PO Box 2522, Iowa City IA 52244.....................319-335-4078
Midgard Press, 2440 O St Ste 202, Lincoln NE 68510..............................402-474-2676
Midlife Musings Publishing, 19 Cannon Point, Lake George NY 12845 ..518-668-9583
Midwest Plan Service, 122 Davidson Hall Iowa St Univ, Ames IA 50011 .515-294-4337
Milady Publishing Corp*, 3839 White Plains Rd, Bronx NY 10467...........212-881-3000
Miles & Weir Ltd, PO Box 1906, San Pedro CA 90733 213-548-5964
R & E Miles Publishers, PO Box 1916, San Pedro CA 90733....................213-833-8856
Milkweed Editions*, PO Box 3226, Minneapolis MN 55403......................612-332-3192
Miller Accounting Publications*, 1250 6th Ave, San Diego CA 92101......619-699-6522
Millers River Publishing Co, Box 159, Athol MA 01331............................617-249-7612
Mills & Sanderson Publ*, 442 Marrett Rd Ste 5, Lexington MA 02173....617-861-0992
Mills Publishing Co, PO Box 6158 King Sta, Santa Ana CA 92706............714-541-5750
John Milton Soc for Blind*, 475 Riverside Dr, New York NY 10115........212-870-3335
Milwaukee Public Museum*, 800 W Wells St, Milwaukee WI 53233.........414-278-2787
Mina Press Publishing, PO Box 854, Sebastopol CA 95472.....................707-829-0854
Mindbody Press, 1749 Vine St, Berkeley CA 94703................................415-644-8242
Minerva Books Ltd, 137 W 14th St, New York NY 10011 212-929-2833
Minnesota Historical Soc Press*, 690 Cedar St, St Paul MN 55101 612-296-2264
Minnesota Scholarly Press Inc*, Box 224, Mankato MN 56001 507-387-4964
Mississippi Dept Archives & History, PO Box 571, Jackson MS 39205 601-359-1424
Misty Hill Press, 5024 Turner Rd, Sebastopol CA 95472.........................415-892-0789
The MIT Press*, 55 Hayward St, Cambridge MA 02142............................617-253-5646
Mitchell Publishing Inc*, 915 River St, Santa Cruz CA 95060.................408-425-3851
MMB Music Inc, 10370 Page Industrial Blvd, St Louis MO 63132.............314-427-5660
Mockingbird Books*, Box 624, St Simons Island GA 31522......................912-638-7212
Modern Books & Crafts Inc*, Box 38, Green Farms CT 06436.................203-366-5495
Modern Curriculum Press*, 13900 Prospect Rd, Cleveland OH 44136 216-238-2222
Modern Handcraft Inc, 4251 Pennsylvania Ave, Kansas City MO 64111 ..816-531-5730
Modern Language Assn*, 10 Astor Pl, New York NY 10003 212-614-6314
Modern Publishing*, 155 E 55th St, New York NY 10022 212-826-0850
Modern World Publishing Co*, PO Box 65766, Los Angeles CA 90065 ...213-221-8044
Mogul Book and FilmWorks, PO Box 2773, Pittsburgh PA 15230 412-461-0705
Momo's Press, 45 Sheridan, San Francisco CA 94103 415-863-3009
Monad Press Anchor Foundation, 410 West St, New York NY 10014......212-741-0690
Monarch Press, 1230 Ave of the Americas, New York NY 10020...............212-245-6400
Mongolia Society, Indiana Univ, Bloomington IN 47405...........................812-335-4078
Monitor Book Co, 9441 Wilshire Blvd, Beverly Hills CA 90212.................213-271-5558
Monroe Press, 16107 Gledhill St, Sepulveda CA 91343............................818-891-6464
Monterey Publishing, 225 Crossroads Blvd #176, Carmel CA 93923 408-625-1818
Montfort Publications, 26 S Saxon Ave, Bay Shore NY 11706...................516-665-0726
Monthly Review Press*, 155 W 23rd St, New York NY 10011 212-691-2555
Moody Press*, 820 N La Salle Dr, Chicago IL 60610 312-973-7800
Moon Publications, 722 Wall St, Chico CA 95928 916-345-5473
Moonsquilt Press, 16401 NE 4th Ave, N Miami Beach FL 33162 305-947-9534
MOP Press, 12890 Rebecca St, Ft Myers FL 33908 813-466-4690
Mor Mac Pub Co, PO Box 985, Daytona Beach FL 32015..........................904-255-4427
Thomas More Press*, 223 W Erie St, Chicago IL 60610............................312-951-2100
Morehouse-Barlow Co*, 78 Danbury Rd, Wilton CT 06897........................203-762-0721
Moretus Press Inc, 274 Madison Ave, New York NY 10016........................212-685-2250
Morgan & Morgan Inc*, 145 Palisade St, Dobbs Ferry NY 10522 914-693-0023
Morgan-Rand Publications, 2200 Sansom St, Philadelphia PA 19103 215-557-8200

Morningside Bookshop*, 260 Oak St, Dayton OH 45410 513-461-6736
Morris County Historical Soc, PO Box 170M, Morristown NJ 07960 201-267-3465
Joshua Morris Publishing Inc*, 167 Old Post Rd, Southport CT 06490 ...203-259-4700
Wm Morrow & Co Inc*, 105 Madison Ave, New York NY 10016 212-889-3050
Morrow Junior Books*, 105 Madison Ave, New York NY 10016 212-889-3050
Morse Press*, Box 24947, Seattle WA 98124 206-282-9988
Mosaic Press*, 358 Oliver Rd, Cincinnati OH 45215 513-761-5977
C V Mosby Co*, 11830 Westline Industrial Dr, St Louis MO 63146...........314-872-8370
Moscow Publishing Enterprise, 1240 W 29th St, Los Angeles CA 90007..213-934-2453
Mother Courage Press, 1533 Illinois St, Racine WI 53405........................414-634-1047
Motorbooks Intl Publ*, 729 Prospect Ave Box 2, Osceola WI 54020.........715-294-3345
Mott Media Inc*, 1000 E Huron St, Milford MI 48042 313-685-8773
Mountain Press Publishing Co*, PO Box 2399, Missoula MT 59806 406-728-1900
Mountain State Press, 2300 MacCorkle, Charleston WV 25304................304-304-9471
Mountaineers Books*, 306 2nd Ave W, Seattle WA 98119........................206-285-2665
Mouton de Gruyter*, 200 Saw Mill River Rd, Hawthorne NY 10532 914-747-0110
Mouvement Publications, 109 E State St, Ithaca NY 14850......................607-272-2157
Moving Parts Press, 419 A Maple St, Santa Cruz CA 95060....................408-427-2271
Moyer Bell Ltd*, Colonial Hill RFD 1, Mount Kisco NY 10549................914-666-0084
Mr Coach Inc, PO Box 9171, Downers Grove IL 60515............................312-964-3090
Mr Cogito Press, UC Box 627 Pacific Univ, Forest Grove OR 97116........503-357-6151
The Mt Aukum Press, Box 483, Mt Aukum CA 95656 209-245-4016
John Muir Publications Inc*, PO Box 613, Santa Fe NM 87504 505-982-4078
The Mulberry Tree Press, 327 N Loudoun St, Winchester VA 22601........703-665-0683
Multi Media Arts, PO Box 14486, Austin TX 78761................................512-837-5503
Multi Media Publishing Inc*, 1393 S Inca St, Denver CO 80223 303-778-1404
Multnomah Press*, 10209 SE Division St, Portland OR 97266..................503-257-0526
Munger Africana Library, Calif Inst of Tech, Pasadena CA 91125 818-356-4468
Muse-ed Co, 14141 Margate St, Van Nuys CA 91401 213-789-3310
Museum of Modern Art*, 11 W 53rd St, New York NY 10019 212-708-9730
Museum of New Mexico Press, PO Box 2087, Santa Fe NM 87503............505-827-6454
Museum of Northern Ariz*, Box 720 Rt 4, Flagstaff AZ 86001 602-774-5211
Music House Publishing, PO Box 2271, Providence RI 02905..................401-941-1417
Music Sales Corp*, 24 E 22nd St, New York NY 10010 212-254-2100
Mustang Publishing Co, PO Box 9327, New Haven CT 06533 203-624-5485
Myrna Publishing Co, PO Box 1104, Statesboro GA 30458 912-764-6076
Mysterious Press*, 129 W 56th St, New York NY 10019...........................212-765-0901
Mystic Marinelife Aquarium, 55 Coogan Blvd, Mystic CT 06355..............203-536-9631
Mystic Seaport Museum, Mystic CT 06355..203-572-0711
Nada, 2782 Dixie SW, Grandville MI 49418 616-531-1442
The Naiad Press Inc*, PO Box 10543, Tallahassee FL 32302....................904-539-9322
Namaste Press, PO Box 4435, Albuquerque NM 87196.............................505-268-4321
Namaste Publications, Box 262, Marshfield MO 65706 417-468-5053
Napsac Reproductions, 646 Pomeroy Rd, Marble Hill MO 63764.............314-238-4273
NAR Productions, PO Box 205, Saddle River NJ 07458...........................201-327-8486
Natl Academy Press*, 2101 Constitution Ave NW, Wash DC 20418..........202-334-3318
Natl Assn of Social Workers*, 7981 Eastern Ave, Silver Spg MD 20910...301-565-0333
Natl Assn of the Deaf, 814 Thayer Ave, Silver Spring MD 20910.............301-587-1788
Natl Book Co*, 333 SW Park Ave, Portland OR 97205.............................503-228-6345
Natl Braille Press*, 88 St Stephen St, Boston MA 02115.........................617-266-6160
Natl Bureau of Economic Res*, 1050 Mass Ave, Cambridge MA 02138...617-868-3900
Natl Conf of State Legislatures*, 1050 17th St, Denver CO 80265.............303-623-7800
Natl Council Teachers of English*, 1111 Kenyon Rd, Urbana IL 61801...217-328-3870

Natl Council Teachers of Math*, 1906 Association, Reston VA 22091 703-620-9840
Natl Ctr for Constitutional Studies, PO Box 37110, Wash DC 20013 801-973-1776
Natl Ctr for Urban Ethnic Affairs, PO Box 33279, Wash DC 20033..........202-232-3600
Natl Education Assn*, 1201 16th St NW, Washington DC 20036 202-822-7250
Natl Gardening Assn, 180 Flynn Ave, Burlington VT 05401 802-863-1308
Natl Geographic Society*, 17th & M Sts NW, Washington DC 20036.......202-857-7000
Natl Learning Corp*, 212 Michael Dr, Syosset NY 11791.......................516-921-8888
Natl Literary Guild Inc, 210 N Pass Ave Ste 204, Burbank CA 91505 818-845-2687
Natl Materials Dev Ctr, Dimond Library UNH, Durham NH 03824 603-862-2429
Natl Poetry Foundation, 302 Neville Univ of Maine, Orono ME 04469 207-581-3814
Natl Press Inc*, 7508 Wisconsin Ave, Bethesda MD 20814.......................301-657-1616
Natl Publ of the Black Hills*, 47 Nepperhan Ave, Elmsford NY 10523....914-592-6006
Natl Publishing Co, 24th & Locust Sts, Philadelphia PA 19101.................215-732-1863
Natl Register Publishing Co*, 3004 Glenview Rd, Wilmette IL 60091 312-256-6067
Natl Retail Merchants Assn*, 100 W 31st St, New York NY 10001...........212-244-8780
Natl Scholarship Research Svc, PO Box 2516, San Rafael CA 94912........415-456-1577
Natl Textbook Co*, 4255 W Touhy Ave, Lincolnwood IL 60646................312-679-5500
Natural World Press, 607 Chiltern Rd, Hillsborough CA 94010 415-344-4154
Naturegraph Publ, 3543 Indian Creek Rd, Happy Camp CA 96039 916-493-5353
Nautical & Aviation Publishing*, 101 W Read St, Baltimore MD 21201..301-659-0220
Naval Institute Press*, Annapolis MD 21402.......................................301-268-6110
Navpress*, 3820 N 30th St PO Box 6000, Colorado Springs CO 80934......303-598-1212
NB Marketing, 9420 Reseda Blvd Ste 442, Northridge CA 91324..............818-993-9161
NBM Publishing Co, 156 E 39th St, New York NY 10016.........................212-661-8129
Neal Schuman Publishers Inc*, 23 Cornelia St, New York NY 10014.......212-620-5990
Negative Capability Press, 6116 Timberly Rd N, Mobile AL 36609..........205-661-9114
William S Nein & Co Inc*, 1285 Main St, Buffalo NY 14209.....................716-882-2600
Nelson Hall Publishers*, 111 N Canal St, Chicago IL 60606.....................312-930-9446
Thomas Nelson Inc*, Nelson Pl at Elm Hill Pike, Nashville TN 37214......615-889-9000
Nevada Publications*, 4135 Badger Circle, Reno NV 89509......................702-747-0800
New Age Press, PO Box 2089, Keala Kekua HI 96750 808-328-8031
New American Library*, 1633 Broadway, New York NY 10019 212-397-8000
New Bedford Press, 5800 W Century Blvd, Los Angeles CA 90009............213-281-6023
New Century Publ*, 220 Old New Brunswick, Piscataway NJ 08854 201-981-0820
New City Press, 206 Skillman Ave, Brooklyn NY 11211...........................718-782-2844
New Directions Publishing Corp*, 80 8th Ave, New York NY 10011........212-255-0230
The New England Press*, Box 575, Shelburne VT 05482............................802-863-2520
New Era Press Inc, Box 29, Farmingdale NY 11735 516-277-9708
New Hampshire Publishing Co*, Box 70, Somersworth NH 03878............603-692-3727
New Harbinger Publications, 5674 Shattuck Ave, Oakland CA 94609.......415-465-1435
New Haven Publishers, 1703 N Tyland Blvd, New Haven IN 46774..........219-746-2646
New Horisons Publishers, 737 10th Ave E, Seattle WA 98102...................206-323-1102
New Horizon Press*, PO Box 669, Far Hills NJ 07931..............................201-234-9546
New Lifestyle Publishing, PO Box 4419, Los Angeles CA 90051 213-660-8201
New Plays Inc, Box 273, Rowayton CT 06853 203-866-4520
New Puritan Library Inc, 91 Lytle Rd, Fletcher NC 28732.......................704-628-2185
New Readers Press*, PO Box 131, Syracuse NY 13210 315-422-9121
New Rivers Press, 1602 Selby Ave, St Paul MN 55104..............................612-645-6324
New Sage Press, PO Box 41029, Pasadena CA 41029 818-791-4122
New Seed Press, PO Box 9488, Berkeley CA 94709 415-540-7576
New Society Publishers*, 4722 Baltimore Ave, Philadelphia PA 19143 215-726-6543
New Victoria Publishers, PO Box 27, Norwich VT 05055.........................802-649-5297
New World Publ Eric L Gibson, 20511 S Blythe, Riverdale CA 93656.......209-867-4653

New York Academy of Sciences*, 2 E 63rd St, New York NY 10021..........212-838-0230
New York Graphic Society Books*, 34 Beacon ST, Boston MA 02106......617-227-0730
NY State Inst Glaze Resrch, 511 N Hamilton, Painted Post NY 14870.....607-962-1671
New York Univ Press*, 70 Washington Sq S, New York NY 10012.............212-598-2886
New York Zoetrope*, 838 Broadway, New York NY 10003.....................212-420-0590
Newbury House Publishers Inc*, 54 Warehouse Ln, Rowley MA 01969...617-948-2704
Newcastle Publishing Co*, 13419 Saticoy St, N Hollywood CA 91605.......213-873-3191
Newmarket Press*, 18 E 48th St, New York NY 10017.............................212-832-3575
Nexus Press, 608 Ralph McGill Blvd, Atlanta GA 30312......................404-544-3579
Nicholas Publishing Co*, 155 W 72nd St, New York NY 10023.................212-580-8079
Night Tree Press, 414 W Thomas St, Rome NY 13440.............................315-337-4142
Nikmal Publishing, 698 River St, Boston MA 02126.............................617-361-2101
Nilgiri Press, PO Box 477, Petaluma CA 94953.................................707-878-2369
Nitty Gritty Cookbooks, 447 E Channel Rd, Benicia CA 94510...............707-746-0800
Nok Publishers International, 150 5th Ave, New York NY 10011............212-675-5785
Nolo Press*, 950 Parker St, Berkeley CA 94710................................415-549-1976
Norfleet Press, 527 E 84th St, New York NY 10028.............................212-472-0864
Norseman Publishing Co, PO Box 6617, Lubbock TX 79493....................806-795-9875
North Amer Students Coop, PO Box 7715, Ann Arbor MI 48107...............313-663-0889
North Atlantic Books*, 2320 Blake St, Berkeley CA 94704....................415-540-7934
North Carolina Div Archives & Hist*, 109 E Jones, Raleigh NC 27611....919-733-7442
North Carolina Museum Nat Science, Box 27647, Raleigh NC 27611......919-733-7450
North Country Press*, One Mile Rd, Thorndike ME 04986.....................207-948-2962
North County Books Inc, 18 Irving Place, Utica NY 13501...................315-733-7915
North Dakota Inst of Regional Studies, NDSU, Fargo ND 58105.............701-237-8338
North Light Publishers*, 1507 Dana Ave, Cincinnati OH 45207..............513-531-2222
North Point Press*, 850 Talbot Ave, Berkeley CA 94706.....................415-527-6260
North Ridge Books, PO Box 13401, Akron OH 44313.............................216-864-8786
North River Press Inc, Box 241, Croton-on-Hudson NY 10520...............914-941-7175
North Star Press, Box 451, St Cloud MN 56301................................612-253-1636
Northeast Sportsmans Press, PO Box 188, Tarrytown NY 10591.............914-762-7193
Northeastern University Press*, PO Box 116, Boston MA 02117.............617-437-5480
Northern Cartographic Inc, PO Box 133, Burlington VT 05402...............802-655-4321
Northern Illinois University Press*, De Kalb IL 60115.....................815-753-1826
Northland Press*, Box N, Flagstaff AZ 86002..................................602-774-5251
Northstar-Maschek AG, PO Box 810, Lakeville MN 55044.....................612-469-5433
Northwest Trails Association, 16812 36th Ave W, Lynwood WA 98037....206-743-3947
Northwestern University Press, 1735 Benson Ave, Evanston IL 60201......312-491-5313
Northwood, PO Box 5634, Madison WI 53705....................................608-231-2355
Northwoods Press*, Box 88, Thomaston ME 04861.............................207-354-6550
Northword*, PO Box 128, Ashland WI 53705....................................608-231-2355
W W Norton & Co Inc*, 500 5th Ave, New York NY 10110.....................212-354-5500
Norwegian Amer Hist Assn, St Olaf College, Northfield MN 55057.........507-663-3221
Not Polyoptics Publ*, 13721 Lynn St #15, Woodbridge VA 22191............703-491-5543
Noyes Publications*, Mill Rd & Grand Ave, Park Ridge NJ 07656...........201-391-8484
O'Connor House Publ, PO Box 64098, Virginia Beach VA 23464.............804-420-2551
O'Sullivan Woodside & Co*, 2218 E Magnolia, Phoenix AZ 85034..........602-244-1000
O2 Press, Rt 1 Box 317, Pandora OH 45877....................................419-384-3332
Oak Tree Publications Inc*, 9601 Aero Dr, San Diego CA 92123.............619-560-5163
Oakwood Publications, 616 Knob Hill, Redondo Beach CA 90277.............213-378-9245
Oasis Press*, 720 S Hillview Dr, Milpitas CA 95035..........................408-263-9671
Occasional Papers*, 500 W Baltimore St, Baltimore MD 21201...............301-538-3870
Ocean Tree Books, PO Box 1295, Santa Fe NM 87504.........................505-983-1412

Ocean View Publications, 2420 Main St, Stratford CT 06497 203-377-7606
Oceana Publications Inc*, 75 Main St, Dobbs Ferry NY 10522...................914-693-1394
Octagon Books*, 171 Madison Ave, New York NY 10016...........................212-685-4371
Octameron Assoc*, 820 Fontaine St, Alexandria VA 22302 703-823-1882
Oddo Publishing, 819 Redwine Rd, Fayetteville GA 30214.........................404-461-7627
Oelgeschlager Gunn & Hain Inc*, 131 Clarendon St, Boston MA 02116..617-437-9620
Of Course Publications, PO Box 70732, Houston TX 77270..........................713-863-0250
Ohara Publications Inc*, 1813 Victory Pl, Burbank CA 91504....................818-843-4444
Ohio Psychology Publishing, 131 N High St, Columbus OH 43125.............614-224-3288
Ohio State Univ Press*, 1050 Carmack Rd, Columbus OH 43210 614-422-6930
Ohio Univ Press*, Scott Quad, Athens OH 45701 614-593-1153
Ohsawa Macrobiotic Found, 1511 Robinson St, Oroville CA 95965 916-533-7702
Okefenokee Press, Rt 3 Box 142 C, Folkston GA 31537...............................912-496-7401
The Old Army Press, PO Box 2243, Ft Collins CO 80522...........................303-484-5535
Old Warren Road Press, 141 W 17th St Loft F, New York NY 10011.......212-242-5762
Olympic Publishing Inc, PO Box 353, Port Ludlow WA 98365....................206-437-2277
Olympus Publishing Co, 1670 E 13 S, Salt Lake City UT 84105.................801-583-3666
Omega Star Inc*, PO Box 87413, Houston TX 77287 713-998-9226
OMF Books*, 404 S Church St, Robesonia PA 19551 215-693-5881
On Da Bayou Press, PO Box 52467, New Orleans LA 70152 504-943-7041
On The Move Press, 655 Oakland Ave, Oakland CA 94611 415-588-8316
One World Enterprises, PO Box 13 Kenmore Sta, Boston MA 02215.......617-731-2775
Oness Press, Box 92, Williams OR 97544...503-942-8221
Open Court Publishing Co*, 315 5th St, Peru IL 61354 815-223-1500
Open My World Publishing, PO Box 15011, San Diego CA 92115 619-265-0908
Oracle Press Ltd*, 5323 Heatherstone Dr, Baton Rouge LA 70820 504-766-5577
Orafa Publishing Co, 3055 La Pietra Cir, Honolulu HI 96815...................808-922-5177
Orbis Books*, Walsh Bldg, Maryknoll NY 10545....................................914-941-7590
Oregon Historical Soc Press*, 1230 SW Park Ave, Portland OR 97205....503-222-1741
Oregon State Univ Press*, 101 Waldo Hall, Corvallis OR 97331 503-754-3166
Oriental Institute Publications, 1155 E 58th St, Chicago IL 60637 312-962-9508
Ortho Information Services*, 575 Market St, San Francisco CA 94105 415-894-0277
The Oryx Press*, 2214 N Central at Encanto, Phoenix AZ 85004 602-254-6156
Osborne Enterprises, PO Box 28312, Tempe AZ 85282.............................602-437-3461
Ottenheimer Publishers*, 300 Reisterstown Rd, Baltimore MD 21208.....301-484-2100
Our Child Press, 800 Maple Glen Ln, Wayne PA 19087.............................215-964-1837
Our Sunday Visitor Inc*, 200 Noll Plaza, Huntington IN 46750..................219-356-8400
Out Of Your Mind, 3031 Colt Way #233, Fullerton CA 92633 704-739-1777
Outdoor Empire Publishing Inc*, PO Box C-19000, Seattle WA 98109....206-624-3845
The Overlook Press*, 12 W 21st St, New York NY 10010 212-807-7300
Richard C Owen Publishers, PO Box 819, New York NY 10185.................212-864-7849
Owl Creek Press*, 1620 N 45th St, Seattle WA 98103 206-633-5929
Ox Box Press, PO Box 4045, Woodbridge CT 06525 203-387-5900
Oxford University Press Inc*, 200 Madison Ave, New York NY 10016 212-679-7300
Oxmoor House INc*, PO Box 2262, Birmingham AL 35201.......................205-877-6534
Ozark Society Foundation, PO Box 3503, Little Rock AR 72203 501-847-3738
Jerome S Ozer Publisher, 340 Tenafly Rd, Englewood NJ 07631...............201-567-7040
Pace Gallery Publications*, 32 E 57th St, New York NY 10022 212-421-3292
Pachart Publishing House, PO Box 35549, Tucson AZ 85740 602-297-4797
Pacific Books*, PO Box 558, Palo Alto CA 94302....................................415-856-0550
Pacific Information, 11684 Ventura Blvd, Studio City CA 91604.............818-797-7654
Pacific Press Publishing Assn*, PO Box 7000, Boise ID 83707 208-465-2595
Pacific Publishing House, PO Box 5756, Newport Beach CA 92662.........714-673-8546

Pacific Scientific Press Inc, 3506 Pennsylvania, Longview WA 98632........206-425-8592
Pacific Search Press*, 222 Dexter Ave N, Seattle WA 98109.....................206-682-5044
Packet Press, 14704 Seneca Castle Ct, Gaithersburg MD 20878.................301-762-7145
Packrat Press, 4366 N Diana Ln, Oak Arbor WA 98277 206-675-6016
Paddlewheel Press, PO Box 230220, Tigard OR 97223............................503-639-5637
Countrywoman Press, PO Box 1275, San Luis Obispo CA 93406.............805-543-5404
Paganiniana Publications*, 3rd & Union Ave, Neptune NJ 07753 201-988-8400
Pal Publishing, 10755 Bachelor Valley Rd, Witter Springs CA 95493........707-275-2777
Palace Publishing, RD 1 Box 320, Moundsville WV 26041.....................304-843-1600
Paladin Press*, PO Box 1307, Boulder CO 80306..................................303-443-7250
Palm Publications, 1850 Union St #294, San Francisco CA 94123 415-928-3369
Palmer Method Handwriting, 1720 W Irving Pk, Schaumburg IL 60193...800-323-9563
Pandora Press*, 29 W 35th St, New York NY 10001................................212-244-3336
Pangloss Press, PO Box 18917, Los Angeles CA 90018 213-663-1950
Panjandrum Books, 11321 Iowa Ave Ste 7, Los Angeles CA 90025...........213-477-8771
Panoptic Enterprises, PO Box 1099, Woodbridge VA 22193.....................703-670-2812
Panorama West Books, 2002 N Gateway #102, Fresno CA 93727.............209-251-7801
Pantheon Books Inc*, 201 E 50th St, New York NY 10022 212-751-2600
The Paper Bag Players, 50 Riverside Dr, New York NY 10024 212-362-0431
The Paperbook Press Inc*, PO Box 1776, Westwood MA 02090................617-329-4344
PAR Inc*, 290 Westminster St, Providence RI 02903 401-331-0130
Para Publishing Co*, PO Box 4232, Santa Barbara CA 93140....................805-968-7277
Para Research Inc*, 85 Eastern Ave, Gloucester MA 01930.......................617-283-3438
Paraclete Press*, Box 1568 Hilltop Plz Rt 6A, Orleans MA 02653 617-255-4685
Paradise Publications, 8110 SW Wareham, Portland OR 97223 503-246-1555
Paragon House Publ*, 2 Hammarskjold Plaza, New York NY 10017........212-223-6433
Paragon Productions, 817 Pearl St, Denver CO 80203.............................303-832-7687
Parent Scene, PO Box 2222, Redlands CA 92373....................................714-792-2412
Parenting Press, 7744 31st Ave NE PO Box 15163, Seattle WA 98115......206-527-2900
Parents Magazine Press, 685 3rd Ave, New York NY 10017 212-878-8700
Parker & Son Publications*, PO Box 60001, Los Angeles CA 90060 213-727-1088
Parker Brothers Publishing*, 190 Bridge St, Salem MA 01970..................617-927-7600
Parker Publishing Co*, PO Box 500, Englewood Cliffs NJ 07631.............201-592-2440
Parnassus Imprints, 21 Canal Rd PO Box 335, Orleans MA 02653 617-255-2932
Partner Press, PO Box 124, Livonia MI 48152 313-681-3350
Partners In Publishing, PO Box 50347, Tulsa OK 74150...........................918-584-5906
The Passive Solar Institute, Box 722, Bascom OH 44809.........................419-937-2226
Passport Press, PO Box 1346, Champlain NY 12919 514-937-8155
The Past In Glass, 515 Northridge Dr, Boulder City NV 89005..................702-565-8741
That Patchsork Place Inc, PO Box 118, Bothell WA 98041........................206-483-3313
Path Press Inc, 53 W Jackson Blvd Ste 1040, Chicago IL 60604 312-663-0167
Pathfinder Press, 410 West St, New York NY 10014................................212-741-0690
Pathway Press*, 1080 Montgomery Ave, Cleveland TN 37311....................615-476-4512
Patio Publications, 850 Woodhollow Ln, Buffalo Grove IL 60090 312-541-2009
Patmos Press Inc, PO Box V, Shepherdstown WV 25443..........................304-876-2086
The Patrice Press, Box 42, Gerald MO 63037..314-764-2801
Patriotic Publishers, 159 Woodland Ave, Verona NJ 07044 201-239-7299
Paulist Press*, 997 Macarthur Blvd, Mahwah NJ 07430............................201-825-7300
PBC Intl Inc*, 1 School St, Glen Cove NY 11542 516-676-2727
Peabody Museum Publications, 11 Divinity Ave, Cambridge MA 02138 ..617-495-3938
Peace & Pieces Press, PO Box 640394, San Francisco CA 94164...............415-771-3431
Peachtree Publishers Ltd*, 494 Armour Cir NE, Atlanta GA 30324.........404-876-8761
F E Peacock Publishers Inc*, 115 N Prospect Ave, Itasca IL 60143...........312-773-1155

Peak Skill Publishing, PO Box 5489, Playa Del Rey CA 90296 213-306-6403
Peanut Butter Publishing*, 911 Western Ave #401, Seattle WA 98104 206-628-6200
J Michael Pearson, PO Box 402844, Miami Beach FL 33140 305-538-0346
Pedipress, 125 Red Gate Ln, Amherst MA 01002..413-549-7798
Peek Publications, PO Box 50123, Palo Alto CA 94303 415-962-1010
Pegus Press, 648 W Sierra Ave PO Box 429, Clovis CA 93612......................209-299-2263
Pelican Publishing Co Inc*, 1101 Monroe St, Gretna LA 70053 504-368-1175
Pella Publishing Co, 337 W 36th St, New York NY 10018............................212-279-9586
Pen-Dec Press, 1724 Georgia Ave, Marysville MI 48040 313-364-8024
Pendle Hill Publications*, 338 Plucsh Mill Rd, Wallingford PA 19086......215-566-4507
Pendragon Press*, 162 W 13th St, New York NY 10011................................212-243-3494
Pendulum Press Inc*, Box 509 Saw Mill Rd, W Haven CT 06516.............203-933-2551
Penguin Books, 40 W 23rd St, New York NY 10010......................................212-807-7300
Peninsula Publishing, PO Box 867, Los Altos CA 94023..............................415-948-2511
The Penkevill Publishing Co*, PO Box 212, Greenwood FL 32443............904-569-2811
Pennsylvania Acad of Science, Lafayette College, Easton PA 18042........215-252-5464
Penn Historical Commission, PO Box 1026, Harrisburg PA 17108 717-787-8312
Penn State Univ Press*, 215 Wagner Bldg, Univ Park PA 16802 814-865-1327
PennWell Books*, PO Box 1260, Tulsa OK 74101..918-835-3161
Pennypress Inc, 1100 23rd Ave E, Seattle WA 98112 206-325-1419
Pensacola Historical Society, 405 S Adams St, Pensacola FL 32501 904-433-1559
Pentagram, PO Box 379, Markesan WI 53946 414-398-2161
Pentecostal Publishing House*, 8855 Dunn Rd, Hazelwood MO 63042 ...314-837-7300
The Penumbra Press, 920 S 38th St, Omaha NE 68105................................402-346-7344
Peregrine Press*, 1168 Boston Post Rd, Old Saybrook CT 06475 203-388-0285
Perfection Form Co*, 8350 Hickman Rd #15, Des Moines IA 50322........515-278-0133
Pergamon Press, Maxwell House Fairview Pk, Elmsford NY 10523..........914-592-7700
Pergot Press, 1001 Bridgeway Ste 227, Sausalito CA 94965......................415-332-0279
Perinatoloty Press*, PO Box 6827, Ithaca NY 14851..................................607-257-3278
The Permanent Press, RD 2 Noyac Rd, Sag Harbor NY 11963................516-725-1101
Permelia Publishing, PO Box 650, Keystone SD 57751................................605-666-4449
Persea Books Inc*, 225 Lafayette St, New York NY 10012 212-431-5270
Persistence Press, 4734 Wentworth Blvd, Indianapolis IN 46201................317-367-9071
Perspectives Press, 905 W Wildwood Ave, Ft Wayne IN 46807................219-456-8411
Peter Pauper Press Inc, 202 Mamaroneck Ave, White Plains NY 10601...914-681-0144
Peterson's Guides Inc*, PO Box 2123, Princeton NJ 08543 609-924-5338
Petrocelli Books Inc*, 251 Wall St, Princeton NJ 08540............................609-924-5851
Petroglyph Press Ltd, 201 Kinoole St, Hilo HI 96720..................................808-935-6001
Pflaum Press, 2451 E River Rd, Dayton OH 45439......................................513-294-5785
Phanes Press, PO Box 6114, Grand Rapids MI 49516..................................616-949-7307
Pharos Books*, 200 Park Ave, New York NY 10166 212-692-3824
Phillie Dee Enterprises, 515 12 High St, Port Jefferson NY 11777............516-928-5876
Phillips Publications Inc, Box 168, Williamstown NJ 08094........................609-567-0695
Philomel Books*, 51 Madison Ave, New York NY 10010............................212-689-9200
Philosophical Library Inc*, 200 W 57th St, New York NY 10019 212-265-6050
Phoenix Books Publishers, PO Box 32008, Phoenix AZ 85064 602-952-0163
Phoenix Publishing, PO Box 3546, Redmond WA 98073..............................206-827-8433
The Photographic Arts Center, 127 E 59th St, New York NY 10022........212-838-8640
Photopia Press, PO Box 1844, Corvallis OR 97339......................................503-757-8761
Pi Press Inc, 3169 Alika Ave Box 23371, Honolulu HI 96822....................808-595-3426
Pickwick Publications*, 4137 Timberlane Dr, Allison Park PA 15101......412-487-2159
Pictorial Histories Pub Co*, 713 S 3rd St, Missoula MT 59801 406-549-8488
The Pierian Press Inc*, PO Box 1808, Ann Arbor MI 48106 313-434-5530

Pigwidgeon Press, Box 76, Derby Line VT 05830................819-876-2538
Pilgrim Press*, 132 W 31st St, New York NY 10001................212-239-8700
Pilgrim Publications, PO Box 66, Pasadena TX 77501................713-477-2329
Pilot Books*, 103 Cooper St, Babylon NY 11702................516-422-2225
Pine Mountain Press Inc, 2440 O St Ste 202, Lincoln NE 68510................402-474-2676
Pineapple Press Inc*, PO Box 314, Englewood FL 33533................813-475-2238
Pinetree Publishing Inc, 3601 Locust Walk, Philadelphia PA 19104................215-222-2845
Pinnacle Books Inc*, 1430 Broadway, New York NY 10018................212-719-5900
Pistil Press, PO Box 91386, Long Beach CA 90809................213-439-0687
Pitman Publishing Inc*, 1020 Plain St, Marshfield MA 02050................617-837-1331
PJD Publications Ltd*, PO Box 966, Westbury NY 11590................516-626-0650
Placebo Press, 4311 Bayou Blvd T-199, Pensacola FL 32503................904-477-3995
Plain View Press Inc, PO Box 33311, Austin TX 78764................512-441-2452
The Plan, PO Box 7800, Santa Cruz CA 95061................408-458-3365
Plantagenet House Inc, Box 271, Blackshear GA 31516................912-449-6601
Players Press*, PO Box 1132, Studio City CA 91604................818-789-4980
Playmore Inc Publishers*, 200 5th Ave, New York NY 10010................212-924-7447
Plays Inc*, 120 Boylston St, Boston MA 02116................617-423-3157
Please Press Ltd, PO Box 3036, Flint MI 48502................313-239-3110
Plenum Publishing Corp*, 233 Spring St, New York NY 10013................212-620-8018
Plexus Publishing Inc, 143 Old Marlton Pike, Medford NJ 08055................609-654-6500
Plum Hall, 1 Spruce Ave, Cardiff NJ 08232................609-927-3770
Pluribus Press Inc*, 160 E Illinois St, Chicago IL 60611................312-467-0424
Plus-Kent Publishing*, 20 Park Plaza, Boston MA 02116................617-543-3377
Pocahontas Press Inc, 2805 Wellesley Ct, Blacksburg VA 24060................703-951-0467
Pocket Books*, 1230 Ave of the Americas, New York NY 10020................212-698-7565
Poets For Peace Publications, Ft Mason Ctr, San Francisco CA 94123................415-621-3073
Polestar Publications, 620 S Minnesota Ave, Sioux Falls SD 57104................605-338-2888
Poly Tone Press, 16027 Sunburst St, Sepulveda CA 91343................818-892-0044
Ponderosa Publishers, Airport Rd Box 68, St Icnatius MT 59865................406-745-4455
Poplar Books, Box 62, Shiloh TN 38376................901-632-1289
The Popular Press*, Popular Culture Ctr, Bowling Green OH 43403................419-372-2981
Porcupine Press Inc*, 1926 Arch St Ste 3R, Philadelphia PA 19103................215-563-2288
Porter Sargent Publishers Inc, 11 Beacon St, Boston MA 02108................617-523-1670
Poseidon Press*, 1230 Ave of the Americas, New York NY 10020................212-698-7290
Positive Feedback Comm, 3744 Applegate Ave, Cincinnati OH 45211................513-661-1690
Positive Press, PO Box 3133, Joliet IL 60436................815-729-4302
The Post Apollo Press, 35 Marie St, Sausalito CA 94965................415-332-1458
Potala Publications, 107 E 31st St 4th fl, New York NY 10016................212-213-5011
Potentials Development Inc, 775 Main St, Buffalo NY 14203................716-842-2658
Potes & Poets Press Inc, 181 Edgemont Ave, Elmwood CT 06110................203-233-2023
Potshot Press, PO Box 1117, Pacific Palisade CA 90272................213-454-9393
Clarkson N Potter Inc*, 225 Park Ave, New York NY 10003................212-254-1600
PPI Publishing*, 835 E Congress Park PO Box 335, Dayton OH 45459....513-433-2709
Praeger Publishers*, 521 5th Ave, New York NY 10175................212-599-8400
Prakken Publications Inc, 416 Longshore Dr, Ann Arbor MI 48107................313-769-1211
Prayer Book Press Inc, 1363 Fairfield Ave, Bridgeport CT 06605................203-384-2284
Precedent Publishing Inc, 737 N LaSalle St, Chicago IL 60610................312-944-2525
Preferred Press, 5702 Research Dr, Huntington Beach CA 92649................714-895-1083
Prema Books, 310 West End Ave, New York NY 10023................212-874-7692
Premier Publishers Inc, PO Box 330309, Ft Worth TX 76163................817-293-7030
Prentice Hall Inc, Englewood Cliffs NJ 07632................201-592-2000
Prentice-Hall Press*, One Gulf + Western Plaza, New York NY 10023..212-373-8125

Presbyterian & Reformed Publishing*, Box 817, Phillipsburg NJ 08865 ...201-454-0505
Prescott Street Press, PO Box 40312, Portland OR 97240.....................503-254-2922
Preservation Press, 1785 Massachusetts Ave NW, Wash DC 20036 202-673-4058
Presidio Press*, 31 Pamaron Way, Novato CA 94947 415-883-1373
The Press of the Third Mind, 932 W Oakdale, Chicago IL 60657 312-929-3387
The Press of Ward Schori, 2716 Noyes St, Evanston IL 60201....................312-475-3241
Press Pacifica, Box 47, Kailua HI 96734 808-261-6594
Pressworks Publishing Inc, PO Box 12606, Dallas TX 75225 214-369-3113
Prestwick Poetry Publ Co, 2235 Calle Guay Mas, La Jolla CA 92037 619-456-2366
Price/Stern/Sloan Inc*, 360 N La Cienega, Los Angeles CA 90048.........213-657-6100
Prima Publ & Communications, PO Box 1260, Rocklin CA 95677............916-624-5718
Princess Publishing, PO Box 386, Beaverton OR 97075.............................503-643-5806
Princeton Architectural Press, 2 Research Way, Princeton NJ 08540 609-924-7911
Princeton Book Co Publishers, PO Box 109, Princeton NJ 08542..............609-737-8177
Princeton Press Publ, 2838 Lakeridge Ln, Westlake Vlg CA 91362...........805-496-3204
Princeton Technical Publ, 301 N Harrison St, Princeton NJ 08540 609-924-6428
Princeton Univ Press*, 41 William St, Princeton NJ 08540 609-452-4900
Principia Press, 5743 S Kimbark Ave, Chicago IL 60637............................312-962-9531
Printed Editions, Box 27 Station Hill Rd, Barrytown NY 12507.................914-758-6488
Printemps Books Inc, PO Box 746, Wilmette IL 60091................................312-251-5418
PRO ED*, 5341 Industrial Oak Blvd, Austin TX 78735..............................512-892-3142
Pro Lingua Assoc*, 15 Elm St, Brattleboro VT 05301................................802-257-7779
ProActive Press, 64 Via La Cumbre, Greenbrae CA 94904.........................415-461-7854
Probus Publishing Co*, 118 N Clinton St, Chicago IL 60606 312-346-7985
Proctor Jones Publ, 3401 Sacramento St, San Francisco CA 94118............415-922-9222
Productivity Inc*, PO Box 814, Cambridge MA 02238................................617-497-5146
Professional Press*, PO Box 1384, Mount Dora FL 32757 904-383-1200
Professional Publications Inc, 1250 5th Ave, Belmont CA 94002............415-593-9119
Professional Resource Exchange*, 635 S Orange, Sarasota FL 33577 813-366-7913
Progenesys Press, PO Box 2623, Christianburg VA 24068...........................703-382-5493
Progresiv Publishr, 401 E 32nd St #1002, Chicago IL 60616 312-225-9181
Progressive Science Inst, PO Box 5335, Berkeley CA 94705 415-654-1619
Project Share, PO Box 2309, Rockville MD 20852.......................................301-231-9539
ProLingua Assoc, 15 Elm St, Brattleboro VT 05301.....................................802-257-7779
Promenade Publishing, PO Box 2092, Boulder CO 80306.............................303-449-6923
Prometheus Books*, 700 E Amherst St, Buffalo NY 14215 716-837-2475
Promethian Press*, PO Box 6827, Ithaca NY 14851....................................607-257-3278
Promontory Publishing Inc, PO Box 117213, Carrollton TX 75011 214-394-6020
Proscenium Publishers Inc*, 118 E 30th St, New York NY 10016...............212-532-5525
Prospect Hill, 216 Wendover Rd, Baltimore MD 21218................................301-235-1026
Prosper Press, PO Box 7033, Boca Raton FL 33431......................................305-391-1429
Prosperity Press, PO Box 230, Glendale CA 91209 213-257-0395
ProStar Publications, 4051 Glencoe Ave, Marina Del Rey CA 90292.......213-306-2094
Prosveta USA, PO Box 49614, Los Angeles CA 90049 213-820-7478
Pruett Publishing Co*, 2928 Pearl St, Boulder CO 80301............................303-449-4919
PSG Publishing Co Inc*, 545 Great Rd, Littleton MA 01460 617-486-8971
Psychohistory Press, 2315 Broadway, New York NY 10024.........................212-873-5900
Psychological Dimensions Inc*, 10 W 66th St 4H, New York NY 10023 ..212-877-2313
The Psychology Society, 100 Beekman St, New York NY 10038...................212-285-1872
The Pterodactyl Press, PO Box 205, Cumberland IA 50843 712-774-2244
Ptolemy Press Ltd, PO Box 243, Grove City PA 16127 412-458-5145
Public Affairs Press*, 419 New Jersey Ave SE, Washington DC 20003.....202-544-3024
Publishers Assoc*, PO Box 160361, Irving TX 75016...................................817-572-7400

Publishers Media, PO Box 546, El Cajon CA 92022.................................619-282-5822
Publishers Press, 1935 S E 59th Ave, Portland OR 97215 503-232-9293
Publishers Services*, 6318 Vesper Ave, Van Nuys CA 91411 818-785-8039
Publishing Horizons Inc, PO Box 02190, Columbus OH 43202................614-261-6565
Publitec Editions, PO Box 4342, Laguna Beach CA 92652........................714-497-6100
Puckerbrush Press, 76 Main St, Orono ME 04473 207-581-3832
Pudding Publications, 2384 Hardesty Dr, S Columbus OH 43204............614-279-4188
Pueblo Publ Press*, 401 Vandament Ave 204G, Yukon OK 73099..........405-354-7825
Puma Publishing, 1670 Coral Dr, Santa Maria CA 93454 805-925-3216
Purdue University Press*, S Campus Courts D, W Lafayette IN 47906....317-494-2035
Purple Mouth Press, 713 Paul St, Newport News VA 23605.....................804-380-6595
Pushcart Press, PO Box 380, Wainscott NY 11975.....................................516-324-9300
Putnam Publishing Group*, 200 Madison Ave, New York NY 10016.......212-576-8900
QED Information Sciences*, 170 Linden St, Wellesley MA 02181............617-237-5656
QED Press, 1012 Hill St #6, Ann Arbor MI 48104 313-994-0371
QSKY Publishing, PO Box 6960, Dearborn Heights MI 62708..................217-753-1995
Quaker Press, 3218 O St NW, Washington DC 20007.................................202-338-3391
Quantal Publishing, 375 Moreton Bay Lane, Goleta CA 93117 805-964-7293
Quarter Books Inc, 215 Park Ave S Ste 2005, New York NY 10003 212-254-2277
Quarterman Publications Inc*, Box 156, Lincoln MA 01773....................617-259-8047
Quartet Books Inc*, 215 Park Ave S Ste 2500, New York NY 10003.........212-254-2277
Quartzite Books, PO Box 1931, Mount Vernon WA 98273 206-336-3345
Quarto Publishing*, 15 W 26th St, New York NY 10010...........................212-685-6610
Que Corp*, 7999 Knue Rd, Indianapolis IN 46250.....................................317-842-7162
The Questor Group, 16215 9th NE, Seattle WA 98155................................206-364-4672
Quill*, 105 Madison Ave, New York NY 10016...212-889-3050
Quintessence Publ, 356 Bunker Hill Mine Rd, Amador City CA 95601....209-267-5470
Quintessence Publishing Co*, 8 S Michigan Ave, Chicago IL 60603 312-782-3221
R & D Services, PO Box 644, Des Moines IA 50303....................................515-276-2131
R & E Publishers*, PO Box 2008, Saratoga CA 95070 408-866-6303
R & M Publishing Co Inc, PO Box 1276, Holly Hill SC 29059...................804-732-4094
REP Publishers, 12703 Red Fox Ct, Maryland Hts MO 63043 314-878-9311
Racz Publishing Co, PO Box 287, Oxnard CA 93041 702-795-8922
Radio & Records, 1930 Century Park W, Los Angeles CA 90067...............213-553-4330
Radio Shack*, 900 Two Tandy Ctr, Ft Worth TX 76102...........................817-390-3919
The Rain Umbrella, 1135 SE Salmon, Portland OR 97214 503-249-7218
Rainbow Books, PO Box 1069, Moore Haven FL 33471 813-946-0293
Rainbow Press, Box 855, Clackamas OR 97015...503-657-9839
Raintree Publishers Inc, 310 W Wisconsin Ave, Milwaukee WI 53203 414-273-0873
Rainy Day Press, 1147 E 26th St, Eugene OR 97403 503-484-4626
Rajneesh Foundation Intl*, Box 9, Rajneeshpuram OR 97741...................503-489-3301
Rama Publishing Co, Box 793, Carthage MO 64836 417-358-1093
Ramparts Press Inc, PO Box 50128, Palo Alto CA 94303 415-325-7861
Ramsco Publishing Co, Box N, Laurel MD 20707 301-953-3699
Rand Mcnally & Co*, 8255 Central Park Ave, Skokie IL 60076 312-673-9100
Random House Inc*, 201 E 50th St, New York NY 10022...........................212-751-2600
Raven Press*, 1140 Ave of the Americas, New York NY 10036 212-575-0335
Rawson Assoc*, 115 5th Ave, New York NY 10003 212-614-1403
Rayid Publications, 115 S La Cumbre #2, Santa Barbara CA 93105.........805-968-3857
RE Search, 20 Romolo #B, San Francisco CA 94133..................................415-362-1465
Re/Search Publications, 20 Romolo Ste B, San Francisco CA 94133........415-362-1465
Reader's Digest Assn, Pleasantville NY 10570 914-769-7000
Reader's Digest Condensed Books*, Pleasantville NY 10570 914-769-7000

Reader's Digest General Books, 750 3rd Ave, New York NY 10017 212-953-0030
Reader's Digest Press, 200 Park Ave, New York NY 10166 212-907-6625
The Real Comet Press, 3131 Western Ave #410, Seattle WA 98121.........206-283-7827
Real Estate Education Co*, 520 N Dearborn St, Chicago IL 60610 312-836-4400
Real Estate Publishing Co*, PO Box 41177, Sacramento CA 95841 916-677-3864
Real Estate Solutions Inc, 2609 Klingle Rd NW, Washington DC 20008..202-362-9854
Realtor Natl Marketing Inst, 430 N Michigan Ave, Chicago IL 60611......312-670-3780
Recap Publications, 201 W 92nd St, New York NY 10025...........................212-724-1711
Record Rama Sound Archives, 4981 McKnight, Pittsburgh PA 15237.......412-367-7330
Red Dust Inc, PO Box 630 Gracie Sta, New York NY 10028 212-348-4388
Red Hen Press, PO Box 3774, Santa Barbara CA 93130 805-682-1278
Red Herring Press, 1209 W Oregon, Urbana IL 61801 217-344-1176
Red Key Press, Box 551, Port St Joe FL 32456 904-277-1305
Redbird Press, PO Box 11441, Memphis TN 38111.....................................901-323-2233
Redbird Productions, Box 363, Hastings MN 55033....................................612-437-3179
Redgrave Publishing Co, 380 Adams St, Bedford Hills NY 10507 914-241-7100
Reed & Cannon Communications, 1446 6th St, Berkeley CA 94710.........415-527-1586
I Reed Books, 1446 6th St Ste D, Berkeley CA 94710 415-527-1586
Reference Publications, 218 St Clair River Dr, Algonac MI 48001.............313-794-5722
Reference Service Press*, 3540 Wilshire Blvd, Los Angeles CA 90010......213-251-3743
Reference Service Press, 10 Twin Dolphin Dr, Redwood City CA 94065..415-594-0743
Regal Books*, PO Box 3875, Ventura CA 93006...805-644-9721
Regents Publishing Co Inc*, 2 Park Ave, New York NY 10016.................212-889-2788
Regnery Gateway Inc*, 950 N Shore Dr, Lake Bluff IL 60044....................312-295-8088
Reiff Press, 120 S 8th St Apt 3, Indiana PA 15701..412-349-3347
Reiman Publications Inc*, PO Box 643, Milwaukee WI 53201...................414-423-0100
Religious Education Press, 1531 Wellington, Birmingham AL 35209........205-879-4040
Renaissance House Publ*, 541 Oak St Box 177, Frederick CO 80530 303-833-2030
Nancy Renfro Studios, 1117 W 9th St, Austin TX 78703.............................512-472-2140
The Report Store, 910 Massachusetts St Ste 503, Lawrence KS 66044.......913-842-7348
Reprint Co Publishers*, 601 Hillcrest Ofcs, Spartanburg SC 29304..........803-582-0732
Research Press*, 2612 N Mattis Ave, Champaign IL 61821 217-352-3273
Research Publications*, 12 Lunar Dr, Woodbridge CT 06525....................203-397-2600
Resource Publications*, 160 E Virginia St #290, San Jose CA 95112 408-286-8505
Resources for the Future*, 1616 P St NW, Washington DC 20036............202-328-5006
Restoration Research, Box 547, Bountiful UT 84010 801-298-4058
Fleming H Revell Co*, 184 Central Ave, Old Tappan NJ 07675 201-768-8060
Review & Herald Publ*, 55 W Oak Ridge Dr, Hagerstown MD 21740 301-791-7000
RGM Publications, H-28 Miriam St, Key West FL 33040..............................305-294-5710
The Rhinos Press Inc*, PO Box 3520, Laguna Hills CA 92654....................714-997-3217
Rhode Island Publications Soc, 189 Wicken St, Providence RI 02903.......401-272-1776
Rice University Press, PO Box 1892, Houston TX 77251...............................713-527-6035
Richboro Press, Box 1, Richboro PA 18954 215-355-6084
Ridge Times Press, Box 90, Mendocino CA 95460...707-937-1188
Ridgeline Press, 1136 Orchard Rd, Lafayette CA 94549 415-283-5836
Lynne Rienner Publishers Inc*, 948 North St Ste 8, Boulder CO 80302 ...303-444-6684
Rio Grande Press Inc*, Box 33 La Casa Escuela, Glorieta NM 87535 505-757-6275
Rising Publishing, PO Box 72478, Los Angeles CA 90002 213-589-4578
River Basin Publishing Co, PO Box 75573, St Paul MN 55175.................612-291-0980
River Road Publishing, 830 E Savidge, Spring Lake MI 49456 616-842-6920
Riverdale Co Publ*, 5506 Kenilworth Ave, Riverdale MD 20737.............301-864-2029
Riverrun Press*, 500 Piermont Ave, Piermont NY 10968 914-359-2629
Riverside Publishing Co*, 8420 W Bryn Mawr Ave, Chicago IL 60631.....312-693-0040

Rizzoli Intl Publications*, 597 5th Ave, New York NY 10017 212-223-0100
Roberts Rinehart Inc Publishers, PO Box 3161, Boulder CO 80303 303-449-3221
Roblin Press, PO Box 152, Yonkers NY 10710..914-337-4576
Robus Books, PO Box 13819, Wauwatosa WI 53213 414-774-3630
Rock Tech Publ, 171 W Putnam Ferry Rd, Woodstock GA 30188 404-926-1311
Rockdale Ridge Press, 8501 Ridge Rd, Cincinnati OH 45236.....................513-891-9900
Rocky Mountain Research Center, PO Box 4694, Missoula MT 59806.....406-549-6330
Rocky Point Press, PO Box 4814, N Hollywood CA 91607............................818-761-3386
Rod and Staff Publishers Inc*, Hwy 172, Crockett KY 41413.....................606-522-4348
Rodale Press Inc*, 33 E Minor St, Emmaus PA 18049 215-967-5171
Ronin Publishing Inc, PO Box 1035, Berkeley CA 94701............................415-540-6278
Roscher House, PO Box 201390, Austin TX 78720.......................................512-258-2288
Rose Publishing Co Inc, 301 Louisiana, Little Rock AR 72201...................501-372-1666
The Rosen Publishing Group Inc*, 29 E 21st St, New York NY 10010 212-777-3017
Ross Books*, PO Box 4340, Berkeley CA 94704 415-841-2474
Rossel Books*, Box 87, Chappaqua NY 10514...914-238-8954
Roth Publishing Inc*, 185 Great Neck Rd, Great Neck NY 11021 516-466-3676
Fred B Rothman & Co*, 10368 W Centennial Rd, Littleton CO 80127.....303-979-5657
Rotzinger Enterprises Inc, 2000 11th St, Rock Island IL 61201................309-786-5370
Roundtable Publishing*, 933 Pico Blvd, Santa Monica CA 90405.................213-450-9777
Routledge & Kegan Paul Inc*, 29 W 35th St, New York NY 10001 212-244-3336
Rovern Press, 185 Birch St, Willimantic CT 06226.....................................203-423-6388
Rowan Tree Press, 124 Chestnut St, Boston MA 02108..............................617-523-7627
Alan Rowe Publications, 3906 N 69th St, Milwaukee WI 53216 414-438-0685
Rowman & Littlefield Publishers*, 81 Adams Dr, Totowa NJ 07512 201-256-8600
Roxbury Publishing Co*, PO Box 491044, Los Angeles CA 90049..............213-458-3493
Royal House Publishing*, 9465 Wilshire Blvd, Beverly Hills CA 90212 213-550-7170
Royall Press, PO Box 9022, San Rafael CA 94912 415-885-1484
Rubes Publishers, 14447 Titus St, Panorama City CA 91402 818-782-0800
Ruddy Duck Press, 4429 Gibraltar Dr, Fremont CA 94536.........................415-797-9096
Runaway Publications, PO Box 1172, Ashland OR 97520 503-482-2578
Running Press Book Publ*, 125 S 22nd St, Philadelphia PA 19103...........215-567-5080
Russell Sage Foundation*, 112 E 64th St, New York NY 10021..................212-750-6000
Russica Publishers*, 799 Broadway, New York NY 10003............................212-473-7480
Rutgers Univ Press*, 109 Church St, New Brunswick NJ 08901................201-932-7762
Rutledge Hill Press*, 513 3rd Ave S, Nashville TN 37210..........................615-244-2700
Ryan Research International, 1593 Filbert Ave, Chico CA 95926...............916-343-2373
Rynd Communications*, 99 Painters Mill Rd, Owings Mills MD 21117...301-363-6400
Sachem Press, Box 9, Old Chatham NY 12136..518-794-8327
William H Sadlier Inc*, 11 Park Pl, New York NY 10007.............................212-227-2120
Sagapress Inc, Rt 100, Millwood NY 10546...914-762-2200
Sage Publications Inc*, 2111 W Hillcrest Dr, Newbury Park CA 91320....805-499-0721
St Andrews Press, St Andrews College, Laurinburg NC 28352....................919-276-3652
St Anthony Messenger Press*, 1615 Republic St, Cincinnati OH 45210 ...513-241-5615
St Bedes Publications*, Box 545, Petersham MA 01366 617-724-3407
St James Press*, 425 N Michigan Ave, Chicago IL 60611 312-329-0806
St John's Publishing Co, 6824 Oaklawn Ave, Edina MN 55435..................612-920-9044
St Josephs University Press*, 5600 City Ave, Philadelphia PA 19131........215-879-7325
St Luke's Press*, 1407 Union Ave, Memphis TN 38104...............................901-357-5441
St Martin's Press*, 175 5th Ave, New York NY 10010 212-674-5151
St Mary's Press*, Terrace Heights, Winona MN 55987 507-452-9090
St Vladimirs Seminary Press*, 575 Scarsdale Rd, Crestwood NY 10707..914-961-8313
Salem House*, 462 Boston St, Topsfield MA 01983......................................617-887-2440

Salem Press Inc*, PO Box 1097, Englewood Cliffs NJ 07632......................201-871-3700
The Salesman's Guide Inc*, 1140 Broadway, New York NY 10001 212-684-2985
Salt-Works Press, RFD 1 Box 141, Granada MS 38901.............................601-237-6863
Salyer Publishing Co, 3111 NW 19th St, Oklahoma City OK 73107............405-943-3841
Samisdat*, Box 129, Richford VT 05476 514-263-4439
Sammis Publishing Corp*, 122 E 25th St, New York NY 10010 212-598-6976
Howard W Sams & Co*, 4300 W 62nd St, Indianapolis IN 46268................317-298-5400
San Francisco Press Inc*, PO Box 6800, San Francisco CA 94101............415-524-1000
San Luis Quest Press, PO Box 998, San Luis Obispo CA 93406 805-543-8500
Sand Pond Publishers, Box 405, Hancock NH 03449.............................603-525-6615
Sandlapper Publishing Inc, PO Box 1932, Orangeburg SC 29116.............803-531-1658
Sandpiper Press, PO Box 286, Brookings OR 97415.............................503-469-5588
Sandpiper Publishing, PO Box 5143, Stateline NV 89449 916-544-3506
Santa Barbara Press, 815 Dela Vina St, Santa Barbara CA 93101...........805-966-2060
Santillana Publishing Co Inc*, 257 Union St, Northvale NJ 07647...........201-767-6961
Sasquatch Publishing Co, 1931 2nd Ave, Seattle WA 98101 206-441-5555
Sassafras Junior League, 2574 E Bennett, Springfield MO 65804 417-887-3563
Satchell's Publishing, 3124 5th Ave, Richmond VA 23222 804-329-2130
Saturday Evening Post*, 1100 Waterway Blvd, Indianapolis IN 46202......317-634-1100
Saturday Press Inc, PO Box 884, Upper Montclair NJ 07043..................201-256-1731
W B Saunders Co*, 210 W Washington Sq, Philadelphia PA 19105...........215-574-4700
Saunders College Publ*, 210 W Washington Sq, Philadelphia PA 19105 ..215-574-4700
K G Saur Inc*, 175 5th Ave, New York NY 10010.................................212-982-1302
Saybrook Publishing, 4223 Cole Ave, Dallas TX 75205 214-521-2375
Scarecrow Press Inc*, 52 Liberty St, Metuchen NJ 08840......................201-548-8600
Schenkman Books*, PO Box 1570 Harvard Sq, Cambridge MA 02238.....617-492-4952
Schiffer Publishing Ltd*, 1469 Morstein Rd, West Chester PA 19380......215-696-1001
Schirmer Books*, 866 3rd Ave, New York NY 10022.............................212-702-5629
Schmul Pub Co Inc*, 3583 New Garden Rd, Salem OH 44460..................216-222-2249
D Schneider, World Peace Univ 35 SE 60th, Portland OR 97215................503-231-3771
Schocken Books Inc*, 62 Cooper Sq, New York NY 10003......................212-475-4900
Scholarly Resources Inc*, 104 Greenhill Ave, Wilmington DE 19805.......302-654-7713
Scholars Facsimiles & Reprints*, Box 344, Delmar NY 12054 518-439-5978
Scholars Press*, PO Box 1608, Decatur GA 30031 404-329-6950
Scholarships Fellowships & Loans, Box 34937, Bethesda MD 20817........301-897-0033
Scholastic Inc*, 730 Broadway, New York NY 10003.............................212-505-3000
Scholium Intl Inc*, 265 Great Neck Rd, Great Neck NY 11021................516-466-5181
School Zone Publishing*, 1819 Industrial Dr, Grand Haven MI 49417.....616-846-5030
Abner Schram Ltd*, 36 Park St, Montclair NJ 07042.............................201-744-7755
Science & Behavior Books, PO Box 60519, Palo Alto CA 94306 415-326-6465
Science Assoc Intl Inc*, 1841 Broadway, New York NY 10023..................212-265-4995
Science Research Assoc Inc*, 155 N Wacker Dr, Chicago IL 60606 312-984-7000
Scientific American Books*, 41 Madison Ave, New York NY 10010..........212-532-7660
The Scientific Press*, 540 University Ave, Palo Alto CA 94301.................415-322-5221
Scott & Foresman & Co*, 1900 E Lake Ave, Glenview IL 60025 312-729-3000
Scott Publishing Co*, Box 828, Sidney OH 45365.................................513-498-0802
Chas Scribner's Sons*, 866 3rd Ave, New York NY 10022.......................212-702-7885
Scripta Humanistica, 1383 Kersey Ln, Potomac MD 20854....................301-340-1095
Scripture Press Publications*, 1825 College Ave, Wheaton IL 60187.......312-668-6000
Sea Challengers, 4 Somerset Rise, Monterey CA 93940 408-373-6306
Seablom Design Books, PO Box 2546, Seattle WA 98111.......................206-285-2308
Seaforth Publications, 1211 Coit Rd, Bratenahl OH 44108......................216-681-4561
Seal Press*, 312 S Washington, Seattle WA 98104.................................206-624-5262

Search, 106 Sterling Ave, Mt Sterling KY 40353 606-498-0661
Seattle Art Museum, Volunteer Park, Seattle WA 98112 206-443-4710
Essai Seax Publications*, PO Box 55, E St Louis IL 62202....................618-271-5323
Second Chance Press, RD 2 Noyac Rd, Sag Harbor NY 11963.................516-725-1101
Security Letter Inc, 166 E 96th St, New York NY 10128........................212-348-1553
Self-Counsel Press Inc*, 1303 N Northgate Way, Seattle WA 98133 206-522-8383
Semiotext(E), Columbia Univ Philosophy Hall, New York NY 10027.......212-280-3956
Sepher Hermon Press Inc*, 53 Park Pl, New York NY 10007 212-349-1860
Serendipity Press, 3801 Kennett Park Bldg C, Wilmington DE 19807.......302-655-4002
Serpent & Eagle Press, 1 Dietz St, Oneonta NY 13820...........................607-432-5604
Servant Publications*, PO Box 8617, Ann Arbor MI 48107......................313-761-8505
Seth Press Inc, PO Box 1370, Bryn Mawr PA 19010 215-642-8633
Seven Hills Books, 49 Central Ave, Cincinnati OH 45202 513-381-3881
Seven Locks Press Inc, PO Box 27, Cabin John MD 20818.....................301-320-2130
Seven Oaks Press, 405 S 7th St, St Charles IL 60174.............................312-584-0187
Seven Seas Press Inc, 2 Dean Ave, Newport RI 02840...........................401-847-1683
Sew Fit Co, PO Box 565, La Grange IL 60525 312-579-3222
Kirit N Shah, 980 Moraga Ave, Piedmont CA 94611 415-653-2076
Shambhala Publications Inc*, PO Box 308, Boston MA 02117.................617-424-0030
Shameless Hussy Press, PO Box 3092, Berkeley CA 94703......................415-547-1062
Shamrock Press & Publishing Co, PO Box 7256, Alexandria VA 22307...703-725-9322
Shapolsky Books*, 56 E 11th St, New York NY 10003............................212-505-2505
Sharon Publications Inc*, 105 Union Ave, Cresskill NJ 07626.................201-568-8800
M E Sharpe Inc*, 80 Business Park Dr, Armonk NY 10504....................914-273-1800
Shasta Abbey Press, PO Box 199, Mt Shasta CA 96067.........................916-926-4208
Harold Shaw Publishers*, 388 Gundersen Dr, Wheaton IL 60189............312-665-6700
Li Kung Shaw, 2530 33rd Ave, San Francisco CA 94116........................415-731-0829
Shearer Publishing, 406 Post Oak Rd, Fredericksburg TX 78624............512-997-6529
Sheed and Ward, 115 E Armour Blvd, Kansas City MO 64141..................816-531-0538
Sheep Meadow Press, PO Box 1345, Riverdale-Hudson NY 10471...........212-549-3321
Shelton Publications, PO Box 391, Sausalito CA 94966..........................415-332-1165
Shengold Publishers Inc*, 23 W 45th St, New York NY 10036 212-944-2555
Shepherd Publishers, 118 Pinepoint Rd, Williamsburg VA 23185 804-229-0661
Sheridan House Inc*, 145 Palisade St, Dobbs Ferry NY 10522 914-693-2410
Sherwood Sugden & Co Publishers, 315 5th St, Peru IL 61354...............815-223-1231
Shining Star Publications*, PO Box 1329, Jacksonville OR 97530 503-899-7121
Ship To Shore, 10500 Mount Holly Rd, Charlotte NC 28214 704-392-4740
The Shoe String Press*, 925 Sherman Ave, Hamden CT 06514 203-248-6307
Shoe Tree Press, 405 Front St PO Box 356, Belvidere NJ 07823..............201-475-4751
Sierra Club Books*, 730 Polk St, San Francisco CA 94109 415-776-2211
Signpost Books, 8912 192nd St SW, Edmonds WA 98020 206-776-0370
Signs of the Times Publ, 407 Gilbert Ave, Cincinnati OH 45202................513-421-2050
Sigo Press, 77 N Washington St, Boston MA 02114................................617-523-2321
Silhouette Books*, 300 E 42nd St, New York NY 10017..........................212-682-6080
Silver Burdett Co*, 250 James St, Morristown NJ 07960 201-285-8100
Silverback Books Inc, 323 Franklin Bldg S Ste 804, Chicago IL 60606 219-736-2112
Simmons Boardman Books, 1809 Capitol Ave, Omaha NE 68102.............402-346-4300
Simon & Schuster*, 1230 Ave of the Americas, New York NY 10020.......212-698-7000
Simply Elegant Cookbook, PO Box 74, Winnetka IL 60093 312-564-2221
Sinauer Assoc Inc*, N Main St, Sunderland MA 01375 413-665-3722
Sincere Press Inc, PO Box 10422, Phoenix AZ 85064.............................602-956-3640
Singer Press, 1540 Rollins Drive, Los Angeles CA 90063........................213-263-2640
Singlejack Books, PO Box 1906, San Pedro CA 90733 213-548-5964

Singular Speech Press, 10 Hilltop Dr, Canton CT 06019.............................203-693-6059
Skyline West Press, 4311 Woodland Park Ave N, Seattle WA 98103.........206-633-2485
Slack Inc*, 6900 Grove Rd, Thorofare NJ 08086.......................................609-848-1000
Slavica Publishers Inc*, PO Box 14388, Columbus OH 43214 614-268-4002
Slawson Communications Inc*, 3719 6th Ave, San Diego CA 92103.........619-291-9126
C S Slaybaugh & Assoc, 285 Manning Rd, Mogadore OH 44260.................216-699-4578
Sleepy Hollow Press, 150 White Plains Rd, Tarrytown NY 10591 914-631-8200
Small Helm Press, 622 Baker St, Petaluma CA 94952................................707-763-5757
SMEAC Info Reference Ctr, 1200 Chambers Rd, Columbus OH 43212....614-292-6717
The Allen Smith Co*, 1435 N Meridian St, Indianapolis IN 46202 317-634-4098
Gibbs M Smith Inc*, Box 667, Layton UT 84041......................................801-544-9800
Peter Smith Publisher Inc*, 6 Lexington Ave, Magnolia MA 01930 617-525-3562
W H Smith Publishers Inc*, 80 Distribution Blvd, Edison NJ 08817.........212-532-6600
Patterson Smith Publishing, 23 Prospect Ter, Montclair NJ 07042 201-744-3291
Smith Smith & Smith, 17515 SW Blue Heron, Lake Oswego OR 97034 ..503-636-2979
Grey Pubs Smith, 26355 Palomita Cir, Mission CA 92691..........................714-951-9009
Smithsonian Inst Press*, 955 L'Enfant Plz, Washington DC 20560...........202-287-3738
Smoky Valley Publications, PO Box 255, Lindsborg KS 67456...................913-227-2302
SMS Publishing Corp, PO Box 2276, Glenview IL 60025...........................312-724-1427
Snow Lion Publications Inc*, PO Box 6483, Ithaca NY 14851...................607-273-8506
Helen F Snow, 148 Mungertown Rd, Madison CT 06443 203-245-9714
Snyder Inst Research, 508 N Pac Coast Hwy, Redondo Bch CA 90277 213-372-4469
Soccer Assoc*, PO Box 634, New Rochelle NY 10802................................914-235-2347
Soc for Technical Comm, PO Box 28130, San Diego CA 92128...................619-746-4005
Society of Actuaries, 500 Park Blvd, Itasca IL 60143.................................312-773-3010
Soc Automotive Eng*, 400 Commonwealth, Warrendale PA 15096 412-776-4841
Society/Transaction*, Rutgers Univ, New Brunswick NJ 08903.................201-932-2280
Solano Press, PO Box 7629, Berkeley CA 94707.......................................415-526-8928
Solaris Press Inc, PO Box 1009, Rochester MI 48063................................313-656-0667
Soldier Creek Press*, 642 S Hunt St, Lake Crystal MN 56055...................507-726-2985
Solidarity Publications, PO Box 40874, San Francisco CA 94140 415-626-6626
Soma Press, PO Box 416, Yelow Springs OH 45387..................................513-767-1573
Somesuch Press, PO Box 188, Dallas TX 75201.......................................214-922-8080
Sophia Press, PO Box 533, Durham NH 03824...603-868-2318
Sore Dove Publishers, PO Box 6332, San Mateo CA 94403 415-344-9798
SOS Publications*, 4223 W Jefferson Blvd, Los Angeles CA 90016..........213-730-1815
Soul Publications, 6041 Cleveland Ave, Columbus OH 43229 614-891-9322
Sound Enterprises Publishing*, Box 722D, Frazer PA 19355.....................215-431-4512
Sound View Press, 36 Webster Pt, Madison CT 06443 203-245-2246
Source Productions, 2635 Griffith Park Blvd, Los Angeles CA 90039 213-660-5976
The Source View Press, Box 390, Martinez CA 94553 415-228-6228
Sourdough Enterprises, 16401 3rd Ave SW, Seattle WA 98166..................206-244-8115
S Dakota Archaeological Soc, 2032 S Grange, Sioux Falls SD 57105 605-336-5493
South End Press, 116th St Botolph, Boston MA 02115...............................617-266-0629
South Group Publishers*, 30 Main St, Port Washington NY 11050 516-883-2221
South Western Publishing*, 5101 Madison Rd, Cincinnati OH 45227 513-271-8811
Southeast Asia Program Cornell Univ, 120 Uris Hall, Ithaca NY 14853 ..607-255-2378
Southern Illinois Univ Press*, PO Box 3697, Carbondale IL 62902 618-453-2281
Southern Methodist Univ Press*, Box 415 SMU, Dallas TX 75275...........214-739-5959
Southern Press, Carthage College, Kenosha WI 53141...............................414-551-8500
Southwest Research & Info Ctr, PO Box 4524, Albuquerque NM 87106..505-262-1862
Southwest Scientific Publ, Drawer 3AM, University Park NM 88003........505-525-1370
Sovereignty Inc., #3 Wausau Sta PO Box 909, Eastsound WA 98245........206-376-2177

The Soyfoods Center, Box 234, Lafayette CA 94549 415-283-2991
SP Med & Sci Books*, 175-20 Wexford Ter, Jamaica NY 11432 718-658-0888
Space & Time, 138 W 70th St 4B, New York NY 10023 212-595-0894
Spanish Lit Publications Co Inc, Box 707, York SC 29745 803-366-9763
Sparrow Press, 103 Waldron St, W Lafayette IN 47906 317-743-1991
Special Learning Corp*, Box 306, Guilford CT 06437 203-453-6525
Special Libraries Assn*, 1700 18th St NW, Washington DC 20009 202-234-4700
Specialized Studies Inc, PO Box 854, Frederick MD 21701 301-694-5530
The Speech Bin, 231 Clarksville Rd, Princeton Jct NJ 08550 609-799-3935
Speer Books, PO Box 1277, Cave Junction OR 97523 503-592-4382
Robt Speller & Sons Publ*, 30 E 23rd St, New York NY 10010 212-477-5524
The Spencer Group, 377 Elliot St, Newton Upper Falls MA 02164 617-965-8388
Daniel Spencer Publisher, PO Box 4130, Malibu CA 90265 213-457-1904
Sphinx Press Inc*, 59 Boston Post Rd, Madison CT 06443 203-245-4000
Spinsters/Aunt Lute Books, PO Box 410687, San Francisco CA 94141 415-558-9655
Spirit Mountain Press, PO Box 1214, Fairbanks AK 99707 907-452-7585
SPL Group, PO Box 31, Fountaintown IN 46130 317-835-7683
Spoken Language Services Inc*, PO Box 783, Ithaca NY 14851 607-257-0500
The Spoon River Press, PO Box 3635, Peoria IL 61614 309-673-2266
The Sporting New Publishing Co*, PO Box 56, St Louis MO 63166 314-997-7111
Spring Publications Inc*, PO Box 222069, Dallas TX 75222 214-943-4093
Springer Publishing Co Inc*, 536 Broadway, New York NY 10012 212-431-4370
Springer Verlag New York Inc*, 175 5th Ave, New York NY 10010 212-460-1500
Springhouse Corp*, 1111 Bethlehem Pike, Springhouse PA 19477 215-646-8700
Spuyten Dyvil, 817 West End Ave 4A, New York NY 10025 212-666-3648
Spyde Enterprises Inc, RFD 1682, Laurel Hollow NY 11791 516-349-3222
Square One Publishers, PO Box 4385, Madison WI 53711 608-255-8425
Sri Shirdi Sai Publications*, 251 Wilbur Ave, Pittsburgh PA 15145 412-823-1296
SRL Publishing Co, PO Box 2277 Sta A, Champaign IL 61820 217-356-1523
ST Publications, 407 Gilbert Ave, Cincinnati OH 45202 513-421-4050
Stackpole Books*, PO Box 1831, Harrisburg PA 17105 717-234-5041
Stage Guild Publications, 820 E Genesee St, Syracuse NY 13210 315-423-4008
Standard Educational Corp*, 200 W Monroe, Chicago IL 60606 312-346-7440
Standard Publishing*, 8121 Hamilton Ave, Cincinnati OH 45231 513-931-4050
Stanford Univ Press*, Stanford CA 94305 415-723-9434
Stanton & Lee Publishers Inc, 44 E Mifflin St, Madison WI 53703 608-255-3254
Star Books Inc*, 408 Pearson St, Wilson NC 27893 919-237-1591
Star Publications, 1211 W 60th Terrace, Kansas City MO 64113 816-523-8228
Star Publishing Co*, PO Box 68, Belmont CA 94002 415-591-3505
Star Rover House*, 1914 Foothill Blvd, Oakland CA 94606 415-532-8408
Star Street Press, Box 252, Pittsford NY 14534 716-244-4850
Starblaze*, 5659 Virginia Beach Blvd, Norfolk VA 23502 804-461-8090
Starlog Press*, 475 Park Ave S, New York NY 10016 212-689-2830
State Historical Society Wisconsin, 816 State St, Madison WI 53706 608-262-1368
State Univ of NY Press*, State Univ Plaza, Albany NY 12246 518-472-5000
Station Hill Press*, Station Hill Rd, Barrytown NY 12507 914-758-5840
Steam Press, 56 Commonwealth, Watertown MA 02172 617-923-1046
Steck Vaughn Co*, PO Box 2028, Austin TX 78768 512-476-6721
Steelstone Press, 4607 Claussen Ln, Valparaiso IN 46383 219-464-1792
Stein & Day Publ*, Scarborough House, Briarcliff Manor NY 10510 914-762-2151
Stemmer House Publ*, 2627 Caves Rd, Owings Mills MD 21117 301-363-3690
Stephanie Ann Books, 3960 Laurel Canyon, Studio City CA 91604 818-509-8110
Stephens Engineering Assoc, 7030 220th St SW, Mtlake Ter WA 98043 ...206-771-2182

Steppingstone Press, PO Box 2757, Boise ID 83701.....................................208-384-1577
Steppingstone Publishing, 2108 S University Dr, Fargo ND 58103.............701-237-4742
Sterling Publishing Co Inc*, 2 Park Ave, New York NY 10016....................212-532-7160
Stewart Tabori & Chang*, 740 Broadway, New York NY 10003.................212-460-5000
George F Stickley Co*, 210 W Washington Sq, Philadelphia PA 19106.....215-922-7126
Still Point Press, 4222 Willow Grove Rd, Dallas TX 75220.........................214-352-8282
H Stillman Publishers*, 21405 Woodchuck Ln, Boca Raton FL 33428.....305-482-6343
Stillpoint Publishing*, Meetinghouse Rd Box 640, Walpole NH 03608....603-756-3508
Stillwell Promotion, PO Box 2862, Savannah GA 31401..............................912-234-5994
Stipes Publishing Co*, 10-12 Chester St, Champaign IL 61820 217-356-8391
Stoeger Publishing Co*, 55 Ruta Ct, S Hackensack NJ 07606 201-440-2700
Stoneydale Press, 205 Main St, Stevensville MT 59870 406-777-2729
Storie Mcowen Publishers Inc, PO Box 308, Manteo NC 27954...................919-473-5881
Stormline Press Inc, PO Box 593, Urbana IL 61801......................................217-328-2665
Stravon Educational Press*, 845 3rd Ave, New York NY 10022.................212-371-2880
Strawberry Hill Press*, 2594 15th Ave, San Francisco CA 94127............415-664-8112
Strugglers' Community Press, PO Box 15155, Savannah GA 31406 912-354-7499
Lyle Stuart Inc*, 120 Enterprise Ave, Secaucus NJ 07094.........................201-866-0490
Studio Press, PO Box 1268, Twain Harte CA 95383.....................................209-533-4222
H S Stuttman Inc*, 333 Post Rd W, Westport CT 06889...............................203-226-7841
Suburban Wilderness Press, 430 S 21st Ave E, Duluth MN 55812.............218-724-6153
Success Publishing*, 10258 Riverside Dr, Palm Bch Gdns FL 33410 305-626-4643
Success With Youth Publ*, PO Box 261129, San Diego CA 92126............619-578-4700
Sufi Islamia/Prophecy Publ, 65 Norwich St, San Francisco CA 94110......415-285-0562
Sherwood Sugden & Co*, 1117 8th St, La Salle IL 61301............................815-223-1231
Summa Publications*, 1801 Mission Rd, Birmingham AL 35216................205-822-0463
Summak Publishing, PO Box 3622, Duluth MN 55803 218-724-8991
Summer Stream Press, PO Box 6056, Santa Barbara CA 93160 805-964-1727
Summit Books*, 1230 Ave of the Americas, New York NY 10020.............212-698-7000
Summit University Press, Box A, Malibu CA 90265 818-991-4751
Sun & Moon Press*, 6363 Wilshire Blvd #115, Los Angeles CA 90048....213-653-6711
Sun Designs, 173 E Wisconsin Ave, Oconomowoc WI 53066........................414-567-4255
Sun Publishing Co*, PO Box 5588, Santa Fe NM 87502................................505-988-2033
Sunbelt Publications, PO Box 191126, San Diego CA 92119 619-697-4811
Sunbelt Publishing, 8330 Meadow Rd Ste 130, Dallas TX 75231 214-363-3824
Sunflower Ink, 10 Murry Grade Palo Colorado Rd, Carmel CA 93923.....408-625-0588
Sunflower Univ Press, 1531 Yuma St, Manhattan KS 66502 913-532-6733
Sunrise Press, 9700 Fair Oaks Blvd Ste C, Fair Oaks CA 95628 916-961-5551
Sunscope Publishing Co, 9 Sunrise Rd, Danbury CT 06810.........................203-743-6943
Sunset Books*, 80 Willow Rd, Menlo Park CA 94025...................................415-321-3600
Sunshine Press, 4984 Arboleda Rd, Fair Oaks CA 95628............................916-961-5551
The Sunstone Press*, PO Box 2321, Santa Fe NM 87504 505-988-4418
Support Source, 420 Rutgers Ave, Swarthmore PA 19081...........................215-544-3605
Sure-Fire Business Success, 50 Follen St, Cambridge MA 02138 617-547-6372
Surrey Books Inc, 500 N Michigan Ave Ste 1940, Chicago IL 60611..........312-661-0050
Survival News Service, PO Box 42152, Los Angeles CA 90042....................213-255-9502
The Susedik Method Inc, PO Box 997, Cambridge OH 43725.......................614-432-5204
Susquehanna University Press*, 440 Forsgate Dr, Cranbury NJ 08512 609-655-4770
Sutherland Publishing, 169566 McGregor Blvd, Ft Myers FL 33908.........813-466-1626
Sutton Aviation Press*, 3631 22nd Ave S, Minneapolis MN 55407 612-729-1175
Swallow's Tale Press, PO Box 930040, Norcross GA 30093.........................404-224-8859
Swansea Press Cresheim Publ, PO Box 27785, Philadelphia PA 19118......215-836-1400
Swedenborg Foundation*, 139 E 23rd St, New York NY 10010 212-673-7310

Sweet Chi Press, 662 Union St, Brooklyn NY 11215.....................................718-857-0449
Sweet Publishing Co*, 3934 Sandshell Dr, Ft Worth TX 76137 817-232-5661
The Switz Press, RR 3 Box 311, Vevay IN 46403...812-427-2529
Sybex Inc*, 2021 Challenger Dr, Alameda CA 94501 415-848-8233
Syentek Books Co Inc, PO Box 26588, San Francisco CA 94126 415-928-0471
Synergy Group Inc, 4766 Park Granada Ste 106, Calabasas CA 91302......818-887-9100
Syntheseis Publications*, 2703 Folsom St, San Francisco CA 94110 415-550-1284
Syntony Publishing, 1450 Byron St, Palo Alto CA 94301 415-324-4450
Syracuse Cultural Workers, PO Box 6367, Syracuse NY 13217 315-474-1132
Syracuse Univ Press*, 1600 Jamesville Ave, Syracuse NY 13244................315-423-2596
Sysygy, Box 428, Rush NY 14543 716-226-2127
SZ/Press, PO Box 20075 Cathedral Finance Sta, New York NY 10025 212-749-5906
TAB Books Inc*, Blue Ridge Summit PA 17214...717-794-2191
The Taft Group*, 5130 MacArthur Blvd NW, Washington DC 20016 202-966-7086
Tahrike Tarsile Quran Inc, PO Box 1115, Elmhurst NY 11373...................718-779-6505
Tam Assoc Ltd, 911 Chicago, Oak Park IL 60302 312-848-6760
Tamarack Editions, 131 Fellows Ave, Syracuse NY 13210 315-478-6495
Tanam Press, 40 White St, New York NY 10013 212-431-9183
Lance Tapley Publisher*, 86 Winthrop St, Augusta ME 04330....................207-622-1179
Taplinger Publishing Co*, 132 W 22nd St, New York NY 10011 212-741-0801
Taproot Publishers, PO Box 15153, Dallas TX 75201 214-296-5187
Jeremy P Tarcher Inc*, 9110 Sunset Blvd, Los Angeles CA 90069.............213-273-3274
Target Communications, 7626 W Donges Bay Rd, Mequon WI 53092.....414-242-3990
Targeted Communications, PO Box 1148, Cleveland OH 44120 216-921-8074
Taylor & Ng*, PO Box 8888, Fairfield CA 94533 707-422-8888
Taylor & Francis*, 3 E 44th St, New York NY 10017 212-867-1490
Taylor Publishing Co*, 1550 W Mockingbird Ln, Dallas TX 75235...........214-637-2800
TBW Books Inc, 36 Old Mill Rd, Falmouth ME 04105 207-781-3002
Teachers College Press*, 1234 Amsterdam Ave, New York NY 10027 212-678-3929
Lawton Teague Publications*, PO Box 12353, Oakland CA 94604 415-369-0153
Technical Publishing Co*, 875 3rd Ave, New York NY 10022.....................212-605-9400
The Technology Press Inc, Box 380, Fairfax Station VA 22039.....................703-978-5299
Technomic Publishing Co*, 851 New Holland Ave, Lancaster PA 17604..717-291-5609
Techwest Publications, 560 S Hartz Ave #447, Danville CA 94526 415-838-2670
Telephone Books, 109 Dunk Rock Rd, Guilford CT 06437...........................203-453-1921
Temple University Press*, Broad & Oxford Sts, Philadelphia PA 19122...215-787-8787
Templegate Publishers*, 302 E Adams St, Springfield IL 62705.................217-522-3353
Ten Mile River Press, 2155 Eastman Lane, Petaluma CA 94952.................707-964-5579
Ten Penny Players Inc, 799 Greenwich St, New York NY 10014.................212-929-3169
Ten Speed Press*, PO Box 7123, Berkeley CA 94707....................................415-845-8414
Test Corp of America*, 330 W 47th St Ste 205, Kansas City MO 64112....816-756-1490
Texas A&M Univ Press*, Drawer C, College Station TX 77843.................409-845-1436
Texas Christian Univ Press*, PO Box 30783 TCU, Ft Worth TX 76129...817-921-7822
Texas Monthly Press Inc*, PO Box 1569, Austin TX 78767 512-476-7085
Texas Tech Press*, PO Box 4240, Lubbock TX 79409..................................806-742-2768
Texas Western Press*, Univ of Texas at El Paso, El Paso TX 79968.........915-747-5688
TFH Publications*, 3rd & Union Ave, Neptune City NJ 07753 201-988-8400
Thames & Hudson Inc*, 500 5th Ave, New York NY 10110 212-354-3763
Theatre Arts Books, 29 W 35th St, New York NY 10001 212-244-3336
Theatre Bay Area, 2940 16th St #102, San Francisco CA 94116 415-621-0427
Theatre Communications Group*, 355 Lexington, New York NY 10017..212-697-5230
Paul Theobald & Co, 5 N Wabash Ave Ste 1406, Chicago IL 60602...........312-236-3994
Theosophical Book Assn for the Blind, Krotona 54, Ojai CA 93023..........805-646-2121

Theosophical Publ House*, 306 W Geneva Rd, Wheaton IL 60189 312-665-0123
Thieme Stratton Inc*, 381 Park Ave S, New York NY 10016 212-683-5088
The Think Shop, PO Box 3754, Albuquerque NM 87190.............................505-831-5029
Third Line Press, 4751 Viviana Dr, Tarzana CA 91356 818-996-0076
Thirteen Colonies Press, 710 S Henry St, Williamsburg VA 23185.............804-229-1775
Thirty-Three Publishing, 26941 Pebblestone Rd, Southfield MI 48034 313-355-3686
The Thomas Co, PO Box 71B, Solvang CA 93463.....................................805-688-7026
Thomas Publications*, PO Box 33244, Austin TX 78764...........................512-832-0355
Charles C Thomas Publisher*, 2600 S 1st St, Springfield IL 62717...........217-789-8980
Thompson & Co Inc*, 1313 5th St SE Ste 301, Minneapolis MN 55414 612-331-3963
Thor Publishing Co, PO Box 1782, Ventura CA 93002.............................805-648-4560
Thorndike Press*, One Mile Rd, Thorndike ME 04986.............................207-948-2962
Thorsons Publishers Inc*, 377 Park Ave S 6th fl, New York NY 10016....212-889-8350
Three Continents Press*, 1636 Connecticut Ave NW, Wash DC 20009 202-457-0288
Three Dimensional Thinking, 1420 Iroquois, Long Beach CA 90815........213-423-1441
Threshold Books, Box 1350 Dusty Ridge Rd RD 3, Putney VT 05346 802-254-8300
Thunder's Mouth Press*, 95 Greene St Ste 2A, New York NY 10012.......212-226-0277
Thurau Press, PO Box 8482, Asheville NC 28814 704-254-5000
Ticker Co, 3801 Mission Ave, Carmichael CA 95608.................................916-489-7757
Ticknor & Fields*, 52 Vanderbilt Ave, New York NY 10017.....................212-687-8996
Tide Press, PO Box 4224, Linden NJ 07036 201-862-0762
Tidewater Publishers*, Box 456, Centreville MD 21617 301-758-1075
Tilted Planet Press, PO Box 8646, Austin TX 78713 512-447-7619
Timber Press*, 9999 SW Wilshire, Portland OR 97225.............................503-292-0745
Time Life Books Inc*, Alexandria VA 22314 703-838-7000
Time Warp Publishing, 7956 White Oak Ave, Northridge CA 91325 818-344-2286
Timeless Books, Box 160, Porthill ID 83853..604-277-9224
Times Books*, 201 E 50th St, New York NY 10022..................................212-872-8110
Tiptoe Publishing, PO Box 206, Nasselle WA 98638 206-484-7722
Tire Management Consultants Press, PO Box 1069, Eugene OR 97440...503-683-0163
TL Enterprises Book Div, 29901 Agoura Rd, Agoura CA 91301 818-991-4980
TLC Publishing Co, PO Box 21508, Oklahoma City OK 73156 405-840-5511
Top Of The Mountain Publ*, 2980 E Bay Dr, Largo FL 34641...................813-535-6854
Toadwood Publishers, RR 6 Box 63, Edwardsville IL 62025 618-656-0531
Tombouctou, Box 265, Bolinas CA 94924..415-868-2738
Tompson & Rutter Inc, Box 297 Dunbar Hill Rd, Grantham NH 03753...603-863-4392
Tonsure Press, 1452 Stroup Rd, Atwater OH 44201.................................216-947-3625
Topping Intl Institute, 4291 Rural Ave, Bellingham WA 98226 206-647-2703
Tor Books*, 49 W 24th St, New York NY 10010 212-564-0150
Total Concepts, PO Box 90607, Honolulu HI 96835.................................808-595-4410
Tower Press, 410 Penn St, Hollidaysburg PA 16648.................................814-696-1311
Track & Field News, PO Box 296, Los Altos CA 94023 415-948-8188
Trad Publishing Co Inc, 1110 NW 8th Ave, Gainesville FL 32601.............904-373-5308
Trado Medic Books*, 102 Norman Ave, Buffalo NY 14213 716-885-3686
Transaction Books*, Rutgers Univ, New Brunswick NJ 08903 201-932-2280
Transatlantic Arts Inc*, PO Box 6086, Albuquerque NM 87197................505-898-2289
Transnational Publ*, PO Box 7282, Ardsley-on-Hudson NY 10503 914-693-0089
Travel Keys, PO Box 160691, Sacramento CA 95816...............................916-452-5200
Travel Text Assoc, 12605 State Fair, Detroit MI 48205 313-527-6971
Travel/Photography Press, PO Box 4486, Inglewood CA 90309 213-296-4565
Trempealeau Press, 800 Hillcrest Dr, Santa Fe NM 87501........................505-983-1947
Triad Publishing Co, 1110 NW 8th Ave Ste C, Gainesville FL 32601........904-373-5308
Tribeca Communications Inc*, 44 W 74th St, New York NY 10023..........212-496-1923

Triglav Press, 1181 Pinetree Grove Ave, Atlanta GA 30319 404-262-2629
Trillium Press*, PO Box 209, Monroe NY 10950 914-783-2999
Trinity University Press, 715 Stadium Dr, San Antonio TX 78284..........512-736-7619
Triple A Press, 12 Country Meadow, Rolling Hills Est CA 90274................213-541-3497
Troll Assoc*, 320 Rt 17, Mahwah NJ 07430 201-529-4000
Troubador Press, 410 N La Cienega Blvd, Los Angeles CA 90048 213-657-6100
True-To-Form Press, 1300 Conwed Tower, St Paul MN 55101...................612-228-7669
TSR Inc*, Box 756, Lake Geneva WI 53147...414-248-3625
Tuffy Books Inc*, 333 Dalziel Rd, Linden NJ 07036.............................914-835-5603
Tundra Books of Northern NY, PO Box 1030, Plattsburgh NY 12901.......514-932-5434
Turnbull & Willoughby Publ*, 1151 W Webster, Chicago IL 60614 312-348-3181
Charles E Tuttle Co Inc*, Box 410, Rutland VT 05701.............................802-773-8930
Twayne Publishers*, 70 Lincoln St, Boston MA 02111..............................617-423-3990
Twelvetrees Press, PO Box 188, Pasadena CA 91102.................................818-798-5207
Twenty-Third Publications*, 185 Willow St, Mystic CT 06355.................203-536-2611
Twin Peaks Press*, PO Box 8097, Portland OR 97207...............................206-694-2462
Tyndale House Publishers*, 336 Gundersen Dr, Wheaton IL 60188 312-668-8300
UCLA Business Forecasting, School of Mgmt, Los Angeles CA 90024.....213-825-1623
Ultralight Publications Inc*, PO Box 234, Hummelstown PA 17036..........717-566-0468
Ultramarine Publishing Co, Box 303, Hasting-on-Hudson NY 10706.......914-478-2522
UMI Research Press*, 300 N Zeeb Rd, Ann Arbor MI 48103....................313-761-4700
Unarius Light*, 145 Magnolia Ave, El Cajon CA 92020............................619-447-4170
Underwood/Miller*, 515 Chestnut St, Columbia PA 17512.......................717-684-7335
Frederick Unger Publishing*, 36 Cooper Sq, New York NY 10003............212-473-7885
Unicon Enterprises, 3602 W Glen Branch, Peoria IL 61614.......................309-688-3772
Unicorn Press Inc*, PO Box 3307, Greensboro NC 27402 919-272-0281
Unicorn Publ House*, 1148 Parsippany Blvd, Parsippany NJ 07054...........201-334-0353
UNIFO Publishers Ltd, PO Box 37, Pleasantville NY 10570......................914-941-1330
Union College Press, College Grounds, Schenectady NY 12308.................518-370-6097
Union Amer Hebrew Congregation*, 838 5th Ave, New York NY 10021..212-249-0100
Union Square Books, PO Box 1150, Novato CA 94948 415-883-8771
Unipub*, 205 E 42nd St, New York NY 10017...212-916-1650
Unique Graphics, 1025 55th St, Oakland CA 94608..................................415-655-3024
Unique Publications*, 4201 W Vanowen Place, Burbank CA 91505..........818-845-2656
United Nations*, Publishing Services, New York NY 10017.......................212-754-8303
United Shannon Publ Co, 6015 Rod Ave, Woodland Hills CA 91367.......818-703-8815
United Synagogue Book Service, 155 5th Ave, New York NY 10010..........212-533-7800
Univelt Inc*, PO Box 28130, San Diego CA 92128...................................619-746-4005
The Universal Black Writer, PO Box 5, New York NY 10101 718-774-4379
Universal Developments, 2855 Velasco Ln, Costa Mesa CA 92626............714-641-0188
Universal Press, Box 113, Somerville MA 02144......................................617-625-2561
Universe Books*, 381 Park Ave S, New York NY 10016............................212-685-7400
Universities Field Staff Intl*, 620 Union Dr, Indianapolis IN 46202 317-274-4122
University Assoc Inc*, 8517 Production Ave, San Diego CA 92121 619-578-5900
University Books Inc*, 120 Enterprise Ave, Secaucus NJ 07094.................201-866-0490
University Editions*, 4937 Humphrey Rd, Huntington WV 25704 304-429-7204
University Microfilms Intl*, 300 N Zeeb Rd, Ann Arbor MI 48103...........313-761-4700
University of Alabama Press*, PO Box 2877, University AL 35486 205-348-5180
University of Alaska Press, Signers' Hall, Fairbanks AK 99701.................907-474-6389
University of Arizona Press*, 1615 E Speedway Blvd, Tucson AZ 85719..602-621-1441
University of Arkansas Press*, 201 Ozark St, Fayetteville AR 72701.........501-575-3246
University of Calif Press*, 2120 Berkeley Way, Berkeley CA 94720..........415-642-4247
University of Chicago Press*, 5801 Ellis Ave, Chicago IL 60637................312-962-7700

University of Delaware Press*, 326 Hullihen Hall, Newark DE 19711 302-738-1149
University of Georgia Press*, Terrell Hall, Athens GA 30602....................404-542-2830
University of Hawaii Press*, 2840 Kolowalu St, Honolulu HI 96822 808-948-8694
University of Idaho Press*, Box 3368 University Sta, Moscow ID 83843 ..208-885-6245
University of Illinois Press*, 54 E Gregory Dr, Champaign IL 61820 217-333-0950
University of Iowa Press*, Westlawn, Iowa City IA 52242...........................319-353-3181
University of Massachusetts Press*, Box 429, Amherst MA 01004...........413-545-2217
University of Michigan Press*, 839 Greene St, Ann Arbor MI 48106 313-764-4394
University of Minn Press*, 2037 Univ Ave, Minneapolis MN 55414..........612-373-3266
University of Missouri Press*, 200 Lewis Hall, Columbia MO 65211 314-882-7641
University of Nebraska Press*, 901 N 17th St, Lincoln NE 68588.............402-472-3581
University of Nevada Press*, Reno NV 89557..702-784-6573
University of New Mexico Press*, Jour Bldg, Albuquerque NM 87131 505-277-2346
University of North Carolina Press*, Box 2288, Chapel Hill NC 27514....919-966-3561
University of Notre Dame Press*, Notre Dame IN 46556.............................219-239-6346
University of Oklahoma Press*, 1005 Asp Ave, Norman OK 73019 405-325-5111
University of Pennsylvania Press*, 418 Service Dr, Phila PA 19104..........215-898-6261
University of Pittsburgh Press*, 127 N Bellefield, Pittsburgh PA 15260 ...412-624-4110
University of Puerto Rico Press*, Box X UPR, Rio Piedras PR 00931 809-763-0812
University of South Carolina Press*, Columbia SC 29208 803-777-5243
University of Tennessee Press*, Comm Bldg, Knoxville TN 37996 615-974-3321
University of Texas Film Library, Box W, Austin TX 78713......................512-471-3572
University of Texas Press*, PO Box 7819, Austin TX 78713 512-471-7233
University of the Trees Press, Box 66, Boulder Creek CA 95006 408-338-2161
University of Utah Press*, 101 USB, Salt Lake City UT 84112...................801-581-6771
University of Washington Press*, PO Box C-50096, Seattle WA 98145....206-543-4050
University of Wisconsin Press*, 114 N Murray St, Madison WI 53715......608-262-4928
University Press of Amer Inc*, 4720 Boston Way, Lanham MD 20706 301-459-3366
University Press of Kansas*, 329 Carruth, Lawrence KS 66045 913-864-4154
University Press of Kentucky*, Lafferty Hall, Lexington KY 40506...........606-257-2951
University Press of Mississippi*, 3825 Ridgewood, Jackson MS 39211 601-982-6205
University Press of New England*, 3 Lebanon St, Hanover NH 03755 603-646-3349
University Press of Virginia*, PO Box 3608, Charlottesville VA 22903.....804-924-3468
University Press of Wash DC, Univ Press Bldg, Riverton VA 22651.........703-635-4029
University Presses of Florida*, 15 NW 15th St, Gainesville FL 32603.......904-392-9275
University Publications of Amer*, 44 Market St, Frederick MD 21701.....301-694-0100
University Science Books, 20 Edgehill Rd, Mill Valley CA 94941 415-383-1430
Unlimited Publishing Co*, Rt 17K Box 240, Bullville NY 10915...............914-361-1299
Unspeakable Visions of the Individual, Box 439, California PA 15419......412-938-8956
Upper Access Publishers, 1 Upper Access Rd, Hinesburg VT 05461........802-482-2988
Upstart Publishing Co, 12 Portland St, Dover NH 03820............................603-749-5071
Urban & Schwarzenberg Inc*, 7 E Redwood St, Baltimore MD 21202......301-539-2550
Urban Institute Press*, 2100 M St NW, Washington DC 20037.................202-857-8724
Urban Land Inst*, 1090 Vermont Ave NW, Washington DC 20005 202-289-8500
The Urbana Free Library, 201 S Race St, Urbana IL 61801.......................217-367-4057
US Catholic Conference*, 1312 Mass Ave NW, Washington DC 20005 202-659-6755
US Directory Services*, 655 NW 128th St Box 68-1700, Miami FL 33168.305-769-1700
US Games Systems Inc*, 38 E 32nd St, New York NY 10016......................212-685-4300
USA Publishing Co, 2929 Castro, San Pablo CA 94806..............................415-236-4960
Utah State University Press*, Logan UT 84322 801-750-1362
UW Publications, PO Box 3315 University Sta, Laramie WY 82061..........307-766-2379
Valentine Publishing & Drama Co, 23 Mill St, Rhinebeck NY 12572........914-876-3589
Valeur Publishing Ltd, Box 4482, Kailua-Kona HI 96745.............................808-329-8653

Valley of the Sun Publishing Co*, PO Box 38, Malibu CA 90265.............213-457-1547
Valuation Press, 13160 Mindanao Wy #274, Marina del Rey CA 90292...213-301-1879
Value Communications Inc, 9601 Aero Dr, San Diego CA 92123.............619-560-5163
Alfred Van Der Marck Editions*, 1133 Broadway, New York NY 10010..212-645-5150
Van Nostrand Reinhold Co Inc*, 115 5th Ave, New York NY 10003 212-254-3232
Vance Bibliographies*, 112 N Charter, Monticello IL 61856......................217-762-3831
Vanderbilt University Press, 1211 18th Ave S, Nashville TN 37212 615-322-3585
The Vanessa-Ann Collection*, PO Box 9113, Ogden UT 84409..................801-621-2777
Vanessapress, PO Box 81335, Fairbanks AK 99708.....................................907-479-0172
Vanguard Press Inc*, 424 Madison Ave, New York NY 10017..................212-753-3906
VCH Publishers Inc*, 303 NW 12th Ave, Deerfield Beach FL 33442 305-428-5566
Velo-News, PO Box 1257, Brattleboro VT 05301 802-254-2305
Vend-o-books*, PO Box 3736, Ventura CA 93006.......................................805-642-2355
Venture Perspectives Inc, 4300 Stevens Creek Blvd, San Jose CA 95129 ..408-247-1325
Venture Publishing Inc, 1640 Oxford Circle, State College PA 16803 814-234-4561
Vera-Reyes Inc, 433 Airport Blvd Ste 103, Burlingame CA 94010 415-344-0374
Verbatim Books, 4 Laurel Heights, Essex CT 06371.....................................203-434-2104
Verlag Chemie Intl Inc*, 303 NW 12th Ave, Deerfield Beach FL 33442 ...305-428-5566
Vertinary Medicine Publishing Co, 9073 Lenexa Dr, Lenexa KS 66215 913-492-4300
Vestal Press Ltd*, 320 N Jensen PO Box 97, Vestal NY 13850.................607-797-4872
VGM Career Horizons*, 4255 W Touhy Ave, Lincolnwood IL 60646........312-679-4210
The Viceroy Press Inc, 645 5th Ave, New York NY 10022............................212-826-3900
Vichitra Press, 10582 Cheviot Drive, Los Angeles CA 90064.....................213-837-8547
Victor Books*, 1825 College Ave, Wheaton IL 60187.................................312-668-6000
Viking Penguin Inc*, 40 W 23rd St, New York NY 10010...........................212-807-7300
Vimach Assoc, 3039 Indianola Ave, Columbus OH 43202 614-262-0471
Vincente Books Inc, PO Box 7388, Berkeley CA 94707................................415-528-5648
Vintage '45 Press, PO Box 266, Orinda CA 94563.......................................415-254-7266
Virginia State Library, 11th St at Capitol Sq, Richmond VA 23219...........804-786-2312
Vishwa Dharma Publications, 174 Santa Clara Ave, Oakland CA 94610..415-654-4683
Visual Education Corp*, 14 Washington Rd, Princeton NJ 08540 609-799-9200
Vitaerobics Inc, 4403 Manchester Ave #109, Encinitas CA 92024.............619-753-9171
Vitality Assoc, PO Box 2154, Saratoga CA 95070.......................................408-867-1241
Vocational & Career Assessment, PO Box 1566, Lakeside CA 92040........619-561-2092
Volcano Press Inc, PO Box 270, Volcano CA 95689.....................................209-296-3445
Voluntad Publishers Inc*, 4255 W Touhy Ave, Lincolnwood IL 60646.....312-679-5500
Volunteers In Asia, PO Box 4543, Stanford CA 94305 415-725-1805
Vongrutnorv Og Press, Randall Flat Rd PO Box 411, Troy ID 83871 208-835-4902
VORT Corp, PO Box 60132, Palo Alto CA 94306..415-965-4000
W W Publications, Box 277, Union Lake MI 48085 313-887-4703
Wadsworth Inc*, 10 Davis Dr, Belmont CA 94002 415-595-2350
Paul Wahl Corp, Bogota NJ 07603 201-342-9245
Wake Forest Univ Press*, PO Box 7333, Winston-Salem NC 27101..........919-761-5448
Wake-Brook House*, 2609 NE 29th Ct, Ft Lauderdale FL 33306.................305-563-9301
Waldron Enterprises, 371 Kings Hwy W, Haddonfield NJ 08033................609-428-3742
Walker & Co*, 720 5th Ave, New York NY 10019 212-265-3632
Wallace-Homestead Book*, 580 Waters Edge Rd, Lombard IL 60148 312-953-1100
Wampeter Press, Box 512, Green Harbor MA 02041....................................617-834-4137
Wanderer Books*, 1230 Ave of the Americas, New York NY 10020 212-245-6400
Warner Books Inc*, 666 5th Ave, New York NY 10103...............................212-484-2900
Warner Press Inc*, 1200 E 5th St, Anderson IN 46018..............................317-644-7721
Warren Gorham & Lamont Inc*, 1 Penn Plaza, New York NY 10019......212-971-5000
Warthog Press, 29 S Valley Rd, W Orange NJ 07052...................................201-731-9269

Washington Researchers Publ, 2612 P St NW, Washington DC 20007 202-333-3533
Washington State Univ Press*, Cooper Publ Bldg, Pullman WA 99164 ...509-335-3518
Watab Marketing Inc, 832 N 1st St, Sartell MN 56377................................612-253-3032
Water Mark Press, 138 Duane St, New York NY 10013................................212-285-1609
Water Row Press, Box 438, Sudbury MA 01776 617-443-8910
Waterfront Books, 98 Brookes Ave, Burlington VT 05401 802-658-7477
Waterfront Center, 1536 44th St NW, Washington DC 20007.....................202-337-0356
Waterfront Press, 52 Maple Ave, Maplewood NJ 07040............................201-762-1565
Waters Publishing, PO Box 442, Brevard NC 28712...............................704-884-4495
Watershed Tapes, PO Box 50145, Washington DC 20004............................202-347-4823
Watson Publishing International*, Box 493, Canton MA 02021 617-828-8450
Watson-Guptill Publications*, 1515 Broadway, New York NY 10036.......212-764-7300
Franklin Watts Inc*, 387 Park Ave S, New York NY 10016 212-686-7070
Waveland Press Inc*, Box 400, Prospect Heights IL 60070 312-634-0081
Waverly Press Inc*, 428 E Preston St, Baltimore MD 21202 301-528-4000
Wayne State University Press*, 5959 Woodward Ave, Detroit MI 48202..313-577-4600
Weber Systems Inc*, 8437 Mayfield Rd 102D, Chesterland OH 44026 216-729-2858
Weinberg Author Publisher, 4377 Clayton Ave, Los Angeles CA 90027 ...213-661-9844
Samuel Weiser, Box 612, York Beach ME 03910 207-363-4393
Wellbeing Books, Box 396, Newtonville MA 02160 617-332-7845
Wescott Cove Publishing Co, PO Box 130, Stamford CT 06904 203-322-0998
Wesleyan University Press*, 110 Mt Vernon St, Middletown CT 06457....203-344-7918
West Family Publishers, PO Box 1912, Beavertown OR 97075 503-641-0113
West Press, PO Box 99717, San Diego CA 92109...................................619-270-9096
West Publishing Co*, 50 W Kellogg Blvd Box 3526, St Paul MN 55166 612-228-2500
Westburg Assoc Publishers, 1745 Madison St, Fennimore WI 53809 608-822-6237
Westcliffe Publishers Inc*, Box 1261, Englewood CO 80150 303-935-0900
Western Assn of Map Libraries, Univ of Calif, Santa Cruz CA 95064 408-429-2364
Western Enterprises, 3538 Oak Cliff Dr, Fallbrook CA 92028 619-728-6465
Western Imprints*, 1230 SW Park Ave, Portland OR 97205 503-222-1741
Western Marine Enterprises Inc, Box Q, Ventura CA 93002...................805-644-6043
Western Psychological Svcs, 12031 Wilshire, Los Angeles CA 90025 213-478-2061
Western Publishing Co Inc*, 1220 Mound Ave, Racine WI 53404.............414-633-2431
Western Tanager Inc, 1111 Pacific Ave, Santa Cruz CA 95060...................408-425-1111
Western World Press, PO Box 366, Sun City CA 92381............................714-652-8288
Westernlore Press*, PO Box 35303, Tucson AZ 85740 602-297-5491
Westin Communications, 5760 Owensmouth, Woodland Hls CA 91367...818-340-6515
The Westminster Press*, 925 Chestnut St, Philadelphia PA 19107 215-928-2700
The Westphalia Press, Rt 1 Box 96, Loose Creek MO 65054.....................314-897-3526
Westview Press Inc*, 5500 Central Ave, Boulder CO 80301.......................303-444-3541
Wetherall Publishing Co, 4421 Portland Ave S, Minneapolis MN 55440 ..612-823-9228
Whatever Publishing Inc, 58 Paul Dr, San Rafael CA 94903 415-472-2100
Wheat Forders Press*, PO Box 6317, Washington DC 20015.....................202-362-1588
Whitaker House*, Pittsburgh & Colfax Sts, Springdale PA 15144.............412-274-4440
White Rose Press*, 61 Cherokee Dr, Memphis TN 38111............................901-525-1836
Whitehall Press, Rt 1 Box 603, Sandersville GA 31082 912-552-7455
Albert Whitman & Co*, 5747 W Howard St, Niles IL 60648 312-647-1355
Whitmore Publishing Co, 35 Cricket Terrace, Ardmore PA 19003............215-896-6116
The Whitney Library of Design*, 1515 Broadway, New York NY 10036...212-764-7318
Whitston Publishing Co*, PO Box 958, Troy NY 12181 518-283-4363
Geo Whittell Memorial Press, 3722 South Ave, Youngstown OH 44502...216-788-1064
Who's Who Amer Restaurants, 1841 Broadway, New York NY 10023......212-581-0360
Whole Person Assoc, PO Box 3151, Duluth MN 55803 218-728-6807

Wide World Publ/Tetra House*, PO Box 476, San Carlos CA 94070........415-593-2839
Markus Wiener Publishing*, 2901 Broadway, New York NY 10025 212-678-7138
Wild Rose Books, 500 E 77th St Ste 1832, New York NY 10021.................212-744-2867
Wild Trees Press, PO Box 378, Navarro CA 95463.....................................707-895-3681
Wilderness Adventure Books, 320 Garden Ln, Fowlerville MI 48836........517-223-9581
Wilderness Press, 2440 Bancroft Way, Berkeley CA 94704.......................415-843-8080
John Wiley & Sons Inc*, 605 3rd Ave, New York NY 10158.....................212-850-6000
Wilkerson Assoc, 5418 Wollochet Dr NW, Gig Harbor WA 98335.............206-858-9076
Williams & Wilkins*, 428 E Preston St, Baltimore MD 21202 301-528-4000
J Williams Book Co*, PO Box 783, Jenks OK 74037 918-299-8224
Williamson Publ*, Church Hill Rd Box 185, Charlotte VT 05445...............802-425-2102
Willow Creek Press, PO Box 300, Wautoma WI 54982 414-787-3005
Wilshire Book Co*, 12015 Sherman Rd, N Hollywood CA 91605 213-875-1711
The H W Wilson Co*, 950 University Ave, Bronx NY 10452.......................212-588-8400
B L Winch & Assoc, 45 Hitching Post Dr, Rolling Hills Est CA 90274......213-539-6430
Winchester Press*, 220 Old New Brunswick Rd, Piscataway NJ 08854.....201-981-0820
Windgate Press, PO Box 1715, Sausalito CA 94966..................................415-332-0912
Windsor Books, PO Box 280, Brightwaters NY 11718................................516-666-4631
Windsor Publications Inc*, 8910 Quartz Ave, Northridge CA 91324........818-709-0200
Windstar Books, PO Box 1643, Virginia Beach VA 23451 804-479-4502
Wine Appreciation Guild*, 155 Connecticut, San Francisco CA 94107.....514-864-1202
Wine Publications, 96 Parnassus Rd, Berkeley CA 94708.........................415-843-4209
Wingbow Press, 2929 5th St, Berkeley CA 94710......................................415-549-3030
Wings of Faith Publ House, 2401B Horne Dr, Charlotte NC 28206 704-332-8923
Winmar Press, 5800 W Century Blvd, Los Angeles CA 90009 213-672-0735
Winn Books, 5700 6th Ave S, Seattle WA 98108.......................................206-763-9544
Winsome Publishers, PO Box 2876, Torrance CA 90509............................213-515-2814
Winston Press Inc*, 600 1st Ave, Minneapolis MN 55403 612-338-3000
Winston-Derek Publishers*, PO Box 90883, Nashville TN 37209.............615-329-1319
Winter Soldier Archive, PO Box 9462, Berkeley CA 94709 415-527-0616
Wintergreen Press S Isle Assoc, 4105 Oak St, Long Lake MN 55356........612-476-1303
Wittenborn Art Books Inc*, 1018 Madison Ave, New York NY 10021......212-288-1558
Wizards Bookshelf, PO Box 6600, San Diego CA 92106............................619-235-0340
Alan Wofsy Fine Arts, PO Box 2210, San Francisco CA 94126 415-986-3030
Wolcotts Legal Form Publ, 15124 Downey Ave, Paramount CA 90723.....213-630-0911
Merlon Wolfe, 575 Madison Ave, New York NY 10022 212-605-0568
Women's Aglow Fellowship*, Box 1, Lynnwood WA 98046 206-775-7282
Women's Art Registry of Minn, 414 1st Ave, Minneapolis MN 55401........612-332-5672
Women's Legal Defense Fund, 2000 P St NW, Washington DC 20036.......202-887-0364
Women's Studio Workshop Print Center, Box V, Rosendale NY 12472...914-658-9133
Wonder View Press, Box 3301, Mililani HI 96789.....................................808-623-5337
Wood Thrush Books, 18 N Winooski Ave, Burlington VT 05401 802-862-6088
Woodbine House*, 10400 Connecticut Ave, Kensington MD 20895...........301-949-3590
Woodbridge Press Publ Co, PO Box 6189, Santa Barbara CA 93160........805-965-7039
Woodland Books*, 500 N 1030 W, Lindon UT 84603................................801-785-8100
Woodsong Graphics Inc, PO Box 238, New Hope PA 18938 215-794-8321
The Word for Today, PO Box 8000, Costa Mesa CA 92628........................714-979-0706
Word Inc*, 4800 W Waco Dr, Waco TX 76703 817-772-7650
Word Lab Inc, PO Box 53462, Houston TX 77052.....................................713-621-4984
Word of Mouth Press, PO Box 824, Yonkers NY 10701.............................202-554-0442
Wordware Publishing Inc*, 1506 Capital, Plano TX 75074 214-423-0090
Work At Home Press, PO Box 5520, Ocala FL 32678.................................904-629-1220
Workman Publishing Co Inc*, 1 W 39th St, New York NY 10018..............212-398-9160

World Book Inc*, 510 Merchandise Mart Plaza, Chicago IL 60654............312-245-3456
World Books, 1915 Las Lomas Rd NE, Albuquerque NM 87106 505-242-9983
World Exonumia, PO Box 4143, Rockford IL 61110 815-226-0771
World of Modeling Inc, PO Box 100, Croton on Hudson NY 10520.........914-737-8512
Worldwatch Inst*, 1776 Massachusetts Ave NW, Wash DC 20036.............202-452-1999
Worth Publishers Inc, 444 Park Ave S, New York NY 10016 212-689-9630
Wright Publishing Co, 1422 W Peachtree St, Atlanta GA 30309................404-876-1900
The Writer Inc*, 120 Boylston St, Boston MA 02116...................................617-423-3157
Writer's Digest Books*, 1507 Dana Ave, Cincinnati OH 45207 513-531-2222
Writer's Journal, PO Box 65798, St Paul MN 55165....................................612-221-0326
Writers & Readers Publishing Inc*, 500 5th Ave, New York NY 10110...212-354-5500
Writers Guide Publications, 5045 W Oakton St #7, Skokie IL 60077........312-675-1146
Writers House Press, PO Box 3071, Iowa City IA 52244 319-337-6430
Writers Publishing Service Co*, 1512 Western Ave, Seattle WA 98101....206-284-9954
The Writing Works*, 3441 Thorndyke W, Seattle WA 98119.....................206-282-3888
WTI Publishing Co, PO Box 42216, Los Angeles CA 90042........................213-254-1326
WWW Publishers, PO Box 42224, Tucson AZ 85733 602-299-6105
Wyrick & Co*, 1A Pinckney St, Charleston SC 29401 803-722-0881
Xavier Press, PO Box 11074, Dallas TX 75223..214-826-5835
Xavier Society for the Blind*, 154 E 23rd St, New York NY 10010 212-473-7800
Xerox Education Publ*, 245 Long Hill Rd, Middletown CT 06457............203-638-2400
Yale University Press*, 92A Yale Sta, New Haven CT 06520 203-436-7584
Yankee Books*, Main St, Dublin NH 03444...603-563-8111
Ye Galleon Press*, PO Box 287, Fairfield WA 99012.................................509-283-2422
Year Book Medical Publishers*, 35 E Wacker Dr, Chicago IL 60601 312-726-9733
Yee Wen Publishing Co, 21 Vista Ct, San Francisco CA 94080.................415-873-7167
Yellow Moon Press, PO Box 1316, Cambridge MA 02238.........................617-628-7894
Yeshiva University Press, 500 W 185th St, New York NY 10033................212-960-5400
Yoga Research Foundation, 6111 SW 74th Ave, Miami FL 33143.............305-666-2006
The Yolla Bolly Press, Box 156, Covelo CA 95428.....................................707-983-6130
Yourdon Press*, 1501 Broadway, New York NY 10036 212-391-2828
Z Press Inc, Box Z, Calais VT 05648..203-467-4257
Zahra Publications, Box 730, Blanco TX 78606 512-833-5334
Zaner-Bloser Inc*, 2300 W 5th Ave Box 16724, Columbus OH 43216.......614-486-0221
Zebra Books*, 475 Park Ave S, New York NY 10016..................................212-889-2299
A M Zimmermann, 2210 Jackson St #404, San Francisco CA 94115........415-929-7577
Zondervan Corp*, 1415 Lake Dr SE, Grand Rapids MI 49506....................616-698-6900
Zoom Publishing, PO Box 730, El Toro CA 92630 714-951-1631
Zoryan Institute, 85 Fayerweather St, Cambridge MA 02138.....................617-497-6713
John T Zubal Inc, 1969 W 25th St, Cleveland OH 44113.............................216-241-7640

BOOK REVIEWERS

See also Magazines, Newspapers, News Services & Feature Syndicates, and TV & Radio Networks for other book review media.

AB Bookman's Weekly, Box AB, Clifton NJ 07015.....................................201-772-0020
Academic Library Book Review, 290 Broadway, Lynbrook NY 11563 516-593-1195
Ad-Lib Publications, 51 N 5th St, Fairfield IA 52556................................515-472-6617
All-Media Services, 13415 Ventura Blvd, Sherman Oaks CA 91423..........213-995-3329
Amer Book Collector, PO Box 1080, Ossining NY 10562..........................914-941-0409

Amer Book Review, Univ of Colo Box 226, Boulder CO 80309 303-492-8947
American Book Review, PO Box 188, New York NY 10003........................212-713-5016
Applied Science & Technology Index, 950 University, Bronx NY 10452....212-588-8400
Appraisal: Science Books, 605 Commonwealth Ave, Boston MA 02215 ...617-353-4150
Art Index, 950 University Ave, Bronx NY 10452 212-588-8400
John Austin, PO Box 49957, Los Angeles CA 90049 714-678-6237
Banking Literature Index, 1120 Connecticut Ave NW, Wash DC 20036...202-467-4180
Gary P Baranik, 1272 Prospect Ave, Brooklyn NY 11218.........................718-435-2729
Joseph Barbato, 40-13 82nd St, Elmhurst NY 11373 718-424-0694
John Barkham Reviews, 27 E 65th St, New York NY 10021 212-879-9705
Barnhardt Dictionary Companion, Box 247, Cold Spring NY 10516........914-265-2822
Diana Barth, 535 W 51st St 3A, New York NY 10019.............................212-307-5465
Marion Benasutti, 885 N Easton Rd 6A3, Glenside PA 19038 215-884-6395
Best Sellers, Univ of Scranton Library, Scranton PA 18510.....................717-961-7530
Biography Index, 950 University Ave, Bronx NY 10452 212-588-8400
Biological & Agricultural Index, 950 University Ave, Bronx NY 10452.....212-588-8400
Black Books Bulletin, 7524 S Cottage Grove, Chicago IL 60619..............312-651-0700
The Bloomsbury Review, PO Box 8928, Denver CO 80201......................303-892-0620
Book Chatter, PO Box 184, Brooklyn NY 11214 718-837-3484
Book Forum, 38 E 76th St, New York NY 10021 212-861-8328
Book Review Digest, 950 University Ave, Bronx NY 10452......................212-588-8400
Book Review Index, Book Tower, Detroit MI 48226................................313-961-2242
Book World, 1150 15th St NW, Washington DC 20071 202-334-7882
Booklist, 50 E Huron St, Chicago IL 60611...312-944-6780
Books & Religion, Duke Univ Divinity School, Durham NC 27706............919-684-3569
Books for Children, Clemson Univ Dept of English, Clemson SC 29634..803-656-3151
The Bookwatch, 166 Miramar Ave, San Francisco CA 94112 415-587-7009
R R Bowker Co, 249 W 17th St, New York NY 10011 212-645-0067
Millicent Braverman, 1517 Schuyer Rd, Beverly Hills CA 90210 213-274-5204
Bulletin of Ctr for Children's Books, 1100 East 57 St, Chicago IL 60637..312-962-8284
Burnham-Kidwell Indexer, 3661 Abrigo Rd, Kingman AZ 86401 602-565-3796
Business Periodicals Index, 950 University Ave, Bronx NY 10452.............212-588-8400
Katy McGuire Caire, 413 Livingston, Pass Christian MS 39571...............601-452-2077
Robert M Cammarota, 215 W 92nd St 12E, New York NY 10025 212-724-3775
Alan Caruba, Box 40, Maplewood NJ 07040...201-763-6392
Catholic Periodical/Lit Index, 461 W Lancaster, Haverford PA 19041.....215-649-5250
Choice, 100 Riverview Ctr, Middletown CT 06457 203-347-6933
Coast Book Review Service, PO Box 7414, Fullerton CA 92634................714-990-0432
Computer Book Review, PO Box 37127, Honolulu HI 96837 808-595-7089
Conch Review of Books, 102 Normal Ave, Buffalo NY 14213 716-885-3686
Contemporary Psychology, Univ of Minn, Minneapolis MN 55455...........612-625-3477
Carole Cook, 304 W 107th St, New York NY 10025 212-866-6275
Ralph Corsel, 932 2nd Ave, New York NY 10022....................................212-371-2777
Cowles Syndicate, 715 Locust St, Des Moines IA 50304..........................515-284-8244
Cumulative Book Index, 950 University Ave, Bronx NY 10452...................212-588-8400
Current Biography, 950 University Ave, Bronx NY 10452..........................212-588-8400
Curriculum Review, 517 S Jefferson St, Chicago IL 60607.......................312-939-3010
Louise A DeVillier, 6305 Pickens, Houston TX 77007 713-862-2952
ECA Assoc, PO Box 15004, Chesapeake VA 23320.................................804-547-5542
ERC Reviews, 1107 Lexington, Dayton OH 45407..................................513-275-6879
Feminist Bookstore News, PO Box 882554, San Francisco CA 94188........415-626-1556
Copywriters Council of Amer, Middle Island NY 11953 516-924-8555
History: Review of New Books, 4000 Albemarle, Washington DC 20016...202-362-6445

Horn Book, 31 St James Ave, Boston MA 02116.................................617-482-5198
Illinois Writers Review, Box 1087, Champaign IL 61820.........................217-398-8526
Indpendent News Alliance, 255 W 84th St, New York NY 10024.................212-692-3713
A Heath Jarrett, PO Box 184, Brooklyn NY 11214.............................718-837-3484
Joan Kain, 235 W 102nd St Apt 16E, New York NY 10025.......................212-850-0768
Thomas Kemp, PO Box 4050, Stamford CT 06907...............................203-323-2826
Kirkus Reviews, 200 Park Ave S, New York NY 10003..........................212-777-4554
Kliatt Paperback Book Guide, 425 Watertown, Newton MA 02158..........617-965-4666
Law Books in Review, 75 Main St, Dobbs Ferry NY 10522......................914-693-5956
Library Journal, 249 W 17th St, New York NY 10011 212-645-0067
LA Times Book Review, Times Mirror Sq, Los Angeles CA 90053............213-972-7777
Jerry Mack Book Review Svc, Box 5200, San Angelo TX 76902 915-653-1795
Lilyan Mastrolia, 4706 Cameron Ranch, Sacramento CA 95841...............916-488-2722
Carole Terwilliger Meyers, PO Box 6061, Albany CA 94706....................415-527-5849
Mary Mueller, 108 Forest Rd, Moorestown NJ 08057...........................609-778-4769
Natl Book Critics Circle, 756 S 10th St, Philadelphia PA 19147 215-925-8406
New Age Book Review, PO Box 324, New York NY 10156........................212-683-7684
New Pages, Box 438, Grand Blanc MI 48439...................................313-742-9583
New York Review of Books, 250 W 57th St, New York NY 10107.............212-757-8070
Albert Nussbaum, Box 746, Tarzana CA 91356.................................213-881-1375
Omni Online Reviews, 1965 Broadway, New York NY 10023 212-496-6100
Evelyn Oppenheimer, 7929 Meadow Park Dr Apt 201, Dallas TX 75230..214-369-0904
Joan Orth, 401 E 65th St Ste 14J, New York NY 10021.........................212-734-9497
Pathfinder Reports, 66 Market St, Seville OH 44273 216-769-2249
Pathway Press, 1080 Montgomery Ave, Cleveland TN 37311.....................615-476-4512
Patrician Productions, 145 W 58th St, New York NY 10019.....................212-265-5612
Paulus Feature Synd, Box 1662, Pittsburgh PA 15230...........................412-562-4067
Pediatric Projects Inc, Box 1880, Santa Monica CA 90406.....................213-828-8963
Postroad Press Inc, PO Box 1212, Roanoke VA 24006...........................703-342-9797
John Preston, Box 5314, Portland ME 04101..................................207-774-3865
Publishers Weekly, 249 W 17th St, New York NY 10011 212-645-0067
Rainbo Electronic Reviews, 8 Duran Ct, Pacifica CA 94044....................415-993-6029
Reference Book Review, PO Box 190954, Dallas TX 75219.......................214-690-5882
Review in Amer History, 701 W 40th St, Baltimore MD 21211 301-338-6983
Review of Education, 380 Adams St, Bedford Hills NY 10507 914-241-7100
Review of Psychoanalytic Books, 315 5th Ave, New York NY 10016 212-684-7900
RQ, 50 E Huron St, Chicago IL 60611 312-944-6780
Sage Publications Inc, 2111 W Hillcrest Dr, Newbury Park CA 91320......805-499-0721
San Francisco Review of Books, 1117 Geary, San Francisco CA 94109.....415-771-1252
Carl Schleier Review, 646 Jones Rd, River Vale NJ 07675 201-391-7135
Sci Tech Book News, 5600 NE Hassalo, Portland OR 97213 503-281-9230
Science Books & Films, 1333 H St NW, Washington DC 20005 202-326-6463
Chronicle Book Review Suppl, 901 Mission, San Francisco CA 94119.......415-777-7042
Doris P Shalley, General Sullivan Rd Box 166, Wash Crossing PA 18977.215-493-3521
Ed Shearer, 312 Deckor St, Jewell IA 50130..................................515-827-5089
Shooting Star Review, 7123 Race St, Pittsburgh PA 15208 412-731-7039
Show/Book Week, 401 N Wabash, Chicago IL 60611 312-321-3000
Small Press Book Review, Box 176, Southport CT 06490........................203-268-4878
The Small Press Book Review, PO Box 176, Southport CT 06490.............203-268-4878
Small Press Review, Box 100, Paradise CA 95969...............................916-877-6110
Helene Taylor, 149 Crescent St, Northampton MA 01060........................413-584-2647
Douglas L Thompson, 12009 Glen Mill Rd, Potomac MD 20854...............301-251-1179
Sunny Tiedemann, 1019 King Cir, Bartlesville OK 74006 918-335-3054

George H Tweney, 16660 Marine View, Seattle WA 98166 206-243-8243
Voice Literary Supplement, 842 Broadway, New York NY 10003 212-475-3300
Wall St Review of Books, 380 Adams St, Bedford Hills NY 10507 914-241-7100
Hans H Wellisch, 5015 Berwyn Rd, College Park MD 20740.....................301-345-3477
West Coast Review of Books, 6331 Hollywood, Hollywood CA 90028 213-464-2662
Women's Review of Books, Wellesley MA 02181..617-431-1453

BOOK STORES & DISTRIBUTORS

This section lists selected major book store chains and distributors. An asterisk (*) denotes a wholesale book distributor. See Associations for national and regional booksellers' organizations.

Baker & Taylor Co*, 50 Kirby Ave, Somerville NJ 08876 201-722-8000
Baptist Book Stores, 127 9th Ave N, Nashville TN 37234 615-251-2011
Barnes & Noble Bookstores, 105 5th Ave, New York NY 10003 212-206-8800
The Book & Record, Commerce St, Poughkeepsie NY 12603......................914-471-2740
Book Bag Stores, Drawer 40, Charleston SC 29402.....................................803-744-1611
The Book Cache, 325 W Potter, Anchorage AK 99502...................................907-561-1438
Book Emporium, 1301 SW Washington, Peoria IL 61602...............................309-673-2327
Book Rack Mgmt Inc, 2703 E Commercial, Ft Lauderdale FL 33308........305-771-4310
Book World Inc, 2420 W 4th St, Appleton WI 54914.....................................414-731-9521
Bookland Stores, 202 N Court St, Florence AL 35630....................................205-764-6150
Bookpeople, 2929 5th St, Berkeley CA 94710..415-549-3030
Bookslinger*, 213 E 4th St, St Paul MN 55101 612-221-0429
Bookstop Inc, 9205 Brown Ln, Austin TX 78754...512-834-9951
Brennan College Service, 45 Island Pond Rd, Springfield MA 01118.........413-781-2296
Brodart Inc*, 500 Arch St, Williamsport PA 17705 717-326-2461
Century Bookstores, PO Box 788, Ft Worth TX 76101 817-927-5811
Cokesbury, 201 8th Ave N, Nashville TN 37202..615-749-6352
College Stores Assoc, 37 River St, Waltham MA 02154 617-899-7154
Crown Books, 3300 75th Ave, Landover MD 20785..301-731-1400
B Dalton Bookseller, 7505 Metro Blvd, Minneapolis MN 55435..................612-893-7000
Dillard's Book Dept, PO Box 486, Little Rock AR 72203 501-376-5200
The Distributors*, 702 S Michigan, S Bend IN 46618....................................219-232-8500
Doubleday Book Shops, 673 5th Ave, New York NY 10022 212-953-4828
Encore Books, 34 S 17th St, Philadelphia PA 19103......................................215-563-2919
Follett College Stores, PO Box 268, Elmhurst IL 60126................................312-279-2330
Gateway Books Inc, 211 W Young High Pike, Knoxville TN 37920.............615-573-9923
Hall of Cards & Books, 2232 S 11th St, Niles MI 49120................................616-684-3013
Hastings Books & Records, 2101 S Western St, Amarillo TX 79109 806-355-0061
Hatch's Inc, 15677 E 17th Ave, Aurora CO 80011..303-341-7234
Ingram Book Co*, 347 Reedwood Dr, Nashville TN 37217 615-361-5000
Joslins, 595 W Hampden, Englewood CO 80110 303-762-8310
Kampmann & Co*, 9 E 40th St, New York NY 10016 212-685-2928
Kroch's & Brentano's, 29 S Wabash Ave, Chicago IL 60603 312-332-7500
Lauriat's Books Inc, 10 Pequot Way, Canton MA 02021 617-828-8300
Little Professor Book Ctrs, 110 N 4th St, Ann Arbor MI 48104...................313-994-1212
Mr Paperback, 1135 Hammond St, Bangor ME 04401 207-942-8237
Pacific Pipeline*, 19215 66th Ave S, Kent WA 98032 206-872-5523
Publishers Group West*, 5855 Beaudry St, Emeryville CA 94608................415-658-3453

Readmor Bookstore Inc, 1131 W 5th Ave, Columbus OH 43212................614-294-7526
Readmore Book, PO Box 9127, Paducah KY 42002........................502-442-1372
Readmore Books, Box 598, Lima OH 45802........................419-225-5826
Taylors Inc, 5455 Beltline Rd, Dallas TX 75240........................214-934-1500
Tower Books, 2500 Del Monte Ave, Sacramento CA 95691.................916-321-2500
United College Bookstore Co, 1590 Concord, Framingham MA 01701.....617-877-7583
Waldenbooks Inc, 201 High Ridge Rd, Stamford CT 06904................203-356-7500
Wallace's Bookstores, PO Box 11518, Lexington KY 40576..............606-255-0886
Western Merchandisers*, 421 E 34th St, Amarillo TX 32270............806-376-6251
Zondervan Bookstores, 1420 Robinson, Grand Rapids MI 49506.........616-698-6900

COMPUTER SOFTWARE PUBLISHERS

See Word Processing Equipment & Supplies for computers and accessories.

Aardvark Techinical Services, 1690 Bolton, Walled Lake MI 48088.........313-669-3110
Abacus Software Inc, Box 7211, Grand Rapids MI 49510..................616-241-5510
Academy Software, Box 6277, San Rafael CA 94903......................415-499-0850
Access Technology, 6 Pleasant St, South Natick MA 01760..............617-655-9191
Accountants Microsystems Inc, 3633 136th Pl SE, Bellevue WA 98006....206-643-2050
ACS Consultants, 199 California Dr, Millbrae CA 94030.................415-697-3861
Activision Inc, Drawer 7286, Mountain View CA 94039..................415-960-0410
Ad-Lib Publications, 51 N 5th St, Fairfield IA 52556.................515-472-6617
Addison Wesley Publishing, Jacob Way, Reading MA 01867...............617-944-3700
Addison Wesley Publishing, 2725 Sand Hill Rd, Menlo Park CA 94025 ...415-854-0300
Advanced Analytical Computer Sys, 19301 Ventura, Tarzana CA 91356..818-708-3917
Advanced Data Institute, 8001 Fruitridge Rd, Sacramento CA 95820.......916-381-8334
Advanced Digital Microsystems, Box 203, Dayton OH 45406..............513-439-1775
Advanced Ideas Inc, 2902 San Pablo Ave, Berkeley CA 94702............415-526-9100
Advanced Logic Systems, 1195 E Argues Ave, Sunnyvale CA 94086.........408-730-0307
Advertising Data Systems Inc, 606 S Mendenhall, Memphis TN 38117....901-761-4740
AHA Inc, Box 8405, Santa Cruz CA 95061...............................408-458-9119
Aldus Corp, 411 1st Ave S, Seattle WA 98104.........................206-622-5500
Alpha Microsystems, 3501 Sunflower Box 25059, Santa Ana CA 92704....714-957-8500
Alpha Software Corp, 30 B St, Burlington MA 01803....................617-229-2924
Alphabit Communications, 13349 Michigan Ave, Dearborn MI 48126.....313-581-2896
The Alternate Source, 704 N Pennsylvania, Lansing MI 48906...........517-484-8270
Altsys Corp, 720 Avenue F Ste 108, Plano TX 75074...................214-424-4888
American Compusoft, 23272 De Lago, Laguna Hills CA 92653.............714-472-8186
American Eagle Software Co, PO Box 46080, Lincolnwood IL 60646.......312-792-1227
American Microware Corp, 1264 Deer Trail, Libertyville IL 60048.......312-367-1811
American Small Business Computers, 118 S Mill, Pryor OK 74361.........918-825-4844
American Systems Development Inc, Box 362, Germantown MD 20874...301-972-2724
American Training Intl Inc, 12638 Beatrice St, Los Angeles CA 90066....213-823-1129
The Amulet Consulting Group, PO Box 241713, Los Angeles CA 90024..213-824-9047
Analytics Intl Inc, 1365 Massachusetts Ave, Arlington MA 02174............617-641-0400
Anchor Systems Inc, 13850 Bellevue Redmond Rd, Bellevue WA 98005..206-644-7111
And All Inc, 8009 Harwin Dr, Houston TX 77036.......................713-780-3124
Andent Inc, 100 North Ave, Waukegan IL 60085........................312-223-5077
Antech Inc, 788 Myrtle St, Roswell GA 30075.........................404-993-7270
Apex Resources Inc, 17 St Marys Ct, Brookline MA 02146..............617-232-9686

Apollo Software, Box 6434, Kent WA 98064 206-852-1215
Apple Computer, 20525 Mariani Ave, Cupertino CA 95014 408-973-2222
Apple For The Teacher, 2331 Rainbow Ave, Sacramento CA 95821..........916-485-1690
Applied Business Software, 2847 Gundry Ave, Long Beach CA 90806......213-426-2188
Aquarius Enterprises, 801 Harbor Dr, Forked River NJ 08731..................609-693-0513
Aquarius People Materials Inc, Box 128, Indian Rocks Bch FL 33535.....813-595-7890
Arlington Software Systems, 400 Massachusetts, Arlington MA 02174.....617-641-0290
M Arman Publishing Inc, PO Box 785, Ormond Beach FL 32074 904-673-5576
Artsci Inc, 5547 Satsuma Ave, North Hollywood CA 91601 818-985-5763
Artworx Software Co Inc, 150 N Main St, Fairport NY 14450...................716-425-2833
Ashton-Tate, 20101 Hamilton Ave, Torrance CA 90502 213-329-8000
Assimilation Inc, 485 Alberto Way, Los Gatos CA 95030.........................408-395-7679
Martha Austin, 5535 Edlen, Dallas TX 75220 214-696-6170
Automation Management, 5718 Westheimer #410, Houston TX 77057 ...713-781-5941
Automation Resources, 2901 W Busch Blvd, Tampa FL 33618..................813-935-8844
Avalon Hill Game Co, 4517 Harford Rd, Baltimore MD 21214................301-254-9200
Avant Garde Publishing, 37 B Commercial Blvd, Novato CA 94947 415-883-8083
Aviation Analysis Inc, Box 3570, Carson City NV 89702.........................202-246-5023
Avinco Corp, Box 189, Sharpsburg MD 21782 301-432-4118
Avocet Systems Inc, 120 Union St Box 490, Rockport ME 04856 800-448-8500
Award Software, 236 N Santa Cruz Ave, Los Gatos CA 95030...................408-395-2773
BT Computing Corp, Box 1465, Euless TX 76039.....................................817-267-1415
BT Enterprises, 10 B Carlough Rd, Bohemia NY 11716.............................516-567-8155
B5 Software, 1024 Bainbridge Pl, Columbus OH 43228 614-276-2752
Bob Baker Software, 3668 Halter Ct, Sacramento CA 95821 916-972-1931
Barclay Bridge Supplies Inc, 8 Bush Ave, Port Chester NY 10573 914-937-4200
Baudville, 1001 Medical Park Dr SE, Grand Rapids MI 49506..................616-957-3036
Bearly Limited, 149 York St, Buffalo NY 14213......................................716-883-4571
Beechwood Software Inc, 975 Ebner Dr, Webster NY 14580 716-872-6450
Popular Programs, 135 Lake St, Kirkland WA 98033 206-822-7065
Berman Assoc Inc, 101 E Holly Ave Ste 14, Sterling VA 22170................703-450-5000
Best Programs, 5134 Leesburg Pike, Alexandria VA 22302 703-931-1300
BI Tech Enterprises Inc, 10 Carlough Rd, Bohemia NY 11716..................516-567-8155
Blue Cap Inc, 349 Paseo Tesoro, Walnut CA 91789 714-594-3317
Borland Intl, 4585 Scotts Valley Dr, Scotts Vly CA 95066........................800-543-7543
Boston Systems Office, 128 Technology Center, Waltham MA 02254.......617-894-7800
BrainBank Inc, 220 5th Ave, New York NY 10001 212-686-6565
Brantex Inc, Box 1708, Greenville TX 75401 214-454-3674
Briley Software, Box 2913, Livermore CA 94550.....................................415-455-9139
Broadway Software, 660 Amsterdam, New York NY 10025 212-580-7508
Broderbund Software, 17 Paul Dr, San Rafael CA 94903 415-479-1170
Brooks Cole Publishing Co, 555 Abrego, Monterey CA 93940..................408-373-0728
E Arthur Brown Co, 3404 Pawnee Dr, Alexandria MN 56308..................612-762-8847
Bruce & James Prog Publ, 2355 Leavenworth, San Francisco CA 94133 ..415-775-8400
Budget Computer Inc, 160 S 2nd St, Milwaukee WI 53204......................414-332-1222
Busi Math Corp, 545 Fond du Lac St, Ripon WI 54971............................414-748-3422
Business & Professional Software, 143 Binney, Cambridge MA 02142.....617-491-3377
Business Computer Design, 900 Jorie Blvd, Oak Brook IL 60521.............312-920-1175
Businessman's Computer Advisor, 15103 Jose St, Van Nuys CA 91405....818-782-1692
Businessmaster Inc, 6443 Coleman Rd, East Lansing MI 48823 517-337-7423
BV Engineering, 2200 Business Way, Riverside CA 92501........................714-781-0252
CALICO Inc, PO Box 15916, St Louis MO 63114.....................................314-863-8028
CAMS Inc, Box 488, Plantsville CT 06479..203-574-4224

CAP Software Inc, 100 Quartz Way, Syracuse NY 13219 315-488-0485
Car Soft Co, Box 28313, Tempe AZ 85282..602-820-3775
Cardco Inc, 300 S Topeka, Wichita KS 67202 316-267-3807
Cardinal Point Inc, Box 596, Ellettsvile IN 47429 812-876-7811
Cawthon Scientific Group, 24224 Michigan Ave, Dearborn MI 48124 313-565-4000
CBS College Publishing, 383 Madison Ave, New York NY 10017 212-872-2597
CBS School Publishing, 383 Madison Ave, New York NY 10017...............212-872-1857
CBS Software, 51 W 52nd St, New York NY 10019 203-622-2613
CDEX Corp, 1885 Lundy Ave, San Jose CA 95131 415-964-7600
CE Software, 801 73rd St, Des Moines IA 50312...515-224-1995
CED Software Development Corp, 3051 India St, San Diego CA 92103....619-295-4145
Celestial Software, 125 University Ave, Berkeley CA 94710................................415-420-0300
Central Point Software, 9700 SW Capital Hwy, Portland OR 97219..........503-244-5782
Charles River Data Systems, 983 Concord St, Framingham MA 01701 617-626-1000
Checkmate Technology Inc, 509 S Rockford, Tempe AZ 85281 602-966-5802
Chem-Al Inc, 2417 Summit Ave, Racine WI 53404 414-637-4338
Chip Taylor Communications, 15 Spollett Dr, Derry NH 03038...............603-434-9262
Chronicle Guidance Publications, PO Box 1190, Moravia NY 13118........315-497-0330
Cimarron Corp, 1502 Brookhollow Dr B, Santa Ana CA 92705....................714-241-5600
Cisco Computer Systems Co, 1117 Loop 304 E, Crockett TX 75835.........409-544-2257
CMA Micro Computer, 55722 Santa Fe Trail, Yucca Valley CA 92284.....619-365-9718
CMV Software Specialists Inc, 2720 W 12th St, Sioux Falls SD 57104.......605-338-6650
Code Writer Corp, 5605 W Howard, Niles IL 60648..312-647-1270
Colorcorp, 208 N Berkshire, Bloomfield Hills MI 48013..................................313-335-2255
Combase Inc, 333 Sibley St Ste 890, St Paul MN 55101.....................................612-221-0214
Commodore Business Machines, 1200 Wilson, King Prussia PA 19380 215-431-9180
Compal Inc, 8500 Wilshire Blvd, Beverly Hills CA 90211 213-652-2263
Comprep Corp, 4418 Chapman Ave Ste 318, Orange CA 92669.....................714-997-2989
ComPress Div of Wadsworth Inc, PO Box 102, Wentworth NH 03282 603-764-5831
Compu U Sports Inc, Box 1340, Frederick MD 21701 301-663-3257
Compu-Tations Inc, Box 502, Troy MI 48099..313-689-5059
Compudata Inc, 5301 Tacony St, Philadelphia PA 19137....................................215-535-2800
CompuLaw Inc, 3520 Wesley St, Culver City CA 90232 213-558-3360
Computer Accounting Consult, 554 Washington, Wellesley MA 02181 617-237-6058
Computer Assoc Intl, 2195 Fortune Dr, San Jose CA 95131 408-942-1727
Computer Consulting Services, 611 Druid Rd E, Clearwater FL 33516....813-446-2643
Computer Continuum, 75 Southgate Ave #6, Daly City CA 94025............415-326-3416
Computer Decisions Corp, 705 Mission Ave, San Rafael CA 94901 415-258-9590
Computer Innovations Inc, 980 Shrewsbury Ave, Tinton Falls NJ 07724..201-542-5920
Computer Island, 227 Hampton Green, Staten Island NY 10312...............212-948-2748
Computer Products Intl, 3225 Danny Park, New Orleans LA 70002.........504-455-5330
Computer Science Press, 11 Taft Ct, Rockville MD 20850....................................301-251-9050
Computer Software for Prof, 1615 Broadway, Oakland CA 94612..............415-444-5316
Computer Solutions, 4801 Fredericksburg Rd, San Antonio TX 78229.....512-341-8851
Computer Systems Consultants, 1454 Latta Ln, Conyers GA 30207.........404-483-4570
Computer Systems House, 2525 S Main, Salt Lake City UT 84115...........801-483-1000
Computers Plus Inc, 3430 Dodge, Dubuque IA 52001.......................................319-556-6150
Computerware, Box 668, Encinitas CA 92024...619-436-3512
Computing, 2519 Greenwich, San Francisco CA 94123....................................415-567-1634
Computx, 14 Pierce Ave, Oak Ridge NJ 07438..201-697-3141
Concept Educational Software, Box 6184, Allentown PA 18001.................215-266-1679
Condor Computer Corp, 2051 S State St, Ann Arbor MI 48104.................313-769-3988
Conduit, Univ of Iowa Oakdale Campus, Iowa City IA 52242 319-353-5789

Context Management Systems, Box 3010, Aguora CA 91301......................818-706-3141
Continental Software, 11223 S Hindry Ave, Los Angeles CA 90045 213-410-3977
Contract Services Assoc, 507 Lead, Kingman AZ 86401................................602-753-1133
Control Systems, 2855 Anthony Ln, Minneapolis MN 55418......................612-789-2421
Core Concepts, Box 24157, Tempe AZ 85282..602-968-3756
Cornwall Computer Sys, 1499 W Palmatto Pk, Boca Raton FL 33432......305-368-0850
Corona Data Systems, 275 E Hillcrest, Thousand Oaks CA 91360............805-495-5800
Countryside Data Inc, 718 N Skyline Dr Ste 201, Idaho Falls ID 83402....208-529-8576
Cow Bay Computing, Box 515, Manhasset NY 11030................................516-356-4423
Creative Software, 960 Hamlin Ct, Sunnyvale CA 94089............................408-745-1655
Crestwood Micro Systems Inc, Box 366, Woodstock NY 12498 914-679-6622
Cross Educational Software, Box 1536, Ruston LA 71270 318-255-8921
Custom Data, Box 1869, Alamogordo NM 88310..505-434-1096
Custom Data, Box 1408, Salt Lake City UT 84110......................................801-322-0708
Custom Software, 1308 Western, Wellington KS 67152 316-326-6197
Cybertek Agency Services, 1408 E University, College Sta TX 77840 409-260-9980
Cynthia Publishing Co, 4455 Los Feliz Blvd, Los Angeles CA 90027 213-664-3165
Cynwyn, 4791 Broadway, New York NY 10034..212-567-8493
CZ Software, 358 Forest Rd, S Yarmouth MA 02673..................................617-771-4155
Data Access Corp, 8525 SW 129 Terrace, Miami FL 33156........................305-238-0012
Data Command, PO Box 548, Kankakee IL 60901......................................815-933-7735
Data Systems, 2301 Churchill Dr, Oxnard CA 93033..................................805-483-3464
Data Systems Northwest, 3421 Kitsup Way, Bremerton WA 98312............206-377-2266
Datalex Co, 650 5th St Ste 406, San Francisco CA 94107 415-541-0780
Datamatics Mgmt Services, 330 New Brunswick, Fords NJ 08863 201-738-9600
Datasafe Corp, 10502 Telephone Rd Ste 394, Houston TX 77075..............713-485-8470
Datasoft Inc, 19808 Nordhoff Pl, Chatsworth CA 91311............................818-701-5161
DataSoft of New Hampshire, 22 Stevens Ave, Merrimack NH 03054........603-424-5217
E David & Assoc, 22 Russett Ln, Storrs CT 06268......................................203-429-1785
DBI Software Products, 1 Energy Place, Mt Pleasant MI 48858..................517-772-5055
DBINC, PO Box 20628, Alburquerque NM 87154......................................505-291-0628
DDA Software, Box 26, Hamburg NJ 07419 201-764-6677
Decision Support Sortware, 1300 Vincent Pl, McLean VA 22101..............703-442-7900
Deegan Learning Materials, Box 245, Mankato MN 56001........................507-625-6500
Delta Farming Systems, 11427 Front Nine Dr, Ft Collins CO 80522........303-223-8804
Denby Scheer & Co, 3580 Alana, Sherman Oaks CA 91430 818-906-7166
Des Data Equipment Supply, 8315 Firestone Blvd, Downey CA 90241.....213-923-9361
Design Trends Ltd, 525 S Washington St, Naperville IL 60540..................312-357-2664
Designer Software, 12777 Jones Rd Ste 100, Houston TX 77060................713-955-8880
Designware Inc, 185 Berry, San Francisco CA 94107..................................415-546-1866
Desktop Composition Systems Inc, PO Box 5279, Reno NV 89513............702-322-1884
Development Learning Materials, 1 DLM Park, Allen TX 75002 214-248-6300
Diamond Head Software, 841 Bishop St, Honolulu HI 96813 808-537-4972
Diamond Systems Inc, Box 48301, Niles IL 60648......................................312-763-1722
Digisoft Computers Inc, 1501 3rd Ave, New York NY 10028......................212-734-3875
Digital Marketing Corp, 2363 Boulevard Cir, Walnut Creek CA 94595....415-947-1000
Digital Software Corp, 200 W Douglas Ste 930, Wichita KS 67202 316-262-1040
Dilithium Press, Box 606, Beaverton OR 97075..503-243-3313
Direct Aid Inc, PO Box 4420, Boulder CO 80306..303-442-8080
Discwasher, Box 6021, Columbia MO 65205..314-449-0941
Walt Disney Telecom, 4563 Colorado, Los Angeles CA 90039....................818-956-3008
Distributed Computing Systems, Box 185, Lombard IL 60148 312-495-0121
Diversified Educational Ent Inc, 725 Main St, Lafayette IN 47901............317-742-2690

Dreams of The Phoenix Inc, PO Box 10273, Jacksonville FL 32247 904-396-6952
Duosoft Corp, 1803 Woodfield Dr, Savoy IL 61874 217-356-7542
Dynacomp, PO Box 18129, Rochester NY 14618.....................................716-442-8960
EMA Inc, Box 339, Los Altos CA 94022 415-969-4679
Earthware Computer Services, PO Box 30039, Eugene OR 97403 503-344-3383
Educational Activities Inc, 1937 Grand Ave, Baldwin NY 11510................516-223-4666
Educational Computing Systems, 136 Fairbanks, Oak Ridge TN 37830 ...615-483-4915
Educational Curriculum Software, PO Box 1120, Riverhead NY 11901...516-727-2242
Educational Media Corp, PO Box 21311, Minneapolis MN 55421.............612-636-5098
Educational Micro Inc, 1926 Hollywood Blvd, Hollywood FL 33020.........305-920-2222
Educomp, 919 W Canadian St, Vinita OK 74301......................................918-256-8995
Edusoft, PO Box 2560, Berkeley CA 94702..800-338-7638
Edutech Inc, 303 Lamartine St, Jamaica Plain MA 02130..........................617-524-1774
Electronic Arts, 2755 Campus Dr, San Mateo CA 94403.............................415-571-7171
Electronic Courseware Systems, 1210 Lancaster, Champaign IL 61821 217-359-7099
Elite Software Development Inc, Drawer 1194, Bryan TX 77806................409-846-2340
Elliam Assoc, 24000 Bessemer St, Woodland Hills CA 91367.....................818-348-4278
Eltech Assoc, 2466 Moreno Dr, Los Angeles CA 90039..............................213-663-0347
EMC Publishing, 300 York Ave, St Paul MN 55101 612-771-1555
En Fleur Corp, 2494 Sun Valley Circle, Silver Spring MD 20906 301-598-4532
Enercom Inc, 3225 S Hardy #101, Tempe AZ 85282 602-894-2279
Enertec Inc, 19 Jenkins Ave, Lansdale PA 19446 214-362-0966
Engineering Software Co, 8800 N Central Expwy, Dallas TX 75231 214-361-2431
Entelek, Box 1303, Portsmouth NH 03801...603-436-0439
Epyx Inc, 1043 Kiel Court, Sunnyvale CA 94086..408-745-0700
Esecsoftware, Box 216, Lexington MA 02173..617-641-2930
Esha Research, 606 Juntura Way SE, Salem OR 97302 503-585-6242
Excalibur Systems Inc, 1512 E Katella Ave, Anaheim CA 92805 714-385-1211
Execuware, 3640 Westgate Center Cir, Winston-Salem NC 27103..............919-760-3676
Extended Software Co, 11987 Cedar Creek Dr, Cincinnati OH 45240.......513-825-6645
Eyring Research Institute Inc, 1455 W 820 N, Provo UT 84601 801-375-2434
EZ Tax Computer Systems Inc, 5 Eagle View Ct, Monsey NY 10952 914-356-7780
Far West Laboratory, 2855 Folsom St, San Francisco CA 94103.................415-565-3000
FBS Systems Inc, Box 248, Aledo IL 61231...309-582-5628
Fitness Planning & Programming, 68 Olive, Chagrin Fls OH 44022.........216-247-5298
Focus Media Inc, 839 Stewart Ave, Garden City NY 11530 516-794-8900
Fox & Geller Inc, 604 Market St, Elmwood Park NJ 07407.......................201-794-8883
Freline Inc, Box 889, Hagerstown MD 21740..301-797-9760
FriendlySoft Inc, 3638 W Pioneer Pkwy, Arlington TX 76013....................817-277-9378
Frontline Publications, 22386 Sunlight Creek, El Toro CA 92630 714-837-6258
Frontrunner Computer Industries, 316 California, Reno NV 89509..........702-786-4600
FS! Software, PO Box 7096, Minneapolis MN 55407.................................612-871-4505
G&G Software Inc, 610 Park Blvd, Austin TX 78751.................................512-458-5760
G&Z Systems Inc, 187 Main St, Eastchester NY 10707 914-961-1613
Gamestar Inc, 1302 State St, Santa Barbara CA 93101 805-963-3487
Gander Software, 3223 Bross Rd, Hastings MI 49058 616-945-2821
Gavel Computing Systems Inc, Rt 2 Box 466, Alachua FL 32615..............904-462-4564
Allen Gelder Software, PO Box 11721, San Francisco CA 94101 415-681-9371
General Universal Systems, 8303 Southwest Fwy, Houston TX 77074 713-981-6634
Generic Computer Products, PO Box 790, Marquette MI 49855 906-249-9801
Generic Software, Dept 205 Box 790, Marquette MI 49855........................906-249-9801
Genium Publishing Corp, 1145 Catalyn St, Schenectady NY 12303 518-377-8855
Gessler Educational Software, 900 Broadway, New York NY 10003.........212-673-3113

James O Godwin & Assoc Inc, 9930 Albory Rd, Sandy UT 84092..............801-571-7590
Good Software Corp, 12900 Preston Rd, Dallas TX 75230...........................214-239-6085
Great Plains Computer Co Inc, Box 916, Idaho Falls ID 83402..................208-529-3210
Greenleaf Software Inc, 2101 Hickory Dr, Carrollton TX 75006 214-446-8641
Greentree Publishers, 5364 Ashwood, Camarillo CA 93010.......................805-483-5375
Guardian Automated Systems, 420 Main St, Buffalo NY 14202..................716-842-6410
Hammer Computer Systems, 900 Larkspur Ldg, Larkspur CA 94939.......415-461-7633
J L Hammett Co, Hammett Place Box 545, Braintree MA 02184................617-848-1000
H J Hansen Co, 545 W Golf Rd, Arlington Height IL 60005........................312-870-8708
Hansen Research & Development, 6042 W Bellfort, Houston TX 77035 ..713-723-8129
Harloff Inc, 725 Market St, Wilmington DE 19801.....................................615-482-7197
Have Computer Will Travel, 13222 Louvre St, Pacoima CA 91331............818-896-3572
HEL Custom Software, 127 Gaither Dr Ste 6, Mt Laurel NJ 08054..........609-234-3800
Hewlett Packard, 3404 E Harmony Rd, Ft Collins CO 80525 303-226-3800
Hewlett Packard, 3410 Central Expressway, Santa Clara CA 95051..........408-749-9500
Hexcraft Inc, Box 39, Cambridge MA 02238...617-354-4451
High Caliber Systems, 165 Madison Ave, New York NY 10016 212-684-5553
Hypergraphics Corp, 308 N Carroll, Denton TX 76201...............................817-565-0004
IBM, 2000 Purchase St, Purchase NY 10577 914-697-7221
ICMS, 1150 Bayhill Dr, San Bruno CA 94066...415-583-7909
ICR FutureSoft, 1730 Kingsey Ave Ste B, Orange Park FL 32073.............904-269-1918
Imagic, 2400 Bayshore Frontage Rd, Mountain View CA 94043 415-940-6030
IMSI, 1299 4th St, San Rafael CA 94901 415-454-4101
Inacomp Computer Center Inc, 1824 W Maple, Troy MI 48084 313-649-0910
Individualized Operand, PO Box 3030, San Rafael CA 94912..................415-459-3323
Info Designs, 445 Enterprise Ct, Bloomfield Hills MI 48013.....................313-334-9790
Information Resource Consult, 11920 Hargrove, St Louis MO 63131.......314-822-7072
Information Solutions Inc, Box 198, Charlottesville VA 22902 919-846-9665
Innovative Software Inc, 9300 W 110th St, Overland Park KS 66210.........913-345-2424
Institute for Scientific Analysis, 36 E Baltimore Pike, Media PA 19063...215-566-0801
Instructional Comm Tech, 10 Stepar Pl, Huntington Sta NY 11746..........516-549-3000
Integral Computer Systems Inc, 136 Main St, Putnam CT 06260 203-928-0451
Intellectual Software, 798 North Ave, Bridgeport CT 06606 203-333-7268
Intelligent Machines, 1440 W Broadway, Missoula MT 59802....................406-728-0332
Intelligent Micro Systems, 1249 Greentree Ln, Narberth PA 19072..........215-664-1207
Intentional Educations, 341 Mt Auburn St, Watertown MA 02172 617-923-7707
Interface Technology Inc, Box 3040, Laurel MD 20708...............................301-490-3608
Interstate Digital Elec, 103 Sandwich St, Plymouth MA 02360 617-747-1462
Interstel Corp, PO Box 57825, Webster TX 77598..713-333-3909
Intl Computer Products, 346 N Western Ave, Los Angeles CA 90004......213-462-8381
Investment Evaluations Corp, 2000 Goldenview Dr, Golden CO 80401 ...303-278-3464
Investments Software Concept, 295 Jessamine Ave, Yonkers NY 10701...914-476-1280
IOTC Inc, Box 1365, Laramie WY 82070 307-721-5818
IPS Publishing, 31225 La Baya Dr #205, Westlake Vlg CA 91362 818-706-1646
J&J Software Services, 212 W Seminole Ave, Melbourne FL 32901..........305-725-8015
Jagdstaffel Software, 645 Brenda Lee Dr, San Jose CA 95123....................408-578-1643
Jamestown Publishers, PO Box 9168, Providence RI 02940........................401-351-1915
Jefferson Software, 723 Kanawha Blvd E, Charleston WV 25301............304-344-8550
Johnson Laird Inc, 6441 SW Canyon Ct, Portland OR 97221.....................503-292-6330
K Waves Financial Services, Box 1675, Sausalito CA 94965........................415-388-9474
Kastel Technology Corp, 621 Minna St, San Francisco CA 94103..............415-863-5636
Kidco Educational Software, PO Box 977, Huntington NY 11743 516-348-1577
KJ Software Inc, 3420 E Shea Blvd Ste 161, Phoenix AZ 85028 602-953-1544

Klug Computer Software, 1730 Arlington Dr, Oshkosh WI 54904 414-235-6205
Krell Software Corp, 1320 Stony Brook Rd, Stony Brook NY 11790 516-751-5139
Krentek Software, PO Box 3372, Kansas City KS 66103.....................913-362-9267
Labsoft, 701 7th Ave 5th Floor, New York NY 10036.......................212-840-1233
Lake Avenue Software, 77 N Oak Knoll Ste 105, Pasadena CA 91101 818-792-1844
The Laser Edge, 360 17th St Ste 203, Oakland CA 94612...................415-835-1581
Lassen Software Inc, Box 1190, Chico CA 95927 916-891-6957
Learnco Inc, 128 High St, Greenland NH 03840 603-778-0813
The Learning Co, 545 Middlefield Rd Ste 170, Menlo Park CA 94025......415-328-5410
Learning Seed Co, 21250 N Andover Rd, Kildeer IL 60047..................312-438-3251
Learning Well, 200 S Service Rd, Roslyn Heights NY 11577................516-621-1540
Lexisoft Inc, 712 5th St, New York NY 95617............................916-758-3630
Life Science Assoc, 1 Fenimore Rd, Bayport NY 11705 516-472-2111
Lifeboat Assoc, 1651 3rd Ave, New York NY 10128 212-860-0300
Lifetree Software, 411 Pacific St, Monterey CA 93949...................408-373-4718
Lighthouse Publishing Svcs, 575 Madison Ave, New York NY 10022.......212-605-0296
Logic Industries Inc, 1685 W Hamlin Rd, Rochester MI 48063 313-852-5294
Lotsabytes, 15445 Ventura Ste 10, Sherman Oaks CA 91413 805-252-5781
Lotus Development Corp, 55 Cambridge Pkwy, Cambridge MA 02142 617-577-8500
Rick Lutowski, 76 Flintwell Way, San Jose CA 95138 408-226-4122
M&T Publishing Inc, 2464 Embarcadero Way, Palo Alto CA 94303.........415-424-0600
Hugh C Maddocks, 10807 Oldfield Dr, Reston VA 22091....................703-476-4860
Major Software, 66 Sylvian Way, Los Altos CA 94022 415-941-1924
Mark Data Products, 24001 Alicia Pkwy, Mission Viejo CA 92691 714-768-1551
Market Directions, 20 E Milwaukee St Ste 304, Janesville WI 53545.........608-754-7818
Mathematical Software Co, PO Box 12349, El Cajon CA 92022 619-940-0333
Matrix Software, 315 Marion Ave, Big Rapids MI 49307...................616-796-2483
Mayday Software, Box 66 Rock Creek Rd, Phillips WI 54555...............715-339-3966
McGraw-Hill Inc, 1221 Ave of the Americas, New York NY 10020...........212-512-2000
McKelvie Programs, 621 Delaware Ave, Delanco NJ 08075 609-461-5587
MECC, 3490 Lexington Ave N, St Paul MN 55112...........................612-481-3560
Medcomp Data Systems, 15502 Hwy 3, Webster TX 77598..................713-488-6667
Media Computer Ent, 880 Sibley Mem Hwy, Mendota Hts MN 55118 612-451-7360
Medical Logic Intl, 5 Pathfinder Dr, Sumter SC 29150 803-469-9180
Melcher Software, 412 Hollybrook Dr, Midland MI 48640.................517-631-7607
Memory Systems Inc, 5212 Hoffman, Skokie IL 60077 312-674-4833
Merry Bee Software, 547 N Washington, Papillion NE 68046 402-592-3479
Metier, PO Box 51204, San Jose CA 95151 408-270-3011
Micro Computer, 34 Maple Ave, Armonk NY 10504 914-273-6480
Micro Ed Inc, Box 444005, Eden Prairie MN 55344 612-944-8750
Micro Intergration Inc, Box 335, Friendsville MD 21531 301-746-5888
Micro Investment Software Inc, 9621 Bowie Way, Stockton CA 95209.....209-952-8833
Micro L Inc, 16803 Davenport Rd, Dallas TX 75248.......................214-248-1498
Micro Learningware, Box 307, Mankato MN 56001.........................507-625-2205
Micro Mikes Inc, 814 S Lamar, Amarillo TX 79106 806-372-3633
Micro Power & Light Co, 12810 Hillcrest Rd #120, Dallas TX 75230.......214-239-6620
Micro Software Distributors, Box 674, Grand Blanc MI 48439 313-694-8730
Micro Solutions Inc, Box 5549, Richmond VA 23220 804-282-0082
Micro Tech Resources Inc, 2533 Banning Rd, Bath OH 44313...............216-666-7962
Micro Universe Inc, 12 Rt 12N Ste 111, Paramus NJ 07652 516-248-8901
Microbase Software Inc, PO Box 34163, Indianapolis IN 46234 317-241-9699
Microcomp Engineering Software, 1408A Encinal, Alameda CA 94501 ...415-865-2308
Microcomputer Investors, 902 Anderson, Fredericksburg VA 22405........703-371-5474

Microdex Corp, 1212 N Sawtelle, Tucson AZ 85716.................................602-326-3502
Micrografx Inc, 1820 N Greenville Ave, Richardson TX 75081 214-234-1769
Micromedx, 187 Gardiners Ave, Levittown NY 11756...............................516-735-8979
Micromint Inc, 25 Terrace Dr, Vernon CT 06066....................................203-871-6170
Micronetics Inc, 1926 Hollywood Blvd, Hollywood FL 33020 305-925-2333
Micropi, Box 5524, Bellingham WA 98227...206-733-9265
MicroPro Intl Corp, 33 San Pablo Ave, San Rafael CA 94903....................415-499-1200
Microproducts, 24627 Watt Rd, Ramona CA 92065..................................619-789-6510
Microprose Software Inc, 120 Lake Front Dr, Hunt Valley MD 21030.....301-667-1151
Microsoft Corp, 16011 NE 36th Way Box 97017, Redmond WA 98073.....206-882-8080
MicroSparc Inc, 45 Winthrop St, Concord MA 01742................................617-371-1660
Microspec, PO Box 863085, Plano TX 75086 214-867-1333
Microtech Exports Inc, 644 Emerson St Ste 8, Palo Alto CA 94301 415-324-9114
Milliken Publishing Co, 1100 Research Blvd, St Louis MO 63132..............314-991-4220
Mindscape Inc, 3444 Dundee Rd, Northbrook IL 60062............................312-480-7667
Miracle Computing, 313 Clayton Ct, Lawrence KS 66044 913-843-5863
Mishtrom, 576 S Telegrath, Pontiac MI 48053 313-334-5700
Tom Mix Software, 4285 Bradford NE, Grand Rapids MI 49506 616-957-0444
MLI Microsystems, Box 825, Framingham MA 01701 617-926-2055
MMG Micro Software, Manalapan 1000 Bldg, Englishtown NJ 07726 201-431-5372
Molecular Inc, 251 River Oaks Pkwy, San Jose CA 95134.......................800-327-6779
Money Tree Software, Box 54, Corvallis OR 97339................................503-757-1178
Morgan Computing Co, PO Box 112730, Carrollton TX 75011 214-245-4763
Mount Castor Industries, 51 Harborview Ln, E Orleans MA 02643.........413-255-9520
Mountain View Press Inc, Box 4656, Mountain View CA 94040.................415-961-4103
Nancy Mulvany, 265 Arlington Ave, Kensington CA 94707......................415-524-4195
Muse Software, 347 N Charles St, Baltimore MD 21201.........................301-659-7212
Natural Software Ltd, 7 Lake St Ste 7E, White Plains NY 10603.............914-761-9329
NEC Home Electronics, 1401 Estes Ave, Elk Grove Vilge IL 60007..........312-228-5900
New Classics Software, 239 Fox Hill Rd, Denville NJ 07834 201-625-8838
Newline Software, Box 289, Tiverton RI 02878 401-624-3322
B A Nicholson & Co Inc, 271 Madison Ave, New York NY 10016 212-889-7535
Nordic Software, 4910 Dudley, Lincoln NE 68504 402-466-6502
Not Polyoptics Publ, 13721 Lynn St, Woodbridge VA 22191....................703-491-5543
Noumenon Corp, 512 Westline Dr, Alameda CA 94501 415-521-2145
Oakland Group, 675 Massachusetts Ave, Cambridge MA 02139 617-491-7311
Omega Star Inc, PO Box 87413, Houston TX 77287 713-998-9226
Omni Software Systems Inc, 146 N Broad St, Griffith IN 46319...............219-924-3522
Omnitronix Inc, Box 43, Mercer Island WA 98040..................................206-236-2066
On Going Ideas, RD #1 Box 810, Starksboro VT 05487...........................802-453-4442
Optimized Systems Software, 1221 B Kentwood, San Jose CA 95129 408-446-3099
Optionware Inc, 4 Barnard Ln, Bloomfield CT 06002...............................203-243-5554
Orange Cherry Media, 52 Griffin Ave, Bedford Hills NY 10507................914-666-8434
Oregon Software Inc, 6915 SW Macadam Ave, Portland OR 97219 503-245-2202
Organic Computing, 96 Caddo Peak, Joshua TX 76058............................817-645-8193
Organizational Software Corp, 2655 Campus Dr, San Mateo CA 94403 ..415-571-0222
Origin Systems Inc, 136 Harvey Rd Bldg B, Londonderry NH 03053........603-644-3360
Osborne Computer Corp, 42680 Christy St, Fremont CA 94538................415-490-6885
Outstanding Software Corp, PO Box 490, Franklin Sq NY 11010.............516-328-3433
P Cubed Inc, 949 Parklane Center, Wichita KS 67218............................316-686-2000
P&B Computer Services Inc, 13701 Bel Red Rd, Bellevue WA 98005 206-641-7390
Pacific Coast Software, 7334 Hollister Ave, Santa Barbara CA 93117.......805-682-7940
Pacific Medsoft Inc, Box 7049, Tahoe City CA 95730..............................916-583-2994

Packaged Solutions Inc, 1 Huntington Quad, Melville NY 11747 516-752-1640
Paladin Software Corps, 2895 Zanker Rd, San Jose CA 95134 408-946-9000
Palantir Software, 12777 Jones Rd Ste 100, Houston TX 77070..............713-955-8880
Paperback Software Intl, 2612 8th St, Berkeley CA 94710.....................415-644-2116
Pasadena Technology Press, 3543 E California, Pasadena CA 91107.......818-442-3141
Passport Designs Inc, 625 Miramontes St, Half Moon Bay CA 94019 415-726-0280
PC Art, 3101 Oak, Terre Haute IN 47803...812-235-4185
Peachtree Software Inc, 4355 Intl Blvd, Norgross GA 30093.....................404-564-5700
Pearlsoft Inc, 25195 S W Parkway, Wilsonville OR 97070 503-682-3636
Penguin Software, 830 4th Ave Box 311, Geneva IL 60134.....................312-232-1984
Persimmon Software, 502 C Savannah St, Greensboro NC 27406.............919-275-5824
Personics Corp, 2352 Main St, Concord MA 01742.....................................617-897-1575
Pfremco Inc, 34 Maxwell Ln, Englishtown NJ 07726 201-431-5372
Photon Software, 14021 NE 8th St, Bellevue WA 98007 800-446-2263
Piedmont Software Co, 5200 Park Rd, Charlotte NC 28209 704-527-0117
Pinnell Engineering, 5331 SW Macadam #270, Portland OR 97201.........503-243-2246
PM Software, 19731 Providence Ln, Huntington Beach CA 92646.............714-963-2221
Polytron Corp, Box 787, Hillsboro OR 97123...503-648-8595
Powerbase Systems Inc, 12 W 37th St, New York NY 10018.....................212-947-3590
Practial Programs, 1104 Aspen Dr, Toms River NJ 08753.....................201-349-6070
Practical Data Corp, 169 S Main St, New City NY 10956.........................914-638-2420
Practical Programs, PO Box 93104, Milwaukee WI 53203 414-278-0829
Procedamus, 8655 Landas View, Rosemead CA 91770.............................213-288-0132
Professional Software Inc, 51 Fremont St, Needham MA 02194...............617-444-5224
Program Innovations, Box 1368, Lumberton NC 28359.............................919-739-3680
Programmming & Sys Mgmt, 3866 Indian Ripple, Dayton OH 45440 513-426-8644
Progressive Peripherals & Software, 2186 S Holly, Denver CO 80222......303-759-5713
Prosoft, 7248 Bellaire Ave, N Hollywood CA 91605 818-765-4444
PSI Systems, Research Park Box 3100, Andover MA 01810 617-475-9030
Psychological Assessment Resources, Box 98, Odessa FL 33556...............813-968-3408
Psychotechnics Inc, 1900 Pickwick Ave, Glenview IL 60025...................312-729-5850
QEI Inc, 119 The Great Road, Bedford MA 01730.....................................617-275-6800
Quadram Corp, 4355 Intl Blvd, Norcross GA 30093 404-923-6666
Quality 99 Software, 1884 Columbia Rd #500, Washington DC 20009 202-667-3574
Quality Input Inc, Box 1383, Orangevale CA 95662.................................916-988-7097
Que Corp, 7999 Knue Rd, Indianapolis IN 46250.....................................317-842-7162
Quest Computing, Box 1323, Freeport Ctr UT 84016 801-825-0968
Questionnaire Service, PO Box 778, East Lansing MI 48823 517-641-4428
Quorum Intl Unlimited, PO 2134, Oakland CA 94614...............................800-222-2824
RD Software, 1290 Monument St, Pacific Palisade CA 90272 213-454-8270
Red Wing Business Systems, 610 Main St Box 19, Red Wing MN 55066..612-388-1106
Regents Educational Software, 2 Park Ave, New York NY 10016 212-889-2788
Resort Management Systems, 1625 Broadway, Denver CO 80202.............303-333-6505
Resource Software Intl Inc, 330 New Brunswick Ave, Fords NJ 08863......201-738-8500
RG Computer Workshops Inc, 37 Marcia Lane, New York NY 10956 914-638-4762
Right On Programs, 1737 Veterens Hwy, Central Islip NY 11722.............516-348-1577
RightSoft Inc, 2033 Wood St #218, Sarasota FL 34237...............................813-952-9211
Rocky Mtn Software Systems, 1280C Newell, Walnut Crk CA 94596........415-680-8378
RTCS, PO Box 3000-886, Camarillo CA 93011...805-987-9781
Rubicon Publishing, 6300 La Calma Dr Ste 100, Austin TX 78752............512-454-5004
Ruff Software Inc, Box 98, Plant City FL 33566...813-681-0194
S&H Software Inc, 58 Van Orden Rd, Harrington Park NJ 07640.............201-768-3144
Sabre System Corp, 19925 Stevens Creek Blvd, Cupertino CA 95014.......408-973-7809

Saddler Engineers Consult, 4170 Canyon Crest, Altadena CA 91001........213-794-2683
Sadtler Research Laboratories, 3316 Spring Garden, Phila PA 19104......215-382-7800
SAIL Systems, 86 W University #14, Mesa AZ 85201 602-962-1876
Samna Corp, 2700 NE Expressway, Atlanta GA 30345....................................404-321-5006
Howard W Sams Inc, 4300 W 62nd St, Indianapolis IN 46268 317-298-5728
Santa Barbara Software, 1400 Dover Rd, Santa Barbara CA 93103..........805-963-4886
Sapana Micro Software, 1305 South Rouse, Pittsburg KS 66762................316-231-5023
W B Saunders, West Washington Square, Philadelphia PA 19105 215-574-4700
Scholastic Inc, 730 Broadway, New York NY 10003..212-505-3325
Science Research Assoc Inc, 155 N Wacker Dr, Chicago IL 60606 312-984-7000
Screenplay Brown Bag, 1095 Airport Rd, Minden NV 89423......................702-782-9731
Selfware Inc, 3545 Chain Bridge Rd #3, Fairfax VA 22030.........................703-352-2977
Sentient Software Inc, Box 4929, Aspen CO 81612...303-925-9293
Seven Hills Software Corp, 2310 Oxford Rd, Tallahassee FL 32304..........904-576-9415
Shannon Software Ltd, PO Box 6126, Falls Church VA 22046 703-573-9274
Shenandoah Software, Box 776, Harrisonburg VA 22801..............................703-433-9485
Sierra On Line Inc, PO Box 485, Coarsegold CA 93614 209-683-6858
Significant Statistics, 3336 N Canyon Rd, Provo UT 84604..........................801-377-4860
Simon & Schuster Inc, 1230 Ave of the Americas, New York NY 10020..212-698-7000
Simulusion, Box 2382, La Jolla CA 92038...619-454-1023
Sir Tech Software, PO Box 245, Ogdenburg NY 13669..................................315-393-6633
The 6502 Program Exchange, 2920 W Moana, Reno NV 89509 702-825-8413
Skyles Electric Works, 231 S Whisman Rd Ste E, Mtn View CA 94041....415-965-1735
Smart Communications Inc, 655 3rd Ave, New York NY 10017.................212-486-1894
SMC Software Systems, Box 600, Basking Ridge NJ 07920..........................201-647-7000
Smith Micro Software Inc, Box 7137, Huntington Beach CA 92615 714-964-0412
Tom Snyder Productions, 123 Mt Auburn St, Cambridge MA 02138........617-876-4433
Soft Images, 200 Rt 17, Mahwah NJ 07430...201-529-1440
The Softa Group, 778 Frontage Rd, Northfield IL 60093................................312-446-7638
SoftCraft Inc, 222 State St, Madison WI 53703 608-257-3300
Softshoppe II, 1558 E Tara Ct, Chanoler AZ 85225 602-821-9178
The Software Bottling Co, 6600 Long Island Expwy, Maspeth NY 11378..718-458-3700
Software Concepts Inc, 1116 Summer St, Stamford CT 06905 203-357-0522
Software Connections Inc, 1435 Knoll Circle #112, San Jose CA 95112...408-293-3400
Software Development Corp, 270 Amity Rd, Woodbridge CT 06525.........203-397-0500
Software Link Inc, 8601 Dunwoody Place, Atlanta GA 30338....................404-998-0700
Software Masters, Box 570417, Houston TX 77257 713-266-5771
Software Publishing Corp, 1901 Landings Dr, Mtn View CA 94043..........415-962-8910
Software Research Tech, 3757 Wilshire Blvd, Los Angeles CA 90010 213-384-5430
The Software Store, 706 Chippewa Sq, Marquette MI 49855 906-228-7622
Software Systems Co Inc, 1 Dubuque Plaza, Dubuque IA 52001 319-556-2323
Software Toolworks, 15233 Ventura Blvd, Sherman Oaks CA 91403.........818-986-4885
Software Wizardry Inc, 1106 1st Capital Dr, St Charles MO 63301 314-946-1968
Softway Inc, 500 Sutter St, San Francisco CA 94102.....................................415-397-4666
Solartek, RD #1 Box 255A, West Hurley NY 12491 914-679-5366
Solution Softworks, 260 Laurel Lane, Bloomingdale IL 60108 312-893-5468
Solution Systems, 541 Main St Ste 410, S Weymouth MA 02190................617-659-1571
Solutions Inc, PO Box 989, Montpelier VT 05602 802-229-0368
Sony Corp of America, Sony Dr, Park Ridge NJ 07656..................................201-930-1000
The Sourceview Software Intl, Box 578, Concord CA 94522 800-443-0100
Southeastern Software, 7743 Briarwood Dr, New Orleans LA 70128........504-246-8438
Southwest Data Systems, 3017 San Fernando Blvd, Burbank CA 91504 ...818-841-1610
Southwest Edpsych Services, PO Box 1870, Phoenix AZ 85001..................602-253-6528

Soyfoods Center, PO Box 234, Lafayette CA 94549 415-282-2991
Specialized Data Systems Inc, PO Box 8278, Madison WI 53708...............608-241-5050
Spectral Assoc, 3418 S 90th, Tacoma WA 98409 206-581-6938
Spectrum Software, 75 Todd Pond Rd, Lincoln MA 01773 617-893-9130
Spinnaker Software, 1 Kendall Sq, Cambridge MA 02139...........................617-494-1200
SPSS Inc, 444 N Michigan Ave, Chicago IL 60611......................................312-329-2400
SSR Corp, 1600 Lyell Ave, Rochester NY 14606...716-254-3200
Sterling Swift Publishing Co, 7901 South IH 35, Austin TX 78744 512-282-6840
Stone+ Assoc, 7910 Ivanhoe Ave, La Jolla CA 92037.................................619-459-9173
Strategic Simulations, 1046 N Rengstorff, Mtn View CA 94043 415-964-1353
Strategy Assoc Inc, 3120 W 29th St, Minneapolis MN 55416 612-927-5044
Structural Research & Analysis, 1661 Lincoln, Santa Monica CA 90404..213-452-2158
STSC Inc, 2115 E Jefferson St, Rockville MD 20852....................................301-984-5000
Sunset Software, 1613 Chelsea Rd Ste 153, San Marino CA 91108 818-284-4763
Superior Graphic Software Products, Box 451, Canton NC 28716 704-648-6015
Supersoft Inc, Box 1628, Champaign IL 61820 217-359-2112
Sympathetic Software, 9531 Telhan Dr, Huntington Beach CA 92646 714-380-3360
Systech Inc, 5410 Baylor Dr, Bartlescille OK 74006.....................................918-333-9693
Systek Inc, Box 6234, Mississippi State MS 39762.......................................601-323-6905
System Aid Computer Control Inc, Box 929, Flushing NY 11354 212-539-6500
Systems Plus Inc, 500 Clyde Ave, Mountain View CA 94043......................415-969-7047
T&W Systems Inc, 7372 Prince Dr #106, Huntington Beach CA 92647....714-847-9960
Tall Tree Systems, 1120 San Antonio, Palo Alto CA 94303.........................415-964-1980
Tara Ltd, 1 Reeves Rd, Point Jefferson NY 11777..516-331-2537
Taxcalc Software Inc, 4210 W Vickery, Ft Worth TX 76107.........................817-738-3122
TCI Software, 6107 W Mill Rd, Flourtown PA 19031 215-836-1406
TCS Software Inc, 6100 Hillcroft Ste 600, Houston TX 77081 713-771-6000
Teach Yourself Comp Software, 2128 W Jefferson, Pittsford NY 14534....716-427-7065
The Teaching Assistant, 22 Seward Dr, Dix Hills NY 11746.......................516-499-8397
Techdata, 6615 La Mora, Houston TX 77083 713-498-0797
Techland Systems Inc, 25 Waterside Plaza, New York NY 10010...............212-684-7788
Technical Data Corp, 330 Congress St 6th fl, Boston MA 02210................617-482-3341
Technological Systems Group, 5044 Haley Ct, Lilburn GA 30247 404-923-4980
The Technology Press Inc, Box 380, Fairfax Station VA 22039...................703-978-5299
Tektronix Inc, PO Box 4600, Beaverton OR 97075......................................503-629-1723
Tele Vend Inc, 111 Croydon Rd, Baltimore MD 21212................................301-532-9079
Telexpress Inc, Box 217, Willingboro NJ 08046...609-877-4900
Terrapin Inc, 222 3rd St, Cambridge MA 02142...617-492-8816
Texas Instruments Inc, 13500 N Central Expwy, Dallas TX 75243 214-995-2011
Texas Systems Inc, 634 S Central Expwy, Richardson TX 75080................214-699-0262
Thoughtware Publishing Co, Box 669, Grants Pass OR 97526....................503-476-1467
Tiger Electronic Inc, 909 Orchard, Mundelein IL 60060.............................312-949-8100
Timeworks Inc, 444 Lake Cook Rd, Deerfield IL 60015 312-948-9200
TLB Inc, 267 Great Valley Pkwy, Malvern PA 19355 215-644-3344
TMQ Software Inc, 1110 Lake Cook Rd, Buffalo Grove IL 60090 312-520-4440
Transcontinental Health Data, 4912 Maplewood, Wichita Fls TX 76308..817-696-2586
Transend Corp, 1887 OToole Ave, San Jose CA 95131 408-435-0701
Trinity Solutions Inc, 5406 Thornwood, San Jose CA 95123......................408-226-0170
Tulsa Computer Consortium, Box 707, Owasso OK 74055.........................918-747-0151
2B Enterprises, 1252 Columbia Rd NW, Washington DC 20009.................202-234-2117
United Pro Com Systems, 1237 4th St Apt #6, St Paul Park MN 55071....612-459-8605
United Software Indus, 1880 Century Park E, Los Angeles CA 90067......213-556-2211
Univair Inc, 9024 St Charles Rock Rd, St Louis MO 63114..........................314-426-1099

US Robotics Inc, 8100 N McCormick, Skokie IL 60076 312-982-5010
User Friendly Software, 1625 S 21st Ave, Hollywood FL 33020..................305-949-8319
Valpar Intl Corp, PO Box 5767, Tucson AZ 85703......................................602-293-1510
The Vax Professional, 921 Bethlehem Pike, Springhouse PA 19477..........215-542-7008
Ventura Educational Systems, 3440 Brokenhill, Newbury Pk CA 91320...805-499-1407
Ventura Software, 1188 Padre Dr Ste 201, Salinas CA 93901.....................408-422-0500
J Vilkaitis Consultants, Box 26, Thomaston CT 06787................................203-283-4232
VIP Technologies, 132 Aero Comino, Santa Barbara CA 93117..................805-968-4364
Virtual Microsystems, 2150 Shattuck Ave #300, Berkeley CA 94704........415-841-9594
Roger Wagner Publishing, Box 582, Santee CA 92071................................619-562-3670
J Weston Walch Publisher, PO Box 658, Portland ME 04104......................207-772-2846
Wall Street Consulting Group Inc, 89 Milburn Ave, Milburn NJ 07041 ...201-762-6652
WB Ctr Self Directed Learning, Box 27616, San Francisco CA 94127.......415-334-3196
Wenger Corp, 555 Park Dr, Owatonna MN 55060......................................507-451-3010
John Wiley & Sons Inc, 605 3rd Ave, New York NY 10158.........................212-850-6540
Hamlin Williams & Assoc Inc, PO Box 34488, Memphis TN 38184 901-388-6120
The Winchendon Group Inc, PO Box 10339, Alexandria VA 22310...........703-960-2587
Winnebago Software Co, 115 W Main, Caledonia MN 55921......................507-724-5411
Winterhalter Inc, 3853 Research Pk Dr, Ann Arbor MI 48106....................313-662-2002
Wood & Clay Hi Tech Gameware, 3134 Orange St, San Jose CA 95127....408-258-5279
Woolf Software Systems Inc, 6754 Eton Ave, Conoga Park CA 91303......818-703-8112
WordPerfect Corp, 288 W Center St, Orem UT 84057 801-227-4000
Workbase Data Systems, Box 3448, Durham NC 27702.............................919-544-5408
Wrapped Up For Kids, 2811 N Thompson Ln, Murfreesboro TN 37130..615-890-5694
Wyman Assoc Inc, 181 2nd Ave Ste 321, San Mateo CA 94401....................415-345-0380
Xerox Corp, 1301 Ridgeview Dr, Lewisville TX 75067 214-436-2616
Xiox Corp, 1720 S Amphlett Blvd Ste 120, San Mateo CA 94402...............415-571-7911
XyQuest, PO Box 372, Bedford MA 01730...617-275-4439
Zephyr Services, 1900 Murray Ave, Pittsburgh PA 15217 412-422-6600
Zypcom, Box 3421, Boise ID 83702...208-345-2387

CONFERENCES & WORKSHOPS

This section lists writer's workshops, conferences, and seminars and sponsors of special programs for writers. See also Schools for other educational programs. For playwriting workshops, see Theatrical Workshops. Also see Associations, as many organizations sponsor conventions and special events for writers.

Ray Abel Productions, Short Dr, Port Chester NY 10573............................914-939-2818
About Books Self-Publishing Retreats, Box 538, Saguache CO 81149.......303-589-8223
Adult Inst in the Arts, PO Box 18154, Okla City OK 73154 405-842-0890
Advanced Freelance Writers, 17372 Evener, Eden Prairie MN 55344......612-934-7042
Akron Manuscript Club Annual, Box 510, Barberton OH 44203...............216-896-2138
Alabama Writers Conclave, 334 Felder Ave, Montgomery AL 36104........205-262-8024
Alaska Experience Travel Writing, 1120 Glacier, Juneau AK 99801..........907-586-3067
Amer Business Consultants, 1540 Nuthatch Ln, Sunnyvale CA 94087 408-738-3011
Amer River College, 4700 College Oak, Sacramento CA 95841..................916-484-8102
Amer Soc Journalists & Authors, 1501 Broadway, New York NY 10036 .212-997-0947
American Film Inst, 2021 N Western, Los Angeles CA 90027.....................213-856-7690
Anderson College Writers Conf, Special Prog, Anderson SC 29621...........803-231-2001
Antioch Writers Conf, 504 Phillips St, Yellow Springs OH 45387 513-767-7129

Appalachian Writers Wkshp, Box 844, Hindmanson KY 41822..................606-785-5475
Arizona Christian Writers Seminar, 648 S Pima, Mesa AZ 85202............602-962-6694
Arkansas Writers Conf, 1115 Gillette Dr, Little Rock AR 72207................501-225-0166
Art of Interviewing, Univ of Calif Ext, Santa Barbara CA 93106.................805-961-4200
Article Writing, Gordon Burgett PO Box 706, Carpenteria CA 93013.......805-684-2469
Arts & Humanities Council of Tulsa, 2210 S Main, Tulsa OK 74114........918-584-3146
Aspen Writers Conf, Drawer 7726 C, Aspen CO 81612.....................................303-925-3122
Astro Psychology Inst, 2640 Greenwich #403, San Francisco CA 94123...415-921-1192
Atlantic Ctr for Arts, 1414 Art Ctr Ave, New Smyrna Bch FL 32069.........904-427-6975
Austin Writers League Wkshps, 1501 W 5th St #108, Austin TX 78703...512-499-8914
Authors Resource Ctr, 4001 E Ft Lowell Rd, Tucson AZ 85712.................602-325-4733
Autumn Conf on Romance Writing, PO Box 684, Hammond IN 46320....312-862-9797
Avila College Writers Conf, 11901 Wornall, Kansas City MO 64145........816-942-8400
Bay Area Writers Conf, 1520 Grand Ave, San Rafael CA 94901...............415-457-4440
Bay de Noc Writers Conf, Bay de Noc College, Escanaba MI 49829.........906-786-5802
Before You Write That Book, PO Box 706, Carpenteria CA 93013............805-684-2469
Beginning Writers Conf, Forest Home, Forest Falls CA 92339..................714-794-1127
Bennington College Writing Wkshps, Bennington VT 05201.....................802-442-5401
Beyond Baroque Literary/Arts Ctr, 681 Venice, Venice CA 90291...........213-822-3006
Biola Univ Writers Inst, 13800 Biola Ave, La Mirada CA 90639................213-944-0351
Black Hills Writers Conf, 444 Lakeside Dr, Burbank CA 91505.................818-845-4500
The Black Think Tank, 1801 Bush St Ste 127, San Francisco CA 94109....415-474-1707
Black Writers Conf, PO Box 43576, Los Angeles CA 90043.........................415-532-6179
Blackhawk Technical Inst, 6004 Prairie Rd, Janesville WI 53545................608-756-4121
Blue Ridge Christian Writers Conf, Box 188, Black Mtn NC 28711...........704-669-8421
Blue Ridge Romance Writers Wkshp, Box 188, Black Mtn NC 28711.......704-669-8421
Book Publishing Weekend, Box 40500, Santa Barbara CA 93140.............805-968-7277
Book Writing, George Burgett PO Box 706, Carpinteria CA 93013...........805-684-2469
Boston Ctr for Adult Educ, 5 Commonwealth Ave, Boston MA 02116.....617-267-4430
Boulder River Wkshp, Box 1143, Big Timber MT 59011..............................406-932-5710
Brainerd College Writers Wkshp, College Dr, Brainerd MN 56401...........218-828-2503
Bread Loaf Writers Conf, Middlebury College, Middlebury VT 05753.....802-388-3711
Brockport Writers Forum, SUNY College, Brockport NY 14420................716-395-2503
Brooklyn Writers Club, PO Box 184, Brooklyn NY 11214...........................718-837-3484
Brun Press Inc, 701 N E 67th St, Miami FL 33138......................................305-756-6249
Bucknell Univ Seminar for Younger Poets, Lewisburg PA 17837.............717-524-1944
Butler Cty Community College, 901 S Haverhill, El Dorado KS 67042.....316-321-5083
Cabrillo Suspense Writers Conf, Box 851, Aptos CA 95001.......................408-462-6304
Cape Arts Workshops, Box 12, Cummaquid MA 02637.............................617-362-2686
Cape Cod Writers Conf, Box 111, West Hyannisport MA 02672................617-775-4811
Carter Caves State Resort Writers, Box 1098, Chautauqua NY 14722.....716-357-4411
Carter Caves Writers Wkshp, Capital Plz Twr, Frankfort KY 40601........502-564-3350
Cassell Communications, PO Box 9844, Ft Lauderdale FL 33310.............305-485-0795
Catholic Univ of Amer, Dept of English, Washington DC 20064................202-635-5488
Central Penn Writers Organization, Box 214, Bainbridge PA 17502.........717-426-3240
Chautauqua Inst Writers Wkshp, PO Box 1098, Chautauqua NY 14722..716-357-6234
Chesapeake Writers Conf, Rappahannock College, Gleens VA 23149.....804-758-5324
Children's Book Writing & Illus, 460 E 79th St, New York NY 10021.......212-744-3822
Children's Lit Writing Wkshp, Box 1158, Port Townsend WA 98368........206-385-3102
Chisholm Trail Writers Wkshp, Box 32927 TCU, Ft Worth TX 76129.....817-921-7134
Christian Writers Conf, 1775 Eden Rd, Lancaster PA 17601......................717-394-6758
Christian Writers Conf, 20800 Marine Dr NW, Stanwood WA 98292......206-652-7575
Christian Writers Conf, 388 E Gundersen Dr, Wheaton IL 60188............312-653-4200

Christian Writers Conf, Box 413, Mount Hermon CA 95041 408-335-4466
Christian Writers Conf, Marion College, Marion IN 46953.......................317-674-6901
Christian Writers Conf, Eastern College, St David's PA 19087...................215-384-8125
Christian Writers Wkshp, 6511 Currywood, Nashville TN 37205..............605-356-1197
Christian Writers Wkshp, Andrews Univ, Berrien Springs MI 49104.......616-471-3125
Christopher Newport College Writers Conf, Newport News VA 23606....804-599-7158
Clarion Sci-Fi-Fantasy Wkshp, MSU Briggs, E Lansing MI 48824 517-353-6480
Clinton Community College, 1000 Lincoln Blvd, Clinton IA 52732.............319-242-6841
College of Dupage, 22nd & Lambert Rd, Glen Ellyn IL 60137....................312-858-2800
Colo Mtn Writers Wkshp, 3000 Cty Rd 114, Glenwood Spgs CO 81601...303-945-7481
Communicating With Pictures, 212 S Chester, Swarthmore PA 19081 215-544-7977
Communication Unlimited, PO Box 706, Carpenteria CA 93013 805-684-2469
Communicom Publishing, 548 NE 43rd Ave, Portland OR 97213..............503-239-5141
Connecticut Writers League, 9 Hiram Ln, Bloomfield CT 06002...............203-242-9942
Conservatory of Amer Letters, PO Box 123, S Thomaston ME 04858.......207-354-6550
CCLM Literary Magazine Wkshp, 666 Broadway, New York NY 10012..212-614-6554
Cornell Univ Writers Program, B12L Ives Hall, Ithaca NY 14853.............607-256-4987
Copywriters Council of Amer, Middle Island NY 11953 516-924-8555
Craft of Fiction Conf, Napa Valley College, Napa CA 94558.....................707-253-1445
Creative Writing Conf, Eastern Kentucky Univ, Richmond KY 40475......606-622-5861
Creative Writing Day, PO Box 801, Abingdon VA 24210 703-628-3411
CRRT Seminar for Writers, 8116 St Lawrence, Chicago IL 60619............312-262-8100
Cummington Community of the Arts, Cummington MA 01026 413-634-2172
Cuyahoga Writers Conf, 4250 Richmond Rd, Cleveland OH 44122 216-987-2046
Deaf Playwrights' Conf, 5 W Main St, Chester CT 06412............................203-526-4971
Decision School of Christian Writing, Box 779, Minneapolis MN 55440..612-338-0500
Deep South Writers Conf, USL Box 44691, Lafayette LA 70504 318-231-6908
Denver Free Univ, PO Box 18455, Denver CO 80218 303-393-6706
District One Tech Inst, 620 W Clairemont Ave, Eau Claire WI 54701......715-833-6200
Dixie Council Authors & Jour, 2826 Evansdale Cir, Atlanta GA 30340....404-939-1924
Dorland Mountain Colony, PO Box 6, Temecula CA 92390......................714-676-5039
Duke University Writers Conf, The Bishop's House, Durham NC 27708..919-684-6259
Eastern Writers Conf, Salem State College, Salem MA 01870 617-745-0556
Edison Community College, Human Resources, Ft Myers FL 33907 813-489-9226
Editor's Desk Writers Conf, 709 SE 52nd Ave, Ocala FL 32761.................904-694-2303
Editorial Experts, 85 S Bragg St Ste 400, Alexandria VA 22312.................703-642-3040
Emory Univ Summer Writing Inst, Atlanta GA 30322 404-329-6048
Face to Face/The Folio Show, 6 River Bend, Stamford CT 06907..............203-358-9900
Feminist Women's Writing Wkshp, Box 456, Ithaca NY 14851 607-273-9040
Festival of Poetry, Robt Frost Place, Fanconia NH 03580 603-823-5510
Fiesta/Siesta Writers Conf, 1120-172 Pepper Dr, El Cajon CA 92021......619-449-0968
Fine Arts Work Ctr, 24 Pearl St, Provincetown MA 02657.........................617-487-9960
Flight of the Mind Wkshp, 622 SE 28th Ave, Portland OR 97214.............503-236-9862
Florida Intl Univ, Bay Vista Campus, N Miami FL 33181...........................305-940-5646
Florida State Writers Conf, PO Box 9844, Ft Lauderdale FL 33310..........305-485-0795
Florida Suncoast Writers Conf, Univ of S Florida, Tampa FL 33620........813-974-2421
Florida Writers Conf, 8320 Sands Point Blvd, Tamarac FL 33321 305-726-2555
Joan Follendore, 13376 Washington Blvd, W Los Angeles CA 90066........213-306-3986
Francis Marion College Writers Retreat, Florence RH 29501 803-661-1500
Free Will Baptist Writers Conf, Box 17306, Nashville TN 37217...............615-361-1221
From Pen to Paycheck, PO Box 292, Grand Canyon AZ 86023 602-638-2597
George Washington Univ, Journalism Dept, Washington DC 20052..........202-676-6225
Paul Gillette's Writing Wkshp, 6515 Sunset, Los Angeles CA 90028.........213-461-9437

Golden Rod Writers Conf, 525 Grove St, Morgantown WV 26505 304-296-7564
Great Lakes Writers Wkshp, 3401 S 39th St, Milwaukee WI 53215..........414-382-6181
Green Lake Christian Writers, Am Baptist Assy, Grn Lk WI 54941 414-294-3323
Greeting Cards Fillers & Humor, PO Box 706, Carpenteria CA 93013 805-684-2469
Hambidge Ctr for Creative Arts, Box 339, Rabun Gap GA 30568 404-746-5718
Hannibal Writers Seminar, La Grange College, Hanibal MO 63401 314-221-2462
Harvard Summer Writing Prog, 20 Garden St, Cambridge MA 02138 617-495-2921
Hauser Productions, 475 No Ferndale Rd, Wayzata MN 55391 612-473-1173
Haystack Program in the Arts, Box 1491 PSU, Portland OR 97207 503-464-4812
Hemingway Western Studies Ctr, Boise State Univ, Boise ID 83725.........208-385-1999
Highland Summer Conf, Box 5917 Radford Univ, Radford VA 24142......703-831-5366
Highlights for Children Wkshp, 803 Church St, Honesdale PA 18431......707-233-1080
Hofstra Univ Writers Conf, Memorial Hall 232, Hempstead NY 11550...516-560-5016
Holy City Zoo Comedy Writing, 408 Clement, San Francisco CA 94108...415-751-6725
Houston Community College, 1401 Alabama, Houston TX 77004 713-630-7287
Idaho Writers League, 423 N 11th St, Pocatello ID 83201.....................208-232-3038
Idyllwild School of Music & the Arts, Box 38, Idyllwild CA 92349........714-659-2171
Illinois Wesleyan Univ Writers Conf, Bloomington IL 61702 309-828-5092
Indian Hills Comm College, Grandview & Elm, Ottumwa IA 52501.........515-683-5111
Indian Univ Writers Conf, 464 Ballantine Hall, Bloomington IN 47405....812-335-1877
Inspirational Romance Writers Conf, Box 188, Black Mtn NC 28711.......704-669-8421
Intl Writers & Translaters Conf, 239 Wynsum Ave, Merrick NY 11566...516-868-5635
Interstate Religious Writers Assn, Box 453, Molville IA 51039.................712-873-3678
Intl Black Writers Conf, PO Box 1030, Chicago IL 60640 312-624-3184
Intl Poetry & Fiction Wkshps, 194 Soundview, Rocky Point NY 11778.....516-744-6160
Intl Technical Communication Conf, 815 15th St NW, Wash DC 20005...202-737-0035
Intl Women's Writing Guild, PO Box 810, New York NY 10028................212-737-7536
Investigations Institute, 53 W Jackson Blvd, Chicago IL 60604................312-939-6050
Investigative Reporters & Editors, PO Box 838, Columbia MO 65205 314-882-2042
Iowa Central Community College, 330 Ave M, Ft Dodge IA 50501.........515-576-7201
Irvine Writers Conf, Univ of CA Extension/Box AZ, Irvine CA 92716 714-856-5192
Johns Hopkins Univ, Summer Writing Conf, Baltimore MD 21218 301-338-8490
Johnson County Community College, Overland Park KS 66210................913-469-3836
Journal Writing, Box 98 Dillman's Lodge, Lac du Flambeau WI 54538....715-588-3143
Just Buffalo, 111 Elmwood Ave, Buffalo NY 14201................................716-885-6400
Katy Night Writers, PO Box 495, Katy TX 77492 713-391-9239
Keys to Professional Writing, 2214 Derby St, Berkeley CA 94705 415-841-1217
Kirkwood Community College, Cedar Rapids IA 52406 319-398-5692
Konglomerati Florida Foundation, Box 5001, Gulfport FL 33737 813-323-0386
L/A House Seminars, 5822 Uplander Way, Culver City CA 90230 213-216-5812
Letters Magazine, Box 905 RD1, Stonington ME 04681 207-367-2484
Life Skills Training Assoc, PO Box 48133, Chicago IL 60648 312-986-0070
Theotes Logos Research, 4318 York Ave S, Minneapolis MN 55410.........612-922-3202
Longboat Key Writers Conf, 5100 Rockhill Rd, Kansas City MO 64110...816-932-4499
Louisiana Writers Conf, Box 4633, Shreveport LA 71104 318-868-1750
Loyola Marymount Univ, English Dept, Los Angeles CA 90045 213-642-2854
Loyola Univ Writers Wkshp, 820 N Michigan Ave, Chicago IL 60611.......312-670-3014
The MacDowell Colony, 100 High St, Peterborough NH 03458 603-924-3886
Magazine Writers Wkshp, SFSU Journalism, San Francisco CA 94117....415-469-2094
Maine Photographic Workshops, 2 Central St, Rockport ME 04856 207-236-8581
Maine Writers Wkshp, Box 905 RD1, Stonington ME 04681.....................207-367-2484
Manhattan Fiction Writers Wkshp, 300 E 51st St, New York NY 10022..212-355-3723
Manhattanville College Writers Week, Purchase NY 10577 914-694-3425

Jim Mann & Assoc, 9 Mt Vernon Dr, Gales Ferry CT 06335 203-464-2511
Maple Woods Comm College, 2601 NE Barry, Kansas City MO 64156.....816-436-6500
Marantha Writers Seminar, 4759 Lake Harbor, Muskegon MI 49441......616-798-2161
Martha's Vineyard Writers Wkshp, Box 1125, Vinyrd Hvn MA 02568 617-693-6603
The Master Teacher, PO Box 1207, Manhattan KS 66502 913-539-0555
McKendree Writers Conf, 4 Fox Creek Rd, Belleville IL 62223 618-397-5388
Medical Writing Conf, UNY 708 Irving Ave, Syracuse NY 13210..............315-473-6560
Metro Community College, PO Box 3777, Omaha NE 68103 402-449-8400
Mich Northwoods Writers Conf, Leelanau Ctr, Glen Arbor MI 49636.....616-334-3072
Midland Writers Conf, 1710 W St Andrews Rd, Midland MI 48640..........517-835-7157
Midnight Sun Writers Conf, Univ of Alaska, Fairbanks AK 99775..........907-474-7800
Midwest Mystery Writers of Amer, PO Box 8, Techny IL 60082................312-588-4833
Midwest Writers Conf, KSU 6000 Frank Ave NW, Canton OH 44720......216-499-9600
Midwest Writers Conf, Univ of Wisc North Hall, River Falls WI 54022 ...715-425-3169
Midwest Writers Wkshp, Ball State Univ, Muncie IN 47306......................317-285-8200
The Millay Colony for the Arts, Steepletop, Austerlitz NY 12017.............518-392-3103
Minnesota Writers Conf, 1200 S Broadway, Rochester MN 55904............612-373-2851
Miss River Writing Wkshp, St Cloud Univ, St Cloud MN 56301 612-255-0121
Mississippi Valley Writers Conf, 3403 45th St, Moline IL 61265..............309-794-7000
Missouri Valley Writers Conf, 5216 Rockhill, Kansas City MO 64110......816-276-2558
Missouri Writers Guild Conf, Box 1069, Branson MO 65616....................417-546-4010
Monmouth Inst, Western Oregon College, Monmouth OR 97361..............503-838-1220
Montalvo Ctr for the Arts, PO Box 158, Saratoga CA 95071.....................408-867-3421
Moody Bible Inst, 820 N LaSalle Dr, Chicago IL 60610............................312-329-4030
Carolyn J Mullins, Virginia Tech Williams Hall, Blacksburg VA 24061...703-951-9711
Murder California Style, 4205 Franklin Ave, Burbank CA 91505 818-845-2051
Natl Entertainment Journalists, PO Box 24021, Nashville TN 37202........615-327-9419
Natl Poetry Foundation, 302 Neville Univ of Maine, Orano ME 04469 207-581-3814
Natl Soc of Newspaper Columnists, PO Box 6955, Louisville KY 40206...502-426-3943
Natl Writers Club Wkshp, 1450 S Havana Ste 620, Aurora CO 80012......303-751-7844
Nazarene Writers Conf, PO Box 419527, Kansas City MO 64141 816-931-1900
Nazarene Writers Conf, Box 527, Kansas City MO 64141 816-931-1900
New England Writers Conf, Simmons College, Boston MA 02115.............617-738-3131
New Jersey Romance Writers, PO Box 107, Hightstown NJ 08520.............609-387-1975
New Jersey Writers Conf, NJ Inst of Tech, Newark NJ 07102....................201-596-3441
New Poetry Wkshp, Napa Valley College, Napa CA 94558.......................707-253-1445
NY State Writers Inst, SUNY 1400 Washington, Albany NY 12222..........518-442-5620
Northeastern Univ, College of Arts & Sciences, Boston MA 02115............617-437-3980
Northern Waters Writers Conf, Univ of Wisc, Eau Claire WI 54701 715-836-2031
NWC Fall Cruise, 1450 S Havana #620, Aurora CO 80012 303-751-7844
NYU School of Cont Educ, 332 Shimkin Hall, New York NY 10038..........212-598-3091
Oakland Univ Writers Conf, Continuing Educ, Rochester MI 48309........313-370-3120
Ohio River Writers Conf, 16 1/2 SE 2nd St, Evansville IN 47708.............812-422-2111
Oklahoma Writers Federation, PO Box 96054, Weatherford OK 73096...405-772-2878
Omega Writing Workshops, RD 2 Box 377, Rhinebeck NY 12572............914-338-6030
Our Lady of the Lake Univ, 411 SW 24th St, San Antonio TX 78285 512-434-6711
Outdoor Writers Assn Conf, 2017 Cato #101, State College PA 16801....814-234-1011
OWAG Writers Showcase, Crowder College, Neosho MO 64850 417-451-4280
Ozark Creative Writers, 6817 Gingerbread, Little Rock AR 72204...........501-565-8889
Ozark Writers & Artists Guild, Crowder College, Neosho MO 64850 417-451-3226
Pacific Northwest Writers Conf, 1811 NE 199th, Seattle WA 98155..........206-364-1293
PAL Bookfair, PO Box 640394, San Francisco CA 94164..........................415-771-3431
Panhandle Pen Women, 129 N Beverly St, Amarillo TX 79106..................806-376-5111

Panhandle-Plains Writers Wkshp, 1900 W 7th St, Plainview TX 79072....806-396-5521
Paris-Amer Acad Writing Wkshp, Box 102 HC 01, Plainview TX 79072...806-889-3533
Pasadena Writers Forum, 1570 E Colorado Blvd, Pasadena CA 91106 818-578-7261
Pathway Press, 1080 Montgomery Ave, Cleveland TN 37311.......................615-476-4512
Patriotic Publishers, 159 Woodland Ave, Verona NJ 07044 201-239-7299
Pendle Hill Publications, 338 Plucsh Mill Rd, Wallingford PA 19086........215-566-4507
The Julie Penrose Ctr, 1661 Mesa Ave, Colorado Springs CO 80906 303-632-2451
Photopia Press, Box 1844, Corvallis OR 97339.......................................503-757-8761
Pikes Peak Christian Writers Seminar, Box 6000, Colo Spgs CO 80934 ..303-598-1212
Pittsburgh Theological Sem, 616 N Highland, Pittsburgh PA 15206..........412-362-5610
Plymouth State College, 3 Reed House, Plymouth NH 03264....................603-536-1550
Pope Writers Conf, Manhattanville College, Purchase NY 10577 914-694-2200
Port Townsend Writers Conf, Box 1158, Port Townsend WA 98368 206-385-3102
Posey International, PO Box 338, Orum UT 84057.....................................801-377-5504
Professional Writers League, 473 E 55th St #3, Long Beach CA 90805 ...213-423-0042
Professional Writers Wkshp, Univ of Okla, Norman OK 73037 405-325-5101
Psychological Dimensions, 10 W 66th St 4H, New York NY 10023 212-877-2313
Publishing Inst, Univ of Penn, Philadelphia PA 19104.............................215-898-6493
Ragdale Foundation, 1260 N Green Bay Rd, Lake Forest IL 60045 312-234-1063
Randall House Writers Conf, PO Box 17306, Nashville TN 37217.............615-361-1221
Mildred I Reid Writers Colony, Penacook Rd, Contoocook NH 03229 603-746-3625
Rhinelander School of Arts, Univ of Wisc, Madison WI 53703 608-263-3494
Rhode Island Creative Arts Ctr, Roger Wms College, Bristol RI 02809...401-255-2210
Rocky Mountain Book Conf, PO Box 1837, Santa Fe NM 87504.................505-983-7434
Romance Writers Conf, 5206 FM 1960 W #208, Houston TX 77069 713-440-6885
The Roundup, 156 W 300 N, American Fork UT 84003...............................801-756-2135
San Diego County Writers Guild, Box 1171, El Cajon CA 92022................619-748-0565
Sandhills Writers Wkshp & Conf, Augusta College, Augusta GA 30910..404-737-1636
Santa Barbara Writers Conf, PO Box 304, Carpenteria CA 93013.............805-684-2250
Santa Fe Writers Conf, 27 E Palace Dept C, Santa Fe NM 87501 505-982-9301
SCBW Rocky Mtn Humor Retreat, 1336 Clayton, Denver CO 80206........303-322-8325
SCBW Rocky Mtn Chapter, 178 Emerald St, Broomfield CO 80020.........303-466-1678
Scholarly Publications Wkshp, N Ariz Univ, Flagstaff AZ 86011 602-523-3559
School of Christian Writing, Forest Home, Forest Falls CA 92339............714-794-1127
Scott Community College, 500 Belmont St, Bettendorf IA 52722...............319-359-4141
Screenplay Enterprises, 270 N Canon #103, Beverly Hills CA 90210 213-273-6432
Screenwriting A to Z, Univ of Okla, Norman OK 73037 405-325-7378
Seacoast Writers Conf, RFD 1 Wadleigh Falls, Newmarket NH 03857 603-659-3393
Seattle Pacific Univ Christian Writers Conf, Seattle WA 98119 206-281-2089
Selling Your Writing, 11684 Ventura Blvd #807, Studio City CA 91604 ...818-789-9175
Sierra Writing Camp, 18293 Crystal St, Grass Valley CA 95949 916-272-8047
Sinclair Community College, 444 W 3rd St, Dayton OH 45402 513-226-2594
Sinipee Writers Wkshp, PO Box 902, Dubuque IA 52004 319-556-0366
Sitka Summer Writers Symposium, Box 1827, Sitka AK 99835 907-747-8808
Skyline Writers Conf, PO Box 33343, N Royalton OH 44133 216-237-6985
Soc for Southwestern Authors, PO Box 41897, Tucson AZ 85717 602-325-0529
Soc of Children's Book Writers, PO Box 296, Los Angeles CA 90066.......213-347-2849
Southampton Writers Conf, Long Island Univ, Southampton NY 11968..516-283-4000
Southeast Community College, Hwy 406, W Burlington IA 52655.............319-752-2731
Southeastern Writers Assn, 4021 Gladesworth Ln, Decatur GA 30035 404-288-2064
Southern Baptist Writers Wkshp, 127 9th Ave N, Nashville TN 37234.....615-251-2939
SW Christian Writers Assn, Box 2635, Farmington NM 87401 505-325-3240
Southwest Writers Conf, Univ of Houston, Houston TX 77004 713-749-7676

Southwest Writers Wkshp, PO Box 14632, Albuquerque NM 87191 505-296-3000
Split Rock Arts Program, 77 Pleasant St SE, Minneapolis MN 55455.......612-624-6800
Squaw Valley Community of Writers, Box 2352, Olympic Vly CA 95730..916-583-5200
State of Maine Writers Conf, Box 296, Ocean Park ME 04063 207-934-5034
Steamboat Spgs Arts Council, Box 771913, Steamboat Spgs CO 80477....303-879-4434
Stonecoast Writers Conf, Univ of Southern Maine, Portland ME 04103..207-780-4291
Suffolk Long Island Writers Conf, 194 Soundview, Rocky Pt NY 11778...516-744-6160
Summer Women's Writing Wkshp, 622 S E 28th, Portland OR 97214 506-236-9862
Summer Writers Workshops, Univ of Mass, Amherst MA 01003.............413-545-0475
Summer Writing Program, 2130 Arapahoe Ave, Boulder CO 80302.........303-444-0202
Sylvan Institute, 7104 N E Hazel Dell Ave, Vancouver WA 98665............206-694-0911
Technical Communication Conf, Univ of Mich, Ann Arbor MI 48109......313-764-1817
Technical Writers Inst, Rensselaer Polytechnic Inst, Troy NY 12181........518-266-6442
Texas Publishers Assn, 2315 Briarwood, San Antonio TX 78209 512-828-1605
Tidewater Writers Conf, 1415 Meads Rd, Norfolk VA 23505 804-423-3135
Touch of Success Photo Sem, PO Box 51532, Indianapolis IN 46251.........317-271-7423
Trenton State College Conf, Hillwood Lakes, Trenton NJ 08625 609-771-3254
Tucson Writers Conf, PO Box 27470, Tucson AZ 85726 602-791-4131
Mark Twain Sesquicentennial, Box 1985, Hannibal MO 63401................314-221-2462
UCLA Ext Writers Program, 10995 LaConte, Los Angeles CA 90024.......213-825-9415
UCSD Writers Conf, Univ Extension X-001, La Jolla CA 92093 619-452-3422
Unblocking Workshops, 24 Concord Ave, Cambridge MA 02138...............617-547-4434
Univ of Alabama Special Studies, Birmingham AL 35294....................205-934-7451
Univ of Alabama Writing Prog, Dept of English, University AL 35486.....205-348-5666
Univ of Bridgeport, 234A North Hall, Bridgeport CT 06601....................203-576-4292
Univ of Calif Berkeley Extension, 2223 Fulton St, Berkeley CA 94720......415-642-1061
Univ of Calif Davis Extension, Writing Workshops, Davis CA 95616........916-752-8253
Univ of Calif Riverside, Extension Ctr, Riverside CA 92521 714-787-4101
Univ of Chicago Publishing Prog, 5835 S Kimbark, Chicago IL 60637......312-702-1722
Univ of Hawaii at Monoa, Summer Writing Conf, Honolulu HI 96822.....808-948-7837
Univ of Iowa Summer Writing Program, Iowa City IA 52242................319-335-2534
Univ of Minn Conf Dept, 315 Pillsbury Dr SE, Minneapolis MN 55455....612-625-3369
Univ of Missouri Cont Educ, 8001 Natural Bridge, St Louis MO 63121...314-553-5961
Univ of North Dakota, English Dept, Grand Forks ND 58202....................701-777-3321
Univ of Okla Continuing Education, 1700 Asp Ave, Norman OK 73037..405-325-1921
Univ of Okla Program Development, 1700 Asp Ave, Norman OK 73037..405-325-5101
Univ of Penn Special Prog, 3808 Walnut, Philadelphia PA 19104.............215-898-6479
Univ of Rochester Writers Wkshp, Special Prog, Rochester NY 14627....716-275-2347
Univ of Texas Dallas, PO Box 830688, Richardson TX 75083..................214-690-2204
Univ of Toledo, Div of Continuing Education, Toledo OH 43606...............419-537-2031
Univ of Virginia Creative Writing, Box 801, Abingdon VA 24210..............703-628-6327
Univ of Wash Summer Writers Conf, UW G-21, Seattle WA 98195.........206-543-2300
Univ of Wisc Communication Programs, Madison WI 53703....................608-262-2368
Univ of Wisconsin Communications, 929 N 6th St, Milwaukee WI 53203 414-224-4186
Upper Midwest Writers Conf, Box 48, Bemidji MN 56601.....................218-755-2813
Urban Journalism, N Arizona Univ, Flagstaff AZ 86001.........................602-523-2232
UT Dallas Writers Conf, PO Box 830688, Richardson TX 75083 214-690-2204
Vassar Inst of Publishing & Writing, Box 300, Poughkeepsie NY 12601..914-452-7000
Villanove University, Villanova PA 19085 215-645-4618
Virginia Ctr for Creative Arts, Mt San Angelo, Sweet Briar VA 24595....804-946-7236
Waldron Enterprises, 371 Kings Hwy W, Haddonfield NJ 08033.............609-428-3742
Warner Pacific College, 2219 SE 68th Ave, Portland OR 97215 503-775-4366
Webster Univ Media Dept, 470 E Lockwood, St Louis MO 63119 314-968-6924

Weekend Retreats for Writers, 11 Mosswood Cir, Cazodew CA 95421.....707-632-5571
Wesleyan Writers Conf, Wesleyan University, Middletown CT 06457.......203-347-9411
W Mich Christian Writers Wkshp, 3000 Ivanrest, Grandville MI 49418...616-538-3470
Western Iowa Tech, Box 265, Sioux City IA 51102......................712-276-0380
Western Maryland Writers Wkshp, Frostburg State College MD 21532..301-689-4238
Western Montana College Writers Conf, Dillon MT 59725.........................406-683-7537
Western Wisconsin Tech Inst, 6th & Vine, La Crosse WI 54601.................608-785-9160
Westroots Business Writing, 3131 A Via Alicante, La Jolla CA 92037 619-450-9272
Wildbranch Writing Wkshp, Sterling College, Craftsbury VT 05827.........802-586-7711
Willamette Writers Conf, PO Box 2485, Portland OR 97208.......................503-233-1877
Women In Communications, PO Box 9561, Austin TX 78766 512-346-9875
Women Writers Conf, Univ of Kentucky, Lexington KY 40506 606-257-3295
Women's Voices Writing Conf, 1312 Addison St, Berkeley CA 94702........415-849-2126
Women's Writing Conf & Retreats, PO Box 810, New York NY 10028 212-737-7536
Workshop Under the Sky, 47 Hyde Blvd, Ballston Spa NY 12020..............518-885-7397
World Humor & Irony, Ariz State Univ, Tempe AZ 85287......................602-965-7592
World of Freelance Writing, 9409 Voss Rd, Marengo IL 60152 312-858-2800
Write Associates Conf, 328 Bramblewood, East Amherst NY 14051........716-689-7222
The Write Business, 769 B Hope St, Providence RI 02906...........................401-274-9330
Write to Be Read Wkshp, 260 Fern Ln, Hume CA 93628...........................209-335-2333
The Writers Center, 4800 Sangamore Rd, Bethesda MD 20816 301-229-0930
Writers at Work, PO Box 8857, Salt Lake City UT 84108 801-355-0264
Writers Connection, 1601 Saratoga Sunnyvale Rd, Cupertino CA 95014..408-973-0227
Writers in the Rockies, 1980 Glenwood Dr, Boulder CO 80302.................303-443-4636
Writers Key West Seminar, 700 Fleming St, Key West FL 33040...............305-745-3640
Writers of Children's Lit, Box 16355 Cameron Univ, Lawton OK 73505..405-248-2200
Writers Retreat, Box 275, Canadensis PA 18325.....................................717-595-2532
Writers Retreat, 404 Crestmont Ave, Hattiesburg MS 39401......................601-264-7034
Writers Retreat Wkshp, PO Box 139, S Lancaster MA 01561....................617-368-0287
Writers Workshop, 2969 Baseline Rd, Boulder CO 80303 303-444-4100
Writers Wkshp in Science Fiction, Univ of Kansas, Lawrence KS 66045..913-864-4520
Writers World of Fact & Fiction, 4245 Calder, Beaumont TX 77076........409-892-3078
Writers World Wkshp, Box 510, Barberton OH 44203 216-666-6673
Writers Workshop, 127 9th Ave N, Nashville TN 37234 615-251-2939
The Writers Wkshp, School Office Box 1098, Chautauqua NY 14722.......716-357-4411
The Writers Wkshp, 2969 Baseline Rd, Boulder CO 80303........................303-444-4100
Writers/Artists Retreat, Rt 1 Box 120, Hot Springs SD 57747...................605-745-4224
Writing for Children Wkshp, Drury College, Springfield MO 65802.........417-865-8731
Writing for Publication, Western Michigan Univ, Kalamazoo MI 49008..616-383-0795
Writing for Publication Seminar, PO Box 322, Fitchburg MA 01420........617-343-4645
Writing for Computer Indus, Mass Inst Tech, Cambridge MA 02139.......617-253-7894
A Writing Retreat, PO Box 9109, Santa Fe NM 87504 505-984-2268
Writing Retreat: River as Metaphor, Box 9109, Santa Fe NM 87504.........505-984-2268
Writing Wkshp for People Over 57, Univ of KY, Lexington KY 40506.....606-257-8314
Writing/Photo Seminar, 21671 Abedul, Mission Viejo CA 92691..............714-583-1074
Writing/Publising Romance Novel, 610 Langdon, Madison WI 53703......608-262-2368
Wyoming Writers, Box 802, Green River WY 82935 307-382-2121
Yale Summer Programs, 53 Wall St, New Haven CT 06520........................203-432-2430
Yellow Springs Inst, Box 340 RR 1, Chester Springs PA 19425.................215-827-9111
Young Authors Conf, 140 7th Ave S, St Petersburg FL 33701.....................813-893-9155

CONTESTS & AWARDS

This section lists writing contests and sponsors of writing awards and competitions. An asterisk (*) denotes a playwriting competition or theatrical contest.

A&C Limerick Contest, Amelia 329 E St, Bakersfield CA 93304 805-323-4064
AAP Education Research Awards, 220 E 23rd St, New York NY 10010 ...212-689-8920
AAUW North Carolina Div, 109 E Jones St, Raleigh NC 27611 919-733-7305
About Books Inc, PO Box 538, Saguache CO 81149 303-589-8223
Acad of Amer Poets Fellowship, 177 E 87th St, New York NY 10128........212-427-5665
ACE Charlotte's Repertory Theatre*, 127 E Trade, Charlotte NC 28202.704-375-4796
Actors Alley Rep Theatre*, 4334 Van Nuys, Sherman Oaks CA 91403......818-986-7440
Actors Repertory Theatre*, 303 E 44th St, New York NY 10017 212-687-6430
Actors Theatre of Louisville*, 316 W Main St, Louisville KY 40202..........502-584-1265
Maude Adams Comp*, Stephens College Theatre, Columbia MO 65201.314-876-7193
Jane Addams Peace Assn, 5477 Cedonia, Baltimore MD 21206 301-488-6987
Adriatic Award*, PO Box 1310, Miami FL 33153.......................................305-756-8513
AIM Magazine Story Contest, PO Box 20554, Chicago IL 60619.................312-874-6184
Alaska State Council on Arts, 619 Warehouse, Anchorage AK 99501.......907-279-1558
The Nelson Algren Award, 33 E Wacker Dr, Chicago IL 60601.................312-565-5000
Algren Award, 568 Broadway PEN Amer Ctr, New York NY 10012 212-334-1660
Amelia Awards for Poetry, 329 E St, Bakersfield CA 93304 805-323-4064
Amelia French Form Prizes, 329 E St, Bakersfield CA 93304......................805-323-4064
Amelia Photo Awards, 329 E St, Bakersfield CA 93304 805-323-4064
Amelia Short Short Fiction Awards, 329 E St, Bakersfield CA 93304.......805-323-4064
Amer Acad Inst Arts & Letters, 633 W 155th St, New York NY 10032.....212-368-5900
ABA Silver Gavel Awards, 750 N Lake Shore, Chicago IL 60611 312-988-6137
Amer Book Award, 1446 6th St Ste D, Berkeley CA 94710 415-527-1586
The Amer Book Awards, 220 E 23rd St, New York NY 10010 212-689-8920
Amer College Theater Festival*, Kennedy Ctr, Wash DC 20566.................202-254-3437
Amer Health Story Contest, 60 5th Ave, New York NY 10011 212-242-2460
Amer Inst of Physics, 335 E 45th St, New York NY 10017 212-661-9404
Amer Institute of Graphic Arts, 1059 Third Ave, New York NY 10021 212-752-0813
Amer Legion 4th Estate Award, 700 N Pennsylvania, Indpls IN 46204 317-635-8411
Amer Musical Theatre Festival*, Box I, Carmel CA 93921.......................408-625-9900
Amer Psychological Assn, 1200 17th St NW, Washington DC 20036.........202-955-7710
Amer Radio Theatre*, 1616 W Victory Blvd #104, Glendale CA 91201....213-857-8494
Amer Sociological Assn, 1722 N St NW, Washington DC 20036 202-833-3410
Amer Stage Directions*, 808 Post St Ste 715, San Francisco CA 94109.....415-851-3304
Amer Translators Assn, 109 Croton Ave, Ossining NY 10562.....................914-941-1500
Amer-Scandinavian Foundation, 127 E 73rd St, New York NY 10021.....212-879-9779
American Univ, Dept of Literature, Washington DC 20016 202-885-2971
Amy Writing Awards, PO Box 16091, Lansing MI 48901.............................517-323-3181
Hans Christian Andersen Prize, 800 Barksdale Rd, Newark DE 19714....302-731-1600
Apsey Playwriting Comp*, Univ of AL Theatre, Birmingham AL 35294 ..205-934-3236
Arizona Authors Assn, PO Box 10492, Phoenix AZ 85064............................602-948-2354
Art Museum Assn of Amer, 270 Sutter St, San Francisco CA 94108 415-392-9222
The Artists Foundation Inc, 110 Broad St, Boston MA 02110....................617-482-8100
Arts & Humanities Council of Tulsa, 2210 S Main, Tulsa OK 74114 918-584-3146
Arvon Foundation Intl Poetry, 50 Cross St, Winchesteron MA 01890.......617-721-1427

ASHA Natl Media Award, 10801 Rockville Pike, Rockville MD 20852......301-897-5700
ASJA Outstanding Author, 1501 Broadway, New York NY 10036............212-997-0947
Assn for Educ in Journalism, Loyola College, Baltimore MD 21210........301-323-1010
Athenaeum Literary Award, 219 S 6th St, Philadelphia PA 19106............215-925-2688
Avon/Flare YA Novel Comp, 105 Madison #814, New York NY 10016....212-481-5609
AWP Award Series, Old Dominion University, Norfolk VA 23508............804-440-3840
BACA Performing Showcase*, 111 Willoughby, Brooklyn NY 11201.........718-596-2222
Emily Clark Balch Prizes, 1 W Range, Charlottesville VA 22903............804-924-3124
Baltimore Playwright's Festival*, 2201 Brookhaven, Fallston MD 21047..301-597-4709
Bancroft Prizes, 202A Low Library, New York NY 10027.....................212-280-3810
Bandon Youth Theatre*, 820 1st St SE, Bandon OR 97411.....................503-347-9011
Banta Literary Award, 1922 University Ave, Madison WI 53705............608-231-1513
Susie Barker Playwrighting Prize*, 3504 Center St, Omaha NE 68105.....402-345-4852
Barn Theatre Playwriting Comp*, 281 W Clinton 31A, Dover NJ 07801..201-334-9320
Mildred L Batchelder Award, 50 E Huron St, Chicago IL 60611.................312-944-6780
Curtis Benjamin Award, 220 E 23rd St, New York NY 10010.....................212-689-8920
Bennett Award, 684 Park Ave, New York NY 10021.................................212-650-0020
Bensalem Assoc of Women Writers, Box 236, Croydon PA 19020..............215-244-0525
ASA Jessie Bernard Award, 1722 N St NW, Washington DC 20036...........202-833-3410
Beta Phi Mu Award, 50 E Huron St, Chicago IL 60611.............................312-944-6780
Beverly Hills Theatre Guild*, 2815 Beachwood, Los Angeles CA 90068...213-273-3033
Colonial Players*, 108 East St, Annapolis MD 21037...............................301-268-7373
Big Brothers/Sisters of Amer, 230 N 13th St, Philadelphia PA 19107.......215-567-7000
Irma Simonton Black Award, 610 W 112th St, New York NY 10025.........212-663-7200
Black Warrior Review Awards, Box 2936 UA, Tuscaloosa AL 35487........205-348-4518
Howard Blakeslee Award, 7320 Greenville, Dallas TX 75231.....................214-706-1340
Theodore C Blegen Award, 701 Vickers Ave, Durham NC 27701............919-682-9319
Oscar Blumenthal Prize, 601 S Morgan St Box 4348, Chicago IL 60680...312-996-7803
BMI Univ Musical Show Comp*, 320 W 57th St, New York NY 10019....212-586-2000
Elmer H Bobst Awards, 25 W 4th St, New York NY 10012.......................212-598-2458
Frederick Bock Prize, 601 S Morgan St Box 4348, Chicago IL 60680.........312-996-7803
Boston Globe Literary Press Comp, 135 Morrissey, Boston MA 02107....617-929-2000
Brandeis Creative Arts Awards, Gryzmish 201, Waltham MA 02254........617-736-4499
L W Brannan Mem Essay Contest, 6116 Timberly N, Mobile AL 36609..205-661-9114
Brooklyn Poetry Circle, 61 Pierrepont St, Brooklyn NY 11201.................718-875-8736
John Nicholas Brown Prize, 1430 Mass Ave, Cambridge MA 02138.........617-491-1622
Burroughs Medal, 15 W 77th St, New York NY 10024.............................212-873-1300
Bush Artist Fellowships, 1st Natl Bank Bldg E900, St Paul MN 55101.....612-227-0891
Witter Bynner Foundation for Poetry, Box 2188, Santa Fe NM 87504......505-988-3251
Randolph Caldecott Medal, 50 E Huron St, Chicago IL 60611..................312-944-6780
Calif Story Comp, Nob Hill Gazette Pier 5, San Francisco CA 94114.......415-788-3120
Calif Writers Club, 2214 Derby St, Berkeley CA 94705............................415-841-1217
Calif Book Medal Awards, 681 Market St, San Francisco CA 94105..........415-362-4903
Campion Award, 106 W 56th St, New York NY 10019.............................212-581-4640
Melville Cane Award, 15 Gramercy Park, New York NY 10003.................212-254-9628
Canterbury Press, 5540 Vista Del Amigo, Anaheim CA 92807..................714-637-1266
Carey-Thomas Award, 249 W 17th St, New York NY 10011.....................212-645-0067
Carter Award Lit Criticism, Box 722, Lexington VA 24450......................704-463-8765
Joel H Cavior Book Awards, 165 E 56th St, New York NY 10022..............212-751-4000
CCLM Grants, 2 Park Ave, New York NY 10016.....................................212-481-5245
CCLM Haider Mem Contest, 666 Broadway, New York NY 10012..........212-614-6551
CCT Playwriting Contest*, 8021 E 129th Ter, Grandview MO 64030.......816-761-5775
CEBA Award, 10 Columbus Cir, New York NY 10019.............................212-586-1771

Celtic Arts Center*, 5651 Hollywood Blvd, Hollywood CA 90028...............213-462-6844
Ctr for Children's Books, Univ of Chicago JRL 473, Chicago IL 60637....312-702-8284
Center Stage*, 3010 R St, Omaha NE 68107...402-444-6199
Chambers Intl Gay Playwriting*, 137 W 22nd St, New York NY 10011....212-942-8861
Chicago Book Clinic, 664 N Michigan Ave, Chicago IL 60611.....................312-951-8254
Children's Science Book Awards, 2 E 63rd St, New York NY 10021 212-838-0230
Christina Crawford Awards*, S Illinois Univ, Carbondale IL 62901 618-453-5741
The Christopher Awards, 12 E 48th St, New York NY 10017.....................212-759-4050
Clark New Playwright Contest*, Box 248273, Coral Gables FL 33124.......305-284-6439
Clauder Competition*, 551 Tremont St, Boston MA 02116 617-357-5667
Gertrude Claytor Mem Award, 15 Gramercy Pk, New York NY 10003....212-254-9628
Fred Cody Award, 901 Mission St, San Francisco CA 94119 415-777-7042
Colorado Council on the Arts, 770 Pennsylvania St, Denver CO 80203 303-866-2617
Columbia College*, 72 E 11th St, Chicago IL 60605 312-663-9462
Columbia/Embassy Award*, Kennedy Ctr ACTF, Wash DC 20566...........202-254-3437
Congregation Emu El*, 1500 Sunset Blvd, Houston TX 77005 713-529-5771
Conn Commission on the Arts, 190 Trumbull St, Hartford CT 06103.......203-566-4770
Conservatory of Amer Letters, PO Box 123, S Thomaston ME 04858.......207-354-6550
Copywriters Council of Amer, Middle Island NY 11953 516-924-8555
Cornerstone*, 270 N Kent St, St Paul MN 55102 612-224-4601
Council for Wisc Writers, PO Box 55322, Madison WI 53705 414-336-2424
Country Playhouse Comp*, Box 218124, Houston TX 77218....................713-467-4497
CSS Publications, PO Box 23, Iowa Falls IA 50126..................................515-648-2716
Dalton Little Theatre*, PO Box 841, Dalton GA 30722............................404-226-6618
Dartmouth Medal, 50 E Huron St, Chicago IL 60611 312-944-6780
David Library Award*, Kennedy Ctr, Washington DC 20566 202-254-3437
Gustav Davidson Award, 15 Gramercy Park, New York NY 10003..........212-254-9628
Mary Carolyn Davies Award, 15 Gramercy Park, New York NY 10003....212-254-9628
Dayton Playhouse*, 1301 E Siebenthaler, Dayton OH 45414....................513-222-7000
De La Torre Bueno Prize, 29 E 9th St, New York NY 10003 212-777-1594
Deep South Writers Contest, Box 4469 USL, Lafayette LA 70504.............318-231-6908
Delacorte Press Prize, 245 E 47th St, New York NY 10017.......................212-605-3000
Delaware State Arts Council, 820 N French St, Wilmington DE 19801.....302-571-3540
DeLong & Assoc Poetry Review, PO Box 1732, Annapolis MD 21404.......301-263-5592
Billee Murray Denny Poetry Award, Lincoln College, Lincoln IL 62656...217-732-3155
Denver Center Productions*, Box 8446, New Haven CT 06530..................303-893-4000
Devins Award for Poetry, 200 Lewis Hall, Columbia MO 65211................314-882-7641
Melvil Dewey Medal, 50 E Huron St, Chigago IL 60611.............................312-944-6780
Alice Fay Di Castagnola Award, 15 Gramercy Pk, New York NY 10003 ..212-254-9628
Emily Dickinson Award, 15 Gramercy Park, New York NY 10003.............212-254-9628
Disabled Experience Playwriting*, 339 11th St, Richmond CA 94801 415-234-5624
Discovery, 1395 Lexington Ave, New York NY 10128 212-427-6000
Dobie-Paisano Writing Fellowships, Univ of Texas, Austin TX 78712......512-471-7213
The Dog Ear Press, PO Box 143, S Harpswell ME 04079 207-729-7791
Dog Writer's Assn of Amer, Box 48, Manassas VA 22110.........................703-369-2384
John Dos Passos Prize, Longwood College, Farmville VA 23901 804-392-9371
Double Image Theatre*, 444 W 56th St, New York NY 10019 212-245-2489
Doubleday-Columbia Fellowship, 245 Park Ave, New York NY 10167.....212-984-7561
Dow Creativity Ctr, Northwood Inst, Midland MI 48640 517-832-4478
Drama Workshop*, 2710 Woodland, Des Moines IA 50312 515-244-8877
Druid Press Fiction Comp, 2724 Shades Crest, Birmingham AL 35216....205-967-6580
Drury College*, 900 N Benton Ave, Springfield MO 65802......................417-865-8731
Dubuque Fine Arts Players*, 1089 S Grandview, Dubuque IA 52001.......319-582-3034

Oscar Dystel Fellowship, 715 Broadway NYU, New York NY 10003........212-998-7370
Eaton Literary Assoc Awards, PO Box 49795, Sarasota FL 34230 813-355-4561
Editors Book Award, Box 380, Wainscott NY 11975 516-324-9300
Educator's Award, Box 1589, Austin TX 78767 512-478-5748
T S Eliot Award for Creative Writing, 934 N Main, Rockford IL 61103....815-964-3242
Elliott Prize, 1430 Massachusetts Ave, Cambridge MA 02138 617-491-1622
Elmira College Theatre*, Elmira NY 14901...607-734-3911
Ralph Waldo Emerson Award, 1811 Q St NW, Washington DC 20009.....202-265-3808
Euclid Little Theatre*, 291 E 222nd St, Euclid OH 44123..........................216-261-6399
Eve of St Agnes Poetry Comp, 6116 Timberly Rd N, Mobile AL 36609.....205-661-9114
Faulkner Award, 568 Broadway PEN Amer Ctr, New York NY 10012.....212-334-1660
Feat Playwriting Festival*, 37 E 9th St, Indianapolis IN 46204...................317-635-7529
Ferndale Repertory Theatre*, PO Box 892, Ferndale CA 95536................707-725-2378
Festival of Firsts Playwriting Comp*, Box 5066, Carmel CA 93921..........408-624-3996
Festival of New Works*, 900 Camp, New Orleans LA 70130 504-523-1216
Festival of Southern Theatre*, Univ of Miss, University MS 38677...........601-232-5816
Festival Theatre of Biography*, 600 W 58th St, New York NY 10019.......212-874-6147
Fiction Network, PO Box 5651, San Francisco CA 94101............................415-391-6610
Fine Arts Work Center, Box 565, Provincetown MA 02657........................617-487-9960
Robt L Fish Award MWA, 150 5th Ave, New York NY 10011......................212-255-7005
Dorothy C Fisher Children's Book, 138 Main St, Montpelier VT 05605 ...802-658-0238
Florida Dept of State, Div of Cultural Affairs, Tallahassee FL 32399........904-488-3976
Florida Intl Univ*, Theatre Dept Tamiami Campus, Miami FL 33199 305-554-2895
Florida State Writing Comp, PO Box 9844, Ft Lauderdale FL 33310 305-485-0795
Fonda Young Playwrights Project*, Kennedy Ctr, Wash DC 20566...........202-662-8899
Consuelo Ford Award, 15 Gramercy Park, New York NY 10003 212-254-9628
Forest History Soc Book Award, 701 Vickers Ave, Durham NC 27701.....919-682-9319
Foster City Comm for the Arts, 650 Shell Blvd, Foster City CA 94404......415-341-8051
Free Press Assn, PO Box 15548, Columbus OH 43215 614-236-1908
Geo Freedley Mem Award, 111 Amsterdam Ave, New York NY 10023 212-870-1670
SCBW Don Freeman Mem Award, PO Box 296, Los Angeles CA 90066..218-347-2849
Friends of Amer Writers Awards, 5901 Sheridan Rd, Chicago IL 60660...312-275-6666
FS Drama Award*, PO Box 5187, Bloomington IN 47402 812-334-0325
Christian Gauss Award, 1811 Q St NW, Washington DC 20009 202-265-3808
General Electric Foundation Award, 2 Park Ave, New York NY 10016 ...212-481-5245
Gold Medallion Book Awards, Box 2439, Vista CA 92083..........................619-941-1636
Gold Medals, AAIAL 633 W 155th St, New York NY 10032 212-368-5900
Golden Kite Awards, PO Box 296, Los Angeles CA 90066 818-347-2849
Goodhart Prize for Fiction, Shenandoah Box 722, Lexington VA 24450...703-463-8765
Goshen College Peace Play Contest*, 1700 S Main, Goshen IN 46526 217-533-3161
Great Alaskan Playrush*, 914 3rd St, Douglas AK 99824............................907-364-2421
Great American Play Contest*, 316 W Main St, Louisville KY 40202 502-584-1265
Great Lakes Colleges Assn, Albion College, Albion MI 49224 517-629-5511
John R Gregg Award, 1221 Ave of Americas, New York NY 10020...........212-997-2166
Grolier Foundation Award, 50 E Huron St, Chicago IL 60611 312-944-6780
Group Repertory Theatre*, 10900 Burbank, N Hollywood CA 91601 213-760-9368
Gulf Coast Play Comp*, 1000 College Blvd, Penascola FL 32504 904-476-5410
Sarah Josepha Hale Award, 58 N Main St, Newport NH 03773.................603-863-3430
Harian Creative Awards, 47 Hyde Blvd, Ballston Spa NY 12020...............518-885-6699
Haskins Medal Award, 1430 Massachusetts Ave, Cambridge MA 02138..617-491-1622
Haslam Intl Scholarship, 137 W 25th St, New York NY 10001...................212-463-8450
R R Hawkins Award, 220 E 23rd St, New York NY 10010 212-689-8920
Drue Heinz Lit Prize, Univ of Pittsburgh Press, Pittsburgh PA 15260.......412-624-4110

Hemingway Days Festival, Box 4045, Key West FL 33041 305-294-4440
Hemingway Found Award, 568 Broadway PEN, New York NY 10012 212-334-1660
Cecil Hemley Mem Award, 15 Gramercy Park, New York NY 10003 212-254-9628
Daniel Whitehead Hicky Award, 1399 Vista Leaf, Decatur GA 30033.......404-636-1316
Sidney Hillman Foundation Inc, 15 Union Sq, New York NY 10003 212-242-0700
Bess Hokin Prize, 601 S Morgan St Box 4348, Chicago IL 60680.................312-996-7803
Horn Book Awards, The Boston Globe, Boston MA 02107............................617-929-2000
Houghton Mifflin Literary Fellowship, 2 Park St, Boston MA 02108 617-725-5923
Darrell Bob Houston Price, 1931 2nd Ave, Seattle WA 98101 206-441-6239
Hugo Awards, Box 8442, Van Nuys CA 91409 213-559-1622
Humanist Magazine, 7 Harwood Dr, Amherst NY 14226 716-839-5080
Humbolt State Univ*, Theatre Arts Dept, Arcata CA 95521 707-826-3566
Idaho Comm on the Arts, 304 W State, Boise ID 83720 208-334-2119
Illinois Arts Council, 100 Randolph Ste 10-500, Chicago IL 60601 312-917-6750
Illinois Playwriting Comp*, W Illinois Univ, Macomb IL 61455 309-298-1543
Illinois State Univ*, Fine Arts Playwriting Contest, Normal IL 61761.......309-438-8783
Individual Artists Fellowship, 312 Wickenden, Providence RI 02903........401-277-3880
Ingersoll Foundation, 934 N Main St, Rockford IL 61103............................815-964-3242
Jamestown Prize, Box 220, Williamsburg VA 23187....................................804-229-2771
Imitation Hemingway Comp, 2020 Ave of Stars, Los Angeles CA 90067 ..213-277-2333
Integrated Young Playwrights Proj, Kennedy Ctr, Wash DC 20566 202-332-6960
Intl Literary Awards, 408 E Main St, Dayton WA 99328..............................509-382-2436
Intl Reading Assn, 800 Barksdale Rd, Newark DE 19714.............................302-731-1600
Intl Society of Dramatists*, PO Box 1310, Miami FL 33513 305-756-8313
Iowa Arts Council, State Capitol Complex, Des Moines IA 50319 515-281-4451
Ironbound Theatre*, 179 Van Buren, Newark NJ 07105 201-792-3524
IUPUI Children's Theatre*, 525 N Blackford St, Indianapolis IN 46202...317-274-2095
J H Jackson Award, 500 Washington St 8th fl, San Francisco CA 94111...415-392-0600
Jacksonville Univ*, College of Fine Arts, Jacksonville FL 32211.................904-744-3950
Jane Addams Peace Assn Award, 5477 Cedonia, Baltimore MD 21206 301-488-6987
Japan Foundation, 342 Madison #1702, New York NY 10173....................212-949-6360
Japan Soc Friendship Fund*, 333 E 47th St, New York NY 10017 212-832-1155
JCC Theatre*, 3505 Mayfield Rd, Cleveland OH 44118................................216-382-4000
Jewish Book Council, 15 E 26th St, New York NY 10010.............................212-532-4949
Anson Jones Award, TMA 1801 N Lamar, Austin TX 78701 512-477-6704
The Chester H Jones Foundation, PO Box 498, Chardon OH 44024.........216-286-6310
Margo Jones Playwriting Comp*, PO Box 23865, Denton TX 76204 817-383-3586
Juniper Prize for Poetry, Univ of Mass, Amherst MA 01003......................413-545-2217
Kanin Playwriting Awards*, Kennedy Ctr ACTF, Wash DC 20566...........202-254-3437
Kansas Quarterly Seaton Awards, KSU, Manhattan KS 66505....................913-532-6716
Kempsville Playhouse*, 800 Monmouth Ln, Virgina Bch VA 23464..........804-495-1892
Robt F Kennedy Book Awards, 1031 31st St NW, Wash DC 20007 202-333-1880
Geo Kernodle Playwriting Comp*, Univ of Ark, Fayetteville AR 72701 ...501-575-2953
Roger Klein Editing Award, 568 Broadway PEN, New York NY 10012....212-334-1660
Marc A Klein Award*, CWRU Theatre Dept, Cleveland OH 44106 216-368-2858
KTCA TV Drama Series Comp*, 1640 Como Ave, St Paul MN 55108......612-646-4611
La Pensee Discovery Theater*, 511 N 179th Pl, Seattle WA 98133.............206-542-8648
Ruth Lake Memorial Award, 15 Gramercy Park, New York NY 10003 212-254-9628
Lamont Poetry Selection, 177 E 87th St, New York NY 10128 212-427-5665
Landon Translation Award*, 177 E 87th St, New York NY 10128 212-427-5665
D H Lawrence Fellowship, Univ of NM, Albuquerque NM 87131...............505-277-6347
Laymen's Natl Bible Committee, 815 2nd Ave, New York NY 10017 212-687-0555
Levinson Prize, 601 S Morgan St Box 4348, Chicago IL 60680....................312-996-7803

Libertarian Futurist Soc, 68 Gebhardt Rd, Penfield NY 10027.................716-288-6137
Lieberman Poetry Award, 15 Gramercy Pk, New York NY 10003 212-254-9628
Light & Life Writing Contest, 901 College Ave, Winona Lake IN 46590 ..219-267-7656
Linden Lane Magazine, Box 2384, Princeton NJ 08543...............................609-924-1413
Joseph W Lippincott Award, 50 E Huron St, Chicago IL 60611 312-944-6780
Little Nashville Playwriting Award*, PO Box 606, Nashville IN 47448......812-334-0325
Little Theatre of Alexandria*, 600 Wolfe St, Alexandria VA 22314............703-683-5778
Lockert Library of Poetry in Trans, 41 William, Princeton NJ 08540........609-452-4900
The Loft Writers Awards, 2301 E Franklin, Minneapolis MN 55406 612-341-0431
Lone Wolf Productions*, 120 W 28th St, New York NY 10001....................212-807-1590
Lorien House, PO Box 1112, Black Mountain NC 28711 704-669-6211
Lorraine Hansberry Award*, Kennedy Ctr ACTF, Wash DC 20566 202-254-3437
LA Times Book Prizes, Times Mirror Sq, Los Angeles CA 90053...............213-972-5000
Louisiana Literary Award, Box 131, Baton Rouge LA 70821.....................504-342-4928
Louisville Experimental Theatre*, 1601 Bernheim, Louisville KY 40210..502-637-8843
James Russell Lowell Prize, MLA 10 Astor Place, New York NY 10003..212-614-6314
The Lyric, 307 Dunton Dr SW, Blacksburg VA 24060...................................703-552-3475
Mac-Haydn Theatre New Works*, PO Box 204, Chatham NY 12037........518-392-9292
MacArthur Fellowships, 140 S Dearborn St Ste 700, Chicago IL 60603 312-726-8000
Edward MacDowell Medal, 100 High St, Peterborough NH 03458 603-924-3886
Mademoiselle Fiction Comp, 350 Madison Ave, New York NY 10017......212-880-8690
Margaret Mann Citation, 50 E Huron St, Chicago IL 60611 312-944-6780
Marilyn Steinbright Award*, 39 Conestoga Rd, Malvern PA 19355 215-647-1900
Marshall Musical Theatre Award*, Univ of Mich, Ann Arbor MI 48109.313-763-5213
Lenore Marshall Prize for Poetry, 72 5th Ave, New York NY 10011 212-242-8400
Maryland State Arts Council, 15 W Mulberry St, Baltimore MD 21201...301-685-6740
John Masefield Mem Award, 15 Gramercy Park, New York NY 10003 212-254-9628
Geo Mason Univ, English Dept, Fairfax VA 22030................................703-323-1055
Mayflower Society Award, 109 E Jones St, Raleigh NC 27611 919-733-7305
McClure 1-Act Play Award*, Amelia 329 E St, Bakersfield CA 93304.......805-323-4064
Mary McNulty Award, 220 E 23rd St, New York NY 10010......................212-689-8920
Lucille Medwick Mem Award, 15 Gramercy Pk, New York NY 10003......212-254-9628
Melcher Book Award UUA, 25 Beacon St, Boston MA 02108.....................617-742-2100
Mercury Awards Larimi Comm, 5 W 37th St, New York NY 10018..........212-819-9310
Meridian Theatre Group*, 137 W 22nd St, New York NY 10011................212-942-8861
Michigan Council on the Arts, 1200 Sixth St, Detroit MI 48226................313-256-3719
Michigan Foundation for the Arts, 1703 Fisher Bldg, Detroit MI 48202 ..313-871-0559
Mid-South Playwrights Comp*, 51 S Cooper, Memphis TN 38104............901-725-0776
Midwest Poetry Review, PO Box 776, Rock Island IL 61201.....................319-391-1874
Midwest Writers Conf, KSU 6000 Frank Ave NW, Canton OH 44720......216-499-9600
Mildenberger Medal, MLA 10 Astor Pl, New York NY 10003 212-614-6314
Mill Mountain Theatre*, 1 Market Sq, Roanoke VA 24011.......................703-342-5730
Milner Award, 1 Margaret Mitchell Sq NW, Atlanta GA 30303 404-688-4034
Minn State Arts Board Awards, 432 Summit Ave, St Paul MN 55102.......612-297-2603
Miss Historical Soc McLemore Prize, Box 571, Jackson MS 39205..........601-359-1424
Missouri Arts Council, 111 N 7th St Ste 105, St Louis MO 63101...............314-444-6845
Mixed Blood vs America*, 1501 S 4th St, Minneapolis MN 55454.............612-338-0937
Modern Language Assn (MLA), 10 Astor Pl, New York NY 10003............212-614-6314
Modern Poetry Assn, 60 W Walton, Chicago IL 60610 312-413-2210
James Mooney Award, Univ of NC, Greensboro NC 27412 919-379-5132
Morse Poetry Prize, Northeastern Univ, Boston MA 02115 617-437-2512
Mott-KTA Research Award, 107 Sondra, Columbia MO 65202..................314-443-3521
Natl Book Critics Cir Awards, 756 S 10th St, Philadelphia PA 19147........215-925-8406

Natl Cartoonists Soc Reuben Award, 9 Ebony Ct, Brooklyn NY 11229 718-743-6510
Natl Endowment for the Arts, 1100 Penn Ave NW, Wash DC 20506.........202-682-5451
Natl Historical Soc, 2245 Kohn Rd Box 8200, Harrisburg PA 17105.........717-657-9555
Natl Inst for Music Theater*, Kennedy Ctr, Washington DC 20566.........202-965-2800
Natl Marine Mfrs Assn, 353 Lexington, New York NY 10016.................212-684-6622
Natl Playwrights Showcase*, 501 E 38th St, Erie PA 16546 814-825-0200
Natl Poetry Foundation, 302 Neville Univ of Maine, Orano ME 04469 207-581-3814
Natl Poetry Series, 26 W 17th St, New York NY 10001.............................212-685-2214
Natl Rep Theatre Foundation*, PO Box 71011, Los Angeles CA 90071 ...213-629-3762
Natl Scholarship Research Service, 122 Alto St, San Rafael CA 94901 415-456-1577
Natl Scholarship Research Service, PO Box 2516, San Rafael CA 94912.415-456-1577
Natl Soc of Prof Engineers, 1420 King St, Alexandria VA 22314.................703-684-2852
Natl Writers Club, 1450 S Havana #620, Aurora CO 80012......................303-751-7844
Nebraska Review Awards, Univ of Neb ASH 212, Omaha NE 68182........402-554-2700
Nebula Awards SFWA, Box 27, Hatfield MA 01038 413-247-5016
Negative Capability Press, 6116 Timberly Rd N, Mobile AL 36609...........205-661-9114
The Pablo Neruda Prize, 2210 S Main, Tulsa OK 74114..............................918-584-3333
Nevada Project Grants, 329 Flint St, Reno NV 89501................................702-784-6231
Allan Nevins Prize, 610 Fayerweather Hall, New York NY 10027...............212-280-2555
New England Review, Middlebury College, Middlebury VT 05753.............802-388-3711
New England Theatre Conf*, 50 Exchange St, Waltham MA 02154...........617-893-3120
New Jersey Inst of Tech, Poetry Contest, Newark NJ 07102.....................201-596-3441
NJ State Council on the Arts, 109 W State St, Trenton NJ 08625 609-292-6130
New Voice Award, 485 Lexington Ave, New York NY 10017......................212-867-4300
New World Theatre*, 7600 Red Rd #212, South Miami FL 33143.............305-663-0223
NY Foundation for the Arts, 5 Beekman St #600, New York NY 10038 ..212-233-3900
New York State Historical Assn, PO Box 800, Cooperstown NY 13326....607-547-2508
John Newbery Medal, 50 E Huron St, Chicago IL 60611 312-944-6780
NHS Book Prize in Amer History, 2245 Kohn, Harrisburg PA 17105........717-657-9555
No Empty Space Theatre*, PO Box 422, Staten Island NY 10310 718-720-6378
Nook News Short Fiction Contest, 10957 Chardon, Chardon OH 44024...216-285-0942
N Amer Mentor Magazine Poetry, 1745 Madison, Fennimore WI 53809 ..608-822-6237
North Dakota Council on the Arts, Black Bldg #606, Fargo ND 58102....701-237-8962
Northern Kentucky Univ*, Dept of Theatre, Highland Hts KY 41076 606-572-5560
NWC Book Contest, 1450 S Havana #620, Aurora CO 80012......................303-751-7844
O'Connor Short Fiction Award, Univ of Ga Press, Athens GA 30606.......404-542-2830
Ohio Arts Council Grants, 727 E Main St, Columbus OH 43205...............614-466-2613
Ohioana Book Awards, 65 S Front St, Columbus OH 43266......................614-466-3831
Ommation Press Book Contest, 5548 N Sawyer, Chicago IL 60625 312-539-5745
Open Book Awards, 1507 Broadway Rm 1907, New York NY 10036...........212-997-0947
Open Circle Theatre*, Goucher College, Towson MD 21204 301-337-6275
Oregon Arts Commission, 835 Summer St NE, Salem OR 97301..............503-378-3625
Stuart Ostrow Foundation*, Box 188, Pound Ridge NY 10576 914-764-4412
Pacific NW Young Readers, 133 Suzzallo Library, Seattle WA 98195........206-543-1794
Paris Review, 541 E 72nd St, New York NY 10021.....................................718-539-7085
Francis Parkman Prize, 610 Fayerweather Hall, New York NY 10027.....212-280-2555
Alicia Patterson Foundation, 655 15th St NW, Washington DC 20005......202-639-4203
PEN American Center, 568 Broadway, New York NY 10012......................212-334-1660
PEN Medal for Translation, 568 Broadway, New York NY 10012.............212-334-1660
PEN Publisher Citation, 568 Broadway, New York NY 10012 212-334-1660
PEN Syndicated Fiction Project, Box 6303, Washington DC 20015...........301-656-7484
PEN Award for Prisoners, 568 Broadway, New York NY 10012................212-334-1660
Penn Council on Arts & Lit, Finance Bldg #216, Harrisburg PA 17120 ...717-787-6883

Perkins Playwriting Contest*, PO Box 1310, Miami FL 33153.................305-756-8313
Jas D Phelan Award, 500 Washington 8th fl, San Francisco CA 94111......415-392-0600
Phi Betta Kappa, 1811 Q St NW, Washington DC 20009 202-265-3808
Playboy College Fiction Contest, 919 N Michigan, Chicago IL 60611........312-751-8000
Playwright's Forum Awards*, PO Box 7150, Colo Spgs CO 80933.............303-593-3232
Edgar Allan Poe Awards, 150 5th Ave, New York NY 10011......................212-255-7005
Poetry Center Book Award, 1600 Holloway, San Francisco CA 94132.......415-338-2227
Poetry Ctr of 92nd St Y, 1395 Lexington, New York NY 10128.................212-427-6000
Poetry Magazine Awards, 60 W Walton, Chicago IL 60610.........................312-413-2210
Poetry Series Award, Princeton Univ Press, Princeton NJ 08540................609-452-4883
Renato Poggioli Award, 568 Broadway PEN, New York NY 10012..........212-334-1660
Geo Polk Awards, Brooklyn Campus Univ Plaza, Brooklyn NY 11201......718-403-1050
Katherine Anne Porter Prize, 2210 S Main, Tulsa OK 74114....................918-584-3333
Portland New Plays In Progress*, PO Box 751, Portland OR 97207 503-229-4612
Princeton Univ Press, 41 William St, Princeton NJ 08540..........................609-452-4900
Prize Stories: O Henry Awards, 245 Park Ave, New York NY 10017........212-953-4561
Project Censored, Sonoma State Univ, Rohnert Park CA 94928..................707-664-2149
Publishers Awards, 901 Mission St, San Francisco CA 94109 415-777-7043
Publishing Hall of Fame, 125 Elm St, New Canaan·CT 06840.....................203-972-3818
Pulitzer Prizes, Columbia Univ Journalism Bldg, New York NY 10027....212-280-3841
Pushcart Prize, PO Box 380, Wainscott NY 11975 516-324-9300
Sir Walter Raleigh Award, 109 E Jones St, Raleigh NC 27611 919-733-7305
Rambunctious Review, 1221 W Pratt Blvd, Chicago IL 60626.....................312-973-3529
Redbook's Story Contest, 224 W 57th St, New York NY 10019 212-262-8284
Regina Medal Award, 461 W Lancaster Ave, Haverford PA 19041..............215-649-5250
Rhyme Time Writing Comp, Box 2377, Coeur d'Alene ID 83814 208-667-7511
Roanoke-Chowan Award, 109 E Jones St, Raleigh NC 27611......................919-733-7305
Roberts/Shiras Inst Award*, N Mich Univ, Marquette MI 49855.............906-227-2553
Rodgers Production Award*, 633 W 155th St, New York NY 10032.........212-368-5900
Romance Writers Awards, 5206 FM 1960 W #208, Houston TX 77069....713-440-6885
Cornelius Ryan Award, 52 E 41st St, New York NY 10017........................212-679-9650
San Francisco Foundation, 500 Washington 8th fl, San Fran CA 94111 ...415-392-0600
Carl Sandburg Awards, 78 E Washington St, Chicago IL 60602.................312-269-2922
SCBW Work-In-Progress Grants, PO Box 296, Los Angeles CA 90066 ...818-347-2849
Scholastic Writing Awards*, 730 Broadway, New York NY 10003...........212-505-3000
Henry Schuman Prize, 215 S 34th St, Philadelphia PA 19104....................215-898-4896
Science Award, 1811 Q St NW, Washington DC 20009.............................202-265-3808
Scripps Howard Foundation, PO Box 5380, Cincinnati OH 45201 513-977-3036
Sequoyah Children's Book Award, 2500 Lincoln, Okla City OK 73105......405-521-2956
Sergel Drama Prize*, 5706 S University Ave, Chicago IL 60637.................312-753-4484
Seventeen Magazine, 850 3rd Ave, New York NY 10022............................212-759-8100
Mina P Shaughnessy Medal, MLA 10 Astor Pl, New York NY 10003......212-614-6314
Shelley Memorial Award, 15 Gramercy Park, New York NY 10003 212-254-9628
Signpost Press, 412 N State St, Bellingham WA 98225..............................206-734-9781
Fannie Simon Award, 1700 18th St, Washington DC 20009........................202-234-4700
Sitka Playwriting Comp*, PO Box 2882, Sitka AK 99835 907-747-6234
Smith Prize for Sonnets, Amelia 329 E St, Bakersfield CA 93304.............805-323-4064
Soc of Midland Authors Drama*, 851 Warrington, Deerfield IL 60015....312-945-6351
Source Theatre Co Playwriting*, 1809 14th St NW, Wash DC 20009 202-462-7782
South Carolina Arts Comm, 1800 Gervais St, Columbia SC 29201............803-734-8696
S Coast Poetry Jour Contest, CSUF English Dept, Fullerton CA 92634 ..714-773-2454
Southern Illinois Univ*, Theatre Dept, Carbondale IL 62901 618-453-5741
Southwest Review, 6410 Airline Rd, Dallas TX 75275 214-373-7440

Southwest Theatre Assn*, Univ Of Oklahoma, Norman OK 73019 405-325-4021
Bryant Spann Mem Prize, ISU History Dept, Terre Haute IN 47809........812-237-2121
Stanley Drama Award*, 631 Howard Ave, Staten Island NY 10301...........718-390-3256
Sydney Taylor Book Awards, 137 W 25th St, New York NY 10001.............212-463-8450
Marvin Taylor Playwriting Award*, PO Box 3030, Sonora CA 95370 209-532-3120
Tenn Arts Comm Fellowship, 320 6th Ave N #100, Nashville TN 37219 ..615-741-1701
Texas Bluebonnet Award, 3355 Bee Cave Rd Ste 603, Austin TX 78746...915-658-6571
Texas Commission on the Arts, PO Box 134067, Austin TX 78711............512-463-5535
Texas Inst of Letters, PO Box 8594, Waco TX 76710...............................817-772-0095
Texas Western Press, Univ of Texas El Paso, El Paso TX 79968 915-747-5688
Theatre Library Assn Award, 111 Amsterdam, New York NY 10023........212-870-1670
Theatre Memphis New Play*, 630 Perkins Ext, Memphis TN 38117..........901-682-8323
Theatreworks/USA*, 131 W 86th St, New York NY 10024 212-595-7500
Thorntree Press Goodman Award, 547 Hawthorne, Winnetka IL 60093...312-446-8099
Eunice Tietjens Prize, 601 S Morgan St Box 4348, Chicago IL 60680 312-966-7803
Towngate Theatre*, Oglebay Inst Perf Arts, Wheeling WV 26003............304-242-4200
Towson State University Prize*, Towson MD 21204...............................301-321-2128
Translation Ctr Award, Columbia Univ Math, New York NY 10027.........212-280-2305
Tri Lakes Community Theatre*, Box 1301, Branson MO 65616 417-334-1380
21st St Theatre Co*, PO Box 67958, Los Angeles CA 90067.....................213-827-5655
Ucross Foundation, Box 19, Ucross WY 82835.......................................307-737-2291
UFO Research Ctr, Box 277, Mt Rainer MD 20712 301-779-8683
Unicorn Theatre*, 3514 Jefferson, Kansas City MO 64111......................816-531-7529
Univ of Arkansas*, KH-406 Drama Dept, Fayetteville AR 72701 501-575-2953
Univ of Hawaii at Monoa*, Dept of Drama, Honolulu HI 96822 808-948-7677
Univ of Miami*, Box 248273, Coral Gables FL 33124.............................305-284-6439
Univ of Pittsburgh Press, 127 N Bellefield, Pittsburgh PA 15260............412-624-4110
Univ of Rochester, English Dept Kafka Prize, Rochester NY 14627..........716-275-2347
Univ of Wisconsin Press, 114 N Murray, Madison WI 53715..................608-262-4750
University Productions*, 911 N University, Ann Arbor MI 48109 313-763-5213
US Naval Inst Essay Contest, Preble Hall, Annapolis MD 21402 301-268-6110
US Ski Writers Assn Hirsch Awards, 514 Franklin, Denver CO 80218.....303-321-4292
Utah Arts Council, 617 E South Temple, Salt Lake City UT 84102 801-533-5895
Uvalde Area Community Theatre*, Box 1451, Uvalde TX 78801 512-278-4082
Irita Van Doren Book Award, 137 W 25th St, New York NY 10001...........212-463-8450
Verbatim Competition, 4 Laurel Hts, Old Lyme CT 06371 203-434-2104
Vermont Council on Arts Grants, 136 State St, Montpelier VT 05602......802-828-3291
Very Special Arts*, Kennedy Ctr, Washington DC 20566 202-662-8899
Virginia Prize for Lit, 101 N 14th St 17th fl, Richmond VA 23219 804-225-3132
Wabash College Theatre*, Crawfordsville IN 47933................................317-362-1400
Celia Wagner Mem Award, 15 Gramercy Park, New York NY 10003.......212-254-9628
Edward Lewis Wallant Book Award, 3 Brighton, W Hartford CT 06117 ..203-236-3372
Richard Weaver Award, 934 N Main St, Rockford IL 61103 815-964-3242
West Coast Ensemble Theatre*, PO Box 38728, Los Angeles CA 90038 ..213-871-8673
Western Illinois Univ*, Brown Hall, Macomb IL 61455 309-298-1543
Western States Book Awards, 207 Shelby St, Santa Fe NM 87501 505-988-1166
WWA Spur Awards, 1753 Victoria, Sheridan WY 82801...........................307-672-2079
Weyerhaeuser Award, 701 Vickers Ave, Durham NC 27701....................919-682-9319
White Childrens Book Award, 1200 Commercial, Emporia KS 66801.......316-343-1200
Walt Whitman Award, 177 E 87th St, New York NY 10128......................212-427-5665
Walt Whitman Citation of Merit, 915 Broadway, New York NY 10010....212-614-2909
Laural Ingalls Wilder Medal, 50 E Huron St, Chicago IL 60611...............312-944-6780
Wm Carlos Williams Prize, 15 Gramercy Park, New York NY 10003.......212-254-9628

Williams/Derwood Award, 415 Madison Ave, New York NY 10017 212-758-0100
Wilson Co Library Perodical Award, 50 E Huron St, Chicago IL 60611...312-944-6780
Robt Winner Mem Award, 15 Gramercy Park, New York NY 10003 212-254-9628
L L Winship Book Award, The Boston Globe, Boston MA 02107.............617-929-2649
Wisconsin Arts Board, 131 W Wilson Ste 301, Madison WI 53702.............608-266-0190
Wo/Man's Showcase*, 6000 NE 22nd Way, Ft Lauderdale FL 33308........305-772-9962
Women in Film*, 8775 Wonderland Ave, Los Angeles CA 90046 213-650-4637
Work-in-Progress Grants, 15 W Mulberry St, Baltimore MD 21201.........301-685-6740
World Book-ALA Goal Awards, 50 E Huron St, Chicago IL 60611............312-944-6780
World Inst of Black Comm, 10 Columbus Cir, New York NY 10019 212-586-1771
Writer's Digest Writing Comp, 1507 Dana Ave, Cincinnati OH 45207......513-531-2222
The Writer's Exchange, PO Box 394, Society Hill SC 29593.........................803-378-4556
Writer's Journal, PO Box 65798, St Paul MN 55165.................................612-221-0326
Writer's Refinery, PO Box 47786, Phoenix AZ 85068 602-944-5268
Writers Guild of Amer*, 8955 Beverly Blvd, Los Angeles CA 90048 213-550-1000
Writers of Tomorrow Awards, Box 13, Rickreall OR 97371....................503-623-6889
WSU Playwriting Contest*, Box 31 WSU, Wichita KS 67208...................316-689-3185
Young Performers Theatre*, Ft Mason Ctr, San Francisco CA 94123.......415-346-5550
Young Playwrights Festival*, 234 W 44th St, New York NY 10036............212-575-7796

DATA BASES & ELECTRONIC MAIL SYSTEMS

This section lists on-line electronic data base services and electronic mail systems. See Researchers for firms that provide research services.

ABI/INFORM, 620 S 5th St, Louisville KY 40202.....................................502-582-4111
ABLEDATA, 4407 8th St NE, Washington DC 20017 202-635-6060
Academic Amer Encyclopedia, 95 Madison Ave, New York NY 10016 212-696-9750
Accident/Incident Data Sys, 800 Independence SW, Wash DC 20591 202-426-4000
Accountants, 1211 Ave of the Americas, New York NY 10036 212-575-6200
ACORN, 8260 Willow Oaks Corporate Dr, Fairfax VA 22031 703-876-2334
ACROPAC, 1600 Peachtree St, Atlanta GA 30302...................................404-885-8000
Act Plus, 2115 E Jefferson St, Rockville MD 20852.................................301-984-5000
ADP Network Services Inc, 175 Jackson Plaza, Ann Arbor MI 48106........313-769-6800
ADP-AUDATEX, 2380 W Winston Ave, Hayward CA 94545 800-227-2074
ADTRACK, PO Box 16073, St. Paul MN 55116 612-698-3543
Aerospace Structures Info Analysis, Patterson AFB, Dayton OH 45433..513-255-6688
AGNET, Univ of Nebraska, Lincoln NE 68583 404-472-1892
AGR, 150 Monument Rd, Bala Cynwyd PA 19004 215-667-6000
AGRICOLA, 10301 Baltimore Blvd, Beltsville MD 20705.........................301-344-3813
Agricompute, 205 W Highland Ave, Milwaukee WI 53203 800-588-9044
Agricultural Forecast, 1211 Connecticut NW, Wash DC 20036..................202-467-4900
Agricultural Market News, 14th & Independence, Wash DC 20250 202-447-7047
AgriData Resources Inc, 205 W Highland Ave, Milwaukee WI 53202.......800-558-9044
AGRITEXT, 300 W 2nd Box 356, Hutchinson KS 67501 316-662-8667
AIM/ARM Ohio State Univ, 1960 Kenny Rd, Columbus OH 43210.........614-486-3655
Air Water Pollution Report, 951 Pershing Dr, Silver Spring MD 20910....301-587-6300
Aircraft Technical Publishers, 655 4th St, San Francisco CA 94107 415-777-1515
Alternative Fuel Data Bank, PO Box 1389, Bartlesville OK 74005.............918-377-4248
Amer Men & Women of Sci, 1180 Ave of Amer, New York NY 10036......212-764-5107
Amer Medical Computing Ltd, 535 N Dearborn St, Chicago IL 60610 312-645-5085

Amer Profile, 1351 Washington Blvd, Stamford CT 06902............................203-965-5454
Amer History & Life, ABC Clio Box 4397, Santa Barbara CA 93140.........805-963-4221
AMI, Mead Data Central Box 1830, Dayton OH 45401 800-227-4908
The Anderson Report, 4505 E Industrial St, Simi Valley CA 93063 805-581-1184
Aneuploidy, Box Y, Oak Ridge TN 37803 615-574-0601
API/AAPG Well Data, Box 3030 Oklahoma Univ, Norman OK 73070......405-360-1600
APIDIST, 2101 L St NW, Washington DC 20037 202-457-7141
APiLIT/American Petroleum Inst, 156 William, New York NY 10038.....212-587-9660
Aquaculture, College of William & Mary, Gloucester Point VA 23062.....804-642-2112
AQUIRE, 401 M St SW, Washington DC 20460 800-424-9065
ARBITRON, 1350 Ave of the Americas, New York NY 10019 212-262-2600
Artbibliographies Modern, 17 Acorn Pk, Cambridge MA 02140 617-684-5770
ASFA, River Rd, Bethesda MD 20816...301-951-1400
ASI, 4520 East-West Hwy Ste 800, Bethesda MD 20814 301-654-1550
Assn of Intl Bond Dealers (DRI), 1750 K St NW, Wash DC 20006...........202-673-7720
AT&T Mail, 1 Speedwell Ave, Morristown NJ 07960 800-367-7225
Australia, 150 Monument Rd, Bala Cynwyd PA 19004 215-667-6000
AUTO-CITE, 50 Broad St, Rochester NY 14694...716-546-5530
Automated Info Transfer Sys, 14th & Constitution, Wash DC 20230........202-377-3181
Automated Minerals Info Sys, 2401 E St NW, Wash DC 20241 202-634-1187
Automotive News, 1750 K St NW, Washington DC 20006...........................202-663-7720
Autopricing, 60 Hudson St, New York NY 10013 212-227-5082
AVCOM, 655 4th St, San Francisco CA 94107 415-777-1515
Avery Index Arch Periodicals, Columbia Univ, New York NY 10027........212-280-8404
BANCOMPARE, 74 Trinity Pl, New York NY 10006 212-964-7002
Bank Administration Inst, 60 Gould Ctr, Rolling Meadows IL 60008.......312-228-6200
Bank Network News, 225 W Ohio St Ste 410, Chicago IL 60610.................312-649-0905
Banker, Bell & Howell Old Mansfield Rd, Wooster OH 44691.................800-321-9881
Banking Regulator, 700 Orange St Box 1992, Wilmington DE 19899.........800-441-7098
BAR, 500 5th Ave, New York NY 10036..212-221-2630
A M Best Co, Ambest Rd, Oldwick NJ 08858 201-439-2200
BI Data Forecasts, 1 Dag Hammarskjold Plaza, New York NY 10017......212-750-6300
Bibliographic Data Base Glaciology, Univ of Colo, Boulder CO 80309 303-492-5171
Bilingual Educ Biblio Abstract, 1300 Wilson, Arlington VA 22209 800-336-1560
Billboard Publications Inc, 1515 Broadway, New York NY 10036..............212-764-7424
BIN, 1515 Broadway, New York NY 10036...212-764-7424
Bioethicsline, Georgetown Univ, Wash DC 20057.......................................202-625-2383
Biography Master Index, Gale Research Co, Detroit MI 48226....................313-961-2242
Patuxent Wildlife Research Ctr, Laurel MD 20708....................................301-498-0205
Black's Guide, 332 Broad St, Red Bank NJ 07701..201-842-6060
Black's Research Service, 332 Broad St Box 2090, Red Bank NJ 07701.....201-842-6060
BLS Consumer Price Index, Dept of Labor, Wash DC 20212.......................202-523-1154
BLS Electronic News, Bureau of Labor Statistics, Wash DC 20212.............202-523-1913
BLS Employment Hours-Earnings, US Dept of Labor, Wash DC 20212.202-523-1154
BLS Labor Force, US Dept Labor 441 G St NW, Wash DC 20212............202-523-1154
BLS Producer Price Index, 600 E St NW, Wash DC 20212...........................202-272-5113
Boating Accident Data Base, G BP 2 US Coast Guard, Wash DC 20593..202-426-1062
Boeckh Computerized Bldg, 615 E Michigan, Milwaukee WI 53202.........414-271-5544
Bogart Inc, 1609 Memorial Ave, Williamsport PA 17705.............................717-326-2416
Book Express Plus, 1609 Memorial Ave, Williamsport PA 17705 717-326-2461
Book Review Index, Gale Research Co, Book Tower, Detroit MI 48226...313-961-2242
Bookline, 121 E 78th St, New York NY 10021..212-737-2715
Books In Print, 1180 Ave of the Americas, New York NY 10036..............212-764-5107

Books Information, 1609 Memorial Ave, Williamsport PA 17701..............717-326-2461
R R Bowker Co, 245 W 17th St, New York NY 10011 212-645-9700
Bowne Info Systems, 435 Hudson St, New York NY 10014.......................212-807-7280
Bridge Info System, 10050 Manchester Rd, St. Louis MO 63122.................314-821-5660
Brookhaven Natl Laboratory, Upton NY 11973.......................................516-282-2902
BRS, 1200 Route 7, Latham NY 12110 518-783-1161
BSI, 8745 E Orchard Rd Ste 518, Englewood CO 80111.......................303-779-8930
Budgetrack, 1750 K St NW, Washington DC 20006..................................202-663-7720
Building Costs, 1617 Beverly Blvd Box 26307, Los Angeles CA 90026......213-624-6451
Bunker Ramo Info Systems, 35 Nutmeg Dr, Trumbull CT 06609 203-377-4141
Bureau of Natl Affairs, 1231 25th St NW Ste 6015, Wash DC 20037 202-785-6892
Business Conditions Digest, US Dept of Commerce, Wash DC 20230.....202-523-0541
Business Dateline, 620 S 5th St, Louisville KY 40202...............................502-582-4111
Business Development Report, Dept of Commerce, Wash DC 20230.......202-377-5999
CA Search, 2540 Olentangy River Rd, Columbus OH 43210.......................614-421-3600
CACI, 8260 Willow Oaks Corporate Dr, Arlington VA 22031 703-876-2334
Cadence Series, 11501 Georgia Ave, Silver Spring MD 20902....................301-942-1700
California Data Base, 1750 K St NW, Wash DC 20006................................202-663-7720
Canadian Agriculture, 150 Monument Rd, Bala Cynwyd PA 19004.........215-667-6000
Canadian Construction (DRI), 1750 K St NW, Wash DC 20006.................202-673-7720
Canadian Data Base, 60 Hudson St, New York NY 10013.......................212-227-5082
Cancer Info Clearinghouse, 9000 Rockville, Bethesda MD 20205.............301-496-4070
Cansim Mini Base (DRI), 1750 K St NW, Wash DC 20006.........................202-673-7720
Capital Publications Inc, 1300 N 17th St Ste 1500, Arlington VA 22209...703-528-1100
Carcinogenesis Bioassay Data, 7901 Woodmont, Bethesda MD 20205.....301-496-1152
Carline Specifications, 150 Monument Rd, Bala Cynwyd PA 19004.........215-667-6000
CBD Plus, 1750 K St NW, Washington DC 20006......................................202-663-7720
CBW, Box 5294 FDR Station, New York NY 10150 212-559-6755
CCRIS, 333 Ravenswood Ave, Menlo Park CA 94025................................415-859-6308
Cellular Radio News, 4041 University Dr Ste 304, Fairfax VA 22030 703-352-1200
Census Plus, 1351 Washington Blvd, Stamford CT 06902..........................203-965-5454
CESARS, PO Box 30028, Lansing MI 48909 517-373-2190
Chase Econometrics, 150 Monument Rd, Bala Cynwyd PA 19004.............215-896-4772
Chemical Abstracts Services, PO Box 3012, Columbus OH 43210 614-421-3600
Chemical Exposure, Box X, Oakridge TN 27830.......................................615-574-7772
Chemical Prices (DRI), 1750 K St NW, Washington DC 20006...................202-673-7720
Chemical Propulsion Info, Johns Hopkins Rd, Laurel MD 20707 301-953-7100
Chemical Regulations Guidelines, EPA 401 M St SW, Wash DC 20460...202-382-3393
CHEMLAB, USEPA Indus Assistance Ofc, Washington DC 20460...........800-424-9065
CHEMLINE, 5333 Westbard Ave, Bethesda MD 20205 301-496-7403
Chemsearch, 3460 Hillview Ave, Palo Alto CA 94304................................800-334-2564
ChemShare Corp, PO Box 1885, Houston TX 77001 713-627-8945
Chemsis, 3460 Hillview Ave, Palo Alto CA 94304......................................800-334-2564
Child Abuse & Neglect, PO Box 1182, Washington DC 20013.....................202-251-5157
Chronolog Newsletter, 3460 Hillview Ave, Palo Alto CA 94304.................415-858-2700
Church & Society, 341 Mark W Station Rd, Windsor CA 95492..................415-707-7819
CINDA, Natl Nuclear Data Ctr, Upton NY 11973 516-282-2902
Cineman Movie Review, 7 Charles Ct, Middletown NY 10940...................914-692-4572
CIS, 4520 East-West Hwy Ste 800, Bethesda MD 20814 301-654-1550
CiSi Energy Data Bases, 12th & Penn Ave, Wash DC 20461.......................202-556-6061
CISI Network Corp PSC Div, 16625 Saticoy St, Van Nuys CA 91406........213-781-8221
CITIBASE, PO Box 5294, New York NY 10150...212-559-5312
CITIQUOTE, 850 3rd Ave, New York NY 10043...212-572-9623

CitiShare, PO Box 1127, New York NY 10043 212-559-0787
CITY/CITM/CITQ, PO Box 5294, New York NY 10150 212-559-6755
Claims Citations, 2001 Jefferson Davis Hwy, Arlington VA 22202............703-979-7230
Claims US Patent Abstracts, 302 Swann Ave, Alexandria VA 22301........703-683-1085
Clearinghouse on Health, 3700 E-W Hwy, Hyattsville MD 20782................301-436-7035
Climate Assessment Data, NOAA W353 WWB 201, Wash DC 20233 301-763-8071
CLINPROT, 9000 Rockville Pike Bldg 82, Bethesda MD 20205 301-496-7403
ClusterPlus, 1351 Washington Blvd, Stamford CT 06902 203-965-5454
CNN Moneyline On Line, 2404 Princess Anne, Virginia Bch VA 23456....804-427-1555
CNPPSDP, Federal Bldg Rm 654, Hyattsville MD 20782 301-436-6404
Coalink, 1750 K St NW, Washington DC 20006 202-663-7720
COAND, 1825 Connecticut Ave NW, Washington DC 20248 202-673-5990
Coastal Engineering Info Analysis Ctr, Box 631, Vicksburg MS 39180.....601-634-2000
Coastal Zone Color Scanner, NOAA Rm 100 WWB, Wash DC 20233.....301-763-8111
COLD, 72 Lyme Rd, Hanover NH 03755 603-643-3200
The College Market, 219 E 42nd St, New York NY 10017...............................212-867-1414
College Press Service, 2505 W 2nd Ave, Denver CO 80219..........................303-936-9930
COMDAT, 1929 Harlem Ave, Chicago IL 60635..312-622-6666
COMDAT CISCO, 327 South LaSalle 800, Chicago IL 60604 312-922-3661
Commerce Business Daily, 433 W Van Buren St, Chicago IL 60607..........312-353-2951
Commodity Info Services, 327 S LaSalle Ste 800, Chicago IL 60604..........312-922-3661
Commodity Systems Inc, 200 W Palmetto Pk, Boca Raton FL 33432........305-392-8663
Comp-U-Card, 777 Summer St, Stamford CT 06901....................................203-324-9261
COMPACT, 1929 Harlem Ave, Chicago IL 60635..312-622-6666
COMPASS, 605 Bloomfield Ave, Montclair NJ 07042....................................201-746-5060
COMPENDEX, 345 E 47th St, New York NY 10017..800-221-1044
COMPMARK Online, 850 3rd Ave, New York NY 10017...............................212-559-3636
Compuguide, 990 Washington St, Dedham MA 02026..................................617-965-1111
CompuServe, 5000 Arlington Centre Blvd, Columbus OH 43220................614-457-8650
CompuServe EasyPlex, 5000 Arlington Ctr Blvd, Columbus OH 43220....800-848-8199
CompuShare Inc, 5000 Arlington Ctr Blvd, Columbus OH 43220................614-457-8600
Compustat (DRI), 1750 K St NW, Washington DC 20006..............................202-673-7720
Compustat, 7400 S Alton Ct, Englewood CO 80112......................................303-771-6510
Computer Aided Environ Legis, 909 W Nevada, Urbana IL 61801 217-333-1369
The Computer Company, 1905 Westmorland St, Richmond VA 23230.....804-358-2171
Computer Direction Advisors, 11501 Georgia, Silver Spring MD 20902...301-942-1700
Computer Farming Newsletter, PO Box 22642, Memphis TN 38122.........901-274-9030
Computer Intelligence, 3344 N Torrey Pines Ct, La Jolla CA 92037..........619-450-1667
Computer Sciences Corp Infonet, 1616 N Ft Myer, Arlington VA 22209..703-841-3500
Computer Sharing Services, 7535 E Hampden, Denver CO 80231............303-695-1500
COMSHARE Inc, PO Box 1588, Ann Arbor MI 48106.................................313-994-4800
The Conference Board (DRI), 1750 K St NW, Wash DC 20006....................202-673-7720
Conference Board Data Bank, 845 3rd Ave, New York NY 10022..............212-759-0900
Conference Papers Index, 5161 River Rd, Bethesda MD 20816 301-951-1400
CONPSPEC, 160 Water St, New York NY 10038 212-952-4400
CONQUIP, 1290 Ridder Park Dr, San Jose CA 95131..................................800-538-9700
Consumer Price Index, US Dept of Labor, Wash DC 20212.........................202-523-1324
Consumer Price Index Data, 1211 Connecticut Ave, Wash DC 20036........202-467-4900
Conticurrency Financial Risk, 277 Park Ave, New York NY 10172............212-826-5628
Control Data Corp BIS, 500 W Putnam Ave, Greenwich CT 06836.........203-622-2000
Conversion Ratio Data Base, 60 Hudson St, New York NY 10013.............212-227-5082
Cook's Underground, 1716 Locust St, Des Moines IA 50336.......................515-284-3000
Copper Development Assn, Greenwich Ofc Pk 2, Greenwich CT 06836...203-625-8210

Corporate Angel Network, 2404 Princess Ann, Virginia Bch VA 23456 804-427-1555
Corporate Bond Model, 60 Hudson St, New York NY 10013 212-227-5082
Corporate Shareholder, 271 Madison Ave, New York NY 10016 212-685-7740
Corps of Engineers Master Guide, 435 Hudson St, New York NY 10014.212-807-7280
Council for Exceptional Children, 1920 Association, Reston VA 22091 ...703-620-3660
Country Evaluation Indicator, 150 Monument, Bala Cynwyd PA 19004...215-896-4772
County Employment & Wages, 150 Monument, Bala Cynwyd PA 19004..215-667-6000
CPBIB, Brookhaven Natl Laboratory, Upton NY 11973.............................516-282-2902
CRDS, 6845 Elm St Ste 500, McLean VA 22101 703-790-0400
CRECORD, 415 2nd St NE Ste 200, Wash DC 20002.................................202-546-5600
The Credit Bureau, 1600 Peachtree St, Atlanta GA 30302 404-885-8000
Credit Union Regulator, 1001 Connecticut Ave, Wash DC 20036.............202-393-6397
CRGS, 4020 Williamsburg Court, Fairfax VA 22032.................................703-385-0440
Criminal Justice Archive Dir, Box 1248, Ann Arbor MI 48106 313-764-2570
Criminal Justice Periodical, 300 N Zeeb Rd, Ann Arbor MI 48106 313-761-4700
CRIS/USDA, NAL Bldg, Beltsville MD 20745...301-344-3846
Cross Info, 934 Pearl Ste B, Boulder CO 80302.......................................303-444-7740
Crude Oil Analysis Data Bank, Box 1398, Bartlesville OK 74003............918-336-2400
CSISRS & CPDAT, Brookhaven Natl Laboratory, Upton NY 11973.........516-282-2902
CSS/QUOTEST, 187 Danbury Rd, Wilton CT 06897 203-762-2511
CTCP, 5600 Fishers Lane, Rockville MD 20857 301-443-3380
CTCP, USEPA 401 M St SW MS-TS799, Washington DC 20460................800-424-9065
CTCP, 9000 Rockville Pike, Rockville MD 20205.......................................301-496-4235
CULP, 1415 Koll Cir Ste 101, San Jose CA 95112 408-289-1756
Currency, 2033 K St NW Ste 305, Washington DC 20006 202-293-2915
Current Research File, 4676 Columbia Pkwy, Cincinnati OH 45226..........513-684-8328
Data Resources Chemicals Service, 29 Hartwell, Lexington MA 02173 617-863-5100
Data Resources Inc (DRI), 1750 K St NW, Washington DC 20006.............202-663-7720
Datacable News, Box 1218, McLean VA 22101...703-442-8616
DATALINX, 15 Southwest Park St, Westwood MA 02090............................617-329-3350
DataQuest Info Systems, 1290 Ridder Park Dr, San Jose CA 95131 800-538-9700
DBI, 2500 Colorado Ave, Santa Monica CA 90406 213-820-4111
DCP, 1221 Ave of the Americas, New York NY 10020.................................212-997-1221
Deadline Data on World Affairs, Box 1830, Dayton OH 45401 800-227-4908
DEBS Confectionary Marketing, Box 1508, Ann Arbor MI 48106.............313-663-4214
Defense & Aerospace Info, 1750 K St NW, Wash DC 20006 202-673-7720
Defense Pest Mgmt Info, Forest Glen Sect WRAMC, Wash DC 20307....301-427-5365
Defense Technical Info, Cameron Sta Bldg 5, Alexandria VA 22314 202-274-6434
Defense Technical Info, 5285 Port Royal Rd, Springfield VA 22161...........703-487-4660
Delphi/General Videotex, 3 Blackstone St, Cambridge MA 02139.............617-419-3393
Dept of Energy, Box Y, Oak Ridge TN 37830...615-574-0601
Dept of Energy Data Base, Box 62, Oak Ridge TN 37830..........................615-576-1155
DERMAL, 401 M St SW MS-TS799, Washington DC 20460.......................800-424-9065
Dialcom Inc, 1109 Spring St Ste 410, Silver Spring MD 20910 301-588-1572
DIALINDEX, 3460 Hillview Ave, Palo Alto CA 94304.................................800-334-2564
Dialmail Knowledge Index, 3460 Hillview Ave, Palo Alto CA 94304 415-858-3796
Dialog Info Services, 3460 Hillview Ave, Palo Alto CA 94304 800-334-2546
Dialog Publications, 3460 Hillview Ave, Palo Alto CA 94304......................415-858-2700
Digestive Diseases Educ & Info, 1555 Wilson, Rosslyn VA 22209.............301-496-9707
Direction of Trade Data Bank, 700 19th St NW, Wash DC 20431..............202-477-3243
DISC, 1200 Route 7, Latham NY 12110...800-883-4707
Disclosure, 5161 River Rd, Bethesda MD 20816..301-951-1300
Disclosure II, 5161 River Rd, Bethesda MD 20816....................................301-951-1300

Discount Corp of NY Data Base, 58 Pine St, New York NY 10005.............212-248-8900
Dissertation Abstracts Intl, 300 N Zeeb Rd, Ann Arbor MI 48106..........313-761-4700
Dividend Data Base, 60 Hudson St, New York NY 10013.......................212-227-5082
DMAHTC, 5285 Port Royal Rd, Springfield VA 22161...................703-487-4600
DMP, 1221 Ave of the Americas, New York NY 10020..........................212-997-1221
DMS, 201 San Antonio Cir Ste 280, Mountain View CA 94040..................415-948-3919
The DMV Group, 2020 Hogback Rd, Ann Arbor MI 48104.....................313-971-5234
Document Info Dir Sys, 4676 Columbia Pkwy, Cincinnati OH 45226........513-684-8328
Dodge Construction Analysis System, 1750 K St NW, Wash DC 20006....202-663-7720
F W Dodge Division, 1221 Ave of the Americas, New York NY 10020......212-997-1221
Dodge/DRI Building Stock, 1750 K St NW, Washington DC 20006.........202-673-7720
DOE RECON, Box 62, Oak Ridge TN 37830..............................615-576-1272
DORIS, 8260 Willow Oaks Corporate Dr, Fairfax VA 22031.....................703-876-2334
Dow Jones News Retrieval, 200 Liberty St, New York NY 10281...............212-416-2000
DRI (Data Resources Inc), 1750 K St NW, Washington DC 20006.........202-673-7720
Drug & Medicine News, 2404 Princess Anne, Virginia Bch VA 23456.......804-427-1555
Drug Info Services, 308 Harvard SE, Minneapolis MN 55455.................612-624-7695
Dun & Bradstreet, 99 Church St, New York NY 10007.....................212-285-7642
Dun's Market Identifiers 10+, 3 Century Dr, Parsippany NJ 07054.........201-455-0900
DunsPrint, 99 Church St, New York NY 10007................................212-285-7642
DwightLine, 1201 Exchange Dr, Richardson TX 75081.......................214-783-8002
EARLYOPT, 11 Broadway, New York NY 10004................................212-269-5460
Earth Resources Observation System, EROS, Sioux Falls SD 57198........605-594-6511
Earthquake Data File, 325 Broadway, Boulder CO 80303.....................303-497-6472
EBIB, PO Box 2068, Houston TX 77001......................................713-529-4301
EBSCO Subscription Services, Box 1943, Birmingham AL 35201............205-991-6600
EBSCONET Serials Control System, Box 1943, Birmingham AL 35201...800-633-4604
ECHO, 4739 All Rd, Marina del Rey CA 90291................................213-823-8415
Economic Social Data System, 1601 N Kent, Washington DC 20523.........703-235-2754
Economic Impact Forecast System, Univ of Illinois, Urbana IL 61801.....217-333-1369
EDR, 1110 Vermont Ave NW Ste 210, Washington DC 20005................202-466-6240
Education Daily Online, 1300 N 17th St Ste 1500, Arlington VA 22209....703-528-1100
EEI Financial Data, 1211 Connecticut Ave NW, Wash DC 20036.........202-467-4900
EI Engineering Meetings, 345 E 47th St, New York NY 10017................212-705-7600
EIS Data Base, 310 Madison Ave Rm 201, New York NY 10017...............212-697-6080
Electric Power Data Base, PO Box 10412, Palo Alto CA 94303..................415-855-2411
Electronic Yellow Pages, Ketchum Pl, Westport CT 06880.....................203-266-8941
Emergency Programs Info Ctr, 6505 Belcrest, Hyattsville MD 20782........301-436-8087
EMI Aerocorp Flight Planning, 7 N Brentwood, Clayton MO 63105.......314-727-9600
Encyclopedia Britannica, 425 N Michigan Ave, Chicago IL 60611.............312-321-7000
Encyclopedia of Associations, Gale Research Co, Detroit MI 48226........313-961-2242
ENDSF Natl Nuclear Data Service, Brookhaven Lab, Upton NJ 11973....516-282-2902
ENERGY, 150 Monument Rd, Bala Cynwyd PA 19004...........................215-667-6000
Energy & Environment, CEEI Park Ridge Lab, Oak Ridge TN 37830......615-574-7470
Energy & Minerals Resources, 951 Pershing, Silver Spg MD 20910.........301-587-6300
Energy Info Data Base, 21093 IRE Control Ctr, Eagan MN 55121...........612-888-9635
Energyline/Environline, 48 W 38th St, New York NY 10018.....................212-944-8500
Environmental Bibliography, 2060 A P Serra, Santa Barbara CA 93103..805-965-5010
Environmental Health Plus, 515 Madison Ave, New York NY 10022.......212-752-4530
Environmental Tech Info System, 909 W Nevada, Urbana IL 61801.........217-333-1369
Environmental Teratology, Box Y, Oak Ridge TN 37830.......................615-574-7871
EPA Chemical Activities, 401 M St NW, Wash DC 20460......................202-382-3415
EPIA, 2011 I St NW, Washington DC 20006..................................202-466-3660

EPIC Ford Data Base, 11722 Sorrento Vly Rd, San Diego CA 92121 714-755-1327
ERIC, 4833 Rugby Ave Ste 301, Bethesda MD 20814.................................301-656-9273
ESTEL, Univ of Maryland, College Park MD 20742 301-454-4848
ETAIRS, 601 D St NW Rm 6517, Washington DC 20213 202-376-3406
EURABANK, 77 Water St, New York NY 10005...212-437-4300
Europe Satellites (DRI), 1750 K St NW, Washington DC 20006...............202-673-7720
European Forecast, 150 Monument Rd, Bala Cynwyd PA 19004...............215-667-6000
Exchange, Mead Data Central Box 1830, Dayton OH 45401.......................800-227-4908
Exchange Master, 605 3rd Ave, New York NY 10158 212-986-1919
Executive Productivity, 10076 Boca Entrada Blvd, Boca Raton FL 33433.305-483-2600
FAA Info & Stats, 800 Independence Ave SW, Washington DC 20591 202-426-3053
FAA Master Guide, 435 Hudson St, New York NY 10014...........................212-807-7280
Family Resources Data, 1219 University Ave, Minneapolis MN 55414 612-331-2774
FAPRS, 726 Jackson Place NW, Washington DC 20503................................202-395-3112
Farm Market Infodata, 14th & Independence, Wash DC 20250 202-447-7047
Farm Software Developments, PO Box 22642, Memphis TN 38122..........901-274-9030
FASTOCK, 111 Broadway, New York NY 10006 212-766-1700
F W Faxon Company Inc, 15 Southwest Park, Westwood MA 02090 617-329-3350
FDIC, 550 17th St NW, Washington DC 20420...202-393-8400
The Fearless Taster, 341 Mark West Station Rd, Winsor CA 95492..........707-542-7819
Federal Index, 415 2nd St NE, Washington DC 20002 202-546-5699
Federal Procurement Data, 4040 N Fairfax Dr, Arlington VA 22203 703-235-1634
Federal Regulatory Search System, 401 M St SW, Wash DC 20460 202-382-3393
Federal Research Report, 951 Pershing Dr, Silver Spring MD 20910 301-587-6300
Federal Reserve Board, 20th & Constitution, Washington DC 20551........202-452-3482
FEDEX, NEIC EI-20 Forrestal Bldg, Washington DC 20585......................202-252-8800
FEDREG, 415 2nd St NE Ste 200, Washington DC 20002 202-546-5600
FEDWATCH/FEDWIR, 490 El Camino Real, Belmont CA 94002............415-595-0610
Fertilizer Forecast, 150 Monumont Rd, Bala Cynwyd PA 19004...............215-667-6000
FHLMC Online Quote System, 1 State St Plaza, New York NY 10004.....212-943-8411
Fiber Optics & Communications, 167 Corey Rd, Brookline MA 02146....617-739-2022
Financial, 150 Monument Rd, Bala Cynwyd PA 19004 215-667-6000
Financial Disclosure Data Base, 1325 K St NW, Wash DC 20436 202-523-4181
Financial Mgmt Advisor, 10076 Boca Entrada, Boca Raton FL 33433......305-483-2600
Financial Post Investement (DRI), 1750 K St NW, Wash DC 20006.........202-673-7720
FIND/SVP Reports & Studies Index, 500 5th Ave, New York NY 10010.212-354-2424
FINDB, 74 Trinity Pl, New York NY 10006..212-964-7002
Fiscal, 60 Hudson St, New York NY 10013..212-227-5082
Fish & Wildlife Reference Service, 3840 York St, Denver CO 80205.........301-571-4656
Fishery Statistics, Natl Marine Fishery Service, Wash DC 20235 202-634-7415
Flash, 605 Bloomfield Ave, Montclair NJ 07042...201-746-5060
Flow of Funds, 1750 K St NW, Wash DC 20006 202-673-7720
FNMA Online Quote System, 1 State St Plaza, New York NY 10004........212-943-8411
Food & Drug Bulletin Board, 600 Maryland Ave SW, Wash DC 20024....202-488-0550
Food & Nutrition Info, Natl Agri Library, Beltsville MD 20705.................301-344-3719
Foods Adlibra, 2000 Frankfort Ave, Louisville KY 40206............................502-897-6736
Ford Investment Review, 11722 Sorrento Vly Rd, San Diego CA 92121 ...619-755-1327
Foreign Exchange, 150 Monument Rd, Bala Cynwyd PA 19004 215-896-4772
Foreign Exchange (FX), 100 Gold St, New York NY 10273 212-791-4654
Foreign Traders Index, Dept of Commerce, Wash DC 20230 202-377-2665
Foundation Directory, 888 7th Ave 26th fl, New York NY 10106...............212-975-1120
FRY9, 74 Trinity Pl, New York NY 10006 212-964-7002
FSLIC, 490 El Camino Real, Belmont CA 94002...800-227-7304

Futures Contracts, 60 Hudson St, New York NY 10013..............................212-227-5682
FX, 175 Jackson Plaza, Ann Arbor MI 48106..313-769-6800
GACIAC, 10 West 35th St, Chicago IL 60616..312-567-4519
GAO, Box 6015, Gaithersburg MD 20877...202-275-6241
GE Quik-Comm, 401 N Washington St, Rockville MD 20850 800-638-9636
GENBANK, 10 Moulton St, Cambridge MA 02238.......................................617-497-2742
GE Info Service, 401 N Washington St, Rockville MD 20850.......................800-638-9636
GENIE, 401 N Washington St, Rockville MD 20850......................................301-340-4000
GEOREF, 1 Skyline Plaza, Falls Church VA 22041 703-379-2480
GIPSY, PO Box 3030 Oklahoma Univ, Norman OK 73070 405-360-1600
Global Finance Info, 33 Riverside Dr. Apt 7F, New York NY 10023..........212-580-9084
Globe/Globe Star, 605 Bloomfield Ave, Montclair NJ 07042.....................201-746-5060
GNMA Online Quote System, 1 State St Plaza, New York NY 10004........212-943-8411
GNMA Pool Data Base, 60 Hudson St, New York NY 10013.......................212-227-5082
The Gold Sheet, 2316 216th Pl NE, Redmond WA 98052.............................206-883-2030
Government Industry Data, GIDEP Oper Ctr, Corona CA 91720 714-736-4677
GPO Publications Ref File, US Gov Printing Ofc, Wash DC 20401...........202-275-3299
Grants/Oryx Press, 2214 N Central at Encanto, Phoenix AZ 85281.........602-254-6156
Graphic Profile, 1351 Washington Blvd, Stanford CT 06902.....................203-965-5454
Grolier Electronic Publishing, 95 Madison Ave, New York NY 10016 212-696-9750
GTE Info Systems Inc, East Park Dr, Mount Laurel NJ 08054.....................609-235-7300
GTE Telemail, 12490 Sunrise Valley Dr, Reston VA 22096..........................703-689-6000
Guidance Info System, Dept S64 Box 683, Hanover NH 03755 603-448-3838
HW Systems, 16134 Hart St, Van Nuys CA 91406.......................................213-988-1830
Handy-Whitman Index (DRI), 1750 K St NW, Wash DC 20006...................202-673-7720
Harfax Industry Data Sources, 54 Church St, Cambridge MA 02138........617-492-0670
Harris Electronic News, Box 356, Hutchinson KS 67501 316-662-8667
Harvard Business Review, 605 3rd Ave, New York NY 10158.....................212-850-6168
Hazardline, 515 Madison Ave, New York NY 10022....................................212-752-4530
Health AV Online Catalog, Northwestern Univ, Rootstown OH 44272.....216-325-2511
Health Benefit Cost Cont, 2404 Princess Anne, Virginia Bch VA 23456...804-427-1555
Health Planning & Admin, 840 N Lakesport Dr, Chicago IL 60611...........312-280-6000
HFO, Natl Energy Info Ctr EI-20, Washington DC 20585 202-252-8800
HI Tech Patents, 101 Verndale St, Brookline MA 02146 617-566-2373
Historical Abstracts, 2040 APS Box 4397, Santa Barbara CA 93103 805-963-4221
Hollywood Hotline, Box 1945, Burbank CA 91560 213-843-2837
Homs Reference Hydrology Tech, 8060 13th St, Silver Spg MD 20910.......310-427-7658
Honeywell Data Network, 6400 France Ave S, Edina MN 55435.................800-328-5200
Horse, Box 4097, Lexington KY 40504 606-278-0411
Hot Specs Advisory, 15 Inverness Way East, Englewood CO 80150 303-790-0600
Hotline Energy Reports, 70 W 6th Ave Ste 415, Denver CO 80204............303-623-7130
HTC, 1110 Vermont Ave NW Ste 200, Washington DC 20005....................202-466-6240
HUD User, Box 280, Germantown MD 20874 301-251-5154
Hydrocomp Inc, 201 San Antonio Cir #280, Mtn View CA 94040.............212-227-5082
IATA, 1730 K St NW, Washington DC 20006...202-822-3929
IBES (DRI), 1750 K St NW, Washington DC 20006 202-673-7720
IBRD World Tables Data Bank, 1818 H St NW, Washington DC 20006 ..202-477-1234
ICARUS, 135 S LaSalle St Rm 1903, Chicago IL 60603................................321-236-1464
IFI/Plenum Data Corp, 302 Swann Ave, Alexandria VA 22301 703-683-1085
IFS, Bureau of Stats 700 19th St NW, Washington DC 20431 202-477-3243
IMF Balance of Payments, Hinman Box 6101, Hanover NH 03755 202-477-3243
IMF Financial Stats, 700 19th St NW, Washington DC 20431......................202-477-7000
IMF Intl Financial Statistics (DRI), 1750 K St NW, Wash DC 20006 202-673-7720

Imports, P.O.Box 19267, Washington DC 20036 202-653-3445
IMS America Ltd, Butler & Maple Avenues, Ambler PA 19002 215-283-8500
IMSPACT, Butler & Maple Aves, Ambler PA 19002 215-283-8500
Index to Trade Catalogs, Smithsonian Inst Lib Rm 25, Wash DC 20560 ..202-357-2163
Industrial Application Centers, Box 647, Indianapolis IN 46223..............317-264-4644
Industrial Forecast Data Bank, 1211 Connecticut Ave, Wash DC 20036..202-467-4900
Industry & Intl Standards, 15 Inverness Way E, Englewood CO 80150 ...303-790-0600
Industry File, 401 M St SW, Washington DC 20460 202-382-2249
Industry Price Index, 1211 Connecticut Ave NW, Wash DC 20036 202-467-4900
Inflation Planner Forecast, 150 Monument Rd, Bala Cynwyd PA 19004..215-667-6000
InfoPlex, 5000 Arlington Centre Blvd, Columbus OH 43220 800-848-8990
Info & Tech Trans of Data, 21098 IRE Control Ctr, Eagan MN 55121.....612-888-9635
Information Bank, Mead Data Central Box 1830, Dayton OH 45401........800-227-4908
Info Handling Services, 15 Inverness Way East, Englewood CO 80150 303-790-0600
Info Intelligence Inc, PO Box 31098, Phoenix AZ 85046............................602-996-2283
Info Science Abstracts, 302 Swann Ave, Alexandria VA 22301 703-683-1085
Info USA Inc, PO Box 15700, Chevy Chase MD 20815 301-657-1200
Inforonics Inc, 550 Newtown Rd, Littleton MA 01460 617-486-8976
Infoserve, 15 Southwest Pk, Westwood MA 02090...................................617-329-3350
INFOTERRA, Rm 2903 211 A US EPA, Washington DC 20460.................202-382-5914
Infrared Info System, 3316 Spring Garden St, Philadelphia PA 19104 215-382-7800
Innerline, 60 Gould Ctr, Rolling Meadows IL 60008 312-228-6200
Inpadoc PFS/PRS Online, 302 Swann Ave, Alexandria VA 22301 703-683-1085
Insight, 490 El Camino Real, Belmont CA 94002 800-227-7304
Inspec, 445 Hoes Lane PO Box 1331, Piscataway NJ 08855......................201-981-0060
InstantChex, Box 1749, Ormond Beach FL 32074....................................904-677-7033
Inst for Scientific Info, 3501 Market St, Philadelphia PA 19104 215-386-0100
Insurance Abstracts, 300 N Zeeb Rd, Ann Arbor MI 48106.......................313-761-4700
Insure, 1 Penn Plaza Ste 2428, New York NY 10119 212-594-8090
Intellimation 10, 35 Nutmeg Dr, Trumbull CT 06609................................203-368-2000
Interactive Market Systems Inc, 22 Cortland St, New York NY 10036 212-869-8810
Interactive Video Technology, 223 Sunrise Dr, Shreve OH 44676 216-587-3732
Intl Data Base, US Bureau of Census, Washington DC 20233.....................301-763-4221
Intl Data Bases, 1211 Connecticut Ave NW Ste 710, Wash DC 20036.......202-467-4900
Intl Financial Statistics, 1211 Connecticut Ave NW, Wash DC 20036......202-467-4900
Intl Medical Tribune Syndicate, 600 New Hampshire, Wash DC 20036 ...202-338-8866
Intl Petroleum Annual, NEIC EI-20 Forrestal Bldg, Wash DC 20585.......202-252-8800
Intl Research & Evaluation, 21093 IRE Control Ctr, Eagan MN 55121 ...612-888-9635
Intl Software Data Base, 1520 S College Ave, Ft Collins CO 80524...........303-482-5574
Intl SOS Assistance, 2402 Princess Anne Rd, Virginia Beach VA 23456..804-427-1555
INTLINE, 150 Monument Rd, Bala Cynwyd PA 19004..............................215-896-4772
Investment News & Views, PO Box 30214, Bethesda MD 20814...............301-762-7145
Investments, 111 Broadway, New York NY 10017.....................................212-487-0101
IPA Info Systems, 4630 Montgomery Ave, Bethesda MD 20814 301-657-3000
ISI, 3501 Market St Science Ctr, Philadelphia PA 19104............................215-386-0100
ISMEC, 5161 River Rd, Bethesda MD 20816 301-951-1400
ISYS, 934 Pearl Ste B, Boulder CO 80302...303-444-7740
ITT Dialcom, 1109 Spring St, Silver Spring MD 20910 800-435-7342
J Schedule, 2033 K St NW Ste 305, Washington DC 20006........................202-293-2915
JAS, 1110 Vermont Ave NW Ste 700, Washington DC 20005 202-466-6240
JForum, c/o Jim Cameron 117 Prospect Park W, Brooklyn NY 11215.....718-788-8528
Journal of Economic Literature, PO Box 7320, Pittsburgh PA 15213........412-268-3869
Journal Soc Architectural Historians, 1700 Walnut, Phila PA 19103........215-735-0224

Kentucky Economic Info, 451 Commerce Bldg, Lexington KY 40506 606-257-7675
Kirk Othmer Online, 605 3rd Ave, New York NY 10158.............................212-850-6360
Labor Statistics, 441 G St NW, Washington DC 20212..............................202-523-1975
LaborLaw, 1231 25th St NW, Washington DC 20037................................202-785-6892
LAN, 167 Corey Rd, Brookline MA 02146...617-739-2022
Land Use Planning Report, 951 Pershing, Silver Spg MD 20910................301-587-6300
Latin Amer Energy Report, 951 Pershing, Silver Spg MD 20910 301-587-6300
Latin Amer Forecast, 150 Monument Rd, Bala Cynwyd PA 19004.............215-896-4772
Law Enforcement-Crim Just, 21098 IRE Ctrl Ctr, Eagan MN 55121 612-888-9635
LC/LINE, 2500 Colorado Ave, Santa Monica CA 90406 213-820-4111
The Legal Resource Index, 404 6th Ave, Menlo Park CA 94025.................800-227-8431
Legi-Slate, 444 N Capitol St NW, Washington DC 20001 202-737-1888
Legislative Info, 3rd & D St SW Rm 696, Wash DC 20515 202-225-1772
LEXIS Mead Data Central Inc, PO Box 933, Dayton OH 45401 513-865-6800
Life Sciences Collection, 5161 River Rd, Bethesda MD 20816...................301-951-1400
Linquistic & Language Behavior, PO Box 22206, San Diego CA 92122....619-565-6603
Lloyd Bush & Assoc, 1 State St Plaza, New York NY 10004 212-943-8411
Login, Box O, Minneapolis MN 55440 612-328-1921
Logistics Systems, 990 Washington St, Dedham MA 02026 617-965-1111
LPGS, 2101 L St NW, Washington DC 20037...202-457-7141
LSI Database (DRI), 1750 K St NW, Washington DC 20006 202-673-7720
Lundberg, 12041 Strathern St, North Hollywood CA 91205 213-768-5111
Macro Forecast Data Base, 1211 Connecticut Ave, Wash DC 20036........202-467-4900
Macroeconomic Forecast, 150 Monument's Rd, Bala Cynwyd PA 19004 215-667-6000
Management Contents, 2265 Carlson Dr, Northbrook IL 60062 800-323-5354
Management Decision Systems, 200 5th Ave, Waltham MA 02254...........617-890-1100
Management Info Div, USDA 3101 Park Ctr, Alexandria VA 22302.........703-756-3100
Management Science Assoc Inc, 5100 Centre Ave, Pittsburg PA 15232....412-683-9533
Marine Industry Data Bases, 300 Broad St, Stamford CT 06901 203-327-6433
Market-America, 8260 Willow Oaks Corp Dr, Arlington VA 22031 703-876-2334
Market Decision System 7, 35 Nutmeg Dr, Trumbull CT 06609................203-386-2000
Market Potential, 1351 Washington Blvd, Stamford CT 06902 203-965-5454
Market Science Assoc Inc, 1560 Broadway 3rd fl, New York NY 10036....212-398-9100
Marshall & Swift, 1617 Beverly Blvd, Los Angeles CA 90026....................213-624-6451
MAS MILS, 2401 E St NW, Washington DC 20241.................................202-632-1138
Massachusetts Health Data (DRI), 1750 K St NW, Wash DC 20006 202-673-7720
Material Properties Data, 2595 Yeager, W Lafayette IN 47906.................317-494-9393
Materials Business File, ASM Intl, Metals Park OH 44073........................216-338-5151
Math/Sci, PO Box 6248, Providence RI 02940 401-272-9500
Matrix Transactions Exchange, PO Box 1773, Boulder CO 80306 303-444-7740
Maxway Data Corp, 225 W 34th St, New York NY 10001 212-947-6100
May Aerial Survey Data, Patuxent Research Ctr, Laurel MD 20708 301-498-9295
MBANK, 2035 K St NW Ste 305, Washington DC 20006 202-293-2915
McDonnell Douglas, 20705 Valley Green, Cupertino CA 95014.................408-446-6000
McGraw-Hill Cost Info, Box 28, Princeton NJ 08540 609-921-6500
MCI Mail, 2000 M St NW Ste 300, Washington DC 20036........................800-624-2255
MDF/I Metals Datafile, Materials Info ASM Intl, Metals Pk OH 44073..216-338-5151
MDR, 1110 Vermont Ave NW Ste 700, Washington DC 20005.................202-466-6240
Mead Data Central Inc, PO Box 933, Dayton OH 45401............................513-865-6800
Media General Data Base, Box C-23293, Richmond VA 23293..................804-649-6587
Media General Financial Services, 301 E Grace, Richmond VA 23219 804-649-6587
Media Science Reports, 324 E 35th St, New York NY 10016 212-344-0870
MEDLARS Library of Medicine, 8600 Rockville, Bethesda MD 20894.....301-496-6193

Mental Health Abstracts, 302 Swann Ave, Alexandria VA 22301 703-683-1085
MER, NEIC EI-20 Forrestal Bldg, Washington DC 20585 202-252-8800
Mergers & Acquisitions, 62 Williams St 6th fl, New York NY 10005 212-668-0940
Merlin, 1044 Northern Blvd, Roslyn NY 11576 516-484-4545
Merrill Lynch Economics, 165 Broadway, New York NY 10080 212-637-6200
Merrill Lynch Pricing (DRI), 1750 K St NW, Wash DC 20006...................202-673-7720
Metadex, Materials Info ASM Intl, Metals Park OH 44073.....................216-338-5151
Metals Data Base, 1211 Connecticut Ave NW Ste 710, Wash DC 20036...202-467-4900
Metals Week, 1221 Ave of the Americas, New York NY 10020 212-997-1221
Metals Week (DRI), 1750 K St NW, Washington DC 20006.......................202-673-7720
Meteorological & Geoastrophysical, 45 Beacon St, Boston MA 02103......617-227-2425
The Micro Advisor, PO Box 30214, Bethesda MD 20814..........................301-762-7145
Military-Federal Specs & Stds, 15 Inverness E, Englewood CO 80150.....303-790-0600
Million Dollar Directory, Three Century Dr, Parsippany NJ 07054...........201-455-0900
Minerals Data System, Box 3030 Oklahoma Univ, Norman OK 73070.....405-360-1600
MISTI II, 60 Hudson St, New York NY 10013 212-227-5082
MJK Data Services, 122 Saratoga Ave Ste 11, Santa Clara CA 95051 408-247-5102
MLA Bibliography, 10 Astor Place, New York NY 10003 212-614-6348
MMI TTI, 219 East 42nd St, New York NY 10017.....................................212-867-1414
Monitor, Old Mansfield Rd, Wooster OH 44691 800-321-9881
Monthly Latin America, 150 Monument Rd, Bala Cynwyd PA 19004 215-896-4772
Moody's Investors Services, 99 Church St, New York NY 10007 212-553-0300
Morgan Stanley Capital Intl (DRI), 1750 K St NW, Wash DC 20006 202-673-7720
MPPR, 1110 Vermont Ave NW Ste 700, Washington DC 20005...............202-466-6240
MRATE, 2033 K St NW Ste 305, Washington DC 20006.........................202-293-2915
MRI, 341 Madison Ave, New York NY 10017 212-599-0444
MSSS, NBS A323 Physics Bldg, Gaithersburg MD 20899.......................301-975-2208
Municipal Debt, 62 Williams St 6th fl, New York NY 10005......................212-668-0940
Muniprice, 60 Hudson St, New York NY 10013.......................................212-227-5082
NAARS, 1211 Ave of the Americas, New York NY 10036 212-575-6326
NAARS, 9333 Springboro Pike Box 933, Dayton OH 45401......................513-859-1611
NARC, 4407 8th St NE, Washington DC 20017 202-635-5822
NASA Sci & Tech Info, Box 8757 BWI Airport, Baltimore MD 21240 202-621-0140
NASTOCK, 2033 K St NW Ste 305, Wash DC 20006................................202-293-2915
Natl Space Svc Data, Goddard Space Flight Ctr, Greenbelt MD 20771....301-344-6695
Nationwide Exam of XRay Trends, 5600 Fishers, Rockville MD 20857.....301-443-3446
Natl Arthritis Info, PO Box 9782, Arlington VA 22209............................703-558-4999
Natl Cartographic & Geographic Ctr, 507 Natl Ctr, Reston VA 22092 703-860-6045
Natl Clearinghouse Alcohol Info, Box 2345, Rockville MD 20852 301-468-2600
Natl Clearinghouse Bilingual Ed, 1300 Wilson, Rosslyn VA 22209 703-522-0710
Natl Clearinghouse Family Planning, Box 2225, Rockville MD 20852......301-881-9490
Natl Computer Network of Chicago, 1929 N Harlem, Chicago IL 60635 ..312-622-6666
Natl Crime Info Ctr, 10th St & Pennsylvania Ave NW, Wash DC 20535 ..202-324-2606
Natl Crime Survey, 633 Indiana Ave NW Rm 1242, Wash DC 20531........202-724-7782
Natl CSS Inc, 187 Danbury Rd, Wilton CT 06897....................................203-762-2511
Natl Diabetes Info, Box NDIC, Bethesda MD 20892.................................301-468-2162
Natl E-Mail Registry, 3 Neshaminy Interplex #302, Trevose PA 19047 800-843-6088
Natl Energy Info Ctr, Forrestal Bldg, Washington DC 20585 202-586-8800
Natl Environmental Data Referral, 3300 Whitehaven, Wash DC 20235 ...202-634-7722
Natl Foundations, 888 7th Ave 26th fl, New York NY 10106 212-975-1120
Natl Highway Traffic Safety Adm, 400 7th St SW, Wash DC 20590 202-426-2768
Natl Injury Info Clearinghouse, 5401 Westbard Ave, Wash DC 20207.....301-492-6424
Natl Library of Medicine, 8600 Rockville Pike, Bethesda MD 20894 301-496-6193

Natl Library Svcs for the Blind, Library of Congress, Wash DC 20542 202-287-5100
Natl Newspaper Index, 404 6th Ave, Menlo Park CA 94025.....................415-367-7171
Natl Nuclear Data Ctr, Brookhaven Natl Laboratory, Upton NY 11973...516-282-2902
Natl Pesticide Info, Purdue Univ, W Layfayette IN 47907 317-494-6616
Natl Rehabilitation Info Ctr, 4407 8th St NE, Washington DC 20017.......202-635-5822
Natl Std Ref Data, NBS A 320 Physics Bldg, Gaithersburg MD 20899......301-975-2208
Natl Study Local Newspaper Rate, 219 E 42nd St, New York NY 10017..212-867-1414
Natl Technical Info Svc, 5285 Port Royal Rd, Springfield VA 22161.........703-487-4640
Natl Telecomputing Co, 70 N Main St PO Box 108, Nyack NY 10960.......914-358-2335
Natural Gas Div Mgmt, 1000 Independence Ave SW, Wash DC 20580....202-252-9482
Natural Gas Planning System, 5757 Bellaire Blvd, Houston TX 77081.....713-660-9033
Natural Resource Mgmt System, 20 Mass Ave NW, Wash DC 20314.......202-272-2034
Natural Resources Library & Info, 18th & C NW, Wash DC 20240..........202-343-5815
NAVFAC Master Guide, 435 Hudson St, New York NY 10014 212-807-7280
NCJRS, NCJRS Box 6000, Rockville MD 20850 301-251-5500
NDEX, Bell & Howell Old Mansfiled Rd, Wooster OH 44691 216-264-6666
NEMA, 2101 L St NW, Washington DC 20037 202-457-8400
NERAC, Mansfield Professional Park, Storrs CT 06268.............................203-486-4533
New Issues, 62 Williams St, New York NY 10005 212-668-0940
New York Regional Economic, 20 New Dutch Lane, Fairfield NJ 07006...201-227-0035
New York Times Online, Mead Data Box 1830, Dayton OH 45401............800-227-4908
Newsbeat, GTE East Park Drive, Mount Laurel NJ 08054 609-235-7300
NewsNet Inc, 945 Haverford Rd, Bryn Mawr PA 19010.............................215-527-8030
NewsSearch, 404 6th Ave, Menlo Park CA 94025 415-367-7171
NEXIS, Mead Data Central Box 1830, Dayton OH 45401..........................800-227-4908
NHTSA Auto Safety Hotline, 400 7th St SW, Washington DC 20590.........800-424-9393
NICEM, NICEM 3716 S Hope St Ste 301, Los Angeles CA 90007............213-743-6681
NIGSEM/NIMIS, Univ of Southern California, Los Angeles CA 90007...800-421-8711
NIH EPA Chemical Info System, Box 2227, Falls Church VA 22046.........703-237-2000
NIKKEI Economic Statistics, 1750 K St NW, Wash DC 20006.................202-673-7720
NIMH Data Base, 5600 Fishers Ln, Rockville MD 20857 301-443-4517
NINCDS, 7550 Wisconsin Ave, Bethedsa MD 20205................................301-496-9244
NIOSHTIC, 4676 Columbia Pkwy, Cincinnati OH 45226..........................513-684-8328
NISH, Dept of Education, Switzer 3119, Washington DC 20202................202-245-0080
Nite Line, 1929 N Harlem Ave, Chicago IL 60635......................................312-622-6666
NMRLIT, 9000 Rockville Pile, Bethesda MD 20205..................................301-496-4235
NPIRS, Purdue Univ Entomology Hall, West Lafayette IN 47907 317-494-6616
NTIS, 5285 Port Royal Rd, Springfield VA 22161.....................................703-487-4640
NUC Codes, 2500 Colorado Ave, Santa Monica CA 90406........................213-820-4111
Nuclear Waste News, 951 Pershing Dr, Silver Spring MD 20910.................301-587-6300
Nutrition Analysis System, 6400 France Ave S, Edina MN 55435.............800-328-5200
OAG2, 2000 Clearwater Dr, Oakbrook IL 60521..312-654-6000
Occupational Health Services, 515 Madison Ave, New York NY 10022...212-752-4530
Oceanic Abstracts, 5161 River Rd, Bethesda MD 20816 301-951-1400
OCLC, 6565 Frantz Rd, Dublin OH 43017...614-764-6390
OECD Economic Ind (DRI), 1750 K St NW, Wash DC 20006....................202-673-7720
Office Automation Update, 10076 Boca Entrada, Boca Raton FL 33433 ..305-483-2600
Official Airline Guide, 2000 Clearwater, Oak Brook IL 60521....................312-654-6000
OLIS, Oregon State Capitol S408, Salem OR 97310..................................503-378-8104
On Line Research Inc, 200 Railroad Ave, Greenwich CT 06830 203-661-1395
Online Auto Rates, 1350 E Touhy Ave, Des Plaines IL 60018...................312-635-0200
Online Chronicle, 11 Tannery Ln, Weston CT 06883 203-227-8466
Online Data Base Report, 215 Park Ave South, New York NY 10003.......212-473-5600

Online Job Hotline, PO Box 31098, Phoenix AZ 85046.................................602-996-2283
Online Stock & Industry Filter, 11501 Georgia, Silver Spg MD 20902.......301-942-1700
Online Tariff Guide, 2020 Hogback Rd, Ann Arbor MI 48104.....................313-971-5234
Online Training & Practice, 3460 Hillview Ave, Palo Alto CA 94304........800-334-2564
Online Well Activity, PO Box 1702, Houston TX 77001................................713-961-5660
Onsite, PO Box 25953, Los Angeles CA 90025..213-820-8931
OnTyme, 20705 Valley Green Dr, Cupertino CA 95014..............................800-435-8880
OPDAT, 175 W Jackson Blvd A1024, Chicago IL 60604.............................312-431-0440
OPRM Interactive Data Base, 1800 G St NW, Washington DC 20550.......202-357-9540
ORBCHEM/ORBPAT, 2500 Colorado Ave, Santa Monica CA 90406.......213-820-4111
Orr System Constr Cost Mgmt, 131 E Exchange, Ft Worth TX 76106.....817-625-1177
OSchedule, 2033 K St NW Ste 305, Washington DC 20006..........................202-293-2915
OTSC Inc, 2115 E Jefferson St, Rockville MD 20852....................................301-984-5444
P/E News/Amer Petroleum Inst, 156 William St, New York NY 10038 ...212-587-9660
Pacific West Oil (DRI), 1750 K St NW, Washington DC 20006....................202-673-7720
PAIS Intl, 11 W 40th St, New York NY 10018...212-736-6629
Paperchem, PO Box 1039, Appleton WI 54912..414-734-9251
Parts Control Automated Sup, 1507 Wilmington, Dayton OH 45444........513-296-5116
PAT PTR, US Patent & Trademark Office, Washington DC 20231...........703-557-2982
PATDATA, 1200 Route 7, Latham NY 12110..800-833-4707
The Patent Data Base, US Dept of Commerce, Washington DC 20231....202-557-3080
PATREACH, 1340 Old Chain Bridge Rd, McLean VA 22101....................703-442-0900
PBM/STIRS, 605 3rd Ave, New York NY 10158...212-850-6331
PC World Online, 2404 Princess Anne, Virginia Bch VA 23456.................804-427-9991
PDB, 7535 E Hampden Ave Ste 200, Denver CO 80231................................303-695-1500
PDQ, 9000 Rockville Pike Bldg 82, Bethesda MD 20205.............................301-496-7403
Pergamon Infoline, 1340 Old Chain Bridge Rd, McLean VA 22101..........703-442-0900
PESTDOC/PESTDOC II, 6845 Elm St Ste 500, McLean VA 22101.........703-790-0400
PETROEX, PO Box 58408, Houston TX 77058...713-332-4511
Petroflash (DRI), 1750 K St NW, Washington DC 20006..............................202-673-7720
Petroleum Data System, Box 3030 Oklahoma Univ, Norman OK 73070...405-360-1600
Petroleum Info Intl, PO Box 1702, Houston TX 77251.................................713-961-0236
PETROSCAN, 8701 Georgia Ave Ste 800, Silver Spring MD 20910...........301-589-8875
Pharmaceutical Futures, 76 Eastern Blvd, Glastonbury CT 06033.............203-633-3501
Pharmaceutical News Index, 620 S 5th St, Louisville KY 40202.................502-582-4111
Pharmaceutical Prospects, 76 Eastern Blvd, Glastonbury CT 06033.........203-633-3501
Philosopher's Index, BGSU, Bowling Green OH 43403...............................419-372-2419
PIE, US Fish & Wildlife 18th & C NW, Washington DC 20204....................202-653-8732
PIW, 1 Times Sq Plz, New York NY 10036...212-575-1242
Platt's Data Bank, 1750 K St NW, Washington DC 20006............................202-663-7720
Poison Control Case Reports, 5600 Fishers Ln, Rockville MD 20857.......301-443-6260
Pollution Abstracts, 5161 River Rd, Bethesda MD 20816............................301-951-1400
Pollution Incident Reporting System, 2100 2nd St, Wash DC 20593.........202-267-0452
Popline, 624 North Broadway, Baltimore MD 21205.....................................301-955-8200
Population Bibliography, Univ Sq E 300A, Chapel Hill NC 27514...........919-966-2157
Power, US Dept Energy MA232 2GTN, Washington DC 20545....................301-353-2855
J D Power Auto Consumer, 31225 La Baya Dr, Westlake Vlg CA 91362..213-889-6330
PR Newswire, 150 East 58th St, New York NY 10155....................................212-832-9400
Pre Med, 1200 Rt 7, Latham NY 12110...800-833-4707
Predicasts, 11001 Cedar Ave, Cleveland OH 44106......................................800-321-6388
Private Placement Data Base, 62 Williams St, New York NY 10005..........212-668-0940
PRIZM, 219 E 42nd St, New York NY 10017..212-867-1414
Procurement Automated Source Sys, 1441 L St NW, Wash DC 20416......202-653-6586

Producer Price Data Base, 1211 Connecticut Ave NW, Wash DC 20036..202-467-4900
PROFILE, Dept of Commerce, Wash DC 20230 202-377-2414
Program Improvement Data, 1960 Kenny Rd, Columbus OH 43210........614-486-3655
Project Share, PO Box 2309, Rockville MD 20852.............................301-231-9539
Proprietary Computer Systems, 16625 Saticoy St, Van Nuys CA 91406....201-227-0035
PSA Data Base, 110 Vermont Ave NW, Washington DC 20005 202-659-5850
Public Affairs Info, 1024 10th St Ste 300, Sacremento CA 95814...............415-444-0676
Public Comments DOE Rule Making, Box X, Oak Ridge TN 37830........615-574-7763
QBANK, 2033 K St NW Ste 305, Washington DC 20006..........................202-293-2915
Quotron 800, 5454 Beethoven St, Los Angeles CA 90066......................213-827-4600
Quotron Systems Inc, 5454 Beethoven St, Los Angeles CA 90066.............213-827-4600
R&T WUIS, DTIC Cameron Station Bldg 5, Alexandria VA 22314..........202-274-6434
Radiation Experience Data, 5600 Fishers Ln, Rockville MD 20857 301-443-1002
Rainbo Electronic Reviews, 8 Duran Ct, Pacifica CA 94044....................415-993-6029
Random Lengths Data Bank, 1750 K St NW, Wash DC 20006..................202-663-7720
Rapidata Div Natl Data Corp, 20 New Dutch Ln, Fairfield NJ 07006 201-227-0035
RapidQuote, 60 Hudson St, New York NY 10013................................212-227-5082
Rare-Earth Info Ctr, EMRRI Iowa State Univ, Ames IA 50011 515-294-2272
RCA Mail, 201 Centennial Ave, Piscataway NJ 08854 800-526-3969
Real Estate Analysis & Planning, 1750 K St NW, Wash DC 20006..........202-673-7720
Real Estate Info Systems Network, 430 N Michigan, Chicago IL 60611....313-329-8200
Recreation Info Management, PO Box 2417, Washington DC 20013.........202-447-4313
Regional & Urban Studies, CEEI Bldg 4500 N, Oak Ridge TN 37830......615-574-7470
Regional Data SMSA, 150 Monument, Bala Cynwyd PA 19004...................215-667-6000
Registry Toxic Effects Chem, 4676 Columbia, Cincinnati OH 45226 513-684-8317
Religion Index, 5600 S Woodlawn Ave, Chicago IL 60637 312-947-9417
RELS, 13464 Washington Blvd, Marina del Rey CA 90291 800-423-6377
REMARC, 1911 N Ft Myer Dr, Arlington VA 22209.............................800-386-3008
Remote Computing Corp, 1044 Northern Blvd, Roslyn NY 11576 516-484-4545
Resources in Computer Educ, 300 SW 6th Ave, Portland OR 97204.........503-248-6800
Resources in Vocational Educ, Ohio State Univ, Columbus OH 43210 800-848-4815
RFC News Service, 341 Mark West Station Rd, Windsor CA 95492 707-542-7819
RILM Abstracts, 33 West 42nd St, New York NY 10036........................212-790-4214
RINGDOC/RING6475, 6845 Elm St, McLean VA 22101.......................703-790-0400
RISI Pulp & Paper Data Banks, 110 Great Rd, Bedford MA 01730 617-271-0030
RLIN Data Base, Research Libraries Group, Stamford CA 94305..............415-328-0920
Robotics Info, 4701 Marburg Ave, Cincinnati OH 45209 513-841-8110
Rock Analysis Storage Sys, Oklahoma Univ, Norman OK 73070...............405-360-1600
ROME, Ohio State U 1960 Kenny Rd, Columbus OH 43210 800-848-4815
RRC, 1110 Vermont Ave NW, Washington DC 20005 202-466-6240
RTECS, 1600 Clifton Rd, Atlanta GA 30333.....................................404-329-3771
Sadtler Research Lab, 3316 Spring Garden, Philadelphia PA 19104.........215-382-7800
Safety Recommendation Data, 800 Independence, Wash DC 20594.........202-382-6817
Savings & Loan, 1700 G St NW, Washington DC 20006.........................202-377-6000
SCAN, FHLBB 320 1st St NW, Washington DC 20552 202-377-6000
SCAN200, 175 Jackson Plaza, Ann Arbor MI 48106..............................313-769-6800
SCC, 1110 Vermont Ave NW Ste 700, Washington DC 20005 202-466-6240
Schedule, 1602 South Parker Rd, Denver CO 80231.............................303-750-7417
SCIPIO, Research Libraries Group, Stanford CA 94305 415-328-0920
SciSearch, 3501 Market St, Philadelphia PA 19104................................215-386-0100
SDC Info Services, 2500 Colorado Ave, Santa Monica CA 90406 213-820-4111
SDR, FAA 800 Independence Ave SW, Washington DC 20591.................202-426-4000
Securities Data Inc, 62 Williams St 6th fl, New York NY 10005................212-668-0940

Securities Industry (DRI), 1750 K St NW, Wash DC 20006.......................202-673-7720
SEDS, DE EI-20 Forrestal Bldg, Washington DC 20585 202-252-8800
SEEDIS, Lawrence Berkeley Lab UC, Berkeley CA 94720 415-486-5307
I P Sharp Assoc, 1200 1st Federal Plz, Rochester NY 14614.......................716-546-7270
Shaw Data Services, 122 E 42nd St, New York NY 10168 212-682-8877
Simmons Market Research, 219 E 42nd St, New York NY 10017..............212-867-1414
Site-Potential, 8260 Willow Oaks Corporate Dr, Arlington VA 22031 703-876-2334
SJRUNDT, 130 E 63rd St, New York NY 10021......................................212-838-0141
SLUDGE, 951 Pershing Dr, Silver Spring MS 20910.................................301-587-6300
SMART, 1929 Harlem Ave, Chicago IL 60635.......................................312-622-6666
Smoking & Health, 5600 Fishers Ln Rm 116, Rockville MD 20857 301-443-1690
SMR, 4041 University Dr Ste 304, Fairfax VA 22030................................703-352-1200
Soils Info Retrieval Systems, 909 W Nevada St, Urbana IL 61801.............312-333-1269
Solar Energy Intelligence Report, 951 Pershing, Silver Spg MD 20910 301-587-6300
Source, 10076 Boca Entrada Blvd, Boca Raton FL 33433 305-483-2600
Source Telecomputing Corp, 1616 Anderson Rd, McLean VA 22102.......703-734-7500
SpecText, 601 Madison St, Alexandria VA 22312....................................705-684-0300
SpecText Master Guide, 435 Hudson St, New York NY 10014.................212-807-7280
Spectrum, 11501 Georgia Ave, Silver Spring MD 20902 301-942-1700
SPIN, 335 E 45th St, New York NY 10017 212-661-9404
Spinner Program, NOAA Rm 100 WWB, Wash DC 20233 301-763-8111
SSIC/SSCB, 3501 Market St, Philadelphia PA 19104 215-386-0100
St Louis Post Dispatch Classified, 900 N Tucker, St Louis MO 63101 314-622-7459
Standard & Poor's Daily News, 25 Broadway, New York NY 10004..........212-205-5377
Standard & Poor's Industry Financial, 1750 K St NW, Wash DC 20006..202-663-7720
Standard & Poor's News Online, 25 Broadway, New York NY 10004.......212-208-8622
STARGRAM, 205 W Highland Ave, Milwaukee WI 53203....................800-588-9044
StarText, 400 W 7th St, Ft Worth TX 76102 817-429-2655
State Agriculture, 150 Monument Rd, Bala Cynwyd PA 19004 215-667-6000
Stock Broker Terminal Service, 35 Nutmeg Dr, Trumbull CT 06609 203-386-2000
StockPort, 850 3rd Ave, New York NY 10043 212-559-3189
StockVue, 301 East Grace St, Richmond VA 23219..................................804-649-6587
STP/LTP, 1 NY Plaza Ste 3507, New York NY 10004..............................212-943-9515
STSC, 2115 E Jefferson St, Rockville MD 20852......................................301-984-5000
Study of Media & Markets, 219 E 42nd St, New York NY 10017 212-867-1414
Sudden Infant Death Syndrome, 1555 Wilson Blvd, Rosslyn VA 22209....703-522-0870
SUPERSITE, 8260 Willow Oaks Corporate Dr, Arlington VA 22031........703-876-2334
Survey Methodology Info Sys, Univ of Michigan, Ann Arbor MI 48106 ...301-764-2570
Survey of Doctorate Recipients, 2101 Constitution, Wash DC 20418.........202-334-3155
Survey of Income & Education, US Bureau of Census, Wash DC 20233 ..301-763-4100
Tax Shelter Insider, 10076 Boca Entrada Blvd, Boca Raton FL 33433......305-483-2600
Tech Net, 15 Inverness Way East, Englewood CO 80150 303-790-0600
Technical Reports, DTIC Cameron Sta Bldg 5, Alexandria VA 22314......202-274-6434
TECLAB/TECTRA, CSU School of Business, Sacramento CA 95819.......916-278-6640
Telecommunications Network Svcs, 1750 K St NW, Wash DC 20006........202-673-7720
Telegen, 48 W 38th St, New York NY 10018 212-944-8500
TeleSearch, 8310 Capital of Texas Hwy, Austin TX 78731........................512-343-9066
TeleTax/TeleTitle, 16134 Hart St, Van Nuys CA 91406 213-988-1830
Telmar Media Systems Inc, 90 Park Ave, New York NY 10016 212-949-4640
Telstat Systems Inc, 60 Hudson St, New York NY 10013...........................212-227-5082
TERM, 1200 Route 7, Latham NY 12110 800-833-4707
Textile Technology Digest, PO Box 391, Charlottesville VA 22902...........804-296-5511
TICK, 1929 N Harlem Ave, Chicago IL 60635...312-622-6666

Time Sharing Resources, 777 Northern Blvd, Great Neck NY 11021........516-487-0101
Toxic Materials News, 951 Pershing Dr, Silver Spring MD 20910 301-587-6300
ToxLine/Natl Library Medicine, 8600 Rockville, Bethesda MD 20209 301-496-6193
Trade & Industry Index, 404 6th Ave, Menlo Park CA 94025.....................800-227-8431
Trade Opportunities, US Dept of Commerce, Washington DC 20230......202-377-2667
Trade Opportunities Prog, Dept of Commerce, Wash DC 20230 202-377-2665
Transportation Satellites (DRI), 1750 K St NW, Wash DC 20006...............202-673-7720
Trinet (DRI), 1750 K St NW, Washington DC 20006 202-673-7720
TRIS, 2101 Constitution Ave NW, Washington DC 20418..........................202-334-3250
TSC Corporate Office, Box 683, Hanover NH 03755..................................603-448-3838
TSCA Plus, Office Toxic Sub 401 M St SW, Washington DC 20460 800-424-9065
Tulsa, Tulsa Univ 600 S College, Tulsa OK 74104 918-592-6000
UCLA Business Forecasting, Los Angeles CA 90024..................................213-825-1623
Ulrich's Intl Periodical Dir, 1180 Ave of Amer, New York NY 10036.......212-764-5107
UMI/Data Courier, 620 S 5th St, Louisville KY 40202................................502-582-4111
Umler, 1930 L St NW, Washington DC 20036 202-835-9100
UN Natl Income Account, 150 Monument Rd, Bala Cynwyd PA 19004.....215-667-6000
Uni Coll Corp, 3401 Science Ctr, Philadelphia PA 19104...........................215-387-3890
UNISTOX, 200 E 42nd St, New York NY 10007..212-655-7000
United Communication Group, 8701 Georgia, Silver Spg MD 20901........301-589-8875
United Info Services Inc, PO Box 8551, Kansas City MO 64114.................913-341-9161
Universal Serial & Book Exchange, 3335 V St NE, Wash DC 20018..........202-636-8723
UPI News, 200 E 42nd St, New York NY 10007 212-655-7500
US Board on Geographic Names, US Naval Observ, Wash DC 20016......202-653-1428
US Census of Agriculture, US Bureau of Census, Wash DC 20233............301-763-4100
US Energy Forecast, 150 Monument Rd, Bala Cynwyd PA 19004.............215-667-6000
US Exports, Bureau of Census, Washington DC 20233...............................301-763-5140
US Macroeconomics, 150 Monument Rd, Bala Cynwyd PA 19004 215-667-6000
US Car-Light Truck, 150 Monument Rd, Bala Cynwyd PA 19004 215-667-6000
US Political Science Documents, Pittsburg Univ, Pittsburg PA 15260.......412-624-5212
US Public School Director, 400 Maryland Ave, Wash DC 20202.................202-245-8653
USARDEC, Plastics Tech Eval Ctr, Picatinny Ars NJ 07806.......................201-724-2778
USClass, 6845 Elm St Ste 500, McLean VA 22121 703-790-0400
USDA Online, US Dept of Agriculture Rm 536A, Wash DC 20250...........202-477-7454
USECON, 175 Jackson Plaza, Ann Arbor MI 48106....................................313-769-6800
USGCA, PO Box 1215, Falls Church VA 22041..703-845-0666
USNO ADS, US Naval Observatory, Washington DC 20390 202-254-4548
USOPT, 22 Cortland St, New York NY 10007 212-285-0700
USPA/USP77/USP70, 6845 Elm St Ste 500, McLean VA 22101 703-790-0400
Value Line Data Base, 711 3rd Ave, New York NY 10017............................212-687-3965
VETDOG, 6845 Elm St Ste 500, McLean VA 22101 703-790-0400
ViewData Videotex Report, 215 Park Ave S, New York NY 10003..............212-473-5600
Vocational Educ Curriculum, Ohio State Univ, Columbus OH 43210......614-486-3655
Wall Street Journal, Box 300, Princeton NJ 08540......................................800-257-5114
Wall Street Week Online, Nonita Ave, Owings Mills MD 21117 301-356-5600
Ward's Autoinfobank, 28 W Adams, Detroit MI 48226................................313-962-4433
Warner Computer Systems Inc, 605 3rd Ave, New York NY 10158...........212-986-1919
Washington Credit Letter, 951 Pershing Dr, Silver Spring MD 20910........301-587-6300
Washington Library Network, Wash State Library, Olympia WA 98504...206-753-5595
Waste Mgmt & Resource Rec, 21093 IRE Ctrl Ctr, Eagan MN 55121.......612-888-9635
Water Data Sources Directory, 421 Natl Ctr, Reston VA 22092..................703-860-6031
Water Resources Abstracts, Dept of Interior, Washington DC 20240.......202-343-8435
WaterNet, 6666 W Quincy Ave, Denver CO 80235 303-794-7711

WATSTORE, 421 Natl Ctr, Reston VA 22092 703-860-6031
WBANK, 2033 K St NW Ste 305, Washington DC 20006 202-293-2915
WDEBT, 150 Monument Rd, Bala Cynwyd PA 19004 215-667-6000
Weekly Economic Survey, 490 El Camino Real, Belmont CA 94002.........415-595-0610
Weekly Economic Update, Box 300, Princeton NJ 08540 800-257-5114
Well History, PO Box 1702, Houston TX 77001 713-961-5660
Western Data Base, 50 W Kellogg Blvd, St Paul MN 55165 612-228-2500
Western Union, 1 Lake St, Upper Saddle Riv NJ 07458 201-825-5000
Western Union EasyLink, 1 Lake St, Upper Saddle Riv NJ 07458 800-336-3797
Wharton US Data Base Files, 3624 Science Ctr, Philadelphia PA 19104...215-823-5237
Who's Who Resource File, Dept of Commerce, Wash DC 20230 202-377-5997
John Wiley & Sons Inc, 605 3rd Ave, New York NY 10158.....................212-850-6331
Windsor Systems Development, 545 5th Ave, New York NY 10017 212-697-5390
Women in Development, Census Bureau, Wash DC 20233.......................301-763-4221
World Agri Supply, 150 Monument Rd, Bala Cynwyd PA 19004...............215-667-6000
World Aluminum Abstracts, ASM Intl, Metals Park OH 44073................216-338-5151
World Best Tables, 1818 H St NW, Washington DC 20433 202-473-2942
World Energy Industry, 4202 Sorrento Valley, San Diego CA 92121 619-452-7675
World Fertilizer Mkt, Natl Fertilzer Dev Ctr, Muscle Shoals AL 35660 ...205-386-2821
World Forecast, 150 Monument Rd, Bala Cynwyd PA 19004 215-896-4772
World Info Library, 605 Bloomfield Ave, Montclair NJ 07042 201-746-5060
World Population, Scuderi Bldg Rm 407 Census Bur, Wash DC 20233...301-763-4086
WPI/WPIL, 6845 Elm St Ste 500, McLean VA 22101 703-790-0400
WSB, 2101 L St NW, Washington DC 20037......................................202-457-7141
X Census Plus, 5161 River Rd, Bethesda MD 20816.............................301-951-1300
X Market, 310 Madison Ave, New York NY 10017 212-697-6080
X Profile, 1351 Washington Blvd, Stamford CT 06902...........................203-965-5454
X Religion, 36 Boylston St, Cambridge MA 02138 617-661-1550
XTAL, NBS A323 Physics Bldg, Gaithersburg MD 20899 301-975-2208
YBANK, 2033 K St NW Ste 305, Washington DC 20006 202-293-2915
Zacks Earnings Estimates (DRI), 1750 K St NW, Wash DC 20006...........202-673-7720
Zip Code, 233 Wilshire Blvd, Santa Monica CA 90401...........................213-451-8583
Zoological Record, BIS 2100 Arch St, Philadelphia PA 19103.................215-587-4800

EDITORS & PROOFREADERS

This section lists firms providing general manuscript editing services, including copy editing, line editing, and proofreading. See Manuscript Analysts for firms providing manuscript evaluation services. Also see Bibliographers, Ghost Writers & Collaborators, and Indexers

AA's & PE's, 428 Lafayette St, New York NY 10003.................................212-228-8707
Kimball Aamodt, 35 W 92nd St, New York NY 10025 212-663-1017
ABC Writing & Editing, 1328 A St SE, Washington DC 20003...................202-543-3442
About Books Inc, PO Box 538, Saguache CO 81149 303-589-8223
Abrams Editorial/Design, 129 Stanford Ave, Emerson NJ 07630..............201-262-4709
Action Research Assoc, 2111 Edinburg Ave, Cardiff-by-Sea CA 92007.....619-944-0752
Rose A Adkins, 741B Robinson Rd, Topanga CA 90290.........................213-455-3823
ADR Typing Service, PO Box 184 Bath Beach Sta, Brooklyn NY 11214....718-837-3484
Advanced Design Corp, 5515 Cherokee Ave, Alexandria VA 22312..........703-354-3390
AEIOU Inc, 74 Memorial Plaza, Pleasantville NY 10570 914-769-1135

Rodelinde Albrecht, 250 Columbus Ste 203, San Francisco CA 94133 415-362-5949
Allen Press Inc, 1041 New Hampshire St, Lawrence KS 66044.................913-843-1234
Carol L Allison, 4848 S Alameda #1804, Corpus Christi TX 78412..........512-992-9496
Ampersand, 16 Forest Dr, Morris Plains NJ 07950................................201-538-9407
Joyce L Ananian, 204 Church St, Waltham MA 02154 617-894-4330
David Leif Anderson, 331 W 20th Street, New York NY 10011 212-741-3121
Denice A Anderson, 328 E 93rd St Apt 2A, New York NY 10128.............212-348-6061
Andujar Communication Tech, 17 E 45th St, New York NY 10017..........212-883-9098
Deborah Annan, 3201 N W 70th St, Seattle WA 98117........................206-789-4663
The Art Works, PO Box 407, Carefree AZ 85331 602-488-2510
Associated Editors, 49 Hazelwood Ln, Stamford CT 06905 203-322-3836
The Author's Friend, 160 W 71st St Apt 11E, New York NY 10023..........212-877-1510
The Authors Resource Ctr, 4001 E Ft Lowell Rd, Tucson AZ 85712 602-325-4733
Faren Bachelis, 1628 Chorro St, San Luis Obispo CA 93401.................805-543-8297
Janet H Baker, 115 Glen Riddle Rd, Media PA 19063..........................215-566-3542
Baldwin Literary Services, 935 Hayes St, Baldwin NY 11510................516-546-8338
Bernice & Leo Balfour, 1219 Ralston St, Anaheim CA 92801 714-774-4944
Baran Tech Writing, 641 27th St, San Francisco CA 94131 415-641-0113
Kathleen Barnes, 238 W 4th St #3C, New York NY 10014...................212-924-8084
Diana Barth, 535 W 51st St Apt 3A, New York NY 10019 212-307-5465
Loris Battin, 98-20 62nd Dr Apt 10E, Rego Park NY 11374.................718-459-3417
Priscilla Battis, RFD 4 Box 3550, Skowhegan ME 04976 207-643-2643
Beaver Wood Enterprises, 11585 Links Dr, Reston VA 22090................703-437-4527
Beatrice Beckman, 2220 N Halsted St, Chicago IL 60614 312-975-7213
Jean B Bernard, 1717 Lanier Pl N W, Washington DC 20009.................202-332-3373
Barbara M Beyda, Box 222763, Carmel CA 93922.............................408-624-6636
Carol Billman, Box 114, Landenburg PA 19350................................215-274-2145
Marjorie M Bitker, 2330 E Back Bay, Milwaukee WI 53202.................414-276-5462
Susan N Bjorner, 10 Cannongate, Tyngsborough MA 01879 617-649-9746
Gilbert J Black, 399 West St, Harrison NY 10528.............................914-835-3160
Samuel R Blate Assoc, 10331 Watkins Mill, Gaithersburg MD 20879 301-840-2248
Jolene M Blozis, 1600 M St NW Natl Geographic, Wash DC 20036.........202-857-7056
Blue Pencil Group, PO Box 3392, Reston VA 22090 202-471-1998
Hazel Blumberg-McKee, 136 S Oxford, St Paul MN 55105...................612-292-1680
The Book Studio Inc, 3 Louis Ln, Croton on Hudson NY 10520.............914-739-9228
The Bookmill, 234 12th St, Santa Monica CA 90402 213-393-3843
The Bookmill, 3610 Moore St, Los Angeles CA 90066 213-398-4645
The Bookworks Inc, PO Box 1189, Chicago IL 60690.........................312-236-8472
Steve Boone, 516 Cramer Ave, Pnt Pleasant Bch NJ 08742..................201-899-6515
Adrienne Holmes Bradford, 18 E Lyon Farm Dr, Greenwich CT 06831...203-531-6766
Linda Bradford, 222 E 10th St, New York NY 10003..........................212-473-1578
Elsa Branden, 222 W 77th St Ste 1218, New York NY 10024................212-362-1100
Robert Brightman, 5 Sussex Rd, Great Neck NY 11020 516-482-2074
Norman Brown & Assoc, 21 Luzon Ave, Providence RI 02906 401-751-2641
Barbara L Bryan, Box 73, Kelly WY 83011......................................307-733-4189
Business Media Resources, 150 Shoreline Hwy, Mill Valley CA 94941.....415-331-6021
BZ/Rights & Permissions Inc, 145 W 86th St, New York NY 10024........212-580-0615
Luis R Caceres/Trans Data Intl, 8711 SW 20th Ter, Miami FL 33165 305-552-8433
Shirley Camper, 40 W 77th St 15B, New York NY 10024.....................212-787-8722
Richard Carlin, 25 Oleander Ct, Lawrenceville NJ 08648 609-896-4465
Carlisle Graphics, Box 834 2530 Kerper Blvd, Dubuque IA 52001...........319-557-1500
Carlsbad Publications, 3242 McKinley St, Carlsbad CA 92008 619-729-9543
Carnes Publication Svcs, 23811 Chagrin Blvd, Beachwood OH 44122......216-292-7959

Anne Carson Assoc, 3323 Nebraska Ave, Washington DC 20016................202-244-6679
Donald Cart, PO Box 65044, Lubbock TX 79464.......................................806-793-0734
Claudia Caruana, PO Box 20077, Elmont NY 10017......................................516-488-5815
Cassell Communications Inc, PO Box 9844, Ft Lauderdale FL 33310......305-485-0795
John Charnay, 19961 Stratern St, Canoga Park CA 91306...........................818-998-2652
Charles Choset, 90 Bedford St, New York NY 10014......................................212-243-0035
James Chotas, 265 E 78th St, New York NY 10021...212-243-0035
Tina Clark, 318 Harvard St Ste 10, Brookline MA 02146...........................617-734-0807
Zipporah W Collins, 2140 Shattuck Ave Rm 404, Berkeley CA 94704......415-848-1442
Comp-Type Inc, 155 Cypress St, Ft Bragg CA 95437......................................707-964-9520
Frances G Conn Assoc, 8320 Woodhaven Blvd, Bethesda MD 20817........301-365-5080
Claire Connelly Editorial Services, 232 Plains Rd, Coventry CT 06238....203-277-6366
Connexions, 14011 Brookgreen Dr, Dallas TX 75240.....................................214-234-4519
Conservatory of Amer Letters, PO Box 123, S Thomaston ME 04858.......207-354-6550
Contemporary Educ Services, 85 Bouvant Dr, Princeton NJ 08540...........609-683-0155
Maria Coughlin, 31 Maryland Ave, Annapolis MD 21401.............................301-269-0978
Paul Covington, 206 Pierron St, Northvale NJ 07647....................................201-768-6386
Contemporary Perspectives Inc, 223 E 48th St, New York NY 10017.......212-753-3800
Creative Freelancers Inc, 62 W 45th St, New York NY 10036....................212-398-9540
Crown Communications, PO Box 11626, St Paul MN 55111.......................612-698-0051
Ernestine R Daniels, 610B Gadd Rd, Hixson TN 37343...............................615-870-1473
Nancy L Daniels, Box 68, Lemont PA 16851..814-237-7711
Dell-Naatz Publication Arts, 106 Pinion Ln, Manitou Springs CO 80829..303-685-9719
Depot Press, PO Box 60072, Nashville TN 37206...615-226-1890
Dr Erwin DiCyan, 1486 E 33rd St, Brooklyn NY 11234..............................718-252-8844
May Dikeman, 70 Irving Pl, New York NY 10003..212-475-4533
A H Drummond Jr, 323 Springs Rd, Bedford MA 01730...............................617-275-1481
Valerie Eads Et Al, Box 1459 Grand Central Sta, New York NY 10016....212-228-0900
Easy Writer, 1400 63rd St, Des Moines IA 50311..515-279-3491
Edit Aids, 241-20 Northern Blvd Ste 6C, Douglaston NY 11362.................718-423-2867
Edit Productions, Box 29527, Oakland CA 94604..415-763-3510
Editcetera, 2490 Channing Way Rm 507, Berkeley CA 94704......................415-849-1110
Editech, 4827 Davenport St NW, Washington DC 20016...............................202-244-8882
Editing & Publishing Services, Pleasant Point Rd, Cushing ME 04563.....207-354-2467
Editing Design & Production, 400 Market St 7th fl, Phila PA 19106.........215-592-1133
Editing Unlimited, 196 Wykagyl Terr, New Rochelle NY 10804................914-636-2637
Editmasters/Mizelle, 4545 Connecticut Ave NW, Wash DC 20008...........202-686-7252
The Editor's Bureau Ltd, Box 68, Westport CT 06881.................................203-227-9275
Editorial & Graphic Services, Martinsville NJ 08836..................................201-469-2195
Editorial Consultants Inc, 1605 12th Ave Ste #7, Seattle WA 98122........206-323-6475
Editorial Consultants Inc, 1728 Union St, San Francisco CA 94123..........415-474-5010
Editorial Consultation Services, 2427 29th St, Lubbock TX 79411............806-793-0881
The Editorial Department, 541 Rt 9W, Grandview NY 10960.....................914-358-1158
Editorial Experts Inc, 85 S Bragg St Ste 400, Alexandria VA 22312..........703-642-3040
Editorial Inc, Box 267, Rockport MA 01966...617-546-7346
Editorial Services, 501 S Cortez Ste F-3, Prescott AZ 86301.....................602-445-8627
Editorial Services, Rt 1 Box 188, Bull Shoals AR 72619.............................501-224-4793
Editorial Services, 531 N 66th St, Seattle WA 98103...................................206-782-4085
Education Systems Inc, Box 337, Gales Ferry CT 06335...............................203-464-0391
Educational Challenges Inc, 1009 Duke St, Alexandria VA 22314.............703-683-1500
Educational Media Co, 6021 Wish Ave, Encino CA 91316............................818-708-0962
J M B Edwards Writer & Editor, 2432 California, Berkeley CA 94703.....415-644-8287
Effective Learning, 7 N MacQuesten Pkwy, Mt Vernon NY 10550...........914-664-7944

Roger E Egan, 7 Lincoln Pl, New Brunswick NJ 08902 201-821-0106
Joyce W Ellis, 89 W Lakeview Ave, Columbus OH 43202 614-263-7946
Irene Elmer, 2806 Cherry, Berkeley CA 94705 415-841-0466
Ruth Elwell & Donald Smith, 87 E 2nd St, New York NY 10003................212-260-6148
Henry W Engel, 441 E 20th St, New York NY 10010.......................................212-477-2597
Jeri Engh, Pine Lake Farm Rt 2, Osceola WI 54020...................................715-248-3800
Ensemble Productions Inc, 175 W 93rd St #5-J, New York NY 10025 212-866-2016
Pearl Eppy, 201 E 79th St, New York NY 10021 212-737-0354
Herta Erville, 320 W End Ave, New York NY 10023 212-874-3988
David R Esner Editorial Consultant, 16 Willow Pl, Brooklyn NY 11201..718-855-0792
Etcetera Enterprises, 269 Lake Rd, Congers NY 10920.................................914-268-9323
Karen Feinberg, 5755 Nahant Ave, Cincinnati OH 45224.............................513-542-8328
Lillian Mermin Feinsilver, 510 McCartney St, Easton PA 18042 215-252-7005
Betsy Feist Resources, 140 E 81st St, New York NY 10028............................212-861-2014
Janice J Feldstein Editorial Svcs, 860 N Lake Shore, Chicago IL 60611...312-951-6215
Jerry Felsen, 84-13 168th St, Jamaica NY 11432...718-739-4242
First Editions, PO Box 1158, Sedona AZ 86336..602-282-1989
Joan Follendore, 13376 Washington Blvd, W Los Angeles CA 90066........213-306-3986
Charles Radley Force, 2076 Southwood Rd, Jackson MS 39211 601-366-3748
Linda E Forlifer, 315 E 33rd St, Baltimore MD 21218.................................301-243-1287
Catherine Fox, RR1 Box 237, Spencer IN 47460...812-829-3297
Sandi Frank, 95 Furnace Dock Rd, Croton on Hudson NY 10520.............914-271-6293
Free Lance Exchange Inc, 150 5th Ave, New York NY 10011.....................212-741-8020
Helena Frost Assoc, 301 E 21st St, New York NY 10010...............................212-475-6642
Norma R Fryatt, 227 Granite St, Rockport MA 01966...................................617-546-6490
Gabriel House Inc, 5045 W Oakton St, Skokie IL 60077................................312-675-1146
Diane Gallo, Box 231 RD 1, Mount Upton NY 13809 607-764-8139
Diane R Gambino, 150-23 24 Rd, Whitestone NY 11357................................718-939-6668
The Garber Group, 420 E 55th St Ste 2R, New York NY 10022....................212-421-4097
Mary-Stuart Garden, 17 Stuyvesant Oval, New York NY 10009 212-477-2597
Albert D Geller, 9127 Luna Ave, Morton Grove IL 60053 312-966-9133
Joan German, West Mountain Rd, Cheshire MA 01225...............................413-743-2036
Susan M Gerstein, 10 Brockway Rd, Hanover NH 03755.............................603-643-2519
Audrey C Gilmour, 9 Mt Pleasant Rd, Morristown NJ 07960 201-895-3047
Martha & Dennis Gleason, Box 540, Boothbay Harbor ME 04538...........207-633-2336
Linda Gluck Graphic Design, 81 N Ohioville Rd, New Paltz NY 12561....914-255-0381
Hadassah Gold, 222 W 83rd St, New York NY 10024......................................212-787-5668
Ellen Gordon, 17 Byron Ln, Larchmont NY 10538 914-834-7089
Chet & Susan Gottfried, Box 9, Kew Gardens NY 11415 212-847-1464
David B Gracy II, 2313 Tower Dr, Austin TX 78703..512-474-2784
Rudolph F Graf, 111 Van Etten Blvd, New Rochelle NY 10804...................914-632-7393
Genevieve S Gray, 8932 E Calle Norlo, Tucson AZ 85710.............................602-886-7829
Tony Greenberg, 3633 Malibu Vista Dr, Malibu CA 90265 213-454-3386
Nancy J Gregg, Box 6524, Springfield IL 62708 217-793-2517
Linda M Gregonis, 3426 E Glenn #7, Tucson AZ 85716................................602-323-9338
George D Griffin, 11 E 9th St, New York NY 10003...212-254-7527
Georgia Griggs, 2636 Kansas Ave, Santa Monica CA 90404.........................213-828-4948
Myra Gross & Assoc Inc, 6930 NW 83rd St, Tamarac FL 33321 305-428-4477
Judith S Grossman, 26 Blancoyd Rd, Merion PA 19066 215-664-3732
Isabel S Grossner, 61 Tuxedo Rd, Montclair NJ 07042.................................201-746-5371
Lesley Gudehus, 200 Berkshire Rd, Hasbrouck Hts NJ 07604 212-303-6784
Polly Guerin, 15 Park Ave, New York NY 10016 212-725-0977
The Guilford Group, Box 981 124 Jerry Ln, Davisville RI 02854................401-884-3101

Michael Haldeman, Box 4494 1014 Adams Circle, Boulder CO 80306 303-442-2518
Hallberg Hallmundsson, 30 5th Ave, New York NY 10011.........................212-982-0407
Harkavy Publishing Service, 33 W 17th St, New York NY 10011................212-929-1339
Harriett, 135 54th St, New York NY 10022 212-688-0094
Daniel J Harrison, 336 Costa Mesa Dr, Toms River NJ 08757...................201-341-8996
James E Hartman, 303 Cambridge Dr Apt C, Clearwater FL 33575 813-797-0396
Marian Hartsough, 1533 Camino Verde, Walnut Creek CA 94596 415-935-8238
Anne Hebenstreit, Box 2292, Elizabeth NJ 07207....................................201-351-6528
Mary L Hey, 1919 Grove St, Boulder CO 80302...303-442-3638
History Assoc, 2686 Claythorne Rd, Cleveland OH 44122.........................216-321-9193
Diane Hodges, 220 E 87th St, New York NY 10128 212-722-0856
Marcia Holly PhD, 214 Maple St, New Haven CT 06511.............................203-787-9699
Burnham Holmes, 51 E 97th St #6E, New York NY 10029 212-831-1939
Peggy Hoover, 501 Somerton Ave, Philadelphia PA 19116.........................215-677-1691
Ruth H Hoover, 20421 Lorne St, Canoga Park CA 91306 818-341-7551
Jeanne Howe, Box 1137, Cullowhee NC 28723...704-293-5842
Avery Hudson, 314 E 78th St Apt 12, New York NY 10021.........................212-897-5117
Eric Hughes, c/o Matagiri, Mount Tremper NY 12457 914-679-8322
Janet M Hunter, 411 Rose Ave, Mill Valley CA 94941 415-388-8788
Miriam Hurewitz, 445 Riverside Dr, New York NY 10027............................212-866-3693
Bernhardt J Hurwood, 440 E 79th St 11E, New York NY 10021..................212-744-6191
Impact Publications, PO Box 1896, Evanston IL 60204 312-475-5748
In Plain English Inc, 25 Fox Ridge Ln, Locust Valley NY 11560 516-676-5219
JJ Editorial Services, 20 El Bonito Way, Millbrae CA 94030.....................415-697-8670
Cliff Johnson & Assoc, 10867 Fruitland Dr, Studio City CA 91604............818-761-5665
Curt Johnson, 3093 Dato, Highland Park IL 60035 312-432-6804
James A Johnson, 675 Academy St Apt 2J, New York NY 10034 212-942-6670
Camille Joslyn, 1763 Wainwright Dr, Reston VA 22090 703-471-1641
Samuel Kaufman, 144 W 86th St, New York NY 10024................................212-787-3628
Christopher Kaylor Company, PO Box 737, Huntsville AL 35804...............205-534-6156
Betty Keim, 26 W 17th St 8th Fl, New York NY 10011.................................212-206-1442
Aidan A Kelly, 2250 Central Ave Ste 332, Alameda CA 94501....................415-521-6126
Carol Kennedy, 3336 Aldrich Ave S, Minneapolis MN 55408 612-823-2784
A Kessler Editorial Services, 10 E 85th St, New York NY 10028................212-772-8864
Frances Kianka, 2352 Generation Dr, Reston VA 22091 703-860-5115
Joyce Megginson Kircher MBA, 545 Patrick, Merritt Is FL 32953 305-452-4894
Kirchoff Wohlberg, 866 United Nations Plz #525, New York NY 10017..212-644-2020
H L Kirk Assoc, 233 E 69th St, New York NY 10021.....................................212-737-6626
Jessie Kitching, 72-61 113th St, Forest Hills NY 11375...............................718-544-3279
W Scott Knoke, 178 N Bridge St, Somerville NJ 08876................................201-526-4682
Deborah Kopka, 3208 S Barrington Ste G, Los Angeles CA 90066 213-391-4300
KPL & Assoc, 1090 Generals Hwy, Crownsville MD 21032............................301-923-6611
John Kremitske, 111 8th Ave Ste 1507, New York NY 10011 212-989-4783
Kristin Kuester, 2115 S Carrollton Ave #F, New Orleans LA 70118 504-866-8243
Ellie Kurtz, Box 610173, North Miami FL 33261...305-891-3960
L/A House Editorial, 5822 Uplander Way, Culver City CA 90230................213-216-5812
Janet Laib, 169 E 69th St PH 17A, New York NY 10021...............................212-772-7866
Becky Laman-Hynes, 688 N E 1st St, Dania FL 33004................................305-920-2738
Burton Lasky Assoc Inc, 111 8th Ave Ste 1507, New York NY 10011 212-989-4783
Lazy Brown Assoc, 2800 Quebec St NW #618, Wash DC 20008 202-686-0975
Learning Design Assoc Inc, 106 Short St, Gahanna OH 43230................614-476-1894
S Lenninger, Box 292, Geneseo IL 61254 309-944-2274
Cynthia Lewin, 35 E 85th St, New York NY 10028......................................212-861-1602

Cindy Lieberman, 18436 Lemarsh St #37, Northridge CA 91325..............818-885-6171
Ligature Inc, 165 N Canal St, Chicago IL 60606.............................312-648-1233
Elaine Linden, 838 15th St, Santa Monica CA 90403.........................213-395-5731
Dalia Lipkin, 39 Chestnut St, Boston MA 02108..............................617-227-8077
E Trina Lipton, 60 E 8th St Box 310, New York NY 10003....................212-533-3148
Literary Consultants, 340 E 52nd St, New York NY 10022....................212-758-4213
Pamela Loeser, 612 Stratford Rd, Baldwin NY 11510 516-867-0940
Susan Lohmeyer, 712 Cedarcroft Rd, Baltimore MD 21212 301-435-5196
William Lurie, 1005 145 Place S E, Bellevue WA 98007 206-747-2022
Donald MacLaren Assoc, 6713 Homestake Dr, Bowie MD 20715............301-262-0444
Joyce Madison, 14600 Saticoy St #204, Van Nuys CA 91405 818-780-6363
Makeready Inc, 233 W 77th St, New York NY 10024 212-595-5083
Jim Mann & Assoc, 9 Mt Vernon Dr, Gales Ferry CT 06335 203-464-2511
Manuscripts Intl, 408 E Main St, Dayton WA 99328...........................509-382-2436
Daniel Marcus Editorial Services, 125 Boyd St, Watertown MA 02172....617-926-1697
Frank H Marks, 4940 East End Ave, Chicago IL 60615 312-684-3124
Frances Martin, 2154 W 73rd St, New York NY 10023 212-877-8160
Hugh & Kate Mason, RD 3 Box 261 Williams Rd, Addison NY 14801.....607-458-5584
J M Matthew, 920 E University, Bloomington IN 47401 812-339-8304
Adrienne Mayor Editorial Svcs, 1432 S 3rd Ave, Bozeman MT 59715......406-586-8476
Lisa McGaw, 15 Willow Terrace Apts, Chapel Hill NC 27514 919-929-7322
Anne V McGravie, 7035 N Greenview, Chicago IL 60626 312-274-1835
Pat McNees, 5708 33rd St N W, Washington DC 20015 202-362-8694
Judith H McQuown & Co, 127 E 59th St #201, New York NY 10022.......212-688-1291
MDZ Communications, 1136 E Stuart, Ft Collins CO 80525 303-493-5532
Barbara Mele, 2525 Holland Ave, Bronx NY 10467 212-654-8047
Tom Mellers, 849 E 12th St, New York NY 10003...............................212-254-4958
Roger Menges, Box 28 Church St Ext, Saratoga Springs NY 12866...........518-583-1166
Barbara Mary Merson, 14 Heathrow Ln, Old Bridge NJ 08857................201-591-0882
Metropolitan Editorial, 301 W 105th St #4F, New York NY 10025 212-549-5518
Metropolitan Research Co, 100 Haven Ave, New York NY 10032 212-781-0264
Robert J Milch, 9 Millbrook Dr, Stony Brook NY 11790........................516-689-8546
Sondra Mochson, 18 Overlook Dr, Port Washington NY 11050................516-883-0984
Mount Ida Press, Box 87, Troy NY 12181.......................................518-272-4597
MS/Smiths Editorial Consult, RR 1 Box 447, Bridgewater CT 06752......203-354-0866
MSS Manuscript Services, 408 S High St, Galena IL 61036 815-777-0831
Mary Mueller, 108 Forest Rd, Moorestown NJ 08057...........................609-778-4769
Kathleen Mulvihill, 830 Louisiana Ave, New Orleans LA 70115...............504-891-3496
J William Myers, 109 Fulton St, Lyons OH 43533 614-927-9719
Natl Evaluation Systems, 30 Gatehouse Rd, Amherst MA 01004 413-256-0444
Charles Neighbors, 7600 Blanco Rd Ste 3607, San Antonio TX 78216......512-342-5324
Lois Newman, 6545 Hollywood Blvd #201, Hollywood CA 90028............213-464-8382
The T R Nugent Agency, 1058 Main St Ste 10, Malden MA 02148............617-322-7273
Naomi Ornest, 173 W 78th St, New York NY 10024 212-873-9128
Orovan Computer Assoc, PO Box 6082, Honolulu HI 96818....................808-841-7992
Pacific Publishing Services, 533 Stagg Ln, Santa Cruz CA 95062.............408-475-6527
Karen Papagapitos, 12 E 81st St, New York NY 10028 212-472-2524
Dick Pawelek, 57-12 66th St, Maspeth NY 11378...............................718-446-2189
Pecalhen Co, 14401 SW 85th Ave, Miami FL 33158............................305-235-3858
Phoenix Writer's Service, 57 Main St, Littlefork MN 56653 218-278-6626
Postroad Press Inc, PO Box 1212, Roanoke VA 24006..........................703-342-9797
Deborah Pritzker, 2676 Grand Concourse, Bronx NY 10458 212-364-3832
Pro-Edit, PO Box 3312, Glendale CA 91201 213-245-0296

Professional Editorial Svcs, 5531 Bubbling Wells, Ravenna OH 44266 216-682-5362
Programs on Change, 784 Columbus Ave Ste 1C, New York NY 10025...212-222-4606
Proofmark Editorial Service, 306 Busse Hwy, Park Ridge IL 60068.........312-696-1109
Generosa Gina Protano, 16 N Chatsworth #104, Larchmont NY 10538...914-834-8896
PS Assoc Inc, PO Box 959, Brookline MA 02146 617-277-9158
Publishers Editorial Services, 23 McQueen St, Katonah NY 10536 914-232-7816
Publishers Media, 5507 Morella Ave, North Hollywood CA 91607 818-980-2666
Publishers Workshop Inc, 63 Montague St, Brooklyn Hts NY 11201........718-855-1525
Publishing Resources Inc, Box 41307, San Juan PR 00940 809-724-0318
Publishing Synthesis Ltd, 425 Broome St, New York NY 10013.................212-966-4904
Shirley Radl, 220 Miramonte Ave, Palo Alto CA 94306................................415-327-3070
Mary H Raitt, 3024 Tilden St N W, Washington DC 20008.........................202-966-1154
Marian Reiner, 71 Disbrow Ln, New Rochelle NY 10804.............................914-235-7808
Reitt Editing Services, 3505 Hampton Hall Way, Atlanta GA 30319.........404-255-5790
Research Findings in Print, 26 W Jefferson Rd, Pittsford NY 14534 716-248-3947
Frank Reuter PhD, Rt 5 Box 243, Berryville AR 72616...............................501-423-2498
Rickreall Creek House, Box 13, Rickreall OR 97371...................................503-623-6889
Richard Roffman Assoc, 697 West End Ave 6A, New York NY 10025 212-749-3647
Carol Z Rothkopf, 16 Rotary Ln, Summit NJ 07901 201-273-1255
Royal Literary Publications, PO Box 6794, Laguna Niguel CA 92677.......714-495-5049
Harold J Salemson, 12 Brookdale Rd, Glen Cove NY 11542.......................516-676-2894
Sanders Editorial, 2029 Century Park E #1060, Los Angeles CA 90067 ..213-543-4268
Joanne Sandstrom, 1958 Manzanita Dr, Oakland CA 94611 415-643-6325
Karen Sardinas-Wyssling, 164 Horizon Dr, Edison NJ 08817 201-287-4075
Keith Schiffman, 117 Bank St Apt 1C, New York NY 10014.......................212-989-5582
Schroeder Editorial Svcs, 2606 Old Mill, Rolling Meadows IL 60008 312-303-0989
Michael Scofield, 3323 Bryant, Palo Alto CA 94306 415-856-1478
Nancy Bell Scott, Textstyle Flinnaean St, Cambridge MA 02138...............617-661-6327
Scripta Medica & Technica, 71 Valley St, South Orange NJ 07079...........201-762-4844
Richard Selman, 14 Washington Pl, New York NY 10003...........................212-473-1874
Service to Publishers Inc, Box 591, Lewisburg PA 17837..........................717-524-4315
Sarah Shaftman, 2433 Superior St, Madison WI 53704...............................608-241-7153
Doris P Shalley, Genl Sullivan Box 166, Wash Crossing PA 18977............215-493-3521
Sherwin Assoc, 2616 N Dayton, Chicago IL 60614 312-935-1581
Jean M Shirhall, 2700 N Norwood St, Arlington VA 22207 703-528-2617
Monica Shoffman-Graves, 101600 Overseas Hwy, Key Largo FL 33037...305-451-1462
Benita Sirkin, 10 Park Ave 16R, New York NY 10016.................................212-683-8580
Smith Editorial Services, PO Box 15153, Dallas TX 75201 214-296-5187
Roger W Smith, 33-45 90th St Apt 5H, Jackson Heights NY 11372 718-565-2855
SMS Publishing Corp, PO Box 2276, Glenview IL 60025............................312-724-1427
Nancy Snyder-Weinstock, 427 16th St, Brooklyn NY 11215......................718-768-4593
Shirley Camper Soman, 40 W 77th St 15B, New York NY 10024 212-787-8722
Special Press, Box 2524, Columbus OH 43216 614-297-1281
Jennifer Sperry, 1454 W Fargo Ave, Chicago IL 60626...............................312-465-6166
SSR Incorporated, 116 4th St S E, Washington DC 20003 202-543-1800
Julia Stair, Box 123, Kingston MA 02364..617-585-2686
Sheila Steinberg, 42 Littlebrook Rd, Springfield NJ 07081 201-273-9388
Ruth Steyn, Box 222 Star Rt, Hancock ME 04640......................................207-422-3373
Jeri L Stolk, 280 Highland St, Worcester MA 01602...................................617-757-3120
Barbara Cohen Stratyner, 300 Riverside Dr, New York NY 10025 212-222-2172
Ralph Strauch, 300 W 55th St Apt 9P, New York NY 10019 212-247-3574
Marjorie Stromquist, 333 E 46th St, New York NY 10017...........................212-883-1269
Elizabeth Peirce Swift, Pleasant Point Rd, Cushing ME 04563..................207-354-2467

Syentek Books Co Inc, PO Box 26588, San Francisco CA 94126 415-928-0471
Synthegraphics Corp, 940 Pleasant Ave, Highland Park IL 60035 312-432-7699
Elaine F Tankard, 3003 Cherry Ln, Austin TX 78703 512-472-5837
Helene Taylor, 149 Crescent St, Northampton MA 01060..........................413-584-2647
Susan Thornton, 464 Minne Wa Wa St, Vermilion OH 44089 216-967-1757
M A Timmons Comm Svcs, 555 Evening St, Worthington OH 43085........614-846-2887
Turner & Winston, 5306 38th St N W, Washington DC 20015....................202-363-6459
Arlene S Uslander, 9406 Kilbourn, Skokie IL 60076.................................312-674-3701
Veritas Communications, 2301 W Las Lomitas, Tucson AZ 85741..........602-293-3111
Carlson Wade, 49 Bokee Ct Rm 4K, Brooklyn NY 11223 718-743-6983
Durrett Wagner, 614 Ingleside Pl, Evanston IL 60201.............................312-236-8472
Gladys H Walker, 21 Thorburn Ave, Trumbull CT 06611 203-261-3085
Walking Bird Publication Services, PO Box 19499, Seattle WA 98109 206-285-1575
Warner-Cotter Co, 49 Water St, San Francisco CA 94133.........................415-441-4011
Andrea Warren, 814 Alabama, Lawrence KS 66044 913-841-2654
Weidner Assoc Inc, Box C-50, Cinnaminson NJ 08077.............................609-486-1755
Bella Hass Weinberg, 1441 Pelham Pkwy N, Bronx NY 10469....................212-547-5159
Toby Wertheim, 240 E 76th St, New York NY 10021 212-472-8587
Western Reserve Publ Services, 1640 Franklin Ave, Kent OH 44240........216-673-2577
Westgate Press, 8 Bernstein Blvd, Center Moriches NY 11934....................516-878-2901
Eleanor B Widdoes, 417 W 120th St, New York NY 10027 212-686-1100
W G Williams Assoc, 1100 17th St NW #1000, Wash DC 20036 703-451-5544
Bayla Winters, 2700 Scott Rd, Burbank CA 91504...................................818-846-1879
Wordcraft Inc, Box 258, Haddonfield NJ 08033 609-428-2525
Wordsmith Inc, 11433 Valley Rd, Fairfax VA 22033 703-691-0660
Wordsworth Assoc, 9 Tappan Rd, Wellesley MA 02181 617-237-4761
Wordsworth Communication, Box 9781, Alexandria VA 22304 703-642-8775
The Write Way, 2512 Orchard Rd, Toledo OH 43606 419-531-2944
Writers Connection, 1601 Saratoga Sunnyvale Rd, Cupertino CA 95014..408-973-0227
Writers: Free-Lance Inc, 12 Cavalier Dr, Ambler PA 19002 215-646-7550
The Writing Service, 315 W 102nd St Ste 7B, New York NY 10025 212-866-5930
Joan Yarfitz Photo Env, 2021 Vista del Mar, Los Angeles CA 90068.........213-465-9947
York Production Services, 3600 W Market St, York PA 17404....................717-792-3551
Beverly Zegarski, 207 Washington, Half Moon Bay CA 94019 415-726-1253
John Ziemer, 1854 Anthony Ct, Mtn View CA 94040................................415-941-6714

FILM, TV & AUDIO-VISUAL PRODUCERS

A&G Productions, 1660 Hotel Circle N Ste 107, San Diego CA 92108......619-291-7031
A&M Films, 1416 N La Brea, Los Angeles CA 90018 213-469-2411
Abacus Pictures, 9336 Washington Blvd, Culver City CA 90230..................213-559-0346
ABC Circle Films, 9911 W Pico Blvd, Los Angeles CA 90035....................213-557-6860
ABC Television Center, 4151 Prospect Ave, Los Angeles CA 90027..........213-557-7777
Abdreizzi/Toback & Co, 6532 Sunset Blvd, Hollywood CA 90028 213-464-2157
Ray Abel Productions, Short Dr, Port Chester NY 10573...........................914-939-2818
Robt Abel & Assoc, 953 N Highland Ave, Los Angeles CA 90036.............213-462-8100
Aberdeen Video, 3349 Cahuenga Blvd W, Los Angeles CA 90068.............213-874-3050
Abraham & Dunn Ltd, PO Box 27025, Honolulu HI 96827........................808-537-3542
Abrams Creative Services, 369 S Crescent Dr, Beverly Hills CA 90212 213-277-2410
ABS & Assoc, Box 5127, Evanston IL 60204...312-328-8697
Academy Film Productions, 3918 W Estes Ave, Lincolnwood IL 60645....312-674-2122

Academy Productions, 10000 Riverside Dr, Toluca Lake CA 91602 818-985-5988
Accolade Productions Ltd, 8686 Franklin Ave, Los Angeles CA 90069.....213-656-0925
Ackerman Benson, 800 S Robertson Blvd, Los Angeles CA 90035.............213-659-9422
The Act Factory, 1314 N Hayworth Ave Ste 402, Los Angeles CA 90046 ..213-851-1400
Action Audio, 367 Windsor Hwy, New Windsor NY 12550....................914-565-8740
Ad Astra Assoc, 2033 Kerwood Ave, Los Angeles CA 90025 213-659-9422
ADCO Productions, 7101 Biscayne Blvd, Miami FL 33138.......................305-751-3118
ADL Video, 3311 Rowena St Ste 18, Los Angeles CA 90027.....................213-662-8385
ADM Productions, 1347 N Caheunga Blvd, Los Angeles CA 90028............213-466-8336
Admaster Inc, 95 Madison Ave, New York NJ 10016..............................212-679-1134
Adventist Media Prod, 1100 Rancho Conejo, Hollywood CA 91320..........213-850-0116
AGS&R Communications, 425 N Michigan, Chicago IL 60611...................312-836-4500
Ahremess Inc, 12839 Marlboro St, Los Angeles CA 90049........................213-395-6479
AIA Productions Inc, 15132 La Maida, Sherman Oaks CA 91403.................818-501-4406
AIE Studios Inc, 3905 Braxton, Houston TX 77063................................713-781-2110
AIM Productions Inc, 7212 McNeil Dr Ste 206, Austin TX 78729 512-250-5535
Aims Media, 6901 Woodley Ave, Van Nuys CA 91406..............................818-785-4111
AIP, 9000 Sunset Blvd Ste 1000, Los Angeles CA 90069..........................213-278-7600
Airfax Productions, 727 N Hudson, Chicago IL 60610 312-944-5577
Airline Film & TV Promotions, 13246 Weidner, Pacoima CA 91331.........818-899-1151
AKO Productions, 20531 Plummer St, Chatsworth CA 91311 818-998-0443
Alan Industries Inc, New Seabury Rotary, Mashpee MA 02649..................617-477-1083
Alaska Film Studios, 700 H St Ste 1, Anchorage AK 99801 907-267-4600
Alaska Picture Inc, PO Box 33741, Juneau AK 99801...............................907-789-9431
Alban Bruce Communication, 1055 Taylor Ave, Baltimore MD 21204 301-828-1220
The Albert Company, 22704 Ventura Blvd, Woodland Hills CA 91367 818-348-0020
Alcom Video Film Prod, 950 Battery St, San Francisco CA 94111..............415-397-0490
Aldan Co Inc, 355 S Mansfield Ave, Los Angeles CA 90036 213-936-1032
The Aldrich Co, 556 S Norton St, Los Angeles CA 90004.........................213-462-6511
Alexander Media Services, 355 Commerce Cir, Sacramento CA 95815 916-925-7111
Alexi Productions, PO Box 8482, Universal City CA 91608.......................818-843-3443
Alive Films, 8271 Melrose, Los Angeles CA 90046 213-852-1100
All State Productions, 1605 N Ivar Ave, Hollywood CA 90028..................213-461-3094
All Video Productions, 4 Beaumont Dr, Melville NJ 11747 516-643-4889
Alladin Productions, 2400 Oxnard St, Woodland Hills CA 91367 818-348-3020
Richard H Allen Films, 1716 Lafayette Rd, Los Angeles CA 90019............213-931-0974
Irwin Allen Productions, Columbia Plaza, Burbank CA 91505.................818-954-3601
Allend'or Productions, 15036 Valley Vista, Sherman Oaks CA 91423 818-986-4622
Alliance Pictures, 7877 State Rd, Cincinnati OH 45230 513-232-4311
Allied Intl Production, 9903 Santa Monica, Beverly Hills CA 90212...........213-201-0800
Alpha Communications, 5408 N Main St, Dayton OH 45415....................513-276-2081
The Alpha Corp, 13063 Ventura Blvd, North Hollywood CA 91604...........818-788-5750
Alpha Media, 22 Dobie Ave, Huntington NJ 11743 516-757-6193
Alpine Film & Video Exchange, 1024 N 250 E, Orem UT 84057 801-226-8209
Alshire Intl Inc, 1015 Isabel St, Burbank CA 91510................................213-849-4671
AM Productions, 46 S DeLacey Ave Ste 15, Pasadena CA 91105...............818-449-0683
Albert J Amateau, 7046 Hollywood Blvd, Los Angeles CA 90028 213-467-5128
Amatulli & Assoc Inc, 1600 Central Pkwy, Cincinnati OH 45210..............513-621-5083
Amazing Picture Prod, 1640 S La Cienega, Los Angeles CA 90035............213-271-6543
Amblin Entertainment, 100 Universal Plz, Universal City CA 91608........818-777-3600
AmCorp Video Production, Box 477, Willingsboro NJ 08046.....................609-871-3636
Amer Audio Prose Library, Box 842, Columbia MO 65205......................314-443-0361
Amer Film Movement, 729 N Victory Blvd, Burbank CA 91502.................818-843-1920

Amer Learning Systems, 1015 Broadway, Shelby MS 38774..........................601-348-7423
American Media, 1454 30th St, W Des Moines IA 50265.............................515-224-0919
Amer Video Factory, 4150 Glencoe Ave, Marina del Rey CA 90292..........213-823-8622
Amicus Productions, 1012 N Sycamore, Los Angeles CA 90038 213-874-3073
Amoya Productions, Box 390, Hollywood CA 90078 213-876-4265
Ampac Video, 3637 Cahuenga, Hollywood CA 90068..............................213-851-7200
Amritraj Productions, 11846 Ventura Blvd, Studio City CA 91604...........818-766-7100
ANCO/Boston Inc, 441 Stuart St, Boston MA 02116 617-267-9700
J E Andary Filmworks, 7080 Hollywood Blvd, Los Angeles CA 90028......213-466-3379
Anderson Filmworks, 6362 Hollywood Blvd, Los Angeles CA 90028.........213-464-0386
Paul L Anderson Productions, 2107 Constitution, Ft Collins CO 80526 ...303-484-3535
Anderson Vidcom, 8028 Meadowbrook Dr, Ft Worth TX 76112 817-261-7886
Glenn Andrew Communications, 320 W 89th St, New York NJ 10024 212-874-7330
Gene Andrews Assoc, 26 Fremont, Battle Creek MI 49017.......................616-963-8333
Ralph Andrews Prod, Columbia Pictures Bldg 86, Burbank CA 91505 818-954-4262
Andromeda Productions, Box 3456 Westside Sta, Elmira NY 90560.........607-732-1090
Animation Arts Assoc, 1100 E Hector, Conshohocken PA 19428.............215-563-2520
Animation Filmakers Corp, 7000 Romaine Ave, Hollywood CA 90038 213-851-5526
Animedia Productions, PO Box 7733, Burbank CA 91510..........................213-851-4777
Another Production Co, 1422 Delgany St, Denver CO 80202.....................303-623-6616
Anson Productions, 1440 S Sepulveda, Los Angeles CA 90025..................213-444-8176
Apollo Films,6071 Bristol Pkwy, Culver City CA 90230..............................213-568-8496
Apple Fox Productions, 9430 Washington Blvd, Culver City CA 90230.....213-204-0520
Apple Productions Inc, 6240 Afton Pl, Hollywood CA 90028 213-462-0995
Appledown Film & Video, 8383 Wilshire Blvd, Beverly Hills CA 90211 213-274-2891
Applied Science Assoc Inc, Box 1072, Butleria PA 16003 412-586-7771
Aprogee Inc, 6842 Valjean Ave, Van Nuys CA 91406................................818-989-5757
Araness Communications, 244 W 49th St Ste 400, New York NY 10019 ..212-582-6246
Arena Productions Inc, 22146 Pacific Coast Hwy, Malibu CA 90265.........213-456-2991
Argus Productions, 15212 La Maida, Sherman Oaks CA 91043 818-788-1055
Arkay Video Productions, 1425 Frontier Rd, Bridgewater NJ 08807 201-560-8373
Arkoff Intl Pictures, 9000 Sunset Blvd Ste 1100, Los Angeles CA 90069...213-278-7600
Armin Productions, 3518 Cahuenga Blvd W, Los Angeles CA 90068........213-278-7600
Arnold & Assoc Productions, 2159 Powell St, San Francisco CA 94133....415-989-3490
Artanis Productions, 8501 Wilshire Blvd, Beverly Hills CA 90211............213-278-1103
Arthur Productions Inc, 20010 Wells Dr, Woodland Hills CA 91634........818-887-1007
Artists Consultants Prod, 11777 San Vicente, Los Angeles CA 90049......213-273-5050
ASC Films Inc, Box 1101, Malibu CA 90265..213-456-2687
Hal Ashby Productions, 21323 Pacific Coast Hwy, Malibu CA 90265........213-456-1358
Ashira Assoc, 441 S Beverly Dr, Beverly Hills CA 90212 213-551-0457
ASK Productions, 4508 Granny White Pike, Nashville TN 37204..............615-385-0295
Askari Television Productions, 7441 Glade Pl, Anchorage AK 99502.......907-344-7901
Aspen Productions, 10100 Santa Monica Blvd, Los Angeles CA 90067.....213-653-6870
Asselin Productions, 8489 W 3rd St, Los Angeles CA 90048.....................213-653-6190
Associated Audio Services, 181 Westchester, Port Chester NY 10573.......914-937-5129
Associated Communications, 32554 Pacific Coast, Malibu CA 90213 213-457-7611
Associated Film Enterprises, Box 2879, Beverly Hills CA 90213.................213-273-5844
Astrofilm Service, 932 N La Brea Ave, Los Angeles CA 90038..................213-851-1673
Athletic Inst Inc, 200 Castlewood Dr, N Palm Beach FL 33408...................305-842-3600
Atkins & Reilly Inc, 316 Steuart St, Boston MA 02116..............................617-482-0232
Atlantic Releasing, 8255 Sunset Blvd, Los Angeles CA 90046..................213-650-2500
Atticus Corp, 9171 Wilshire Blvd Ste 530, Beverly Hills CA 90210 213-274-5847
Audio Vistas Inc, 333 W 52nd St, New York NY 10019 212-586-2177

Audio Visual Consultants, 1440 Broadway Ste 422, Oakland CA 94612 ...415-653-9567
Audio Visual Productions, 111 Midstreams Place, Brick NJ 08724............201-899-4342
Audio Visual Unlimited, 6115 Selma Ave, Los Angeles CA 90028.............213-467-9155
Audio-Video Craft, 7000 Santa Monica Blvd, Los Angeles CA 90038........213-466-6475
Audio-Video Recorders of Arizona, 3830 N 7th St, Phoenix AZ 85014......602-277-4723
Audiovisual Design Studios, 1823 Silas Deane, Rocky Hill CT 06067.......203-529-2581
Aura Productions Inc, 7911 Willoughby Ave, Los Angeles CA 90046........213-656-9373
Aurora Films, PO Box 020164, Juneau AK 99802.............................907-586-6696
Aurora Productions, 8642 Melrose Ste 200, Los Angeles CA 90069.........213-854-5742
Bruce Austin Productions, 6110 Santa Monica, Hollywood CA 90038......213-462-4844
AV Communications, 513 Conti St, New Orleans LA 70130.....................504-522-9769
AV Media Craftsman, 110 E 23rd St Ste 600, New York NY 10010...........212-228-6644
Avalon Group Ltd, 8833 Sunset Blvd Ste 307, Hollywood CA 90069.........213-652-6654
Avanti Films, 6855 Santa Monica Blvd Ste 404, Los Angeles CA 90038....213-465-3154
Avion Communications, 200 Madison Ave, New York NY 10016..............212-532-6660
Avocet Two, Box 56, Millwood VA 22646...703-837-2152
AVP Communication, Box 454, Westborough MA 01581.......................617-366-4694
AVP Inc, 2330 Byrd Dr, Kalamazoo MI 49002.....................................616-382-5030
AVTECH, 6023 N Dixie Dr, Dayton OH 45414.....................................513-890-7600
AVW Audio Visual Inc, 2241 Irving Blvd, Dallas TX 75207....................214-634-9060
Azevedo Intl, 6716 Hillpark Dr Ste 307, Los Angeles CA 90068..............213-874-5016
Azteca Films Inc, 555 N La Brea Ave, Los Angeles CA 90036..................213-938-2413
Bachner Productions Inc, 360 1st Ave 5D, New York NY 10010...............212-673-2946
Fred Badiyan Productions, 720 W 94th St, Minneapolis MN 55420..........612-888-5507
Doug Bailey Films Inc, 140 Congressional Ln, Rockville MD 20852..........301-881-0200
Jacques Bailhe, 4967 Franklin Ave, Los Angeles CA 90027.....................213-466-5544
Bob Baker Productions, 1345 W 1st St, Los Angeles CA 90026.................213-250-9995
Clyde Baldschun & Assoc, 8522 La Tuna Canyon, Sun Valley CA 91352..818-352-9888
Ball Communications Inc, 1101 N Fulton, Evansville IN 47710.................812-428-2300
Lucille Ball Productions, Box 900, Beverly Hills CA 90213.....................213-203-3650
George Bamber Productions, 3886 Altura Ave, La Crescenta CA 91214..818-249-7566
Bandera Enterprises, Box 1107, North Hollywood CA 91604.....................818-985-5050
Bob Banner Assoc Inc, 8687 Melrose Mez 20, Los Angeles CA 90069......213-657-6800
Chuck Barbee Productions, 5235 Woodlake, Woodland Hills CA 91367..818-703-7269
Bard Productions, 280 S Beverly Dr Ste 501, Beverly Hills CA 90212.......213-550-7444
Bardott Co Inc, 1 Madison St, East Rutherford NJ 07073......................201-470-0202
Bob Barker Productions, 9201 Wilshire Blvd, Beverly Hills CA 90210......213-278-1160
Barnaby Productions, 816 N La Cienega Ave, Los Angeles CA 90027......213-657-6150
Slim Barnard Enterprises, 1543 N Serrano, Los Angeles CA 90027.........213-465-9111
Barr Films, 3490 E Foothill Blvd, Pasadena CA 91107..........................818-793-6153
Barris Industries Inc, 9100 Wilshire Blvd, Beverly Hills CA 90212..........213-278-9550
Barry & Knight Prod, 1888 Century Park E, Los Angeles CA 90067.........213-556-1000
Hall Bartlett Productions, 9200 Sunset Blvd, Los Angeles CA 90069........213-278-8883
Billy Barty Productions, 10954 Moorpark, N Hollywood CA 91602.........818-980-4700
Bass Sail Herb Yager & Assoc, 709 Sunset Blvd, Los Angeles CA 90028..213-466-9701
Bassinson Productions, 723 N Cahuenga Blvd, Hollywood CA 90038.......213-466-2171
Batjac Productions, 9570 Wilshire Blvd, Beverly Hills CA 90212.............213-278-9870
Bay Area Video Coalition, 1111 17th St, San Francisco CA 94107.............415-861-3282
BBZ Films Ltd, 321 Hampton Dr Ste 209, Venice CA 90291.....................213-399-7793
Marjori Bean Films, 4172 Minnecota Dr, Thousand Oaks CA 91360........805-529-2767
Chris Bearde Productions, 225 Santa Monica, Santa Monica CA 90401...213-394-9609
Beth Beatty Productions, 5555 Melrose Ave, Los Angeles CA 90038........213-467-3778
Warren Beatty Productions, 5555 Melrose Ave, Los Angeles CA 90038...213-468-5000

Beaux Arts Prod & Ent, Box 1004, Beverly Hills CA 90213...........................213-874-2200
Bel-Air-Gradison Prod, 10100 Santa Monica, Los Angeles CA 90067.......213-874-2200
Alan Belkin Productions, 148 Beverly Dr, Beverly Hills CA 90212.............213-276-4065
Dave Bell Assoc, 3211 Cahuenga Blvd West, Los Angeles CA 90068.........213-851-7801
Gil Bellin Productions, 175 Westminster Dr, Yonkers NY 10710.............914-968-2892
Ben Av Productions, 9200 Sunset Blvd Ste 1220, Los Angeles CA 90069..213-271-5171
Brian Bender Prod, 6331 Hollywood Blvd, Hollywood CA 90028............213-461-9697
Bill Benenson Productions, 321 Hampton Dr, Venice CA 90291............213-399-7793
Bennett Laboratory, 2553 Cleveland Ave, Columbus OH 43211 614-267-7007
Bennett Productions, 6922 E Ocean Blvd, Long Beach CA 90803 213-433-4478
Berg & Assoc, 8334 Clairmont Mesa Blvd Ste 203, San Diego CA 92111..619-292-8257
Aaron Berger Enterprises, 1024 N La Brea Ave, Hollywood CA 90038....213-464-0180
Bergwall Productions, Box 238, Uniondale NY 11553................................516-222-1111
Berkofsky/Barrett Prod, 813 N La Brea Ave, Los Angeles CA 90038.........818-954-3961
Ralph Berliner Audio/Music, 35 W 90th St, New York NY 10024 212-873-6390
Harvey Bernhard Enterprises, 4000 Warner Blvd, Burbank CA 91522.....818-954-3961
The Bernstein Co, 1124 N Citrus Ave, Hollywood CA 90038......................213-461-5100
Jay Bernstein Productions, Producer's Bldg 8, Burbank CA 91505...........818-954-3791
Best Intl Films, 9200 Sunset Blvd PH22, Los Angeles CA 90069................213-550-7311
Beverly Hills Screen Ent, 8949 Sunset Blvd, Los Angeles CA 90069...........213-275-3088
Beyond Sound, 6253 Hollywood Blvd, Hollywood CA 90028....................213-463-8181
BFM Enterprises, 1347 N Cahuenga Blvd, Los Angeles CA 90028............213-466-8336
BGP Productions, 10637 Burbank Blvd, North Hollywood CA 91601 818-506-4925
Bibas-Redford Inc, 11 Rye Ridge Plaza, Port Chester NY 10573................914-937-4320
Jerry Bick Prod, 1413 Greenfield, Los Angeles CA 90025........................213-473-1769
Big Deal Inc, 8500 Wilshire Blvd Ste 506, Beverly Hills CA 90211............213-657-5562
Big Mac Enterprises, Box 1073, Studio City CA 91604 818-506-5621
Big Zig Video, 1216 1/2 Spruce St, Berkeley CA 94709..............................415-644-3565
Bijou Film, 1015 N Cahuenga Blvd, Los Angeles CA 90038.......................213-461-2721
Tony Bill Productions, 73 Market St, Venice CA 90291 213-396-5937
Billy Jack Productions, 11693 San Vicente, Los Angeles CA 90049...........213-394-0286
Biomedical Communications, 4200 E 9th St, Denver CO 80262................303-394-7342
Biomedical Communications, 650 E 25th St, Kansas City MO 64108........816-234-0443
Black Stallion Country Prod, PO Box 2250, Culver City CA 90231...........213-419-8142
Blaise Media, 3400 J St, Sacramento CA 95816...916-446-3126
Blanc Communications, 9454 Wilshire Blvd, Beverly Hills CA 90212 818-784-5452
Samuel R Blate Assoc, 10331 Watkins Mill, Gaithersburg MD 20879 301-840-2248
Blockbusters, Box 1474, Studio City CA 91604...818-784-5452
Blondheim Productions, 14560 Round Vly, Sherman Oaks CA 91403 213-467-5316
The Blue Group Inc, 494 Tuallitan Rd, Los Angeles CA 90049..................213-476-2229
Bluebird Inc, 8451 Melrose Ave, Los Angeles CA 90069............................213-651-5180
Stanford Blum Enterprises, 4222 Woodman, Sherman Oaks CA 90025...213-501-3555
Garry Blye Enterprises, 11620 Wilshire Blvd, Los Angeles CA 90025.......213-657-8740
BMA Audio Cassettes, 200 Park Ave S, New York NY 10003 212-674-1900
The Bolen Productions, 19706 Pacific Coast Hwy, Malibu CA 90265.........213-456-1339
Eric D Boltax Assoc, 230 E 44th St, New York NY 10017 212-687-0963
Bonjo Productions Ltd, 1 Transglobal Sq, Long Beach CA 90807 213-426-3622
Bonneville Productions, 7755 Sunset Blvd, Los Angeles CA 90046............213-273-6400
Booke & Co, Box 66, Winston-Salem NC 27102 919-748-1120
Pat Boone Productions, 9255 Sunset Blvd, Los Angeles CA 90069............213-274-0751
Seymour Borde & Assoc, 1800 N Highland Ave, Hollywood CA 90028.....213-461-3936
Bosustow Video, 2207 Colby Ave, West Los Angeles CA 90064 213-478-0821
Walton Productions Bouchard, Bishops Rd, Kingston MA 02364 617-585-6893

Bob Boyett Productions, 3970 Overland Ave, Culver City CA 90230 213-202-6490
Bradfors-La Riviere Inc, 709 Lapeer Ave, Saginaw MI 48607......................517-754-2453
Jack Brady Productions, 32554 Pacific Coast Hwy, Malibu CA 90265 213-457-7611
Brandman Productions Inc, 2062 N Vine St, Hollywood CA 90068 213-463-3224
Brandon Productions, 13126 Valleyheart Dr, Studio City CA 91604 818-995-8036
John Bransby Productions Ltd, 221 W 57th St, New York NY 10019 212-333-5656
Zev Braun Pictures Inc, 291 S La Cienega Blvd, Beverly Hills CA 90211.213-659-8032
Braverman Productions, 6290 Sunset Blvd, Hollywood CA 90028 213-466-4111
Robert Braverman Productions, 366 N Broadway, Jericho NY 11753.......516-935-2801
Bravo Productions, 947 Hillsdale Ave, West Hollywood CA 90069............213-855-0708
BRB Entertainment & Mgmt, 666 N Robertson, Los Angeles CA 90069..213-652-5581
Bregman Productions, 100 Universal Plz, Universal City CA 91608..........818-777-4950
Martin Brest Prod, 5555 Melrose, Los Angeles CA 90038 213-468-4404
he Brillstein Co, 9200 Sunset Blvd Ste 428, Los Angeles CA 90069 213-275-6135
Brookfield Productions, 11600 Washington Pl, Los Angeles CA 90066.....213-390-9767
Stanley J Brooks Co, 1416 Westwood Blvd, Los Angeles CA 90024 213-470-2849
Brooksfilms Ltd, 10201 W Pico Blvd, Los Angeles CA 90035.....................213-203-3688
Peter S Brown Productions, 3450 Sawtelle Blvd, Los Angeles CA 90066..213-390-4205
Kevin Bruce Productions, 9000 W Sunset Blvd, Los Angeles CA 90069 ...213-859-7252
Bryer Patch Productions, 15363 Mulholland Dr, Los Angeles CA 90077..818-789-6998
Bryna Co, 141 El Camino Dr Ste 209, Beverly Hills CA 90212 213-274-5294
Werner H Buck Ent, 3031 W Burbank Blvd, Burbank CA 91505...............818-841-9850
Burbank Intl Pictures, 3412 W Olive Ave, Burbank CA 91505...................818-846-8441
Burch Communications, 825 Forest Arms Ln, Mound MN 55364 612-472-7426
Burns Media, 5701 Main St, Buffalo NY 14221.......................................716-632-1632
Bill Burrud Productions, 1100 S La Brea Ave, Los Angeles CA 90019.....213-641-6028
Burst Video/Film, PO Box 5354, Atlanta GA 30307 404-523-8023
Alden Butcher Prod, 6331 Hollywood Blvd, Hollywood CA 90028............213-467-6045
Butler Learning Systems, 1325 W Dorothy Lane, Dayton OH 45409 513-298-7462
Caruth C Byrd Productions, 1900 W Olive Ave, Burbank CA 91506 213-463-3175
C&A Films Inc, 1334 Westwood Blvd, Los Angeles N9 90024 213-470-1315
Cablenglish, 11500 W Olympic Blvd Ste 385, Los Angeles CA 90064........213-477-1997
Cabscott Broadcast Production, 517 7th Ave, Lindenwold NJ 08021 609-346-2724
Cactus Tree Productions, 6123 Glenoak, Los Angeles CA 90068...............213-466-2825
Caedmon, 1995 Broadway, New York NY 10023.......................................212-580-3400
Cal Motion Picture Video, 3494 Hancock St, San Diego CA 92110...........619-297-1621
Cal Vista Intl Ltd, 6649 Odessa Ave, Van Nuys CA 91460.......................818-780-9000
Cali-Filmery, 18625 Cassandra St, Tarzana CA 91365..............................818-881-7128
Calico Creations Ltd, 8843 Shirley Ave, Northridge CA 91324...................818-885-6663
Calif Communications, 6900 Santa Monica, Los Angeles CA 90038 213-466-8511
Calif Marin Video, Box 9029, San Rafael CA 94912.................................415-924-6400
Calliope Films, 12140 Olympic Blvd, Los Angeles CA 90064.....................213-826-3666
Calliope Productions, 825 Boone Ave N, Minneapolis MN 55427 612-544-8669
Cambridge Films, 4827 Sepulveda Blvd, Sherman Oaks CA 91403............818-789-8141
Campbell Films Inc, Corey Hill, Saxtons River VT 05154...........................802-869-2547
Campbell-Powell-Thompson, 7421 Beverly, Los Angeles CA 90036 213-857-1214
Camrac Studios, 1775 Kuenzli St, Reno NV 89502...................................702-323-0965
Stephen J Cannell Prod, 7083 Hollywood Blvd, Los Angeles CA 90028 ...213-465-5800
Cannon Group, 640 San Vicente, Los Angeles CA 90048............................213-658-2100
Capito Communications, 14576 Charmeran Ave, San Jose CA 95124.......408-371-4379
Capitol Pictures Inc, 1438 Fower St, Los Angeles CA 90028 213-467-7226
Cardinal Entertainment Corp, 814 S Westgate, Los Angeles CA 90049 ...213-207-5646
Anthony Cardoza Enterprises, Box 4163, North Hollywood CA 91607.....818-985-5550

Care Video Productions, 25730 Hilliard Blvd, Westlake OH 44145 216-835-5872
Carlin Company, 8721 Sunset Blvd, Los Angeles CA 90069........................213-652-9354
Mark Carliner Productions, 11700 Laurelwood, Studio City CA 91604....818-763-4783
Kevin Carlisle & Assoc, 1647 Woods Dr, Los Angeles CA 90069 213-650-1020
Carman Productions, 15456 Cabrito Rd, Van Nuys CA 91406....................213-873-7370
Carmel Enterprises, 9200 Sunset Blvd Ste 908, Los Angeles CA 90069 213-278-8883
Carmel Production Co, 10 Dell Glen Ave PO Box 3, Lodi NJ 07644.........201-546-3500
Carolco Inc, 9255 Sunset Blvd #910, Los Angeles CA 90069......................213-273-0284
Allan Carr Enterprises, PO Box 691670, Los Angeles CA 90069..............213-278-2490
William Carruthers Co, 200 N Larchmont Blvd, Los Angeles CA 90004..213-465-0669
Carson Productions Group, 10045 Riverside, Toluca Lake CA 91602......818-506-5333
Linda Carter Productions, Box 5973, Sherman Oaks CA 91413 818-884-1433
Cartwright & Assoc, 4437 Camino Cardenal, Tucson AZ 85718 602-299-0195
Carwin-Bayless Productions, 1235 24th St, Santa Monica CA 90404.........213-278-2484
Jack Cash Productions, 650 N Bronson Ave, Los Angeles CA 90004........213-462-5885
Cassell Photographic Products, 2950 E 55th Pl, Indianapolis IN 46220....317-251-1201
Cassiatore Productions, 300 S Olive St Ste 711, Los Angeles CA 90012...213-680-1850
Castalian Assoc, 2525 Hyperion Ave, Los Angeles CA 90027.....................213-662-8141
Catalina Productions, 15301 Ventura Blvd, Sherman Oaks CA 91403......213-907-6300
Catalyst Communications, 2816 Rowena Ave, Los Angeles CA 90039 213-664-4410
Cates Brothers Co, 195 S Beverly Dr Ste 412, Beverly Hills CA 90212......213-273-0966
Cathedral Films, 5310 Derry, Agoura CA 91301.......................................818-991-3290
Thomas Catsell & Assoc, 2207 Colby Ave, Los Angeles CA 90064............213-824-2700
Cattani Films Inc, 9494 Wilshire Blvd, Beverly Hills CA 90212 213-274-5892
Cavalcade Pictures Inc, 959 N Fairfax Ave, Los Angeles CA 90046 213-824-2700
Cavalcade Productions Inc, 7360 Potter Valley Rd, Ukiah CA 95482.......707-743-1168
CBS/Fox Video, 1930 Century Park W Ste 400, Los Angeles CA 90067....213-556-1862
CEAVCO Audio Visual Co, 1650 Webster St, Denver CO 80215.................303-238-6493
Celebrity Commercials Inc, 1400 Braeridge Dr, Beverly Hills CA 90210..213-278-4574
Center for Communications Inc, 110 Cabot St, Beverly MA 01915 617-922-3773
Centre Film Inc, 1103 El Centro Ave, Los Angeles CA 90038 213-466-5123
Centre Productions Inc, 1800 30th St Ste 207, Boulder CO 80301 303-444-1166
Centron Productions Inc, 1621 W 9th St, Lawrence KS 66044....................913-843-0400
Century Video Corp, 280 S Beverly Dr Ste 501, Beverly Hills CA 90212...213-550-7444
John Cestare Productions, Box 5286, Beverly Hills CA 90210.....................213-659-4134
Challenge Productions, 469 N Crescent Dr, Beverly Hills CA 90213.........818-986-9681
Ernest Chambers Productions, 1438 N Gower, Hollywood CA 90028......213-464-6158
Channel 1 Video, PO Box 1437, Seabrook NH 03874 603-474-5046
Chapple Films & Video, Rt 198, Chaplin CT 06235.....................................203-455-9779
B G Charles Inc, 9291 Flicker Pl, Los Angeles CA 90069.............................213-273-3283
Chartoff-Winkler Prod, 10125 W Washington, Culver City CA 90230.......213-204-0474
R B Chenoweth Films, 1860 E North Hills Dr, La Habra CA 90631..........213-691-1652
Cherokee Productions, 6420 Wilshire Blvd, Los Angeles CA 90048.........213-651-1601
Cheshire Country Co, 6060 N Larchmont, Los Angeles CA 90004.............213-462-6511
Chiaramonte Films, 120 S Elm St, Beverly Hills CA 90210.........................213-275-5313
Chicago Board of Rabbis, 1 S Franklin, Chicago IL 60606 312-444-2896
Children's Media Productions, PO Box 40400, Pasadena CA 91104 818-797-5469
China Telepictures Intl, PO Box 5155, Beverly Hills CA 90210..................213-276-8196
Chip Taylor Communications, 15 Spollett Dr, Derry NH 03038................603-434-9262
Chocolate Chip Productions, 6515 Sunset Blvd, Los Angeles CA 90028...213-465-4512
Harold Chohen Productions, 9200 Sunset Blvd, Los Angeles CA 90069...213-550-0570
Christian Broadcasting Network, Virginia Beach VA 23463 804-424-7777
Christian Church, Box 1986, Indianapolis IN 46206...................................317-353-1491

Christiania Productions, 1801 Ave of Stars, Los Angeles CA 90067 213-879-2811
Christopher Enterprises, 2029 Century Park E, Los Angeles CA 90067...213-553-6666
Churchill Films, 662 N Robertson Blvd, Los Angeles CA 90069................213-657-5110
Cimarron Productions, 6875 Evans Ave, Denver CO 80224......................303-753-0988
Cimarron Productions, 846 N Cahuenga Blvd, Los Angeles CA 90038.....213-464-1011
Cinaco Film Co, 9056 Santa Monica Blvd, Los Angeles CA 90069............213-278-3302
Cine Design Films, 255 Washington St, Denver CO 80202.....................303-777-4222
Cine Enterprises, 2811 Wilshire Blvd, Santa Monica CA 90403 213-829-9514
Cine Guild, 1015 N Cahuenga Blvd, Los Angeles CA 90038 213-461-2721
Cine Mark, 303 E Ohio St, Chicago IL 60611......................................312-337-3303
Cine-Magic Productions, 1134 N Formosa Ave, Los Angeles CA 90046...213-876-2939
Cine-Media Intl, 1 Transglobal Sq, Long Beach CA 90807......................213-426-3622
Cine-Paris, 7616 Hollywood Blvd Ste 205, Los Angeles CA 90046............213-851-2888
Cinecan Film Productions, Box 8601, University City CA 91608................818-763-5428
Cinecorp, 10100 Santa Monica Blvd Ste 1500, Los Angeles CA 90067.......213-552-9977
Cinema Arts Productions, 4041 Woking Way, Los Angeles CA 90027......213-666-2244
Cinema Dynamics, PO Box 2926, Hollywood CA 90078.........................213-301-8433
Cinema Features, 3000 Sparr Blvd, Glendale CA 91208.........................818-240-2425
Cinema Group Inc, 8758 Venice Blvd, Los Angeles CA 90034..................213-204-0102
Cinema Payments Inc of Calif, 20440 Tiara, Woodland Hills CA 91367...818-703-1312
Cinema Pictures Inc, 10212 Noble Ave, Mission Hills CA 91345...............818-892-6797
Cinema Samples Productions, 1545 Point View, Los Angeles CA 90035..213-932-8161
Cinema Sound Ltd, 311 W 75th St, New York NY 10023 212-799-4800
Cinemakers Inc, 330 W 42nd St, New York NY 10036............................212-563-6545
Cinemaphile Amalg Pictures, Box 8054, Universal City CA 91608..............213-656-9061
Cinesong Corp, 3989 Weslin Ave, Sherman Oaks CA 91423.....................818-905-1298
Cinetel Productions, 9200 Sunset Blvd Ste 1215, Los Angeles CA 90069 ..213-550-1067
Cinevid Inc, Box 246, Beverly Hills CA 90213 213-465-9078
Cineworks, 124 Great Bay Rd, Greenland NH 03840..............................603-431-4241
Circle Video Productions, 2901 W 16th St, Indianapolis IN 46222 317-638-1066
City Film Center Inc, 6412 65 Place, Middle Village NY 11379..................718-456-5050
Tom Clay Commercial Prod, 6515 Sunset Blvd, Hollywood CA 90028......213-464-6566
Clearvue Inc, 5711 N Milwaukee Ave, Chicago IL 60646.........................312-775-9433
Joseph Cleary Prod, 1624 W Ocean Front, Newport Beach CA 92663......714-675-8888
CMI, 612 Hampton Dr, Venice CA 90291...213-392-8771
Coast Productions, 1001 N Poinsettia Pl, Hollywood CA 90046................213-876-2021
Coastline Films, 6860 Canby St Ste 101, Reseda CA 91335......................818-996-3114
Cobe Sandy Productions, 9000 Sunset Blvd, Los Angeles CA 90069 213-550-8710
Coe Communications, 5813 Wicomico Ave, Rockville MD 20852...............301-881-2820
Coe Film Assoc Inc, 65 E 96th St, New York NY 10128 212-831-5355
Herman Cohen Productions, 650 N Bronson, Hollywood CA 90004.........213-466-3388
Robert Cohn Productions, 100 S Donheny Dr, Los Angeles CA 90048.....213-274-6738
Charles Colarusso Prod, 3801 Barham Blvd, Los Angeles CA 90068........213-960-2407
Color Film Corp, 1741 Resthaven Lane, Mound MN 55364......................612-644-7700
Color Stock Library Inc, 4718 Euclid Ave, Tampa FL 33629.....................813-253-0248
Columbia Pictures, Columbia Plaza, Burbank CA 91505 818-954-3595
Comart Aniforms Inc, 21 Penn Plaza, New York NY 10001 212-714-2550
Coming Attractions, 8265 Sunset Blvd, Los Angeles CA 90046.................213-656-9021
Command Performance Prod, 710 N Seward St, Hollywood CA 90038 213-467-4000
Commercial Video Inc, 2800 Superior Ave, Cleveland OH 44114 216-771-3233
Commonwealth Comm, 1215 W 6th St, Los Angeles CA 90017..................213-482-9899
Communications Concepts, 7980 N Atlantic, Cape Canaveral FL 32920 ..305-783-5232
Communications Corp of America, 11 W Illinois St, Chicago IL 60610 312-467-9575

Communications Group West, 1640 5th St, Santa Monica CA 90401 213-451-2522
Communications Resources, 45 Field Point Rd, Greenwich CT 06830 203-629-1500
Communicreations Inc, 2130 S Bellaire St, Denver CO 80222....................303-759-1155
Company of Artists Prod, 3518 Cahuenga W, Los Angeles CA 90068.......213-851-5811
Compass Intl Pictures, 9229 Sunset Blvd, Los Angeles CA 90069 213-858-1655
Complete Post Inc, 6087 Sunset Blvd, Hollywood CA 90028....................213-467-1244
Comprenetics Inc, 5819 Uplander Wy, Culver City N9 90230 213-204-2081
Compro Productions, 2080 Peachtree Industrial Ct, Atlanta GA 30341....404-455-1943
Compton Communications, 112 N Washington St, Hillsdale IL 312-4 312-467-9575
Computer Productions, 1556 Hudson St, Denver CO 80220....................303-393-6240
Computer Video Prod, 1317 Clover Dr S, Minneapolis MN 55420............612-888-2388
Concept 80's, 3409 W Chester Pike, Newtown Square PA 19073 215-353-5900
Concept Video Productions, 1533 Magnolia Blvd, Burbank CA 91506.....818-841-7030
Inc Conda Enterprises, Box 1344, Loomis CA 95650................................818-247-3671
Manuel S Conde, 1135 N Cole Ave, Los Angeles CA 90038....................213-464-4537
Condyne/Oceana Group, 75 Main, Dobbs Ferry NY 10522....................914-693-5944
Conly Productions, 1556 Hudson St, Denver CO 80220............................303-393-6240
Connections, 1422 W Lake St Apt 312, Minneapolis MN 55408 612-827-2995
Consolidated/Barton, 5407 Roosevelt Blvd, Jacksonville FL 32210............904-389-4541
Contact! Visual Communications, 1306 Main St, Evanston IL 60202........312-475-4656
Contempo Communications, 1841 Broadway, New York NY 10023..........212-247-4373
Continental Film Prod, 4220 Amnicola Hwy, Chattanooga TN 37406.......615-622-1193
Harper Conway Productions, Box 2493, Toluca Lake CA 91602.............818-762-8184
Cooga Mooga Inc, 9255 Sunset Blvd, Los Angeles CA 90069....................213-274-0751
Cooper Video Communications, 2125 Millburn, Maplewood NJ 07040.....201-763-6147
Corday Productions, Columbia Pictures TV Bldg 8, Burbank CA 91505..818-954-6000
Cordero Productions, 138 N Swall Dr, Los Angeles CA 90049..................213-276-5222
Core Communications Inc, 565 5th Ave, New York NY 10017..................212-557-2540
Cornell Communications Co, 32 S Lansdowne, Lansdowne PA 19050......215-622-4600
Cornell Univ Educational TV Ctr, NB13 MVR Hall, Ithaca NY 14853 ...607-256-5565
Cornerstone Productions, 6430 W Sunset Blvd, Hollywood CA 90028......213-871-2255
Coronado Studios, 4500 Biscayne Blvd, Miami FL 33137........................305-573-7250
Coronet MTI Film & Video, 108 Wilmot Rd, Deerfield IL 60015 312-940-1260
Corporate Comm, 2950 E Jefferson St, Detroit MI 48207 313-259-3585
Corporate Comm, 32969 Hamilton, Farmington Hls MI 48018 313-553-4747
Corporate Media Comm, 1530 Cooledge Rd, Tucker GA 30085................404-491-6300
Corporate Media Concepts, 2720 Stemmons Fwy, Dallas TX 75207 214-631-4291
Corporate Productions Inc, 4516 Mariota Ave, Toluca Lake CA 91602 ...818-760-2622
Corri Films Intl, 2049 Century Park E, Los Angeles CA 90067..................213-557-0173
Cosmicircus Productions, 414 S 41st St, Richmond CA 94804 415-451-5818
Pierre Cossette Productions, 8899 Beverly Blvd, Los Angeles CA 90048..213-278-3366
Robert A Costa Productions, 1615 Colorado, Los Angeles CA 90041 213-255-1841
Cotton Candy/Eye On Video, 224 N Juanita, Los Angeles CA 90004........213-382-4048
Country Harvest Productions, 629 E Keefe Ave, Milwaukee WI 53212....414-372-1832
Country Music Entertainment, Box 4234, Panorama City CA 91412 818-786-6957
Courier Productions, 4121 Wilshire Blvd, Los Angeles CA 90010 213-382-3009
The Cousteau Society, 8440 Santa Monica Blvd, Los Angeles CA 90069 ..213-656-4422
Coventry Productions, PO Box 2548, Hollywood CA 90078.....................213-464-2220
CQ Productions, 3755 C Cahuenga Blvd W, Studio City CA 91604 818-508-0664
Craig Productions, 6314 La Mirada Ave, Los Angeles CA 90038 213-467-7146
Douglas S Cramer Co, 1041 N Formosa Ave, Los Angeles CA 90046.......213-850-2661
Crandall Communications, 155 W 23rd St, New York NY 10001..............212-255-2200
Thomas Craven Film Corp, 114 E 25th St, New York NY 10010...............212-777-7433

Craven Productions, 727 N Victory Blvd, Burbank CA 91502 818-843-6009
Creative Communications, 13700 Tahiti, Marina del Rey CA 90292 213-821-5866
Creative Enterprise Intl, 6630 Sunset Blvd, Hollywood CA 90028 213-463-9929
Creative Media Arts, 1708 Livonia Ave, Los Angeles CA 90035 213-839-4490
Creative Options Inc, 1730 K St NW Ste 719, Washington DC 20006 302-658-7301
Creative Partnership Inc, 6815 Willoughby, Hollywood CA 90028 213-461-3548
Creative Productions, 20 E 53rd St, New York NY 10022............................212-935-1111
Creative Productions Inc, 200 Main St, Orange NJ 07050...........................201-676-4422
Creative Productions, 2610 Van Marter Rd Ste 1, Spolane WA 99206......509-922-2885
Creative Selling Inc, 422 Logan St, Carnegie PA 15106 412-276-7750
Creative Talent Management, 595 E Broad St, Columbus OH 43215........614-224-6180
Creative Technology, 853 Copley Rd, Akron OH 44320................................216-535-5778
Creative Video Services, 500 Ventu Park Rd, Newbury Park CA 91320....818-707-2424
Creative Visuals Inc, 731 Harding St NE, Minneapolis MN 55413 612-378-1621
Creatividideo, 3433 Pierce Dr, Ellicott City MD 21043 301-465-0200
CRM McGraw Hill Prod, 2999 Overland, Los Angeles CA 90064...............213-870-5912
Cross Current Comm, 11240 Magnolia, N Hollywood CA 91606...............818-509-0951
Cross-Cultural Communications, 239 Wynsum, Merrick NY 11566 516-868-5635
Crossover Programming Co, 1237 7th St, Santa Monica CA 90401 213-451-9762
Crossword Productions, 11337 Havenhurst, Granada Hills CA 91344......818-366-1958
Crown Intl Pictures, 292 S La Cienega, Beverly Hills CA 90211 213-657-6700
Croydon Productions Ltd, 1079 E Olive Ave, Burbank CA 90211 818-954-9341
Cruse & Company, 7000 Romaine St, Hollywood CA 90038....................213-851-8814
Crystalite Productions, Box 1940, Santa Monica CA 90406 213-459-8552
CSI Productions, 1709 Utica Sq, Tulsa OK 74114 918-743-7881
CTA Film Production, 23730 Clarendon St, Woodland Hills CA 91367....818-992-1304
Culp Communications, 1259 A Folsom St, San Francisco CA 94103.........415-558-9000
Culver City Studios, 9336 W Washington Blvd, Culver City CA 90230 213-871-0360
Cumberland Mountain Film Co, 620 Lincoln Blvd, Venice CA 90291......213-396-4543
Cally Curtis Co, 1111 N Las Palmas Ave, Los Angeles CA 90038...............213-467-1101
Dan Curtis Production Inc, 9911 W Pico Blvd, Los Angeles CA 90035 213-557-6910
Custom Productions, Box 8045, Universal City CA 91608............................213-877-2557
Custom Video, 1401 W Paces Ferry Rd Ste E 115, Atlanta GA 30327.......404-231-3585
CVM Productions Inc, 13 E 16th St, New York NY 10003............................212-691-0040
Cybern Film System Inc, 7257 W Touhy Ave, Chicago IL 60648.................312-774-2550
Cypress Point Productions, 3952 Overland, Culver City CA 90230...........213-202-4272
Cypress Publishing Group, 1763 Gardena Ave, Glendale CA 91204.........818-244-8651
Czar Productions Inc, 39 Princeton St, West Hartford CT 06110 203-233-2034
D Productions, 7213 Melrose Ave, Hollywood CA 90046................................213-930-2800
D'Angelo Productions, 6420 Wilshire Blvd, Los Angeles CA 90028 213-651-1601
Da Silva Assoc, 137 E 38th St, New York NY 10016 212-696-1657
Dagonet Productions Inc, 214 S Bedford Dr, Beverly Hills CA 90212.......213-277-3361
Dana Productions, 6249 Babcock Ave, North Hollywood CA 91606 213-977-9246
Nicholas Dancy Prod, 333 W 39th St, New York NY 10018 212-564-9140
Darby Media Group, 4015 N Rockwell St, Chicago IL 60618......................312-583-5090
DAT Productions Inc, 83 S Front St Cotton Row, Memphis TN 38103.....901-525-2621
Dave & Dave Inc, 7033 Sunset Blvd Ste 225, Hollywood CA 90028 213-469-2107
Davis Color Slides Inc, 355 Lexington Ave, New York NY 10017..............212-986-0199
Bill Davis Productions, 1313 N Vine St Ste 7, Los Angeles CA 90028.......213-462-2554
Davis Pictures, 10201 W Pico Blvd, Los Angeles CA 90035.......................213-203-3540
Davis-Panzer Prod, 1438 N Gower #174, Los Angeles CA 90028.............213-463-2343
Davis-Glick Productions, 1231 Lincoln Blvd, Santa Monica CA 90401 213-458-9200
Day Productions, 1016 N Fairview St, Burbank CA 91505............................213-877-6510

DCA Film/Video Productions, 1424 Easton Rd, Horsham PA 19044........215-443-5580
DD & B Studios, 401 S Woodward Ave, Birmingham MI 48011.................313-642-0640
DDL Omni Engineering, 15 Koger Executive Ctr, Norfolk VA 23502.......804-461-1158
Walt De Faria Productions, 427 N Canon Dr, Beverly Hills CA 90210.....213-275-9392
De Laurentiis Ent Group, 8670 Wilshire Blvd, Beverly Hills CA 90211....213-854-7000
Harry De Ligter Productions, 2258 20th St, Santa Monica CA 90405........213-450-5324
Alfred De Martini Educ Films, 414 4th Ave, Haddon Hts NJ 08035..........609-547-2800
De Sort/Films, 2017 Pacific Ave, Venice CA 90291 213-822-2400
The Debin-Locke Co, 1119 N McCadden Pl, Hollywood CA 90038............213-462-2608
Degeto Film, 1295 Ozeta Terrace, Los Angeles CA 90069............................213-659-8558
Delaney Films, 483 Mariposa Dr, Ventura CA 93001................................805-653-2699
Delphi Productions Ltd, 1800 30th St Ste 309, Boulder CO 80301 303-443-2100
Delta Productions, 3333 Glendale Blvd Ste 3, Los Angeles CA 90039.......213-663-8754
Delta Video Productions, 3412 W Olive Ave, Burbank CA 91505 818-846-8441
Dena Pictures Inc, 9100 Sunset Blvd Ste 140, Los Angeles CA 90069........818-846-8441
Hal Dennis Productions, 6314 La Mirada Ave, Los Angeles CA 90038 213-467-7146
Derio Productions Inc, 1865 N Fuller Ave, Los Angeles CA 90046 213-851-8140
Destiny Productions Ltd, Box 2389, Los Angeles CA 90078 213-276-2063
Detrick Lawrence, 580 Tremont St, Duxbury MA 02332.............................617-934-6561
Jerry Dexter Productions Inc, Box 105, Beverly Hills CA 90213 213-278-9510
Diamond P Sports Inc, 4621 Cahuenga Blvd, Toluca Lake CA 91602.......818-508-5211
Diamond Jim A/V Prod, 5929 Hillview Park, Van Nuys CA 91401............818-988-4969
Dibie-Dash Productions, 4985 Hollywood Blvd, Los Angeles CA 90027...213-663-1915
A Different Eye, 1807 N Gramercy Pl Ste 3, Hollywood CA 90028..............213-461-7804
Digital Productions, 3416 S La Cinega Blvd, Los Angeles CA 90016.........213-938-1111
Digital Video Corp, 369 N Orange Ave, Orlando FL 32801.........................305-425-1999
Dimension Film, 666 N Robertson Blvd, Los Angeles CA 90069 213-657-2910
Direct Broadcast Programs, 11632 Ventura, Studio City CA 91604 818-890-3034
Direct Cinema Ltd Inc, Box 69589, Los Angeles CA 90060........................213-656-4700
Directions Inc, 5530 Coltsfoot Ct, Columbia MD 21045 301-596-4689
Walt Disney Pictures, 500 S Buena Vista St, Burbank CA 91521 818-840-1000
William Ditzel Productions, 933 Shroyer Rd, Dayton OH 45419 513-298-5381
Diverse Industries Inc, 7651 Haskell Ave, Van Nuys CA 91405 818-782-7201
Diversity Productions, Box 726, Beaverton OR 97075 503-642-1777
Christopher Dixon Inc, 116 E 63rd St, New York NY 10021 212-838-9069
Stefan Dobert Productions, 5214 Wissioming Rd, Bethesda MD 20816....301-229-5083
Dogwood Productions, 5451 Marathon St, Los Angeles CA 90038..............213-468-5000
Dolphin Multi-Media, 1137D San Antonio Rd, Palo Alto CA 94303.........415-962-8310
Dolphin Productions, 140 E 80th St, New York NY 10021.........................212-628-5930
Dolphin Productions, 8350 Melrose Ave, Los Angeles CA 90069 213-655-7431
Domain TeleMedia Inc, 289 Main Pl, Carol Stream IL 60188....................312-668-5300
John Doremus Inc, 875 N Michigan, Chicago IL 60611 312-664-8944
Stanley Dorfman Prod, 1556 Dearborn Dr, Los Angeles CA 90068...........213-460-4396
Harry Dorsey & Assoc, 6333 Espanade, Playa Del Rey CA 90291 213-823-9180
Doswell Productions, 311 W 43rd St, New York NY 10036........................212-757-1600
Double D Assoc, N 85 W 16282 May Ave, Menomonee Falls WI 53051....414-255-5879
Double J Productions, 6310 Heather Dr, Hollywood CA 90068..................213-462-0604
Michael Douglas Prod, 10201 W Pico, Los Angeles CA 90035 213-203-1595
Dove Films, 672 S Lafayette Pl Studio 8, Los Angeles CA 90057..............213-461-3737
Victor Drai Productions, 10202 W Washington, Culver City CA 90232.....213-558-6951
Dreamlight Images Inc, 932 La Brea Ave Ste C, Hollywood CA 90038.....213-850-1996
Mark Druck Productions, 300 E 40th St, New York NY 10016................212-682-5980
DSM Producers Ent Publ, 161 W 54th St, New York NY 10019 212-245-0006

Dubois/Ruddy Audio Visual Prod, 2145 Crooks, Troy MI 48084...............313-643-0320
Duck Soup Productions, 1026 Montana, Santa Monica CA 90403.............213-451-0771
Dudkowski-Lynch Assoc, 150 Shoreline Hwy, Mill Valley CA 94941.........415-332-5825
Dudley Enterprises, 9200 Sunset Blvd Ste 607, Los Angeles CA 90069.....213-273-6167
Richard H Dunlap Productions, 444 N La Brea, Los Angeles CA 90036..213-936-1611
Cal Dunn Studios Inc, 229 W Illinois St, Chicago IL 60610........................312-644-7600
Durasell Corp, 360 Lexington Ave, New York NY 10017.....................212-687-1010
DWJ Assoc, 1 Robinson Ln, Ridgewood NJ 07450.................................201-445-1711
DY Productions, Box 1724, Burbank CA 91507....................................818-841-6072
E & A Design, 101 2nd St, Liverpool NY 13088..................................315-457-9360
EagleVision Inc, Box 3347, Stamford CT 06905.................................203-359-8777
Charles Eames & Ray, Box 268, Venice CA 90291.............................213-396-5991
Richard Earl Production, PO Box 925, Pacific Palisade CA 90272............213-454-1248
Eastern Airlines, Bldg 30 Miami Inter Airport R105, Miami FL 33148.....305-873-7091
ECA Inc, 221 W 57th St 11th fl, New York NY 10019 212-333-5656
Ed-Venture Films, 1122 Calada St, Los Angeles CA 90023 213-261-1885
Edge City Prod, 2323 Corinth, Los Angeles 90025 213-477-8539
Edgeware Assoc, 150 9th Ave, New York NY 10011............................212-807-7509
EDR/Media, 3592 Lee Rd, Shaker Heights OH 44120..........................216-751-7300
Educational Communications, 761 5th Ave, King of Prussia PA 19406 215-337-1011
Educational Filmstrips & Video, 1401 19th St, Huntsville TX 77340.........409-295-5767
Educational Images Ltd, Box 3456, Elmira NY 14905 607-732-1090
Educational Insights, 19560 S Rancho Way, Dominguez Hls CA 90220...213-637-2131
Educational Video Group, 1235 Sunset Plaza, Los Angeles CA 90069 213-659-8831
Blake Edwards Prod, 1888 Century Park E, Los Angeles CA 90067.........213-553-6740
Ralph Edwards Prod, 1717 N Highland, Los Angeles CA 90028.............213-462-2212
HM Edwards, Box 3132, Englewood CO 80155.................................303-771-3537
EFC Film & Video Production, Box 1017, Annandale VA 22003 703-750-0560
Effective Communication Arts, 221 W 57th St, New York NY 10019........212-333-5656
Eggers Films, 6345 Fountain Ave, Los Angeles CA 90028.....................213-856-0060
Einfield & Assoc, 1515 N Las Palmas Ave, Los Angeles CA 90028..........213-461-3731
Eisenlohr Productions, 1543-B N Serrano Ave, Los Angeles CA 90027 ...213-465-9111
Richard Elfman Productions, 723 Ocean Front, Venice CA 90291 213-399-9118
Elfo Productions, 1607 Pacific Ave Ste 202, Venice CA 90201...............213-396-9404
The Elliott Concern, 932 N Ka Brea Ave, Los Angeles CA 90038..............213-874-9400
Elmar Productions, 5746 Sunset Blvd, Hollywood CA 90028....................213-856-1170
Charles Elms Productions, 1260 S 350 W, Bountiful UT 84010 801-298-2727
Elsboy Inc, 9128 Sunset Blvd, Los Angeles CA 90069 213-271-4473
Embassy Home Ent, 1901 Ave of Stars, Los Angeles CA 90067 213-553-3600
EMC Corp, 300 York Ave, St Paul MN 55101.....................................612-771-1555
Emerald Studios Inc, Box 1647, Orange CA 92668 714-771-7394
Empire Entertainment, 1551 N La Brea Ave, Hollywood CA 90028..........213-856-5900
Endler Assoc, 3920 Sunny Oaks Road, Sherman Oaks CA 91403...........818-783-7110
Energy Productions, 2690 Beachwood Dr, Los Angeles CA 90068 213-462-3310
Ray Engel Productions, 7557 Hampton Ave, Los Angeles CA 90046........213-850-5411
Ensemble Productions Inc, 175 W 93rd St #5-J, New York NY 10025.....212-866-2016
Entermark Corp, 1511 N Ogden Dr, Los Angeles CA 90046....................213-851-8700
Enterprises Productions Inc, 5912 Ramirez Canyon, Malibu CA 90265..213-457-8081
Enterprises Unlimited, Box 31 FDR Sta, New York NY 10150.................212-832-6659
Entertainment Arts Inc, 210 N Pass Ave Ste 104, Burbank CA 91505.......818-841-0225
Entertainment Network, 11111 Santa Monica, Los Angeles CA 90025......213-478-1266
Entertainment Productions Inc, Box 554, Malibu CA 90265 213-456-3143
Entertainment Ventures Inc, 1654 Cordova St, Los Angeles CA 90007 213-731-7236

Environmental Video, PO Box 577, Manhattan Beach CA 90266................213-546-4581
Era 21 Productions, 2525 Hyperion Ave, Los Angeles CA 90027...............213-662-8141
Essex Intl, 8841 Wilbur Ave, Northridge CA 91324.......................................818-993-7739
Essex Pictures, Box 2548, Los Angeles CA 90078..213-464-5977
Essex Video Inc, Box 1055, Northridge CA 91328..818-993-5322
ETC Inc, 2307 Castillian Dr, Hollywood CA 90068..213-874-9803
Eue/Screen Gems Ltd, 3701 W Oak St, Burbank CA 91505 818-954-3000
Euramco Intl Inc, Box 5434, Beverly Hills CA 90210....................................213-820-6666
Eureka Productions, 11940 San Vicente Blvd, Los Angeles CA 90049......213-820-6666
Robt Evans Prod, 5555 Melrose, Los Angeles CA 90038................................213-468-5855
Eveslage Film & Video, 39 Dorman, San Francisco CA 94124.....................415-821-9416
Expanding Images, 14 Hughes B105, Irvine CA 92718..................................714-770-2342
Martin Ezra & Assoc, 48 Garrett Rd, Upper Darby PA 19082......................215-352-9595
F P & Assoc Productions, 6362 Hollywood Blvd, Hollywood CA 90028....213-467-8742
F-M Productions, 1811 W Magnolia Blvd, Burbank CA 91506.....................213-849-7618
F/O Productions, 14937 Ventura Blvd, Sherman Oaks CA 91403 818-784-8231
Jerry Fairbanks Productions, PO Box 38696, Hollywood CA 90038.........213-462-1101
Fairview Video, 222 Haws Ave, Norristown PA 19401..................................215-277-6500
Falcon Communications, 800 S Date Ave, Alhambra CA 91402.................818-997-7500
Family Films Inc, 14622 Lanark St, Panorama City CA 90046....................213-874-6633
Fannon/Osmond Inc, 1071 Ave of the Americas, New York NY 10018 ...212-391-8368
Fast Forward Productions, 540 Brooklyn Mtn, Hopatcong NJ 07843........201-398-2536
Faultline Films, 8444 Wilshire Blvd 5th Fl, Beverly Hills CA 90211 213-653-2324
Doris Faye Productions, 325 W 45th St, New York NY 10036......................212-246-0430
Don Fedderson Productions, 16255 Ventura Blvd, Encino CA 91436 818-986-3118
Edward Feil Productions, 4614 Prospect Ave, Cleveland OH 44103...........216-771-0655
Edward Feldman Co, 9336 W Washington, Culver City CA 90230.............213-202-3505
Feline Productions, 1125 Veronica Spgs, Santa Barbara CA 93105 805-682-4047
Fenady Assoc Inc, Box 9000, Beverly Hills CA 90213....................................213-203-3148
Festival Productions, 849 E Charleston Rd, Palo Alto CA 94306 415-494-9366
The FHM Co, 3525 Berry Dr, Studio City CA 91604 818-769-2395
Freddie Fields Prod, 10202 W Washington, Culver City CA 90230.............213-558-5411
50/50 Productions, 3217 Dona Emilla Dr, Studio City CA 91604 213-650-1685
Film & General Prod, 9601 Wilshire Blvd, Beverly Hills CA 90210 213-585-7700
Film America Inc, 3132 Randolph Rd NE, Atlanta GA 30345.....................404-261-3735
Film Center, 12444 Victory Blvd Ste 307, North Hollywood CA 91606......818-760-1700
Film Consortium, 9165 Sunset Blvd Ste 300, Los Angeles CA 90069.........213-550-0190
Film Effects Intl, 1140 Citrus Ave, Los Angeles CA 90038............................213-460-2001
The Film Group Inc, 2400 Massachusetts Ave, Cambridge MA 02140......617-354-5695
Film Packages Intl, 9000 Sunset Blvd Ste 615, Los Angeles CA 90069......213-274-5251
The Film Tree, 8554 Melrose Ave, Los Angeles CA 90069............................213-659-9350
Film Ventures Intl, 11908 Ventura Blvd Ste 201, Studio City CA 91604....818-769-4210
Film-Fair/Carousel Prod, 10900 Ventura Blvd, Studio City CA 91604.....818-766-9441
Film-Tel, 4800 S Sepulveda Blvd, Culver City CA 90230...............................213-391-7175
Film/Jamel Productions, 195 S Beverly Dr, Beverly Hills CA 90212.........213-273-0966
Filmaccord Inc, 2271 Roscomare Rd, Los Angeles CA 90077 213-476-8543
Filmack Studios, 1327 S Wabash, Chicago IL 60605 312-427-3395
Filmagic, 6362 Hollywood Blvd, Los Angeles CA 90028..............................213-464-5333
Filmation Studios, 18107 Sherman Way, Reseda CA 91335.........................818-345-7414
Filmcorp Group Inc, 8758 Venice Blvd, Los Angeles CA 90034..................213-558-0071
Filmcrafters, PO Box 45572, Los Angeles CA 90045......................................213-641-6028
Filmline Productions Assoc, 1467 Tamarind, Los Angeles CA 90028........213-466-8667
Filmrite Assoc Inc, 1040 N McCadden Pl, Hollywood CA 90038 213-464-7491

Films Intl, 4230 Ben Ave, Studio City CA 91604...818-762-2181
Financial News Network, 2525 Ocean Park Blvd, Studio City CA 90405 ...213-450-2412
Fine Arts Films, 11632 Ventura Blvd Ste 201, Studio City CA 91604.........818-980-3034
Finnegan Assoc, 4225 Coldwater Canyon, Studio City CA 91604 818-985-0430
Imero Fiorentino Assoc, 7060 Hollywood Blvd, Los Angeles CA 90028....213-467-4020
Fire Prevention Through Films, Box 11, Newton Highlands MA 02161....617-965-4444
Firelight Publishing, 9028 Sunset Blvd Ste 203, Los Angeles CA 90069....213-278-6999
Firesign Productions, 1155 N La Cienega Blvd, Hollywood CA 90069......213-652-6376
First Artists Prod Co, 2029 Century Park E, Los Angeles CA 90067 213-557-0838
First Natl Bank of Chicago, 2 1st Natl Bank Pl, Chicago IL 60670 312-407-4048
Hyman W Fisher Inc, Box 655, Livingston NJ 07039 201-994-9480
David Fisher Productions, 14144 Dickens, Sherman Oaks CA 91423........818-907-1368
James Fitzgerald Ent, 1061 Ravoli Dr, Pacific Palisade CA 90272............213-454-1160
Five-Twenty Corp, 1900 Ave of Stars Ste 1630, Los Angeles CA 90067 213-277-3373
FJC Intellimedia Inc, 8332 Zenith, Baldwinsville NY 13027 315-622-1683
Flagg Films, 10943 Burbank Blvd, North Hollywood CA 91601 213-985-5050
Flamingo Films Inc, 7026 Santa Monica Blvd, Hollywood CA 90038 213-466-5111
Flattery-Halperin-Cole, 8258 Fountain Ave, Los Angeles CA 90046 213-650-6388
Flaum-Grinberg Prod, 1040 McCadden Pl, Los Angeles CA 90038............213-464-7491
Flint Productions Inc, 7758 Sunset Blvd, Los Angeles CA 90046 213-851-1060
FlipTrack Learning Systems, 999 Main, Glen Ellyn IL 60137....................312-790-1117
Florida Production Center, 150 Riverside Dr, Jacksonville FL 32202 904-354-7000
Florida Vidcom, 3685 N Federal Hwy, Pompano Bch FL 33064..................305-943-5590
Flying Camera Inc, 114 Fulton St, New York NY 10038.............................212-725-0658
Flying Eye Graphics, 208 5th Ave, New York NY 10010 212-725-0658
FMS Productions Inc, 1777 Vine St, Los Angeles CA 90028 213-461-4567
FOCUS, Box 340, Mishawaka IN 46544...219-259-7801
Focus III Productions, 7805 Sunset Blvd, Hollywood CA 90046 213-850-1855
Focus Tele-Productions, PO Box 9342, New Orleans LA 70115................504-837-2020
Fonda Films, PO Box 491355, Hollywood CA 90049..................................213-458-4545
Foothill Productions, 70 W 83rd St, New York NY 10024..........................212-877-0973
Forerunner Television Show, PO Box 1799, Gainesville FL 32602..............904-375-6000
Forrest Productions, PO Box 1245, Beverly Hills CA 90213 213-557-2615
Forsher Collection, 650 N Bronson, Los Angeles CA 90004 213-461-0178
40 Share Productions, 1800 Ave of the Stars, Los Angeles CA 90067 213-203-7947
Robert H Forward Prod, 550 S Barrington, Los Angeles CA 90049............213-476-3605
Foster Communications, 910 Race St, Cincinnati OH 45202.....................513-241-9937
Four D Productions, 9200 Sunset Blvd Ste 920, Los Angeles CA 90069....213-550-7022
Four Star Intl Inc, 931 Cole Ave, Los Angeles CA 90038 818-469-2102
Sonny Fox Productions, 1447 N Kings Rd, Los Angeles CA 90069............213-650-0606
Foxcroft Productions, 1501 Skylark Ln, Los Angeles CA 90069 213-271-6087
Redd Foxx Productions, 933 N La Brea Ave, Los Angeles CA 90038........213-874-6610
Frager Productions, 4119 Brentler Rd, Louisville KS 40222 502-893-6654
Franciscan Communication Ctr, 1229 S Santee, Los Angeles CA 90015..213-746-2916
Sandy Frank Productions, 5800 Sunset Blvd, Hollywood CA 90028..........213-460-5735
Frankel Film Inc, 13418 Ventura Blvd, Sherman Oaks CA 91423...............818-501-5044
Karen Frankel Productions, 520 E 48th St, New York NY 10028...............212-744-6446
John Frankenheimer Prod, 2800 Olympic, Santa Monica CA 90404 213-829-0404
Franklin Film Production Co, Box 1994, Los Angeles CA 90028...............213-464-6838
Frankovich Productions, 9200 Sunset Blvd, Los Angeles CA 90069 213-278-0920
Freberg Ltd, 8730 Sunset Blvd Ste 503, Los Angeles CA 90069 213-657-6550
Free Lance Exchange Inc, 150 5th Ave Ste 854, New York NY 10011 212-741-8020
Joel Freeman Prod, 150 El Camino #205, Beverly Hills CA 90212.............213-274-0200

Doug Freeman Sound-Edit, 6362 Hollywood, Hollywood CA 90028 213-467-8742
Freese & Friends Inc, 1429 N Wells St, Chicago IL 60610.....................312-642-4475
Paul French & Partners, 505 Gabbettville Rd, La Grange GA 30240 404-882-5581
Freund & Kleppel, 6290 Sunset Blvd Ste 603, Los Angeles CA 90028 213-469-1444
Fried Productions, 768 Farmington Ave, Farmington CT 06032.................203-674-8221
Rick Friedberg & Assoc, 5225 Wilshire Blvd, Los Angeles CA 90036........213-937-5743
Charles Fries Production, 9200 Sunset Blvd, Los Angeles CA 90069 213-859-9957
Fruition Publications Inc, Box 103, Blawenburg NJ 08504....................609-466-3196
FTG Intl, 1141 Lodi Pt, Los Angeles CA 90038.............................213-467-7210
Full Circle Communications Inc, 73 Leeds Ct E, Danville CA 94526........415-820-6258
Full Circle Entertainment, 1901 Ave of Stars, Los Angeles CA 90067 213-556-2450
Fuller Productions, 905 Hillgrove Ste 7, La Grange IL 60525................312-579-9578
Funky Punky & Chic, PO Box 601 Cooper Sta, New York NY 10276 212-533-1772
Furia/Oringer Prod, 5800 Owensmouth, Woodland Hls CA 91367...........818-702-0230
Furman Films Inc, 3466 21st St, San Francisco CA 94110....................415-824-8500
Fusion Films, 9157 Sunset Blvd Ste 206, Los Angeles CA 90069.............213-276-3122
GH Productions Inc, 9911 W Pico Blvd, Los Angeles CA 90035 213-277-9711
GN Productions, 2007 N Hobart, Los Angeles CA 90027.....................213-463-5693
GTA West, 116 S La Brea Ave, LosAngeles CA 90036.........................213-937-6100
George Gage Productions, 31316 Broad Beach Rd, Malibu CA 90265 213-457-1170
Galaxy Releasing, 9336 W Washington, Los Angeles CA 90230 213-202-3393
Galia Intl Inc, Box 5778, Sherman Oaks CA 91403 818-789-2221
Gannett Productions Inc, 304 E 45th St, New York NY 10017................212-286-0770
Gardian Productions, 1717 W Highland Ave, Los Angeles CA 90028.......213-462-6414
Garen/Albrecht Productions, 1351 3rd St, Santa Monica CA 90401..........213-458-1723
Greg Garrison Productions, 3400 Alameda St, Burbank CA 91505...........213-849-2471
Gateway Productions, 3011 Magazine St, New Orleans LA 70115 504-891-2600
Gaylord Productions, 9255 Sunset Blvd Ste 800, Los Angeles CA 90069 ..213-274-7769
GBF Productions, 1040 N Las Palmas Ave, Hollywood CA 90038...........213-462-6081
John L Gean Productions, 1041 N Formosa, Hollywood CA 90046...........213-850-3111
David Geffen Co, 9130 Sunset Blvd, Los Angeles CA 90069....................213-278-9010
Bo Gehring Assoc, 13431 Beach Ave, Venice CA 90291 213-823-8577
General Educational Media, 701 Beaver Valley, Wilmington DE 19803...302-478-1994
General Music Corp, 6210 Sunset Blvd Ste 202, Los Angeles CA 90028...213-462-0715
Geoffrey Productions, 1888 Century Park E, Los Angeles CA 90067.........213-553-6741
Georgetown TV Productions, 3900 Reservoir Rd NW, Wash DC 20007 ...202-625-2351
Georgian Bay Productions, 3815 W Olive, Burbank CA 95105..................818-843-7704
David Gerber Co, 10202 W Washington Blvd, Burbank CA 90230............213-558-6400
German Television Films, 2354 N Canyon Dr, Hollywood CA 90068........213-467-6664
Gervino Beker Assoc, 90 Hilltop Dr, Trumbull CT 06611......................203-377-2180
Gessler Publishing, 900 Broadway, New York NY 10003 212-673-3113
Gideon Productions, 9696 Culver Rd #203, Culver City CA 90232 213-558-8110
Gifford Animation Inc, 548 E 87th St, New York NY 10128....................212-986-2826
Gileon Assoc Inc, 5609 Sunset Blvd, Los Angeles CA 90028 213-467-1131
Vern Gillum & Friends, 8630 Pinetree Pl, Los Angeles CA 90069............213-659-6100
Giraldi/Suarez Productions, 329 N Wetherly, Beverly Hills CA 90212 213-859-8930
Gladden Productions, 9454 Wilshire Blvd, Beverly Hills CA 90212...........213-202-0202
Glaston-Tor Ltd, 4565 Sherman Oaks Ave, Sherman Oaks CA 91403 818-783-4450
Glazer Entertainment Co, 9903 Santa Monica, Beverly Hills CA 90212....213-201-0800
Cary Glieberman, 972 Miramonte Dr #2, Santa Barbara CA 93109 805-966-2355
Global Pictures Inc, 4774 Melrose Ave, Los Angeles CA 90029.................213-665-5257
GMA Audio Visual Inc, 30 N Park, Lombard IL 60148........................312-377-0004
GMT Productions, 5751 Buckingham Pkwy, Culver City CA 90230..........213-649-3733

Goal Productions, 2027 N Lake Ave, Altadena CA 90029 818-797-7668
Gary Goddard Prod, 6834 Hollywood Blvd, Hollywood CA 90028 213-877-1088
Jeff Gold Productions, 300 E 51st St, New York NY 10022 212-759-8785
The Leonard Goldberg Co, 5555 Melrose Ave, Los Angeles CA 90038.....213-468-4806
Golden Harvest Films, 9884 Santa Monica, Beverly Hills CA 90212 213-203-0722
Golden Pictures Ltd, 125 S Racine, Chicago IL 60607 312-226-8240
Golden West Video Tape Div, 5800 Sunset Blvd, Los Angeles CA 90028 ..213-460-5866
Goldfarb Distributors, 914 S Robertson, Los Angeles CA 90035...............213-652-5693
Goldsholl Film Group, 420 Frontage Rd, Northfield IL 60093 312-446-8300
Milt Goldstein Enterprises, 260 S Beverly Dr, Beverly Hills CA 90212 213-273-5450
The Samuel Goldwyn Co, 10203 Santa Monica, Los Angeles CA 90067....213-552-2255
Golin Productions, 4207 Troost Ave, Studio City CA 91604 818-505-0191
Norman Gollin Prod, 9048 Wonderland Park, Los Angeles CA 90046......213-656-2398
Goodson-Todman Prod, 6430 Sunset Blvd, Los Angeles CA 90028 213-464-4300
Googolplex Inc, 77 Bleecker St, New York NY 10012 212-475-3990
Gerald Gordon Enterprises, 15525 Leadwell St, Van Nuys CA 91406.......818-994-8684
Marc Gordon Production, Box 2155, Beverly Hills CA 90213 213-934-6416
Alex Gordon Productions, Box 36676, Los Angeles CA 90036...................213-936-1874
Lawrence Gordon Co, 10201 W Pico Blvd, Los Angeles CA 90035.............213-203-3608
Gorman Multimedia Comm, 2 W 45th St, New York NY 10036 212-840-2092
Gornick Film Productions, 4200 Camino Real, Los Angeles CA 90065....213-223-8914
Joe Gottfried Management, 15456 Cabrito Rd, Van Nuys CA 91406.........213-873-7370
James Graham & Assoc, 4028 W California Ave, Glendale CA 91203......818-956-6646
Bob Graham Productions, 1926 Hillcrest Rd, Los Angeles CA 90068.......212-874-7004
Grand Slam Productions, 4028 Colfax Ave, Studio CIty CA 91604 818-877-2797
Roy Grandey Productions, Box 4224, Burlingame CA 94010 415-692-0500
Granite Productions, 2222 Sherman Way, Canoga Park CA 91303............818-999-3223
Leonard Grant & Assoc, PO Box 69405, Los Angeles CA 90069 213-274-9483
Sherry Grant Productions, 17915 Ventura Blvd, Encino CA 91316...........818-705-2535
Grapevine Productions Ltd, 5055 E Broadway, Tucson AZ 85711...........602-747-3115
Graphic Films Inc, 3341 Cahuenga Blvd W, Los Angeles CA 90068 213-938-9436
Graphic Media Inc, 421 Summitt St, Winston-Salem NC 27101 919-722-8951
Graphic Media Inc, 373 Rte 46 W, Fairfield NJ 07006................................201-227-5000
Graphics One Fifty Co, 150 Speedwell Ave, Morris Plains NJ 07950.........201-267-6446
Grayson Productions, 7315 Melrose Ave, Los Angeles CA 90068 213-938-9436
Great American Cinema Co, 10711 Wellworth, Los Angeles CA 90024....213-475-0937
Bob Green Productions, 7950 Westglen, Houston TX 77063 713-977-1334
Craig Green Productions, 3518 Cahuenga Blvd, Los Angeles CA 90068 ..213-874-2305
Greenberg/R Inc, 350 W 39th St, New York NY 10018 212-239-6767
Greentree Prod, 10835 Santa Monica, Los Angeles CA 90067 213-970-7557
Larry Greene Productions, 1151 Sunset Hills, Los Angeles CA 90069 213-273-0673
The Greif-Dore Co, 1888 Century Park E, Los Angeles CA 90067 213-201-7174
Abner J Greshler Prod, 9200 Sunset Blvd, Los Angeles CA 90069.............213-278-8146
Greyfalcon House, 124 Waverly Place, New York NY 10011 212-777-9042
Griffin Media Design Inc, 802 Wabash Ave, Chesterton IN 46304............219-926-8602
Gary Griffin Productions, 12667 Memorial Dr, Houston TX 77024 713-465-9017
Merv Griffin Productions, 1541 N Vine St, Los Angeles CA 90028 213-461-4701
Sherman Grinberg Prod, 1040 N McCadden Pl, Los Angeles CA 90038 ..213-464-7491
David Grober Prod, 616 Venice Blvd, Marina del Rey CA 90291 213-822-4656
Group Five Communications Inc, 671 Elm St, Manchester NH 03101......603-627-2599
Group One Films, 9200 Sunset Blvd Ste 1105, Los Angeles CA 90069 213-550-8767
Group One Productions, 1 China Basin Bldg, San Francisco CA 94107....415-777-5777
Group Two, 428 E 25th St, Baltimore MD 21218 301-467-9000

Group Visionary Productions, 13046 Greenleaf, Studio City CA 91604....818-995-6050
Group W Productions, 3801 Barham Blvd, Los Angeles CA 90068 818-850-3800
Reg Grundy Productions, 9911 W Pico Blvd, Los Angeles CA 90035........213-557-3571
Guber-Peters, 4000 Warner Blvd, Burbank CA 91522...............................818-954-2994
Robt Guenette Productions, 8489 W 3rd St, Los Angeles CA 99006..........213-658-8450
Guymark Inc Studios, Box 5037, Hamden CT 06518 203-248-9323
Gwynbly Inc, 9911 W Pico Blvd PH-A, Los Angeles CA 90035..................213-277-9711
The Haboush Co, 6611 Santa Monica Blvd, Hollywood CA 90038 213-466-4111
Brad Hagert, PO Box 18642, Irvine CA 92713...714-261-7266
Geoff Haines-Stiles Prod, 776 S Madison Ave, Pasadena CA 91106..........818-449-3570
Halcyon Productions, 9200 Sunset Blvd Ste 808, Los Angeles CA 90069 ..213-550-0570
H B Halicki Productions, 17902 S Vermont Ave, Gardena CA 90248.......213-770-1744
Paula Lee Haller Production, 8489 W 3rd St, Los Angeles CA 90048 213-651-0948
Hallmark Communications, 51 New Plant Ct, Owings Mills MD 21117...301-363-4500
Jim Halsey Co, 1930 Century Park W, Los Angeles CA 90067 213-552-1100
Joe Hamilton Productions, 141 El Camino Dr, Beverly Hills CA 90212...213-278-2661
Armand Hammer Prod, 10889 Wilshire Blvd, Los Angeles CA 90024.......213-879-3786
Handel Film Corp, 8730 Sunset Blvd, Los Angeles CA 90069.....................213-657-8990
Hanna-Barbera Prod, 3400 Cahuenga W, Los Angeles CA 90068 213-851-5000
Hansen & Gervasoni Prod, 1454 Seward, Hollywood CA 90028 213-467-5085
Ed Hansen Assoc, 1454 N Seward St, Hollywood CA 90028.......................213-467-5085
Har D Har Productions Inc, 19525 Braewood Dr, Tarzana CA 91356......818-345-2363
Harcon Productions, Box 2493, Toluca Lake CA 91602 818-345-2363
Harding Productions, 4782 Unity Line Rd, New Waterford OH 44445 216-475-7352
Hardman Eastman Studios, 1400 E Carson St, Pittsburg PA 15203..........412-481-4450
Larry Harmon Pictures Corp, 650 N Bronson, Hollywood CA 90004 213-463-2331
Harmony Gold USA, 8831 Sunset Blvd Ste 300, Los Angeles CA 90069....213-652-8720
Harmony Pictures, 2921 W Alameda Ave, Burbank CA 91505..................818-846-6700
Harremas Productions, 9720 Wilshire Blvd, Beverly Hills CA 90212.........213-274-0151
Denny Harris Inc, 12166 W Olympic Blvd, Los Angeles CA 90064.............213-826-6565
James B Harris Productions, 248 S Lasky, Beverly Hills CA 90212...........213-273-4270
Ken Harris Video Prod, 3960 Laurel Canyon, Beverly Hills CA 91604......818-780-0320
Harris-Tuchman Productions, 1226 W Olive Ave, Burbank CA 91506.....818-841-4100
Rich Harrison & Co Inc, 6000 Sunset Blvd, Los Angeles CA 90028 213-463-2189
Hatos-Hall Productions, 7833 Sunset Blvd, Los Angeles CA 90046..........213-874-3000
Haycox Photoramic Inc, 1531 Early St, Norfolk VA 23502........................804-855-1911
Hayden Productions, 2029 Sunset Blvd 6th fl, Los Angeles CA 90067.......213-879-3257
Hayes School Publishing, 321 Pennwood, Wilkinsburg PA 15221 412-371-2373
Bruce Hayes Productions, 380 Chestnut St, San Francisco CA 94133........415-956-1542
Headliner Productions Inc, 6221 Afton Pl, Los Angeles CA 90028.............213-462-5050
Headoc Productions, 1516 Westwood Blvd, Los Angeles CA 90024 213-470-8080
Heaping Teaspoon Animation, 4002 19th St, San Francisco CA 94114......415-626-1893
Paul Heller Productions, 1666 N Beverly Dr, Beverly Hills CA 90210 213-275-4477
Hemdale Film Corp, 1118 N Wetherly Dr, Los Angeles CA 90069.............213-550-6894
Henderson Productions, 4201 W Alameda St, Burbank CA 91505 818-985-6417
Hennessy Productions, 900 Palm Ave, South Pasadena CA 91505............213-682-2353
Bob Henry Productions, 11940 San Vincente, Los Angeles CA 90049.......213-879-0012
Hephaestus Productions, 1790 N Orange Grove, Hollywood CA 90046 ...213-850-5607
Heritage Entertainment, 9229 Sunset Blvd, Los Angeles CA 90069..........213-278-1566
Hermes Productions, 9601 Wilshire Blvd, Beverly Hills CA 90210 213-273-2141
Robert M Hertzberg, 57 W 75th St, New York NY 10023..........................212-873-3211
Milan Herzog, Box 206, Hollywood CA 90078...213-466-8496
Hess Productions, 55 Greenwich Ave Ste 1, New York NY 10014.............212-255-1995

Christopher Hibler Prod, 16133 Ventura Blvd, Encino CA 91436 818-981-5492
Hickmar Productions, 4000 Warner Blvd, Burbank CA 91522 818-954-5104
Hickox-Daniel Productions, 4000 Warner Blvd, Burbank CA 91522.........818-854-3034
Alfred Higgins Productions, 9100 Sunset Blvd, Los Angeles CA 90069 213-272-6500
High Country Films, 6865 E Arizona, Denver CO 80224 303-756-8030
High Seas Presentation, 2347 Eastern Canal, Venice CA 90291 213-821-7669
Hill-Daves Productions, 6430 Variel Ave, Woodland Hills CA 91367 818-364-3933
Hill-Obst Prod, 5555 Melrose, Los Angeles CA 90038.............................213-468-4516
Hillmann & Carr, 2121 Wisconsin Ave NW, Washington DC 20007.........202-342-0001
HISK, 10950 Ventura Blvd, Studio CIty CA 60481.................................213-277-9711
Steve Hitter & Assoc, 10799 Northgate St, Culver City CA 90230 213-204-1517
Holland-Wegman Productions, 1545 Bronson, Grand Island NY 14072 ...716-853-7477
Hollywood & Vine Productions, 1777 Vine St, Hollywood CA 90028 213-461-4567
Hollywood Artists Productions, 691 S Irolo St, Los Angeles CA 90005.....213-384-5269
Hollywood Blues/Lucrecia Ent, 1680 Vine St, Hollywood CA 90028.........213-460-4036
Hollywood Cinema Center, Box 2026, North Hollywood CA 91602 213-851-6532
Hollywood Intl Film Corp, 1044 S Hill St, Los Angeles CA 90015 213-749-2067
Hollywood Newsreel Syndicate, 1622 N Gower, Los Angeles CA 90028....213-469-7307
Burton Holmes Inc, 1004 Karrabee St, W Hollywood CA 90069 213-652-0970
Home Box Office, 1100 Ave of the Americas, New York NY 10019 212-664-0023
Homer & Assoc Inc, 1420 N Beachwood Dr, Los Angeles CA 90028 213-462-4710
Dennis Hommel Assoc, 3540 Middlefield Rd, Menlo Park CA 94025.......415-365-4565
Hope Enterprises Inc, 3808 Riverside Dr Ste 100, Burbank CA 91505......818-841-2020
Harry Hope Productions, 3122 Arrowhead Dr, Menlo Park CA 90068.....213-469-5596
Hormel Geordie Film Ent, 8822 Oakwilde Ln, Los Angeles CA 90025 213-478-8227
Hornstein Entertainment, 3808 Riverside Dr, Burbank CA 91505............213-655-2494
Howard Intl Film Group, 9255 Sunset Blvd, Los Angeles CA 90069 213-274-3106
Howl Productions, 1474 N Kings Rd, Los Angeles CA 90069 213-656-4787
Ice Capades Inc, 6121 Santa Monica Blvd, Los Angeles CA 90038 213-469-2769
Icom Inc, 278 N 5th St, Columbus OH 43215.......................................614-224-4400
Icon Communications Ltd, 717 Lexington Ave, New York NY 10022........212-688-5155
Icon R & D, 2619 B Hyperion Ave, Los Angeles CA 90027.....................213-660-8457
Idea Factory, 2212 Lakeshore Ave, Los Angeles CA 90039.....................213-661-5911
Ie Inc, 736 S Eddy St, South Bend IN 46615.......................................219-282-2551
Image Dynamics, 84 Burnham Rd, Morris Plains NJ 07652 201-538-7149
Image Engineering Inc, 632 N Victory Blvd, Burbank CA 91502...............818-847-5885
Image Imagination, PO Box 4136, Los Angeles CA 90078 213-937-1314
Image Innovation Inc, 14 Buttonwood Dr, Somerset NJ 08873 201-256-2622
Image Integration, 2418 Stuart St, Berkeley CA 94705 415-841-8524
Image Makers, 916 N Charles St, Baltimore MD 21201..........................301-727-8800
Image Makers of Pittsford, 6 Wood Gate, Pittsford NY 14534 716-385-4567
Image Productions, 1812 W Victory Blvd, Burbank CA 91506 818-846-2047
Image Stream Inc, 5450 W Washington Blvd, Los Angeles CA 90016.......213-933-9196
Image-Maker Inc, 928 E Carpenteria St, Santa Barbara CA 93103...........805-965-8546
ImageMatrix/Cincinnati, 2 Garfield Pl, Cincinnati OH 45202.................513-381-1380
Images Inc, 1662 Stockton St, Jacksonville FL 32204.............................904-388-3300
Imagesmith Inc, 290 Cypress St, Rochester NY 14620 716-473-4010
Imagine Ent/Ron Howard, 4000 Warner Blvd, Burbank CA 91522 818-954-1884
Impact Communications, 11 Pine Ridge Rd, Port Chester NY 10573.......914-937-0900
Imperial Intl Learning, 329 E Court St, Kankakee IL 60901....................815-933-7735
In-Sight Into Communication, 288 Fillow St, Norwalk CT 06850...............203-853-1115
In-Sync, 4572 Marston, Encino CA 91316 818-708-0539
Inage West Ltd, 11846 Ventura Blvd, Los Angeles CA 91604 213-466-4181

Independent Producers Service, 7370 Melrose, Los Angeles CA 213-6 213-466-4181
Independent Video, 92 Horatio St, New York NY 10014 212-242-2581
Indianer Multi Media, 16201 SW 95 Ave, Miami FL 33157 305-235-6132
Indie Prod Co, Columbia Plaza, Burbank CA 91505 818-954-2600
Indigo Productions, Columbia Plaza, Burbank CA 91505 818-954-3417
Industrial Communications Assoc, 17 Gables Dr, Hicksville NY 11801...516-433-2035
Industrial Media, 6660 28th St SE, Grand Rapids MI 49506 616-949-7770
Industrial Training Systems Corp, 20 W Stow Rd, Marlion NJ 08054......609-983-7300
Infamous Films, 1252 S Orange Grove Ave, Los Angeles CA 90019 213-937-4372
Infinity Filmworks, 2160 Lakeshore Ave Ste B, Los Angeles CA 90039....213-666-2020
InfoCom Productions Inc, 4614 Prospect Ave, Cleveland OH 44103.........216-431-9163
Ingels Inc, 8322 Beverly Blvd Ste 207, Los Angeles CA 90048 213-852-0300
Inland Audio Visual Co, N 2325 Monroe St, Spokane WA 99205 509-328-0706
Innerquest Comm, 6383 Rose Ln, Carpinteria CA 93013 805-684-9977
Innovation Unlimited, 4444 Via Marina, Marina del Rey CA 90291.........213-823-4251
Insight!, 100 E Ohio St, Chicago IL 60611 312-467-4350
Instructional Comm Ctr, Univ of Louisville, Louisville KY 40292..............502-589-6461
Instructional Systems, 11899 W Pico Blvd, Los Angeles CA 90064 213-477-8541
Inter-Planetary Prod, 14225 Ventura Blvd, Sherman Oaks CA 91423.......818-981-4950
Inter-Television Prod, 15050 Sherman Way, Van Nuys CA 91505............818-785-3052
Interactive Production Assoc, 11385 Exposition, Los Angeles CA 90064..213-390-9466
Intercomcon Inc, 1022 N Palm Ave, Los Angeles CA 90069 213-933-4544
Intercontinental Media Services, PO Box 75127, Wash DC 20013.............202-638-5595
Intercontinental Releasing, 10351 Santa Monica, Los Angeles CA 90025.213-552-3800
Intermix Inc, 2505 S Robertson Blvd, Los Angeles CA 90034....................213-870-2121
Intl Cable Telecomm, 316A N Euclid, St Louis MO 63108.......................314-361-3335
Intl Home Entertainment, 650 N Bronson Ave, Los Angeles CA 90004 ...213-460-4545
Intl Media Services Inc, 718 Sherman Ave, Plainfield NJ 07060................201-756-4060
Intl Medifilms, 3393 Barnham Blvd, Los Angeles CA 90068......................213-851-4555
Intl Producers Services, 3518 Cahuenga Blvd W, Hollywood CA 90068...213-851-3595
Intl Rainbow Pictures, 933 N La Brea Ave #202, Hollywood CA 90038...818-888-2277
Intl Video Entertainment, 7920 Alabama Ave, Canoga Park CA 91304....818-888-3040
Interscope Communications, 10900 Wilshire, Los Angeles CA 90024.......213-208-8525
Interurban Films, PO Box 6444, Glendale CA 91205................................818-240-9130
Intervision, 400 Woodvine Ct, Roswell GA 30076 404-992-9292
Iota Productions, 1220 Sunset Plaza Dr, Los Angeles CA 90069................213-652-3223
Ishi Company Ltd, 9220 Sunset Plaza D, Los Angeles CA 90069..............213-275-5351
Isis Productions, 9601 Wilshire Blvd Ste 526, Beverly Hills CA 90210......213-278-6060
Island Films, 9000 Sunset Blvd, Los Angeles CA 90069...........................213-276-4500
ITC Productions Inc, 12711 Ventura Blvd 3rd fl, Studio City CA 91604...818-760-2110
IXION, 1335 N Northlake Way, Seattle WA 98103.................................206-547-8801
J P Video Services, 9538 W Pico Blvd, Los Angeles CA 90035..................213-271-1209
David J Jackson Prod, 646 Barrington, Brentwood CA 90049 213-471-8316
Riley Jackson Prod, 6353 Homewood Ave, Los Angeles CA 90028 213-464-4708
Jacob & Gerber Inc, 731 N Fairfax Ave, Los Angeles CA 90046 213-655-4082
Jacoby/Storm Productions Inc, 22 Crescent Rd, Westport CT 06880.......203-227-2220
JAG Productions, 11684 Ventura Blvd, Studio City CA 91604..................818-985-6817
JAD Films Intl, 11900 Avenue of Stars Ste 1535, Los Angeles CA 90067..213-203-0288
Henry Jaffe Enterprises, 1420 N Beachwood Dr, Hollywood CA 90028 ...213-466-3543
Jaffe-Lansing, 5555 Melrose, Los Angeles CA 90038 213-468-4575
Jaguar Productions, 7000 Santa Monica Blvd, Hollywood CA 90038........213-466-7021
Jalem Productions, 141 El Camino Dr Ste 201, Beverly Hills CA 90212...213-278-7750
James Communications, 7508 Maria Ave, Louisville KY 40222..................502-426-2654

Jamieson & Assoc Inc, 5200 Willson Rd, Minneapolis MN 55424..............612-920-3770
Jayell Enterprises, PO Box 2616 Ft Dearborn Sta, Dearborn MI 48123 ...313-565-9687
The Jaypat Studio, 1081 Westwood Blvd, Los Angeles CA 90024..............213-208-1659
Jeffries Films Intl, 3855 Lankershim Blvd, North Hollywood CA 91604...818-760-6666
Jemmin Inc, 205 Hill St, Santa Monica CA 90405....................................213-392-9711
Jenkins Covington Newman Rath, 7175 Sunset, Hollywood CA 90046......213-850-5561
Jenner/Wallach Productions, 1400 Brawridge, Beverly Hills CA 90210 ...213-278-4574
Ray Jewell Productions, 11136 Weddington, N Hollywood CA 91601 818-766-3747
JJH Productions Inc, 900 Palm Ave, South Pasadena CA 91030.................213-682-3611
JLP Pictures, PO Box 5155, Beverly Hills CA 90210 213-276-8196
JM Production Co, 2208 Union St, San Francisco CA 94123 415-346-3261
The JN Co, 20 Crossways Park N, Woodbury NY 11797...............................516-364-8557
Johns Hopkins Univ, 1721 E Madison St, Baltimore MD 21205 301-955-3562
Johnson Nyquist Prod, 23854 Via Fabricante, Mission Viejo CA 92691 ...714-770-5777
Jerry Johnson Productions, 8489 W 3rd St, Los Angeles CA 90048 213-655-2563
Johnson/Cowen Inc, 1601 N El Centro Ave, Los Angeles CA 90028.........213-466-5301
Jones Productions Inc, 517 Chester, Little Rock AR 72201 501-372-4285
JSK Enterprises Inc, 470 S Bedford Dr, Beverly Hills CA 90212................213-553-1525
Junior Black Academy, 3800 Commerce St, Dallas TX 75210 214-827-6242
Ken Jurek Assoc Inc, 4284 W Streetsboro Rd, Richfield OH 44286 216-659-3961
Paul Justman Productions, 6169 Glen Holly, Los Angeles CA 90068.......213-464-6195
K&H Productions, 4141 Office Pkwy, Dallas TX 75204..............................214-826-8952
Kake Productions, 1621 W 9th St, Wichita KS 67201 316-943-4221
Kaleidoscope Films Ltd, 844 N Seward St, Los Angeles CA 90038.............213-465-1151
Kaleidoscope Productions, 160 W 95th St, New York NY 10025 212-749-7624
Kamstra Communications Inc, 370 Selby Ave, St Paul MN 55102 612-228-1419
Paul S Karr Prod, 2949 W Indian School, Phoenix AZ 85017....................602-266-4198
Karson/Higgins/Shaw Comm, 729 N Seward, Hollywood CA 90038........213-461-3030
Kartes Video Communications, 10 E 106th St, Indianapolis IN 46280 317-844-7403
Peter Kasloff Productions, Box 106, Topanga CA 90290...........................213-455-3026
Leonard Katzman, 10201 W Washington Blvd, Culver City CA 90230......213-826-3000
Kavich/Reynolds Prod, 6381 Hollywood Blvd, Hollywood CA 90028........213-466-2490
Kaye Entertainment Ent, 1680 N Vine St, Los Angeles CA 90028 213-462-6001
Stacy Keach Productions, 5216 Laurel Canyon, N Hollywood CA 91607..818-877-0472
Keefco, 1961 N Van Ness Ave, Los Angeles CA 90068.................................213-467-6766
Keller Productions, 1800 N Highland Ave, Hollywood CA 90028 213-463-2186
Michael P Kellerman Prod, 6777 Hollywood, Hollywood CA 90028..........213-469-9880
Don Kelley Organization, 1474 N Kings Rd, Los Angeles CA 90069 213-656-4787
Kenwood Group, One China Basin Bldg, San Francisco CA 94107............415-777-5777
Kenworthy Snorkel Films, PO Box 49581, Los Angeles CA 90049.............213-476-4100
Kerner-Avnet, 505 N Robertson, Los Angeles CA 90048.............................213-271-7408
Kestral Films, 3903 W Olive, Burbank CA 91522 818-954-6460
Key Films, 812 N Highland Ave, Los Angeles CA 90038 213-464-4100
Keyboard Workshop, Box 192, Medford OR 97501......................................503-664-6751
Paul W Keys Prod, 32123 W Lindero Canyon, Westlake Vlg CA 91361....818-889-9130
KHNL, 150 B Puuhale Rd, Honolulu HI 96819 808-847-3246
Kids Matter Inc, PO Box 3460, Ashland OR 97520.....................................503-484-0088
Kimbo Educational, 10-16 N 3rd Ave, Long Branch NJ 07740 201-229-4949
Kimmel/Lucas Productions, 932 N La Brea, Los Angeles CA 90038........213-874-0436
King Intl Corp, 124 S Laksy Dr, Beverly Hills CA 90212...........................213-274-0333
Kings Road Productions, 1901 Ave of Stars, Los Angeles CA 90067.........213-552-0057
KK Communications, 205 W 54th St, New York NY 10019 212-581-1840
Klasky/Csupo, 729 Seward St, Hollywood CA 90038...................................213-463-0145

Klein & Friends Inc, 3855 Lankershim Blvd, N Hollywood CA 91604.......818-766-0452
Aladar Klein, 7266 Franklin Ave, Los Angeles CA 90046.....................213-876-7852
KLS Tele-Productions Inc, 5011 S 16th St Ste 101, Lincoln NE 68512 402-423-4600
KMST TV, 2200 Garden Rd, Monterey CA 93940 408-649-0460
Knicar Productions, Box 2539, Toluca Lake CA 91602 213-556-2220
Koala Inc, PO Box 66100, Houston TX 77006....................................713-640-3593
Howard W Koch, 5555 Melrose Ave, Los Angeles CA 90038.................818-468-5996
Koch/Marschall Productions, 1718 N Mohawk St, Chicago IL 60614 312-664-6482
Kodiak Films Inc, 11075 Santa Monica Blvd, Los Angeles CA 90025........213-479-8575
KOOL AM-FM Radio CBS, 2196 E Camelback Rd, Phoenix AZ 85016...602-956-9696
Korean Television Prod, 5225 Wilshire Blvd, Los Angeles CA 90036........213-935-1289
Jon Koslowsky Productions, 8489 W 3rd St, Los Angeles CA 90048 213-893-0164
Kostyk Productions, PO Box 25286, Nashville TN 37202 615-329-4419
Kounis Productions, 7906 Santa Monica Blvd, Los Angeles CA 90046 213-656-2072
Kragen Productions, 1112 N Sherbourne Dr, Los Angeles CA 90069 213-854-4400
Jerry Kramer & Assoc, 1312 La Brea Ave, Hollywood CA 90028 213-462-2680
Kristofferson Film Prod, 1607 N El Centro, Hollywood CA 90028...........213-467-5216
Kriton Productions, 7906 Santa Monica Blvd, Los Angeles CA 90046......213-656-5964
Sid & Marty Krofft Prod, 1040 Las Palmas, Hollywood CA 90038..........213-467-3125
KTHV TV Arkansas 11, Box 269, Little Rock AR 72203......................501-376-1111
KTVU Retail Services, 2 Jack London Sq, Oakland CA 94607................415-874-0228
KTXL TV, 4655 Fruitridge Rd, Sacramento CA 95820........................916-454-4422
Kurtz & Friends, 2312 W Olive Ave, Burbank CA 91506 818-841-8188
Daniel Kutt, 921 10th St, Santa Monica CA 90403 213-394-6008
L&M Productions, 2110 Superior Ave, Cleveland OH 44144................216-621-0754
The LA Effects Group, 13034 Saticoy St, North Hollywood CA 91605.......818-982-0217
La Loggia Productions Inc, 2700 Rinconia, Los Angeles CA 90028..........213-462-3055
LA Trax Inc, 8033 Sunset Blvd Ste 1010, Los Angeles CA 90046............213-852-1980
N Lee Lacy & Assoc, 8446 Melrose Pl, Los Angeles CA 90069 213-852-1414
Cheryl Lad Productions, 1800 Century Park E, Los Angeles CA 90067....213-553-6700
Lagacy Productions, Box 477, Willingboro NJ 08046 609-871-3636
Laird Intl Studios, 9336 W Washington Blvd, Culver City CA 90230 213-836-5537
Laissez-Faire Films, 937 N Cole Ste 6, Hollywood CA 90038.................213-938-1567
Lajon Productions Inc, 2907 W Olive Ave, Burbank CA 91505...............818-841-1440
Edie & Ely Landau Inc, 2029 Century Park E, Los Angeles CA 90067......213-553-5010
The Landsburg Co, 11811 W Olympic Blvd, Los Angeles CA 90064 213-208-2111
Don Lane Picture Inc, 35 W 45th St, New York NY 10016....................212-686-1818
Lanoas Productions, 4259 Michael Ave, Los Angeles CA 90066.............213-822-6761
Walter Lantz Productions, 100 Universal Plz, Universal City CA 91608...818-985-4321
Larry Larry Co, Columbia Plaza East Ste 246, Burbank CA 91505 818-954-2526
Las Palmas Productions, 2238 N Las Palmas, Hollywood CA 90038........213-467-5222
Laurel Video Productions, 1999 E Rt 70, Cherry Hill NJ 08003 609-424-3300
Donna Lawrence Productions, Box 4608, Louisville KS 40204..............502-589-9617
Susanne & Bernard Lax, 9105 Carmelita, Beverly Hills CA 90210 213-550-4550
Lazan/Jerod Productions, 17073 Mooncrest St, Encino CA 91316...........818-989-2726
Le Mond/Zetter Prod, 8370 Wilshire Blvd, Beverly Hills CA 90211........213-658-8320
Learning Resources Network, PO Box 3416, Durham NC 27702 919-683-8050
Learning Systems Inc, 1535 Fen Park Dr, Fenton MO 63026.................314-343-1000
Brian Lee & Co, 2025 N Summit, Milwaukee WI 53202......................414-277-7600
Lee Lee Intl Productions, 1717 N Highland, Los Angeles CA 90028 213-466-2177
Alan Lee Productions, 5334 Donna Ave, Tarzana CA 91356.................818-344-9631
Leech Ian & Assoc, 3701 Oak St, Burbank CA 91505.........................818-954-5390
Legend Productions, Box 1034 Hollywood Sta, Los Angeles CA 90078.....213-871-0474

Leibovit Productions Ltd, Box 2019, Beverly Hills CA 90213 213-306-1909
Lemorande Production Co, 207 E Michigan Ave, Milwaukee WI 53202...414-271-3358
Herbert Leonard Entertainment, 5300 Fulton, Van Nuys CA 91401 818-783-0457
J K Lesser Productions, 5319 Hollywood Blvd, Los Angeles CA 90027....213-466-8149
Gene Lester Productions, 4918 Alcove Ave, N Hollywood CA 91607........818-769-6160
Sidney H Levine Prod, 8833 Sunset Blvd, Los Angeles CA 90069 213-652-6654
Wm V Levine Assoc, 31 E 28th St, New York NY 10016.............................212-683-7177
Levinson Entertainment, 650 N Bronson, Los Angeles CA 90004.............213-460-4545
Levy-Gardner-Laven Prod, 9570 Wilshire Blvd, Beverly Hills CA 90212 ..213-278-9820
Libens-Johnson Prod, 6253 Hollywood Blvd, Los Angeles CA 90028........213-463-3606
Mort Libov Productions, 1438 N Gower, Los Angeles CA 90028 213-827-1537
Jack Lieb Productions Inc, 200 E Ontario St, Chicago IL 60611 312-943-1440
Light-House Productions, 427 Linnie Canal, Venice CA 90291.................213-827-1537
Lilac Productions, 4507 Auckland, North Hollywood CA 91602 818-506-5130
Lilyan Productions Inc, 524 Ridge Rd, Watchung NJ 07090......................201-561-5528
Lima Productions, Box 2548, Hollywood CA 90078 213-464-2220
The Lind Organization, 225 E 47th St, New York NY 10017....................212-751-6800
Lindberg Productions Inc, 49 W 46th St, New York NY 10036..................212-719-2060
Linhoff Color Photo, 4400 Frances Ave S, Edina MN 55410....................612-927-7333
Richard Linke Assoc, 417 Colorado Ave, N Hollywood CA 40121..............818-760-2500
Lion's Gate Studios, 1861 S Bundy Dr, Los Angeles CA 90025 213-394-9697
E Trina Lipton, 60 E 8th St Box 310, New York NY 10003.......................212-533-3148
Lirol Productions, 6334 Homewood Ave, Hollywood CA 90028 213-467-8111
Litewaves Inc, 1119 1st Ave Ste 315, Seattle WA 98101 206-623-4004
Little Joey Inc, 11331 Ventura Blvd Ste 300, Studio City CA 91604 818-980-9411
The Little Red Filmhouse, PO Box 691083, Los Angeles CA 90069...........213-855-0241
Little Sister Pictures, 1958 Glencoe Way, Hollywood CA 90068................213-850-0473
Wm Littlejohn Productions, 23435 Malibu Colony, Malibu CA 90265......213-456-8620
Livingston 5, 1516 Formosa Ave, Los Angeles CA 90046 213-851-5051
LMI Productions, Box 532, Malibu CA 90265...213-463-5998
Lodestar Productions, 1336 N Citrus Ave Ste 9, Los Angeles CA 90028 ..213-466-9938
Logos Films, 149 Maple St, Wilmington DE 19808..................................302-994-5459
The Londonderry Co, Box 1305, Woodland Hills CA 19364.......................818-710-0216
Lone Star Pictures Intl Inc, 6430 Sunset Blvd, Hollywood CA 90028........213-463-3175
Long Reign Entertainment, 11508 Wyoming, Los Angeles CA 90025........213-477-8387
Longridge Enterprises, 5150 Wilshire Blvd, Los Angeles CA 90036..........213-938-0109
Lord & Lady Enterprises Inc, 4999 Kahala Ave, Honolulu HI 96816........213-858-2013
Lori Productions, 3347 Laurel Canyon, Studio City CA 91604 213-466-7567
Karl Lorimar Home Video, 17942 Cowan, Irvine CA 92714.......................714-474-0355
Lorimar Productions Inc, 3970 Overland Ave, Culver City CA 90230........213-202-2000
Lorimar Telepictures, 10202 W Washington, Culver City CA 90230 213-558-5000
Abby Lou Entertainment, 3855 Lankershim, Los Angeles CA 91604.........818-506-8199
Louisiana State Univ Medical Center, Box 33932, Shreveport LA 71130..318-674-5260
Louisville Productions, 520 Chestnut St, Louisville KY 40202....................502-582-7744
Lumeni Productions, 1727 N Ivar Ave, Hollywood CA 90028...................213-462-2110
A C Lyles Productions, 5555 Melrose Ave, Los Angeles CA 90038 213-468-5819
Lynch/Biller Productions, 6430 Sunset Blvd, Hollywood CA 90028 213-469-7166
Fed Lyon Pictures, 237 Clara St, San Francisco CA 94107 415-974-5645
Lyons Inc, 715 Orange St, Wilmington DE 19801 302-654-6146
M&M's Entertainment, 6600 Santa Monica Blvd, Hollywood CA 90038...213-469-6600
M2 Ltd, 5 Bethany Ct, Gaithersburg MD 20879......................................301-977-4281
Mac of Knap Productions, 6305 Yucca St, Hollywood CA 90028...............213-461-1955
Mace Neufeld Prod, 10202 W Washington, Culver City CA 90230 213-858-2929

MacGillivray Freeman Films, Box 205, South Laguna CA 92677................714-494-1055
Malcolm Mackenzie & Assoc, Box 25123, Wilmington DE 19899..............302-764-6755
Lee Madden Assoc, 16918 Marquez Ave, Pacific Palisade CA 90272.........213-459-5198
Madison Pacific Inc, Box 5597, Sherman Oaks CA 91430 818-990-6196
Madonna College Media Services, 36600 Schoolcraft, Livonia MI 48150..313-591-5118
Douglas Mador Prod, 804 N Sierra Bonita, Los Angeles CA 90046...........213-651-1278
Magic Lantern Prod, 100 Universal Plz, Universal City CA 91608.............818-508-4165
Lee Magid Productions Inc, Box 532, Malibu CA 90265 213-463-5998
Mercedes Maharis Prod, 8841 Exposition Blvd, Culver City CA 90232.....213-202-1555
Mai Tai Productions, Box 8460, Universal City CA 91608 213-874-3565
Major Media Inc, 3326 Commercial Ave, Northbrook IL 60062 312-498-4610
Malco Electronics, S Wolcott Ave, Lawrence MA 01843.............................617-685-4383
Leo Malcom Productions, 6536 Sunset Blvd, Hollywood CA 90028...........213-464-4448
Adrian Malone Prod, 3574 Cahuenga Blvd W, Los Angeles CA 90068.....213-850-1414
Malpaso Productions, 4000 Warner Blvd, Burbank CA 91522 818-954-1228
Management Three, 9744 Wilshire Blvd, Beverly Hills CA 90212.............213-550-7100
Manhattan Video Prod, 12 W 27th St, New York NY 10001.......................212-683-6565
Manion Outdoors Publishing Co, PO Box 188, Delafield WI 53018..........414-646-4196
Mann & Goldstein Co, 7046 Hollywood Blvd, Los Angeles CA 90028......213-462-7528
Ted Mann Productions, 9200 Sunset Blvd, Los Angeles CA 90069............213-273-3336
Thomas J Manning, 691 S Irolo St, Los Angeles CA 90005 213-384-5269
Martin Manulis Productions Inc, Box 818, Beverly Hills CA 90212..........213-476-2709
Carl R Mappes, Box 759, Kimberling City MO 65686................................417-739-4982
Maraday Productions, 9744 Wilshire Blvd, Beverly Hills CA 90212.........213-859-7202
Marcelo Montealegre Inc, 512 Broadway, New York NY 10012.................212-226-2796
Marchack Productions, 1041 N Manfield Ave, Hollywood CA 90038 213-461-3200
Mariah Productions, 545 8th Ave 3rd fl, New York NY 10018..................212-947-0090
Maritz Communications Co, 4925 Cadieux Rd, Detroit MI 48224............313-259-7660
Maritz Communications Co, 1100 High Ridge Rd, Stamford CT 06905...203-329-2363
Marjon Productions, 3518 Cahuenga Blvd W, Los Angeles CA 90068......213-851-7715
Market St Prod, 73 Market St, Venice CA 90291 213-396-5937
Marketing Support Films, Box 278, St Joseph MO 64506..........................816-279-5869
Markowitz Chesler Producing, 6565 Sunset Blvd, Hollywood CA 90028 ..213-659-9703
Paul D Marks Productions, PO Box 67831, Los Angeles CA 90067..........213-553-0076
Mars Production Corp, 10635 Riverside Dr, N Hollywood CA 90067.......818-980-8011
MARSAC, 9228 Camino Lago Vista, Spring Valley CA 92077 714-267-3961
Marsden Productions, 30 E 33rd St, New York NY 10016...........................212-725-9220
Peter Marshall Enterprises, 9931 Melvin Ave, Northridge CA 91324......818-90707776
Marshfilm Enterprises, PO Box 8082, Shawnee Mission KS 66208...........816-523-1059
Martel Media Productions, 9255 Sunset Blvd, Los Angeles CA 90069......213-274-7170
R J Martin Co, 315 Rt 17, Paramus NJ 07652 201-592-0952
Quinn Martin Films, 1041 N Formosa Ave, Los Angeles CA 90046.........213-850-2653
Pete Martin Productions, 3740 Evans St, Los Angeles CA 90027 213-664-7765
Martin Video Productions, 188 Mount Joy Ave, Freeport NY 11520........516-223-4054
Martin-Garrison Productions, 4040 Vineland, Studio City CA 91604.......818-509-0881
Martin/Arnold Color Systems Inc, 150 5th Ave, New York NY 10011.....212-675-7270
Maryland Public TV, 11767 Bonita, Owings Mills MD 21117 301-337-4052
Ed Marzola & Assoc, 11846 Ventura Blvd, Studio City CA 91604..............818-506-7788
Masai Films, 6922 Hollywood Blvd Ste 401, Hollywood CA 90028...........213-466-5451
Gene Massey Films, 550 S Barrington, Los Angeles CA 90049...................213-476-3668
Master Digital, 1749 14th St, Santa Monica CA 90404................................213-452-1511
Jim Mathers Video/Film, 4739 Lankershim, N Hollywood CA 91602.......818-762-2214
Matrixx Productions, 11434 Ventura Blvd, North Hollywood CA 90602 ..818-760-0357

Mattingly Productions, 10100 Main St, Fairfax VA 22031...........................703-385-6625
Maverick Pictures Intl, 9033 Ventura Blvd, Studio City CA 91604 213-271-3622
Max Films, 2525 Hyperion Ave, Los Angeles CA 90027................................213-662-3285
Maxima II, 436 11 Ave, San Diego CA 92101 619-232-8963
The Mayer Co, 182 S Detroit St, Los Angeles CA 90036................................213-936-6783
Stephen Maynard Media Svcs, 50 Foxwood Ct, Bedminster NJ 07921......201-234-1009
Maynor Enterprises, Box 1641, Beverly Hills CA 90213................................213-277-5881
MB Productions Inc, 451 W 54th St, New York NY 10019..............................212-586-8854
MCA TV Intl, 100 Universal City Plaza, Universal City CA 91608..............818-508-4275
MCA-TV Universal Studios, 100 Universal Plz, Univ City CA 91608.......818-985-4321
Gene McCabe Productions, Box 4156, Burbank CA 91503............................818-841-2030
McCall/Coppola At Filmfair, 10900 Ventura, Studio City CA 91604.......818-766-8770
McCanse/Newby Prod, 6356 Fountain Ave, Los Angeles CA 90028..........213-464-7677
Teri McCarthy, 16250 Ventura Blvd Ste 335, Encino CA 91436.................818-986-3860
B F McClain Productions Inc, Box 5813, Asheville NC 28803.....................704-274-1431
John E McDonald Prod, 1548 Oak Grove Dr, Los Angeles CA 90041......213-256-0299
Tom McGowan Productions, 7023 Fernhill Dr, Malibu CA 90265..............213-552-1928
Cameron McKay Productions, 1101 N Cole, Los Angeles CA 90038........213-463-6073
McKown & Co, PO Box 25134, Los Angeles CA 90025.................................213-479-1941
Rod McKuen Enterprises, Box G, Beverly Hills CA 90038 213-657-7311
MDC Teleproductions, 15282 Newsboy Cir, Huntington Bch CA 92647...714-896-2495
Kenneth R Meades, PO Box 71098, Los Angeles CA 90071 213-666-9570
Meadowlane Enterprises, 15201 Burbank Blvd, Van Nuys CA 91441........213-873-2717
Mecs Laszlo Films, 1140 N Beachwood Dr, Los Angeles CA 90038.........213-465-8290
Medallion TV Entertainment, 8831 Sunset Blvd, Los Angeles CA 90069..213-652-8100
Media Concepts Inc, 331 N Broad St, Philadelphia PA 17403.....................717-848-4850
The Media Dept, 3030 N Park, Lombard IL 60148..312-377-0005
Media Design Group Inc, 1133 Morse Blvd, Winter Park FL 32789..........305-628-1755
Media Dimensions, 1850 York Rd, Timonium MD 21093............................301-561-4550
Media Forum Intl, RFD 1 Box 107, West Danville VT 05873......................802-592-3444
Media Four Productions, 6519 Fountain Ave, Los Angeles CA 90028......213-466-2266
Media Learning Systems, 120 W Colorado Blvd, Pasadena CA 91105......818-499-0006
Media Network Systems, PO Box 40296, San Francisco CA 94110 415-821-7800
Media Resources, 201 Lyons Ave, Newark NJ 07112...................................201-926-7305
Media West, 10244 SW Arctic Dr, Beaverton OR 97005.............................503-626-7002
The Media Works Inc, 300 W Washington, Chicago IL 60606.....................312-332-4441
Mediacom Development, Box 1926, Simi Valley CA 93062...........................818-991-5452
Mediterraneo Productions, 1712 N Vermont, Los Angeles CA 90027.......213-663-7654
Meeting Media Enterprises Ltd, 3330 Dundee Rd, Northbook IL 60002..312-564-8160
Mega Productions Inc, 1714 N Wilton Pl, Hollywood CA 90028................213-462-6342
Melear Multi Media, 1344 Johnson Ferry Rd, Marietta GA 30067...........404-971-5665
Bill Melendez Productions, 439 N Larchmont, Los Angeles CA 90004.....213-463-4101
Mellodan Productions Inc, 3115 W Olive Ave, Burbank CA 91505...........818-843-3741
Daniel Melnick, 838 N Doheny Dr Ste 406, Los Angeles CA 90069..........213-859-1571
Memphis Communications Corp, PO Box 41735, Memphis TN 38174.....901-725-9271
Menter Worldwide, 1911 Lakeshore Dr, St Joseph MI 49085.....................616-983-7476
Mentor Productions, 9533 Brighton Way, Beverly Hills CA 90210 213-278-2210
Mercedes Entertainment, 1301 Summit Ridge, Beverly Hills CA 90210 ...213-859-8454
Mercury Entertainment, 1901 Ave of Stars, Los Angeles CA 90067..........213-556-7408
Arthur Meriwether Inc, 1529 Brook Dr, Downers Grove IL 60090............312-495-0600
Meta-4 Productions, 8300 Santa Monica Blvd, Los Angeles CA 90069 213-654-6686
Metavision, 347 S Ogden Dr Ste 220, Los Angeles CA 90036.....................213-936-8281
Metcalfe Film & Videotape, 3709 Locksley, Birmingham AL 35223...........205-967-1661

Metro Video Productions Inc, 1075 Rankin St, Troy MI 48083 313-588-7600
Metromedia Producers Corp, 5746 Sunset Blvd, Los Angeles CA 90028..213-462-7111
Ron Meyers & Assoc, 1438 Gower St, Los Angeles CA 90028 213-462-7429
MFI Video, 1905 Grace Ave, Hollywood CA 90068 213-874-8527
MGM Studios, 10000 W Washington, Culver City CA 90232....................213-280-6000
MGM Entertainment Co, 10202 W Washington, Culver City CA 90232 ...213-558-5000
Miami Audio Visual Co, 555 NW 95th St, Miami FL 33150 305-757-5000
Michael/Daniel Prod, 7025 Santa Monica Blvd, Los Angeles CA 90038...213-464-7307
Michaeljay Inc, 2849 Executive Dr Ste 200, Clearwater FL 34622..............813-577-2993
Michigan Media, 400 4th St, Ann Arbor MI 48103 313-764-8298
Mid-America Audio Visual Inc, PO Box 11428, Columbus OH 43211.......614-268-3300
Midland Video Productions, 11820 W Ripley, Wauwatosa WI 53226........414-778-1990
Midwest Visuals Inc, Box 38, Brimson MN 55602 612-698-0962
Mikas Films Inc, 6000 Canterbury Dr Ste D308, Culver City CA 90230 ...213-641-5461
Ted V Mikels Productions, 3000 Sparr Blvd, Glendale CA 91208 818-240-2425
Milas-Hinshaw Prod, 13759 Ventura Blvd, Sherman Oals CA 91423........213-466-5588
Mileham Entertainment Inc, Box 1865, Hollywood CA 90028..................213-464-7116
Deke Miles & Assoc Prod, 6123 Glen Oak, Los Angeles CA 90068 213-466-2825
Miles & Co, 1418 Dodson Ave, San Pedro CA 90732..............................213-548-0462
The Miles Co, 2062 N Vine St #5, Hollywood CA 90068..........................213-463-3224
Reid Miles Inc, 1136 N Las Palmas, Los Angeles CA 90038 213-462-6106
Edward K Milkis Prod, 5451 Marathon St, Los Angeles CA 90038............213-468-5000
Robin Miller Filmaker, 606 W Broad St, Bethlehem PA 18018..................215-691-0900
Warren Miller Productions, 505 Pier Ave, Hermosa Beach CA 90254 213-376-2494
Milner Fenwick Inc, 2125 Greenspring Dr, Timmonium MD 21093............301-252-1700
Miracle Productions, Box 4621, Westlake Village CA 90038 818-889-9714
Miracle Films Inc, 6311 Romaine St, Los Angeles CA 90038 213-468-8867
Mirage Enterprises, 100 Universal Plz, Universal City CA 91608 818-777-1000
Mirisch Co, 100 Universal Plz, Universal City CA 91608..........................818-777-1271
Mirkin & Assoc, 13416 Magnolia Blvd, Sherman Oaks CA 91423............818-784-4177
MITA, 4115 Charlene Dr, Los Angeles CA 90043....................................213-291-6063
Mitam Productions, 1607 N El Centro Ste 3, Los Angeles CA 90028........213-462-1251
Mobile Video One, 111 S 108 Ave, Omaha NE 68154..............................402-330-0110
Mobile Visual Prod, 5251 Lampson Ave, Garden Grove CA 92645 714-894-3133
Moctesuma Esparza Prod, 1036 Lemoyne Ave, Los Angeles CA 90026 ...212-660-5292
Modupe Prince All-African Prod, 1103 Hobart, Los Angeles CA 90006 ...213-733-7216
Moffit/Lee Productions, 1438 N Gower St, Los Angeles CA 90028............213-467-1000
Mojo Productions, 650 N Bronson Ave Bldg 100, Hollywood CA 90004...213-465-6776
Monad Trainer's Aid, 163060 22nd Ave, Whitestone NY 11357................718-352-3227
Mondello Assoc Inc, 320 E 38th St, New York NY 10016..........................212-661-5020
Montana State Univ TV Center, Bozeman MT 59717................................406-994-3437
Monument Pictures, 5555 Melrose, Los Angeles CA 90038......................213-468-5692
Moody Inst of Science, 12000 W Washington Blvd, Whittier CA 90606 213-698-8256
Moonbase Productions, 2025 Stanley Hills Blvd, Los Angeles CA 90046..213-654-7471
Gary Moore & Assoc, 1125 E Orange Ave, Los Angeles CA 91016 818-359-9414
Morse Entertainment Group, 205 S Beverly, Beverly Hills CA 90212.......213-276-9021
Jack Morton Productions Inc, 830 3rd Ave, New York NY 10022............212-758-8400
Dann Moss Assoc, 9220 Sunset Blvd Ste 306, Los Angeles CA 90069........213-278-8090
Moss Communications Inc, 1521 Green Oaks Pl, Kingwood TX 77339....713-358-7700
Mother Dubbers Inc, 13626 Gamma, Dallas TX 75234............................214-980-4840
Motion Control Systems, 658 N Larchmont, Los Angeles CA 90004........213-465-3104
Motion Picture Marine, 616 Venice Blvd, Marina Del Ray CA 90291 213-822-1100
Motion Picture Photography, PO Box 1859, Los Angeles CA 90078.........213-462-4266

Motion Picture Production Svc, 932 N La Brea, Los Angeles CA 90038 ..213-874-9516
Motion Picture Recording, 7060 Hollywood, Los Angeles CA 90028 213-462-6897
Motivation Media Inc, 1245 Milwaukee Ave, Glenview IL 60025................312-297-4740
Motivational Media, 6855 Santa Monica Blvd, Los Angeles CA 90038 213-465-3168
Motown Productions, 6255 Sunset Blvd 18th fl, Los Angeles CA 90028....213-461-9954
Mount Company, Columbia Plaza, Burbank CA 91505 818-954-1905
Moustache Productions, 3501 Terrace View Dr, Encino CA 91436...........818-501-0299
The Movie Machine, 838 N Doheny Dr, Los Angeles CA 90069 213-273-3838
The Movie Store, 11111 Santa Monica Blvd, Los Angeles CA 90025 213-478-4230
Movie Tech Studios, 832 N Seward St, Hollywood CA 90038 213-467-8491
Moving Images, 1117 N 19th St Rm 750, Rosslyn VA 22209 703-524-2600
Moving Targets Inc, 2111 Woodland Way, Hollywood CA 90068 213-867-9693
Mr. Wizard Studios, Box 83, Canoga Park CA 91305 818-703-1227
MTM, 4024 Radford Ave, Studio City CA 91604..818-760-4000
MTV & Nickelodeon Networks, 1775 Broadway, New York NY 10019 212-713-6409
Mugwump Productions, 4000 Warner Blvd, Burbank CA 91522 818-954-3767
Multi Media Works, 7227 Beverly Blvd, Los Angeles CA 90036 213-939-1185
Multivision Intl, 340 W Huron St, Chicago IL 60610 312-337-2010
Mulvehill Productions, 1994 Lucille Ave, Los Angeles CA 90039.............213-664-4049
Kathleen Mulvihill, 830 Louisiana Ave, New Orleans LA 70115................504-891-3496
Burt Munk & Co, 666 Dundee Rd Ste 503, Northbrook IL 60042...............312-564-0855
Jack Murphy Assoc, 12746 Tiarra St, North Hollywood CA 91607............213-776-4330
Myriad Productions, 1314 N Hayworth Ave, Los Angeles CA 90046 213-851-1400
Naomi Productions Inc, 1438 N Gower St, Hollywood CA 90028 213-465-2027
Gary Nardino Prod, 5555 Melrose, Los Angeles CA 90038.........................213-826-0978
Natl Education TV, 2715 Packard Rd, Ann Arbor MI 48104........................313-971-3600
Natl Educational Media, 21601 Devonshire St, Chatsworth CA 91311......818-709-6009
Natl General Pictures, 9601 Wilshire Blvd, Beverly Hills CA 90201...........213-273-1228
Natl Photographic Laboratories, 1926 W Gray St, Houston TX 77019.....713-527-9300
Natl Telefilm Assoc Inc, PO Box 66903, Los Angeles CA 90066 213-306-4040
Natl Television News, 23480 Park Sorrento, Calabasas CA 91303.............818-883-6121
Natl Video Industries Inc, 15 W 17th St, New York NY 10011.....................212-691-1300
Neila Incorporated, 1410 N Curson Ave, Los Angeles CA 90046................213-876-7826
The Nelson Co, 5400 Shirley Ave, Tarzana CA 91356...................................213-873-2431
Paul Nemiroff Productions Inc, 227 E 59th St, New York NY 10022........212-832-7600
New & Unique Videos, 2336 Sumac Dr, San Diego CA 92105.....................619-282-6126
New Breed Productions Inc, PO Box 15367, Long Beach CA 90815 213-431-8221
New Empire Films, 650 N Bronson Ave, Los Angeles CA 90004.................213-461-8535
New England Slide Service Ltd, Box 231, Rutland VT 05701.....................802-773-2581
New Horizons Picture Corp, 11600 San Vicente, Los Angeles CA 90049..213-820-6733
New Media Group Ltd, 11846 Ventura Blvd, Studio City CA 91604 818-506-7227
New Orient Media Inc, Box 333, West Dundee IL 60118.............................312-428-6000
New Orleans Video Access Ctr, 2010 Magazine, New Orleans LA 70130..504-524-8626
New Regency Films, 10202 W Washington, Culver City CA 90232 213-558-5065
New Seed Press, PO Box 9488, Berkeley CA 94709 415-540-7576
New World Pictures, 1440 S Sepulveda, Los Angeles CA 90025 213-444-8100
New Zoo Revue Co, 9401 Wilshire Blvd Ste 620, Beverly Hills CA 90212..213-278-5325
Newland-Raynor Prod, 8480 W Beverly Blvd, Los Angeles CA 90048.......213-655-2222
Nexus Productions, 4049 C Radford Ave, Studio City CA 91604................818-760-4651
Fred A Niles Comm Ctr, 1028 W Washington Blvd, Chicago IL 60607 312-738-4181
Wendell Niles Productions, 4555 Ledge Ave, N Hollywood CA 91602......818-985-2252
Noble Productions Inc, 1615 S Crest Dr, Los Angeles CA 90035 213-552-2934
L Randall Nogg Prod, 1301 N Havenhurst, Los Angeles CA 90046 213-650-2303

Nor-X Productions, 739 N Croft Ave Ste 301, Los Angeles CA 90068......213-655-4852
The Norkat Co Ltd, 148 S Beverly Dr Ste 200, Beverly Hills CA 90212.....213-276-6741
Northeast Video Inc, 420 Lexington Ave, New York NY 10017....................212-611-8830
Harry Novak Productions, 4774 Melrose Ave, Los Angeles CA 90029 213-665-5257
Novcom Inc, 1545 N Wilcox Ave Ste 201, Hollywood CA 90028 213-461-3688
November Productions, 204 S Clark Dr, Beverly Hills CA 90211.................213-652-1996
NRW Company, 5746 Sunset Blvd, Hollywood CA 90028...........................213-856-1746
NSR Productions Inc, 366 N Broadway, Jericho NY 11753.........................516-433-1135
Nu Videa Inc, 9155 Sunset Blvd Ste 7, Los Angeles CA 90069 213-659-4037
NYCOM, 101 Bryn Mawr Ste 300, Bryn Mawr PA 19010...........................215-527-5100
Nystrom, 333 N Elston, Chicago IL 60618...312-463-1144
Danny O'Donovan Ent, 9000 Sunset Blvd, Los Angeles CA 90069 213-276-4181
O'Neil & Jeffries, 3855 Lankershim Blvd, North Hollywood CA 91604 818-760-6666
Oak Woods Media Inc, PO Box 527, Oshtemo MI 49077 616-375-5621
October Productions, 6644 Santa Monica, Hollywood CA 90038 213-469-9377
Off Broadway Video Prod, 8319 Halls Ferry Rd, St Louis MO 63147.......314-389-9711
Ohlmeyer Communications, 150 E Camino Dr, Beverly Hills CA 90212..213-276-9699
Oklahoma State University, Audiovisual Center, Stillwater OK 74078......405-624-7216
David Oliver Productions, 8805 Skyline Dr, Los Angeles CA 90046...........213-654-9335
Omega Entertainment, 8780 Shoreham Dr, Los Angeles CA 90069 213-855-0516
Omega Star Inc, PO Box 87413, Houston TX 77287 713-998-9226
OMNI Communications, 101 E Carmel, Carmel IN 46032 317-844-6664
Omnicom Productions Inc, 4700 Ardmore, Okemos MI 48864 517-349-6303
Omstar Productions, 1714 N Ivar Ave N Wing, Hollywood CA 90028.......213-464-6699
One Inch Video Productions, 4710 W Magnolia, Burbank CA 91505........818-760-6900
One Pass Productions, 1 China Basin Bldg, San Francisco CA 94106.......415-777-5777
One Way Productions, 2048 Century Park E, Los Angeles CA 90067 213-553-6918
Optasonics Productions, 186 8th St, Cresskill NJ 07626 201-871-4192
Oriol Productions, 175 N Sycamore, Los Angeles CA 90036 213-933-1812
Orion Pictures Corp, 1875 Century Park East, Los Angeles CA 90067.....213-557-8700
Other Factors/Insight Media, PO Box 42810, Los Angeles CA 90042.......213-258-2300
Glenn Otto Productions, 937 N Cole Ave Ste 2, Los Angeles CA 90038...213-461-0222
Our Sunday Visitor, 200 Noll Plz, Huntington IN 46750.............................219-356-8400
Owen Electric Pictures, 355 E 86th St, New York NY 10028 212-410-0882
Owen Murphy Productions, 49 Richmondville Ave, Westport CT 06880..203-226-4241
P&P Studios Inc, Box 4185, Stamford CT 06907..203-359-9292
PDK Pictures Inc, 3712 Barnham Blvd, Los Angeles CA 90068 213-851-0572
Pace Films, 411 E 53rd Ave, New York NY 10022.....................................212-755-5486
Pacific Arts, 50 N La Cienega, Beverly Hills CA 90211..............................213-657-2233
Pacific Coast Productions, 629 Terminal Way, Costa Mesa CA 92627 714-645-1640
Pacific Films, 2530 N Ontario St, Burbank CA 91504 818-848-5579
Pacific Productions, Box 2881, Honolulu HI 96802....................................808-531-1560
Pacific Standard Television, 1126 SW 13, Portland OR 97205...................503-222-1471
Del Paeske Productions Inc, 5820 W St Paul Ave, Milwaukee WI 53213..414-778-1070
Paisley Productions Inc, 6063 Sunset Blvd, Los Angeles CA 90028...........213-461-2871
Pakula Co, 10889 Wilshire Blvd, Los Angeles, CA 90024 213-208-3046
Palance-Levy Productions Inc, 1438 N Gower, Hollywood CA 90028.......213-467-7226
Palardo Productions, 1807 Taft Ave Ste 4, Hollywood CA 90028.............213-469-8991
Palms Productions, 5862 Tujunga Ave, North Hollywood CA 91601 818-509-0371
Pan Arts Prod, 4000 Warner Blvd, Burbank CA 91522..............................818-954-3631
Pan American Pictures, 9033 Wilshire Blvd, Beverly Hills CA 90211........213-271-2191
Pantechnicon Productions, 2011 Pontius Ave, Los Angeles CA 90025......213-473-0914
Pantomime Pictures, 12144 Riverside Dr, N Hollywood CA 91607 818-980-5555

David Paradine Television, 9000 Sunset Blvd, Los Angeles CA 90069 213-275-5644
Paragon Productions, 817 Pearl St, Denver CO 80203.................................303-832-7687
Parallax Studio Ltd, 5 Fox Hill, Stony Brook NY 11790.............................516-751-1105
Paramount Pictures Corp, 5555 Melrose Ave, Los Angeles CA 90038 213-468-5000
Paramount Video, 5555 Melrose Ave, Los Angeles CA 90038 213-468-5519
Tom Parker Motion Pictures, 18653 Ventura Blvd, Tarzana CA 91356....818-342-9115
Parkinson-Friendly Prod, 9200 Sunset Blvd, Los Angeles CA 90069.........213-274-7800
Parriott Productions Inc, 5159 Anestoy, Encino CA 91316...........................818-986-5240
Pasetta Productions, 8322 Beverly Blvd Ste 205, Los Angeles CA 90048..213-655-8500
Paisano Productions, 9911 W Pico Blvd, Los Angeles Lo 90035 213-277-9482
Jim Passin Productions, 756 Waveland, Chicago IL 60613 312-248-9534
Pathological Comm Group, 9100 Wilshire, Beverly Hills CA 90212 213-273-4581
Patterson & Hall, 425 Tamal Plaza, Corte Madera CA 94925 415-924-1055
Paul Entertainment, 8776 Sunset Blvd, Los Angeles CA 90069 213-652-9320
Paulist Productions, 17575 Pac Coast Hwy, Pacific Palisades CA 90272...213-454-0688
Paulist Communications, 2257 Barry Ave, Los Angeles CA 90064.............213-477-2559
PCA Teleproductions, 801 Crestdale Ave, Matthews NC 28105 704-847-8011
Peak Productions Inc, Box 329, Winter Park CO 80482 303-726-5881
Peanut Butter & Jelly Prod, 7631 Lexington, Los Angeles CA 90046........213-851-9175
Peckham Productions Inc, 65 S Broadway, Tarrytown NY 10591 914-631-5050
Pegasus, 14306 Hortense St, Sherman Oaks CA 91423 818-906-8829
Penguin Productions, 1725 SW 17th St, Ocala FL 32674 813-577-2993
Pendragon Films Ltd, 9336 Washington Blvd, Culver City CA 91202........213-599-0346
Penfield Productions Ltd, 35 Springfield St, Agawam MA 01001...............413-786-4454
Penland Productions Inc, 1333 Virginia Ave, Glendale CA 91202.............818-241-7564
Peregrine Entertainment, 9229 Sunset Blvd, Los Angeles CA 90069 213-859-8350
Performance Designs Inc, 16 Allen Dr, Woodcliff Lake NJ 07675.............201-391-8588
Personal Communication, 48-05 Browvale Ave, Flushing NY 11362.........718-229-3254
Phase III, 3222 La Cienega Blvd Ste 106, Culver City CA 90230 213-670-0005
Phelan/Schreiner Productions, 1540 Race St, Denver CO 80206...............303-399-4580
Phipps & Co Productions, 5807-E S Garnett Rd, Tulsa OK 74146............918-250-7371
Phoenix Entertainment, 310 N San Vicente, Los Angeles CA 90048..........213-657-7502
Phoenix Videofilms, 2949 W Indian School, Phoenix AZ 85017..................602-266-4198
Photo Art Inc, 1105 Jefferson St, Wilmington DE 19801 302-658-7301
Photo Communications Services, 6410 Knapp NE, Ada MI 49301.............616-676-1499
Photocom Productions, 147 N 13th St, Grover City CA 93433....................805-481-6550
PIC-TV Inc, 10933 Camarillo St, North Hollywood CA 91602 818-985-1100
Mary Pickford Co, Box 10059, Beverly Hills CA 90213...............................213-272-9035
Pierre Enterprises Inc, 1164 S La Brea Ave, Hollywood CA 90019.............213-937-6764
Pike Productions Inc, 97 Lake Ave PO Box 309, Newton MA 02159.........617-332-5560
Ping Pong Productions, 7471 Melrose Ave, Los Angeles CA 90046 213-653-7028
Pix Productions Inc, 3843 S Main St, Santa Ana CA 92707.........................714-957-1749
Playboy Productions, 8560 Sunset Blvd Ste 501, Los Angeles CA 90069...213-659-4080
Playhouse Pictures, 1401 N La Brea Ave, Los Angeles CA 90028................213-851-2112
PM Media/Image Comm, 320 W 30th St, New York NY 10001.................212-695-1656
Po'Boy Productions, 5907 W Pico Blvd, West Los Angeles CA 90035.........213-855-1285
Point of View Productions, 2477 Folsom St, San Francisco CA 94110.......415-821-0435
Hal Polaire Assoc, 12301 Wilshire Blvd, Los Angeles CA 90025 213-820-8872
Police Science Prod, 4789 Vineland Ave, N Hollywood CA 91602...............213-820-8872
The Polished Apple, 3742 Seahorn Dr, Malibu CA 90265.............................213-459-2630
Sydney Pollack Productions, 4000 Warner Blvd, Burbank CA 91522........818-954-6000
Polycom Teleproductions, 142 E Ontario St 4th fl, Chicago IL 60611........312-337-6000
Polygram Pictures, 3940 Overland Ave, Culver City CA 90230 213-202-4400

Harry M Poplin Enterprises, 346 N Larchmont, Los Angeles CA 90004..213-462-5610
Positive Feedback Comm, 3744 Applegate Ave, Cincinnati OH 45211......513-661-1690
Positive Media, 5422A Fair Ave, N Hollywood CA 91601 818-761-5192
Ken Post Communication Services, 33 W 87th St, New York NY 10024 ..212-580-1931
Power Video Prod, 2828 Woodland Ridge, Baton Rouge LA 70816...........504-293-0225
Praxix Film Works, 6918 Tujunga Blvd, North Hollywood CA 91605........818-508-0402
Preface Publications Inc, 811 Grass Ct, Chico CA 95926 916-893-9023
Premier Video & Film, 3033 Locust, St Louis MO 63103.............................314-531-3555
Premore Inc, 5130 Klump Ave, N Hollywood CA 91601 818-506-7714
Presentation Inc, 1422 N 44th St, Phoenix AZ 85008 602-275-0303
Edward R Pressman Prod, 4000 Warner Blvd, Burbank CA 91522 818-954-6000
Price Filmakers, 3393 Barham Blvd, Los Angeles CA 90068 213-851-4555
John M Price Films Inc, Box 81, Radnor PA 19087 215-687-6699
PrimaLux Video Inc, 30 W 26th St, New York NY 10010..............................212-206-1402
Prism Entertainment, 1888 Century Park E, Los Angeles CA 90067.........213-277-3270
Prism Productions Inc, Box 83, Canoga Park CA 91305 818-703-1227
Pro Video, 801 N La Brea Ave Ste 104, Hollywood CA 90038....................213-934-8840
Pro Video, 3348 Louise Ave, Salt Lake City UT 84109 801-467-3740
Process Communications, PO Box 1068, Bridgehampton NY 11932........516-725-2646
ProComm, 1868 Lincoln Ctr 5420 LBJ Fwy, Dallas TX 75240 214-233-7296
Producers Assoc, 7243 Santa Monica, Hollywood CA 90046......................213-851-4123
Producers East Media, 535 Broadhollow Rd Rt 110, Melville NY 11747..516-420-5680
Producers Group Ltd, 405 N Wabash Ave, Chicago IL 60611 312-467-1830
The Producers Inc, 1095 E Indian School Rd, Phoenix AZ 85014..............602-297-7767
Producers Pictures Corp, Box 3473, Van Nuys CA 91407 818-891-9546
Producers Sales Org, 10100 Santa Monica, Los Angeles CA 90067..........213-552-9977
Production 8, 1800 N Highland Ste 410, Los Angeles CA 90028................213-469-5165
Production Consultants, 11 Sherman St Box 151, Fairfield CT 06430.......203-259-3696
Production Services Unltd, 10000 Riverside Dr, Toluca Lake CA 91602..818-761-6699
Production West, 6223 Selma Ave, Los Angeles CA 90028 213-464-0169
Professional Artists Group, 845 N Highland, Los Angeles CA 90038 213-871-2222
Program House, 67 The Crossway, Butler NJ 07405....................................201-492-0864
Project Films, 9744 Wilshire Blvd Ste 207, Beverly Hills CA 90212 213-274-8708
Promedia, 459 Pine Hill Rd, Leonia NJ 07605...201-592-1829
Promedia AV Productions, 237 Cleveland Ave, Columbus OH 43215.......614-221-0700
Promotional Films & Video, 1313 Cambridge St, Hopkins MN 55343 612-935-2183
PSO Delphi, 10100 Santa Monica Blvd Ste 150, Los Angeles CA 90067....213-522-9977
Pulsar Video, 5205 S 113 Plaza, Omaha NE 68501.....................................402-472-3611
John Purdy Inc, 2307 Castilian Dr, Hollywood CA 90212 213-877-9802
Pure Gold Productions, 4774 Melrose Ave, Los Angeles CA 90029 213-665-5257
Bob Quinn Q Productions, 4731 Vineland Ave, N Hollywood CA 91602..818-761-0211
QED Enterprises, 4802 5th Ave, Pittsburg PA 15213 412-622-1322
QM Productions, 1041 N Formosa Ave, Los Angeles CA 90046..................213-850-2653
Quality Five Productions, 13134 Hartsook, Sherman Oaks CA 91423.......818-981-7083
The Quantum Leap Corp, 9601 Wilshire Blvd, Beverly Hills CA 90210....213-859-8300
Quartet Films Inc, 12345 Ventura Blvd Ste M, Studio City CA 91614......818-509-0100
R&B EFX and Animation Inc, 1802 Victory Blvd, Glendale CA 91201.....818-956-8406
RL Labs Inc, 916 N Charles St, Baltimore MD 21201 301-727-8800
R/Greenberg Assoc Inc, 350 W 39th St, New York NY 10018......................212-239-6767
Radiance Films Intl, 9200 Sunset Bvd Ste 530, Los Angeles CA 90069 213-652-2260
Radiovision, 8833 Sunset Blvd Ste 408, Los Angeles CA 90069 213-659-2780
Radler Productions, 6041 Morella Ave, North Hollywood CA 91606........818-506-7998
Carl Ragsdale Assoc Inc, 4725 Stillbrooke, Houston TX 77035..................713-729-6530

Rainbow TV Works, 1420 N Beachwood Dr, Los Angeles CA 90028.........213-469-1611
Raintree Productions, 666 N Robertson Blvd, Los Angeles CA 90069......213-652-8330
Randken Corp, 1041 N Mansfield Ave, Hollywood CA 90038 213-464-1682
Random Productions, 5437 Laurel Canyon, N Hollywood CA 91607 818-760-7333
Martin Ransohoff Productions, Columbia Plz W, Burbank CA 91505......818-954-3491
Rapid Eye Movement Prod, 1478 S Cardiff, Los Angeles CA 90035 213-557-1491
Bill Rase Productions Inc, 955 Venture Ct, Sacramento CA 95825 916-929-9181
Rastar Productions Inc, Columbia Plaza West, Burbank CA 91505..........818-954-6000
Elia Ravasz Productions, Box 1859, Hollywood CA 90078........................213-462-4266
RCA/Columbia Home Video, 2901 W Alameda, Burbank CA 91505 818-954-4950
RDB Productions, 118 N Mulberry, Muncie IN 47305 317-284-3311
Brooks Read & Assoc Inc, 236 Napoleon St, Baton Rouge LA 70802 504-343-1715
The Reading Laboratory Inc, Box 28, Georgetown CT 06829.....................203-834-2478
Reality Productions, 9978 Holder St, Buena Park CA 90620 714-828-2199
Rearguard Productions, 6030 Wilshire Blvd, Los Angeles CA 90036 213-937-1570
Recorded Sound Ltd, 630 Fulton Bldg, Pittsburg PA 15222 412-288-9998
Red Car Editing, 1040 N Las Palmas Ave, Los Angeles CA 90038 213-937-1570
Red River Enterprises, Box 859, Monrovia CA 91016..............................818-303-4118
Reedy Productions, 16626 Arminta St, Van Nuys CA 91406 818-901-1944
Marian Rees Assoc, 4125 Redford Ave, Studio City CA 91604.....................818-508-5599
Reeves Corporate Services, 708 3rd Ave, New York NY 10017.....................212-573-8570
Reibold Company Inc, 3410 N Knoll Dr, Los Angeles CA 90028 213-462-3209
Reider Film & Television, 1189 Virginia Ave NE, Atlanta GA 30306........404-874-8436
Rick Reinert Productions, 201 N Hollywood Way, Burbank CA 91505.....818-769-2566
Renan Productions, 2253 Pontius Ave, Los Angeles CA 90064 213-478-0393
Renovare Co, 1615 N Laurel Ave, Los Angeles CA 90046 213-656-4420
RESCO, 99 Draper Ave, Meriden CT 06450...203-238-4709
Resources for Educ & Mgmt, 544 Medlock Rd, Decatur GA 30030 404-373-7743
Resources Inc, 187th St Paul St, Burlington VT 05401 802-862-0550
Joe Reynolds Filmaker, 1136 N Tamarind Ave, Los Angeles CA 90038....213-469-4375
RFG Assoc Inc, 1530 N Gower St Ste 204, Los Angeles CA 90028...............213-466-2648
Rham Film & Video Production, 905 N Cole, Hollywood CA 90038 213-465-3932
Bert Rhine Productions, 7073 Vineland Ave, Hollywood CA 91605 818-764-1225
Rhodes Productions, 124 11th St, Manhattan Beach CA 90266 213-379-3686
John Rich Productions, 1801 Ave of Stars, Los Angeles CA 90067...............213-277-0700
Rich/Sato Productions, 1242 N Beachwood Dr, Los Angeles CA 90038 ..213-464-5709
Richter Productions, 330 W 42nd St, New York NY 10036.........................212-947-1395
Rick Bell Productions, 5435 E Lewis, Phoenix AZ 85008 602-840-5232
Jocelyn Riley, Box 5264 Hilldale, Madison WI 53705 608-271-7083
Riviera Productions, 31628 Saddletree Br, Westlake Village CA 91361....818-889-5778
RKO Pictures, 1900 Avenue of Stars Ste 1562, Los Angeles CA 90067 213-277-3133
RKO Pictures Archives, 129 N Vermont Ave, Los Angeles CA 90004 213-383-5525
RM Films Intl Inc, Box 3748, Los Angeles CA 90078 213-466-7791
Roar of Laughter Prod, 6331 Hollywood Blvd, Hollywood CA 90028 213-461-9697
Herold Robbins Intl, 9220 Sunset Blvd, Los Angeles CA 90069 213-276-1011
Fred Roberts Productions, 94 S Sunnyside, Sierra Madra CA 91024..........818-355-7863
Dar Robinson & Co, 11754 Vanowen St, North Hollywood CA 91605 818-765-0110
Rock Solid Productions, 801 S Main St, Burbank CA 91506.......................818-841-8220
Richard H Roffman Prod, 697 West End Ave 6A, New York NY 10025 ..212-749-3647
Rogers Samuels Prod, 120 El Camini Dr, Beverly Hills CA 90212...............213-273-8964
Rolling Hills Productions, 204 S Beverly Dr, Beverly Hills CA 90212........213-462-6677
Joffe Rollins Morra & Brezner, 5555 Melrose, Los Angeles CA 90038.....213-462-6677
Romax Production Inc, 11836 Ventura Blvd, Studio City CA 91604 818-763-5540

Rosamond Productions, 7461 Beverly Blvd, Los Angeles CA 90036.........213-933-7508
Rose & Asseyev Prod, 10202 W Washington, Culver City CA 90203.........213-836-3000
Rose/Dunnell & Mellini, 8281 Melrose Ave, Los Angeles CA 90046.......213-653-9240
Rosebud Pictures Co Inc, 1438 Gower St, Los Angeles CA 90028.............213-461-7198
Rosemont Productions, 1990 Westwood Blvd, Los Angeles CA 90025......213-474-4700
Robert Rosenthal Prod, 10100 Santa Monica, Los Angeles CA 90067.......213-553-9049
Ross McCanse & Assoc, 6356 Fountain Ave, Los Angeles CA 90028........213-464-7677
Ross-Gaffney Inc, 21 W 46th St, New York NY 10036 212-719-2744
Ted Roter Film & Stage Prod, 12211 Malone, Los Angeles CA 90066......213-473-3559
Peter Rothenberg Comm, 19041 Braemore, Northridge CA 91326 818-368-8269
Roto Effects of America, 737 N Seward St, Hollywood CA 90038 213-463-2989
Roundtable Film & Video, 113 N San Vicente, Beverly Hills CA 90211....213-657-1402
Jack Rourke Productions, Box 1705, Burbank CA 91507 818-843-4839
Royalty Reels, 650 N Bronson Ave, Los Angeles CA 90004.........................213-467-5386
RSO Films, 1041 N Formasa, Los Angeles CA 90046 213-850-2601
Ruby-Spears Enterprises, 3255 Cahuenga W, Hollywood CA 90068.........213-874-5100
Ruddy-Morgan Productions, 120 El Camino, Beverly Hills CA 90212......213-271-7698
Russell-McCartney Productions, 5220 N Clark, Lakewood CA 90712......213-866-3422
Russell-Manning Productions, 905 Park Ave, Minneapolis MN 55404.....612-338-7761
Aaron Russo Prod, 13009 Valleyheart Dr, Studio City CA 91604............818-501-8794
RWB Productions, 6499 Ivarene Ave, Hollywood CA 90068......................213-469-0860
Paul Ryan Films, 538 Hill St, Santa Monica CA 90405 213-392-2169
RZR Television Productions, 42 Carriage Way, Pomono CA 91766.........714-865-1987
S & S Pictures Corp, 190 N Cannon Dr, Beverly Hills CA 90210..............213-274-8407
S-L Film Productions, PO Box 41108, Los Angeles CA 90041 213-254-8528
Saban Productions, 11724 Ventura Blvd Ste A, Studio City CA 90210......818-985-3805
Leo Salkin Films Inc, 6305 Yucca St, Los Angeles CA 90028 213-463-4513
N J Sambul & Co Inc, 5 E 16th St, New York NY 10003.............................212-924-2800
Samuels Artists & Prod, 9046 Sunset Blvd, Los Angeles CA 90069...........213-278-5050
San Francisco Light Works, 509 6th St, San Francisco CA 94103..............415-989-1255
San Francisco Video, PO Box 42189, San Francisco CA 94142...................415-648-0745
Alan Sands Productions, 225 E 74th St, New York NY 10021....................212-697-6135
Sandy Corp, 1500 W Big Beaver Rd, Troy MI 48084................................313-649-0800
Sanrio Communications, 10474 Santa Monica, Los Angeles CA 90025 213-470-8500
Jim Sant'Andrea Inc, 320 W 57th St, New York NY 10019 212-974-5400
H G Saperstein & Assoc, 1875 Century Park E, Los Angeles CA 90067 ...213-556-3800
Sarley/Cashman Inc, 6464 Sunset Blvd Ste 805, Hollywood CA 90028.....213-464-7404
Saturn Intl Pictures, 20611 Plummer St, Chatsworth CA 91311.................818-407-1188
Herman Saunders Ent, 1777 Vine St, Los Angeles CA 90028....................213-461-4567
Pierre Sauvage Productions, 8760 Wonderland, Los Angeles CA 90046...213-605-8986
Save the Children, 54 Wilton Rd, Westport CT 06880 203-226-7272
Ken Sax Productions, 1814 Parnell Ave, W Los Angeles CA 90025...........213-475-4433
Saxton Communications, 124 E 40th St, New York NY 10016 212-867-2210
Saxton Films Ltd, 1422 N Sweetzer Ave, Los Angeles CA 90068..............213-654-4364
Schaefer Karpf Eckstein, 3500 W Olive Ave #730, Burbank CA 91505....818-953-7770
Schaeffer Buchfuehrer Prod, PO Box 1308, Los Angeles CA 90078.........213-846-5885
Schenck Enterprises, 190 N Canon Dr Ste 306, Beverly Hills CA 90210...213-274-8439
Edgar J Scherick & Assoc, 10960 Wilshire Blvd, Los Angeles CA 90024..213-473-7730
Lawrence Schiller Prod, 4827 N Sepulveda, Sherman Oaks CA 91403......818-906-0926
Schine Productions, 626 S Hudson Ave, Los Angeles CA 90005.................213-937-5000
George Schlatter Prod, 8321 Beverly Blvd, Los Angeles CA 90048............213-655-1400
Peter Schleger Co, 135 W 58th St, New York NY 10019 212-765-7129
William Schlottmann Productions, PO Box 193, New York NY 10009.....212-473-1916

Gerald Schnitzer Prod, 8033 Sunset Blvd, Los Angeles CA 90046 213-461-2989
Schorr Assoc, 112 S 16th St Penthouse A, Philadelphia PA 19102 215-569-2221
Schulman Video Center, 861 Seward St, Hollywood CA 90038..................213-465-8110
Cheryl A Schwartz Productions, Box 1248, Beverly Hills CA 90213 213-274-1061
SCL Communications, 702 Lincolnway W, South Bend IN 46616..............219-232-3545
Scorpio Productions Ltd, 8330 W 3rd St, Los Angeles CA 90048 213-655-5580
Screen Gems Inc, Columbia Plaza, Burbank CA 91522.............................818-954-6000
Screen Images Inc, 1041 N Orange Dr, Hollywood CA 90038 213-462-4383
Screen Presentations Inc, 309 Massachusetts Ave NE, Wash DC 20002...202-546-8900
Screen Trade Films, 10584 Wellworth Ave, Westwood CA 90024..............213-470-2848
Screenware, 21 Stetson Ave, Kentfield CA 94904.....................................415-457-2741
Searchlight Films, Fox Hill Rd, Bernardston MA 01337 413-648-9464
Sebastian Intl Pictures, 10584 Wellworth Ave, Westwood CA 90024........818-889-3697
Seemann Video Productions, 44 Beachwood, New Hartford NY 13413 315-793-0013
Sefton Assoc Inc, 3351 Claystone SE, Grand Rapids MI 49506 616-957-0600
Daniel A Segal Prod, 19433 Pacific Coast Hwy, Malibu CA 90265............213-456-2687
Stan Seiden Productions, 6233 Hollywood Blvd, Los Angeles CA 90028..213-468-1700
Bob Seizer Productions, 257 S Rodeo Dr, Beverly Hills CA 90212............213-277-7050
Sell Pictures Inc, 9701 Wilshire Blvd, Beverly Hills CA 90212..................213-874-5402
Walter Seltzer Productions, 4172 Stanbury, Sherman Oaks CA 91423......818-788-1268
SG/Greg Harrison Prod, 4040 Vineland Ave, Studio City CA 91604 818-509-0881
Shadoevision, 9100 Sunset Blvd Ste 113, Los Angeles CA 90069.............818-788-1268
The Shana Corp, 34751 Seven Mile Rd, Livonia MI 48152.......................313-477-6812
Jerry Shanks Productions, 4 Quarterback, Marina del Rey CA 90292......213-392-2595
Shapiro Entertainment Corp, 3883 Fredonia St, Los Angeles CA 90068..213-851-2952
Bea Shaw Productions, 10527 Sarah St, North Hollywood CA 91602.......818-761-9357
Edward Shaw Productions, Box 709, Woodland Hills CA 91365................818-888-0168
Sheen/Greenblatt Prod, 956 N Seward St, Los Angeles CA 90038 818-888-0168
Tom Shelly Enterprises, 6253 Hollywood Blvd, Los Angeles CA 90028....213-466-4650
Shelton Leigh Plamer & Co, 360 E 57th St, New York NY 10022.............212-980-3445
Sheridan-Elson Communications, 20 W 37th St, New York NY 10018.....212-239-2000
Sherway Publishing Co, PO Box 3096, Chatsworth CA 91313 818-700-9049
Robert Short Productions, 4228 Glencoe, Marina del Rey CA 90291 213-306-6842
The Show Biz, 3040 W Market St, Akron OH 44313.................................216-864-5433
Showmedia, 444 N Maple Dr, Beverly Hills CA 90210.............................213-271-6716
Showpiece Productions, Box 79 Main Sta, Yonkers NY 10702 914-965-0801
Showscan Film Corp, 4503 Glencoe Ave, Marina del Rey CA 90292........213-827-7541
The Sidaris Co, 1819 Carla Ridge, Beverly Hills CA 90210.......................213-275-2682
Joseph Siegman Inc, 9200 Sunset Blvd Ste 1000, Los Angeles CA 90069..213-276-1014
Sight & Sound Inc, 6969 Grover St, Omaha NE 68106 402-393-0999
Signal Productions Inc, 6223 Selma Ave, Los Angeles CA 90028 213-463-4173
Silver Bullet Pictures, 28140 Everett Dr, Southfield MI 48076 313-443-1553
Silver Image, 11025 Seven Hill Ln, Potomac MD 20854 301-983-3366
Joel Silve Prod, 10201 W Pico Blvd, Los Angeles CA 90035 213-203-3017
Silver/Regan, 9336 Washington Blvd, Culver City CA 90230......................213-559-0346
Silvercup Studios, 42-25 21st St, Long Island City CA 11101.....................718-784-3390
Silvermine Films Inc, 630 9th Ave, New York NY 10036 212-582-4056
Jerry Sim Productions, 3765 Cahuenga Blvd W, Studio City CA 91604 718-784-3390
Simmons Productions, 660 Main St, Woburn MA 01901............................617-933-6377
Jamil Simon Assoc, 2 Tyler Ct, Cambridge MA 02140 617-491-4300
Nicholas Simone, 1524 N Courtney Dr, Los Angeles CA 90046 213-661-7777
Simpson-Bruckheimer Prod, 5555 Melrose, Los Angeles CA 90038 213-468-4518
Greg H Sims Co, 1801 Century Park E, Los Angeles CA 90067..................213-201-0634

Sitting Bull Enterprises, 7285 Franklin Ave, Los Angeles CA 90046.........213-876-3527
Size Inc, 600 Moulton Ave Ste 405, Los Angeles CA 90031.......................213-223-2312
Skouras Films, 1040 Las Palmas, Los Angeles CA 90046...........................213-467-3000
Skylight Production Inc, 6815 W Willoughby, Los Angeles CA 90038 213-464-4500
SLR Productions, PO Box 3266, Los Angeles CA 90078 213-876-6336
SM Productions, 16115 Vanowen St, Van Nuys CA 92406...........................818-994-8840
Smeloff Teleproductions, 8201 E Pacific Pl Ste 502, Denver CO 80231.....303-750-5000
Smith-Hemion Productions, 1438 N Gower St, Los Angeles CA 90028....213-871-1200
Smithline Productions Inc, 9255 Sunset Blvd, Los Angeles CA 90069 213-274-7769
Smothers Inc, 8489 W 3rd St Ste 38, Los Angeles CA 90048.......................213-651-0200
Phoebe T Snow Prod, 240 Madison Ave, New York NY 10016....................212-679-8756
Ken Snyder Enterprises, 485 Hot Springs Rd, Santa Barbara CA 93108..805-969-1807
Jerry Socher Prod, 12150 W Olympic Blvd, Los Angeles CA 90064 213-820-6867
Andrew Solt Productions, 9113 Sunset Blvd, Los Angeles CA 90069.........213-276-9522
Richard Soltys Productions, 1615 W Burbank Blvd, Burbank CA 91506..818-843-0373
Sonoma Video Productions, 1717 Darby Rd, Sebastopal CA 95472...........707-829-1016
Sony Inst Applied Video Tech, PO Box 29906, Los Angeles CA 90029 213-462-1982
Sound Enterprises Publishing, Box 722D, Frazer PA 19355.......................215-431-4512
Leonard South Productions, 4500 Forman Ave, Toluca Lake CA 91602..213-760-8383
South Seas Safari Co, Box 815, Hollywood CA 90078 213-465-1768
South Street Productions, 2347 Glendon Ave, Los Angeles CA 90064 213-273-8666
Southbrook Entertainment, 9601 Wilshire, Beverly Hills CA 90210...........213-274-8021
Southby Productions, 5000 E Anaheim St, Long Beach CA 90804 213-498-8834
Southern Illinois Univ, School of Medicine, Springfield IL 62702.............217-785-2135
Rick Spalla Video Prod, 301 W 45th St, New York NY 10036 212-756-4646
Rick Spalla Video Prod, 1622 N Gower St, Los Angeles CA 90028 213-469-7307
Jack Spear Productions, 7243 Santa Monica, Hollywood CA 90046..........213-851-4123
Specification Video, 824 Keeler St, Boone IA 50036..................................515-432-8256
Spectra Image Inc, 540 N Hollywood Way, Burbank CA 91505 818-842-1111
Spectrum Productions Inc, 532 Madison Ave, New York NY 10022..........212-319-8610
Speed Communication Inc, 359 Wildwood Rd, Stamford CT 06903 203-329-0411
Aaron Spelling Productions, 1041 N Formosa, Los Angeles CA 90046.....213-850-3911
Spender Productions, 234 5th Ave, New York NY 10001............................212-697-5895
Sperling & Richards, 8760 Sunset Blvd, Los Angeles CA 90069 213-855-1366
Milton Sperling Prod, 13701 Riverside Dr, Sherman Oaks CA 91423.......818-981-4313
Ed Spiegel Co, 8489 W 3rd St, Los Angeles CA 90048................................213-522-0577
Spiegel-Bergman Prod, 2029 Century Park E, Los Angeles CA 90067 213-522-0577
Spindler Productions, 1501 Broadway, New York NY 10036 212-730-1255
Martin Spinelli Assoc Inc, 12 E 86th St, New York NY 10028 212-288-4649
Spoken Arts Inc, Box 289, New Rochelle NY 10802...................................914-636-5482
Spots Alive Consultants Inc, 342 Madison Ave, New York NY 10173......212-953-1677
Spotwise Productions, 1170 Commonwealth Ave, Boston MA 02134.......617-232-2002
Spungbuggy Works Inc, 8506 Sunset Blvd, Los Angeles CA 90069...........213-657-8070
Square Wheel Productions, PO Box 675, Van Nuys CA 91408....................818-508-0332
SRS Productions Inc, 4224 Ellenita Ave, Tarzana CA 91356.....................213-996-5337
Stage Fright Productions, 8817 Amboy Ave, Sun Valley CA 91352...........818-768-3333
Stage Two Productions, 713 S 3rd St, Minneapolis MN 55415...................612-333-3302
Stamford Sobel, 515 Madison Ave, New York NY 10022 212-355-5330
Jay S Stanley & Assoc, 5301 McClanahan Dr, N Little Rock AK 72116....501-758-8029
Stanton Films, 2417 Artesia Blvd, Redondo Beach CA 90278 213-542-6573
Star Entertainment, 6253 Hollywood Blvd, Los Angeles CA 90028...........213-463-2000
Starborn Filmworks, 3884 Franklin Ave, Los Angeles CA 90027...............213-662-3121
Starquest Productions, 2780 Outpost Dr, Hollywood CA 90068.................213-467-8277

Peter Starr Productions, 23320 Oxnard St, Woodland Hills CA 91367 818-888-2500
Starr/Ross Corp Comm, 2727 Ponce de Leon, Coral Gables FL 33134 ...305-446-3300
Starwest Productions, 1391 N Speer Blvd Ste 409, Denver CO 80204 303-623-0636
State Fair College Media Ctr, 1900 Clarendon Rd, Sedalia MO 65301.....816-826-7100
Steckler Productions, 9530 Heather Rd, Beverly Hills CA 90210................213-275-8647
Stegman Productions Inc, 1715 S Boston Ave, Tulsa OK 74119....................918-585-8194
Stereovision Intl Inc, 3421 Burbank Blvd, Burbank CA 91505.....................818-841-1127
Don Stern Productions, 13743 Victory Blvd, Van Nuys CA 91401.............818-994-7000
Kris Stevens Ent, 14241 Ventura Blvd, Sherman Oaks CA 91423 818-981-8255
Shadow Stevens Inc, 9100 Sunset Blvd Ste 113, Los Angeles CA 90069 213-274-1244
E J Stewart Inc, 525 Mildred Ave, Primos PA 19018....................................215-626-6500
Bob Stewart Productions, 1717 N Highland, Hollywood CA 90028 213-461-3721
Stiletto Ltd, PO Box 69180, Hollywood CA 90069 213-650-8560
Bob Stivers Assoc, 710 N Seward St, Los Angeles CA 90038 213-467-4000
Andre Stojka Productions, 1246 S La Cienega, Los Angeles CA 90035 213-934-5906
Stokes & Kohne, 738 Cahuenga Blvd, Hollywood CA 90038.......................213-469-8176
Jim Stokes Comm, 453 S Cedar Lake, Minneapolis MN 55405 612-377-6251
Andrew L Stone Inc, 10478 Wyton Dr, Los Angeles CA 90024....................213-279-2427
Stoney Point Prod, 8322 Beverly Blvd, Los Angeles CA 90048 213-852-0300
Storeyline Prod, 1875 Century Park E, Los Angeles CA 90067...................213-201-2300
Straightley Films, 1438 N Gower St Box 8, Los Angeles CA 90028 213-462-8117
Herbert L Strock Productions, 6500 Barton, Los Angeles CA 90038........213-461-1298
Stuart Hersh Productions, 306 W 38th St, New York NY 10018................212-947-7780
Studio 5 Productions, 5 TV Place, Boston MA 02192.................................617-449-0400
Studio 932 Ltd, 932 12 Ave, Seattle WA 98122..206-322-9010
Studio Center Corp, 200 W 22nd St, Norfolk VA 23517..............................804-622-2111
Studio Television Services, 7550 Sunset Blvd, Los Angeles CA 90046.......213-851-7556
Kent Stumpell, 1316 Santa Monica Mall, Santa Monica CA 90401.............213-396-3875
Milton B Suchin Co, 201 N Robertson Blvd, Beverly Hills CA 90211........213-550-1133
Burt Sugarman Inc, 150 El Camino Ste 303, Beverly Hills CA 90212 213-274-7451
John M Sullivan Assoc, 880 Commonwealth Ave, Boston MA 02215 617-277-1710
Summerhouse Films, 10820 Ventura Blvd, Studio City CA 91604...............818-980-5833
The Sun Group, 1133 Broadway Rm 1527, New York NY 10010 212-255-1000
Sun Television, 1040 N Las Palmas Ave, Hollywood CA 90038.................213-461-5001
Sunbreak Productions, 256 S La Cienega Blvd, Beverly Hills CA 90211...213-855-0364
Sundance Productions, 1888 Century Park E, Los Angeles CA 90067 818-980-5833
Sunlight Pictures Corp, 8009 Santa Monica, Los Angeles CA 90046.........213-659-2324
Sunwest Productions, 1021 N McCadden Pl, Los Angeles CA 90038 213-461-2957
Supe 'N Dupe, 278 N 5th St, Columbus OH 43215 614-224-4400
Supercolossal Pictures, 3413 Cahuenga Blvd W, Los Angeles CA 90068..213-876-6770
Superior Video Services, 13423 Saticoy St, North Hollywood CA 91605 ...818-768-6770
Survival Anglia Ltd, 10100 Santa Monica, Los Angeles CA 90067..............213-553-8383
Suski-Fallick Prod West, 6671 Sunset Blvd, Los Angeles CA 90028..........213-464-2171
Sutherland Learning Assoc, 8700 Reseda Blvd, Northridge CA 91324 818-701-1344
Hack Swain Productions, 1185 Cattlemen Rd, Sarasota FL 34232..............813-371-2360
Swanson Productions, 2811 Cahuenga Blvd W, Hollywood CA 90068.......213-851-8930
Swenson Productions, 40 Winsor Place, Glen Ridge NJ 07028....................201-744-7880
Sygma Television, 8833 Sunset Blvd Ste 407, Los Angeles CA 90069.........213-855-1349
Synchronous Media Intl, 1217 Turner St, Lansing MI 48906......................517-482-3333
Syscon Video Productions, 133 Gaither Dr, Mount Laurel NJ 08054........609-234-5510
Taft Entertainment, 1800 Century Park E, Los Angeles CA 90067.............213-551-1911
Martin Tahse Productions, 6230 Sunset Blvd, Hollywood CA 90028 213-466-9710
Takwa Bay Films Inc, 1462 N Stanley Ave, Los Angeles CA 90046 213-874-2882

Talco Productions, 279 E 44th St, New York NY 10017 212-697-4015
Talking Rings Entertainment, PO Box 2019, Beverly Hills CA 90213 213-306-1909
Tamarand Inc, 1124 N Citrus, Los Angeles CA 90067 213-461-5100
Tandem Productions, 1901 Ave of the Stars, Los Angeles CA 90067 213-553-3600
Tantalus Inc, 3876 Carpenter Ave, Studio City CA 91604 818-766-2789
Tantra Productions, 350 N Crescent Dr, Beverly Hills CA 90210 213-937-9900
Tapper Productions Inc, 330 W 42nd St Ste 2420, New York NY 10036...212-947-0930
Tartan Productions, 6063 Sunset Blvd, Los Angeles CA 90028 213-461-2877
TAT Communications Co, 12970 Bradley St, Sylmar CA 91342 818-367-2154
Tauro Productions, 5324 Melrose Ave, Los Angeles CA 90038....................213-467-8505
Alfred Taylor, 442 S Almont Dr, Beverly Hills CA 90212 213-275-0706
TBS Productions, 4000 Warner Blvd, Burbank CA 91522............................818-954-6000
Teitzell Film Inc, 5967 W 3rd St Ste 301, Los Angeles CA 90036 213-934-3644
Tel-Air Interests Inc, 1755 NE 149th St, Miami FL 33181 305-944-3268
Telco Productions, 6525 Sunset Blvd Ste 401, Hollywood CA 90028..........213-461-2888
Telecine Inc, Box 2390, North Hollywood CA 91602 818-846-5386
Teleklew Productions, 1299 Ocean Ave Ste 800, Santa onica CA 90401 ...213-451-5727
Telemated Motion Pictures, Box 176 Prince Sta, New York NY 10012.....212-475-8050
Telematic Systems, 55 Wheeler St, Cambridge MA 02138 617-492-2881
Telemation Productions, 834 N 7th Ave, Phoenix AZ 85007.......................602-254-1600
Telemation Productions, 3210 W Westlake Ave, Glenview IL 60025..........312-729-5215
Telemation Productions, 7700 E Iliff St, Denver CO 80231 303-751-6000
Telemedia Productions, 18321 Ventura Blvd, Tarzana CA 91356 818-708-2005
Telepictures Productions, 415 N Crescent Dr, Beverly Hills CA 90212 213-859-3300
TeleTechniques, 1 W 19th St, New York NY 10011 212-206-1475
Television Assoc Inc, 2410 Charleston Rd, Mountain View CA 94043 415-967-6040
Television Matrix, 1438 N Gower St, Hollywood CA 90028 213-465-9616
Television Production Services, Box 1233, Edison NJ 08818......................201-287-3626
TeleVisual Productions, 1287 Wabash Ave, Springfield IL 62704................217-787-4757
Ten-Four Productions Inc, 5555 Melrose, Los Angeles CA 90038...............213-468-5900
Texas Heart Inst TV, PO Box 20269, Houston TX 77225 713-791-4276
Theme Song, 396 Watchogue Rd, Staten Island NY 10314 718-698-4178
Third Eye Production Co, 100 S Doheny Dr, Los Angeles CA 90048........213-858-4939
Third Wave Productions, 7130 Hollywood Blvd, Los Angeles CA 90046..213-851-7080
Catzel Thomas & Assoc, 10994 Washington, Culver City CA 90230 213-558-7100
Danny Thomas Prod, 11350 Ventura Blvd, Studio City CA 91604.............818-985-2940
Larry Thompson Co, 1440 S Sepulveda, Los Angeles CA 90025 213-478-6100
Thompson-Paul Prod, 13444 Ventura Blvd, Sherman Oaks CA 90067......818-789-5114
Thorn EMI Films Inc, 9489 Dayton Way, Beverly Hills CA 90210 213-278-4770
Fred G Thorne Productions, 2780 Outpost Dr, Beverly Hills CA 90210...213-467-8277
Threshold Films, 2025 N Highlland Ave, Los Angeles CA 90068................213-874-8413
Thunder Music Inc, 2033 Kerwood Ave, Los Angeles CA 90025 213-556-0061
T Thure Video Productions, PO Box 5443, Tucson AZ 85703 602-252-5021
Thursday's Child Prod, 7245 Franklin Ave, Los Angeles CA 90045 213-874-4427
Rodger Tilton Films Inc, 315 6th Ave, San Diego CA 92101.....................619-233-6513
Timely-Lively Productions, 12198 Ventura Blvd, Studio City CA 91604....818-766-6800
Timestream Video, 11821 N Circle Dr, Whittier CA 90601 213-699-8797
Steve Tisch Co, 515 N Robertson, Los Angeles CA 90048...........................213-278-7680
Titan Films, 73 Market St, Venice CA 90291...213-399-9319
C Tobalina Productions Inc, 1044 S Hill St, Los Angeles CA 90015...........213-749-2067
Todd-AO, 1021 N Seward St, Los Angeles CA 90028 213-463-1136
The Toho Co Ltd, 2049 Century Park E, Los Angeles CA 90067.................213-277-1081
Total Involvement Inc, 190 Main St, Westport CT 06880 203-227-9558

Total Video Co, 220 E Grand Ave Ste D, S San Francisco CA 94080.........415-583-8236
Total Visuals, 145 W 45th St, New York NY 10036.....................................212-944-8788
Touchstone Films, 500 S Buena Vista, Burbank CA 91521.........................818-840-1000
TPS Video Services, Box 1233, Edison NJ 08818.......................................201-287-3626
TR Productions, 1031 Commonwealth Ave, Boston MA 02215...................617-783-0200
Trancas Intl Films, 9229 Sunset Blvd Ste 415, Hollywood CA 90069.........213-657-7670
Trans World Airlines, 5550 Wilshire Blvd, Los Angeles CA 90036............213-935-6266
Trans World Intl, 6464 Sunset Blvd, Los Angeles CA 90046......................213-461-0467
Trans-American Video Inc, 1541 N Vine St, Los Angeles CA 90028 213-466-2141
Trans-Atlantic Enterprises, 101 Ocean Ave, Santa Monica CA 90402......213-454-6515
Transcon Intermedia Prod, 650 N Bronson, Los Angeles CA 90004.........213-464-2279
Translight Media Assoc Inc, 931 W Liberty, Wheaton IL 60187.................312-690-7780
Translor Films, 9200 Sunset Blvd Ste 303, Los Angeles CA 90069 213-274-8483
Transtar Productions, 9520 E Jewell, Denver CO 80231.............................303-695-4207
Travellers World Comm, 400 Main St, Stamford CT 06901 203-869-9561
Travelling Image Co, PO Box 14261, Portland OR 97214...........................503-234-9192
Don Trevor Assoc Inc, 20 E 9th St, New York NY 10003 212-473-0868
Tri Video Teleproduction, Box 8822, Incline Village NV 89450..................702-323-6868
Trigon Productions, 9454 Wilshire Blvd, Beverly Hills CA 91602.............818-760-3150
Triplane Films Inc, 183 N Martell Ave Ste 220, Los Angeles CA 90036 ...213-937-1320
Tri-Star Pictures, 1875 Century Park E, Los Angeles CA 90067.................213-201-2300
Troll Assoc, 100 Corporate Dr, Mahwah NJ 07430......................................201-529-4000
Trump Films Ltd, 1128 N Las Palmas Ave, Hollywood CA 90038..............213-462-4444
TTC Productions Inc, 5746 Sunset Blvd, Hollywood CA 90028....................213-856-1746
Tuley-Brevelle Productions, 1730 Purdue Ste 3, Los Angeles CA 90025 ...213-479-0380
Turman-Foster Co, 10202 W Washington, Culver City CA 90232.............213-558-6906
Howard R Turner, 57 W 75th St, New York NY 10023.................................212-873-3211
Turquoise Square Prod, 8226 Sunset Blvd, Los Angeles CA 90046 213-650-6911
TV Computer Graphic, 30800 Telegraph Rd, Birmingham MI 48010........313-646-0200
TV Gems Inc, 7244 Hillside Ave, Los Angeles CA 90046.............................213-876-2077
TVL Productions, 221 E Walnut St, Pasadena CA 91101.............................213-681-1111
Twentieth Century Fox, 10201 W Pico Blvd, Los Angeles CA 90035 213-277-2211
Twenty-First Century Prod, 439 Western Ave, Glendale CA 91201...........818-244-2133
Bill Udell Productions, 6006 Vantage Ave, North Hollywood CA 91606 ..818-985-6866
Ufland-Roth Prod, 9454 Wilshire Blvd, Beverly Hills CA 90210.................213-558-5455
Ultra Film Service, 1159 N Highland Ave, Los Angeles CA 90038 213-466-7972
Ultra Image, 211 N Victory Blvd, Burbank CA 91502 818-848-7673
Ultra Media Comm, 9056 Santa Monica, Los Angeles CA 90069................213-271-7279
UMS TV Productions, 3212 East 8th St, Long Beach CA 90804..................213-434-3453
Unger Productions Inc, 2029 Century Park E, Los Angeles CA 90067......213-553-5010
Unicorn Productions, 7656 Sunset Blvd, Hollywood CA 90046 213-874-3400
Unifilms Inc, 6748 Clybourn Ave Ste 124, North Hollywood CA 91606 818-506-4205
United Artists, 450 N Roxbury Dr, Beverly Hills CA 90210 213-281-4000
United Mgmt & Production, PO Box 69554, Los Angeles CA 90069.........213-274-9839
United Odyssey Inc, 21417 Evalyn Ave, Torrance CA 90503.......................213-540-2165
United Producers, 327 S Ogden Dr Ste 209, Los Angeles CA 90036.........818-931-1811
United States Audio-Visuals, Box 5686, Hilton Head Is SC 29938.............803-681-5000
United States Pictures, 13701 Riverside Dr, Sherman Oaks CA 91423.....818-981-4313
United TV Broadcasting, 6601 Hollywood Blvd, Los Angeles CA 90028...213-467-4044
United Video Industries Inc, 5533 Sunset Blvd, Los Angeles CA 90028....213-465-1000
Unity Pictures Corp, 11661 San Vicente Blvd, Los Angeles CA 90049......213-826-1026
Univ of Mississippi, Communications Resources, University MS 38677....601-232-5917
Univ of Missouri Kansas City, 650 E 25th St, Kansas City MO 64108......816-234-0442

Univ of Northern Iowa, Educational Media Ctr, Cedar Falls IA 50614 319-273-2309
Univ of Vermont, 223 Rowell Bldg UVM, Burlington VT 05405 802-656-2927
Univ of Wash, SB-56 T281 HSB, Seattle WA 98195 206-545-1186
Univ of Wisconsin Stout, 800 S Broadway, Menomonie WI 54751............. 715-232-2624
Universal Pictures, 100 Universal Plz, Universal City CA 91608................ 818-777-1000
Universal Learning Systems, 1800 N Highland, Los Angeles CA 90028 ...213-467-7141
Universal Training Systems, 255 Revere Dr, Northbrook IL 60062........... 312-498-9700
Unix Enterprises Inc, 650 N Bronson Ave, Hollywood CA 90004............... 213-876-8393
Unlimited Solutions AV, 15785 W Ryerson Rd, New Berlin WI 53151...... 414-784-3113
UPA Prod of Amer, 1875 Century Park E, Los Angeles CA 90067............. 213-556-3800
Utritronics Inc, 733 N Victory Blvd East 7th fl, Burbank CA 91502 818-843-2288
Vabs Multi-Image, 705 Hinman, Evanston IL 60202 312-328-8697
S A Vail & Assoc, 1351 N Crescent Hts Blvd, Los Angeles CA 90046........ 213-650-0224
Renee Valente Productions, 10201 W Pico Blvd, Los Angeles CA 90064 .. 213-277-2211
Valiant Intl Pictures, 4774 Melrose Ave, Los Angeles CA 90029................ 213-665-5257
Francis G Valuskis, 1839 Deloz Ave, Los Angeles CA 90027 213-663-4424
Vanguard Video Productions, 7084 Huntley Rd, Columbus OH 43229..... 614-436-4610
Various Stages, 1314 Benton Way, Los Angeles CA 90026 213-413-0368
VCA Teletronics, 231 E 55th St, New York NY 10022................................ 212-355-1600
Vector Productions Inc, Box 7000-645, Redondo Beach CA 90277........... 213-757-0520
Venice Studios, 2017 Pacific Ave, Venice CA 90291 213-822-2400
Vestron Video, 60 Long Ridge Rd, Stamford CT 06907 203-968-0000
Vestron Video, 9255 Sunset Blvd, Los Angeles CA 90069 213-858-3990
Via Vision Productions, 5919 Franklin Ave, Los Angeles CA 90028.......... 213-460-4864
Viacom Enterprises, 10900 Wilshire Blvd 4th fl, Los Angeles CA 90024...213-208-2700
Vicom Entertainment, 812 N Highland Ave, Hollywood CA 90038........... 213-469-3434
Victor-Grais Prod, 450 N Roxbury, Beverly Hills CA 90210 213-281-4510
Vidcom Production Facility, 2426 Townsgate, Westlake Vlg CA 91361 818-991-1974
Vide-U Productions, 612 N Sepulveda Blvd, Los Angeles CA 90049.......... 213-472-7023
Videa Ltd, 200 Guaranty Bldg, Cedar Rapids IA 52401 319-366-0404
Video Aided Instruction Inc, 182 Village Rd, East Hills NY 11577............ 516-621-6176
Video Arts Inc, 185 Berry St Ste 265, San Francisco CA 94107 415-546-0331
Video Communication Ctr, George Fox College, Newberg OR 97132...... 503-538-6621
Video Communication Services, 208 Linden Ave, Riverton NJ 08077 608-768-1775
Video Communicators Intl, 1830 16th St, Newport Beach CA 92663......... 714-953-8097
The Video House, 201 N Hollywood Way Ste 202, Burbank CA 91505 818-954-9559
Video in Phoenix, 2311 W Royal Palm Rd, Phoenix AZ 85021 602-995-4448
Video Park Inc, 11316 Penny wood, Baton Rouge LA 70809.................... 504-292-0840
Video Pioneers Corp, 1636 E Edlinger St, Santa Ana CA 92705................ 714-547-1503
Video Presentations Corp, 23311 Commerce Pk, Beachwood OH 44122..216-464-5115
Video Production Co of Amer, 1201 Central Ave, Charlotte NC 28204..... 704-376-1191
Video Resources, 1805 E Dyer Rd, Santa Ana CA 92705........................... 714-261-7266
Video Tape Enterprises Inc, 8610 Sunset Blvd, Los Angeles CA 90069..... 213-659-4801
Video Vacation Guide, 1091 E Commercial, Ft Lauderdale FL33334 305-491-8802
The Video Troupe, Box 67, Windham NH 03087....................................... 603-893-4554
Video Vision Inc, 2033 Kerwood Ave, Los Angeles CA 90025 213-556-0061
Video-It Inc, 1016 N Sycamore Ave, Hollywood CA 90038....................... 213-876-4055
Videoactive, PO Box 24032, Santa Barbara CA 93121 805-966-9247
Videoasis, 317 S Verdugo Rd, Glendale CA 91205 818-507-1037
Videocom Inc, 502 Sprague St, Dedham MA 02026 617-329-4080
Videographics, 2918 Champa St, Denver CO 80205 303-297-1614
VideoMasters Inc, 620 N Broadway Ste 203, Milwaukee WI 53202........... 414-273-8686
Videomedia, 211 Weddell Dr, Sunnyvale CA 94089................................. 408-745-1700

Videotic Productions, PO Box 12192, Austin TX 78711............................512-467-0701
Videovision Corp, 27285 Las Ramblas Ste 130, Mission Viejo CA 92692..714-831-7700
Videoworks Inc, 24 W 40th St, New York NY 10018 212-869-2500
Vidi Ltd, 420 Marine St Ste 4, Santa Monica CA 90405 213-399-3089
Vidistrib Inc, 4209 Troost Ave, Studio City CA 91604................................818-762-2559
Viewpoint, 1630 Old Oakland Rd Ste 8213, San Jose CA 95131..............408-370-0211
Vik-Winkle Productions, 729 N Victory Blvd, Burbank CA 91502 818-843-1920
Norm Virag Productions, 3415 N East St, Lansing MI 48906.....................517-374-8193
Vision II Films, 1543 W Olympic Blvd, Los Angeles CA 90015 213-385-6363
Vista Films, 9336 W Washington, Culver City CA 90230 213-202-3310
Visual Communications Group, 3300 Mitchell Ln, Boulder CO 80301.....303-443-6003
Visual Information Systems, 1 Harmon Plaza, Secaucus NJ 07094............201-867-7600
Visual Projects Ltd, 67 Yale St, Roslyn Heights NY 11577 516-621-5285
Visual Promotions, 6442 Santa Monica Blvd, Los Angeles CA 90038........213-465-4079
Visual Services, 1 W 19th St, New York NY 10011.....................................212-580-9551
Visual Studies, 49 Rivoli St, San Francisco CA 94117 415-664-4699
VRA Teleplay Pictures, Box 8471 Univ Plz, Universal City CA 91608 213-462-1099
WK Productions Inc, 999 N Doheny Dr Ste 309, Los Angeles CA 90069..213-271-5903
WT Productions, 1438 N Gower St, Los Angeles CA 90028...........................213-464-1333
Roger Wade Productions Inc, 15 W 44th St, New York NY 10036 212-575-9111
Bill Wadsworth Productions, 2404 Rio Grande, Austin TX 78705............512-478-2971
Raymond Wagner Productions, Box 900, Beverly Hills CA 90213 213-203-1925
Brad Waisbren Enterprises, Box 8741, Universal City CA 91608 818-506-3000
Kent Wakeford & Assoc, 927 N La Cienega, Los Angeles CA 90069.........213-659-9863
Ken Wales Productions, 211 19th St, Santa Monica CA 90402 213-395-4850
Wallach/Seizer Productions, 1400 Braeridge, Beverly Hills CA 90210 213-278-4574
Hal Wallis Productions, 9200 Sunset Blvd, Los Angeles CA 90069 213-273-3381
Jay Ward Productions Inc, 8218 Sunset Blvd, Los Angeles CA 90046.......213-654-3050
Warner Bros Inc, 4000 Warner Blvd, Burbank CA 91522.............................818-954-6000
Glen Warren Productions, 9911 W Pico Blvd, Los Angeles CA 90035 213-553-9233
Waters Productions, 8450 DeLongpre Ave, Los Angeles CA 90069 213-656-2393
WATL TV 36, 575 Ponce de Leon Ave, Atlanta GA 30308 404-892-3636
Waveland Software Inc, 756 Waveland Ave, Chicago IL 60613...................312-248-9534
WB Ctr Self Directed Learning, Box 27616, San Francisco CA 94127.......415-334-3196
WCPX TV Channel 6, PO Box 66000, Orlando FL 32853 305-291-6000
WDIV TV, 550 Lafayette Blvd, Detroit MI 48231 313-222-0444
WDR/West German TV, 1295 Ozeta Ter, Los Angeles CA 90069 213-659-8558
Eric Weaver Enterprises Inc, 315 Harvey Dr, Glendale CA 91206............213-245-0308
Jerry Webb & Assoc, 801 N La Brea Ave, Los Angeles CA 90038 213-245-0308
Mimi Weber, 9738 Arby Dr, Beverly Hills CA 90210....................................213-278-8440
Wed Enterprises, 1401 Flower St, Glendale CA 91201................................818-956-6500
Tom Weigand Inc, 717 N 5th St, Reading PA 19601 215-374-4431
Ed Weinberger Productions, 5555 Melrose Ave, Los Angeles CA 90038..213-468-5871
Jerry Weintraub Prod, 11111 Santa Monica, Los Angeles CA 90067.........213-477-8900
Fred Weintraub Prod, 10202 W Washington, Culver City CA 90232 213-558-6428
Lennie Weinrib Productions, 9255 Sunset Blvd, Los Angeles CA 90069 ...213-278-4831
Jacob Weisbarth & Assoc, 9903 Santa Monica, Beverly Hills CA 90212 ...213-475-0668
Ken Weisbrod Productions Inc, PO Box 5359, Chatwsworth CA 91313....818-718-0644
Barry Weitz Films Inc, 4024 Radford Ave, Studio City CA 91604.............213-760-6125
Wescom Productions, 9000 Sunset Blvd Ste 415, Los Angeles CA 90069..213-278-0112
West Entertainment, PO Box 16567, Los Angeles CA 90046.....................213-654-1096
West Wind Productions, 12206 Magnolia, N Hollywood CA 91607...........818-508-9800
Westbrook Films Ltd, 2821 Westbrook Ave, Los Angeles CA 90046.........213-876-8052

Western America Films Inc, Box 21543, Billings MT 59104 406-656-0965
Western Audio Visual, 835 2nd Ave, Durango CO 81301 303-247-1576
Western Video Systems, 8050 Ronson Rd, San Diego CA 92111................619-292-0337
Western World Press, Box 366, Sun City CA 92381.....................................714-652-8288
Westlake Audio Intl, 7265 Santa Monica Blvd, Los Angeles CA 90046 213-851-9800
Westport Communications Group, 155 Post Rd E, Westport CT 06880...203-226-3525
Westwind Productions Ltd, 11934 Tabor St, Los Angeles CA 90066.........213-391-9834
Wexler Film Production Inc, 801 N Seward St, Los Angeles CA 90038.....213-462-6671
WGAN Productions, Box 1731, Portland ME 04104 207-797-9330
White Eagle Prod, 10202 W Washington, Culver City CA 90232 213-558-6706
Ruth White Films, PO Box 34485, Los Angeles CA 90034 213-836-4678
Bill White Productions, 5907 W Pico Blvd, Los Angeles CA 90035 213-934-1412
Thelma White Productions, 8431 N Western, Panorama City CA 91420 ..818-894-3336
White Star Prof Film Service, 16641 Airport Rd, Lansing MI 48906 517-321-1776
White-Pix Productions, 1600 N Western Ave, Los Angeles CA 90028.......213-462-4352
Whitefeather Prod, 8455 Beverly Blvd, Los Angeles CA 90048....................213-937-3737
Whitefire Inc, 13440 Ventura Blvd, Sherman Oaks CA 91423......................818-907-5316
Wilder Brothers Prod, 10327 Santa Monica, Los Angeles CA 90025.........213-557-3500
Wildwood/Redford, 100 Universal Plz, Universal City CA 91608................818-777-5505
Wiley Sound Business, 605 3rd Ave, New York NY 10158................................212-850-6000
Wilhite Productions, 3742 Seahorn Dr, Malibu CA 90265............................213-459-2630
Richard Williams Animation, 3193 Cahuenga, Los Angeles CA 90068.....213-851-8060
W G Williams Assoc, 1100 17th St NW Ste 1000, Wash DC 20036..............202-463-8017
Wilson Learning Corp, 6950 Washington S, Eden Prairie CO 55344.........612-944-2880
Winchester Productions, 315 S Beverly Dr, Beverly Hills CA 90212 213-553-0171
Wingstar Film Production Inc, 114 E 32nd St, New York NY 10016 212-685-5031
Winkler/Daniel Productions, 5555 Melrose, Los Angeles CA 90038 213-468-4343
Bryan WInter Productions, 1131 Altadena Rd, Los Angeles CA 90069 213-854-1040
Winters Productions, Box 920, Montrose CA 91020 818-790-4201
Winterset Productions Inc, Box 757, Malibu CA 90265...............................213-278-1333
Wirth-Howard Productions, 5706 Ostin St, Woodland Hills CA 91367.....818-888-6198
Robert Wise Prod, 815 S Beverly Dr, Beverly Hills CA 90212 213-284-7932
Witt-Thomas Prod, 1438 N Gower Ste 475, Los Angeles CA 90028...........213-464-1333
Witzend Productions, 1600 N Highland Ave, Los Angeles CA 90028........213-462-6185
Wizard/Spectrum Video, 6461 Sunset Blvd, Hollywood CA 00282............213-462-6185
WKYT Productions, Box 5037, Lexington KY 70130....................................504-522-9769
WMW-Brzezinski Video, 6253 Hollywood Blvd, Hollywood CA 90028......213-465-3503
Wollin Production Services, 666 N Robertson, Los Angeles CA 90069....213-659-0175
David L Wolper Productions, 4000 Warner Blvd, Burbank CA 91522......818-954-1707
Women's Interart Ctr, 549 W 52nd St, New York NY 10019 212-246-1050
World Stage, 7765 Lemona St, Van Nuys CA 91405......................................818-902-2205
World Wide Pictures, 2520 W Olive Ave, Burbank CA 91505 818-843-1300
Worldwide Entertainment, 5912 Ramirez Canyon, Malibu CA 90265.......213-457-8081
David Worth Productions, 1807 19th St, Santa Monica CA 90404 213-450-2694
Frank Worth Productions, 1850 Whitley Ave, Hollywood CA 90028 213-462-2311
Marvin Worth Productions, 4000 Warner Blvd, Burbank CA 91522........818-954-3651
WPHL Productions, 5001 Wynnefield Ave, Philadelphia PA 19131 215-878-1700
Wren Assoc Inc, 5 Independence Way, Princeton NJ 08540 609-924-8085
Carter Wright Ent, 6533 Hollywood Blvd, Los Angeles CA 90028..............213-469-0944
Bob Wright Productions, 247 N Goodman St, Rochester NY 14607 716-271-2280
Douglas Wright Productions, PO Box 69308, Hollywood CA 90069..........213-656-5470
The Write Place, 1306 Main St, Evanston IL 60202.......................................312-869-1956
Yasney Productions, 8885 Hollywood Hilld Rd, Los Angeles CA 90046 ...213-650-4401

Ed Yelin Productions, 1020 Riverside Dr Ste 45, Burbank CA 91506........818-843-5951
Yellow Cat Productions, 8720 Georgia Ave, Silver Spring MD 20910........301-565-3589
YLS Productions, Box 54, Los Alamitos CA 90720.............................213-430-2890
Bud Yorkin Prod, 9336 W Washington, Culver City CA 90230...................213-202-3230
Yorktown Prod, 9336 W Washington, Culver City CA 90230 213-202-3402
Young & Assoc/Phrammis Prod, 11434 Ventura, Studio City CA 91403..818-509-8970
Dick Young Productions Ltd, 118 Riverside Dr, New York NY 10024......212-787-8954
Charles Yulish Assoc, 799 Broadway Rm 325, New York NY 10003.........212-777-8383
Larry Yust Productions, 520 S Rossmore Ave, Los Angeles CA 90020.....213-936-7044
Neil Zachary, PO Box 4136, Los Angeles CA 90078............................213-937-1314
Zachry Assoc Inc, 709 N 2nd, Abilene TX 79601 915-677-1342
Zanuck-Brown Co, 202 N Canon Dr, Beverly Hills CA 90210..................213-274-0261
Zelman Studios Ltd, 623 Cortelyou Rd, Brooklyn NY 11218..................718-941-5500
Tom Zenanko Outdoors, 5420 71st Cir N, Brooklyn Ctr MN 55429..........612-566-4797
Zenith Intl Pictures, 1537 Benedict Canyon, Beverly Hills CA 90210........213-274-6033
ZI Ltd, 600 N McClurg Ct Ste 1712A, Chicago IL 60611 312-337-0902
Zielinski Productions, 7850 Slater Ave, Huntington Beach CA 92647.......714-842-5050
Galanty Zimmerman Fiman, 1640 5th St, Santa Monica CA 90401 213-451-2522
M J Zink Productions, 245 W 19th St, New York NY 10011 212-929-2949
ZM Squared, 903 Edgewood Ln PO Box C-30, Cinnaminson NJ 08077....609-786-0612
Zupnick Enterprises, 9229 Sunset Blvd, Los Anglles CA 90069 213-273-9125

GHOST WRITERS & COLLABORATORS

About Books Inc, PO Box 538, Saguache CO 81149 303-589-8223
Action Research Assoc, 2111 Edinburg Ave, Cardiff-by-Sea CA 92007 619-944-0752
Alternative Research, PO Box 432, New York NY 10015 212-683-3478
Irene Atney-Yurdin, 2 Harborview Rd, Port Washington NY 11050 516-944-7814
Baldwin Literary Services, 935 Hayes St, Baldwin NY 11510...............516-546-8338
Kathleen Barnes, 238 W 4th St #3C, New York NY 10014...................212-924-8084
Diana Barth, 535 W 51st St Apt 3A, New York NY 10019 212-307-5465
Gilbert J Black, 399 West St, Harrison NY 10528.............................914-835-3160
Barbara J Bloch, 21 Dupont Ave, White Plains NY 10605 914-946-7715
The Bookmill, 3610 Moore St, Los Angeles CA 90066 213-398-4645
The Bookworks Inc, PO Box 1189, Chicago IL 60690 312-236-8472
Bookwright, PO Box 7119, Ann Arbor MI 48107 313-995-1470
Boston Word Works, 6354 Van Nuys #420, Van Nuys CA 91401 818-787-8646
Elsa Branden, 222 W 77th St Ste 1218, New York NY 10024................212-362-1100
Robert Brightman, 5 Sussex Rd, Great Neck NY 11020 516-482-2074
Norman Brown & Assoc, 21 Luzon Ave, Providence RI 02906 401-751-2641
Nan & Vincent Buranelli, Box 6297, Lawrenceville NJ 08648 609-896-2180
Business Media Resources, 150 Shorline Hwy, Mill Valley CA 94941.......415-331-6021
Luis R Caceres Jr, 8711 SW 20th Ter, Miami FL 33165 305-552-8433
Richard Carlin, 25 Oleander Ct, Lawrenceville NJ 08648 609-896-4465
Diane Carlson, 1215 Hull Terrace, Evanston IL 60202 312-869-7642
John Charnay, 19961 Stratern St, Canoga Park CA 91306.....................818-998-2652
Tina Clark, 318 Harvard St Ste 10, Brookline MA 02146 617-734-0807
E R Cole, PO Box 91277, Cleveland OH 44101.................................216-234-1775
Frances G Conn Assoc, 8320 Woodhaven Blvd, Bethesda MD 20817........301-365-5080
Paul Covington, 206 Pierron St, Northvale NJ 07647..........................201-768-6386
Contemporary Perspectives Inc, 223 E 48th St, New York NY 10017.......212-753-3800

Nancy L Daniels, Box 68, Lemont PA 16851...814-237-7711
May Dikeman, 70 Irving Pl, New York NY 10003 212-475-4533
A H Drummond Jr, 323 Springs Rd, Bedford MA 01730...............................617-275-1481
Valerie Eads Et Al, PO Box 1459, New York NY 10016 212-228-0900
Editmasters/Mizelle, 4545 Connecticut Ave NW, Wash DC 20008...........202-686-7252
Editorial & Graphic Services, Martinsville NJ 08836.....................................201-469-2195
Editorial Consultants Inc, 3221 Pierce St, San Francisco CA 94123..........415-931-7239
Editorial Excelsior Corp, 15 N Market St, San Jose CA 95113....................408-293-3734
Editorial Services, 501 S Cortez Ste F-3, Prescott AZ 86301 602-445-8627
Educational Challenges Inc, 1009 Duke St, Alexandria VA 22314..............703-683-1500
J M B Edwards Writer & Editor, 2432 California, Berkeley CA 94703.....415-644-8287
Pearl Eppy, 201 E 79th St, New York NY 10021...212-737-0354
First Editions, PO Box 1158, Sedona AZ 86336..602-282-1989
Free Lance Exchange Inc, 111 E 85th St, New York NY 10028 212-722-5816
Fromer Writing & Editing Service, 1508 13th St NW, Wash DC 20005 201-232-6915
David Frost PhD, 1229 E 7th St, Plainfield NJ 07062......................................201-755-3286
Gabriel House Inc, 5045 W Oakton St, Skokie IL 60077................................312-675-1146
Diane Gallo, Box 231 RD 1, Mount Upton NY 13809......................................607-764-8139
Jack Galub, 27 W 96th St, New York NY 10025...212-865-7886
Albert D Geller, 9127 Luna Ave, Morton Grove IL 60053 312-966-9133
Chet & Susan Gottfried, Box 9, Kew Gardens NY 11415 212-847-1464
Isabel S Grossner, 61 Tuxedo Rd, Montclair NJ 07042...................................201-746-5371
The Guilford Group, 124 Jerry Ln Box 981, Davisville RI 02854.................401-884-3101
Hardin Publishing Co, Box 269, Avera GA 30803...404-598-2312
Harriett, 135 54th St, New York NY 10022...212-688-0094
Emilie C Harting, 7143 Ardleigh St, Philadelphia PA 19119 215-247-5673
Daniel W Hill, 3023 Honeysuckle Way NE, Salem OR 97303 503-364-9210
Diane Casella Hines, 2366 Live Oak Meadow Rd, Malibu CA 90265........213-456-3220
Janet M Hunter, 411 Rose Ave, Mill Valley CA 94941 415-388-8788
Curt Johnson, 3093 Dato, Highland Park IL 60035 312-432-6804
Deborah Kopka, 3208 S Barrington Ste G, Los Angeles CA 90066.............213-391-4300
John Kremitske, 111 8th Ave Ste 1507, New York NY 10011 212-989-4783
L/A House Editorial, 5822 Uplander Way, Culver City CA 90230..............213-216-5812
Burton Lasky Assoc Inc, 111 8th Ave Ste 1507, New York NY 10011.......212-989-4783
Lazy Brown Assoc, 2800 Quebec St NW Ste 618, Wash DC 20008.............202-686-0975
Donald MacLaren Assoc, 6713 Homestake Dr, Bowie MD 20715 301-262-0444
Makeready Inc, 233 W 77th St, New York NY 10024.......................................212-595-5083
Manuscripts Intl, 408 E Main St, Dayton WA 99328......................................509-382-2436
Frank H Marks, 4940 East End Ave, Chicago IL 60615 312-684-3124
Anne V McGravie, 7035 N Greenview, Chicago IL 60626 312-274-1835
Pat McNees, 5708 33rd St NW, Washington DC 20015 202-362-8694
Judith H McQuown & Co, 127 E 59th St #201, New York NY 10022.......212-688-1291
MDZ Communications, 1136 E Stuart #220, Ft Collins CO 80525.............303-493-5532
Tom Mellers, 849 E 12th St, New York NY 10003 212-254-4958
Barbara Mary Merson, 14 Heathrow Ln, Old Bridge NJ 08857 201-591-0882
MS/Smiths Editorial Consult, RR 1 Box 447, Bridgewater CT 06752.......203-354-0866
Mary Mueller, 108 Forest Rd, Moorestown NJ 08057....................................609-778-4769
Kathleen Mulvihill, 830 Louisiana Ave, New Orleans LA 70115 504-891-3496
Charles Neighbors, 7600 Blanco Rd Ste 3607, San Antonio TX 78216......512-342-5324
Lois Newman, 6545 Hollywood Blvd #201, Hollywood CA 90028................213-464-8382
Postroad Press Inc, PO Box 1212, Roanoke VA 24006....................................703-342-9797
Deborah Pritzker, 2676 Grand Concourse, Bronx NY 10458 212-364-3832
Professional Editing & Typing, 410 E 20th St 3A, New York NY 10009...212-477-0615

Professional Editorial Svcs, 5531 Bubbling Wells, Ravenna OH 44266 216-682-5362
Programs on Change, 784 Columbus Ave Ste 1C, New York NY 10025...212-222-4606
Publishing Resources Inc, Box 41307, San Juan PR 00940 809-724-0318
Research Findings in Print, 26 W Jefferson Rd, Pittsford NY 14534 716-248-3947
Carol Z Rothkopf, 16 Rotary Ln, Summit NJ 07901 201-273-1255
Lynn Sonberg Book Services, 166 E 56th St, New York NY 10022 212-758-9604
SSR Incorporated, 116 4th St SE, Washington DC 20003.............................202-543-1800
Autumn Stanley, 241 Bonita los Trancos Wds, Portola Vly CA 94025.......415-851-1847
Sheila Steinberg, 42 Littlebrook Rd, Springfield NJ 07081 201-273-9388
Kiel Stuart, 12 Skylark Ln, Stony Brook NY 11790.....................................516-751-7080
Thump Records Hennings, 807 W 25th St #4, Minneapolis MN 55405 612-872-7329
Turner & Winston, 5306 38 St NW, Washington DC 20015 202-363-6459
Arlene S Uslander, 9406 Kilbourn, Skokie IL 60076 312-674-3701
Gladys H Walker, 21 Thorburn Ave, Trumbull CT 06611 203-261-3085
Walking Bird Publication Services, PO Box 19499, Seattle WA 98109 206-285-1575
Bess Wallace Assoc, 1502 N Mitchell, Payson AZ 85541............................602-474-2983
Bayla Winters, 2700 Scott Rd, Burbank CA 91504.....................................818-846-1879
The Wordsmith, 106 Mason Rd, Durham NC 27712 919-477-8430
Betty Wright & Assoc, PO Box 1069, Moore Haven FL 33471....................813-946-0293
Writers Alliance Ltd, 104 E 40th St, New York NY 10016 212-986-2830
Writers Connection, 1601 Saratoga Sunnyvale Rd, Cupertino CA 95014..408-973-0227
Writers: Free-Lance Inc, 12 Cavalier Dr, Ambler PA 19002 215-646-7550
The Writing Service, 315 W 102nd St Ste 7B, New York NY 10025............212-866-5930
Joan Yarfitz Photo Env, 2021 Vista del Mar, Los Angeles CA 90068 213-465-9947

GRAMMAR HOT LINES

This list contains agencies that will answer questions about grammar and punctuation. Most are staffed by volunteers and operate during limited hours.

Academic Support Center, Cedar Crest College, Allentown PA 18104 215-437-4471
Barnhart Dictionary Hotline, Box 247, Cold Spring NY 10516...................516-265-2822
Burger Associates, Robert S Burger, Glen Mills PA 19342 215-399-1130
Business English Helpline, Cosumnes Rvr Col, Sacramento CA 95823 916-686-7444
Dial-A-Grammar, Raymond Walters College, Cincinnati OH 45236 513-745-4312
Grammar Crisis Line, Ball State Univ Writing Ctr, Muncie IN 47306 317-285-8387
Grammar Hotline, Lincoln Univ, Lincoln Univ PA 19352 215-932-8300
Grammar Hotline, Purdue Univ Writing Lab, West Lafayette IN 47907...317-494-3723
Grammar Hotline, C S Mott Community College, Flint MI 48503..............313-762-0229
Grammar Hotline, Univ School of Nova Univ, Ft Lauderdale FL 33314...305-475-7697
Grammar Hotline, NE Wisconsin Tech Inst, Green Bay WI 54307 414-498-5427
Grammar Hotline, Methodist College, Fayetteville NC 28301 919-488-7110
Grammar Hotline, Univ of Wisconsin, Platteville WI 53818 608-342-1615
Grammar Hotline, The Citadel Writing Center, Charleston SC 29409......803-792-3194
Grammar Hotline, Missouri Southern State College, Joplin MO 64801....417-624-0171
Grammar Hotline, Illinois State Univ, Normal IL 61761 309-438-2345
Grammar Hotline, Northeastern Univ English Dept, Boston MA 02115 ..617-437-2512
Grammar Hotline, North Shore Community College, Lynn MA 01915....617-593-7284
Grammar Hotline, USL English Dept, Lafayette LA 70504.........................318-231-5224
Grammar Hotline, EIU Writing Center, Charleston IL 61920....................217-581-5929
Grammar Hotline, Tidewater Comm College, Virginia Bch VA 23456.....804-427-7170

Grammarphone, Triton College, River Grove IL 60171 312-456-0300
Grammarphone, Frostburg State College, Frostburg MD 21532.............301-689-4327
IUPUI Writing Hotline, Indiana Univ/Purdue, Indianapolis IN 46202......317-274-3000
Learning Line, San Antonio College, San Antonio TX 78284 512-733-2503
Natl Grammar Hotline, Moorpark College, Moorpark CA 93021 805-529-2321
Rewrite, York College of City Univ of NY, Jamaica NY 11451................718-739-7483
UHD Grammar Line, Univ of Houston Downtown, Houston TX 77002...713-221-8670
Virginia Lee Underwood, 1801 Dakota Av, Chickasha OK 73018................405-224-8622
USC Grammar Hotline, Univ of Southern Colo, Pueblo CO 81001.........303-549-2787
Writer's Hotline, Univ of Missouri at KC, Kansas City MO 64110.............816-276-2244
Writer's Hotline, Univ of South Carolina, Columbia SC 29208..................803-777-7020
Writer's Hotline, Emporia State Univ, Emporia KS 66801 316-343-1200
Writer's Hotline, Univ of Maryland, Baltimore MD 21228.....................301-455-2585
Writer's Hotline, W Mich Univ 1044 Moore Hall, Kalamazoo MI 49008..616-383-8122
The Writer's Hotline, Univ of Arkansas, Little Rock AR 72204 501-569-3162
Writer's Remedies, Univ of Cincinnati, Cincinnati OH 45221 513-475-2493
Writing Center, Georgia State Univ, Atlanta GA 30303 404-658-2906
Writing Center Hotline, Cincinnati Tech College, Cincinnati OH 45223 ..513-569-1737
Writing Center Hotline, Auburn Univ, Auburn AL 36830.....................205-826-5749
Writing Lab & Grammar Hotline, Univ of W Fla, Pensacola FL 32514....904-474-2129
Writing Resource Center, Ohio Wesleyan Univ, Delaware OH 43015......614-369-4431

GREETING CARD PUBLISHERS

Accord Publications, 1 Mt Vernon St, Ridge Field Park NJ 07660.............201-440-3210
Amberley Greeting Card Co, 11510 Goldcoast, Cincinnati OH 45249 513-489-2775
American Greetings, 10500 American Rd, Cleveland OH 44144 216-252-7300
Andrews McMeel & Parker, 4900 Main St, Kansas City MO 64112...........816-932-6700
Argus Communications, 1 DLM Park, Allen TX 75002.....................214-248-6300
Carolyn Bean Publishing, 2230 W Winton Ave, Hayward CA 94545.........415-957-9774
Blue Mountain Arts Inc, PO Box 4549, Boulder CO 80306.....................303-449-0536
Buzza Cards, 2100 Section Rd, Cincinnati OH 45237.....................513-841-6600
The Calligraphy Collection, 2939 NW 43rd Ave, Gainesville FL 32605.....904-378-0748
Carlton Cards, 8200 Carpenter Fwy, Dallas TX 75247 214-638-4800
Colortype, 1640 Market St, Corona CA 91720 714-734-7410
Comstock Cards, 1205 Industrial Way, Sparks NV 89431.....................702-359-9441
Create-A-Craft, PO Box 330008, Ft Worth TX 76163.....................817-292-1855
Crystal Group, 4375 Brainy Boro Sta, Metuchen NJ 08840.....................201-654-4400
Current Inc, PO Box 2559, Colorado Springs CO 80901.....................303-594-4100
Freedom Greeting Card Co, PO Box 715, Bristol PA 19007.....................215-945-3300
Gibson Greeting Cards, 2100 Section Rd, Cincinnati OH 45237 513-841-6600
Grand Slam Greetings, 35 York St, Brooklyn NY 11201 718-797-1204
Hallmark Cards, 2501 McGee PO Box 419580, Kansas City MO 64141 ...816-274-5111
Kalan Inc, 521 Walnut St, Darby PA 19023.....................215-586-7122
Kimball Miles Co, 41 W 8th St, Oshkosh WI 54901.....................414-231-3800
Leanin' Tree Publishing, PO Box 9500, Boulder CO 80301.....................303-530-1442
Loonart Designs, 423 West St PO Box 610, Suttons Bay MI 49682...........616-271-6828
Maine Line Co, PO Box 418, Rockport ME 04856.....................207-236-8536
New Bo-Tree, 1137 San Antonio Rd, Palo Alto CA 94303.....................415-967-1817
Oatmeal Studios, PO Box 138, Rochester VT 05767.....................802-767-3171
Paper Moon Graphics, 4060 Ince Blvd, Culver City CA 90232 213-202-4800

Paramount Cards, PO Box 1225, Pawtucket RI 02862.................................401-726-0800
Pegasus Greeting Card Co, 1611 Edith St, Berkeley CA 94703.................415-849-3535
Portal Publications, 707 Tamalpais Dr, Corte Madera CA 94925.............415-924-5652
Recycled Paper Products, 3636 N Broadway, Chicago IL 60613.................800-621-9894
Red Farm Studio, 334 Pleasant St PO Box 347, Pawtucket RI 02862........401-728-9300
Redleterkardz, PO Box 231015, Pleasant Hill CA 94523.............................415-792-1200
Renaissance Greeting Cards, PO Box 126, Springvale ME 04083.............207-324-4153
Rockshots, 632 Broadway, New York NY 10012...212-420-1400
Rousana Cards, 28 Sager Place, Hillside NJ 07205....................................201-373-1000
Royce Intl Corp, 6924 Canby Ave, Reseda CA 91335.................................818-342-8900
Rust Craft Greeting Cards, PO Box 351, Dedham MA 02026....................617-329-6000
Sagamon Co, Rt 48 W, Taylorville IL 62568..217-824-2264
Silver Visions, 301 Elliot St, Newton MA 02164..617-244-9504
Strings Attached, PO Box 132, Mill Valley CA 94942................................415-459-5300
Sunrise Publications, PO Box 2699, Bloomington IN 47402.....................812-336-9900
Vagabond Creations, 2560 Lance Dr, Dayton OH 45409...........................513-298-1124
Warner Press, PO Box 2499, Anderson IN 46018......................................317-644-7721
Carol Wilson Fine Arts, PO Box 17394, Portland OR 97217......................503-281-0780

ILLUSTRATORS & DESIGNERS

Abisch-Kaplan, 166 W Waukena Ave, Oceanside NY 11572......................516-764-9828
Ad Infinitum, 7 N MacQuesten Pkwy, Mt Vernon NY 10550....................914-664-7944
Ad Win Display Co, 9 E 19th St, New York NY 10003................................212-254-1118
Norman Clark Adams, 10 Hitzell Ter, Rutland VT 05701..........................802-775-4288
Dwight Edward Agner, 320 Snapfinger Dr, Athens GA 30605...................404-353-7719
AIMS Intl Marketing Svcs, 629 Market St, Troy OH 45373.......................513-339-2600
Rodelinde Albrecht, 250 Columbus Ste 203, San Francisco CA 94133.......415-362-5949
All In Graphic Arts, 10550 NW 77th Ct #303, Hialeah Gdns FL 33016....305-558-3454
Judy Allan, 301 E 69th St 6C, New York NY 10021...................................212-744-0076
Allen-Wayne Communications, 44 Cooper Sq, New York NY 10003.........212-674-2900
Amer Living, PO Box 901, Allston MA 02130...617-522-7782
Lee Ames & Zak Ltd, 6500 Jericho Tpke, Commack NY 11725.................516-499-2222
Anco/Boston, 441 Stuart St, Boston MA 02116...617-267-9700
Doug Anderson, 347 E 50th St, New York NY 10022..................................212-838-7242
Antler & Baldwin Design Group Inc, 7 E 47th St, New York NY 10017...212-751-2031
Michael J Artell, 2809 LaQuinta Dr, Plano TX 75023................................214-964-0901
The Artwerks Group, 6116 N Central Expy Ste 305, Dallas TX 75206.......214-361-7750
Mary Anne Asciutto, 99 Madison Ave 5th fl, New York NY 10016............212-679-8660
Ann Atene, 2341 S Woodstock St, Philadelphia PA 19145.........................215-468-1461
Autospec Inc, Box 1037, Pacific Grove CA 93950.......................................408-649-0890
Award Design, 520 5th Ave Suite 412, Fairbanks AK 99701......................907-456-8212
Paul Bacon Studios, 881 7th Ave Rm 1202, New York NY 10019..............212-247-4760
Carol Bancroft & Friends, 185 Goodhill Rd, Weston CT 06883................203-226-7674
Esther J Baran, Industrial Center Bldg Rm 278, Sausalito CA 94965........415-641-0113
Ray Barber, 295 Washington Ave, Brooklyn NY 11205.............................718-857-2941
Karin Batten, 240 W 98th St, New York NY 10025...................................212-222-1873
Joe Bauch Design, 920 Broadway, New York NY 10010.............................212-473-7637
Barbara Bedick, 382 3rd St Apt 4, Brooklyn NY 11215.............................718-499-2947
Suzanne Bennett & Assoc, 251 5th Ave, New York NY 10016....................212-686-6452
Betty Binns Graphics, 31 E 28th St, New York NY 10016..........................212-679-9200

Edgar & Barbara Blakeney Design, 61 Horatio, New York NY 10014......212-243-0109
The Book Department Inc, 648 Beacon St, Boston MA 02215.....................617-266-1116
Bookmakers Inc, 305 N Main St, Westport CT 06880....................................203-226-4293
The Bookmakers Inc, 298 E South St, Wilkes-Barre PA 18702...................717-823-9183
The Bookmill, 3610 N Moore St, Los Angeles CA 90066............................213-394-4069
The Bookworks Inc, PO Box 1189, Chicago IL 60690...................................312-236-8472
Bootstrap Economic Publ, 292 W Washington, Pasadena CA 91103.........818-797-5551
Clarice Borio, 72 University Place, New York NY 10003..............................212-777-7434
The Borja Studio, 5136 S Dorchester Ave, Chicago IL 60615....................312-493-0665
H Shaw Borst Inc, 149 Kisco Ave, Mount Kisco NY 10549.......................914-666-6366
Ray Boultinghouse Inc, 153 E 30th St, New York NY 10016......................212-679-7950
Brazos Graphics, 303 Anderson St, College Station TX 77840....................409-693-8784
Alice Brickner, 4720 Grosvenor Ave, Bronx NY 10471.............................212-549-5909
James F Brisson Book Design & Prod, Williamsville VT 05362..................802-348-7802
Pema Browne Ltd, 185 E 85th St, New York NY 10028...............................212-369-1925
Burmar Technical Corp, 175 IU Willets Rd, Albertson NY 11507.............516-484-6000
Michele Butchko, 430 Lafayette St, New York NY 10003............................212-260-6658
Cabat Studio, 627 N 4th Ave, Tucson AZ 85705...602-622-6362
Eric Carle, West Hill Rd, West Hawley MA 01339.......................................413-339-4066
Carlisle Graphics, Box 834, Dubuque IA 52001..319-557-1500
Carlson Graphic Services, 75 Priscilla Dr, Lincroft NJ 07738.....................201-530-1911
Cartoons By Johns, PO Box 1300, Pebble Beach CA 93953.........................408-649-0303
L R Caughman & Caughman, 1256 Harvard Ave, Claremont CA 91711..714-624-5246
Charthouse Maps, Box 214 Main St, Canaan NH 03741..............................603-523-4320
Chestnut House Group Inc, 540 N Lake Shore Dr, Chicago IL 60611.......312-222-9090
Cobb/Dunlop Publisher Services, 401 Broadway, New York NY 10013...212-226-3361
Columbia Publishing Co Inc, 234 E 25th St, Baltimore MD 21218............301-366-7070
Compuscript, 1210 Forest Ln, Mount Pleasant MI 48858............................517-773-5724
Connexions, 14011 Brookgreen Dr, Dallas TX 75240..................................214-234-4519
Robt Cooney Graphic Design, 11201 State Rt 1, Pt Reyes CA 94956.........415-663-8230
Cover to Cover Inc, 210 E 86th St Ste 501, New York NY 10028................212-734-1800
Todd Crawshaw, 345-D Folsom St, San Francisco CA 94105.....................415-777-3939
Create-A-Craft, PO Box 330008, Ft Worth TX 76163.................................817-292-1855
Creative Ad/Ventures Inc, 331 Madison Ave, New York NY 10017...........212-682-1280
Creative Group Inc, 22 Marsh Hill Rd, Orange CT 06477..........................203-795-0505
Creative Media Services, PO Box 5955, Berkeley CA 94705......................415-843-3408
Creative Services, Box 5162, Carmel CA 93921...408-624-7573
Curriculum Concepts Inc, 770 Broadway, New York NY 10003..................212-475-6500
Vincent Curulli, 1944 E 23rd St, Brooklyn NY 11229.................................718-998-9496
Alex D'Amato Graphic Designer, 32 Bayberry St, Bronxville NY 10708....914-779-6264
Janet P D'Amato Illustration, 32 Bayberry St, Bronxville NY 10708..........914-779-6264
Danmark & Michaels Inc, 378 S Oyster Bay Rd, Hicksville NY 11801......516-931-6500
Brigitte De Wever, 769 Union St Apt 3R, Brooklyn NY 11215....................718-638-2022
Joseph Del Gaudio Design Group, 215 W 98th St, New York NY 10025..212-222-7432
Joseph B Del Valle, 41 Union Sq W, New York NY 10003............................212-989-4120
Delgado Design Inc, 114 E 32nd St, New York NY 10016.............................212-685-5925
Dell Naatz Publication Arts, 106 Pinion Ln, Manitou Springs CO 80829..303-685-9719
The Design Element, 8624 Wonderland Av, Los Angeles CA 90046...........213-656-3293
The Design Source, 14 E 4th St, New York NY 10012...................................212-475-8080
Designworks Inc, 5 Bridge St, Watertown MA 02172..................................617-926-6286
Jennifer Dewey, 102 W San Francisco St Ste 16, Santa Fe NM 87501........505-988-2924
Diamond Art Studio Ltd, 11 E 36th St, New York NY 10016.......................212-355-5444
DMV/DRS Creative Services Inc, 301 York St, Jersey City NJ 07302.......201-435-3548

DockxDesign, 108 Fulton St, Boston MA 02109..617-367-5775
Don O Tech, 23811 Chagrin Blvd, Beachwood OH 44122............................216-765-8058
Donnelley Cartographic Services, 700 N Duke St, Lancaster PA 17602....717-393-9707
Lisa Vey Dubbert, 7359 Kerry Hill, Columbia MD 21045 301-381-2565
Adrianne Onderdonk Dudden, 829 Old Gulph, Bryn Mawr PA 19010......215-525-6584
Cecile Duray-Bito, 1040 Stearns Ave, Boulder CO 80303 303-499-6292
Audrey Dyer, Box 615, Homewood CA 95718..916-525-4561
Editcetera, 2490 Channing Way Rm 507, Berkeley CA 94704 415-849-1110
Editing Design & Production, 400 Market St 7th fl, Phila PA 19106 215-592-1133
Editorial & Graphic Services, Martinsville NJ 08836.................................201-469-2195
Educational Challenges Inc, 1009 Duke St, Alexandria VA 22314.............703-683-1500
Ehn Graphics Inc, 244 E 46th St, New York NY 10017...............................212-661-5947
Fritz Eichenberg, 142 Oakwood Dr, Peace Dale RI 02883 401-783-5638
Eldolon Press, 18 Narrow Rocks Rd, Westport CT 06880...........................203-227-8732
Elkin Assoc, 44 Burnett Place, Nutley NJ 07110...201-667-1317
Emerson Wajdowicz Studios Inc, 1123 Broadway, New York NY 10010..212-807-8144
Deborah England, 210 W 17th St, New York NY 10011 212-989-0253
Mel Erikson/Art Service, 31 Meadow Rd, Kings Park NY 11754 516-544-9191
Eugene M Ettenberg, 435B Heritage Village, Southbury CT 06488 203-264-7420
Joseph Feld, 44 Darling Ave, New Rochelle NY 10804.................................914-633-7642
Finegold Direct Marketing, 41 Union Sq W, New York NY 10003 212-620-3980
Wladislaw Finne, Mayberry Ln, Yarmouth ME 04096.................................207-846-3570
Quentin Fiore, Box 216 Reservoir Rd, Hopewell NJ 08525 609-466-2332
The Flack Studio, 288 Lexington St, Watertown MA 02172 617-926-5160
Henri Fluchere, 21 Oak St, Irvington NY 10533...914-591-9090
The Four Corners Press, 2056 College SE, Grand Rapids MI 49507.........616-243-2015
Mel Fowler, 463 West St G 224 Westbeth, New York NY 10014 212-691-9214
Stan Fraydas, 60 Locust Ave, New Rochelle NY 10801................................914-632-2444
Free Lance Exchange Inc, 111 E 85th St, New York NY 10028 212-722-5816
Irene Friedman, 225 W 12 St, New York NY 10011 212-243-4882
Froehlich Advertising Services, 8 Wanamaker Ave, Mahwah NJ 07430....201-529-1737
Leslie Stevenson Fry, 567 St Paul St Apt 5, Burlington VT 05401 802-862-4034
G&H/Soho Ltd, 39 W 14th St, New York NY 10011.....................................212-684-0850
Geary Consulting, 300 W Schuster Apt 22, El Paso TX 79902....................915-533-5777
Klaus Gemming Book Design, 49 Autumn St, New Haven CT 06511........203-562-0289
General Cartography, 321 S Riverside, Croton-on-Hudson NY 10520......914-271-6100
Arnold Genkins, 301 E 48th St Ste 14E, New York NY 10017....................212-758-4907
Helen Gentry, 1170 Camino Delora, Santa Fe NM 87501 505-982-0677
George Giusti Designer, 20 Chalburn Rd, West Redding CT 06896 203-938-3370
Howard T Glasser, 28 Forge Rd, Assonet MA 02702....................................617-644-5714
Ned Glattauer, 343 E 30th St, New York NY 10016.....................................212-686-6927
Linda Gluck Graphic Design, 81 N Ohioville Rd, New Paltz NY 12561....914-255-0381
Ragna Tischler Goddard, Box 306 RR 1, Higganum CT 06441.................203-345-4290
A Good Thing Inc, 230 Park Ave, New York NY 10017.................................212-687-8155
Bruce Gore, 1614 Woodlands St, Nashville TN 37206.................................615-298-3588
A Graphic Method Inc, 3285 Long Beach Rd, Oceanside NY 11572.........516-764-1144
Graphics Etcetera, 176 Federal St, Boston MA 02110 617-425-3107
The Graphics Place, 2038 Colorado Blvd, Los Angeles CA 90041 213-256-4605
The Graphix Group Inc, 209 S Water St, Champaign IL 61820 217-351-6262
Marian Gravelle, 81-05 35th Ave, Jackson Hts NY 11372 718-429-5039
Mina Greenstein, 605 E 82nd St, New York NY 10028.................................212-737-9203
Ann Grifalconi, 496 Hudson St, New York NY 10014...................................212-777-9042
Andrew J Grossman, 3912 Ingomar St NW, Washington DC 20015 202-686-0480

Philip Grushkin Inc, 86 E Linden Ave, Englewood NJ 07631.....................201-568-6686
Haan Graphic Publ Svcs, PO Box 1296, Middletown CT 06457.................203-344-9137
M Haas, Sander Rd, Jeffersonville NY 12748...914-482-4209
Robert Hagenhofer, 273A Wertsville Rd RD 1, Flemington NJ 08822......201-548-6000
Ernie Haim, 69 Walling Rd, Warwick NY 10990..914-258-4480
Harriett, 135 E 54th St, New York NY 10022...212-688-0094
Joseph Denis Harrington, 26268 Carmelo St, Carmel CA 93923..............408-624-0425
Harris Studio, 2310 E 101st Ave, Crown Point IN 46307............................219-769-4460
Marian Hartsough, 1533 Camino Verde, Walnut Creek CA 94596...........415-935-8238
HeBo Inc, 4741 Guerley Rd, Cincinnati OH 45238.....................................513-471-0825
Heidelberg Graphics, 1116 Wendy Way, Chico CA 95926...........................916-342-6582
Heritage Books, 1445 E 2nd St, Plainfield NJ 07062..................................201-753-4000
Hofmann Visual Communications, 337 E 81st St, New York NY 10028...212-535-3767
Horvath & Cuthbertson Illustrators, Box 1141, Rockland ME 04841.......207-594-4534
Raymond F Houlihan, 41 Union Sq W, New York NY 10003.....................212-929-5996
Hunter Graphics, Berrien Springs MI 49103..616-429-4087
Inkstone Books, Box 22172, Carmel CA 93950..408-375-3296
Interdisciplinary Design Team, 75 Toll Dr, Southampton PA 18966.........215-364-3218
Reggie Jackson, 135 Sheldon Ter, New Haven CT 06511............................203-787-5191
Anna F Jacobs, 23 Caplewood Dr, Tuscaloosa AL 35401............................205-758-2279
Louise E Jefferson, Buell Rd, Litchfield CT 06759.....................................203-567-8076
JL Design Assoc Inc, 134 W 26th St, New York NY 10001..........................212-206-6970
JMH Corp, 247 S Meridian Ste 300, Indianapolis IN 46225.......................317-639-2535
Justdesign, 160 5th Ave Ste 613, New York NY 10010................................212-620-4672
Walter Kern & Assoc, 386 Park Ave S, New York NY 10016.......................212-532-7711
Kirchoff Wohlberg, 866 United Nations Plz #525, New York NY 10017..212-644-2020
Kitchen Sink Art Studio, 2 Swamp Rd, Princeton WI 54968.......................414-295-6922
Kudelka Illustration & Design, 13616 43rd St, Phoenix AZ 85032..........602-996-3266
Lake End Graphics Ltd, 21 Prince St, New York NY 10012.........................212-226-7086
Bob Laurie Studios Inc, 386 Park Ave S Rm 201, New York NY 10016...212-972-1922
Wolfgang Lederer, 2 Sunset Ter, Kensington CA 94707..............................415-528-7893
Ledo Graphics, 666 Springfield Ave, Summit NJ 07901..............................201-273-8390
Lee Words/Graphics, 15 Maritta Ave, Lee MA 02138.................................413-243-1581
Jerry Leff Assoc Inc, 420 Lexington Ave, New York NY 10170...................212-697-8525
Leoleen-Durck Creations, 35 Lennon Cove, Jackson TN 38305...................901-668-1205
Abe Lerner, 101 W 12th St, New York NY 10011..212-243-2803
Karen Levy Calligraphy, 370 E 76th St, New York NY 10021.....................212-472-1669
Stan Levy, 2500 Walters Ct, Bellmore NY 11710...516-221-0856
Ted Lewin, 152 Willoughby Ave, Brooklyn NY 11205................................718-622-3882
Richard Lewis, 90 Dean St, Brooklyn NY 11201...718-852-8078
Libra Graphics Inc, 150 5th Ave Ste 400, New York NY 10011...................212-929-3170
Al Lichtenbert, 10 E 40th St, New York NY 10016......................................212-689-5400
Ligature Inc, 165 N Canal St, Chicago IL 60606..312-648-1233
Forbes Linkhorn, 201 E 21 St, New York NY 10010....................................212-473-3767
E Trina Lipton, 60 E 8th St Box 310, New York NY 10003..........................212-533-3148
LMD Service for Publishers, 315 W 23rd St, New York NY 10011.............212-691-6411
Joseph Low, RFD 278 Middle Rd, Chilmark MA 02535..............................617-645-2610
Jack Lucey, 84 Crestwood Dr, San Rafael CA 94901...................................415-453-3172
Tim J Luddy Conceptions, 366 W 23rd St 4W, New York NY 10011.........212-243-9254
Sheila Lynch, 365 W 20th St Apt 12A, New York NY 10011........................212-255-3222
Nancy Lou Makris Studio, 45 Seely Rd, Wilton CT 06897..........................203-762-5921
Marker II Studio, 270 Park Ave S Ste 8C, New York NY 10010.................212-982-1390
Barbara Marks Graphic Design, 15 Flying Pt, Stony Creek CT 06405......203-481-3361

Marsh Communications Inc, 149 Kisco Ave, Mount Kisco NY 10549 914-666-6366
R Masheris Assoc Inc, 1338 Hazel Ave, Deerfield IL 60015 312-945-2055
MassMarket Books, 872 Massachusetts Ave, Cambridge MA 02139.........617-864-2126
Michael McCurdy, RFD 2 Box 145, Great Barrington MA 01230..............413-528-2749
J W McDaniel Studio, 20 Brookside Dr, Greenwich CT 06830...................212-760-7811
Media Distribution Co-op, 1745 Louisiana St, Lawrence KS 66044...........913-842-3176
James Mennick, 238 Merrydale Rd, San Rafael CA 94903...........................415-472-3410
Robert Mentken Concept & Design, 51 E 97th St, New York NY 10029...212-534-5101
Arthur Meriwether Inc, 1529 Brook Dr, Downers Grove IL 60090.............312-495-0600
Merlin Communications Inc, 61 Kansas St, Hackensack NJ 07601............201-488-1712
Metier Industrial Inc, 315 Riverside Dr, New York NY 10025....................212-866-8488
Metrographics Ltd Inc, 242 W 38th St 11th fl, New York NY 10018...........212-840-7130
David Miller, 530 West End Ave, New York NY 10024...............................212-787-8304
Mirenburg & Co, 301 E 38th St, New York NY 10001.................................212-971-4006
Richard Moss, 151 W 16th St, New York NY 10011....................................212-691-2588
Andrew Mudryk Inc, 31 Oakwood Ave, Upper Montclair NJ 07043..........201-746-9683
Nancy Dale Muldoon, 29 High Ridge Rd, Brookfield Ctr CT 06805..........203-775-2816
The Murton Press, 26 Anderson Rd, Greenwich CT 06830.........................203-869-4434
Music Book Assoc Inc, 711 Amsterdam Ave, New York NY 10025...........212-222-1611
Bob & Faith Nance, 1811 Windsor Blvd, Homewood AL 35209 205-871-1613
Fran Gazze Nimeck, 358A RD 4, North Brunswick NJ 08902.....................201-821-8741
North Plains Books and Art, PO Box 1830, Aberdeen SD 57402...............605-226-3548
Nostradamus Advertising, 250 W 57th St 1128A, New York NY 10019....212-581-1362
Tom O'Sullivan, 202 Riverside Dr, New York NY 10025............................212-865-0229
John Okladek, 1226 16th St, Fort Lee NJ 07024...201-224-3309
Olivestone Publishing Services, 6 W 18th St, New York NY 10011 212-691-8420
Packrat Press, 4366 N Diana Ln, Oak Arbor WA 98277 206-675-6016
Perfectplot, 600 Central Ave Ste 333, Highland Park IL 60023 312-831-6633
Pictograph Corp, Box 856, New York NY 10056 212-260-1630
Herbert Pinzke Design Inc, 1935 N Kenmore, Chicago IL 60614...............312-528-2277
Berenice Chaplan Pliskin, 94 Woodcrest Ave, White Plains NY 10604.....914-761-8915
Port Studios Inc, 510 N Dearborn St, Chicago IL 60610............................312-787-0595
Precision Graphics, 119 W Washington, Champaign IL 61820 217-359-6655
Press In Tuscany Alley, 1 Tuscany Alley, San Francisco CA 94133............415-986-0641
Jane Preston, 750 Main St, Greenport NY 11944.......................................516-477-0729
Publications Illust & Pres, 149 W Merrick Rd, Freeport NY 11520..........516-546-6996
Publishers Graphics, 251 Greenwood Ave, Bethel CT 06801 203-797-8188
Publishing Resources Inc, Box 41307, San Juan PR 00940.........................809-724-0318
Publishing Synthesis Ltd, 425 Broome St, New York NY 10013.................212-219-0135
Purnell Co Inc, 20 East St, Boston MA 02111 617-482-6767
The Pushpin Group Inc, 67 Irving Place, New York NY 10003 212-674-8080
Arlene Putterman, 7865 Spring Ave, Elkins Park PA 19117 215-635-0169
The Quarasan Group Inc, 1845 Oak St Ste 7, Northfield IL 60093 312-446-4777
Repro Art Service, 102 Swinick Dr, Dunmore PA 18512.............................717-961-5410
Arthur Ritter Inc, 45 W 10th St, New York NY 10011 212-505-0241
Ron Logan, 52 Eastern Ave, Brentwood NY 11717 718-624-1488
Chris Roth, Box 967, Racine WI 53405...414-554-8668
Roxbury Publishing Co, PO Box 491044, Los Angeles CA 90049...............213-458-3493
Rudra Press, Box 1973, Cambridge MA 02238...617-576-3394
Thomas S Ruzicka Inc, 167 N Cedar Brook Rd, Boulder CO 80302 303-447-2740
The Savage Group, 142 E 16th St, New York NY 10003.............................212-260-0786
Jack Schecterson Assoc Inc, 6 E 39th St, New York NY 10016..................212-889-3950
Bernard Schleifer Co, 200 W 20th St, New York NY 10011 212-675-2615

Jacqueline Schuman, 838 West End Ave, New York NY 10025 212-865-3258
Robert Schwartz & Assoc, 34 E 30th St, New York NY 10016.................212-689-8482
Science Fantasy Assoc, 2495 Glendower Ave, Hollywood CA 90027 213-666-6326
Seablom Design Books, PO Box 2546, Seattle WA 98111......................206-285-2308
Art Seiden, 380 Howard Ave, Woodmere NY 11598.............................516-295-0285
SI International, 43 E 19th St, New York NY 10003 212-254-4996
Sirius House, 473 20th Ave, San Francisco CA 94121 415-668-0925
Sisson Foss & Co, Box 282 Rte 2, Charlottesville VA 22901.................804-823-4610
Lynne Skreczko, 225 Sterling Place, Brooklyn NY 11238.....................718-638-7889
Edward Smith Design Inc, 114 E 32nd St, New York NY 10016 212-686-5818
Gary Smith Design, Box 2621, Manassas VA 22110 703-368-2489
Society of Illustrators, 128 E 63rd St, New York NY 10021.................212-838-2560
Kelly Solis-Navarro, 1051 Santa Cruz Ave, Menlo Park CA 94025 415-322-6937
Spec Graph Corp, 637 Manchester Rd, Norristown PA 19403..................215-539-4530
Special Press, Box 2524, Columbus OH 43216...............................614-297-1281
J J Spector & Assoc, 4250 Galt Ocean Dr, Ft Lauderdale FL 33308..........305-563-4093
Spectragraphics, 1515 John St, Fort Lee NJ 07024.........................201-592-1829
Star Valley Publications, Box 421, Noti OR 97461.........................503-935-2974
Charlotte Staub, 9 E 13th St, New York NY 10003..........................212-255-8173
Douglas Steel, 565 West End Ave, New York NY 10024 212-580-0219
Mark Stein Studios, 83-15 116th St Apt 1F, Jamiaca NY 11418...............718-441-3439
Ruth H Steinberger, Box 132 Rt 1, Check VA 24072.........................703-651-8429
Kiel Stuart, 12 Skylark Ln, Stony Brook NY 11790.........................516-751-7080
Taly Design Group, 430 Oak Grove Ste 408, Minneapolis MN 55403........612-338-2260
Jean Tamburine, 73 Reynolds Dr, Meriden CT 06450 203-235-1800
Tenth Avenue Editions, 885 10th Ave, New York NY 10019 212-307-6780
Thirteen Colonies Press, 710 S Henry St, Williamsburg VA 23185...........804-229-1775
Stan Tusan, 3418 Perada Dr, Walnut Creek CA 94598........................415-937-9424
Muriel Underwood, 173 W Madison St Ste 1011, Chicago IL 60602...........312-236-8472
Unique Graphics, 1025 55th St, Oakland CA 94608..........................415-655-3024
Vantage Art Inc, 875 Broadway, Massapequa NY 11758.......................516-799-0100
Steven Vegh Jr, 1191 Clay Ave, Bronx NY 10456 212-588-1690
Joseph Vesely Production Svcs, 84A Lower Rd, Deerfield MA 01342 413-772-0002
Visual Services, 99 Dalmeny Rd, Briarcliff Manor NY 10510................914-941-5225
Alice Wadowski-Bak, 482 23rd St, Niagara Falls NY 14303 716-285-9774
Walking Bird Publication Services, PO Box 19499, Seattle WA 98109 206-285-9774
Walnut Grove Assoc, 1601 Sheridan Ln, Nossistown PA 19403 215-539-3010
Warner-Cotter Co, 49 Water St, San Francisco CA 94113....................415-441-4011
Aldren A Watson, Box 128, North Hartland VT 05052........................802-295-5339
Werner Graphics, 101 W 85th St Ste 4-4, New York NY 10024................212-724-2941
Frank O Williams, 1426 W Rascher, Chicago IL 60640 312-728-7426
Adrian Wilson, 1 Tuscany Alley, San Francisco CA 94133 415-986-0641
Ursula Wolf-Rottkay, Box 1025, Camarillo CA 93011........................805-484-7533
Jeanyee Wong, 131 E 19th St, New York NY 10003...........................212-674-3121
Lili Cassel Wronker, 144-44 Village Rd, Jamaica NY 11435.................718-380-3990
York Production Services, 3600 W Market St, York PA 17404................717-792-3551
Franco Zavani, 246 W 11th St, New York NY 10014..........................212-255-5234

INDEXERS

AA's & PE's, 428 Lafayette St, New York NY 10003 212-228-8707
About Books Inc, PO Box 538, Saguache CO 81149 303-589-8223
Rose A Adkins, 741B Robinson Rd, Topanga CA 90290 213-455-3823
AEIOU Inc, 74 Memorial Plaza, Pleasantville NY 10570 914-769-1135
Victoria Agee, 1701 Overlook Dr, Silver Spring MD 20903 301-434-7073
Alternative Research, PO Box 432, New York NY 10015 212-683-3478
Wm T Amatruda, 9506 St Andrews Way, Silver Spring MD 20901 301-585-3570
Amer Soc of Indexers (ASI), 1700 18th St NW, Washington DC 20009 203-323-2826
Joyce L Ananian, 204 Church St, Waltham MA 02154 617-894-4330
Mary Jane Anderson, 1737 Colonial Ln, Northfield IL 60093 312-441-5673
Cheryl B Archer, 52A Robbins Ave, Newington CT 06111 203-566-7532
Sheila M Ary, 526 Russell Rd, DeKalb IL 60115 815-758-1985
Associated Editors, 49 Hazelwood Ln, Stamford CT 06905 203-322-3836
Astor Indexers, 170 E 83rd St, New York NY 10028 212-734-0714
Robin Mayper Balaban, 6134 Woodman #205, Van Nuys CA 91401 213-277-9012
Baran Tech Writing, 641 27th St, San Francisco CA 94131 415-641-0113
Jean E Barton, 4632 SW Elevation Ln, Topeka KS 66604 913-478-9045
Priscilla Battis, RFD 4 Box 3550, Skowhegan ME 04976 207-643-2643
David Batty CDB Entprises, 11608 Gilsan St, Silver Spring MD 20902 301-593-8901
Beaver Wood Enterprises, 11585 Links Dr, Reston VA 22090 703-437-4527
Linda Berman, 2037 Oliver Way, Merrick NY 11566 516-546-2663
Rose M Bernal, 510 E 20th St Apt 5C, New York NY 10009 212-702-3570
Julia J Bewsey, 176 Sunset Rd, Lake Ozark MO 65049 314-365-3541
Barbara M Beyda, Box 222763, Carmel CA 93922 408-624-6636
Susan N Bjorner, 10 Cannongate, Tyngsborough MA 01879 617-649-9746
Gilbert J Black, 399 West St, Harrison NY 10528 914-835-3160
Jolene M Blozis, 1600 M St NW Natl Geographic, Wash DC 20036 202-857-7056
Blue Pencil Group, PO Box 3392, Reston VA 22090 202-471-1998
Hazel Blumberg-McKee, 136 S Oxford, St Paul MN 55105 612-292-1680
The Book Studio Inc, 3 Louis Ln, Croton on Hudson NY 10520 914-739-9228
The Bookmill, 234 12th St, Santa Monica CA 90402 213-393-3843
The Bookworks Inc, PO Box 1189, Chicago IL 60690 312-236-8472
Bookwright, PO Box 7119, Ann Arbor MI 48107 313-995-1470
Becky Brass, 18830 5th Ave N, Plymouth MN 55447 612-340-2997
Mary M Brintle, 150-17 12th Rd, Whitestone NY 11357 718-767-7240
Agnes Brite, 242 Beacon St Apt 10, Boston MA 02116 617-267-0369
Catherine M Brosky, 4614 5th Ave Apt 813, Pittsburgh PA 15213 412-682-0837
Norman Brown & Assoc, 21 Luzon Ave, Providence RI 02906 401-751-2641
Sue Brown, 1601 Shady Grove, Bossier City LA 71112 318-746-9593
Gordon Brumm, 2 Inman St, Cambridge MA 02139 617-547-5673
Barbara L Bryan, Box 73, Kelly WY 83011 307-733-4189
Jo Burke, 710 A St SE, Washington DC 20003 202-623-7044
Burnham-Kidwell Indexer, 3661 Abrigo Rd, Kingman AZ 86401 602-565-3796
Nancy S Cannon, HC 87 Box 313A, Delhi NY 13753 607-746-6037
Richard Carlin, 25 Oleander Ct, Lawrenceville NJ 08648 609-896-4465
Carlisle Graphics, 2530 Kerper Blvd, Dubuque IA 52001 319-557-1500
Charles Carmony, 250 W 105th St Apt 2A, New York NY 10025 212-749-1835
Carnes Publication Svcs, 23811 Chagrin Blvd, Beachwood OH 44122 216-292-7959

Anne Carson Assoc, 3323 Nebraska Ave, Washington DC 20016...............202-244-6679
Rose M Caruso, 306 Carr Ave, Rockville MD 20850.....................................301-424-8133
Ann Cassar, Brinton Lake Rd RD 5, West Chester PA 19382....................215-459-2380
Chestnut House Group Inc, 540 N Lake Shore Dr, Chicago IL 60611.......312-222-9090
Charles Choset, 90 Bedford St, New York NY 10014....................................212-243-0035
Wendy Lee Chow, 856 Humewick Way, Sunnyvale CA 94087.....................408-736-7310
E R Cole, PO Box 91277, Cleveland OH 44101..216-234-1775
Joan Callahan Compton, Box 246, Kula Maui HI 96731 714-842-6977
Connecticut Periodical Index, PO Box 4050, Stamford CT 06907 203-323-2826
Connexions, 14011 Brookgreen Dr, Dallas TX 75240..................................214-234-4519
Maria Coughlin, 31 Maryland Ave, Annapolis MD 21401...........................301-269-0978
Dr Carol Cubberley, PO Box 1207, Oviedo FL 32765..................................305-365-9556
Nancy L Daniels, Box 68, Lemont PA 16851..814-237-7711
John G Deaton, PO Box 26559, Austin TX 78755..512-345-1465
Charles Decker, 45-35 44th St, Long Island City NY 11104 718-786-0897
Joseph R DeMarco, 496 N 19th St, Philadelphia PA 19130.........................215-567-5028
Louise A DeVillier, 6305 Pickens, Houston TX 77007 713-862-2952
Amy L Dibartolo, 128 Killewald Ave, Tonawanda NY 14150 716-695-2936
Maria Virginia Dooley, PO Box 161, East Marion NY 11939......................516-477-2420
Marion H & Wm S Downey, 130 Constitution Blvd, Whiting NJ 08759 201-350-5376
A H Drummond Jr, 323 Springs Rd, Bedford MA 01730..............................617-275-1481
Norman Duren Jr, 618 Clara Barton Dr Ste 5, Garland TX 75042 214-494-0086
Valerie Eads Et Al, PO Box 1459, New York NY 10016 212-228-0900
Easy Writer, 1400 63rd St, Des Moines IA 50311..515-279-3491
Editcetera, 2490 Channing Way Rm 507, Berkeley CA 94704....................415-849-1110
Editing & Publishing Services, Pleasant Point Rd, Cushing ME 04563.....207-354-2467
Editing Design & Production Inc, 400 Market St 7th fl, Phila PA 19106...215-592-1133
Editing Unlimited, 196 Wykagyl Terr, New Rochelle NY 10804................914-636-2637
The Editor's Bureau Ltd, Box 68, Westport CT 06881 203-227-9275
Editorial & Graphic Services, Martinsville NJ 08836..................................201-469-2195
Editorial Consultants Inc, 1605 12th Ave Ste #7, Seattle WA 98122........206-323-6475
Editorial Consultants Inc, 3221 Pierce St, San Francisco CA 94123..........415-931-7239
Editorial Consultation Services, 2427 29th St, Lubbock TX 79411 806-793-0881
Editorial Excelsior Corp, 15 N Market St, San Jose CA 95113...................408-293-3734
Editorial Experts Inc, 85 S Bragg St Ste 400, Alexandria VA 22312 703-642-3040
Editorial Inc, Box 267, Rockport MA 01966...617-546-7346
Educational Challenges Inc, 1009 Duke St, Alexandria VA 22314.............703-683-1500
Educational Media Co, 6021 Wish Ave, Encino CA 91316...........................818-708-0962
Effective Learning, 7 N MacQuesten Pkwy, Mt Vernon NY 10550 914-664-7944
Roger E Egan, 7 Lincoln Pl, New Brunswick NJ 08902 201-821-0106
Elisabetha S Eliason, 30 Mayne Ave, Stanhope NJ 07874 201-347-8215
Joyce W Ellis, 89 W Lakeview Ave, Columbus OH 43202 614-263-7946
Irene Elmer, 2806 Cherry, Berkeley CA 94705 415-841-0466
Ruth Elwell & Donald Smith, 87 E 2nd St, New York NY 10003...............212-260-6148
Henry W Engel, 441 E 20th St, New York NY 10010.....................................212-477-2597
Roberta Engleman, 3232 Brandywine Rd, Chapel Hill NC 27514...............919-967-3047
Sylvia Stark Farrington, 50 E 89th St, New York NY 10128........................212-860-3242
Dr Hilda Feinberg, 1812 Wellbourne Dr NE, Atlanta GA 30324 404-875-0077
Janice J Feldstein Editorial Svcs, 860 N Lake Shore, Chicago IL 60611...312-951-6215
Heidi Finkbeiner, 9500 Dunbrook Ct, Gaithersburg MD 20879 301-330-8285
Gerri Flanzraich, 34 Daley St, New Hyde Park NY 11040 516-741-2831
Catherine Fox, RR1 Box 237, Spencer IN 47460 812-829-3297
Theodore P Francis, 1490 Sacramento St, San Francisco CA 94109 415-673-1388

Sandi Frank, 95 Furnace Dock Rd, Croton on Hudson NY 10520.............914-271-6293
Free Lance Exchange Inc, 111 E 85th St, New York NY 10028 212-722-5816
Norma R Fryatt, 227 Granite St, Rockport MA 01966...............................617-546-6490
Gabriel House Inc, 5045 W Oakton St, Skokie IL 60077...........................312-675-1146
Kathleen J Garcia, 165 Woodlane, Newark NY 14513 315-331-4070
Gazelle Publications, 5580 Stanley Dr, Auburn CA 95603.......................916-878-1223
Audrey C Gilmour, 9 Mt Pleasant Rd, Morristown NJ 07960 201-895-3047
Martha & Dennis Gleason, Box 540, Boothbay Harbor ME 04538...........207-633-2336
Goins Indexing Services, 17 Lexington Green, S Burlington VT 05403.....802-658-0103
David B Gracy II, 2313 Tower Dr, Austin TX 78703 512-474-2784
Gravity Publishing, 6324 Heather Ridge Way, Oakland CA 94611...........415-339-3774
Genevieve S Gray, 8932 E Calle Norlo, Tucson AZ 85710........................602-886-7829
Tony Greenberg, 3633 Malibu Vista Dr, Malibu CA 90265 213-454-3386
Linda M Gregonis, 3426 E Glenn #7, Tucson AZ 85716...........................602-323-9338
Grinstead/Feik Indexers, 1623-29 3rd Ave, New York NY 10128.............212-369-3480
Susan J Grodsky, 622 Andamar Way, Goleta CA 93117...........................805-967-7735
Nancy A Guenther, 543 Spring Oak Dr, West Chester PA 19382 215-436-4049
Michael Haldeman, 1014 Adams Cir, Boulder CO 80306..........................303-442-2518
Robin M Haller, 7860 S Hudson St, Littleton CO 80122...........................303-220-1031
Daniel J Harrison, 336 Costa Mesa Dr, Toms River NJ 08757...................201-341-8996
Heritage Books, 1445 E 2nd St, Plainfield NJ 07062 201-753-4000
Herr's Indexing Service, Star Rt, Washington VT 05675...........................802-883-2272
Mary L Hey, 1919 Grove St, Boulder CO 80302.....................................303-442-3638
Daniel W Hill, 3023 Honeysuckle Way N E, Salem OR 97303 503-364-9210
Diane Hodges, 220 E 87th St, New York NY 10128..................................212-722-0856
Rhonda J Holland, 3313 Alabama Ave, Alexandria VA 22305 804-683-3753
Ruth H Hoover, 20421 Lorne St, Canoga Park CA 91306.........................818-341-7551
Jeanne Howe, Box 1137, Cullowhee NC 28723.......................................704-293-5842
Nancy Humphreys, 2415 12th Ave, Oakland CA 94606............................415-642-4786
Janet M Hunter, 411 Rose Ave, Mill Valley CA 94941 415-388-8788
Information on Demand Inc, PO Box 9550, Berkeley CA 94709 415-644-4500
Inforonics Inc, 550 Newtown Rd, Littleton MA 01460..............................617-486-8976
Thomas Jackrell, 12 Campbell Ave, Belleville NJ 07109...........................201-759-5318
Harold R Jenkins & Assoc, 5700 Wyandotte St, Kansas City MO 64113...816-444-2590
Curt Johnson, 3093 Dato, Highland Park IL 60035...................................312-432-6804
Camille Joslyn, 1763 Wainwright Dr, Reston VA 22090 703-471-1641
Joan Kain, 235 W 102nd St Apt 16E, New York NY 10025........................212-850-0768
Marie Kascus, 207 Ridgewood Rd, W Hartford CT 06107.........................203-521-8417
Julie Kawabata, 927 SE Clatsop St, Portland OR 97202...........................503-231-8029
Carol R Kelm, 432 N Elmwood Ave, Oak Park IL 60302...........................312-386-8752
Thomas Kemp, PO Box 4050, Stamford CT 06907...................................203-323-2826
Carol Kennedy, 3336 Aldrich Ave S, Minneapolis MN 55408 612-823-2784
Frances Kianka, 2352 Generation Dr, Reston VA 22091 703-860-5115
Mary L Kirk, 4813-10 Atlantis Ct, Wilmington NC 28403 919-392-2419
Jessie Kitching, 72-61 113th St, Forest Hills NY 11375...........................718-544-3279
W Scott Knoke, 178 N Bridge St, Somerville NJ 08876.............................201-526-4682
Bill Koehnlein, 236 E 5th St, New York NY 10003 212-674-9145
James Kohl, 1317 Dorsh Rd, Cleveland OH 44121...................................216-381-3255
Deborah Kopka, 3208 S Barrington Ste G, Los Angeles CA 90066............213-391-4300
KPL & Assoc, 1090 Generals Hwy, Crownsville MD 21032......................301-923-6611
Ellie Kurtz, PO Box 610173, North Miami FL 33261................................305-891-3960
L/A House Editorial, 5822 Uplander Way, Culver City CA 90230............213-216-5812
Burton Lasky Assoc Inc, 111 8th Ave Ste 1507, New York NY 10011 212-989-4783

Lazy Brown Assoc, 2800 Quebec St NW Ste 618, Wash DC 20008..............202-686-0975
Anne Leach, 140 Stuyvesant Dr, San Anselmo CA 94960........................415-485-5571
Cindy Lieberman, 18436 Lemarsh St #37, Northridge CA 91325................818-885-6171
Ligature Inc, 165 N Canal St, Chicago IL 60606.................................312-648-1233
Elinor Lindheimer Indexing Services, 558 N State St, Ukiah CA 95482 ...707-468-0464
Elliot Linzer, 36-40 Bowne St Apt 3J, Flushing NY 11354......................718-353-1261
Carolee Lipsey, 370-C Park Ave, Highland Park IL 60035......................312-433-8844
Eli & Gail Liss, 800 Yerry Hill Rd RR2 Box 800, Woodstock NY 12498..914-679-7173
Barbara S Littlewood, 5102 Manor Cross, Madison WI 53711 608-238-0929
Wm O Lively, 410 Schley Rd, Annapolis MD 21401...............................301-268-0530
Lockwood Indexers, 8 W 13th St, New York NY 10011 212-924-4604
Auralie Phillips Logan, 232 Watch Hill Rd, Peekskill NY 10566............914-739-3469
Susan Lohmeyer, 712 Cedarcroft Rd, Baltimore MD 21212 301-435-5196
Lombardi Indexing & Info Svcs, 2900 Sandy Ln, Santa Cruz CA 95062....408-476-1131
Ruthanne Lowe, Box 193, Pacific Grove CA 93950 408-649-4309
Marsha Luevane, PO Box 36326, Denver CO 80236...............................303-989-1036
F J Lumpkin, 9554 Loyston Rd, Knoxville TN 37928............................615-992-3051
William Lurie, 1005 145 Place S E, Bellevue WA 98007 206-747-2022
Dick Luxner, 145-B Park Ave, Park Ridge NJ 07656 201-391-5935
Paul Machlis, Bancroft Library UC Berkeley, Berkeley CA 94720............415-642-3781
Hugh C Maddocks, 10807 Oldfield Dr, Reston VA 22091........................703-476-4860
Kristina Masiulis, 282 Boyd Ave, Elmhurst IL 60126............................312-833-2163
Hugh & Kate Mason, RD 3 Box 261 Williams Rd, Addison NY 14801.....607-458-5584
Adrienne Mayor Editorial Svcs, 1432 S 3rd Ave, Bozeman MT 59715......406-586-8476
Janet Mazefsky, 234 E 88th St Apt A, New York NY 10128 212-427-7375
Lisa McGaw, 15 Willow Terrace Apts, Chapel Hill NC 27514 919-929-7322
Judith H McQuown & Co, 127 E 59th St #201, New York NY 10022.......212-688-1291
MDZ Communications, 1136 E Stuart #220, Ft Collins CO 80525............303-493-5532
Robert J Milch, 9 Millbrook Dr, Stony Brook NY 11790.........................516-689-8546
Rhea Milhalisin, 600 Honey Run Rd, Ambler PA 19002.........................215-646-3814
Suzanna Moody, 5942 Dellwood Ave, Shoreview MN 55126....................612-481-7275
Mount Ida Press, Box 87, Troy NY 12181...518-272-4597
MSS Manuscript Services, 408 S High St, Galena IL 61036 815-777-0831
Mary Mueller, 108 Forest Rd, Moorestown NJ 08057............................609-778-4769
Nancy Mulvany, 265 Arlington Ave, Kensington CA 94707......................415-524-4195
Nancy Myers, 905 Prairie Park Dr, Beresford SD 57004.........................605-763-5364
Jo-Anne Naples, 719 S 3rd St, Dekalb IL 60115...................................815-758-4295
Natl Evaluation Systems, 30 Gatehouse Rd, Amherst MA 01004..............413-256-0444
Mary G Neumann, 2312 S Rogers 2E, Bloomington IN 47401................312-333-6189
Lois Newman Lit Svcs, 6545 Hollywood Blvd, Hollywood CA 90028.........213-464-8382
Nancy Noda, 2182 27th Ave, San Francisco CA 94116...........................415-661-7027
Northwind Editorial Services, 7962 Cole Rd, Colden NY 14033................716-941-5777
Lynn Nutwell, 1771 Greensward Quay, Virgina Beach VA 23454..............804-496-7439
Mary O'Leary, 2701 Grand Ave S, Minneapolis MN 55408.....................612-872-4399
Robert J Palmer, 601 E 11th St, New York NY 10009.............................212-505-6127
Karen L Pangallo, 27 Buffum St, Salem MA 01970................................617-744-8796
Kathleen J Patterson, 34 Maple Ave, Hastings-Hudson NY 10706............914-478-0881
Carol Penne, 10625 Greenacres Dr, Silver Spring MD 20903...................301-434-7415
Perry Roe & Assoc, 111 Acorn St, Millis MA 02154 617-376-8459
Dr Eloise S Pettus, 203 N Wilmot Rd Apt 208, Tucson AZ 85711 602-790-7056
James P Pilarski, 2734 W Leland #3, Chicago IL 60625 312-769-2714
Wm Pitt, PO Box 356, Riverdale MD 20737 301-454-6003
David Pofelski, 10941 Ave D, Chicago IL 60617...................................312-768-9228

Alex V Popovkin, 85 E 10th St Apt O, New York NY 10003.......................212-777-0340
Edythe C Porpa, 2637 Valmont Rd #37, Boulder CO 80302....................303-442-2847
Paula Presley, Thos Jefferson Univ LB 115, Kirksville MO 63501 816-785-4525
Primary Sources, 124 E 79th St, New York NY 10021 212-472-0419
Professional Editing & Typing, 410 E 20th St 3A, New York NY 10009...212-477-0615
Professional Editorial Svcs, 5531 Bubbling Wells, Ravenna OH 44266 216-682-5362
Professional Indexing, 405 E 3rd St Ste 393, Long Beach CA 90802........213-435-3492
Proofmark Editorial Service, 306 Busse Hwy, Park Ridge IL 60068..........312-696-1109
Generosa Gina Protano, 16 N Chatsworth #104, Larchmont NY 10538...914-834-8896
Publishers Editorial Services, 23 McQueen St, Katonah NY 10536 914-232-7816
Publishing Resources Inc, Box 41307, San Juan PR 00940 809-724-0318
Quinn's Record Mgmt Service, 614 Pershing Dr, Silver Spg MD 20910 301-589-4461
Mary H Raitt, 3024 Tilden St NW, Washington DC 20008.......................202-966-1154
Research Findings in Print, 26 W Jefferson Rd, Pittsford NY 14534 716-248-3947
Wm J Richardson Assoc, 152 W Hoffman Ave, Lindenhurst NY 11757 ...516-957-3440
Riofrancos & Co Indexes, 236 W 27th St Ste 704, New York NY 10001....212-929-8249
Linda E Rogers, 1350 County Road 83, Boulder CO 80302.......................303-444-8150
Peter & Erica Rooney, 65 Morton St Apt 5-I, New York NY 10014............212-675-0904
Barbara J Roos, 2041 Pierce St Apt 1, San Francisco CA 94115 415-567-0460
Shirley Roth, 551 Firlock #3, Sunnyvale CA 94086.................................408-773-8469
Carol Z Rothkopf, 16 Rotary Ln, Summit NJ 07901................................201-273-1255
Marilyn J Rowland, 40 Upland Rd, Duxbury MA 02331 617-934-6756
Martin Russell, 61 Kincaid Dr, Yonkers NY 10710.................................914-793-5296
Santa Barbara Software, 1400 Dover Rd, Santa Barbara CA 93103.........805-963-4886
Schroeder Editorial Svcs, 2606 Old Mill, Rolling Meadows IL 60008.......312-303-0989
David H Scott, Box 141, Blue Hill ME 04614...207-374-9933
Edward J Serdziak, PO Box 856, Jamul CA 92035..................................619-468-3874
Service to Publishers Inc, Box 591, Lewisburg PA 17837 717-524-4315
Sarah Shaftman, 2433 Superior St, Madison WI 53704...........................608-241-7153
Doris P Shalley, Genl Sullivan Box 166, Wash Crossing PA 18977...........215-493-3521
Sherwin Assoc, 2616 N Dayton, Chicago IL 60614 312-935-1581
Monica Shoffman-Graves, 101600 Overseas Hwy, Key Largo FL 33037...305-451-1462
Benita Sirkin, 10 Park Ave 16R, New York NY 10016.............................212-683-8580
Smith Editorial Services, PO Box 15153, Dallas TX 75201 214-296-5187
Nancy Snyder-Weinstock, 427 16th St, Brooklyn NY 11215....................718-768-4593
Sourcenet, PO Box 6767, Santa Barbara CA 93160................................805-964-6066
Special Press, PO Box 2524, Columbus OH 43216.................................614-297-1281
SSR Incorporated, 116 4th St SE, Washington DC 20003.........................202-543-1800
Noreen Stackpole, 3 Ellen Ct, Centereach NY 11720..............................516-981-6634
Julia Stair, Box 123, Kingston MA 02364..617-585-2686
Sylvia M Stark, 50 E 89 St, New York NY 10128....................................212-860-3242
Sheila Steinberg, 42 Littlebrook Rd, Springfield NJ 07081 201-273-9388
Betty Steinfeld, 5 Woodridge Ln, Westford MA 01886............................617-692-8569
Ruth Steyn, Box 222 Star Rt, Hancock ME 04640..................................207-422-3373
Paul Stimler, 1546 Dolores St, San Francisco CA 94104.........................415-285-6279
Kenneth W Summers, 2748 W Cattail Pl, Tucson AZ 85745.....................602-743-9583
Loren Sumner, PO Box 1309, Biddeford ME 04005 207-283-9684
Elaine Svenonius, 5380 Village Green, Los Angeles CA 90016 213-299-2523
Elizabeth Peirce Swift, Pleasant Point Rd, Cushing ME 04563................207-354-2467
Elaine F Tankard, 3003 Cherry Ln, Austin TX 78703 512-472-5837
Helene Taylor, 149 Crescent St, Northampton MA 01060.........................413-584-2647
Bettie Jane Third, 2077 Center Ave Apt 11B, Ft Lee NJ 07024 201-461-6511
Dorothy Thomas, 123 W 74th St, New York NY 10023.............................212-799-0970

Douglas L Thompson, 12009 Glen Mill Rd, Potomac MD 20854................301-251-1179
Gary B Thompson, 106 Hamilton St, Geneva NY 14456..............................315-789-2792
Mary F Tomaselli, 146-05 14th Ave, Whitestone NY 11357 718-767-3541
Charles H Troutman, Ofc of Atty General, Agana GU 96910....................671-472-6841
Turner & Winston, 5306 38 St NW, Washington DC 20015 202-363-6459
Twin Oaks Indexing Collective, Rt 4 Box 169, Louisa VA 23093................703-894-5126
Walking Bird Publication Services, PO Box 19499, Seattle WA 98109 206-285-1575
A Cynthia Weber Inquiry Inc, 195 Sunny Hill, Northampton PA 18067....215-837-9615
Judith Weedman, UC School of Library & Info, Berkeley CA 94720........415-642-6775
Weidner Assoc Inc, Box C-50, Cinnaminson NJ 08077..............................609-486-1755
Bella Hass Weinberg, 1441 Pelham Pkwy N, Bronx NY 10469................212-547-5159
Alexandra L Weir Indexing, 640 Allenby 204B, Pittsburgh PA 15218........412-247-0207
Hans H Wellisch, 5015 Berwyn Rd, College Park MD 20740....................301-345-3477
Sylvia Welygan, 4194 Salem Dr, Woodbury MN 55125 612-459-0764
Western Reserve Publ Services, 1640 Franklin Ave, Kent OH 44240.........216-673-2577
Thomas J Whitby, 6983 S Washington St, Littleton CO 80122....................303-798-7049
Patrice S White, 606 N Chester Rd, Swarthmore PA 19081 215-328-9829
Eleanor B Widdoes, 417 W 120 St, New York NY 10027..........................212-686-1100
Laurie R Winship, 729 Crawford Ave, Syracuse NY 13224 315-446-4975
Wayne Witt, PO Box 1039 Inst of Paper Chem, Appleton WI 54912.........414-738-3269
The Wordsmith, 106 Mason Rd, Durham NC 27712................................919-477-8430
Wordsworth Assoc, 9 Tappan Rd, Wellesley MA 02181 617-237-4761
Writers Alliance Ltd, 104 E 40th St, New York NY 10016 212-986-2830
Writers: Free-Lance Inc, 12 Cavalier Dr, Ambler PA 19002.......................215-646-7550
The Writing Service, 6306 Pepper Hill Dr, West Bloomfield MI 48033.....313-851-7377
Barbara Wurf/Indexpert Svcs, 3122 Cardiff, Los Angeles CA 90034........213-837-1654
York Production Services, 3600 W Market St, York PA 17404...................717-792-3551
Robert Zolnerzak, 167 Hicks St, Brooklyn Hts NY 11201...........................718-522-0591

LEGAL SERVICES

This section lists organizations that can offer legal assistance or referrals for writers and other artists, including the Volunteer Lawyers for the Arts (VLA) program and related agencies.

Albany League of Arts VLA Program, 19 Clinton, Albany NY 12207 518-449-5380
Amer Bar Assn, 750 N Lake Shore Dr, Chicago IL 60611 312-988-5000
Amer Civil Liberties Union, 142 W 43rd St, New York 10032.....................212-944-9800
The Artists Foundation, 110 Broad St, Boston MA 02169............................617-482-8100
Arts Council Buffalo & Erie County, 700 Main St, Buffalo NY 14202.......716-856-7520
Austin Lawyers for the Arts, PO Box 2577, Austin TX 78768 512-476-7573
Broward Arts Council, 100 S Andrews Ave, Ft Lauderdale FL 33301 305-357-7457
Business Volunteers for the Arts, 1601 Biscayne Blvd, Miami FL 33132...305-350-7700
Calif Lawyers for the Arts, Ft Mason Ctr, San Francisco CA 94123..........415-775-7200
Cedar Rapids-Marion Arts Council, 424 1st Ave, Cedar Rpds IA 52407..319-398-5322
Cincinnati Lawyers for the Arts, Univ of Cin, Cincinnati OH 45221 513-475-4383
Cleveland Bar Assn VLA Prog, 118 St Clair Ave, Cleveland OH 44114 216-696-3525
Colorado Lawyers for the Arts, PO Box 300428, Denver CO 80203 303-830-0379
Community Arts Council, 609 W Main St, Louisville KY 40202.................502-582-1821
Connecticut Comm on the Arts, 190 Trumbull St, Hartford CT 06103......203-566-4770
Copyright Information Svcs, PO Box 1460, Friday Harbor WA 98250 206-378-5128

Duchess County Arts Council, 39 Market St, Poughkeepsie NY 12601.....914-454-3222
Georgia VLA, PO Box 1131, Atlanta GA 30301..404-586-4945
Arnold Gottlieb, 421 N Michigan St Ste D, Toledo OH 43624....................419-243-3125
Huntington Arts Council Inc, 213 Main St, Huntington NY 11743............516-271-8423
La Costa Music Business Consultants, PO Box 147, Cardiff CA 92007 ...619-436-7219
Lawyers for the Arts/VLA DC, 918 16th St NW #503, Wash DC 20006 ...202-429-0229
Lawyers for the Creative Arts, 623 S Wabash #300N, Chicago IL 60605..312-427-1800
Legal Video Services/Teleview, 301 N Alpine, Beverly Hills CA 90210 213-271-2340
Lexington Council of Arts, 161 N Mill St, Lexington KY 40507.................606-255-2951
Barry Lindahl, 491 W 4th St PO Box 741, Dubuque IA 52201....................319-583-4113
Lousiana VLA/Arts Council, 2 Canal St #936, New Orleans LA 70130 ...504-523-1465
Maine VLA/Commission on Arts, 55 Capitol St, Augusta ME 04333........207-289-2724
Maryland VLA, Univ of Balt School of Law, Baltimore MD 21201............301-685-0600
Minnesota VLA, 100 S 5th St #1500, Minneapolis MN 55402....................612-337-1500
Montana VLA, c/o Joan Jonkel PO Box 8687, Missoula MT 69807...........406-721-1835
North Carolina VLA, PO Box 590, Raleigh NC 27602 919-890-3195
Ocean State Lawyers for Arts, 96 Sachem Rd, Narrangansett RI 02882 ...401-789-5686
Philadelphia VLA, 251 S 18th St, Philadelphia PA 19103............................215-545-3385
Pinellas County Arts Council, 400 Pierce Blvd, Clearwater FL 33516.......813-462-3327
Practicing Law Institute, 810 7th Ave, New York NY 10019......................212-765-5700
San Diego Lawyers for Arts, 1205 Prospect #400, La Jolla CA 92037.......619-454-9696
South Carolina Lawyers for Arts, PO Box 10023, Greenville SC 29603....803-232-6970
St Louis VLA/Regional Arts Comm, 329 N Euclid, St Louis MO 63108...314-361-7686
State Arts Council of Okla, Thorpe Bldg #640, Okla City OK 73105........405-521-2931
Tennessee Arts Commission, 320 6th Ave N, Nashville TN 37219 615-741-1701
Texas Lawyers for the Arts, 1540 Sul Ross, Houston TX 77006..................713-526-4876
Utah Lawyers for the Arts, 50 S Main Ste 900, Salt Lake City UT 84144..801-521-5800
VLA NJ Ctr for Non-Profit Corp, 36 W Lafayette, Trenton NJ 08608.......609-695-6422
Volunteer Lawyers for Arts, 1285 Ave of Amer, New York NY 10019......212-977-9270
Los Angeles VLA, PO Box 57008, Los Angeles CA 90057............................213-489-4060
Wash Area Lawyers for Arts, 2025 I St NW #608, Wash DC 20006 202-861-0055
Washington VLA, 1402 3rd Ave 428 Vance Bldg, Seattle WA 98101 206-223-0502

LIBRARIES

This list contains selected major libraries and research facilities with special collections. Contact the Inter-Library Loan Department of your local library for information on the holdings of these and other libraries.

Acad Motion Picture Arts & Sci, 8949 Wilshire, Beverly Hls CA 90211....213-278-4313
Akron-Summit County Public Library, 55 S Main St, Akron OH 44326...216-762-7621
Albuquerque Public Library, 501 Copper Ave NW, Albuq NM 87102......505-766-5100
Allen County Public Library, 900 Webster St, Ft Wayne IN 46801...........219-424-7241
Anthenaeum of Philadelphia, 219 S 6th St, Philadelphia PA 19106............215-925-2688
Arriaga Publications, PO Box 652, Booneville AR 72927............................501-675-3478
Atlanta-Fulton Public Library, 1 Mitchell Sq NW, Atlanta GA 30303......404-688-4636
Austin Public Library, 800 Guadalupe St, Austin TX 78768 512-473-4244
Birmingham Public Library, 2100 Park Pl, Birmingham AL 35203 205-226-3600
Boston Public Library, Copley Sq, Boston MA 02117................................617-536-5400
Brooklyn Public Library, Grand Army Plz, Brooklyn NY 11238 718-780-7700
Buffalo & Erie County Public Library, Lafayette Sq, Buffalo NY 14203...716-856-7525

Carnegie Library of Pittsburgh, 4400 Forbes Ave, Pittsburgh PA 15213 ..412-622-3100
Center for Holocaust Studies, 1609 Ave J, Brooklyn NY 11230 718-338-6494
Center for Migration Studies, 209 Flagg Pl, Staten Island NY 10304 718-351-8800
Central Iowa Regional Library, 4715 Grand, Des Moines IA 50312..........515-277-0220
Chicago Public Library, 425 N Michigan Ave, Chicago IL 60611...............312-269-2900
Cleveland Public Library, 325 Superior Ave, Cleveland OH 44114.............216-623-2800
Columbia Univ Library, 535 W 114th St, New York NY 10027.................212-280-2271
Copyright Information Ofc, Library of Congress, Washington DC 20559.202-479-0700
Cornell Univ Libraries, Ithaca NY 14853...607-255-4144
Crouse Library Publ Arts, CUNY 33 W 42nd St, New York NY 10036....212-764-6338
Dallas Public Library, 1515 Young St, Dallas TX 75201............................214-670-1400
Dayton & Montgomery Cty Library, 215 E 3rd St, Dayton OH 45402.......513-224-1651
Denver Public Library, 1357 Broadway, Denver CO 80203 303-571-2000
Detroit Public Library, 5201 Woodward Ave, Detroit MI 48202...............313-833-1000
District of Columbia Public Library, 901 G St NW, Wash DC 20001 202-727-2255
Duke Univ, Wm R Perkins Library, Durham NC 27706.............................919-684-2034
E Baton Rouge Parish Library, 7711 Goodwood, Baton Rge LA 70806 ...504-389-3360
El Paso Public Library, 501 N Oregon St, El Paso TX 79001 915-541-4864
Enoch Pratt Free Library, 400 Cathedral St, Baltimore MD 21201 301-396-5430
Erie County Library System, 3 S Perry Sq, Erie PA 16501........................814-452-2333
Evansville-Vanderburgh Library, 22 SE 5th St, Evansville IN 47708........812-428-8200
Forsyth Cty Public Library, 860 W 5th St, Winston-Salem NC 27101 919-727-2556
Fort Worth Public Library, 300 Taylor St, Ft Worth TX 76102..................817-870-7700
Free Library of Philadelphia, Logan Sq, Philadelphia PA 19103................215-686-5322
Grand Rapids Public Library, 60 Library Plz, Grand Rapids MI 49503 ...616-456-3600
Greenville County Library, 300 College St, Greenville SC 29601 803-242-5000
Harvard Univ Library, Cambridge MA 02138...617-495-3650
Hawaii State Library System, 465 S King St, Honolulu HI 96813 808-548-5596
Holt-Atherton Ctr Western Studies, Univ Pacific, Stockton CA 95211 209-946-2404
Houston Public Library, 500 McKinney Ave, Houston TX 77002...............713-224-5441
Indiana Univ Libraries, 10th St & Jordan Ave, Bloomington IN 47405 812-335-3403
Indianapolis-Marion County Library, 40 E St, Indianapolis IN 46206......317-269-1700
Jackson Metropolitan Library, 301 N State St, Jackson MS 39201 601-944-1120
Jacksonville Public Library, 122 N Ocean St, Jacksonville FL 32202.........904-633-6870
Kanawha County Public Library, 123 Capitol St, Charleston WV 25301..304-343-4646
Kansas City Public Library, 311 E 12th St, Kansas City MO 64106...........816-221-2685
Knox County Public Library, 500 W Church Ave, Knoxville TN 37902.....615-523-0781
Library of Congress, Cataloging in Publication, Washington DC 20540....202-287-6372
Library of Congress, Information Ofc, Washington DC 20540....................202-287-5000
Library of Congress, Prints & Photographs Div, Washington DC 20540 ..202-287-6394
Library of Congress, Reference Section, Washington DC 20540.................202-287-5522
Lincoln City Libraries, 136 S 14th St, Lincoln NE 68508.........................402-435-2146
Long Beach Public Library, 101 Pacific Ave, Long Beach CA 90802.........213-437-2949
Los Angeles Public Library, 630 W 5th St, Los Angeles CA 90071............213-612-3200
Louisville Free Public Library, 4th & York Sts, Louisville KY 40203........502-584-4154
Madison Public Library, 201 W Mifflin St, Madison WI 53703..................608-266-6300
MEDOC, Univ of Utah Bldg 89, Salt Lake City UT 84112 801-581-5268
Memphis-Shelby County Library, 1850 Peabody, Memphis TN 38104......901-725-8855
Metropolitan Library System, 131 McGee Ave, Okla City OK 73102.......405-235-0571
Miami-Dade Public Library System, 101 W Flagler St, Miami FL 33130..305-375-2665
Michigan State Univ Library, East Lansing MI 48824.................................517-355-2344
Mid-Continent Library, 15616 E 24 Hwy, Independence MO 64050 816-836-5200
Milwaukee Public Library, 814 W Wisconsin Ave, Milwaukee WI 53233 .414-278-3000

Minneapolis Public Library, 300 Nicollet Mall, Minneapolis MN 55401 ..612-372-6500
Mississippi Dept of Archives & Hist, Box 571, Jackson MS 39205 601-359-1424
Multnomah County Library, 801 SW 10th Ave, Portland OR 97205 503-223-7201
Museums at Stony Brook, 1208 Rt 25A, Stony Brook NY 11790................516-751-0066
Natl Baseball Library, Main St, Cooperstown NY 13326 607-547-9988
New Orleans Public Library, 219 Loyola Ave, New Orleans LA 70140 504-596-2550
New York Public Library, 5th Ave & 42nd St, New York NY 10018..........212-930-0800
New York Univ Library, 70 Washington Sq S, New York NY 10012..........212-598-2484
Newark Public Library, 5 Washington St, Newark NJ 07101....................201-733-7800
Norfolk Public Library, 301 E City Hall Ave, Norfolk VA 23510...............804-441-2887
Northwestern Univ Library, 1935 Sheridan Rd, Evanston IL 60201..........312-491-7658
Ohio State Univ Libraries, 1858 Neil Ave Mall, Columbus OH 43210......614-422-6151
Omaha Public Library, 215 S 15th St, Omaha NE 68102.......................402-444-4800
J Michael Pearson, PO Box 402844, Miami Beach FL 33140 305-538-0346
Pennsylvania State Univ, Pattee Library, Univ Park PA 16802.................814-865-0401
Phoenix Public Library, 12 E McDowell Rd, Phoenix AZ 85004 602-262-6451
Princeton Univ Library, Princeton NJ 08540 609-452-3180
Providence Public Library, 150 Empire St, Providence RI 02903.............401-521-7722
Public Library of Annapolis, 5 Truman Pkwy, Annapolis MD 21401 301-224-7371
Public Library of Charlotte, 310 N Tryon St, Charlotte NC 28202............704-336-2725
Public Library of Cincinnati, 800 Vine St, Cincinnati OH 45202 513-369-6000
Public Library of Columbus, 28 S Hamilton Rd, Columbus OH 43213.....614-864-8050
Public Library of Nashville, 8th Ave N & Union, Nashville TN 37203......615-244-4700
Public Library of Youngstown, 305 Wick Ave, Youngstown OH 44503.....216-744-8636
Queens Borough Public Library, 89-11 Merrick, Jamaica NY 11432.........718-990-0700
Richmond Public Library, 101 E Franklin St, Richmond VA 23219 804-780-4256
Rochester Public Library, 115 South Ave, Rochester NY 14604 716-428-7300
Rosenbach Museum & Library, 2010 Delancey Pl, Phila PA 19103............215-732-1600
Sacramento Public Library, 101 8th St, Sacramento CA 95823 916-440-5926
St Louis Public Library, 1301 Olive St, St Louis MO 63103....................314-241-2288
St Paul Public Library, 90 W 4th St, St Paul MN 55102........................612-292-6311
St Petersburg Public Library, 3745 9th Ave N, St Petersburg FL 33713 ...813-893-7724
Salt Lake City Public Library, 209 E 5th S, Salt Lake City UT 84111 801-363-5733
San Antonio Public Library, 203 S St Mary's, San Antonio TX 78205.......512-299-7790
San Diego Public Library, 820 E St, San Diego CA 92101......................619-236-5800
San Francisco Public Library, Civic Center, San Francisco CA 94102......415-558-4235
San Jose Public Library, 180 W San Carlos St, San Jose CA 95113...........408-277-4822
Seattle Public Library, 1000 4th Ave, Seattle WA 98104......................206-625-4931
Braun Research Library, 234 Museum Dr, Los Angeles CA 90065 213-221-2164
Springfield Public Library, 220 State St, Springfield MA 01103.................413-739-3871
Stanford Univ Libraries, Stanford CA 94305 415-723-9108
Tampa-Hillsborough County Library, 900 N Ashley, Tampa FL 33602....813-223-8945
Tucson Public Library, 111 E Pennington, Tucson AZ 85726....................602-791-4391
Tulsa City-County Library, 400 Civic Center, Tulsa OK 74103 918-592-7977
Univ of Arizona Library, Tucson AZ 85721......................................602-621-2101
Univ of Calif Berkeley, Univ Library, Berkeley CA 94720 415-642-3773
Univ of Calif LA, Univ Library 405 Hilgard, Los Angeles CA 90024 213-825-1201
Univ of Chicago Library, 1100 E 57th St, Chicago IL 60637...................312-962-7874
Univ of Illinois Library, 1408 W Gregory Dr, Urbana IL 60801..................217-333-0790
Univ of Iowa Libraries, Iowa City IA 52242......................................319-353-4450
Univ of Michigan, Univ Libraries, Ann Arbor MI 48109 313-764-9356
Univ of Minnesota Libraries, 309 19th Ave S, Minneapolis MN 55455.....612-373-3097
Univ of North Carolina, Davis Library, Chapel Hill NC 27514................919-962-1301

Univ of Pennsylvania Libraries, 3420 Walnut St, Phila PA 19104 215-898-7091
Univ of Pittsburgh, Univ Libraries, Pittsburgh PA 15260 412-624-4437
Univ of Southern Calif, Doheny Mem Library, Los Angeles CA 90089 213-743-2543
Univ of Texas Libraries, Box P, Austin TX 78713.......................................512-471-3811
Univ of Virginia, Alderman Library, Charlottesville VA 22903....................804-924-3026
Univ of Washington Libraries, FM 25, Seattle WA 98195...........................206-543-9153
Univ of Wisconsin Library, 728 State St, Madison WI 53706......................608-262-3521
Virginia Library Assn, 80 S Early St, Alexandria VA 22304.......................703-370-6020
Waukesha Cty Historical Museum, 101 W Main, Waukesha WI 53186....414-548-7186
Wichita Public Library, 223 S Main, Wichita KS 67202..............................316-262-0611
Worcester Public Library, Salem Square, Worcester MA 01608................617-799-1655
Yale Univ Library, 120 High St, New Haven CT 06520................................203-436-8335

MAGAZINES

This section lists publishers of magazines, journals and newsletters. See also
Newspaper Magazine Supplements.

A+, 11 Davis Dr, Belmont CA 94002...415-594-2290
A/C Flyer, 7200 Corporate Center Dr Ste 610, Miami FL 33126................305-591-2147
AAA World, 1999 Shepard Rd, St Paul MN 55116 612-690-7238
AAA World Hawaii/Alaska, 730 Ala Moana Blvd, Honolulu HI 96813.....808-528-2600
AANA Journal, 216 Higgins Rd, Park Ridge IL 60068 312-692-7050
AAR Times, 1720 Regal Row, Dallas TX 75235.....................................214-630-3540
AARP News Bulletin, 1909 K St NW, Washington DC 20049 202-872-4700
AB Bookman's Weekly, Box AB, Clifton NJ 07015................................201-772-0020
Abacus, 175 5th Ave, New York NY 10010 212-460-1500
ABC Star Service, 131 Clarendon St, Boston MA 02116......................617-262-5000
Aboard, 135 Madeira Ave, Coral Gables FL 33134...............................305-442-0752
Abraxas, 2518 Gregory St, Madison WI 53711......................................608-238-0175
Absolute Reference, 7999 Knue Rd Ste 202, Indianapolis IN 46250...........317-842-7162
The Absolute Sound, PO Box 115, Sea Cliff NY 11579 516-676-2830
Abyss, 921 E 49th St, Austin TX 78751 512-467-2806
ACA News, 6619 N Scottsdale Rd, Scottsdale AZ 85253 602-951-9191
Academe/AAUP, 1012 14th St NW Ste 500, Washington DC 20005 202-737-5900
Academic Financier, 28974 Harmony Ranch Rd, Tollhouse CA 93667.....209-855-3643
Academic Technology, 1311 Executive Ctr Dr, Tallahassee FL 32301........904-878-4178
Academic Therapy, 20 Commercial Blvd, Novato CA 94947......................415-883-3314
Accent, 1720 Washington PO Box 10010, Ogden UT 84409......................801-394-9446
Accent On Living, PO Box 700, Bloomington IL 61702............................309-378-2961
Access, 8310 Capital of Texas Hwy, Austin TX 78731.............................512-343-9066
Accident Analysis & Prevention, Maxwell House, Elmsford NY 10523.....914-592-7700
Accounts of Chemical Research, 1155 16 St NW, Wash DC 20036 202-872-4546
Aceto Bookmen, 5721 Antietam Dr, Sarasota FL 33581 813-924-9170
Achievement, 925 NE 122st St, North Miami FL 33161...........................305-895-0153
Acres USA, PO Box 9547, Kansas City MO 64133 816-737-0064
Across the Board, 845 3rd Ave, New York NY 10022 212-759-0900
Acta Cytologica, 2 Jacklynn Ct, St Louis MO 63132...............................314-991-4440
Action, 901 College Ave, Winona Lake IN 46590....................................219-267-7656
Action Sport Retailer, 31652 2nd Ave, South Laguna CA 92677.................714-499-5374
Activewear Magazine, PO Box 5400, Denver CO 80217..........................303-295-0900

ACTS, 324 Bartless St #9, San Francisco CA 94110 415-647-2961
Ad-Lib Publications, 51 N 5th St, Fairfield IA 52556...........................515-472-6617
ADA Data/Intl Resource Dev, 6 Prowitt St, Norwalk CT 06855 203-866-7800
Adirondack Life, Rt 86 Box 97, Jay NY 12941 518-946-2191
Adirondack Mountain Club, 174 Glen St, Glens Falls NY 12801............518-793-7737
Administrative Law Review, 1900 Olive St, Denver CO 80220...............303-753-2560
Administrative Science Quarterly, Cornell Univ, Ithaca NY 14853 607-255-5581
Adolescence, 4901 Morena Blvd Ste 330, San Diego CA 92117.................619-581-9449
ADS Magazine, 130 5th Ave, New York NY 10011................................212-243-0700
Adult Education Quarterly, 1201 16th St NW, Washington DC 20036......202-822-7866
Advances in Astronautical Sciences, Box 28130, San Diego CA 92128.....619-746-4005
Advances in Biosciences, Maxwell House, Elmsford NY 10523................914-592-7700
Advantage Magazine, 1719 West End, Nashville TN 37203 615-229-1973
Adventure Magazine, 12910 Totem Lake Blvd, Kirkland WA 98034..........206-821-7766
Adventure Road, 200 E Randolph Dr, Chicago IL 60601.........................312-856-2583
Advertising Age, 740 N Rush, Chicago IL 60611 312-649-5200
Advertising Techniques, 10 E 39th St 6th fl, New York NY 10016 212-889-6500
Advertising World, 150 Fifth Ave, New York NY 10011...........................212-807-1660
The Advocate, 22761 Pacific Coast Hwy, Malibu CA 90265.....................213-871-1225
Adweek, 820 Second Ave, New York NY 10017......................................212-661-8080
Aerial, Box 1901, Manassas VA 22110 703-368-5614
AERO, 5509 Santa Monica Blvd, Los Angles CA 90038 213-466-1166
Aero, PO Box 6050, Mission Viejo CA 92690.......................................714-240-6001
Aerosol Age, 10 Canfield Rd, Cedar Grove NJ 07009 201-239-5800
Aerospace, 1725 De Sales St NW, Washington DC 20036.......................202-429-4600
Aerospace America, 1633 Broadway, New York NY 10019 212-581-4300
Aerospace Historian, Eisenhower Hall, Manhattan KS 66506 913-532-6733
Affaire de Coeur, 5660 Roosevelt Pl, Fremont CA 94538 415-656-4804
AFFILIA: Women in Social Work, 311 E 94th St, New York NY 10128 ...212-360-5790
Affirmative Action Register, 8356 Olive Blvd, St Louis MO 63132............314-991-1335
Africa News, Box 3851, Durham NC 27702 919-286-0747
Africa Report, 833 United Nations Plaza, New York NY 10017 212-949-5731
Afro-Hispanic Review, Univ of Missouri, Columbia MO 65211...............314-882-6229
AFTA, 153 George St 2nd fl, New Brunswick NJ 08901..........................201-828-5467
Afterimage, 31 Prince St, Rochester NY 14607......................................716-442-8676
AFTRA/Dick Moore & Assoc, 1560 Broadway, New York NY 10036 212-719-9570
Ag Review, 16 Grove St, Putnam CT 06260 203-928-7778
Ag-Pilot Intl, Drawer R, Walla Walla WA 99362 509-522-4311
Agada, 2020 Essex St, Berkeley CA 94703..415-848-0965
Agape, 6940 Oporto Dr, Los Angeles CA 90068.....................................213-876-6295
Age of Achievement, 835 Securities Bldg, Seattle WA 98101 206-622-3538
The Agencies, PO Box 3044, Hollywood CA 90078................................213-466-4297
Agenda for Citizen Involvement, 9 Murray St, New York NY 10007.........212-349-6460
The Agincourt Irregular, 65 Eckerson Rd, Harrington Pk NJ 07640.........201-768-2489
Aglow, PO Box I, Lynnwood WA 98046..206-775-7282
The Agni Review, 236 Bay State Rd, Boston MA 02115..........................617-354-8522
Agri Finance, 5520-G Touhy Ave, Skokie IL 60077...............................312-676-4060
Agri Marketing, 5520-G Touhy Ave, Skokie IL 60077............................312-676-4060
Agri-Practice, 7 Ashley Ave S, Santa Barbara CA 93103........................805-965-1028
Agribusiness Worldwide, PO Box 29155, Shawnee Mission KS 66201.....913-236-7300
Agrichemical Age, 83 Stevenson St, San Francisco CA 94105..................415-495-3340
AgriComp, 103 Outdoors Bldg, Columbia MO 65201............................314-443-4316
Agricultural History, Univ of California Press, Berkeley CA 94720 415-642-4191

Agronomy Journal, 677 S Segoe Rd, Madison WI 53711 608-273-8080
Agway Cooperator, PO Box 4933, Syracuse NY 13221 315-477-6231
AHA! Hispanic Arts News, 200 E 87th St 2nd fl, New York NY 10028......212-369-7054
Ahoy!, 45 W 34th St Ste 407, New York NY 10001...................................212-239-0855
AI Magazine, 445 Burgess Dr, Menlo Park CA 94025................................415-328-3123
Aim Magazine, 7308 S Eberhart Ave, Chicago IL 60619...........................312-874-6184
AIMplus Arthritis Info Magazine, 45 W 34th St, New York NY 10001 212-239-0855
Air & Space, 900 Jefferson Dr, Washington DC 20560...............................202-357-4414
Air Cargo News, Box 527 Borough Hall Sta, Jamaica NY 11424 718-479-0716
Air Cargo World, 6255 Barfield Rd, Atlanta GA 30328 404-256-9800
Air Cond Heating & Refrig, 755 W Big Beaver Rd, Troy MI 48007...........313-362-3700
Air Force, 1750 Pennsylvania Ave NW, Washington DC 20026...................202-637-3300
Air Force Times, Times Journal Bldg, Springfield VA 22159 703-750-2000
Air Line Pilot, 535 Herndon Pkwy PO Box 1169, Herndon VA 22069.......703-689-4176
Air Progress, 7950 Deering Ave, Canoga Park CA 91304...........................818-887-0550
AirCal, 12955 Biscayne Blvd, North Miami FL 33181................................305-893-1520
Airfair Interline Magazine, 25 W 39th St, New York NY 10018................212-840-6714
Airline & Travel Food Service, 665 La Villa Dr, Miami Spgs FL 33166 305-887-1701
Airline Executive, 6255 Barfield Rd, Atlanta GA 30328 404-256-9800
Airport Services Management, 50 S 9th St, Minneapolis MN 55402..........612-333-0471
Akerkon Literary Journal, Box 223, Haganburg NY 13655.......................518-358-9531
Akwesasne Notes, Box 196, Rooseveltown NY 13683 518-358-9531
Alabama Alumni, PO Box 1928, University AL 35486................................205-348-1548
Alabama Game & Fish, PO Box 741, Marietta GA 30061 404-953-9222
Alaska, 808 E St, Anchorage AK 99501..907-272-6070
Alaska Airlines, 1932 1st Ave Ste 503, Seattle WA 98101..........................206-682-5871
Alaska Construction & Oil, 109 W Mercer St, Seattle WA 98119................206-285-2050
Alaska Flying, Pouch 112010, Anchorage AK 99511.................................907-344-3331
Alaska Outdoors, Box 6324, Anchorage AK 99502....................................907-276-2672
Alaska Quarterly Review, Univ of Alaska, Anchorage AK 99508................907-786-1731
Alaskafest, 1932 1st Ave Ste 503, Seattle WA 98101.................................203-682-5871
Albatross, 4014 SW 21st Rd, Gainseville FL 32607...................................904-377-8594
Albuquerque Senior Scene, 8421 Osuna NE, Albuquerque NM 87111......505-299-4401
Albuquerque Singles Scene, 8421 Osuna NE, Albuquerque NM 87111.....505-299-4401
Alcalde, PO Box 7278, Austin TX 78713...512-471-3799
Alcoholism & Addiction, 1005 NE 72nd St, Seattle WA 98115 206-527-8999
Alfred Hitchcock's Mystery Mag, 380 Lexington, New York NY 10017 212-557-9100
ALI-ABA Course Material Jour, 4025 Chestnut, Philadelphia PA 19104..215-243-1600
Alive, 444 Market St, San Francisco CA 94111 415-954-3000
Alive! for Young Teens, Beaumont & Pine Blvd, St Louis MO 63166........314-371-6900
All About Beer, 2154 W La Palma, Anaheim CA 92801.............................714-635-9040
All Around the Editor's Desk, 709 SE 52nd Ave, Ocala FL 32671.............904-694-2303
All Terrain Vehicle Industry, 2201 Cherry Ave, Long Beach CA 90801 213-595-4753
Allegheny Review, Box 32, Meadville PA 16335..814-724-6553
Alliance Life, 350 N Highland Ave, Nyack NY 10960 914-353-0750
Alma Magazine, Box 89, Alalmosa CO 81101..303-589-6641
Aloha The Magazine of Hawaii, 828 Fort St Mall, Honolulu HI 96813......808-523-9871
Alps Monthly, PO Box 640394, San Francisco CA 94164...........................415-771-3431
Alternate Press Index, PO Box 33109, Baltimore MD 21218 301-243-2471
Alternate Routes, PO Box 367, Los Angeles CA 90041..............................213-259-2704
Alternative Energy Retailer, PO Box 2180, Waterbury CT 06722................203-755-0158
Alternative Media, PO Box 1347 Ansonia Sta, New York NY 10023 212-974-1990
The Alternative Part Paper, 8123 19th Pl, Adelphi MD 20783....................301-434-4559

Alternative Sources of Energy, 107 S Central, Milaca MN 56353 612-983-6892
Altman & Weil Report to Legal Mgmt, Box 472, Ardmore OK 19003.......215-649-4646
Alura, 29371 Jacquelyn, Livonia MI 48154 313-427-2911
Amaryllis Review, 1906 Sir James Dr, Salt Lake City UT 84116 801-596-8871
Amateur Boxer, PO Box 249, Cobalt CT 06414..203-342-4730
Amateur Golf Register, 2843 Pembroke Rd, Hollywood FL 33020 305-921-0881
Amazing Heroes, 4359 Cornell Rd, Agoura CA 91301 818-706-7606
Amazing Stories, PO Box 110, Lake Geneva WI 53147................................414-248-3625
Amelia Magazine, 329 E St, Bakersfield CA 93304......................................805-323-4064
America, 106 W 56th St, New York NY 10019...212-581-4640
America West, 7500 N Dreamy Draw Dr, Phoenix AZ 85020 602-997-7200
American Agent & Broker, 408 Olive St, St Louis MO 63102 314-421-5445
American Agriculturist, 710 W Clinton St, Ithaca NY 14851 607-273-3507
American Annals of the Deaf, 814 Thayer Ave, Silver Spring MD 20910 ..301-585-4363
American Anthropologist, 1703 New Hampshire Ave, Wash DC 20009....202-232-8800
American Antiquity, 1511 K St NW, Washington DC 20005.........................202-638-6079
American Artist, 1515 Broadway, New York NY 10036................................212-764-7300
American Astrology, 475 Park Ave S, New York NY 10016 212-689-2830
American Athiest, PO Box 2117, Austin TX 78768 512-458-1244
Amer Automatic Merchandiser, 7500 Old Oak, Cleveland OH 44130.......216-243-8100
American Baby Magazine, 575 Lexington Ave, New York NY 10022........212-752-0775
American Banker, 1 State St Plaza, New York NY 10004..............................212-943-0400
American Baptist, Box 851, Valley Forge PA 19482.....................................215-768-2000
American Bar Assn Journal, 750 N Lake Shore Dr, Chicago IL 60611.....312-988-5000
American Bee Journal, 51 S 2nd St, Hamilton IL 62341................................217-847-3324
American Bible Society Record, 1865 Broadway, New York NY 10023.....212-581-7400
American Bicyclist, 80 8th Ave, New York NY 10011 212-206-7230
Amer Biology Teacher, 11250 Roger Bacon Dr #19, Reston VA 22090....703-471-1134
Amer Biotechnology Laboratory, 808 Kings Hwy, Fairfield CT 06430.......203-576-0500
American Birds, 950 3rd Ave, New York NY 10022 212-546-9189
American Book Collector, PO Box 1080, Ossining NY 10562 914-941-0409
American Book Review, Univ of Colo Box 226, Boulder CO 80309............303-492-8947
American Bookseller, 137 W 25th St, New York NY 10001............................212-463-8450
American Brewer, PO Box 713, Hayward CA 94541......................................415-886-9823
American Buddist, 301 W 45th St, New York NY 10036 212-489-1075
American Business, 1775 Broadway, New York NY 10019.............................212-581-2000
American Cage Bird Magazine, 1 Glamore Ct, Smithtown NY 11787.......516-979-7962
American Cemetary, 1501 Broadway, New York NY 10036 212-398-9266
American Cinematographer, 1782 N Orange Dr, Hollywood CA 90078 ...213-876-5080
American Citizen Italian Press, 13681 V St, Omaha NE 68137..................402-896-0403
Amer City & County Magazine, 6255 Barfield Rd, Atlanta GA 30328.......404-256-9800
American Clay Exchange, PO Box 2674, La Mesa CA 92041......................619-697-5922
American Clean Car, 500 N Dearborn St, Chicago IL 60610 312-337-7700
American Coin-Op, 500 N Dearborn St, Chicago IL 60610 312-337-7700
American Collectors Jour, PO Box 407, Kewanee IL 61443........................308-853-8441
American Council on Education, 1 Dupont Cir, Washington DC 20036 ...202-939-9300
American Craft, 45 W 45th St, New York NY 10036......................................212-869-9422
Amer Dance Guild Newsletter, 570 7th Ave 20th fl, New York NY 10018.212-944-0557
American Dane, 3717 Harney St PO Box 31748, Omaha NE 68131 402-341-5049
American Demographics, PO Box 68, Ithaca NY 14851................................607-273-6343
American Druggist, 555 W 57th St, New York NY 10019 212-399-2890
American Drycleaner, 500 N Dearborn St, Chicago IL 60610 312-337-7700
Amer Economic Review, 1313 21st Ave S Ste 809, Nashville TN 37212......615-322-2595

American Educator, 555 New Jersey Ave NW, Washington DC 20001 202-879-4420
American Family Physician, 1740 W 92nd St, Kansas City MO 64114.......816-333-9700
American Farriers Jour, 63 Great Rd, Maynard MA 01754 617-897-5552
American Field, 222 W Adams St, Chicago IL 60606.................................312-372-1383
American Film, 3 E 54th St, New York NY 10022 212-355-5432
American Fire Journal, 9072 E Artesia Blvd #7, Bellflower CA 90706.....213-866-1664
Amer Firearms Industry, 2801 E Oakland Pk, Ft Lauderdale FL 33306...305-561-3505
American Fitness, 15250 Ventura Blvd, Sherman Oaks CA 91403..........818-905-0040
American Forests Magazine, 1319 18th St NW, Washington DC 20036....202-467-5810
American Fruit Grower, 37841 Euclid Ave, Willoughby OH 44094 216-942-2000
American Glass Review, PO Box 2147, Clifton NJ 07015............................201-779-1600
American Handgunner, 591 Camino de la Reina, San Diego CA 92108...619-297-5352
American Health, 80 5th Ave, New York NY 10011...................................212-242-2460
Amer Health Care Assn Jour, 1200 15th St NW, Washington DC 20005 ..202-833-2050
American Heart Jour, 11830 Westline Indus Dr, St Louis MO 63146........314-827-8370
American Heritage Magazine, 60 5th Ave, New York NY 10011................212-206-5500
American Historical Review, 400 A St SE, Washington DC 20003.............202-544-2422
American History Illustrated, 2245 Kohn Rd, Harrisburg PA 17105.........717-657-9555
American Hockey, 2997 Broadmoor Valley, Colorado Spgs CO 80906......303-576-4990
American Horticulturist, Box 105, Mount Vernon VA 22121.....................703-768-5700
American Hunter, 470 Spring Park Pl, Herndon VA 22070.......................202-828-6230
American Indian Art, 7314 E Osborn Dr, Scottsdale AZ 85251 602-994-5445
American Indian Basketry, PO Box 66124, Portland OR 97266.................503-233-8131
American Indian Culture & Research, UCLA, Los Angeles CA 90024....213-825-4777
American Industrial Hygiene Assn, 475 Wolf Ledges, Akron OH 44311..216-762-7294
American Inst of Architects, 1735 New York Ave NW, Wash DC 20006..202-626-7300
American Jewelry Manufacturer, 825 7th Ave, New York NY 10019........212-245-7555
Amer Jour Obstetrics/Gynecology, 11830 Westline, St Louis MO 63146..314-872-8370
Amer Jour of Sociology, 1130 E 59th St, Chicago IL 60637 312-702-8580
Amer Jour of Botany, Univ of Texas, Austin TX 78713............................512-471-5487
Amer Jour of Cardiology, 875 3rd Ave, New York NY 10022.....................212-605-9400
Amer Jour of Clinical Pathology, E Washington Sq, Phila PA 19105 215-238-4200
Amer Jour of Emergency Medicine, W Washington Sq, Phila PA 19105...215-574-4700
Amer Jour of Hosp Pharmacy, 4630 Montomery, Bethesda MD 20814 301-657-3000
Amer Jour of Law & Medicine, 765 Commonwealth, Boston MA 02215 ..617-353-2912
Amer Jour of Medicine, 875 3rd Ave, New York NY 10022 212-605-9769
Amer Jour of Nursing, 555 W 57th St, New York NY 10019.....................212-582-8820
Amer Jour of Occup Therapy, 1383 Piccard, Rockville MD 20850............301-948-9626
Amer Jour of Orthodontics, 11830 Westline, St Louis MO 63146.............314-872-8370
Amer Jour of Pathology, E Washington Sq, Philadelphia PA 19105 215-238-4200
Amer Jour of Physics, Univ Missouri Benton Hall, St Louis MO 63121 ...314-553-5921
Amer Jour of Psychiatry, 1400 K St NW, Washington DC 20005...............202-682-6020
Amer Jour of Public Health, 1015 15th St NW, Washington DC 20005.....202-789-5600
Amer Jour of Surgery, 875 3rd Ave, New York NY 10022.........................212-605-9400
Amer Jour Diseases of Children, 535 N Dearborn, Chicago IL 60610.......312-645-5000
Amer Jour on Infection Control, 11830 Westline, St Louis MO 63146......314-872-8370
Amer Jour on Intl Law, 40 Washington Sq S, New York NY 10012...........212-589-2494
American Karate, 351 W 54th St, New York NY 10019 212-586-4432
American Laboratory, 808 Kings Hwy, Fairfield CT 06430 203-576-0500
American Land Forum, 1319 18th St NW, Washington DC 20036.............202-331-0637
American Laundry Digest, 500 N Dearborn St, Chicago IL 60610.............312-337-7700
American Lawyer, 205 Lexington Ave, New York NY 10016......................212-696-8900
American Legion Magazine, PO Box 1055, Indianapolis IN 46206.............317-635-8411

American Libraries, 50 E Huron St, Chicago IL 60611.................................312-944-6780
American Literature, 210 W Duke Bldg, Durham NC 27708......................919-684-3948
Amer Machinist & Automated Mfg, 11 W 19th St, New York NY 10011..212-337-7942
Amer Mathematical Monthly, 1529 18th St NW, Washington DC 20036..202-387-5200
American Medical News, 535 N Dearborn St, Chicago IL 60610.................312-645-5000
American Mining Congress Jour, 1920 N St NW, Wash DC 20036............202-861-2800
Amer Motorcyclist, 33 Collegeview Rd, Westerville OH 43081....................614-891-2425
American Mover, 2200 Mill Rd, Alexandria VA 22314...............................703-838-1938
American Nurse, 2420 Pershing Rd, Kansas City MO 64108......................816-474-5720
American Office Dealer, 49 E 21st St, New York NY 10010........................212-529-3344
American Organist, 815 2nd Ave Ste 318, New York NY 10017...................212-687-9188
Amer Paint & Coatings Jour, 2911 Washington, St Louis MO 63103........314-534-0301
American Pharmacy, 2215 Constitution Ave NW, Wash DC 20037............202-628-4410
American Photographer, 1515 Broadway, New York NY 10036...................212-719-6122
American Poetry, Box 611, Jefferson NC 28640...919-246-4460
American Poetry Review, 1616 Walnut St #405, Philadelphia PA 19103...215-732-6770
American Politics, 810 18th St NW, Washington DC 20006.........................202-347-1110
American Postal Worker, 1300 L St NW, Washington DC 20005.................202-842-4200
American Printer & Lithographer, 300 W Adams, Chicago IL 60606........312-726-2802
American Psychologist, 1200 17th St NW, Washington DC 20036...............202-955-7600
American Public Opinion Index, PO Box 70205, Louisville KY 40270......502-893-2527
American Quarterly, Univ of Penn, Philadelphia PA 19104.......................215-898-6252
Amer Rev Respiratory Disease, 1740 Broadway, New York NY 10019.....212-315-8700
American Rifleman, 1600 Rhode Island Ave NW, Wash DC 20036............202-828-6200
American Rose, Box 30000 Jefferson Paige Rd, Shreveport LA 71130......318-938-5402
American Salesman, 424 N 3rd St, Burlington IA 52601...........................319-753-6888
American Salon Eighty-Five, 100 Park Ave, New York NY 10017.............212-532-5588
American Scholar, 1811 Q St NW, Washington DC 20009..........................202-265-3808
American School & University, 401 N Broad St, Philadelphia PA 19108..215-238-5300
American School Board Jour, 1680 Duke St, Alexandria VA 22314..........703-838-6722
American Scientist, 345 Whitney Ave, New Haven CT 06517.....................203-624-2566
American Screenwriter, PO Box 67, Manchaca TX 78652..........................512-282-2749
American Shipper, 33 S Hogan St 2nd fl, Jacksonville FL 32201...............904-355-2601
American Shotgunner, PO Box 3351, Reno NV 89505................................702-826-3825
American Skating World, 2545 Brownsville Rd, Pittsburgh PA 15210.......412-885-7600
Amer Soc Personnel Admin, 606 N Washington, Alexandria VA 22314....703-548-3440
American Sociological Review, 1722 N St NW, Washington DC 20036.....202-833-3410
American Spectator, 1969 W 6th St, Bloomington IN 47402......................812-334-2715
American Squaredance, PO Box 488, Huron OH 44839.............................419-433-2188
American Survival Guide, 2145 W La Palma Ave, Anaheim CA 92801....714-635-9040
American Taste, 10 E 40th St, New York NY 10017....................................212-689-5400
American Teacher, 555 New Jersey Ave NW, Washington DC 20001........202-879-4430
American Theatre, 355 Lexington Ave, New York NY 10017......................212-697-5230
American Theatre Magazine, 355 Lexington Ave, New York NY 10017...212-697-5230
American Towman, Box 205, Metuchen NJ 08840......................................201-549-5444
Amer Transcendental Quar, Univ of Rhode Island, Kingston RI 02881...401-792-5931
Amer Transportation Builder, 525 School St SW, Wash DC 20024...........202-488-2722
Amer Tree Farmer, 1619 Massachusetts Ave NW, Wash DC 20036..........202-797-4500
American Trucker Magazine, PO Box 9159, Brea CA 92622......................714-528-6600
Amer Veterinary Med Assn, 930 N Meacham, Schaumburg IL 60196.......312-885-8070
American Voice, Broadway at 4th Ave, Louisville KY 40202......................502-562-0045
American Way, PO Box 61616 MD 2G23, DFW Airport TX 75261...........817-355-1583
American West, 3033 N Campbell Ave, Tucson AZ 85719..........................602-881-5850

American Zionist, 4 E 34th St, New York NY 10016......................................212-481-1500
Americana, 29 W 38th St, New York NY 10018 212-398-1550
Americans for Legal Reform, 201 Mass Ave NE, Wash DC 20002 202-546-4258
Americas, 1889 F St NW, Washington DC 20006......................................202-789-3278
Americas Review, Univ of Houston 4800 Calhoun, Houston TX 77004.....713-749-4768
AMHCA Jour, 5999 Stevenson Ave, Alexandria VA 22304......................703-823-9800
The Amicus Jour, 122 E 42nd St Rm 4500, New York NY 10168................212-949-0049
AmigaWorld, 80 Elm St, Peterborough NH 03458......................................603-924-9471
AMIT Women, 817 Broadway, New York NY 10003 212-477-4720
Ampersand, 303 N Glenoaks Blvd Ste 600, Burbank CA 91502...................818-848-4666
Amtrak Express, 140 E Main St, Huntington NY 11743......................516-385-9299
Amusement Business, 14 Music Circle E, Nashville TN 37202 615-748-8120
ANALOG Computing, 565 Main St, Cherry Valley MA 01611......................617-892-3488
Analog Science Fiction, 380 Lexington Ave, New York NY 10017 212-557-9100
Analysis Press, Box 228, Chappaque NY 10514 914-238-3641
Analytical Chemistry, 1155 16th St NW, Washington DC 20036 202-872-4576
Ancestry Newsletter, PO Box 476, Salt Lake City UT 84110......................801-531-1790
Ancient Truth, 704 S 25th St, Mt Vernon IL 62864......................................618-242-5867
Androgyne, 930 Shields, San Francisco CA 93132......................................415-586-2697
Anesthesiology, E Washington Sq, Philadelphia PA 19105 215-574-4200
Anesthesiology News, 148 W 24th St, New York NY 10011 212-620-4600
Anesthesiology Review, 116 W 32nd St 8th fl, New York NY 10001...........212-736-6688
Angelstone, 316 Woodland Dr, Birmingham AL 35209 205-870-7281
Angeltread, 102 S Second Apt 114, Grayville IL 62844 502-965-4842
Angle Orthodonist, 100 W Lawrence Ste 406, Appleton WI 54911 414-739-5882
The Anglican Digest, Hillspeak, Eureka Springs AR 72632......................501-253-9701
Angus Jour, 3201 Frederick Blvd, St Joseph MO 64501......................816-233-0508
Anima, 1053 Wilson Ave, Chambersburg PA 17201......................................717-263-8303
Animal Kingdom Magazine, NY Zoological Park, Bronx NY 10460 212-220-5121
Animals, 350 S Huntington Ave, Boston MA 02130......................................617-522-7400
The Animals' Agenda, PO Box 5234, Westport CT 06881 203-226-8826
ANNA Jour, Box 56 N Woodbury Rd, Pitman NJ 08071......................609-589-2319
Annals of Emergency Medicine, PO Box 619911, Dallas TX 75261...........214-659-0911
Annals of Internal Medicine, 4200 Pine St, Philadelphia PA 19104 215-243-1200
Annals of Neurology, 34 Beacon St, Boston MA 02108 617-227-0730
Annals of Sports Medicine, PO Box 4704, North Hollywood CA 91607....818-989-3432
Annals of Surgery, E Washington Sq, Philadelphia PA 19105......................215-238-4200
Annals of Thoracic Surgery, 34 Beacon St, Boston MA 02106 617-227-0730
Annals of Otology, 4507 Laclede, St Louis MO 63108......................314-367-4987
Another Chicago Magazine, PO Box 11223, Chicago IL 60611...................312-524-1289
Antaeus, 26 W 17th St, New York NY 10011 212-645-2214
Antic: The Atari Resource, 524 2nd St, San Francisco CA 94107...............415-957-0886
Antietam Review, 33 W Washington St, Hagerstown MD 21740...................301-791-3132
Antimicrobial Agents & Chemotherapy, 1913 I St NW, Wash DC 20006..202-833-9680
The Antioch Review, PO Box 148, Yellow Springs OH 45387 513-767-7386
The Antiquarian, PO Box 798, Huntington NY 11743......................516-271-8990
Antique Automobile, 501 W Governor Rd, Hershey PA 17033 717-534-1910
Antique Dealer, 1115 Clifton Ave, Clifton NJ 07013 201-779-1600
Antique Monthly, Drawer 2, Tuscaloosa AL 35402......................................205-345-0272
Antique Phonograph Monthly, 502 E 17th St, Brooklyn NY 11226...........718-941-6835
Antique Review, PO Box 538, Worthington OH 43085 614-885-9757
Antique Trader Weekly, 100 Bryant St, Dubuque IA 52001......................319-588-2073
Antique Week, 27 N Jefferson St, Knightstown IN 46148......................317-345-5133

Antiques & Auction News, Rt 230 W Box 500, Mt Joy PA 17552.................717-653-9797
Antiques & Collecting Hobbies, 1006 S Michigan, Chicago IL 60605.........312-939-4767
AOA News, 243 N Lindbergh Blvd, St Louis MO 63141 314-991-4100
AOPA Pilot, 421 Aviation Way, Frederick MD 21701....................................301-695-2350
AORN Jour, 10170 E Mississippi Ave, Denver CO 80231.............................303-755-6300
APA Monitor, 1200 17th St NW, Washington DC 20036................................202-955-7690
APCO Bulletin, 930 3rd Ave, New Smyrna Beach FL 32070.........................904-427-3461
Aperture, 20 E 23rd St, New York NY 10010...212-505-5555
APharmacy Weekly, 2215 Constitution Ave NW, Washington DC 20037..202-628-4410
Appalachian Heritage, Berea College, Bereaa KY 40404 606-986-9341
Appalachian Trailway News, PO Box 807, Harpers Ferry WV 25425 304-535-6331
Appaloosa News, 309 S Ann Arbor Ste 100, Oklahoma City OK 73127.....405-949-2288
Appaloosa World, PO Box 1035, Daytona Beach FL 32029.........................904-767-6284
Apparel Industry, 180 Allen Rd South Bldg #300, Atlanta GA 30328 404-252-8831
Apparel Merchandising, 425 Park Ave, New York NY 10022.....................212-371-9400
The Apple Blossom Connection, PO Box 325, Stacyville IA 50476.............515-737-2269
Appleton & Lange, 25 Van Zant St, East Norwalk CT 06855.....................203-838-4400
Appliance, 1000 Jorie Blvd, Oak Brook IL 60521 312-789-3484
Appliance Manufacturer, 6200 Som Center Rd, Solon OH 44139 216-349-3060
Appliance Service News, 110 W St Charles Rd, Lombard IL 60148 312-932-9550
Applied Cardiology, 825 S Barrington Ave, Los Angeles CA 90049..........213-826-8388
Applied Radiology, 1640 5th St PO Box 2178, Santa Monica CA 90406 213-395-0234
Applied Research in Mental Retardation, Elmsford NY 10523.................914-592-7700
The Appraisal Journal, 430 N Michigan Ave, Chicago IL 60611 312-329-8559
APWA Reporter, 1313 E 60th St, Chicago IL 60637.....................................312-947-2541
Aquaculture Magazine, 23 Sunset Terrace, Ashville NC 28801..................704-254-7334
Arabian Horse Times, Rt 3, Waseca MN 56093 507-835-3204
Arachne, 162 Sturges St, Jamestown NY 14701 716-488-0417
Ararat Quarterly, 585 Saddle River Rd, Saddle Brook NJ 07662 201-797-7600
Arbor Age, PO Box 122, Encino CA 91316..813-343-5961
ARC Rural Arts Services, Box 1547, Meddocino CA 95460 717-937-4494
Archaeogogy, 15 Park Row, New York NY 10038..212-732-5154
Archaeological News, Univ of Georgia, Athens GA 30602 404-542-1261
Archery Business, 11812 Wayzata Blvd, Minnetonka MN 55343 612-545-2662
Archery World, 11812 Wayzata Blvd, Minnetonka MN 55343......................612-545-2662
Architectural Designs, 380 Lexington Ave, New York NY 10017................212-557-9100
Architectural Digest, 5900 Wilshire Blvd, Los Angeles CA 90036..............213-937-5486
Architectural Record, 1221 Ave of the Americas, New York NY 10020....212-512-4565
Architectural Technology, 1735 New York Ave NW, Wash DC 20006......202-626-7471
Architecture, 1735 New York Ave NW, Washington DC 20006....................202-626-7300
Architecture California, 1303 J St Ste 200, Sacramento CA 95814............916-448-9082
Archives of Internal Medicine, 535 N Dearborn St, Chicago IL 60610......312-645-5000
Archives of Ophthalmology, 535 N Dearborn St, Chicago IL 60610...........312-645-5000
Archives of Otolaryngology, 535 N Dearborn St, Chicago IL 60610...........312-645-5000
Archives of Pathology, 535 N Dearborn, Chicago IL 60610 312-645-5000
Archives of Surgery, 535 N Dearborn St, Chicago IL 60610 312-645-5000
Archives Physical Medicine/Rehab, 30 N Michigan, Chicago IL 60602 312-236-9543
Area Auto Racing News, 2829-31 S Broad St, Trenton NJ 08610 609-888-3618
Area Development, 525 Northern Blvd, Great Neck NY 11021....................516-829-8990
Arete: Jour of Sport Lit, SDSU Press, San Diego CA 92182.......................619-265-5200
Arithmetic Teacher, 1906 Association Dr, Reston VA 22091.......................703-620-9840
Arizona Highways, 2039 W Lewis Ave, Phoenix AZ 85009...........................602-258-6641
Arizona Living, 5046-C N 7th St, Phoenix AZ 85014 602-264-4295

Arizona Monthly, 3136 N 3rd Ave, Phoenix AZ 85013.................................602-279-7999
Arizona Quarterly, Univ of Arizona Main Library, Tucson AZ 85721.......602-621-6396
Arizona Senior World, 2207 S 48th St Ste A, Tempe AZ 85282....................602-438-1566
Arizoo, PO Box 5155, Phoenix AZ 85010...602-273-1341
The Ark, 20 Tufts St, Cambridge MA 02139 617-876-0064
Arkansas Sportsman, PO Box 741, Marietta GA 30061 404-953-9222
Arkansas Times, 201 E Markham, Little Rock AR 72203 501-375-2985
The Armchair Detective, 129 W 56th St, New York NY 10019....................212-765-0902
Armed Forces & Society, Box 27, Cabin John MD 20818 301-320-2130
Armed Forces Comptroller, Box 91, Mount Vernon VA 22121...................703-780-6164
Armed Forces Jour Intl, 1414 22 St NW Ste 104, Washington DC 20037..202-296-0450
Armenian Numismatic Soc, 8511 Beverly Park, Pico Rivera CA 90660.....213-695-0390
Arms & Outdoor Digest, 2801 E Oakland Pk, Ft Lauderdale FL 33306....305-561-3505
D Armstrong Co Inc, 2000-M Govenors Circle, Houston TX 77092..........713-688-1441
Army Magazine, 2425 Wilson Blvd, Arlington VA 22201..............................703-841-4300
Army Times, 6883 Commercial Dr, Springfield VA 22159.............................703-750-2000
Army-Navy Store/Outdoor Merch, 567 Morris, Elizabeth NJ 07208.........201-353-7373
Arrival Magazine, 48 Shattuck Sq, Berkeley CA 94704 415-655-0878
Art & Antiques, 89 5th Ave, New York NY 10003 212-206-7050
Art & Artists, 280 Broadway Ste 412, New York NY 10007 212-227-3770
Art & Auction, 250 W 57th St Ste 215, New York NY 10107.......................212-582-5633
Art Business News, 60 Ridgeway Plaza, Stamford CT 06905.....................203-356-1745
Art Com, PO Box 3123 Rincon Annex, San Francisco CA 94119.................415-431-7672
Art Direction, 10 E 39th St 6th fl, New York NY 10016 212-889-6500
Art Education, 1916 Association Dr, Reston VA 22091 703-860-8000
Art Hazards News, 5 Beekman St, New York NY 10038 212-227-6220
Art in America, 980 Madison Ave, New York NY 10021 212-734-9797
Art Material Trade News, 6255 Barfield Rd, Atlanta GA 30328...................404-256-9800
Art Papers, 972 Peachtree St NE, Atlanta GA 30309 404-885-1273
Art Product News, Drawer 117, St Petersburg FL 33731..............................813-821-6064
Art Times, PO Box 730, Mt Marion NY 12456 914-246-5170
Art West, 303 E Main St, Bozeman MT 59715 406-586-5411
The Artcophile, 20 Beharrell St, Concord MA 01742.....................................617-369-1167
Artemis, PO Box 945, Roanoke VA 24005 703-774-4341
Artex Press, 1917 Center St, Stevens Point WI 54481 715-341-6959
Artforum, 65 Bleecker St, New York NY 10012 212-475-4000
Artful Dodge, PO Box 1473, Bloomington IN 47402 812-966-2096
Arthritis & Rheumatism, 17 Executive Pk Dr #480, Atlanta GA 30329 ...404-633-3777
Artichoke Publications, 5809 Harvest Hill, Dallas TX 75230 214-233-2486
The Artilleryman, 4 Water St Box C, Arlington MA 02174 617-646-2010
The Artist's Magazine, 1507 Dana Ave, Cincinnati OH 45207 513-531-2222
Artists' Publications In Print, PO Box 3692, Glendale CA 91201 213-797-0514
ARTlines, PO Box 2671, Taos NM 87571 505-758-4519
ARTnews, 5 W 37th St, New York NY 10018..212-398-1690
Artpolice, 133 E 25th St, Minneapolis MN 55404 612-825-3673
Arts, 12 S 6th St Ste 1030, Minneapolis MN 55402...612-339-7571
Arts & Activities, 591 Camino de la Reina #200, San Diego CA 92108 619-297-5352
Arts & Architecture, 1147 S Hope St, Los Angeles CA 90015......................213-749-6982
Arts Magazine, 23 E 26th St, New York NY 10010..212-685-8500
Arts Management, 408 W 57th St, New York NY 10019...................................212-245-3850
Artsline, 2518 Western Ave, Seattle WA 98121 206-441-0786
Artweek, 1628 Telegraph Ave, Oakland CA 94612..415-763-0422
ASC Newsletter, University of Kansas, Lawrence KS 66045 913-864-4867

ASHA, 10801 Rockville Pike, Rockville MD 20852 301-897-5700
Ashlee Publishing Co Inc, 310 Madison Ave, New York NY 10017 212-682-7681
ASHRAE Jour, 1791 Tullie Cir NE, Atlanta GA 30093................................404-636-8400
Ashton-Tate Quarterly, 20101 Hamilton Ave, Torrance CA 90502...........213-538-7579
Asia-Pacific Defense Forum, Box 13, Camp HM Smith HI 96861..............808-477-6924
Asian Survey, Univ of Calif Press, Berleley CA 94720................................415-642-0978
ASM News, 1931 I St NW, Washington DC 20006 202-833-9680
ASM News, Rte 87, Metals Park OH 44073 216-338-5151
Assembly Engineering, 25 W 550 Geneva Rd, Wheaton IL 60187.............312-665-1000
Associate Reformed Presbyterian, 1 Cleveland St, Greenville SC 29601 ...803-232-8297
Association & Society Mgr, 825 S Barrington, Los Angeles CA 90049 213-826-8388
Assn for Systems Management, 24587 Bagley, Cleveland OH 44138.........216-243-6900
Association Management, 1575 I St NW, Washington DC 20005 202-626-2708
Association Info & Image Mgmt, 1100 Wayne, Silver Spg MD 20910........301-587-8202
Astro Psychology Inst, 2640 Greenwich #403, San Francisco CA 94123...415-921-1192
Astro Signs, 566 Westchester Ave, Rye Brook NY 10573.............................914-939-2111
Astronomy Magazine, 625 E St Paul Ave, Milwaukee WI 53202.................414-276-2689
The Astronomy Quarterly, PO Box 35549, Tucson AZ 85740.....................602-297-4797
ASU Travel Guide, 1325 Columbus Ave, San Francisco CA 94133.............415-441-5200
Asymptotical World, 341 Lincoln Ave, Williamsport PA 17703 717-322-7841
ATA Magazine of Martial Arts, PO Box 240835, Memphis TN 38124.......901-761-2821
Atari Explorer, PO Box 3427, Sunnyvale CA 94088....................................408-745-4787
ATC Cablevision Program Guide, 332 Congress St, Boston MA 02210 617-574-9400
Athena Incognito Magazine, 1442 Judah St, San Francisco CA 94122.......415-665-0219
Athletic Jour, 1719 Howard St, Evanston IL 60202....................................312-328-8545
Atlanta, PO Box 5502, Atlanta GA 30307...404-378-9769
Atlanta Art Papers Inc, 927 Peachtree St NE, Atlanta GA 30309..............404-885-1273
Atlanta Magazine, 6255 Barfield Rd, Atlanta GA 30328.............................404-256-9800
Atlanta Singles, 3423 Piedmont Rd NE, Atlanta GA 30305 404-239-0642
Atlanta Women's News, 2810 New Spring Rd #106, Atlanta GA 30339 404-434-5966
Atlantic City Magazine, 1637 Atlantic Ave, Atlantic City NJ 08401 609-348-6886
The Atlantic, 8 Arlington St, Boston MA 02116 617-536-9500
The ATO Palm, 4001 W Kirby Ave, Champaign IL 61821............................217-351-1865
Atomic Spectroscopy, 901 Ethan Allen Hwy, Ridgefield CT 06877............203-431-7740
Attage, 11754 Jollyville Rd, Austin TX 78759..512-250-1255
Attenzione, 152 Madison Ave, New York NY 10016....................................212-683-9000
Atticus Review, 720 Herber Ave, Calexico CA 92231 619-357-3721
ATV News, 2201 Cherry Ave, Long Beach CA 90801...................................213-595-4753
ATV Sports, PO Box 2260, Costa Mesa CA 92626......................................714-979-2560
Auction & Surplus, 1250 W Glenoaks Blvd, Glendale CA 91201 818-545-0333
Audecibel, 20361 Middlebelt, Livonia MI 48152...313-478-2610
Audio, 1515 Broadway 11th fl, New York NY 10036....................................212-719-6331
Audio Amateur, PO Box 576, Peterborough NH 03458..............................603-924-9464
Audio Times, 345 Park Ave S, New York NY 10010.....................................212-686-7744
Audio-Visual Communications, 50 W 23rd St, New York NY 10010.........212-645-1000
Audio/Visual Poetry Found, 400 Fish Hatchery, Marianna FL 32446 904-482-3890
AudioVideo Intl/DEMPA Publ, 400 Madison Ave, New York NY 10017 .212-752-3003
Audubon, 950 3rd Ave, New York NY 10022..212-546-9250
Aufbau, 2121 Broadway, New York NY 10023...212-873-7400
Austin Homefinder, 4501 Spicewood Springs, Austin TX 78759 512-343-2241
Austin Homes & Gardens, 900 West Ave, Austin TX 78701 512-479-8936
Austin Magazine, PO Box 4368, Austin TX 78765......................................512-339-9955
Authors Resource Ctr News, 4001 E Ft Lowell Rd, Tucson AZ 85712......602-325-4733

Auto Glass Jour, 303 Harvard E PO Box 12099, Seattle WA 98102...........206-322-5120
Auto Laundry News, 370 Lexington Ave, New York NY 10017 212-532-9290
Auto Merchandising News, 234 Greenfield St, Fairfield CT 06430 203-384-9323
Auto Racing Digest, 1020 Church St, Evanston IL 60201 312-491-6440
Auto Trim News, 1623 Grand Ave, Baldwin NY 11510 516-223-4334
Autobuff, 4480 N Shallowford Rd Ste 100, Atlanta GA 30338.....................404-394-0010
Automatic Machining, 100 Seneca Ave, Rochester NY 14621 716-338-1522
Automation In Housing, PO Box 120, Carpinteria CA 93013 805-684-7659
Automobile Intl, 368 Park Ave S, New York NY 10016 212-689-0120
Automobile Quarterly Magazine, 221 Nassau St, Princeton NJ 08540.......609-924-7555
Automotive Aftermarket News, 65 E South Water St, Chicago IL 60601...312-332-0210
Automotive Age, 6931 Van Nuys Blvd, Van Nuys CA 91405.......................818-997-0644
Automotive Body Repair News, 65 E South Water St, Chicago IL 60601..312-332-0201
Automotive Booster of Calif, PO Box 765, LaCanada CA 91011 213-790-6554
Automotive Cooling Jour, 1709 N Broad St, Lansdale PA 19446................215-362-5800
Automotive Fleet, 2500 Artesia Blvd, Redondo Beach CA 90278 213-376-8788
Automotive Industries, Chilton Way, Radnor PA 19089...........................215-964-4243
Automotive Messenger, 320 Brooks, Hazelwood MO 63042.......................314-731-4040
Automotive News, 1400 Woodbridge Ave, Detroit MI 48207.....................313-446-6000
Autosound & Communications, 345 Park Ave S, New York NY 10010 212-686-7744
AutoWeek, 1400 Woodbridge Ave, Detroit MI 48207.................................313-446-6000
AV Video, 25550 Hawthorne Blvd, Torrance CA 90505..............................213-373-9993
AV: Audio-Visual Magazine, 204 Noble Plz, Jenkintown PA 19046...........215-887-0816
Aviation Digest Magazine, 49 Miry Brook Rd, Danbury CT 06810............203-792-5800
Aviation Mechanics Jour, 1000 College View Dr, Riverton WY 82501.....307-856-1582
Aviation Week & Space Tech, 1221 Ave of Amer, New York NY 10020 ...212-512-2000
Aviation/USA, PO Box 2029, Tuscaloosa AL 35403 205-349-2990
Avionics, PO Box 5100, Westport CT 06881...203-227-2280
Aviva Press, PO Box 1357, Brookline MA 02146 617-739-1537
The Awakener Magazine, 938 18th St, Hermosa Beach CA 90254 213-379-2656
Awards Shopper, PO Box 8784, Jacksonville FL 32239 904-725-6320
Awards Specialist, 26 Summit St PO Box 1230, Brighton MI 48116..........313-227-2614
Away ALA, 888 Worcester St, Wellesley MA 02181 617-237-5200
Axios, 800 S Euclid St, Fullerton CA 92632..714-526-2131
Aztlan, 405 Hilgard Ave, Los Angeles CA 90025..213-825-2642
B'nai B'rith Jewish Monthly, 1640 Rhode Island, Wash DC 20036..........202-857-6645
B-City, 619 West Surf St, Chicago IL 60657..312-871-6175
Baby Talk, 185 Madison Ave, New York NY 10016.....................................212-679-4400
Backpacker, One Park Ave, New York NY 10016 212-719-6000
The Backstretch, 19363 James Couzens Hwy, Detroit MI 48235..............313-342-6144
Badger Sportsman, 19 E Main, Chilton WI 53014......................................414-849-4651
Bakersfield Lifestyle, 123 Truxtun Ave, Bakersfield CA 93301 805-325-7124
Bakery Production & Marketing, 5725 E River Rd, Chicago IL 60631 312-693-3200
Baking Equipment, 9000 W 67th St, Merriam KS 66202...........................913-236-7300
Baking Industry, 301 E Erie St, Chicago IL 60611......................................312-644-2020
Ball State Univ Forum, Ball State Univ English Dept, Muncie IN 47306..317-285-8456
Ballroom Dancing USA, 10870 Mississippi, Minneapolis MN 55443.........612-427-5942
Balls & Strikes, 2801 NE 50th St, Oklahoma City OK 73111 405-424-5266
Baltimore Gay Paper, PO Box 22575, Baltimore MD 21203 301-837-5445
Baltimore Magazine, 26 S Calvert St, Baltimore MD 21202......................301-752-7375
BAM Magazine, 5951 Canning St, Oakland CA 94609 415-652-3810
Bamboo Ridge, PO Box 61781, Honolulu HI 96822...................................808-395-7098
Banjo Newsletter, PO Box 364, Greensboro MD 21639 301-482-6278

Bank Loan Officers Report, 1 Penn Plaza 40th fl, New York NY 10119 ...212-971-5000
Bank Note Reporter, 700 E State St, Iola WI 54990......................................715-445-2214
Bank Operations Report, 1 Penn Plaza 40th fl, New York NY 10119........212-971-5000
Bank Personnel Report, 1 Penn Plaza 40th fl, New York NY 10119..........212-971-5000
Bank Systems & Equipment, 1515 Broadway, New York NY 10036..........212-869-1300
Bankers Monthly, 870 7th Ave, New York NY 10019....................................212-399-1084
Banking Software Rev, 9100 Keystone, Indianapolis IN 46240...................317-844-7461
Baptist Leader, Valley Forge PA 19482..215-768-2153
Barbie, 300 Madison Ave, New York NY 10017...212-687-0680
The Bare Foot Review, PO Box 15182, San Diego CA 92115.......................619-583-2020
The Barnhart Dictionary Companion, Box 247, Cold Spring NY 10516 ...914-265-2822
Barrister, 750 N Lake Shore Dr, Chicago IL 60611 312-988-6047
Barron's Business/Financial Wkly, 200 Liberty, New York NY 10028 212-416-2759
Barter Communique, PO Box 2527, Sarasota FL 33578................................813-349-3300
Baseball America, PO Box 2089, Durham NC 27702....................................919-682-9635
Baseball Cards, 700 E State St, Iola WI 54990 715-445-2214
Baseball Digest, 1020 Church St, Evanston IL 60201..................................312-491-6440
Baseball: Our Way, 3211 Milwaukee St #1, Madison WI 53714................608-241-0549
Basic Society News, PO Box 815099, Dallas TX 75381................................214-484-9900
Basketball Digest, 1020 Church St, Evanston IL 60201 312-491-6440
Bassin', 15115 S 76th E Ave, Bixby OK 74008...918-366-4441
Bassmaster Magazine, PO Box 17900, Montgomery AL 36141 205-272-9530
The Battery Man, 100 Larchwood Dr, Largo FL 33540................................813-586-1409
Bay & Delta Yachtsman, 2019 Clement Ave, Alameda CA 94501..............415-865-7500
BBW: Big Beautiful Woman, PO Box 1305, Woodland Hills CA 91364 818-986-5130
The Beast, Box 789, Wainscott NY 11975..516-324-2027
Beatlefan, 2819 Hollywood Dr, Decatur GA 30033.....................................404-296-1197
Beauty & Grooming Intl, 157 W 57th St Ste 803, New York NY 10019.....212-315-2700
Beauty Fashion, 48 E 43rd St, New York NY 10017......................................212-687-6190
Beauty Handbook Magazine, 420 Lexington Ave, New York NY 10017 ...212-687-7344
Bed & Breakfast Update, PO Box 4814, North Hollywood CA 91607 818-761-3386
Beef, 1999 Shepard Rd, St Paul MN 55116 612-690-7374
Beef Magazine, 659 Haight St, San Francisco CA 94117 415-626-3817
Behavior Today, 2315 Broadway, New York NY 10024................................212-873-5900
Behavioral Disorders Jour, 1920 Association Dr, Reston VA 22091..........703-620-3660
Behind Small Business Newsletter, Box 37147, Minneapolis MN 55431 ...612-881-5364
Bell Assn for the Deaf, 3417 Volta Pl NW, Washington DC 20007.............202-337-5220
Belles Lettres, PO Box 987, Arlington VA 22216 301-294-0278
The Bellingham Review, 412 N State St, Bellingham WA 98225 206-734-9781
Bellowing Ark, PO Box 45637, Seattle WA 98145 206-545-8302
Beloit Fiction Jour, Box 11 Beloit College, Beloit WI 53511.....................608-365-3391
Beloit Poetry Jour, Box 154 RFD 2, Ellsworth ME 04605 207-667-5598
Bend of the River, 143 W 3rd St PO Box 239, Perrysburg OH 43551.........419-874-7534
The Bent of Tau Beta Pi, Box 8840 Univ Sta, Knoxville TN 37996 615-546-4578
The Berkeley Monthly, 1301 59th St, Emeryville CA 94608 415-658-9811
Berkeley Works, 2206 M L King Way Apt C, Berkeley CA 94704 415-849-3979
Bern Porter Intl, 22 Salmond Rd, Belfast ME 04915...................................207-338-3763
Bestways, PO Box 2028, Carson City NV 89702 702-883-7311
Better Buildings, 12 W 37th St, New York NY 10018...................................212-563-6460
Better Business, 235 E 42nd St, New York NY 10017 214-573-2385
Better Health, 1485 Chapel St, New Haven CT 06511 203-789-3974
Better Health & Living, 800 2nd Ave, New York NY 10017.........................212-986-9026
Better Homes & Gardens, 1716 Locust St, Des Moines IA 50336 515-284-3000

Better Investing, Box 220, Royal Oak MI 48068..313-543-0612
A Better Life for You, 424 N 3rd St, Burlington IA 52601...........................319-752-5415
Better Living, 1775 Broadway, New York NY 10019.................................212-581-2000
Better Nutrition, 390 5th Ave, New York NY 10018..................................212-613-9700
Better Roads, Box 558, Park Ridge IL 60068..312-693-7710
Beverage Industry, 7500 Old Oak Blvd, Cleveland OH 44130....................216-243-1800
Beverage Media, 161 Ave of the Americas, New York NY 10013...............212-620-0100
Beverage Retailer, 1661 Rt 23, Wayne NJ 07470.......................................201-696-8105
Beverly Hills 213, 9570 Wilshire Blvd Mezz, Beverly Hills CA 90212........213-275-5848
Beyond, PO Box 1124, Fair Lawn NJ 07410..201-791-6721
Beyond Baroque Newsletter, PO Box 2727, Venice CA 90291...................213-822-3006
Bible of Weather Forecasting, PO Box 63302, Los Angeles CA 90063......213-263-2640
Biblical Archaeologist, Box HM Duke Station, Durham NC 27706..........919-684-3075
Biblical Archaeology Rev, 3000 Connecticut Ave NW, Wash DC 20008....202-387-8888
Biblical History, 105 Loudoun St SW, Leesburg VA 22075.........................703-771-9400
Bicycle Business Jour, 1904 Wenneca Ave, Ft Worth TX 76102...............817-870-0341
Bicycle Guide, 711 Boylston St, Boston MA 02116....................................617-236-1885
Bicycle Rider, 29901 Agoura Rd, Agoura CA 91301..................................818-991-4980
Bicycling, 33 E Minor St, Emmaus PA 18098..215-967-5171
Big Scream Nada, 2782 Dixie SW, Grandville MI 49418.............................616-531-1442
Big Two-Hearted, 424 Stephenson Ave, Iron Mountain MI 49801.............906-774-3305
Bike Tech, 33 E Minor St, Emmaus PA 18049..215-967-5171
Bikereport, PO Box 8308, Missoula MT 59807..406-721-1776
Bile: Press of the Third Mind, 932 W Oakdale, Chicago IL 60657.............312-929-3387
Bilingual Review/Press, Ariz State Univ, Tempe AZ 85287.......................602-965-3867
Bill Communications, 110 N Miller Rd, Akron OH 44313............................216-867-4401
Billboard, 1515 Broadway, New York NY 10036...212-764-7300
Biochemical-Biophysical Research, 111 5th Ave, New York NY 10003.....212-741-6800
Biochemical Education, Maxwell House, Elmsford NY 10523....................914-592-7700
Biochemistry, 1155 16th St NW, Washington DC 20036.............................202-872-4546
Biology Digest, 143 Old Marlton Pike, Medford NJ 08055.........................609-654-6500
Biomedical Products, PO Box 1952, Dover NJ 07801................................201-361-9060
Bioscience, 1401 Wilson Blvd, Arlington VA 22209....................................703-527-6776
BioTechniques, 2 Woodland St, Natick MA 01760......................................617-655-8282
Biotechnology, 65 Bleecker St, New York NY 10012...................................212-477-9600
Bird Talk, PO Box 6050, Mission Viejo CA 92690.......................................714-240-6001
Bird Watcher's Digest, PO Box 110, Marietta OH 45750...........................614-373-5285
Birding, PO Box 4335, Austin TX 78765...512-474-4804
Birmingham, 2027 1st Ave N, Birmingham AL 35203..................................205-323-5461
Birth, 110 El Camino Real, Berkeley CA 94705...415-658-5099
Black & White, PO Box 47318, Chicago IL 60647..312-278-1778
Black Amer Literature, ISU Parsons Hall 237, Terre Haute IN 47809......812-237-2968
Black Bear Review, 1916 Lincoln St, Croydon PA 19020............................215-788-3543
Black Belt, 1813 Victory Pl, Burbank CA 91504..818-843-4444
Black Books Bulletin, 7524 S Cottage Grove Ave, Chicago IL 60619........312-651-0770
Black Buzzard Press, 4705 S 8th Rd, Arlington VA 22204.........................703-521-0142
Black Careers, PO Box 8214, Philadelphia PA 19101.................................215-387-1600
The Black Collegian, 1240 S Broad St, New Orleans LA 70125.................504-821-5694
Black Confession, 355 Lexington Ave, New York NY 10017........................212-391-1400
Black Enterprise, 130 5th Ave, New York NY 10011...................................212-242-8000
Black Family, PO Box 1046, Herndon VA 22070..703-860-3411
Black Fly Review, Univ of Main Ft Kent, Ft Kent ME 04743......................207-834-3162
Black Mountain Review, PO Box 1112, Black Mountain NC 28711............704-669-6211

Black New Orleans, 1240 S Broad St, New Orleans LA 70125 504-827-5578
Black Romance, 355 Lexington Ave, New York NY 10017 212-391-1400
The Black Scholar, PO Box 2869, Oakland CA 94609 415-547-6633
Black Warrior Review, PO Box 2936, Tuscaloosa AL 35487 205-348-4518
Black Willow Poetry, 401 Independence Dr, Harleysville PA 19438...........215-368-0163
Blackjack Forum RGE, 2000 Center St #1067, Berkeley CA 94704 415-540-5209
The Blade Magazine, PO Box 22007, Chattanooga TN 37422 615-894-0339
Blair & Ketchum's Country Jour, 2245 Kohn Rd, Harrisburg PA 17105..717-657-9555
Blake, Univ of Rochester, Rochester NY 14627 716-275-4091
Blind Alleys, PO Box 13224, Baltimore MD 21203 301-342-3092
Blitz, PO Box 48124, Los Angeles CA 90048...213-851-9384
Blood, 6277 Sea Harbor Dr, Orlando FL 32887.....................................305-345-4200
The Blood-Horse, 1736 Alexandria Dr, Lexington KY 40544 606-278-2361
Bloodroot, Box 891, Grand Forks ND 58206..701-775-6079
The Bloomsbury Review, PO Box 8928, Denver CO 80201.......................303-892-0620
Blow, 4820 SE Boise, Portland OR 97206..503-774-6304
Blue & Gray, 130 Galloway Rd, Galloway OH 43119..............................614-870-1861
Blue Buildings, 1215 25th St #F, Des Moines IA 50311...........................515-274-9103
Blue Coud Quarterly, Box 98, Marvin SD 57251....................................605-432-5528
The Blue Glow/Egad!, 21738 S Avalon Blvd, Carson CA 90745 213-835-5474
Blue Horse, PO Box 6061, Augusta GA 30906..404-798-5628
The Blue Sky Jour, 1710 Decker Rd, Malibu CA 90265.........................213-457-4613
Blue Unicorm, 22 Avon Rd, Kensington CA 94707.................................415-526-8439
Bluefish, PO Box 1601, Southampton NY 11968.....................................516-283-8811
Bluegrass Unlimited, PO Box 111, Broad Run VA 22014 703-361-8992
BM/E, 295 Madison Ave, New York NY 10017.......................................212-685-5320
BMX Action, 3162 Kashiwa St, Torrance CA 90505.................................213-539-9213
BMX Plus, 10600 Sepulveda Blvd, Mission Hills CA 91345......................714-545-6012
Board & Administrator, PO Box 259, Akron IA 51001............................712-568-2418
Boardroom Reports, 330 W 42nd St, New York NY 10036 212-239-9000
Boat & Motor Dealer, 3945 Oakton St, Skokie IL 60076.........................312-982-1810
Boat Pennsylvania, PO Box 1673, Harrisburg PA 17105..........................717-657-4520
Boating Industry, 850 3rd Ave, New York NY 10022................................212-715-2600
Boating Magazine, 1 Park Ave, New York NY 10016................................212-725-3972
Boating Product News, 850 3rd Ave, New York NY 10022........................212-715-2732
Bobbin, 1110 Shop Rd, Columbia SC 29202..803-771-7500
Boca Raton, 114 NE 2nd St, Boca Raton FL 33432.................................305-392-3406
Body Fashion/Intimate Apparel, 545 5th Ave, New York NY 10017 212-503-2900
Bodyshop Business, 11 S Forge St, Akron OH 44304..............................216-535-6117
Bogus Review, 120 W 97th St #10A, New York NY 10025........................212-222-1731
Bomb Magazine, PO Box 2003 Canal Sta, New York NY 10013................212-431-3943
Bon Appetit, 5900 Wilshire Blvd, Los Angeles CA 90036.........................213-937-1025
Book Business Mart, 16254 Wedgewood, Ft Worth TX 76133 817-293-7030
Book Dealers World, PO Box 2525, La Mesa CA 92041 619-462-3297
Book Forum, 38 E 76th St, New York NY 10021 212-861-8328
Book News, PO Box 330309, Ft Worth TX 76163....................................817-293-7030
The Book Report, 2950 N High St, Columbus OH 43214..........................614-261-6584
Book Talk, 8632 Horacio Pl NE, Albuquerque NM 87111........................505-299-8940
Booklist, 50 E Huron St, Chicago IL 60611..312-944-6780
BookLover, 151 W 75th St, New York NY 10023 212-362-8096
BookNotes, PO Box 42265, Portland OR 97242......................................503-233-2637
Books of the Southwest, Univ of Ariz Library, Tucson AZ 85721 602-621-2101
Bookstore Jour, 2620 Venetucci Blvd, Colorado Springs CO 80901..........303-576-7880

The Bookwatch, 166 Miramar Ave, San Francisco CA 94112 415-587-7009
Bop, 7060 Hollywood Blvd Ste 720, Hollywood CA 90028 414-295-6922
Boro Park Voice, 4616 13th Ave, Brooklyn NY 11219 718-436-1800
Boston Business Jour, 393 D St, Boston MA 02210 617-268-9880
Boston Magazine, 300 Massachusetts Ave, Boston MA 02115....................617-262-9700
Boston Observer, 8 Newbury St, Boston MA 02116.....................................617-267-4345
The Boston Phoenix, 100 Massachusetts Ave, Boston MA 02115 617-536-5390
Boston Review, 33 Harrison Ave, Boston MA 02111 617-350-5353
Bostonia Magazine, 10 Lenox St, Brookline MA 02146 617-353-3081
Both Sides Now, Rt 6 Box 28, Tyler TX 75704...214-592-4263
The Bottom Line, 1120 E Oakland Ave, Lansing MI 48906.........................517-487-9276
Bottomfish Magazine, 21250 Stevens Creek Blvd, Cupertino CA 95014....408-996-4550
Bottomline, 1101 15th St NW Ste 400, Washington DC 20005 202-851-3100
Boulder Co Business Report, PO Box 8005-265, Boulder CO 80306 303-440-4950
Bow & Arrow Hunting, Box HH, Capistrano Beach CA 92624.....................714-493-2101
Bow Waves Boating, 1405 3rd Ave, Spring Lake NJ 07762 201-449-3225
Bowhunter, 3808 S Calhoun St, Ft Wayne IN 46807....................................219-456-3580
Bowlers Jour, 101 E Erie St, Chicago IL 60611 312-266-7171
Bowling, 5301 S 76th St, Greendale WI 53129...414-421-6400
Bowling Digest, 1020 Church St, Evanston IL 60201....................................312-491-6440
Box 749: Printable Arts Soc, PO Box 749, New York NY 10011.................212-980-0519
Boxboard Containers, 300 W Adams St, Chicago IL 60606.........................312-726-2802
Boxoffice, 1800 N Highland Ave, Hollywood CA 90028 213-465-1186
Boys' Life, 1325 Walnut Hill Ln, Irving TX 75038 214-580-2000
BPME Image, 1528A Granite Hills Dr, El Cajon CA 92019........................619-447-1227
Brahman Jour, Box 220, Eddy TX 76524 817-859-5451
Braille Forum, 1010 Vermont Ave NW, Washington DC 20005...................202-393-3666
Brain/Mind Bulletin, PO Box 42211, Los Angeles CA 90042......................213-223-2500
Brake & Front End, 11 S Forge St, Akron OH 44304 216-535-6117
Bravo, 1081 Trafalgar St, Teaneck NJ 07666..201-836-5922
Bread, 6401 The Paseo, Kansas City MO 64131 816-333-7000
Bread Loaf Quarterly, Middlebury College, Middlebury VT 05753............802-388-3711
Breathless, 910 Broad St, Endicott NY 13760...212-785-7790
Brennan Partners Inc, 485 5th Ave, New York NY 10017............................212-867-9291
Brick & Clay Record, 6200 SOM Ctr Rd, Solon OH 44139.........................216-349-3060
Bridal Guide, 441 Lexington Ave, New York NY 10017 212-949-4040
Bridal Trends, PO Box 10010, Ogden UT 84409..801-394-9446
Bride's, 350 Madison Ave, New York NY 10017 212-880-8800
Bridge: Asian-Amer Perspective, 32 E Broadway, New York NY 10002 ...212-925-8685
Brigham Young Univ Studies, 3168 JKHB BYU, Provo UT 84602............801-378-4647
Brilliant Ideas for Publishers, 4709 Sherwood Rd, Madison WI 53711 608-271-6867
British Defence Dir, Maxwell House, Elmsford NY 10523 914-592-7700
British Heritage, 2245 Kohn Rd, Harrisburg PA 17105 717-657-9555
Broadcast Engineering, Box 12901, Overland Park KS 66212....................913-888-4664
Broadcasting, 1735 De Sales St NW, Washington DC 20036 202-638-1022
Broadway Magazine, 332 W 57th St, New York NY 10019..........................212-315-0800
Broiler Industry, Sandstone Bldg, Mount Morris IL 61054.........................815-734-4171
Broken Streets, 57 Morningside Dr E, Bristol CT 06010.............................203-582-2943
Bronze Thrills, 355 Lexington Ave, New York NY 10017.............................212-391-1400
Broomstick, 3543 18th St #3, San Francisco CA 94110...............................415-552-7460
Carol Bryan Magazines, 1000 Byus Dr, Charleston WV 25311 304-345-2378
Buckeye Farm News, 35 E Chestnut St, Columbus OH 43216.....................614-225-8905
Bucknell Review, Bucknell Univ English Dept, Lewisburg PA 17837........717-524-1184

Buddy Orig Texas Music Mag, 501 N Good-Latimer, Dallas TX 75204 ...214-826-8742
Buffalo Spree Magazine, 4511 Harlem Rd, Buffalo NY 14226....................716-893-3405
Builder Insider, PO Box 191125, Dallas TX 75219 214-871-2913
Builder/Dealer, 16 1st Ave, Corry PA 16407 814-664-8624
Building Blocks, PO Box 33279, Washington DC 20033 202-232-3600
Building Design Jour, 6255 Barfield Rd, Atlanta GA 30328 404-256-9800
Building Material Retailer, 1111 Douglas Dr, Minneapolis MN 55442.....612-544-1597
Building Operating Mgmt, 2100 W Florist, Milwaukee WI 53201............414-228-7701
Building Services Contractor, 101 W 31st St, New York NY 10001...........212-279-4455
Building Supply News, 1350 E Touhy Ave, Des Plaines IL 60018 312-635-8800
Buildings Design & Constr, 1350 E Touhy, Des Plaines IL 60018..............312-635-8800
Bulletin of Clinical Neurosciences, 111 5th Ave, New York NY 10003 305-345-4100
Bulletin of Medical Library Assn, 919 N Michigan, Chicago IL 60611......312-266-2456
Bulletin of the Atomic Scientist, 5801 S Kenwood, Chicago IL 60637.......312-363-5225
Bulletin Sci/Tech Handicapped, 1776 Mass Ave NW, Wash DC 20036....202-467-4496
Bus Ride, PO Box 1472, Spokane WA 99210 509-328-9181
Bus Tours, 9698 W Judson Rd, Polo IL 61064...815-946-2341
Business Aviation, Westchester Airport, White Plains NY 10604 914-948-1912
Business Age, PO Box 11597, Milwaukee WI 53211...................................414-332-7507
Business Atlanta, 6255 Barfield Rd, Atlanta GA 30328 404-256-9800
Business Computer Systems, 221 Columbus Ave, Boston MA 02116........617-536-7780
Business Digest of Delaware Valley, 2442 Golf Rd, Phila PA 19131 215-477-8620
Business Digest of Lehigh Valley, 112 E Broad St, Bethlehem PA 18018 .215-861-0766
Business Digest of Southern NJ, 2449 Golf Rd, Philadelphia PA 19131 ...215-477-8620
Business Facilities, PO Box 2060, Red Bank NJ 07701................................201-842-7433
Business Forms & Systems, 401 N Broad St, Philadelphia PA 19108........215-238-5300
Business Horizons, Indiana University, Bloomington IN 47405..................812-335-5507
Business Insurance, 740 N Rush St, Chicago IL 60611 312-649-5398
Business Jour, 80 S Market St Ste 200, San Jose CA 95113 408-295-3800
The Business Jour, 2025 N Summit Ave, Milwaukee WI 53202..................414-278-7788
Business Marketing, 740 N Rush St, Chicago IL 60611 312-649-5260
Business Month, 875 3rd Ave, New York NY 10022 212-605-9400
Business New Hampshire, 177 E Industrial Dr, Manchester NH 03103....603-668-7330
The Business of Fur, 141 W 28th St, New York NY 10001............................212-279-4250
Business Press of Orange Cty, 9774 W Katella, Anaheim CA 92804.........714-956-4520
Business Software, 501 Galveston Dr, Redwood City CA 94063 415-366-3600
The Business Times, 544 Tolland St, E Hartford CT 06108 203-289-9341
Business to Business, PO Box 6085, Tallahassee FL 32314.........................904-222-7072
Business Today, PO Box 10010, Ogden UT 84409.......................................801-394-9446
Business View, PO Box 9859, Naples FL 33941 813-263-7525
Business Week, 1221 Ave of Americas, New York NY 10020 212-512-1221
Business Week Careers, 1221 Ave of Americas, New York NY 10020 212-512-3409
Business Worcester, PO Box 300, Worcester MA 01614 617-799-0648
Butane-Propane News, 338 Foothill Blvd, Arcadia CA 91006 818-357-2168
Buying Office Products, 8310 Capital of Texas Hwy, Austin TX 78731.....512-343-9066
Byline, PO Box 130596, Edmond OK 73013..405-348-3325
Byte, 70 Main St, Peterborough NH 03458...603-924-9281
Cable Hour TV Magazine, PO Box 15548, Ft Wayne IN 46885...................219-493-4588
Cable Marketing, 352 Park Ave S, New York NY 10010 212-685-4848
Cable Television Business, 6300 S Syracuse Way, Englewood CO 80111..303-220-0600
Cabletime, 332 Congress St, Boston MA 02210 617-574-9400
Cablevision, 600 Grant St, Denver CO 80203 303-860-0111
Cache Review, PO Box 19794, Seattle WA 98109 602-748-0600

Cadence Jazz & Blues Magazine, Cadence Bldg, Redwood NY 13679......315-287-2852
Caesura, Auburn University English Dept, Auburn AL 36849....................205-826-4620
Cafe Solo, 7975 San Marcos, Atascadero CA 93422....................................805-466-0947
Calif Highway Patrolman, 2030 V St, Sacramento CA 95818....................916-452-6751
California Angler, 6200 Yarrow Dr PO Box 1789, Carlsbad CA 92008.....619-967-1942
California Bicyclist, PO Box 210477, San Francisco CA 94121.................415-221-4066
California Builder, 693 Mission St Penthouse, San Francisco CA 94105...415-781-1431
California Business, 4221 Wilshire Blvd #400, Los Angeles CA 90010.....213-937-5820
California Farmer, 731 Market St, San Francisco CA 94103.....................415-495-3340
California Geology, 1416 9th St Rm 1341, Sacramento CA 95814.................916-445-0514
California History, 1090 Jackson St, San Francisco CA 94109..................415-567-1848
California Homes & Lifestyles, 2900 Bristol, Costa Mesa CA 92626.........714-241-9221
California Inntouch, 2550 Fair Oaks Blvd, Sacramento CA 95825..............916-488-1770
California Jour, 1714 Capitol Ave, Sacramento CA 95814.......................916-444-2840
California Lawyer, 555 Franklin St, San Francisco CA 94102..................415-561-8280
California Magazine, 11601 Wilshire Blvd, Los Angeles CA 90025...........213-479-6511
California Pharmacist, 1112 I St, Sacramento CA 95814..........................916-444-7811
California Publisher, 1127 11th St, Sacramento CA 95814.......................916-443-5991
California Real Estate, 525 Virgil Ave, Los Angeles CA 90020................213-739-8234
Call Board, 2940 16th St #102, San Francisco CA 94103.........................415-621-0427
Callaloo, Univ of Virginia English Dept, Charlottesville VA 22903..........804-924-6637
Calligraphy Idea Exchange, 2500 S McGee, Norman OK 73072...............405-364-8794
Calliope, Roger Williams College, Bristol RI 02809...............................401-253-1040
Calliopes Corner, PO Box 110647, Anchorage AK 99511..........................907-349-7170
Calypso Log, 777 3rd Ave, New York NY 10017......................................212-826-2940
Calyx, PO Box B, Corvallis OR 97339..503-753-9384
Caminos Magazine, PO Box 54307, Los Angeles CA 90054.....................213-222-1349
Camper Times, PO Box 6294, Richmond VA 23230.................................804-270-5653
Camperways, 1108 N Bethlehem Pike, Spring House PA 19477.................215-643-2058
Camping Magazine, 5000 State Rd 67 N, Martinsville IN 46151...............317-342-8456
Camping Today, 9425 S Greenville Rd, Greenville MI 48838....................616-754-9179
Campus Life, 465 Gundersen Dr, Carol Stream IL 61088.........................312-260-6183
Campus Voice, 505 Market St, Knoxville TN 37902...............................615-521-0646
Cancer, E Washington Sq, Philadelphia PA 19105..................................215-238-4200
Cancer Investigation, 270 Madison Ave, New York NY 10016..................212-698-9000
Candy Industry, 7500 Old Oak Blvd, Cleveland OH 44130.......................216-243-8100
Candy Marketing Quarterly, 7500 Old Oak Blvd, Cleveland OH 44130...216-243-8100
Candy Wholesaler, 1120 Vermont Ave NW, Washington DC 20005..........202-463-2124
Canoe, PO Box 3146, Kirkland WA 98083...206-827-6363
Cape Cod Compass, 935 Main St PO Box 375, Chatham MA 02633.........617-945-3542
Cape Cod Life, Box 222, Osterville MA 02655.......................................617-428-5706
The Cape Rock, Southeast Missouri State, Cape Girardeau MO 63701....314-651-2151
Capital Region Magazine, 295 Quail St, Albany NY 12208......................518-458-2091
Capper's, 616 Jefferson St, Topeka KS 66607..913-295-1108
Car & Driver, 2002 Hogback Rd, Ann Arbor MI 48104............................313-971-3600
Car & Parts, 911 Vandemark Rd, Sidney OH 45367...............................513-498-2111
Car Collector & Car Classics, 8601 Dunwoody Pl, Atlanta GA 30338......404-998-4603
Car Craft, 8490 Sunset Blvd, Los Angeles CA 90069..............................213-657-5100
Cardio, 500 Howard St, San Francisco CA 94105...................................415-397-1881
Cardiology Management, 1640 5th St, Santa Monica CA 90406................213-395-0234
Cardiology World News, PO Box 1548, Marco Island FL 33937................813-394-0400
Cardiovascular Medicine, 475 Park Ave S, New York NY 10016..............212-686-0555
Career World, 3652 Madeville Canyon, Los Angeles CA 90049................213-208-8025

Careers, 1001 Ave of the Americas, New York NY 10018 212-354-8877
Caribbean Review, Florida Intl Univ Tamiami Trail, Miami FL 33199......305-554-2246
Caribbean Travel & Life, 606 N Washington St, Alexandria VA 22314.....703-683-5496
Carnegie Council on Ethics, 170 E 64th St, New York NY 10021 212-838-4120
Carnegie-Mellon Magazine, Pittsburgh PA 15213......................................412-578-2900
Carolina Business & Finance, PO Box 36639, Charlotte NC 28236...........704-375-8034
Carolina Game & Fish, 2121 Newmarket Pkwy, Marietta GA 30067 404-953-9222
Carolina Quarterly, Univ of North Carolina, Chapel Hill NC 27514.........919-962-0244
Carousel, Writer's Ctr 7815 Old Georgetown Rd, Bethesda MD 20814 301-229-0930
Carta Abierta, Texas Lutheran College, Seguin TX 78155 512-379-4161
Claudia Caruana, PO Box 20077, Elmont NY 10017 516-488-5815
Carville Star, Box 325, Carville LA 70721..504-642-5559
Cascades East, 716 NE 4th St PO Box 5784, Bend OR 97708......................503-382-0127
CASE, 80 Grand St, Jersey City NJ 07302..201-332-7962
Case & Comment, 50 Broad St East, Rochester NY 14694 716-546-5530
Case Analysis, 401 E 32nd St #1002, Chicago IL 60616.............................312-225-9181
Casting Eng & Foundry World, Box 1919, Bridgeport CT 06601 203-377-5566
Casual Living, 370 Lexington Ave, New York NY 10164............................212-532-9290
Cat Fancy, PO Box 6050, Mission Viejo CA 92690 714-240-6001
Catalog Age, 6 River Bend Box 4949, Stamford CT 06907.........................203-358-9900
Catalog Showroom Business, 1515 Broadway, New York NY 10036.........212-869-1300
Catalog Showroom Merch, 1020 W Jericho Tpk, Smithtown NY 11787....516-543-0505
Catechist, 2451 E River Rd Ste 200, Dayton OH 45439..............................513-294-5785
Catering Today, PO Box 222, Santa Claus IN 47579...................................812-937-4464
The Cathartic, PO Box 1391, Ft Lauderdale FL 33302................................305-474-7120
Catholic Digest, PO Bos 64090, St Paul MN 55164....................................612-647-5298
Catholic Forester, 425 W Shuman Blvd, Naperville IL 60566.....................312-983-4920
Catholic Library Assn, 461 W Lancaster Ave, Haverford PA 19041..........215-649-5250
Catholic Near East, 1011 1st Ave, New York NY 10022 212-826-1480
Catholic New York, 1011 1st Ave, New York NY 10022 212-688-2399
Catholic Socialist Review, 2250 Central Ave #322, Alameda CA 94501 ...415-521-6126
Catholic Twin Circle, 6404 Wilshire Blvd, Los Angeles CA 90048 213-653-2200
Cats Magazine, PO Box 290037, Port Orange FL 32029 904-788-2770
The Cattleman, 1301 W 7th St, Ft Worth TX 76102 817-332-7155
Cavalier, 2355 Salzedo St, Coral Gables FL 33134.....................................305-443-2378
Caveat Emptor/Consumers Bulletin, Box 336, South Orange NJ 07079...201-762-6714
CBIA News, 370 Asylum St, Hartford CT 06103...203-547-1661
CD Publications, 8555 16th St, Silver Spring MD 20903 301-588-6380
CEE, 707 Westchester Ave, White Plains NY 10604....................................914-949-8500
Ceilidh, PO Box 6367, San Mateo CA 94403...415-591-9902
Celebration, 2707 Lawina Rd, Baltimore MD 21216 301-542-8785
The Celibate Woman Jour, 3306 Ross Pl NW, Washington DC 20008 202-966-7783
Cell, 292 Main St, Cambridge MA 02142..617-253-2890
Cellular Business, 9221 Quivira Rd, Overland Park KS 66215....................913-888-4664
Censorship News, 132 W 43rd St, New York NY 10036...............................212-944-9899
Centennial Review, Michigan State Univ, E Lansing MI 48824...................517-355-1905
Center for Migration Studies, 209 Flagg Pl, Staten Island NY 10304........718-351-8800
The Center Magazine, 745 W Main, Louisville KY 40202...........................502-584-3126
The Center Magazine, PO Box 4068, Santa Barbara CA 93103 805-961-2611
Central Florida Magazine, 341 N Maitland Ave, Maitland FL 32751........305-628-8850
Central NY Business Review, 719 E Genessee St, Syracuse NY 13210 315-472-3082
Centrum Guide, PO Box 1000, Worcester MA 01614..................................617-799-0511
Ceramic Arts & Crafts, 30595 W Eighth Mile Rd, Livonia MI 48152........313-477-6650

Ceramic Industry, 6200 SOM Ctr, Solon OH 44139.....................................216-349-3060
Ceramic Scope, 3632 Ashworth N, Seattle WA 98103 206-547-7611
Ceramics Monthly, 1609 NW Blvd, Columbus OH 43212..........................614-488-8236
CFI Computer Solutions, 201 W 92nd St, New York NY 10025................212-724-1711
Chain Merchandiser, 65 Crocker Ave, Piedmont CA 94611 415-547-4545
Chain Store Age Executive, 425 Park Ave, New York NY 10022...............212-371-9400
Challenge, 80 Business Park Dr, Armonk NY 10504 914-273-1800
Chamber Music, 215 Park Ave S, New York NY 10003..............................212-460-9030
Chance, 175 5th Ave, New York NY 10010 212-460-1500
Change Magazine, 4000 Albemarle St NW, Washington DC 20016...........202-362-6445
Changing Times, 1729 H St NW, Washington DC 20006............................202-887-6400
Channel X, PO Box 1275, San Luis Obispo CA 93406................................805-543-5404
Channels Magazine, 19 W 44th St, New York NY 10036...........................212-302-2680
Chariot, PO Box 312, Crawfordsville IN 47933..317-362-4500
Charioteer, 337 W 36th St, New York NY 10018 212-279-9586
Charisma, 190 N Westmonte Dr, Altamonte Spring FL 32714..................305-869-5005
Chariton Review, Missouri State Univ, Kirksville MO 63501 816-785-4499
Charlotte, PO Box 36639, Charlotte NC 28236.......................................704-375-8034
Charlotte Business & Finance, PO Box 36639, Charlotte NC 28236..........704-375-8034
Charlotte Business Quarterly, PO Box 36639, Charlotte NC 28236 704-375-8034
Chart Your Course, 350 Weinacker Ave, Mobile AL 36604......................205-478-4700
Charteng Workshop, 226 Linden St, Rumford ME 04276 207-364-7237
Chartering, 830 Pop Tilton's Pl, Jensen Beach FL 33457 305-334-2003
The Chattahoochee Review, 2101 Womack Rd, Dunwoody GA 30338 404-393-3300
Chemical & Engineering News, 1155 16th St NW, Wash DC 20036...........202-872-4600
Chemical Business, 100 Church St, New York NY 10007...........................212-732-9820
Chemical Engineering, 1221 Ave of the Americas, New York NY 10020..212-512-3696
Chemical Equipment, 13 Emery Ave, Randolph NJ 07869.........................201-361-9060
Chemical Marketing Reporter, 100 Church St, New York NY 10007........212-732-9820
Chemical Processing, 301 E Erie St, Chicago IL 60611.............................312-644-2020
Chemical Product News, 301 E Erie St, Chicago IL 60611 312-644-2020
Chemical Times & Trends, 428 E Preston St, Baltimore MD 21202..........301-528-4000
Chemical Week, 1221 Ave of the Americas, New York NY 10020..............212-512-2922
Chemtech, 1155 16th St NW, Washington DC 20036 202-872-4579
Chesapeake Bay Magazine, 1819 Bay Ridge, Annapolis MD 21403...........301-263-2662
Chess Intl, 12414 Hwy 99 Ste 208, Everett WA 98204 206-355-1816
Chess Life, 186 Rt 9W, New Windsor NY 12550......................................914-562-8350
Chevron USA Odyssey, 575 Market St, San Francisco CA 94105 415-894-1952
Chevy Outdoors, 30400 Van Dyke, Warren MI 48093................................800-232-6266
Chic Magazine, 2029 Century Park E, Los Angeles CA 90067...................213-556-9200
Chicago, 414 N Orleans, Chicago IL 60610 312-222-8999
Chicago History, Clark St at North Ave, Chicago IL 60614......................312-642-4600
Chicago Parent News, 7001 N Clark St #217, Chicago IL 60626 312-508-0973
Chicago Review, Univ of Chicago, Chicago IL 60637................................312-753-3571
Chief Fire Executive, 33 Irving Pl, New York NY 10003 212-475-5400
Chief of Police, 1100 NE 125th St, Miami FL 33161................................305-891-9800
Child, 110 6th Ave, New York NY 10011 212-463-1000
Child & Adolescent Social Work, 72 5th Ave, New York NY 10011..........212-243-6000
Child Development, 5801 S Ellis Ave, Chicago IL 60637...........................312-962-7600
Child Life, 1100 Waterway Blvd, Indianapolis IN 46202..........................317-636-8881
Child Welfare, 67 Irving Pl, New York NY 10003 212-254-7410
Childbirth Educator, 575 Lexington Ave, New York NY 10022.................212-752-0755
Childhood Education, 11141 Georgia #200, Wheaton MD 20902 301-942-2443

Children's Album, PO Box 6086, Concord CA 94524......................................415-671-9852
Children's Digest, 1100 Waterway Blvd, Indianapolis IN 46202.....................317-636-8881
Children's House/World, PO Box 111, Caldwell NJ 07006 201-239-3442
Children's Playmate, 1100 Waterway Blvd, Indianapolis IN 46202.............317-636-8881
Chilton's Automotive Marketing, Chilton Way, Radnor PA 19089 215-964-4000
Chimera, 4215 N Marshall Wy, Scottsdale AZ 85251.....................................602-946-7056
China Glass & Tableware, PO Box 2147, Clifton NJ 07015..........................201-779-1600
China Painter, 2641 NW 10th St, Oklahoma City OK 73107.......................405-521-1234
Chiron Review of Jungian Analysis, 400 Linden, Wilmette IL 60091.........312-256-7551
Chocolate Singles, PO Box 333, Jamaica NY 11431......................................718-978-4800
Chocolatier, 45 W 34th St, New York NY 10001...212-239-0855
Choice, 100 Riverview Center, Middletown CT 06457..................................203-347-6933
The Choral Journal, PO Box 6310, Lawton OK 73506..................................405-355-8161
Chouteau Review, PO Box 10016, Kansas City MO 64111 816-444-8693
Christian Adventurer, PO Box 850, Joplin MO 64802 417-624-7050
Christian Bookseller & Librarian, 398 E St Charles, Wheaton IL 60187..312-653-4200
Christian Century, 407 S Dearborn St, Chicago IL 60605 312-427-5380
Christian Herald, 40 Overlook Dr, Chappaqua NY 10514 914-769-9000
Christian Home & School, 3350 E Paris, Grand Rapids MI 49508 616-957-1070
Christian Inquirer, 2002 Main St, Niagra Falls NY 14305............................716-284-5194
Christian Leadership, PO Box 2458, Anderson IN 46018..............................317-642-0257
Christian Life Magazine, 398 E St Charles Rd, Wheaton IL 60187 312-653-4200
Christian Living for Sr Highs, 850 N Grove, Elgin IL 60120 312-741-2400
Christian Ministry, 407 S Dearborn St, Chicago IL 60605 312-427-5380
Christian Single, 127 9th Ave N, Nashville TN 37234..................................615-251-2228
Christianity & Crisis, 537 W 121st St, New York NY 10027........................212-662-5907
Christianity Today, 465 Gundersen Dr, Carol Stream IL 60188.....................312-260-6200
Christmas Annual, 426 S 5th St, Minneapolis MN 55440 612-330-3437
Christopher Street, 249 W Broadway, New York NY 10013...........................212-925-8021
Chronicle of Higher Education, 1255 23rd St NW, Wash DC 20037..........202-466-1000
Chronicle of the Horse, PO Box 46, Middleburg VA 22117 703-687-6341
Chronicles Mag of Amer Culture, 934 N Main, Rockford IL 61103...........815-964-5054
Church & State, 8120 Fenton St, Silver Spring MD 20910............................301-589-3707
Church Educator, 2861 C Saturn St, Brea CA 92621.....................................714-961-0622
The Church Herald, 6157 28th St SE, Grand Rapids MI 49506 616-458-5156
Church Management Clergy Jour, PO Box 1625, Austin TX 78767...........512-327-8501
Church Media Library, 127 9th Ave N, Nashville TN 37234.........................615-251-2752
The Church Musician, 127 9th Ave N, Nashville TN 37234...........................615-251-2961
Church Training, 127 9th Ave N, Nashville TN 37234...................................615-251-2843
The Churchman, 1074 23rd Ave N, Petersburg FL 33704...............................813-894-0097
Cimarron Review, Oklahoma State Univ, Stillwater OK 74078.....................405-624-6573
Cincinnati Bell, 201 E 4th St, Cincinnati OH 45201.....................................513-397-4690
Cincinnati Business Jour, 1212 Sycamore St, Cincinnati OH 45210 513-241-7701
Cincinnati Magazine, 35 E 7th St, Cincinnati OH 45202 513-421-4300
Cincinnati Medicine, 320 Broadway, Cincinnati OH 45202..........................513-421-7010
Cincinnati Poetry Review, Univ of Cincinnati, Cincinnati OH 45221..........513-475-4484
Cineaste, PO Box 2242, New York NY 10009...212-982-1241
Cinefantastique, PO Box 270, Oak Park IL 60303 312-366-5566
Cinemascore Film Music Jour, PO Box 70868, Sunnyvale CA 94086.......415-960-1151
Circle K Intl, 3636 Woodview Trace, Indianapolis IN 46268 317-875-8755
Circle Track, 8490 Sunset Blvd, Los Angeles CA 90069...............................213-657-5100
Circuit Rider, PO Box 801, Nashville TN 37202..615-749-6488
Circuits Manufacturing, 1050 Commonwealth, Boston MA 02215............617-232-5470

Circulation, 7320 Greenville Ave, Dallas TX 75231............214-373-6300
Circus Magazine, 419 Park Ave S, New York NY 10016............212-685-5050
Cite Guide, PO Box 20533, Seattle WA 98102............206-323-7374
City & State, 220 E 42 St, New York NY 10017............212-210-0114
City Limits, 40 Prince St, New York NY 10012............212-925-9820
City Sports Magazine, PO Box 3693, San Francisco CA 94119............415-788-2611
CityGuide, 332 Congress St Ste 500, Boston MA 02210............617-574-9400
Civil Engineering, 345 E 47th St, New York NY 10017............212-705-7463
Civil War Book Exchange, PO Box 15432, Philadelphia PA 19149............609-786-1865
Civil War Times Illustrated, 2245 Kohn Rd, Harrisburg PA 17105............717-657-9555
Classical Calliope, 20 Grove St, Peterborough NH 03458............603-924-7209
The Classical Outlook, Univ of Georgia, Athens GA 30605............404-549-6537
Classroom Computer Learning, 2169 Francisco, San Rafael CA 94901....513-294-5785
Clavier, 200 Northfield Rd, Northfield IL 60093............312-446-5000
Clearwater Journal, 2222 S Louisiana St, Little Rock AR 72206............503-963-9778
Clearwater Navigator, 112 Market St, Poughkeepsie NY 12601............914-454-7673
The Clergy Journal, PO Box 162527, Austin TX 78716............512-327-8501
Cleveland Magazine, 1621 Euclid Ave, Cleveland OH 44115............216-771-2833
The Cliffs of Pendare, Box 3025, Rock Hill SC 29731............803-324-4120
Clinical Chemistry, PO Box 5218, Winston-Salem NC 27113............919-725-0208
Clinical Obstetrics & Gynecology, E Wash Sq, Phila PA 19105............215-238-4200
Clinical Orthopaedic Research, E Wash Sq, Phila PA 19105............215-238-4200
Clinical Pediatrics, E Washington Sq, Philadelphia PA 19105............215-238-4200
Clinical Pharmacology, 11830 Westline, St Louis MO 63146............314-872-8370
Clinical Pharmacy, 4630 Montgomery Ave, Bethesda MD 20814............301-657-3000
Clinical Preventive Denistry, E Washington Sq, Phila PA 19105............215-238-4273
Clinical Psychiatry News, 12230 Wilkins Ave, Rockville MD 20852............301-770-6170
Clinical Research, 6900 Grove Rd, Thorofare NJ 08086............609-848-1000
Clinical Rheumatology, 53 Park Pl, New York NY 10007............212-766-4300
Clinical Social Work Jour, 72 5th Ave, New York NY 10011............212-243-6000
Clinical Symposia, 14 Henderson Dr, West Caldwell NJ 07006............201-882-4816
Clinics In Primary Care, W Washington Sq, Phila PA 19105............215-574-4700
Clinton St Quarterly, PO Box 3588, Portland OR 97208............503-222-6039
Clockwatch Review, 737 Penbrook Way, Hartland WI 53029............414-367-8315
The Closest Penguins, 333 10th St, San Francisco CA 94103............415-431-7861
Closing the Gap, Box 68, Henderson MN 56044............612-248-3294
Clothed With the Sun, Box 132, Oshkosh WI 54902............414-231-9950
Club Costa, 9200 Ward Pkwy, Kansas City MO 64114............816-361-8404
Club House, PO Box 15, Berrien Springs MI 49103............616-471-3701
Club Industry, 1415 Beacon St Ste 320, Brookline MA 02146............617-277-3823
Club Management, 408 Olive St, St Louis MO 63102............314-421-5445
Co-Op News, 1414 University Ave, Berkeley CA 94702............415-526-0440
COA Review, PO Box 190, Rutherford NJ 07070............201-460-7912
Coal Age, 11 W 19th St, New York NY 10017............212-512-1221
Coal Mining, 300 W Adams St, Chicago IL 60606............312-726-2802
Coast Magazine, 5000 B Kings Hwy, Myrtle Beach SC 29577............803-449-5415
Coastal Plains Farmer, 3000 Highwoods #300, Raleigh NC 27625............919-872-5040
Cobblestone, 20 Grove St, Peterborough NH 03458............603-924-7209
CODA Poets & Writers, 201 W 54th St, New York NY 10019............212-757-1766
Coin Prices, 700 E State St, Iola WI 54990............715-445-2214
Coin World, 911 Vandemark Rd, Sidney OH 45367............513-498-2111
Coinage, 2660 E Main St, Ventura CA 92002............213-788-7080
Coins, 700 E State St, Iola WI 54990............715-445-2214

Cold Drill, Boise State Univ English Dept, Boise ID 83725 208-385-1999
Collaboration, Box 372, High Falls NY 12440 914-687-9222
Collage, 1200 S Willis Ave, Wheeling IL 60090..312-541-9290
Collectible Automobile, 3841 W Oakton St, Skokie IL 60076 312-676-3470
Collectors Club Philatelist, 22 East 35th St, New York NY 10016..............212-683-0559
Collectors Motor News, 919 South St, Long Beach CA 90805......................213-423-3063
Collectors News-Antique Rep, 506 2nd St, Grundy Ctr IA 50638..................319-824-5456
Collectors' Showcase, 1018 Rosecrans St, San Diego CA 92106 619-222-0386
College & Research Libraries, 50 E Huron St, Chicago IL 60611 312-944-6780
College & University, Univ of N Colo, Greeley CO 80639............................303-351-2881
College Composition & Comm, 1111 Kenyon Rd, Urbana IL 61801...........217-328-3870
College English, 1111 Kenyon Rd, Urbana IL 61801 217-328-3870
College English, Univ of Alabama, University AL 35486................................205-348-6488
College Entertainment Guide, 303 N Glenoaks, Burbank CA 91502 818-848-4666
College Mathematics Jour, 1529 18th St NW, Wash DC 20036....................202-387-5200
College Media Review, Ball State Univ, Muncie IN 47306............................317-285-8456
College of Physicians, 19 S 22nd St, Philadelphia PA 19118 215-561-6050
College Outlook, PO Box 239, Liberty MO 64068..816-781-4941
College Store Executive, 825 Old Country Rd, Westbury NY 11590 516-334-3030
The College Store Journal, 528 E Lorain St, Oberlin OH 44074 216-775-7777
College Woman, 303 N Glenoaks Blvd, Burbank CA 91502 818-848-4666
Collegiate Career Woman, 44 Broadway, Greenlawn NY 11740 516-261-8917
Colonial Homes, 1790 Broadway 14th fl, New York NY 10019......................212-247-8720
Colorado Business, 1621 18th St, Denver CO 80202 303-295-0900
Colorado Homes & Lifestyles, 2550 31st St, Denver CO 80216 303-455-1944
Colorado North Review, Univ of N Colorado, Greeley CO 80639..............303-351-1350
Colorado Outdoor Journal, PO Box 432, Florence CO 81226......................303-275-3166
Colorado Review, Colo State Univ, Ft Collins CO 80523 303-491-6428
Colorado Sports Monthly, Box 3519, Evergreen CO 80439 303-670-3700
Columbia, 1 Columbus Plaza, New Haven CT 06507 203-772-2130
Columbia Journalism Review, Columbia Univ, New York NY 10027 212-280-5595
Columbus Business Jour, 666 High St, Worthington OH 43085 614-888-6800
Columbus Free Press, PO Box 8234, Columbus OH 43201............................614-481-9499
Columbus Monthly, 171 E Livingston Ave, Columbus OH 43215 614-464-4567
Columbus Single Scene, PO Box 30856, Gahanna OH 43230 614-476-8802
Come-All-Ye, Box 494, Hatboro PA 19040 215-675-6762
Comet Halley Magazine, 1363 Oliver Ave, San Diego CA 92109..................619-270-0327
Comico, 1547 DeKalb St, Norristown PA 19401 215-277-4305
Comics Collector, 700 E State St, Iola WI 54990..715-445-2214
Comics Journal, 1800 Bridgeate #101, Westlake Vlg CA 91361 805-379-1881
The Comics Revue, Box 1763, Wayne NJ 07470..201-628-1259
Commentary, 165 E 56th St, New York NY 10022..212-751-4000
Commercial Carrier Journal, Chilton Way, Radnor PA 19089 215-964-4000
Commercial Fisheries News, Box 37, Stonington ME 04681 207-367-2396
Commercial News, 125 12th St, San Francisco CA 94103..............................415-621-7012
Commodity Journal, 10 Park St, Concord NH 03301......................................603-224-2376
Commodore Magazine, 1200 Wilson Rd, West Chester PA 19380..............215-431-9100
Common Cause Magazine, 2030 M St NW, Washington DC 20036...........202-833-1200
Common Ground, 9 Mono Ave, Fairfax CA 94930..415-459-4900
Common Sense, PO Box 650051, Miami FL 33165 305-221-0154
Common Sense, 50 Mill St, Dover NH 03820 603-749-5071
Commonweal, 232 Madison Ave, New York NY 10016....................................212-683-2042
Communication Age, 55 E Jackson Blvd, Chicago IL 60604........................312-922-2435

Communication Arts, 410 Sherman Ave, Palo Alto CA 94303.....................415-326-6040
Communication Briefings, 806 Westminster, Blackwood NJ 08012...........609-589-3503
Communication World, 870 Market St, San Francisco CA 94102 415-433-3400
Communications Engineering & Design, 600 Grant, Denver CO 80203 ...303-860-0111
Communications News, 124 S 1st St, Geneva IL 60134.....................312-232-1400
Communications Week, 600 Community Dr, Manhasset NY 11030...........516-365-4600
Communicator's Journal, PO Box 602, Omaha NE 68101 402-551-0444
Communities, 105 Sun St, Stelle IL 60919 815-256-2252
Commuter Air, 6255 Barfield Rd, Atlanta GA 30328 404-256-9800
Compact Periodicals, 2500 Hollywood Blvd, Hollywood FL 33020 305-925-5242
Company, 3441 N Ashland Ave, Chicago IL 60657 312-281-1539
Compaq Magazine, 3381 Ocean Dr, Vero Beach FL 32963.....................305-231-6904
Compass Publications Inc, 1117 N 19th St, Arlington VA 22209 703-524-3136
Compendium Cont Educ Dentistry, Box 3153, Princeton NJ 08540...........609-896-0641
Compendium Cont Educ Vetenarian, Box 277, Princeton Jct NJ 08550....609-882-5600
Compensation & Benefits, 135 W 50th St, New York NY 10020 212-903-8069
Complete Hairdos, 300 W 43rd St, New York NY 10036.........................212-397-5200
Complete Woman, 1165 N Clarke, Chicago IL 60610 312-266-8680
Compressed Air, 253 E Washington Ave, Washington NJ 07882.................201-689-4496
Compute!, 324 W Wendover Ave, Greensboro NC 27408.........................919-275-9809
Compute!'s Gazette, 324 W Wendover, Greensboro NC 27408...................919-275-9809
Computer & Elec Mktg, 1050 Commonwealth, Boston MA 02215..............617-739-4750
Computer & Elec Graduate, 44 Broadway, Greenlawn NY 11740 516-261-8917
Computer Advertising News, 155 E 23rd St, New York NY 10160...............212-505-2700
Computer Book Review, PO Box 37127, Honolulu HI 96837 808-595-7089
Computer Consultant, 208 N Townsend St, Syracuse NY 13203 315-472-1008
Computer Dealer, PO Box 1952, Dover NJ 07801................................201-361-9060
Computer Decisions, 10 Mulholland Dr, Hasbrouck Hts NJ 07604 201-393-6000
Computer Design, PO Box 417, Littleton MA 01460 617-486-9501
Computer Entertainer, 12115 Magnolia, N Hollywood CA 91607.............213-761-1516
Computer Entertainment, 460 W 34th St, New York NY 10001.................212-947-6500
Computer Gaming World, 515 S Harbor Blvd, Anaheim CA 92805 714-535-4435
Computer Graphics Today, 2722 Merrilee Dr, Fairfax VA 22031...............703-698-9600
Computer Instructor, 614 Santa Barbara, Santa Barbara CA 93101..........805-963-0439
Computer Language, 500 Howard St, San Francisco CA 94105.................415-397-1881
Computer Merchandising, 15720 Ventura Blvd, Encino CA 91436 818-995-0436
Computer Pictures Magazine, 330 W 42nd St, New York NY 10036.........212-947-0020
Computer Products, 13 Emery Ave, Randolph NJ 07869 201-361-9060
Computer Reseller News, 600 Community, Manhasset NY 11030..............516-365-4600
Computer Retailing, 1760 Peachtree Rd NW, Atlanta GA 30357 404-874-4462
Computer Shopper, 407 S Washington Ave, Titusville FL 32780.................305-269-3211
Computer Systems Equip, 1221 Ave of Americas, New York NY 10020 ..212-512-2000
Computer Systems News, 111 E Shore Rd, Manhasset NY 11030...............516-365-4600
Computer Technology Review, 924 Westwood, Los Angeles CA 90024.....213-208-1335
Computer Update, 1 Center Plaza, Boston MA 02108 617-367-8080
Computer User's Legal Report, 191 Post Rd, Westport CT 06880..............203-227-1360
Computer-Aided Engineering, 1111 Chester, Cleveland OH 44114 216-696-7000
Computers in Accounting, 964 3rd Ave, New York NY 10155....................212-935-9210
Computers in Banking, 150 Broadway, New York NY 10038.....................212-227-1200
Computers in Healthcare, 6300 S Syracuse, Englewood CO 80111.............303-220-0600
Computerworld, 375 Cochituate Rd, Framingham MA 01701 617-879-0700
Computerworld Focus, 375 Cochituate Rd, Framingham MA 01701..........617-879-0700
Computing for Business, 7330 Adams St, Paramount CA 90723.................213-408-0999

Concrete, 111 E Wacker Dr Ste 1775, Chicago IL 60601.............................312-938-2300
Concrete Construction, 426 S Westgate, Addison IL 60101 312-543-0870
Concrete International, 22400 W Seven Mile Rd, Detroit MI 48219 313-532-2600
Concrete Products, 300 W Adams, Chicago IL 60606 312-726-2802
Conde Nast Publications, 350 Madison Ave, New York NY 10017...........212-880-8800
Conditions, PO Box 150056, Brooklyn NY 11215.....................................212-788-8654
Condor Books Inc, 351 W 54th St, New York NY 10019 212-787-9281
The Confectioner, 771 Kirkman Rd, Orlando FL 32811............................305-299-3865
Confident Living, PO Box 82808, Lincoln NE 68501 402-474-4567
Confluent Education, 833 Via Granada, Santa Barbara CA 93103.............805-569-1754
Confrontation, CW Post College LIU, Greenville NY 11548.....................516-299-2391
Congress Monthly, 15 E 84th St, New York NY 10028 212-879-4500
Congressional Digest, 3231 P St NW, Washington DC 20007 202-333-7332
Congressional Quarterly, 1414 22nd NW, Washington DC 20037.............202-887-8500
Connecticut Business/Financial, 595 Franklin, Hartford CT 06114 203-278-3800
Connecticut Magazine, 789 Reservoir Ave, Bridgeport CT 06606.............203-274-5488
Connecticut Periodical Index, PO Box 4050, Stamford CT 06907 203-323-2826
Connecticut Traveler, 2276 Whitney Ave, Hamden CT 06518 203-281-7505
Connexions, 4228 Telegraph, Oakland CA 94609......................................415-654-6725
The Connoisseur, 224 W 57th St, New York NY 10019 212-262-5595
Conscience, 2008 17th St NW, Washington DC 20009................................202-638-1706
Consensus Chigago, 407 E 91st Ste 1D, New York NY 10028 212-410-1111
Conservation Foundation, 1255 23rd St NW, Washington DC 20037........202-293-4800
The Conservationist, 50 Wolf Rd, Albany NY 12233.................................518-457-5547
Conservative Digest, 7777 Leesburg Pike, Falls Church VA 22043 703-893-1411
The Constantian Society, 123 Orr Rd, Pittsburgh PA 15241 412-831-8750
Construction, 7297 R Lee Highway, Falls Church VA 22042.....................703-536-5522
Construction Dimensions, 25 K St Ste 300, Washington DC 20002 202-783-2924
Construction Equipment, 1350 E Touhy Ave, Des Plaines IL 60018 312-635-8800
Construction Industry Press, 58 Paul Dr, San Rafael CA 94903...............415-499-7674
Construction News, 715 W 2nd St, Little Rock AR 72201 501-376-1931
Construction Specifier, 601 Madison St, Alexandria VA 22314.................703-684-0200
Construction Supervisor, 24 Rope Ferry, Waterford CT 06386 203-739-0169
Construction Times, 110 S Greeley, Stillwater MN 55082..........................612-430-1113
Constructioneer, 1 Bond St, Chatham NJ 07928 203-453-3717
Constructive Action Newsletter, 710 Lodi St, Syracuse NY 13203.............315-471-4644
Consultant, 55 Holly Hill Ln, Greenwich CT 06830 203-661-0600
Consulting Engineer, 1301 S Grove Ave, Barrington IL 60010 312-381-1840
Consumer Action News, 1106 E High St, Springfield OH 45505................513-325-2001
Consumer Electronics, 345 Park Ave S, New York NY 10010.....................212-686-7744
Consumer Guide, 3841 W Oakton St, Skokie IL 60076 312-676-3470
Consumer Lending Report, 1 Penn Plaza, New York NY 10119 212-971-5000
Consumer Reports, 256 Washington St, Mount Vernon NY 10553............914-667-9400
Consumers Digest, 5705 N Lincoln Ave, Chicago IL 60659.......................312-275-3590
Consumers Research, 517 2nd St NE, Washington DC 20002 202-546-1713
Contact, PO Box 9248, Berkeley CA 94709...415-644-0696
Contemp Christian, 25231 Paseo de Alicia, Laguna Hills CA 92654 714-951-9106
Contemporary Dialysis, 17901 Ventura Blvd, Encino CA 91316 818-344-4200
Contemporary Long Term Care, 1719 West End, Nashville TN 37203......615-329-1973
Contemporary Orthopaedics, 2500 Artesia, Redondo Bch CA 90278 213-367-8788
Contemporary Psychology, 1200 17th St NW, Washington DC 20036 202-955-7600
Contemporary Social Issues, 511 Lincoln St, Santa Cruz CA 95060 408-426-4479
Contemporary Sociology, 267 19th Ave S, Minneapolis MN 55455............612-376-8429

Contemporary Surgery, 2500 Artesia, Redondo Beach CA 90278..............213-376-8788
Continental, 2525 Wallingwood Ste 804, Austin TX 78746.....................512-328-4560
Continental Cablevision Guide, 332 Congress St, Boston MA 02210 617-574-9400
The Contract Bridge Bulletin, PO Box 161192, Memphis TN 38186 901-332-5586
Contract Magazine, 1515 Broadway, New York NY 10036 212-869-1300
Contracting Bulletin, 7216 Boone Ave, Brooklyn Park MN 55428..............612-537-7730
Contractor, 1301 S Grove Ave, Barrington IL 60010 312-381-1840
Contractors Market Center, PO Box 2029, Tuscaloosa AL 35403 205-349-2990
Control Engineering, 1301 S Grove Ave, Barrington IL 60010 312-381-1840
Controlled Publishing, 2811 Wilshire, Santa Monica CA 90403.................213-829-7863
Convenience Store Merch, 41 E 42nd St, New York NY 10017 212-490-3999
Converting Magazine, 400 N Michigan Ave, Chicago IL 60611 312-222-2000
The Cook's Magazine, 2710 North Ave #200, Bridgeport CT 06604..........203-366-4155
Cookbook Digest, 100 E 50th St, New York NY 10022.............................212-755-6789
Cooking for Profit, 131 S Main St, Fond du Lac WI 54935........................414-923-3700
Cooperative Farmer, PO Box 26234, Richmond VA 23260.........................804-281-1317
Coral Springs Monthly, PO Box 8783, Coral Springs FL 33075 305-344-8090
Cornell Univ College of Engineering, Ithaca NY 14853 607-255-6095
Cornerstone, 4707 N Malden, Chicago IL 60640 312-989-2080
Corona, Montana State Univ History Dept, Bozeman MT 59717.................406-994-5200
Corp & Incentive Travel, 488 Madison Ave, New York NY 10022..............212-888-1500
Corporate Fitness, 1640 5th St, Santa Monica CA 90401.........................213-395-0234
Corp Meetings & Incentives, 7500 Old Oak, Cleveland OH 44130 216-243-8100
Corporate Monthly, 105 Chestnut St, Philadelphia PA 19106 215-629-1611
Corporate Travel, 1515 Broadway, New York NY 10036..........................212-869-1300
Corrections Today, 4321 Hartwick Rd, College Park MD 20740.................301-699-7600
Corvette Fever, PO Box 44620, Ft Washington MD 20744 301-839-2221
Corvette News, 30005 Van Dyke Ave, Warren MI 48090..........................313-575-9400
COSMEP Newsletter, PO Box 703, San Francisco CA 94101......................415-922-9490
Cosmopolitan, 224 W 57th St, New York NY 10019.................................212-262-5700
Cost Engineering, 308 Monongahela Bldg, Morgantown WV 26505.........304-296-8444
Cottonwood, Univ of Kansas Box J, Lawrence KS 66045 913-864-3777
Council on Exceptional Children, 1920 Association, Reston VA 22091....703-620-3660
The Counselor Magazine, 1120 Wheeler Way, Langhorne PA 19047........215-752-4200
Count Dracula Fan Club, 29 Wash Sq W, New York NY 10011 212-533-5018
Counterforce, PO Box 1532, Anderson CA 96007...................................916-365-8026
Counterman, 11 S Forge St, Akron OH 44304.......................................216-535-6117
Country Magazine, 227 S Washington St, Alexandria VA 22313 703-548-6177
Country Music Foundation, 4 Music Sq E, Nashville TN 37203.................615-256-1639
Country Needlecraft, 306 E Parr Rd, Berne IN 46711.............................219-589-8741
Country Song Roundup, Charlton Bldg, Derby CT 06418.........................203-735-3381
Country Woman, PO Box 643, Milwaukee WI 53201 414-423-0100
Countryside, 312 Portland Rd Hwy 19E, Waterloo WI 53594....................414-478-2115
Covenant Companion, 5101 N Fancisco Ave, Chicago IL 60625.................312-784-3000
Coydog Review, 203 Halton Ln, Watsonville CA 95076 408-688-2794
The CPA Journal, 600 3rd Ave, New York NY 10016 212-661-2020
CPI 100, 496 N Kings Hwy, Cherry Hill NJ 08034...................................609-482-6699
CPI Purchasing, 275 Washington St, Newton MA 02158...........................617-964-3030
CQ Radio Amateur's Jour, 76 N Broadway, Hicksville NY 11801..............516-681-2922
Crab Creek Review, 4462 Whitman Ave N, Seattle WA 98103...................206-633-1090
Craft & Needlework Age, Box 420, Englishtown NJ 07726........................201-972-1022
CrafTrends, 6405 Atlantic Blvd, Norcross GA 30071 404-441-9003
Crafts 'N Things, 14 Main St, Park Ridge IL 60068 312-825-2161

Crafts Magazine, PO Box 1790 News Plaza, Peoria IL 61656.....................309-682-6626
The Crafts Report, 3623 Ashworth N, Seattle WA 98103 206-547-7611
Crafts Woman, 1153 Oxford Rd, Deerfield IL 60015 312-945-1769
Craftwoman, Box 848, Libertyville IL 60048 312-362-9186
Crain's Chicago Business, 740 N Rush St, Chicago IL 60611......................312-649-5200
Crain's Cleveland Business, 140 Public Sq, Cleveland OH 44114 216-522-1383
Crain's Detroit Business, 1400 Woodbridge, Detroit MI 48207...................313-446-0419
Crain's New York Business, 220 E 42nd St, New York NY 10017................212-210-0100
Crawlspace, 908 W 5th St, Belevedere IL 61008...815-547-4567
Crazyhorse, Univ Arkansas English Dept, Little Rock AR 72204................501-569-3160
Creation/Evolution Journal, 7 Harwood Dr, Amherst NY 14226 716-839-5083
Creative Child & Adult, 8080 Spring Valley, Cincinnati OH 45236............513-631-1777
Creative Computing, 39 E Hanover Ave, Morris Plains NJ 07950 201-540-0445
Creative Ideas for Living, 820 Shades Creek, Birmingham AL 35209 205-870-6471
Creative Person, 1000 Byus Dr, Charleston WV 25311................................304-345-2378
The Creative Woman, Governors State Univ, Univ Park IL 60466..............312-534-5000
Creative Years, 5010 NE Waldo Rd, Gainesville FL 32609...........................904-373-7445
Credences, 420 Capen Hall NY State Univ, Buffalo NY 14260....................716-673-2917
Credit & Financial Mgmt, 475 Park Ave S, New York NY 10016 212-578-4410
Credit Union Executive, PO Box 431, Madison WI 53701 608-231-4000
Credit Union Magazine, PO Box 431, Madison WI 53701............................608-231-4000
Credit Union News, 150 Nassau St, New York NY 10038.............................212-267-7707
The Credit World, PO Box 27257, St Louis MO 63141 314-991-3030
Creem, 7715 Sunset Blvd, Los Angeles CA 90046..213-851-8771
Creeping Bent, 433 W Market St, Bethlehem PA 18018 215-691-3548
Creole Magazines of America, PO Box 5454, Bossier City LA 71111 318-226-1981
The Crescent Review, PO Box 15065, Winston-Salem NC 27113................919-768-5943
Cricket Magazine for Children, 315 5th St, Peru IL 61354.........................815-224-6643
Crime & Delinquency, 77 Maiden Le 4th fl, San Francisco CA 94108 415-956-5651
Crime and Social Justice, PO Box 40601, San Francisco CA 94140...........415-550-1703
The Crisis, 6515 Sunset Blvd, Los Angeles CA 90028...................................213-465-4512
Critical Care Medicine, 428 E Preston, Baltimore MD 21202 301-528-4000
Critical Care Nurse, 680 Rt 206 N, Bridgewater NJ 08807.........................201-231-0900
Critique, PO Box 11368, Santa Rosa CA 95406...707-525-9401
Crochet World Omnibook, 306 E Parr Rd, Berne IN 46711........................219-589-8741
Crop Dust, Rt 5 Box 75, Warrenton VA 22712..703-347-5523
Crops & Soils Magazine, 677 S Segoe Rd, Madison WI 53711....................608-273-8080
Cross Country Skier, 135 N 6th St, Emmaus PA 18098 215-967-5171
Cross Currents, Mercy College, Dobbs Ferry NY 10522..............................914-693-4500
Cross Timbers Review, Cisco Junior College, Cisco TX 76437....................817-442-2567
Crosscountry, Box 492, Ridgefield CT 06877...203-431-8225
CROW, 153 George St #2, New Brunswick NJ 08901 201-828-5467
Cruise Travel, 1020 Church St, Evanston IL 60201.......................................312-491-6440
Cruising World, 524 Thames St, Newport RI 02840......................................401-847-1588
CTA/NEA Action, 1705 Murchison Dr, Burlingame CA 94010...................415-697-1400
CTB: Cable TV Business, 6530 S Yosemite, Englewood CO 80111............303-694-1522
Culinary Inst of Amer, North Rd, Hyde Park NY 12538 914-452-9600
Cum Notis Variorum, Univ of Calif, Berkeley CA 94720............................415-642-2623
Cumberland Poetry Review, PO Box 120128, Nashville TN 37212 615-373-8948
Current, 4000 Albemarle St NW, Washington DC 20016 202-362-6445
Current Advances in Biochemistry, Elmsford NY 10523............................914-592-7700
Current Advances in Cell & Dev Biology, Elmsford NY 10523...................914-592-7700
Current Advances in Endocrinology, Elmsford NY 10523 914-592-7700

Current Advances in Immunology, Elmsford NY 10523.....................914-592-7700
Current Anthropology, 5801 S Ellis Ave, Chicago IL 60637......................312-962-7600
Current Consumer & Lifestudies, 3500 Western, Highland Pk IL 60035..312-432-2700
Current Health, 3500 Western Ave, Highland Park IL 60035 312-432-2700
Current History, 3740 Creamery Rd, Furlong PA 18925 215-598-7894
Current Literature on Aging, 600 Maryland Ave SW, Wash DC 20024.....202-479-1200
Current Podiatric Medicine, 799 Rt 25A, Rocky Point NY 11778...............516-744-0022
Current Problems in Surgery, 35 E Wacker Dr, Chicago IL 60601 312-726-9733
Current World Leaders, 2060 Alameda PS, Santa Barbara CA 93103.......805-965-5010
Currents, 314 N 20th St, Colorado Springs CO 80904 303-473-2466
Curriculum Product Review, PO Box 4949, Stamford CT 06907.................203-358-9900
Curriculum Review, 517 S Jefferson St, Chicago IL 60607.......................312-939-3010
Custom Applicator, 6263 Poplar Ave, Memphis TN 38119 901-767-4020
Cutis, 875 3rd Ave, New York NY 10022 212-605-9400
Cutting Tool Engineering, 464 Central Ave, Northfield IL 60093..............312-441-7520
CW Communications Inc, 80 Pine St, Peterborough NH 03458 603-924-9471
Cycle Guide, 20916 Higgins Ct, Torrance CA 90501................................213-328-5700
Cycle News, PO Box 498, Long Beach CA 90801......................................213-427-7433
Cycle World, 1499 Monrovia Ave, Newport Beach CA 92663 714-720-5300
Cycling USA, 1750 E Boulder St, Colorado Springs CO 80909 303-578-4581
Cyrano's Journal, Box 68, Westport CT 06881 203-847-5319
D Magazine, 3988 N Central Expwy, Dallas TX 75204.............................214-827-5000
D&B Reports, 299 Park Ave 24th fl, New York NY 10171 212-593-6723
Daedalus, Norton's Woods 136 Irving St, Cambridge MA 02138...............617-491-2600
Daily Development, 12755 State Hwy 55, Minnepolis MN 55441................612-559-2322
Daily Variety, 1400 N Cahuenga Blvd, Hollywood CA 90028 213-469-1141
Daily Word, Unity School of Christianity, Unity Village MO 64065............816-524-3550
Dairy Field, 111 E Wacker Dr 17th fl, Chicago IL 60601 312-938-2370
Dairy Goat Journal, 14415 N 73rd St Ste 101, Scottsdale AZ 85260 602-991-4628
Dairy Herd Management, PO Box 67, Minneapolis MN 55440 612-374-5200
Dairy Record, 5725 E River Rd, Chicago IL 60631 312-693-3200
The Dairyman, PO Box 819, Corona CA 91718.......................................714-735-2730
Dallas Magazine, 1507 Pacific Ave, Dallas TX 75201...............................214-954-1390
Dallas Writers' Newsletter, 2223 Bennett #215, Dallas TX 75206..............214-821-7754
Dallas-Ft Worth Business Jour, 4131 N Central Expy, Dallas TX 75204..214-386-5858
Dallas-Ft Worth Home Buyer, 5501 LBJ Fwy, Dallas TX 75240................214-239-2399
Dance Exercise Today, 2437 Morena Blvd, San Diego CA 92110 619-275-2450
Dance Magazine, 33 W 60th St, New York NY 10023 212-245-9050
Dance Teacher Now, 803 Russell Blvd, Davis CA 95616 916-756-6222
The Dandelion, 1985 Selby Ave, St Paul MN 55104................................612-646-8917
Daring Poetry Quarterly, Box 526, Canton OH 44701 216-454-7519
Darkroom & Creative Camera Tech, 7800 Merrimac, Niles IL 60648 312-965-0566
Darkroom Photography, 9021 Melrose Ave, Los Angeles CA 90069.........415-989-4360
Data Base Monthly, 8310 Capital of Texas Hwy, Austin TX 78731...........512-343-9066
Data Based Advisor, 4010 Morena Blvd, San Diego CA 92117..................619-483-6400
Data Communications, 1221 Ave of Americas, New York NY 10020........212-512-3139
Data Processing Digest, PO Box 1249, Los Angeles CA 90078...................213-851-3156
Data Training, 178 Federal St, Boston MA 02110....................................617-542-0146
Datamation, 249 W 17th St, New York NY 10011.....................................212-645-0067
Daughters of Sarah, 2716 W Cortland, Chicago IL 60647 312-252-3344
Daughters of Amer Revolution, 1776 D St NW, Wash DC 20006.................202-879-3286
Dawn, RR1 Box 400, Honesdale PA 18431..717-253-5551
Dawn, PO Box 6189, Laguna Niguel CA 92677..714-249-1001

Daytime TV, 355 Lexington Ave, New York NY 10017 212-391-1400
Dayton Business Jour, 40 W 4th St, Dayton OH 45402.....................513-228-0000
Dayton Magazine, 1980 Kettering Tower, Dayton OH 45423....................513-226-1444
Dazzle, 1999 Shepard Rd, St Paul MN 55116 612-690-7200
Dimensions in Critical Care Nursing, E Wash Sq, Phila PA 19105...........215-238-4200
Dealer Communicator, 777 S State Rd 7, Margate FL 33068......................305-971-4360
Dealerscope, 115 2nd Ave, Waltham MA 02254...............................617-890-5124
December Magazine, 3093 Dato, Highland Park IL 60035..................312-432-6804
December Rose Assn, 255 S Hill St #407, Los Angeles CA 90012...............213-617-7002
Decision, 1300 Harmon Place, Minneapolis MN 55403..........................612-338-0500
Decorative Artist's Workbook, 1507 Dana Ave, Cincinnati OH 45207.......513-531-2222
Deer & Deer Hunting, PO Box 1117, Appleton WI 54912.........................414-734-0009
Defense Science, 300 Orchard City, Campbell CA 95008 408-370-3509
Defense System Review, 2592 Solano Ave, Napa CA 94558 707-257-8480
Deli News, 12028 Venice Blvd Ste 7, Mar Vista CA 90066.......................213-391-1982
Deli-Dairy Management, Box 373, Cedarhurst NY 11516.........................516-295-3680
Dell Puzzle Publications, 245 E 47th St, New York NY 10017...................212-605-3360
Delta Sky, 12955 Biscayne Blvd, N Miami FL 33181...............................305-893-1520
Democratic Left, 853 Broadway Ste 801, New York NY 10003 212-260-3270
Denistry Today, 20 Church St, Montclair NJ 07042 201-783-3935
Dental Assisting, 5002 Lakeland Cir, Waco TX 76710 817-776-5011
Dental Clinics, W Washington Sq, Philadelphia PA 19105 215-574-4700
Dental Economics, PO Box 3408, Tulsa OK 74101 918-835-3161
Dental Hygiene, 444 N Michigan Ave, Chicago IL 60611 312-440-8900
Dental Laboratory Review, 757 3rd Ave, New York NY 10017..................212-418-4100
Dental Management, 747 3rd Ave, New York NY 10017............................212-418-4100
Dental Products Report, 4849 Golf Rd, Skokie IL 60077..........................312-674-0110
Dentist, 225 N New Rd PO Box 7573, Waco TX 76714............................817-776-9000
Dentists MarketPlace, 600 W Putman Ave, Greenwich CT 06830 203-661-0693
Denver Business, 899 Logan St Ste 611, Denver CO 80203.......................303-832-5400
Denver Housing Guide, 13693 E Iliff Ave, Aurora CO 80014 303-695-8440
Denver Magazine, 899 Logan St Ste 611, Denver CO 80203......................303-832-5400
Denver Quarterly, Univ of Denver, Denver CO 80208...............................303-753-2869
Dermatology Times, 747 3rd Ave, New York NY 10017 212-418-4100
Deros, 6009 Edgewood Ln, Alexandria VA 22310.....................................703-971-2291
Design Book Review, 1418 Spring Way, Berkeley CA 94708.....................415-486-1956
Design Graphics World, 6255 Barfield Rd, Atlanta GA 30328....................404-256-9800
Design News, Cahners Bldg 275 Washington St, Newton MA 02158..........617-964-3030
Design Solutions, 2310 S Walter Reed Dr, Arlington VA 22206 202-671-9100
Designfax, 6521 Davis Industrial Pkwy, Solon OH 44139........................216-248-1125
Designment Review, 10901 Bridgeport Way, Tacomo WA 98499 206-584-6309
Detroit Monthly, 1400 Woodbridge, Detroit MI 48207 313-446-0600
The Detroiter, 150 Michigan Ave, Detroit MI 48226 313-964-4000
Development Sales Catalog, 899 Logan St, Denver CO 80203....................303-832-5400
Developmental Psychology, Univ of Illinois, Champaign IL 61820.............217-333-6371
Diabetes, 2 Park Ave, New York NY 10016..212-683-7444
Diabetes Care, 2 Park Ave, New York NY 10016.......................................212-683-7444
Diabetes Forecast, 2 Park Ave, New York NY 10016.................................212-683-7444
Diabetes Self Management, 42-15 Crescent, Long Island NY 11101 718-937-4283
Diagnostic Imaging, 500 Howard St, San Francisco CA 94105 415-397-1881
Dial, 3000 Harry Hines Blvd, Dallas TX 75201...214-871-2792
Dial-A-Poem Poets LP's, 222 Bowery, New York NY 10012.......................212-925-6372
Dialogue, 3100 Oak Park Ave, Berwyn IL 60402 312-749-1908

Dialysis & Transplantation, 7628 Densmore Ave, Van Nuys CA 91406...818-782-7328
Digital Design, 1050 Commonwealth Ave, Boston MA 02215.....................617-232-5470
Dimension, PO Box 26673, Austin TX 78755..512-345-0622
Dimension Cable Service Guide, 332 Congress St, Boston MA 02210.......617-547-9400
Dimensional Stone, 17901 Ventura Blvd, Encino CA 91316.........................818-344-4200
DIN News Service, PO Box 5115, Phoenix AZ 85010....................................602-257-0797
Directory of Women's Media, 3306 Ross Pl NW, Wash DC 20008.............202-966-7783
Dirt Bike, 10600 Sepulveda Blvd, Mission Hills CA 91345...........................818-365-6831
Dirt Rider Magazine, 8490 Sunset Blvd, Los Angeles CA 90069 213-657-5100
The Disciple, PO Box 179, St Louis MO 63166...314-371-6900
Discipleship Journal, PO Box 6000, Colorado Springs CO 80934..............303-598-1212
Disciplina, 1101 19th Ave S, Nashville TN 37212 615-327-1444
The Discount Merchandiser, 2 Park Ave, New York NY 10016..................212-889-6030
Discount Store News, 425 Park Ave, New York NY 10022...........................212-371-9400
Discover Magazine, 1271 Ave of the Americas, New York NY 10020.......212-586-1212
Discovery, 3701 West Lake Ave, Glenview IL 60025....................................312-467-1157
Discovery YMCA, 101 N Wacker Dr, Chicago IL 60606.............................312-977-0031
Diseases of the Colon & Rectum, E Washington Sq, Phila PA 19105........215-238-4200
Dispensing Optician, 10341 Democracy Ln, Fairfax VA 22030 703-691-8355
Dissociated Press, 584 Castro #332, San Francisco CA 94114...................415-621-7196
Distribution, Chilton Way, Radnor PA 19089 215-964-4389
Distributor, 1098 Milwaukee Ave PO Box 745, Wheeling IL 60090..........312-537-6460
DITN, 58135 Benham Ave, Elkhart IN 46517 312-664-9782
The Diver, PO Box 249, Cobalt CT 06414...203-342-4730
Diversion, 60 E 42nd St, New York NY 10165...212-682-3710
Dixie Contractor, 525 Marshall St, Decatur GA 30031 404-377-2683
The Dixie Trucker, Box 647, Pewee Valley KY 40056 502-241-0146
DIY Retailing, 770 N High School Rd, Indianapolis IN 46224....................317-248-1261
DNR:The Magazine, 7 E 12th St, New York NY 10003...............................212-741-4200
DO, 212 E Ohio St, Chicago IL 60611 312-280-5800
Dog Fancy, PO Box 6050, Mission Viejo CA 92690 714-240-6001
Dog River Review, Box 125, Parkdale OR 97041..503-352-6494
Dog World, 300 W Adams St, Chicago IL 60606..312-726-2802
Doll Crafter, Box 67A, Mukilteo WA 98275 206-347-1414
DollarWiseWare Journal, PO Box 6075, Denver CO 80206......................303-355-1452
Dolls, 170 5th Ave, New York NY 10010 212-989-8700
Dolphin Digest, PO Box 341459, Miami FL 33243 305-662-5614
Dolphin Log, 8440 Santa Monica Blvd, Los Angeles CA 90069 213-656-4422
Donde, 7955 Biscayne, Miami Beach FL 33141..305-866-5968
Doo Daa Florida, 227 Westridge Dr, Tallahassee FL 32304.......................904-575-3339
Door County Almanak, 10905 Bay Shore Dr, Sister Bay WI 54234...........414-854-2742
Doorways To The Mind, PO Box 29396, Sappington MO 63126................314-849-3722
Down Beat, 222 W Adams, Chicago IL 60606 312-346-7822
Down East, Box 679, Camden ME 04843..207-594-9544
Dr Dobb's Journal, 2464 Embarcadero Way, Palo Alto CA 94303.............415-424-0600
Dragon, PO Box 110, Lake Geneva WI 53147..414-248-8044
The Drama Review, 51 W 4th St, New York NY 10003...............................212-598-2597
Dramatics Magazine, 3368 Central Pkwy, Cincinnati OH 45225...............513-559-1996
Dramatika, 429 Hope St, Tarpon Springs FL 33589.....................................813-937-0109
Draperies & Window Coverings, 840 US Hwy 1, N Palm Bch FL 33408...305-627-3393
Dressage & CT, PO Box 12460, Cleveland OH 44112................................216-932-6517
The Drovers Journal, 7950 College Blvd, Shawnee Mission KS 66201 913-451-2200
Drug Facts & Comparisons, 111 W Port Plaza, St Louis MO 63141 314-878-2515

Drug Interaction Newsletter, PO Box 1903, Spokane WA 99210.................509-534-5713
Drug Store News, 425 Park Ave, New York NY 10022....................................212-371-9400
Drug Therapy, 800 2nd Ave, New York NY 10017..212-599-3400
Drug Therapy For The Elderly, PO Box 1903, Spokane WA 99210 509-534-5713
Drug Topics, 680 Kinderkamack Rd, Oradell NJ 07649.............................201-262-3030
Drummer, PO Box 11314, San Francisco CA 94101.......................................415-864-3456
DSM Publishing Inc, 940 Tyler St Studio 17, Benicia CA 94510.................707-745-6897
The Duck Book, Box 1928, Cocoa FL 32923..305-632-8654
The Duckburg Times, 400 Valleyview, Selah WA 98942 509-697-4634
Ducks Unlimited, 1 Waterfowl Way, Long Grove IL 60047........................312-438-4300
Dune Buggies & Hot VWs, 2949 Century Place, Costa Mesa CA 92656 714-979-2560
Dungeon Master, PO Box 11314, San Francisco CA 94101 415-864-3456
The Duplex Planet, Box 1230, Sarasota Springs NY 12866 518-587-5356
DVM/Veterinary Medicine, 7500 Old Oak, Cleveland OH 44130 216-243-8100
Dvorak Developments, PO Box 1895, Upland CA 91785 818-963-3703
Dynamic Years, 215 Long Beach Blvd, Long Beach CA 90801 213-432-5781
E-ITV, 51 Sugar Hollow Rd, Danbury CT 06810 203-743-2120
Eagle, PO Box 447, Sicklerville NJ 08081...609-629-6091
Eagle Communications Inc, 340 W Main St, Missoula MT 59802.............406-721-2063
EAP Digest, 2145 Crooks Rd Ste 103, Troy MI 48084 313-643-9580
Ear Magazine of New Music, 325 Spring St #208, New York NY 10013...212-807-7944
Ear Nose & Throat Journal, 139 Harrison Rd, Glen Rock NJ 07452........201-444-8660
Early Amer Life, 2245 Kohn Rd Box 8200, Harrisburg PA 17105...............717-657-9555
Earnshaw's Girls & Boys Wear, 393 7th Ave, New York NY 10001...........212-563-2742
Earth Shelter Living, 110 S Greely, Stillwater MN 55082 612-430-1113
Earth's Daughters, Johnson Box 143, Lockport NY 14094 716-837-7778
Earthwise Newsletter, PO Box 680-536, Miami FL 33168............................305-688-8558
East European Quarterly, Box 29 Univ of Colo, Boulder CO 80309 303-492-6157
East Village Eye, 611 Broadway Ste 609, New York NY 10012.....................212-777-6157
East West Jour, 17 Station St, Brookline MA 02146......................................617-232-1000
Eastern Aftermarket Journal, Box 373, Cedarhurst NY 11516....................516-295-3680
Eastern Boating, 1405 3rd Ave Ste 4, Spring Lake NJ 07762......................201-449-3225
Eastern Financial Times, 1405 3rd St, Spring Lake NJ 07762 201-449-3225
Eastern Horse World, 114 West Hills Rd, Huntington Sta NY 11746 516-549-3557
Eastern Review, 34 E 51st St, New York NY 10022 212-888-5900
Easy Living, 1999 Shepard Rd, St Paul MN 55116 612-690-7227
Easyriders, Box 52, Malibu CA 90265...213-889-8701
Ebony, 820 S Michigan Ave, Chicago IL 60605 312-322-9200
Ebony Jr, 820 S Michigan Ave, Chicago IL 60605 312-322-9270
Echelon, 12955 Biscayne Blvd, N Miami FL 33181..305-893-1520
Eclipse Comics, PO Box 1099, Forestville CA 95436......................................707-887-1521
Ecology, Cornell University Corson Hall, Ithaca NY 14853........................607-256-3221
The Economic Press Inc, 12 Daniel Rd, Fairfield NJ 07006 201-227-1224
The Ecphorizer, 814 Gail Ave, Sunnyvale CA 94086......................................408-738-0430
Editor & Publisher, 11 W 19th St, New York NY 10011...............................212-675-4380
The Editor's Desk, 709 SE 52nd Ave, Ocala FL 32671 904-694-2303
Editor's Forum, PO Box 411806, Kansas City MO 64141 913-236-9235
The Editorial Eye, 85 S Bragg St, Alexandria VA 22312 703-642-3040
EDN, 221 Columbus Ave, Boston MA 02116ยน..617-536-7780
EDN Career News, 221 Columbus Ave, Boston MA 02116............................617-536-7780
The Education Digest, 416 Longshore Dr, Ann Arbor MI 48107 313-769-1211
Educational Dealer, Box 526, Dansville NY 14437...716-335-3947
Educational Record, 1 Dupont Circle, Washington DC 20036.....................202-833-4788

Educational Technology, 720 Palisade Ave, Englewood Cliffs NJ 07632 ...201-871-4007
EE's Electronics Distributor, 707 Westchester, White Plains NY 10604 ...914-949-8500
EE Electronic Product News, 707 Westchester, White Plains NY 10604 ...914-949-8500
EIDOS, PO Box 96, Boston MA 02137 617-262-0096
80 Micro, 80 Pine St, Peterborough NH 03458 603-924-9471
Eire-Ireland, Box 5026 College of St Thomas, St Paul MN 55105 612-647-5678
El Palacio, PO Box 2087, Santa Fe NM 87504 505-827-6794
El Paso Magazine, 10 Civic Ctr Plaza, El Paso TX 79901 915-544-7880
Elancee, 600 S Dearborn St Ste 704, Chicago IL 60605 312-939-7000
Elastomerics, 6255 Barfield Rd, Atlanta GA 30328 404-256-9800
Eldritch Tales, 1051 Wellington Rd, Lawrence KS 66044 913-843-4341
Electri-Onics, 17730 W Peterson Rd, Libertyville IL 60048 312-362-8711
The Electric Co, 1 Lincoln Plaza, New York NY 10023 212-595-3456
Electric Light & Power, 1301 S Grove, Barrington IL 60010 312-381-1840
The Electric Weenie, PO Box 2715, Quincy MA 02269 617-749-6900
Electrical Apparatus, 400 N Michigan Ave, Chicago IL 60611 312-321-9440
Electrical Constr & Maint, 1221 Ave of Amer, New York NY 10020 212-512-2847
Electrical Contractor, 7315 Wisconsin Ave, Bethesda MD 20814 301-657-3110
Electrical Systems Design, 5123 W Chester Pike, Edgemont PA 19028 215-359-1240
Electrical Wholesaling, 1221 Ave of Americas, New York NY 10020 212-512-4961
Electrical World, 1221 Ave of the Americas, New York NY 10020 212-512-2928
ElectriCity, 262 S 12th St, Philadelphia PA 19107 215-985-1990
The Electron, 4781 E 355th St, Willoughby OH 44094 216-946-9065
Electronic Business, 1350 E Touhy Ave, Des Plaines IL 60018 312-635-8800
Electronic Buyers' News, 600 Community Dr, Manhasset NY 11030 516-365-4600
Electronic Component News, Chilton Way, Radnor PA 19089 215-964-4000
Electronic Design, 10 Mulholland Dr, Hasbrouck Height NJ 07604 201-393-6000
Electronic Education, 1311 Executive Ctr Dr, Tallahassee FL 32301 904-878-4178
Electronic Engineering Mgr, 600 Community, Manhasset NY 11030 516-365-4600
Electronic Engineering Times, 600 Community, Manhasset NY 11030 516-365-4600
Electronic Imaging, 1050 Commonwealth Ave, Boston MA 02215 617-322-5470
Electronic News, 7 E 12th St, New York NY 10003 212-741-4000
Electronic Packaging & Prod, 1350 E Touhy, Des Plaines IL 60018 312-635-8800
Electronic Products, 645 Stewart Ave, Garden City NY 11530 516-222-2500
Electronic Servicing & Tech, PO Box 12901, Overland Pk KS 66212 913-888-4664
Electronics, 1221 Ave of the Americas, New York NY 10020 212-512-2645
Electronics Test, 1050 Commonwealth Ave, Boston MA 02215 617-232-5470
Electronics West, 2250 N 16 St Ste 105, Phoenix AZ 85006 602-253-9086
Electrum, 2222 Silk Tree Dr, Tustin CA 92680 714-730-4046
Elementary School Journal, 5801 Ellis Ave, Chicago IL 60637 314-882-7888
Elevator World, PO Box 6507 Loop Branch, Mobile AL 36606 205-479-4514
Ellery Queen's Mystery Mag, 380 Lexington Ave, New York NY 10017 ...212-557-9100
Elysium Growth Press, 5436 Fernwood Ave, Los Angeles CA 90027 213-455-1000
Emergency, 6200 Yarrow Dr, Carlsbad CA 92009 619-438-2511
Emergency Librarian, Box C34069 Dept 284, Seattle WA 98124 604-734-0255
Emergency Medical Services, 7628 Densmore, Van Nuys CA 91406 818-782-7328
Emergency Medicine, 475 Park Ave S, New York NY 10016 212-686-0555
Emergency Unlimited, PO Box 35637 Sta D, Albuquerque NM 87176 505-867-3834
Emigre, PO Box 175, Berkeley CA 94704 415-841-4161
Emmy Magazine, 3500 W Olive, Burbank CA 91505 213-506-7885
Empire!, 2911 Arthur Kill Road, Staten Island NY 10309 718-356-7333
Employee Relations, 24 Rope Ferry, Waterford CT 06386 203-739-0169
Employee Services Mgmt, 2400 S Downing, Westchester IL 60153 312-562-8130

Encore Arts in Performance, 1410 SW Morrison, Portland OR 97205 503-226-1468
Endless Vacation, PO Box 80260, Indianapolis IN 46280.............................317-871-9500
Energy Engineering, PO Box 411, Brooklyn NY 11202 718-834-8444
Energy Review, 2060 Alameda Padre Serra, Santa Barbara CA 93103.......805-965-5010
Energy User News, 7 E 12th St, New York NY 10003....................................212-741-4400
Enfantaisie, 2603 SE 32nd Ave, Portland OR 97202......................................503-235-5304
Engage/Social Action, 100 Maryland Ave NE, Washington DC 20002......202-488-5632
Engineer's Digest, 2500 Office Ctr, Willow Grove PA 19090......................215-657-3203
Engineered Systems, 755 W Big Beaver Rd, Troy MI 48007......................313-362-3700
Engineering & Mining, 1221 Ave of Americas, New York NY 10020........212-512-1221
Engineering & Science, Caltech 1-17, Pasadena CA 91125...........................818-356-4686
Engineering News-Record, 1221 Ave of Americas, New York NY 10020..212-512-1000
The English Journal, 1111 Kenyon Rd, Urbana IL 61801.............................217-328-3870
Engravers Journal, 26 Summit St PO Box 318, Brighton MI 48116 313-229-5725
Enroute, Box 205, Metuchen NJ 08840 201-549-5444
The Ensign, 1504 Blue Ridge Rd PO Box 31664, Raleigh NC 27622..........919-821-0892
Entree, 7 E 12th St, New York NY 10003..212-741-4009
Entrepreneur, 2311 Pontius Ave, Los Angeles CA 90064 213-478-0437
Environment, 4000 Albemarle St NW, Washington DC 20016......................202-362-6445
Environmental Action, 1346 Connecticut Ave, Washington DC 20036......202-833-1845
Environmental Bibliography, 2060 Alameda, Santa Barbara CA 93103....805-965-5010
Environmental Opportunities, Box 670, Walpole NH 03608 603-756-3422
Epiphany Journal, PO Box 14727, San Francisco CA 94114 415-431-4670
Episcopal Church Facts, 1114 Delaware Ave, Buffalo NY 14209 716-875-8374
The Episcopalian, 1201 Chestnut St, Philadelphia PA 19107.....................215-564-2010
Epoch, Cornell Univ 245 Goldwin Smith, Ithaca NY 14853.......................607-256-3385
EPRI Journal, PO Box 10412, Palo Alto CA 94303 415-855-2258
Equal Opportunity, 44 Broadway, Greenlawn NY 11740.............................516-261-8917
Equipment Guide News, 1290 Ridder Park Dr, San Jose CA 95131...........408-971-9000
Equipment Management, 7300 N Cicero Ave, Lincolnwood IL 60646.......312-588-7300
Equus, 656 Quince Orchard Rd, Gaithersburg MD 20878...........................301-977-3900
Erie & Chautauqua Magazine, 1250 Tower Lane, Erie PA 16505 814-452-6070
Espionage Magazine, PO Box 1184, Teaneck NJ 07666 201-836-9177
Esquire, 1790 Broadway, New York NY 10019..212-459-7500
Essence, 1500 Broadway, New York NY 10036 212-730-4260
Eternity Magazine, 1716 Spruce St, Philadelphia PA 19103 215-546-3696
Eugene O'Neill Newsletter, Univ of Boston, Boston MA 02114 617-723-4700
Europe, 2100 M St NW Ste 707, Washington DC 20037................................202-862-9555
Evangel, 901 College Ave, Winona Lake IN 46590..219-267-7161
Evangelical Beacon, 1515 E 66th St, Minneapolis MN 55423.....................612-866-3343
Evangelizing Today's Child, Child Evangelism, Warrenton MO 63383.....314-456-4321
Everybody's Money, PO Box 431, Madison WI 53701...................................608-231-4087
Excavating Contractor, 1495 Maple Way Ste 500, Troy MI 48083 313-643-8655
Exceptional Children, 1920 Association Dr, Reston VA 22091......................703-620-3660
The Exceptional Parent, 605 Commonwealth Ave, Boston MA 02215 617-536-8961
Exclusively Yours, 161 W Wisconsin Ave, Milwaukee WI 53202................414-271-4270
Executive Administrator, PO Box 259, Akron IA 51001 712-568-2418
The Executive Educator, 1680 Duke St, Alexandria VA 22314 703-838-6722
The Executive Female, 1041 3rd Ave, New York NY 10021..........................212-371-0740
Executive Financial Woman, 500 N Michigan Ave, Chicago IL 60611.......312-661-1700
Executive Golfer, 2171 Campus Dr, Irvine CA 92715 714-752-6474
Executive Report, 3 Gateway Ctr 5th fl, Pittsburgh PA 15222 412-471-4585
Exhibit Builder, Box 920, Great Neck NY 11022 516-466-5750

Exile Press, 765 Sunset Pkwy, Novato CA 94947 415-883-2132
Expecting, 685 3rd Ave, New York NY 10017...212-878-8700
Exploring, 1325 Walnut Hill Ln, Irving TX 75038 214-580-2352
The Exporter, 6 W 37th St, New York NY 10018...212-563-2772
Expresso Tilt, 10 B Chatham Lane, Newark DE 19713....................................303-737-5852
Exquisite Corpse, Louisiana State Univ, Baton Rouge LA 70803...............504-388-2982
The Fabricator, 7811 N Alpine, Rockford IL 61111...815-654-1902
Fabricnews, 360 N Bedford Dr, Beverly Hills CA 90210...............................213-274-6752
Faces Intl, 8833 Sunset Blvd Penthouse, Los Angeles CA 90069 213-463-2237
Faces: Magazine About People, 20 Grove St, Peterborough NH 03458 603-924-7209
Facet Creative Writing Magazine, PO Box 4950, Hualapai AZ 86412.......602-757-7462
Facets, 535 N Dearborn St, Chicago IL 60610 312-645-5000
Facilities Design & Management, 1515 Broadway, New York NY 10036..212-869-1300
Fact Money Management, 305 E 46th St, New York NY 10017....................212-319-6868
Factsheet Five, 41 Lawrence St, Medford MA 02155.....................................617-391-3496
Fag Rag, PO Box 331 Kenmore Sta, Boston MA 02215 617-426-4469
Fair Times, Box 455, Arnold MO 63010..314-464-2616
Fairfield County Woman, 15 Bank St, Stamford CT 06901 203-323-3105
Familia Latina Magazine, PO Box 4958, Los Angeles CA 90051 213-222-1349
Family Circle, 110 5th Ave, New York NY 10011 212-463-1000
Family Computing, 730 Broadway, New York NY 10003 212-505-3580
Family Festivals, PO Box 37, Saratoga CA 95071 408-286-8505
The Family Handyman, 1999 Shepard Rd, St Paul MN 55116 612-690-7328
Family Magazine for Military Wives, Box 4993, Walnut Crk CA 94596....415-284-9093
Family Motor Coaching, 8219 Clough Pike, Cincinnati OH 45244.............513-474-3622
The Family of God, PO Box 19571, Las Vegas NV 89132.............................702-731-4750
Family Planning Perspectives, 111 5th Ave, New York NY 10003.............212-254-5656
Family Practice News, 12230 Wilkins Ave, Rockville MD 20852 301-770-6170
Family Process, 149 E 78th St, New York NY 10021......................................212-861-6059
Family Relations, Miami University, Oxford OH 45056 513-529-2914
Family Therapy, 4901 Morena Blvd Ste 330, San Diego CA 92117 619-581-9449
Family Therapy News, 1717 K St NW Ste 407, Washington DC 20006 202-429-1825
Fancy Food, 1414 Merchandise Mart, Chicago IL 60654...............................312-824-7440
Fandom Unlimited, PO Box 70868, Sunnyvale CA 94086 415-960-1151
Fanfare, 213 Woodland St, Tenafly NJ 07670 201-567-3908
Fangoria, 475 Park Ave S, New York NY 10016 212-689-2830
Fantastic Films, PO Box 1900, Evanston IL 60201..312-883-4445
Fantasy Mongers Quarterly, PO Box 149, Buffalo NY 14226.....................716-839-2415
Fantasy Review, 11 Ferry Lane West, Westport CT 06880............................203-226-6967
Farm & Ranch Guide, 4023 N State St, Bismark ND 58501 701-255-4905
Farm & Ranch Living, 5400 S 60th St, Greendale WI 53129........................414-423-0100
Farm Computer News, Locust at 17th St, Des Moines IA 50336 515-284-3231
Farm Equipment, 1233 Janesville Ave, Ft Atkinson WI 53538....................414-563-6388
Farm Family America, 1999 Shepard Rd, St Paul MN 55116.......................612-690-7200
Farm Futures, 330 E Kilbourn Ave, Milwaukee WI 53202............................414-278-7676
Farm Industry News Midwest, 1999 Shepard Rd, St Paul MN 55116 612-690-7293
Farm Journal, 230 W Washington Sq, Philadelphia PA 19105.....................215-829-4700
Farm Show, 20088 Kenwood Tr PO Box 1029, Lakeville MN 55044 612-469-5572
Farm Store Merchandising, 2501 Wayzata, Minneapolis MN 55440 612-374-5200
Farm Supplier, Sandstone Bldg, Mount Morris IL 61054.............................815-734-4171
Farmer's Digest, 2645 Maple Hill Le, Brookfield WI 53005 414-782-1570
Farmer's Exchange, Box 37, Verona WI 53593..608-845-8836
The Farmer, 1999 Shepard Rd, St Paul MN 55116...612-690-7361

Farmland News, 3315 N Oak, Kansas City MO 64116.................................816-459-6000
The Farmstead Press, 1 Main St PO Box 111, Freedom ME 04941...........207-382-6200
The FASEB Journal, 9650 Rockville Pike, Bethesda MD 20814.................301-530-7100
Fashion Accessories, 65 W Main St, Bergenfield NJ 07621.........................201-384-3336
Fashion Galleria, 4979 Thunder Rd, Dallas TX 75234................................214-386-5228
Fastbook Series, 1509 Dexter, Austin TX 78704.......................................512-441-2452
Fastener Technology Intl, 6521 Davis Indus Pkwy, Solon OH 44139.........216-248-1125
Fat Tuesday, 419 N Larchmont Blvd Ste 104, Los Angeles CA 90004........213-461-0571
Fate, 500 Hyacinth Place, Highland Park IL 60035....................................312-433-4550
FDA Consumer, 5600 Fishers Ln, Rockville MD 20857.............................301-443-3220
Fedco Reporter, 9300 Santa Fe Spgs Rd, Santa Fe Spgs CA 90670............213-946-2511
Federal Credit Union, 1111 N 19th St Ste 700, Arlington VA 22209..........703-522-4770
Federal Times, Times Journal Bldg, Springfield VA 22159.......................703-750-2000
Feed & Grain Times, 1233 Janesville Ave, Ft Atkinson WI 53538.............414-563-6388
Feedlot Management, 580 Waters Edge, Lombard IL 60187.......................312-953-1100
Feedstuffs, 2501 Wayzata Blvd, Minneapolis MN 55440..........................612-374-5200
Feeling Great, 45 W 34th St Ste 407, New York NY 10001.......................212-239-0855
Feline Practice, 7 Ashley Ave S, Santa Barbara CA 93103.........................805-965-1028
Fellowship, Box 271, Nyack NY 10960...212-358-4601
The Female Patient, 400 Plaza Dr, Secaucus NJ 07094.............................201-865-7500
Feminist Bookstore News, PO Box 882554, San Francisco CA 94188........415-626-1556
Feminist Collections, 728 State St, Madison WI 53706.............................608-263-5754
Feminist Periodicals, 728 State St, Madison WI 53706..............................608-263-5754
Feminist Studies, Univ of Maryland, College Park MD 20742...................301-454-2363
Feminist Writers Guild, PO Box 9396, Berkeley CA 94709......................415-524-3692
Fence Industry/Access Control, 6255 Barfield Rd, Atlanta GA 30328......404-256-9800
Fertility & Sterility, 200 1st St SW W-10, Rochester MN 55905...............507-284-3850
Fertilizer Progress, 1015 18th St NW, Washington DC 20036....................202-861-4900
Fessenden Review, PO Box 7272, San Diego CA 92107............................619-488-4991
Festivals, 160 E Virginia St #290, San Jose CA 95112..............................408-286-8505
Fiberarts Magazine of Textiles, 50 College St, Ashville NC 28801............704-253-0467
Fiction Intl, San Diego State Univ, San Diego CA 92182...........................619-265-5443
Fiction Network Magazine, PO Box 5651, San Francisco CA 94101.........415-391-6610
Field & Stream, 1515 Broadway, New York NY 10036.............................212-719-6685
50 Plus, 850 3rd Ave, New York NY 10022...212-715-2600
The Fighter Intl, 1017 Highland Ave, Largo FL 33540..............................813-584-0054
Fighting Stars, 1813 Victory Pl, Burbank CA 91504..................................818-843-4444
Fighting Woman News, PO Box 1459, New York NY 10163.....................212-228-0900
Film Comment, 140 W 65th St, New York NY 10023...............................212-877-1800
Film Quarterly, Univ of Calif Press, Berkeley CA 94720..........................415-642-6333
Film World, 8060 Melrose Ave, Los Angeles CA 90046............................213-653-8060
Films in Review, PO Box 589, New York NY 10021.................................212-628-1594
The Final Draft, PO Box 47786, Phoenix AZ 85068..................................602-944-5268
Finance & Development, IMF Bldg, Washington DC 20431.......................202-473-8290
Financial Computing, 1 River Rd, Cos Cob CT 06807...............................203-661-5000
Financial Freedom Report, 1831 Ft Union, Salt Lake City UT 84121.......801-943-1280
Financial Professional, PO Box 1928, Cocoa FL 32923............................305-632-8654
Financial Services Times, 437 Newtonville Ave, Newton MA 02160.........617-244-1240
Financial Strategies, 250 Piedmont Ave NE, Atlanta GA 30365................404-521-6500
Financial World, 1450 Broadway, New York NY 10018............................212-869-1616
Financier, 355 Lexington Ave, New York NY 10017.................................212-599-0023
Fine Dining, 1897 NE 164th St, Miami FL 33162.....................................305-947-9352
Fine Homebuilding, 63 S Main St PO Box 355, Newtown CT 06470.........203-426-8171

Fine Madness, PO Box 15176, Seattle WA 98115 206-842-1273
Fine Print, PO Box 3394, San Francisco CA 94119 415-776-1530
Fine Times, 5951 Canning St, Oakland CA 94609 415-652-3810
Fine Tuning, 1015 N 6th St, Milwaukee WI 53201 414-278-1468
Fine Woodworking, 63 S Main St PO Box 355, Newtown CT 06470............203-426-8171
Finescale Modeler, 1027 N 7th St, Milwaukee WI 53233.....................414-272-2060
Finnish Connection, PO Box 1531, Vancouver WA 98668 206-695-7807
Fins & Feathers, 318 W Franklin Ave, Minneapolis MN 55404..............612-874-8404
Fire Command Magazine, Batterymarch Pk, Quincy MA 02269 617-770-3000
Fire Engineering, 875 3rd Ave, New York NY 10022 212-605-9640
Fire Journal, Batterymarch Pk, Quincy MA 02269 617-770-3000
Firehouse Magazine, 33 Irving Pl, New York NY 10003 212-475-5400
Firemen's Monthly, 1405 3rd Ave, Silver Lake NJ 07762 201-449-3225
Firepower, PO Box 270, Cornville AZ 86325 602-634-6127
First Comics Inc, 435 N LaSalle St, Chicago IL 60610 312-670-6770
First Hand, 310 Cedar Lane, Teaneck NJ 07666 201-836-9177
The Fish Boat, PO Box 2400, Covington LA 70434..............................504-893-2930
Fisheries Communications Inc, PO Box 37, Stonington ME 04681 207-367-2396
The Fisherman, Bridge St, Sag Harbor NY 11963 516-725-4200
Fishing & Boating Illustrated, Box HH, Capistrano Beach CA 92624......714-493-2101
Fishing & Hunting News, 511 Eastlake E, Seattle WA 98109 206-624-3845
Fishing Facts, Box 609 US Hwy 41-45, Menomonee Falls WI 53051........414-255-4800
Fishing Tackle Retailer, 1 Bell Rd, Montgomery AL 36141.................205-272-9530
Fishing World, 51 Atlantic Ave, Floral Park NY 11001........................516-352-9700
Fitness Management, 215 S Hwy 101, Solano Beach CA 92075..............619-481-4155
Fleet Owner, 1221 Ave of the Americas, New York NY 10020................212-512-4563
Flight Reports, 1280 Saw Mill River Rd, Yonkers NY 10710................914-423-6000
Floor Covering Weekly, 919 3rd Ave, New York NY 10022....................212-759-8050
Flooring, 7500 Old Oak Blvd, Cleveland OH 44130............................216-243-8100
Floral & Nursery Times, PO Box 699, Wilmette IL 60091....................312-256-8777
Flordia Keys Magazine, 2111 O/S Hwy Box 8181, Marathon FL 33050....305-743-3721
Florida Builder, Drawer 6126, Clearwater FL 33518............................813-733-5555
Florida Forum, PO Drawer 4850, Winter Park FL 32793......................305-671-3772
Florida Grocer, PO Box 430760, S Miami FL 33143.............................305-441-1138
Florida Grower & Rancher, 1331 N Mills Ave, Orlando FL 32803 305-894-6522
Florida Gulf Coast Living, 1311 N Westshore Blvd, Tampa FL 33607......813-879-1177
The Florida Horse, PO Box 2106, Ocala FL 32678 904-629-8082
Florida Hotel & Motel Journal, PO Box 1529, Tallahassee FL 32302 904-224-2888
Florida Leader, PO Box 14081, Gainesville FL 32604 904-373-6907
Florida Racquet Journal, PO Box 11657, Jacksonville FL 32239.............904-743-0218
The Florida Review, Univ of Central Florida, Orlando FL 32816 305-275-2038
Florida Sports!, PO Box 18694, Tampa FL 33679.................................813-254-4216
Florida Sportsman, 5901 SW 74th St, Miami FL 33143 305-661-4222
Florida Underwriter, PO Box 320066, Tampa FL 33679........................813-251-8843
Florida Wildlife, 620 S Meridian St, Tallahassee FL 32301 904-488-5563
Florida's Gold Coast, PO Box 70250, Ft Lauderdale FL 33307...............305-782-2104
Florist, 29200 Northwestern Hwy Box 2227, Southfield MI 48037............313-355-9300
Flower & Garden, 4251 Pennsylvania Ave, Kansas City MO 64111.............816-531-5730
Flower News, 549 W Randolph St, Chicago IL 60606............................312-236-8648
Flowers & Magazine, 12233 W Olympic Blvd, Los Angeles CA 90064 213-826-5253
Flute Talk, 200 Northfield Rd, Northfield IL 60093.............................312-446-5000
The Flutist Quarterly, 805 Laguna Dr, Denton TX 76201.....................817-387-9472
Fly Fisherman, 2245 Kohn Rd, Harrisburg PA 17105 717-657-9555

The Flyfisher, 1387 Cambridge, Idaho Falls ID 83401.................................208-523-7300
Flying, 1 Park Ave, New York NY 10016...212-725-3500
The Flying A, 300 S East Ave, Jackson MI 49203 517-787-8121
Focus, 1250 24th St NW, Washington DC 20037 202-778-9505
Focus On the Family, 50 E Foothill Blvd, Arcadia CA 91066...................818-445-1579
Focus-Metro Phila Business News, 1015 Chestnut, Phila PA 19107..........215-925-8545
Focus/Midwest Magazine, 8606 Olive Blvd, St Louis MO 63132 314-991-1698
Folio, 6 River Bend PO Box 4949, Stamford CT 06907 203-358-9900
Folio, American Univ, Washington DC 20016 202-885-2971
Folk Era Today, 6 S 230 Cohasset Rd, Naperville IL 60540...................312-961-3559
Food & Beverage Marketing, 345 Park Ave S, New York NY 10010 212-686-7744
Food & Service, PO Box 1429, Austin TX 78767......................................512-444-6543
Food Engineering International, Chilton Way, Radnor PA 19089 215-964-4453
Food Management, 7500 Old Oak Blvd, Cleveland OH 44130....................216-243-8100
Food People, PO Box 1208, Woodstock GA 30188....................................404-928-8994
Food Processing, 301 E Erie St, Chicago IL 60611 312-644-2020
Food Service Equip Specialist, 1350 E Touhy, Des Plaines IL 60018 312-635-8800
Food Trade News, 119 Sibley Ave, Ardmore PA 19003..............................215-642-7040
Foodservice Product News, 104 5th Ave 20th fl, New York NY 10011......212-206-7440
Football Digest, 1020 Church St, Evanston IL 60201 312-491-6440
The Football News, 17820 E Warren Ave, Detroit MI 48224......................313-881-9554
Football: Our Way, 3211 Milwaukee St #1, Madison WI 53714 608-241-0549
The Footloose Librarian, PO Box 972, Minneapolis MN 55440 612-874-8108
Footwear News, 7 E 12th St, New York NY 10003......................................212-741-4310
Footwork Magazine, Passaic Cty Comm College, Patterson NJ 07509 201-684-6555
For Parents, 7052 West Ln #283500, Eden NY 14057 716-992-3316
For Your Eyes Only, PO Box 8759, Amarillo TX 79114...............................806-655-2009
Forbes, 60 5th Ave, New York NY 10011 212-620-2200
Ford Times, 111 E Wacker Dr, Chicago IL 60601..313-322-2460
Fore, 3740 Cahuenga Blvd, North Hollywood CA 91604..............................818-980-3630
Forecast for Home Economics, 730 Broadway, New York NY 10003........212-505-3000
Forecast Magazine, 1515 Broadway, New York NY 10036...........................212-703-7650
The Forecaster Publishing Co, 19623 Ventura Blvd, Tarzana CA 91356 ..818-345-4421
Foreign Affairs, 58 E 68th St, New York NY 10021.....................................212-734-0400
Foreign Policy, 11 Dupont Circle NW, Washington DC 20036 202-797-6420
Forest Industries, 500 Howard St, San Francisco CA 94105 415-397-1881
Forest Notes, 54 Portsmouth St, Concord NH 03301.................................603-224-9945
Forests & People, Drawer 5067, Alexandria VA 71301 318-443-2558
Format, 405 S 7th St, St Charles IL 60174 312-584-0187
Formations, PO Box 327, Wilmette IL 60091 312-251-5588
Fortune Magazine, Time & Life Bldg, New York NY 10020 212-586-1212
Forum, 1965 Broadway, New York NY 10023 212-496-6100
Foundation for Economic Educ, 30 S Broadway, Irvington NY 10533.......914-591-7230
Foundation For New Literature, 4641 Park Blvd, San Diego CA 92116....619-299-4859
Foundation Grants Index Bimonthly, 79 5th Ave, New York NY 10003...212-620-4230
Foundation News, 1828 L St NW, Washington DC 20036............................202-466-6512
Foundry Management & Tech, Penton Plz, Cleveland OH 44114................216-696-7000
4H Leader, 7100 Connecticut Ave, Chevy Chase MD 20815.......................301-961-2850
Four-Wheel & Off-Road, 8490 Sunset Blvd, Los Angeles CA 90069 213-854-2360
Four Wheeler, 6728 Eton Ave, Canoga Park CA 91303...............................818-992-4777
Fox River Patriot, PO Box 31, Princeton WI 54968 414-295-6252
Foxfire, Box B, Rabun Gap GA 30568 404-746-5318
Foxway, 114 E Wilson, Batavia IL 60510..312-879-9270

FQ, PO Box 11314, San Francisco CA 94101 415-864-3456
Franciscan Herald, 1434 W 51st St, Chicago IL 60609.............................312-254-4455
France Today, 1051 Divisadero, San Francisco CA 95115..........................415-921-5100
Franklin Mint Almanac, Franklin Ctr PA 19091..215-459-7016
Free Inquiry, 3159 Bailey Ave, Buffalo NY 14215.......................................716-834-2921
Free Press Network, PO Box 15548, Columbus OH 43215.......................614-461-5266
Freebies, 407 State St, Santa Barbara CA 93101..805-962-9135
Freedom Magazine, 1301 N Catalina St, Los Angeles CA 90027.............213-663-2058
Freedomways Quarterly Review, 799 Broadway, New York NY 10003......212-477-3985
The Freedonia Gazette, Darien 28, New Hope PA 18938 215-862-9734
Freelance Writer's Report, PO Box 9844, Ft Lauderdale FL 33310............305-485-0795
Freeman Digest, PO Box 31776, Salt Lake City UT 84131.........................801-973-1776
The Freeman, 30 S Broadway, Irvington-Hudson NY 10533......................914-591-7230
French Review, Univ of N Carolina, Chapel Hill NC 27514......................919-962-0158
Frequent Flyer, 888 7th Ave, New York NY 10106....................................212-997-8300
Freshwater & Marine Aquarium, Box 487, Sierra Madre CA 91024 818-355-1476
Freestylin', 3162 Kashiwa St, Torrance CA 90505......................................213-539-9213
Frets, 20085 Stevens Creek, Cupertino CA 95014.....................................408-466-1105
Friday of the Jewish Exponent, 226 S 16th St, Philadelphia PA 19102.......215-893-5745
The Friend, 50 E North Temple, Salt Lake City UT 84150.........................801-531-2210
Friendly Exchange, 1716 Locust St, Des Moines IA 50336 515-284-2008
Friends, 30400 Van Dyke Blvd, Warren MI 48093......................................313-575-9400
Friends Journal, 1501 Cherry St, Philadelphia PA 19102 215-241-7277
The Friends of Wine, 2302 Perkins Place, Silver Spring MD 20910............301-588-0980
Front Page Detective, 460 W 34th St, New York NY 10001.......................212-947-6500
Frontiers Jour of Women Studies, Univ of Colo, Boulder CO 80309........303-492-3025
Fuel Oil News, Box 360, Whitehouse NJ 08888...201-381-7279
Full Cry, Box 10, Boody IL 62514...217-865-2332
Functional Photography, 101 Crossways Park W, Woodbury NY 11797...516-496-8000
Fundamentalist Journal, 2220 Langhorne Rd, Lynchburg VA 24514........804-528-4112
Fur-Fish-Game, 2878 E Main St, Columbus OH 43209 614-231-9585
Furniture Design & Mfg, 400 N Michigan Ave, Chicago IL 60611............312-222-2000
Furniture/Wood Digest, 1233 Janesville Ave, Ft Atkinson WI 53538........414-563-6388
Fusion Magazine, 304 W 58th St 5th fl, New York NY 10019....................212-247-8439
Future Homemakers of Amer, 1910 Association Dr, Reston VA 22091 703-476-4900
Futures & Options Trader, 13618 Scenic Crest, Yucaipa CA 92399..........714-793-5545
Futures Magazine, 219 Parkdale, Cedar Falls IA 50613.............................319-277-6341
Futurific, 280 Madison Ave, New York NY 10016.....................................212-684-4913
The Futurist, 4916 St Elmo Ave, Bethesda MD 20814...............................301-656-8274
Gallery, 800 2nd Ave, New York NY 10017 212-986-9600
Gallery Works, 25 Carlin St, Norwalk CT 06851..203-849-0072
The Galley Sail Review, 1630 University Ave #42, Berkeley CA 94703.....415-486-0187
Gambling Times, 1018 N Cole Ave, Hollywood CA 90038 213-463-4833
Game & Fish Magazines, 2121 New Market Pkwy, Marietta GA 30067....404-953-9222
Games, 1350 Ave of the Americas, New York NY 10019.............................212-421-5984
Gaming Intl, 2515 Pacific Ave, Atlantic City NJ 08401..............................609-345-6848
The Gamut, RT 1216 Cleveland State Univ, Cleveland OH 44115.............216-687-4679
Robert T Garcia Publisher, PO Box 41714, Chicago IL 60641...................312-867-4143
Garden, NY Botanical Gardens, Bronx NY 10458......................................212-220-8657
Garden Design, 1733 Conneticut Ave NW, Washington DC 20009...........202-466-7730
Garden Supply Retailer, PO Box 2400, Minnetonka MN 55343.................612-931-0211
Gargoyle, PO Box 3567, Washington DC 20007 202-333-1544
Gas Industries, PO Box 827, Woodland Hills CA 91365 818-884-1561

Gay Chicago Magazine, 1527 N Wells St, Chicago IL 60606 312-751-0130
Gay Community News, 167 Tremont St, Boston MA 02111........................617-426-4469
GCT, 350 Weinacker Ave, Mobile AL 36604 205-478-4700
The Gem, Churches of God PO Box 926, Findlay OH 45839......................419-424-1961
Gems & Gemology, 1660 Stewart St, Santa Monica CA 90404 213-829-2991
The Genealogical Helper, 3223 S Main St, Nibley UT 84321....................801-752-6022
General Aviation News, 1712 E Belt Line Rd, Carrollton TX 75006 214-446-2502
General Denistry, 211 E Chicago Ave Ste 1200, Chicago IL 60611............312-440-4300
Genesis, 1840 Wilson Blvd Ste 204, Arlington VA 22201 703-524-7802
Genesis, 770 Lexington Ave, New York NY 10021.....................................212-486-8430
Genetics, Box 2427, Chapel Hill NC 27514..919-942-3466
Gent, 2355 Salzedo St, Coral Gables FL 33134 305-443-2378
Gentlemen's Quarterly, 350 Madison Ave, New York NY 10017................212-880-8800
Geology, 3300 Penrose Pl PO Box 9140, Boulder CO 80301.......................303-447-8850
Geophysics, 8801 S Yale, Tulsa OK 74137..918-493-3516
Georgia Jour, PO Box 526, Athens GA 30603 404-548-5269
The Georgia Review, Univ of Georgia, Athens GA 30602............................404-542-3481
Georgia Sportsman, 2121 Newmarket Pkwy #136, Marietta GA 30067....404-953-9222
Geotechnical Fabrics Report, 345 Cedar Bldg #450, St Paul MN 55101...612-222-2508
Geothermal Energy, 5762 Firebird Ct, Camarillo CA 93010.......................805-482-6288
Geotimes, 4220 King St, Alexandria VA 22302 703-379-2480
Geriatric Consultant, PO Box 1548, Marco Island FL 33937.....................813-394-0400
Geriatric Medicine Today, Princeton Meadows, Plainsboro NJ 08536......609-275-1900
Geriatrics, 757 3rd Ave, New York NY 10017...212-418-4100
The Gerontologist, 1411 K St NW Ste 300, Washington DC 20005 202-393-1411
Get PMVI, 227 Westridge Dr, Tallahassee FL 32304..................................904-575-3339
Geyer's Office Dealer, 51 Madison Ave, New York NY 10010 212-689-4411
GFWC Clubwoman, 1734 N St NW, Washington DC 20036..........................202-347-3168
Giant Crosswords, 1772 State Rd, Cuyahoga Falls OH 44223 216-923-2397
The Giants Newsweekly, 43 E Front St Ste 10, Red Bank NJ 07701 201-747-1085
Gifted Children, PO Box 115, Sewell NJ 08080 609-582-0277
Gifts & Decorative Accessories, 51 Madison Ave, New York NY 10010 ...212-689-4411
Giftware Business, 1515 Broadway, New York NY 10036 212-869-1300
Giftware News, 112 Adrossan PO Box 5398, Deptford NJ 08096................609-227-0798
Girl Scout Leader, 830 3rd Ave, New York NY 10022................................212-940-7500
Glamour, 350 Madison Ave, New York NY 10017.......................................212-880-8800
Glass Craft News, 270 Lafayette St Rm 701, New York NY 10012 212-966-6694
Glass Digest, 310 Madison Ave, New York NY 10017 212-682-7681
Glass Magazine, 8200 Greensboro Dr, McLean VA 22102 703-442-4890
Gleaning in Bee Culture, 723 W Liberty St, Medina OH 44256..................216-725-6677
Glider Rider, 1085 Bailey Ave, Chattanooga TN 37401.............................615-629-5375
Global Trade Executive, 401 N Broad St, Philadelphia PA 19108.............215-238-5300
Go West, 1240 Bayshore Hwy, Burlingame CA 94010................................415-579-3511
Go Guide New Orleans, 1826 Constantinople, New Orleans LA 70115 504-897-0040
Gold Prospector, PO Box 507, Bonsall CA 92003 619-728-6620
Golden State, 755 Davis St, San Francisco CA 94111 415-421-6375
Golden Years Magazine, 233 E New Haven Ave, Melbourne FL 32902....305-725-4888
Golf Course Management, 1617 St Andrews Dr, Lawrence KS 66046 913-841-2240
Golf Digest, 5520 Park Ave, Trumbull CT 06611.......................................203-373-7000
Golf Illustrated, 3 Park Ave, New York NY 10016.....................................212-340-9200
Golf Journal, Golf House, Far Hills NJ 07931..201-234-2300
Golf Magazine, 380 Madison Ave, New York NY 10017.............................212-687-3000
Golf Shop Operations, 5520 Park Ave, Trumbull CT 06611.......................203-373-7232

The Golf Traveler, 1137 E 2100 S, Salt Lake City UT 84106 801-486-9391
Golf World, 2100 Powers Ferry Rd, Atlanta GA 30339 404-955-5656
Good Housekeeping, 959 8th Ave, New York NY 10019 212-262-3614
Good News, 1937 10th Ave, Lake Worth FL 33466 305-533-0990
Good News, PO Box 150, Wilmore KY 40390 606-858-4661
Good News Broadcaster, 12th & M Sts, Lincoln NE 68501 402-474-4567
Good Reading, PO Box 40, Litchfield IL 62056 217-324-3425
Good Sam's Hi-Way Herald, 29901 Agoura Rd, Agoura CA 91301 818-991-4980
Good Times, 5951 Canning St, Oakland CA 94609 415-652-3810
Goodlife, 1401 W Paces Ferry Rd Ste D-110, Atlanta GA 30327 404-231-9310
The Goofus Office Gazette, 270 Hobart St, Pearl River NY 10965 914-620-1416
Helen Gordon, PO Box 307, Carmel IN 46032 317-846-7007
Gorham Axios Newsletter, 800 S Euclid St, Fullerton CA 92632 714-526-2131
Gourmet Magazine, 560 Lexington Ave, New York NY 10022 212-888-8800
The Gourmet Retailer, 1545 NE 123rd St, North Miami FL 33161 305-893-8771
Gourmet Telefood Today, 10 E 39th St, New York NY 10016 212-213-8558
Government Computer News, 1620 Elton Rd, Silver Spring MD 20903 301-445-4405
Government Executive, 1725 K St NW, Washington DC 20006 202-785-2593
Government Product News, 1111 Chester Ave, Cleveland OH 44114 216-696-7000
Graduating Engineer, 1221 Ave of the Americas, New York NY 10020 ...212-512-4123
Grammy Pulse, 303 N Glenoaks Blvd Ste 140, Burbank CA 91502 818-849-1313
Grand Rapids Magazine, 40 Pearl St NW, Grand Rapids MI 49503 616-459-4545
Grand Street, 50 Riverside Dr, New York NY 10024 212-496-6088
Grandparenting!, 801 Cumberland Hills Dr, Hendersonville TN 37075 ...615-822-8586
Grapevine's Finger Lakes Magazine, 108 S Albany St, Ithaca NY 14850 ..607-272-3470
Graphic Arts Monthly, 875 3rd Ave, New York NY 10022 212-605-9574
Graphic Arts Product News, 300 W Adams, Chicago IL 60606 312-726-2802
Graphic International, 2922 N State Rd 7, Pompano Beach FL 33063 305-971-4360
Grass & Grain, 1531 Yuma, Manhattan KS 66502 913-539-7558
Gray Panthers Network, 700 Chestnut St, Philadelphia PA 19107 215-545-6555
Gray's Sporting Journal, 205 Willow St, South Hamilton MA 01982 617-468-4486
Great Foods Magazine, 333 Sylvan Ave, Englewood Cliffs NJ 07632 201-569-2424
Great Lakes Fisherman, 921 Eastwind Dr, Westerville OH 43081 614-882-5653
Great Lakes Travel & Living, 108 W Perry St, Pt Clinton OH 43452 419-734-5774
Greater Phoenix Jewish News, PO Box 26590, Phoenix AZ 85068 602-870-9470
Greater Portland, 142 Free St, Portland ME 04101 207-772-2811
Greenfield Review Lit Ctr, RD 1 Box 80, Greenfield Ctr NY 12833 518-584-1728
Greenhouse Grower, 37841 Euclid Ave, Willoughby OH 44094 216-942-2000
Greenhouse Manager, 1268 St Louis Ave, Ft Worth TX 76101 817-332-8236
Greenville Woman, 712 N Main St, Greenville SC 29609 803-232-7799
Greetings Magazine, 309 5th Ave, New York NY 10016 212-679-6677
The Greyhound Review, Box 543, Abilene KS 67410 913-263-4660
The Griffith Observer, 2800 E Observatory Rd, Los Angeles CA 90027 ...213-664-1181
Grimm Press & Publishing, PO Box 1523, Longview WA 98632 206-577-8598
Grocers Journal of Calif, 1636 W 8th St, Los Angeles CA 90017 213-381-5811
Grocers' Spotlight, 25689 Kelly Rd, Roseville MI 48066 313-779-4940
Grocery Distribution, 307 N Michigan Ave, Chicago IL 60601 312-263-1057
Groom & Board, 207 S Wabash Ave, Chicago IL 60604 312-663-4040
Grounds Maintenance, 9221 Quivira Rd, Overland Park KS 66215 913-888-4664
Group, PO Box 481, Loveland CO 80539 303-669-3836
Group Practice Jour, 1422 Duke St, Alexandria VA 22314 703-838-0033
The Grower, 400 Knightsbridge Pkwy, Lincolnshire IL 60069 312-634-2600
Growing Parent, 22 N 2nd St PO Box 1100, Lafayette IN 47902 317-423-2624

Growing Without Schooling, 729 Boylston St, Boston MA 02116..............617-437-1550
GSA Bulletin, 3300 Penrose Pl, Boulder CO 80301.................................303-447-8850
GSA News & Information, 3300 Penrose Pl, Boulder CO 80301 303-447-2020
Guide to the Florida Keys, PO Box 330712, Miami FL 33133.....................305-665-2858
Guideposts, 747 3rd Ave, New York NY 10017......................................212-754-2200
Guitar Player, 20085 Stevens Creek, Cupertino CA 95014 408-446-1105
Guitar World, 1115 Broadway 8th fl, New York NY 10010......................212-807-7100
Gulf Coast Cattleman, 11201 Morning Ct, San Antonio TX 78213............512-344-8300
Gulf Coast Fisherman, 205 Bowie Drawer P, Port Lavaca TX 77979........512-552-8864
Gulf Coast Golfer, 9182 Old Katy Rd, Houston TX 77055 713-464-0308
Gulfshore Life, 3620 Tamiami Tr N, Naples FL 33940..............................813-262-6425
Gun Digest, 4092 Commercial Ave, Northfield IL 60062 312-441-7010
Gun Dog Publication Inc, Box 68, Adel IA 50003 515-993-4006
The Gun Report, 110 S College Ave, Aledo IL 61231..............................309-582-5311
Gun World, 34249 Camino Capistrano, Capistrano Beach CA 92624 714-493-2101
Gung-Ho, Charlton Bldg, Derby CT 06418..203-735-3381
Guns, 591 Camino de la Reina Ste 200, San Diego CA 92108.....................619-297-5350
Guns & Ammo, 8490 Sunset Blvd, Los Angeles CA 90069........................213-657-5100
Gurney's Gardening News, 2nd & Capitol, Yankton SD 57079....................605-665-4451
Hadassah Magazine, 50 W 58th St, New York NY 10019.........................212-355-7900
Haight-Ashbury Literary Jour, PO Box 15133, San Francisco CA 94115..415-552-7064
Hair & Beauty Guide, 300 W 43rd St, New York NY 10036......................212-397-5200
Ham Radio Magazine, Main St, Greenville NH 03048.............................603-878-1441
Handball, 930 N Benton Ave, Tucson AZ 85711.....................................602-795-0434
Handicap News, 3060 E Bridge St, Brighton CO 80601.............................303-659-4463
Handling & Shipping Mgmt, 1111 Chester Ave, Cleveland OH 44114......216-696-7000
Handloader Magazine, 138 N Montezuma St, Prescott AZ 86302 602-445-7810
Handmade Magazine, 50 College St, Asheville NC 28801 704-253-0468
Hands-On Electronics, 500B Bi-County Blvd, Farmingdale NY 11735......516-293-3000
Robin & Russ Handweavers, 533 N Adams St, McMinnville OR 97128....503-472-5760
Handwoven, 306 N Washington Ave, Loveland CO 80537 303-669-7672
Happiness Holding Tank, 9727 SE Reedway, Portland OR 97266.............503-771-6779
Harcourt Brace Jovanovich, 6277 Sea Harbor Dr, Orlando FL 32821 305-345-2000
Hardcopy for DEC Computers, 1061 S Melrose, Placentia CA 92670.......714-632-6924
Hardware Age, Chilton Way, Radnor PA 19089......................................215-964-4275
Hardware Merchandiser, 7300 N Cicero Ave, Lincolnwood IL 60646.......312-674-7300
Hardware Retailing, 770 N High School Rd, Indianapolis IN 46224.........317-248-1261
Hardy Reports, PO Box 98490, Pasadena CA 91109 818-795-1957
The Harmonizer, 6315 3rd Ave, Kenosha WI 53140 414-654-9111
Harper's Bazaar, 1700 Broadway, New York NY 10019 212-903-5300
Harper's Magazine, 666 Broadway, New York NY 10012.........................212-614-6500
Hartford Woman, 595 Franklin Ave, Hartford CT 06114 203-278-3800
The Harvard Advocate, 21 South St, Cambridge MA 02138......................617-495-7820
Harvard Business Review, Soldiers Field, Boston MA 02163.....................617-495-6800
Harvard Educational Review, 13 Appian Way, Cambridge MA 02138......617-495-3432
Harvard Law Review, Gannett House, Cambridge MA 02138 617-495-7888
Harvard Magazine, 7 Ware St, Cambridge MA 02138..............................617-495-5746
Hastings Center Report, 360 Broadway, Hasting-on-Hudson NY 10706...914-478-0500
Haunts, PO Box 3342, Providence RI 02906 401-781-9438
Having Writ, 3039 Indianola Ave, Columbus OH 43202..........................614-262-0471
Hawaii, 36 Merchant St, Honolulu HI 96813...808-524-7400
The Hawaii Hotel Network, 532 Cummins St, Honolulu HI 96814............808-524-8404
Hawaii Review, Univ of Hawaii English Dept, Honolulu HI 96822...........808-948-8548

Health, 3 Park Ave, New York NY 10016...212-340-9200
Health & Social Work, 257 Park Ave S 10th fl, New York NY 10010 212-460-9400
Health Care Financial Mgmt, 1900 Spring Rd, Oak Brook IL 60521.........312-655-4600
Health Care Systems, 1515 Broadway, New York NY 10036 212-869-1300
Health Education, 1900 Association Dr, Reston VA 22091...........................703-476-3400
Health Food Retailing, 6255 Barfield Rd, Atlanta GA 30328......................404-256-9800
Health Foods Business, 567 Morris Ave, Elizabeth NJ 07208.....................201-353-7373
Health Freedom News, Box 688, Monrovia CA 91016................................818-359-8334
Health Industry Today, 454 Morris Ave, Springfield NJ 07081....................201-564-9400
Health Literature Review, 1300 Conwed Twr, St Paul MN 55101...............612-228-7669
Health Progress, 4455 Woodson Rd, St Louis MO 63134...........................314-427-2500
Healthplex, 8303 Dodge St, Omaha NE 68114...402-390-4528
Hearing Instruments, 131 W 1st St, Duluth MN 55802...............................218-723-9345
Hearst Corp, 959 8th Ave, New York NY 10019..212-262-5700
Heart & Lung, 11830 Westline Indus Dr, St Louis MO 63146......................314-872-8370
Heat Transfer Engineering, 1010 Vermont Ave NW, Wash DC 20005 201-783-3958
Heat Treating, 7 E 12th St, New York NY 10003...212-741-6481
Heating Piping & Air Cond News, PO Box 1952, Dover NJ 07801.............201-361-9060
Heating/Piping/Air Conditioning, 2 Illinois Ctr, Chicago IL 60601 312-861-0880
Heavy Duty Distribution, 707 Lake Crook Rd, Deerfield IL 60015.............312-498-3180
Heavy Duty Trucking, 4001 Westerly Pl #106, Newport Bch CA 92660....714-833-0512
Heavy Metal, 635 Madison, New York NY 10022..212-688-4070
Helicon Nine, PO Box 22412, Kansas City MO 64113.................................913-345-0802
Hemlock Quarterly, PO Box 66218, Los Angeles CA 90066........................213-391-1871
Hemlocks & Balsams, Lees-McRae College, Banner Elk NC 28604 704-898-5241
Hennepin Cty Library Cat, 12601 Ridgedale, Minnetonka MN 55343.......612-541-8561
Heresies, 1306 Canal St Sta, New York NY 10013.......................................212-227-2108
HFD Retailing Home Furnishings, 7 E 12th St, New York NY 10003.......212-741-4000
Hicall, 1445 Boonville Ave, Springfield MO 65802.....................................417-862-2781
High Country News, Box 1090, Paonia CO 81428 303-527-4898
High Fidelity, 825 7th Ave, New York NY 10019 212-265-8360
High Performance, 240 S Broadway 5th fl, Los Angeles CA 90012 213-687-7362
The High Plains Journal, 1500 E Wyatt Earp, Dodge City KS 67801.........316-227-7171
High Society, 801 2nd Ave, New York NY 10017...212-661-7878
High Times, 211 E 43rd St, New York NY 10017..212-972-8484
High Volume Printing, PO Box 368, Northbrook IL 60062..........................312-564-5940
High-Tech Manager's Bulletin, 24 Rope Ferry, Waterford CT 06386........203-442-4365
High-Tech Marketing, 1460 Post Rd E, Westport CT 06880.......................203-255-9997
High-Tech Selling, 24 Rope Ferry Rd, Waterford CT 06385 203-442-4365
The Highlander, PO Box 397, Barrington IL 60011 312-382-1035
Highlights for Children, 803 Church St, Honesdale PA 18431 707-233-1080
Highway & Heavy Construction, 1301 S Grove, Barrington IL 60010........312-381-1840
Hiram Poetry Review, Box 162, Hiram OH 44234.......................................216-569-5330
His, 5206 Main St, Downers Grove IL 60515...312-964-5700
Hispania, USC Univ Park, Los Angeles CA 90089 213-743-2516
Hispanic Business, 360 S Hope Ave, Santa Barbara CA 93105 805-682-5843
Hispanic Review of Business, PO Box 75418, Washington DC 20013........202-547-8754
Hispanic Times, 6355 Topanga Canyon, Woodland Hills CA 91367 818-889-3281
Hispanic USA, 161 W Harrison St, Chicago IL 60605 312-427-4045
The Historian, 2801 W Bancroft St, Toledo OH 43606................................419-537-2209
Historic Preservation, 1785 Massachusetts Ave NW, Wash DC 20036......202-673-4084
Historical Studies Physical Sciences, UC Press, Berkeley CA 94720........415-642-4191
Historical Times Inc, 2245 Kohn Rd Box 8200, Harrisburg PA 17105.......717-657-9555

History & Technology, 50 W 23rd St, New York NY 10010..........................212-206-8900
History News, 172 2nd Ave N Ste 102, Nashville TN 37201 615-255-2971
Hit Parader, Charlton Bldg, Derby CT 06418...203-735-3381
Hoard's Dairyman, 28 Milwaukee Ave W, Ft Atkinson WI 53538.............414-563-5551
Hobby Bookwatch, PO Box 52033, Tulsa OK 74152..................................918-743-7048
Hobby Merchandiser, Box 420, Englishtown NJ 07726 201-972-1022
The Hoboken Terminal, Box 841, Hoboken NJ 07030...............................201-798-1696
Hockey Digest, 1020 Church St, Evanston IL 60201 312-491-6440
Hockey Illustrated, 355 Lexington Ave, New York NY 10017....................212-391-1400
Hog Farm Management, 12400 Whitewater Dr, Minneapolis MN 55343..612-931-2900
Holistic Life, 2223 El Cajon Blvd Ste 426, San Diego CA 92104................619-298-4569
Holistic Living News, PO Box 16346, San Diego CA 92116........................619-280-0317
Hollywood Acting Coaches, PO Box 3044, Hollywood CA 90078 213-466-4297
Holy Trinity Monastery, PO Box 36, Jordanville NY 13361 315-858-0940
Home, 140 E 45th St, New York NY 10017 212-682-4040
Home & Auto, 747 3rd Ave, New York NY 10017..212-418-4159
The Home Alter, 2900 Queen Ln, Philadelphia PA 19129...........................215-848-6800
Home Business News, 12221 Beaver Pike, Jackson OH 45640 614-988-2331
Home Center Magazine, 400 Knightsbridge, Lincolnshire IL 60069..........312-634-2600
Home Entertainment, 220 Westbury Ave, Carle Pl NY 11514 516-334-7880
Home Fashions Textiles, 7 E 12th St, New York NY 10003 212-741-6475
Home Furnishings, PO Box 581207, Dallas TX 75258 214-741-7632
Home Healthcare Business, 454 Morris Ave, Springfield NJ 07081 201-564-9400
Home Life, 127 9th Ave N, Nashville TN 37234..615-251-2271
Home Lighting & Accessories, PO Box 2147, Clifton NJ 07015.................201-779-1600
Home Mechanix, 1515 Broadway, New York NY 10036..............................212-719-6630
Home Planet News, Box 415 Stuyvesant Sta, New York NY 10009.............212-769-2854
Home Resource Magazine, PO Box 12061, Boulder CO 80303....................303-447-2665
The Home Shop Machinist, Box 629, Traverse City MI 49685....................616-946-3712
Home Viewer, 11 N 2nd St, Philadelphia PA 19106 215-629-1588
Homebuilt Aircraft, 16200 Ventura Blvd Ste 201, Encino CA 91436........818-986-8400
Homecare Magazine, 2048 Cotner Ave, Los Angeles CA 90025 213-477-1033
The Homemaker, 7375 E Peakview Ave, Englewood CO 80111 303-779-0077
The Homeowner, 3 Park Ave, New York NY 10016......................................212-340-9620
Homeworking Mothers, PO Box 423, East Meadow NY 11554 516-997-7394
Honolulu, 36 Merchant St, Honolulu HI 96813 808-524-7400
Hoof Beats, 750 Michigan Ave, Columbus OH 43215................................614-224-2291
Hoosharar, 585 Saddle River Rd, Saddle Brook NJ 07662 201-797-7600
Hoosier Farmer, 130 E Washington St, Indianapolis IN 46204 317-263-7821
Horizon Magazine, 1305 Greensboro Ave, Tuscaloosa AL 35401 205-345-0272
The Horn Book Magazine, 31 St James Ave, Boston MA 02116.................617-482-5198
Horological Times, 3700 Harrison Ave, Cincinnati OH 45211 513-661-3838
Horoscope, 245 E 47th St, New York NY 10017..212-605-3000
The Horror Show, 14848 Misty Springs Ln, Oak Run CA 96069 916-472-3540
Horse & Horseman, 34249 Cam Capistrano, Capistrano Bch CA 92624...714-493-2101
Horse & Rider, 41919 Moreno, Temecula CA 92390...................................714-676-5712
The Horse Digest, 3 Royal St SE, Leesburg VA 22075................................703-777-6508
Horse Illustrated, PO Box 6050, Mission Viejo CA 92690 714-240-6001
Horseman, 5314 Bingle Rd, Houston TX 77092...713-688-8811
Horseplay, PO Box 130, Gaithersburg MD 20877......................................301-840-1866
Horticulture, 755 Boylston St, Boston MA 02116......................................617-247-4100
HortIdeas, Rt 1 Box 302, Gravel Switch KY 40328 606-332-7606
Hosiery & Underwear, 545 5th Ave, New York NY 10017..........................212-503-2919

Hospital & Community Psychiatry, 1400 K St NW, Wash DC 20005 202-682-6000
Hospital Formulary, 7500 Old Oak Blvd, Cleveland OH 44130 216-243-8100
Hospital Gift Shop Mgmt, 7628 Densmore, Van Nuys CA 91406 818-782-7232
Hospital Medicine, 90 Park Ave 28th fl, New York NY 10016 212-682-5430
Hospital Pharmacy, E Washington Sq, Philadelphia PA 19105 215-238-4200
Hospital Physician, 400 Plaza Dr, Secaucus NJ 07094 201-865-7500
Hospital Practice, 515 Lexington Ave, New York NY 10022 212-421-7320
Hospital Therapy, 800 2nd Ave, New York NY 10017 212-599-3400
Hospital Topics, 1308 Casey Key Rd, Nokomis FL 33555 813-488-0905
Hospital Tribune, 257 Park Ave S, New York NY 10010 212-674-8500
Hospitality Scene, 3301 Como Ave SE, Minneapolis MN 55414 612-645-6311
Hospitals, 211 E Chicago Ave Ste 700, Chicago IL 60611 312-440-6800
Hostelers' Knapsack, PO Box 37613, Washington DC 20013 202-783-6161
Hot Bike, 2145 W La Palma, Anaheim CA 92801 714-635-9040
Hot Boat Magazine, 500 Harrington St Ste I, Corona CA 91720 714-736-3070
Hot CoCo, 80 Pine St, Peterborough NH 03458 603-924-9471
Hot Rod Magazine, 8490 Sunset Blvd, Los Angeles CA 90069 213-657-5100
The Hot Springs Gazette, PO Box 480740, Los Angeles CA 90048 213-856-4867
Hotel & Motel Management, 7500 Old Oak Blvd, Cleveland OH 44130 ...216-243-8100
Hotel & Restaurants Intl, PO Box 5080, Des Plaines IL 60018 312-635-8800
Hotel & Travel Index, 1 Park Ave, New York NY 10016 212-503-5600
Hounds & Hunting, Box 372, Bradford PA 16701 814-368-6154
House & Garden, 350 Madison Ave, New York NY 10017 212-880-8800
House Beautiful, 1700 Broadway, New York NY 10019 212-903-5000
Housewares Merchandising, 21 Locust Ave, New Canaan CT 06840 203-966-9377
Housewives' Handy Hints, Box 66, Mount Dora FL 32757 904-343-8282
Housing, 1221 Ave of the Americas, New York NY 10020 212-512-6909
Houston City Magazine, 1800 W Loop S, Houston TX 77027 713-850-7600
Houston Home & Garden, 5615 Kirby Dr, Houston TX 77265 713-524-3000
Houston Living, 10101 SW Fwy Ste 400, Houston TX 77074 713-541-5075
Houston Monthly Magazine, 6603 Rookin, Houston TX 77074 713-772-1039
Houston Woman, PO Box 66973-148, Houston TX 77006 713-661-1248
How, 6400 Goldsboro Rd, Bethesda MD 20817 212-463-0600
How(ever), 554 Jersey St, San Francisco CA 94114 415-285-7047
HP Design & Mfg, PO Box 399, Cedar Park TX 78613 512-250-5518
Hub Rail, PO Box 1831, Harrisburg PA 17105 717-234-5099
The Hudson Review, 684 Park Avenue, New York NY 10021 212-650-0020
Hudson Valley Magazine, PO Box 425, Woodstock NY 12498 914-679-5100
Human Events, 422 1st St SE, Washington DC 20003 202-546-0856
Human Organization, 1001 Connecticut Ave NW, Wash DC 20036 202-466-8518
Human Pathology, W Washington Sq, Philadelphia PA 19105 215-574-4700
Human Sciences Press, 72 5th Ave, New York NY 10011 212-243-6000
Humane Society of the US News, 2100 L St NW, Washington DC 20037 ..202-452-1100
The Humanist, 7 Hardwood Dr, Amherst NY 14226 716-839-5080
Humboldt Bay Sheep & Wool Newsletter, Box 4392, Arcata CA 95521 707-822-7716
Humpty Dumpty's Magazine, 1100 Waterway, Indianapolis IN 46202 317-636-8881
Hunting, 8490 Sunset Blvd, Los Angeles CA 90069 213-854-2184
Hurricane Alice, 207 Church St SE, Minneapolis MN 55455 612-625-1834
HVAC Product News, 135 Addison Ave, Elmhurst IL 60126 312-530-6160
Hybrid Circuit Technology, 17730 W Peterson, Libertyville IL 60048 312-362-8711
Hydraulics & Pneumatics, 1111 Chester Ave, Cleveland OH 44114 216-696-7000
Hydrocarbon Processing, PO Box 2608, Houston TX 77001 713-529-4301
I & CS, 1 Chilton Way, Radnor PA 19089 215-964-4000

IAN, 1 Chilton Way, Radnor PA 19089..215-964-4000
Iconoclast, 8780 Venice Blvd, Los Angeles CA 90034.....................213-559-3711
ID Systems, 174 Concord St, Petersborough NH 03458....................603-924-9631
Idea Ink, PO Box 4010, Madison WI 53711.....................................608-273-0333
Ideals, Nelson Pl at Elm Hill Pike, Nashville TN 37214....................615-889-9000
IEEE Computer Soc, 10662 Los Vagueros, Los Alamitos CA 90720.........714-821-8380
IEEE Eng in Medicine & Biology, 345 47th St, New York NY 10017........212-705-7900
IEEE Software, 10662 Los Vagueros Cir, Los Alamitos CA 90720.............714-821-8380
IEEE Trans Biomedical Eng, 345 E 47th St, New York NY 10017...........212-705-7900
IEEE Trans Medical Imaging, 345 E 47th St, New York NY 10017...........212-705-7900
Illinois Banker, 205 W Randolph, Chicago IL 60606...........................312-984-1500
Illinois Entertainer, 2200 E Devon, Des Plaines IL 60018....................312-298-9333
Illinois Jour of Pharmacy, 222 W Adams St Ste 1089, Chicago IL 60606..312-236-5288
The Illinois Libertarian, 1111 Church St, Evanston IL 60201.................312-475-0391
Illinois Magazine, PO Box 40, Litchfield IL 62056.............................217-324-3425
Illinois Medical Jour, 20 N Michigan Ave Ste 700, Chicago IL 60602.......312-782-1654
Illinois Writers Review, PO Box 1087, Champaign IL 61820.................217-429-0117
Image Magazine, PO Box 28048, St Louis MO 63119.........................314-296-9662
Image: Jour of Nursing, 1100 Waterway, Indianapolis IN 46202............317-634-8171
Imagine, 89 Massachusetts Ave Ste 270, Boston MA 02115..................617-267-2592
IMC Jour Intl Medical Ctr, 1515 NW 167th St, Miami FL 33169............305-623-1091
Impact:OA, 2360 Maryland Rd, Willow Grove PA 19090......................215-659-4300
Implement & Tractor, 9221 Quivira Rd, Overland Park KS 66215............913-888-4664
Import Automotive Parts, 7637 Fulton, N Hollywood CA 91605..............818-764-0611
Impressions, 15400 Knoll Trail Dr Ste 112, Dallas TX 75248.................214-239-3060
Imprint, 555 W 57th St, New York NY 10019...................................212-581-2211
In Business, 18 S 7th St PO Box 323, Emmaus PA 18049.....................215-967-4135
In Touch For Men, 7216 Varna, N Hollywood CA 91605......................818-764-2288
In-Fisherman, Box 999 Hwy 371 N, Brainerd MN 56401......................218-829-1648
In-Plant Printer & Electronic Publ, PO Box 368, Northbrook IL 60062...312-564-5940
In-Plant Reproductions, 401 N Broad St, Philadelphia PA 19108............215-238-5300
Inago, PO Box 7541, Tuscon AZ 85725...602-294-7031
Inbound Logistics, 1 Penn Plaza 250 W 34 St, New York NY 10119.........212-290-7336
Inc Magazine, 38 Commercial Wharf, Boston MA 02110.....................617-227-4700
Incentive Marketing, 633 3rd Ave, New York NY 10017......................212-986-4800
Incentive Travel Manager, 825 S Barrington, Los Angeles CA 90040........213-826-8388
Incidents of the War, Box 765, Gettysburg PA 17325.........................717-334-0751
InCider, Rt 101 & Elm St, Peterborough NH 03458............................603-924-7138
Income Opportunities, 380 Lexington Ave, New York NY 10017.............212-557-9100
Independent Banker, Box 267, Sauk Centre MN 56378.......................612-352-6546
Independent Film & Video, 625 Broadway, New York NY 10012.............212-473-3400
Independent Restaurants, 2132 Fordem Ave, Madison WI 53701............608-244-3528
Independent School, 18 Tremont St, Boston MA 02108........................617-723-6900
Indian Truth, 1505 Race St, Philadelphia PA 19102...........................215-563-8349
Indiana Business, 1000 Waterway Blvd, Indianapolis IN 46202..............317-633-2026
Indiana Magazine of History, Indiana Univ, Bloomington IN 47405........812-335-4139
Indiana Medicine, 3935 N Meridian St, Indianapolis IN 46208..............317-925-7545
Indiana Review, 316 N Jordon, Bloomington IN 47405.......................812-335-3439
The Indiana Underwriter, 420 E 4th St, Cincinnati OH 45202...............513-721-2140
Indianapolis Monthly, 8425 Keystone Crossing, Indianapolis IN 46260....317-259-8222
Indigenous World, 275 Grand View #103, San Francisco CA 94114.........415-647-1966
Industrial Design Magazine, 330 W 42nd St, New York NY 10036...........212-695-4955
Industrial Development, 1954 Airport Rd NE, Atlanta GA 30341............404-458-6026

Industrial Distribution, 875 3rd Ave, New York NY 10022.........................212-605-9540
Industrial Education, 1495 Maple Wy, Troy MI 48084...............................313-643-8655
Indus Elec Equip Design, 1221 Ave of Americas, New York NY 10020....212-512-2000
Industrial Engineering, 25 Technology Park, Norcross GA 30092..............404-449-0460
Industrial Equipment News, 1 Penn Plaza, New York NY 10119 212-695-0500
Industrial Fabric Products, 345 Cedar Bldg #450, St Paul MN 55101......612-222-2508
Industrial Finishing, 25 W 550 Geneva Rd, Wheaton IL 60188.................312-665-1000
Industrial Heating, 1000 Killarney Dr, Pittsburgh PA 15234 412-885-6550
Industrial Machinery News, 29516 Southfield Rd, Southfield MI 48037 ...313-557-0100
Industrial Photography, 50 W 23rd St 6th fl, New York NY 10010 212-645-1000
Industrial Product Bulletin, PO Box 1952, Dover NJ 07801 201-361-9060
Industrial Safety & Hygiene News, 1 Chilton Way, Radnor PA 19089.......215-964-4000
Industrial West, 4164 N Peck Rd Ste A, El Monte CA 91732.....................818-442-8321
Industry, 441 Stuart St, Boston MA 02116 617-262-1180
Industry Week, 1111 Chester Ave, Cleveland OH 44114 216-696-7000
Infantry, PO Box 2005, Ft Benning GA 31905...404-545-2350
Infection & Immunity, 1913 I St NW, Washington DC 20006 202-833-9680
Infection Control, 6900 Grove Rd, Thorofare NJ 08086 609-848-1000
Infections in Surgery, 134 W 29th St 4th fl, New York NY 10001 212-714-1740
Infectious Diseases, 276 5th Ave Ste 1007, New York NY 10001................212-686-8848
Info 64, 2343 Dubuque Rd, Iowa City IA 52240...319-338-0070
Info Franchise Newsletter, 728 Center St, Lewiston NY 14092.................716-754-4669
Inform, 1100 Wayne Ave, Silver Spring MD 20910 301-587-8202
Information Center, 38 Chauncy St, Boston MA 02111 617-542-0146
Info Retrieval & Library Automation, Box 88, Mt Airy MD 21771............301-892-1496
Information Technology & Libraries, 50 E Huron St, Chicago IL 60611..312-944-6780
Information Today, 143 Old Marlton Pike, Medford NJ 08055 609-654-6266
Information Week, 600 Community Dr, Manhasset NY 11030 516-365-4600
Infosystems Magazine, Hitchcock Bldg, Wheaton IL 60188.......................312-665-1000
InfoWorld, 1060 Marsh Rd Ste C-200, Menlo Park CA 94025 415-328-4602
Infusion, 34 Ridge St, Winchester MA 01890 617-729-7474
Inkblot, 439 49th St #11, Oakland CA 94609...415-652-7127
Inland Architect, 10 W Hubbard St PO Box 10394, Chicago IL 60610 312-321-0583
Inland Mag of Middle West, 18 S Home Ave, Park Ridge IL 60068..........312-346-0300
Inn Room Magazine, 210 S Juniper Ste 205A, Escondido CA 92025 619-489-5252
Inner Light, GPO Box 1994, New York NY 10001 212-685-4080
Inner-View, PO Box 66156, Houston TX 77266 713-523-6397
Innkeeping World, PO Box 84108, Seattle WA 98124 206-284-4247
Inside Chicago, 2501 W Peterson Ave, Chicago IL 60659............................312-784-0800
Inside Detective, 460 W 34th St, New York NY 10001 212-947-6500
Inside MS, 205 E 42nd St, New York NY 10017 212-986-3240
Inside Print, 6 Riverbend PO Box 4949, Stamford CT 06907......................203-358-9900
Inside Running & Fitness, 9514 Bristlebrook Dr, Houston TX 77083.......713-498-3208
Inside Sports, 1020 Church St, Evanston IL 60201 312-491-6440
Inside The Jewish Exponent, 226 S 16th St, Philadelphia PA 19102...........215-893-5700
Insight, 5 N Greenwich Rd, Armonk NY 10504...914-273-6666
Inst of Logotherapy Press, 2000 Dwight Way, Berkeley CA 94704 415-845-2522
Inst of Mind & Behavior, PO Box 522 Vlg Sta, New York NY 10014........718-783-1471
Instant & Small Comm Printer, 425 Huehl Rd, Northbrook IL 60062......312-564-5940
Inst Certified Financial Planners, 3443 S Galena, Denver CO 80321 303-751-7600
Institutional Distribution, 633 3rd Ave, New York NY 10017....................212-986-4800
Institutional Investor, 488 Madison Ave, New York NY 10022..................212-832-8888
Instructor, 545 5th Ave, New York NY 10017...212-503-2888

The Instrumentalist, 200 Northfield Rd, Northfield IL 60093.....................312-446-5000
Insulation Outlook, 1025 Vermont Ave NW Ste 410, Wash DC 20005 202-783-6278
Insurance Review, 110 William St, New York NY 10038 212-669-9200
Insurance Sales Magazine, 1200 N Meridian St, Indianapolis IN 46204....317-634-1541
Insurance Software Review, 9100 Keystone, Indianapolis IN 46240 317-844-7461
Insurance Times, 437 Newtonville Ave, Newton MA 02160 617-244-1240
Insurance Week, Seattle 1st Natl Bank Ste 2322, Seattle WA 98154 206-624-6965
InTech, 67 Alexander Dr, Research Triangle Park NC 27709 919-549-8411
Integral Yoga Magazine, Box 172, Buckingham VA 23921 804-969-4801
The Intellectual Activist, 131 5th Ave, New York NY 10003 212-982-8357
Intercollegiate Review, 14 S Bryn Mawr Ave, Bryn Mawr PA 19010...........215-525-7501
The InterConnection Journal, 363 W Drake, Ft Collins CO 80526.............303-223-9372
Interim, Univ of Nevada English Dept, Las Vegas NV 89154 702-739-3172
Interior Design, 475 Park Ave S, New York NY 10016 212-686-0555
Interior Landscape Industry, 111 N Canal St #545, Chicago IL 60606.....312-782-5505
Interiors, 1515 Broadway, New York NY 10036...212-764-7535
Internal Medicine/Cardiology, 12230 Wilkins, Rockville MD 20852..........301-770-6170
The Intl Advisor, 2211 Lee Rd, Winter Park FL 32789 305-628-5300
Intl Bluegrass, 326 St Elizabeth St, Owensboro KY 42301.........................502-684-9025
Intl Bulletin of Missionary Research, Box 2057, Ventnor NJ 08406 609-823-6671
Intl Business Monthly, PO Box 87339, Houston TX 77287 713-641-0201
Intl Clinical Products Rev, 808 Kings Hwy, Fairfield CT 06430 203-576-0500
Intl Contact Lens Clinic, 633 3rd Ave, New York NY 10017 212-741-4905
Intl Council of Shopping Centers, 665 5th Ave, New York NY 10022.......212-421-8181
Intl Family Planning Perspectives, 111 5th Ave, New York NY 10003......212-254-5656
Intl Gymnast, 410 Broadway Ste A, Santa Monica CA 90401 213-836-2642
Intl Jour of Chinese Medicine, 5266 E Pomona, Los Angeles CA 90022..213-721-0774
Intl Jour Mental Health, 80 Business Park Dr, Armonk NY 10504...........914-273-1800
Intl Jour of Periodontics, 8 S Michigan, Chicago IL 60603 312-782-3221
Intl Living, 824 E Baltimore St, Baltimore MD 21202 301-234-0515
Intl Musician, 1501 Broadway, New York NY 10036 212-869-1330
Intl Olympic Lifter, 3602 Eagle Rock, Los Angeles CA 90065....................213-257-8762
Intl Poetry Review, PO Box 2047, Greensboro NC 24702 919-273-1711
Intl Security, 79 John F Kennedy St, Cambridge MA 02138 617-253-2866
Intl Sport Fishing Publ, 11000 Metro Pkwy #4, Ft Myers FL 33912 813-275-5567
Intl Television, 1 Park Ave, New York NY 10016 212-503-5777
Intl Thespian Society, 3368 Central Pkwy, Cincinati OH 45225..................513-559-1996
Intl Travel News, 2120 28th St, Sacramento CA 95818...............................916-457-3643
Intl Wildlife, 1412 W 16th St NW, Washington DC 20036 703-790-4510
The Internist, 1101 Vermont Ave NW Ste 500, Washington DC 20005.....202-289-1700
Interpretation: Bible & Theology, 3401 Brook, Richmond VA 23227........804-355-0671
Interracial Books for Children, 1841 Broadway, New York NY 10023 212-757-5339
Interspace Books, 4500 Chesapeake St N W, Washington DC 20016 202-363-9082
Interview, 860 Broadway, New York NY 10003 212-477-2222
Intimate Fashion News, 309 5th Ave, New York NY 10016 212-679-6677
Intravenous Therapy News, 83 Peaceable St, Georgetown CT 06829........203-544-9506
Inverted-A Horn, 401 Forrest Hill, Grand Prairie TX 75051.......................214-264-0066
Investigate, 2211 Lee Rd, Winter Park FL 32789 305-628-5300
Investment Decisions, 11 Elm Place, Rye NY 10580 914-967-9100
Iowa Farmer Today, 500 3rd Ave SE, Cedar Rapids IA 52408....................319-398-8461
Iowa Review, 308 EPB Univ of Iowa, Iowa City IA 52242 319-335-0462
Iowa Sports Desk, PO Box 1303, Iowa City IA 52244................................319-337-9321
The Iowan, 214 9th St, Des Moines IA 50309..515-282-8220

IPMS/USA Quarterly & Update, PO Box 480, Denver CO 80201.............303-753-0473
Irish Literary Supplement, 114 Paula Blvd, Selden NY 11784...................516-698-8243
Irish People, 4951 Broadway, New York NY 10034................................212-567-1611
Iron Age, Chilton Way, Radnor PA 19089...215-964-4000
Iron Mountain, PO Box 22872, Boulder CO 80306.............................303-939-9067
Ironwood Press Inc, PO Box 164, Winona MN 55987.........................507-454-7524
The Ironworker, 1750 Network Ave NW #400, Washington DC 20006.....202-383-4800
Irrigation Age, 1999 Shepard Rd, St Paul MN 55116.........................612-690-7203
Isaac Asimov's Science Fiction, 380 Lexington, New York NY 10017.......212-557-9100
ISKCON World Review, 3764 Watseka Ave, Los Angeles CA 90034.........213-204-3646
Island Life, Box X, Sanibel Island FL 33957....................................813-472-4344
Islands, 3886 State St, Santa Barbara CA 93105................................805-682-7177
Israel Horizons, 150 5th Ave Ste 911, New York NY 10011...................212-255-8760
Issue, 3700 20th St #33, San Francisco CA 94110..............................415-771-6921
Issues, PO Box 11250, San Francisco CA 94101.................................415-864-2600
Issues in Science & Technology, 2102 Constitution, Wash DC 20418........202-334-3305
It Will Stand, PO Box 507, Harrisburg NC 28075..............................704-455-2014
Italian Times, PO Box 20241, Baltimore MD 21284...........................301-254-1300
Itinerary: Magazine for Travelers, 137 W 32nd St, Bayonne NJ 07002 201-858-3400
Jack & Jill, 1100 Waterway Blvd, Indianapolis IN 46202 317-636-8881
Jacksonville Magazine, PO Box 329, Jacksonville FL 32201...................904-353-0300
Jacksonville Monthly, 555 Wharfside Way, Jacksonville FL 32207............904-396-0555
Jacksonville Today, 1032 Hendricks Ave, Jacksonville FL 32207..............904-396-8666
Jam Music Magazine, PO Box 110322, Arlington TX 76007...................817-540-2113
JAMA, 535 N Dearborn St, Chicago IL 60601..................................312-645-5000
James White Review, PO Box 3356 Traffic Sta, Minneapolis MN 55403 ...612-291-2913
JAOA, 212 E Ohio St, Chicago IL 60611...312-280-5800
Japan & America, Box 774, Pleasant Grove UT 84062 801-785-4353
Japan Report, 1000 Connecticut Ave NW, Washington DC 20036.............202-296-5633
JAX FAX Travel Marketing, 280 Tokeneke Rd, Darien CT 06820 203-655-8746
Jaycees Magazine, PO Box 7, Tulsa OK 74121 918-584-2481
Jazz Times, 8055 13th St, Silver Spring MD 20910.............................301-588-4114
Jazziz, PO Box 8309, Gainesville FL 32605 904-375-3705
Jean's Journal, PO Box 791693, Dallas TX 75379...............................214-241-9574
The Jefferson Review, 109 E Broadway, Louisville KY 40202 502-584-0181
Jeopardy, Western Wash Univ Humanities 350, Bellingham WA 98225 ...206-676-3118
Jeremiah: I'm Mad As Hell, Box T, Crugers NY 10521.........................914-271-5124
Jesus People USA, 4707 N Malden, Chicago IL 60640 312-561-2450
Jet, 820 S Michigan Ave, Chicago IL 60605......................................312-322-9200
Jet Cargo News, PO Box 920952, Houston TX 77292...........................713-681-4760
Jet Lag Magazine, 8419 Halls Ferry, St Louis MO 63147 314-383-5841
Jewelers' Circular Keystone, Chilton Way, Radnor PA 19089 215-964-4000
Jewish Currents, 22 E 17th St Ste 601, New York NY 10003 212-924-5740
Jewish Vegetarians of N Amer, PO Box 1463, Baltimore MD 21203..........301-752-8348
Jewish Weekly News, 99 Mill St PO Box 1569, Springfield MA 01101........413-739-4771
Jimmy & Lucy's House of K, 2719A Stuart St, Berkeley CA 94705............415-848-8177
Jive, 355 Lexington Ave, New York NY 10017....................................212-391-1400
Jobber & Warehouse Executive, 950 Lee St, Des Plaines IL 60016............312-296-0770
Jobber Topics, 7300 N Cicero Ave, Lincolnwood IL 60646.....................312-588-7300
JOGN Nursing, E Washington Sq, Philadelphia PA 19105......................215-238-4200
John Milton Talking Book, 475 Riverside Dr, New York NY 10115..........212-870-3335
Jones Intercable Program Guide, 322 Congress St, Boston MA 02210 617-574-9400
The Journal, 164 W 17th Ave 421 Denney Hall, Columbus OH 43210......614-292-4076

JOTS: Jour of the Senses, 5436 Fernwood Ave, Los Angeles CA 90027 ...213-465-7121
Jour for Anthroposophy, PO Box 58, Hadley MA 01035...........................413-256-0655
Jour for Research in Math Ed, 1906 Association Dr, Reston VA 22091...703-620-9840
Jour of Abnormal Psychology, 1400 N Uhle St, Arlington VA 22201 202-955-7600
Jour of Accountancy, 1211 Ave of the Americas, New York NY 10036.....212-575-6200
Jour of Allergy & Clinical Immun, 11830 Westline, St Louis MO 63146...314-872-8370
Jour of Amer Acad Dermatology, 11830 Westline, St Louis MO 63146.....314-972-8370
Jour of Amer Acad of Religion, Univ Rochester, Rochester NY 14627.....716-275-5415
Jour of Amer Concrete Inst, 22400 W 7 Mile Rd, Detroit MI 48219 313-532-2600
Jour of Amer Dental Assn, 211 E Chicago Ave, Chicago IL 60611 312-440-2740
Jour of Amer Dietetic Assn, 430 N Michigan Ave, Chicago IL 60611 312-280-5000
Jour of Amer History, 702 Ballantine Hall, Bloomington IN 47405 812-335-3034
Jour of Amer Medical Record Assn, 875 N Michigan, Chicago IL 60611..312-787-2672
Jour Amer Medical Women's Assn, 465 Grand St, New York NY 10002..212-533-5104
Jour of Amer Oil Chemists Soc, 508 S 6th St, Champaign IL 61820 612-926-3589
Jour of Amer Optometric Assn, 243 N Lindbergh, St Louis MO 63141.....314-991-4100
Jour Amer Planning Assn, Hickerson House, Chapel Hill NC 27514........919-962-3074
Jour of Amer Psychoanalytic Assn, 315 5th Ave, New York NY 10016.....212-684-7900
Jour of Amer Soc Info Science, 605 3rd Ave, New York NY 10158.............212-850-6570
Jour of Amer Water Works Assn, 6666 W Quincy, Denver CO 80235 303-794-7711
Jour of Applied Behavior Analysis, Univ Kansas, Lawrence KS 66045 913-843-0008
Jour of Applied Psychology, BGSU, Bowling Green OH 43403 419-372-2301
Jour of Asian Studies, 260 Stephens Hall, Berkeley CA 94720 415-642-3608
Jour Assn Per Severe Handicap, 7010 Roosevelt, Seattle WA 98115.........206-523-8446
Jour of Bacteriology, 1913 I St NW, Washington DC 20006...........................202-833-9680
Jour of Biological Chemistry, 9650 Rockville Pike, Bethesda MD 20814..301-530-7150
Jour of Bone & Joint Surgery, 10 Shattuck St, Boston MA 02115...............617-734-2835
Jour of Borderland Research, Box 549, Vista CA 92083.............................805-724-2043
Jour of Business Strategy, 1 Penn Plaza, New York NY 10119 212-971-5000
Jour of Cardiopulmonary Rehab, 53 Park Pl, New York NY 10007 212-766-4300
Jour of Career Planning, 62 Highland Ave, Bethlehem PA 18017 215-868-1421
Jour of Chiropractic, 8229 Maryland Ave, St Louis MO 63105 314-862-7800
Jour of Christian Nursing, 5206 Main St, Downers Grove IL 60515 312-964-5700
Jour of Clinical Endocrinology, 428 E Preston, Baltimore MD 21202 301-528-4000
Jour of Clinical Investigation, 1230 York Ave, New York NY 10021........212-570-8663
Jour of Clinical Microbiology, 1913 I St NW, Washington DC 20006........202-833-9680
Jour of Clinical Psychiatry, PO Box 240008, Memphis TN 38124..............901-682-1001
Jour of Clinical Ultrasound, 605 3rd Ave, New York NY 10158.................212-692-6000
Jour of Commercial Bank Lending, Phila Natl Bank, Phila PA 19107 215-665-2850
Jour of Communication, 3620 Walnut St, Philadelphia PA 19104 215-898-6685
Jour of Consult-Clinic Psych, W Psychiatric Inst, Pittsburgh PA 15213....412-624-2989
Jour of Continuing Educ in Nursing, 6900 Grove, Thorofare NJ 08086 ...609-848-1000
Jour of Defense & Diplomacy, 6819 Elm St, McLean VA 22101 703-488-1338
Jour of Dental Educ, 1625 Massachusetts Ave NW, Wash DC 20036........202-667-9433
Jour of Dental Research, 1111 14 St NW, Washington DC 20005 202-898-1050
Jour of Dentistry for Children, 211 E College Ave, Chicago IL 60611......312-943-1244
Jour of Dermatologic Surgery, 475 Park Ave S, New York NY 10016.......212-725-5157
Jour of Educational Psychology, Stanford Univ, Stanford CA 94305.........415-723-8698
Jour of Emergency Medical Svc, 215 S Hwy 101, Solana Bch CA 92075 ...619-481-1128
Jour of Emergency Medicine, Maxwell House, Elmsford NY 10523..........914-592-7700
Jour of Emergency Nursing, 11830 Westline Indus, St Louis MO 63146...314-872-8370
Jour of Endodontics, 428 E Preston St, Baltimore MD 21202 301-528-4000
Jour of Environmental Science, 940 E NW Hwy, Mt Prospect IL 60056...312-255-1561

Jour of Family Practice, 25 Van Zant St, East Norwalk CT 06855.............203-838-4400
Jour of Fee-Based Info Svcs, 5106 FM 1960 W, Houston TX 77069 914-679-2549
Jour of Financial Software, 2811 Wilshire, Santa Monica CA 90403 213-829-7385
Jour of Food Science, 221 N La Salle St, Chicago IL 60601.....................312-782-8424
Jour of Forms Management, 1818 SE Division St, Portland OR 97202.....503-232-0232
Jour of Gerontological Nursing, 6900 Grove Rd, Thorofare NJ 08086......609-848-1000
Jour of Gerontology, 1411 K St NW Ste 300, Washington DC 20005 202-393-1411
Jour of Graphoanalysis, 111 N Canal St, Chicago IL 60606.....................312-930-9446
Jour of Hand Surgery, 11830 Westline Indus Dr, St Louis MO 63146.......314-872-8370
Jour of Home Economics, 2010 Mass Ave NW, Wash DC 20036 202-862-8300
Jour of Hospital Supply, 133 E Cook, Libertyville IL 60048 312-680-7878
Jour of Housing, 2600 Virginia Ave NW #404, Washington DC 20037.....202-333-2020
Jour of Immunology, 428 E Preston St, Baltimore MD 21202 301-528-4000
Jour of Infectious Diseases, 5801 S Ellis Ave, Chicago IL 60637.................312-962-7600
Jour of Information System Mgmt, 6560 N Park, Pennsauken NJ 08109..609-662-2070
Jour of Inst Socioeconomic Study, Airport Rd, White Plns NY 10604......914-428-7400
Jour of Learning Disabilities, 6 E 12th St, New York NY 10003.................212-741-5454
Jour of Long-Term Care Admin, 4650 E-W Hwy, Bethesda MD 20814....301-652-8384
Jour of Manipulative & Physio Ther, Box 368, Lawrence KS 66044..........312-629-2000
Jour of Marital & Family Therapy, 1717 K St NW, Wash DC 20006 202-429-1825
Jour of Marketing Research, Univ of Texas, Austin TX 78712....................512-471-3434
Jour of Marriage & Family, Case Western Univ, Cleveland OH 44106....216-368-2705
Jour of Medical Technology, 150 5th Ave Ste 322, New York NY 10011 ..212-929-2174
Jour of Mind & Behavior, PO Box 522 Vlg Sta, New York NY 10014 212-874-6975
Jour of Modern Literature, Temple Univ, Philadelphia PA 19122.............215-787-8505
Jour of Musculoskeletal Medicine, 55 Holly Hill, Greenwich CT 06830...203-661-0600
Jour of Narrative Technique, E Michigan Univ, Ypsilanti MI 48197.........313-487-0151
Jour of Neurosurgery, Dartmouth Medical School, Hanover NH 03755...603-643-4164
Jour of New Jersey Poets, 285 Madison Ave, Madison NJ 07940................201-593-8710
Jour of New World Archaeology, 405 Hilgard, Los Angeles CA 90024......213-825-7411
Jour of Nuclear Medicine, 136 Madison Ave, New York NY 10016 212-889-0717
Jour of Nursing Administration, E Washington Sq, Phila PA 19105.........215-238-4200
Jour of Ocular Therapy & Surgery, 211 E Chicago, Chicago IL 60611 312-787-3335
Jour of Oral & Maxillofacial Surgery, W Wash Sq, Phila PA 19105 215-238-4200
Jour of Pediatrics, 11830 Westline Industrial Dr, St Louis MO 63146.......314-872-8370
Jour of Pharmaceutical Sciences, 2215 Constitution, Wash DC 20037......202-628-4410
Jour of Physical Ed, 1900 Association Dr, Reston VA 22091.....................703-476-3400
Jour of Political Economy, 5801 S Ellis Ave, Chicago IL 60637.................312-702-8421
Jour of Polymorphous Perversity, 10 Waterside, New York NY 10010.....212-689-5473
Jour of Practical Nursing, 10801 Pear Tree Ln, St Louis MO 63074.........314-426-2662
Jour of Property Management, 430 N Michigan Ave, Chicago IL 60611...312-661-1930
Jour of Prosthetic Dentistry, 11830 Westline Indus, St Louis MO 63146..314-872-8370
Jour of Psych Anthropology, 2315 Broadway, New York NY 10024 212-873-3760
Jour of Psychohistory, 2315 Broadway, New York NY 10024....................212-873-5900
Jour of Psychosocial Nursing, 6900 Grove Rd, Thorofare NJ 08086 609-848-1000
Jour of Psychosocial Oncology, 28 E 22nd St, New York NY 10010..........212-228-2800
Jour of Quality Technology, 230 W Wells St, Milwaukee WI 53203............414-272-8575
Jour of Reconstruct Microsurgery, 3331 Bainbridge, Bronx NY 10467.....212-920-5551
Jour of Rehabilitation, 633 S Washington St, Alexandria VA 22314..........703-836-0850
Jour of Reproductive Medicine, 2 Jacklynn St, St Louis MO 63132............314-991-4440
Jour of Respiratory Diseases, 55 Holly Hill Ln, Greenwich CT 06830.......203-661-0600
Jour of School Health, 1521 S Walter St, Kent OH 44240........................216-678-1601
Jour of Sedimentary Petrology, Box 4348 Univ of IL, Chicago IL 60680...312-996-3159

Jour of Shasta Abbey, Box 199, Mt Shasta CA 96067.....................................916-926-4208
Jour of Soil-Water Conservation, 7515 NE Ankeny, Ankeny IA 50021.....515-289-2331
Jour of South Asian Literature, Oakland Univ, Rochester MI 48309........313-370-2154
Jour of Speech & Hearing, 10801 Rockville, Rockville MD 20852.............301-897-5700
Jour of Sport Psychology, PO Box 5076, Champaign IL 61820....................217-351-5076
Jour of Sports Physical Therapy, 428 E Preston, Baltimore MD 21202....301-528-4000
Jour of Systems Management, 24587 Bagley Rd, Cleveland OH 44138.....216-243-6900
Jour of Texture Studies, 155 Post Rd East Ste 6, Westport CT 06880.......203-227-6596
Jour of the Hellenic Diaspora, 337 W 36th St, New York NY 10018.........212-279-9586
Jour of the Philosophy of Sport, PO Box 5076, Champaign IL 61820........217-351-5076
Jour of the West, 1531 Yuma, Manhattan KS 66502....................................913-532-6733
Jour of Thoracic-Cardio Surgery, 11830 Westline, St Louis MO 63146....314-872-8370
Jour of Trauma, 428 E Preston St, Baltimore MD 21202.............................301-528-4000
Jour of Ultrasound in Medicine, W Washington Sq, Phila PA 19105.......215-574-4874
Jour of Urology, 428 E Preston St, Baltimore MD 21202............................301-528-4000
Jour of Visual Impair & Blindness, 15 W 16th St, New York NY 10011..212-620-2150
Journalism Educator, Univ of North Carolina, Chapel Hill NC 27514.....919-962-4084
Journalism Quarterly, Ohio Univ, Athens OH 45701.................................614-594-5013
The Joyful Woman, PO Box 90028, Chattanooga TN 37412.......................615-698-7318
Judicature, 25 E Washington Ste 1600, Chicago IL 60602..........................312-558-6900
Juggler's World, PO Box 443, Davidson NC 28036....................................704-892-1296
Jump Cut, PO Box 865, Berkeley CA 94701...415-658-4482
Junior Scholastic, 730 Broadway, New York NY 10003..............................212-505-3071
Junior Trails, 1445 Boonville Ave, Springfield MO 65802..........................417-862-2781
Jurimetrics Journal, 750 N Lake Shore Dr, Chicago IL 60611....................312-947-3576
Juvenile Merchandising, 370 Lexington Ave, New York NY 10017...........212-532-9290
Kairos, 900 West End Ave Apt 10D, New York NY 10025.........................212-663-8159
Kaldron, Box 7036, Halcyon CA 93420..805-489-2770
Kaleidoscope, 326 Locust St, Akron OH 44302...216-762-9755
Kalliope, 3939 Roosevelt Blvd, Jacksonville FL 32205...............................904-387-8211
Kansas City Magazine, 3401 Main St, Kansas City MO 64111....................816-561-0444
Kansas City Town Squire, PO Box 8593, Kansas City MO 64114..............913-381-8080
Kansas Farmer, 7500 Old Oak Blvd, Cleveland OH 44130........................216-243-8100
Kansas Quarterly, Kansas State Univ, Manhattan KS 66506......................913-532-6716
Karate/Kung-Fu Illustrated, 1813 Victory Pl, Burbank CA 91504............818-843-4444
Kashrus, PO Box 96 Parkville Sta, Brooklyn NY 11204.............................718-998-3201
Kavitha, 4408 Wickford Rd, Baltimore MD 21210.....................................301-467-4316
Keepsake Magazine For Brides, 38 W Wilshire Dr, Phoenix AZ 85003....602-252-9257
Keltica: The Inter-Celtic Jour, 96 Marguerite Ave, Waltham MA 02154..617-899-2204
Kentucky Business Ledger, 1385 S 3rd St, Louisville KY 40208.................502-636-0551
Kentucky Happy Hunting Ground, 1 Game Farm, Frankfort KY 40601...502-564-4336
The Kenyon Review, Kenyon College, Gambier OH 43022.........................614-427-3339
Kettering Review, 5335 Far Hills Ave Ste 300, Dayton OH 45429.............513-434-7300
Keyboard, 20085 Stevens Creek, Cupertino CA 95014................................408-446-1105
Keyboard Classics Magazine, 223 Katonah Ave, Katonah NY 10536........914-232-8108
Keyboards Computers & Software, 299 Main, Northport NY 11768.........516-754-9311
Keynote Magazine, 1180 Ave of the Americas, New York NY 10036........212-730-9626
Keynoter, 3636 Woodview Trace, Indianapolis IN 46268............................317-875-8755
The Kibbutz Journal, 27 W 20th St, New York NY 10011..........................212-255-1338
Kick America's Soccer Mag, 575 Lexington, New York NY 10022.............212-935-8147
Kidney International, 175 5th Ave, New York NY 10010.............................212-460-1500
Kids Fashions, 71 W 35th St, New York NY 10001....................................212-594-0880
Kidstuff, 1307 S Killian Dr, Lake Park FL 33403.......................................305-842-9411

The Kindred Spirit, Rt 2 Box 111, Saint John KS 67567.................................316-549-3933
The Kingdom Press, 105 Chestnut Hill Rd, Amherst NH 03031.................603-673-3208
Kirkus Reviews, 200 Park Ave S, New York NY 10003.....................................212-777-4554
Kitchen & Bath Business, 1515 Broadway, New York NY 10036.....................212-869-1300
Kitchen & Bath Design News, 2 University Place, Hackensack NJ 07601 .201-487-7800
Kite Lines, 7106 Campfield Rd, Baltimore MD 21207 301-484-6287
Kitplanes, PO Box 6050, Mission Viejo CA 92690...714-240-6001
Kiwanis Magazine, 3636 Woodview Trace, Indianapolis IN 46268.................317-875-8755
KLMN, Box 92, Williams OR 97544..503-942-8221
Konglomerati, Box 5001, Gulfport FL 33737 813-323-0386
Korean Culture, 5505 Wilshire Blvd, Los Angeles CA 90036.........................213-936-7141
L'Apache, 713 Sietta Vista Dr Drawer G, Wofford Hts CA 93285..................619-376-3634
LA Dick, 4664 La Mirada, Los Angeles CA 90029 213-665-2470
LA Parent, PO Box 3204, Burbank CA 91504..818-846-0400
LA West, 919 Santa Monica Blvd, Santa Monica CA 90401.............................213-458-3376
Lab Animals, 475 Park Ave S, New York NY 10016..212-725-2300
Labor Education & Research Project, PO Box 20001, Detroit MI 48220..313-883-5580
Laboratory Equipment, PO Box 1952, Dover NJ 07801....................................201-361-9060
Laboratory Investigation, 428 E Preston St, Baltimore MD 21202.............201-528-4000
Laboratory Management, 50 W 23rd St 6th fl, New York NY 10010.........212-645-1000
Laboratory Medicine, 2100 W Harrison St, Chicago IL 60612......................312-738-1336
LACMA Physician, 1925 Wilshire Blvd, Los Angeles CA 90054....................213-483-1581
LaCrosse City Business, 505 King St, La Crosse WI 54601............................608-782-2130
Ladies' Home Journal, 100 Park Ave, New York NY 10017............................212-953-7070
Lady's Circle, 105 E 35th St, New York NY 10016...212-689-3933
Lady's Circle Patchwork Quilts, 23 W 26th St, New York NY 10010 212-689-3933
Ladyslipper Catalog, PO Box 3124, Durham NC 27705..................................919-683-1570
Lake Effect, Box 315, Oswego NY 13126...315-342-3579
Lake Superior, 325 Lake Ave S, Duluth MN 55802..218-722-5002
Lakeland Boating, 1921 St Johns Ave, Highland Park IL 60035 312-432-8477
Lamishpaha, 1841 Broadway, New York NY 10023..212-581-5151
LAN Local Area Network, 12 W 21st St, New York NY 10010........................212-691-8215
Lancaster Independent Press, PO Box 275, Lancaster PA 17604................717-397-7377
Lancet, 34 Beacon St, Boston MA 02106...617-227-0730
Land Mobile Product News, 9221 Quivira Rd, Overland Park KS 66212 ..913-888-4664
Land-Line Magazine, I-70 at Grain, Grain Valley MO 64029.......................816-229-5791
Landmarks, 835 Securities Bldg, Seattle WA 98101 206-622-3538
Landscape Architecture, 1190 E Broadway NW, Louisville KY 40204 502-589-1167
Language, 3421 M St NW, Washington DC 20007..202-298-7120
Language, 464 Amsterdam Ave, New York NY 10024..212-799-4475
Language Arts, 1111 Kenyon Rd, Urbana IL 61801..217-328-3870
Language Speech & Hearing, 10801 Rockville, Rockville MD 20852..........301-897-5700
Lapidary Journal, 3564 Kettner Blvd, San Diego CA 92101 619-297-4841
Lapis, 1438 Ridge Rd, Homewood IL 60430...312-957-5856
Laryngoscope, 9216 Clayton Rd Ste 18, St Louis MO 63124 314-997-5070
The Las Vagas Insider, Box 370, Henderson NV 89015..................................702-564-3895
Laser Chemistry, 50 W 23rd St, New York NY 10010.......................................212-206-8900
Laser Focus, 119 Russell St, Littleton MA 01460...617-486-9501
Lasers & Applications, 23717 Hawthorne #306, Torrance CA 90505 213-378-0261
Late Knocking, Box 336, Forest Hill MD 21050..301-692-5389
Latest Jokes Newsletter, PO Box 3341, Brooklyn NY 11202 718-855-5057
Latin Amer Lit Rev, 1309 Cathedral of Learning, Pittsburgh PA 15260 412-351-1477
Latin American Perspectives, PO Box 5703, Riverside CA 92517...............714-787-5508

Latin New York Magazine, 316 5th Ave Ste 301, New York NY 10001 212-868-3330
The Laughing Man, 750 Adrian Way, San Rafael CA 94903......................415-492-0922
The Laurel Review, WV Wesleyan College, Buckhannon WV 26201.........304-473-8240
Law & Order, 1000 Skokie Blvd, Wilmette IL 60091 312-256-8555
Lawn & Garden Marketing, 9221 Quivira Rd, Overland Park KS 66215...913-888-4664
Lawn Care Industry, 7500 Old Oak Blvd, Cleveland OH 44130 216-243-8100
The D H Lawrence Review, Univ of Delaware, Newark DE 19716 302-454-1480
The Lawyer's PC, PO Box 1108, Lexington SC 29072 803-359-9941
LC Magazine, 320 North A St, Springfield OR 97477...............................503-726-1200
Leadership, 465 Gundersen Dr, Carol Stream IL 60188 312-260-6200
Learning, 19 Davis Dr, Belmont CA 94002 415-646-8700
The Leather Craftsman, PO Box 1386, Ft Worth TX 76036......................817-923-6787
Leatherneck Magazine, Box 1775, Quantico VA 22134...........................703-640-3171
Lector Hispanic Rev Jour, PO Box 4273, Berkeley CA 94704 415-893-8702
The Left Index, 511 Lincoln St, Santa Cruz CA 95060 408-426-4479
Legacy, Univ of Mass English Dept, Amherst MA 01003 413-545-4270
Leisure Time Electronics, 11 W 19th St, New York NY 10011 212-741-7210
Lens Magazine, 645 Stewart Ave, Garden City NY 11530 516-294-7820
Lesbian Connection, PO Box 811, East Lansing MI 48823 517-371-5257
Let's Live, 444 N Larchmont Blvd, Los Angeles CA 90004 213-469-3901
A Letter Among Friends, Box 1198, Groton CT 06340.............................203-889-8074
The Letter Exchange, PO Box 6218, Albany CA 94706 415-526-7412
LGLC Newsletter, 1800 Market St #210, San Francisco CA 94102 415-522-0838
Liars Corner Almanac, Box 657, Athens OH 45701 614-592-2543
The Libertarian Digest, 1920 Cedar St, Berkeley CA 94709 415-548-3776
Liberty, 55 W Oak Ridge Dr, Hagerstown MD 21740...............................202-722-6000
Library Currents, Box 1796, Grass Valley CA 95945 916-272-5212
Library Hi Tech News, PO Box 1808, Ann Arbor MI 48106......................313-434-5530
Library Imagination Paper, 1000 Byus Dr, Charleston WV 25331.............304-345-2378
Library Journal, 249 W 17th St, New York NY 10011 212-645-0067
Library Trends, 505 E Armory St, Champaign IL 61820 217-333-1359
The Licensing Book, 264 W 40 St, New York NY 10018 212-575-4510
Licensing International, 490 Rt 9 Box 420, Englishtown NJ 07726 201-972-1022
Licensing Today, 11 W 19th St, New York NY 10011..............................212-741-7210
Mary Ann Liebert Inc Publishers, 1651 3rd Ave, New York NY 10128 212-289-2300
Life, Time & Life Bldg Rockefeller Ctr, New York NY 10020...................212-522-1212
Life Association News, 1922 F St NW, Washington DC 20006....................202-331-6070
Lifeline, 54 Wilton Rd, Westport CT 06880..203-226-7271
Lifelines Software Magazine, 1651 3rd Ave, New York NY 10128.............212-722-1700
Lifelong Learning, 1201 16th St NW Ste 230, Washington DC 20036 202-822-7866
Lifestyles, 2194 Palou Ave, San Francisco CA 94124 415-824-2900
Liftouts, 1503 Washington Ave S, Minneapolis MN 55454 612-333-0031
Light & Life, 901 College Ave, Winona Lake IN 46590............................219-267-7161
Light Year, Case Western Reserve Univ, Cleveland OH 44106 216-795-2810
Lighted Pathway, 922 Montgomery Ave, Cleveland TN 37311...................615-476-4512
Lightwave Jour of Fiber Optics, 235 Bear Hill Rd, Waltham MA 02154 ..617-890-2700
Lightworks Magazine, PO Box 1202, Birmingham MI 48012.....................313-626-8026
Liguorian, 1 Liguorian Dr, Liguori MO 63057 314-464-2500
Lilith, 250 W 57th St Ste 1328, New York NY 10019 212-757-0818
Linguacode, 1181 Pinetree Grove Ave, Atlanta GA 30319 404-981-8129
Linington Lineup, 1223 Glen Terace, Glassboro NJ 08028.......................609-589-1571
Linking the Dots, HCR 222, Islesboro ME 04848 207-734-6745
Linkup, 143 Old Marlton Pike, Medford NJ 08055 609-654-6266

Linn's Stamp News, 911 Vandermark Rd, Sidney OH 45367 513-489-2111
The Lion & The Unicorn, Brooklyn College, Brooklyn NY 11210...............213-780-5195
The Lion, 300 22nd St, Oak Brook IL 60570..312-986-1700
Listen, 6830 Laurel St NW, Washington DC 20012......................................202-722-6726
Literaria, 1302 East F St, Russellville AR 72801 501-968-8495
Literary Cavalcade, 730 Broadway, New York NY 10003.............................212-505-3000
Literary Magazine Review, Kansas State Univ, Manhattan KS 66506........913-532-6716
Literary Research, Univ of Maryland, College Park MD 20742 301-454-6953
The Literary Review, 285 Madison Ave, Madison NJ 07940 201-377-4050
Literary Sketches, PO Box 810571, Dallas TX 75381 214-243-8776
Liturgy Training Publ, 1800 N Hermitage Ave, Chicago IL 60622..............312-486-8970
Live, 1445 Boonville Ave, Springfield MO 65802..417-862-2781
Live Stream Magazine, PO Box 629, Traverse City MI 49684.....................616-946-3712
The Living Church, 407 E Michigan St, Milwaukee WI 53202.....................414-276-5420
Living Off The Land, PO Box 2131, Melbourne FL 32902............................305-723-5554
Living With Children, 127 9th Ave N, Nashville TN 37234...........................615-251-2229
Living With Preschoolers, 127 9th Ave N, Nashville TN 37234....................615-251-2229
Llamas Magazine, PO Box 100, Herald CA 95638......................................209-748-2620
The Llewellyn New Times, 213 E 4th St, St Paul MN 55164.......................612-291-1970
Loblolly, 1310 Raleigh Rd, Wilson NC 27893...919-237-2642
Locksmith Ledger, 1800 Oakton Blvd, Des Plaines IL 60018 312-298-6210
Locus, PO Box 13305, Oakland CA 94661...415-339-9196
Lodging Hospitality, 1100 Superior Ave, Cleveland OH 44114....................216-696-7000
Logo & Education Computing, 1320 Stony Brk, Stony Brook NY 11790 ..516-751-0271
Lone Star Comedy, PO Box 29000, San Antonio TX 78229.........................512-271-2632
Lone Star Horse Report, PO Box 14767, Ft Worth TX 76117....................817-834-3951
Lone Star Humor, PO Box 29000, San Antonio TX 78229 512-271-2632
Long Island's Nightlife, 1770 Deer Park Ave, Deer Park NY 11729 516-242-7722
Long Shot, PO Box 456, New Brunswick NJ 08903.....................................201-432-5934
The Long Story, 11 Kingston St, North Andover MA 01845 617-686-7638
The Lookout, 8121 Hamilton Ave, Cincinnati OH 45231 513-931-4050
Loonfeather, 426 Bemidji Ave, Bemidji MN 56601 218-751-7570
Loose Change, 1515 S Commerce St, Las Vegas NV 89102.........................702-387-8750
Lorien House, PO Box 1112, Black Mountain NC 28711 704-669-6211
Los Angeles Lawyer, PO Box 55020, Los Angeles CA 90055......................213-627-2727
Los Angeles Magazine, 1888 Century Park E, Los Angeles CA 90067.......213-553-0237
Lost Generation Journal, Rt 5 Box 134, Selma MO 65560.........................314-265-8594
Lost Treasure, 15115 S 76th E Ave, Bixby OK 74008 918-366-4441
Lottery Players Magazine, PO Box 5013, Cherry Hill NJ 08034 609-665-7577
Louisiana Contractor, 18271 Old Jefferson, Baton Rouge LA 70817........504-292-8980
Louisiana Historical Assn, PO Box 42808, Lafayette LA 70504..................318-231-6871
Louisiana Life, 4200 S I-10 Service Rd #220, Matairie LA 70001 504-456-2220
Louisiana Market Bulletin, PO Box 44365, Baton Rouge LA 70804 504-925-4857
Louisville, One Riverfront Plaza, Louisville KY 40202................................502-566-5050
The Louisville Review, 315 Bingham Humanities, Louisville KY 40292.....502-588-6801
LP Gas, 7500 Old Oak Blvd, Cleveland OH 44130......................................216-243-8100
Lubrication Engineering, 838 Busse Hwy, Park Ridge IL 60068 312-825-5536
Lucha/Struggle, PO Box 37 Times Sq Sta, New York NY 10108 212-663-8112
Lucidity, 2711 Watson, Houston TX 77009 713-869-6028
Luna Tack, Box 372, West Branch IA 52358..319-643-7324
Lutheran Forum, 308 W 46th St, New York NY 10036.................................212-757-1292
The Lutheran Standard, 426 S 5th St, Minneapolis MN 55440...................612-330-3300
The Lutheran Witness, 1333 S Kirkwood Rd, St Louis MO 63122.............314-965-9000

The Lutheran, 2900 Queen Ln, Philadelphia PA 19129................215-438-6580
Lynn North Shore Magazine, 45 Forest Ave, Swampscott MA 01907........617-592-0160
The Lyric, 307 Dunton Dr SW, Blacksburg VA 24060....................703-552-3475
M, 7 E 12 St, New York NY 10003 212-741-4000
M/R Magazine, 2600 Dwight Way, Berkeley CA 94704...................415-549-0537
MAAT, 1223 S Selva, Dallas TX 75218...........................214-324-3093
Macazine, 8008 Shoal Creek Blvd, Austin TX 78767 512-467-4550
The MacGuffin, 18600 Haggerty Rd, Livonia MI 48152.................313-591-6400
Mach, PO Box 11314, San Francisco CA 94101....................415-864-3456
Machine & Tool Blue Book, 25 W 550 Geneva Rd, Wheaton IL 60188.....312-665-1000
Machine Design, 1111 Chester Ave, Cleveland OH 44114...............216-696-7000
Macintosh Buyer's Guide, 1660 Beachland Blvd, Vero Beach FL 32963...305-231-6904
MacWeek, 5211 S Washington Ave, Titusville FL 32780 305-269-3211
MacWorld, 501 2nd St, San Francisco CA 94107....................415-546-7822
Mad Magazine, 485 Madison Ave, New York NY 10022 212-752-7685
Mademoiselle, 350 Madison Ave, New York NY 10017 212-880-8800
Madison Avenue Magazine, 369 Lexington Ave, New York NY 10017......212-972-0600
The Madison Review, 600 N Park St, Madison WI 53706................608-263-3303
Magazine & Bookseller, 322 8th Ave, New York NY 10001 212-620-7330
Magazine Age, 125 Elm St, New Canaan CT 06840 203-972-0761
The Magazine Antiques, 980 Madison Ave, New York NY 10021.............212-734-9797
Magazine Fantasy & Science Fiction, Box 56, Cornwell CT 06753 203-672-6376
Magazine for Christian Youth, 201 8th Ave S, Nashville TN 37202..........615-749-6463
Magazine of Fur & Leather Retail, 141 W 28th St, New York NY 10001.212-279-4250
The Mage, Colgate Univ Student Assn, Hamilton NY 13346 315-824-1000
Magic Changes, 2 S 424 Emerald Green Dr #F, Warrenville IL 60555.....312-393-7856
Magna for Big & Tall Men, PO Box 286, Cabin John MD 20818.............301-320-2745
Maine Organic Farmer & Gardener, PO Box 2176, Augusta ME 04330 ..207-622-3118
Mainline Modeler, 5115 Monticello Dr, Edmonds WA 98020 206-743-2607
Mainstream, 5894 S Land Park Dr, Sacramento CA 95822...............916-422-1921
Mainstream Mag of Able-Disabled, 2973 Beech, San Diego CA 92102.....619-234-3138
Maintenance & Modernization, Box 535, Olney MD 20832.................301-924-5490
Making It! Careers News, 2109 Broadway, New York NY 10023.............212-575-9018
Maledicta, 331 S Greenfield Ave, Waukesha WI 53186..................414-542-5853
Mallife, PO Box 1393, Tempe AZ 85821 602-967-4226
Manage, 2210 Arbor Blvd, Dayton OH 45439....................513-294-0421
Management Accounting, 10 Paragon Dr, Montvale NJ 07645.............201-573-9000
Management Review, 135 W 50th St, New York NY 10020 212-903-8393
Management Technology, 12 W 21st St, New York NY 10010 212-206-6660
Management Update, 1355 S Colorado Blvd Ste 900, Denver CO 80222..303-753-1111
Management World, 2360 Maryland Rd, Willow Grove PA 19090............215-659-4300
Manhattan Inc, 420 Lexington Ave Ste 2012, New York NY 10170 212-697-2100
Manhattan Poetry Review, 36 Sutton Pl S #11D, New York NY 10022....212-355-6634
Mankato Poetry Review, Box 53 MSU, Mankato MN 56001 507-389-5511
Manscape 2, PO Box 1314, Teaneck NJ 07666 201-836-9177
Manufacturers Mart, 133 Hillside Rd, Fairfield CT 06430................203-250-1669
Manufacturing Engineering, 1 SME Dr, Dearborn MI 48121 313-271-1500
Manufacturing Systems, 25 W 550 Geneva Rd, Wheaton IL 60188...........312-665-1000
Manuscripts, Univ of S Carolina History Dept, Columbia SC 29208........803-777-6526
Marian Helpers Bulletin, Eden Hill, Stockbridge MA 01263...............413-298-3691
Marine Corps Gazette, PO Box 1775, Quantico VA 22134 703-640-6161
Marine Engineering/Log, 345 Hudson St, New York NY 10014 212-620-7220
Mark, Univ of Toledo English Dept, Toledo OH 43606 419-537-2318

Market Watch, 400 E 51st St, New York NY 10022.................................212-751-6500
Marketing & Media Decision, 1140 Ave of Amer, New York NY 10036 ..212-391-2155
Marketing & Sales Promotion, 1552 Gilmore, Mtn View CA 94040 415-941-7525
Marketing Communications, 50 W 25th St 6th fl, New York NY 10010 ...212-645-1000
Marketing News, 250 S Wacker Dr Ste 200, Chicago IL 60606 312-648-0536
Marketing Times, 6151 Wilson Mills Rd Ste 200, Cleveland OH 44143 216-473-2100
Marquee, 624 Wynne Rd, Springfield PA 19064.......................................215-543-8378
Marriage & Family Living, Abbey Press, St Meinrad IN 47577.................812-357-8011
Marriage & Divorce Today, 2315 Broadway, New York NY 10024............212-873-5900
Mart Magazine, PO Box 1952, Dover NJ 07801..201-361-9060
Marta News, 139 Day St, Newington CT 06111 203-246-8883
Marvel Comics, 387 Park Ave S, New York NY 10016 212-576-9200
Maryknoll, Walsh Bldg, Maryknoll NY 10545 914-941-7590
Maryland Magazine, 45 Calvert St, Annapolis MD 21401 301-269-3507
Maryland Medical Jour, 1211 Cathedral St, Baltimore MD 21201 301-529-0872
Mass High Tech, 755 Mt Auburn St, Watertown MA 02172 617-924-2422
Mass Market Retailers, 1 Park Ave, New York NY 10016...........................212-889-8741
The Massachusetts Review, Univ of Mass, Amherst MA 01003 413-545-2689
Massage, PO Box 1969, Kealakekua HI 96750 808-329-2433
Massife, PO Box 51 Pratt Sta, Brooklyn NY 11205....................................718-237-1299
Master Detective, 460 W 34th St, New York NY 10001...............................212-947-6500
Master Drawings Association, 29 E 36th St, New York NY 10016 212-685-0008
Master Thoughts, PO Box 37, San Marcos CA 92069 619-746-9430
Material Handling Engineering, 614 Superior, Cleveland OH 44113 216-696-0300
Material Handling Product News, 13 Emery Ave, Randolph NJ 07869 210-361-9060
Materials Engineering, 1111 Chester Ave, Cleveland OH 44104................216-696-7000
Materials Evaluation, 4153 Arlingate Plaza, Columbus OH 43228............614-274-6003
Mathematics Magazine, 1529 18th St NW, Washington DC 20036 202-387-5200
Mathematics Teacher, 1906 Association Dr, Reston VA 22091....................703-620-9840
Matrix, 1209 W Oregon, Urbana IL 61801...217-344-6922
A Matter of Crime, 2006 Sumter St, Columbia SC 29201............................803-771-4642
Mature Living, 127 9th Ave N, Nashville TN 37209...................................615-251-2191
Mature Outlook, 3701 W Lake Ave, Glenview IL 60025..............................312-291-4739
Mature Years, 201 8th Ave S, Nashville TN 37202.....................................615-749-6438
May Trends, 111 S Washington St, Park Ridge IL 60068 312-825-8806
Mayo Alumnus, 200 SW 1st St, Rochester MN 55905 507-284-2511
Mayo Clinic Proceedings, Plummer Bldg, Rochester MN 55905.................507-284-2154
MBA, 18 N Main St PO Box 8001, Chagrin Falls OH 44022........................216-622-4444
MBM Magazine for Black Men, 1123 Broadway, New York NY 10010 212-924-5480
McCall's, 230 Park Ave, New York NY 10169 212-551-9500
McCall's Needlework & Craft, 230 Park Ave, New York NY 10169 212-551-9500
McGraw-Hill Inc, 1221 Ave of the Americas, New York NY 10020............212-512-2000
MCN, 555 W 57th St, New York NY 10019...212-582-8820
MD Computing, 175 5th Ave, New York NY 10010 212-460-1500
MD Magazine, 30 E 60th St, New York NY 10022..212-355-5432
MDA News, 810 7th Ave, New York NY 10019 212-586-0808
ME Magazine, PO Box 182, Bowdoinham ME 04008...................................207-666-5774
Measurements & Control, 2994 W Liberty, Pittsburgh PA 15216 412-343-9666
Meat Industry, 90 Throckmorton Ave, Mill Valley CA 94942......................415-388-7575
Meat Processing, 7500 Old Oak Blvd, Cleveland OH 44310.........................216-243-8100
Mechanical Engineering, 345 E 47th St, New York NY 10017.....................212-705-7722
Media & Methods, 1511 Walnut St, Philadelphia PA 19102.........................215-563-3501
Media History Digest, 11 W 19th St, New York NY 10011............................212-675-4380

Media Impact, 7510 Old Chester Rd, Bethesda MD 20817 301-229-1740
Media Management Monographs, 9 Mt Vernon, Gales Ferry CT 06335..203-464-2511
Media Profiles, 550 1st St, Hoboken NJ 07030 201-963-1600
Media Report To Women, 10606 Mantz Rd, Silver Spring MD 20903 301-445-3230
Media Spotlight, PO Box 1288, Costa Mesa CA 92628 714-953-2900
Media: Library Service Jour, 127 9th Ave N, Nashville TN 37234 615-251-2752
Mediafile, Ft Mason Ctr, San Francisco CA 94123 415-441-2557
Medical Aspects Human Sexuality, 90 Park Ave, New York NY 10016 212-682-5430
Medical Business Jour, 3461 Rt 22 E, Somerville NJ 08876......................201-231-9695
Medical Care Products, PO Box 1952, Dover NJ 07801 201-267-6040
Medical Clinics of N Amer, W Washington Sq, Philadelphia PA 19105 215-574-4700
Medical Economics, 680 Kinderkamack Rd, Oradell NJ 07649 201-262-3030
Medical Electronics, 2994 W Liberty Ave, Pittsburgh PA 15216 412-343-9666
Medical Electronics & Equip, 532 Busse Hwy, Park Ridge IL 60068.........312-693-3773
Medical Grand Rounds, 233 Spring St, New York NY 10013 212-620-8000
Medical Group Management, 1355 Colorado Blvd, Denver CO 80222 303-753-1111
Medical Instrumentation, 1901 N Ft Myer #602, Arlington VA 22209.....703-525-4890
Medical Marketing & Media, 31 Bailey Ave, Ridgefield CT 06877............305-368-9301
Medical Products Sales, 550 Frontage Rd, Northfield IL 60093..................312-446-1622
Medical Self-Care, Box 1000, Point Reyes CA 94956 415-663-8462
Medical Times, 80 Shore Rd, Port Washington NY 11050..........................516-883-6350
Medical Tribune, 257 Park Ave S, New York NY 10010............................212-674-8500
Medical Ultrasound, 605 3rd Ave, New York NY 10158............................212-692-6026
Medical World News, 7676 Woodway Ste 112, Houston TX 77063 713-780-2299
Medicenter Management, PO Box 2178, Santa Monica CA 90406.............213-395-0234
Medicine, 428 E Preston St, Baltimore MD 21202 301-528-4000
Medicine & Computer, 470 Mamaroneck Ave, White Plains NY 10605....914-681-0040
Medicine & Science in Sports, PO Box 1440, Indianapolis IN 46206 317-637-9200
The Meeting Manager, 3719 Roosevelt Blvd, Middletown OH 45044........513-424-6827
Meeting News, 1515 Broadway, New York NY 10036................................212-869-1300
Meetings & Conventions, 1 Park Ave, New York NY 10016......................212-503-5700
Members Health & Racquet Club, 15 Bank St, Stamford CT 06901..........203-964-0084
Memphis Business Jour, 88 Union, Memphis TN 38103............................901-523-0437
Memphis Magazine, 460 Tennessee St, Memphis TN 38101......................901-521-9000
Memphis State Review, MSU English Dept, Memphis TN 38152................901-454-2668
Men's Retailer/Western Retailer, PO Box 586398, Dallas TX 75258........214-631-6089
Menninger Perspective, PO Box 829, Topeka KS 66601............................913-273-7500
Mental Retardation, 1719 Kalorama Rd NW, Washington DC 20009.......202-387-1968
Merchandising, 1515 Broadway, New York NY 10036................................212-869-1300
Mercury, 1290 24th Ave, San Francisco CA 94122....................................415-661-8660
The Meridian, 630 N College Ste 423, Indianapolis IN 46204 317-638-8228
MERIP Middle East Report, PO Box 43445, Washington DC 20010 202-667-1188
The Message, Rt 15 Box 270, Tucson AZ 85715..505-988-4411
Metal Building Review, 1800 Oakton, Des Plaines IL 60018 312-298-6210
Metal Fabricating News, 710 S Main St, Rockford IL 61101....................815-965-4031
Metal Progress, Rt 87, Metals Park OH 44073..216-338-5151
Metalworking Digest, 13 Emery Ave, Randolph NJ 07869 201-361-9060
Metalworking News, 7 E 12th St, New York NY 10003..............................212-741-4140
Metaphor, 109 Minna St Ste 153, San Francisco CA 94501 415-641-7231
Metlfax, 6521 Davis Industrial Pkwy, Solon OH 44139............................216-248-1125
Metro Singles Lifestyles, PO Box 28203, Kansas City MO 64118..............816-436-8424
Metropolis, 177 E 87th St, New York NY 10128..212-722-5050
Metropolitan, 2500 Artesia Blvd, Redondo Beach CA 90278......................213-376-8788

Metropolitan Detroit Magazine, 422 W Congress, Detroit MI 48226........313-963-8500
Metropolitan Home, 750 3rd Ave, New York NY 10017.............................212-557-6600
Metrosphere, Box 32 Metropolitan State Col, Denver CO 80204................303-556-2495
Mexican Studies, Univ of Calif Press, Berkeley CA 94720 415-642-0978
Mexico West!, 2424 Newport Blvd #91, Costa Mesa CA 92627....................714-662-7616
Miami Today, PO Box 1368, Miami FL 33101...305-358-2663
Miami/South Florida Mag, PO Box 340008, Coral Gables FL 33134 305-856-5011
Michigan Dental Assn Journal, 230 N Washington, Lansing MI 48933.....517-372-9070
Michigan Farmer, 7500 Old Oak Blvd, Cleveland OH 44130.....................216-243-8100
Michigan Food News, 221 N Walnut, Lansing MI 48933............................517-372-6800
Michigan Living AAA, 17000 Executive Plaza, Dearboarn MI 48126.........313-336-1211
Michigan Medicine, 120 W Saginaw, East Lansing MI 48823 517-337-1351
The Michigan Municipal Review, PO Box 1487, Ann Arbor MI 48106 313-662-3246
Michigan Natural Resources, PO Box 30034, Lansing MI 48909 517-373-9267
Michigan Nurse, 120 Spartan Ave, East Lansing MI 48823........................517-337-1653
Michigan Out-of-Doors, PO Box 30235, Lansing MI 48909........................517-371-1041
Michigan Quarterly Review, Univ of Mich, Ann Arbor MI 48109.............313-764-9265
Michigan Sportsman, PO Box 33502, Detroit MI 48232.............................414-231-9338
The Michigan Woman, PO Box 1171, Birmingham MI 48012......................313-851-5755
Micro Cornucopia, 155 NW Hawthorne, Bend OR 97701............................503-382-8048
Micro MarketWorld, 1060 Marsh Rd Ste C-200, Menlo Park CA 94025 ..415-328-8220
MicroAge Quarterly, PO Box 1920, Tempe AZ 85281 602-968-3168
Microbiological Reviews, 1913 I St NW, Washington DC 20006.................202-833-9680
Microelectronic Mfg, 17730 W Peterson, Libertyville IL 60048 312-362-8711
Micropendium, PO Box 1343, Round Rock TX 78664...................................512-255-1512
MicroPublishing Report, 2004 Curtis Ave #A, Redondo Bch CA 90278..213-376-5724
Microthought, 2811 Wilshire Blvd Ste 640, Santa Monica CA 90403.........213-829-7385
Microwave Journal, 610 Washington St, Dedham MA 02026 617-326-8220
Microwave Systems News, 1170 E Meadow Dr, Palo Alto CA 94303 415-494-2800
Microwaves & RF, 10 Mulholland Dr, Hasbrouck Hts NJ 07604................201-393-6285
Mid-American Review, BGSU English Dept, Bowling Green OH 43403..419-372-2725
Mid-Atlantic Country, PO Box 246, Alexandria VA 22313..........................703-548-6177
Mid-Continent Banker, 408 Olive St, St Louis MO 63102 314-421-5445
Mid-Continent Bottler, 10741 El Monte, Overland Park KS 66207............913-341-0020
Mid-Peninsula News, 424 Stephenson Ave, Iron Mtn MI 49801 906-774-3005
Middle Eastern Dancer, PO Box 1572, Casselberry FL 32707 305-788-0301
Midstream Monthly Jewish Rev, 515 Park Ave, New York NY 10022 212-752-0600
Midway Magazine, 9600 SW Oak St, Portland OR 97223 503-244-2299
Midwest Chaparral, 1309 2nd Ave SW, Waverly IA 50677..........................319-352-1716
Midwest Contractor, 3170 Mercier PO Box 766, Kansas City MO 64141..816-931-2080
Midwest Living, 1912 Grand Ave, Des Moines IA 50336.............................515-284-3006
Midwest Motorist AAA, 12901 N 40 Dr, St Louis MO 63141 314-851-3315
Midwest Outdoors, 111 Shore Dr, Hinsdale IL 60521 312-887-7722
Midwest Poetry Review, PO Box 776, Rock Island IL 61201......................319-391-1874
Midwest Purchasing, 25000 Euclid Ave, Cleveland OH 44117...................216-261-9500
The Midwest Quarterly, Pittsburg State Univ, Pittsburg KS 66762............316-231-7000
Mike Shayne Mystery Mag, 6660 Reseda Blvd #108, Reseda CA 91335...818-343-2992
The Militant, 14 Charles Ln, New York NY 10014......................................212-243-6392
The Military Engineer, 607 Prince St, Alexandria VA 22314......................703-549-3800
Military Images, RD2 Box 2542, E Stroudsburg PA 18301 717-476-1388
Military Lifestyle, 1732 Wisconsin Ave NW, Washington DC 20007 202-944-4000
Military Living, PO Box 2347, Falls Church VA 22042................................703-237-0203
Military Logistics Forum, 15 Ketchum St, Westport CT 06881...................203-226-7463

Military Market, 6883 Commercial Dr, Springfield VA 22159 703-750-8676
Military Review, Ft Leavenworth KS 66027...913-684-5642
Military/Space Elec Design, 1221 Ave of Amer, New York NY 10020 212-512-2000
Mill Hunk Herald, 916 Middle St, Pittsburgh PA 15212 412-321-4767
Milling & Baking News, 9000 W 67th St, Merriam KS 66202.................913-236-7300
Millmeter, 826 Broadway, New York NY 10003......................................212-477-4700
Milwaukee Magazine, 312 E Buffalo St, Milwaukee WI 53202 414-273-1101
Minas Tirith Evening-Star, Box 277, Union Lake MI 48085.....................313-887-4703
Mind In Motion, Box 1118, Apple Valley CA 92307................................619-242-2780
Mind Your Own Business At Home, PO Box 14850, Chicago IL 60614.....312-472-8116
Mini Magazine for IBM Systems, 85 Eastern, Gloucester MA 01930 617-283-3438
Mini-Micro Systems, 275 Washington St, Newton MA 02158...................617-964-3030
Miniature Collector, 170 5th Ave, New York NY 10010 212-989-8700
Miniatures Dealer, Clifton House, Clifton VA 22024................................703-830-1000
Ministries, 190 N Westmonte Dr, Altamonte Springs FL 32714................305-869-5005
Minkus Stamp & Coin Journal, 41 W 25th St, New York NY 10010 212-741-1334
Minne Ha! Ha!, PO Box 14009, Minneapolis MN 55414............................612-332-5315
Minnesota History, 690 Cedar St, St Paul MN 55101 612-296-2264
Minnesota Literature Newsletter, 1 Nord Circle, St Paul MN 55127.........612-483-3904
Minnesota Medicine, 2221 University #400, Minneapolis MN 55414.........612-378-1875
Minnesota Sportsman, PO Box 741, Marietta GA 30061 404-953-9222
Minnesota Women's Press, 2395 University Ave, St Paul MN 55114.........612-646-3968
Minn Science Fiction Reader, 3806 Glenhurst, St Louis Pk MN 55416 612-925-2726
Minority Engineer, 44 Broadway, Greenlawn NY 11740............................516-261-8917
Miorita, Univ of Rochester Dewey Hall, Rochester NY 14627....................716-275-4258
The Miraculous Medal, 475 E Chelten Ave, Philadelphia PA 19144 215-848-1010
MIS Week, 7 E 12th St, New York NY 10003 212-741-4000
Mississippi, Downhome Publications Inc, Jackson MS 39236....................601-982-8418
Mississippi Business Jour, Highland Vlg #254, Jackson MS 39211..........601-982-8418
Mississippi Mud, 1336 SE Marion St, Portland OR 97202........................503-236-9962
The Mississippi Rag, 5644 Morgan Ave S, Minneapolis MN 55419...........612-920-0312
Mississippi Review, PO Box 5144, Hattiesburg MS 39406........................601-266-4321
Mississippi State Univ Alumnus, PO Box 5328, Miss State MS 39762......601-325-3442
Mississippi Valley Review, Western Illinois Univ, Macomb IL 61455........309-298-1514
Missouri Life, 1205 University Ave, Columbia MO 65201...........................314-342-1281
Missouri Medicine, 113 Madison St, Jefferson City MO 65102 314-636-5151
The Missouri Review, Univ of Missouri, Columbia MO 65211 314-882-6066
Missouri Ruralist, 2401 A Vandiver, Columbia MO 65202........................314-474-9557
Mister Production Enterprise, 11822 Rosecrans, Norwalk CA 90650 213-863-2179
MIX Magazine, 2608 9th St, Berkeley CA 94710......................................415-843-7901
MLA News, 919 Michigan Ave, Chicago IL 60611....................................312-266-2456
MLO Medical Lab Observer, 680 Kinderkamack, Oradell NJ 07649.........201-262-3030
Mobile Mfd Home Merchandiser, 203 N Wabash, Chicago IL 60601........312-236-3528
Mobius, 2120 Berkeley Way, Berkeley CA 94720.....................................415-642-7485
Model Airplane News, 837 Post Rd, Darien CT 06820 203-655-7737
Model Railroader, 1027 N 7th St, Milwaukee WI 53233 414-272-2060
Model Retailer, Clifton House, Clifton VA 22024......................................703-830-1000
Modern Brewery Age, 22 S Smith St, Norwalk CT 06855 203-853-6015
Modern Bulk Transporter, 1602 Harold St, Houston TX 77006 713-523-8124
Modern Dentalab, 60 Ridgeway Plaza Ste 3, Stamford CT 06905.............203-327-0031
Modern Drummer, 870 Pompton Ave, Cedar Grove NJ 07009...................201-239-4140
Modern Electronics, 76 N Broadway, Hicksville NY 11801.......................516-681-2922
Modern Floor Coverings, 345 Park Ave S, New York NY 10010 212-686-7744

Modern Healthcare, 740 N Rush, Chicago IL 60611......................312-649-5341
Modern Horse Breeding, 656 Quince Orch, Gaithersburg MD 20878.......301-977-3900
Modern Intl Drama, Theatre Dept SUNY, Binghamton NY 13901..........607-777-2704
Modern Jeweler, 400 Knightsbridge Pkwy, Lincolnshire IL 60069.............312-634-2600
Modern Language Jour, 114 N Murray St, Madison WI 53715..................614-422-6277
Modern Language Quar, 4045 Brooklyn Ave NE, Seattle WA 98105........206-543-2992
Modern Liturgy, PO Box 444, Saratoga CA 95071...............................408-252-4195
Modern Machine Shop, 6600 Clough Pike, Cincinnati OH 45244................513-231-8020
Modern Materials Handling, 221 Columbus Ave, Boston MA 02116.........617-536-7780
Modern Maturity, 3200 E Carson, Lakewood CA 90712......................213-496-2277
Modern Medicine, 757 3rd Ave, New York NY 10017.......................212-243-8100
Modern Office Technology, 1100 Superior Ave, Cleveland OH 44114.......216-696-7000
Modern Percussionist, 870 Pompton Ave, Cedar Grove NJ 07009.............201-239-4140
Modern Photography, 825 7th Ave, New York NY 10019......................212-265-8360
Modern Plastics, 1221 Ave of the Americas, New York NY 10020............212-512-6241
Modern Railroads, 1350 E Touhy Ave, Des Plaines IL 60018....................312-399-0202
Modern Recording Music, 1120 Old Country Rd, Plainview NY 11803....516-433-6530
Modern Romances, 215 Lexington Ave, New York NY 10016...............212-340-7500
Modern Salon, Box 400, Prairie View IL 60069................................312-634-2600
Modern Tire Dealer, 110 N Miller Rd PO Box 5417, Akron OH 44313....216-867-4401
Modern Veterinary Practice, 5782 Thornwood Dr, Goleta CA 93117.......805-963-6561
Modern Woodmen, Miss River at 17th St, Rock Island IL 61201.............309-786-6481
Modern World Publishing Co, PO Box 65766, Los Angeles CA 90065.....213-221-8044
Mom Guess What?, 1400 S St Ste 100B, Sacramento CA 95814..................916-441-6397
Moment Magazine, 462 Boylston St, Boston MA 02116......................617-536-6252
Money Magazine, 1271 Ave of the Americas, New York NY 10020...........212-841-4621
Money Maker, 5705 N Lincoln Ave, Chicago IL 60659......................312-275-3590
Moneysworth, 1775 Broadway, New York NY 10019.........................212-581-2000
The Monist, Box 600, La Salle IL 61301...................................815-223-1231
Monographics Press, Rt 1 Box 81, Puposky MN 56667......................218-243-2402
Montana Magazine, 3020 Bozeman, Helena MT 59601......................406-443-2842
Montana Mag of Western History, 225 N Roberts, Helena MT 59620......406-449-2694
The Montana Review, 1620 N 45th St, Seattle WA 98103.................406-543-5307
Monterey Life, PO Box 2107, Monterey CA 93942.........................408-372-9200
Monthly Detroit, 1400 Woodbridge, Detroit MI 48207....................313-446-6000
Moody Monthly, 820 N LaSalle Dr, Chicago IL 60610.....................312-508-6820
Moody Street Irregulars, Box 157, Clarence Center NY 14032.............716-741-3393
Moose Magazine, Loyal Order of Moose, Mooseheart IL 60539...............312-859-2000
The Morgan Horse, Box 1, Westmoreland NY 13490.........................315-735-7522
Morrow Owner's Review, PO Box 5487, Berkeley CA 94705...............415-644-2638
The Mother Earth News, PO Box 70, Hendersonville NC 28791.............704-693-0211
Mother Jones, 1663 Mission St, San Francisco CA 94103................415-558-8881
Mother of Ashes Press, PO Box 135, Harrison ID 83833..................208-689-3738
Mothering, PO Box 8410, Santa Fe NM 87504.............................505-984-8116
Motheroot Journal, PO Box 8306, Pittsburgh PA 15218...................412-731-4453
Mothers Today, 441 Lexington Ave, New York NY 10017..................212-867-4820
Motocross Action, 16200 Sepuveda Blvd, Mission Hills CA 91345..........818-365-6831
Motor, 555 W 57th St 17th fl, New York NY 10019.......................212-399-5660
Motor Age, Chilton Way, Radnor PA 19089..............................215-964-4000
Motor Press Magazine, 555 W 57th St, New York NY 10019...............212-399-5658
Motor Service, 950 Lee, Des Plaines IL 60016..........................312-296-0770
Motor Trend, 8490 Sunset Blvd, Los Angeles CA 90069..................213-657-5100
Motorboating & Sailing, 224 W 57th St, New York NY 10019.............212-262-8768

Motorcycle Product News, 6931 Van Nuys Blvd, Van Nuys CA 91405.......818-997-0644
Motorcyclist Magazine, 8490 Sunset Blvd, Los Angeles CA 90069 213-657-5100
MotorHome, 29901 Agoura Rd, Agoura CA 91301.................................818-991-4980
Motorland, 150 Van Ness Ave, San Francisco CA 94101....................415-565-2448
Movie Collector's World, 151 E Birch St, Annandale MN 55302................612-274-5230
Movie Mirror, 355 Lexington Ave, New York NY 10017.........................212-391-1400
Moviegoer, 505 Market St, Knoxville TN 37902................................615-521-0600
Movieline Magazine, 1141 S Beverly Dr, Los Angeles CA 90035 213-282-0711
Moving Up, 303 N Glenoaks Blvd, Burbank CA 91502 818-848-4666
Mpls St Paul Magazine, 12 S 6th St, Minneapolis MN 55402 612-339-7571
Mr Cogito, UC Box 627 Pacific Univ, Forest Grove OR 97116 503-357-6151
Ms., 119 W 40th St, New York NY 10018......................................212-719-9800
Mt Aukum Review, Box 483, Mt Aukum CA 95656 209-245-4016
Mudfish, 184 Franklin St, New York NY 10013 212-219-9278
Multichannel News, 300 S Jackson St, Denver CO 80209 303-393-6397
Multi-Housing News, 1515 Broadway, New York NY 10036....................212-869-1300
Multi-Level Marketing News, 10236 Fair Oaks, Fair Oaks CA 95628........916-965-9594
Multis, 211 E Chicago Ave, Chicago IL 60611................................312-951-1100
Muppet Magazine, 300 Madison Ave, New York NY 10017 212-687-0680
Muscadine, 1111 Lincoln Place, Boulder CO 80302..........................303-443-9748
Muscle & Fitness, 21100 Erwin St, Woodland Hills CA 91367 818-884-6800
Muscle Training Illustrated, 209-10 S Conduit Ave, Queens NY 11413 ...718-978-4200
Muscular Development, Box 1707, York PA 17405 717-767-6481
Muse's Brew Poetry Review, Box 9484, Forestville CT 06010 203-589-5039
Museum News, 1225 I St NW, Washington DC 20005.........................202-289-1818
Music & Sound Output, 220 Westbury Ave, Carle Place NY 11514 516-334-7880
Music City News, 50 Music Sq W Ste 601, Nashville TN 37202...............615-329-2200
Music Educators Journal, 1902 Association Dr, Reston VA 22091...........703-860-4000
Musical America, 825 7th Ave, New York NY 10019 212-265-8360
Musician Magazine, 1515 Broadway, New York NY 10036....................212-764-7395
MusicLine, 25231 Paseo de Alicia Ste 201, Laguna Hills CA 92653 714-951-9106
Muslim Star, 25341 Five Mile Rd, Redford Township MI 48239 313-535-0014
The Mustard Seed, 38 Sunrise Ave, Katonah NY 10536 914-232-7577
Mutual Fund Sourcebook, 53 W Jackson Blvd, Chicago IL 60604 312-427-1985
Myrtle Beach, PO Box 1474, N Myrtle Beach SC 29598.......................803-272-8150
Mystery Fancier, 1711 Clifty Dr, Madison IN 47250..........................812-273-6908
Mystery Time Anthology, PO Box 2377, Coeur d'Alene ID 83814.............208-667-7511
Mythlore, 740 S Hobart Blvd, Los Angeles CA 90005 213-384-9420
Na'Amat Woman, 200 Madison Ave, New York NY 10016 212-725-8010
NACLA Report on the Americas, 151 W 19th St, New York NY 10011.....212-989-8890
NADTP Journal, PO Box 508 Kenmore Sta, Boston MA 02215 617-437-6472
NALS Docket, 3005 E Skelly Dr Ste 120, Tulsa OK 74105 918-749-6423
Nancy's Magazine, 336 E Torrence Rd, Columbus OH 43214 614-267-8183
Narrow Gauge & Shortline Gazette, 1 1st St Ste N, Los Altos CA 94022..415-941-3823
Nashville!, 1719 West End Ave, Nashville TN 37203..........................615-329-1973
Nation's Business, 1615 H St NW, Washington DC 20062 202-463-5650
Nation's Health, 1015 15th St NW, Washington DC 20005 202-789-5600
Nation's Restaurant News, 425 Park Ave, New York NY 10022.................212-371-9400
The Nation, 72 5th Ave, New York NY 10011 212-242-8400
Nationwide Careers, PO Box 15727, Little Rock AR 72231 501-374-4315
Natl Acad of Science, 2101 Constitution Ave, Washington DC 20418 202-334-2000
Natl Assn of Parents & Professionals, Box 646, Marble Hill MO 63764...314-238-2010
Natl Assn of Social Workers, 7981 Eastern Ave, Silver Spg MD 20910.....301-565-0333

Natl Beauty School Journal, 3839 White Plains Rd, Bronx NY 10467.......212-881-3000
Natl Bus Trader, 9698 W Judson Rd, Polo IL 61064.................................815-946-2341
Natl Business Woman, 2012 Massachusetts Ave NW, Wash DC 20036 202-293-1100
Natl Ctr for Constitutional Studies, PO Box 37110, Wash DC 20013.......801-973-1776
Natl Christian Reporter, PO Box 222198, Dallas TX 75222......................214-630-6495
Natl Conf of State Legislatures, 1050 17th St #2100, Denver CO 80265...303-623-7800
Natl Defense Magazine, 1700 N Moore St Ste 900, Arlington VA 22209...703-522-1820
Natl Development, PO Box 5017, Westport CT 06880.................................203-226-7463
Natl Doll World, 306 E Parr Rd, Berne IN 46711......................................219-589-8741
Natl Dragster, 10639 Riverside Dr, North Hollywood CA 91602................818-985-6472
Natl Fisherman, 21 Elm St, Camden ME 04843..207-236-4342
Natl Forum, Phi Kappa Phi 216 Petrie Hall, Auburn Univ AL 36849........205-279-9110
The Natl Future Farmer, PO Box 15130, Alexandria VA 22309.................703-360-3600
Natl Gardening, 180 Flynn Ave, Burlington VT 05401..............................802-863-1308
Natl Geographic Magazine, 17th & M Sts NW, Washington DC 20036....202-857-7000
Natl Greenhouse Industry, Box 217, Mills WY 82644.............................307-472-3107
Natl Guard, 1 Massachusetts Ave NW, Washington DC 20001...................202-789-0031
Natl Hog Farmer, 1999 Shepard Rd, St Paul MN 55116............................612-690-7452
Natl Home Center, 425 Park Ave, New York NY 10022.............................212-371-9400
Natl Jeweler, 1515 Broadway, New York NY 10036.................................212-869-1300
Natl Journal, 1730 M St NW, Washington DC 20036.................................202-857-1400
Natl Lampoon, 635 Madison Ave, New York NY 10022.............................212-688-4070
Natl Law Journal, 111 8th Ave, New York NY 10011 212-741-8300
Natl Masters News, PO Box 2372, Van Nuys CA 91404.............................818-785-1895
Natl Motorist, 1 Market Plaza, San Francisco CA 94105...........................415-777-4000
The Natl Notary, 23012 Ventura Blvd, Woodland Hills CA 91365 818-347-2035
Natl NOW Times, 1401 New York Ave NW #800, Wash DC 20005...........202-347-2279
Natl Parks Magazine, 1015 31st St NW, Washington DC 20007.................202-944-8530
Natl Petroleum News, 950 Lee St, Des Plaines IL 60016...........................312-296-0770
Natl Racquetball, PO Drawer 6126, Clearwater FL 33518 813-733-5555
The Natl Reporter, PO Box 647, Washington DC 20044.............................202-328-0178
Natl Review, 150 E 35th St, New York NY 10016.....................................212-679-7330
Natl Rural Letter Carrier, 1750 Penn Ave NW, Wash DC 20006 202-393-5840
Natl Safety News, 444 N Michigan Ave, Chicago IL 60611 312-527-4800
The Natl Sheriff, 1450 Duke St, Alexandria VA 22314..............................703-836-7827
Natl Shoe Retailers Assn, 9861 Broken Land, Columbia MD 21046..........301-381-8282
Natl Show Horse, 10401 Linn Sta Rd, Louisville KY 40233 502-423-1902
Natl Trade Publications, 8 Stanley Cir, Latham NY 12110 518-783-1281
Natl Wildlife, 8925 Leesburg Pike, Vienna VA 22184 703-790-4510
Natl Wildlife Magazine, 8925 Leesburg Pike, Vienna VA 22184................703-790-4510
NATSO Trucker's News, PO Box 1285, Alexandria VA 22313....................703-549-2100
Natural History, Central Park W at 79th St, New York NY 10024.............212-769-5500
Nature, 65 Bleecker St, New York NY 10012 212-477-9600
Nautica, Pickering Wharf, Salem MA 01970...617-745-6905
Nautical Brass, Box 744DB, Montrose CA 91020......................................818-248-2616
Nautical Quarterly, 373 Park Ave S 10th fl, New York NY 10016..............212-685-9114
The Nautilus, PO Box 3430, Silver Spring MD 20901................................202-357-2019
Naval Affairs, 1303 New Hampshire Ave NW, Washington DC 20036......202-785-2768
Navy News, 2429 Bowland Pkwy Ste 155, Virginia Beach VA 23454 804-486-8000
Navy Times, 6885 Commercial Dr, Springfield VA 22159...........................703-750-8636
NCFE Motivator, 50 Fremont St, San Francisco CA 94105........................415-777-0460
NCR Monthly, Box 399, Cedar Park TX 78613..512-250-9023
ND REC Magazine, Box 727, Mandan ND 58554 701-663-6501

Nebo, Arkansas Tech Univ, Russellville AR 72801 501-968-0256
The Nebraska Review, Univ of Nebraska ASH 212, Omaha NE 68182 402-554-2700
Needlepoint News, PO Box 5967, Concord CA 94524................................415-671-9852
Negative Capability, 6116 Timberly Rd N, Mobile AL 36609....................205-661-9114
The Negro Educational Review, PO Box 2895, Jacksonville FL 32203 904-646-2870
The Negro History Bulletin, 1401 14th St NW, Washington DC 20005......202-667-2822
Nemo/Fantagraphics, 1800 Bridgegate #101, Westlake Vlg CA 91361 805-379-1881
Network, PO Box 810 Gracie Sta, New York NY 10028................................212-737-7536
Network, 349 S 600 E, Salt Lake City UT 84102......................................801-532-6095
Network for Public School, 10840 Little Patuxent, Columbia MD 21044 ..301-997-9300
Neurology, 7500 Old Oak Blvd, Cleveland OH 44130................................216-243-8100
Neurosurgery, 428 E Preston St, Baltimore MD 21202............................301-528-4000
Nevada Businss Jour, 2375 E Tropicana, Las Vegas NV 89109...................702-454-1669
Nevada Magazine, Capitol Complex, Carson City NV 89710 702-885-5416
New Age Digest, PO Box 1373, Leala Kekua HI 96750 808-328-8031
New Age Journal, 342 Western Ave, Brighton MA 02135..........................617-787-2005
New Age Media Resource Directory, PO Box 419, New York NY 10002...212-777-4220
New America, Univ of New Mexico, Albuquerque NM 87131......................505-277-6347
The New American, 395 Concord Ave, Belmont MA 02178.........................617-489-0605
New Art Examiner, 230 E Ohio, Chicago IL 60611 312-642-6236
New Body, 888 7th Ave, New York NY 10106..212-541-7100
New Books on Women & Feminism, 728 State St, Madison WI 53706.......608-263-5754
New Breed, 30 Amarillo Dr, Nanuet NY 10954...914-623-8426
New Business, PO Box 3312, Sarasota FL 33581 813-366-8225
New Catholic World, 997 Macarthur Blvd, Mahwah NJ 07430....................201-825-7300
New Cleveland Woman, 104 E Bridge St, Berea OH 44017........................216-243-3740
New Covenant, PO Box 7009, Ann Arbor MI 48107 313-761-8505
The New Criterion, 850 7th Ave, New York NY 10019.............................212-247-6980
New Dimensions, 111 NE Evelyn St, Grants Pass OR 97526....................503-479-0549
New Directions for Women, 108 W Palisade Ave, Englewood NJ 07631 ...201-568-0226
New Disciples, PO Box 801, Nashville TN 37202......................................615-749-6000
New England Out-of-Doors, 510 King St, Littleton MA 01460................617-486-4785
New England Bride, 21 Pocahontas Dr, Peabody MA 01960.......................617-535-4186
New England Builder, 25 Hubbard St, Montpelier VT 05602 802-223-6123
New England Church Life, 88 Tremont St, Boston MA 02108....................617-523-3579
New England Construction, 27 Muzzey St, Lexington MA 02173.................617-862-2355
New England Farm Bulletin, Box 147, Cohasset MA 02025 617-383-9023
New England Farmer, Box 391, St Johnsbury VT 05819 802-748-8908
New England Getaways, 21 Pocahontas Dr, Peabody MA 01960.................617-535-4186
New England Jour of Medicine, 10 Shattuck St, Boston MA 02115 617-734-9800
New England Monthly, 132 Main St, Haydenville MA 01039 413-268-7262
New England Quarterly, Northeastern Univ, Boston MA 02115 617-437-2734
New England Review, Middlebury College, Middlebury VT 05753.............802-388-3711
New England Sampler, Box 306, Belfast ME 04915.................................207-525-4482
New England Senior Citizen, 470 Boston Post Rd, Weston MA 02193......617-899-2702
New Equipment Digest, Penton Plaza, Cleveland OH 44114.....................216-696-7000
The New Era, 50 E N Temple, Salt Lake City UT 84150...........................801-531-2951
New Expression, 207 S Wabash Ave, Chicago IL 60604 312-663-0543
The New Farm, 222 Main St, Emmaus PA 18049 215-967-5171
New Frontier, 129 N 13th St, Philadelphia PA 19107 215-567-1685
New Hampshire Alumnus, Univ of NH, Durham NH 03824......................603-862-2040
New Hampshire Profiles, PO Box 4638, Portsmouth NH 03801 603-433-1551
New Haven County Woman, 2969 Whitney Ave, Hamden CT 06518.........203-288-7774

New Jersey Business, 310 Passaic Ave, Fairfield NJ 07006 201-882-5004
New Jersey Dental Assn Jour, 1 Dental Plaza, N Brunswick NJ 08902......201-821-9400
New Jersey Monthly, 7 Dumont Rd, Morristown NJ 07960 201-539-8230
New Jersey Reporter, 16 Vandeventer Ave, Princeton NJ 08542 609-924-9750
New Jersey Success, 1138 N Broad St, Hillside NJ 07205............................201-352-3282
The New Kent Quarterly, Kent State Univ, Kent OH 44242........................216-672-2676
The New Laurel Review, 828 Lesseps St, New Orleans LA 70117................504-947-6001
The New Leader, 275 7th Ave, New York NY 10001.....................................212-807-8240
New Letters, Univ of Missouri, Kansas City MO 64110................................816-276-1168
New Methods Journal, PO Box 22605, San Francisco CA 94122.................415-664-3469
New Mexico Business Journal, PO Box 1788, Albuquerque NM 87120 505-243-5581
New Mexico Humanities Review, NM Tech, Socorro NM 87801.................505-835-5445
New Mexico Magazine, 1100 St Francis Dr, Santa Fe NM 87503.................505-827-6180
New Moon, PO Box 2056, Madison WI 53701..608-251-6226
New Orleans Business, 2520 Belle Chasse Hwy, Gretna LA 70054..............504-362-4310
New Orleans City Business, 111 Veterans Hwy, Metairie LA 70005...........504-834-9292
New Orleans Magazine, PO Box 26815, New Orleans LA 70186..................504-246-2700
New Orleans Review, PO Box 195, New Orleans LA 70118.........................504-865-2152
New Pages, Box 438, Grand Blanc MI 48439..313-743-8055
New Pathways Into Science Fiction, PO Box 863994, Plano TX 75068......214-272-6780
The New Physician, 1890 Preston White Dr, Reston VA 22091 703-620-6600
The New Poets Series, 541 Piccadilly Rd, Baltimore MD 21204..................301-321-2863
The New Press, 127 Ludlow St 4C, New York NY 10002..............................212-254-8763
New Realities, 680 Beach Ste 408, San Francisco CA 94109 415-776-2600
The New Republic, 1220 19th St NW Ste 200, Washington DC 20036 202-331-7494
New Research Traveler & Conv, 11717 S Vincennes, Chicago IL 60643....312-881-3712
New Southern Literary Messenger, 400 S Laurel, Richmond VA 23220 ...804-780-1244
New Thought, 7314 E Stetson Dr, Scottsdale AZ 85251 602-945-0744
New Unionist, 621 West Lake St Rm 210, Minneapolis MN 55408.............612-823-2593
New Ventura County Woman, 812 Links View, Simi Valley CA 93065......805-583-1894
New Vistas, 1111 S Bayshore Dr, Miami FL 33131......................................305-350-1256
New Voices, 24 Edgewood Terrace, Methuen MA 01844 617-685-3087
New Wilderness, 325 Spring St Rm 208, New York NY 10013.....................212-807-7944
New Woman, 215 Lexington Ave, New York NY 10016................................212-685-4790
New Women's Times, PO Box 39561, Rochester NY 14604..........................716-271-5523
New World Outlook, 475 Riverside Dr, New York NY 10115.......................212-870-3758
New Writer's Magazette, PO Box 15126, Sarasota FL 34277.......................813-485-1036
New York, 755 2nd Ave, New York NY 10017 212-880-0700
New York Acad Medicine Bulletin, 2 E 103rd St, New York NY 10029.....212-876-8200
New York Alive, 152 Washington Ave, Albany NY 12210............................518-465-7511
New York Antique Almanac, PO Box 335, Lawrence NY 11559 516-371-3300
New York City Business, 122 E 42nd St Ste 2701, New York NY 10168....212-682-3830
New York Habitat Magazine, 928 Broadway, New York NY 10010 212-505-2030
New York Journal Japan, 545 5th Ave Ste 602, New York NY 10017........212-557-5547
New York Native, 249 W Broadway, New York NY 10013............................212-925-8021
The New York Review of Books, 250 W 57th St, New York NY 10107.......212-757-8070
New York Running News, 9 E 89th St, New York NY 10128.........................212-860-2280
New York Sports, 812 Carroll St, Brooklyn NY 11215.................................718-622-3547
New York State Dental Journal, 30 E 42nd St, New York NY 10017.........212-986-3937
NY State Jour of Medicine, 420 Lakeville, Lake Success NY 11042...........516-488-6100
NY State Nurses Assn Jour, 2113 Western Ave, Guilderland NY 12084...518-456-5371
New York's Finest, 250 Broadway, New York NY 10007..............................212-233-5531
New York's Nightlife, 1770 Deer Park Ave, Deer Park NY 11729 516-242-7722

The New Yorker, 25 W 43rd St, New York NY 10036..................................212-840-3800
Newe America CASE, 80 Grand St, Jersey City NY 07302.....................201-332-9191
The News Basket, PO Box 220, Bayside CA 95524.....................................707-822-6009
The News Circle, 1250 W Glenoaks Blvd, Glendale CA 91201....................818-545-0333
The News Media & The Law, 800 18th St NW, Wash DC 20006.................202-466-6313
Newsreal, PO Box 40323, Tucson AZ 85717..602-887-3982
Newsweek, 444 Madison Ave, New York NY 10022......................................212-350-4000
Nibble, 52 Domino Dr, Concord MA 01742..617-371-1660
The Nightmare Express, 262 Sherburne #2, St Paul MN 55103.................612-290-2068
Nightmoves, 105 W Madison, Chicago IL 60602..312-346-7765
Nimrod, 2210 S Main, Tulsa OK 74114..918-584-3333
19th Century Literature, Univ of Calif Press, Berkeley CA 94720..............415-642-4191
19th Century Music, Univ of Calif Press, Berkeley CA 94720....................415-642-4191
Nissan Discovery, PO Box 4617, North Hollywood CA 91607.....................213-877-4406
Nit & Wit, Box 627, Geneva IL 60134...312-232-9496
NITA, E Washington Sq, Philadelphia PA 19105..215-238-4200
NJEA Review, 180 W State St PO Box 1211, Trenton NJ 08607...................609-599-4561
NMEA News, 49 Delwood Lane, Tinton Falls NJ 07724................................201-542-2666
Noah's Ark, 7726 Portal, Houston TX 77071...713-771-7143
Nolo News, 950 Parker St, Berkeley CA 94710..415-549-1976
NOMDA Spokesman, 12411 Wornall Rd, Kansas City MO 69145...............816-941-3100
Nomos, 9857 S Damen Ave, Chicago IL 60643...312-663-9595
Non-Foods Merchandising, 345 Park Ave S, New York NY 10011..............212-686-7744
North Amer Hunter, 7901 Flying Cloud Dr, Minneapolis MN 55435..........612-941-7654
North Amer Mentor Magazine, 1745 Madison St, Fennimore WI 53809 ..608-822-6237
North Amer Publishing Co, 401 N Broad St, Philadelphia PA 19108.........215-238-5300
The North Amer Review, Univ of Northern Iowa, Cedar Falls IA 50614...319-273-2681
North Amer Whitetail, 2121 Newmarket Ste 136, Marietta GA 30067.......404-953-9222
North Carolina Libraries, 7101 Winding Way, Wake Forest NC 27587....919-556-2940
North Country Anvil, PO Box 37, Millville MN 55957 507-798-2366
North Dakota REC, PO Box 727, Mandan ND 58554 701-663-6501
North Light, 32 Berwick Ct, Fairfield CT 06430...203-336-4225
North Shore, 874 Green Bay Rd, Winnetka IL 60093...................................312-441-7892
North Shore Women's News, PO Box 1056, Huntington NY 11743.............516-271-0832
North Texas Golfer, 9182 Old Katy Rd, Houston TX 77055.........................713-464-0308
Northcoast View, PO Box 1374, Eureka CA 95502 707-443-4887
Northeast Outdoors, PO Box 2180, Waterbury CT 06722 203-755-0158
The Northern Engineer, Univ of Alaska, Fairbanks AK 99775 907-474-7798
Northern Lights Studies, Univ of Maine, Presque Isle ME 04769 207-764-0311
Northern Literature Quar, Univ of Minn, Minneapolis MN 55455............612-373-3381
Northern Logger & Timber Processor, Box 69, Old Forge NY 13420.......315-369-3078
Northern Review, Wisconsin Univ, Stevens Point WI 54481.......................715-346-3568
Northern Virginian, 135 Park St PO Box 1177, Vienna VA 22180..............703-938-0666
Northweat Chess, 4715 9th Ave NE, Seattle WA 98105..............................206-392-7760
Northwest Living, 130 2nd Ave S, Edmonds WA 98020................................206-774-4111
Northwest Review, 369 PLC Univ of Oregon, Eugene OR 97404.................503-686-3957
Northwest Wine Almanac, PO Box 85595, Seattle WA 98145......................206-789-8922
Nostalgia World, PO Box 231, North Haven CT 06473................................203-269-8502
Not Man Apart, 1045 Sansome St, San Francisco CA 94111.......................415-433-7373
Notre Dame Magazine, 415 Admin Bldg, Notre Dame IN 46556.................219-239-5335
Now And Then, Box 19180A ETSU, Johnson City TN 37614........................615-929-6173
Now Comics, 525 S Dearborn, Chicago IL 60605...312-786-9013
NSBE Journal, 1240 S Broad St, New Orleans LA 70125..............................504-822-3533

NSGA Sports Retailer, 1699 Wall St, Mt Prospect IL 60056 312-439-4000
NSS Today, 7628 Densmore Ave, Van Nuys CA 91406................................818-782-7328
Nuclear News, 555 N Kensington Ave, La Grange Park IL 60525................312-352-6611
Nuclear Plant Safety, 799 Roosevelt Rd, Glen Ellyn IL 60137....................312-932-4999
Nuclear Times, 298 5th Ave, New York NY 10001 212-563-5940
Nuestro, 461 Park Ave S, New York NY 10016..212-684-5999
Nugget, 2355 Salzedo St, Coral Gables FL 33134 305-443-2378
Numismatic News, 700 E State St, Iola WI 54990 715-445-2214
The Numismatist, 818 N Cascade Ave, Colorado Springs CO 80903.........303-632-2646
The Nurse Practitioner, 109 W Mercer St, Seattle WA 98119 206-285-2050
Nursery Manager, 1268 St Louis Ave, Ft Worth TX 76101 817-332-8236
Nursing, 1111 Bethlehem Pike, Springhouse PA 19477................................215-646-8700
Nursing & Health Care, 10 Columbus Circle, New York NY 10019..........212-582-1022
Nursing Clinics, W Washington Sq, Philadelphia PA 19105.......................215-574-4700
Nursing Forum, PO Box 218, Hillsdale NJ 07642 201-391-7845
Nursing Homes, 5 Willowbrook Ct, Potomac MD 20854............................301-983-1152
Nursing Life, 1111 Bethlehem Pike, Springhouse PA 19477........................215-646-8700
Nursing Management, 600 S Federal St, Chicago IL 60605..........................312-341-1014
Nursing Outlook, 555 W 57th St, New York NY 10019................................212-582-8820
Nursing Research, 555 W 57th St, New York NY 10019................................212-582-8820
Nursingworld Journal, 470 Boston Post Rd, Weston MA 02193 617-899-2702
Nutrition Action Health Letter, 1501 16th St NW, Wash DC 20036 202-332-9110
Nutrition Health Review, 171 Madison Ave, New York NY 10016.............212-697-3590
Nutrition Research, Maxwell House Fairview Pk, Elmsford NY 10523.....914-592-7799
Nutrition Today, 111 Chinquapin Rd, Annapolis MD 21401................301-267-8616
Nutritional Consultant, 2375 E Tropicana #270, Las Vagas NV 89109....702-454-1665
Nutritional Support Services, 7628 Densmore, Van Nuys CA 91406 818-782-7328
Nutshell News, Clifton House, Clifton VA 22024......................................703-830-1000
NY Talk, 1133 Broadway, New York NY 10010..212-807-7100
NYC-New Youth Connection, 16 W 22nd St #805, New York NY 10010..212-242-3270
Nycticorax, PO Box 8444 Grace Sta, Asheville NC 28814 704-254-1359
O & A Marketing News, PO Box 765, LaCanada CA 91011 213-790-6554
O.ARS, PO Box 179, Cambridge MA 02238..603-529-1060
OB Gyn News, 770 Lexington Ave, New York NY 10021 212-421-0707
Ober Income Letter, Box 888, Mill Hill Rd, Woodstock NY 12498............914-679-2300
Oblates Magazine, 15 S 59th St, Belleville IL 62222 618-233-2238
Obsidian II, Box 8105 North Carolina State Univ, Raleigh NC 27695.......919-737-3870
Obstetrical & Gyn Survey, 428 E Preston, Baltimore MD 21202 301-528-4000
Occupational Hazards, 1111 Chester Ave, Cleveland OH 44114 216-696-7000
Occupational Health & Safety, 225 N New Rd, Waco TX 76714................817-776-9000
Occupational Health Nursing, 6900 Grove Rd, Thorofare NJ 08086.........609-848-1000
Ocean Industry, 3301 Allen Pkwy, Houston TX 77001................................713-529-4301
Ocean Navigator, 18 Danforth St, Portland ME 04101................................207-772-2466
Ocean State Business, 10 Davol Square, Providence RI 02903 401-274-5400
Oceanus, Woods Hole Oceanographic Inst, Woods Hole MA 02543.........617-548-1400
Ocular Surgery News, 6900 Grove Rd, Thorofare NJ 08086 609-848-1000
Odessa Poetry Review, RR 1 Box 39, Odessa MO 64076 816-633-4067
Odyssey, 1027 N 7th St, Milwaukee WI 53233..414-276-2689
OEA Communique, 5454 Cleveland Ave, Columbus OH 43229..................614-895-7277
Off Hours, 800 2nd Ave, New York NY 10017 212-599-3400
Off Lead Dog Training, Box A 13 Clinton St, Clark Mills NY 13321 315-853-8375
Off Our Backs, 1841 Columbia Rd NW Rm 212, Washington DC 20009..202-234-8072
Off-Road's Thunder Trucks, 12301 Wilshire, Los Angeles CA 90025........213-820-3601

Office Admin & Automation, 51 Madison Ave, New York NY 10010........212-689-4411
Office Guide to Tampa Bay, 1111 N Westshore, Tampa FL 33607............813-877-3427
Office Magazine, PO Box 1231, Stamford CT 06904...............................203-327-9670
Office Products Dealer, 25 W 550 Geneva Rd, Wheaton IL 60188............312-665-1000
Office Systems, Danbury Rd Box 150, Georgetown CT 06829....................203-544-9526
Office Systems Dealer, Danbury Rd Box 150, Georgetown CT 06829.......203-544-9526
Office Systems Ergonomics, 3029 Wilshire, Santa Monica CA 90403........213-453-1844
The Office, 1600 Summer St, Stamford CT 06904...............................203-327-9670
The Officer, 1 Constitution Ave, Wash DC 20002.................................202-479-2200
Official Detective Stories, 460 W 34th St, New York NY 10001.................212-947-6500
Official Karate, 351 W 54th St, New York NY 10019.............................203-735-3381
Offshore, 220-9 Reservoir St, Needham MA 02194...............................617-449-6204
Ohio Business, 1720 Euclid Ave, Cleveland OH 44115...........................216-621-1644
Ohio Chess Bulletin, 303 W Merry Ave, Bowling Green OH 43402.........419-352-6307
The Ohio Farmer, 7500 Old Oak Blvd, Cleveland OH 44130....................216-243-8100
Ohio Fisherman, 921 Eastwind Dr, Westerville OH 43081.......................614-882-5658
Ohio Magazine, 40 S 3rd St, Columbus OH 43215...............................614-461-5083
The Ohio Motorist, PO Box 6150, Cleveland OH 44101..........................216-361-6216
Ohio Renaissance Review, Box 804, Ironton OH 45638...........................614-532-0846
The Ohio Review, Ohio Univ Ellis Hall, Athens OH 45701......................614-593-1900
Ohio State Univ College of Medicine, Columbus OH 43210....................614-422-5674
Ohio State Medical Journal, 600 S High St, Columbus OH 43215............614-228-6971
The Ohio Underwriter, 420 E 4th St, Cincinnati OH 45202....................513-721-2140
Ohioana Quarterly, 65 S Front St, Columbus OH 43266.........................614-466-3831
Oil & Gas Investor, 1900 Grant St Ste 400, Denver CO 80203.................303-832-1917
Oil & Gas Journal, PO Box 1260, Tulsa OK 74101...............................918-835-3161
Oil Gas & Petrochemical Equip, 1421 S Sheridan, Tulsa OK 74112.........918-835-3161
The Oklahoma Farmer-Stockman, 10111 N Central, Dallas TX 75231.....214-363-7651
Oklahoma Today, PO Box 53384, Oklahoma City OK 73152....................405-521-2496
Old Bottle & Popular Archeology, PO Box 243, Bend OR 97709............503-382-6978
Old Cars Weekly & Price Guide, 700 E State St, Iola WI 54990.................715-445-2214
Old Mill News, 604 Ensley Dr Rt 29, Knoxville TN 37920......................615-577-7757
The Old Red Kimono, Box 1864, Rome GA 30163................................404-295-6312
Old Sturbridge Visitor, Old Sturbridge Inc, Sturbridge MA 01566...........617-347-3362
Old West Quarterly, PO Box 2107, Stillwater OK 74076........................405-743-3370
The Old-House Journal, 69A 7th Ave, Brooklyn NY 11217......................718-636-4514
Omega Star Inc, PO Box 87413, Houston TX 77287.............................713-998-9226
Omni, 1965 Broadway, New York NY 10023..212-496-6100
On Cable, 25 Van Zant St, Norwalk CT 06855.....................................203-866-6256
On Communications, 375 Cochituate Rd, Framingham MA 01701..........617-879-0700
On The Line, 616 Walnut Ave, Scottdale PA 15683................................412-887-8500
On Track, 17165 Newhope St Unit M, Fountain Valley CA 92708.............714-966-1131
Oncology Nursing Forum, 3111 Banksville Rd, Pittsburgh PA 15216........412-344-3899
1001 Home Ideas, 3 Park Ave, New York NY 10016..............................212-340-9250
1199 News, 330 W 42nd St, New York NY 10036.................................212-947-1944
One Shot, 3379 Morrison Ave, Cincinnati OH 45220.............................513-861-1532
Onion World, 111C S 7th Ave PO Box 1467, Yakima WA 98907.............509-248-2452
Online Data Access, 11754 Jollyville Rd Ste 103, Austin TX 78759...........512-250-1255
Online Today, 5000 Arlington Centre Blvd, Columbus OH 43220.............614-457-8600
Only Music, 2530 Republic Bank Ctr, Houston TX 77002........................713-227-0095
Open Court Publishing Co, 315 5th St, Peru IL 61354............................815-223-1500
Open Magazine/Laundry Press, 215 North Ave W, Westfield NJ 07090..201-654-3092
Open Places, Box 2085 Stephens College, Columbia MO 65215.................314-442-2211

Open Wheel, PO Box 715, Ipswich MA 01938..............................617-356-7030
Openers, 50 E Huron St, Chicago IL 60611.................................312-944-6780
The Opera Companion, 40 Museum Way, San Francisco CA 94114..........415-626-2741
Opera News, 1865 Broadway, New York NY 10023.....................212-582-3285
Operations Forum, 2626 Pennsylvania Ave, Washington DC 20037.........202-337-2500
Ophthalmic Forum, 456 Clinic Dr, Columbus OH 43210...................614-421-4960
Ophthalmic Surgery, 6900 Grove Rd, Thorofare NJ 08086................609-848-1000
Ophthalmology, E Washington Sq, Philadelphia PA 19105................215-238-4200
Ophthalmology Management, 5 N Greenwich Rd, Armonk NY 10504.....914-273-6666
Ophthalmology Times, 747 3rd Ave, New York NY 10017.................212-418-4100
Opossum Holler Tarot, Rt 2, Campbellsburg IN 47108....................812-755-4788
Opportunity Magazine, 6 N Michigan Ave, Chicago IL 60602.............312-346-4790
Optical Engineering, 1022 19 St, Bellingham WA 98225..................206-676-3290
Optical Index, 11 E Adams Rm 1209, Chicago IL 60603..................312-337-7800
Optics Letters, 1816 Jefferson Place NW, Washington DC 20036.................202-233-8130
Optimal Health, 1842 Hoffman St Ste 201, Madison WI 53704.............608-249-0186
The Optimist Magazine, 4494 Lindell Blvd, St Louis MO 63108.............314-371-6000
Options, 7628 Densmore Ave, Van Nuys CA 91406.......................818-782-7328
Options, PO Box 470, Port Chester NY 10573.............................914-939-2111
Optometric Monthly, 11 E Adams Rm 1209, Chicago IL 60603.............312-337-7800
Optometry Times, 747 3rd Ave, New York NY 10017.....................212-418-4100
Oracle Sci-Fiction & Fantasy, 21111 Mapleridge, Southfield MI 48075....313-355-9827
Oral Surgery Medicine Pathology, 11830 Westline, St Louis MO 63146...314-872-8370
Orange Coast Magazine, 245-D Fischer, Costa Mesa CA 92626.............714-545-1900
Orange County Business Jour, 1112 Chestnut, Santa Ana CA 92701........714-835-9692
Orange County South, 23706 Birtcher Dr Ste A, El Toro CA 92630.........714-472-1133
Orben's Current Comedy, 1200 N Nash St, Arlington VA 22209............703-522-3666
Oregon Business, 208 SW Stark, Portland OR 97204.....................503-223-0304
Oregon Historical Quarterly, 1230 SW Park Ave, Portland OR 97205.....503-222-1741
Oregon Magazine, 280 SW Stark, Portland OR 97204....................503-223-0304
Organic Gardening, 33 E Minor St, Emmaus PA 18049....................215-967-5171
Organizational Dynamics, 135 W 50th St, New York NY 10020.............212-586-8100
Origin, 302 Neville Hall Univ of Maine, Orano ME 04469.................207-581-3814
Orlando Magazine, PO Box 2207, Orlando FL 32802.....................305-644-3355
Ornament, 1221 S La Cienega PO Box 35029, Los Angeles CA 90035......213-652-9914
Oro Madre, 4429 Gibraltar Dr, Fremont CA 94536.......................415-797-9096
ORT Reporter, 315 Park Ave S, New York NY 10010......................212-505-7700
Orthopaedic Review, 116 W 32nd St, New York NY 10001................212-736-6688
Orthopedics Today, 6900 Grove Rd, Thorofare NJ 08086.................609-848-1000
Osteopathic Annals, 139 Harristown Rd, Glen Rock NJ 07452.............201-444-8660
Ostomy Quarterly, 36 Executive Park, Irvine CA 92714..................213-413-5510
OTC Review, 110 Pennsylvania Ave, Oreland PA 19075...................215-887-9000
The Other Side, 300 W Apsley St, Philadelphia PA 19144................215-849-2178
Other Voices, 820 Ridge Rd, Highland Park IL 60035....................312-831-4684
Otolaryngology, 11830 Westline Industrial Dr, St Louis MO 63146........314-872-8370
Oui Magazine, 300 W 43rd St, New York NY 10036......................212-397-5200
Our Little Friend, PO Box 7000, Boise ID 83707.........................208-465-2581
Our Sunday Visitor, 200 Noll Plaza, Huntington IN 46750................219-356-8400
Our Town Newspaper, 451 E 83rd St, New York NY 10028................212-439-7799
Outdoor America, 1701 N Ft Myer Dr Ste 1100, Arlington VA 22209.......703-528-1818
Outdoor Life, 380 Madison Ave, New York NY 10017....................212-687-3000
The Outerbridge, College of Staten Island, Staten Island NY 10301.........212-390-7654
Outreach Pre-College Prog, 800 Florida Ave NE, Wash DC 20002.............202-651-5341

Outside Magazine, 1165 N Clark St, Chicago IL 60610....................................312-951-0990
Outside Plant, PO Box 183, Cary IL 60013 312-639-2200
Ovation, 33 W 60th St, New York NY 10023 212-765-5110
Overland Journal, Box 42, Gerald MO 63037 314-764-2801
Owlflight, 1025 55th St, Oakland CA 94608...415-655-3024
The Owner Builder, 1516 5th St, Berkeley CA 94710..................................415-526-9222
Owner Operator, Chilton Way, Radnor PA 19089 215-964-4000
Oyez Review, 430 S Michigan Ave, Chicago IL 60614 312-341-2017
Ozark, 5900 Wilshire Blvd Ste 800, Los Angeles CA 90036 213-937-5810
Ozarks Mountaineer, Box 868 Rt 3, Branson MO 65616............................417-546-5390
Pace Magazine, 338 N Elm St, Greensboro NC 27401 919-378-6065
Pacific Arts and Letters, PO Box 640394, San Francisco CA 94164...........415-771-3431
Pacific Banker, 109 W Mercer St, Seattle WA 98119.................................206-285-2050
Pacific Boating Almanac, 4051 Glencoe, Marina del Rey CA 90292.........213-306-2094
Pacific Bridge, PO Box 883903, San Francisco CA 94188 415-641-4788
Pacific Builder & Engineer, 109 W Mercer St, Seattle WA 98119.............206-285-2050
Pacific Coast Journal, PO Box 25482, Sacramento CA 95825 916-924-7265
Pacific Discovery, Golden Gate Park, San Francisco CA 94118.................415-221-5100
Pacific Express Magazine, 9600 SW Oak Ste 310, Portland OR 97223......503-244-2299
Pacific Fishing, 1515 NW 51st St, Seattle WA 98107................................206-789-5333
Pacific Northwest, 222 Dexter Ave, Seattle WA 98109.............................206-682-2704
Pacific Travel News, 100 Grant Ave, San Francisco CA 94108...................415-781-8240
Package Printing, 401 N Broad St, Philadelphia PA 19108.........................215-238-5300
Packaging, 1350 E Touhy Ave, Des Plaines IL 60018 312-635-8800
Packaging Digest, 400 N Michigan Ave Ste 1216, Chicago IL 60611 312-222-2000
The Packer, 400 Knightsbridge Pkwy, Lincolnshire IL 60069 312-634-2600
Paddlewheel Press, PO Box 230220, Tigard OR 97223..............................503-639-5637
Pages, 3610 Country Club, Wichita KS 67208 316-684-9497
Paideuma, 302 Neville Hall Univ of Maine, Orono ME 04469....................207-581-3814
Paint Horse Journal, PO Box 18519, Ft Worth TX 76118 817-439-3400
Paintbrush, Georgia Southwestern College, Americus GA 31709...............912-928-1350
Painted Bride Quarterly, 230 Vine St, Philadelphia PA 19106...................215-925-9914
Painters & Allied Trades, 1750 New York Ave NW, Wash DC 20006.......202-637-0700
Painting & Wallcovering Contr, 130 W Lockwood, St Louis MO 63119 ...314-961-6644
The Palimpsest, 402 Iowa Ave, Iowa City IA 52240 319-338-5471
Palm Springs Life, 303 N Indian Ave, Palm Springs CA 92262..................619-325-2333
Pan Am Clipper, 34 E 51st St, New York NY 10022....................................212-888-5900
Pan Erotic Review, PO Box 2992, Santa Cruz CA 95063............................408-426-7082
Panache, 45-50 38th St, Long Island City NY 11101..................................718-937-8813
Pangloss Papers, PO Box 18917, Los Angeles CA 90018...........................213-663-1950
The Panhandler, Univ West Florida English Dept, Pensacola FL 32514...904-474-2923
Panjandrum Poetry Jour, 11321 Iowa Ave #7, Los Angeles CA 90025.....213-477-8771
Paper Age, 70 Oak St, Norwood NJ 07648..201-767-6800
Paper Film & Foil Converter, 300 W Adams St, Chicago IL 60606...........312-726-2802
Paper Industry Equipment, 610 S McDonald, Montgomery AL 36197 205-834-1170
Paper Sales, 7500 Old Oak Blvd, Cleveland OH 44130 216-243-8100
Paper Trade Journal, 400 Knightsbridge Pkwy, Lincolnshire IL 60069 312-634-2600
Paperbound Packaging, 7500 Old Oak Blvd, Cleveland OH 44130............216-243-8100
Papercutting World, 584 Castro St, San Francisco CA 94114 415-346-2473
The Paperworker, 3340 Perimeter Hill Dr, Nashville TN 37202 615-254-6666
Parabola Magazine, 656 Broadway, New York NY 10012..........................212-505-6200
Parachutist, 1440 Duke St, Alexandria VA 22314.......................................703-836-3495
The Paralegal, 10 S Pine St PO Box 629, Doylestown PA 18901................215-348-5575

Parameters, US Army War College, Carlisle Barrack PA 17013.................717-245-4943
Parents, 685 3rd Ave, New York NY 10017...212-878-8700
The Paris Review, 541 E 72nd St, New York NY 10021 718-539-7085
Parish Family Digest, 200 Noll Plaza, Huntington IN 46750........................219-356-8400
Park Maintenance, Box 1936, Appleton WI 54913...414-733-2301
Parking, 1112 16th St NW Ste 2000, Washington DC 20036.........................202-296-4336
Parnassus, 205 W 89th St, New York NY 10024..212-787-3569
Partisan Review, 141 Bay State Rd, Boston MA 02215 617-353-4260
Partnership, 465 Gundersen Dr, Carol Stream IL 60188................................312-260-6200
Passages North, Wm Bonifas Fine Arts Center, Escanaba MI 49829.......906-786-3833
Passaic Review, 195 Gregory Ave, Passaic NJ 07055 201-460-1774
Passenger Train Journal, Box 860, Homewood IL 60430..............................312-957-7245
Pastoral Life, Rt 224, Canfield OH 44406...216-533-5503
Pathologist, 7400 N Skokie Blvd, Skokie IL 60077 312-677-3500
Pathway Press, 1080 Montgomery Ave, Cleveland TN 37311......................615-476-4512
Patient Care, 690 Kinderkamack Rd, Oradell NJ 07649................................201-599-8000
Paunch, 123 Woodland Ave, Buffalo NY 14214...716-836-7332
Pavement, Student Activity Ctr Univ of Iowa, Iowa City IA 52242.............319-351-6361
Pay Phone Exchange, PO Box 22134, Knoxville TN 37933............................615-690-9530
PC Digest, 1 Winding Dr, Philadelphia PA 19131 215-878-9300
PC Magazine, 1 Park Ave, New York NY 10016..212-503-5255
PC Publishing, 1800 Market St, San Francisco CA 94102.............................415-864-0560
PC Retailing, 115 2nd Ave, Waltham MA 02154..617-890-5124
PC Tech Journal, World Trade Center Ste 211, Baltimore MD 21202......301-576-0770
PC Week, 1 Park Ave, New York NY 10016...212-503-5110
PC World, 555 De Haro St, San Francisco CA 94107......................................415-861-3861
PCM, 9529 US Hwy 42, Prospect KY 40059..502-228-4492
The Peace Newsletter, 924 Burnet Ave, Syracuse NY 13203 315-472-5478
Peacework, 2161 Massachusetts Ave, Cambridge MA 02240........................617-661-6130
Peanut Butter, 730 Broadway, New York NY 10003..212-505-3000
Pebble, Univ of Nebraska, Lincoln NE 68588 402-826-4038
Pediatric Annals, 6900 Grove Rd, Thorofare NJ 08086 609-848-1000
Pediatric Clinics, W Washington Sq, Philadelphia PA 19105......................215-574-4700
Pediatric Mental Health, PO Box 1880, Santa Monica CA 90406 213-828-8963
Pediatric News, 12230 Wilkins Ave, Rockville MD 20852............................301-770-6170
Pediatric Nursing, Box 56 N Woodbury Rd, Pitman NJ 08071 609-589-2381
Pediatrics, Box 927, Elk Grove IL 60007 312-228-5005
Pediatrics for Parents, 176 Mt Hope Ave, Bangor ME 04401 207-942-6212
The Pegasus Review, PO Box 134, Flanders NJ 07836.................................201-927-0749
Pembroke Magazine, Box 60 PSU, Pembroke NC 28372................................919-521-4214
Pennsylvania, PO Box 576, Camp Hill PA 17011 717-761-6620
Pennsylvania Angler, PO Box 1673, Harrisburg PA 17105 717-657-4518
Pennsylvania Farmer, 705 Lisburn Rd, Camp Hill PA 17011 717-761-6050
Pennsylvania Food Merchants Assn, 224 Pine St, Harrisburg PA 17108..717-234-6031
Pennsylvania Game News, 8000 Derry St, Harrisburg PA 17105................717-787-3745
Pennsylvania Heritage, PO Box 1026, Harrisburg PA 17108.......................717-787-8312
Pennsylvania Lawyer, 100 South St PO Box 186, Harrisburg PA 17108 717-238-6715
Pennsylvania Outdoors, 801 Oregon St, Oshkosh WI 54901........................414-233-7470
Pennsylvania Review, Univ of Pittsburgh, Pittsburgh PA 15260..................412-624-0026
The Pennsylvania Sportsman, PO Box 5196, Harrisburg PA 17110...........717-233-4797
Penny Power, 256 Washington St, Mount Vernon NY 10553.........................914-667-9400
Pensacola Historical Society, 405 S Adams St, Pensacola FL 32501.........904-433-1559
Pension World, 6255 Barfield Rd, Atlanta GA 30328.....................................404-256-9800

Pensions & Investment Age, 740 Rush St, Chicago IL 60611.......................312-649-5200
Pentecostal Evangel, 1445 Boonville, Springfield MO 65802.......................417-862-2781
The Pentecostal Messenger, 4901 Pennsylvania, Joplin MO 64802..............417-625-7050
Penthouse, 1965 Broadway, New York NY 10023...212-496-6100
People In Action, PO Box 10010, Ogden UT 84409 801-394-9446
People Weekly, Time-Life Bldg Rockefeller Ctr, New York NY 10020 212-586-1212
Percision Metal, 1111 Chester Ave, Cleveland OH 44114 216-696-7000
Performance, 1020 Currie St, Ft Worth TX 76107 817-338-9444
Performance Horseman, Gum Tree Corner, Unionville PA 19375............215-857-1101
Perinatal Press, 52nd & F Sts, Sacramento CA 95819....................................916-733-1750
Perinatology-Neonatology, 825 S Barrington, Los Angeles CA 90049........213-826-8388
Personal Computing, 10 Mulholland Dr, Hasbrouck Hts NJ 07604...........201-393-6187
Personnel Administrator, 606 N Washington St, Alexandria VA 22314....703-548-3440
Personnel Advisory Bulletin, 24 Rope Ferry Rd, Waterford CT 06386.....203-442-4365
Personnel Journal, 245 Fischer Ave Ste B2, Costa Mesa CA 92626...........714-751-1883
Personnel Magazine, 135 W 50th St, New York NY 10020............................212-903-8067
Perspective, PO Box 788, Wheaton IL 60189 312-293-1600
Perspectives in Psych Care, 194B Kinderkamack, Park Ridge NJ 07656...201-391-7845
Pest Control, 7500 Old Oak Rd, Cleveland OH 44130 216-243-8100
Pet Age, 207 S Wabash Ave, Chicago IL 60604 312-663-4040
Pet Business, 5400 NW 84th Ave, Miami FL 33166 305-591-1629
Pet Dealer, 567 Morris Ave, Elizabeth NJ 07208...201-353-7373
Petersen's Photographic, 8490 Sunset Blvd, Los Angeles CA 90069 213-854-2200
Petroleum Engineer Intl, PO Box 1589, Dallas TX 75221.............................214-691-3911
Petroleum Equipment, PO Box 360, Whitehouse NJ 08888...........................201-381-7279
Petroleum Independent, 1101 16th St NW, Washington DC 20036.............202-857-4775
Pets/Supplies/Marketing, 1 E 1st St, Duluth MN 55802.............................218-723-9303
PGA Magazine, 100 Ave of Champions, Palm Beach Gdns FL 33418........305-626-3600
Pharmaceutical & Cosmetic Equip, 15 S 9th St, Minneapolis MN 55402..612-370-0413
Pharmaceutical Engineering, 8910 N Dale Mabry, Tampa FL 33614 813-932-6069
Pharmaceutical Executive, 320 North A St, Springfield OR 97477.............503-726-1200
Pharmaceutical Mfg, 2416 Wilshire Blvd, Santa Monica CA 90403 213-829-0315
Pharmaceutical Representative, 550 Frontage Rd, Northfield IL 60093 ...312-446-1622
Pharmaceutical Technology, 320 North A St, Springfield OR 97477..........503-726-1200
The Pharmacy Student, 2215 Constitution Ave NW, Wash DC 20037.......202-628-4410
Pharmacy Times, 80 Shore Rd, Port Washington NY 11050 516-883-6350
The Pharos, 525 Middlefield Rd Ste 130, Menlo Park CA 94025.................415-329-0291
Phi Delta Kappan, 8th & Union PO Box 789, Bloomington IN 47402........812-339-1156
Philadelphia Business Jour, 2300 Market St, Philadelphia PA 19103........215-569-0202
Philadelphia Magazine, 1500 Walnut St, Philadelphia PA 19102................215-545-3500
Philadelphia Medicine, 2100 Spring Garden St, Philadelphia PA 19130....215-563-5343
Philadelphia Poets, 1919 Chestnut St Apt 1701, Philadelphia PA 19103 ...215-568-1145
Philatelic Journalist, 154 Laguna Ct, St Augustine Shores FL 32086 904-797-3513
Philosophy In Science, PO Box 35549, Tucson AZ 85740................................602-297-4797
Phoebe, 4400 University Dr, Fairfax VA 22030...703-323-3730
Phoenix Home & Garden, 3136 N 3rd Ave, Phoenix AZ 85013...................602-234-0840
Phoenix Metro Magazine, 4707 N 12th St, Phoenix AZ 85014 602-248-8900
Phoenix Quarterly, 1627 K St NW, Washington DC 20006............................202-466-4050
Photo Lab Management, 1312 Lincoln Blvd, Santa Monica CA 90406 213-451-1344
Photo Review, 301 Hill Ave, Langhorne PA 19047...215-757-8921
Photo Weekly, 1515 Broadway, New York NY 10036 212-764-7396
Photo/Design, 1 Park Ave, New York NY 10016 212-685-8520
Photobulletin, Osceola WI 54020...715-248-3800

Photogrammetric Engine, 210 Little Falls St, Falls Church VA 22046.......703-534-6617
The Photoletter, Osceola WI 54020..715-248-3800
Photomarket, Osceola WI 54020...715-248-3800
Photomethods, 1 Park Ave, New York NY 10016...212-725-3942
Photonics Spectra, Box 1146 Berkshire Common, Pittsfield MA 01202....413-499-0514
Physical Review Letters, 1 Research Rd, Ridge NY 11961.............................516-924-5533
Physical Therapy, 1111 N Fairfax St, Fairfax VA 22314................................703-684-2782
The Physician & Sportsmedicine, 4530 W 77th St, Edina MN 55435.........612-835-3222
Physician Assistant, 400 Plaza Dr, Secaucus NJ 07094..................................201-865-7500
Physician's Management, 7500 Old Oak Rd, Cleveland OH 44130.............216-243-8100
Physician's Sportlife, 15-22 Fair Lawn Ave, Fair Lawn NJ 07410................201-796-6500
Physicians & Computers, 2333 Waukegan, Bannockburn IL 60015...........312-940-8333
The Physics Teacher, SUNY Dept of Physics, Stony Brook NY 11794......516-246-6058
Physics Today, 335 E 45 St, New York NY 10017..212-661-9404
Physiological Chem & Phys, 7101 Winding Wy, Wake Forest NC 27587..919-556-2940
Physiologist, 9650 Rockville Pike, Bethesda MD 20814.................................301-530-7164
Piano Quarterly, Box 815, Wilmington VT 05363...802-464-5149
Pickups & Mini-Trucks, 8490 Sunset Blvd, Los Angeles CA 90069...........213-657-5100
Pico Jour of Portable Computing, 7 School St, Peterborough NH 03458..603-924-7859
Piedmont Literary Review, PO Box 3656, Danville VA 24543......................804-793-0956
Pig In A Pamphlet, PO Box 81925, Pittsburgh PA 15217..............................814-664-9404
Pig Iron Press, PO Box 237, Youngstown OH 44501......................................216-783-1269
The Pikestaff Forum, Box 127, Normal IL 61761...309-452-4831
PIMA Magazine, 2400 E Oakton St, Arlington Hts IL 60005.......................312-956-0250
Pinchpenny, 4851 Q St, Sacramento CA 95819..916-451-3042
Pioneer, 1548 Poplar Ave, Memphis TN 38104...901-272-2461
PIP College Helps Newsletter, PO Box 50347, Tulsa OK 74150..................918-584-5906
Pipe Line Industry, 3301 Allen Pkwy, Houston TX 77019............................713-529-4301
Pipe Smoker, 6172 Airways Blvd, Chattanooga TN 37422.............................615-892-7277
Pipeline & Gas Journal, 7500 Old Oak Blvd, Cleveland OH 44130.............216-243-8100
Pit & Quarry, 111 E Wacker Dr Ste 1775, Chicago IL 60601..........................312-938-2300
Pittsburgh Magazine, 4802 5th Ave, Pittsburgh PA 15213............................412-622-1360
Pizza Today, PO Box 114, Santa Claus IN 47579...812-937-4464
Place Stamp Here, Box 250, Farmingdale NY 07727.......................................201-938-4297
Plain Truth, Box 111, Pasadena CA 91123..818-304-6000
Plainsong, Box U245 West Kentucky Univ, Bowling Green KY 42101......502-745-5708
Plainswoman, PO Box 8027, Grand Forks ND 58202......................................701-777-8043
Plan & Print, 9931 Franklin Ave PO Box 879, Franklin Park IL 60131.....312-671-5356
Plane & Pilot Magazine, 16200 Ventura Blvd Ste 201, Encino CA 91406..818-986-8400
Planning, 1313 E 60th St, Chicago IL 60637...312-955-9100
Plant Disease, 3340 Pilot Knob Rd, St Paul MN 55121.................................612-454-7250
Plant Engineering, 1301 S Grove Ave, Barrington IL 60010.........................312-381-1840
Plant Services, 301 E Erie St, Chicago IL 60611..312-644-2020
Plants & Gardens, 1000 Washington Ave, Brooklyn NY 11225...................718-622-4433
Plastic & Reconstructive Surgery, 428 E Preston, Baltimore MD 21202..301-528-4000
Plastics Compounding, 1129 E 17th Ave, Denver CO 80218.......................303-832-1022
Plastics Design Forum, 1129 E 17th Ave, Denver CO 80218........................303-832-1022
Plastics Machinery & Equipment, 1129 E 17th Ave, Denver CO 80218....303-832-1022
Plastics Technology, 633 3rd Ave, New York NY 10017.................................212-986-4800
Plastics World, 221 Columbus Ave, Boston MA 02116..................................617-536-7780
The Plate Collector, 100 N Edward Gary, San Marcos TX 78667................512-396-1888
Plate World, 6054 W Touhy Ave, Chicago IL 60648..312-763-7773
Plating & Surface Finishing, 12644 Research Pkwy, Orlando FL 32826...305-281-6441

Playbill, 71 Vanderbilt Ave, New York NY 10169...212-557-5757
Playboy, 919 N Michigan Ave, Chicago IL 60611...312-751-8000
Players, 8060 Melrose Ave, Los Angeles CA 90046 213-653-8060
Playgirl, 801 2nd Ave, New York NY 10017..212-986-5100
Plays, 120 Boylston St, Boston MA 02116..617-423-3157
Playthings, 51 Madison Ave, New York NY 10010..212-689-4411
Pleasure Boating, 1995 NE 150th St, N Miami FL 33181.................................305-945-7403
Pleiades Publications, 6677 W Colfax Ave, Lakewood CO 80214 303-237-3398
Plexus, 545 Athol Ave, Oakland CA 94606...415-451-2585
The Plough: N Coast Review, Firelands College, Huron OH 44839 419-433-5560
Plumbing & Mechanical, 7574 Lincoln Ave, Skokie IL 60077.....................312-677-2707
Plus, Rt 22 Box FCL, Pawling NY 12564..914-855-5000
PMLA, 62 5th Ave, New York NY 10011..212-741-5588
POB Point of Beginning, PO Box 810, Wayne MI 48184.................................313-729-8400
Pockets, 1908 Grand Ave PO Box 189, Nashville TN 37202 615-340-7240
Podiatry Management, PO Box 50, Island Sta NY 10044.................................212-355-5216
Poesis, Bryn Mawr College, Bryn Mawr PA 19010 215-645-5306
Poet & Critic, 203 Ross Hall Iowa State Univ, Ames IA 50011.....................515-294-2180
Poet Forum, 3120 Old Mobile Hwy, Pascagoula MS 39567 601-264-6644
Poet Lore, 4000 Albemarle St NW, Washington DC 20016............................202-362-6445
Poet News, 2791 24th St #8, Sacramento CA 95818..916-739-1885
Poetic Justice, 8220 Rayford Dr, Los Angeles CA 90045 213-649-1491
Poetics Journal, 2639 Russell St, Berkeley CA 94705.......................................415-548-1817
Poetry, 60 W Walton St, Chicago IL 60610..312-280-4870
Poetry East, Star Rt 1 Box 50, Earlysville VA 22936...804-973-5299
Poetry Flash, PO Box 4172, Berkeley CA 94704...415-548-6871
The Poetry Miscellany, Univ of Tenn, Chattanooga TN 37403 615-755-4629
Poetry Motel, 430 S 21st Ave E, Duluth MN 55812..218-724-6153
Poetry Newsletter, PO Box 18326, Philadelphia PA 19120 215-787-1778
Poetry On Tape, 121 6th St, Petaluma CA 94952...415-863-4577
Poetry Resource Center, 621 S Washington, Royal Oak MI 48067.............313-399-6163
Poetry Today, PO Box 20822, Portland OR 97220 503-231-7628
Poetry/LA, PO Box 84271, Los Angeles CA 90073 213-472-6171
Poetry: San Francisco Quar, Ft Mason Ctr, San Francisco CA 94123.......415-621-3073
Poets On, Box 255, Chaplin CT 06235..203-455-9671
Poets' Roundtable, 826 South Center St, Terre Haute IN 47807.....................812-234-0819
The Poisoned Pen, 50 1st Pl, Brooklyn NY 11231...718-596-7739
Poker Chips, Rt 2 Box 2845, Manistique MI 49854...906-341-5468
Poker Player, 1018 N Cole Ave, Hollywood CA 90038.....................................213-466-5261
Police, 6200 Yarrow Dr, Carlsbad CA 92008..619-438-2511
Police and Security Bulletin, Box 88, Mt Airy MD 21771.............................301-829-1496
Police Times, 1100 NE 125th St, N Miami FL 33161...305-891-1700
Political Affairs, 235 W 23rd St, New York NY 10011 212-989-4994
Political Science Quarterly, 2852 Broadway, New York NY 10025.............212-866-6754
Political Woman, 4521 Campus Dr, Irvine CA 92715 714-854-3506
Polled Hereford World, 4700 E 63rd St, Kansas City MO 64130 816-333-7731
Pollution Engineering, 1935 Shermer Rd, Northbrook IL 60062..................312-498-9840
Polo, 656 Quince Orchard Rd, Gaithersburg MD 20878 301-977-0200
Polyhedron, Box 509, Lake Geneva WI 53147 414-248-3625
Pool & Spa News, 3923 W 6th St, Los Angeles CA 90020 213-385-3926
Popular Cars, 2145 W La Palma, Anaheim CA 92801 714-635-9040
Popular Ceramics, 3639 San Fernando Rd, Glendale CA 91204.................818-246-8145
Popular Communications, 76 N Broadway, Hicksville NY 11801 516-681-2922

Popular Computing, 70 Main St, Peterborough NH 03458 603-924-9281
Popular Hot Rodding, 12301 Wilshire Blvd, Los Angeles CA 90025..........213-820-3601
Popular Lures, 15115 S 76th E Ave, Bixby OK 74008.................................918-366-4441
Popular Mechanics, 224 W 57th St, New York NY 10019 212-262-4815
Popular Photography, 1 Park Ave, New York NY 10016.............................212-503-3700
Popular Science, 380 Madison Ave, New York NY 10017 212-687-3000
Popular Woodworking, 1300 Galaxy Way #8, Concord CA 94520.............415-671-9852
Population Bulletin, 2213 M St NW, Washington DC 20037......................202-785-4664
Pork, PO Box 2939, Shawnee Mission KS 66201 913-451-2200
Portable Companion, 42680 Christy St, Fremont CA 94538........................415-490-6885
Portable Lower East Side, 463 West St #344, New York NY 10014 212-929-5606
Portland Review, PO Box 751, Portland OR 97207.................................503-229-4468
Ports O' Call, PO Box 530, Santa Rosa CA 95402...................................707-542-0898
A Positive Approach, 1600 Malone St, Millville NJ 08332..........................609-327-4040
Possibilities: The Magazine of Hope, 2029 P St NW, Wash DC 20036 202-296-3760
Post Electricity, 1621 18th St, Denver CO 80202.....................................303-295-0900
Postcard Collector, 700 E State St, Iola WI 54990 715-445-2214
Postgraduate Medicine, 4530 W 77th St, Minneapolis MN 55435 612-835-3222
Potato Grower of Idaho, PO Box 981, Idaho Falls ID 83402 208-522-5187
Potentials in Marketing, 50 S 9th St, Minneapolis MN 55402....................612-333-0471
Poultry Digest, Sandstone Bldg, Mount Morris IL 61054.........................815-734-4171
Poultry Tribune, Sandstone Bldg, Mount Morris IL 61054.......................815-734-4171
Powder The Skier's Magazine, Box 1028, Dana Point CA 92629 714-496-5922
Powder/Bulk Solids, 15 S 9th St, Minneapolis MN 55402 612-370-0413
Power, 11 W 19th St, New York NY 10011...212-337-4060
Power Engineering Magazine, 1301 S Grove Ave, Barrington IL 60010....312-381-1840
Powerboat, 15917 Strathern St, Van Nuys CA 91406 818-989-1820
Powerlifting USA, Box 467, Camarillo CA 93011 805-482-2378
Practical Cardiology, 50 Rt 9, Morganville NJ 07751 201-536-3600
Practical Gastroenterology, 42-15 Crescent St, Long Island NY 11101 718-937-4283
Practical Homeowner, 33 E Minor St, Emmaus PA 18049 215-967-5171
Practical Horseman, Gum Tree Corner, Unionville PA 19375 215-857-1101
Practical Knowledge, 111 N Canal St, Chicago IL 60606..........................312-930-9446
The Practical Lawyer, 4025 Chestnut St, Philadelphia PA 19104...............215-243-1620
Prairie Farmer, 580 Waters Edge, Lombard IL 60187 312-953-1100
Prairie Rose, 212 N 4th St Green Tree Sq, Bismarck ND 58501................701-223-1385
Prairie Schooner, Univ of Nebraska Andrews Hall, Lincoln NE 68588.....402-472-7211
The Prairie Wool Companion, 126 S Phillips Ave, Sioux Falls SD 57102..605-338-4333
Preaching, 1529 Cesery Blvd, Jacksonville FL 32211 904-743-5994
Prelude To Fantasy, 2351 NW 3rd St #203, New Brighton MN 55112......612-781-8997
Premium/Incentive Business, 1515 Broadway, New York NY 10036........212-869-1300
The Presbyterian Outlook, 512 E Main St, Richmond VA 23219 804-649-1371
Presbyterian Survey, 341 Ponce de Leon Ave NE, Atlanta GA 30365.......404-873-1549
Present Tense, 165 E 56th St, New York NY 10022..................................212-751-4000
Preservation News, 1785 Massachusetts Ave NW, Wash DC 20016...........202-673-4075
Press De Laplantz, 899 Bayside Cutoff, Bayside CA 95524 707-822-6009
Press Magazine, PO Box 5400, Denver CO 80217 303-295-0900
Pressure, 25875 Jefferson, St Claire Shores MI 48081.............................313-774-8180
Presumptions, 1442A Walnut St #58, Berkeley CA 94709 415-653-4925
Prevention, 33 E Minor St, Emmaus PA 18049 215-967-5171
Price Club Journal, PO Box 85466, San Diego CA 92138........................619-581-4977
The Priest, 200 Noll Plaza, Huntington IN 46750...................................219-356-8400
Primary Cardiology, 400 Plaza Rd, Secaucus NJ 07094 201-865-7500

Primary Care & Cancer, 79 Powerhouse Rd, Roslyn Heights NY 11577..516-621-1080
Primary Treasure, PO Box 7000, Boise ID 83707 208-465-2581
Primary Writing, 1545 18th St NW #116, Washington DC 20036 202-232-2472
Primavera, 1212 E 59th St, Chicago IL 60637 312-324-5920
Prime Natl Publishing, 470 Boston Post Rd, Weston MA 02183................617-899-2702
Prime Time Sports & Fitness, PO Box 6091, Evanston IL 60204 312-869-6434
Princeton Alumni Weekly, 41 William St, Princeton NJ 08540....................609-452-4885
The Princeton Journal, 40 Witherspoon St, Princeton NJ 08540 609-924-7911
Princeton Parents, Nassau St Stanhope Hall, Princeton NJ 08544 609-452-5734
Print & Graphics, PO Box 25498, Washington DC 20007 202-337-6815
Printing Impressions, 401 N Broad St, Philadelphia PA 19108 215-238-5300
Printing News, 468 Park Ave S, New York NY 10016 212-689-9690
Printing Views, 8328 N Lincoln, Skokie IL 60077 312-539-8540
Prints Magazine, PO Box 1468, Alton IL 62002..................................618-462-1468
Privacy Journal, PO Box 15300, Washington DC 20003 202-547-2865
Private Pilot, PO Box 6050, Mission Viejo CA 92690..............................714-240-6001
Private Practice, 3535 NW 58th Ste 470, Oklahoma City OK 73112............405-943-2318
Pro Bass, 15115 S 76th E Ave, Bixby OK 74008 918-366-4441
Pro Football, 350 Madison Ave, New York NY 10017 212-880-8252
Pro Football Weekly, 2501 W Peterson Ave, Chicago IL 60659 312-989-0920
Pro Sound News, 2 Park Ave, New York NY 10016 212-213-3444
Proceedings, US Naval Inst, Annapolis MD 21402 301-268-6110
Processed Prepared Foods, 5725 E River Rd, Chicago IL 60631................312-693-3200
Processed World, 55 Sutter St #829, San Francisco CA 94104 415-495-6823
Product Design & Development, Chilton Wy, Radnor PA 19089................215-964-4000
Product Marketing, 11 W 19th St, New York NY 10011............................212-741-7210
Production, Box 101, Bloomfield Hills MI 48303 313-647-8400
Production Engineering, 1100 Superior Ave, Cleveland OH 44114..............216-696-7000
Production Supervisor's Bulletin, 24 Rope Ferry, Waterford CT 06386 ...203-442-4365
Productivity Improvement, 24 Rope Ferry, Waterford CT 06386................203-442-4365
Productivity Inc, 750 Summer St, Stamford CT 06901 203-967-3500
Products Finishing, 6600 Clough Pike, Cincinnati OH 45244 513-231-8020
Professional & Corp Publishing, 549 Hawthorne, Bartlett IL 60103 312-837-8088
Professional Agent, 400 N Washington St, Alexandria VA 22314................703-836-9340
Professional Builder, 1350 E Touhy Ave, Des Plaines IL 60018...................312-635-8800
Professional Carwashing, 8 Stanley Circle, Latham NY 12110....................518-783-1281
Professional Furniture Merchant, 180 Allen Rd NE, Atlanta GA 30328..305-753-7400
Professional Medical Assistant, 20 N Wacker Dr, Chicago IL 60606 312-899-1500
Professional Photographer, 1090 Executive Way, Des Plaines IL 60018...312-299-8161
Professional Pilot, West Bldg Wash Natl Airport, Wash DC 20001...........703-684-8270
Professional Psychology, 1200 17 St NW, Washington DC 20036................202-955-7600
Professional Quilter, PO Box 4096, St Paul MN 55104............................612-488-0974
Professional Safety, 850 Busse Hwy, Park Ridge IL 60068 312-692-4121
Professional Selling, 24 Rope Ferry Rd, Waterford CT 06386....................203-442-4365
Professional Stained Glass, 270 Lafayette St, New York NY 10012 212-966-6694
Profile Magazine, PO Box 52247, Lafayette LA 70505 318-981-0859
Profiles, 533 Stephens Ave, Solano Beach CA 92075..............................619-481-4353
Profit, 208 SE 3rd Ave, Ft Lauderdale FL 33301...................................305-463-4500
Profit Investment Oppor, 13410 E Cypress Forest, Houston TX 77070 713-890-4329
The Profit, PO Box 1132, Studio City CA 91604..................................818-789-4980
Profitable Craft Merchandising, PO Box 1790, Peoria IL 61656................309-682-6626
Progress in Cardiovascular Diseases, HBJ Publ, Orlando FL 32887 305-345-4200
Progress in Food Nutrition & Science, Elmsford NY 10523 914-592-7700

Progress in Neuro Psychopharmacology, Elmsford NY 10523 914-592-7700
Progress in Neurobiology, Maxwell House, Elmsford NY 10523.................914-592-7700
Progress Report, 1111 N Fairfax St, Alexandria VA 22314....................703-684-2782
Progressive Architecture, 600 Summer St, Stamford CT 06904 203-348-7531
Progressive Farmer, 820 Shades Creek Pkwy, Birmingham AL 35202 205-877-6000
Progressive Grocer, 1351 Washington Blvd, Stamford CT 06902 203-325-3500
Progressive Platter, PO Box 638, Boston MA 02215 617-247-1144
The Progressive, 409 E Main St, Madison WI 53703 608-257-4626
Proofs Magazine of Dental Sales, PO Box 3408, Tulsa OK 74101............918-835-3161
Prophet Newsline, 1015 N El Centro Ave, Los Angeles CA 90038.............213-463-7876
PSA Jour, 2005 Walnut St, Philadelphia PA 19103 215-563-1663
PSA Magazine, 5900 Wilshire Blvd, Los Angeles CA 90036....................213-937-5810
Psychiatric Annals, 6900 Grove Rd, Thorofare NJ 08086......................609-848-1000
Psychic Guide Magazine, 1408 Atwood Ave, Johnston RI 02919...............401-351-4320
Psychological Bulletin, Vanderbilt Univ, Nashville TN 37240...................615-322-8494
Psychological Review, NYU Dept of Psychology, New York NY 10003 212-598-3730
Psychology Today, 1200 17th St NW, Washington DC 20036 202-955-7800
Psychosomatics, 55 Holly Hill Lane, Greenwich CT 06830 203-661-0600
Psychotherapy, Mather Memorial Bldg, Cleveland OH 44106..................216-368-2841
PsycScan Clinical Psychology, 1200 17th St NW, Wash DC 20036............202-955-7600
Ptolemy/Brown Mills Review, Box 908, Browns Mills NJ 08015................609-893-7594
Public Administration Review, 1120 G St NW #500, Wash DC 20005......202-393-7878
Public Citizen, 2000 P St NW PO Box 19404, Washington DC 20036........202-293-9142
The Public Historian, Univ of California Press, Berkeley CA 94720 415-642-4191
The Public Interest, 10 E 53rd St, New York NY 10022 212-207-7123
Public Management, 1120 G St NW, Washington DC 20005....................202-626-4600
Public Opinion, 1150 17th St NW, Washington DC 20036......................202-862-5906
Public Opinion Quarterly, 52 Vanderbult Ave, New York NY 10017........212-867-9040
Public Personnel Management, 1850 K St NW #870, Wash DC 20006.....202-833-5860
Public Power, 2301 M St NW, Washington DC 20037 202-775-8300
Public Property, 1350 Florida, San Francisco CA 94110........................415-641-7227
Public Relations Journal, 845 3rd Ave, New York NY 10022 212-826-1757
Public Welfare, 1125 15th St NW, Washington DC 20005......................202-293-7550
Publish!, 501 2nd St, San Francisco CA 94107................................415-243-0600
Publisher's Report, PO Box 850, Moore Haven FL 33471......................813-946-0283
Publishers Weekly, 249 W 17th St, New York NY 10011......................212-645-0067
Publishing In Output Mode, Box 1275, San Luis Obispo CA 93406 805-543-5404
Publishing Northwest, 5770 Franson Ct, North Bend OR 97459..............503-756-5757
Publishing Trade, 1680 SW Bayshore Blvd, Ft St Lucie FL 34984............305-879-6666
Pudding Magazine, 2384 Hardesty Dr, S Columbus OH 43204................614-279-4188
Puerto Del Sol, Box 3E NM State Univ, Las Cruces NM 88003................505-646-2345
Pulp & Paper, 500 Howard St, San Francisco CA 94105........................415-397-1881
Pulpit Helps, 6815 Shallowford Rd, Chattanooga TN 37422 615-894-6060
Pulpsmith, 5 Beekman St, New York NY 10038 212-732-4822
Pulse!, 2500 Del Monte, Sacramento CA 95691................................916-321-2450
Pulse Transamerica Ins, 1149 S Broadway, Los Angeles CA 90015..........213-741-7226
Pumper Publications, PO Drawer 220, Three Lakes WI 54562..................715-546-3347
The PUN, PO Box 536-583, Orlando FL 32853................................305-898-0463
Puncture, 1674 Filbert #3, San Francisco CA 94123 415-771-5127
Purchasing Executive's Bulletin, 24 Rope Ferry, Waterford CT 06386 203-442-4365
Purchasing Magazine, 275 Washington St, Newton MA 02158..................617-964-3030
Purchasing World, 6521 Davis Industrial Pkwy, Solon OH 44139 216-248-1125
Purdue Alumnus, Purdue Memorial Union 160, W Lafayette IN 47907....317-494-5184

Pure-Bred Dogs, 51 Madison Ave, New York NY 10010 212-696-8330
Purple Cow Newspaper for Teens, 3423 Piedmont, Atlanta GA 30305......404-239-0642
Purple Pegasus, 800 Niles Rd, Port St Joe FL 32456....................................904-229-8251
Purpose, 616 Walnut Ave, Scottdale PA 15683..412-887-8500
Purrrrr! Newsletter for Cat Lovers, HCR 227 Rd, Islesboro ME 04949...207-734-6745
Quality, 25 W 550 Geneva Rd, Wheaton IL 60188...312-665-1000
Quality Control Supervisor, 24 Rope Ferry Rd, Waterford CT 06836......203-442-4365
Quality Progress, 230 W Wells St Ste 7000, Milwaukee WI 53202.............414-272-8575
Quality Review Bulletin, 875 N Michigan Ave, Chicago IL 60611..............312-642-6061
Quality Woodwork & Furniture, 1233 Janesville, Ft Atkinson WI 53538..414-563-6388
Quarter Horse Jour, PO Box 32470, Amarillo TX 79120 806-376-4811
Quarterly Jour of Speech, USC Comm Arts, Los Angeles CA 90089........413-545-0293
Quarterly Review of Literature, 26 Haslet Ave, Princeton NJ 08540 609-921-6976
Quarterly West, Univ of Utah, Salt Lake City UT 84112.............................801-581-3938
Queen of All Hearts, 26 S Saxon Ave, Bay Shore NY 11706.......................516-665-0726
Quercus, 2791 24th St Ste 8, Sacramento VA 95818 916-739-1885
Quest, PO Box 5076, Champaign IL 61820..217-351-5076
Quick Frozen Foods Intl, 80 8th Ave, New York NY 10011.........................212-989-1101
Quick Printing, 3255 S US 1, Ft Pierce FL 33482..305-465-9450
Quill & Scroll, Univ of Iowa, Iowa City IA 52242..319-353-4475
The Quill, 55 W Jackson, Chicago IL 60604..312-922-7424
Quilt, 1446 6th St #D, Berkeley CA 94701..415-527-1586
Quintessence Intl, 8 S Michigan Ave, Chicago IL 60603..............................312-782-3221
R & D Management Digest, Box 88, Mt Airy MD 21771 301-829-1496
R/C Modeler, 144 W Sierra Madre, Sierra Madre CA 91024 818-355-1476
Rabbits, Box 7 Rte 1, Waterloo WI 53594...414-478-2115
Raccoon, 3387 Poplar Ave Ste 205, Memphis TN 38111 901-323-8858
Racing Pictorial, PO Box 500, Indianapolis IN 46206.................................317-291-7900
Racing Wheels, 7502 NE 133 Ave, Vancouver WA 98662.............................206-892-5590
RaJAH, Univ of Mich Modern Language Bldg, Ann Arbor MI 48109.......313-763-2351
Radar, 8121 Hamilton Ave, Cincinnati OH 45231..513-931-4050
Radiance Mag for Large Women, PO Box 31703, Oakland CA 94604.......415-482-0680
Radical America, 1 Summer St, Somerville MA 02143................................617-628-6585
Radio World, 5827 Columbia Park Ste 310, Falls Church VA 22041..........703-998-7600
Radio-Electronics, 500-B Bi-County Blvd, Farmingdale NY 11735.............516-293-3000
Radiologic Clinics, W Washington Sq, Philadelphia PA 19105 215-547-4700
Radiologic Technology, 15000 Central Ave SE, Albuquerque NM 87123..505-298-4500
Radiology, 21700 Northwestern Hwy Tower 14, Southfield MI 48075........313-559-7844
Railfan & Railroad, Box 700, Newton NJ 07860..201-383-3355
Railroad Model Craftsman, PO Box 700, Newton NJ 07860........................201-383-3355
Railway Age, 345 Hudson St NW, New York NY 10014................................212-620-7200
Railway Track & Structures, 345 Hudson St, New York NY 10014...........212-620-7200
Rain, 1135 SE Salmon, Portland OR 97214...503-249-7218
Rainbow Magazine, 9529 US Hwy 42, Prospect KY 40059 502-228-4492
RAM, 1830 81st St #2, Brooklyn NY 11214...718-256-5008
Rambunctious Review, 1221 W Pratt Blvd, Chicago IL 60626....................312-973-3529
The Rangefinder, 1312 Lincoln Blvd, Santa Monica CA 90406 213-451-8506
Ranger Rick, 1412 16th St NW, Washington DC 20036................................703-790-4274
Raritan, 165 College Ave, New Brunswick NJ 08903.....................................201-932-7852
Rave, 40 Prince St, New York NY 10012 212-925-7560
RDH Magazine for Dental Hygiene, 225 N New Rd, Waco TX 76714.......817-776-9000
Re/Search, 20 Romolo Ste B, San Francisco CA 94133 415-362-1465
Re:Sources, 1346 Connecticut Ave NW Ste 912, Washington DC 20036 ...202-822-6800

Read America!, 3900 Glenwood Ave, Golden Valley MN 55422.................612-374-2120
Read Magazine, 245 Long Hill Rd, Middletown CT 06457.........................203-347-7251
Reader's Digest, Pleasantville NY 10570...914-769-7000
Readers Review, 424 N 3rd St, Burlington IA 52601 319-752-5415
The Reading Teacher, 800 Barksdale Rd, Newark DE 19714.....................302-731-1600
Real Estate Review, 390 Plandome Rd, Manhasset NY 11030 516-627-4810
Real Estate Today, 430 N Michigan Ave, Chicago IL 60611......................312-329-8277
Real Estate West, 909 17th St Ste 607, Denver CO 80202........................303-295-6001
Real Fun, Box 15243, Philadelphia PA 19125...215-423-3481
Real West, Charlton Bldg, Derby CT 06418 203-735-3381
Realtor Magazine, 10400 Connecticut Ave, Kensington MD 20895 202-949-4781
Realty & Building, 311 W Superior St Ste 316, Chicago IL 60610 312-944-1204
Reason, 2716 Ocean Park Blvd, Santa Monica CA 90405 213-392-0443
Rebirth of Artemis, 24 Edgewood Ter, Methuen MA 01844......................617-685-3087
Reconstructionist, 270 W 89th St, New York NY 10024 212-496-2960
Record, 745 5th Ave, New York NY 10151...212-350-1298
Record Collector's Monthly, PO Box 75, Mendham NJ 07945...................201-543-9520
Recreation News, PO Box 32335, Washington DC 20007...........................202-965-6960
Recreation Sports & Leisure, 50 S 9th St, Minneapolis MN 55402 612-333-0471
Red Bass, PO Box 10258, Tallahassee FL 32302 904-222-1328
Red Cedar Review, Mich State Univ, E Lansing MI 48824 517-355-9656
The Red Pagoda, 125 Taylor St, Jackson TN 38301.................................901-427-7714
Redbook, 224 W 57th St, New York NY 10019 212-262-8284
Redgrave Publishing Co, 380 Adams St, Bedford Hills NY 10507 914-241-7100
The Redneck Review of Literature, Rt 1 Box 1085, Fairfield ID 83327......208-764-2536
Reeves Journal, PO Box 7001, Laguna Hills CA 92654 714-830-0881
Referee, PO Box 161, Franksville WI 53126...414-632-8855
Reference Service Review, PO Box 1808, Ann Arbor MI 48106 313-434-5530
Reflect, 3306 Argonne Ave, Norfolk VA 23509.....................................804-857-1097
Reflections, Box 368, Duncan Falls OH 43734.......................................614-674-4121
The Reformed Journal, 255 Jefferson St, Grand Rapids MI 49503 616-459-4591
Refrigerated Transporter, 1602 Harold St, Houston TX 77006..................713-523-8124
Regardies Business of Wash, 1010 Wisconsin Ave, Wash DC 20007.........202-342-0410
Regulation, 1150 17th St NW, Washington DC 20036 202-862-5800
Relix Magazine, PO Box 94, Brooklyn NY 11229....................................718-258-0009
REMark, Hilltop Rd, St Jopeph MI 49085..616-982-3463
Remodeling, 655 15th St NW, Washington DC 20005..............................202-737-0717
Remodeling Contractor, 300 W Adams St, Chicago IL 60614....................312-726-2802
Remodeling World, 308 N Wolf Rd, Wheeling IL 60090...........................312-520-3322
Renegade Press, 3908 E 4th St, Long Beach CA 90814 213-433-4874
Rcnews, 707 Lakc Crook Rd, Deerfield IL 60015.....................................312-498-3180
Rental Products News, 1233 Janesville Ave, Ft Atkinson WI 53538...........414-563-6388
Representations, Univ of California Press, Berkeley CA 94720...................415-642-4191
Republic Scene, 5900 Wilshire Blvd Ste 800, Los Angeles CA 90036 213-937-5810
Research & Development, 1301 S Grove Ave, Barrington IL 60010...........312-381-1840
Research News, 241 W Engineering, Ann Arbor MI 48109 313-763-5587
Research on Aging, 275 S Beverly Dr, Beverly Hills CA 90212 213-274-8003
Resident & Staff Physician, 80 Shore Rd, Port Washington NY 11050 516-883-6350
Resolve Newsletter, 1255 23rd St NW, Washington DC 20037 202-293-4800
Resort Management, 2431 Morena Blvd, San Diego CA 92110 619-275-3666
Resource Recycling, PO Box 10540, Portland OR 97210...........................503-227-1319
Respiratory Therapy, 825 S Barrinton Ave, Los Angeles CA 90049 213-826-8388
Response, 475 Riverside Dr, New York NY 10115....................................212-870-3755

Response!, 215 S Hwy 101 PO Box 1026, Solana Beach CA 92075 619-481-1128
Restaurant & Hotel Design, 633 3rd Ave, New York NY 10017.................212-986-4800
Restaurant Business, 633 3rd Ave, New York NY 10017 212-986-4800
Restaurant Hospitality, 1111 Chester Ave, Cleveland OH 44114...............216-696-7000
Restaurant Management, 7500 Old Oak Blvd, Cleveland OH 44130.........216-243-8100
Restaurants & Institutions, 1350 E Touhy, Des Plaines IL 60018 312-635-8800
Restaurants USA, 311 1st St NW, Washington DC 20001 202-638-6100
Restoration, PO Box 50046, Tucson AZ 85703.................................602-622-2201
Retailer & Marketing News, PO Box 191105, Dallas TX 75219.................214-871-2930
Retailer News, 249 E Emerson, Orange CA 92665..............................714-921-0600
The Retired Officer, 201 N Washington St, Alexandria VA 22314..............703-549-2311
Retirement Life, 1531 New Hampshire Ave NW, Washington DC 20036..202-232-4000
Review, 1338 Military St PO Box 5020, Port Huron MI 48061.................313-985-5191
Review for Religious, 3601 Lindell Blvd Rm 428, St Louis MO 63108 314-535-3048
Review of Infectious Diseases, 5801 S Ellis Ave, Chicago IL 60637...........312-962-7700
Review of Intl Broadcasting, PO Box 49756, Ft Lauderdale FL 33349 305-731-4016
Review of Optometry, 201 King of Prussia Rd, Radnor PA 19089 215-964-4000
Review of the Graphic Arts, 2401 Charleston Rd, Mtn View CA 94043 415-962-8976
ReVision Journal, PO Box 316, Cambridge MA 02238 617-354-5827
RFD, Rt 1 Box 127E, Bakersville NC 28705 704-688-4791
RFDA, Rt 1 Box 127E, Bakersville NC 28705 704-688-2447
Rhino, 3915 Foster St, Evanston IL 60203 312-675-6814
Rhode Island Woman, 942 Park Ave, Cranston RI 02910.....................401-461-1830
Rider, 29901 Agoura Rd, Agoura CA 91301 818-991-4980
Ridge Review, Box 90, Mendocino CA 95460................................707-937-1188
Rifle, 138 N Montezuma St, Prescott AZ 86302...............................602-445-7810
Right of Way, 9920 La Cienega Blvd Ste 515, Inglewood CA 90301...........213-649-5323
Right On!, 105 Union Ave, Cresskill NJ 07626 201-569-5055
Righting Words, PO Box 6811 FDR Sta, New York NY 10150 718-761-0235
Rights, 175 5th Ave, New York NY 10010....................................212-673-2040
Rio Grande Writers Quar, PO Box 25543, Albuquerque NM 87125 505-247-8736
Ripon College Magazine, PO Box 248, Ripon WI 54971.......................414-748-8115
Ripon Forum, 6 Library Ct SE, Washington DC 20003.........................202-546-1292
Rising Star, 47 Byledge Rd, Manchester NH 03104 603-623-9796
Risk & Benefits Management, 1640 5th St, Santa Monica CA 90401.........213-395-0234
Risk Insurance Mgmt Soc, 205 E 42nd St 15th fl, New York NY 10017....212-286-9292
River Rat Review, PO Box 24198, Lexington KY 40524 606-277-8601
River Runner, PO Box 697, Fallbrook CA 92028 619-723-8155
River Styx, 14 S Euclid, St Louis MO 63108.................................314-361-0043
Riverrun, 62249 Shimmel Rd, Centreville MI 49032...........................616-467-9945
Riverside Quarterly, PO Box 833-044, Richardson TX 75083 214-231-9024
Riverwind, Hocking Technical College, Nelsonville OH 45764................614-753-3591
RN, 680 Kinderkamack Rd, Oradell NJ 07649 201-262-3030
Road & Track, 1499 Monrovia Ave, Newport Beach CA 92663................714-720-5300
Road King Magazine, PO Box 250, Park Forest IL 60466 312-481-9240
Road Rider Magazine, PO Box 6050, Mission Viejo CA 92690 714-240-6001
Roads Magazine, 380 Northwest Hwy, Des Plaines IL 60616.....................312-298-6622
Roadwerk, 110 Masonic #5, San Francisco CA 94117.........................415-558-8316
The Roanoke Review, Roanoke College English Dept, Salem VA 24153 ..703-375-2367
The Roanoker, 3424 Brambleton Ave, Roanoke VA 24026 703-989-6138
The Robb Report, 1 Acton Pl, Acton MA 01720...............................617-263-7749
Roberts Publishing Corp, 45 John St, New York NY 10038.....................212-233-3768
Robotics World, 6255 Barfield Rd, Atlanta GA 30328 404-256-9800

Rock & Soul, 441 Lexington Ave, New York NY 10017 212-370-0986
Rock Magazine, 1112 N LaCienega Blvd, Los Angeles CA 90069 213-659-7567
Rock Products, 300 W Adams, Chicago IL 60606 312-726-2802
RockBill, 850 7th Ave, New York NY 10019 212-977-7745
The Rocket, 5951 Canning St, Oakland CA 94609.................................415-652-3810
The Rockford Review, PO Box 858, Rockford IL 61105 815-399-9595
Rocky Mountain Construction, 2203 Champa St, Denver CO 80205.........303-295-0630
Rocky Mountain Motorist, 4100 E Arkansas Ave, Denver CO 80222 303-753-8800
Rod Serling's Twilight Zone, 800 2nd Ave, New York NY 10017 212-986-9600
Rodeo News, Box 587, Pauls Valley OK 73075......................................405-238-3310
Rolling Stone, 745 5th Ave, New York NY 10151 212-758-3800
The Romantist, 3610 Meadowbrook Ave, Nashville TN 37205 615-292-9695
Roof Design, 7500 Old Oak Blvd, Cleveland OH 44130 216-243-8100
Roofer, PO Box 06253, Ft Myers FL 33906 813-275-7663
Rose Sheet FDC Report, 5550 Friendship, Chevy Chase MD 20815 301-657-9830
Rosicrucian Digest, Rosicrucian Park, San Jose CA 95191 408-287-9171
Ross Reports Television, 40-29 27th St, Long Island City NY 11101..........718-937-3990
The Rotarian, 1600 Ridge Ave, Evanston IL 60211................................312-328-0100
Rotary Rocket, 4020 Palos Verdes #108, Rolling Hls Est CA 90274 213-544-0822
Rotor & Wing Intl, PO Box 1790 News Plaza, Peoria IL 61656 309-682-6626
Rotzinger Enterprises Inc, 2000 11th St, Rock Island IL 61201 309-786-5370
RQ, 50 E Huron St, Chicago IL 60611 312-944-6780
RSC, PO Box 7021, Troy MI 48007 313-362-3700
RSI: Roofing/Siding/Insulation, 545 5th Ave, New York NY 10017 212-503-2927
RSVP Magazine of Good Living, 828 Fort St Mall, Honolulu HI 96813....808-523-9871
Rubber & Plastics News, 34 N Hawkins Ave, Akron OH 44313 216-836-9180
Rubberstampmadness, Box 168, Newfield NY 14867...............................607-564-7673
RUN, 80 Pine St, Peterborough NH 03458 603-924-7138
Runaway, Box 610, Alta Loma CA 91701 800-824-7888
Runner's World, PO Box 366, Mountain View CA 94042..........................415-965-8777
The Runner, 1 Park Ave, New York NY 10016 212-503-4244
Running Times, 14416 Jefferson Davis Hwy, Woodbridge VA 22191........703-491-2044
Rural Georgia, 148 International Blvd Ste 845, Atlanta GA 30043..............404-659-3430
Rural Heritage, 29 & College Box 7, Cedar Falls IA 50613......................319-277-3475
Rural Kentuckian, 4515 Bishop Lane, Louisville KY 40232 502-451-2430
Rural Living, 5061 Chamberlayne Ave, Richmond VA 23227.....................804-264-2801
Ruralite, Box 558, Forest Grove OR 97116...503-357-2105
RV Business, 29901 Agoura Rd, Agoura CA 91301 818-991-4980
Rx Being Well, 800 2nd Ave, New York NY 10017 212-599-3400
Rx Home Care, 1640 5th St, Santa Monica CA 90401.............................213-395-0234
Sacramento Magazine, PO Box 2424, Sacramento CA 95811 916-446-7548
Saddle & Bridle, 375 N Jackson Ave, St Louis MO 63130 314-725-9115
Safari, 5151 E Broadway, Tucson AZ 85711 602-747-0260
Safety Compliance, 24 Rope Ferry Rd, Waterford CT 06386.....................203-442-4365
Sagetrieb, 302 Neville Hall Univ of Maine, Orono ME 04469.....................207-581-3814
Sail, 100 1st Ave, Charleston MA 02129 617-241-9500
Sailboard News, 2 S Park Pl PO Box 159, Fair Haven VT 05743................802-265-8153
Sailing, 125 E Main St, Port Washington WI 53074................................414-284-3494
Sailing World, 111 East Ave, Norwalk CT 06851 215-238-5300
Sailor, 25 Van Zant, East Norwalk CT 06855 203-866-8598
Sailors' Gazette, 337 22nd Ave N Ste 110, St Petersburg FL 33704 813-823-9172
Saint Andrews Review, Saint Andrews College, Laurinburg NC 28352......919-276-3652
Sales & Marketing Management, 633 3rd Ave, New York NY 10017 212-986-4800

Sales Manager's Bulletin, 24 Rope Ferry Rd, Waterford CT 06386...........203-442-4365
Salmagundi, Skidmore College, Saratoga Springs NY 12866......................518-584-5000
Salt Water Sportsman, 186 Lincoln St, Boston MA 02111 617-426-4074
SAM Advanced Mgmt Jour, 2331 Victory Pkwy, Cincinnati OH 45206.....513-751-4566
Samisdat, Box 129, Richford VT 05476 514-263-4439
The Sample Case, 632 N Park St, Columbus OH 43215...............................614-228-3276
San Angelo Magazine, 34 W Harris, San Angelo TX 76903 915-653-1221
San Antonio Homes & Garden, 900 West Ave, Austin TX 78701................512-479-8936
San Antonio Monthly, PO Box 17554, San Antonio TX 78217....................512-829-9200
San Antonio Today, 1911 Radium, San Antonio TX 78216 512-349-1281
San Diego Business Jour, 3444 Camino del Rio, San Diego CA 92108.....619-283-2271
San Diego Home/Garden, 655 4th Ave, San Diego CA 92101 714-233-4567
San Diego Magazine, PO Box 85409, San Diego CA 92138.........................619-225-8953
San Diego Woman, 2171 India St Ste H, San Diego CA 92101 619-234-3644
San Francisco Focus, 680 8th St, San Francisco CA 94103........................415-553-2800
San Francisco Review of Books, 1117 Geary, San Francisco CA 94109.....415-771-1252
The San Francisco Sports Review, PO Box 4520, Berkeley CA 94704.......415-845-2062
Sandcript, Box 333, Cunnaquid MA 02637 617-362-6078
Sanitary Maintenance, 2100 W Florist Ave, Milwaukee WI 53209.............414-228-7701
Sasquatch Publishing Co, 1931 2nd Ave, Seattle WA 98101 206-441-5555
Sat Guide Cable's Satellite Magazine, 418 N River, Hailey ID 83333........208-788-9531
Satellite Business, PO Box 2772, Palm Springs CA 92263 619-323-2000
Satellite Cmmunications, 6500 S Syracuse Way, Englewood CO 80220....303-220-0600
Satellite Direct, PO Box 53, Boise ID 83707 208-322-2800
Satellite Dish Magazine, PO Box 8, Memphis TN 38101............................901-521-1580
Satellite Orbit, PO Box 53, Boise ID 83707 208-322-2800
Satellite World, PO Box 53, Boise ID 83707 208-322-2800
The Saturday Evening Post, 1100 Waterway, Indianapolis IN 46202 317-636-8881
Saturday Review, 214 Massachusetts Ave NW #460, Wash DC 20002......202-547-1106
Savings Institutions, 111 E Wacker Dr, Chicago IL 60601.........................312-644-3100
Savvy Magazine, 3 Park Ave, New York NY 10016 212-340-9200
Scandinavian Review, 127 E 73rd St, New York NY 10021.........................212-879-9779
Scavenger's Newsletter, 519 Ellinwood, Osage City KS 66523....................913-528-3538
Scholastic Inc, 730 Broadway, New York NY 10003....................................212-505-3000
Scholastic Scope, 730 Broadway, New York NY 10003................................212-505-3000
Scholastic Update, 730 Broadway, New York NY 10003 212-505-3000
School Arts Magazine, 50 Portland St, Worcester MA 01608 617-754-7201
School Bus Fleet, 2500 Artesia Blvd, Redondo Beach CA 90278................213-376-8788
School Business Affairs, 1760 Reston Ave Ste 411, Reston VA 22090 703-478-0405
School Food Service Journal, 4101 E Iliff Ave, Denver CO 80222.............303-757-8555
School Library Journal, 249 W 17th St, New York NY 10011 212-645-0067
School Musician Dir/Teacher, 4049 W Peterson, Chicago IL 60649 312-463-3400
School Product News, 1111 Chester Ave, Cleveland OH 44114....................216-696-7000
School Science & Math Assn, BGSU, Bowling Green OH 43403 419-372-7393
School Shop, 416 Longshore Dr PO Box 8623, Ann Arbor MI 48107........313-769-1211
Science & Children, 1742 Connecticut Ave NW, Washington DC 20009....202-328-5800
Science & Society, 445 W 59th St Rm 4331, New York NY 10019..............212-775-3556
Science Challenge, 3500 Western Ave, Highland Park IL 60035.................312-432-2700
Science Fiction Chronicle, PO Box 4175, New York NY 10163.................718-643-9011
Science News, 1719 N St NW, Washington DC 20036..................................202-785-2255
The Science Teacher, 1742 Connecticut Ave NW, Wash DC 20009...........202-328-5800
Science World, 730 Broadway, New York NY 10003....................................212-505-3000
The Sciences, 2 E 63rd St, New York NY 10021...212-838-0230

Scientific American, 415 Madison Ave, New York NY 10017 212-754-0550
Scientific Computing & Automation, PO Box 1952, Dover NJ 07801........201-361-9060
Scope, 426 S 5th St, Minneapolis MN 55440..612-330-3413
Score, 491 Mandana Blvd #3, Oakland CA 94610 415-268-9284
Scorecard, 9509 US Hwy 42 PO Box 385, Prospect KY 40059 502-228-4492
Scott Stamp Monthly, 911 Vandermark PO Box 828, Sidney OH 45365...513-498-2111
Scouting, 1325 Walnut Hill Ln, Irving TX 75038 214-580-2355
SCP Newsletter, PO Box 4308, Berkeley CA 94707 415-540-0300
Scree, Box 1047, Fallon NV 89406 702-423-6643
Screen Printing, 407 Gilbert Ave, Cincinnati OH 45202 513-421-2050
Scripts & Concepts, 548 NE 43rd Ave, Portland OR 97213 503-239-5141
Scuba Times, PO Box 6268, Pensacola FL 32503 904-478-5288
Sculpture Review, 15 E 26th St, New York NY 10010 212-889-6960
Sea Frontiers, 3979 Rickenbacker Causeway, Miami FL 33149 305-361-5786
Sea Heritage News, 254-26 75th Ave, Glen Oaks NY 11004 212-343-9575
Sea History, 132 Maple St, Croton-on-Hudson NY 10520 914-271-2177
Sea Magazine, PO Box 1337, Newport Beach CA 92664.............................213-854-2222
Sea of Amythest, Box 410, Chatham MA 02633...617-896-5613
Sea Power, 2300 Wilson Blvd, Arlington VA 22201....................................703-528-1775
Sea Technology, 1117 N 19 St, Arlington VA 22209....................................703-524-3136
Seacoast Life, 220 Lafayette Rd PO Box 594, N Hampton NH 03862........603-964-9898
Seafood Leader, 1115 NW 45th St, Seattle WA 98107................................206-789-6506
The Search, Box 543, Crattleboro VT 05301 802-257-0872
Seatrade Week, 40 Rector St Ste 1805, New York NY 10006 212-422-6470
Seattle's Child, PO Box 22578, Seattle WA 98122.....................................206-322-2594
Seaway Review, 221 Water St, Boyne City MI 49712...................................616-582-2814
Second Coming Inc, PO Box 31249, San Francisco CA 94131....................415-647-3679
Secondary Mortgage Markets, PO Box 37348, Washington DC 20013......202-789-4700
Secretary Magazine, 301 E Armour Ste 200, Kansas City MO 64111 816-531-7010
Secrets, 215 Lexington Ave, New York NY 10016..212-340-7500
Securities Traders Monthly, 150 Broadway, New York NY 10038..............212-227-1200
Security Distrib & Mktg, 1350 E Touhy, Des Plaines IL 60018 312-635-8800
Security Management, 1655 N Ft Myer Dr, Arlington VA 22209................800-368-5685
Security Management, 24 Rope Ferry Rd, Waterford CT 06386 203-442-4365
Security World, 1350 E Touhy Dr, Des Plaines IL 60018............................312-635-8800
Seed Savers Exchange, Box 70, Decorah IA 52101 319-382-3949
Seek, 8121 Hamilton Ave, Cincinnati OH 45231..513-931-4050
The Seeker Magazine, PO Box 7601, San Diego CA 92107 619-225-0133
Selected Reading, 424 N 3rd St, Burlington IA 52601................................319-752-5415
Self, 350 Madison Ave, New York NY 10017..212-880-8834
Self-Help Update, Box 38, Malibu CA 90265 213-457-1547
Self-Improvement Journal, Box 564, Mableton GA 30059 404-944-0917
Selling Direct, 6255 Barfield Rd, Atlanta GA 30328..................................404-256-9800
Semaphore Signal, 207 Granada Dr, Aptos CA 95003 408-685-9200
Semiconductor Intl, 1350 E Touhy Ave, Des Plaines IL 60018 312-635-8800
Semiotext(E), Columbia Univ Philosophy Hall, New York NY 10027 212-280-3956
Seneca Review, Hobart & William Smith Colleges, Geneva NY 14456......315-789-5500
Senior, 3565 S Higuera St, San Luis Obispo CA 93401...............................805-544-8711
Senior American News, 470 Boston Post Rd, Weston MA 02193 617-899-2702
Senior Citizen World, 1020 Broad St, Newark NJ 07102............................201-642-3149
Senior Citizens Today, 1930 Alhambra Blvd, Sacramento CA 95816.........916-451-7265
Senior Edition, 1660 Lincoln, Denver CO 80264..303-837-9100
Senior Times, 12 S 1st St, San Jose CA 95113..408-289-9604

Senior Voice, 6541 44th St, Pinellas Park FL 33565................813-521-4026
The $ensible Sound, 403 Darwin Dr, Snyder NY 14226................716-839-4590
Sensors, 174 Concord St, Peterborough NH 03458................603-924-9631
Serials Review, PO Box 1808, Ann Arbor MI 48106................313-434-5530
The Sertoman, 1912 E Meyer Blvd, Kansas City MO 64132................816-333-8300
Service Business, 1916 Pike Pl, Seattle WA 98101................206-622-4241
Service Reporter, 1098 S Milwaukee Ave, Wheeling IL 60090................312-537-6460
Sesame Street, 1 Lincoln Plaza, New York NY 10023................212-595-3456
The Sesquipedalian, 5007 Woodland Way, Annandale VA 22003................405-528-7598
Seven Lifestyle/Caesars, 1801 Century Park E, Los Angeles CA 90067....213-552-2711
Seventeen Magazine, 850 3rd Ave, New York NY 10022................212-759-8100
73 Magazine for Radio Amateurs, 80 Pine St, Peterborough NH 03458 ...603-525-4201
Sew Business, 1515 Broadway, New York NY 10036................212-869-1300
Sew News, PO Box 1790, Peoria IL 61656................309-682-6626
Sewanee Review, Univ of the South, Sewanee TN 37375................615-598-1246
Sextant, 716 E St SE, Washington DC 20003................202-544-0900
Sexual Medicine Today, 257 Park Ave S, New York NY 10010................212-674-8500
Sexuality Today, 2315 Broadway, New York NY 10024................212-873-5900
Sez/A Multi-Racial Journal, PO Box 8803, Minneapolis MN 55408................612-822-3488
The Shakespeare Newsletter, 1217 Ashland Ave, Evanston IL 60202................312-475-7550
Shape, 21100 Erwin St, Woodland Hills CA 91367................818-715-0600
Sharing, Box 1470, Yuma AZ 85364................602-782-9511
Sharing Ideas, PO Box 1120, Glendora CA 91740................818-335-8069
Sharing the Victory, 8701 Leed Rd, Kansas City MO 64129................816-921-0909
Shaw, 234 Burrowes Bldg Univ of Penn, University Park PA 16802................814-865-4242
Sheep! Magazine, Rt 1 Box 78, Helenville WI 53137................414-674-3029
Sheet Music Magazine, 223 Katonah Ave, Katonah NY 10536................914-232-8108
Shenandoah, Box 722, Lexington VA 24450................703-463-8765
Shipmate, Alumni House USNA, Annapolis MD 21402................301-263-4469
Shipping Digest, 51 Madison Ave, New York NY 10010................212-689-4411
Shoe Service, 112 Calendar Ct Mall, La Grange IL 60525................312-482-8010
Shoe Tree, Box 452, Belvidere NJ 07823................201-475-4819
Shooting Industry, 591 Camino de la Reina #200, San Diego CA 92108..619-297-5350
Shooting Star Review, 7123 Race St, Pittsburgh PA 15208................412-731-7039
Shooting Times, PO Box 1790 News Plaza, Peoria IL 61656................309-682-6626
Shopping Center World, 6255 Barfield Rd, Atlanta GA 30328................404-256-9800
Short Story Intl, 6 Sheffield Rd, Great Neck NY 11021................516-466-4166
Shotgun Sports, PO Box 340, Lake Havasu City AZ 86403................602-855-0100
Show Business, 1501 Broadway, New York NY 10036................212-354-7600
Showboat, 213 Broadway Ste 5, San Antonio TX 78205................512-227-4262
Shutterbug Ads/Photo News, 407 S Washington, Titusville FL 32780................305-269-3211
Shuttle Spindle & Dyepot, 65 La Salle Rd, West Hartford CT 06107................203-233-5124
Sibyl-Child, Box 1773, Hyattsville MD 20788................301-362-1404
Sierra, 730 Polk St, San Francisco CA 94109................415-923-5656
Sierra View, 22450 Dekalb Dr, Woodland Hills CA 91364................818-347-7998
Sight & Sound Marketing, 51 E 42nd St, New York NY 10017................212-867-2270
Sightlines, 45 John St, New York NY 10038................212-227-5599
Sightsaving, 79 Madison Ave, New York NY 10016................212-684-3505
Sign Of The Times, PO Box 70672, Seattle WA 98107................206-784-8999
The Sign Writer Newspaper, PO Box 7344, Newport Beach CA 92658................714-644-8342
Signature Magazine, 641 Lexington Ave 2nd fl, New York NY 10022................212-888-9450
Signcraft, 1939 Grove Ave PO Box 06031, Ft Myers FL 33906................813-939-4644
Signpost Magazine, 1305 4th Ave #518, Seattle WA 98101................206-625-1367

Signs, 105 East Duke Building, Durham NC 27708 919-497-0970
Signs of the Times, PO Box 7000, Boise ID 83707 208-465-2500
Signs of the Times, 407 Gilbert Ave, Cincinnati OH 45202 513-421-2050
Signs: Jour of Women in Culture, Duke Univ, Durham NC 27701...........919-684-2783
Silent Advocate, 1720 Glendale-Milford Rd, Cincinnati OH 45215...........513-771-7600
Silver Wings, PO Box 5201, Mission Hills CA 91345................................818-893-2889
Silverfish Review, PO Box 3541, Eugene OR 97403 503-342-2344
Sing Heavenly Muse!, PO Box 13299, Minneapolis MN 55414 612-822-8713
Sing Out!, PO Box 1071, Easton PA 18044 215-253-8105
Singer Press, 1540 Rollins Dr, Los Angeles CA 90063...........................213-263-2640
The Singing News, 2611 W Cervantes St, Pensacola FL 32523...................904-434-2773
Single Impact, 7245 College St, Lima NY 14485 716-582-2790
The Single Parent, 8807 Colesville Rd, Silver Spring MD 20910..................301-588-9354
SingleLife Magazine, 606 W Wisconsin Ave, Milwaukee WI 53203 414-271-9700
Sinsemilla Tips, 217 SW 2nd St PO Box 2046, Corvallis OR 97339...........503-757-8477
16 Magazine, 157 W 57th St, New York NY 10019 212-489-7220
68000! Computing, Box 390, Martinez CA 94553...................................415-228-6228
Sipapu, Box 216, Winters CA 95694...916-662-3364
Skating Magazine, 20 1st St, Colorado Springs CO 80906 303-635-5200
Ski Business, 537 Post Rd, Darien CT 06850...203-655-3216
Ski Magazine, 380 Madison Ave, New York NY 10017..............................212-687-3000
Ski Racing, 2 Bentley Ave, Poultney VT 05764..802-287-9090
Skies Amer Publishing, 9600 SW Oak St, Portland OR 97223....................503-244-2299
Skiing, 1 Park Ave, New York NY 10016 212-503-3920
Skiing Trade News, 1 Park Ave, New York NY 10016 212-503-3900
Skin & Allergy News, 770 Lexington Ave, New York NY 10022.................212-421-0707
Skin Diver, 8490 Sunset Blvd, Los Angeles CA 90069 213-854-2960
Sky & Telescope, 49 Bay State Rd, Cambridge MA 02238..........................617-864-7360
Skydiving, PO Box 1520, Deland FL 32721 904-736-9779
Skylark, 2233 171st St Purdue Univ Calumet, Hammond IN 46323.............219-844-0520
Skylines, 1250 I St NW, Washington DC 20005 202-289-7000
Skylite, 12955 Biscayne Blvd, North Miami FL 33181..............................305-893-1520
Slimmer, 801 2nd Ave, New York NY 10017 212-986-5100
Slipstream, PO Box 2071 New Market Sta, Niagara Falls NY 14301...........716-282-2616
Sloan Management Review, 50 Memorial Dr, Cambridge MA 02139........617-253-7170
Slow Mountain, Box 8 West View Sta, Binghamton NY 13905....................607-798-9893
Small Boat Journal, PO Box 1066, Bennington VT 05201..........................802-442-3101
Small Businesswoman's Newsletter, PO Box 66, Mt Dora FL 32757...........904-343-8282
Small Pond Magazine of Literature, Box 664, Stratford CT 06497 203-378-4066
Small Press, 11 Ferry Lane West, Westport CT 06880................................203-226-6967
The Small Press Book Review, PO Box 176, Southport CT 06490...............203-268-4878
Small Press Review, Box 100, Paradise CA 95969....................................916-877-6110
Small World, 225 W 34th St #1212, New York NY 10001...........................212-563-2742
The Small-Towner, Box 182, Glen Arbor MI 49636...................................616-334-4968
Smithsonian, 900 Jefferson Dr, Washington DC 20560..............................202-381-6195
SMPTE Journal, 862 Scarsdale Ave, Scarsdale NY 10583...........................914-472-6606
Snack Food, 131 W 1st St, Duluth MN 55802 218-723-9343
Snips, 407 Mannheim Rd, Bellwood IL 60104 312-544-3870
Snow Week, 11812 Wayzata Blvd Ste 100, Minnetonka MN 55343...........612-545-2662
Snowmobile, 11812 Wayzata Blvd Ste 100, Minnetonka MN 55343...........612-545-2662
Snowmobile West, 520 Park Ave PO Box 981, Idaho Falls ID 83402 208-522-5187
Snowy Egret, 205 S 9th St, Williamsburg KY 40769 606-549-0850
Soap Opera Digest, 254 W 31st St, New York NY 10001............................212-947-6300

Soap Opera World, 1 World Trade Ctr, New York NY 10048....................212-608-3459
Soap/Cosmetics/Chemical Spec, 101 W 31st St, New York NY 10001.....212-279-4456
Soccer America, PO Box 23704, Oakland CA 94623....................................415-549-1414
Soccer Digest, 1020 Church St, Evanston IL 60201....................................312-491-6440
Social Anarchism, 2743 Maryland Ave, Baltimore MD 21218.....................301-243-6987
Social Education, 3501 Newark St, Washington DC 20016..........................202-966-7840
Social Forces, UNC 168 Hamilton Hall 070A, Chapel Hill NC 27514......919-962-5502
Social Justice Review, 3835 Westminster Pl, St Louis MO 63108..............314-371-1653
Social Order Series, 7899 St Helena Rd, Santa Rosa CA 95404.................707-539-0569
Social Policy, 33 W 42nd St Rm 620N, New York NY 10036......................212-840-7619
Social Theory, 511 Lincoln St, Santa Cruz CA 95060...................................408-426-4479
Social Work, 257 Park Ave S, New York NY 10010......................................212-460-9400
Society/Transaction, Rutgers Univ, New Brunswick NJ 08903.................201-932-2280
SOF's Combat Weapons, 5735 E Arapahoe Ave, Boulder CO 80303........303-449-3750
Soft Sector, 9529 US Hwy 42, Prospect KY 40059......................................502-228-4492
Software, 2803 Ocean Park Blvd Ste K, Santa Monica CA 90405.............213-450-6646
Software Developer's Monthly, PO Box 390, Martinez CA 94553.............415-228-6228
Software Digest, 1 Winding Dr, Philadelphia PA 19131.............................215-878-9300
Software in Healthcare, 323 Richmond St, El Segundo CA 90245............213-322-5434
Software Merchandising, 15720 Ventura Blvd #222, Encino CA 91436....818-995-0436
Software News, 5 Kane Industrial Dr, Hudson MA 01749..........................617-562-9808
Sojourner, 143 Albany St, Cambridge MA 02139.......................................617-661-3567
Sojourners, PO Box 29272, Washington DC 20017......................................202-636-3637
Solar Age Magazine, Church Hill, Harrisville NH 03450............................603-827-3347
Solar Engineering & Contracting, 755 W Big Beaver, Troy MI 48084......313-362-3700
Soldier of Fortune, PO Box 693, Boulder CO 80306...................................303-499-3750
Solid State Technology, 14 Vanderventer, Port Washington NY 11050.....516-883-6200
Solidarity, 1 Old Country Rd Drawer 74, Carle Place NY 11514...............516-742-0600
Soloing for Christian Singles, PO Box 15523, W Palm Beach FL 33416...305-967-7739
Solution Journal, 11 Greenfield Ave, Stratford CT 06497..........................203-377-7954
Solutions (Unisys), PO Box 1804, West Chester PA 19382..........................215-542-4011
Song, 1333 Illinois Ave, Stevens Point WI 54481..715-344-6836
Song Hits Magazine, Charlton Bldg Division St, Derby CT 06418.............203-735-3381
Sonoma Mandala, Sonoma State Univ, Rohnert Park CA 94928................707-664-2140
Sonora Review, Univ of Ariz English Dept, Tucson AZ 85721...................602-621-1387
The Sons of Norway Viking, 1455 W Lake St, Minnepolis MN 55408........612-827-3611
Sooner LPG Times, 2910 N Walnut, Oklahoma City OK 73105...................405-525-9386
Sound & Video Contractor, PO Box 12901, Overland Park KS 66212.......913-888-4664
Sound & Vibration, 27101 E Oviatt Rd, Bay Village OH 44140..................216-835-0101
Sound Choice, Box 1251, Ojai CA 93023...805-646-6814
Sound Management, 304 Park Ave S, New York NY 10010..........................212-254-4800
Soundings, Pratt St, Essex CT 06426..203-767-0906
Soundings East, Salem State College, Salem MA 01970...............................617-741-6000
The Sounds of Poetry, 2076 Vinewood, Detroit MI 48216..........................313-841-9742
Source, 200 Smith St, Waltham MA 02154..617-895-6000
Source View, 835 Castro St Box 390, Martinez CA 94553...........................415-228-6228
South American Explorer, 1510 York St, Denver CO 80206.......................303-320-0388
South Carolina Review, Clemson Univ, Clemson SC 29631........................803-656-3229
South Coast Poetry Jour, CSUF English Dept, Fullerton CA 92634.........714-773-2454
South Dakota Review, Box 111 Univ Exchange, Vermillion SD 57069......605-677-5229
South Florida Home & Garden, 75 SW 15th Rd, Miami FL 33129.............305-374-5011
South Florida Poetry Review, PO Box 5945, Ft Lauderdale FL 33310.......305-742-5624
South Texas Housing Guide, 4242 Medical Dr, San Antonio TX 78229....512-691-2923

Southeastern FRONT, 565 17th St NW, Cleveland TN 37311.....................615-479-3244
Southern Accents, 1760 Peachtree Rd, Atlanta GA 30357...........................404-874-4462
Southern Agitator, PO Box 52467, New Orleans LA 70152........................504-943-7041
The Southern Banker, 6195 Crook Creek Rd, Norcross GA 30092.............404-448-1011
Southern Beverage Journal, PO Box 561107, Miami FL 33256 305-233-7230
The Southern California Anthology, USC, Los Angeles CA 90089............213-743-8255
Southern Coalition Jails/Prisons, PO Box 12044, Nashville TN 37212.....615-383-9610
Southern Exposure, PO Box 531, Durham NC 27702 919-688-8167
Southern Golf, Northwood Plz Sta, Clearwater FL 33519.............................813-796-3877
Southern Humanities Review, Auburn Univ, Auburn AL 36849 205-826-4606
Southern Lifestyle, PO Box 10932, Raleigh NC 27605 919-832-3059
Southern Living, 820 Shades Creek Pkwy, Birmingham AL 35201..............205-877-6000
Southern Lumberman, 128 Holiday Ct, Franklin TN 37064..........................615-791-1961
Southern Magazine, 201 E Markham, Little Rock AR 72201 501-375-4114
Southern Medical Jour, 35 Lakeshore Dr, Birmingham AL 35219 205-945-1840
Southern Outdoors, 1 Bell Rd, Montgomery AL 36141................................205-272-9530
Southern Pharmacy Jour, 3030 Peachtree Rd NW, Atlanta GA 30305 404-231-1267
Southern Poetry Review, UNCC English Dept, Charlotte NC 28223.........704-597-4225
Southern Pulp & Paper, 75 3rd St NW, Atlanta GA 30365 404-881-6442
Southern Quarterly, Box 5078 USM, Hattiesburg MS 39406......................601-266-4370
The Southern Review, LSU 43 Allen Hall, Baton Rouge LA 70803 504-388-5108
Southern Supermarketing, 820 Shades Creek, Birmingham AL 35209 205-877-6306
Southern Travel, 5520 Park Ave PO Box 395, Trumbull CT 06611.............203-373-7000
Southwest Art, 9 Greenway Plaza Ste 2010, Houston TX 77046 713-850-0990
Southwest Banker/Texas Banker, 320 N Glenwood, Tyler TX 75702 214-595-5304
Southwest Floor Covering, PO Box 810195, Dallas TX 75381 214-484-4474
Southwest Hotel-Motel Review, 8602 Crownhill, San Antonio TX 78209 ..512-828-3566
Southwest Real Estate News, 18601 LBJ Fwy, Mesquite TX 75150............214-270-6651
Southwest Review, 6410 Airline Rd, Dallas TX 75275 214-373-7440
Southwest Spirit, 5900 Wilshire Blvd, Los Angeles CA 90036 213-937-5810
Souvenirs & Novelties, 401 N Broad St #226, Phila PA 19108 215-925-9744
Soviet Economy, 7961 Eastern Ave, Silver Spring MD 20910.....................301-587-3356
Soviet Life, 1706 18th St NW, Washington DC 20009.................................202-328-3224
SOW, Keith at 25th St NW, Cleveland TN 37311 615-476-5197
Soybean Digest, 777 Craig Rd PO Box 41309, St Louis MO 63141.............314-432-1600
Soyfoods, PO Box 511, Encinitas CA 92024 619-753-5979
Space & Time, 138 W 70th St 4B, New York NY 10023...............................212-595-0894
Space For All People, 1724 Sacramento St #9, San Francisco CA 94109 ..415-673-1079
The Space Press, 645 West End Ave, New York NY 10025............................212-724-5919
Space World, 600 Maryland Ave SW, Washington DC 20024 202-484-1111
Speaker Builder, Box 494, Peterborough NH 03458....................................603-924-9464
Spec-Data/Manu-Spec System, 601 Madison, Alexandria VA 22314 703-684-0300
Special Care in Dentistry, 211 E Chicago Ave, Chicago IL 60611..............312-440-2774
Special Interest Autos, PO Box 196, Bennington VT 05201 802-442-3101
Special Libraries, 235 Park Ave S, New York NY 10003..............................212-477-9250
Specialty Automotive, 7637 Fulton Ave, North Hollywood CA 91605........818-764-0611
Specialty Travel Index, 9 Mono Ave, Fairfax CA 94930...............................415-459-4900
Specifying Engineer, 1350 E Touhy Ave, Des Plaines IL 60018 312-635-8800
Spector Magazine of the Triad, 211 N Greene, Greensboro NC 27401.....919-272-7379
Spectrum Magazine, 345 E 47th St, New York NY 10017 212-705-7555
Speculum, Medieval Acad 1430 Mass Ave, Cambridge MA 02138.............617-491-1622
Speedhorse, PO Box 1000, Norman OK 73070...405-288-2391
SPIE Optical Engineering Rep, 1022 19th St, Bellingham WA 98225........206-676-3290

Spin-Off, 306 N Washington Ave, Loveland CO 80537 303-669-7672
Spine, E Washington Sq, Philadelphia PA 19105...................................215-238-4200
Spirit, PO Box 1231, Sisters OR 97759 503-549-0443
Spirit of Aloha, 36 Merchant St, Honolulu HI 96813..............................808-524-7400
Spirits Wine & Beer Mktg, 4504 Excelsior, Minneapolis MN 55416..........612-920-7711
Spiritual Life, 2131 Lincoln Rd NE, Washington DC 20002 202-832-6622
Spitball, 6224 Collegevue, Cincinnati OH 45224.................................606-261-3024
Splash, 561 Broadway #4B, New York NY 10012 212-966-3218
Spoon River Quarterly, Box 1443, Peoria IL 61655 507-537-6463
Sport Aviation, Wittman Airfield, Oshkosh WI 54903.............................414-426-4800
Sport Fishing, 809 S Orlando Ave PO Box 2456, Winter Park FL 32790 ..305-628-4802
Sport Flyer, PO Box 98786, Tacoma WA 98498...................................206-588-1743
Sport Magazine, 119 W 40th St, New York NY 10018 212-869-4700
Sporting Classics, Hwy 521 S PO Box 1017, Camden SC 29020...................803-425-1003
Sporting Goods Business, 1515 Broadway, New York NY 10036................212-869-1300
The Sporting Goods Dealer, 1212 N Lindbergh, St Louis MO 63132.........314-997-7111
Sports & Recreation, 9100 Cottonwood Land, Osseo MN 55369 612-545-9182
Sports Afield, 250 W 55th St, New York NY 10019 212-262-8835
Sports Collectors Digest, 700 E State St, Iola WI 54990 715-445-2214
Sports Fitness, 21100 Erwin St, Woodland Hills CA 91367.....................818-884-6800
Sports History, 105 Loudon St SW, Leesburg VA 22075..........................203-771-9400
Sports Illustrated, 1271 Ave of the Americas, New York NY 10020 212-586-1212
Sports Inc, 755 3rd Ave 20th fl, New York NY 10017 212-755-7160
Sports Marketing News, 1460 Post Rd, Westport CT 06880 203-255-9997
Sports Merchandiser, 1760 Peachtree Rd NW, Atlanta GA 30357...........404-874-4462
Sports-Nutrition News, PO Box 986, Evanston IL 60204.........................312-251-5950
Sports Parade, PO Box 10010, Ogden UT 84409 801-394-9446
Sportscan, 141 5th Ave, New York NY 10010 212-505-7600
Sportscape, 1415 Beacon St, Brookline MA 02146 617-277-3823
Sportsman Magazine, 2121 New Market #136, Marietta GA 30067 404-953-9222
The Spotlight, 300 Independence Ave SE, Washington DC 20003 202-546-3787
Spring, PO Box 222069, Dallas TX 75222 214-943-4093
Springfield!, PO Box 4749, Springfield MO 65808 417-882-4917
Sproutletter, PO Box 62, Ashland OR 97520.....................................503-488-2326
Spur, PO Box 85, Middleburg VA 22117..703-687-6314
Square Dancing, 462 N Robertson Blvd, Los Angeles CA 90048................213-652-7434
St Anthony Messenger, 1615 Republic St, Cincinnati OH 45210 513-241-5615
St Croix Review, Box 244, Stillwater MN 55082.................................612-439-7190
St Joseph's Messenger & Advocate, PO Box 288, Jersey City NJ 07303 201-798-4141
St Louis Business Journal, 712 N 2nd St, St Louis MO 63102...................314-421-6200
St Louis Journalism Review, 8380 Olive Blvd, St Louis MO 63132............314-991-1699
St Louis Magazine, PO Box 88908, St Louis MO 63118............................314-231-7200
ST-Log for Atari ST Owners, PO Box 23, Worcester MA 01603...................617-892-9230
Stagebill, 144 E 44th St, New York NY 10017....................................212-687-9275
Stallion Magazine, 351 W 54th St, New York NY 10019 212-586-4432
Standard, 6401 The Paseo, Kansas City MO 64131................................816-333-7000
The Star Blazers Fandom Report, PO Box 4912, Clifton NJ 07015 516-623-2833
Starlight, 408 Pearson St, Wilson NC 27893.....................................919-237-1591
Star*Line, PO Box 1764, Cambridge MA 02238 617-876-0928
Starlog, 475 Park Ave S, New York NY 10016 212-689-2830
Stars & Stripes Natl Tribune, PO Box 1803, Washington DC 20013.........202-789-0422
StarWeb Paper, PO Box 40029, Berkeley CA 94704................................415-845-2740
Starwind, Box 98, Ripley OH 45167 513-392-4549

State Government, PO Box 11910, Lexington KY 40578.............................606-252-2291
The State of Art, 13910 Champion Forest Dr, Houston TX 77069 713-440-8025
Stateways, 352 Park Ave S, New York NY 10010.....................................212-685-4848
Steppingstones, PO Box 1856, New York NY 10027 718-474-5063
Stereo Review, 1515 Broadway, New York NY 10036................................212-719-6000
Stereo World, PO Box 14801, Columbus OH 43214 614-263-4296
Steve Canyon Magazine, 2 Swamp Rd, Princeton WI 54968 414-295-6922
Stickers! Magazine, 10 Columbus Circle Ste 1300, New York NY 10019..212-541-7300
Stock Car Racing Magazine, PO Box 715, Ipswich NY 01938 617-356-7030
The Stock Market Magazine, 16 School St, Yonkers NY 10701 914-423-4566
Stone Country, PO Box 132, Menemsha MA 02552 617-693-5832
Stone In America, 6902 N High St, Worthington OH 43085.......................614-885-2713
Stone Review, 1415 Elliot Pl NW, Washington DC 20007 202-342-1100
Stone Soup, PO Box 83, Santa Cruz CA 95063...408-426-5557
The Stone, 1112 B Ocean, Santa Cruz CA 95060..408-429-9988
Stonehenge Viewpoint, 2821 De La Vina St, Santa Barbara CA 93105......605-687-9350
Stony Hills/Small Press News, Weeks Mills, New Sharon ME 04955 207-778-3436
Stores, 100 W 31st St, New York NY 10001..212-244-8780
Stories, 14 Beacon St Ste 614, Boston MA 02108.....................................617-742-3345
Straight, 8121 Hamilton Ave, Cincinnati OH 45231 513-931-4050
Strategic Health Care Marketing, 211 Midland Ave, Rye NY 10580.........914-967-6741
Strategies, PO Box 838, Montclair NJ 07042...201-783-5480
Strategy & Tactics Magazine, Box 110, Lake Geneva WI 53147................414-248-3625
Stream Lines, 207 Lind Hall SE, Minneapolis MN 55414..........................612-373-3539
Street Rodder, 2145 W La Palma, Anaheim CA 92801 714-635-9040
Strelets, 80 Grand St, Jersey City NJ 07302..201-332-7962
Stroke, 7320 Greenville Ave, Dallas TX 75231 214-750-5300
Struggle, PO Box 8261 Harper Sta, Detroit MI 48213................................313-824-6258
Student Lawyer, 750 N Lake Shore Dr, Chicago IL 60611..........................312-988-6048
Studies in Family Planning, 1 Hammarskjold Plz, New York NY 10017..212-644-1300
Studio Photography, 210 Crossways Park Dr, Woodbury NY 11797..........516-496-8000
The Subcontractor, 8401 Corporate Dr Ste 540, Landover MD 20785 703-684-3950
Suburban West Business, 840 E St Rd Box 31, Westtown PA 19393.........215-399-1720
Success and Money!, 173 SE 5th Ave #2, Delray Beach FL 33444 305-492-4025
Success Magazine, 342 Madison Ave, New York NY 10173........................212-503-0700
Successful Dealer, 707 Lake Cook Rd, Deerfield IL 60015 312-498-3180
Successful Farming, 1716 Locust St, Des Moines IA 50336........................515-284-2897
Successful Magazine Publishing, 1 Main St, Freedom ME 04941................207-382-6200
Successful Meetings, 633 3rd Ave, New York NY 10017 212-986-4800
The Sugar Producer, 520 Park PO Box 981, Idaho Falls ID 83402.............208-522-5187
Sun Dog, Florida State Univ English Dept, Tallahassee FL 32306 904-644-1248
Sun Up Energy News Digest, Drawer S, Yucca Valley CA 92284.................619-365-0604
The Sun, 412 W Rosemary, Chapel Hill NC 27514 919-942-5282
Sunbelt Executive, PO Box 26815, New Orleans LA 70168 504-246-2700
Suncoast, 2070 Sunset Pt Ste 115, Clearwater FL 33575 813-442-5090
Sunday School Counselor, 1445 Boonville, Springfield MO 65802.............417-862-2781
Sunset, 80 Willow Rd, Menlo Park CA 94025..415-321-3600
Sunshine Artists USA, 1700 Sunset Dr, Longwood FL 32750 305-323-5937
Sunshine Magazine, PO Box 40, Litchfield IL 62056.................................217-324-3425
Sunshine Mag of S Florida, PO Box 14430, Ft Lauderdale FL 33302........305-761-4017
Sunshine Service News, PO Box 29100, Miami FL 33102 305-552-3887
Super Chevy, 12301 Wilshire Blvd, Los Angeles CA 90025 213-820-3601
Super Service Station, 7300 N Cicero Ave, Lincolnwood IL 60646............312-588-7300

Super Stock & Drag Illus, 602 Montgomery St, Alexandria VA 22314 703-836-5881
Super Teen, 355 Lexington Ave, New York NY 10017 212-391-1400
Superintendent's Profile, 220 Central Ave, Dunkirk NY 14048 716-366-4774
Supermarket Business, 25 W 43 St, New York NY 10036 212-354-5169
Supermarket News, 7 E 12th St, New York NY 10003 212-741-4343
Supervision, 424 N 3rd St, Burlington IA 52601 319-752-5415
Supervisory Management, 135 W 50th St, New York NY 10020 212-903-8075
Supervisory Sense, 135 W 50th St, New York NY 10020 212-903-8075
Surfer, 33046 Calle Aviador, San Juan Capistrano CA 92675.....................714-496-5922
Surfing, 2720 Camino Capistrano, San Clemente CA 92672 714-492-7873
Surgery, 11830 Westline Industrial Dr, St Louis MO 63146 314-872-8370
Surgical Clinics of N Amer, W Washington Sq, Philadelphia PA 19105....215-574-4700
Surgical Practice News, 183 Peaceable St, Georgetown CT 06829 203-544-9506
Surgical Products, PO Box 1952, Dover NJ 07801.....................................201-361-9060
Surgical Rounds, 80 Shore Rd, Port Washington NY 11050 516-883-6350
Survey of Ophthalmology, 7 Kent St Ste 4, Brookline MA 02146................617-566-2138
Surveyor, 65 Broadway, New York NY 10006..212-440-0537
Survive, 5735 E Arapahoe Ave, Boulder CO 80303 303-449-2064
Suzuki Assn of the Americas, PO Box 354, Muscatine IA 52761.................319-263-3071
Swank, 888 7th Ave, New York NY 10106..212-541-7100
SWAT, PO Box 270, Cornville AZ 86325..602-634-6127
Swedish Information Service, 825 3rd Ave, New York NY 10022 212-751-5900
Sweet Potato, 5951 Canning St, Oakland CA 94609 415-652-3810
Swim, PO Box 45497, Los Angeles CA 90045 213-674-2120
Swimming Pool Age, 6255 Barfield Rd, Atlanta GA 30328 404-256-9800
Swimming Technique, 116 W Hazel St, Inglewood CA 90302......................213-674-2120
Swimming World & Jr Swimmer, 116 W Hazel, Inglewood CA 90302......213-674-2120
Sylvia Porter's Personal Finance, 380 Lexington, New York NY 10017....212-557-9100
Synergy, PO Box 4790 Grand Central Sta, New York NY 10017 212-865-9595
Synthesis, PO Box 1858, San Pedro CA 90733...213-833-2633
Synthesis Journal, PO Box 9803, San Jose CA 95157................................503-479-9086
Systems & Software, 10 Mulholland Dr, Hasbrouck Hts NJ 07604.............201-393-6000
Systems/3X World, 950 Lee St, Des Plaines IL 60016................................312-296-0770
T-J Today Jazz Dir, Box 533, Watsonville CA 95077 408-728-3948
T-Shirt Retailer & Screen Printer, 195 Main St, Metuchen NJ 08840 201-494-2889
Tai Chi, PO Box 26156, Los Angeles CA 90025 213-665-7773
Talisman, PO Box 44320, Columbus OH 43204 614-276-0671
Tallahassee Magazine, PO Box 12848, Tallahasses FL 32317 904-385-3310
Tampa Bay Metro Magazine, 2502 Rocky Point Rd, Tampa FL 33607 813-885-9855
Tampa Bay The Suncoast's Mag, 2531 Landmark, Clearwater FL 33519..813-791-4800
TAPPI, PO Box 105113 Technology Park, Atlanta GA 30348 404-446-1400
Taproot, Box 488, Stony Brook NY 11790..516-632-6635
Tar River Poetry, East Carolina Univ, Greenville NC 27834......................919-752-6041
The Tax Adviser, 1211 Ave of the Americas, New York NY 10036...........212-575-6317
Tea & Coffee Trade Journal, 130 W 42nd St, New York NY 10036 212-661-5980
Teacher Update, PO Box 429, Belmont MA 02178....................................617-484-7327
Teachers & Writers Magazine, 5 Union Sq W, New York NY 10003........212-691-6590
Teaching & Computers, 730 Broadway, New York NY 10003 212-505-3000
Teaching/K-8, 325 Post Rd W PO Box 3330, Westport CT 06880..............203-454-1020
Technical Analysis of Stocks, 9131 California Ave, Seattle WA 98136 206-983-0570
Technical Photography, 101 Crossways Park Dr, Woodbury NY 11797....516-496-8000
Technicalities, 2214 North Central at Encanto, Phoenix AZ 85004...........602-254-6156
Technology & Conservation of Art, 1 Emerson Pl, Boston MA 02114.......617-227-8581

Technology Review, Mass Inst of Tech, Cambridge MA 02139 617-253-8250
TechTrends, 1126 16th St NW, Washington DC 20036...............................202-466-4780
Teen, 8490 Sunset Blvd, Los Angeles CA 90069...213-657-5100
Teen Beat, 2 Park Ave, New York NY 10016...212-532-6444
Teen Set, 18455 Burbank Blvd Ste 309, Tarzana CA 91356.........................818-705-1951
Teenage, 928 Broadway, New York NY 10010...212-505-5350
Teens & Boys Magazine, 71 W 35th St, New York NY 10001 212-594-0880
Teens Today, 6401 The Paseo, Kansas City KS 64131..................................816-333-7000
Telecommunications, 610 Washington St, Dedham MA 02026....................617-326-8220
Teleconnect Magazine, 12 W 21st St, New York NY 10010 212-691-8215
Telemarketing, 1 Technology Plaza, Norwalk CT 06854 203-852-6800
Telephone Engineer & Management, 124 S 1st St, Geneva IL 60134.........312-232-1400
Telephony, 55 Jackson Blvd, Chicago IL 60604..312-922-2435
Telescope, 15201 Wheeler Land, Sparks MD 21152....................................301-771-4544
Television Broadcast, 4551 W 107th St, Overland Park KS 66207..............913-642-6611
Television Intl, Box 8471 Universal Plaza, Universal City CA 91608 213-462-1099
Television Quarterly, 110 W 57th St, New York NY 10019 212-586-8424
Telos, 431 E 12th St, New York NY 10009 212-228-6479
Tempest, PO Box 680-536, Miami FL 33168...305-688-8558
Tempo Life in Northeastern PA, 610 Mulberry St, Scranton PA 18510.....717-961-3355
10 Million Flies Can't Be Wrong, 116 Northwood Apt, Storrs CT 06268 ..203-429-7516
Tendril, Box 512, Green Harbor MA 02041...617-834-4137
Tennessee Bar Journal, 3622 West End Ave, Nashville TN 37205 615-383-7421
The Tennessee Magazine, 710 Spence Ln, Nashville TN 37210...................615-367-9284
Tennessee Medical Assn Jour, 112 Louise Ave, Nashville TN 37203.........615-327-1451
Tennessee Sportsman, 2121 Newmarket #136, Marietta GA 30067 404-953-9222
Tennis, 5520 Park Ave, Trumbull CT 06611..203-373-7000
Tennis USA, 1515 Broadway, New York NY 10036.......................................212-719-6323
Texas Banker's Record, PO Box 2007, Austin TX 78768..............................512-472-7980
Texas Business, 5757 Alpha Rd Ste 400, Dallas TX 75240 214-239-4481
Texas Child Care Quarterly, Box 2960, Austin TX 78769............................512-450-4167
Texas College Student, PO Box 162464, Austin TX 78716............................512-472-3893
The Texas Farmer-Stockman, 10111 N Central, Dallas TX 75231 214-363-7651
Texas Fisherman, 5314 Bingle Rd, Houston TX 77092.................................713-688-8811
Texas Gardener, PO Box 9005, Waco TX 76714..817-772-1270
Texas Heart Inst Jour, PO Box 20269 Drawer 268, Houston TX 77225....713-791-4209
Texas Highways Magazine, 11th & Brazos, Austin TX 78701......................512-463-8581
Texas Land Use Journal, PO Box 1663, Ft Worth TX 76101 817-834-5242
Texas Monthly, PO Box 1569, Austin TX 78767..512-476-7085
The Texas Observer, 600 W 7th St, Austin TX 78701...................................512-477-0746
Texas Professional Engineer, PO Box 2154, Austin TX 78768.....................512-472-9286
Texas Sportsman, 2121 Newmarket Pkwy Ste 136, Marietta GA 30067 404-953-9222
The Texas Woman's News, 15790 Dooley Rd, Dallas TX 75244....................214-960-6397
Texas Writers Newsletter, Midwestern St Univ, Wichita Falls TX 76309..817-692-6611
Textile Products & Proc, 4170 Ashford-Dunwoody, Atlanta GA 30319.....404-252-0626
Textile World, 4170 Ashford-Dunwoody Rd Ste 420, Atlanta GA 30319...404-252-0626
Textiles Panamericanos, 2100 Powers Ferry Rd, Atlanta GA 30339..........404-955-5656
TFR The Freelancers' Report, PO Box 93, Poquonock CT 06064 203-688-5496
THE Journal, Box 17239, Irvine CA 92713..714-261-0366
Theater, 222 York St, New Haven CT 06520..203-432-1568
Theater Week, 28 W 25th St, New York NY 10010 212-627-2120
Theatre Crafts, 135 5th Ave, New York NY 10010 212-677-5997
Theatre Design and Tech, 330 W 42nd St #1702, New York NY 10036 212-563-5551

Theatre News, 1010 Wisconsin Ave NW, Washington DC 20007................202-342-7530
Theatre Times, 325 Spring St, New York NY 10013.....................................212-989-5257
Theatrical Faces, 136 S 4th St, Allentown PA 18102.......................................215-435-2207
Theologia 21, PO Box 37, San Marcos CA 92069 619-746-9430
Theological Studies, Georgetown Univ, Washington DC 20057.................202-338-0754
Theology Digest, 3634 Lindell Blvd, St Louis MO 63108............................314-658-2859
Theology Today, Box 29, Princeton NJ 08542...609-921-8300
Therapaeia, 257 Park Ave S, New York NY 10010 212-674-8500
Third Coast, PO Box 592, Austin TX 78767 512-472-2016
Third Rail, PO Box 46127, Los Angeles CA 90046.....................................213-850-7548
Third Woman, Indiana Univ BH849, Bloomington IN 47401.....................812-335-5257
Third World Resources, 464 19th St, Oakland CA 94612 415-536-1876
Thirteen, Box 392, Portlandville NY 13834...607-286-7500
13th Moon, PO Box 309 Cathedral Sta, New York NY 10025.....................212-678-1973
33 Metal Producing, 1221 Ave of the Americas, New York NY 10020......212-512-3330
This People, 5 Triad Ctr, Salt Lake City UT 84180 801-575-6900
The Thoroughbred Record, 2265 Harrodsburg, Lexington KY 40544........606-276-5311
Thought, Univ Box L, Bronx NY 10458 212-579-2322
Thoughts For All Seasons, SUNY Geneseo, Geneseo NY 14454................716-245-5336
The Threepenny Review, PO Box 9131, Berkeley CA 94709 415-849-4545
3-2-1 Contact, 1 Lincoln Plaza, New York NY 10023 212-595-3456
Threshold Magazine, PO Box 922, Columbia MO 65205.............................314-442-6134
Threshold of Fantasy, PO Box 70868, Sunnyvale CA 94086 415-960-1151
Thrust Publications, 8217 Langport Ter, Gaithersburg MD 20877............301-948-2514
Thrust: For Educational Leadership, 1517 L St, Sacramento CA 95814...916-444-3216
Thursday Publishers, 1846N Pine Bluff Rd, Stevens Point WI 54481........715-344-6441
TI Professional Computing, 12416 Hymeadow Dr, Austin TX 78750........512-250-9023
Tic, PO Box 350, Albany NY 12201 518-434-3147
Ticket Central Calendar, 325 Spring St, New York NY 10013....................212-989-5257
Tidewater Virginian, 711 W 21st St, Norfolk VA 23517 804-625-4233
Tiger Beat Star, 1086 Teaneck Rd, Teaneck NJ 07666................................201-833-1800
Tile & Decorative Surfaces, 17901 Ventura Blvd D, Encino CA 91316 818-344-4200
Time Inc, Time & Life Bldg Rockefeller Ctr, New York NY 10020...........212-586-1212
Timeline, 1985 Velma Ave, Columbus OH 43211 614-297-2360
The Toastmaster, PO Box 10400, Santa Ana CA 92711 714-542-6793
Today, 800 Barksdale Rd, Newark DE 19714...302-731-1600
Today's Arizona Woman, 7140 6th Ave, Scottsdale AZ 85251....................602-941-4299
Today's Catholic Teacher, 26 Reynolds Ave, Ormond Beach FL 32074....904-672-9974
Today's Chiropractic, 1269 Barclay Circle, Marietta GA 30060..................404-581-9917
Today's Christian Woman, 184 Central Ave, Old Tappan NJ 07675..........201-768-8060
Today's Executive, 1251 Ave of the Americas, New York NY 10020..........212-489-8900
Today's Living, 6255 Barfield Rd, Atlanta GA 30328 404-256-9800
Today's Nursing Home, 550 Frontage Rd, Northfield IL 60093 312-446-1622
Today's Office, 645 Stewart Ave, Garden City NY 11530............................516-222-2500
Today's OR Nurse, 6900 Grove Rd, Thorofare NJ 08086............................609-848-1000
Today's Parish, 185 Willow St PO Box 180, Mystic CT 06355.....................203-536-2611
Tole World, PO Box 5968, Concord CA 94524 415-671-9852
Toledo Business Journal, 136 N Summit St, Toledo OH 43604................419-244-8200
Toledo Poets Ctr Press, UH 5070C Univ of Toledo, Toledo OH 43606....419-537-2983
Toledot, 155 E 93rd St Ste 3C, New York NY 10128 212-427-5395
Tom Mann's Junior Outdoor, Rte 2 Box 84C, Eufaula AL 36027.............205-687-7044
Tooling & Production, 6521 Davis Industrial Pkwy, Solon OH 44139........216-248-1125
Top Line, 505 Market St, Knoxville TN 37902 615-521-0600

Top of the News, 50 E Huron St, Chicago IL 60611 312-944-6780
Top Shelf, 30 W Mifflin St Ste 301, Madison WI 53703.............................608-233-0160
Topical Time, 4145 Glendale Rd, Dale City VA 22193..............................415-548-3776
Topics in Health Care Finan, 1600 Research, Rockville MD 20850...........301-251-8500
Torch Romances, PO Box 3307, McLean VA 22103.................................703-734-5700
Torso, 155 Ave of the Americas, New York NY 10013................................213-850-5400
Total Fitness, 15115 S 76th E Ave, Bixby OK 74008...................................918-366-4441
Total Health, 6001 Topanga Cyn Blvd, Woodland Hills CA 91367.............818-887-6484
Touchdown Illustrated, 450 Samsome St, San Francisco CA 94111...........415-398-1919
Tourist Attractions & Parks, 401 N Broad St, Philadelphia PA 19108......215-925-9744
Tours & Resorts, 990 Grove St, Evanston IL 60201....................................312-491-6440
Towards, 3442 Grant Park Dr, Carmichael CA 95608..................................916-485-9274
Towers Club USA Newsletter, PO Box 2038, Vancouver WA 98668..........206-574-3084
Town & Country, 1700 Broadway, New York NY 10019..............................212-903-5000
Town Forum Jour, Box 569, Cottage Grove OR 97424................................503-942-7720
Towpaths, 1341 W 112th St, Cleveland OH 44102......................................216-226-7890
Toy & Hobby World, 124 E 40th St, New York NY 10016............................212-741-7210
Toys Hobbies & Crafts, 545 5th Ave Ste 1403, New York NY 10017........212-687-1185
TPT Magazine, 119 Russell St PO Box 1425, Littleton MA 01460.............617-486-9501
TQ Teen Quest, PO Box 82808, Lincoln NE 68501......................................402-474-4567
Tracer Magazine, 937 Reinli Ste 1, Austin TX 78751................................512-452-3877
Track & Field News, PO Box 296, Los Altos CA 94023 415-948-8188
Tradeshow & Exhibit Manager, 1640 5th St, Santa Monica CA 90401......213-395-0234
Tradeswomen Magazine, PO Box 40664, San Francisco CA 94140.............415-821-7334
Tradition, 106 Navajo, Council Bluffs IA 51501 712-366-1136
Traffic Management, 221 Columbus Ave, Boston MA 02116......................617-536-7780
Traffic Safety, 444 N Michigan Ave, Chicago IL 60611 312-527-4800
Traffic World, 1325 G St NW Ste 900, Washington DC 20005....................202-626-4500
Trailblazer, 4800 S 188 Way, Seattle WA 98188..206-644-1100
Trailer Boats, 16427 S Avalon, Gardena CA 90248 213-323-9040
Trailer Life, 29901 Agoura Rd, Agoura CA 91301......................................818-991-4980
Trails-A-Way, 9425 S Greenville Rd, Greenville MI 48838.......................616-754-9179
Training, 50 S 9th St, Minneapolis MN 55402..612-333-0471
Trains, 1027 N 7th St, Milwaukee WI 53233 414-272-2060
Tranet, Box 567, Rangeley ME 04970 207-864-2252
Trans-Species Unltd, PO Box 1553, Williamsport PA 17703......................717-322-3252
Transaction, Rutgers Univ, New Brunswick NJ 08903 201-932-2280
Transactional Analysis Jour, 1772 Vallejo St, San Francisco CA 94123 ...415-885-5992
Transfusion, E Washington Sq, Philadelphia PA 19105.............................215-238-4200
Transitions Abroad, PO Box 344, Amherst MA 01004 413-256-0373
Translation, Columbia Univ Math Bldg, New York NY 10027....................212-280-2305
Translation Review, PO Box 830688, Richardson TX 75083 214-690-2093
Transmission & Distribution, 1 River Rd, Cos Cob CT 06807....................203-661-5000
Transport Topics, 1616 P St NW, Washington DC 20036.............................202-797-5251
Transportation Quarterly, PO Box 2055, Westport CT 06880....................203-227-4852
The Trapper, 213 N Saunders PO Box 550, Sutton NE 68979 402-773-4343
Travel & Learning Abroad, Box 1122, Brattleboro VT 05301....................802-257-5253
Travel & Leisure, 1120 Ave of the Americas, New York NY 10036...........212-382-5600
Travel Business Manager, 90 W Montgomery, Rockville MD 20850..........301-424-3347
Travel Digest, 342 Madison Ave, New York NY 10017................................212-661-0656
Travel Smart for Business, 40 Beechdale Rd, Dobbs Ferry NY 10522......914-693-8300
Travel Weekly, 1 Park Ave, New York NY 10016...212-503-3600
Travel-Holiday Magazine, 51 Atlantic Ave, Floral Park NY 11001 516-352-9700

Travelage, 320 N Michigan, Chicago IL 60601................................312-346-4952
Travelhost Magazine, 8080 N Central Expwy, Dallas TX 75206................214-691-1163
Traveling Times, 23929 W Valencia Blvd, Valencia CA 91355..................805-255-0230
Travelore Report, 1512 Spruce St, Philadelphia PA 19102....................215-735-3838
Travelwriter Marketletter, Plaza Hotel Rm 1723, New York NY 10019 ...212-759-6744
Treasure Found, 6280 Adobe Rd, 29 Palms CA 92277..........................619-367-3531
Tree Trimmers Log, PO Box 833, Ojai CA 93023.............................805-646-9688
Tri-Athlete, 1127 Hamilton St, Allentown PA 18102..........................215-821-6864
Triathalon Magazine, 8461 Warner Dr, Culver City CA 90230 213-558-3321
The Tribune, 777 United Nations Plaza 3rd fl, New York NY 10011.........212-687-8633
Trifle, PO Box 182, Dover NH 03820..603-749-5114
TriQuarterly, Northwestern Univ 1735 Benson, Evanston IL 60208.........312-491-7614
Trivia, Box 606, North Amherst MA 01059..................................413-367-2254
Trivia Quest, 566 Westchester Ave, Rye Brook NY 10573 914-939-2111
Tropical Fish Hobbyist, 3rd & Union Ave, Neptune City NJ 07753...........201-988-8400
Truckers/USA, PO Box 2029, Tuscaloosa AL 35403..........................205-349-2990
Truckin', 2145 W La Palma, Anaheim CA 92801 714-635-9040
Trucks, 20 Waterside Plaza, New York NY 10010.............................212-532-1392
True Confessions, 215 Lexington Ave, New York NY 10016 212-340-7500
True Detective, 460 W 34th St, New York NY 10001..........................212-947-6500
True Experience, 215 Lexington Ave, New York NY 10016 212-340-7500
True Love, 215 Lexington Ave, New York NY 10016...........................212-340-7500
True Romance, 215 Lexington Ave, New York NY 10016 212-340-7537
True Story, 215 Lexington Ave, New York NY 10016 212-340-7500
True West Monthly, PO Box 2107, Stillwater OK 74076......................405-743-3370
Trumpeter, 1512 Lancelot, Borger TX 79007.................................806-273-7225
Trustee, 211 E Chicago Ave, Chicago IL 60611 312-951-1100
Truth & Life, PO Box 6697, Torrance CA 90504..:..........................213-371-2494
Truth Journal, Lake Rubun Rd, Lakemont GA 30552.........................404-782-4723
The Truth, Box 582, Plymouth NH 03264....................................603-536-3992
Tucson Lifestyle, 7000 E Tangue Verde Rd, Tucson AZ 85715................602-721-2929
Tulsa Studies in Women's Literature, 600 S College, Tulsa OK 74104 918-592-6000
Tun's Tales, PO Box 1118, Kulpsville PA 19443 215-362-8397
Turf & Sport Digest, 511-513 Oakland Ave, Baltimore MD 21212 301-323-0300
Turkey, 3941 N Paradise Rd, Flagstaff AZ 86001.............................602-774-6913
Turkey Call, PO Box 530, Edgefield SC 29824 803-637-3106
Turkey World, Sandstone Bldg, Mount Morris IL 61054 815-734-4171
Turn-On Letters, PO Box 470, Port Chester NY 10573 914-939-2111
Turtle Mag for Preschool Kids, 1100 Waterway, Indianapolis IN 46202...317-636-8881
Turtle Quarterly, 25 Rainbow Mall, Niagara Falls NY 14303 716-284-2427
TV & Movie Screen, 355 Lexington Ave, New York NY 10017................212-391-1400
TV Guide, PO Box 500, Radnor PA 19088 215-293-8500
TV Technology, 5827 Columbia Pile Ste 310, Falls Church VA 22041........703-998-7600
TWA Ambassador, 284 E 5th St Ste 209, St Paul MN 55101 612-291-1720
Twilight Zone, 800 2nd Ave, New York NY 10017............................212-986-9600
Twin Cities, 7831 E Bush Lake Rd, Minneapolis MN 55435 612-835-6855
Twins Magazine, PO Box 12045, Overland Park KS 66212..................913-722-1090
2 AM Magazine, PO Box 50444, Chicago IL 60605 312-652-0013
Two Way Radio Dealer, 600 Grant St, Denver CO 80203 303-860-0111
TWT Magazine, 3900 Lemmon Ave, Dallas TX 75219 214-521-0622
The Typographer, 2262 Hall Pl NW, Washington DC 20007.................202-965-3400
U & lc/ITC, 2 Dag Hammarskjold Plaza, New York NY 10017................212-371-0699
U Magazine, PO Box 1450, Downers Grove IL 60515 312-964-5700

UFO Review, PO Box 1994, New York NY 10001 212-685-4080
Ultra Magazine, 2000 Bering Dr Ste 200, Houston TX 77057 713-961-4132
Ultralight Aircraft, 16200 Ventura Blvd Ste 201, Encino CA 91436 818-986-8400
Ultralight Planes, PO Box 6050, Mission Viejo CA 92690 714-240-6001
Ultrasport, 11 Beacon St, Boston MA 02108 617-227-1988
Umbrella, PO Box 40100, Pasadena CA 91104 818-797-0514
Uncensored Letters, PO Box 470, Port Chester NY 10573 914-939-2111
Underwater USA, 3185 Lackawanna Ave, Bloomsburg PA 17815 717-784-6081
Underwriters' Report, 667 Mission St, San Francisco CA 94105 415-981-3221
The Unexplained, PO Box 8042, Van Nuys CA 91409 818-366-1090
Unfinished Furniture, 1850 Oak St, Northfield IL 60093 312-446-8434
Unique Homes, 1 Park Ave, New York NY 10016 212-503-3780
United, 34 E 51st St, New York NY 10022 212-888-5900
The United Brethren, 302 Lake St, Huntington IN 46750 219-356-2312
United Evangelical Action, PO Box 28, Wheaton IL 60189 312-665-0500
United Lumbee Nation Times, Box 512, Fall River Mills CA 96028 916-336-6701
United Methodist Reporter, PO Box 660275, Dallas TX 75266 214-630-6495
United Polka Boosters, PO Box 681, Glastonbury CT 06033 203-537-1880
United States Banker, 1 River Rd, Cos Cob CT 06807 203-661-5000
United Synagogue Review, 155 5th Ave, New York NY 10010 212-533-7800
Unity Magazine, Unity School of Christianity, Unity Village MO 64065 ...816-524-3550
University Journal, CSU Graduate School, Chico CA 95929 916-895-5700
Unix/World, 444 Castro St, Mountain View CA 94041 415-940-1500
Unknowns, 1900 Century Blvd NE Ste One, Atlanta GA 30345 404-636-3145
Unsound, 801 22nd St, San Francisco CA 94107 415-550-8143
Unspeakable Visions of Individual, PO Box 439, California PA 15419 412-938-8956
Up Against The Wall Mother, 6009 Edgewood, Alexandria VA 22310 703-971-2219
The Upper Room, 1908 Grand Ave, Nashville TN 37202 615-327-2700
Urban Health, 1814 Washington Ave, East Point GA 30344 404-762-7668
Urban Land, 1090 Vermont Ave NW, Washington DC 20005 202-289-8500
Urban Media Inc, 220 Bagley Ave Ste 830, Detroit MI 48226 313-965-0388
Uremia Investigation, 270 Madison Ave, New York NY 10016 212-696-9000
Urologic Clinics, W Washington Sq, Philadelphia PA 19105 215-574-4700
Urology, Box 643, Ridgewood NJ 07451 201-864-4000
US Jour Drug-Alcohol Depend, 1721 Blount, Pompano Bch FL 33069 305-979-5408
Us Magazine, 1 Dag Hammarskjold Plaza, New York NY 10017 212-836-9200
US Medicine, 2033 M St NW, Washington DC 20036 202-463-6000
US News & World Report, 2400 N St NW, Washington DC 20037 202-955-2000
US Pharmacist, 352 Park Ave S, New York NY 10010 212-685-4848
US Tobacco & Candy Journal, 254 W 31st St, New York NY 10001 212-594-4120
US Woman Engineer, 345 E 46 St Ste 305, New York NY 10017 212-705-7855
US1 Worksheets, 21 Lake Dr, Roosevelt NJ 08555 609-448-5096
USAir Magazine, 600 3rd Ave, New York NY 10016 212-697-1460
Used Equipment Directory, 70 Sip Ave, Jersey City NJ 07306 201-653-4440
User's Guide, 2055 Woodside Rd Ste 180, Redwood City CA 94063 415-364-0108
Utah Holiday Magazine, 419 E 1st South, Salt Lake City UT 84111 801-532-3737
Utility Supervision, 24 Rope Ferry Rd, Waterford CT 06386 203-442-4365
Utne Reader, 2732 W 43rd St, Minneapolis MN 55410 612-929-2670
VA Practitioner, 320 North A St, Springfield OR 97477 503-726-1200
Vacation Industry Review, PO Box 431920, S Miami FL 33243 305-667-0202
Vail, 899 Logan St Ste 30, Denver CO 80203 303-832-5400
Valley Magazine, 16800 Devonshire St, Granada Hills CA 91344 818-368-3353
Valley Women's Voice, 40 Every Woman's Center, Amherst MA 01003 413-545-2436

Van Digest, PO Box 25583, Chicago IL 60625...312-539-1936
Vanity Fair, 350 Madison Ave, New York NY 10017....................................212-880-8800
Vantage Point, 1285 Ave of Americas, New York NY 10019.......................212-245-4510
Variety, 154 W 46th St, New York NY 10036..212-869-5700
Vegetarian Jour, PO Box 1463, Baltimore MD 21203.................................301-752-8348
Vegetarian Times, PO Box 570, Oak Park IL 60303....................................312-848-8120
Velo-News, PO Box 1257, Brattleboro VT 05301...802-254-2305
Ventura County & Coast Reporter, 1583 Spinnaker, Ventura CA 93001..805-656-0707
Venture, 521 5th Ave, New York NY 10175...212-682-7373
Venture, PO Box 150, Wheaton IL 60189...312-665-0630
Venture Inward, Box 595, Virginia Beach VA 23451..................................804-428-3588
Verbatim The Language Quarterly, 4 Laurel Hts, Old Lyme CT 06371....203-434-2104
Verdict, 123 Truxtun Ave, Bakersfield CA 93301.......................................805-325-7124
Vermont Business, The Square, Bellows Falls VT 05101............................802-463-9933
Vermont Life Magazine, 61 Elm St, Montpelier VT 05602.........................802-828-3241
Vermont Woman, 200 Main St Ste 15, Burlington VT 05401......................802-863-6688
Verse, College of Wm & Mary English Dept, Williamsburg VA 23185.....803-792-7901
The Very Beginning, PO Box 3071, Iowa City IA 52244.............................319-337-6430
A Very Small Magazine, Box 24, Boone NC 28607......................................919-297-1938
The Veteran, 2001 S St NW, Washington DC 20009......................................202-332-2700
Veterinary Clinics, W Washington Sq, Philadelphia PA 19105..................215-574-4700
Veterinary Computing, PO Drawer KK, Santa Barbara CA 93102..............805-963-6561
Veterinary Economics, 9073 Lenexa Dr, Lenexa KS 66215.........................913-492-4300
Veterinary Forum, 1610 A Frederica Rd, St Simons Island GA 31522.......912-638-4848
Veterinary Medicine, 690 S 4th St, Edwardsville KS 66111........................913-422-5010
Veterinary Practice Management, 505 Market St, Knoxville TN 37902.....615-595-5211
Vette, 175 Hudson St, Hackensack NJ 07601...201-488-7171
VFW Magazine, 406 W 34th St, Kansas City MO 64111.............................816-756-3390
Vibrant Life, 55 W Oak Ridge Dr, Hagerstown MD 21740..........................301-791-7000
Vicatimology An Intl Jour, PO Box 39045, Washington DC 20016.............703-528-8872
Victimology, 5535 Lee Hwy, Arlington VA 22207.......................................703-536-1750
Video Arts, 650 Missouri, San Francisco CA 94107.....................................415-863-8434
Video Business, 345 Park Ave S, New York NY 10010.................................212-686-7744
Video Extra, 11 N 2nd St, Philadelphia PA 19106.......................................215-629-1588
Video Magazine, 460 W 34th St, New York NY 10001.................................212-947-6500
Video Marketing, 1680 Vine St Ste 820, Hollywood CA 90028....................213-462-6350
Video Now, 375 N Broadway, Jericho NY 11753...516-933-6800
Video Product News, 441 S Calle Encillia, Palm Springs CA 92263...........619-323-2000
Video Review, 902 Broadway, New York NY 10010.....................................212-477-2200
Video Store, 1700 E Dyer Rd, Santa Ana CA 92705.....................................714-250-8060
Video Systems, PO Box 12901, Overland Park KS 66212............................913-888-4664
Video Times, 3841 W Oakton St, Skokie IL 60076.......................................312-676-3470
Videography, 50 W 23rd St, New York NY 10010..212-645-1000
VideoPro, 902 Broadway, New York NY 10010...212-477-2200
VideoSat News, 418 N River, Hailey ID 83333..208-788-4936
Vietnam War Newsletter, Box 122, Collinsville CT 06022..........................203-582-9784
Vineyard & Winery Management, 103 3rd St, Watkinsglen NY 14891.......607-535-7133
Vintage '45, Box 266, Orinda CA 94563..415-254-7266
Vinyl, 201 Weatern Ave N, St Paul MN 55102..612-291-7156
Virginia Bar News, 700 Bldg Ste 1622, Richmond VA 23219......................804-786-2061
Virginia Cavalcade, Virginia State Library, Richmond VA 23219.............804-786-2312
Virginia Forests, 1205 E Main St, Richmond VA 23219..............................804-644-8462
The Virginia Quarterly Review, 1 W Range, Charlottesville VA 22903.....804-924-3124

Virginia State Library, 11th St at Capitol Sq, Richmond VA 23219...........804-786-2312
Virginia Wildlife, PO Box 11104, Richmond VA 23230 804-257-1000
The Virginian, Box 8, New Hope VA 24469..703-885-0388
Virtue, 548 Sisters Pkwy, Sisters OR 97759 503-549-8261
Vision Lifestyles, 1333 Alger SE PO Box 7259, Grand Rapids MI 49510..616-241-5616
Visions, 4705 S 8th Rd, Arlington VA 22204...703-521-0142
Vista, PO Box 50434, Indianapolis IN 46250 317-842-0444
Vista/USA Exxon Travel Club, PO Box 161, Convent Sta NJ 07961...........201-538-7600
Visual Merchandising-Store Design, 407 Gilbert, Cincinnati OH 45202...513-421-2050
Vital Christianity, 1200 E 5th St, Anderson IN 46018 317-644-7721
VLSI Design Magazine, 600 Community Dr, Manhasset NY 11030............516-365-4600
Vocational Education Journal, 2020 N 14th St, Arlington VA 22201.........703-522-6121
Vogue, 350 Madison Ave, New York NY 10017..212-880-8800
Vogue Patterns, 161 Ave of the Americas, New York NY 10013 212-620-2500
Vol No Magazine, 24721 Newhall Ave, Newhall CA 91321 805-254-0851
Volkswagen's World, 888 W Big Beaver Rd, Troy MI 48007 313-362-6770
Volleyball Monthly, PO Box 3137, San Luis Obispo CA 93403 805-541-2294
Volunteer Leader, 211 E Chicago Ave Ste 700, Chicago IL 60611 312-440-6893
Vongrutnorv Og Press, Randall Flat Rd PO Box 411, Troy ID 83871 208-835-4902
The Vortex, 800 S Euclid, Fullerton CA 92632...714-526-6257
Voyager, 1909 N Enterprise St, Orange CA 92665 714-921-0624
VW & Porsche, 12301 Wilshire Blvd, Los Angeles CA 90025....................213-820-3601
VW Trends, 2145 W La Palma Ave, Anaheim CA 92801 714-635-9040
W, 7 E 12th St, New York NY 10003...212-741-4000
Walker's Estimating & Constr, 5030 N Harlem, Chicago IL 60656 312-867-7070
Walking Tours of San Juan, 301 1st Federal Bldg, Santurce PR 00909.....809-722-1767
Walking World, PO Box 509 Gracie Sta, New York NY 10028....................212-355-3231
Walkways, 733 15th St NW, Washington DC 20005 202-737-9555
Wall Street Computer Review, 150 Broadway, New York NY 10038.........212-227-1200
The Wall Street Transcript, 99 Wall St, New York NY 10005 212-747-9500
The Wallace Stevens Journal, Clarkson Univ, Potsdam NY 13676 315-268-3987
Wallaces Farmer, 1501 42nd St, Des Moines IA 50265 515-224-6000
Walls & Ceilings, 14006 Ventura Blvd, Sherman Oaks CA 91423 213-789-8733
Walt Whitman Quarterly Review, Univ of Iowa, Iowa City IA 52240 319-335-0592
Wang Solutions, 3381 Ocean Dr, Vero Beach FL 32960................................305-231-6904
War Cry, 799 Bloomfield Ave, Verona NJ 07044 201-239-0606
Ward's Auto World, 28 W Adams, Detroit MI 48226 313-962-4433
Wards Communications Inc, 28 W Adams St, Detroit MI 48226................313-962-4433
Warehousing Supervisor, 24 Rope Ferry, Waterford CT 06386 203-442-4365
Warm Fuzzy Newsletter, 45 Hitching Post, Rolling Hls Est CA 90274 213-539-6430
WARM Journal, 414 1st Ave N, Minneapolis MN 55401 612-332-5672
Washington Business Review, 138 Church St NE, Vienna VA 22180 703-281-4681
Washington Dossier, 3301 New Mexico Ave NW, Wash DC 20016............202-362-4040
Washington Evergreen State Magazine, 901 Lenora, Seattle WA 98121...206-328-5000
Washington Intl Arts Letter, PO Box 15240, Washington DC 20003.........202-328-1900
Wash Journalism Review, 2233 Wisconsin Ave NW, Wash DC 20007 202-333-6800
The Washington Monthly, 1711 Connecticut Ave, Wash DC 20009...........202-462-0128
Washington Quarterly, 1800 K St NW Ste 400, Washington DC 20006.....202-887-0200
The Washington Report, PO Box 10309, St Petersburg FL 33733..............813-866-1598
Washington Review, PO Box 50132, Washington DC 20004........................202-638-0515
Washington Trooper, PO Box 1523, Longview WA 98632............................206-577-8598
Washington Wildlife, 600 N Capitol Way, Olympia WA 98504....................206-753-5707
Washington Woman, 1911 N Ft Meyer Dr, Arlington VA 22209................703-522-3477

The Washingtonian, 1828 L St NW, Washington DC 20036..........................202-296-3600
Waste Age, 1730 Rhode Island Ave NW, Washington DC 20036.................202-861-0708
Watch & Clock Review, 2403 Champa St, Denver CO 80205 303-296-1600
Water & Wastes Digest, 380 Northwest Hwy, Des Plaines IL 60016..........312-298-6622
Water Equipment News, 813 N Lincoln Ave, Urbana IL 61801 217-344-7443
The Water Skier, PO Box 191, Winter Haven FL 33882 813-324-4341
Water Engineering & Mgmt, 380 NW Hwy, Des Plaines IL 60016..............312-298-6622
Waterbed, 2512 Artesia Blvd, Redondo Beach CA 90278 213-376-8788
Waterfowler's World, PO Box 38306, Germantown TN 38183 901-767-7978
Waterfront, 1760 Monrovia Ave, Costa Mesa CA 92627...............................714-646-3963
Waterfront News, 1224 SW 1st Ave, Ft Lauderdale FL 33315.....................305-524-9450
Waterways, 799 Greenwich St, New York NY 10014 212-929-3169
Waterworld News, 6666 W Quincy Ave, Denver CO 80235 303-794-7711
The Wave, 95 Tussel Lane, Scotch Plains NJ 07076.....................................201-382-8450
Wavelength, 5951 Canning St, Oakland CA 94609 415-652-3810
Waystation for the Sci-Fi Writer, 1025 55th St, Oakland CA 94608............415-655-3024
WDS Forum, 1507 Dana Ave, Cincinnati OH 45207.......................................513-531-2222
We The People of N Carolina, PO Box 2508, Raleigh NC 27602 919-828-0758
Wealth, 4425 W Napoleon Ave, Metairie LA 70001..504-456-9034
Weatherwise, 4000 Albemarle St NW, Washington DC 20016 202-362-6445
The Weaver's Journal, PO Box 14238, St Paul MN 55114.............................612-646-7445
Webb Traveler Magazine, 1999 Shepard Rd, St Paul MN 55116 612-690-7228
Webster Review, 470 E Lockwood, Webster Groves MO 63119.....................314-432-2657
Wee Wisdom, Unity School of Christianity, Unity Village MO 64065 816-524-3550
Weeds Trees & Turf, 7500 Old Oak Blvd, Cleveland OH 44130 216-243-8100
Weighing & Measurement, PO Box 5867, Rockford IL 61125 815-399-6970
Weight Watchers Magazine, 360 Lexington Ave, New York NY 10017.....212-370-0644
Weirdbook, PO Box 149 Amherst Branch, Buffalo NY 14226.......................716-839-2415
Welding Design & Fabrication, 1111 Chester Ave, Cleveland OH 44114..216-696-7000
Welding Distributor, 1111 Chester Ave, Cleveland OH 44114......................216-696-7000
WES Window Treatment Indus, 345 Cedar Bldg, St Paul MN 55101 612-222-2508
The Wesleyan Advocate, PO Box 50434, Indianpolis IN 46250.....................317-842-0444
West Branch, Bucknell Univ, Lewisburg PA 17837...717-524-1440
West Coast Rev of Books, 6331 Hollywood Blvd, Hollywood CA 90028....213-464-2662
West Hills Review, 246 Old Walt Whitman, Huntington Sta NY 11746.....516-427-5240
West Michigan Magazine, 7 Ionia SW, Grand Rapids MI 49503.................616-774-0204
Westart, PO Box 6868, Auburn CA 95604..916-885-0969
Westburg Assoc Publishers, 1745 Madison St, Fennimore WI 53809 608-822-6237
Western & English Fashions, 2403 Champa, Denver CO 80205 303-296-1600
Western Assn of Map Libraries, Univ of Calif, Santa Cruz CA 95064 408-429-2364
Western Boatman, 16427 S Avalon Blvd, Gardena CA 90248 213-323-9040
Western Business, 401 N Broadway, Billings MT 59101 406-252-4788
Western City, 1400 K St, Sacramento CA 95814...916-444-8960
Western Electronics, 4164 N Peck Rd Ste A, El Monte CA 91732.............818-442-8321
Western Flyer, 8415 Steilacoom Blvd SW, Tacoma WA 98498 206-588-1743
Western Horse, Box FF, Sun City CA 92381..714-679-2963
The Western Horseman, PO Box 7980, Colorado Spgs CO 80933.............303-633-5524
Western Humanities Review, Univ of Utah, Salt Lake City UT 84112.......801-581-6070
Western Investor, 400 SW 6th Ave, Portland OR 97204 503-222-0577
The Western Jour of Medicine, 44 Gough St, San Francisco CA 94103.....415-863-5522
Western New York Magazine, 107 Delaware Ave, Buffalo NY 14202........716-852-7100
Western Outdoors, 3197-E Airport Loop Dr, Costa Mesa CA 92626........714-546-4370
Western Publisher, PO Box 591012, San Francisco CA 94159 415-661-7964

Western Real Estate Directory, 6255 Barfield Rd, Atlanta GA 30328 404-256-9800
Western Reserve, PO Box 2780, N Canton OH 44720 216-452-1820
Western Roofing/Insulation, 27202 Via Burgos, Msn Viejo CA 92691.....714-951-1653
Western RV Traveler, 2019 Clement Ave, Alameda CA 94501....................415-865-7500
Western Sun Publications, Box 1470, Yuma AZ 85364...............................602-782-9511
Western's World, 5900 Wilshire Blvd Ste 800, Los Angeles CA 90036.......213-937-5810
Westways, 2601 S Figueroa St, Los Angeles CA 90007...............................213-741-4760
What Makes People Successful, 424 N 3rd St, Burlington IA 52601 319-752-5415
What's New, 11 Allen Rd, Boston MA 02135 617-787-3636
Wheat Grower, 415 2nd St NE Ste 300, Washington DC 20002...................202-547-7800
Wheel & Off-Road, 8490 Sunset Blvd, Los Angeles CA 90069 213-854-2360
Wheels of Time, 201 Office Park Dr, Birmingham AL 35223 205-879-2131
Whiskey Island, Cleveland State Univ, Cleveland OH 44115 216-687-2056
Whispering Wind Magazine, 8009 Wales St, New Orleans LA 70126........504-241-5866
The White Light, PO Box 93124, Pasadena CA 91109 818-794-6013
Whole Earth Review, 27 Gate Five Rd, Sausalito CA 94965......................415-332-1716
Whole Life, 89 5th Ave, New York NY 10003 212-741-7274
The Wholesaler, 135 Addison Ave, Elmhurst IL 60126 312-530-6160
Wholistic Living News, PO Box 16346, San Diego CA 92116....................619-280-0317
Wide Open Magazine, 326 I St, Eureka CA 95501.....................................707-445-3847
The Widener Review, Widener Univ, Chester PA 19013 215-499-4266
Wilderness, 1400 I St NW 10th fl, Washington DC 20005..........................202-842-3400
Wildfire, PO Box 9167, Spokane WA 99209...509-326-6561
Wildlife Photography, PO Box 691, Greenville PA 16125..........................412-588-3492
Williams & Wilkins, 428 E Preston St, Baltimore MD 21202 301-528-4000
Willow Springs, Box 1063 E Wash Univ, Cheney WA 99004......................509-458-6429
Wilson Library Bulletin, 950 University Ave, Bronx NY 10452..................212-588-8400
The Wilson Quarterly, 600 Maryland Ave SW #430, Wash DC 20560......202-287-3400
WIN News, 187 Grant St, Lexington MA 02173..617-862-9431
Wind, Box 809K, Pikeville KY 41501..606-631-1129
Wind Power Digest, Box 700, Bascom OH 44809 419-937-2299
Wind Surf, Box 561, Dana Point CA 92629..714-661-4888
Windfall, Univ of Wisc English Dept, Whitewater WI 53190 414-472-1036
Windless Orchard, English Dept Indiana Univ, Ft Wayne IN 46805 219-481-6764
The Windless Orchard, Indiana Univ, Ft Wayne IN 46805 219-482-5441
Windrider, 809 S Orlando Ave, Winter Park FL 32789 305-628-4802
Wine & Spirits Buying Guide, PO Box 1548, Princeton NJ 08542.............609-921-2196
The Wine Spectator, 601 Van Ness Ave, San Francisco CA 94102.............415-673-2040
Wines & Vines, 1800 Lincoln Ave, San Rafael CA 94901............................415-453-9700
The Winged Foot, 180 Central Park S Rm 1223, New York NY 10019 212-247-5100
Winning, 15115 S 76th E Ave, Bixby OK 74008 918-366-4441
Wire Tech, 6521 Davis Industrial Pkwy, Solon OH 44139 216-248-1125
Wisconsin Acad Review, 1922 Univ Ave, Madison WI 53705 608-263-1692
Wisconsin Agriculturist, PO Box 4420, Madison WI 53711 608-274-9400
Wisconsin Business Jour, 7535 Office Ridge, Eden Prairie MN 55344 612-941-5822
Wisconsin Grocer, 802 W Broadway, Madison WI 53713...........................608-222-4515
Wisconsin Natural Resources, 101 S Webster St, Madison WI 53703 608-266-1510
Wisconsin Restaurateur, 122 W Washington, Madison WI 53703..............603-251-3663
Wisconsin Review, Univ of Wisconsin Box 158, Oshkosh WI 54901..........715-424-2267
Wisconsin Silent Sports, PO Box 152, Waupaca WI 54981........................715-258-7731
Wisconsin Sportsman, PO Box 2266, Oshkosh WI 54903...........................414-233-1327
Wisconsin Trails, 6225 Univ Ave PO Box 5650, Madison WI 53705..........608-231-2444
The Wise Woman, 2441 Cordova St, Oakland CA 94602 415-536-3174

Wittenberg Door, 1224 Greenfield Dr, El Cajon CA 92021 619-440-2333
WittyWorld Intl Cartoon Mag, PO Box 1458, N Wales PA 19454.............215-699-2626
Wohl Associates, 555 City Line Ave Ste 240, Bala Cynwyd PA 19004........215-667-4842
Woman Bowler, 5301 S 76th St, Greendale WI 53129.............................414-421-9000
The Woman Engineer, 44 Broadway, Greenlawn NY 11740....................516-261-8917
Woman Magazine, 1115 Broadway, New York NY 10010 212-807-7100
Woman of Power, 15 Leland St, Cambridge MA 02238............................617-491-6204
Woman's Art Journal, 7008 Sherwood Dr, Knoxville TN 37919 615-584-7467
Woman's Day, 1515 Broadway, New York NY 10036 212-719-6755
The Woman's Newspaper, PO Box 1303, Princeton NJ 08542....................609-890-0999
Woman's Touch, 1445 Boonville, Springfield MO 65802............................417-862-2781
Woman's World, 177 N Dean St, Englewood NJ 07631............................201-569-0006
Women & Co, 505 King St, La Crosse WI 54601 608-782-2130
Women Artists News, PO Box 3304, New York NY 10163 212-666-6990
Women In Business, PO Box 8728, Kansas City MO 64114 816-361-6621
Women in the Arts Bulletin, 325 Spring St #200, New York NY 10013 ...212-691-0988
Women's Circle, 306 E Parr Rd, Berne IN 46711 219-589-8741
Women's Circle Home Cooking, PO Box 198, Henniker NH 03242...........603-474-2404
Women's Household Crochet, 306 E Parr Rd, Berne IN 46711 219-589-8741
Women's League Outlook, 48 E 74th St, New York NY 10021...................212-628-1600
Women's News, PO Box 829, Harrison NY 10528 914-835-5400
Women's Quarterly Review, PO Box 708, New York NY 10150 212-675-7794
The Women's Record, PO Box 7, Roslyn Hts NY 11577 516-625-3033
Women's Review of Books, Wellesley College, Wellesley MA 02181.........617-431-1453
Women's Sports & Fitness, 501 2nd St, San Francisco CA 94107.............415-442-0220
Women's Studies Quarterly, 311 E 94th St, New York NY 10128 212-360-5790
Women's Voice of Columbus, 638 Oak St, Columbus OH 43215 614-221-1022
Women's Words, 8 Fort Point St #12, East Norwalk CT 06855.................203-852-8031
Women-In-Literature, PO Box 60550, Reno NV 89506.............................702-972-1671
Womens Aglow Fellowship, PO Box I, Lynnwood WA 98406....................206-775-7282
WomenWise, 38 S Main St, Concord NH 03301 603-225-2739
Wonder Time, 6401 The Paseo, Kansas City MO 64131...........................816-333-7000
Wood & Wood Products, 400 Knightsbridge, Lincolnshire IL 60069.........312-634-2600
Wood 'N Energy, PO Box 2008, Laconia NH 03247 603-528-4285
Woodall's Campground Mgmt, 11 N Skokie Hwy, Lake Bluff IL 60044....312-295-7799
WoodenBoat Magazine, PO Box 78, Brooklin ME 04616 207-359-4651
Woodmen of the World Magazine, 1700 Farnam St, Omaha NE 68102 402-342-1890
Woodsmith, 2200 Grand Ave, Des Moines IA 50312..............................515-282-7000
Woodwind Brass & Precussion, 138 Front St, Deposit NY 13754..............607-467-3000
Woodworker's Journal, 25 Town View Dr, New Milford CT 06776...........203-355-2697
The Wooster Review, The College of Wooster, Wooster OH 44691..........216-263-2000
Word Dynamics Concept, PO Box 5256, Sacramento CA 95817 916-427-6836
Word from Washington, 425 I St NW Ste 141, Washington DC 20001......202-842-1266
The Word In Season, 2900 Queen Ln, Philadelphia PA 19129..................215-848-6800
Word of Mouth A Newspaper, PO Box 8872, Jacksonville FL 32205 904-724-2779
Workbasket, 4251 Pennsylvania Ave, Kansas City MO 64111 816-531-5730
Workbench, 4251 Pennsylvania Ave, Kansas City MO 64111 816-531-5730
The Workbook, PO Box 4524, Albuquerque NM 87106 505-262-1862
Working Classics, 298 9th Ave, San Francisco CA 94118 415-387-3412
Working Mother, 230 Park Ave, New York NY 10169.............................212-551-9412
Working Parents, 441 Lexington Ave, New York NY 10017 212-867-4820
Working Woman, 342 Madison Ave, New York NY 10173 212-309-9800
Workout, 18455 Burbank Blvd Ste 309, Tarzana CA 91356 818-345-6362

Worksteader News, 2396 Coolidge Way, Rancho Cordova CA 95670........916-635-8764
World Coin News, 700 E State St, Iola WI 54990 715-445-2214
World Grain, PO Box 29155, Merriam KS 66202...913-236-7300
World Humor & Irony, Ariz State Univ, Tempe AZ 85287........................602-965-7592
World Market Perspective, 2211 Lee Rd, Winter Park FL 32789................305-628-5300
The World of Banking, 2550 Golf Rd, Rolling Meadows IL 60008..............312-228-6200
World of Poetry, 2431 Stockton Blvd, Sacramento CA 95817......................916-731-8463
World Oil, PO Box 2608, Houston TX 77001..713-529-4301
World Order, 415 Linden Ave, Wilmette IL 60091 312-251-1854
World Police & Fire Games, 6200 Yarrow Dr, Carlsbad CA 92008 619-438-2511
World Policy Jour, 777 United Nations Plaza, New York NY 10017 212-490-0010
World Press Review, 230 Park Ave, New York NY 10169 212-697-6162
World Progress, 200 W Monroe St, Chicago IL 60606 312-346-7440
World Tennis, 3 Park Ave, New York NY 10016 212-340-9683
World Traveling, 30943 Club House Ln, Farmington Hills MI 48018........313-626-6068
World War II, 105 Loudoun St SW, Leesburg VA 22075.............................703-771-9400
World Wastes, 6255 Barfield Rd, Atlanta GA 30328 404-256-9800
World Wide Printer, 401 N Broad St, Philadelphia PA 19108.....................215-238-5300
World's Fair, PO Box 339, Corte Madera CA 94925 415-924-6035
Worldwide Challenge, Arrowhead Springs, San Bernardino CA 92414.....714-886-9711
The Wormwood Review Press, PO Box 8840, Stockton CA 95208.............209-466-8231
WPI Jour, 100 Institute Rd, Worcester MA 01609...617-793-5410
Wrestling World, 355 Lexington Ave, New York NY 10017.........................212-391-1400
The Writer Inc, 120 Boylston St, Boston MA 02116.....................................617-423-3157
Writer's Digest, 1507 Dana Ave, Cincinnati OH 45207 513-531-2222
The Writer's Exchange, PO Box 394, Society Hill SC 29593 803-378-4556
Writer's Info, PO Box 2377, Coeur d'Alene ID 83814...................................208-667-7511
Writer's Inspirational Market News, PO Box 5650, Lakeland FL 33807...813-644-3548
Writer's Journal, PO Box 65798, St Paul MN 55165....................................612-221-0326
Writer's Newsletter, 1530 7th St, Rock Island IL 61201...............................309-788-3980
The Writer's Nook News, 10957 Chardon Road, Chardon OH 44024 216-285-0942
Writer's Yearbook, 1507 Dana Ave, Cincinnati OH 45207...........................513-531-2222
The Writer, 120 Boylston St, Boston MA 02116 617-423-3157
Writers Connection, 1601 Saratoga Sunnyvale Rd, Cupertino CA 95014..408-973-0227
Writers on Writing, PO Box 2222, Cocoa FL 32923 305-639-3162
Writers Forum, Univ of Colorado, Colorado Springs CO 80907.................303-593-3155
Writers Grapevine, 4425 Indianola Ste 4, Columbus OH 43214 614-263-4825
Writers West, PO Box 16097, San Diego CA 92116......................................619-278-6108
Writers-In-Waiting Newsletter, 837 Archie St, Eugene OR 97402.............503-688-5400
Writing!, 3500 Western Ave, Highland Park IL 60035...................................312-432-2700
Written Communication, 275 S Beverly Dr, Beverly Hills CA 90210.........213-274-8003
Wyoming Rural Electric News, 340 W B St, Casper WY 82601 307-234-6152
Wyoming the Hub of the Wheel, Box 9, Saratoga WY 82331.......................307-326-5214
Xanadu, Box 773, Huntington NY 11743...516-691-2376
YABA World, 5301 S 76th St, Greendale WI 53129.....................................414-421-4700
Yacht Racing & Cruising, 23 Leroy Ave, Darien CT 06820........................203-655-2531
The Yacht, Box 329, Newport RI 02840 401-849-7814
Yachting, 5 River Rd, Cos Cob CT 06807...203-629-8300
The Yale Review, 1902A Yale Sta, New Haven CT 06520 203-432-0499
Yankee, Main St, Dublin NH 03444..603-563-8111
Yankee Homes, Main St, Dublin NH 03444..603-563-8111
Yard & Garden, 1233 Janesville Ave, Ft Atkinson WI 53538......................414-563-6388
Yarrow, Kutztown State U English Dept, Kutztown PA 19530 215-683-4353

Ye Olde Newes, Box 1508, Lufkin TX 75901...409-637-7468
Yellow Silk, PO Box 6374, Albany CA 94706..415-841-6500
Yesteryear, PO Box 2, Princeton WI 54968...414-787-4808
Yoga Journal, 2054 University Ave, Berkeley CA 94704.................................415-841-9200
Young & Alive, 4444 S 52nd St, Lincoln NE 68506..402-488-0981
Young Ambassador, PO Box 82808, Lincoln NE 68501.................................402-474-4567
Young Author's Magazine, 3015 Woodsdale Blvd, Lincoln NE 68502........402-421-3172
Young Children, 1834 Connecticut Ave NW, Washington DC 20009.........202-232-8777
Young Miss, 685 3rd Ave, New York NY 10017..212-878-8700
Your Church, 198 Allendale Rd, King of Prussia PA 19406.........................215-265-9400
Your Health, PO Box 10010, Ogden UT 84409...801-394-9446
Your Health & Fitness, 3500 Western Ave, Highland Park IL 60035.........312-432-2700
Your Home, PO Box 10010, Ogden UT 84409..801-394-9446
Your Virginia State Trooper, PO Box 2189, Springfield VA 22152............703-451-2524
The Youth Report, 226 W Pensacola St Ste 301, Tallahassee FL 32301.....904-681-0019
Youth Update, 1615 Republic St, Cincinnati OH 45210...............................513-241-5615
Zero to Three, 733 15th St NW Ste 912, Washington DC 20005...................202-347-0308
Ziff-Davis Publishing Co, 1 Park Ave, New York NY 10016.........................212-725-3500
Zip Magazine, 322 8th Ave, New York NY 10022..212-620-7330
Zip Target Marketing, 322 8th Ave, New York NY 10001.............................212-620-7330
Zone 3, PO Box 4565 Austin Peay State Univ, Clarksville TN 37044..........615-648-7031
Zoonooz, PO Box 551, San Diego CA 92112..619-231-1515
Zyzzyva, 41 Sutter St, San Francisco CA 94104...415-387-8389

MANUSCRIPT ANALYSTS

These firms provide manuscript evaluation services. See Editors & Proofreaders for
firms offering copy and line editing services.

AA's & PE's, 428 Lafayette St, New York NY 10003.....................................212-228-8707
About Books Inc, PO Box 538, Saguache CO 81149......................................303-589-8223
Rose A Adkins, 741B Robinson Rd, Topanga CA 90290...............................213-455-3823
All-Media Services, 13415 Ventura Blvd, Sherman Oaks CA 91423...........818-995-3329
Carol L Allison, 4848 S Alameda #1804, Corpus Christi TX 78412...........512-992-9496
Elaine Andrews, 225 W 12th St, New York NY 10011.....................................212-675-5185
Andujar Communication Tech, 17 E 45th St, New York NY 10017...........212-883-9098
Deborah Annan, 3201 N W 70th St, Seattle WA 98117...................................206-789-4663
Baldwin Literary Services, 935 Hayes St, Baldwin NY 11510......................516-546-8338
Diana Barth, 535 W 51st St Apt 3A, New York NY 10019.............................212-307-5465
Carol Billman, Box 114, Landenburg PA 19350..215-274-2145
Marjorie M Bitker, 2330 E Back Bay, Milwaukee WI 53202..........................414-276-5462
Samuel R Blate Assoc, 10331 Watkins Mill, Gaithersburg MD 20879.......301-840-2248
Blue Pencil Group, PO Box 3392, Reston VA 22090.......................................202-471-1998
The Book Studio Inc, 3 Louis Ln, Croton on Hudson NY 10520.................914-739-9228
The Bookmill, 3610 Moore St, Los Angeles CA 90066.................................213-398-4645
Bookwright, PO Box 7119, Ann Arbor MI 48107...313-995-1470
Boston Word Works, 6354 Van Nuys Blvd Ste 420, Van Nuys CA 91401..818-787-8646
D W Bourne, Box 613, Woods Hole MA 02543...617-548-3705
Elsa Branden, 222 W 77th St Ste 1218, New York NY 10024.......................212-362-1100
Robert Brightman, 5 Sussex Rd, Great Neck NY 11020...............................516-482-2074
Norman Brown & Assocs, 21 Luzon Ave, Providence RI 02906.................401-751-2641

Business Media Resources, 150 Shorline Hwy, Mill Valley CA 94941.......415-331-6021
Carlsbad Publications, 3242 McKinley St, Carlsbad CA 92008 619-729-9543
Diane Carlson, 1215 Hull Terrace, Evanston IL 60202 312-869-7642
Anne Carson Assoc, 3323 Nebraska Ave, Washington DC 20016...............202-244-6679
Donald Cart, PO Box 65044, Lubbock TX 79464....................................806-793-0734
Claudia Caruana, PO Box 20077, Elmont NY 10017 516-488-5815
Curtis Casewit, PO Box 19039, Denver CO 80219..................................303-935-0277
Charles Choset, 90 Bedford St, New York NY 10014................................212-243-0035
Tina Clark, 318 Harvard St Ste 10, Brookline MA 02146 617-734-0807
Mollie L Cohen, 8 Grammercy Park S, New York NY 10003.....................212-533-1798
E R Cole, PO Box 91277, Cleveland OH 44101.......................................216-234-1775
Zipporah W Collins, 2140 Shattuck Ave Rm 404, Berkeley CA 94704 415-848-1442
Frances G Conn Assoc, 8320 Woodhaven Blvd, Bethesda MD 20817........301-365-5080
Connexions, 14011 Brookgreen Dr, Dallas TX 75240..............................214-234-4519
Contemporary Educ Services, 85 Bouvant Dr, Princeton NJ 08540 609-683-0155
Contemporary Perspectives Inc, 223 E 48th St, New York NY 10017 212-753-3800
Nancy L Daniels, Box 68, Lemont PA 16851..814-237-7711
May Dikeman, 70 Irving Pl, New York NY 10003 212-475-4533
Drennan Communications, 6 Valley Forge Ln, Weston CT 06883.............203-454-8652
A H Drummond Jr, 323 Springs Rd, Bedford MA 01730..........................617-275-1481
Ed It, PO Box 29527, Oakland CA 94604 415-763-3510
Edit Productions, PO Box 29527, Oakland CA 94604 415-763-3510
Editing & Publishing Services, Pleasant Point Rd, Cushing ME 04563.....207-354-2467
Editing Design & Production, 400 Market St, Philadelphia PA 19106.......215-592-1133
Editmasters/Mizelle, 4545 Connecticut Ave NW, Wash DC 20008 202-686-7252
The Editor's Bureau Ltd, Box 68, Westport CT 06881 203-227-9275
Editorial & Graphic Services, Martinsville NJ 08836...............................201-469-2195
Editorial Consultants Inc, 1605 12th Ave Ste #7, Seattle WA 98122........206-323-6475
Editorial Consultants Inc, 3221 Pierce St, San Francisco CA 94123..........415-931-7239
The Editorial Department, 541 Rt 9W, Grandview NY 10960 914-358-1158
Editorial Experts Inc, 85 S Bragg St Ste 400, Alexandria VA 22312 703-642-3040
Editorial Services, 531 N 66th St, Seattle WA 98103 206-782-4085
Editorial Services, 501 S Cortez Ste F-3, Prescott AZ 86301 602-445-8627
Editorial Services, Rt 1 Box 188, Bull Shoals AR 72619 501-224-4793
Educational Challenges Inc, 1009 Duke St, Alexandria VA 22314.............703-683-1500
J M B Edwards Writer & Editor, 2432 California, Berkeley CA 94703.....415-644-8287
Effective Learning, 7 N MacQuesten Pwy, Mt Vernon NY 10550 914-664-7944
Roger E Egan, 7 Lincoln Pl, New Brunswick NJ 08902 201-821-0106
Henry W Engel, 441 E 20th St, New York NY 10010...............................212-477-2597
Pearl Eppy, 201 E 79th St, New York NY 10021 212-737-0354
David R Esner Editorial Consultant, 16 Willow Pl, Brooklyn NY 11201..718-855-0792
Feedback Services, PO Box 5187, Bloomington IN 47402........................812-334-0325
Karen Feinberg, 5755 Nahant Ave, Cincinnati OH 45224.......................513-542-8328
Lillian Mermin Feinsilver, 510 McCartney St, Easton PA 18042 215-252-7005
Elane Feldman & Assoc, 101-A Clark St Apt 17B, Brooklyn NY 11201 718-875-3383
Janice J Feldstein Editorial Svcs, 860 N Lake Shore, Chicago IL 60611...312-951-6215
First Editions, PO Box 1158, Sedona AZ 86336......................................602-282-1989
Daniel Fliegler, 2741 Wallace Ave, Bronx NY 10467 212-654-5672
Charles Radley Force, 2076 Southwood Rd, Jackson MS 39211 601-366-3748
Free Lance Exchange Inc, 111 E 85th St, New York NY 10028 212-722-5816
Fromer Writing & Editing Service, 1508 13th St NW, Wash DC 20005 201-232-6915
David Frost PhD, 1229 E 7th St, Plainfield NJ 07062 201-755-3286
Gabriel House Inc, 5045 W Oakton St, Skokie IL 60077..........................312-675-1146

Diane Gallo, Box 231 RD 1, Mount Upton NY 13809 607-764-8139
The Garber Group, 420 E 55th St Ste 2R, New York NY 10022.................212-421-4097
Mary-Stuart Garden, 17 Stuyvesant Oval, New York NY 10009 212-477-2597
Martha & Dennis Gleason, Box 540, Boothbay Harbor ME 04538............207-633-2336
Gravity Publishing, 6324 Heather Ridge Way, Oakland CA 94611............415-339-3774
George D Griffin, 11 E 9th St, New York NY 10003....................................212-254-7527
Shelley Gross Assoc, PO Box 2415, Hollywood CA 90078.........................213-465-2630
Judith S Grossman, 26 Blancoyd Rd, Merion PA 19066 215-664-3732
Isabel S Grossner, 61 Tuxedo Rd, Montclair NJ 07042...............................201-746-5371
The Guilford Group, 124 Jerry Ln, Davisville RI 02854 401-884-3101
Linda Hardcastle, 13707 FM 149 Ste 218, Houston TX 77086...................713-440-8876
Harkavy Publishing Service, 33 W 17th St, New York NY 10011...............212-929-1339
Harriett, 135 54th St, New York NY 10022...212-688-0094
Jean Highland, 12 E 97th St, New York NY 10029......................................212-289-5318
Daniel W Hill, 3023 Honeysuckle Way NE, Salem OR 97303 503-364-9210
Diane Casella Hines, 2366 Live Oak Meadow Rd, Malibu CA 90265........213-456-3220
Lee M Hoffman, 8320 Sands Point Blvd Apt 203, Tamarac FL 33321........305-726-2555
Marcia Holly PhD, 214 Maple St, New Haven CT 06511............................203-787-9699
Janet M Hunter, 411 Rose Ave, Mill Valley CA 94941 415-388-8788
Jean Wiley Huyler Comm, 922 N Pearl A27, Tocoma WA 98406................206-759-1579
E H Immergut & Assoc, 2 Sidney Pl, Brooklyn NY 11201 718-625-1364
Island Press Publishing, 175 Bahia Via, Ft Meyers Beach FL 33931.........813-463-9482
Dorri Jacobs, 784 Columbus Ave, New York NY 10025 212-222-4606
Cliff Johnson & Assoc, 10867 Fruitland Dr, Studio City CA 91604.............818-761-5665
Curt Johnson, 3093 Dato, Highland Park IL 60035 312-432-6804
Aidan A Kelly, 2250 Central Ave Ste 332, Alameda CA 94501....................415-521-6126
A Kessler Editorial Services, 10 E 85th St, New York NY 10028.................212-772-8864
H L Kirk Assoc, 233 E 69th St, New York NY 10021 212-737-6626
W Scott Knoke, 178 N Bridge St, Somerville NJ 08876...............................201-526-4682
Deborah Kopka, 3208 S Barrington Ste G, Los Angeles CA 90066 213-391-4300
John Kremitske, 111 8th Ave Ste 1507, New York NY 10011 212-989-4783
L/A House Editorial, 5822 Uplander Way, Culver City CA 90230............213-216-5812
Larsen/Pomada, 1029 Jones St, San Francisco CA 94109 415-673-0939
Lazy Brown Assoc, 2800 Quebec St NW Ste 618, Wash DC 20008.............202-686-0975
Judith Lechner, 1314 Ocean Pwy, Brooklyn NY 11230 718-336-5649
Ligature Inc, 165 N Canal St, Chicago IL 60606...312-648-1233
Elaine Linden, 838 15th St, Santa Monica CA 90403 213-395-5731
Literary Consultants, 340 E 52nd St, New York NY 10022.........................212-758-4213
Donald MacLaren Assoc, 6713 Homestake Dr, Bowie MD 20715 301-262-0444
Manuscripts Intl, 408 E Main St, Dayton WA 99328..................................509-382-2436
Anne V McGravie, 7035 N Greenview, Chicago IL 60626 312-274-1835
Pat McNees, 5708 33rd St NW, Washington DC 20015 202-362-8694
Judith H McQuown & Co, 127 E 59th St #201, New York NY 10022.......212-688-1291
Tom Mellers, 849 E 12th St, New York NY 10003 212-254-4958
Barbara Mary Merson, 14 Heathrow Ln, Old Bridge NJ 08857 201-591-0882
Metropolitan Research Co, 100 Haven Ave, New York NY 10032..............212-781-0264
Sondra Mochson, 18 Overlook Dr, Port Washington NY 11050.................516-883-0984
MS/Smiths Editorial Consult, RR 1 Box 447, Bridgewater CT 06752......203-354-0866
MSS Manuscript Services, 408 S High St, Galena IL 61036 815-777-0831
J William Myers, 109 Fulton St, Lyons OH 43533 614-927-9719
Natl Evaluation Systems, 30 Gatehouse Rd, Amherst MA 01004...............413-256-0444
Natl Poetry Foundation, 302 Neville Univ of Maine, Orano ME 04469 207-581-3814
Lois Newman, 6545 Hollywood Blvd #201, Hollywood CA 90028..............213-464-8382

Rebecca Newman, 8360 Ridpath Dr, Los Angeles CA 90046........................213-654-0659
The T R Nugent Agency, 1058 Main St Ste 10, Malden MA 02148 617-322-7273
Pacific Publishing Services, 533 Stagg Ln, Santa Cruz CA 95062..............408-475-6527
Karen Papagapitos, 12 E 81st St, New York NY 10028 212-472-2524
Edith Messing Pavese, 2 Grace Ct, Brooklyn NY 11201 718-875-6250
Picture Research, 6307 Bannockburn Dr, Bethesda MD 20817 301-229-6722
Deborah Pritzker, 2676 Grand Concourse, Bronx NY 10458 212-364-3832
Pro-Edit, PO Box 3312, Glendale CA 91201 213-245-0296
Professional Editorial Svcs, 5531 Bubbling Wells, Ravenna OH 44266 216-682-5362
Programs on Change, 784 Columbus Ave Ste 1C, New York NY 10025...212-222-4606
Generosa Gina Protano, 16 N Chatsworth #104, Larchmont NY 10538...914-834-8896
Publishers Media, 5507 Morella Ave, North Hollywood CA 91607 818-980-2666
Publishers Workshop Inc, 63 Montague St, Brooklyn Hts NY 11201........718-855-1525
Publishing Resources Inc, Box 41307, San Juan PR 00940......................809-724-0318
Publishing Synthesis Ltd, 425 Broome St, New York NY 10013................212-966-4904
Reitt Editing Services, 3505 Hampton Hall Way, Atlanta GA 30319.........404-255-5790
Research Findings in Print, 26 W Jefferson Rd, Pittsford NY 14534 716-248-3947
Carol Z Rothkopf, 16 Rotary Ln, Summit NJ 07901.................................201-273-1255
Harold J Salemson, 12 Brookdale Rd, Glen Cove NY 11542.....................516-676-2894
Michael Scofield, 3323 Bryant, Palo Alto CA 94306 415-856-1478
David H Scott, Box 141, Blue Hill ME 04614..207-374-9933
Richard Selman, 14 Washington Pl, New York NY 10003...........................212-473-1874
Doris P Shalley, Genl Sullivan Box 166, Wash Crossing PA 18977...........215-493-3521
Sherwin Assoc, 2616 N Dayton, Chicago IL 60614....................................312-935-1581
Jean M Shirhall, 2700 N Norwood St, Arlington VA 22207 703-528-2617
Monica Shoffman-Graves, 101600 Overseas Hwy, Key Largo FL 33037...305-451-1462
Signum Books Ltd, Box 5057, Oregon City OR 97045 503-655-7092
Lynn Sonberg Book Services, 166 E 56th St, New York NY 10022 212-758-9604
Autumn Stanley, 241 Bonita los Trancos Wds, Portola Vly CA 94025.......415-851-1847
Sheila Steinberg, 42 Littlebrook Rd, Springfield NJ 07081 201-273-9388
Ruth Steyn, Box 222 Star Rt, Hancock ME 04640.....................................207-422-3373
Barbara Cohen Stratyner, 300 Riverside Dr, New York NY 10025 212-222-2172
Alfred Sundel, 400 C High Point Dr, Hartsdale NY 10530 914-948-3799
Elizabeth Peirce Swift, Pleasant Point Rd, Cushing ME 04563.................207-354-2467
Synthegraphics Corp, 940 Pleasant Ave, Highland Park IL 60035 312-432-7699
M A Timmons Comm Svcs, 555 Evening St, Worthington OH 43085........614-846-2887
Turner & Winston, 5306 38th St NW, Washington DC 20015.....................202-363-6459
Arlene S Uslander, 9406 Kilbourn, Skokie IL 60076 312-674-3701
Durrett Wagner, 614 Ingleside Pl, Evanston IL 60201................................312-236-8472
Gladys H Walker, 21 Thorburn Ave, Trumbull CT 06611 203-261-3085
Walking Bird Publication Services, PO Box 19499, Seattle WA 98109 206-285-1575
Lehman Weichselbaum, 83 Harrison Ave, Brooklyn NY 11206..................718-388-6486
Weidner Assoc Inc, Box C-50, Cinnaminson NJ 08077..............................609-486-1755
Bayla Winters, 2700 Scott Rd, Burbank CA 91504....................................818-846-1879
Helen Witty, 57 Lion Head Rock Rd, East Hampton NY 11937...................516-324-1503
Women In Communications, PO Box 9561, Austin TX 78766......................512-346-9875
The Wordsmith, 81 Club Rd, Upper Montclair NJ 07043............................201-783-4087
Wordsworth Communication, Box 9781, Alexandria VA 22304 703-642-8775
Wordworth Assoc, 9 Tappan Rd, Wellesley MA 02181 617-237-4761
Betty Wright & Assoc, PO Box 1069, Moore Haven FL 33471....................813-946-0293
Writers Alliance Ltd, 104 E 40th St, New York NY 10016 212-986-2830
Writers Publishing Service Co, 1512 Western Ave, Seattle WA 98101......206-284-9954
The Writing Service, 315 W 102nd St Ste 7B, New York NY 10025...........212-866-5930

The Writing Service, 6306 Pepper Hill Dr, West Bloomfield MI 48033.....313-851-7377
Joan Yarfitz Photo Env, 2021 Vista del Mar, Los Angeles CA 90068.......213-465-9947
York Production Services, 3600 W Market St, York PA 17404....................717-792-3551
Donald Young, 166 E 61st St Apt 3C, New York NY 10021.........................212-593-0010

NEWSPAPERS

This section lists daily and weekly newspapers in state order. An asterisk (*) denotes a daily newspaper. A plus (+) indicates a newspaper with a circulation of over 50,000.

ALABAMA

Advertiser-Free Press, 704 E Laurel St, Scottsboro AL 35768 205-574-5922
Alabama Journal*+, 200 Washington Ave, Montgomery AL 36104..........205-262-1611
Alexander City Outlook*, 139 Church St, Alexander City AL 35010..........205-234-4281
Andalusia Star-News, 209 Dunson, Andalusia AL 36420..............................205-222-1101
Anniston Star*, 216 W 10th St, Anniston AL 36202...................................205-236-1551
Arab Tribune, S Brindles Mountain Pkwy, Arab AL 35016 205-831-3771
Athens News Courier*, Houston & Green Sts, Athens AL 35611 205-232-2720
Atmore Advance, 301 S Main St, Atmore AL 36502 205-368-2123
Azalea City News & Review, 4430 Government, Mobile AL 36609.............205-666-9115
Baldwin Times, Box 571, Bay Minette AL 36507..205-937-2511
Birmingham News*+, 2200 4th St N, Birmingham AL 35202......................205-325-2222
Birmingham Post-Herald*+, 2200 4th Ave N, Birmingham AL 35203 205-325-2222
Boaz News Leader, Box 600, Boaz AL 35957..205-593-3361
Brewton Standard, Box 887, Brewton AL 36426.......................................205-867-4876
Butler Choctaw Advocate, 210 N Mulberry, Butler AL 36904..................205-459-2858
Central Alabama Ind Advertiser, Main St, Columbiana AL 35051..........205-669-3131
Centreville Press, 119 Court Sq, Centreville AL 35042 205-926-9769
Cherokee County Herald, 107 W 1st St, Centre AL 35960..........................205-927-5037
Clarke County Democrat, Box 39, Grove Hill AL 36451 205-275-3375
Colbert County Reporter, 106 W 5th St, Tuscumbia AL 35674....................205-383-8471
Community News, Main St, Sumiton AL 35148..205-648-3231
Cullman Tribune, 413 1st Ave SW, Cullman AL 35055................................205-739-1351
Daily Home*, 4 Sylacauga Hwy, Talladega AL 35160 205-362-1000
Decatur Daily*, 201 1st Ave SE, Decatur AL 35602 205-353-4612
Demopolis Times, 315 E Jefferson St, Demopolis AL 36732......................205-289-3791
Dothan Eagle*, 203 N Oates, Dothan AL 36302..205-792-3141
Eagle, 122 Tichenor Ave, Auburn AL 36830 601-821-7150
East Lauderdale News, E Lee St, Rogersville AL 35652................................205-247-5565
Eastern Shore Courier, 325 Fairhope Ave, Fairhope AL 36533 205-928-2321
Enterprise Ledger*, 106 N Edwards St, Enterprise AL 36330 205-347-9533
Eufaula Tribune, E Barbour St, Eufaula AL 36027 205-687-3506
Evergreen Courant, Box 440, Evergreen AL 36401.....................................205-578-1492
Fayette County Broadcaster, 735 E Columbus St, Fayette AL 35555.........205-932-3300
Florence Times*, 219 W Tennessee St, Florence AL 35630...........................205-766-3434
Ft Payne Times-Journal*, 200 8th St S E, Ft Payne AL 35967 205-845-2550
Franklin County Times, Box 1088, Russellville AL 35653 205-332-1881
Gadsden Times*, 401 Locust St, Gadsden AL 35902...................................205-547-7521
Greenville Advocate, 103 Hickory St, Greenville AL 36037 205-382-3111
Guntersville Advertiser-Gleam, Taylor St, Guntersville AL 35976.............205-582-3232

Haleyville Northwest Alabamian, Highway 195, Haleyville AL 35565........205-486-9461
Hamilton Journal-Record, Drawer N, Hamilton AL 35570 205-921-3106
Hartselle Enquirer, Box 929, Hartselle AL 35640.....................................205-773-6566
Heflin Cleburne News, Box 6, Heflin AL 36264..205-463-2872
Herald-Picture, 861 Florence Blvd, Florence AL 35631.............................205-764-1511
Huntsville News*, 2117 W Clinton Ave, Huntsville AL 35801....................205-532-4500
Huntsville Times*+, 2317 Memorial Pkwy SW, Huntsville AL 35807.......205-532-4000
Islander, 215 N McKenzie, Foley AL 36535..205-943-2151
Jacksonville News, 203 N Pelham Rd, Jacksonville AL 36265...................205-435-5021
Jasper Daily Mountain Eagle*, 2026 3rd Ave, Jasper AL 35501................205-221-2840
Lanett Valley Times-News*, 220 N 12th St, Lanett AL 36863....................205-644-1101
Leeds News, 720 Parkway Dr, Leeds AL 35094..205-699-2214
Linden Democrat-Reporter, Drawer G, Linden AL 36748 205-295-5224
Madison County Record, Box 175, Madison AL 35758..............................205-772-8666
Mobile Beacon, 2311 Costarides, Mobile AL 36617 205-479-0629
Mobile County News, PO Box 396, Byu La Batre AL 36509......................205-824-2280
Mobile Inner City News, 551 Summerville St, Mobile AL 36633 205-473-2767
Mobile Press*+, 304 Government St, Mobile AL 36630............................205-433-1551
Mobile Register*+, 304 Government St, Mobile AL 36630........................205-433-1551
Monroe Journal, 126 Hines St PO Box 826, Monroeville AL 36461 205-575-3282
Montgomery Advertiser*+, 200 Washington, Montgomery AL 36104......205-262-1611
Montgomery Independent, 880 S Court St, Montgomery AL 36104...........205-264-7323
Moulton Advertiser, 217 Walnut St, Moulton AL 35650............................205-974-1114
News-Herald, Box 809, Saraland AL 36571 205-675-8885
Opelika-Auburn News*, 3505 Pepperell Pkwy, Opelika AL 36801 205-749-6271
Opp News, Covington Ave, Opp AL 36467...205-493-3595
Oxford Sun, 112 Hwy 78 W, Anniston AL 36201.......................................205-831-3771
Phenix Citizen-Extra, 1507 5th Ave, Phenix City AL 36867......................205-298-0679
Piedmont Journal-Independent, 124 N Center, Piedmont AL 36067.........205-365-6739
Randolph Leader, Box 232, Roanoke AL 36274...205-863-2819
River City Shopper, 701 B 2nd Ave SE, Decatur AL 35601.......................205-355-2717
St Clair News-Aegis, Box 748, Pell City AL 35125....................................205-884-2310
Sand Mountain News, Main St, Rainsville AL 35986 205-638-2079
Sand Mountain Reporter, 2240 Hooper Dr, Albertville AL 35950.............205-878-1311
Selma Times-Journal*, 1018 Water Ave, Selma AL 36701.........................205-875-2110
South Alabamian, 1064 Coffeeville Rd, Jackson AL 36545........................205-246-4494
Southern Democrat, Washington Ave at 3rd St, Oneonta AL 35121..........205-625-3231
Tallassee Tribune, 301 Gilmer Ave, Tallassee AL 36078 205-283-6568
Troy Messenger*, 113 Market St, Troy AL 36081......................................205-566-4270
Tuscalossa News*, 2001 6th St, Tuscalossa AL 35402...............................205-345-0505
Tuskegee Inst Tuskegeean+, 1907 Washington St, Tuskegee AL 36088....205-727-2840
Vernon Lamar Democrat, 124 1st St NW, Vernon AL 35592.....................205-695-7029
Wetumpka Herald, 300 Green St, Wetumpka AL 36092.............................205-567-7811

ALASKA

Anchorage Daily News*, 821 W 5th Ave, Anchorage AK 99510...................907-272-8561
Anchorage Times*+, 820 4th St, Anchorage AK 99501.............................907-263-9000
Fairbanks Daily News-Miner*, 200 N Cushman, Fairbanks AK 99707......907-456-6661
The Frontiersman, Box D, Palmer AK 99645...907-745-3288
Juneau Empire*, 3100 Channel Dr, Juneau AK 99801...............................907-586-3740
Ketchikan Daily News*, Box 7900, Ketchikan AK 99901...........................907-225-3157
Kodiak Daily Mirror*, 216 W Rezanof, Kodiak AK 99615.........................907-486-3227

ARIZONA

Apache Junction Independent, 2066 W Apache, Apache AZ 85220...........602-982-7799
Arizona Daily Sun*, 417 W Santa Fe Ave, Flagstaff AZ 86002 602-774-4545
Arizona Republic*+, 120 E Van Buren St, Phoenix AZ 85004 602-271-8000
Arizona Silver Belt, 298 N Pine, Globe AZ 85501.....................................602-425-7121
Arizonan Tribune*, 35 W Boston, Chandler AZ 85224...............................602-963-6666
Casa Grande Dispatch*, 200 W 2nd St, Casa Grande AZ 85222.................602-836-7461
Central Phoenix Independent, 4717 N Central Ave, Phoenix AZ 85012....602-263-9176
Copper Era, Box 1357, Clifton AZ 85533 602-865-3162
The Courier*, 147 N Cortez, Prescott AZ 86302 602-445-3333
Daily News-Sun*, 10020 Santa Fe Dr, Sun City AZ 85372 602-972-6397
Desert Airman, 1 W Orange Grove Rd, Tucson AZ 85704...........................602-297-1107
Eastern Arizona Courier, 301 E Hwy 70, Safford AZ 85546 602-428-2560
Gilbert Independent, 4210 E Main St No 10, Mesa AZ 85205 602-830-3862
Green Valley News, Box 567, Green Valley AZ 85614...............................602-625-5511
Holbrook Tribune News-Snowflake, 200 E Hopi, Holbrook AZ 86025 602-524-6203
Kingman Daily Miner*, 3015 Stockton Hill Rd, Kingman AZ 86401.........602-753-6397
Lake Havasu City Herald, 2225 W Acoma, Lake Havasu AZ 86403.........602-855-2197
Mesa Tribune*, 120 W 1st Ave, Mesa AZ 85201..602-833-1221
Mohave Valley News, Box 567, Bullhead City AZ 86430 602-754-2233
New Times+, PO Box 2510, Phoenix AZ 85002..602-271-0040
North Scottsdale Rancher, Box 5424, Scottsdale AZ 85261 602-483-0977
Paradise Valley Independent, 10854 N 32nd St, Phoenix AZ 85028 602-992-0741
Parker Pioneer, Box N, Parker AZ 85344...602-669-2275
Payson Roundup & Rim Country News, Box 1460, Payson AZ 85541.......602-474-5251
Phoenix Gazette*+, 120 E Van Buren St, Phoenix AZ 85004 602-271-8000
Red Rock News, 114 Van Deren, Sedona AZ 86336 602-282-7795
Scottsdale Independent, Box 5424, Scottsdale AZ 85261............................602-483-0977
Scottsdale Progress*, PO Box 1150, Scottsdale AZ 85252..........................602-941-2300
Sierra Vista Herald*, 102 Fab Ave, Sierra Vista AZ 85635........................602-458-9440
Sun Cities Independent, 10327 W Coggins Dr, Sun City AZ 85351 602-972-6101
Tempe Daily News*, 607 Mill Ave, Tempe AZ 85281................................602-829-4700
Tucson Arizona Daily Star*+, 4850 S Park Ave, Tucson AZ 85726 602-573-4400
Tucson Citizen*+, 4850 S Park Ave, Tucson AZ 85726..............................602-294-4433
Tucson Weekly, PO Box 2429, Tucson AZ 85702.......................................602-792-3630
Verde Independent, 116 S Main St, Cottonwood AZ 86326..........................602-634-2241
Verde View, Box 1187, Camp Verde AZ 86322...602-567-3162
Wampum Saver & Ind Shopper, Ed Van Ctr, Show Low AZ 85901..........602-537-5721
Weekly Territorial, 1 W Orange Grove Rd, Tucson AZ 85704 602-297-1107
Westsider, 195 Lamar Blvd, Goodyear AZ 85338 602-932-2170
White Mountain Independent, Ed Van Center, Show Low AZ 85901.......602-537-5721
Wickenburg Sun, Box 1298, Wickenburg AZ 85358....................................602-684-5454
Yuma Daily Sun*, 2055 S Arizona Ave, Yuma AZ 85364.............................602-783-3333

ARKANSAS

Advance Monticellonian, 314 N Main, Monticello AR 71655....................501-367-5325
Arkadelphia Daily Siftings Herald*, 26th St, Arkadelphia AR 71923........501-246-5525
Arkansas Democrat*+, Capitol Ave & Scott St, Little Rock AR 72201....501-378-3400
Arkansas Gazette*+, 112 W 3rd, Little Rock AR 72201............................501-371-3700
Ashley News Observer, 102 Pine St, Crossett AR 71635............................501-364-5186

Batesville Guard*, 258 W Main St, Batesville AR 72501 501-793-2383
Baxter Bulletin, 16 W 6th St, Mountain Home AR 72653.............................501-425-3133
Benton County Daily Democrat*, 209 N W A, Bentonville AR 72712 501-273-7781
Benton Daily Courier*, 322 N Main St, Benton AR 72015 501-778-8228
Berryville Star-Progress, Oakview Dr, Berryville AR 72616 501-423-6636
Brinkley Argus, 308 W Cedar, Brinkley AR 72021.......................................501-734-1056
Camden News*, 113 Madison Ave, Camden AR 71701................................501-836-8192
Carroll County Tribune, 123 E Main, Green Forest AR 72638.....................501-438-5221
Cleburne County Times, 107 N 4th St, Heber Springs AR 72543 501-362-2425
Clinton Van Buren County Democrat, 114 S Court, Clinton AR 72031 501-745-5175
Conway Log Cabin Democrat*, 1058 Front St, Conway AR 72032................501-327-6621
Courier News*, N Broadway & Moultrie, Blytheville AR 72316...................501-763-4461
Courier-Democrat*, 201 E 2nd St, Russellville AR 72801 501-968-5252
Daily Citizen*, 3000 E Race Ave, Searcy AR 72143.....................................501-268-8621
DeQueen Daily Citizen*, 404 DeQueen Ave, DeQueen AR 71832...............501-642-2111
Dumas Clarion, 136 E Waterman, Dumas AR 71639.....................................501-382-4925
El Dorado News-Times*, 111 N Madison, El Dorado AR 71730...................501-862-6611
Forrest City Times-Herald*, 222 N Izard St, Forrest City AR 72335..........501-633-3130
Harrison Times*, 111 W Rush Ave, Harrison AR 72601...............................501-741-2325
Helena-West Helena World*, 417 York St, Helena AR 72342 501-338-9181
Herald & Democrat, 101 N Mt Olive, Siloam Springs AR 72761..................501-524-5144
Hope Star*, W 3rd & Grady Sts, Hope AR 71801 501-777-8841
Hot Springs Sentinel Record*, 300 Spring, Hot Spgs AR 71901..................501-623-7711
Interstate News, 1225 Hwy 68 Bypass W, Siloam Springs AR 72761...........501-524-5030
Jacksonville Daily News*, 116 W Hickory, Jacksonville AR 72076...............501-982-6506
Johnson County Graphic, 203 E Cherry, Clarksville AR 72830.....................501-754-2005
Jonesboro Sun*, 518 Carson, Jonesboro AR 72401......................................501-935-5525
Lincoln Ledger, Town Square, Star City AR 71667.......................................501-628-4161
Little Rock Southern Mediator+, PO Box 1257, Little Rock AR 72201 ...501-376-3000
Madison County Record, 109 Court St, Huntsville AR 72740.......................501-738-2141
Magnolia Banner-News*, Box 100, Magnolia AR 71753 501-234-5130
Malvern Daily Record*, 219 Locust, Malvern AR 72104 501-337-7523
Marianna Courier Index, 12 W Chestnut, Marianna AR 72360 501-295-2521
Marshall Mountain Wave, 103 E Main, Marshall AR 72650 501-448-3321
Mena Star, 501 Mena St, Mena AR 71953 501-394-1900
Nashville News, 418 N Main, Nashville AR 71852...501-845-2010
Newport Daily Independent*, 2111 Highway 67 N, Newport AR 72112 501-523-5855
North Little Rock Times, 26rh & Willow, N Little Rock AR 72115.............501-758-2571
Northwest Arkansas Times*, 212 N East Ave, Fayetteville AR 72701........501-442-6242
Osceola Times, 112 N Poplar, Osceola AR 72370..501-563-2615
Paragould Daily Press*, Highway 49 at Hunt St, Paragould AR 72450.....501-239-8562
Petit Jean Country Headlight, 908 W Broadway, Morrilton AR 72110 501-354-2451
Piggott Times, 209 W Main St PO Box 59, Piggott AR 72454 501-598-2201
Pine Bluff Commercial*, 300 Beech St, Pine Bluff AR 71601 501-534-3400
Pine Bluff News, 421 W Barraque, Pine Bluff AR 71611...............................501-534-8803
Pocahontas Star-Herald, Box 608, Pocahontas AR 72455 501-892-4554
Prescott Nevada County Picayune, 125 W Main, Prescott AR 71857..........501-887-2002
Sheridan Headlight, 101 E Center, Sheridan AR 72150................................501-942-2142
Southwest Times Record*, 920 Rogers, Ft Smith AR 72901 501-782-7770
Springdale News*, 514 E Emma Ave, Springdale AR 72764..........................501-751-6200
Stuttgart Daily Leader*, 111 W 6th St, Stuttgart AR 72160 501-673-8533
Trumann Democrat, 106 E Main, Trumann AR 72472..................................501-483-6317
Van Buren Press Argus, 213 Main St, Van Buren AR 72956 501-474-3443

Walnut Ridge Times Dispatch, 225 W Main, Walnut Ridge AR 72476.....501-886-2464
West Memphis Evening Times*, 111 E Bond, W Memphis AR 72301......501-735-1010
Wynne Progress, 702 N Falls Blvd, Wynne AR 72396 501-238-2375
Yellville Mountain Echo, PO Box 528, Yellville AR 72687.........................501-449-4257

CALIFORNIA

Agoura Valley News, Box 236, Agoura CA 91301 213-889-1230
Alameda Times Star*, 1516 Oak St, Alameda CA 94501 415-523-1200
Altadenan-Pasadenan Chronicle, 2396 N Lake, Altadena CA 91001.........213-798-8954
Alturas-Modoc County Record, 201 W Carlos, Alturas CA 96101 916-233-2632
Anaheim Bulletin*, 1771 S Lewis St, Anaheim CA 92805........................714-634-1567
Anaheim Independent, 13261 Century Blvd, Garden Grove CA 92643......714-537-7510
Antelope Valley Ledger*, 44815 Fig Ave, Lancaster CA 93534....................805-948-4701
Antioch Daily Ledger*, 1700 Cavallo Rd, Antioch CA 94509 415-757-2525
Arcadia Tribune, 10 N 1st Ave, Arcadia CA 91006................................818-446-0111
The Argus*, 37427 Centralmont Pl, Fremont CA 94536.............................415-794-0111
The Ark, 1606 Juanita Ln, Belevedere CA 94920.....................................415-435-2652
Artesia/Cerritos Community Advocate, Box 95, Artesia CA 90701...........213-402-4463
Atascadero News, 5660 El Camino Real, Atascadero CA 93422.................805-466-2585
Atwater Signal, 927 Atwater Blvd, Atwater CA 95301................................209-358-6431
Auburn Journal, 1030 High St, Auburn CA 95603....................................916-885-5656
Azusa Herald, 234 E Foothill Blvd, Azusa CA 91702 213-969-1711
Bakersfield Californian*+, Bin 440, Bakersfield CA 93302....................805-395-7500
Banning Record Gazette*, 218 N Murray St, Banning CA 92220 714-849-4586
Barstow Desert Dispatch*, 130 Coolwater, Barstow CA 92311 619-256-2257
Beacon March AFB, 3512 14th St, Riverside CA 92501.............................714-684-1200
Bell Gardens Review, Box 2158, Bell CA 90201..............:.....................213-869-3585
Bell-Maywood-Cudahy Industrial Post, 6415 Atlantic, Bell CA 90201......213-771-2222
Bellflower Herald American+, 117000 Bellflower, Bellflower CA 90706 ..213-925-7475
Belmont Courier Bulletin, 640 Roble Ave, Menlo Park CA 94025.............415-326-5580
Belvedere Citizen, 5420 N Figueroa St, Los Angeles CA 90042 213-254-5111
Berkeley Press, Grand Lake Sta, Oakland CA 94610................................415-893-8000
Beverly Hills Courier, 8840 Olympic Blvd, Beverly Hills CA 90211 213-278-1322
Beverly Hills Independent, 1920 Colorado, Santa Monica CA 90404.........213-829-6811
Beverly Hills Post, 1433 S Robertson Blvd, Los Angeles CA 90035 213-552-3364
Big Bear Life & The Grizzly, Box 1789, Big Bear Lake CA 92315.............714-866-3456
Brawley News*, 135 S Plaza, Brawley CA 92227......................................619-344-1220
Brentwood Westwood Press, 1920 Colorado, Santa Monica CA 90404......213-829-6811
Brooklyn-Belvedere Comet, 2912 E Brooklyn, Los Angeles CA 90033 213-265-5743
Buena Park News, 13261 Century Blvd, Garden Grove CA 92643.............714-537-7510
Burbank Daily Review*, 220 E Magnolia Blvd, Burbank CA 91502............213-843-8700
Burbank Scene, 10001 Commerce Ave, Tujunga CA 91042.......................213-352-3131
Burlingame Leader, 205 Broadway, Millbrae CA 94030 415-697-5335
Butterfield Express-Valley, 24231 Sunnymead, Sunnymead CA 92388......714-653-7614
Campbell Press, 10950 N Blaney Ave, Cupertino CA 95014 408-255-7500
Carmarillo Daily News*, 99 S Glenn Dr, Carmirillo CA 93010 805-987-5001
Carmel Valley Outlook, Ocean & San Carlos, Carmel CA 93921..............408-624-0162
Carmichael Citizen, Box 38, Fair Oaks CA 95628....................................916-635-3300
Carousel, 687 1st St, Encinitas CA 92024 619-753-6543
Carson Star & Harbor Mail, 5215 Torrance Blvd, Torrance CA 90509....213-540-5511
Central Coast Times, PO Box 1561, San Luis Obispo CA 93406.................805-544-6500
Century City Post, 1433 S Robertson Blvd, Los Angeles CA 90035 213-552-3364

Ceres Courier, 2940 4th St, Ceres CA 95307..209-537-5932
Chico Enterprise-Record*, 700 Broadway, Chico CA 95926......................916-891-1234
Chico News & Review+, 353 E 2nd St, Chico CA 95928...........................916-894-2300
Citrus Heights Bulletin, Box 38, Fair Oaks CA 95628.................................916-635-3300
City News, 1660 Beverly Blvd, Los Angeles CA 90026..............................213-484-2840
City Press, 1660 Beverly Blvd, Los Angeles CA 90026..............................213-484-2840
City Terrace Comet, 2912 E Brooklyn Ave, Los Angeles CA 90033...........213-263-5743
Claremont Courier, 112 Harvard Ave, Claremont CA 91711......................714-621-4761
Cloverdale Revellie, 112 W 1st St, Cloverdale CA 95425..........................707-894-3339
Clovis Independent, 1321 Railroad Ave, Clovis CA 93612.........................209-298-8081
Coalinga Record, Box 496, Coalinga CA 93210...209-935-1517
Coast Dispatch, 687 1st St, Encinitas CA 92024..619-753-6543
Coastside Chronicle, 1331 San Mateo, S San Fran CA 94080.....................415-952-4105
Colton Courier, 333 E Valley Blvd, Colton CA 92324................................714-825-1145
Colusa County Sun Herald*, 210 6th St PO Box 89, Colusa CA 95932.....916-458-2121
Concord Transcript*, Box 308, Concord CA 94522....................................415-682-6440
Construction Labor News, 2101 Almaden Rd #303, San Jose CA 95125..408-265-6280
Contra Costa Independent*, 164 Harbour Way, Richmond CA 94801.....415-234-6262
Contra Costa Sun, Box 599, Lafayette CA 94549..415-284-4444
Contra Costa Times*+, 2640 Shadelands Dr, Walnut Creek CA 94598....415-935-2525
Coronado Journal, 1125 Loma Ave, Coronado CA 92118............................619-435-3141
Costa Mesa News+, 1609 Babcock Ave, Newport Beach CA 92663..........714-631-8120
Country Almanac, PO Box 620029, Redwood City CA 94062......................415-851-0200
Culver City News+, 4043 Irving Pl, Culver City CA 90232.......................213-893-5271
Cupertino Courier, 10950 N Blaney Ave, Cupertino CA 95014....................408-255-7500
Daily Californian*, 1000 Pioneer Way, El Cajor CA 92022........................619-442-4404
Daily Democrat*, 702 Court St, Woodland CA 95695.................................916-662-5421
Daily Independent*, 739 N China Lake Rd, Ridgecrest CA 93555.............619-375-4481
Daily News*+, 14539 Sylvan St, Van Nuys CA 91411..............................818-997-4111
Daily Press*, PO Box 427, Paso Robles CA 93447.....................................805-238-0330
Daily Review*, 116 W Winton Ave, Hayward CA 94544............................415-783-6111
Daily Star Progress*, 600 S Palm St, La Habra CA 90632.........................213-697-1734
Daily Sun-Post*, 1542 N El Camino Real, San Clemente CA 92672..........714-492-5121
Daily Tribune*+, 1210 Azusa Canyon, W Covina CA 91790......................213-962-8811
Daly City Record, 1331 San Mateo Ave, S San Francisco CA 94080..........415-952-4105
Danville Valley Pioneer, Box 68N Blaney Ave, Danville CA 94526............415-837-4267
Davis Enterprise*, 315 G St, Davis CA 95616..916-756-0800
Del Norte Triplicate, 312 H St, Crescent City CA 95531............................707-464-2141
Desert Sentinel, 66538 E 8th St, Desert Hot Spgs CA 92240......................714-329-1411
Desert Sun*, 611 S Palm Canyon Dr, Palm Springs CA 92263...................619-325-8666
Desert Trail, Box 159, 29 Palms CA 92277..714-367-3577
Desert View, 255 N El Cielo, Palm Spgs CA 92262...................................619-327-6205
Diamond Bar Bulletin, Box 4000, Ontario CA 91761.................................714-984-2468
Dispatch, 6400 Monterey St, Gilroy CA 95020...408-842-6411
Eagle Rock Sentinel, 5420 N Figueroa St, Los Angeles CA 90042.............213-254-5111
East Bay Express+, PO Box 3198, Berkeley CA 94703..............................415-652-4610
East Los Angeles Gazette, 2100 W Beverly Blvd, Montebello CA 90640...213-727-1117
East Los Angeles Tribune, 2100 W Beverly Blvd, Montebello CA 90640..213-727-1117
East San Jose Sun, 10950 N Blaney Ave, Cupertino CA 95014....................408-255-7500
East Yolo Record, Box 38, Fair Oaks CA 95628.......................................916-635-3300
Eastside Journal, 5420 N Figueroa St, Los Angeles CA 90042...................213-254-5111
Eastside Sun, 2912 E Brooklyn Ave, Los Angeles CA 90033......................213-263-5743
Easy Reader+, 1233 Hermosa Ave, Hermosa Beach CA 90254....................213-372-4611

Edwards AFB The Shuttle, 6298 Curtis Pl, California City CA 93505........619-373-8686
El Mundo, 630 20th St, Oakland CA 94612..415-763-1120
El Segundo Herald, 107 Sierra St, El Segundo CA 90245.............................213-322-1830
El Segundo-Hawthorne Beacon, 5215 Torrance, Torrance CA 90509........213-540-5511
El Sereno Star, 5420 N Figueroa St, Los Angeles CA 90042.........................213-254-5111
Elk Grove Citizen, 8998 Elk Grove Blvd, Elk Grove CA 95624.....................916-685-3945
Enterprise, 232 S Main St, Fallbrook CA 92028..714-728-6116
Enterprise, 6298 Curtis Pl, Califoria City CA 93505......................................619-373-8686
Escondido News Reporter, 395 N Hale, Escondido CA 92025......................619-489-1901
Escondido Times-Advocate*, 207 E Pennsylvania, Escondido CA 92025..619-745-6611
Eureka Times Standard*, 930 6th St, Eureka CA 95501................................707-442-1711
Extraprize, 232 S Main St, Fallbrook CA 92028...714-728-6116
Fairfield Daily Republic*, 1250 Texas St, Fairfield CA 94533.....................707-425-4646
Five Cities Times, 1052 Grand Ave, Arroyo Grande CA 93420.....................805-489-4206
Folsom Telegraph, 825 Sutter St, Folsom CA 95630......................................916-985-2581
Fontana Herald News*, 16920 Spring St, Fontana CA 92335......................714-822-2231
Foster City Progress, 1261 E Hillsdale Blvd, San Mateo CA 94404............415-574-9292
Fresno Bee*+, 1626 E St, Fresno CA 93786...209-441-6111
Fresno Guide*+, Box 11907, Fresno CA 93775.....:.......................................209-268-8611
Ft Bragg Advocate-News, Box 1188, Ft Bragg CA 95437...............................707-964-5642
Fullerton Daily News Tribune*, 655 W Valencia, Fullerton CA 92632......714-871-2345
Galt Herald, 604 N Lincoln Way, Galt CA 95632..209-745-1551
Gardena Breeze Advertiser, 5215 Torrance Blvd, Torrance CA 90509......213-540-5511
Gardena Valley News, 16417 S Western Ave, Gardena CA 90247.................213-329-6351
Glendale News-Press*, 111 N Isabel, Glendale CA 91209.............................213-241-4141
Glendora Press, 234 E Foothill Blvd, Azusa CA 91702..................................213-969-1711
Grass Valley Union*, 11464 Sutton Way, Grass Valley CA 95945................916-273-9561
Gridley Herald, 630 Washington St, Gridley CA 95948.................................916-846-3661
Griffith Park News, 1660 Beverly Blvd, Los Angeles CA 90026....................213-484-2840
Half Moon Bay Review, 714 Kelly Ave, Half Moon Bay CA 94019..............415-726-4424
Hanford Sentinel*, 418 W 8th St, Hanford CA 93232....................................209-582-0471
Hawthorne Press Tribune, 4043 Irving Pl, Culver City CA 90232.............213-839-5271
Healdsburg Tribune Enterprise, Box 518, Healdsburg CA 95448.............707-433-4451
Hemet News*, 123 Carmalita St, Hemet CA 92343.......................................714-925-0555
Hesperia Resorter, 16925 Main St, Hesperia CA 92345................................619-244-0021
Hi-Desert Star, 7333 Apache Trail, Yucca Valley CA 92284.........................619-365-3315
Highland Park News-Herald, PO Box 1031, Los Angeles CA 90042..........213-254-5111
Highlander+, 19331 E Walnut, La Puente CA 91748.....................................714-594-6886
Hollister Evening Free Lance*, 350 6th St, Hollister CA 95023...................408-637-5566
Hollywood Citizen News, PO Box 1031, Los Angeles CA 90026 213-484-2840
Humboldt Beacon & Fortuna Advance, 928 Main, Fortuna CA 95540......707-725-6166
Huntington Bch Independent+, 13261 Century, Gdn Grove CA 92643....714-537-7510
Huntington Harbour Sun, 216 Main St, Seal Beach CA 90704....................213-430-7555
Huntington Park Bulletin, 6415 Atlantic Ave, Bell CA 90201......................213-771-2222
Huntington Park Daily Signal*, 12130 Paramount, Downey CA 90242....213-862-1645
Imperial Beach Reminder, 1231 Palm Ave, Imperial Beach CA 92032.....714-424-8162
Imperial Beach Star News, 835 3rd, Chula Vista CA 92010 619-427-3000
Imperial Valley Press*, 205 N 8th St, El Centro CA 92243 619-352-2211
Independent & Gazette*+, 164 Harbour Way, Richmond CA 94801........415-234-6262
Independent & Star News, 1920 Colorado, Santa Monica CA 90404.........213-829-6811
Indio Daily News*, 45140 Towne, Indio CA 92201..619-347-3313
Indio Merchant, 74-405 Hwy 111, Palm Desert CA 92260............................619-346-1181
Inglewood News+, 4043 Irving Pl, Culver City CA 90232.............................213-839-5271

Inglewood-Hawthorne Wave, 2621 W 54th St, Los Angeles CA 90043.......213-294-4111
Inter-City Express+, 1210 Azusa Canyon Rd, W Covina CA 91790.........213-962-8811
Intermountain News, 1075 Main St, Burney CA 96013 916-335-4533
Irvine Today, 1609 Babcock Ave, Newport Beach CA 92663 714-631-8120
Irvine World News, 16630 Aston St, Santa Ana CA 92713.........................714-979-6865
Kelseyville Lake Sun & Sun Sampler, Box 972, Kelseyville CA 95451 707-279-1775
Kern Valley Sun, 41 Big Blue Rd, Kernville CA 93238..............................714-376-2213
King City Rustler, Box J, King City CA 93930...408-385-3222
La Canada Valley Sun, 1 Valley Sun Ln, La Canada CA 91011...................213-790-8774
La Jolla Light, 450 Pine St, La Jolla CA 92037..619-459-4201
La Mirada Lamplighter, 13261 Century Blvd, Garden Grove CA 92643 ..714-537-7510
La Verne Courier, 112 Harvard Ave, Claremont CA 91711........................714-621-4761
La Verne Leader, Box 4000, Ontario CA 91761..714-984-2468
Laguna Niguel News, 384 Forest Ave #22A, Laguna Beach CA 92651 714-497-6555
Lake Arrowhead Mountain News, Box 310, Lake Arrowhead CA 92352 ..714-337-6145
Lake County Record-Bee, Box 848, Lakeport CA 95453 707-263-5636
Lake Tahoe News, 3330 Lake Tahoe Blvd, S Lake Tahoe CA 95705..........916-544-8904
Lakewood Clarion, Box 586, Paramount CA 90723 213-633-0731
Lamont Reporter, 9717 Main St, Lamont CA 93241..................................805-845-3704
Las Virgenes Independent, Box 236, Agoura CA 91301.............................213-889-1230
Las Virgenes News Enterprise, 23961 Craftsman, Calabasas CA 91302....213-346-8822
Lassen Advocate, 1803 Main St, Susanville CA 96130 916-257-4106
Lawndale Tribune+, 4043 Irving Pl, Culver City CA 90232.....................213-839-5271
Leisure World News, 23522 Paseo de Valencia, Laguna Hills CA 92653...714-837-5200
Livermore Tri Valley Herald*, 6207 Sierra Ct, Dublin CA 94568................415-447-2111
Locus*+, 34 Ridgewood Lane, Oakland CA 94611 415-339-9196
Lodi News-Sentinel*, PO Box 1360, Lodi CA 95241.................................209-369-2761
Lompoc Record*, 115 N H St, Lompoc CA 93436 805-736-2313
Los Alamitos News-Enterprise, 3729 Catalina, Los Alamitos CA 90720 ...213-431-1397
Los Altos Town Crier, 10950 N Blaney Ave, Cupertino CA 95014 408-255-7500
Los Angeles Daily Journal*, 210 S Spring St, Los Angeles CA 90012........213-625-2141
Los Angeles Enterprise, PO Box 2522, Los Angeles CA 90054...................213-625-5844
LA Herald Examiner*+, 1111 S Broadway, Los Angeles CA 90015 213-744-8000
LA Metropolitan Gazette+, 812 N Fair Oaks, Pasadena CA 91103............213-792-4165
Los Angeles Opinion*+, 1436 S Main St, Los Angeles CA 90015..............213-748-1191
LA Reader+, 12224 Victory Blvd, N Hollywood CA 91606 818-763-3555
Los Angeles Reporter, 8300 W 3rd St, Los Angeles CA 90048...................213-653-3344
Los Angeles Sentinel, 1112 E 43rd St, Los Angeles CA 90011 213-232-3261
Los Angeles Star Review, 1421 S Stanely Ave, Los Angeles CA 90019 213-937-3754
Los Angeles Times*+, Times Mirror Sq, Los Angeles CA 90053.................213-972-5000
Los Angeles Weekly+, 2140 Hyperion Ave, Los Angeles CA 90027..........213-667-2620
Los Banos Enterprise, 525 J St, Los Banos CA 93635................................213-631-1155
Los Feliz Hills News, 1660 Beverly Blvd, Los Angeles CA 90026 213-484-2840
Los Gatos Times-Observer, 10950 N Blaney Ave, Cupertino CA 95014....408-255-7500
Lynwood Press & Tribune, Box 70, Lynwood CA 90262............................213-631-1155
Madera Daily Tribune*, 100 E 7th, Madera CA 93637...............................209-674-2424
Malibu Surfside News, 28925 Pacific Coast Hwy, Malibu CA 90265..........213-457-2112
Malibu Times, 3864 Las Flores Canyon Rd, Malibu CA 90265....................213-456-8016
Manhattan Beach Reporter, 500 S Sepulveda, Manhatn Bch CA 90266.....213-374-4040
Manteca Bulletin, 531 E Yosemite Ave, Manteca CA 95336........................209-239-3531
Marin Independent Jour*, 150 Alameda del Prado, Novato CA 94947.....415-883-8600
Mariposa Gazette, 5081 Jones St, Mariposa CA 95338 209-966-2500
Martinez News Gazette*, 615 Estudillo St, Martinez CA 94553..................415-228-6400

Mather Air Force-Wingtips, Box 38, Fair Oaks CA 95628 916-635-3300
McClellan AFB Spacemaker, Box 38, Fair Oaks CA 95628........................916-635-3300
Mendocino Beacon, 45066 Ukiah St, Mendocino CA 95460 707-937-5874
Merced County Times, PO Box 772, Merced CA 95341...............................209-358-5311
Merced Sun-Star*, 3033 N G St, Merced CA 95340......................................209-722-1511
Messenger & Advertiser, 5215 Torrance Blvd, Torrance CA 90509 213-540-5511
Metro, 410 S 1st St, San Jose CA 95113..408-298-8000
Mexican American Sun, 2912 E Brooklyn Ave, Los Angeles CA 90033 213-263-5743
Mid Valley News, 3622 Center Ave, El Monte CA 91731..............................818-443-1753
Mill Valley Record, 438 Miller Ave, Mill Valley CA 94941........................415-388-3211
Milpitas Post, 20 Corning Ave, Milpitas CA 95035.....................................408-262-2454
Modesto Bee*+, 1325 H St, Modesto CA 95354 209-578-2000
Montclair Courier, 111 S College Ave, Claremont CA 91711.....................714-621-4761
Montclair Press, Grand Lake Station, Oakland CA 94610 415-893-8000
Montclair Tribune, Box 4000, Ontario CA 91761 714-984-2468
Montebello Comet, 2912 E Brooklyn Ave, Los Angeles CA 90033...............213-262-5743
Monterey Park Comet, 2912 E Brooklyn Ave, Los Angeles CA 90033 213-262-5743
Monterey Peninsula Herald*, Pacific at Jefferson, Monterey CA 93940 ...408-372-3311
Morgan Hill Times, 30 E 3rd St, Morgan Hill CA 95037.............................408-779-4106
Morning Press Enterprise*+, 3512 14th St, Riverside CA 92592...............714-684-1200
Morning Press*, 425 W Vista Way, Vista CA 92083 619-724-7161
Morro Bay Sun-Bulletin, 1149 Market St, Morro Bay CA 93442 805-772-7346
Morthwest Leader, 1660 Beverly Blvd, Los Angeles CA 90026...................213-484-2840
Mount Shasta Herald, Box 127, Mount Shasta CA 96067 916-926-5214
Mountain Courier, Drawer B D, Crestline CA 92325 714-338-4449
Mountain View Sun, 10950 N Blaney Ave, Cupertino CA 95014 408-255-7500
Napa County Record, 520 3rd St PO Box 88, Napa CA 94558 707-252-8877
Napa Register*, 1615 2nd St, Napa CA 94558 707-226-3711
Natl City Star News, 835 3rd, Chula Vista CA 92010 619-427-3000
Needles Desert Star, 911 3rd St, Needles CA 92363 714-326-2222
Newhall Signal & Saugus Enterprise, PO Box 877, Newhall CA 91322 805-259-1234
Newport Ensign+, 1609 Babcock Ave, Newport Beach CA 92663 714-631-8120
News-Chronicle*, 2595 Thousand Oaks, Thousand Oaks CA 91359 805-496-3211
News-Post, 384 Forest Ave #22A, Laguna Beach CA 92651 714-497-6555
News-Press*+, De La Guerra Plz, Santa Barbara CA 93101 805-966-3911
Nonrovia News-Post, 10 N 1st Ave, Arcadia CA 91006 213-446-0111
North County News, 8044 San Miguel Canyon, Salinas CA 93907...............408-663-3000
North County Post, 1331 San Mateo, San Bruno CA 94066 415-952-4102
North Highlander, Box 38, Fair Oaks CA 95628...916-635-3300
North Shore Shopper, 839 Via De La Paz, Pacific Palisade CA 90272.......213-454-1321
Northeast Star-Review, 5420 N Figueroa St, Los Angeles CA 90042..........213-254-5111
Northridger, 18137 Parthenia St, Northridge CA 91325.............................213-886-1611
Novato Advance, 1068 Machin Ave, Novato CA 94947................................415-892-1516
Oaceanside Blade-Tribune*, 1722 S Hill St, Oceanside CA 92054 714-433-7333
Oakdale Leader, 122 S 3rd St, Oakdale CA 95361 209-847-3021
Oakland California Voice, 814 27th St, Oakland CA 94607..........................415-465-8552
Oakland Montclarion, 6208 La Salle Ave, Oakland CA 94611 415-339-3953
Oakland Post+, 630 20th St, Oakland CA 94612 415-763-1120
Oakland Tribune*+, 409 13th St, Oakland CA 94623..................................415-645-2000
Observer-American, 4474 Old Hwy 53, Clearlake Highlands CA 95422....707-994-6444
Ojai Valley News Inc, 1016 W Ojai Ave, Ojai CA 93023 805-646-1476
Ontario Daily Report*, 212 E B St, Ontario CA 91761 714-983-3511
Orange Coast Daily Pilot*+, 330 W Bay St, Costa Mesa CA 92627 714-642-4321

Orange County News+, 13261 Century Blvd, Garden Grove CA 92643....714-537-7510
Orange County Register*+, 625 N Grand Ave, Santa Ana CA 92711.......714-835-1234
Orangevale News, 825 Sutter St, Folsom CA 95630 916-985-2581
Oroville Mercury-Register*, 2081 2nd St, Oroville CA 95965....................916-533-3131
Outlook Mail, 1920 Colorado Ave, Santa Monica CA 90404....................213-829-6811
Oxnard Press Courier*, 300 W 9th St, Oxnard CA 93030 805-483-1101
Pacific Sun, PO Box 5553, Mill Valley CA 94942.......................................415-383-4500
Pacifica Record, 1331 San Mateo, S San Francisco CA 94080....................415-952-4102
Pacifica Tribune, 59 Aura Vista, Pacifica CA 94044 415-359-6666
Palm Springs Magazine, 74-405 Hwy 111, Palm Desert CA 92260 619-346-1181
Palmdale Antelope Valley Press, Box 880, Palmdale CA 93550 805-273-2700
Palo Verde Valley Times, 231 N Spring St, Blythe CA 92225....................714-922-3181
Palos Verdes Peninsula News, 900 Silver Spur, Pls Vrd Pnsla CA 90274 ..213-377-6877
Paradise Post, Box 70, Paradise CA 95969..916-877-4413
Parkside Journal, 1660 Beverly Blvd, Los Angeles CA 90026....................213-484-2840
Pasadena Star-News*, 525 E Colorado Blvd, Pasadena CA 91109.............818-578-6300
Pasadena Weekly, 300 S Raymond Ave #12, Pasadena CA 91105 818-584-1500
Peninsula Breeze, 5215 Torrance Blvd, Torrance CA 90509....................213-540-5511
Peninsula Times Tribune*+, 245 Lytton Ave, Palo Alto CA 94301............415-853-1200
Petaluma Argus-Courier*, 830 Pataluma Blvd, Petaluma CA 94952 707-762-4541
Pico Post, 1433 S Robertson Blvd, Los Angeles CA 90035 213-552-3364
Pico Rivera News, 4928 Whittier Blvd, Los Angeles CA 90022 213-268-7177
Pico/Beverlywood Post+, 1433 S Robertson, Los Angeles CA 90035........213-552-3370
Piedmont Press, Grand Lake Station, Oakland CA 94610.........................415-893-8000
Pittsburg Post-Dispatch*, 515 Railroad Ave, Pittsburg CA 94565 415-432-7336
Placentia Highlander, 1227 E Yorba Linda, Placentia CA 92670 714-524-8520
Placentia News-Times+, 1227 E Yorba Linda Blvd, Placentia CA 92670..714-524-8520
Placerville Mountain Democrat, 443 Main St, Placerville CA 95667 916-622-1255
Placerville Sierra Breeze, Box 446, Placerville CA 95667.........................916-622-2280
Pomona Progress-Bulletin*, 300 S Thomas St, Pomona CA 91766.............714-622-1201
Porterville Recorder*, 115 E Oak Ave, Porterville CA 93257 209-784-5000
Post Newspaper Group+, 630 20th St, Oakland CA 94612.........................415-763-1120
Press-Enterprise*+, 1534 N Palm Canyon, Palm Spgs CA 92262.............619-325-1151
Press-Enterprise*+, 3512 14th St, Riverside CA 92502 714-684-1200
Press-Telegram*+, 604 Pine Ave, Long Beach CA 90844 213-435-1161
Rancho Bernardo Journal, 16776 Bernardo Ctr, San Diego CA 92128.....714-487-5757
Rancho Cordovan, Box 38, Fair Oaks CA 95628..916-635-3300
Rancho Cucamonga Times, Box 4000, Ontario CA 91761 714-984-2468
Ravenswood Post, 640 Roble Ave, Menlo Park CA 94025..........................415-326-5580
Record Ledger, 10001 Commerce Ave, Tujunga CA 91042 213-352-3131
Red Bluff Daily News*, 545 Diamond Ave, Red Bluff CA 96080..............916-527-2151
Redding Record Searchlight*, 1101 Twin View, Redding CA 96099 916-243-2424
Redlands Daily Facts*, 700 Brookside Ave, Redlands CA 92373................714-793-3221
Reedley Exponent, Box 432, Reedley CA 93654...209-638-2244
Reflex & Advertiser, 5215 Torrance Blvd, Torrance CA 90509 213-540-5511
Reporter*, PO Box 1509, Vacaville CA 95696 707-448-2200
Review/Mono Herald, 1566 Tavern Rd, Mammoth Lakes CA 93546 619-934-8544
Rialto Record, 130 S Riverside Ave, Rialto CA 92376................................714-875-3456
Richmond Post, 630 20th St, Oakland CA 94612...415-763-1120
Rio Linda World, 4225 Northgate Blvd, Sacramento CA 95834..................916-929-1143
Rohnert Park Cotati Clarion, Box 218, Cotati CA 94928 707-795-5451
Roseville Press-Tribune*, 413 N Lincoln St, Roseville CA 95678..............916-783-0451
Sacramento Bee*+, 21st & Q Sts, Sacramento CA 95813 916-321-1111

Sacramento Suburban, Box 38, Fair Oaks CA 95628 916-635-3300
Sacramento Union*+, 301 Capitol Mall, Sacramento CA 95814................916-442-7811
Saddleback Valley News, 23811 Via Fabricante, Msn Viejo CA 92691 714-768-3631
St Helena Star, 1328 Main St, St Helena CA 94574....................................707-963-2731
Salinas Californian*, 123 W Alisal St, Salinas CA 93901 408-424-2221
San Bernardino Sun*+, 399 D St, San Bernardino CA 92401....................714-889-9666
San Carlos Enquirer, 640 Roble Ave, Menlo Park CA 94025.....................415-326-5580
San Diego Reader+, PO Box 80803, San Diego CA 92138..........................619-231-7821
San Diego Sentinel+, 7750 Convoy Ct, San Diego CA 92111.....................619-571-0288
San Diego Transcript*, 2131 3rd Ave, San Diego CA 92101.......................619-232-4381
San Diego Union*+, 350 Camino De La Reina, San Diego CA 92108......619-299-3131
San Diego Uptown Examiner, 3740 El Cajon, San Diego CA 92105 714-263-3171
San Dimas Press, Box 4000, Ontario CA 91761 714-984-2468
San Fernando Vly Chron+, 7133 Owensmouth, Canoga Pk CA 91303.....213-884-0800
San Francisco Bay Guardian+, 2700 19th St, San Francisco CA 94110....415-824-7660
San Francisco Chronicle*+, 901 Mission St, San Francisco CA 94103.....415-777-1111
San Francisco Examiner*+, 110 5th St, San Francisco CA 94103..............415-777-2424
San Francisco Post, 630 20th St, Oakland CA 94612.................................415-763-1120
San Francisco Progress+, 851 Howard, San Francisco CA 94103.............415-982-8022
San Francisco Sun Reporter, 1366 Turk St, San Francisco CA 94115.......415-931-5778
San Francisco Today, 1331 San Mateo Ave, S San Francisco CA 94080 ...415-952-4102
San Jose Mercury News*+, 750 Ridder Park Dr, San Jose CA 95190.......408-920-5000
San Juan Record+, Box 38, Fair Oaks CA 95628 916-635-3300
San Marino Tribune, 2260 Huntington Dr, San Marino CA 91108...........213-282-5707
San Mateo Times*, 1080 S Amphlett Blvd, San Mateo CA 94402..............415-348-4321
San Pedro News-Pilot*, 362 W 7th St, San Pedro CA 90731 213-832-0221
San Rafael Terra Linda News, 31 Joseph Ct, San Rafael CA 94903 415-472-1200
San Ramon Valley Herald*, Box 907, Danville CA 94526............................415-837-0214
San Ramon Valley Herald, Box 907, Danville CA 92014.............................619-753-6543
Santa Barbara Independent, 607 State St, Santa Barbara CA 93101 805-965-5205
Santa Clara Sun, 10950 N Blaney Ave, Cupertino CA 95014......................408-255-7500
Santa Cruz Sentinel*, 207 Church St, Santa Cruz CA 95060......................408-423-4242
Santa Maria Times*, 3200 Skyway Dr, Orcutt CA 93455 805-925-2691
Santa Maria Times*, 3200 Skyway Dr, Santa Maria CA 93454...................805-925-2691
Santa Monica Outlook*, 1920 Colorado Ave, Santa Monica CA 90404 213-829-6811
Santa Paula Daily Chronicle*, 116 N 10th St, Santa Paula CA 93060........805-525-5555
Santa Rosa News Herald, 83 Brookwood Ave, Santa Rosa CA 95402.......707-546-6584
Santa Rosa Press Democrat*+, 427 Mendocino, Santa Rosa CA 95402...707-546-2020
Seal Beach Journal, 216 Main St, Seal Beach CA 90704.............................213-430-7555
Seaside Post News-Sentinel, Box 670, Seaside CA 93955.............................408-394-6632
Seaside Post, 630 20th St, Oakland CA 94612..415-763-1120
Sebastopol Times-Guide, 115 S Main St, Sebastopol CA 95472..................707-823-7845
Sherman Oaks Sun, Box 257, Encino CA 91316 213-907-5449
Sierra Madre News, 9 Kersting Ct, Sierra Madre CA 91024 818-355-3324
Sierra Sun, Box 2973, Truckee CA 95734...916-587-6061
Solvang Santa Ynez Valley News, Box 647, Solvang CA 93463....................805-688-5522
Sonoma Index Tribune, 117 W Napa St, Sonoma CA 95476.......................707-938-2111
South Gate Press, 8808 National Ave, South Gate CA 90280 213-869-3585
S Lake Tahoe Daily Tribune*, 3079 Harrison, S Lake Tahoe CA 95705 ...916-541-3880
South Pasadena Journal, 5420 N Figueroa St, Los Angeles CA 90042......213-254-5111
South Pasadena Review, 1024 Mission St, S Pasadena CA 91030 213-799-1161
South Sacramento News, Box 38, Fair Oaks CA 95628...............................916-635-3300
South SF Enterprise-Journal, 1331 San Mateo, S San Fran CA 94080 415-952-4102

Southwest News & Champion*, 12130 Paramount, Downey CA 90242.....213-862-1656
Stockton Record*+, 530 E Market St, Stockton CA 95202 209-943-6397
Sun City News, 27070 Sun City Blvd, Sun City CA 92381.............................714-679-1191
Sun Independent+, 1131 E Las Tunas, San Gabriel CA 91776....................213-285-2233
Sun Reporter, 4326 Tweedy Blvd, South Gate CA 90280.............................213-567-1258
Sunnyvale Scribe, 10950 N Blaney Ave, Cupertino CA 95014....................408-255-7500
Suttertown News+, 1731 L St, Sacramento CA 95814.................................916-448-9881
Taft Daily Midway Driller*, 800 Center St, Taft CA 93268 805-763-3171
Tahoe World, 241 N Lake Tahoe, Tahoe City CA 95730 916-583-3488
Tehachapi News, Box 230, Tehachapi CA 93561 805-822-4223
Telegram-Tribune*, 1321 Johnson Ave, San Luis Obispo CA 93406.........805-595-1111
Temple City Times, 9224 E Las Tunas, Temple City CA 91780 818-287-0419
Tolucan, 10001 Commerce Ave, Tujunga CA 91042.....................................213-352-3131
Torrance Daily Breeze*+, 5215 Torrance Blvd, Torrance CA 90509.........213-540-5511
Travis AFB Tailwind, 1250 Texas St, Fairfield CA 94533 707-425-4646
The Tribune*+, PO Box 191, San Diego CA 92112.....................................714-299-3131
Tulare Advance-Register*, 388 E Cross Ave, Tulare CA 93274..................209-688-0521
Turlock Daily Journal*, 138 S Center St, Turlock CA 95380 209-634-9141
Tustin News, 649 B St, Tustin CA 92680...714-544-4110
Twin Cities Times, Box 65, Corte Madera CA 94925 415-924-8552
Ukiah Daily Journal*, 590 S School St, Ukiah CA 95482............................707-468-0123
Union, 613 H St, Arcata CA 95521 707-822-3661
Upland Courier, 112 Harvard Ave, Claremont CA 91711.............................714-621-4761
Upland News, Box 4000, Ontario CA 91761 714-984-2468
Vallejo Times-Herald*, 500 Curtola Pkwy, Vallejo CA 94590....................707-644-1141
Valley Journal, 298 S Sunnyvale Ave Ste 104, Sunnyvale CA 94086 408-736-9090
Valley Scent, 10001 Commerce Ave, Tujunga CA 91042............................213-352-3131
Venice-Marina Ness Vangrd, 1920 Colorado, Santa Monica CA 90404.....213-829-6811
Ventura County Star-Free Press*+, 5250 Ralson, Ventura CA 93003......805-656-4111
Victor Valley Daily Press*, PO Box 1389, Victorville CA 92392 619-241-7744
Visalia Times-Delta*, 330 N West St, Visalia CA 93277 209-734-5821
Vista News, Box 218, Vista CA 92083...714-724-5421
Watsonville Register-Pajaronian*, 1000 Main, Watsonville CA 95076......408-724-0611
The Wave Newspaper+, 2621 W 54th St, Los Angeles CA 90043.................213-290-3000
Weaverville Weekly Trinity Journal, Box 340, Weaverville CA 96093 916-623-2055
Weekend Desert Post, 74-405 Hwy 111, Palm Dsrt CA 92260 619-346-1181
Weekly Breeze, 5215 Torrance Blvd, Torrance CA 90509 213-540-5511
Weekly Calistogan, PO Box 385, Calistoga CA 94515 707-942-6242
West County Times+, 1660 San Pablo Ave, Pinole CA 94564 915-724-8400
West Hollywood Post, 1433 S Robertson Blvd, Los Angeles CA 90035 213-552-3364
West LA Independent, 1920 Colorado, Santa Monica CA 90404 213-829-6811
West Sacramento News-Ledger, 816 W Acres, W Sacto CA 95691 916-371-8030
Westchester News+, 4043 Irving Pl, Culver City CA 90232 213-839-5271
Westchester-Ladera Observer, 1920 Colorado, Santa Monica CA 90404..213-829-6811
Westlake Post, 1660 Beverly Blvd, Los Angeles CA 90026 213-484-2840
White Sheet, 73400 Hwy 111, Palm Desert CA 92260.................................619-346-0601
Whittier Daily News*, 7037 Comstock Ave, Whittier CA 90608 213-698-0955
Whittier East Whittier Review, Box 4647, Whittier CA 90608 213-693-7771
Wilshire Independent, 1660 Beverly Blvd, Los Angeles CA 90026.............213-484-2840
Wilshire Press, 1660 Beverly Blvd, Los Angeles CA 90026........................213-484-2840
Woodland Calif Farm Observer, Box 1204, Woodland CA 95695.............916-662-1274
World, 413 N Lincoln St, Roseville CA 95678..916-786-8742
Wyvernwood Chronicle, 2912 E Brooklyn Ave, Los Angeles CA 90033.....213-263-5743

Yreka Siskiyou Daily News*, 309 S Broadway, Yreka CA 96097 916-842-5777
Yuba-Sutter Appeal-Democrat*, 319 G St, Marysville CA 95901 916-741-2345
Yucaipa-Calimesa News-Mirror, 35154 Yucaipa, Yucaipa CA 92399 714-797-9101

COLORADO

Arkansas Valley Journal, 7 W 5th St, La Junta CO 81050 303-384-8121
Arvada Sentinel, 8100 Ralston Rd, Arvada CO 80003 303-424-5525
Aspen Times, 310 E Main, Aspen CO 81611 303-925-3414
Aurora Sun, Box 95, Wheat Ridge CO 80034 303-332-4846
Boulder Daily Camera*, 1048 Pearl St, Boulder CO 80302 303-442-1202
Boulder Town & Country Review, Box 2210, Boulder CO 80306 303-443-3800
Brighton Blade, 139 N Main St, Brighton CO 80601 303-659-1141
Broomfield Enterprise, 11946 Quay St, Canon City CO 81212 303-275-8663
Canon City Daily Record*, 523 Main, Canon City CO 81212 303-275-7565
Colo Spgs Gazette Telegraph*+, 30 S Prospect, Colo Spgs CO 80903 303-632-5511
Colorado Springs Sun*+, 104 S Cascade Ave, Colo Spgs CO 80901 303-633-3881
Colorado Statesman, 1710 Lafayette, Denver CO 80218 303-832-3667
Colorado Transcript*, Box 987, Golden CO 80401 303-279-5541
Coloradoan*, 1212 Riverside Ave, Ft Collins CO 80522 303-224-7730
Cortez Montezuma Valley Journal, 37 E Main, Cortez CO 81321 303-565-8527
Daily Sentinel*, 734 S 7th St, Grand Junction CO 81501 303-242-5050
Delta County Independent, 353 Main St, Delta CO 81416 313-874-4421
Denver Herald Dispatch, 312 Federal, Denver CO 80219 303-935-2453
Denver Post*+, 650 15th St, Denver CO 80202 303-820-1010
Durango Herald*, 1275 Main Ave, Durango CO 81301 303-247-3504
Englewood Sentinel, 14062 Denver W Pkwy, Lakewood CO 80215 303-279-0810
Estes Park Trail-Gazette, 251 Moraine Ave, Estes Park CO 80517 303-586-3356
Evergreen Canyon Courier, Box 430, Evergreen CO 80439 303-674-5534
Ft Morgan Times*, 329 Main St, Ft Morgan CO 80701 303-867-5651
Fountain Security & Advertiser, 120 E Ohio, Fountain CO 80817 303-382-5613
Free Weekly Newspaper, 922 Colorado, Glenwood Springs CO 81601 303-945-7493
Fremont Trader, Box 1151, Canon City CO 81212 303-275-8663
Glenwood Springs Post*, 2014 Grand Ave, Glenwood Spring CO 81601..303-945-8515
Golden Advertiser, 900 11th St, Golden CO 80401 303-279-6636
Golden Outlook, 900 11th St, Golden CO 80401 303-279-6636
Greeley Tribune*, 714 8th St, Greeley CO 80632 303-352-0211
Gunnison Country Times, 218 N Wisconsin, Gunnison CO 81230 303-641-1414
Jefferson County Shopper, 900 11th St, Golden CO 80401 303-279-6636
La Junta Tribune-Democrat*, 422 Colorado Ave, La Junta CO 81050 303-384-4475
Lakewood South Jefferson Sun, 900 11th St, Golden CO 80401 303-279-6636
Lakewood-Jefferson Sentinel, 14062 Denver W, Lakewood CO 80215......303-279-0810
Littleton Sentinel, 14062 Denver W Pkwy, Lakewood CO 80215................303-279-0810
Littleton Times, 2546 Main, Littleton CO 80120 303-797-3841
Longmont Times-Call*, 717 4th Ave, Longmont CO 80501 303-776-2244
Loveland Daily Reporter-Herald*, 450 Cleveland, Loveland CO 80537....303-669-5050
Meeker Herald, 4th & Main, Meeker CO 81641 303-878-4016
Montrose Daily Press*, 535 S 1st St, Montrose CO 81401.........................303-249-3444
Northglenn-Thornton Sentinel, 431 W 84th Ave, Denver CO 80221 303-428-4999
Northwest Colorado Daily Press*, 466 Yampa Ave, Craig CO 81625 303-824-7031
Paonian-Herald, Box P, Paonia CO 81428 303-527-4155
Pikes Peak Jour, 22 Ruxton, Manitou Spgs CO 80829.................................303-685-9201
Pueblo Chieftain*+, 825 W 6th St, Pueblo CO 81002 303-544-3520

Rocky Mountain News*+, 400 W Colfax Ave, Denver CO 80204 303-892-5000
Salida Mountain Mail*, 125 E 2nd St, Salida CO 81201.............................303-539-6691
The Sentinel, 431 W 84th Ave, Denver CO 80221 303-428-4999
Steamboat Springs Pilot, 1041 Lincoln, Steamboat Spgs CO 80477...........303-879-1502
Sterling Journal-Advocate*, 504 N 3rd St, Sterling CO 80751 303-522-1990
Summit County Journal, 213 N Main, Breckenridge CO 80424 303-453-2331
Summit County Sentinel, Box 279, Dillon CO 80435.................................303-468-2831
Trinidad Chronicle News*, 200 Church, Trinidad CO 81082 303-846-3311
Vail Trail, 2211 N Frontage Rd, Vail CO 81657 303-476-2444
Valley Courier*, 401-407 State, Alamosa CO 81101...................................303-589-2553
Westminster Sentinel, 431 W 84th Ave, Denver CO 80221 303-428-4999
Westword, 2401 15th St #220, Denver CO 80202..303-458-6616
Wheatridge & Arvada E Jefferson Star, 900 11th St, Golden CO 80401 ...303-279-6636
Wheatridge Sentinel, 14062 Denver W Pkwy, Lakewood CO 80215 303-279-0810
Wray Gazette, 411 Main, Wray CO 80758 303-332-4846
Yuma Pioneer Inc, Box 326, Yuma CO 80759...303-848-2174

CONNECTICUT

Advertiser, 11 Boardman Terrace, New Milford CT 06776 203-354-2261
The Advocate*, 75 Tresser Blvd, Stamford CT 06901 203-327-1600
American*, 389 Meadow St, Waterbury CT 06722......................................203-574-3636
Ansonia Evening Sentinel*, 241 Main, Ansonia CT 06401.........................203-734-2546
Brandford Review, 332 Federal Rd, Brandford CT 06405............................203-488-2535
Bridgeport Post Telegram*+, 410 State St, Bridgeport CT 06604..............203-333-0161
Bridgeport Telegram*, 410 State St, Bridgeport CT 06604.........................203-333-0161
Bristol Press*, 99 Main St, Bristol CT 06010...203-584-0501
Cheshire Herald, 133 Highland Ave, Cheshire CT 06410 203-272-5316
Clinton Recorder, Box 239, Clinton CT 06413..203-669-5727
Compass, 19 E Main St, Mystic CT 06355...203-572-0544
Danbury News-Times*, 333 Main St, Danbury CT 06810 203-744-5100
Danielson Best Deal, 23 Center St, Danielson CT 06239 203-774-5563
Darien News-Review, 6 Squab Ln, Darien CT 06820...................................203-655-7476
Darien Review, 20 West Ave, Darien CT 06820...203-655-1474
Enfield Northern Conn Bazaar, 71 Church St, Enfield CT 06082 203-745-3348
Enfield Press, 71 Church St, Enfield CT 06082...203-745-3348
Fairfield Citizen News, 136 Main St, Westport CT 06880 203-226-6311
Fairfield County Advocate, 1090 Black Rock Tpke, Fairfield CT 06430....203-366-0000
Fairpress+, 250 Westport Ave, Norwalk CT 06856.....................................203-846-3451
Farmington Valley Herald, 1 Old Mill Ln, Simsbury CT 06070 203-658-4471
Gazette, 182 Sound Beach Ave, Old Greenwich CT 06870 203-637-1774
Glastonbury Citizen, 87 Nutmeg Ln, Glastonbury CT 06033 203-633-4691
Greenwich Time*, 20 E Elm, Greenwich CT 06830 203-869-8300
Hamden Chronicle, 20 Isham Rd, W Hartford CT 06107 203-236-5884
Hartford Advocate+, 470 Capitol Ave, Hartford CT 06106 203-527-8600
Hartford Courant*+, 285 Broad St, Hartford CT 06115 203-241-6272
Journal-Courier*, 40 Sargent Dr, New Haven CT 06511.............................203-562-1121
Lakeville Journal, Bissell St, Lakeview CT 06039 203-435-9873
The Ledger, Box 397, Ridgefield CT 06877 203-438-6545
Litchfield Enquirer, 11 Boardman Terrace, New Milford CT 06776..........203-354-2261
Longmeadow News, 71 Church St, Enfield CT 06082...................................203-745-3348
Manchester Herald*, Herald Square, Manchester CT 06040......................203-643-2711
Middletown Press*, 2 Main St, Middletown CT 06457................................203-347-3331

Milford Citizen*, 349 New Haven Ave, Milford CT 06460 203-874-1691
Milford Daily Citizen*, 349 New Haven Ave, Milford CT 06460................203-874-1691
Monroe Courier, Box 216, Monroe CT 06468...203-268-6234
Naugatuck Daily News*, 195 Water St, Naugatuck CT 06770 203-729-2228
New Britain Herald*, 1 Herald Square, New Britain CT 06050 203-225-4601
New Canaan Advertiser, 42 Vitti St, New Canaan CT 06840.......................203-966-9541
New Haven Advocate+, 1184 Chapel St, New Haven CT 06511...................203-789-0010
New Haven Register*+, 40 Sargent Dr, New Haven CT 06511.....................203-562-1121
New London Day*, 47 Eugene O'Neill Dr, New London CT 06320.............203-442-2200
New Milford Times, 11 Boardman Terrace, New Milford CT 06776.........203-354-2261
Newington Town Crier, 20 Isham Rd, W Hartford CT 06107......................203-236-5884
Newtown Bee, 5 Church Hill Rd, Newtown CT 06470.................................203-426-3141
Niantic News, Box 349, Guilford CT 06437 203-453-2711
North Haven Post, 174 Center St, Wallingford CT 06492 203-269-1464
Norwalk Hour*, 346 Main Ave, Norwalk CT 06852...................................203-846-3281
Putnam Observer-Patriot, 80 Main St, Putnam CT 06260...........................203-928-7943
Record-Journal*, 11 Crown St, Meriden CT 06450 203-255-1661
Register Citizen*, 190 Water St, Torrington CT 06790 203-489-3121
Ridgefield Press, 16 Bailey Ave, Ridgefield CT 06877................................203-438-6546
Shelton Suburban News, 100 Bridgeport Ave, Shelton CT 06484................203-735-6404
Southbury Voice, PO Box 383, Southbury CT 06488....................................203-263-2116
Southington Observer, 132 Main St, Southington CT 06489 203-621-6751
Stafford Press, Box 26, Stafford Springs CT 06076 203-684-2306
Stratford Bard, 2083 Main St, Stratford CT 06497 203-377-3809
Trumbull Times, White Plains Rd, Trumbull CT 06611................................203-268-6234
Waterbury Republican*+, 389 Meadow St, Waterbury CT 06722 203-574-3636
West Hartford News, 20 Isham Rd, W Hartford CT 06107 203-236-5884
West Haven News, 666 Savin Ave, W Haven CT 06516 203-933-1000
Wethersfield Post, 20 Isham Rd, W Hartford CT 06107 203-236-5884
Willimantic Chronicle*, Chronicle Rd, Willimantic CT 06226....................203-423-8466
Wilton Bulletin, 16 Bailey Ave, Ridgefield CT 06877 203-438-6546

DELAWARE

Brandywine-Wilmington West, 2209 Silverside, Wilmington DE 19810.....302-475-0300
Delaware Beachcomber, Box 309, Rehoboth Beach DE 19971 302-227-9466
Delaware Coast Press, Box 309, Rehoboth Beach DE 19971.......................302-227-9466
Delaware State News*, Webbs Ln & New Burton Rd, Dover DE 19901...302-647-3600
Delmarva News, Box 665, Millsboro DE 19966 302-934-8011
Milford Chronicle, 10 SW Front St, Milford DE 19963 302-422-4521
Newark Weekly Post, 153 Chestnut Hill Rd, Newark DE 19711 302-738-7200
News Journal+, 831 Orange St, Wilmington DE 19899 302-573-2000
Seaford Leader-State Register, 616 Water St, Seaford DE 19973 302-629-5505
State Register & BiState Wkly, 111 E Market, Laurel DE 19956.................302-875-7563
Sussex Countian, 115 N Race, Georgetown DE 19947 302-856-0026
Sussex Post, Box 117, Millsboro DE 19966 302-934-9261
The Wave, PO Box 1467, Bethany Beach DE 19930....................................302-227-9466
Wilmington Defender, 1702 Locust St, Wilmington DE 19802....................302-656-3252

DISTRICT OF COLUMBIA

City Paper+, 917 6th St NW, Washington DC 20001 202-289-0520
Country News, 440 1st St NW, Washington DC 20001 202-393-6226
Wash Afro-American Newspaper, 2002 11th St NW, Wash DC 20001.......202-332-0080
Washington Blade, 724 9th St NW, Washington DC 20001 202-347-2038
Washington Informer, 3117 M L King Jr Ave SE, Wash DC 20032............202-561-4100
Washington News Observer, 811 Florida Ave NW, Wash DC 20001 202-232-3060
Washington Post*+, 1150 15th St NW, Washington DC 20071...................202-334-6000
Washington Times*+, 3600 New York Ave NE, Washington DC 20002..202-636-3000

FLORIDA

Anna Maria Islander, 314 Pine, Anna Maria FL 33501 813-778-0751
The Arcadian, 209 W Oak, Arcadia FL 33821..813-494-2434
Auburndale Star, 213 E Lake St, Auburndale FL 33823 813-967-4134
Avon Park Sun, 203 W Main St, Avon Park FL 33825...............................813-453-4355
Baker County Press, Box 598, MacClenny FL 32063................................904-259-2400
Beaches Leader, 712 3rd St N, Jacksonville FL 32250................................904-249-9033
Belleview Leader, 7490 43rd St N, Pinellas Park FL 33565........................813-544-5733
Boca Raton News*, 34 SE 2nd St, Boca Raton FL 33432 305-395-8300
Boynton Beach News Jour, 54 NE 4th Ave, Delray Beach FL 33444..........305-276-6321
Brandon News, 402 Oakfield Dr, Brandon FL 33511................................813-689-1201
Brooksville Sun Journal, 702 Lamar Ave, Brooksville FL 33512...............904-796-4925
Carol City-Opa-Locka News, Box 43-1010, Miami FL 33143 305-667-7481
Central County Courier, 27 Lilac Dr, Debary FL 32713 305-668-4820
Citrus County Chronicle, 130 Heights Ave, Inverness FL 32650 904-726-1441
Clay County Crescent, 806 W Walnut, Green Cove Springs FL 32043 904-284-3166
Clearwater Sun*+, Box 2078, Clearwater FL 33517..................................813-448-2011
Clewiston News, 109 Central Ave, Clewiston FL 33440 813-983-9148
Coral Gables News+, 6796 SW 62nd Ave, Miami FL 33143......................305-667-7481
Countrywide Shopper, 7490 43rd St N, Pinellas Park FL 33565................813-544-5733
Dade Home News, 4694 Palm Ave, Hialeah FL 33012................................305-556-1155
Daily Breeze*, 2510 Del Prado Blvd, Cape Coral FL 33904......................813-574-1110
Daily Clay Today*, 1564 Kingsley Ave, Orange Park FL 32073 904-264-3200
Daily Highlander*, 33 W Orange Ave, Lake Wales FL 33853......................813-676-2571
Daytona Pennysaver, 454 S Yonge St, Ormond Beach FL 32074................904-677-4262
Deland Sun News*, 111 S Alabama Ave, Deland FL 32720........................904-734-3661
Delray Beach News Jour, 54 NE 4th Ave, Delray Beach FL 33444............305-276-6321
Diario Las Americas*+, 2900 NW 39th St, Miami FL 33142 305-633-3341
Englewood Herald, Box 988, Englewood FL 33533................................813-474-3346
Eustis Lake Region News, 501 N Bay St, Eustis FL 32726 904-357-3199
Evening Times*, Drawer T, W Palm Beach FL 33402..............................305-837-4700
Fernandina Beach News Leader, Box 766, Fernandina Beach FL 32034...904-261-3686
Florida Times-Union*+, 1 Riverside Ave, Jacksonville FL 32202..............904-359-4111
Forest Bugle Leader, 7490 43rd St N, Pinellas Park FL 33565 813-544-5733
Ft Lauderdale News*+, 101 N New River, Ft Lauderdale FL 33302 305-761-4000
Ft Lauderdale Shopper, 1711 N State Rd, Margate FL 33063 305-971-0111
Ft Myers News-Press*+, 2442 Anderson Ave, Ft Myers FL 33901 813-335-0200
Gainsville Sun*, 2700 SW 13th St, Gainsville FL 32607 904-378-1411
The Globe+, 5401 NW Broken Sound Blvd, Boca Raton FL 33431 305-997-7733
Haines City Herald, Box 247, Haines City FL 33844 813-422-4991

Hallandale Digest Inc, 224 S Dixie, Hallandale FL 33009............................305-457-8029
Herald Coastal Observer, 130 South H St, Lake Worth FL 33460 305-585-9387
Herald-Advocate, 115 S 7th Ave, Wauchula FL 33873.................................813-773-3255
Hi-Riser, 4009 NE 5th Terr, Ft Lauderdale FL 33334 305-563-3311
Hialeah Home News, 4694 Palm Ave, Hialeah FL 33012 305-556-1155
Hialeah-Miami Springs News, 6796 SW 62nd Ave, Miami FL 33143........305-667-7481
Holmes County Advertiser, Box 7, Bonifay FL 32425.................................904-547-2270
Home News, 4694 Palm Ave, Hialeah FL 33012 305-556-1155
Homestead-Florida City News, 6796 SW 62nd Ave, Miami FL 33143........305-667-7481
Independent Farmer & Rancher, 620 N Main St, Gainesville FL 32601....904-377-2444
Island Reporter, 2075 Periwinkle Way, Sanibel FL 33957 813-472-1587
Jackson County Floridan*, 104 E Lafeyette, Marianna FL 32446...............904-526-3614
Jacksonville Journal*, 1 Riverside Ave, Jacksonville FL 32202 904-359-4111
Jewish Journal, 4036 NE 5th Ter, Ft Lauderdale FL 33334........................305-563-3200
Jupiter Courier-Journal, 800 Indiantown Rd, Jupiter FL 33458................305-746-5111
Kendall-South Miami News, 6796 SW 62nd Ave, Miami FL 33143............305-667-7481
Key West Citizen*, 515 Greene St, Key West FL 33040 305-294-6641
Keynoter Publishing Co Inc, 3015 Overseas Hwy, Marathon FL 33050 305-743-5551
Lake City Reporter*, 126 E Duval St, Lake City FL 32055 904-752-1293
Lake News, Box 527, Leesburg FL 32748...904-456-7720
Lake Placid Journal, 232 N Main St, Lake Placid FL 33852........................813-465-2423
Lake Wales News, 138 Stuart Ave, Lake Wales FL 33853 813-676-3467
Largo & Florida Sentinel, 424 W Bay Dr, Largo FL 33540 813-581-2600
Ledger*+, Lime & Missouri Sts, Lakeland FL 33802................................813-687-7000
Leesburg Commercial*, 212 E Main St, Leesburg FL 32748......................813-787-4515
Lehigh Acres Suburban Reporter, Box 05864, Ft Myers FL 33905 813-694-7911
Lehigh News, Box 908, Lehigh Acres FL 33970 813-369-2191
Longboat Islander, 314 Pine, Anna Maria FL 33501 813-778-0751
Madison County Carrier, Drawer 772, Madison FL 32340 904-973-4141
Marco Island Eagle, Box 579, Marco FL 33937......................................813-394-7596
Marion Leader, 7490 43rd St N, Pinellas Park FL 33565.........................813-544-5733
Melbourne Times, Box 1870, Melbourne FL 32901 305-723-7661
Miami Beach Home News, 4694 Palm Ave, Hialeah FL 33012..................305-556-1155
Miami Beach Sun-Reporter*, 1771 West Ave, Miami FL 33139.................305-532-4531
Miami Herald*+, 1 Herald Plaza, Miami FL 33132..................................305-350-2111
Miami News*+, 1 Herald Plaza, Miami FL 33101 305-376-3300
Miami Review*, 100 NE 7th St, Miami FL 33101....................................305-377-3721
The Mirror+, Box 787, Jensen Beach FL 33457......................................305-334-3345
Naples Star, 1010 Central Ave, Naples FL 33940....................................813-262-7601
The Natl Enquirer*+, 600 SE Coast Ave, Lantana FL 33464 305-586-1111
Natl Examiner+, 5401 NW Broken Sound Blvd, Boca Raton FL 33431....305-997-7733
News Chief*, 650 6th St SW, Winter Haven FL 33880 813-294-7731
News Tribune*, 600 Edwards Rd, Ft Pierce FL 34982..............................305-461-2050
News-Journal*+, 901 6th St, Daytona Beach FL 32017 904-252-1511
North Miami Beach News, Box 43-1010, Miami FL 33143........................305-667-7481
North Miami Neighbors Newspaper, 1926 NE 149 St, Miami FL 33161 ...305-949-0871
North Miami News+, Box 43-1010, Miami FL 33143 305-949-0871
Noticias Latinas+, Box 43-1010, Miami FL 33143...................................305-949-0871
Ocala Star Banner*, 819 SE 1st Ter, Ocala FL 32670.............................904-629-0011
Okaloosa News Journal, 480 US 90 E, Crestview FL 32536 904-682-2704
Okeechobee News, 404 NW 3rd St, Okeechobee FL 33972 813-763-3134
Orlando Sentinel*+, 633 N Orange Ave, Orlando FL 32801 305-420-5000
Orlando Sun of Pine Hills, Box 416, Winter Park FL 32790 305-647-1217

Palatka Daily News*, 1825 St Johns Ave, Palatka FL 32077 904-328-2721
Palm Beach Daily News*, 265 Royal Poinciana, Palm Beach FL 33480.....305-837-4763
Panama City News-Herald*, 501 W 11th St, Panama City FL 32401..........904-763-7621
Pasco News, 1606 US 301 S, Dade City FL 33525.....................................904-567-5639
Pensacola News-Journal*+, 1 News-Journal Plz, Pensacola FL 32501......904-435-8500
Pensacola Woman, PO Box 15362, Pensacola FL 32514 904-453-6227
Perry News-Herald, Box 888, Perry FL 32347..904-584-7819
Perry Taco Times, 108 E Main St, Perry FL 32347 904-584-5513
Plant City Courier, 101 N Thomas St, Plant City FL 33566.........................813-752-3113
Playground Daily News*, 200 Racetrack, Ft Walton Beach FL 32513........904-863-1111
Polk County Democrat, 190 S Florida Ave, Barstow FL 33830 813-533-4183
Punta Gorda Herald News*, Box 1808, Punta Gorda FL 33950....................813-639-2151
Quincy Gadsden County Times, Box 790, Quincy FL 32351.........................904-627-7649
St Augustine Record*, 158 Cordova St, St Augustine FL 32085....................904-829-6562
St Cloud News/Kissimmee Gazette, Box 578, Saint Cloud FL 32769.........305-892-2823
St Petersburg Times*+, 490 1st Ave S, St Petersburg FL 33701.................813-893-8111
Santa Rosa Press Gazette, 531 E Elva St, Milton FL 32570 904-623-3131
Sarasota Bulletin, 2003 Princeton St, Sarasota FL 33579.............................813-366-5821
Sarasota Herald Tribune*+, 801 S Tamiami Trail, Sarasota FL 33578 813-953-7755
Sebring News, 2714 SE Lakeview Dr, Sebring FL 33870 813-385-6155
Shopper & Observer News, 100 Shell Pt Rd E, Ruskin FL 33570................813-645-3111
South Dade News Leader*, 15-17 NE 1st Rd, Homestead FL 33030 305-245-2311
South Dade News, 6796 SW 62nd Ave, Miami FL 33143.............................305-667-7481
South West News, Box 43-1010, Miami FL 33143..305-949-0871
Southern Jewish Weekly, PO Box 3297, Jacksonville FL 32206..................904-634-1469
Starke Bradford County Telegraph, 135 W Call St, Starke FL 32091........904-964-6305
Stuart News*, 111 E Ocean Blvd, Stuart FL 34994 305-287-1550
Sumter County Times, Box 668, Bushnell FL 33513 904-697-2572
Sun Coast Times, 200 Miami Ave, Venice FL 33595....................................813-484-2611
Sun-Tattler*, 2600 N 29th Ave, Hollywood FL 33020.................................305-929-8100
Suncoast News+, 607 W Main St, New Port Richy FL 33552 813-849-7500
Suwannee County's Independent Post, Box 336, Live Oak FL 32060.........904-362-1734
Tallahassee Democrat*+, 277 N Magnolia Dr, Tallahassee FL 32301......904-599-2100
Tampa Florida Sentinel-Bulletin, 2207 21st St, Tampa FL 33605 813-248-1921
Tampa News Reporter, PO Box 2539, Tampa FL 33601 813-258-1741
Tarpon Springs Holiday Herald, Box 1028, Tarpon Springs FL 33589......813-937-2538
Tarpon Springs Leader, 11 E Orange St, Tarpon Springs FL 33589..........813-937-6101
Titusville Star-Advocate, 1100 S Hopkins Ave, Titusville FL 32780 305-267-4711
Today*+, 308 Forrest Ave, Cocoa FL 32922..305-632-8700
Tribune, 4009 NE 5th Terr, Ft Lauderdale FL 33334 305-563-3311
Valparaiso Bayou Times, Box 37, Valparaiso FL 32580................................904-678-1031
Vero Beach Press-Journal, 1801 S US 1, Vero Beach FL 32960..................305-562-2315
Wakulla News, Box 307, Crawfordville FL 32327 904-926-7102
Weekly News, 901 NE 79th St, Miami FL 33138 305-757-6333
Winter Garden Times, 720 S Dillard St, Winter Garden FL 32787 305-656-2121
Winter Haven Herald, Box 899, Winter Haven FL 33880.............................813-293-6339
Zephyrhills News, 611 5th Ave, Zephyrhills FL 33599.................................813-782-1558

GEORGIA

Acworth Neighbor, 580 Fairground St, Marietta GA 30060 404-428-9411
Adel News, 131 S Hutchinson Ave, Adel GA 31620 912-896-2233
Albany Herald*, 126 N Washington PO Box 48, Albany GA 31703............912-888-9300
Albany Journal, Box 1628, Albany GA 31702...912-435-6222
Alpharetta Neighbor, 580 Fairground St, Marietta GA 30060......................404-428-9411
Americus Times-Recorder*, Vienna Rd, Americus GA 31709....................912-924-2750
Athens Daily News*, 1 Press Place, Athens GA 30601 404-549-0123
Athens Observer, 288 N Lumpkin, Athens GA 30603....................................404-548-6346
Atlanta Daily World*, 145 Auburn Ave NE, Atlanta GA 30335 404-659-1110
Atlanta Inquirer, 947 M L King Jr Dr NW, Atlanta GA 30314....................404-523-6086
Atlanta Journal-Constitution*+, 72 Marietta St, Atlanta GA 30303.........404-526-5151
Atlanta Voice+, 633 Pryor St SW, Atlanta GA 30314...................................404-524-6426
Augusta Chronicle*+, 725 Board St, Augusta GA 30913 404-724-0851
Augusta Herald*, 725 Broad St, Augusta GA 30903......................................404-724-0851
Austell Neighbor, 580 Fairground St, Marietta GA 30060 404-428-9411
Bainbridge Post-Searchlight, 301 N Crawford, Bainbridge GA 31717.......912-246-2827
Banner Herald*, 1 Press Place, Athens GA 30605..404-549-0123
Banner-Herald & Daily News*, 1 Press Place, Athens GA 30613...............404-549-0123
Baxley News-Banner, Box 409, Baxley GA 31513 912-367-2468
Blairsville North Georgia News, Box 748, Blairsville GA 30512 404-745-6343
Cairo Messenger, 31 1st Ave NE, Cairo GA 31728..912-377-2032
Calhoun Times, 111 N Park Ave, Calhoun GA 30701 404-629-2230
Camilla Enterprise, 13 S Scott St, Camilla GA 31730 912-336-5265
Cedartown Standard, Box 308, Cedartown GA 30125......................................404-748-1520
Chamblee Neighbor, 580 Fairground St, Marietta GA 30060 404-428-9411
Chatsworth Times, N 3rd Ave, Chatsworth GA 30705....................................404-695-4646
Cherokee Tribune, 64 Academy St, Canton GA 30114....................................404-479-1441
Clarkston Neighbor, 580 Fairground St, Marietta GA 30060.........................404-428-9411
Clayton Neighbor, 6435 B Tara Blvd, Jonesboro GA 30236 404-471-9700
Clayton Tribune, Main & Oak Crescent, Clayton GA 30525 404-782-3312
Coffee County Progress, 202 N Madison Ave; Douglas GA 31533.............912-384-5152
Columbus Enquirer*+, 17 W 12th St, Columbus GA 31902........................404-324-5526
Columbus Ft Benning Bayonet, 17 W 12th St, Columbus GA 31994 404-324-5526
Columbus Ledger*, 17 W 12th St, Columbus GA 31994................................404-324-5526
Columbus Times*, 2230 Buena Vista Rd, Columbus GA 31906....................404-324-2404
Commerce News, 35 S Broad St, Commerce GA 30529 404-335-5121
Cordele Dispatch*, 306 13th Ave W, Cordele GA 31015...............................912-273-2277
Cornelia Northeast Georgian, Box 190, Cornelia GA 30531 404-778-4215
Covington News, 4132 Hwy 278 W, Covington GA 30209 404-786-3401
Creative Loafing+, PO Box 54223, Atlanta GA 30308...................................404-688-5623
Daily Sun*, 1553 Watson Blvd, Warner Robins GA 31093.............................912-923-6432
Daily Tribune News*, 251 S Tennessee St, Cartersville GA 30120 404-382-4545
Dallas New Era, Box 246, Dallas GA 30132...404-445-3379
Dalton Daily Citizen-News*, 308 S Thornton Ave, Dalton GA 30720........404-278-1011
Decatur-DeKalb News/Era, 1 Town Ctr, Decatur GA 30033.......................404-343-4488
DeKalb News Sun+, 739 DeKalb Industrial Way, Decatur GA 30033.......404-292-3536
Doraville Neighbor, 580 Fairground St, Marietta GA 30060 404-428-9411
Douglas Enterprise, S Madison Ave, Douglas GA 30133 404-942-6571
Dublin Courier Herald*, 115 S Jefferson St, Huber GA 31040...................912-222-5522
Dunwoody Neighbor, 580 Fairground St, Marietta GA 30060 404-428-9411

Eastman Times Journal-Spotlight, Drawer 707, Eastman GA 31023........912-374-5562
Elberton Star, 14 N Oliver St, Elberton GA 30635 404-283-3100
Fayette County News, 210 E Lanier Ave, Fayetteville GA 30214 404-461-6317
Forsyth County News, 107 Dahlonega St, Cumming GA 30130....................404-887-3126
Ft Valley Leader-Tribune, 205 Main St, Ft Valley GA 31030 912-825-2432
Franklin County Citizen, Box 148, Lavonia GA 30553............................404-356-8557
Gainsville Times*, 345 Green St NW, Gainsville GA 30501......................404-532-1234
Gwinnett Daily News*, 394 Clayton St NE, Lawrenceville GA 30246.........404-963-0311
Haralson Gateway-Beacon, 222 Tallapoosa St, Bremen GA 30110...........404-537-2434
Henry Herald, Box 233, McDonough GA 30253 404-957-9161
Herald-Leader, 111 E Central Ave, Fitzgerald GA 31750........................912-423-9331
Herald-Tribune, 251 S Tennessee St, Cartersville GA 30120 404-382-4545
Jackson Herald, 147 Lee St, Jefferson GA 30549..............................404-367-5233
Jackson Progress-Argus, 129 Mulberry St, Jackson GA 30233..................404-775-3107
Jeff Davis County Ledger, Railroad St, Hazlehurst GA 31539...................912-375-4225
Jonesboro News Daily*, 138 Church St, Jonesboro GA 30236 404-478-5500
Kennesaw Neighbor, 580 Fairground St, Marietta GA 30060....................404-428-9411
Lanier Tribune, 490 B S Enota Dr NE, Gainesville GA 30501 404-535-2503
Lawrenceville Home Weekly, 232 Crogan St, Lawrenceville GA 30245......404-963-9205
Lithonia Observer, 739 DeKalb Industrial Way, Decatur GA 30033 404-292-3536
Mableton Neighbor, 580 Fairground St, Marietta GA 30060.....................404-428-9411
Macon News*, 120 Broadway, Macon GA 31201..............................912-744-4200
Macon Telegraph & News*+, 120 Braodway, Macon GA 31213................912-744-4200
Madison Madisonian, Box 191, Madison GA 30650............................404-342-2424
Manchester Star-Mercury, Box 426, Manchester GA 31816...................404-846-3188
Marietta Daily Journal*, 580 Fairground St, Marietta GA 30060 404-428-9411
Martinez Columbia News, 3919 Roberts Rd, Augusta GA 30907..............404-863-6165
Mashville Barrien Press, 200 E McPherson Ave, Nashville GA 31639......912-686-7771
Monroe Walton Tribune, 124 N Broad, Monroe GA 30655 404-267-8371
Moultrie Observer*, 27 N Main St, Moultrie GA 31768 912-985-4545
Multi-County Star, 4132 Hwy 278 W, Covington GA 30209.....................404-786-3401
Newman Times-Herald, 16 Jefferson St, Newman GA 30264....................404-253-1576
News-Reporter, 116 W Robt Toombs, Washington GA 30673..................404-678-2636
Northside Neighbor, 120 Copeland Rd NE 122, Atlanta GA 30342.............404-256-3100
Pelham Journal, 207 McLaughlin Ave, Pelham GA 31779 912-294-3661
Perry Houston Home Journal, 1010 Carroll St, Perry GA 31069................912-987-1823
Roswell Neighbor, 580 Fairground St, Marietta GA 30060......................404-428-9411
Sandersville Progress, 118 E Haynes St, Sandersville GA 31082................912-552-3161
Savannah News-Press*+, 111 W Bay St, Savannah GA 31402.................912-236-9511
Southline+, 761 Peachtree St NE #B, Atlanta GA 30308 404-872-8206
Southside & Fayette Sun, 1614 Thompson Ave, Atlanta GA 30334............404-762-8446
Springfield Herald, Box 247, Springfield GA 31329.............................912-754-6123
Statesboro Herald*, 1 Herald Square, Statesboro GA 30458....................912-764-9031
Statesboro Southern Beacon, 1 Herald Square, Statesboro GA 30458......912-764-9031
Summerville News, Box 310, Summerville GA 30747 404-857-2494
Swainsboro Forest-Blade, E Moring St, Swainsboro GA 30401................912-237-9971
Sylvester Local, Box 387, Sylvester GA 31791.................................912-776-3991
Telegraph & News*+, 120 Braodway, Macon GA 31213 912-744-4200
This Week in Peachtree City, 406 Line Crk, Peachtree City GA 30269 404-487-7729
Thomaston Times, Box 430, Thomaston GA 30286.............................404-647-5414
Thomson McDuffie Progress, 101 Church St SW, Thomson GA 30824....404-595-1601
Tifton Gazette*, 211 N Tift Ave, Tifton GA 31794................................912-382-4321
Times Courier, Box 306, Ellijay GA 30540.....................................404-635-4313

Times-Enterprise*, 119 N Madison, Thomasville GA 31792......................912-226-2400
Union Recorder, 1 Union Recorder Plaza, Milledgeville GA 31061...........912-452-0567
Valdosta Daily Times*, 201 N Troup St, Valdosta GA 31601......................912-244-1880
Walker County Messenger, 119 Public Square E, Lafayette GA 30728 404-638-1859
Waycross Journal Herald*, 400 Isabella St, Waycross GA 31501................912-283-2244
Waynesboro True Citizen, 610 Academy Ave, Waynesboro GA 30830 404-554-2111
Winder News, 510 W Athens St, Winder GA 30680......................................404-867-7557

HAWAII

Garden Island, 3137 Kuhio Hwy, Lihue HI 96766 808-245-3681
Hawaii Hochi*, 917 Kokea St, Honolulu HI 96817................................808-845-2255
Hawaii Sun Press+, 46-016 Alaloa, Kaneohe HI 96744........................808-235-5881
Hawaii Tribune-Herald*, 355 Kinoole St, Hilo HI 96721......................808-935-6621
Maui News, Box 550, Wailuku HI 96793...801-244-3981
Star-Bulletin & Advertiser*+, 605 Kapiolani, Honolulu HI 96813 808-525-8000
Waikiki Beach Press+, 777 Ala Moana, Honolulu HI 96813.....................808-536-1881

IDAHO

Blackfoot Morning News*, 27 NW Main, Blackfoot ID 83221 208-529-4919
Boise Journal of Commerce, Box 7337, Boise ID 83707.............................208-343-3626
Burley South Idaho Press*, 230 E Main, Burley ID 83318.........................208-678-2202
Central Idaho Star-News, Box 984, McCall ID 83638 208-634-2123
Clearwater Tribune, Box 71, Orofino ID 83544..208-476-4571
Coeur d'Alene Press*, 2nd & Lakeside Ave, Coeur D Alene ID 83814 208-664-8176
Emmett Messenger Index, 120 Washington, Emmett ID 83617................208-365-2241
Gooding County Leader, 442 Main St, Gooding ID 83330.........................208-934-4449
Idaho County Free Press, Mill & Main, Grangeville ID 83530 208-983-1070
Idaho Falls Post-Register*, 333 Northgate Mile, Idaho Falls ID 83401.....208-522-1800
Idaho Press-Tribune*, 1618 N Midland, Nampa ID 83657.........................208-467-9251
Idaho Press-Tribune*, 1618 N Midland, Ola ID 83657 208-467-9251
Idaho Register, 420 W Idaho, Boise ID 83701 208-342-2997
Idaho State Journal*, 305 S Arthur Ave, Pocatello ID 83201.....................208-232-4161
Idaho Statesman*+, 1200 N Curtis Rd, Boise ID 83706.............................208-377-6200
Idahonian*, 409 S Jackson, Moscow ID 83843...208-882-5561
Jefferson Star, 134 W Main, Rigby ID 83442..208-745-8701
Kellogg Evening News*, 401 Main St, Kellogg ID 83837 208-783-1107
Lewiston Morning Tribune*, 505 C St, Lewiston ID 83501 208-743-9411
Mountain Home News, 195 S 3rd E, Mountain Home ID 83647 208-587-3331
North Side News, Box 468, Jerome ID 83338...208-324-3391
Palouse Shopper, Box 8187, Moscow ID 83843 208-882-5561
St Maries Gazette Record, 127 S 7th, St Maries ID 83861..........................208-245-4538
Salmon Recorder-Herald, 519 Van Dreff St, Salmon ID 83467..................208-756-2221
Sandpoint Daily Bee*, 310 Church, Sandpoint ID 83864.............................208-263-9534
Sandpoint News-Bulletin, 310 Church, Sandpoint ID 83864......................208-263-5151
Sunday Journal*, 305 S Arthur Ave, Pocatello ID 83201.............................208-232-4161
Twin Falls Times-News*, 132 3rd St W, Twin Falls ID 83301.....................208-733-0931
Valley News, 30 E Franklin, Meridian ID 83642 208-888-1941
Wallace North Idaho Press*, 506 6th St, Wallace ID 83873........................208-556-1561
Wood River Journal, 112 S Main, Hailey ID 83333 208-788-3444

ILLINOIS

Addison Press, 112 S York St, Elmhurst IL 60126 312-834-0900
Albany Park News, 7519 N Ashland Ave, Chicago IL 60626.......................312-761-7200
Algonquin Countryside, 200 James St, Barrington IL 60010 312-381-9200
Alsip Edition, 3840 W 147th St, Midlothian IL 60445.................................312-388-2425
Alton Citizen Newspaper, 329 Belle St, Alton IL 62002 618-462-2100
Alton Telegraph*, 111 E Broadway, Alton IL 62002...................................618-463-2500
Anna Gazette-Democrat, 112 Lafayette St, Anna IL 62906.........................618-833-2158
Antioch News & Reporter, 30 S Whitney St, Grayslake IL 60030...............312-223-8161
Aurora Beacon-News*, 101 S River St, Aurora IL 60506.............................312-844-5844
Back of the Yards Journal, 4625 S Ashland Ave, Chicago IL 60609...........312-927-7200
Bartlett Township Times, 316 S Schmale Rd, Wheaton IL 60187................312-892-5600
Bartonville Limestone Independent, 911 W Garfield, Peoria IL 61607 309-697-1851
Belleville News-Democrat*, 120 S Illinois St, Belleville IL 62222 618-234-1000
Beverly News, 3840 W 147th St, Midlothian IL 60445 312-388-2425
Bi-State Reporter, 30 S Whitney St, Grayslake IL 60030............................312-223-8161
Bloomingdale Press, 112 S York St, Elmhurst IL 60126.............................312-834-0900
Blue Island Sun Standard, 5959 S Harlem Ave, Chicago IL 60638............312-586-8800
Bolingbrook Sun, 349 N Schmidt Rd, Bolingbrook IL 60439 312-759-9169
Bourbonnais Herald, 536 N Convent Ave, Bourbonnais IL 60914 815-933-1131
Breese Journal, 623 N 2nd St, Breese IL 62203 618-526-7211
Bridgeport Independent, 3840 W 147th St, Midlothian IL 60445................312-388-2425
Brighton Park-McKinley Park Life, 2949 W 43rd St, Chicago IL 60632....312-523-3663
Brookfield Times, 6894 W 47th St, Lyons IL 60534....................................312-442-9300
Buffalo Grove Countryside*+, 200 James St, Barrington IL 60010............312-381-9200
Burbank Stickney Independent, 3840 W 147th St, Midlothian IL 60445....312-388-2425
Bureau Country Republican, 316 S Main St, Princeton IL 61356 815-875-4461
Cahokia-Dupo Herald, 1256 Camp Jackson Rd, E Saint Louis IL 62206..618-337-7300
Calumet Day, 18127 William St, Lansing IL 60438......................................312-895-3700
Canton Daily Ledger*, 53 W Elm, Canton IL 61520...................................309-746-5100
Carlinville Democrat, 118 N West St, Carlinville IL 62626.........................217-845-2561
Carlyle Union Banner, 671 10th St, Carlyle IL 62231 618-594-3131
Carmi Times*, 323 E Main St, Carmi IL 62821...618-382-4176
Carol Stream Press, 112 S York St, Elmhurst IL 60126..............................312-834-0900
Carroll County Review, 809 Main St, Thomson IL 61285 815-259-2131
Cary-Grove Countryside, 200 James St, Barrington IL 60010 312-381-9200
Centralia Sentinel*, 232 E Broadway, Centralia IL 62801 618-532-5604
Champaign-Urbana News Gazette*+, Box 677, Champaign IL 61820.......217-351-5252
Chatham-Southeast Citizen, 412 E 87th St, Chicago IL 60619...................312-487-7700
Chicago Bridgeport News, 3506 S Halsted St, Chicago IL 60609 312-927-3118
Chicago Daily Defender*, 2400 S Michigan Ave, Chicago IL 60616...........312-225-2400
Chicago El Informador, 1510 W 18th St, Chicago IL 60608 312-421-7702
Chicago Evergreen Gazette, 3201 N Broadway, Chicago IL 60057 312-472-2000
Chicago Good News Weekly, 4731 N Western Ave, Chicago IL 60625.......312-878-7334
Chicago Hegewisch News, 3150 E 133rd St, Chicago IL 60633 312-646-1100
Chicago Heights Star, 1526 Otto Blvd, Chicago Heights IL 60411............312-755-6161
Chicago Independent Bulletin+, 2041 W 95th St, Chicago IL 60643 312-783-1040
Chicago Near North News, 26 E Huron St, Chicago IL 60611 312-787-2677
Chicago Racing Form*, 731 Plymouth Ct, Chicago IL 60605 312-922-0366
Chicago Reader+, PO Box 11101, Chicago IL 60611 312-828-0350
Chicago Reporter, 4941 N Milwaukee, Chicago IL 60630..........................312-286-6100

Chicago Ridge Citizen, 3840 W 147th St, Midlothian IL 60445 312-388-2425
Chicago Sun Times*+, 401 N Wabash Ave, Chicago IL 60611....................312-321-3000
Chicago Tribune*+, 435 N Michigan Ave, Chicago IL 60611 312-222-3232
Chicago West Side Times, 4941 W Cermak Rd, Chicago IL 60608 312-247-8500
Chicago's Northwest Side Press, 4941 N Milwaukee, Chicago IL 60630....312-286-6100
Chicago-Lawndale News, 2711 W Cermak Rd, Chicago IL 60608 312-247-8500
Chicagoland Community Reporter, 4355 W 26th St, Chicago IL 60623 312-277-4200
Chillicothe Bulletin, 1016 N 2nd St, Chillicothe IL 61523 309-274-2185
Cicero Life, 2601 S Harlem, Berwyn IL 60402 312-484-1234
Clarendon Hills Progress, 922 Warren, Downers Grove IL 60515.............312-969-0188
Clay City County Advocate-Press, 105 W North Ave, Flora IL 62839........618-662-8392
Clear Ridge Times, 6894 W 47th St, Lyons IL 60534 312-442-9300
Clinton Daily Journal*, 117 Main, Clinton IL 61727 217-935-3171
Coles County Daily Times-Courier*, 307 6th St, Charleston IL 61920.......217-345-7085
Collinsville Herald, 113 E CLay St, Collinsville IL 62234 618-344-0264
Columbia Monroe County Clarion, 212 W Locust, Columbia IL 62236....618-281-4292
Crete-Park Forest South Star, 1526 Otto Blvd, Chicago Hts IL 60411......312-755-6161
Crystal Lake Mirror, 200 James St, Barrington IL 60010 312-381-9200
Crystal Lake Morning Herald*, 7803 Pyott Rd, Crystal Lake IL 60014 815-459-4040
Crystal Lake News, 404 Virginia St, Crystal Lake IL 60014..........................815-459-1456
Daily Calumet*, 18127 William St, Lansing IL 60438 312-895-3700
Daily Clay County Advocate-Press*, 105 W North Ave, Flora IL 62839....618-662-2108
Daily Courier-News*, 300 Lake St, Elgin IL 60120......................................312-888-7800
Daily Herald*+, PO Box 280, Arlington Hts IL 60006..................................312-870-3600
Daily Reporter*, 216 S Central, Casey IL 62420...217-932-5211
Daily Sentinel*, 109 S Jefferson, Woodstock IL 60098 815-338-1300
Daily Southtown Economist*+, 5959 S Harlem Ave, Chicago IL 60638 ...312-586-8800
Danville Commercial-News*, 17 W North St, Danville IL 61832 217-446-1000
Darien Progress, 922 Warren, Downers Grove IL 60515...............................312-969-0188
Decatur Herald-Review*+, 601 E William, Decatur IL 62525 217-429-5151
Deerfield Review, 400 Lake Cook Rd, Deerfield IL 60015 312-948-9100
DeKalb Daily Chronicle*, Barber Green Rd, DeKalb IL 60115 815-756-4841
Democrat Message, 120 E Main St, Mt Sterling IL 62353.............................217-773-3371
Des Plaines Journal, 1368 Webford Ave, Des Plaines IL 60016 312-299-5511
Des Plaines Times, 1000 Executive Way, Des Plaines IL 60018...................312-824-1111
Dixon Evening Telegraph*, 113 Peoria Ave, Dixon IL 61021.......................815-284-2222
Downers Grove Reporter, 922 Warren, Downers Grove IL 60515.............312-969-0188
Du Page Progress, 922 Warren, Downers Grove IL 60515 312-969-0188
East Peoria Courier, 100 Detroit Ave, Morton IL 61550 309-264-2211
Economist Shopper, 5959 S Harlem, Chicago IL 60638 312-586-8800
Edwardsville Intelligencer*, 117 N 2nd St, Edwardsville IL 62025.............618-656-4700
Edwardsville Journal, 1990 Troy Rd, Edwardsville IL 62025 618-656-8000
Effingham Daily News*, 201 N Banker, Effingham IL 62401 217-347-7151
Elgin Herald, Box 811, Elgin IL 60120...312-888-3555
Elgin News Magazine, 250 Williams Rd, Carpentersville IL 60110.............312-426-1600
Elm Leaves, 137 S Marion, Oak Park IL 60302...312-383-3200
Elmhurst Press, 112 S York St, Elmhurst IL 60126......................................312-834-0900
Enterprise, 519 W Lockport St, Plainfield IL 60544......................................815-436-2431
Evanston Review, 1569 Sherman Ave, Evanston IL 60201 312-866-6500
Evergreen Park Courier, 3840 W 147th St, Midlothian IL 60445.................312-388-2425
Family Journal, 1368 Webford Ave, Des Plaines IL 60016............................312-299-5511
Farmers Weekly Review, 100 Manhattan Rd, Joliet IL 60433......................815-727-4811
Forest Leaves, 1232 Central Ave, Wilmette IL 60091 312-251-4300

Fort Sheridan Tower, 30 S Whitney St, Grayslake IL 60030.........................312-223-8161
Fox Lake Press, 30 S Whitney St, Grayslake IL 60030..............................312-223-8161
Fox Valley Sun, 9 W Jackson, Naperville IL 60540.................................312-355-0063
Franklin Park Herald, 1232 Central Ave, Wilmette IL 60091......................312-251-4300
Free Press Progress, 112 W State, Nokomis IL 62075.............................217-563-2115
Freeport Journal-Standard*, 27 S State Ave, Freeport IL 61032..............815-232-1171
Galena Gazette Publications Inc, 309 S Main St, Galena IL 61036...........815-777-0019
Galesburg Post, 80 S Cherry St, Galesburg IL 61404...............................309-343-5617
Geneseo Republic, 108 W 1st St, Geneseo IL 61254................................309-944-2119
Geneva Chronicle, 410 W State, Geneva IL 60134..................................312-232-9666
Geneva Republican, 17 N 1st St, Geneva IL 60134.................................312-232-7400
Gibson City Courier, 115 N Sangamon Ave, Gibson City IL 60936...........217-784-4244
Gillespie Area News, 112 W Chestnut St, Gillespie IL 62033....................217-839-2139
Glen Ellyn News, 460 Pennsylvania Ave, Glen Ellyn IL 60137..................312-469-0100
Glencoe News, 1232 Central Ave, Wilmette IL 60091 312-251-4300
Glendale Heights Press, 112 S York St, Elmhurst IL 60126 312-834-0900
Glenview Announcements, 1806 Glenview Rd, Glenview IL 60025............312-724-4300
Glenview Glenviews, 30 S Whitney St, Grayslake IL 60030 312-223-8161
Golden Prairie News, 301 S Chestnut, Assumption IL 62510 217-226-3721
Golf Mill Journal, 1368 Webford Ave, Des Plaines IL 60016....................312-299-5511
Grayslake Times, 30 S Whitney St, Grayslake IL 60030 312-223-8161
Great Lakes Bulletin, 30 S Whitney St, Grayslake IL 60030.....................312-223-8161
Greenville Advocate, 305 S 2nd St, Greenville IL 62246 618-664-3144
Hardin County Independent, Box 328, Elizabethtown IL 62931...............618-287-2361
Harrisburg Daily Register*, 35 S Vine, Harrisburg IL 62946....................618-253-7146
Harvard Herald, 201 S Ayer St, Harvard IL 60033 815-943-4411
Harwood Heights News*+, 130 S Prospect, Park Ridge IL 60068.............312-696-3133
Hazel Crest-Country Club Hills Star, 1526 Otto, Chicago Hts IL 60411..312-755-6161
Henry News Republican, Box 190, Henry IL 61537................................309-364-3250
The Herald, 179 S Northwest Hwy, Cary IL 60013.................................312-639-2301
The Herald, 7803 Pyott Rd, Crystal Lake IL 60014 815-459-4040
Hickory Hills Citizen, 3840 W 147th St, Midlothian IL 60445..................312-388-2425
Highland News Leader, 822 Broadway, Highland IL 62249 618-654-2366
Highland Park News, 444 Central Ave, Highland Park IL 60035...............312-433-4300
Hillsboro-Montgomery Cty News, 106 W Seward, Hillsboro IL 62049 217-523-3929
Hinsdale Doings, 118 W 1st St, Hinsdale IL 60521 312-887-0600
Hinsdale Suburban Tribune+, 765 N York Rd, Hinsdale IL 60521 312-887-4070
Homewood-Flossmoor Star, 1526 Otto Blvd, Chicago Heights IL 60411..312-755-6161
Hyde Park Herald, 5240 S Harper Ave, Chicago IL 60615 312-643-8533
Illinoian-Star*, 1210 Wall St, Beardstown IL 62618 217-323-1010
Illinois State Journal*+, 313 S 6th St, Springfield IL 62705 217-788-8600
Illinois Times, PO Box 3524, Springfield IL 62708.................................217-753-2226
Iroquois County Daily Times*, 1492 E Walnut St, Watseka IL 60970.......815-432-5227
Jacksonville Journal Courier*, 235 W State, Jacksonville IL 62651...........217-245-6121
Joliet Herald-News*, 300 Caterpillar Dr, Joliet IL 60436.......................815-729-6161
The Journal*, 8 Dearborn Sq, Kankakee IL 60901 815-937-3355
Journal-Pilot, 31 N Washington, Carthage IL 62321 217-357-2149
Kendall County Record, 222 S Bridge St, Yorkville IL 60560...................312-553-7034
Kewanee Star-Courier*, 105 E Central Blvd, Kewanee IL 61443.............309-852-2181
La Grange Countryside Citizen, 19 E 31st St, La Grange IL 60525 312-354-0600
Lake Forester, 1232 Central Ave, Wilmette IL 60091.............................312-251-4300
Lake Forester, 444 Central Ave, Highland Park IL 60035........................312-433-4300
Lawrenceville Daily Record*, 1209 State St, Lawrenceville IL 62439.........618-943-2331

Libertyville Independent Register, 345 Milwaukee, Libertyvle IL 60048...312-362-2090
Libertyville Review*+, 1232 Central Ave, Wilmette IL 60091......................312-251-4300
Lincoln Courier*, McLean & Pulaski Sts, Lincoln IL 62656 217-732-2101
Lisle Sun, 4745 Main St Ste 109, Lisle IL 60532......................................312-968-8200
Litchfield News-Herald*, 112 E Ryder St, Litchfield IL 62056....................217-324-2121
Lombard Lombardian, 613 S Main, Lombard IL 60148...............................312-627-7010
Lombard Spector, 112 S York St, Elmhurst IL 60126................................312-834-0900
Lombard Villa Park Review, 613 S Main, Lombard IL 60148 312-627-7010
Loves Park Post & Buyers Guide, 518 Merrill Ave, Rockford IL 61111....815-877-4044
Lyons Times, 6894 W 47th St, Lyons IL 60534.......................................312-442-9300
Macomb Journal*, 128 N Lafayette, Macomb IL 61455.............................309-833-2114
Macoupin County Enquirer, 125 E Main, Carlinville IL 62626....................217-854-2534
Macoupin County Shopper, 431 S Main St, Hillsboro IL 62049 217-532-3933
Manito Review, 106 N Broadway PO Box 709, Manito IL 61546 309-968-6705
Marion Daily Republican*, 111 Franklin, Marion IL 62959 618-993-2626
Mascoutah Herald, 314 E Church St, Mascoutah IL 62258........................618-566-8282
Mason County Democrat, 217 W Market St, Havana IL 62644 309-543-3311
Matterson-Richton Park Star, 1526 Otto Blvd, Chicago Hts IL 60411......312-755-6161
Mattoon Journal Gazette*, 100 Broadway, Mattoon IL 61938....................217-235-5656
Maywood Herald, 1440 W North Ave, Melrose Park IL 60106 312-251-4300
McLeansboro Times Leader, 137 S Jackson, McLeansboro IL 62859........618-643-2387
Melrose Park Herald*+, 208 W Harrison, Oak Park IL 60304 312-383-3200
Mendota Reporter, 702 Illinois Ave, Mendota IL 61342 815-539-9396
Metropolis Planet, 101 W 7th St, Metropolis IL 62960.............................312-388-2425
Midlothian-Bremen Messenger, 3840 W 147th St, Midlothian IL 60445...312-388-2425
Moline Daily Dispatch*, 1720 5th Ave, Moline IL 61265 309-764-4344
Monmouth Review Atlas*, 400 S Main, Monmouth IL 61462 309-734-3176
Morris Herald*, 1804 Division St, Morris IL 60450................................815-942-3221
Morton Grove Champion, 130 S Prospect, Park Ridge IL 60068...............312-696-3133
Morton-Tazewell News, 100 Detroit Ave, Morton IL 61550 309-264-2211
Mt Carmel Republican Register*, 115 E 4th St, Mt Carmel IL 62863.......618-262-5144
Mt Greenwood Express, 3840 W 147th St, Midlothian IL 60445 312-388-2425
Mt Prospect Journal, 1368 Webford Ave, Des Plaines IL 60016...............312-299-5511
Mt Vernon Register News*, 116 N 9th St, Mt Vernon IL 62864................618-242-0113
Mundelein Review*+, 1232 Central Ave, Wilmette IL 60091......................312-251-4300
Naperville Sun, 9 W Jackson, Naperville IL 60540..................................312-355-0063
Nashville News, 130 W St Louis St, Nashville IL 62263 618-327-3411
Near South Herald, 5240 S Harper Ave, Chicago IL 60615......................312-643-8533
Near West Gazette, 1335 W Harrison St, Chicago IL 60607....................312-243-4288
News Journal, 519 S State St, Jerseyville IL 62052 618-498-5551
News-Tribune*, 426 2nd St, La Salle IL 61301 815-223-3200
Newton Press Mentor, 101 S Jackson St, Newton IL 62448 618-783-2324
Niles Bugle Publications, 8746 N Shermer Rd, Chicago IL 60648..............312-966-3900
Niles Spectator, 130 S Prospect, Park Ridge IL 60068...........................312-696-3133
North Central Associated Publishers, 406 Center St, Durand IL 61024....815-248-2121
North Chicago Tribune, 30 S Whitney St, Grayslake IL 60030....................312-223-8161
North County News, 122 S Main, Red Bud IL 62278 618-282-3803
North Loop News, 800 N Clark St, Chicago IL 60610 312-787-5396
North Town News, 7519 N Ashland Ave, Chicago IL 60626......................312-761-7200
Northbrook Star, 1240 Meadeow Rd, Northbrook IL 60062.......................312-272-4300
Northwest Herald*+, 4005 Kane Ave Ste F, McHenry IL 60050................815-385-0170
Northwest Journal, 1368 Webford Ave, Des Plaines IL 60016....................312-299-5511
Northwestern Illinois Dispatch, 419 Main St, Savanna IL 61074................815-273-2277

Northwestern Illinois Farmer, 119 W Railroad, Lena IL 61048 815-369-2811
Oak Forest Star Herald, 1526 Otto Blvd, Chicago Heights IL 60411.........312-755-6161
Oak Lawn Independent, 3840 W 147th St, Midlothian IL 60445..................312-388-2425
Oak Leaves, 208 Harrison St, Oak Park IL 60302......................................312-383-3200
Ogle County Life, 401 N Main, Rochelle IL 61068.....................................815-562-4171
Olney Daily Mail*, 206 Whittle Ave, Olney IL 62450 618-393-2931
Olympia Review, 108 S Main St, Minier IL 61759 309-392-2414
Orland Park Messenger, 3840 W 147th St, Midlothian IL 60445.................312-388-2425
Palatine Countryside, 200 James St, Barrington IL 60010 312-381-9200
Palos Citizen, 3840 W 147th St, Midlothian IL 60445................................312-388-2425
Pana News Palladium, 205 S Locust St, Pana IL 62557..............................217-562-2113
The Pantagraph*+, 301 W Washington, Bloomington IL 61701 309-829-9411
Park Forest Star, 1526 Otto Blvd, Chicago Heights IL 60411 312-755-6161
Park Ridge Advocate, 130 S Prospect, Park Ridge IL 60068......................312-696-3133
Pekin Daily Times*, 22 S 4th, Pekin IL 61554...309-346-1111
Penny Saver Publications Inc+, 6775 W 174th St, Tinley Park IL 60477 ..312-429-6400
Peoria Journal Star*+, 1 News Plaza, Peoria IL 61643..............................309-686-3000
Peoria Observer, 1625 W Candletree Dr, Peoria IL 61614 309-692-4810
Peoria Penny Press, 9011-C N University, Peoria IL 61614 309-692-6600
Petersburg Observer, 235 E Sangamon, Petersburg IL 62675....................217-632-2236
Piatt County Journal Republican, 503 W Center, Monticello IL 61856 217-762-2511
Pointer Economist, 18241 West St, Lansing IL 60438.................................312-895-5600
Pontiac Daily Leader*, 318 N Main St, Pontiac IL 61764...........................815-842-1153
Proviso Star Sentinel, 130 D Broadway, Melrose Park IL 60106.................312-345-1750
Pulaski Enterprise, 315 1st St, Mounds IL 62964......................................618-745-6267
Quincy Herald-Whig*, 130 S 5th, Quincy IL 62301 217-223-5100
Rantoul Pacesetter, 1332 E Harmon Dr, Rantoul IL 61866 217-892-9613
Rantoul Press, 1332 E Harmon Dr, Rantoul IL 61866.................................217-892-9613
Regional News, 12243 S Harlem Ave, Palos Heights IL 60463 312-448-4000
Register Star*+, 99 E State St, Rockford IL 61105 815-987-1200
Register-Mail*, 140 S Prairie St, Galesburg IL 61401................................309-343-7181
The Reporter, 10139 S Harlem Ave, Chicago Ridge IL 60415.....................312-424-7660
The Review, 6712 N Olympia Ave, Chicago IL 60631.................................312-824-1111
River Grove Messenger*+, 208 W Harrison, Oak Park IL 60304.................312-383-3200
Riverdale-Dolton Pointer Economist, 18241 West St, Lansing IL 60438 ...312-895-5600
Robinson Daily News*, 302 S Cross St, Robinson IL 62454........................618-544-2101
Rochelle News/Leader, 401 N Main, Rochelle IL 61068 815-562-4171
Rock Island Argus*, 1724 4th Ave, Rock Island IL 61201 309-786-6441
Rogers Park-Edgewater News, 7519 N Ashland Ave, Chicago IL 60626....312-761-7200
Romeoville Sun, 349 N Schmidt Rd, Bolingbrook IL 60439.......................312-759-9169
Roselle Record, 316 S Schmale Rd, Wheaton IL 60187..............................312-892-5600
Rosemont Progress*+, 208 W Harrison, Oak Park IL 60304......................312-383-3200
Rushville Times, 110 E LaFayette, Rushville IL 62681...............................217-322-3321
St Charles Chronicle, 2601 E Main, St Charles IL 60174 312-584-3873
Salem Times-Commoner, 120 S Broadway, Salem IL 62881.......................618-548-3330
Schiller Park Independent*+, 208 W Harrison, Oak Park IL 60304 312-383-3200
Scottsdale-Ashburn Independent, 3840 147th St, Midlothian IL 60445 312-388-2425
Shelbyville Union*, 100 W Main St, Shelbyville IL 62565 217-774-2161
Skokie Life Newspaper Group, 5158 W Main St, Skokie IL 60077.............312-673-7700
Skokie News, 7870 Lincoln Ave, Skokie IL 60077.....................................312-673-5000
Skokie Review, 130 S Prospect, Park Ridge IL 60068.................................312-696-3133
South Holland Star-Tribune, 1526 Otto Blvd, Chicago Hts IL 60411........312-755-6161
Southern Illinoisan*, 710 N Illinois St, Carbondale IL 62901 618-529-5454

Southtown Economist*+, 5959 S Harlem, Chicago IL 60638......................312-586-8800
Southwest News-Herald+, 6225 S Kedzie Ave, Chicago IL 60629...............312-476-4800
Sparta News-Plaindealer, 116 W Main St, Sparta IL 62286......................618-443-2154
Staunton Star-Times, 108 W Main, Staunton IL 62088............................618-635-2000
Steamwood Township Times, 316 S Schmale Rd, Wheaton IL 60187........312-892-5600
Sterling Daily Gazette*, 312 2nd Ave, Sterling IL 61081.........................815-625-3600
Streator Daily Times-Press*, 122 S Bloomington St, Streator IL 61364....815-672-2111
Suburban Journal, 1368 Webford Ave, Des Plaines IL 60016 312-299-5511
Suburban Life Graphic, 239 Ogden Ave, Downers Grove IL 60515 312-969-1100
Suburbanite Economist, 5959S Harlem Ave, Chicago IL 60638.................312-586-8800
Sullivan News-Progress, 100 W Monroe St, Sullivan IL 61951..................217-728-7381
Summit Valley Times, 6894 W 47th St, Lyons IL 60534...........................312-442-9300
Sun Newspapers, 19 E 31st St, La Grange IL 60525 312-352-8030
Sunday Star, 7519 N Ashland Ave, Chicago IL 60626 312-761-7200
Taylorville Breeze-Courier*, 212 S Main St, Taylorville IL 62568 217-824-2233
Thrif-T-Nikel Weekly, 801 Canal St, Ottawa IL 61350.............................815-433-5595
Tinley Part Star Herald, 1526 Otto Blvd, Chicago Heights IL 60411.........312-755-6161
Tri-County Today, Box 72, Sandwich IL 60548..815-786-2125
Tuscola Review, 115 W Sale St, Tuscola IL 61953 217-253-2358
US Suburban Press*+, 929 N Plum Grove, Schaumburg IL 60195 312-882-8262
Vandalia Leader-Union, 229 S 5th St, Vandalia IL 62471 618-283-3374
Vernon Hills Review*+, 1232 Central Ave, Wilmette IL 60091 312-251-4300
Vienna Times, Box 457, Vienna IL 62995 618-658-4321
Villa Park Argus, 112 S York St, Elmhurst IL 60126 312-834-0900
Warren-Newport Press, 30 S Whitney St, Grayslake IL 60030 312-223-8161
Washington Courier, 1220 Washington Sq, Washington IL 61571..............309-444-3139
Washington Reporter, 100 Detroit Ave, Morton IL 61550 309-264-2211
Waterloo Republic-Times, 222 S Main, Waterloo IL 62298.......................618-939-6318
Wauconda Leader, 30 S Whitney St, Grayslake IL 60030..........................312-223-8161
Wayne County Press, 213 E Main St, Fairfield IL 62837...........................618-842-2662
Weekend Booster, 7519 N Ashland Ave, Chicago IL 60626 312-761-7200
West Chicago Press, 100 Arbor Ave, West Chicago IL 60185.....................312-231-0500
West Cook County Press, 112 S York St, Elmhurst IL 60126......................312-834-0900
West Frankfort Daily American*, 111 S Emma, W Frankfort IL 62896....618-932-2146
West Proviso Herald, 1440 W North Ave, Melrose Park IL 60106..............312-251-4300
Westmont Progress, 922 Warren Ave, Downers Grove IL 60515 312-969-0188
Wheaton Daily Journal*, Box 360, Wheaton IL 60187.............................312-653-1100
Wheaton Leader, 460 Pennsylvania Ave, Glen Ellyn IL 60137 312-469-0100
Wheeling Countryside*+, 200 James St, Barrington IL 60010....................312-381-9200
Wilmette Life, 1232 Central Ave, Wilmette IL 60091...............................312-256-7642
Winnetka Talk, 1232 Central Ave, Wilmette IL 60091..............................312-256-7642
Woodridge Progress, 922 Warren Ave, Downers Grove IL 60515...............312-969-0188
Worth Citizen, 3840 W 147th St, Midlothian IL 60445 312-388-2425
Worth Township Times, 12243 S Harlem Ave, Palos Heights IL 60463 312-448-4000
Zion-Benton News, 2719 Elisha Ave, Zion IL 60099 312-746-9000

INDIANA

Alexandria Times-Tribune, 116 E Church St, Alexandria IN 46001 317-724-4469
Anderson Herald-Bulletin*, 1133 Jackson St, Anderson IN 46015.............317-643-5371
Angola Herald-Republican, 12 Minument Pl, Angola IN 46703.................219-665-3117
Auburn Evening Star*, 118 W 9th St, Auburn IN 46706............................219-925-2611
Banner-Gazette, Grove & Hwy 60, Pekin IN 47165 812-967-3176

Batesville Herald-Tribune, 4 W Pearl St, Batesville IN 47006..................812-934-4343
Bloomington Herald-Telephone*, 1900 Walnut, Bloomington IN 47401...812-332-4401
Boonville Standard, 204 W Locust St, Boonville IN 47601 812-897-2330
Brazil Times*+, 100 Times Square, Brazil IN 47834....................................812-446-2216
Brookville American-Democrat, Box 38, Brookville IN 47012....................317-645-4221
Brown County Democrat, 136 N Van Buren St, Nashville IN 47448..........812-988-2221
Brownstown Banner, 116 E Cross St, Brownstown IN 47220 812-358-2111
Calumet Press, 8411 Kennedy Ave, Highland IN 46322..............................219-838-0717
Carmel News Journal, Box 95, Carmel IN 46032...317-846-5809
Carmel Tribune, 9615 N College Ave, Indianapolis IN 46280 317-844-3311
Cedar Lake Journal, 116 Clark St, Lowell IN 46356.....................................219-696-7711
Charlestown Courier, Main-Cross, Charlestown IN 47111..........................812-256-6243
Charlestown Leader, 844 High St, Charlestown IN 47111 812-256-3377
The Clarion, 301 N Capitol Ave, Corydon IN 47112......................................812-738-4552
Columbus Republic*, 333 2nd St, Columbus IN 47201.................................812-372-7811
Connersville News-Examiner*, 406 Central Ave, Connersville IN 47331 ..317-825-0585
Corydon Democrat, 301 N Capitol Ave, Corydon IN 47112.........................812-738-4552
Crawford County Democrat*+, PO Box 99, English IN 47118...................812-338-2113
Crawfordsville Journal-Review*, 119 N Green, Crawfordsvle IN 47933....317-362-1200
Daily Clintonian*, 422 S Main St, Clinton IN 47842...................................317-832-2443
Daily Journal*, 2575 N Morton St, Franklin IN 46131 317-736-7101
Daily Reporter*, 212 E Main St, Greenfield IN 46140..................................317-462-5528
Decatur Democrat*, 141 S 2nd St, Decatur IN 46733 219-724-2121
DeKalb County Advertiser, 105 N Randolph St, Garrett IN 46738 219-357-3806
East Chicago Calumet-Globe, 2005 Broadway, East Chicago IN 46312.....219-397-2211
East Side Herald, 4309 E Michigan St, Indianapolis IN 46201...................317-356-2487
Evansville Courier*+, 201 N W 2nd St, Evansville IN 47708 812-424-7711
Evansville Press*, 201 N W 2nd St, Evansville IN 47703.............................812-464-7601
Farmweek, 27 N Jefferson St, Knightstown IN 46148..................................317-345-5133
Fishers Sun-Herald, 9615 N College Ave, Indianapolis IN 46280..............317-844-3311
Fort Wayne Journal-Gazette*+, 600 W Main St, Ft Wayne IN 46802.......219-423-3311
Fort Wayne News-Sentinel*+, 600 W Main St, Ft Wayne IN 46802..........219-461-8222
Fowler Benton Review, Box 668, Fowler IN 47944 317-884-0100
Gary Crusader, 1549 Broadway, Gary IN 46407..219-885-4357
Gary Info, 1953 Broadway PO Box M587, Gary IN 46401 219-882-6711
Gary Post-Tribune*+, 1065 Broadway, Gary IN 46402................................219-881-3000
The Giveaway, 890 N Gardner, Scottsburg IN 47170....................................812-752-3171
Goshen News*, 114 S Main St, Goshen IN 46526...219-533-2151
Greensburg Daily News*, 135 S Franklin, Greensburg IN 47240 812-663-3111
The Guide, 516 E Main St, Brownsville IN 46112..317-852-2500
Hobart Gazette, 413 Main St, Hobart IN 46342...219-942-6575
Huntington Herald-Press*, 7 N Jefferson, Huntington IN 46750 219-356-6700
Indianapolis News*+, 307 N Pennsylvania St, Indianapolis IN 46206........317-633-1240
Indianapolis Recorder, 2901 N Tacoma Ave, Indianapolis IN 46218.........317-924-5143
Indianapolis Spotlight, 1469 S Meridian St, Indianapolis IN 46225 317-631-3402
Indianapolis Star*+, 307 N Pennsylvania St, Indianapolis IN 46206.........317-633-1240
Jasper Herald*, 216 4th St, Jasper IN 47546...812-482-2424
Jeffersonville Evening News*, 221 Spring St, Jeffersonville IN 47130 812-283-6636
Journal & Austin Chronicle, 39 E Wardell St, Scottsburg IN 47170..........812-752-2611
Journal Press, 414 3rd St, Aurora IN 47001...812-537-0063
Journal-Democrat, 541 Main St, Rockport IN 47635....................................812-649-4440
Kokomo Tribune*, 300 N Union St, Kokomo IN 46901 317-459-3121
La Porte Herald-Argus*, 701 State St, La Porte IN 46350............................219-362-2161

Lafayette Journal and Courier*, 217 N 6th St, Layfayette IN 47902..........317-423-5511
Lafayette Leader, 512 Columbia St, Lafayette IN 47901.....................317-742-7700
LaGrange Standard News, State Rd 9 S, LaGrange IN 46761 219-463-2166
Lake County Star Register, 15 N Court, Crown Point IN 46307................219-663-4212
Lake Station Herald, 3161 E 84th Pl, Merrillville IN 46342.................219-942-0521
Lawrence Ad-Courier, 7962 Pendleton Pike, Lawrence IN 46226............317-542-8149
Lawrence Journal, 7962 Pendleton Pike, Lawrence IN 46226 317-542-8149
The Leader, 21 N Main St PO Box 38, Knox IN 46534 219-772-2101
The Leader, 382 Main Cross, Charlestown IN 47111 812-256-3377
Lebanon Reporter*, 117 E Eashington, Lebanon IN 46052....................317-482-4650
Ledger Tribune*, 303 W 2nd St, New Albany IN 47150 812-944-6481
Linton Daily Citizen*, 79 S Main, Linton IN 47441 812-847-4487
Logansport Pharos-Tribune*, 517 E Broadway, Logansport IN 46947 219-722-5000
Madison Courier*, 310 Courier Sq, Madison IN 47250 812-265-3641
Mail-Journal, 206 S Main, Milford IN 46542....................219-658-4111
Martinsville Daily Reporter*, 60 S Jefferson, Martinsville IN 46151.........317-342-3311
Merrillville Herald, 3161 E 84th Pl, Merrillville IN 46342....................219-942-0521
Michigan City News-Dispatch*, 121 W Michigan, Mich City IN 46360.....219-874-7211
Mishawaka Enterprise-Record, 126 Lincolnway E, N Liberty IN 46554....219-255-4789
Monticello Daily Herald-Journal*, 114 S Main St, Monticello IN 47960 ..219-583-5121
Mooresville Times, 23 E Main St, Mooresville IN 46158 317-831-0280
Mount Vernon Democrat*, 430 Main St, Mt Vernon IN 47620....................812-838-4811
Muncie Evening Press*, 125 S High St, Muncie IN 47305 317-747-5700
Muncie Star*, PO Box 2408, Muncie IN 47307 317-747-5762
New Castle Courier-Times*, 201 S 14th St, New Castle IN 47362 317-529-1111
The News, Hwy 256, Austin IN 47102....................812-794-3924
News-Gazette*, 224 W Franklin St, Winchester IN 47394 317-584-4501
Noblesville Daily Ledger*, 957 Logan St, Noblesville IN 46060 317-773-1210
Noblesville Telegraph, 871 Conner St, Noblesville IN 46060 317-773-5000
North East Topics, 9615 N College Ave, Indianapolis IN 46280....................317-844-3311
N Manchester News-Journal, 112 W Main, N Manchester IN 46962.........219-982-2178
North Vernon Sun, PO Box 410, North Vernon IN 47265 812-346-3973
Northeast Reporter, 4309 E Michigan St, Indianapolis IN 46201 317-356-2487
Osgood Journal, 115 S Washington St, Versailles IN 47042....................812-689-6364
Paoli News & Republican, Court St PO Box 190, Paoli IN 47454 812-723-2572
Peru Daily Tribune*, 26 W 3rd St, Peru IN 46970....................317-473-6641
Petersburg Press Dispatch, Box 68, Petersburg IN 47567 812-354-8500
Pike Register, 9615 N College Ave, Indianapolis IN 46280 317-844-3311
Pilot-News*, 217 N Center St, Plymouth IN 46563....................219-936-3101
Portage Journal, 2583 Portage Mall, Portage IN 46368 219-762-9564
Portland Commercial Review*, 309 W Main St, Portland IN 47371...........219-726-8141
Post & Mail*, 116 N Chauncey St, Columbia City IN 46725....................219-244-5153
Princeton Daily Clarion*, Gibson & Broadway, Princeton IN 47670.........812-385-2525
Pulaski County Journal, 114 W Main St, Winamac IN 46996 219-946-6628
Putnam County Banner*, 100 N Jackson St, Greencastle IN 46135 317-653-5151
Regional News, Box 358, La Crosse IN 46348....................219-754-2432
Rensselaer Republican*, 117 N Van Rensselaer, Rensselaer IN 47978.....219-866-5111
Richmond Graphic, 621 NW 1st St, Richmond IN 47374....................317-966-8211
Richmond Palladium-Item*, 1175 N A St, Richmond IN 47374....................317-962-1575
Rochester Sentinel*, 118 E 8th St, Rochester IN 46975 219-223-2111
Rockport Democrat, Box 27, Rockport IN 47635 812-649-2411
Rockville Parke County Sentinel, 125 W High St, Rockville IN 47872.......317-569-2033
Rushville Republican*, 219 N Perkins St, Rushville IN 46173....................317-932-2222

Salem Leader, 117 E Walnut St, Salem IN 47167...812-883-3281
Seymour Tribune*, 1215 E Tipton, Seymour IN 47274 812-522-4871
Shelbyville News*, 123 E Washington, Shelbyville IN 46176......................317-398-6631
South Bend Tribune*+, 223 W Colfax Ave, South Bend IN 46626 219-233-6161
South Lake County Advertiser, 116 Clark St, Lowell IN 46356....................219-696-7711
Spencer Evening World*, 114 E Franklin St, Spencer IN 47460 812-829-2255
Sullivan Daily Times*, PO Box 130, Sullivan IN 47882...........................812-268-6356
Tell City News, 537 Main St, Tell City IN 47586 812-547-3424
Thorntown Hossier Graphic, Box 128, Thorntown IN 46071 317-676-5525
The Times*+, 417 Fayette St, Hammond IN 46325 219-933-3223
Times-Mail*, 813 16th St, Bedford IN 47421...812-275-3355
Tipton Tribune*, 110 W Madison, Tipton IN 46072 317-675-2115
Tri-County Banner, 27 N Jefferson St, Knightstown IN 46148....................317-345-5133
Tri-County News, 1410 S Michigan St, South Bend IN 46613....................219-289-2455
Tri-County Weekly News, 153 S Jefferson St, Berne IN 46711 219-589-2101
Tribune-Star*, 721 Wabash Ave, Terre Haute IN 47808 812-232-0581
Valparaiso Vidette-Messenger*, 1111 Glendale, Valparaiso IN 46383 219-462-5151
Versailles Republican, 115 S Washington St, Versailles IN 47042 812-689-6364
Vevay Reveille-Enterprise, 111 W Market St, Vevay IN 47043.................812-427-2311
Vincennes Sun-Commercial*, 702 Main St, Vincennes IN 47591 812-886-9955
Vincennes Valley Advance, 1103 N 3rd, Vincennes IN 47591....................812-885-4271
Warrick Enquirer, 204 W Locust St, Boonville IN 47601...........................812-897-2330
Washington Patriot, 9615 N College Ave, Indianapolis IN 46280..............317-844-3311
Washington Times-Herald*, 102 E Van Trees, Washington IN 47501 812-254-0480
West Side Messenger, 516 E Main St, Brownsville IN 46112......................317-852-2500
Westfield Enterprise, 9615 N College Ave, Indianapolis IN 46280..............317-844-3311
Westside Enterprise, 1750 W Morris St, Indianapolis IN 46221 317-639-6477
Westville Indicator, 156 Flynn Rd, Westville IN 46391 219-785-2234
Zionville Eagle, 9615 N College Ave, Indianapolis IN 46280.....................317-844-3311

IOWA

Adair County Free Press, 108 E Iowa St, Greenfield IA 50849....................515-743-6121
Algona Upper Des Moines, 111 E Call St, Algona IA 50511......................515-295-3535
Altoona Herald, 116 2nd St SE, Altoona IA 50009.................................515-967-4224
Ames Daily Tribune*, 317 5th St, Ames IA 50010..................................515-232-2160
Anamosa Journal-Eureka, 113 N Ford, Anamosa IA 52205.....................319-462-3511
Atlantic News-Telegraph*, 410 Walnut St, Atlantic IA 50022....................712-243-2624
Bettendorf News, 1704 State St, Bettendorf IA 52772.............................319-355-2644
Boone News-Republican*, 812 Keeler St, Boone IA 50036 515-432-1234
Bremer County Independent, 311 W Bremer, Waverly IA 50677 319-352-3335
Carroll Daily Times Herald*, 508 N Court St, Carroll IA 51401 712-792-3573
Cedar Rapids Gazette*+, 500 3rd Ave SE, Cedar Rapids IA 52401..........319-398-8211
Centerville Iowegian*, 105 N Main St, Centerville IA 52544 515-856-6336
Chariton Herald-Patriot, 817 Braden Ave, Chariton IA 50049....................515-744-2137
Chariton Leader, 817 Braden Ave, Chariton IA 50049.............................515-744-2137
Cherokee Daily Times*, 111 S 2nd St, Cherokee IA 51012........................712-225-5111
Clarinda Herald Journal, 215 E Washington St, Clarinda IA 51632..........712-542-2181
Clayton County Register, 106 Cedar NW, Elkader IA 52043 319-245-1311
Clinton Herald*, 221 6th Ave S, Clinton IA 52732..................................319-242-7101
Clinton Town Talk, 612 S 2nd St, Clinton IA 52732................................319-243-1526
Corydon Times-Republican, 205 W Jackson, Corydon IA 50060................515-872-1234
Council Bluffs Daily Nonpareil*, 117 Pearl St, Council Bluffs IA 51501...712-328-1811

Cresco Times-Plain Dealer, 214 N Elm, Cresco IA 52136 319-547-3601
Creston News Advertiser*, 503 W Adams, Creston IA 50801 515-782-2141
Daily Iowan*+, 111 Communications Center, Coralville IA 52242 319-335-6063
Davenport Quad-City Times*+, 124 E 2nd St, Davensport IA 52808........319-383-2200
Decorah Journal, 107 E Water St, Decorah IA 52101 319-382-4221
Decorah Public Opinion, 107 E Water St, Decorah IA 52101.....................319-382-4221
Denison Bulletin & Review, 1410 Broadway, Denison IA 51442.................712-263-2123
Des Moines Register*+, 715 Locust St, Des Moines IA 50309 515-284-8000
Des Moines Tribune*+, 715 Locust, Des Moines IA 50304 515-284-8000
DeWitt Observer, 512 7th St, De Witt IA 52742 319-659-3121
Doon Press, RR 1, Doon IA 51235 712-726-3313
Dubuque Telegraph Herald*, W 8th & Bluff, Dubuque IA 52001..............319-588-5611
Dyersville Commercial, Box 128, Dyersville IA 52040...............................319-875-7231
Eagle Grove Eagle, 314 W Broadway, Eagle Grove IA 50533 515-448-4745
Eldora Herald-Leader, W Washington Ave, Eldora IA 50627 515-858-5051
Emmetsburg Reporter & Democrat, Box 73, Emmetsburg IA 50536 712-852-2323
Estherville Daily News*, 10 N 7th St, Estherville IA 51334......................712-362-2622
Fairfield Ledger*, 112 E Broadway, Fairfield IA 52556 515-472-4129
Forest City Summit, 105 Clark St, Forest City IA 50436............................515-582-2112
Fort Dodge Messenger*, 713 Central Ave, Ft Dodge IA 50501...................515-573-2141
Fort Madison Daily Democrat*, 1226 Ave H, Ft Madison IA 52627 319-372-6421
Glenwood Opinion-Tribune, 116 S Walnut, Glenwood IA 51534.................712-527-3191
Grinnell Herald-Register, 813 5th Ave, Grinnell IA 50112..........................515-236-3113
Grundy Register, 601 G Ave, Grundy Center IA 50638 319-824-6958
Hardin County Times, 406 Stevens, Iowa Falls IA 50126............................515-648-2521
Harlan News Advertiser, Box 721, Harlan IA 51537..................................712-755-3111
Harlan Tribune, 1114 7th St, Harlan IA 51537 712-755-3111
Hawk Eye*, 800 S Main, Burlington IA 52601...319-754-8461
Highland Park News, Box 4050, Des Moines IA 50333 515-279-3049
Humboldt Independent, 727 Summer Ave, Humboldt IA 50548 515-332-2514
Humboldt Republican, 727 Summer Ave, Humboldt IA 50548 515-332-2514
Independence Bulletin-Journal, 505 1st St, Independence IA 50644...........319-334-2557
Independence Conservative, 505 1st St, Independence IA 50644.................319-334-2557
India•.ola Record-Herald & Tribune, 203 W Salem, Indianola IA 50125..515-961-2511
Iowa City Press-Citizen*, 319 E Washington St, Iowa City IA 52240.........319-337-3181
Iowa Falls Citizen, 406 Stevens, Iowa Falls IA 50126 515-648-2521
Jefferson Bee, 214 N Wilson Ave, Jefferson IA 50129 515-386-4161
Jefferson Herald, 214 N Wilson Ave, Jefferson IA 50129 515-386-4161
Knoxville Express, 122 E Robinson, Knoxville IA 50138 515-842-2155
Knoxville Journal, 122 E Robinson, Knoxville IA 50138.............................515-842-2155
Kossuth County Advance, 111 E Call St, Algona IA 50511 515-295-3535
Le Mars Daily Sentinel*, 41 1st Ave NE, Le Mars IA 51031......................712-546-7031
Lee Town News, 2611 E University, Des Moines IA 50317 515-262-5651
Leon Journal-Reporter, 114 N Main St, Leon IA 50144.............................515-446-4151
Lyon County Reporter Inc, 310 1st St, Rock Rapids IA 51246....................712-472-2525
Manchester Democrat-Radio, 109 E Delaware, Manchester IA 52057......319-927-2020
Manchester Press, 109 E Delaware St, Manchester IA 52057.....................319-927-2020
Maquoketa Sentinel-Press, 108 W Quarry St, Maquoketa IA 52060..........319-652-2441
Missouri Valley Times-News, 109 N 5th St, Missouri Valley IA 51555 712-642-2791
Mitchell County Press-News, 112 N 6th St, Osage IA 50461 515-732-3721
Monticello Express, 111 E Grand, Monticello IA 52310.............................319-465-3555
Mount Ayr Record-News, 119 N Taylor, Mt Ayr IA 50854 515-464-2440
Mount Pleasant News*, 215 W Monroe, Mt Pleasant IA 52641..................319-385-3131

Muscatine Journal*, 301 E 3rd St, Muscatine IA 52761 319-263-2331
Nevada Journal*, 1133 6th St, Nevada IA 50201.............................515-382-2161
New Hampton Economist, 10 N Chestnut Ave, New Hampton IA 50659..515-394-2111
New Hampton Tribune, 10 N Chestnut Ave, New Hampton IA 50659 515-394-2111
Newspapers of Benton County, 832 12th St, Belle Plaine IA 52208............319-444-2520
Newspapers of Iowa County, 100 W Main St, Marengo IA 52301 319-642-5506
Newton Daily News*, 200 1st Ave E, Newton IA 50208..............................515-792-3121
North Scott Press, 208 N 2nd St, Eldridge IA 52748................................319-285-8111
Oelwein Daily Register*, 25 1st St SE, Oelwcin IA 50662.........................319-283-2144
Osceola Sentinel-Tribune, 115 E Washington, Osceola IA 50213............515-342-2131
Oskaloosa Herald*, 1901 A Ave W PO Box 530, Oskaloosa IA 52577 515-672-2581
Ottumwa Courier*, 213 E 2nd St, Ottumwa IA 52501.............................515-684-4611
Pella Chronicle, 739 Franklin St, Pella IA 50219.....................................515-628-3882
Perry Chief, 1323 2nd, Perry IA 50220 515-465-4666
Pilot Tribune, 111 W 7th, Storm Lake IA 50588.....................................712-732-3130
Red Oak Express, 2012 Commerce Dr, Red Oak IA 51566.........................712-623-2568
Republican Standard, 15 1st St NW, W Des Moines IA 52172.....................319-568-3431
Sheldon Sun, Box 160, Sheldon IA 51201 712-324-2514
Shenandoah Sentinel*, 118 S Elm, Shenandoah IA 51601.........................712-246-1100
Sioux City Journal*+, 6th & Pavonia St, Sioux City IA 51102.....................712-279-5072
Slater Tri-County Times, 312 Main St, Slater IA 50244 515-685-3412
Spencer Daily Reporter*, 416 1st Ave W, Spencer IA 51301......................712-262-6610
Spirit Lake Beacon, 1706 Ithaca St, Spirit Lake IA 51360.........................712-336-1211
Story City Herald, 511 Broad, Story City IA 50248..................................515-733-4318
Tama News-Herald, 202 W 3rd St, Tama IA 52339....................................515-484-2841
Times Guthrian, 205 State, Guthrie Center IA 50115 515-747-3511
Times Republican*, 135 W Main, Marshalltown IA 50158.........................515-753-6611
Tipton Conservative & Advertiser, W 5th St, Tipton IA 52772..................319-886-2131
Traer Star Clipper, 625 2nd St, Traer IA 50675.......................................319-478-2323
Urbandale News, 3805 68th St, Des Moines IA 50322 515-276-9265
Vinton Cedar Valley Daily Times*, 108 E 5th St, Vinton IA 52349 319-472-2311
Washington Evening Journal*, 111 N Marion, Washington IA 52353.......319-653-2191
Waterloo Courier*+, 501 Commercial St, Waterloo IA 50704 319-291-1400
Waukon Democrat, 15 1st St NW, W Des Moines IA 52172 319-568-3431
Waverly Democrat, 311 W Bremer, Waverly IA 50677................................319-352-3335
West Union Union, Box 153, W Union IA 52175.......................................319-422-3888
Winterset Madisonian, 112 W Court Ave, Winterset IA 50273 515-462-2101

KANSAS

Abilene Reflector-Chronicle*, 303 N Broadway, Abilene KS 67410 913-263-1000
Anderson Countian, 112 W 6th, Garnett KS 66032.................................913-448-3121
Arkansas City Traveler*, 200 E 5th Ave, Arkansas KS 67005.....................316-442-4200
Atchison Daily Globe*, 1015 Main St, Atchison KS 66002.........................913-367-0583
Augusta Daily Gazette*, 204 E 5th St, Augusta KS 67012.........................316-775-2218
Baxter Springs Citizen, 1036 Military Ave, Baxter Springs KS 66713........316-856-2115
Belleville Telescope, 1817 US 81 Frontage Rd, Belleville KS 66935.........913-527-2244
Beloit Daily Call*, 122 E Court, Beloit KS 67420.....................................913-738-5728
Bonner Springs-Edwardville Chief, Box 256, Bonner Springs KS 66012...913-422-4048
Capital-Journal*+, 616 Jefferson, Topeka KS 66607.............................913-295-1111
Chanute Tribune*, 15 N Evergreen, Chanute KS 66720 316-431-4100
Colby Free Press, 155 W 5th, Colby KS 67701 913-462-3963
Columbus Daily Advocate*, 215 S Kansas, Columbus KS 66725.................316-429-2773

Concordia Blade-Empire*, 510 Washington, Concordia KS 66901.............913-243-2424
Daily News of Johnson City*, 514 S Kansas, Olathe KS 66061.................913-764-2211
Dodge City Daily Globe*, 705 2nd Ave, Dodge City KS 67801....................316-225-4151
Emporia Gazette*, 517 Merchant St, Emporia KS 66801............................316-342-4800
Eureka Herald, Box 590, Eureka KS 67045..316-583-5721
Fort Riley Post, 814 N Washington St, Junction City KS 66101....................913-831-1889
Fort Scott Tribune*, 6 E Wall, Ft Scott KS 66701......................................316-223-1460
Garden City Telegram*, 310 N 7th, Garden City KS 67846........................316-275-7105
Garnett Review, 112 W 6th, Garnett KS 66032...913-448-3121
Girard Press, Box 126, Girard KS 66743...316-724-4426
Goodland Daily News*, 1205 Main St, Goodland KS 67735.......................913-899-2338
Grass & Grain, 1531 Yuma, Manhattan KS 66502.....................................913-539-7558
Great Bend Tribune*, 2012 Forest Ave, Great Bend KS 67530...................316-792-1211
Hays Daily News*, 507 Main St, Hays KS 67601.......................................913-628-1081
Hiawatha Daily World*, 607 Utah St, Hiawatha KS 66434.........................913-742-2111
High Plains Journal+, 1500 E Wyatt Earp Blvd, Dodge City KS 67801....316-227-7171
Holton Recorder, 109 W 4th, Holton KS 66436...913-364-3141
Hutchinson News*, 300 W 2nd, Hutchinson KS 67501...............................316-662-3311
Independence Daily Reporter*, Box 869, Independence KS 67301.............316-331-3550
Iola Register*, 302 S Washington, Iola KS 66749......................................316-365-2111
Junction City Daily Union*, 814 N Washington, Junction City KS 66441..913-762-5000
Kansas City Kansan*, 901 N 8th St, Kansas City KS 66101........................913-371-4300
Kingman Journal, Box 353, Kingman KS 67068...316-531-3151
Larned Tiller & Toiler*, 115 W 5th St, Larned KS 67550...........................316-285-3111
Lawrence Journal World*, 6th & N H Sts, Lawrence KS 66044...................913-843-1000
Levenworth Times*, 418 Seneca St, Leavenworth KS 66048......................913-682-0305
Lyons Daily News*, 210 W Commercial, Lyons KS 67554...........................316-257-2368
Manhattan Mercury*, 5th & Osage, Manhattan KS 66502...........................913-776-8805
Marion County Record, 117 S 3rd, Marion KS 66861.................................316-382-2165
Marysville Advocate, 107 S 9th, Marysville KS 66508................................913-562-2317
McPherson Sentinel*, 310 S Main St, McPherson KS 67460.......................316-241-2422
Miami Republican, 121 S Pearl, Paola KS 66071......................................913-294-2311
Newton Kansan*, 121 W 6th, Newton KS 67114.......................................316-283-1500
Norton Daily Telegram*, 215 S Kansas, Norton KS 67654..........................913-877-3361
Osawatomie Graphic, 635 Main St, Osawatomie KS 66064.........................913-755-4151
Ottawa Herald*, 104 S Cedar, Ottawa KS 66067......................................913-242-4700
Paola Western Spirit, 121 S Pearl, Paola KS 66071...................................913-294-2311
Parsons Sun*, 221 S 18th, Parsons KS 67357...316-421-2000
Phillips County Review, 257 F St, Phillipsburg KS 67661...........................913-543-5242
Pittsburg Morning Sun*, Drawer H, Pittsburg KS 66762.............................316-231-2600
Pratt Tribune*, 319 S Ninnesch, Pratt KS 67124......................................316-672-5511
Record Publications, 3206 Strong Ave, Kansas City KS 66106....................913-362-1988
Russell Daily News*, 802 N Maple St, Russell KS 67665............................913-483-2116
Salina Journal*, 333 S 4th St, Salina KS 67401..913-823-6363
Smith County Pioneer, 201 S Main, Smith Center KS 66067.......................913-282-3371
Southwest Daily Times*, 16 S Kansas, Liberal KS 67901............................316-624-2541
TeleGraphics Inc, Box 66, Baldwin City KS 66006....................................913-594-6424
Washington County News, Box 316, Washington KS 66968.........................913-325-2219
Wellington Daily News*, 113 W Harvey, Wellington KS 67152....................316-326-3326
Wichita Eagle-Beacon*+, 825 E Douglas, Wichita KS 67202.....................316-268-6000
Wilson County Citizen, 706 Madison, Fredonia KS 66736...........................316-378-3812
Winfield Courier*, 201 E 9th St, Winfield KS 67156..................................316-221-1050
Wyandotte West, PO Box 12003, Kansas City KS 66112.............................913-788-5565

KENTUCKY

Advertiser, 40 S Bank St, Mt Sterling KY 40353..606-498-2222
Advocate Messenger*, 330 S 4th St PO Box 149, Danville KY 40422.........606-236-2551
Appalachian News-Express, 201 Caroline, Pikeville KY 41501.....................606-437-4054
Barbourville Mountain Advocate, 214 Knox St, Barbourville KY 40906...606-546-9225
Bath County News-Outlook, Box 577, Owingsville KY 40360.......................606-674-2181
Benton Tribune Courier, 308 E 12th St, Benton KY 42025 502-527-3162
Big Sandy News, 101 Main Cross, Louisa KY 41230.....................................606-638-4581
Breckenridge County Herald-News, Box 6, Hardinsburg KY 40143............502-756-2109
Cadiz Record, Public Square, Russellville KY 42276....................................502-726-9507
Caldwell County Times, 607 W Washington, Princeton KY 42445 502-365-5588
Campbell County Recorder, 654 Highland, Ft Thomas KY 41075.................606-781-4421
Carrollton News-Democrat, 111 5th St, Carrollton KY 41008......................502-732-4261
Central City Times Argus, 204 W Broad St, Central City KY 42330..........502-754-2331
Central Kentucky News, 428 Woodlawn Ave, Campbellsville KY 42718...502-465-8111
Citizen Advertiser, 123 W 8th St, Paris KY 40361.......................................606-987-1870
Clay City Times, 616 6th Ave, Clay City KY 40312......................................606-663-5540
Clinton Co News, 116 Washington St, Albany KY 42602 606-387-5144
Commonwealth Journal*, 110 E Mt Vernon, Somerset KY 42501..............606-678-8191
Corbin Times-Tribune*, Kentucky at Monroe, Corbin KY 40701...............606-528-2464
Courier-Journal*+, 525 W Broadway, Louisville KY 40202 502-582-4011
Crittenden Press, 123 E Bellville St, Marion KY 42064...............................502-965-3191
Cumberland County News, Box 307, Burkesville KY 42717 501-864-3891
Cumberland Tri-City News, Box 490, Cumberland KY 40823 606-589-4321
Cynthiana Democrat, Webster St, Cynthiana KY 41031...............................606-234-1035
Daily Independent*, 224 17th St, Ashland KY 41101....................................606-329-1717
Dawson Springs Progress, Box 404, Dawson Springs KY 42408..................502-797-3271
Dixie News, 6603 Dixie Hwy, Florence KY 41042..606-371-6177
Doone County Recorder, 2986 Union Sq, Burlington KY 41005....................606-586-6123
Elizabethtown News-Enterprise*, 408 Dixie, Elizabethtown KY 42701.....502-769-2312
Falmouth Outlook, 210 Main St, Falmouth KY 41040 606-654-3333
Floyd County Times, 3rd Ave, Prestonsburg KY 41653.................................606-886-8506
Ft Knox Inside the Turret, Box 127, Elizabethtown KY 42701 502-769-1200
Franklin Favorite, 103 High St, Franklin KY 42134 502-586-4481
Fulton Leader*, State Line St, Fulton KY 42041...502-472-1121
Georgetown News & Times, 218 E Main, Georgetown KY 41324...............502-863-1111
Glasgow Republican, 100 Commerce Dr, Glasgow KY 42141.......................502-678-5171
Grant County News, 102 S Main St, Williamstown KY 41097 606-824-3344
Grayson County News Gazette, Box 305, Leitchfield KY 42754....................502-259-3627
Grayson Journal-Enquirer, 113 Hord St, Grayson KY 41143 606-474-5101
Green River Republican, W Ohio St, Morgantown KY 42261 502-526-3811
Greenup News, 207 Harrison St, Greenup KY 41144 606-473-9851
Harlan Daily Enterprise*, US 421 By-Pass, Harlan KY 40831 606-573-4510
Harrodsburg Herald, 101 W Broadway, Harrodsburg KY 40330 606-734-2726
Hawesville Hancock Clarion, Main St, Hawesville KY 42348 502-927-6945
Hazard Herald-Voice, 341 Main St, Hazard KY 41701.................................606-436-5771
Henderson Gleaner*, 455 Klutey Park Plaza, Henderson KY 42420..........502-827-2000
Interior Journal, 111 E Main St, Stanford KY 40484 606-365-2104
Irvine Citizen Voice & Times, Box 118, Irvine KY 40336.............................606-723-5161
The Jeffersonian, Box 7432, Louisville KY 40207..502-895-5436
Jessamine Journal, 131 E Brown St, Nicholasville KY 40356 606-885-5381

Kenton County Recorder, 22 Commonwealth Ave, Erlanger KY 41018....606-727-9200
Kentucky Advocate*, W Walnut, Danville KY 40422..................................606-236-2551
Kentucky New Era*, 1618 E 9th St, Hopkinsville KY 42240 502-886-4444
Kentucky News, 118 S 5th, Paducah KY 42001 502-442-7380
Kentucky Post*, 421 Madison Ave, Covington KY 41011 606-292-2600
Kentucky Standard, 110 W Foster Ave, Bardstown KY 40004 502-348-9003
LaRue County Herald News, 114 N Lincoln, Hodgenville KY 42748 502-358-3524
Lawrenceburg Anderson News, 133 Main St, Lawrenceburg KY 40342.....502-839-6906
Ledger-Independent*, 43 W 2nd St, Maysville KY 41056...........................606-564-9091
Leitchfield News-Gazette, Public Square, Russellville KY 42276 502-726-9507
Leslie County News, Box 967, Hyden KY 41749.......................................606-672-2841
Letcher County Community Press, Box 156, Cromona KY 41810..............606-855-4541
Lexington Herald-Leader*+, Main and Midland, Lexington KY 40507....606-231-3100
Liberty Casey County News, Box 40, Liberty KY 42539 502-783-7171
Licking Valley Courier, 115 Main St, West Liberty KY 41472 606-743-3551
Logan Leader, Public Square, Russellville KY 42276 502-726-9507
London Sentinel-Echo, 123 W 5th St, London KY 40741...........................606-878-7400
Louisville Defender, 1720 Dixie Hwy, Louisville KY 40210 502-772-2591
Ludlow News Enterprise, 235 Elm St, Covington KY 41016......................606-261-9660
Madison County Newsweek, Box 732, Richmond KY 40475......................606-623-5957
Madisonville Messenger*, 221 S Main, Madisonville KY 42431 502-821-6833
Manchester Enterprise, 110 Court St, Manchester KY 40962....................606-598-2319
Martin Countian, Box 1029, Inez KY 41224 606-298-7570
Mayfield Messenger*, 201 N 8th St, Mayfield KY 42066...........................502-247-5223
McCreary County Record, Box 9, Whitley City KY 42653.........................606-376-5356
Meade County Messenger, 235 Main St, Brandenburg KY 40108 502-422-2155
Messenger-Inquirer*, 1401 Frederica, Owensboro KY 42301....................502-926-0123
Middlesboro Daily News*, 120 N 11th St, Middlesboro KY 40965.............606-248-1010
The Mirror, PO Box 7432, Louisville KY 40207 502-895-5436
Morehead News, 722 West 1st St, Morehead KY 40351.............................606-784-4116
Murray Ledger & Times*, Whitnell at Glendale, Murray KY 42071 502-753-1916
The Neighbor, 3715 Bardstown Rd, Louisville KY 40218...........................502-458-0100
New Castle Henry County Local, PO Box 209, New Castle KY 40050.......502-845-2850
Ohio County Messenger, 220 N Main St, Beaver Dam KY 42320 274-927-8274
Ohio County Times News, 108 W Center St, Hartford KY 42347...............502-298-7100
Ohio County Times, 108 W Center St, Hartford KY 42347 502-298-7100
Oldam Era, 204 S 1st St, La Grange KY 40031 502-222-7183
Paducah Sun*, 408 Kentucky Ave, Paducah KY 42001 502-443-1771
Paintsville Herald, W 3rd St, Paintsville KY 41240..................................606-789-5315
Park City Daily News*, 813 College St, Bowling Green KY 42101.............501-843-4321
Pineville Sun-Cumberland Courier, 103 Pine St, Pineville KY 40977........606-337-2333
Providence Journal-Enterprise, Box 197, Providence KY 42450 502-667-2068
The Reporter, PO Box 7432, Louisville KY 40207....................................502-895-5436
Richmond Register*, 380 Big Hill Ave, Richmond KY 40475....................606-623-1669
Russell Springs Times Journal, 120 Wilson St, Russell Spgs KY 42642....502-866-3191
Russellville News Democrat, Public Square, Russellville KY 42276..........502-726-9507
Salyersville Independent, 7 Maple St, Salyersville KY 41465 606-349-2915
Scottsville Citizen-Times, Box 308, Scottsville KY 42164.........................502-237-3441
The Sentinel, 1558 Hill St, Radcliff KY 40160...502-351-4407
Shelbyville Sentinel-News, 702 Washington, Shelbyville KY 40065...........502-633-2526
Shepherdsville Pioneer News, 1105 Beech St, Shepherdsville KY 40165 ...502-543-2288
Shively Newsweek, 4639 Dixie Hwy, Louisville KY 40216 502-448-4581
Springfield Sun, 117 Cross Main, Springfield KY 40069............................606-336-3716

Sturgis News, 615 Adams, Sturgis KY 42459 501-333-5545
The Times*+, 525 W Broadway, Louisville KY 40202.....................502-582-4641
Tompkinsville News, 105 N Main, Tompkinsville KY 42167 502-487-5576
Union County Advocate, 214 W Main, Morganafield KY 42437.....501-389-1833
Versailles Woodford Sun, Box 29, Versailles KY 40383....................606-873-4131
Wayne County Outlook, 109 E Columbia Ave, Monticello KY 42633........606-348-5776
Whitesburg Mountain Eagle, Box 808, Whitesburg KY 41858...........606-633-2252
Wickliffe Advance Ycoman, Box 8, Wickliffe KY 42087 502-335-3194
Williamsburg Whitley Republican, Box 418, Williamsburg KY 40769.......606-549-0643
Winchester Sun*, Wall & Cleveland, Winchester KY 40391.............606-744-3123

LOUISIANA

Abbeville Meridional, 318 N Main St, Abbeville LA 70510....................318-893-4223
Alexandria Daily Town Talk*, 1201 3rd St, Alexandria LA 71306 318-487-6397
Alexandria News Weekly, 706 Lee St, Alexandria LA 71301.................318-443-7664
Avoyelles Journal, 100 N Main St, Marksville LA 71351.......................318-253-5413
Baker Observer, Box 539, Baker LA 70714 504-775-2340
Bastrop Daily Enterprise*, 119 E Hickory, Bastrop LA 71220 318-281-4421
Baton Rouge Advocate*+, 525 Lafayette St, Baton Rouge LA 70902........504-383-1111
Baton Rouge Comm Leader, 1210 North Blvd, Baton Rge LA 70802........504-343-0544
Baton Rouge State-Times*, 525 Layfayette St, Baton Rouge LA 70802 504-383-1111
Beauregard Times News, 122 Shirley St, De Ridder LA 70634 318-463-6204
Bienville Democrat, 117 N Maple, Arcadia LA 71001 318-263-2922
Bogalusa Daily News*, 525 Ave V, Bogalusa LA 70427 504-732-2565
Bossier Press, 409 Barksdale Blvd, Bossier City LA 71111...................318-747-4010
Clinton Watchman, Box 368, Clinton LA 70722.................................504-683-5195
Concordia Sentinel, N 1st St, Ferriday LA 71334.................................318-757-3001
Crowley Post-Signal*, 601 N Parkerson Ave, Crowley LA 70526 318-783-3450
Daily Iberian*, Lewis & Main, New Iberia LA 70560...........................318-365-6773
Daily Review*, 1014 Front St, Morgan City LA 70380 504-384-8370
DeRidder Enterprise, 125 N Washington Ave, De Ridder LA 70634..........318-463-4431
Donaldsonville Chief, Box 309, Donaldsonville LA 70346 504-473-3101
East Orleans Guide, 8917 W Judge Perez Dr, Chalmette LA 70043..........504-279-4336
Eunice News, 251 N 2nd St, Eunice LA 70535....................................318-457-3061
Franklin Banner*, 111 Wilson, Franklin LA 70538.............................318-828-3706
Franklin Post, 810 Iberia St, Franklin LA 70538 318-828-2671
Franklin Sun, 604 Prarie, Winnsboro LA 71295..................................318-435-4521
Gonzales Community Mirror, Box 38, Gonzales LA 70737..................504-644-4569
Gris Gris+, 2431 S Acadian Thruway #590, Baton Rouge LA 70808........504-927-5437
Hammond Daily Star*, PO Box 1149, Hammond LA 70401.................504-345-2333
Hammond Vindicator, 105 S Cate, Hammond LA 70401 504-345-4321
Houma Daily Courier & Terrebonne*, 312 School, Houma LA 70361......504-879-1557
Jackson Independent, 624 Hudson Ave, Jonesboro LA 71251................318-259-2551
Jeanerette Enterprise, 806 E Main St, Jeanerette LA 70554 318-276-5171
Jena Times Olla-Tullos Signal, Drawer M, Jena LA 71342 318-992-4121
Jennings Daily News*, 238 Market St, Jennings LA 70546 318-824-3011
Lafayette Advertiser*, 221 Jefferson St, Lafayette LA 70501.................318-235-8511
Lake Charles American Press*, 327 Broad St, Lake Charles LA 70602....318-439-2781
Laplace L'Observateur, 121 W 6th, Laplace LA 70068.........................504-652-7502
Leesville Leader, 206 E Texas St, Leesville LA 71446...........................318-239-3444
Livingston Parish News, Box 458, Denham Spgs LA 70726 504-665-5176
Louisiana Weekly, 640 S Rampart, New Orleans LA 70113 504-524-5563

Madison Journal, 300 S Chestnut St, Tallulah LA 71282..............................318-574-1404
Mamou Acadian Press, Drawer D, Mamou LA 70554.................................318-468-3333
Mansfield Enterprise-Journal, 202 Adams St, Mansfield LA 71052..........318-872-0317
Metairie East Bank Guide+, 3033 N Causeway, Metairie LA 70002.........318-837-6397
Metarie Guide, 2520 Belle Chasse Hwy, Gretna LA 70054...........................504-363-4310
Minden Press-Herald*, 109 Dixie St, Minden LA 71055.............................318-377-1866
Monroe Dispatch, 2301 Desiard St, Monroe LA 71203................................318-387-3001
New Orleans Guide, 8001 Chief Menteur Hwy, New Orleans LA 70126...504-241-6353
News-Star*+, 411 N 4th St, Monroe LA 71201 318-322-5161
Oakdale Journal, Box 668, Oakdale LA 71463...318-335-0635
Opelousas Daily World*, Hwy 167, Opelousas LA 70570..............................318-942-4971
Pineville Red River Journal, Box 973, Pineville LA 71360............................318-445-0241
Plaquemine Post/Iberville South, Box 589, Plaquemine LA 70764.............504-687-3288
Plaquemines Gazette, 801 Belle Chasse Hwy N, Belle Chasse LA 70037..504-392-1619
Pointe Coupee Banner, 123 St Mary St, New Roads LA 70760 504-638-7155
Quachita Citizen, 810 Natchitoches St, West Monroe LA 71291.................318-322-3161
Rayne Acadian-Tribune, 108 N Adams PO Box 260, Rayne LA 70578......318-334-3186
Rayne Independent, Box 428, Rayne LA 70578 318-334-2128
Rayville Richland Beacon-News, Box 209, Rayville LA 71269.....................318-728-2250
Ruston Daily Leader*, 208 W Park Ave, Ruston LA 71270...........................318-255-4353
Sabine Index, 850 San Antonio Ave, Many LA 71449.................................318-256-3495
St Bernard Guide, 8917 W Judge Perez Dr, Chalmette LA 70043 504-279-4336
St Bernard Voice, 234 Mehle Ave, Arabi LA 70032.....................................504-279-7488
St Martinville Teche News, 214 N Main St, St Martinville LA 70582.........318-394-6232
St Tammany Farmer, 321 N New Hampshire St, Covington LA 70433.....504-892-2323
St Tammany Guide, 2520 Belle Chasse Hwy, Gretna LA 70054 504-363-4310
St Tammany News-Banner, Drawer 90, Covington LA 70433.....................504-892-7980
St Tammany News-Banner, Box 673, Mandeville LA 70448.........................504-626-7130
Shreveport Journal*, 222 Lake St, Shreveport LA 71130 318-459-3200
Shreveport Sun, 2224 Jewella Rd, Shreveport LA 71107 318-631-6222
Slidell Daily Sentry-News*, 3648 Pontchartrain Dr, Slidell LA 70459........504-643-4918
Slidell Daily Times*, 1441 Shortcut Rd, Slidell LA 70459..........................504-643-5236
Southwest Builder News, 716 E Napoleon, Sulpher LA 70663.....................318-527-7075
Sunday Advocate*+, 525 Lafayette St, Baton Rouge LA 70821..................504-383-1111
Thibodaux Daily Comet*, 705 W 5th St, Thibodaux LA 70301 504-447-4055
Times of Acadiana, 201 Jefferson St, Lafayette LA 70501 318-237-3560
The Times*+, 222 Lake St, Shreveport LA 71130..318-459-3200
Times-Picayune/States Item*+, 3800 Howard, New Orleans LA 70140...504-586-3785
Ville Platte Gazette, Box 220, Ville Platte LA 70586...................................318-363-3939
Vivian Caddo Citizen, Box 312, Vivian LA 71082 318-375-3294
West Bank Guide+, 2520 Belle Chasse Hwy, Gretna LA 70054...................504-363-4310
West Carroll Gazette, Drawer G, Oak Grove LA 71263................................318-428-3207
West Side Journal, 668 N Jefferson, Port Allen LA 70767 504-343-2540
Winn Parish Enterprise, Lafayette & Long, Winnfield LA 71483................318-628-2712
Zachary Plainsman-News, Box 279, Zachary LA 70791 504-654-6841

MAINE

American Journal, 820 Main St, Westbrook ME 04092 207-854-2577
Aroostook Republican & News, Access Hwy, Caribou ME 04736................207-496-3251
Bangor Daily News*+, 491 Main St, Bangor ME 04401................................207-942-4881
Bar Harbor Times, 66 Main St, Bar Harbor ME 04609 207-288-3311
Belfast Republican Journal, 4 Main St, Belfast ME 04915............................207-388-3333

Boothbay Register, 95 Townsend Ave, Boothbay Harbor ME 04538.........207-633-4620
Calais Advertiser, Knight's Corner, Calais ME 04619....................................207-454-3561
Camden Herald, Highland Mill Mall, Camden ME 04943.............................207-236-8511
Central Maine Sentinel*, 25 Silver St, Waterville ME 04901 207-873-3341
Courier-Gazette, 1 Park Dr, Rockland ME 04841..207-594-4401
Eastern Gazette, Box 306, Dexter ME 04930...207-924-7402
Ellsworth American, 63 Main St, Ellsworth ME 04605 207-667-2576
Evening Express*, 390 Congress St, Portland ME 04104...............................207-775-5811
Evening Journal*, 104 Park St, Lewiston ME 04240......................................207-784-5411
Farmington Chronicle, Wilton Road, Farmington ME 04938.......................207-778-2075
Franklin Journal, Wilton Road, Farmington ME 04938.................................207-778-2075
Houlton Pioneer Times, 23 Court St, Houlton ME 04730.............................207-532-2281
The Journal*, Alfred St, Biddleford ME 04005..207-282-1535
Kennebec Journal*, 274 Western Ave, Augusta ME 04330...........................207-623-3811
Lewiston Daily Sun*, 104 Park St, Lewiston ME 04240 207-784-5411
Lincoln County News, Mills Rd, Newcastle ME 04553...................................207-563-3171
Lincoln News, Box 35, Lincoln ME 04457 207-794-6532
Livermore Falls Advertiser, Main St, Livermore Falls ME 04254................207-897-2022
Machias Valley News Observer, 31 Broadway, Machias ME 04654............207-255-6561
Maine Sunday Telegram*+, 390 Congress St, Portland ME 04104...........207-775-5811
Maine Times, 41 Main St, Topsham ME 04086..207-729-0126
Norway Advertiser-Democrat, Advertiser Square, Norway ME 04268.......207-743-7011
Old Town-Orono Times, 400 N Main St, Old Town ME 04468....................207-827-4451
Piscataquis Observer, Union Square, Dover Foxcroft ME 04426 207-853-4806
Portland Press Herald*+, 390 Congress St, Portland ME 04104...............207-775-5811
Presque Isle Star-Herald, Box 510, Presque Isle ME 04769.........................207-768-5431
Rumford Falls Times, 56 Congress St, Rumford ME 04276...........................207-364-7893
St John Valley Times, 696 W Main St, Madawaska ME 04756 207-728-3336
Somerset Reporter, Water St, Skowhegan ME 04976......................................207-474-9555
Times Record*, Industry Rd, Brunswick ME 04011.......................................207-729-3311
Weekly Journal, Box 359, Brewer ME 04412 207-989-6100
Winthrop Advertiser, Box 17, Winthrop ME 04364.......................................207-582-2266
York County Coast Star, Rte 1 S, Kennebunk ME 04043...............................207-985-2961

MARYLAND

The Aegis, 10 Hays St, Bel Air MD 21014 301-838-4400
Annapolis Capital*, 213 West St, Annapolis MD 21401 301-268-5000
Anne Arundel Times, 98 Edgewater Ave, Annapolis MD 21401..................301-268-9300
Arbutus Times, Box 312, Elliott City MD 21043 301-465-3333
Baltimore Afro-American News+, 628 N Eutaw, Baltimore MD 21201....301-728-8200
Baltimore Enterprise, 1314 Light St, Baltimore MD 21230...........................301-752-0711
Baltimore Jewish Times, 2104 N Charles St, Baltimore MD 21218.............301-752-3504
Baltimore News American*+, 301 E Lombard St, Baltimore MD 21202..301-528-8000
Baltimore Sun*+, 501 N Calvert St, Baltimore MD 21278............................301-332-6000
Bolling Beam, Box 1272, Rockville MD 20850..301-948-1500
Bowie Blade News, 6806 Laurel-Bowie Rd, Bowie MD 20715.....................301-262-3700
Cambridge Dorchester News, 512 Race St, Cambridge MD 21613.............301-228-5151
Capital Flyer, Box 1272, Rockville MD 20850 301-948-1500
Carroll County Evening Sun*, 11 Liberty St, Westminister MD 21157.....301-848-3388
Carroll County Times*, 201 Railroad Ave, Westminster MD 21157..........301-848-4400
Catonsville Times, Box 312, Elliott City MD 21043 301-465-3333
City Paper+, 2612 N Charles St, Baltimore MD 21218.................................301-889-6600

Columbia Flier, 10750 Little Patuxent Pkwy, Columbia MD 21044.............301-730-3620
Community Times, Box 312, Elliott City MD 21043 301-465-3333
Crofton News-Crier, 6806 Laurel-Bowie Rd, Bowie MD 20715..................301-262-3700
Cumberland News*, 7 S Mechanic St, Cumberland MD 21502...................301-722-4600
Daily & Sunday Times*, PO Box 1937, Salisbury MD 21801....................301-749-7171
Daily Banner*, 302 High St, Cambridge MD 21613............................301-228-3133
Damascus Courier-Gazette, Box 606, Gaithersburg MD 20877..................301-253-6161
Dundalk Eagle, 4 N Center Pl, Baltimore MD 21222..........................301-288-6060
East Baltimore Guide, 526 S Conkling, Baltimore MD 21224..................301-732-6600
Eastern Shore Times, 3316 Coastal Hwy, Ocean City MD 21842................301-289-6834
Easton Star-Democrat*, 1 Airpark Dr, Easton MD 21601 301-822-1500
Elkton Cecil Whig, 601 Bridge St, Elkton MD 21921 301-398-3311
Enterprise, Box 700, Lexington Pk MD 20653................................301-862-2111
Evening Times*, 7 S Mechanic St, Cumberland MD 21502 301-722-4600
Focus: A Buyers Guide, Box 1272, Rockville MD 20850 301-948-1500
Frederick Post*, 200 E Patrick St, Frederick MD 21701.....................301-622-1177
Frostburg Guardian, Box 425, Frostburg MD 21532...........................301-689-9487
Gaithersburg Gazette+, Box 606, Gaithersburg MD 20877 301-253-6161
Greenbelt News Review, PO Box 68, Greenbelt MD 20770 301-474-4131
Hagerstown Herald-Mail*, 100 Summit Ave, Hagerstown MD 21740.......301-733-5131
Harford Democrat, 4 S Parke, Aberdeene MD 21001...........................301-272-2600
Howard County Times, 10750 Little Patuxent, Columbia MD 21044.........301-730-3620
Jeffersonian, 305 Washington St, Baltimore MD 21204.......................301-337-2640
Kent County News, 217 High St, Chestertown MD 21620.......................301-778-2011
Laurel Leader, 357 Main St, Laurel MD 20707 301-725-2000
Laurel Sentinel, Box 1272, Rockville MD 20850 301-948-1500
Living Montgomery+, Box 1272, Rockville MD 20850 301-948-1500
Maryland Coast Press, 33rd St & Coastal Hwy, Ocean City MD 21842....301-289-6834
Maryland Gazette, PO Box 567, Glen Burnie MD 21061........................301-766-3700
Maryland Independent, 7 Industrial Park Dr, Waldorf MD 20601.............301-645-9480
The Messenger, 305 Washington St, Baltimore MD 21204 301-337-2640
Montgomery County Sentinel, Box 1272, Rockville MD 20850..................301-948-1500
Montgomery Journal, 5721 Randolph Rd, Rockville MD 20852 301-984-5995
Natl Edition, 628 N Eutaw St, Baltimore MD 21201 301-728-8200
New Jersey Afro American, 628 N Eutaw St, Baltimore MD 21201............301-728-8200
News*, 200 E Patrick St, Frederick MD 21701...............................301-662-1177
Northwest Star, 23 Walker Ave, Baltimore MD 21208.........................301-653-3800
Preston News & Farmer, Main & Maole, Preston MD 21655.....................301-673-7131
Prince Frederick Recorder, Box F, Prince Frederick MD 20678 301-535-1214
Prince George Sentinel, Box 1272, Rockville MD 20850 301-948-1500
Prince George's Journal*, 9426 Annapolis Rd, Lanham MD 20706...........301-459-3131
Prince George's Post-Sentinel, 4302 Baltimore, Bladensburg MD 20710 ..301-779-2900
Queen Anne's Record-Observer, 114 Broadway, Centreville MD 21617....301-758-1400
The Record, 601 Revolution St, Havr De Grace MD 21078.....................301-939-4040
The Republican, 108 S 2nd St, Oakland MD 21550............................301-334-3963
Salisbury News & Advertiser, Box 831, Salisbury MD 21801 301-749-0272
Silver Spring Suburban Record, 7676 Fenton St, Silver Spg MD 20910....301-589-6400
Stripe, Box 1272, Rockville MD 20850......................................301-948-1500
Sunday Times*, 7 S Mechanic St, Cumberland MD 21502 301-722-4600
Tawson Times, 305 Washington St, Baltimore MD 21204.......................301-337-2640
The Times, 2130 Old Eastern Ave, Baltimore MD 21220 301-687-4224
Times-Crescent, 105 La Grange Ave, La Plata MD 20646......................301-934-4606
Upper Marlboro Enquirer-Gazette, Box 30, Upr Marlboro MD 20870.....301-627-2833

Wheaton News, Box 1656, Silver Spring MD 20902......................................301-949-7333
Worcester County Messenger, 129 Market, Pocomoke City MD 21851 301-957-1700

MASSACHUSETTS

Advocate Newspapers+, 87 School St, Hatfield MA 01038 413-247-9301
Amesbury News, 2 Washington St, Ipswich MA 01938 617-356-5141
Amherst Valley Advocate+, Box 862, Amherst MA 01002 413-549-2700
Andover Townsman, 89 N Main St, Andover MA 01810.............................617-475-1943
Arlington Advocate, 4 Walker St, Arlington MA 02174..............................617-729-8100
Assabet Valley Beacon, 20 Main St, Acton MA 01720 617-263-3761
Athol Daily News*, 225 Exchange St PO Box A, Athol MA 01331 617-249-3535
Auburn News, 7 Main St, Webster MA 01570..617-943-4800
Bay State Banner, 925 Washington St, Dorchester MA 02124 617-288-4900
Bedford Minute-Man, 9 Meriam St, Lexington MA 02173 617-861-9110
Belmont Citizen, 72 Trapelo Rd, Blemont MA 02178 617-484-1500
Berkshire Courier, 268 Main St, Gr Barrington MA 01230..........................413-528-3020
Berkshire Eagle*, 33 Eagle, Pittsfield MA 01202 413-447-7311
Billerica News, 49 Pollard St, N Billerica MA 01862...................................617-667-2013
Blackstone Valley Tribune, 60 Church St, Whitinsville MA 01588 617-234-2107
Boston Globe*+, 135 Morrissey Blvd, Boston MA 02107 617-929-2000
Boston Hellenic Chronicle, 324 Newbury St, Boston MA 02115.................617-262-4500
Boston Herald American*+, 300 Harrison Ave, Boston MA 02106...........617-426-3000
Boston Phoenix+, 100 Massachusetts Ave, Boston MA 02115....................617-536-5390
Boston Post-Gazette, 5 Prince St, Boston MA 02113....................................617-227-8929
Bourne Courier, Trading Post Corners, Buzzards Bay MA 02532.................617-759-7315
Braintree Forum & Observer, 720 Union St, Braintree MA 02184..............617-843-2937
Braintree Star, 239 Shaw St, Braintree MA 02184.......................................617-843-2476
Bulletin, 9 Meriam St, Lexington MA 02173..617-861-9110
Burlington News, 120 Cambridge St, Burlington MA 01803.........................617-272-2369
Burlington Times-Union, 1 Skilton Ln, Burlington MA 01803.....................617-273-2210
Cambridge Chronicle, 145 Elm St, W Somerville MA 02144 617-628-6200
Canton Journal, 484 Washington St, Canton MA 02021................................617-828-0006
Cape Cod News, 349 Main St, Hyannis MA 02601 617-775-1594
Cape Cod Oracle, 84 Cranberry Hwy, Orleans MA 02653............................617-255-3133
Cape Cod Times*, 319 Main St, Hyannis MA 02601.....................................617-775-1200
Cape Codder, 5 Namskaket Rd, Orleans MA 02653......................................617-255-2121
Chelmsford-Westford-Tyngsboro, 5 North Rd, Chelmsford MA 01824 617-256-3311
Chicopee Herald, 53 Springfield St, Chicopee MA 01013 413-592-2651
Christian Science Monitor*+, 1 Norway St, Boston MA 02115.................617-450-2303
Chronicle, 338 Elm St, S Dartmouth MA 02748...617-992-1522
Concord Journal, 81 Middle St, Arlington MA 02174..................................617-861-9110
Daily Evening Item*, 38 Exchange St, Lynn MA 01901...............................617-593-7700
Daily Hampshire Gazette*, 115 Conz St, Northampton MA 01060.............413-584-5000
Daily Item*, 156 Church St, Clinton MA 01510...413-386-0176
Daily News*+, 1860 Main St, Springfield MA 01102 413-788-1300
Daily Times Chronicle*, 25 Montvale Ave, Woburn MA 01801 617-933-3700
Daily Transcript*, 420 Washington St, Dedham MA 02026 617-329-5000
Danvers Herald, 9 Page St, Danvers MA 01923 617-774-0505
Dartmouth Chronicle, 780 Country St, Fall River MA 02726.......................617-674-4656
Dorchester Suburban Record, 1220 Adams, Dorchester Ctr MA 02124...617-298-1900
Enterprise Brockton*+, 60 Main St, Brockton MA 02403 617-586-6200
The Enterprise*, 250 Maple St, Marlborough MA 01752 617-485-5200

The Enterprise, Depot Ave, Falmouth MA 02541............................617-548-4700
Evening Gazette*+, 20 Franklin St, Worcester MA 01612 617-793-9100
Everett Leader Herald-News Gazette, 28 Church St, Everett MA 02149...617-387-4570
Fall River Herald News*, 207 Pocasset St, Fall River MA 02722..............617-676-8211
Fitchburg-Leominster Sentinal*, 808 Main St, Fitchburg MA 01420.........617-343-6911
Ft Devens Dispatch, 83 Fitchburg Rd, Ayer MA 01432............................617-772-0777
Ft Devens Sentry, 83 Fitchburg Rd, Ayer MA 01432 617-772-0777
Foxboro Reporter, 15 Wall St, Foxboro MA 02035.................................617-543-4851
Gardner News*, 309 Central St, Gardner MA 01440................................617-632-8000
Greenfield Recorder*, 14 Hope St, Greenfield MA 01301..........................413-772-0261
Hamilton-Wenham Chronicle, 2 Washington St, Ipswich MA 01938.........617-356-5141
Hansconian, 9 Meriam St, Lexington MA 02173.....................................617-861-9110
Hartford Advocate+, 19 St James Ave, Springfield MA 01109 413-781-1900
Haverhill Gazette*, West Lowell Ave, Haverhill MA 01830......................617-374-0321
Inquirer & Mirror, Milestone, Nantucket MA 02554..............................617-228-0001
Ipswich Chronicle, 2 Washington St, Ipswich MA 01938 617-356-5141
Ipswich Today, 2 Washington St, Ipswich MA 01938...............................617-356-5141
Jewish Advocate, 251 Causeway St, Boston MA 02114.............................617-227-5130
Lawrence Eagle Tribune*+, 100 Turnpike St, N Andover MA 01845........617-685-1000
Lexington Minute-Man, 9 Meriam St, Lexington MA 02173......................617-861-9110
Lowell Sun*+, 15 Kearney Square, Lowell MA 01852..............................617-458-7100
Ludlow Register, 24 Water St, Palmer MA 01069 413-283-8393
Lynn Sunday Post, 617 Chestnut St, Lynn MA 01903..............................617-592-4600
Lynn Times, 8 Atlantic St, Lynn MA 01903...617-599-1155
Maiden Evening News*, 277 Commercial St, Maiden MA 02148 617-321-8000
Mansfield News, 172 N Main St, N Billerica MA 01862............................617-339-8977
Marblehead Reporter, 8 Anderson St, Marblehead MA 01945....................617-631-7700
Medford Daily Mercury*, 277 Commercial St, Maiden MA 02148 617-321-8000
Melrose Free Press, 40 W Foster St, Melrose MA 02176............................617-665-4000
Melrose Shoppers News, 11 Franklin St, Stoneham MA 02180....................617-438-1660
Middleboro Gazette, 780 Country St, Fall River MA 02726 617-674-4656
Middlesex News*+, 33 New York Ave, Framingham MA 01701..................617-872-4321
Milton Record-Transcript, 25 High St, Milton Village MA 02187..............617-698-0190
Montachusett Review, 214 Lunenburg St, Fitchburg MA 01420 617-342-8055
Natick Bulletin & Natick Sun, 2 Summer St, Natick MA 01760 617-653-8080
New Leader, 135 Main St, Spencer MA 01562 617-885-9402
The News*, 25 Elm St, Southbridge MA 01550.......................................617-764-4325
Newton Graphic, 420 Washington St, Dedham MA 02026.........................617-329-5000
Newton Times, Box 239, Newton Center MA 02159 617-965-0122
North Billerica News, 49 Pollard St, N Billerica MA 01862.......................617-667-2014
North Reading Transcript, 1 Lowell Rd, North Reading MA 01864.........617-664-4761
North Shore Sunday+, 9 Page St, Danvers MA 01923...............................617-774-0505
Old Colony Memorial, Long Pond Rd, Plymouth MA 02360 617-746-5555
Palmer Journal Register, 24 Water St, Palmer MA 01069 413-283-8393
Parkway Transcript, 420 Washington St, Dedham MA 02026 617-329-5000
Patriot Ledger*+, 13 Temple St, Quincy MA 02169 617-786-7000
Peabody Times*, Box 628, Peabody MA 01960..617-532-1000
Provincetown Advocate, 100 Bradford St, Provincetown MA 02657...........617-487-1170
Public Spirit, 83 Fitchburg Rd, Ayer MA 01432.....................................617-772-0777
Quincy Sun, 1372 Hancock St, Quincy MA 02169 617-471-3100
Reading Chronicle, 531 Main St, Reading MA 01867..............................617-944-2200
Register, Box 400, Yarmouth Port MA 02675...617-362-2111
The Republican*+, 1860 Main St, Springfield MA 01102.........................413-788-1000

Revere Journal, 327 Broadway, Revere MA 02151 617-284-2400
Salen Evening News*, 155 Washington St, Salem MA 01970........................617-744-0600
Saugus Advertiser, 55 Essex St, Saugus MA 01906......................................617-233-2040
Sharon Advocate, 66 S Main St, Sharon MA 02067 617-784-2131
Somerset Spectator, 780 Country St, Fall River MA 02726 617-674-4656
Somerville Journal, 145 Elm St, W Somerville MA 02144............................617-628-6200
South Boston Tribune, Box 6, South Boston MA 02127 617-268-3440
South County Advertiser, 7 Main St, Webster MA 01570...............................617-943-4800
Springfield Union*+, 1860 Main St, Springfield MA 01102 413-788-1000
Standard-Times*+, 555 Pleasant, New Bedford MA 02742..........................617-997-7411
State Line Shopping Guide, 24 Water St, Palmer MA 01069 413-283-8393
Stoughton Chronicle, 3 Pearl St, Stoughton MA 02072.................................617-344-2100
Sunday Independent+, 20 Main St, Acton MA 01720....................................617-263-3761
Swampscott Reporter, 8 Anderson St, Marblehead MA 01945.....................617-631-7700
Taunton Daily Gazette*, 5 Cohannet, Taunton MA 02780 617-822-7121
Tewksbury Merrimack Valley Adv, Box 8, Tewksbury MA 01876 617-851-3766
Thenicle Beverly Times*, Dunham Rd, Beverly MA 02703 617-922-1234
The Times, 7 Main St, Webster MA 01570..617-943-4800
Topsfield Tri-Town Transcript, 2 Washington St, Ipswich MA 01938 617-356-5141
Town Crier & Fence Viewer, 111 Boston Post, Sudbury MA 01776...........617-443-8948
Town Crier, 364 Middlesex, Wilmington MA 01887 617-658-2346
The Transcript*, American Legion Dr, North Adams MA 01247 413-663-3741
Transcript-Telegram*, 120 Whiting Farms Rd, Holyoke MA 01040..........413-536-2300
Tri-County Advertiser, 60 Church St, Whitinsville MA 01588.....................617-234-2107
Vineyard Gazette, S Summer St, Edgartown MA 02539...............................617-627-4311
Vineyard Grapevine, Main St, Vineyard Haven MA 02568...........................617-693-3915
The Voice, 512 W Main St, Shrewbury MA 01545 617-752-6494
Wachusett People, 512 W Main St, Shrewbury MA 01545 617-752-6494
Walpole Times, 955 Main St, Walpole MA 02081 617-688-0243
Waltham News Tribune*, 18 Pine St, Waltham MA 02154............................617-893-1670
Ware River News, 4 Church St, Ware MA 01082 413-967-3505
Watertown Press, 145 Elm St, W Somerville MA 02144 617-628-6200
Wayland-Weston Town Crier, 111 Boston Post Rd, Sudbury MA 01776...617-443-8948
Weekender, 145 Elm St, W Somerville MA 02144...617-628-6200
Wellesley Townsman, 1 Crest Rd, Wellesley MA 02181.................................617-235-4000
West Roxbury Transcript, 420 Washington St, Dedham MA 02026 617-329-5000
West Springfield Record, 516 Main St, W Springfield MA 01089................413-736-1587
Westfield Evening News*, 62 School St, Westfield MA 01085.....................413-562-4181
Westford Eagle, 13 Alpine Ln, Acton MA 01729...617-256-7196
Weymouth News & Gazette, 720 Union St, Braintree MA 02184.................617-843-2937
Wick-Qua-Boaq Weekly, 135 Main St, Spencer MA 01562 617-885-9402
Winchester Star, 3 Church St, Winchester MA 01890...................................617-729-8100
Worcester Evening Gazette*+, 20 Franklin St, Worcester MA 01613 617-793-9100
Worcester Magazine+, PO Box 1000, Worcester MA 01614 617-799-0511
Worcester News Recorder, 75 W Boylston St, Worcester MA 01606 617-791-9272
Worcester Telegram*+, 20 Franklin St, Worcester MA 01613 617-793-9100

MICHIGAN

Adrian Daily Telegram*, 133 N Winter St, Adrian MI 49221.......................517-265-5111
Alpena News*, 130 Park Pl, Alpena MI 49707 517-354-3111
Ann Arbor News*+, 340 E Huron St, Ann Arbor MI 48104 313-994-6989
Argus-Press*, 201 E Exchange St, Owosso MI 48867.................................517-725-5136
Battle Creek Enquirer*, 155 W Van Buren St, Battle Creek MI 49106.....616-964-7161
Bay City Times*, 311 5th St, Bay City MI 48706.......................................616-964-7161
Big Rapids Pioneer*, 502 N State, Big Rapids MI 49307 616-796-4831
Cadillac News*, 130 N Mitchell, Cadillac MI 49601...................................616-775-6565
Cheboygan Daily Tribune*, 308 N Main St, Cheboygan MI 49721.............616-627-7144
Coldwater Daily Reporter*, 15 W Pearl St, Coldwater MI 49036 517-273-2318
Daily Tribune*, 210 E 3rd St, Royal Oak MI 48067....................................313-541-3004
Detroit Metro Times+, 800 David Whitney Bldg, Detroit MI 48226 313-961-4060
Detroit News*+, 615 Lafayette Blvd, Detroit MI 48231 313-222-2300
Dowagiac Daily News*, 205 Spaulding St, Dowagiac MI 49047 616-782-2101
Escanaba Daily Press*, 600 Lucington St, Escanaba MI 49829 906-786-2021
Flint Journal*+, 200 E 1st St, Flint MI 48501 313-767-0660
Grand Haven Tribune*, 101 N 3rd, Grand Haven MI 49417.......................616-842-6400
Grand Rapids Press*+, 155 Michigan NW, Grand Rapids MI 49503 616-459-1400
Herald-Paladium*, 3450 Hollywood, St Joseph MI 49085 616-429-2400
Hillsdale Daily News*, 33 McCollum, Hillsdale MI 49242..........................517-437-7351
Holland Sentinel*, 54 W 8th, Holland MI 49423.......................................616-392-2311
Huron Daily Tribune*, 211 N Jeisterman, Bad Axe MI 48413 517-269-6461
Ionia Sentinel-Standard*, 114 North Depot, Ionia MI 49931 616-527-2100
Ironwood Daily Globe*, 118 E McLeod Ave, Ironwood MI 49938 906-932-2211
Jackson Citizen Patriot*, 214 S Jackson St, Jackson MI 49204...................517-787-2300
Jewish News, 20300 Civic Ctr Dr, Southfield MI 48076 313-354-6060
Kalamazoo Gazette*+, 401 S Burdick St, Kalamazoo MI 49003 616-345-3511
Lansing State Journal*+, 120 E Lanawee, Lansing MI 48919.....................517-377-1000
Marquette Mining Journal*, 249 W Washington, Marquette MI 49855....906-228-2500
Menominee Herald-Leader*, 122 6th Ave, Menominee MI 49858 906-863-5544
Monroe Evening News*, 20 W 1st St, Monroe MI 48161 313-242-1100
Mt Clemens Macomb Daily*+, 67 Cass Ave, Mt Clemens MI 48043........313-469-4510
Mt Pleasant Morning Sun*, 215 N Main, Mt Pleasant MI 48858................517-772-2971
Muskegon Chronicle*+, 981 3rd St, Muskegon MI 49443...........................616-722-3161
Niles Daily Star*, 217 N 4th St, Niles MI 49120 616-683-2100
Petoskey News-Review*, 319 State St, Petoskey MI 49770..........................616-347-2544
Saginaw News*+, 203 S Washington Ave, Saginaw MI 48605......................517-752-7171
Sault Ste Marie Evening News*, 109 Arlington, Slt St Marie MI 49783 906-632-2235
South Haven Daily Tribune*, 259 Kalamazoo, S Haven MI 49090.............616-637-1104
Sturgis Journal*, 209 John St, Sturgis MI 49091..616-651-5407
Three Rivers Commercial*, 124 N Main St, Three Rivers MI 49093.........616-279-7488
Times Herald*, 911 Military St, Port Huron MI 48060................................313-985-7171
Traverse City Record-Eagle*, 120 W Front St, Traverse City MI 49684....616-946-2000
Ukranian News Inc*+, 19411 W Warren Ave, Detroit MI 48228.................313-336-8291
Ypsilanti Press*, 20 E Michigan, Ypsilanti MI 48197..................................313-482-2000

MINNESOTA

Albert Lea Tribune*, 808 Front St, Albert Lea MN 56007..............................507-373-1411
Austin Daily Herald*, 310 2nd St NE, Austin MN 55912...............................507-433-8851
Bemidji Pioneer*, 1320 Neilson Ave SE, Bemidji MN 56601 218-751-3740
Brainerd Dispatch*, 215 S 6th St, Brainerd MN 56401 218-829-4705
City Pages+, 100 N 6th St 308C Butler Sq, Minneapolis MN 55403...........612-375-1015
Crookston Daily Times*, 124 S Broadway, Crookston MN 56716 218-281-2730
Fairbault Daily News*, 514 Central Ave N, Fairbault MN 55021 507-334-4383
Fairmont Sentinel*, 64 Downtown Plaza, Fairmont MN 56031....................507-235-3303
Fergus Falls Journal*, 914 E Channing, Fergus Falls MN 56537.................218-736-7511
Free Press*, 418 S 2nd St, Mankato MN 56001 507-625-4451
Hibbing Tribune*, Box 38, Hibbing MN 55746 218-262-1011
Intl Falls Daily Journal*, Box 951, Intl Falls MN 56649 218-283-8411
The Journal*, 303 N Minnesota St, New Ulm MN 56073 507-359-2911
Little Falls Transcript*, 50 E Broadway, Little Falls MN 56345................612-632-6627
Marshall Independent*, 508 W Main, Marshall MN 56258.............................507-537-1551
Mesabi Daily News*, 704 7th Ave S, Virginia MN 55792 218-741-5544
News-Tribune & Herald*+, 424 W 1st St, Duluth MN 55802 218-723-5281
Owatonna People's Press*, 135 W Pearl St, Owatonna MN 55060................507-451-2840
Red Wing Republican Eagle*, 433 W 3rd St, Red Wing MN 55066 612-388-8235
Rochester Post-Bulletin*, 18 1st Ave SE, Rochester MN 55901...................507-285-7600
St Cloud Daily Times*, 3000 7th St N, St Cloud MN 56301...........................612-255-8700
Twin Cities Reader, 600 1st Ave N #600, Minneapolis MN 55403 612-338-2900
Waseca County News*, 213 NW 2nd St, Waseca MN 56093.............................507-835-3380
West Central Tribune*, 2208 W Trott Ave, Willmar MN 56201.....................612-235-1150
Winona Daily News*, 601 Franklin St, Winona MN 55987 507-452-7820
Worthington Daily Globe*, 300 11th St, Worthington MN 56187................507-376-9711

MISSISSIPPI

Aberdeen Examiner, 209 E Commerce St, Aberdeen MS 39730..................601-369-4507
Amory Advertiser, 113 S Main, Amory MS 38821..601-256-5647
Batesville Panolian, 218 Watt St, Batesville MS 38606..................................601-563-4591
Booneville Banner-Independent, 210 Main St, Booneville MS 38829.........610-728-6214
Brookhaven Daily Leader*, N Railroad Ave, Brookhaven MS 39601 601-833-6961
Calhoun County Journal, N/S City Square, Bruce MS 38915.....................601-983-2570
Carthaginian, 122 Franklin St, Carthage MS 39051......................................601-267-4501
Clarion-Ledger*+, 311 E Pearl St, Jackson MS 39205.................................601-961-7000
Clarke County Tribune, 101 Main St, Quitman MS 39355 601-776-3726
Clarksdale Press Register*, 123 2nd St, Clarksdale MS 38614 601-627-2201
Cleveland Bolivar Commercial*, 821 N Chrisman, Cleveland MS 38732..601-843-4241
Columbia Columbian-Progress, 318 2nd St, Columbia MS 39429............601-736-2611
Columbian-Progress/Shopper Guide, 318 2nd St, Columbia MS 39429 ...601-736-2611
Commercial Dispatch*, 516 Main St, Columbus MS 39701.......................601-328-2424
Copiah County Courier, 103 S Ragsdale Ave, Hazlehurst MS 39083.........601-894-3141
Corinth Daily Corinthian*, 808 Waldron, Corinth MS 38834.....................601-286-3366
Daily Times Leader*, 227 Court St, West Point MS 39773 601-494-1422
Delta Democrat-Times*, 988 N Broadway, Greenville MS 38701 601-335-1155
Greenwood Commonwealth*, 329 Hwy 82 W, Greenwood MS 38930........601-453-5312
Hattiesburg American*, 825 N Main St, Hattiesburg MS 39401...................601-582-4321
Holly Springs South Reporter, Box 278, Holly Springs MS 38635..............601-252-4261

Houston Times Post, 219 N Jackson, Houston MS 38851............................601-465-3771
Itawamba County Times, 106 W Main, Fulton MS 38843...........................601-862-3141
Jackson Daily News*, 311 E Pearl St, Jackson MS 39205 601-961-7000
Jackson Style, 4016 N State St, Jackson MS 39206....................................601-362-0758
Jasper County News, 5th Ave, Bay Springs MS 39422..............................601-764-2388
Kosciusko Star-Herald, 319 N Madison, Kosciusko MS 39090................601-289-2251
Laurel Leader Call*, 130 Beacon St, Laurel MS 39440 601-428-0551
Macon Beacon, 403 S Jefferson, Macon MS 39341 601-726-4747
Madison County Herald, 159 E Center St, Canton MS 39046 601-859-1221
McComb Enterprise-Journal*, 129 N Broadway, McComb MS 39648......601-684-2421
Meridian Star*, 814 22nd Ave, Meridian MS 39301 601-693-1551
Mississippi Press Register*, 405 Delmas Ave, Pascagoula MS 39567.......601-762-1112
Natchez Democrat*, 503 N Canal St, Natchez MS 39120 601-442-9101
Neshoba Democrat, 39 Beacon St, Philadelphia MS 39350........................601-656-4000
New Albany Gazette, 713 Carter Ave, New Albany MS 38652....................601-534-6321
Newton Record, 120 S Main St, Newton MS 39345 601-683-2001
Northeast Miss Daily Journal*, 1655 S Green, Tupelo MS 38801 601-842-2611
Northside Sun, PO Box 16709, Jackson MS 39236....................................601-957-1122
Ocean Springs Record, 715 Cox Ave, Ocean Springs MS 39564.................601-875-2791
Oxford Eagle*, 916 Jackson Ave, Oxford MS 38655 601-234-4331
Picayune Item*, 214 N Curran Ave PO Box 580, Picayune MS 39466........601-798-4766
Pontotoc Progress, 13 E Jefferson, Pontotoc MS 38863.............................601-489-3511
Rankin County News, 207 Government St, Brandon MS 39042...................601-825-8333
Ripley Southern Sentinel, Box 558, Ripley MS 38668................................601-563-4414
Scott County Times, 311 Smith St, Forest MS 39074 601-469-2561
Sea Coast Echo, 124 Court St, Bay St Louis MS 39520 601-467-5474
Silver Wings, 516 Main St, Columbus MS 39701......................................601-328-2424
South-West Sun, PO Box 16709, Jackson MS 39236..................................601-957-1122
Starkville Daily News*, 316 University Drive, Starkville MS 39759............601-323-1642
Sun Daily Herald*, 320 DeBuys Rd, Gulfport MS 39501..........................601-896-2100
Sun-Herold*, Box 4567, Biloxi MS 39531 601-896-2100
Sunday Mirror, 318 2nd St, Columbia MS 39429......................................601-736-2611
Taylorsville Signal, Box 380, Taylorsville MS 39168 601-785-6525
Tishomingo County News, 120 W Front St, Iuka MS 38852 601-423-3666
Tyler Times, 727 Beulah Ave, Tylertown MS 39667...................................601-876-5111
Vicksburg Evening Post*, 920 South St, Vicksburg MS 39180 601-636-4545
Wayne County News, 608 Station St, Waynesboro MS 39367 601-735-4341
Winston County Journal, 119 N Court Ave, Louisville MS 39339 601-773-6241
Yazoo Herald*, 1053 Grand Ave, Yazoo City MS 39194.............................601-746-4911

MISSOURI

Aurora Advertiser*, Box 509, Aurora MO 65605.......................................417-678-2115
Belton-Raymore Star-Herald, 419 Main, Belton MO 64012.......................816-331-5353
Bethany Republican-Clipper, 214 N 16th, Bethany MO 64424 816-425-6325
Bolivar Herald-Free Press, 335 S Springfield, Bolivar MO 65613 417-326-7636
Bollinger County Banner, Box 45, Marble Hill MO 63764.........................314-238-2831
Boonville Daily News*, 412 High St, Boonville MO 65233.........................816-258-7237
Bowling Green Times, 106 Main St, Bowling Green MO 63334...................314-324-2222
Branson Beacon & Leader, 114 Commercial St, Branson MO 65616 417-334-3161
Bulletin-Journal, Box 1399, Cape Girardeau MO 63701.............................314-334-7181
California Democrat, 319 S High St, California MO 65018 314-796-2135
Canton Press-News Journal, 130 N 4th St, Canton MO 63435 314-288-5668

Carrollton Democrat*, Box 69, Carrollton MO 64633 816-542-0881
Carthage Press*, 527 S Main, Carthage MO 64836 417-358-2191
Cass County Democrat, 310 S Lexington, Harrisonville MO 64701 816-884-3228
Cedar County Republican, 405 SE Arcade, Stockton MO 65785................417-276-4211
Charleston Enterprise-Courier, Box 69, Charleston MO 63834 314-683-3351
Clay Dispatch-Tribune, 7007 NE Parvin Rd, Kansas City MO 64117.......816-454-9660
Clayton Citizen, 12520 Olive Blvd, St Louis MO 63146.............................314-434-9400
Clayton Watchman Advocate*+, 130 S Bemiston, St Louis MO 63105.....314-725-1515
Clinton Daily Democrat*, 212 S Washington, Clinton MO 64735 816-885-2281
Columbia Daily Tribune*, 4th & Walnut, Columbia MO 65205................314-449-3811
Columbia Missourian*, 9th & Elm, Columbia MO 65201 314-442-3161
Constitution-Tribune*, 818 Washington, Chillicothe MO 64601 816-646-2411
Courier News, 7020 Chippewa, St Louis MO 63119..................................314-481-1111
Cuba Free Press, 110 S Buchanan, Cuba MO 65453..................................314-885-7460
Daily American Republic*, 208 Poplar St, Poplar Bluff MO 63901...........314-785-1414
Daily Journal*, 1513 St Joe Dr, Flat River MO 63601 314-431-2010
Daily News*, 116 W North Main St, Richmond MO 64085..........................816-776-5454
Daily Standard*, 417 Thompson, Excelsior Springs MO 64024................816-637-3147
Daily Star-Journal*, 135 E Market, Warrensburg MO 64093.....................816-747-8123
Daily Statesman, 200 W Stoddard, Dexter MO 63841.................................314-624-4545
De Soto Press, Box 670, De Soto MO 63020 314-586-3344
Democrat*, 700 S Massachusetts, Sedalia MO 65301 816-826-1000
Democrat-Argus, 111 E 5th St, Caruthersville MO 63830............................314-333-4336
Democrat-News, 110 N Mine La Motte St, Fredericktown MO 63645.......314-783-3366
Dexter Daily Statesman*, 200 W Stoddard, Dexter MO 63841....................314-624-7448
Dispatch-Tribune, 7007 NE Parvin Rd, Kansas City MO 64117 816-454-9660
Doniphan Prospect-News, 110 Washington, Doniphan MO 63935............314-996-2103
Douglas County Herald, 307 Washington Ave, Ava MO 65608 417-683-4181
Farmington County Advertiser, 28 E Columbia, Farmington MO 63640..314-756-2313
Farmington Press Greensheet*, Box 70, Farmington MO 63640................314-756-8927
Fenton Journal, 7020 Chippewa, St Louis MO 63119.................................314-481-1111
Festus-Crystal City News-Democrat*, 3 Industrial, Festus MO 63028.......314-296-1800
Flat River Lead Belt News, 206 W Main, Flat River MO 63601....................314-431-2195
Florissant Valley Reporter, Box 69, Florissant MO 63031.........................314-839-1111
Fulton Daily Sun-Gazette*, 5th St & Ravine, Fulton MO 65251................314-642-2234
Fulton Sun*, 115 E 5th, Fulton MO 65251...314-642-7272
Gasconade Cty Republican, 106 E Washington, Owensville MO 65066 314-437-2323
Hannibal Courier-Post*, 200 N 3rd St, Hannibal MO 63401 314-221-2800
Herald*, 131 S Cedar, Nevada MO 64772 417-667-3344
Hermann Advertiser-Courier, 136 E 4th St, Hermann MO 65041 314-486-5418
Hermitage Index, Box 127, Hermitage MO 65668.....................................417-745-6404
Houston Newspapers, 113 N Grand, Houston MO 65483............................417-967-2000
Independence Dispatch-Tribune, 7007 NE Parvin, Kans City MO 64117..816-454-9660
Independence Examiner*, 410 S Liberty, Independence MO 64051...........816-254-8600
Independent-Journal, 119 E High St, Potosi MO 63664 314-438-5141
Ironton Mountain Echo, 110 N Main, Ironton MO 63650..........................314-546-3917
Jackson Cash-Book Journal, 210 W Main St, Jackson MO 63755 314-243-3515
Jefferson City Capital News*, 210 Monroe St, Jefferson City MO 65102..314-636-3131
Jefferson County Journal, 7020 Chippewa, St Louis MO 63119 314-481-1111
Jefferson Republic, Box 670, De Soto MO 63020.....................................314-586-3344
Joplin Globe*, 117 E 4th St, Joplin MO 64801..417-623-3480
Journal of Livestock, Livestock Exchange, St Joseph MO 64504................816-238-6450
Journal/Ozark Beacon, 114 N Broadway, Poplar Bluff MO 63901............314-686-1258

Kansas City Star*+, 1729 Grand Ave, Kansas City MO 64108 816-234-4141
Kansas City Times*+, 1729 Grand Ave, Kansas City MO 64108 816-234-4141
Kennett Daily Dunklin Democrat*, 212 N Main St, Kennett MO 63857 ...314-888-4505
Kirksville Express & News*, 110 E McPherson, Kirksville MO 63501 816-665-2808
Lamar Democrat*, 106 W 10th, Lamar MO 64759 417-682-5529
Lawrence County Record, 312 S Hickory, Mt Vernon MO 65712 417-466-2185
Leader & Press*, 651 Boonville Ave, Springfield MO 65801.....................417-836-1111
Lebanon Daily Record*, 290 S Madison, Lebanon MO 65536 417-532-9131
Lee's Summit Journal, 415 S Douglas, Lee's Summit MO 64063................816-524-2345
Lexington News, 926 Main St, Lexington MO 64067....................................816-259-2266
Liberty Tribune, 7007 NE Parvin Rd, Kansas City MO 64117 816-454-9660
Linn Unterrified Democrat, Main St, Linn MO 65051 314-897-3150
Macon Chronicle-Herald*, 217 W Bourke, Macon MO 63552 816-385-3121
Maiden Press-Merit, Box 399, Maiden MO 63863.......................................314-276-4508
Marshall Democrat-News*, 121 N Lafayette, Marshall MO 65340 816-886-2233
Marshfield Mail, 211 N Clay St, Marshfield MO 65706..............................417-468-2013
Maryville Daily Forum*, 111 E Jenkins, Maryville MO 64468....................816-582-3167
Meramec Community Press, 7020 Chippewa, St Louis MO 63119.............314-481-1111
Mexico Ledger*, 300 N Washington, Mexico MO 65265.............................314-581-1111
Milan Standard, 105 S Market, Milan MO 63556..816-265-4244
Moberly Monitor Index*, 218-N Williams St, Moberly MO 65270.............816-263-4123
Moberly Standard, 218 N Williams, Moberly MO 65270.............................816-263-4123
Monett Times*, 505 Broadway, Monett MO 65708......................................417-235-3135
Monroe County Appeal, 114 Main, Paris MO 65275 816-327-4192
Montgomery Standard, 115 W 2nd St, Montgomery MO 63361..................314-564-2339
Mound City News-Independent, 511 State St, Mound City MO 64470 816-442-5423
Mountain Grove News-Journal, 150 E 1st, Mtn Grove MO 65711.............417-926-5148
Naborhood Link News, 416 Lemay Ferry Rd, St Louis MO 63125 314-631-4321
Natl Catholic Reporter+, PO Box 419281, Kansas City MO 64141 816-531-0538
Neosho Daily News*, 1006 W Harmony St, Neosho MO 64850 417-451-1520
Nevada Daily Mail*, 131 S Cedar, Nevada MO 64772................................417-667-3344
Nevada Herald, 131 S Cedar, Nevada MO 64772..417-667-3344
News & Tribune*, 210 Monroe St, Jefferson City MO 65102 314-636-3131
News Press*, 9th & Edmond, S Joseph MO 64502 816-279-5671
News Press, 8630 St Charles Rock Rd, St Louis MO 63114........................314-427-4300
North County News-Press, 8630 St Charles Rock, St Louis MO 63114 314-427-4300
North County Publications+, 9320 Lewis & Clark, St Louis MO 63136 ...314-868-8000
North Side Community News, 5748 Helen Ave, St Louis MO 63136.........314-261-5555
O'Fallon-St Peters County Tribune, 216 E Elm, Ofallon MO 63366.........314-272-4949
Osage Beach Lake Sun-Leader, 3 Stonecrest Mall, Osage MO 65065.......314-348-2751
Ozark Headliner, 427 E South St, Ozark MO 65721 417-485-3541
Pacific Maramec Vly Transcript, 210 N Columbus, Union MO 63084......314-257-3977
Palmyra Spectator, 304 S Main, Palmyra MO 63461..................................314-769-3111
Perry County Republic, 7 N Main St, Perryville MO 63775........................314-547-2525
Platte Dispatch-Tribune, 7007 NE Parvin Rd, Kansas City MO 64117......816-454-9660
Post-Tribune*, 210 Monroe St, Jefferson City MO 65102...........................314-636-3131
Press Dispatch, 7007 NE Parvin Rd, Kansas City MO 64117.....................816-454-9660
Press-Journal, 1130 Manchester Rd, Ballwin MO 63001............................314-481-1111
Pulaski County Democrat, 103 S Benton, Waynesville MO 65583 314-774-6632
Ray County Herald, Box 260, St Charles MO 63301...................................314-724-1111
Raytown Dispatch Tribune, 10227 E 61 St, Kansas City MO 64133..........816-454-9660
Receille, 114 N Hwy 5, Camdenton MO 65020 314-346-2132
Riverfront Times+, 1915 Park Ave, St Louis MO 63104..............................314-231-6666

Rolla Daily News*, 101 W 7th St, Rolla MO 65401.....................................314-364-2468
St Clair Chronicle, 525 N Commercial St, St Clair MO 63077.................314-629-1111
St Genevieve Herald Inc, 330 Market St, St Genevieve MO 63670............314-883-2222
St James Leader Journal, 125 W Springfield, St James MO 65559...........314-265-3321
St Joseph Gazette*+, 9th & Edmond, St Joseph MO 64502.....................816-279-5671
St Joseph News Press*, 9th & Edmond, St Joseph MO 64502....................816-279-5671
St Louis American, 3910 Lindell Ave, St Louis MO 63108.......................314-533-8000
St Louis County Star, 11545 St Charles Rock, Hazelwood MO 63044......314-291-2222
St Louis Crusader, 4371 Finney Ave, St Louis MO 63113.........................314-531-5860
St Louis Globe-Democrat*+, 710 N Tucker, St Louis MO 63101 314-342-1212
St Louis Post-Dispatch*+, 900 N Tucker Blvd, St Louis MO 63101.........314-622-7000
St Peters Courier-Post, Box 496, St Peters MO 63376.............................314-441-2900
Salem News, Box 111, Salem MO 65560...314-729-4126
Salem Press, Box 458, Salem MO 65560...314-729-4721
Savannah Reporter, 410 W Market St, Savannah MO 64485.....................816-324-3149
Sikeston Daily Standard*, 205 S New Madrid, Sikeston MO 63801 314-471-1137
South County Journal+, 2340 Hampton, St Louis MO 63139....................314-781-6397
South St Louis County News+, 9111 Gravois, St Louis MO 63123............314-638-1222
Southeast Missourian*, 301 Broadway, Cape Girardeau MO 63701........314-335-6611
Southwest Missourian, Box 522, Kimberling City MO 65686 417-739-4246
Springfield Daily News*, 651 Boonville Ave, Springfield MO 65801..........417-869-4411
Sullivan Independent News, Springfield Rd, Sullivan MO 63080.............314-486-6511
Sullivan Tri-County News, 226 W Main, Sullivan MO 63080 314-486-6013
Sunday News & Leader*+, 651 Boonville Ave, Springfield MO 65801......417-869-4411
Table Rock Gazette, Theatre Mall, Kimberling City MO 65686................417-793-4695
39th St Neighborhood News, 7020 Chippewa, St Louis MO 63119............314-481-1111
Trenton Republican Times*, 122 E 8th St, Trenton MO 64683 816-359-2212
Tri-County Journal, 113 W St Louis St PO Box 6, Pacific MO 63069........314-227-1272
Tri-County Journal, 7020 Chippewa, St Louis MO 63119...........................314-481-1111
Tri-County Shopper, Box 670, De Soto MO 63020.....................................314-586-3344
Troy Free Press & Silex Index, 175 E Cherry, Troy MO 63379 314-528-4720
Union Franklin Tribune, 104 S McKinley, Union MO 63084.....................314-583-2545
Unionville Republican, 119 N 17th St, Unionville MO 63465.....................816-947-2222
Versailles Leader-Statesman, 109 W Jasper, Versailles MO 65084............314-378-5441
Warrenton News-Journal, 101 E Main, Warrenton MO 63383....................314-456-3481
Warsaw Benton County Enterprise, 107 Main St, Warsaw MO 65355......816-438-6312
Washington Missourian, Box 336, Washington MO 63090 314-239-7701
Wayne County Journal, 101 W Elm, Piedmont MO 63957...........................314-223-7122
Waynesville Ft Gateway Guide*, Ft Wood Spur, Waynesville MO 65583..314-336-3711
Wednesday Magazine, 105 E Gregory, Kansas City MO 64114 816-361-0616
Wentzville Messenger, 700 A Pearce Blvd, Wentzville MO 63385.............314-327-6463
West County Citizen, 12520 Olive Blvd, St Louis MO 63146......................314-434-9400
West County Journal, 7020 Chippewa, St Louis MO 63119.......................314-481-1111
West Plains Daily Quill*, 125 N Jefferson, West Plains MO 65775...........417-256-9191
Windsor Review, 205 S Main, Windsor MO 65360....................................816-647-2121

MONTANA

Agri-News, PO Box 30755, Billings MT 59107...406-259-5406
Anaconda Leader, 121 Main St, Anaconda MT 59711................................406-563-5283
Billings Gazette*+, 401 N Broadway, Billings MT 59103 406-657-1200
Bozeman Chronicle*, 32 S Rouse, Bozeman MT 59771...............................406-587-4491
Glasgow Courier, 341 3rd Ave S, Glasgow MT 59230 406-228-9301

Great Falls Tribune*, Box 5468, Great Falls MT 59403...............................406-761-6666
Hardin Herald, Box R, Hardin MT 59034..307-665-1008
Havre Daily News*, 119 2nd St, Havre MT 59501 406-265-6796
Helena Independent Record*, 317 Allen St, Helena MT 59601 406-427-1900
Herald-News, Box 639, Wolf Point MT 59201..406-653-2222
Hungry Horse News, 926 Nucleus Ave, Columbia Falls MT 59912 406-892-2151
Kalispell Daily Interlake*, 727 E Idaho, Kalispell MT 59901.....................406-755-7000
Kalispell News, 38 6th Ave W, Kalispell MT 59903 406-755-6767
Lewistown News-Argus, 521 W Main, Lewistown MT 59475.......................406-538-3401
Livingston Enterprise*, 401 S Main, Livingston MT 59047 406-222-2000
Miles City Daily Star*, 13 N 6th St, Miles City MT 59301...........................406-232-0450
Missoula Missoulian*, 500 N Higgins Ave, Missoula MT 59807...............406-721-5200
Montana Standard*, 25 W Granite, Butte MT 59701 406-782-8301
Polson Flathead Courier, Box 1091, Polson MT 59860 406-883-4343
Ravalli Republic*, 232 Main St, Hamilton MT 59840.................................406-363-3300
Ronan Pioneer, 123 Main St SW, Ronan MT 59864 406-676-3800
Sidney Herald, Box 1033, Sidney MT 59270..406-482-2706
Western News, 311 California Ave, Libby MT 59923 406-293-4124
WestMont Word, 515 N Ewing, Helena MT 59601.......................................406-442-5820

NEBRASKA

Air Pulse Offutt AFB, 604 Ft Crook Rd N, Bellevue NE 68005 402-733-7300
Albion News, Box 431, Albion NE 68620 402-395-2115
Alliance Times-Herald*, 114 E 4th St, Alliance NE 69301.........................308-762-3060
Auburn Press Tribune, 830 Central Ave, Auburn NE 68305.......................402-274-3187
Aurora News-Register, 1320 K St, Aurora NE 68818...................................402-694-2131
Beatrice Daily Sun*, 200 N 7th St, Beatrice NE 68301..............................402-223-5233
Bellevue Leader, 604 Ft Crook Rd N, Bellevue NE 68005 402-733-7300
Blair Pilot-Tribune, 16th & Front, Blair NE 68008......................................402-426-2121
Central City Republican Nonpareil, 802 C Ave, Central City NE 68826...308-946-3081
Columbus Telegram*, 1254 27th Ave, Columbus NE 68601.......................402-564-2741
Crete News, 1201 Linden, Crete NE 68333..402-826-2147
Custer County Chief, 305 S 10th St, Broken Bow NE 68822 308-872-2471
Daily Independent*, 422 W 1st St, Grand Island NE 68801.......................308-382-1000
David City Banner-Press, 331 E St, Fairbury NE 68352..............................402-729-6141
Dawson County Herald, Box 599, Lexington NE 68850...............................308-324-5511
Douglas County Post Gazette, 209 3rd St, Waterloo NE 68069 402-779-2528
Fremont Tribune*, 135 N Main St, Fremont NE 68025 402-721-5000
Geneva Nebraska Signal, 131 N 9th St, Geneva NE 68361 402-759-3117
Gering Courier, Box 70, Gering NE 69341...308-436-2222
Hastings Tribune*, 908 W 2nd St, Hastings NE 68901...............................402-462-2131
Holdrege Daily Citizen*, PO Box 344, Holdrege NE 68949.......................308-995-4441
Kearney Daily Hub*, 13 E 22nd St, Kearney NE 68847..............................308-237-2152
Lincoln Journal-Star*+, 926 P St, Lincoln NE 68501.................................402-475-4200
McCook Daily Gazette*, W 1st & E Sts, McCook NE 69001 308-345-4500
Nebraska City News-Press*, 123 S 8th St, Nebraska City NE 68410 401-873-3334
Nemaha County Herald, 830 Central Ave, Auburn NE 68305 402-274-3187
Norfolk Daily News*, 525 Norfolk Ave, Norfolk NE 68701 402-371-1020
North Platte Telegraph*, 621 N Chestnut, North Platte NE 69101 308-532-6000
Northeast Lincoln Sun, PO Box 83289, Lincoln NE 68501.........................402-466-8521
Northwest Lincoln Sun, PO Box 83289, Lincoln NE 68501.........................402-466-8521
O'Neill Frontier & Holt County Ind, 114 N 4th St, O'Neill NE 68763........402-336-1220

Ogallala Keith County News, 116 W A St, Ogallala NE 69153 308-284-4046
Omaha Catholic Voice+, 6060 NW Radial, Omaha NE 68104 402-558-6611
Omaha World-Herald*+, World-Herald Square, Omaha NE 68102.........402-444-1000
Ord Quiz, 305 S 16th St, Ord NE 68862...308-728-3262
Papillion Times, 138 N Washington, Papillion NE 68046.............................402-339-3331
Plattsmouth Journal, 410 Main, Plattsmouth NE 68048..............................402-296-2141
Schuyler Sun, 1112 C St, Schuyler NE 68661 402-352-2424
Scottsbluff Star-Herald*, 1405 Broadway, Scottsbluff NE 69361 308-632-0670
Seward County Independent, 129 S 6th St, Seward NE 68434......................402-643-3676
Sidney Newspapers Inc, Box 219, Sidney NE 69162.................................308-254-5555
South Sioux City Star, 2520 Dakota Ave, S Sioux City NE 68776 402-494-4264
Southeast Lincoln Sun, PO Box 83289, Lincoln NE 68501........................402-466-8521
Southwest Lincoln Sun, PO Box 83289, Lincoln NE 68501 402-466-8521
Syracuse Journal-Democrat, 123 W 17th, Syracuse NE 68446....................402-269-2135
Tri-City Trib, 320 W 8th St, Cozad NE 69130...308-784-3644
Valentine Newspaper, 122 W 2nd St, Valentine NE 69201..........................402-376-3742
Wahoo Newspaper, 564 N Broadway, Wahoo NE 68066................................402-443-4162
Wayne Herald, 114 Main, Wayne NE 68787..402-375-2600
West Point News, 134 E Grove St, West Point NE 68788...........................402-272-2461
York News-Times*, 327 Platte Ave, York NE 68467..................................402-362-4478

NEVADA

The Chronicle, Box 2288, Carson City NV 89701 702-882-2111
Eagle Standard*, 40 E Williams St, Fallon NV 89406 702-423-3101
Elko Daily Free Press*, 491 4th St, Elko NV 89801 702-738-3118
Gardnerville Record-Courier, Box 158, Gardnerville NV 89410...................702-782-5121
Lahontan Valley News*, PO Box 1297, Fallon NV 89406............................702-423-6041
Las Vegas Look, 1007 Cheyenne Ave, N Las Vegas NV 89039 702-642-2567
Las Vegas Review-Journal*+, 1111 W Bonanza, Las Vegas NV 89125.....702-383-0211
Las Vegas Sun*+, 121 S Highland, Las Vegas NV 89106...........................702-385-3111
Las Vegas Today+, 1007 Cheyenne Ave, N Las Vegas NV 89039 702-642-2567
Mason Valley News, 41 N Main, Yerington NV 89447 702-463-2856
Nellis AFB Bullseye, 1007 Cheyenne Ave, N Las Vegas NV 89039 702-642-2567
Reno Gazette-Journal*+, 955 Kuenzli St, Reno NV 89520 702-788-6200
Sparks Tribune, 1002 C St, Sparks NV 89431...702-359-3837
Valley Times*, 1007 Cheyenne, N Las Vegas NV 89030.............................702-642-2567

NEW HAMPSHIRE

Argus Champion, Box 509, Newport NH 03773 603-863-1776
Berlin Reporter, 151 Main St, Berlin NH 03570.......................................603-752-1200
Carroll County Independent, Moultonville Rd, Ctr Ossipee NH 03814....603-539-4111
Claremont Eagle-Times*, 19 Sullivan St, Claremont NH 03743...................603-542-5121
Concord Monitor*, 3 N State, Concord NH 03301 603-224-5301
Connecticut Valley Reporter, 10 Bank St, Lebanon NH 03766 603-448-1405
Coos County Democrat, 79 Main St, Lancaster NH 03584 603-788-4939
Courier, 146 Union St, Littleton NH 03561...603-444-3927
Derry News, 46 W Broadway, Derry NH 03038 603-432-3363
Evening Citizen*, 171 Fair St, Laconia NH 03246....................................603-524-3800
Exeter News-Letter, 255 Water St, Exeter NH 03833................................603-772-6000
1590 Broadcaster+, 502 W Hollis St, Nashua NH 03062............................603-889-1590
Foster's Daily Democrat*, 333 Central Ave, Dover NH 03820....................603-742-4455

Granite State News, Endicott St, Wolfeboro NH 03894 603-569-3126
Hampton Union, Depot Square, Hampton NH 03842...................................603-926-4511
Hillsboro Messenger, School St, Hillsboro NH 03244..................................603-464-5588
Journal Transcript, 100 Memorial St, Franklin NH 03235............................603-934-2323
Keene Sentinel*, 60 West St, Keene NH 03431...603-352-1234
Milford Cabinet and Journal, School St, Milford NH 03055 603-673-3100
Nashua Telegraph*, 60 Main St, Nashua NH 03061 603-882-2741
Peterborough Transcript, 43 Grove St, Peterborough NH 03458................603-924-3333
Plymouth Record Citizen, 111 Main St, Plymouth NH 03264.....................603-536-1311
Portsmouth Herald*, 111 Maplewood Ave, Portsmouth NH 03801...........603-436-1800
The Reporter, Seavey St, North Conway NH 03860 603-356-5566
Rochester Courier, 32 Wakefield St, Rochester NH 03867...........................603-332-1182
Salem Observer, 90 Main St, Salem NH 03079..603-893-4356
Somersworth-Berwicks Free Press, Jarvis Ave, Rochester NH 03867 603-332-1182
Valley News*, 7 Interchange Dr, West Lebanon NH 03784 603-298-8711

NEW JERSEY

Advance News, 2048 Hwy 37, Lakehurst NJ 08733 201-657-8936
Advisor+, 915 Hwy 35, Middletown NJ 07748...201-671-5300
Allentown Messenger-Press, 34 S Main St, Allentown NJ 08501 609-259-7171
Asbury Park Press*+, Press Plaza, Asbury Park NJ 07712..........................201-774-7000
Atlantic City Press*+, 1900 Atlantic Ave, Atlantic City NJ 08404 609-345-1234
Bayshore Independent, 81 Broad St, Keyport NJ 07735...............................201-739-1010
Beach Haven Times, 345 East Bay Ave, Manahawkin NJ 08050.................609-597-3211
Beachcomber, 2100 Central Ave, Beach Haven NJ 08008.............................609-494-5900
Beacon, 345 East Bay Ave, Manahawkin NJ 08050 609-597-3211
Beacon-Record, 14 Bridge St, Lambertville NJ 08530..................................609-397-3000
Belleville Telegram, 228 Washington Ave, Belleville NJ 07109 201-759-4065
Bellville Times News, 800 Bloomfield Ave, Adelphia NJ 07710 201-759-3200
Bergen News Publishing+, 111 Grand Ave, Palisades Park NJ 07650 201-947-5000
Berkeley Heights News, 80 South St, New Providence NJ 07974..................201-464-1025
Bernardsville News, 17 Morrison Rd, Bernardsville NJ 07924 201-766-3900
Blairstown Press, Rt 94, Blairstown NJ 07825 201-362-6161
Bloomfield Independent Press, 266 Liberty St, Bloomfield NJ 07003........201-674-8000
Booster News, 2206 Rt 9, Howell NJ 07731 201-370-0666
Bordentown Register News, 137 Farnsworth, Bordentown NJ 08505.........609-298-7111
Bridgeton Evening News*, 100 E Commerce St, Bridgeton NJ 08302........609-451-1000
Burlington County Times*, Route 130, Willingboro NJ 08046 609-871-8000
Camden County Record, 34 S Broadway, Gloucester City NJ 08030..........609-456-1330
Cape May Press, Main St, Cape May Ct House NJ 08210...........................609-465-5055
Cape May Star & Wave, 513 Washington Mall, Cape May NJ 08204 609-884-3466
Central-Bergen News, 111 Grand Ave, Palisades Park NJ 07650.................201-947-5000
Chatham Courier, 353 Main St, Chatham NJ 07928....................................201-377-2000
Chatham Independent, 80 South St, New Providence NJ 07974.................201-464-1025
Cherry Hill News, 1111 Union Ave, Cherry Hill NJ 08034...........................609-663-4200
Clark Patriot, 219 Central Ave, Rahway NJ 07065 201-574-1200
Cliffside Park Palisadian, 629 Palisade Ave, Cliffside Park NJ 07010 201-943-3000
Courier-News*+, 1201 U S Highway W, Somerville NJ 08807....................201-722-8800
Courier-Post*+, Box 5300, Cherry Hill NJ 08034......................................609-663-6000
Cranford Chronicle, 118 South Ave E, Cranford NJ 07016........................201-276-6000
Daily Advance*, Rt 206 S, Dover NJ 07801 201-347-5400
Daily Racing Form*, 10 Lake Dr, Hightstown NJ 08520.............................609-448-9100

Daily Record*+, 55 Park Place, Morristown NJ 07960 201-538-2000
Daily Register*, 1 Register Plaza, Red Bank NJ 07701 201-542-4000
Dateline Journal, 296 Clifton Ave, Clifton NJ 07011 201-773-5010
Delaware Valley News, 207 Harrison St, Frenchtown NJ 08825................201-996-4047
Delaware Valley News, Box 32, Flemington NJ 08822................................201-782-4747
Denville Citizen of Morris County, 425 E Main St, Denville NJ 07834......201-627-0400
Dispatch, 22 Bank St, Summit NJ 07901...201-464-1025
East Orange Record, 17 N Essex Ave, Orange NJ 07050.............................201-674-8000
Egg Harbor News, 144 Philadelphia Ave, Egg Harbor city NJ 08215.........201-568-6600
Elizabeth Journal*, 295 N Broad St, Elisabeth NJ 07207............................201-354-5000
Fair Lawn News Beacon, 12-38 River Rd, Fair Lawn NJ 07410 201-791-8400
Fairfield Herald, 376 Hollywood Ave, Caldwell NJ 07006 201-227-6666
Fairview News, 155 Broad Ave, Fairview NJ 07022.....................................201-945-5596
Fort Dix Post, 17 High St, Mt Holly NJ 08060...609-267-0285
Fort Lee/Sun Bulletin, 111 Grand Ave, Palisades Park NJ 07650 201-947-5000
Franklinville Sentinel, N Delsea Dr, Franklinville NJ 08322.......................609-694-1600
Freehold Central Jersey Leader, Box 349, Freehold NJ 07728....................201-462-9797
Gazette-Leader, 1212 Atlantic Ave, Wildwood NJ 08260 609-522-3423
Gloucester City News, 34 S Broadway, Gloucester City NJ 08030 609-456-1330
Gloucester County Times*, 309 S Broad St, Woodbury NJ 08096................609-845-3300
Greenville News, 155 Broad Ave, Fairview NJ 07022..................................201-945-5596
Hackettstown Forum+, 106 E Moore St, Hackettstown NJ 07840................201-852-1212
Haddon Gazette, 1111 Union Ave, Cherry Hill NJ 08034 609-663-4200
Hammonton News, 12th & West End Ave, Hammonton NJ 08037..............609-561-2300
Hawthorne Press, 417 Lafayette Ave, Paterson NJ 07507 201-427-3330
Hillsborough Beacon, 300 Witherspoon St, Princeton NJ 08540.................609-924-3244
Hillside Times, 166 Long Ave PO Box 250, Hillside NJ 07205....................201-923-9207
Hoboken Pictorial, 155 Broad Ave, Fairview NJ 07022................................201-945-5596
Hudson Reporter+, 1321 Washington St, Hoboken NJ 07030 201-798-7800
Hunterdon Review, 15 E Main St, Clifton NJ 08809 201-735-4081
Jersey Journal*+, 30 Journal Square, Jersey City NJ 07306 201-653-1000
Jersey Pictorial, 155 Broad Ave, Fairview NJ 07022....................................201-945-5596
Jersey Pictorial, 155 Broad Ave, Fairview NJ 07022....................................201-945-5596
The Journal, 1111 Union Ave, Cherry Hill NJ 08034....................................609-663-4200
Kearny Observer, 531 Kearny Ave, Kearny NJ 07032...................................201-991-1600
Kendall Park Central Park, 3530 Rt 27, Kendall Park NJ 08824...................201-297-3434
Lawrence Ledger, 2431 Main St, Trenton NJ 08648......................................609-896-9100
Local Review, 30 Oak St, Ridgewood NJ 07451 201-445-6400
Madison-Florham Park Eagle, 41 Kings Rd, Madison NJ 07940...................201-377-2000
Mainland Journal, 69 E W Jersey Ave, Pleasantville NJ 08232....................609-641-3100
Manville News, 300 Witherspoon St, Princeton NJ 08540 609-924-3244
Maple Shade Progress, 306 E Main St, Maple Shade NJ 08052 609-779-7788
Maywood Our Town, 58 W Pleasant Ave, Maywood NJ 07607 201-843-5700
Medford Central Record, Old Marlton Pike, Medford NJ 08055 609-654-9221
Mercer County Messenger, 2667 Nottingham Way, Trenton NJ 08619 609-586-1210
Middlesex Chronicle, 409 Union Ave, Middlesex NJ 08846 201-469-8123
Middletown Courier, 915 Hwy 35, Middletown NJ 07748............................201-671-5300
Millburn & Short Hills Item, 100 Millburn Ave, Millburn NJ 07041.........201-376-1200
Millville Daily*, 22 E Vine St, Millville NJ 08332..609-825-3456
Montclair Times, 114 Valley Rd, Montclair NJ 07042...................................201-746-1100
Morris News Bee, 310 Speedwell Ave, Morris NJ 07950 201-538-1000
Netcong News-Leader, PO Box 637, Netcong NJ 07857 201-347-0300
New Brunswick Home News*+, 123 How Ln, New Brunswick NJ 08903..201-246-5500

New Jersey Herald*, Box 10, Newton NJ 07860......................................201-383-1500
New Providence Press, 80 South St, New Providence NJ 07974................201-464-1025
Newark Star Ledger*+, Star-Ledger Plaza, Newark NJ 07101.................201-877-4141
News of Paterson*, 1 News Plaza, Paterson NJ 07509.............................201-684-3000
News Report, Black Horse Pike and Freeway, Blackwood NJ 08012..........609-227-1205
News Tribune*+, 1 Hoover Way, Woodbridge NJ 07095..........................201-442-0400
The News, 1111 Union Ave, Cherry Hill NJ 08034..................................609-663-4200
News-Record, 463 Valley St, Maple Shade NJ 07040...............................201-674-8000
NewsWeekly, 2601 River Rd PO Box 242, Cinnaminson NJ 08077............609-829-0628
North Jersey Prospector+, 85 Crooks Ave, Clifton NJ 07011...................201-773-8300
North Jersey Suburbanite, 50 Piermont Rd, Englewood NJ 07631............201-568-6666
Observer, Black Horse Pike and Freeway, Blackwood NJ 08012................609-227-1205
Observer-Tribune, 31 Fairmount Ave, Chester NJ 07930.........................201-879-4100
Ocean County Leader, 600 Arnold Ave, Pt Pleasant Bch NJ 08742...........201-899-1000
Ocean County Observer*, 8 Robbins St, Toms River NJ 08754..................201-349-3000
Ocean County Reporter+, 1184 Fischer Blvd, Toms River NJ 08753........201-270-1300
Ocean County Review, 715 Boulevard, Seaside Heights NJ 08751.............201-973-0147
Orange Transcript, 17 N Essex Ave, Orange NJ 07050.............................201-674-8000
Palisadian, 222 W Palisades Blvd, Palisades Park NJ 07650.....................201-944-8182
Paramus Sunday Post, W 18 E Ridewood Ave, Paramus NJ 07652...........201-261-6400
Passaic Citizen, 298 Passaic St, Passaic NJ 07055...................................201-779-7500
Passaic Herald-News*+, 988 Main Ave, Passaic NJ 07055......................201-365-3000
Phillipsburg Free Press, 198 Chamber St, Phillipsburg NJ 08865.............201-859-4444
Post Eagle, 800 Van Houten Ave, Clifton NJ 07013................................201-473-5414
Press Journal, 21 Grand Ave, Englewood NJ 07631................................201-568-1700
Princeton Packet, 300 Witherspoon St, Princeton NJ 08540....................609-924-3244
Princeton Spectrum, PO Box 3005, Princeton NJ 08540.........................609-799-9559
Princeton Town Topics, 4 Mercer St, Princeton NJ 08540.......................609-924-2200
Progress, 6 Brookside Ave, Caldwell NJ 07006..201-226-8900
Rahway News-Record, 219 Central Ave, Rahway NJ 07065......................201-574-1200
Ramsey Home and Store News, 6 A E Main St, Ramsey NJ 07446............201-327-1212
Ramsey-Mahwah Reporter, 44 N Central Ave, Ramsey NJ 07446............201-825-3737
The Record*+, 150 River St, Hackensack NJ 07602................................201-646-4000
Record-Breeze, 403 White Horse Pike, Clementon NJ 08021....................609-783-5787
Record-Spirit, Black Horse Pike & Freeway, Blackwood NJ 08012...........609-227-1205
Regional Weekly News, 393 Ridgedale Ave, East Hanover NJ 07936........201-887-1323
Retrospect, 732 Haddon Ave, Camden NJ 08108.....................................609-854-1400
Ridgewood News, 30 Oak St, Ridgewood NJ 07451.................................201-445-6400
SandPaper+, 1816 Long Beach Blvd, Surf City NJ 08008........................609-494-2034
Scotch Plains Times, 1600 E 2nd St, Scotch Plains NJ 07076..................201-322-5266
Secaucus Home News, 766 Irving Pl, Secaucus NJ 07094.........................201-867-2071
Secaucus Press, 155 Broad Ave, Fairview NJ 07022................................201-945-5596
Sentinel-Ledger, 112 8th St, Ocean City NJ 08226..................................609-399-5411
The Shield, 155 Broad Ave, Fairview NJ 07022.......................................201-945-5596
Short Hills Independent, 80 South St, New Providence NJ 07974.............201-464-1025
Somerset Messenger Gazette, 36 E Main, Somerville NJ 08876...............201-722-3000
Somerset Spectator, PO Box 5717, Somerset NJ 08875...........................201-875-0035
South Bergenite, 39 Meadow Rd, Rutherford NJ 07070...........................201-933-2700
South Jersey Advisor, 644 W White Horse Pike, Cologne NJ 08213..........609-646-5843
Spolesman, Box 1266, New Brunswick NJ 08901....................................201-249-0012
Springfield Leader, 2667 Nottingham Way, Trenton NJ 08619.................609-586-1210
Stirling Echoes-Sentinel, 254 Mercer St, Stirling NJ 07980.....................201-647-1170
Suburban Life Today+, 132 N Greenbrook, N Caldwell NJ 07006............201-228-7460

Suburban Trends, 1 Boonton Ave, Butler NJ 07405......................................201-838-9000
Suburban, 1111 Union Ave, Cherry Hill NJ 08034..................................609-663-4200
Summit Independent, 80 South St, New Providence NJ 07974....................201-464-1025
Sunday News, 30 Oak St, Ridgewood NJ 07451...201-445-6400
Sunday Post, 30 Oak St, Ridgewood NJ 07451..201-445-6400
The Times*+, 500 Perry St, Trenton NJ 08605...609-396-3232
Today's Sunbeam*, 93 5th St, Salem NJ 08079..609-935-1500
Town News South, 583 Winters Ave, Paramus NJ 07652............................201-261-1404
Ukrainian Weekly, 30 Montomery St, Jersey City NJ 07302........................201-434-0237
Union City Hudson Dispatch*, 409 39th St, Union City NJ 07087.............201-863-2000
Union Irvington Herald, 2667 Nottingham Way, Trenton NJ 08619..........609-586-1210
Valley Star, 21 Grand Ave, Englewood NJ 07631..201-568-1700
Verona Cedar Grove Times, 508 Bloomfield Ave, Verona NJ 07044.........201-239-0900
Vineland Down Jersey Newspaper, 733 Elmer St, Vineland NJ 08360.......609-696-5411
Vineland Times Journal*, 891 E Oak Rd, Vineland NJ 08360....................609-691-5000
West Essex Tribune, 495 S Livingston Ave, Livingston NJ 07039.............201-992-1771
West Orange Chronicle, 17 N Essex Ave, Orange NJ 07050......................201-674-8000
Westfield Leader, 50 Elm St, Westfield NJ 07090......................................201-232-4407
Williamstown Plain Dealer, 19 Clinton Ave, Williamstown NJ 08094........609-227-1205
Windsor-Hights Herald, 504 Mercer St, Hightstown NJ 08520...................609-448-3005
Wrightstown Leader, 137 Farnsworth Ave, Bordentown NJ 08505 609-298-7111
Wyckoff News, 629 Wyckoff Ave, Wyckoff NJ 07481..................................201-891-2222

NEW MEXICO

Alamogordo Daily News*, 518 24th St, Alamogordo NM 88310 505-437-7120
Albuquerque Journal*+, 717 Silver Ave SW, Albuquerque NM 87103.....505-842-2300
Albuquerque Tribune*, PO Drawer T, Albuquerque NM 87103 505-823-3600
Carlsbad Current-Argus*, 620 S Main, Carlsbad NM 88220 505-887-5501
Clovis News-Journal*, 6th & Pile Sts, Clovis NM 88101............................505-763-3431
Deming Headlight*, 219 E Maple, Deming NM 88030...............................505-546-2611
Farmington Daily Times*, 201 N Allen, Farmington NM 87401 505-325-4545
Gallup Independent*, 500 N 9th St, Gallup NM 87301 505-863-8611
Grants Daily Beacon*, 300 N 2nd St, Grants NM 87020.............................505-287-4411
Hobbs Daily News-Sun*, 201 N Thorp, Hobbs NM 88240............................505-393-2123
Hobbs Flare, 114 E Dunnam, Hobbs NM 88240 505-393-5141
Las Cruces Sun-News*, 256 W Las Cruces, Las Cruces NM 88001............505-523-4581
Las Vegas Daily Optic*, 614 Lincoln, Las Vegas NM 87710......................505-425-6796
Los Alamos Monitor*, 256 D P Rd, Los Alamos NM 87544 505-662-4185
Lovington Daily Leader*, 14 W Ave B, Lovington NM 88260....................505-396-2844
Portales News-Tribune*, 101 E 1st, Portales NM 88130 505-356-4481
Raton Range*, 208 S 3rd, Raton NM 87740 505-445-2721
Rio Grande Sun, 238 N Railroad, Espanola NM 87532.............................505-753-2126
Roswell Daily Record*, 2301 N Main, Roswell NM 88201.........................505-622-7710
Ruidoso News, Box 128, Ruidoso NM 88345...505-257-4001
Santa Fe New Mexican*, 202 E Marcy St, Santa Fe NM 87501..................505-983-3303
Sierra County Sentinel, 1729 E 3rd, Truth or Consequences NM 87901...505-894-3088
Silver City Press-Independent*, 300 Market, Silver City NM 88061..........505-388-1576
Taos News, Box U, Taos NM 87571 505-758-2241
Valencia County News-Bulletin, Box 25, Belen NM 87002 505-864-4472

NEW YORK

Albany Times-Union*+, 645 Albany-Shaker Rd, Albany NY 12212 518-454-5694
Albion Advertiser, 8 E Bank St, Albion NY 14411....................................716-589-4455
Altamont Enterprise, 123 Maple Ave, Altamont NY 12009 518-861-6641
Amherst Bee, 5564 Main St, Williamsville NY 14221................................716-632-4700
Amityville Record, 31 Greene St, Amityville NY 11701.............................516-264-0077
Auburn Citizen*, 25 Dill St, Auburn NY 13021......................................315-253-5311
Aufbau, 2121 Broadway, New York NY 10023...212-873-7400
Babylon Beacon, 45 Deer Park Ave, Babylon NY 11702 516-587-5612
Baldwin Citizen, Box 521, Baldwin NY 11510..516-764-2500
Baldwinsville Messenger, 7 E Genesee St, Baldwinsville NY 13027..........315-635-3921
Batavia Daily News*, 2 Apollo Dr, Batavia NY 14020...............................716-343-8000
Bay News, 1733 Sheepshead Bay Rd, Brooklyn NY 11235 718-769-4400
Bayside Times, 214 41st Ave, Flushing NY 11361 718-229-0300
Beacon Free Press, 291 Main St, Beacon NY 12508 914-297-3723
Beacon Light, Box H, Mahopac NY 10541...914-628-8400
Bellmore Life, 2717 Grand Ave, Bellmore NY 11710 516-826-0333
Bellmore-Merrick Observer, 2262 Centre Ave, Bellmore NY 11710 516-679-9888
Blasdell-Woodlawn Front Page, 2703 S Park, Lackawanna NY 14218.......716-823-2222
Boonville Herald, E Schuyler St PO Box 372, Boonville NY 13309 315-942-4449
Bowling Highlights News, 131 Winthrop Ave Ext, Liberty NY 12754 914-292-9114
Brewster Times, Box H, Mahopac NY 10541...914-628-8400
Brighton-Pittsford Post, Drawer C, Fishers NY 14453 716-381-3300
Bronx Co-op City Times, 2049 Bartow Ave, Bronx NY 10475...................212-671-2044
Bronx Parkway News, 970 Woodmansten Pl, Bronx NY 10462...................212-829-0806
Bronxville Review Press, 147 Gramatin, Mt Vernon NY 10550 914-337-7580
Brooklyn Courier, 1733 Sheepshead Bay Rd, Brooklyn NY 11235.............718-769-4400
Brooklyn Daily Bulletin*, 16 Court St, Brooklyn NY 11241 212-624-6181
Brooklyn Graphic, 2054 86th St, Brooklyn NY 11214................................718-266-8900
Brooklyn Phoenix Newspaper, 395 Atlantic Ave, Brooklyn NY 11217.......212-643-1032
Brooklyn Record, 44 Court St, Brooklyn NY 11201 212-875-8230
Brooklyn Spectator, 8320 3rd Ave, Brooklyn NY 11209............................212-283-6603
Brooklyn Times, 618 Brighton Beach Ave, Brooklyn NY 11235 212-648-5600
Buffalo News*+, 1 News Plaza, Buffalo NY 14240 716-849-4444
Camillus Advocate, 57 Genesee St Box 70, Camillus NY 13031 315-672-8192
Canandaigua Daily Messenger*, 73 Buffalo St, Canandaigua NY 14424 ..716-394-0770
Canarsie Courier, 1142 E 92nd St, Brooklyn NY 11236.............................212-257-0600
Canarsie Digest, 1733 Sheepshead Bay Rd, Brooklyn NY 11235...............718-769-4400
Canton St Lawrence Plaindealer, 75 Main St, Canton NY 13617...............315-386-8521
Catskill Mail*, 30 Church St, Catskill NY 12414......................................518-943-2100
Cazenovia Republican, 72 Albany St, Cazenovia NY 13035 315-655-3415
Center Moriches Bay Tide, Box 1281, Center Moriches NY 11934.............516-281-1000
Chatham Courier-Roughnotes, 17 Railroad Ave, Chatham NY 12037......518-392-4141
Cheektowaga Bee, 5564 Main St, Williamsville NY 14221.........................716-632-4700
Cheektowaga Journal, 951 Ridge Rd, Lackawanna NY 14218 716-822-4700
Cheektowaga Times, 343 Maryvale Dr, Cheektowaga NY 14227.................716-892-5323
Chelsea Clinton News, 56 W 22nd St, New York NY 10010 212-989-5761
Chemung Valley Reporter, 205 S Main St, Horseheads NY 14845 607-739-3001
Chenango American, 12 S Chenango St, Greene NY 13778 607-656-4511
Chief-Civil Service Leader+, 150 Nassau St, New York NY 10038............212-962-2690
Chittenango Bridgeport Times, 208 Genesee St, Chittenango NY 13037..315-687-3887

Chronicle Express, 138 Main St, Penn Yan NY 14527 315-536-4422
City Newspaper+, 250 N Goodman St, Rochester NY 14607 716-244-3329
Clarence Bee, 5564 Main St, Williamsville NY 14221 716-632-4700
Cobleskill Times-Journal, 19 Division St, Cobleskill NY 12043...................518-234-2515
Commack News, 1 Brooksite Dr, Smithtown NY 11787 516-265-2100
Community Herald, 30 Irving Pl, New York NY 10003...............................212-777-6810
Coney Island Times, 1029 Brighton Beach Ave, Brooklyn NY 11235 212-769-6000
Cooperstown Freeman's Journal, 1 Otsego Ct, Cooperstown NY 13326...607-547-2545
Courier Gazette, 613 S Main St, Newark NY 14513...................................315-331-1000
Courier Journal, 612 E Main St, Palmyra NY 14522.................................315-597-6655
Courier-Standard-Enterprise, 1 Canal St, Fort Plain NY 13339 518-993-2321
Cross Westchester Weekly, 355 Main St, Armonk NY 10504....................914-273-5651
Democrat & Chronicle*+, 55 Exchange, Rochester NY 14614...................716-232-7100
DeWitt News-Times, 200 Brooklea Dr, Fayetteville NY 13066...................315-637-3121
Downtown Herald, 30 Irving Pl, New York NY 10003.................................212-777-6810
East Aurora Advertiser, 710 Main St, E Aurora NY 14052.........................716-652-0320
East Greenbush Area News, Box 31, East Greenbush NY 12061................518-286-6600
East Hampton Star, 153 Main St, East Hampton NY 11937.......................516-324-0002
East Meadow Beacon, 80 N Franklin St, Hempstead NY 11550..................516-483-4100
East Rockaway/Lynbrook Observer, Box A, E Rockaway NY 11518........516-764-2500
East Side Herald, 30 Irving Pl, New York NY 10003.................................212-777-6810
The Echo, The Echo Bldg, Canaan NY 12029..518-781-4420
Elizabethtown Valley News, Box 338, Elizabethtown NY 12932..................518-873-6368
Ellenville Journal, 101 Main St, Ellenville NY 12428 914-647-3061
Ellenville Press, 7 Cape Ave, Ellenville NY 12428 914-647-7222
Elmira Star Gazette*, 201 Baldwin St, Elmira NY 14902..........................607-734-5151
Elmont Elmonitor, 2054 Hillside Ave, Elmont NY 11003...........................516-352-4258
Elmsford Record of Greenburgh, 70 E Main St, Elmsford NY 10523 914-592-2110
Evening-Observer*, 8 E 2nd St, Dunkirk NY 14048 716-366-3000
Fairport-Perinton Herald-Mail, 2010 Empire Blvd, Webster NY 14580...716-671-1533
Farmingdale Observer, 124 Front St, Massapequa Park NY 11762 516-799-1150
Farmingdale Post, 51 Heisser Ln, Farmingdale NY 11735.........................516-249-0131
Fayetteville Eagle Bulletin, 200 Brooklea Dr, Fayetteville NY 13066.........315-637-3121
Fishkill Standard, Box H, Mahopac NY 10541..914-628-8400
Flatbush Life, 1733 Sheepshead Bay Rd, Brooklyn NY 11235 718-769-4400
Floral Park Bulletin, PO Box 94, Floral Park NY 11002.............................516-775-7700
Floral Park Gateway, 138 Plainfield Ave, Floral Park NY 11002.................516-775-2700
Forum of South Queens, Box 97, Rockaway Beach NY 11693....................718-634-4000
Franklin Sq Bulletin, 107 S Tyson Ave, Floral Park NY 11001...................516-775-7700
Free Press & Herald, 136 Park St, Tupper Lake NY 12986.........................518-359-2166
Fulton Patriot, 186 S 1st St, Fulton NY 13069 315-592-2459
Gates-Chili News, 1635 Brooks Ave, Rochester NY 14624.........................716-436-1200
Gazette-Advertiser, 51 E Market, Rhinebeck NY 12572.............................914-876-3033
Genesee Country Express, 113 Main St, Dansville NY 14437.....................716-335-2272
Glen Cove Guardian, 186 W Main St, Oyster Bay NY 11771.......................516-922-4215
Glen Cove Record Pilot, 29 Continental Pl, Glen Cove NY 11542...............516-676-1200
Glen Falls Post-Star*, Lawrence & Cooper Sts, Glen Falls NY 12801.......518-792-3131
Goshen Independent Republican, Drawer A, Goshen NY 10924.................914-294-6111
Gouverneur Tribune Press, 40 Clinton St, Gouverneur NY 13624.............315-287-2100
Gowanda Penny Saver News, 62 W Main St, Gowanda NY 14070 716-532-2288
Grand Island Dispatch, 1871 Whitehaven Rd, Grand Island NY 14072....716-773-7676
Granville Sentinel, 6 North St, Granville NY 12832..................................518-642-1234
Great Neck News, 375 Great Neck Rd, Great Neck NY 11022 516-482-1100

Great Neck Record, 132 E 2nd St, Mineola NY 11501 516-747-8282
Greece Post, 4 S Main St, Pittsford NY 14534..716-352-6300
Greenburgh Inquirer, 791 Central Ave, Scarsdale NY 10583......................914-723-2226
Greene County News, 391 Main St, Catskill NY 12414...............................518-943-2100
Greenpoint Gazette, 597 Manhattan Ave, Brooklyn NY 11222....................212-398-6067
Greenwich Journal & Salem Press, 1 Hill St, Greenwich NY 12834..........518-692-2266
Greenwood Lake News, PO Box 1117, Greenwood Lake NY 10925...........914-477-2575
Guardian Newsweekly, 33 W 17th St, New York NY 10011.....................212-691-0404
Hamilton County News, Box 338, Elizabethtown NY 12932......................518-873-6368
Hamilton Mid-York Weekly, 3 Madison St, Hamilton NY 13346 315-824-2150
Harlem Valley Times, E Main St, Amenia NY 12501 914-373-9555
Harrison Independent, 213 Harrison Ave, Harrison NY 10528...................914-835-3600
Hempstead Beacon, 80 N Franklin St, Hempstead NY 11550 516-483-4100
Henrietta Post, 4 S Main St, Pittsford NY 14534..716-352-6300
Herald American*+, Clinton Sq, Syracuse NY 13221 315-470-0011
Herald Journal*+, Clinton Sq, Syracuse NY 13221..................................315-470-0011
Herkimer Evening Telegram*, 111 Green St, Herkimer NY 13350...........315-866-2220
Hicksville Centre Island News*, 22 W Nicholai St, Hicksville NY 11800..516-931-0012
Hicksville Mid Island Herald, 1 Jonathan Ave, Hicksville NY 11801........516-931-1400
Home Reporter & Sunset News, 8723 3rd Ave, Brooklyn NY 11209..........212-238-6600
Hornell Evening Tribune*, 85 Canisteo St, Hornell NY 14843 607-324-1425
Hudson Register Star*, 366 Warren St, Hudson NY 12534 518-838-4355
Irondequoit Press, 657 Tius Ave, Rochester NY 14617................................716-342-9450
Islip News, 1 Brooksite Dr, Smithtown NY 11787......................................516-265-2100
Ithaca Journal*, 123 W State St, Ithaca NY 14850 607-272-2321
Ithaca Times+, PO Box 27, Ithaca NY 14851...607-273-6092
Jefferson County Journal, 7 Main St, Adams NY 13605.............................315-232-2141
Journal & Republican, 7556 State St, Lowville NY 13367 315-376-3525
Journal of Commerce*, 110 Wall St, New York NY 10005..........................212-208-0373
Ken-Ton Bee, 5564 Main St, Williamsville NY 14221................................716-632-4700
Kings Courier, 1733 Sheepshead Bay Rd, Brooklyn NY 11235....................718-769-4400
Kingston Daily Freeman*, 79 Hurley Ave, Kingston NY 12401..................914-331-5000
Knickerbocker News*, 645 Albany-Shaker Rd, Albany NY 12212.............518-454-5694
La Grange Independent, Box H, Mahopac NY 10541 914-628-8400
Lackawanna Front Page, 2703 S Park Ave, Lackawanna NY 14218...........716-823-8222
Lackawanna Leader, 951 Ridge Rd, Lackawanna NY 14218.......................716-822-4700
Lake Placid News, Mill Hill, Lake Placid NY 12946 518-523-4401
Lancaster Enterprise, 5564 Main St, Williamsville NY 14221....................716-632-4700
Leader Observer, 70 Jamaica Ave, Woodlawn NY 11421 212-296-2200
Leader, 18 E Sunrise Hwy, Freeport NY 11520...516-378-3133
Levittown Tribune, 2946 Hempstead Turnpike, Levittown NY 11756........516-735-4567
Little Falls Evening Times*, 347 S 2nd St, Little Falls NY 13365...............315-823-3680
Little Neck/Glen Oaks Ledger, 214 41st Ave, Flushing NY 11361 718-229-0300
Liverpool-Salina Review, 7 E Genesse St, Liverpool NY 13088..................315-635-3921
Lockport Tri-County News, 459 S Transit St, Lockport NY 14094 716-439-9222
Lockport Union-Sun & Journal*, 459 S Transit St, Lockport NY 14094...716-439-9222
Locust Valley Leader, 160 Birch Hill Rd, Locust Valley NY 11560............516-676-1434
Long Beach Independent Voice, 120 W Park, Long Beach NY 11561........516-432-0065
Long Island Advance, 20 Medford Ave, Patchogue NY 11772.....................516-475-1000
Long Island News, 9 Front St, Rockville Center NY 11571 516-706-5209
Long Island News, PO Box 422, Coram NY 11727 516-698-0200
Long Island Traveler-Watchman, Traveler St, Southold NY 11971...........516-765-3425
Malone Evening Telegram*, 136 E Main St, Malone NY 12953.................518-483-4700

Mamaroneck Daily Times*, 126 Library Lane, Mamaroneck NY 10543...914-698-5500
Marathon Independent Newspapers, 10 E Main, Marathon NY 13803.....607-849-3278
Marcellus Observer, 44 E Genesee St, Skaneateles NY 13152 315-685-8338
Maspeth Queens Ledger, 65 Grand Ave, Maspeth NY 11378 718-894-8585
Massapequa Post, 1029 Park Blvd, Massapequa Park NY 11762 516-798-5100
Massapequan Observer, 124 Front St, Massapequa Park NY 11762 516-798-5100
Medina Journal-Register*, 413 Main St, Medina NY 14103 716-798-1400
Merrick Beacon, 80 N Franklin St, Hempstead NY 11550..........................516-483-4100
Merrick Life, 1840 Merrick Ave, Merrick NY 11566 516-378-5320
Messena Observer, 56 Main St, Messena NY 13662....................................315-769-2451
Mid-Island News, 1 Brooksite Dr, Smithtown NY 11787.............................516-265-2100
Mineola American, 35 E Jericho Tpke, Mineola NY 11501...........................516-746-3066
Mirror-Recorder, 7 Harper St, Stamford NY 12167 607-652-7303
Moneysaver, 72 W High St, Ballston Spa NY 12020 518-885-4341
Monroe-Woodbury Photo News, 2 Lake St, Monroe NY 10950....................914-782-8391
Moriches Bay Tide, 640 Montauk Hwy, Shirley NY 11967 516-281-1000
Mt Kisco Patent Trader*, N Bedford Rd, Mt Kisco NY 10549....................914-666-8951
Mt Vernon Daily Argus*, 147 Gramatan, Mt Vernon NY 10550.................914-668-3000
New Rochelle Standard-Star*, 92 North Ave, New Rochelle NY 10802....914-636-8900
New York City Tribune*+, 401 5th Ave, New York NY 10016....................212-532-8300
New York Daily News*+, 220 E 42nd St, New York NY 10017....................212-210-2100
New York Heights Inwood, 4780 Broadway, New York NY 10040 212-569-8800
New York India Abroad, 331 Park Ave, New York NY 10010.....................212-254-6622
New York Post*+, 210 South St, New York NY 10002................................212-349-5000
New York Recorder, East New York Sta, Brooklyn NY 11207....................212-636-9500
New York Soho Weekly News, 514 Broadway, New York NY 10003 212-431-3150
NY Staats-Zeitung & Herold, 36-30 37th St, Long Island NY 11101.........718-786-1110
New York Times*+, 229 W 43rd St, New York NY 10036............................212-556-1234
Newburgh Evening News*, 85 Dickson St, Newburg NY 12550 914-562-3000
News-Review, 214 Roanoke Ave, Riverhead NY 11901 516-727-3000
Newsday*+, Long Island NY 11747..516-454-2020
Niagara Gazette*, 310 Niagara St, Niagara Falls NY 14303 716-282-2311
North County News, 1766 Front St, Yorktown Heights NY 10598 914-962-4748
North Syracuse Star News, 7 E Genesee St, Baldwinsville NY 13027........315-635-3921
Northport Observer, 160 Main St, Northport NY 11768.............................516-261-6124
Norwich Evening Sun*, 45 Hale St, Norwich NY 13815..............................607-334-3276
Nyack Journal-News*, 53 Hudson Ave, Nyack NY 10960............................914-358-2200
Oceanside Beacon, 2787 Long Beach Rd, Oceanside NY 11572 516-764-2500
Ogdensburg Journal*, 308 Isabella, Ogdensburg NY 13669 315-393-1000
Olean Times Herald*, 639 Norton Dr, Olean NY 14760.............................716-372-3121
Oneida Daily Dispatch*, 130 Broad St, Oneida NY 13421 315-363-5100
Oneonta Star*, 102 Chestnut St, Oneonta NY 13820 315-432-1000
Onondaga Valley News, 250 Bear St W, Syracuse NY 13204.....................315-472-7825
Our Town+, 435 E 86th St, New York NY 10028 212-289-8700
Owego Tioga County Gazette & Times, 28 Lake St, Owego NY 13827......607-687-3990
Oxford Review-Times, 12 S Chenango St, Greene NY 13778 607-656-4511
Oyster Bay Enterprise Pilot, Box 535, Oyster Bay NY 11771...................516-922-9095
Pawling News-Chronicle, 3 Memorial Ave, Pawling NY 12564..................914-855-1100
Peekskill Star*, 824 Main St, Peekskill NY 10566......................................914-737-1200
Penfield Post Republican, 4 S Main St, Pittsford NY 14534 716-352-6300
Penfield Press, 2010 Empire Blvd, Webster NY 14580................................716-671-1533
People's Daily World*, 239 W 23rd St 3rd fl, New York NY 10011 212-924-2523
Phoenix Register, 821 State St, Phoenix NY 13135....................................315-695-4771

Plattsburgh Press-Republican*, 170 Margaret, Plattsburgh NY 12901 518-561-2300
Polish American World, 3100 Grand Blvd, Baldwin NY 11510...................516-223-6514
Port Chester Daily Item*, 33 New Broad St, Port Chester NY 10573........914-939-0800
Port Jefferson North Shore Record, Box 248, Port Jefferson NY 11777 ...516-473-1370
Port Washington News, 270 Main St, Port Washington NY 11050 516-767-0035
Post-Journal*, 15 W 2nd St, Jamestown NY 14701...............................716-487-1111
Potsdam Courier and Freeman, 71 Market St, Potsdam NY 13676...........315-265-6000
Poughkeepsie Journal*+, 85 Civic Ctr Plz, Poughkeepsie NY 12602 914-454-2000
Press & Sun-Bulletin*+, Vestal Pkwy E, Binghamton NY 13902 607-798-1234
Pulaski Democrat, 40 Clinton St, Gouverneur NY 13624 315-287-2100
Putnam County Courier, 45 Gleneida Ave, Carmel NY 10512.................914-225-3633
Queens Illustrated News, 2054 Hillside Ave, New Hyde Park NY 11040..516-328-3788
Record of Yonkers, 10 Ludlow St, Yonkers NY 10705 914-592-2110
Record-Advertiser, 435 River Rd, N Tonawanda NY 14120....................716-693-1000
Recorder*, 1 Venner Rd, Amsterdam NY 12010 518-843-1100
Reporter, 181 Delaware St, Walton NY 13856....................................607-865-4131
Review Shoppers News, 25 Union Ave, Ronkonkoma NY 11779................516-588-6600
Ridgewood Times, 815A Seneca Ave, Flushing NY 11385 718-821-7500
Riverdale Press, 6155 Broadway, Bronx NY 10471.............................212-543-6065
Riverside Press, 6155 Broadway, Bronx NY 10471.............................212-543-6065
Riverside Review, 946 Hertel Ave, Buffalo NY 14216..........................716-877-8400
Rochester 10th Ward Courier, 495 Emerson, Spencerport NY 14559.......716-254-5200
Rochester Vicinity Post, 495 Emerson St, Rochester NY 14613 716-254-5200
Rockland County Times, 11 New Main St, Haverstraw NY 10927 914-429-2000
Rome Daily Sentinel*, 333 W Dominick St, Rome NY 13440....................315-337-4000
Ronkonkoma Review, 25 Union Ave, Ronkonkoma NY 11779 516-588-6600
Roslyn News, 132 E 2nd St, Mineola NY 11501.................................516-747-8282
Rouses Point North Countryman, Box 338, Elizabethtown NY 12932 518-873-6368
Rye Chronicle, 139 Purchase St, Rye NY 10580 914-967-0065
Salamanca Press*, 36 River St, Salamanca NY 14779...........................716-945-1644
Salmon River News, Jefferson St, Pulaski NY 13142 315-963-7813
Saratoga Springs Saratogian*, 20 Lake St, Saratoga Spring NY 12866 518-584-4242
Saugerties Old Dutch Post-Star, 45 Partition St, Saugerties NY 12477.....914-246-4985
Scarsdale Inquirer, Harwood Building, Scarsdale NY 10583.....................914-725-2500
Schenectady Gazette*+, 332 State St, Schenectady NY 12301 518-374-4141
Scotia-Glenville Journal, 72 W High St, Ballston Spa NY 12020...............518-885-4341
Seaford-Wantagh Observer, 2262 Centre Ave, Bellmore NY 11710.........516-679-9888
Shelter Island Reporter, Box 1000, Shelter Island NY 11965.................516-749-1000
Skaneateles Press, 44 E Genesee St, Skaneateles NY 13152...................315-685-8338
Smithtown Messenger, 1 Brooksite Dr, Smithtown NY 11787.................516-265-2100
Smithtown News, 1 Brooksite Dr, Smithtown NY 11787........................516-265-2100
South Bay Newspaper+, 150 W Hoffman Ave, Lindenhurst NY 11757.....516-226-2636
South Buffalo News, 2703 S Park Ave, Lackawanna NY 14218................716-823-8222
South Buffalo Review, 951 Ridge Rd, Lackawanna NY 14218 716-822-4700
South Shore Record, Hewlett Plaza, Hewlett NY 11557........................516-374-9200
Southampton Press, 30 Nuget St, Southampton NY 11968 516-283-4100
Spackenkill Sentinel, 84 Main St, Wappingers Falls NY 12590.................914-297-3723
Spotlight, 125 Adams St, Delmar NY 12054 518-439-4949
The Star+, 660 White Plains Rd, Tarrytown NY 10591 914-332-5000
Staten Island Advance*+, 950 Fingerboard, Staten Island NY 10305 718-981-1234
Staten Island Register, 2100 Clove Rd, Staten Island NY 10305 212-447-4700
Steuben Courier-Advocate, 10 W Steuben St, Bath NY 14810..................607-776-2121
Suburban News, 1835 N Union St, Spencerport NY 14559.....................716-352-3411

Suburban Press, 6519 E Quaker, Orchard Park NY 14127 716-662-9378
Suffolk County News, Box 367, Sayville NY 11782..............................516-589-6200
Suffolk Times, 429 Main St, Greenport NY 11944....................................516-477-0081
Sun & Erie County Independent, 46 Buffalo St, Hamburg NY 14075 716-649-4040
Sun Telegram*+, 201 Baldwin, Elmira NY 14902.................................607-734-5151
Sunday Record*+, 501 Broadway, Troy NY 12181................................518-272-2000
Syosset Tribune, Box 695, Syosset NY 11791..516-931-1400
Syracuse New Times+, 1415 W Genesee St, Syracuse NY 13204 315-422-7011
Syracuse Post-Standard*+, Clinton Sq, Syracuse NY 13221 315-473-7700
Tarrytown Daily News*, 111 Old White Plains, Tarrytown NY 10591.......914-631-5000
Thousand Islands Sun, 7 Market St, Alexandria NY 13607 315-482-2581
Three Village Herald, PO Box 703, East Setauket NY 11733 516-751-1550
Ticonderoga Times, 20 Putnam St, Ticonderoga NY 12883.......................518-585-6204
Times-Herald-Record*+, 40 Mulberry St, Middletown NY 10940.............914-343-2181
Times-Review Corp, PO Box F, Greenport NY 11944.................................516-477-0081
Tonawanda News*, 435 River Rd, N Tonawanda NY 14120.........................716-693-1000
Town & Country News, 40 Clinton, Gouverneur NY 13624.........................315-287-2100
Tri-County Publications, 286 Main St, Arcade NY 14009 716-492-4472
Tri-State Gazette*, 84 Fowler St, Port Jervis NY 12771.............................914-856-5383
Tri-Town News, 11 Division St, Sidney NY 13838.....................................607-563-3625
Troy Times Record*, 501 Broadway, Troy NY 12181.................................518-272-2000
Ulster County Townsman, Rt 212, Woodstock NY 12498............................914-679-6507
Utica Daily Press*, 221 Oriskany Plaza, Utica NY 13503 315-797-9150
Utica Observer-Dispatch*+, 221 Oriskany St E, Utica NY 13503 315-797-9150
Valley News, 201 Main St, Vestal NY 13850...607-748-3334
Valley News, N 7th & Erie Sts, Fulton NY 13069 315-593-8314
Valley Stream Courier, 244 Whaley St, Freeport NY 11520 516-378-5002
Village Newspaper, 88 7th Ave S, Long Island City NY 10014 212-929-7200
Village Times of Setauket, 185 Rt 25A, East Setauket NY 11733 516-751-7744
Village Voice+, 842 Broadway, New York NY 10003 212-475-3300
Walden Citizen Herald, 39 Main St, Walden NY 12586.............................914-778-2101
Wantagh-Seaford Citizen, 2079 Wantagh Ave, Wantagh NY 11793...........516-826-0812
Warrensburg-Lake George News, 166 Main, Warrensburg NY 12817.......518-623-3411
Warwick Advertiser-Photo News, 25 Railroad Ave, Warwick NY 10990 ...914-986-2061
Warwick Valley Dispatch, 2 Oakland Ave, Warwick NY 10990 914-986-2216
Watertown Daily Times*, 260 Washington St, Watertown NY 13601 315-782-1000
Webster Herald, 2010 Empire Blvd, Webster NY 14580.............................716-671-1533
Weekender, 163 Dreiser Loop, Bronx NY 10475 212-671-1234
Weisbeck Publishing & Printing, 132200 Broadway, Alden NY 14004......716-937-9226
Wellsville Daily Reporter*, 159 N Main St, Wellsville NY 14895 716-593-5300
West Hempstead Beacon, 80 N Franklin St, Hempstead NY 11550 516-483-4100
West Seneca Front Page, 2703 S Park Ave, Lackawanna NY 14218............716-823-8222
West Seneca Observer, 951 Ridge Rd, Lackawanna NY 14218....................716-822-4700
West Side Herald, 30 Irving Pl, Long Island City NY 10003......................212-777-6810
West Side Times, 2503 Delaware, Buffalo NY 14216.................................716-873-2594
Westbury Times, 132 E 2nd St, Mineola NY 11501....................................516-747-8282
Westbury Times, 57 Old Country Rd, Westbury NY 11590 516-334-3362
Westchester Business Journal, 217 Harrison Ave, Harrison NY 10528 914-835-4600
Westchester County Press, 61 Pinecrest, Hastings-Hudson NY 10706 914-478-0006
Westsider, 56 W 22nd St, New York NY 10010 212-989-5761
White Plains Reporter Dispatch*, 1 Gannett, White Plains NY 10604......914-694-9300
Whitehall Times, 6 Williams, Whitehall NY 11978 516-288-1100
Whitney Pt Reporter, 12 S Chenango St, Greene NY 13778........................607-656-4511

Woodside Herald, 45-08 Skillman Ave, Sunnyside NY 11104......................212-937-1234
Yankee Trader+, 1110 Hallock Ave, Port Jefferson Sta NY 11776............516-331-3300
Yonkers Herald Statesman*, 733 Yonkers Ave, Yonkers NY 10704.........914-965-5000
Yonkers Home News & Times, 40 Larkin Plaza, Yonkers NY 10701.........914-965-4000

NORTH CAROLINA

Aberdeen Sandhill Citizen, 202 N Sandhill Blvd, Aberdeen NC 28315......919-944-2356
Anson Messenger & Intelligencer, Box 192, Wadesboro NC 28170...........704-694-2318
Anson Record, Box 959, Wadesboro NC 28170......................................704-694-2161
Asheboro Courier-Tribune*, 152 N Fayeteville St, Asheville NC 27203....919-625-2101
Asheville Citizen*+, 14 O Henry Ave, Asheville NC 28802......................704-252-5611
Bertie Ledger-Advance, 124 S King, Windsor NC 27983............................919-794-3185
Bladen Journal, PO Box 67, Elizabethtown NC 28337................................919-862-4163
Blowing Rocket, Box 1026, Blowing Rock NC 28605................................704-295-7522
Boone Watauga Democrat, Box 353, Boone NC 28607..............................704-264-3612
Brevard Transylvania Times, Box 32, Brevard NC 28712..........................704-883-8156
Brunswick Beacon, Box 470, Shallotte NC 28459....................................919-754-6890
Burlington Daily Times-News*, 707 S Main St, Burlington NC 27215.......919-227-0131
Burnsville Yancey Journal, Box 280, Burnsville NC 28714........................704-682-2120
Butner-Creedmoor News, 418 N Main, Creedmoor NC 27522....................919-528-2393
Carteret County News, 4018 Arendell St, Morehead City NC 28557...........919-726-7081
Cary News, 212 E Chatham St, Cary NC 27511......................................919-467-2231
Caswell Messenger, Box 100, Yanceyville NC 27379................................919-694-4145
Chapel Hill Newspaper*, 505 W Franklin St, Chapel Hill NC 27514.........919-967-7945
Charlotte News*, 600 S Tryon St, Charlotte NC 28202............................704-379-6300
Charlotte Observer*+, 600 S Tryon St, Charlotte NC 28202....................704-379-6300
Clemmons Courier, Box 765, Clemmons NC 27012..................................919-766-4126
Cleveland Publishers, 213 S Washington St, Shelby NC 28150..................710-487-7264
Concord Tribune*, 125 Union St S, Concord NC 28025............................704-782-3155
Davie County Enterprise, S Main St, Mocksville NC 27028......................704-634-2129
Dunn Daily Record*, Box 1448, Dunn NC 28334..................................919-892-3117
Durham Morning Herald*+, 115 Market St, Durham NC 27702...............919-682-8181
Durham Sun*, 115 Market St, Durham NC 27702..................................919-682-8181
Eden Daily News*, 804 Washington St, Eden NC 27288............................919-623-2155
Elizabeth City Daily Advance*, 216 S Poindexter, Eliz City NC 27909......919-335-0841
Elkin-Jonesville Tribune, 113 W Market St, Elkin NC 28621....................919-835-1513
Enfield Progress, Franklin St, Enfield NC 27823....................................919-826-4161
Enquirer-Journal*, 500 W Jefferson St, Monroe NC 28110......................704-289-1541
The Enterprise, 218 W 1st St, Rutherfordton NC 28139............................704-287-3327
The Enterprise, Box 268, Canton NC 28716..704-648-2381
Fayetteville Observer*, 458 Whitfield St, Fayetteville NC 28302................919-323-4848
Fayetteville Times*, 458 Whitfield St, Fayetteville NC 28302....................919-323-4848
Franklin Press, 246 Depot St PO Box 350, Franklin NC 28734..................704-524-2010
Garner News, Box 466, Garner NC 27529..919-722-1166
Gastonia Gazette*, 2500 E Franklin Blvd, Gastonia NC 28053..................704-864-3293
Goldsboro News-Argus*, 310 N Berkeley Blvd, Goldsboro NC 27532.......919-778-2211
Graham Alamance News, 114 W Elm St, Graham NC 27253......................919-228-7851
The Graphic, PO Box 1008, Nashville NC 27856....................................919-459-7101
Greensboro A&T Register, Box E 25, Greensboro NC 27411....................919-379-7700
Greensboro Daily News*+, 200 E Market, Greensboro NC 27420............919-373-7222
Greensboro News & Record*+, 200 E Market, Greensboro NC 27420.....919-373-1000
Greenville Daily Reflector*, 209 Cotanche St, Greenville NC 27834..........919-752-6166

Halifax County, Box 40, Scotland Neck NC 27874 919-826-4161
Henderson Daily Dispatch*, 304 Chestnut St, Henderson NC 27536........919-492-4001
Hendersonville Times-News*, Box 490, Hendersonville NC 28739.............704-692-0505
Hickory Daily Record*, 116 3rd St NW PO Box 968, Hickory NC 28603..704-322-4510
Hickory News, 270 Union Square Common, Hickory NC 28601..................704-328-6164
High Point Enterprise*, 210 Church St, High Point NC 27261...................919-885-2161
Jacksonville Daily News*, Bell Fork Rd, Jacksonville NC 28540.................919-353-1171
Journal-Patriot, 711 Main St, N Wilkesboro NC 28659............................919-838-4117
Kannapolis Daily Independent*, 119 N Main St, Kannapolis NC 28081...704-933-2181
Kernersville News, 300 E Mountain St, Kernersville NC 27284.................919-993-2161
King Times News, PO Drawer 11506, Winston Salem NC 27106...............919-765-2883
Kings Mountain Mirror-Herald, Drawer 752, Kings Mtn NC 28086.........704-739-7496
Kinston Daily Free Press*, 2103 N Queen St, Kinston NC 28501.............919-527-3191
Laurinburg Exchange, 211 Cronly St, Laurinburg NC 28352....................919-276-2311
Lexington Dispatch*, 30 E 1st Ave, Lexington NC 27292........................704-249-3981
Lincoln Times-News, 119 W Water St, Lincolnton NC 28092...................704-735-3031
Louisburg Franklin Times, 109 S Bickett Blvd, Louisburg NC 27549........919-496-6503
Madison Messenger, Box 508, Madison NC 27025...................................919-548-6047
Manteo Coastland Times, 501 Budleigh St, Manteo NC 27954.................919-473-2105
Marshville Union News and Home, 201 E Union, Marshville NC 28103...701-624-5068
McDowell News, N Logan St, Marion NC 28752.....................................704-652-3313
Mecklenburg Gazette, Box 548, Davidson NC 28036..............................704-892-8809
Montgomery Herald, 139 Bruton St, Troy NC 27371.............................919-576-6051
Mooresville Tribune, 147 E Center Ave, Mooresville NC 28115..............704-664-5554
Morganton News-Herald*, 301 Collett St, Morganton NC 28655.............704-437-2161
Mt Airy News, 319 Renfro St, Mt Airy NC 27030..................................919-786-4141
Mt Airy Times, Box 608, Mt Airy NC 27030..919-789-9025
Mt Olive Tribune, Hwy 55 West, Mt Olive NC 28365.............................919-658-9456
Murphy Cherokee & Andrews Journal, 1 Church St, Murphy NC 28906..704-837-5122
New Bern Sun-Journal*, 226 Pollock St, New Bern NC 28560..................919-638-8101
News & Observer*+, 215 S McDowell St, Raleigh NC 27602.....................919-829-4500
News of Orange County, PO Box 580, Hillsborough NC 27278.................919-732-2171
News Outlook, US 1 South, Southern Pines NC 28387.............................919-692-9600
News-Herald, 116 N McGlohon St, Ahoskie NC 27910............................919-332-2123
News-Messenger, 105 E Washington St, Rockingham NC 28379...............919-582-1675
North Carolina Anvil, 821 Morgan St, Durham NC 27701.......................919-688-9544
North Carolina Independent, PO Box 2690, Durham NC 27705................919-286-1815
Northampton News, PO Box 705, Jackson NC 27845..............................919-534-6911
Observer-News-Enterprise*, 307 N College Ave, Newton NC 28658.........704-464-0221
Oxford Public Ledger, Corner of Spring & Wall, Oxford NC 27565.........919-693-2646
Pender Chronicle, 210 Courthouse Ave, Burgaw NC 28245.....................919-259-2351
Pender Post, Fremont & Walker, Burgaw NC 28245...............................919-259-9111
Raeford News-Journal, 119 W Elwood Ave, Raeford NC 28376...............919-875-2121
Raleigh Carolinian, 518 E Martin St, Raleigh NC 27601..........................919-834-5558
Raleigh Times*, 215 S McDowell St, Raleigh NC 27602..........................919-829-4500
Randolph Guide, 431 S Fayetteville St, Asheboro NC 27203....................919-625-5576
Reidsville Review*, 225 Turner Dr, Reidsville NC 27320.........................919-349-4331
Richmond County Journal*, 105 Washington, Rockingham NC 28379.....919-997-3111
Roanoke Beacon, Box 726, Plymouth NC 27962....................................919-793-2123
Roanoke Rapids Daily Herald*, Box 520, Roanoke Rpds NC 27870.........919-537-2505
Robesonian*, 121 W 5th St, Lumberton NC 28359.................................919-739-4322
Rocky Mount Telegram*, 150 Howard St, Rocky Mt NC 27801...............919-446-5161
Roxboro Courier-Times, 109 Clayton Ave, Roxboro NC 27573................919-599-0162

Rutherford County News, 218 W 1st St, Rutherfordton NC 28139.............704-287-3327
Salisbury Post*, 131 W Innes St, Salisbury NC 28144 704-633-8950
Sampson Independent*, 303 Elizabeth St, Clinton NC 28328 919-592-8137
Sanford Daily Herald*, 208 St Clair Ct, Sanford NC 27330.......................919-776-0531
Scotland Neck Commonwealth, Main St, Scotland Neck NC 27874...........919-626-4161
Shelby Star*, 315 E Graham St, Shelby NC 28150.......................................704-484-7000
Siler City Chatham News, Box 290, Siler City NC 27344 919-633-2320
Smithfield Herald, 125 S 4th St, Smithfield NC 27577.................................919-934-2176
Southern Pines Pilot, 145 W Pennslyvania, Southern Pines NC 28387 919-692-7271
Spring Hope Enterprise, 113 Ash St, Spring Hope NC 27882.....................919-478-3651
Spruce Pine Tri-County News, 123 Locust, Spruce Pine NC 28777............710-765-2071
Stanly News & Press, 241 W North St, Albermarle NC 28001 704-982-2121
Star of Zion, 401 E 2nd St, Charlotte NC 28231..704-377-4329
Star-News*+, 1003 S 17th St, Wilmington NC 28403 919-343-2000
State Port Pilot, 105 S Howe St, Southport NC 28461..................................919-457-6473
Statesville Record & Landmark*, 222 E Broad St, Statesville NC 28677..704-873-1451
Sylva Herald & Ruralite, 24 E Main PO Box 307, Sylva NC 28779............704-586-2611
Tabor City Tribune, Hwy 701 N, Tabor City NC 28463 919-653-3153
Tarboro Southerner*, 504 Wilson St, Tarboro NC 27886............................919-823-3106
Taylorsville Times, Box 278, Taylorsville NC 28681....................................704-632-2532
Thomasville Times*, 512 Turner St, Thomasville NC 27360 919-475-2151
Tryon Daily Bulletin*, 106 N Trade St, Tryon NC 28782............................704-859-9151
Wadesboro Messenger & Intelligencer, Box 192, Wadesboro NC 28170...704-694-2318
Wake Weekly, 504 S White St, Wake Forest NC 27587.................................919-556-3182
Wallace Enterprise, 113 N College St, Wallace NC 28466............................919-285-2178
Warrenton Warren Record, 413 N Main, Waynesboro NC 28786.................704-452-0661
Washington Daily News*, 217 Market St, Washington NC 27889.................919-946-2144
West Jefferson Skyland Post, Box 67, W Jefferson NC 28694......................919-246-4121
Whiteville News Reporter, 127 W Columbus St, Whiteville NC 28472.......919-642-4104
Williamston Enterprise, 106 W Main St, Williamston NC 27892 919-792-1181
Wilmington Morning Star*, 1003 S 17th St, Wilmington NC 28403...........919-343-2000
Wilson Daily Times*, 2001 Downing St Extension, Eilson NC 27893 919-243-5151
Winston-Salem Journal*+, 416 N Marshall, Winston-Salem NC 27102 ...919-727-7211
Winston-Salem Suburbanite, 3443 Robinhood, Winston-Slm NC 27106...919-765-2883
Yadkin Enterprise, Drawer 11506, Winston-Salem NC 27106 919-765-2883
Yadkin Rippie, Box 7, Yadkinville NC 27055..919-679-2341

NORTH DAKOTA

Benson County Farmers Press, 4318 B Ave, Minnewaukan ND 58351.....701-473-5436
Bismarck Tribune*, 707 E Front Ave, Bismarck ND 58501 701-223-2500
Bottineau Courant, 419 Main St, Bottineau ND 58318 701-228-2605
Bowman Finder, 212 S Main, Bowman ND 58623.......................................701-523-5623
Cass County Reporter, 122 6th Ave N, Casselton ND 58012.......................701-347-4493
Cavalier County Republican, 306 5th Ave, Langdon ND 58249..................701-256-5311
Dickinson Press*, 127 W 1st St, Dickinson ND 58601................................701-225-8141
Emmons County Record, 201 N Broadway, Linton ND 58552.....................701-254-4537
Fargo Forum*+, 101 N 5th St, Fargo ND 58102...701-235-7311
Grafton Record, 402 Hill Ave, Grafton ND 58237 701-352-0640
Grand Forks Herald*, 114 N 4th St, Grand Forks ND 58201 701-775-4211
Harvey Herald, Box 189, Harvey ND 58341..701-324-4646
Jamestown Sun*, 122 2 St NW, Jamestown ND 58401................................701-252-3120
The Journal, 217 N Main, Crosby ND 58730 701-965-6088

Midweek Eagle, 322 Sheyenne St, West Fargo ND 58078 701-282-2443
Minot Daily News*, 301 4th St SE, Minot ND 58701 701-852-3341
Northwood Gleaner, Box C, Northwood ND 58267 701-587-6126
Pierce County Tribune, 219 S Main, Rugby ND 58368 701-776-5252
Ransom County Gazette, 310 Main St, Lisbon ND 58054 701-683-4128
Turtle Mountain Star, Box 849, Rolla ND 58367 701-477-3182
Valley City Times-Record*, 140 3rd St NE, Valley City ND 58072 701-845-0463
Wahpeton-Breckenridge News*, 601 Dakota, Wahpcton ND 58075 701-642-8585
Walsh County Press, Box 49, Park River ND 58270 701-284-6333
Williston Herald*, 14 W 4th St, Williston ND 58801 701-572-2165

OHIO

Ace News, 409 S 22nd St, Heath OH 43056 614-522-3166
The Advertiser, 1014 N Main St, Bellefontaine OH 43311 513-599-4270
The Advocate*, 25 W Main St, Newark OH 43055 614-345-4053
Akron Beacon Journal*+, 44 E Exchange St, Akron OH 44328 216-375-8111
Alliance Review*, 40 S Linden Ave, Alliance OH 44601 216-821-1300
Anthony Wayne Herald, 1514 W Bancroft St, Toledo OH 43606 419-475-1501
Archbold Buckeye, 207 N Defiance St, Archbold OH 43502 419-445-4466
Ashland Times-Gazette*, 40 E 2nd St, Ashland OH 44805 419-323-1581
Ashtabula County Sentinel, 46 W Jefferson St, Jefferson OH 44047 216-576-9115
Ashtabula Star-Beacon*, 4626 Park Ave, Ashtabula OH 44004 216-998-2323
Athens Messenger*, Rte 33 N & Johnson Rd, Athens OH 45701 614-592-6612
Austintown Leader, 35 W State St, Niles OH 44446 216-530-5449
Barberton Herald, 70 4th St NW, Barberton OH 44203 216-753-1068
Barnesville Enterprise, 162 E Main St, Barnesville OH 43713 614-425-1912
Beavercreek Daily News*, 1342 N Fairfield Rd, Dayton OH 45432 513-426-5222
Bedford Sun Banner, 32914 Solon Rd, Cleveland OH 44139 216-349-0240
Bedford Times-Register, 711 Broadway, Cleveland OH 44146 216-232-4055
Beford Sun Banner, 5510 Cloverleaf Pkwy, Cleveland OH 44125 216-524-0830
Bellefontaine Examiner*, 127 E Chillicothe, Bellefontaine OH 43311 513-592-3060
Bellevue Gazette*, 107 N Sandusky St, Bellevue OH 44811 419-483-4190
Berea News Sun, 5510 Cloverleaf Pkwy, Cleveland OH 44125 216-524-0830
Bluffton News, 103 N Main St, Bluffton OH 45817 419-358-8010
Boardman News, 6221 Market St, Youngstown OH 44512 216-758-2658
Booster, 4100 N High St, Columbus OH 43214 614-267-3175
Brimfield Tribune-Gazette, 3982 St Rt 43, Kent OH 44240 216-673-5040
Brown County Press, 470 W Main, Mt Orab OH 45154 513-732-2511
Brunswick Sun Times, 5510 Cloverleaf Pkwy, Cleveland OH 44125 216-524-0830
Bryan Times*, 127 S Walnut, Bryan OH 43506 419-636-1111
Bucyrus Telegraph Forum*, 117 W Rensselaer St, Bucyrus OH 44820 419-562-3333
Cadiz Harrison News-Herald, 136 S Main St, Cadiz OH 43907 614-942-2118
Caldwell Journal-Leader, 309 Main St, Caldwell OH 43724 614-732-2341
Canal Fulton Signal, 123 N Canal St, Canal Fulton OH 44614 216-854-4549
Canal Winchester Times, 935 Walnut St, Canal Winchester OH 43110 614-837-3441
Canton Repository*+, 500 Market Ave S, Canton OH 44702 216-454-5611
Carey Progressor-Times, 109 W Findley St, Carey OH 43316 419-396-7567
Carrollton Free Press-Standard, Box 37, Carrollton OH 44615 216-627-5591
Celina Daily Standard*, 123 E Market, Celina OH 45822 419-586-2371
Centerville-Bellbrook Times, 54 Marco Ln, Centerville OH 45459 513-435-7273
Chagrin Valley Herald Sun, 32914 Solon Rd, Cleveland OH 44139 216-349-0240
Chagrin Valley Times, 34 S Main St, Chagrin Falls OH 44022 216-274-5335

Chillicothe Gazette*, 50 W Main St, Chillicothe OH 45601........................614-773-2111
Cincinnati Enquirer*+, 617 Vine St, Cincinnati OH 45201......................513-721-2700
Clermont County Review, 6124 Corbly Rd, Cincinnati OH 45230..............513-231-6221
Clermont Courier, 564 Batavia Pike, Cincinnati OH 45224.......................513-528-1111
Clermont Sun, 465 E Main St PO Box 366, Batavia OH 45103....................513-732-2511
Cleveland Plain Dealer*+, 1801 Superior Ave, Cleveland OH 44120........216-344-4500
Cleveland South End News, 8815 Broadway, Cleveland OH 44105.............216-441-2032
Columbus Citizen-Journal*+, 34 S 3rd St, Columbus OH 43216..............614-461-5000
Columbus Dispatch*+, 34 S 3rd St, Columbus OH 43216........................614-461-5000
Columbus Northland News, PO Box 20921, Columbus OH 43220..............614-451-1212
Community Journal North, 564 Batavia Pike, Cincinnati OH 45224.........513-528-1111
Conneaut News-Herald*+, 182 Broad St, Conneaut OH 44030..................216-593-1166
The Courier*, 701 W Sandusky St, Findlay OH 45840................................419-422-5151
Crosrent News*, Perry & 2nd Sts, Defiance OH 43512..............................419-784-5441
Daily Advocate*, W Main at Sycamore, Greenville OH 45331....................513-548-3151
Daily Chief-Union*, 111 W Wyandot, Upper Sandusky OH 43351...........419-294-2331
Daily News & Journal Herald*+, 45 S Ludlow, Dayton OH 45401.........513-225-2421
Daily Sentinel-Tribune*, 300 E Poe, Bowling Green OH 43402................419-352-4611
Darke County Early Bird, 114 W George St, Arcanum OH 45304.............513-692-5102
Delaware Gazette*, 18 E Williams, Delaware OH 43015............................614-363-1161
Delphos Daily Herald*, 405 N Main, Delphos OH 45833.........................419-692-5050
Delta Atlas, 212 Main St, Delta OH 43515..419-822-3231
East Liverpool Evening Review*, 210 E 4th St, E Liverpool OH 43920.....216-385-4545
Eastern Hills Journal, 564 Batavia Pike, Cincinnati OH 45224.................513-528-1111
Elyria Chronicle-Telegram*, 225 East Ave, Elyria OH 44036....................216-329-7000
Erie County Reporter, 615B S Main St PO Box 128, Huron OH 44839.....419-433-5983
Euclid Sun Journal, 5510 Cloverleaf Pkwy, Cleveland OH 44125.............216-524-0830
Evening Independent*, 50 North Ave NW, Massillon OH 44646...............216-833-2631
Fairborn Daily Herald*, 1 Herald Square, Fairborn OH 45324................513-878-3993
Fairfield Echo, 5120 Dixie Hwy, Hamilton OH 45014................................513-829-7900
Fairfield Leader, 108 N Main St PO Box 248, Baltimore OH 43105..........614-862-8223
Fostoria Review Times*, 113 E Center St, Fostoria OH 44830...................419-435-6641
Franklin Chronicle, 522 S Main St, Franklin OH 45005............................513-746-3691
Fremont News-Messenger*, 1700 Cedar St, Fremont OH 43420................419-332-5511
Fulton County Expositer, 201 N Fulton, Wauseon OH 43567....................419-335-2010
Galion Inquirer*, 378 N Market St, Galion OH 44833..............................419-468-1117
Gallipolis Daily Tribune*, 825 3rd Ave, Gallipolis OH 45631...................614-446-2342
Garfield/Maple Hts Sun, 5510 Cloverleaf Pkwy, Cleveland OH 44125.....216-524-0830
Geauga Times Leader*+, 111 Water St, Chardon OH 44024.....................216-286-6101
Greenfield Daily Times*, 345 Jefferson, Greenfield OH 45123..................513-981-2141
Grove City Record, 3451 Grant Ave, Grove City OH 43123.......................614-875-2307
Hamilton-Fairfield Journal-News*, 288 Court St, Hamilton OH 45011....513-863-8200
Herald Sun, 5510 Cloverleaf Pkwy, Cleveland OH 44125.........................216-524-0830
Hillsboro Press Gazette*, 209 S High St, Hillsboro OH 45133.................513-393-3456
Hilltop News, 5505 Cheviot Rd, Cincinnati OH 45247...............................513-661-8352
Holmes County Farmer-Hub, 4 N Clay St, Millersburg OH 44654.............216-674-5676
Huber Heights Courier, 7089 Taylorsville Rd, Dayton OH 45424.............513-236-4990
Indian Lake Advertiser, 395 S High St, Covington OH 45318....................513-473-2028
Ironton Tribune*, 2903 S 5th St, Ironton OH 45638................................614-532-1441
Jackson Journal Herald, 295 Broadway St, Jackson OH 45640.................614-286-2187
The Journal*, 1657 Broadway, Lorain OH 44052.....................................216-245-6901
Kent-Ravenna Record-Courier*, 126 N Chestnut, Ravenna OH 44266.....216-296-9657
Kenton Times*, 201 E Columbus, Kenton OH 43326................................419-674-4066

Kettering-Oakwood Times, 3484 Far Hills Ave, Kettering OH 45429........513-294-7000
Lakewood Sun Post, 5510 Cloverleaf Pkwy, Cleveland OH 44125...............216-524-0830
Lancaster Eagle-Gazette*, 138 W Chestnut St, Lancaster OH 43103.........614-654-1321
The Leader, 71 N Market St, E Palestine OH 44413................................216-426-9481
Lebanon Star, 200 Harmon Ave, Lebanon OH 45036................................513-932-3010
Lima News*, 121 E High St, Lima OH 45802 419-223-1010
Lima Sentinel, 2519 Shawnee Rd, Cridersville OH 45806....................419-991-2242
Lisbon Morning Journal*, 308 W Maple, Lisbon OH 44432.....................216-424-9541
Logan Daily News*, 72 E Main St, Logan OH 43138................................614-385-2107
London Madison Press*, 30 S Oak St, London OH 43140......................614-852-1616
Lorain County Times, Box 516, Lorain OH 44052...............................216-288-1111
Louisville Herald, 308 S Mill St, Louisville OH 44641.........................216-875-5610
Main St Press, 88 N Main St, Rittman OH 44270................................216-925-4040
Manchester Signal, 414 E 7th St, Manchester OH 45144 513-549-2800
Mansfield News Journal*+, 70 W 4th St, Mansfield OH 44901 419-522-3311
Maple Heights Press, 711 Broadway, Cleveland OH 44146...................216-232-4055
Marietta Times*, 700 Channel Lane, Marietta OH 45750.....................614-373-2121
Marion Star*, 150 Court St, Marion OH 43302 614-387-0400
Marysville Journal-Tribune*, 207 N Main St, Marysville OH 43040.........513-644-9111
Maumee Valley Herald, 1514 W Bancroft St, Toledo OH 43606 419-475-1501
Medina County Gazette*, 885 W Liberty St, Medina OH 44256...............216-725-4166
Mercer County Chronicle, Walnut & Market, Coldwater OH 45828.........419-678-2324
Miamisburg News, 230 S 2nd St, Miamisburg OH 45342........................513-866-3331
Middletown Journal*, 52 South Broad, Middletown OH 45044 513-422-3611
Milford-Loveland Area Mailer, Box 366, Batavia OH 45103.................513-732-2511
Millcreek Valley News, 5505 Cheviot Rd, Cincinnati OH 45247...............513-661-8352
Minerva Leader, 111 Short St, Minerva OH 44657 216-868-5164
Monroe County Beacon, 103 E Court St, Woodsfield OH 43793...............614-472-0734
Morgan County Herald, 89 W Main St, McConnelsville OH 43756...........614-962-3377
Morning Journal*, 308 Maple St, Lisbon OH 44432.............................216-424-9541
Morrow County Sentinel, 18 W High St, Mount Gilead OH 43338...........419-946-3010
Mount Vernon News*, Box 791, Mt Vernon OH 43050.........................614-397-5333
Mount Washington Press, 6124 Corbly Rd, Cincinnati OH 45230 513-231-6221
Napoleon Northwest Signal*, East Riverview, Napoleon OH 43545..........419-592-5055
New Philadelphia Times-Reporter*, 629 Wabash, New Phila OH 44663 ..216-364-5577
Newcomerstown News, 140 Main St, Newcomerstown OH 43832............614-498-7117
News-Herald*, 115 W 2nd, Port Clinton OH 43452 419-734-3141
News-Herald*, 38879 Mentor Ave, Willoughby OH 44094 216-951-0004
Niles Daily Times*, 35 W State St, Niles OH 44446.............................216-652-5841
North Ridgeville Light, 35836 Center Ridge Rd, Elyria OH 44039 216-327-2173
Norwalk Reflector*, 61 E Monroe St, Norwalk OH 44857....................419-668-3771
Norwood Enterprise, 5505 Cheviot Rd, Cincinnati OH 45247..................513-661-8352
Oregon News, 2154 Woodville Rd, Toledo OH 43616 419-693-0561
Orrville Courier Crescent, 409 N Main St, Orrville OH 44667................216-682-2055
Ottawa County Exponent, 106 Locust St, Oak Harbor OH 43449............419-898-5361
Oxford Press, 15 S Beech St, Oxford OH 45056................................513-523-4139
Painesville Telegraph*+, 84 N State St, Painesville OH 44077................216-354-4333
Parma Sun Post, 5510 Cloverleaf Pkwy, Cleveland OH 44125...............216-524-0830
Paulding Progress, 113 S Williams St, Paulding OH 45879 419-399-4015
Penny Saver, 395 S High St, Covington OH 45318...............................513-473-2028
Photo Star, 307 State St, Willshire OH 45898....................................419-495-2696
Piqua Daily Call*, 121 E Ash St, Piqua OH 45356...............................513-773-2721
Point & Shoreland Journal, 5198 N Summit St, Toledo OH 43611 419-729-2855

Pomeroy Daily Sentinel*, 111 Court St, Pomeroy OH 45769 614-992-2155
Portage Lakes Herald, 70 4th St NW, Barberton OH 44203 216-753-1068
Portsmouth Daily Times*, 637 6th St, Portsmouth OH 45662 614-353-3101
Press Newspapers+, 1550 Woodville, Millbury OH 43447 419-836-2221
Press-News, 200 W Church, E Canton OH 44730 216-488-1266
Pulse-Journal, 108 W Main St, Mason OH 45040...513-398-8856
Putnam County Sentinel, 232 E Main St, Ottawa OH 45875 419-523-5709
Record Herald*, 138 S Fayette, Washington Ct House OH 43160 614-335-3611
Register-Herald, 105 W Main, Eaton OH 45320 513-456-5553
Rocky Fork Enterprise, 77 Mill St, Columbus OH 43230 614-471-1600
Rural-Urban Record, 24487 Squires Rd, Columbia Station OH 44028......216-236-8982
Saint Marys Leader*, 102 E Spring St, St Marys OH 45885.......................419-394-7414
Salem Farm & Dairy, 185 E State St, Salem OH 44460 216-337-3419
Salem News*, 161 N Lincoln Ave, Salem OH 44460 216-332-4601
Sandusky Register*, 314 W Market St, Sandusky OH 44870 419-625-5500
Shelby Globe*, 37 W Main St, Shelby OH 44875...419-342-4276
Sidney Daily News*, 911 Vandemark Rd, Sidney OH 45365 513-498-2111
Solon Herald Sun, 32914 Solon Rd, Cleveland OH 44139 216-349-0240
Solon Times, 34 S Main St, Chagrin Falls OH 44022....................................216-274-5335
Star Free Press, 25 E Franklin St, Springboro OH 45066..............................513-748-2550
Steubenville Herald-Star*, 401 Herald Sq, Steubenville OH 43952 614-283-4711
Stillwater Valley Advertiser, 395 S High St, Covington OH 45318 513-473-2028
Stow Sentry, 1619 Commerce Dr, Stow OH 44224 216-688-0088
Strongville-N Royalton Sun, 5510 Cloverleaf, Cleveland OH 44125 216-524-0830
Struthers Journal, 23 Lowellville Rd, Struthers OH 44471 216-755-2155
Sugarcreek Budget, 134 N Factory St, Sugarcreek OH 44681 216-852-4634
Sun Banner Pride, 5510 Cloverleaf Pkwy, Cleveland OH 44125.................216-524-0830
Sun Courier, 5510 Cloverleaf Pkwy, Cleveland OH 44125...........................216-524-0830
Sun Herald, 5510 Cloverleaf Pkwy, Cleveland OH 44125 216-524-0830
Sun Messenger, 5510 Cloverleaf Pkwy, Cleveland OH 44125.....................216-524-0830
Sun Observer, 5510 Cloverleaf Pkwy, Cleveland OH 44125........................216-524-0830
Sun Press, 5510 Cloverleaf Pkwy, Cleveland OH 44125..............................216-524-0830
Sun Scoop Journal, 5510 Cloverleaf Pkwy, Cleveland OH 44125 216-524-0830
Sun Times Sentinel, 811 Pearl Rd, Brunswick OH 44212............................216-225-8110
Sunbury News, 40 S Vernon St, Sunbury OH 43074 614-965-3891
Sunday Messenger*, Rte 33 N & Johnson Rd, Athens OH 45701.............614-592-6612
Sunday Times-Sentinel*, 825 3rd Ave, Gallipolis OH 45631......................614-446-2342
Sycamore Messenger News, 9409 Mongomery, Cincinnati OH 45242........513-791-5600
Sylvia Herald, 1514 W Bancroft St, Toledo OH 43606.................................419-475-1501
Tiffin Advertiser-Tribune*, 320 Nelson St, Tiffin OH 44883......................419-447-4455
The Times, 211 Myrtle Ave, Willard OH 44890...419-935-0184
Times-Leader*, 200 S 4th St, Martins Ferry OH 43935 614-633-1131
Tipp City Herald, 1455 W Main St, Tipp City OH 45371.............................513-667-2214
Toledo Blade*+, 541 Superior St, Toledo OH 43660...................................419-245-6000
Tri-Village News, 919 Old W Henderson Rd, Columbus OH 43220...........614-451-1212
Tribune Shopping News, 117 S Main St, New Lexington OH 43764 614-342-4121
The Tribune*, 550 Main St, Coshocton OH 43812..614-622-1122
Troy Daily News*, 224 S Market St, Troy OH 45373 513-335-5634
Upper Arlington News, 919 Old W Henderson, Columbus OH 43220.......614-451-1212
Urbana Daily Citizen*, 220 E Court St, Urbana OH 43078.........................513-652-1231
Van Wert Times-Bulletin*, 700 Fox Rd, Van Wert OH 45891 419-238-6397
Vandalia Chronicle, 319 Kenbrook, Vandalia OH 45377.............................513-898-3977
Vermillion Photojournal, 651 Main St, Vermillion OH 44089 216-967-5268

The Vindicator*+, Vindicator Square, Youngstown OH 44501....................216-747-1471
Vinton County Courier, 100 N Market St, McArthur OH 45651.................614-596-5393
The Voice, 615B S Main St PO Box 128, Huron OH 44839.........................419-433-5983
Wadsworth News-Banner, 115 Watrusa Ave, Wadsworth OH 44281.........216-334-2561
Wapaloneta Daily News*, 8 Willipie St, Wapakoneta OH 45895.................419-738-2128
Warren Tribune Chronicle*, 240 Franklin St SE, Warren OH 44482........216-841-1600
Wellston Sentry, 22 S Ohio Ave, Wellston OH 45692................................614-384-6786
West Life, 26943 Westwood Rd, Cleveland OH 44145................................216-871-5797
West Side Sun News, 5510 Cloverleaf Pkwy, Cleveland OH 44125.............216-524-0830
West Toledo Herald, 1514 W Bancroft St, Toledo OH 43606....................419-475-1501
Western Star, 200 Harmon Ave, Lebanon OH 45036................................513-932-3010
Westerville Public Opinion, 130 Graphic Way, Westerville OH 43081......614-882-2244
Westlaker Times, Box 516, Lorain OH 44052..216-288-1111
Wheelersburg Scioto Voice, 8019 Hayport Rd, Wheelersburg OH 45694..614-574-8494
Wilmington News-Journal*, 47 S South St, Wilmington OH 45177............513-382-2574
Wintersville Citizen, 734 Main St, Steubenville OH 43952........................614-264-4303
Wooster Daily Record*, 212 E Liberty St, Wooster OH 44691..................216-264-1125
Worthington News, 666 High St, Worthington OH 43085.........................614-885-5131
Xenia Daily Gazette*, 37 S Detroit St, Xenia OH 45385...........................513-372-4444
Zanesville Times-Recorder*, 34 S 4th St, Zanesville OH 43701.................614-452-4561

OKLAHOMA

Altus Times*, 218 W Commerce, Altus OK 73521.....................................405-482-1221
Alva Review-Courier*, 620 Choctaw, Alva OK 73717................................405-327-2200
Anadarko Daily News*, 117 E Broadway, Anadarko OK 73005...................405-247-3331
Ardmore Daily Arfmoreite*, 117 W Broadway, Ardmore OK 73402.........405-223-2200
Bethany Tribune-Review, 3813 N College, Bethany OK 73008...................405-789-1962
Blackwell Journal-Tribune*, 113 E Blackwell, Blackwell OK 74631.........405-363-3370
Capitol Hill Beacon+, 124 W Commerce, Oklahoma City OK 73109........405-232-4151
Chandler Lincoln County News, 718 Manvel Ave, Chandler OK 74834....405-258-1818
Cherokee County Chronicle, Grovers Corner, Tahlequah OK 74464.........918-456-5257
Chickasha Daily Express*, 302 N 3rd St, Chickasha OK 73018..................405-224-2600
Clinton Daily News*, 522 Avant Ave, Clinton OK 73601...........................405-323-5151
Cordell Beacon, 115 E Main St, Cordell OK 73632....................................405-832-3333
Coweta Times-Star, Box 40, Wagoner OK 74477......................................918-485-5505
Cushing Daily Citizen*, 115 S Cleveland St, Cushing OK 74023...............918-225-3333
Daily Oklahoman*+, 500 N Broadway, Oklahoma City OK 73125.............405-232-3311
Daily Phoenix & Times Democrat*, 214 Wall St, Muskogee OK 74401.....918-682-3311
Del City News, 513 SE 29th St, Oklahoma City OK 73115.........................405-672-6777
Duncan Banner*, 1001 Elm St, Duncan OK 73533....................................405-255-5354
Durant Daily Democrat*, 200 W Beech, Durant OK 74701.......................405-924-4388
Eastside Times, 8545 E 41st St, Tulsa OK 74145......................................918-663-1414
Edmond Evening Sun*, 123 S Broadway, Edmond OK 73034.....................405-341-2121
El Reno Tribune*, 201 N Rock Island, El Reno OK 73036..........................405-262-5180
Elk City Daily News Inc*, PO Box 1037, Elk City OK 73648.....................405-225-3000
Enid Daily Eagle*, 227 W Broadway, Enid OK 73702...............................405-233-6600
Enid Morning News*, 227 W Broadway, Enid OK 73701...........................405-233-6600
Examiner-Enterprise*, 300 E Frank Phillips, Bartlesville OK 74003.......918-336-1600
Frederick Daily Leader*, 304 W Grand, Frederick OK 73542....................405-335-2188
Grove Sun, 14 W 3rd St, Grove OK 74344...918-786-2228
Guthrie Leader*, 107 W Harrison, Guthrie OK 73044..............................405-282-2222
Guymon Daily Herald*, 515 N Ellison, Guymon OK 73942.......................405-338-3355

Henryetta Daily Free-Lance*, 812 W Main, Henryetta OK 74437..............918-652-3311
Hobart Democrat-Chief*, 216 W 4th, Hobart OK 73651 405-726-3333
Hugo News*, 128 E Jackson, Hugo OK 74743 405-326-3311
Idabel McCurtain Gazette*, 107 S Central, Idabel OK 74745.....................405-286-3321
Jenks Journal, Box 100, Jenks OK 74037 918-299-9463
Kingfisher Times, 323 N Main St, Kingfisher OK 73750.............................405-375-3220
Lawton Constitution*, 102 S 3rd St Box 648, Lawton OK 73501 405-353-0620
Lawton Morning Press*, 102 S 3rd St, Lawton OK 73501 405-353-0620
Le Flore County Sun, 319 Dewey St, Poteau OK 74953 918-647-3188
Madill Record, Box 529, Madill OK 73446..405-795-3355
Moore American, 2324 N Janeway, Oklahoma City OK 73160....................405-794-5555
Norman Transcript*, 215 E Comanche, Norman OK 73070....................405-321-1800
Oklahoma City Friday, 10801 N Quail Plz Dr, Okla City OK 73120..........405-755-3311
Oklahoma City North Star+, 2925 NW 64th, Oklahoma City OK 73156..405-840-3636
Oklahoma City Times*+, 500 N Broadway, Oklahoma City OK 73125 405-232-3311
Oklahoma Gazette+, PO Box 2178, Oklahoma City OK 73101 405-235-0798
Okmulgee Times*, 114 E 7th, Okmulgee OK 74447 918-756-3600
Pauls Valley Democrat*, 108 S Willow, Pauls Valley OK 73075 405-238-6464
Pawhuska Journal-Capital*, 700 Ki-He-Kah, Pawhuska OK 74056...........918-287-1590
Perry Daily Journal*, 714 Delaware, Perry OK 73077 405-336-2222
Pictorial Press, W 2nd St, Tahlequah OK 74464..918-456-8833
Ponca City News*, 300 N 3rd St, Ponca City OK 74601...............................405-765-3311
Poteau News & Sun, 906 Central, Poteau OK 74953...918-647-3188
Pryor Jeffersonian, 32 S Adair, Pryor OK 74362..918-825-1300
Puarcell Register, 225 W Main, Purcell OK 73080..405-527-2126
Sand Springs Times, 303 N McKinley Ave, Sand Springs OK 74063.........918-245-6634
Sapulpa Daily Herald*, 16 S Park, Sapulpa OK 74066....................................918-224-5185
Seminole Producer*, 121 N Main, Seminole OK 74868 405-382-1100
Sequoyah County Times, 111 N Oak, Sallisaw OK 74955 918-775-4433
Shawnee News-Star*, 215 N Bell, Shawnee OK 74801.....................................405-273-4200
Stigler News-Sentinel, Box 310, Stigler OK 74462...918-967-4655
Stillwater News-Press*, 211 W 9th, Stillwater OK 74074 405-372-5000
Stilwell Democrat-Journal, Box 508, Stilwell OK 74960.................................918-696-2228
Tahlequah Star Citizen, West 2nd, Tahlequah OK 74464 918-456-8833
This Week*+, 7430 SE 15th, Oklahoma City OK 73110.....................................405-737-8811
Tulsa County News, 8545 E 41st St, Tulsa OK 74145 918-663-1414
Tulsa Southside Times, 7941 E 57, Tulsa OK 74145..918-665-0770
Tulsa Star, 8939 E 60th St, Tulsa OK 74145 918-584-7314
Tulsa Tribune*+, 315 S Boulder Ave, Tulsa OK 74102..................................918-581-8400
Tulsa World*+, 318 S Main, Tulsa OK 74102..918-581-8300
Vinita Daily Journal*, 138 S Wilson, Vinita OK 74301 918-256-6422
Wagoner Record-Democrat, Box 40, Wagoner OK 74477............................918-485-5505
Wagoner Tribune, Box 40, Wagoner OK 74477...918-485-5505
Watonga Republican, 104 E Main, Watonga OK 73772.................................405-623-4922
Weatherford Daily News*, 118 S Broadway, Weatherford OK 73069 401-772-3301
Woodward Daily Press*, 1023 Main, Woodward OK 73801.......................405-256-6582
Woodward News*+, PO Box 928, Woodward OK 73802.............................405-256-2200
Yukon Review, 110 S 5, Yukon OK 73099..405-354-5264

OREGON

Albany Democrat-Herald*, 138 6th St, Albany OR 97321.............................503-926-2211
Aloha Breeze, 150 SE 3rd Ave, Hillsboro OR 97123...................................503-648-1131
Baker Record-Courier, 1718 Main, Baker OR 97814 503-523-5353
Beaverton Valley Times, 9730 SW Cascade Blvd, Portland OR 97223.......503-684-0360
Bend Bulletin*, 1526 NW Hill St, Bend OR 97701......................................503-382-1811
Canby Herald, 241 N Grant, Canby OR 97013...503-266-6831
Capital Press, 1400 Broadway NE, Salem OR 97308 503-364-4431
Clackamas County Review, 14631 McLoughlin, Milwaukie OR 97222......503-653-1732
Coos Bay World*, 350 Commercial, Coos Bay OR 97420.............................503-269-1222
Corvallis Gazette-Times*, 600 SW Jefferson Ave, Corvallis OR 97330.....503-753-2641
Cottage Grove Sentinel, 116 N 6th St, Cottage Grove OR 97424...............503-942-3325
Curry Coast Pilot, 507 Chetco Ave, Brookings OR 97415............................503-469-3123
Curry County Reporter, Box 766, Gold Beach OR 97444..............................503-247-6643
Daily Astorian*, 949 Exchange St PO Box 210, Astoria OR 97103.............503-325-3211
Daily Journal of Commerce*, 2014 NW 24th Ave, Portland OR 97210.....503-226-1311
Daily Tidings*, 1661 Siskiyou Blvd, Ashland OR 97520 503-482-3456
Dalles Chronicle*, 4th & Federal, The Dalles OR 97058..............................503-296-2141
Democrat-Herald*, 1915 1st St, Baker OR 97814.......................................503-523-3673
Enterprise-Courier*, 10th & Main, Oregon City OR 97045.........................303-656-1911
Grants Pass Daily Courier*, 409 SE 7th St, Grants Pass OR 97526 503-474-3700
Gresham Outlook, Box 880, Gresham OR 97030...503-665-2181
Herald & News*, Pine at Esplanade, Klamath Falls OR 97601.....................503-883-4000
Hermiston Herald, 158 E Main, Hermiston OR 97838.................................503-567-6457
Hood River News, 409 Oak, Hood River OR 97031......................................503-386-1234
Lebanon Express, PO Box 459, Lebanon OR 97355.....................................503-258-3151
Madras Pioneer, 452 6th St, Madras OR 97741..503-475-2275
Medford Mail Tribune*, 33 N Fir St, Medford OR 97501............................503-776-4411
Newberg Graphic, 109 N School St, Newburg OR 97132 503-538-2181
Newport News-Times, Box 965, Newport OR 97365......................................503-265-8571
News Guard, 930 SE Hwy 101, Lincoln City OR 97367...............................503-994-2178
News-Register, 611 3rd St, McMinnville OR 97128......................................503-472-5114
The Observer*, 1406 5th St, La Grande OR 97850 503-963-3161
Ontario Daily Argus Observer*, 1160 SW 4th St, Ontario OR 97914........503-889-5387
Pendleton East Oregonian*, 211 SE Byers Ave, Pendleton OR 97801 503-276-2211
Polk County Itemizer-Observer, 147 SE Court St, Dallas OR 97338.........503-623-2373
Portland Business Today*, 2014 NW 24th Ave, Portland OR 97210 503-226-1311
Portland Observer, 1463 NE Killingsworth, Portland OR 97208 503-283-2486
Portland Oregon Journal*+, 1320 SW Broadway, Portland OR 97201....503-221-8275
Portland Orgonian*+, 1320 SW Broadway, Portland OR 97201...............503-221-8327
Prineville Central Oregonian, 558 N Main, Prineville OR 97754 503-447-6205
Redmond Spokesman, 226 N 6th St, Redmond OR 97756 503-548-2184
Register-Guard*+, 975 High St, Eugene OR 97401......................................503-485-1234
Roseburg News-Review*, 345 NE Winchester, Roseburg OR 97470...........503-672-3321
Saint Helens Chronicle, 195 S 15th St, St Helens OR 97051 503-397-0116
Saint Johns Review, 8410 N Lonbard, Portland OR 97203 503-286-0321
Salem Oregon Statesman*, 280 Church St NE, Salem OR 97309 503-399-6611
Sandy Post, 17270 Bluff Rd PO Box 68, Sandy OR 97055 503-668-5548
Seaside Signal, 113 N Holladay PO Box 848, Seaside OR 97138................503-738-5561
Silverton Appeal-Tribune, Box 35, Silverton OR 97381..............................503-873-8385
Siuslaw News, 148 Maple St, Florence OR 97439...503-997-3441

Springfield News, Box 139, Springfield OR 97477.................................503-746-1671
Statesman Journal*+, 280 Church St NE, Salem OR 97309.......................503-399-6611
Stayton Mail, Box 400, Stayton OR 97383..503-769-6338
Sun-Enterprise, 1697 Monmouth St, Independence OR 97351....................503-838-3467
Sweet Home New Era, 1200 Long St, Sweet Home OR 97386.....................503-367-2135
This Week Magazine+, 6960 SW Sandburg St, Portland OR 97223...........503-620-4121
Tilamook Headlight-Herald, 1908 2nd St, Tillamook OR 97141.................503-842-7535
Valley Times, 12490 SW Main St, Portland OR 97223.............................503-639-2118
Washington County News Times, 12490 SW Main, Portland OR 97223....503-639-2118
Washington County News, 2014 A St, Forest Grove OR 97116 503-357-3181
Willamette Week, 2 NW 2nd Ave, Portland OR 97209..............................503-243-2122
Wilsonville Times+, 12490 SW Main St, Portland OR 97223 503-639-2118

PENNSYLVANIA

Abington Journal, 406 S State St, Clarks Summit PA 18411....................717-587-1148
Advance Leader, 610 Beatty Rd, Monroeville PA 15146 412-856-7400
Advance of Bucks County, 444 S State St, Newtown PA 18940.................215-968-2244
Advertiser, Box 929, Canonsburg PA 15317..412-561-0700
Advisor, 229 Pittsburgh St, Scottdale PA 15683.....................................412-887-7400
Allegany Reporter Shopper, 403 Locust St, Turtle Creek PA 15145 412-823-7163
Allied News, 113 N Broad St, Grove City PA 16127...............................412-458-5010
Altoona Mirror*, 1000 Green Ave, Altoona PA 16601.............................814-946-7411
Ambler Gazette, 95 E Butler Ave, Ambler PA 19002 215-646-5100
Ardmore Main Line Chronicle, 19 E Lancaster, Ardmore PA 19003........215-642-1567
Ardmore Main Line Times, 19 E Lancaster, Ardmore PA 19003...............215-642-1567
Barnesboro Star, 520 Philadelphia Ave, Barnesboro PA 15714................814-948-6210
Beaver County Times*+, 400 Fair Ave, Beaver PA 15009.......................412-775-3200
Bedford County Shoppers Guide, 100 Masters Ave, Everett PA 15537.....814-652-5191
Bedford Gazette*, 424 W Penn St, Bedford PA 15522.............................814-623-1151
Bellevue Suburban Life, 610 Beatty Rd, Monroeville PA 15146 412-856-7400
Bentleyville Courier*, 440 W Main, Monongahela PA 15063....................412-258-7000
Berwick Enterprise*, 3185 Lackawanna Ave, Bloomsburg PA 17815 717-784-2121
Blair County Shopper's Guide, 100 Masters Ave, Everett PA 15537.........814-652-5191
Boyertown Area Times, 124 N Chestnut St, Boyertown PA 19512.............215-367-6041
Braddock Free Press, 725 Talbot Ave, Braddock PA 15104.....................412-271-0622
Bradford Era*, 43 Main St, Bradford PA 16701......................................814-368-3173
Bradford Journal, 165 Interstate Pkwy, Bradford PA 16701....................814-362-6563
Brookville American, 175 Main St, Brookville PA 15825 814-849-5338
Bucks County Advisor, 6220 Ridge Ave, Philadelphia PA 19128..............215-483-7300
Bucks County Courier Times*+, 8400 Rt 13, Levittown PA 19057...........215-752-6701
Bucks County Telegraph, 390 Easton Rd, Horsham PA 19044..................215-675-8250
Bucks County Tribune, Box 365, Langhorne PA 19047............................215-675-6600
Burlington County News Weekly+, 6220 Ridge Ave, Phila PA 19128........215-483-7300
Butler County News, Box 160, Zelienople PA 16063 412-452-7040
Butler Eagle*, 114 W Diamond, Butler PA 16001...................................412-282-8000
Call Chronicle Newspaper*+, 101 N 6th St, Allentown PA 18102............215-820-6500
Cameron County Echo, Box 308, Emporium PA 15834 814-486-3711
Canonsburg Daily Notes*, 112 E Pike St, Canonsburg PA 15317.............412-745-6400
Carbondale News, 41 N Church St, Carbondale PA 18407 717-282-3300
Carlisle Sentinel*, 457 E North St, Carlisle PA 17013.............................717-243-2611
Central Delaware County Town Talk, Box 110, Media PA 19063..............215-566-6755
Centre Daily Times*, 3400 E College Ave, State College PA 16801..........814-238-5000

Centre Democrat, 106 N Allegheny St, Bellefonte PA 16823......................814-355-4881
Chambersburg Public Opinion*, 77 N 3rd St, Chambersburg PA 17201 ..717-264-6161
Chestnut Hill Local, 8434 Germantown Ave, Philadelphia PA 19118........215-248-1880
Citizen-Standard, 100 W Main St, Valley View PA 17983..........................717-682-9081
Clarion News, 645 Main St, Clarion PA 16214..814-226-7000
Columbia News*, 341 Chestnut St, Columbia PA 17512 717-684-2125
Connellsville Daily Courier*, 127 W Apple St, Connellsville PA 15425 412-628-2000
Corry Journal*, 28 W South St, Corry PA 16407 814-655-8291
Cosmopolite-Herald, West High St, Union City PA 16438..........................814-438-7666
County Leader, 3405 West Chester Pike, Newtown Square PA 19073.......215-356-3820
County Observer, Box 521, Reedsville PA 17084 717-667-2611
County Press, 3405 West Chester Pike, Newtown Square PA 19073..........215-356-3820
Courier-Express*, Long & High, Du Bois PA 15801..................................814-371-4200
Daily American*, Box 638, Somerset PA 15501...814-445-9621
Daily Intelligencer*, 333 W Broad St, Doylestown PA 18901.....................215-345-3000
Daily Item*, 200 Marker St, Sunbury PA 17801...717-286-5671
Daily Local News*, 250 N Bradford, West Chester PA 19380 215-696-1776
Daily News*, 13 S Main St, Bangor PA 18013...215-588-2196
Daily Press*, 245 Brussells St, St Marys PA 15857...................................814-781-1596
Daily Review*, 116 Main St, Towanda PA 18848.......................................717-265-2151
Daily Times*+, 205 W 12th St, Erie PA 16534 814-456-8531
Danville News*, 14 Mahoning St, Danville PA 17821 717-275-3235
Delaware County Daily Times*+, 500 Mildred, Clifton Hts PA 19018......215-622-8800
Democrat-Messenger*, 32 S Church St, Waynesburg PA 15370 412-627-6166
Drexel Hill Leader, 3405 West Chester Pike, Newtown Sq PA 19073....215-356-3820
East Penn Free Press, 408 Chestnut St, Emmaus PA 18049......................215-965-6031
Elizabethtown Chronicle, 9 N Market St, Elizabethtown PA 17022........717-367-7152
Ellwood City Ledger*, 835 Lawrence Ave, Ellwood City PA 16117............412-758-7529
Ephrata Review, 50 E Main St, Ephrata PA 17522 717-733-2244
Erie Morning News*, 205 W 12th St, Erie PA 16534 814-456-8531
Evening Times*, 201 N Lehigh Ave, Sayre PA 18840 717-888-9643
The Express*, 30 N 4th St, Easton PA 18042...215-258-7171
Feasterville Spirit, 101 N York Rd, Hatboro PA 19040 215-675-3430
Fishtown Star, 250 W Girard Ave, Philadelphia PA 19123........................215-925-7827
Forest Press, 165 Elm St, Tionesta PA 16353..814-755-4900
Fulton County News, E Market & 5th, McConnellsburg PA 17233............717-485-3811
The Gazette, 610 Beatty Rd, Monroeville PA 15146 412-856-7400
Germantown Paper, 6220 Ridge Ave, Philadelphia PA 19128.....................215-483-7300
Gettysburg Times*, 18 Carlisle St, Gettysburg PA 17325..........................717-334-1131
Girard Cosmopolite-Herald, 106 Vine St, Girard PA 16417 814-774-9648
Girard Home News, 1015 Chestnut, Philadelphia PA 19107......................215-923-8087
Glenside News, 466 Johnson St, Jenkintown PA 19046..............................215-884-4775
Globe Times*, 202 W 4th St, Bethlehem PA 18015....................................215-867-5000
The Globe, 466 Johnson St, Jenkintown PA 19046.....................................215-884-4775
Green Tab+, 2519 Universal Rd, Pittsburgh PA 15235 412-795-3300
Greensburg Tribune Review*+, Cabin Hill Dr, Greensburg PA 15601.....412-834-1151
Greenville Record-Argus*, 10 Penn Ave, Greenville PA 16125..................412-588-5000
Grit+, 208 W 3rd St, Williamsport PA 17701 717-326-1771
Hamburg Item, Box 31, Hamburg PA 19526...215-562-7515
Hanover Evening Sun*, 135 Baltimore St, Hanover PA 17331...................717-637-3736
Harrisburg Patriot-News*+, 812 Market St, Harrisburg PA 17105...........717-255-8278
Hazleton Standard Speaker*, 21 N Wyoming, Hazleton PA 18201 717-455-3636
Hershey Sun, 115 S Water St, Hummelstown PA 17036 717-566-3251

In Pittsburgh, PO Box 4286, Pittsburgh PA 15203......................................412-488-1212
Independent & Enterprise News, Box 704, Edinboro PA 16412 814-734-1234
Independent Observer, 229 Pittsburgh St, Scottdale PA 15683 412-887-6101
The Independent, 350 Walnut, Collegeville PA 19426 215-489-3001
Indiana Gazette*, 899 Water St, Indiana PA 15701 412-465-5555
Irwin Standard-Observer*, Box 280, Irwin PA 15642.............................412-863-3601
Jeannette News-Dispatch*, 227 S 4th St, Jeannette PA 15644....................412-523-5541
Jeannette Spirit, 310 Clay Ave, Jeannette PA 15644.................................412-527-2868
Jeffersonian Democrat, 175 Main St, Brookville PA 15825 814-849-5338
Johnstown Observer, 215 Cambria Savings Bldg, Johnstown PA 15907 814-534-1715
Johnstown Tribune Democrat*+, 425 Locust St, Johnstown PA 15907.....814-535-8651
The Journal, 1049 Brookline Blvd, Pittsburgh PA 15226............................412-531-1505
The Journal, 3623 Brownsville Rd, Pittsburgh PA 15227 412-884-3111
Juniata Sentinel, Old Rt 22 RD 3, Mifflintown PA 17059 717-436-8206
Kane Republican*, 200 N Fraley St PO Box 838, Kane PA 16735 814-837-6000
Kennett News & Advertiser, 107 N Union, Kennett Sq PA 19348 215-444-3678
King of Prussia Today's Post*, 160 N Gulph Rd, Norristown PA 19406...215-337-1700
Kittanning Leader Times*, 115 N Grant Ave, Kittanning PA 16201..........412-543-1303
Lancaster Intelligencer Journal*, 8 W King St, Lancaster PA 17603 717-291-8811
Lansdale Reporter*, 307 Derstine Ave, Lansdale PA 19446 215-855-8440
Latrobe Bulletin*, 1211 Ligonier St, Latrobe PA 15650.............................412-537-3251
Laurel Highlands Scene, 229 Pittsburgh St, Scottdale PA 15683.................412-887-7400
Leader-Vindicator, 435 Broad St, New Bethlehem PA 16242.......................814-275-3131
Lebanon Daily News*, S 8th & Poplar Sts, Lebanon PA 17042....................717-272-5611
Lehighton Times News*, 1st & Iron Sts, Lehighton PA 18235 215-377-2051
Lewistown Sentinel*, 6th & Summitt, Lewistown PA 17044 717-248-6741
Ligonier Echo, 112 W Main St, Ligonier PA 15658....................................412-238-2111
Lock Haven Express*, 9 W Main St, Lock Haven PA 17745 717-748-6791
Marcus Hook Press, 3245 Garret Rd, Drexel Hill PA 19026 215-259-4141
McKeesport Daily News*, 401 Walnut, McKeesport PA 15134....................412-664-9161
Meadville Tribune*, 947 Federal Ct, Meadsville PA 16335 814-724-6370
Middletown Press and Journal, 109 Poplar St, Middletown PA 17057......717-944-4628
Milton Standard*, 19 Arch St, Milton PA 17847 717-742-9671
Monessen Valley Independent*, Eastgate 19, Monessen PA 15062............414-684-5200
Montgomery Transcript, 350 Walnut, Collegeville PA 19426 215-489-3001
Montgomeryville Spirit, 290 Commerce Dr, Ft Washington PA 19034.....215-646-5100
Montomery County Record*, 333 W Broad St, Doylestown PA 18901......215-345-3000
Montrose Independent, 10 S Main St, Montrose PA 18801...........................717-278-1141
Morning Press*, 3185 Lackawanna, Bloomsburg PA 17815 717-784-2121
Morrisons Cove Herald, 113 N Market St, Martinsburg PA 16662.............814-793-2144
Mount Joy Merchandiser, Rt 230 W, Mt Joy PA 17552................................717-653-1833
Mount Pleasant Journal, 23 S Church St, Mt Pleasant PA 15666 412-547-2322
Mountaineer Herald, 113 S Center St, Ebensburg PA 15931 814-472-8240
New Castle News*, 27 N Mercer St, Newcastle PA 16103 412-654-6651
New Era*+, 8 W King St, Lancaster PA 17604...717-291-8811
New Hope Gazette, 6220 Ridge Ave, Philadelphia PA 19128.......................215-483-7300
News Eagle, 522 Spring St, Hawley PA 18428 717-226-4547
News of Delaware Cty, 9138 W Chester Pike, Upper Darby PA 19082.......215-352-5400
The News+, 1181 Airport Rd, Aliquippa PA 15001 412-375-6611
News-Sun, 19 S 3rd St, Newport PA 17074 717-567-6226
Newville Valley Times-Star, 51 Big Spring Ave, Newville PA 17241...........717-776-3197
Norristown Times Herald*, Markley & Airy St, Norristown PA 19401.....215-272-2500
North East Breeze, 35 S Lake St, North East PA 16428 814-725-4557

North Hills News Record, 9825 Perry Hwy, Pittsburgh PA 15237 412-366-0545
North Star, 250 W Girard Ave, Philadelphia PA 19123 215-925-7827
Northeast Advisor, 6220 Ridge Ave, Philadelphia PA 19128.......................215-483-7300
Northeast Breeze, 6220 Ridge Ave, Philadelphia PA 19128.........................215-483-7300
Northeast Times+, 8033 Frankford Ave, Philadelphia PA 19136 215-332-3300
Observer-Reporter*, 122 S Main St, Washington PA 15301 412-222-2200
The Patriot, PO Box 346 Rt 222 & Sharadin Rd, Kutztown PA 19530.......215-683-7343
Pennsburg Town & Country, 4th St & Pottstown, Pennsburg PA 18073 ...215-679-9561
Perkasie News-Herald, 320 S 7th St, Perkasie PA 18944.............................215-257-6839
Perry County Times, Box 128, New Bloomfield PA 17068..........................717-582-4305
Philadelphia Daily News*+, 400 N Broad St, Philadelphia PA 19101........215-854-5900
Philadelphia Guide Newspapers, 3800 Kensington, Phila PA 19124..........215-288-2400
Philadelphia Inquirer*+, 400 N Broad St, Philadelphia PA 19101.............215-854-2000
Philadelphia Jewish Exponent+, 226 S 16th St, Philadelphia PA 19102....215-893-5740
Philadelphia Jewish Times, 2417 Welsh Rd, Philadelphia PA 19114 215-464-3900
Philadelphia News Gleaner+, 1612 Margaret, Philadelphia PA 19124.......215-535-4275
Philadelphia Tribune Co, 520 S 16th St, Philadelphia PA 19146 212-546-1005
Phoenixville Evening Phoenix*, 225 Bridge St, Phoenixville PA 19460 215-933-8926
Pike County Dispatch, 105 W Catherine St, Milford PA 18337 717-296-6641
Pittsburg Oakland News, 234 Meyran Ave, Pittsburgh PA 15213................412-683-4500
Pittsburgh Herald, 1024 Main St, Pittsburgh PA 15215 412-782-2121
Pittsburgh Post Gazette*+, 50 Blvd of the Allies, Pittsburgh PA 15222....412-263-1100
Pittsburgh Union, 1719 Liberty Ave, Pittsburgh PA 15222.........................212-281-8533
Pittston Sunday Dispatch, 109 New St, Pittston PA 18640 717-655-1418
Pocono Shopper+, Rt 7 Box 7497, Stroudsburg PA 18360 717-421-4492
Port Royal Times, 4th & Milford, Port Royal PA 17082 717-527-2213
Portage Dispatch, 709 Caldwell Ave, Portage PA 15946............................814-736-9666
The Post, 29 W Market St Box 356, Middleburg PA 17842..........................717-837-6065
Potter Enterprise, Box 29, Coudersport PA 16915......................................814-274-8044
Pottstown Mercury*, King & Hanover Sts, Pottstown PA 19464...................215-323-3000
Pottsville Republican*, 111 Mahantongo St, Pottsville PA 17901................717-622-3456
The Progress*, 206 E Locust St, Clearfiled PA 16830 814-765-5581
The Progress, 390 Easton Rd, Horsham PA 19044......................................215-675-8250
The Progress, 610 Beatty Rd, Monroeville PA 15146 412-856-7400
Prospect Park Interboro News, 816 11th Ave, Prospect Park PA 19076....215-532-0316
Punxsutawney Spirit*, 107 N Findley St, Punxsutawney PA 15767.............814-938-8740
Quakertown Free Press Journal, 312 W Broad, Quakertown PA 18951 ...215-536-6820
Quakertown Free Press*, 312 W Broad, Quakertown PA 18951 215-536-6820
Ravine Press-Herald, Box 8, Ravine PA 17966..717-345-4455
Reading Berks County Record & Press, 18 S 5th St, Reading PA 19601...215-376-2901
Reading Eagle*+, Box 582, Reading PA 19603..215-373-4221
Reading Times*, 345 Penn St, Reading PA 19603.......................................215-373-4221
The Record*, 204 E Lincoln Hwy, Coatesville PA 19320.............................215-384-4900
The Record, 705 5th Ave, Coraopolis PA 15108 412-264-4140
Record-Outlook, 115 Barr St, McDonald PA 15057.....................................412-926-2111
The Recorder, 813 Fayette St, Conshohocken PA 19428.............................215-828-4600
Reporter of the Spring-Ford Area, 842 Oak St, Royersford PA 19468 215-948-4850
Richmond Star, 250 W Girard Ave, Philadelphia PA 19123.........................215-925-7827
Ridgway Record*, 20 Main St, Ridgway PA 15853.......................................814-773-3151
Ridley Press, 3245 Garret Rd, Drexel Hill PA 19026..................................215-259-4141
Roxborough Review, 6220 Ridge Ave, Philadelphia PA 19128 215-483-7300
Scranton Times*+, Penn Ave & Spruce St, Scranton PA 18505 717-348-9100
Scrantonian*+, 338 N Washington Ave, Scranton PA 18501.......................717-344-7221

Sewickley Herald, 514 Beaver St, Sewickley PA 15143 412-741-8200
Shamokin News-Item*, 707 N Rock St, Shamokin PA 17872 717-648-4641
Sharon Herald*, 34 S Dock St, Sharon PA 16146 412-981-6100
Shenandoah Evening Herald*, Ringtown Road, Shenandoah PA 17976...717-462-2777
Shippensburg News-Chronicle, Box 100, Shippensburg PA 17257 717-532-4101
Signal-Item, 20 E Mall Plaza, Carnegie PA 15106 412-276-4000
Souderton Independent, 21 S Front, Souderton PA 18964 215-723-4801
South Hills Record, 3623 Brownsville Rd, Pittsburgh PA 15227................412-884-3111
South Philadelphia Review, 12th & Porter Sts, Philadelphia PA 19148.....215-467-1100
South Pittsburgh Reporter, 1301 E Carson, Pittsburgh PA 15203 412-481-0266
Southampton Spirit, 101 N York Rd, Hatboro PA 19040 215-675-3430
Southern Delaware County, Box 110, Media PA 19063............................215-566-6755
SW Phila Globe Times, 6408 Woodland Ave, Philadelphia PA 19142........215-727-7777
Springfield Press, 204 Ballymore Rd, Springfield PA 19064 215-544-6660
Springfield Sun, 290 Commerce Dr, Ft Washington PA 19034...................215-646-5100
Stroudsburg Pocono Record*, 511 Lenox St, Stroudsburg PA 18360.........717-421-3000
Suburban Gazette, 421 Locust St, McKees Rocks PA 15136......................412-331-2645
Sullivan Review, Box 305, Dushore PA 18614................................717-928-8403
Sunday Bulletin*+, 30th & Market Sts, Philadelphia PA 19101.................215-662-7550
Sunday News*+, 8 W King St, Lancaster PA 17604 717-291-8811
Susquehanna County Press, 10 S Main St, Montrose PA 18801..................717-278-1141
Tarentum-News Kensington*, 4th & Wood, Tarentum PA 15084..................412-224-4321
Three Star Edition, 250 W Girard Ave, Philadelphia PA 19123 215-925-7827
Times Chronicle, 466 Johnson St, Jenkintown PA 19046 215-884-4775
Times Leader*+, 15 N Main St, Wilkes Barre PA 18701.........................717-829-7100
Times Sun, 201 1st St, West Newton PA 15089 412-872-6800
Times-Express, 610 Beatty Rd, Monroeville PA 15146 412-856-7400
Times-Leader, West High St, Union City PA 16438 814-438-7666
Times-News*+, 205 W 12th St, Erie PA 16534................................814-456-8531
Titusville Herald*, 209 W Spring, Titusville PA 16354 814-827-3634
Today's Post, 160 N Gulph Rd, Norristown PA 19406............................215-337-1700
Today's Spirit*, 101 N York Rd, Hatboro PA 19040............................215-675-3430
Town & Country East & Central, West High St, Union City PA 16438 814-438-7666
Town & Country, 165 Interstate Pkwy, Bradford PA 16701.......................814-362-6563
Town and Country West, Girard PA 16417......................................814-774-9648
Town Talk Aston-Brookhaven, Box 110, Media PA 19063.........................215-566-6755
Town Talk Newspaper+, 1300 MacDade Blvd, Folsom PA 19033 215-583-4432
The Tribune*, 338 N Washington Ave, Scranton PA 18501.......................717-344-7221
Tunkhannock New Age-Examiner, Box 59, Tunkhannock PA 18657..........717-836-2123
Tyrone Daily Herald*, 1018 Pennsylvania Ave, Tyrone PA 16686.............814-684-4000
Union Press-Courier, 452 Magee Ave, Patton PA 16668..........................814-674-3666
Uniontown Herald-Standard*, 8 E Church St, Uniontown PA 15401........412-439-7500
Upper Darby Press, 3245 Garret Rd, Drexel Hill PA 19026......................215-259-4141
Upper Dauphin Sentinel, 510 Union St, Millersburg PA 17061 717-692-3171
Valley Times-Star, 51 Big Spring Ave, Newville PA 17241......................717-776-3197
The Villager, Wilson Dr, Moscow PA 18444 717-842-8789
Warminster Spirit, 101 N York Rd, Hatboro PA 19040 215-675-3430
Warren Times Observer*, 205 Pennsylvania Ave W, Warren PA 16365....814-723-8200
Wayne Independent, 220 8th St, Honesdale PA 18431............................717-253-3055
Waynesboro Record Herald*, 30 Walnut St, Waynesboro PA 17268.........717-762-2151
Weekly Bulletin, 2-4 N Baltimore St, Dillsburg PA 17019......................717-432-5211
Weekly Recorder, 214 Main St, Claysville PA 15323............................412-663-7742
Wellsboro Gazette, 23 East Ave, Wellsboro PA 16901 717-724-2287

West Oak Lane Leader, 6220 Ridge Ave, Philadelphia PA 19128................215-483-7300
West Shore Times, 13 W Main St, Mechanicsbuarg PA 17055.....................717-766-9629
Westfield Free Press-Courier, 119 Main St, Westfield PA 16950 814-367-2230
Wilkes-Barre Independent*+, 90 E Market, Wilkes Barre PA 18701 717-822-3111
Williamsport Sun-Gazette*, 252 W 4th St, Williamsport PA 17701 717-326-1551
Willow Grove Guide, 131 N York Rd, Willow Grove PA 19090.................215-659-5600
Yardley News, 45 E Afton Ave, Morrisville PA 19067 215-493-2794
Yardley News, 6220 Ridge Ave, Philadelphia PA 19128 215-483-7300
York Daily Record*, 1750 Industrial Hwy, York PA 17402.......................717-757-4842
York Dispatch*+, 15 E Philadelphia St, York PA 17401 717-854-1575

RHODE ISLAND

Barrington Times, 1 Bradford St, Bristol RI 02809................................401-253-6000
Bristol Phoenix, 1 Bradford St, Bristol RI 02809...................................401-253-6000
Chariho Times, 854 Main St, Wakefield RI 02880 401-789-9744
Cranston Herald, 798 Park Ave, Cranston RI 02910 401-781-4240
Cranston Mirror, 250 Auburn St, Cranston RI 02910.............................401-467-7474
Cumberland Lincoln Observer, 1285 Mendon Rd, Pawtucket RI 02864...401-723-0404
Eastside Monthly, 305 S Main St, Providence RI 02903...........................401-521-0023
Evening Bulletin*+, 75 Fountain St, Providence RI 02902.......................401-277-7000
Evening Times*, 23 Exchange St, Pawtucket RI 02962..............................401-722-4000
Lincoln-Cumberland Observer News, Box 358, Greenville RI 02828.........401-949-2700
NewPaper, 131 Washington St, Providence RI 02903................................401-273-6397
Newport Daily News*, 101 Malbone Rd, Newport RI 02840......................401-849-3300
Newport Navalog, 101 Malbone Rd, Newport RI 02840............................401-849-3300
The Observer, Box 358, Greenville RI 02828 401-949-2700
The Packet, 101 Malbone Rd, Newport RI 02840.....................................401-849-3300
Pawtucket Valley Daily Times*+, 1353 Main, W Warwick RI 02983.........401-821-7400
Portsmouth Sakonnet Times, 2829 E Main Rd, Portsmouth RI 02871......401-683-1000
Providence Journal*+, 75 Fountain St, Providence RI 02902.....................401-277-7000
Providence Journal-Bulletin*+, 75 Fountain St, Providence RI 02902......401-277-7000
Rhode Island Pendulum, 22 London St, E Greenwich RI 02818 401-884-4662
Seekonk Star, 172 Tauton Ave, E Providence RI 02914...........................401-434-7210
Standard Times, 13 W Main St, N Kingstown RI 02852 401-294-4576
Warren Times Gazette, 1 Bradford St, Bristol RI 02809 401-253-6000
Warwick Beacon, 3288 Post Rd, Warwick RI 02886................................401-732-3100
Westerly Sun*, 56 Main St, Westerly RI 02891..401-596-7791
Woonsocket Call*, 75 Main St, Woonsocket RI 02895 401-762-3000

SOUTH CAROLINA

Aiken Standard*, 124 Rutland Dr, Aiken SC 29801 803-648-2311
Airlift Dispatch, 1929 Maybank Hwy, Charleston SC 29412.....................803-571-3684
Anderson Independent-Mail*, 1000 Williamston, Anderson SC 29622......803-224-4321
Bamberg Advertiser-Herald, 102 McGee St, Bamberg SC 29003 803-245-5204
Barnwell People Sentinel, Drawer 1255, Barnwell SC 29812....................803-259-3501
Batesburg Twin-City News, Box 311, Batesburg SC 29006.......................803-532-6203
Beaufort Gazette*, 1556 Salen Rd, Beaufort SC 29902............................803-524-3183
Bowhook, 1929 Maybank Hwy, Charleston SC 29412 803-571-3684
Charleston Chronicle, PO Box 2548, Charleston SC 29403......................803-723-2785
Charleston News & Courier*+, 134 Columbus, Charleston SC 29402......803-577-7111
Cheraw Chronicle, 114 Front St, Cheraw SC 29520 803-537-5261

Chester News & Reporter, 104 York St, Chester SC 29706 803-385-3177
Chronicle-Independent*, 1115 Broad St, Camden SC 29020.......................803-432-6157
Clemson Messenger, College Ave, Clemson SC 29631...............................803-654-2451
Clinton Chronicle, 513 N Broad St, Clinton SC 29325 803-833-1900
Columbia Record*, Stadium Rd, Columbia SC 29202...............................803-771-6161
Conway Field & Herald, 1025 3rd Ave, Conway SC 29526..........................803-248-6366
Darlington News & Press, 141 S Main, Darlington SC 29532.....................803-393-3811
Dillon Herald, 501 N 2nd Ave Hwy 301 N, Dillon SC 29536 803-774-3311
Dispatch-News, 115 E Main St, Lexington SC 29072 803-359-3195
Easley Progress, 208 Russell St, Easley SC 29640 803-855-0355
Evening Post*+, 134 Columbus St, Charleston SC 29402...........................801-577-7111
Florence Morning News*, 141 S Irby St, Florence SC 29501 803-669-1771
Fort Mill Times, 116 Main St, Ft Mill SC 29715.......................................803-547-2353
Gaffney Ledger, Baker Blvd, Gaffney SC 29342..803-489-1131
Georgetown Times, 615 Front St, Georgetown SC 29442............................803-546-4148
Greenville News*+, 305 S Main St, Geeenville SC 29602 803-298-4100
Greenville Piedmont*, 305 S Main St, Greenville SC 29602 803-298-4100
Greenwood Index-Journal*, Phoenix & Fair, Greenwood SC 29646..........803-223-1411
Greer Citizen, 105 Victoria, Greer SC 29651 803-877-2076
Hartsville Messenger, 207 E Carolina Ave, Hartsville SC 29550 803-332-6545
Herald-Journal*, Drawer 1657, Spartanburg SC 29304.............................803-582-4511
Hilton Head Island Packet, 1 Pope Ave Mall, Hilton Head Is SC 29928 ..803-785-4293
Lancaster News, 701 N White St PO Box 640, Lancaster SC 29720............803-286-2400
Landrum News Leader, 146 Trade, Landrum SC 29356...............................803-457-3337
Laurens County Advertiser, 226 W Laurens, Laurens SC 29360 803-984-2586
Marlboro Herald, 100 Fayetteville Ave, Bennettsville SC 29512................803-479-3815
Moultrie News, 1929 Maybank Hwy, Charleston SC 29412........................803-571-3684
Myrtle Beach Sun News*, PO Box 406, Myrtle Beach SC 29577................803-448-8351
Newberry Observer, 1716 Main St, Newberry SC 29108.............................803-276-0625
North Myrtle Beach Times, 203 N Kings, N Myrtle Bch SC 29582.............803-249-3525
Pickens Sentinel, Garvin St, Pickens SC 29671..803-878-2453
Press & Standard, 113 Washington St, Walterboro SC 29488.....................803-549-2586
Rock Hill Evening Herald*, 132 W Main St, Rock Hill SC 29731 803-329-4000
Sa Luda Standard Sentinel, Box 676, Saluda SC 29138 803-445-2527
Seneca Journal & Tribune, Box 547, Seneca SC 29678 803-882-2375
The Shopper, Box 115, West Columbia SC 29168 803-794-6610
Spartanburg Herald*, Drawer 1657, Spartanburg SC 29304.....................803-582-4511
Spartanburg Journal*, Drawer 1657, Spartanburg SC 29304.....................803-582-4511
The State*+, George Rogers Blvd, Columbia SC 29202.............................803-771-6161
Suburban News, PO Box 12110, Charleston SC 29412 803-762-0004
Sumter Daily Item*, 20 N Magnolia St, Sumter SC 29150 803-775-6331
Times & Democrat*, 211 Broughton SE, Orangeburg SC 29115 803-534-3352
Tribune-Times, 911 SE Main St PO Box 1179, Simpsonville SC 29681......803-963-8934
Union Daily Times*, 414 S Pinckney, Union SC 29379..............................803-427-1234
Weekly Observer, Main St, Hemingway SC 29554......................................803-558-3323

SOUTH DAKOTA

Aberdeen American News*, 124 S 2nd St, Aberdeen SD 57401....................605-225-4100
Argus Leader*+, 200 S Minnesota Ave, Sioux Falls SD 57102 605-331-2200
Belle Fourche Daily Post*, 1004 5th Ave, Belle Fourche SD 57717...........605-892-2528
Brookings Daily Register*, 312 5th St, Brookings SD 57006 605-692-6271
The Guide, 424 Quincy St, Rapid City SD 57709 605-342-0431

Huron Daily Plainsman*, 49 E 3rd St, Huron SD 57350 605-352-6401
Lead Call*, 7 S Main, Lead SD 57754..605-584-2303
Madison Daily Leader*, 218 S Egan Ave, Madison SD 57042 605-256-4555
Meade County Times-Tribune, 1238 Main St, Sturgis SD 57785................605-347-2503
Mitchell Daily Republic*, 120 S Lawler, Mitchell SD 57301........................605-996-5514
Pierre Daily Capital Journal*, 404 E Sioux Ave, Pierre SD 57501.............605-224-7301
Rapid City Guide, 424 Quincy St, Bethlehem SD 57709..............................605-342-0431
Rapid City Journal*, 507 Main, Bethlehem SD 57709 605-342-0280
Redfield Press, 16 E 7th Ave, Redfield SD 57469 605-472-0822
Sisseton Courier, 117 E Oak, Sisseton SD 57262..605-698-7642
Tri-State Livestock News, 1022 Main, Sturgis SD 57785 605-347-2585
Vermillion Plain Talk, 201 W Cherry St, Vermillion SD 57069 605-624-2695
Watertown Public Opinion*, 120 3rd Ave NW, Watertown SD 57201.......605-886-6901
Webster Reporter & Farmer, 624 Main, Webster SD 57274 605-345-3356
Winner Advocate, Box 71, Winner SD 57580 605-842-1481
Yankton Daily Press & Dakotan*, 319 Walnut, Yankton SD 57078...........605-665-7811

TENNESSEE

Alamo Crockett Times, 128 W Main, Alamo TN 38001 901-696-4558
Amusement Business, 14 Music Cir E, Nashville TN 37203 615-748-8120
Appalachian Observer-News, 121 Leinart St, Clinton TN 37716................615-562-7411
Athens Daily Post-Athenian Co Inc*, 320 S Jackson, Athens TN 37303....615-745-5664
Bolivar Bulletin-Times Inc, 410 W Market, Bolivar TN 38008....................901-658-3691
Brownsville States Graphic, 42 S Washington, Brownsville TN 38012.......901-772-1172
Camden Chronicle, 144 W Main, Camden TN 38320..................................901-584-7200
Carroll County News, 163 Court Sq, Huntingdon TN 38344 901-986-2253
Carthage Courier, 504 Main, Carthage TN 37030......................................615-735-1110
Chattanooga Times*, 117 E 10th St, Chattanooga TN 37402.....................615-756-1234
Claiborne Progress, 1001 Main St, Tazewell TN 37879...............................615-626-3222
Cleveland Daily Banner*, 1505 25th St NW, Cleveland TN 37311.............615-472-5041
Clinton Courier News, Box 270, Clinton TN 37716......................................615-457-2515
Collierville Herald, 139 N Main St, Collierville TN 38017 901-853-2241
Covington Leader, 2001 Hwy 51 S, Covington TN 38019 901-476-7116
Crossville Chronicle, 402 S Main St, Crossville TN 38555...........................615-484-5145
Cumberland County Times, Hwy 127 N, Crossville TN 38555....................615-484-7510
Daily Herald*, 1115 S Main St, Columbia TN 38402....................................615-388-6464
Daily News Journal*, 224 N Walnut, Murfreesboro TN 37130 615-893-5860
Democrat-Observer, Cook St, Madisonville TN 37354.................................615-442-4575
The Dispatch*, 1065 E 10th St, Cookeville TN 38501...................................615-528-5405
Dresden Enterprise, Box 139, Dresden TN 38225...901-364-2234
Dyer County Tennessean, 210 Main, Newbern TN 38059 901-627-3247
Dyer Tri-City Reporter, Box 266, Dyer TN 38330 901-692-3506
Elizabethton Star*, 300 Sycamore St, Elizabethton TN 37643 615-542-4151
Elk Valley Times Observer & News, 418 N Elk, Fayetteville TN 37334 615-433-6151
Erwin Record, 218 Gay St, Erwin TN 37650..615-743-4112
Franklin Review Appeal, 412 Main St, Franklin TN 37064 615-794-2555
Gatlinburg Mountain Vistor, Box 160, Pigeon Forge TN 37863................615-428-0746
Germantown News, 2150 S Germantown Rd, Memphis TN 38138.............901-754-0337
Giles County Shopper-Entertainer, 308 W College, Pulaski TN 38478 615-363-3544
Giles Free Press, Box E, Pulaski TN 38478 615-363-4548
Goodlettsville, Box 248, Goodlettsville TN 37748...615-882-1313
Grainger County News, Box 218, Rutledge TN 37861 615-828-5254

Greenville Sun*, 121 W Summer St, Greenville TN 37743 615-638-4181
Grundy County Herald, PO Box 188, Tracy City TN 37387 615-592-2781
Hendersonville Free Press, 131 Sanders Ferry, Hendersnvle TN 37075 615-822-1186
Hendersonville Star News+, Box 68, Hendersonville TN 37075.................615-824-8480
Herald Tribune, Box 277, Jonesboro TN 37659......................................615-753-3136
Humboldt Courier Chronicle, 2606 E End Dr, Humboldt TN 38343 901-784-2531
Jackson Sun*, 245 W Lafayette, Jackson TN 38301.................................901-427-3333
Jasper Journal, Box 398, Jasper TN 37347..615-942-2433
Johnson City Press-Chronicle*, 204 W Main, Johnson City TN 37601......615-929-3111
Kingsport Daily News*, 310 E Sullivan, Kingsport TN 37660....................615-246-4800
Kingsport Times-News*, 701 Lynn Garden Dr, Kingsport TN 37662 615-246-8121
Knoxville Journal*+, 210 W Church Ave, Knoxville TN 37901 615-522-4141
Knoxville News-Sentinel*+, 204 W Church Ave, Knoxville TN 37901.......615-523-3131
La Follette Press, Box 1261, La Follette TN 37766 615-562-8468
Lauderdale County Enterprise, 145 E Jackson Ave, Ripley TN 38063......901-635-1771
Lawrenceburg Democrat-Union, Box 685, Lawrenceburg TN 38464..........615-762-2222
Leaf Chronicle*+, 200 Commerce St, Clarksville TN 37040 615-552-1808
Lewisburg Tribune, 116 E Ewing, Lewisburg TN 37091............................615-359-1526
Lexington Progress, 23 N Broad St, Lexington TN 38351.........................901-968-6397
Livingston Enterprise, Box 129, Livingston TN 38570..............................615-823-1274
Macon County Times, Box 69, Lafayette TN 37083 615-666-2440
Manchester Times, 300 N Spring St, Manchester TN 37355.....................615-728-7577
Marshall Gazette, 116 E Ewing, Lewisburg TN 37091 615-359-1526
Maryville-Alcoa Times*, 307 S Harper Ave, Maryville TN 37801.............615-983-0260
McKenzie Banner, 255 Banner Row, McKenzie TN 38201........................901-352-3323
Memphis Commercial Appeal*+, 495 Union Ave, Memphis TN 38103 ...901-529-2345
Milan Mirror-Exchange, Box 549, Milan TN 38358.................................901-686-8114
Millington Star, 5107 Easley, Millington TN 38053 901-872-2286
Morning Times Dispatch, 1065 E 10th St, Cookeville TN 38502.............615-528-5405
Morristown Citizen Tribune*, 1609 W 1st N, Morristown TN 37814.........615-581-5630
Mountain City Tomahawk, PO Box 90, Mountain City TN 37683.............615-727-6121
Nashville Banner*+, 1100 Broadway, Nashville TN 37202.......................615-259-8800
Nashville Suburban News, 2700 Franklin Rd, Nashville TN 37204............615-383-6189
News Herald, 508 E Broadway, Lenoir City TN 37771 615-986-6581
News-Examiner, 360 Summer Hall Dr, Gallatin TN 37066.......................615-452-2561
News-Free Press*+, 400 E 11th St, Chattanooga TN 37401 615-756-6900
Oak Ridger*, 785 Oak Ridge Tpke, Oak Ridge TN 37830.......................615-482-1021
Paris Post-Intelligencer*, 208 E Wood St, Paris TN 38242 901-642-1162
Parsons News Leader, Box 339, Parsons TN 38363..................................901-847-2000
Pulaski Citizen, Box E, Pulaski TN 38478...615-363-4548
Robertson County Times, W Public Sq, Springfield TN 37172..................615-384-3567
Rockwood Times, Box 297, Rockwood TN 37854....................................615-354-9162
Rogersville Review, 207 Washington St, Rogersville TN 37857 615-272-7422
Rutherford Courier, Box 127, Smyrna TN 37167 615-459-3868
Savannah Courier, 801 Main St, Savannah TN 38372 901-925-6397
Scott County News, 224 Alberta Ave, Oneida TN 37841..........................615-569-8351
Selmer Independent Appeal, 111 N 2nd St, Selmer TN 38375...................901-645-5346
Sevier County News-Record, Commerce St, Sevierville TN 37862.............615-453-2895
Shelbyville Times-Gazette*, 323 E Depot St, Shelbyville TN 37160 615-684-1200
Smithville Review, 106 S 1st St, Smithville TN 37166...............................615-597-5485
South Pittsburg Hustler, 307 Elm Ave, S Pittsburg TN 37380...................615-837-7382
Sparta Expositor, 16 Liberty Square, Sparta TN 38583.............................615-836-3718
Springfield Herald, West Public Square, Springfield TN 37172..................615-384-3567

Standard Banner, 139 Andrew Johnson, Jefferson City TN 37760.............615-475-2081
State Gazette*, Hwy 51 By Pass, Dyersburg TN 38024.................................901-285-4091
Sullivan County News, 627 Central Ave, Blountville TN 37617 615-323-5700
The Tennessean*+, 1100 Broadway, Nashville TN 37202............................615-259-8000
Tennessee Republican, 108 2nd Ave, Huntingdon TN 38344.......................901-986-3751
Trenton Herald Gazette, 111 E 1st St, Trenton TN 38382...........................901-855-1711
Tri-County News, Chapman Hwy, Seymour TN 37865..................................615-577-5935
Union City Daily Messenger*, 613 E Jackson, Union City TN 38261 901-885-0744
Wayne County News, East Hollis St, Waynesboro TN 38485.......................615-722-5429
Weakley County Press, Box 410, Martin TN 38237......................................901-587-3144
Winchester Herald-Chronicle, 808 1st Ave NE, Winchester TN 37398.....615-967-2272

TEXAS

Abilene Reporter-News*+, North 1st & Cypress, Abilene TX 79604.........915-673-4271
Addison/North Dallas Today, 1712 Beltline, Carrollton TX 75006............214-446-0303
Alice Echo-News*, Box 1610, Alice TX 78332...512-664-6588
Alpine Avalanche, Box 719, Alpine TX 79830..915-837-3334
Alvin Sun, PO Box 1407-D, Alvin TX 77511 713-331-4421
Amarillo Daily News*+, 900 Harrison St, Amarillo TX 79166...................806-376-4488
Amarillo Globe-News*, 900 Harrison St, Amarillo TX 79166.....................806-376-4488
Andrews County News, 210 E Broadway, Andrews TX 79714.....................915-523-2085
Angleton Times, 700 Western Ave, Angleton TX 77515...............................713-849-8581
Arlington Citizen-Journal, 1111 W Abram, Arlington TX 76010 817-277-4131
Arlington Daily News*, 400 W Abram St, Arlington TX 76010....................817-277-5511
Athens Daily Review*, 201 S Prairieville St, Athens TX 75751....................214-675-5626
Atlanta Citizen Journal, 306 W Main, Atlanta TX 75551 214-796-7133
Austin American-Statesman*+, 166 E Riverside Dr, Austin TX 78704....512-445-3500
Austin Citizen*, 621 N St Hohns Ave, Austin TX 78761................................512-453-6633
Azle News Advertiser, 1121 SE Parkway, Azle TX 76020.............................817-237-1184
Bay City Daily Tribune*, 3013 7th St, Bay City TX 77414...........................409-245-5555
Baylor County Banner, 109 E Morris St, Seymour TX 76380........................817-888-2616
Beaumont Enterprise*+, 380 Walnut St, Beaumont TX 77704 713-833-3311
Beeville Bee-Picayune, 206 W Corpus Christi, Beeville TX 78102...............512-358-2550
Bellville Times, 106 E Palm, Bellville TX 77418 409-865-3131
Benbrook News, 7820 Wyatt Dr, Ft Worth TX 76108 817-246-2473
Big Spring Herald*, 710 Scurry, Big Spring TX 79720 915-263-7331
Bonham Daily Favorite*, 314 N Center, Bonham TX 75418.......................214-583-2124
Borger News-Herald*, 207 N Main, Borger TX 79007 806-273-5611
Bowie News, 218 W Tarrant, Bowie TX 76230...817-972-2247
Brady Standard-Herald Publishers, 201 S Bridge, Brady TX 76825..........915-597-2959
Brazoria County News, 113 E Bernard, West Columbia TX 77486.............713-345-3127
Bridgeport Index, 1001 Halsell, Bridgeport TX 76026.................................817-683-4021
Brownfield News, 409 W Hill St, Brownfield TX 79316...............................806-683-4021
Brownsville Herald*, 1135 E Van Buren, Brownsville TX 78520................512-542-4301
Brownsville Times, 1225 N Expressway Ste 108, Brownsville TX 78520 512-542-3504
Brownwood Bulletin*, 700 Carnegie, Brownwood TX 76801.......................915-646-2541
Bryan-College Station Eagle*, 1729 Briercreat, Bryan TX 77802 409-779-4444
Burleson County Citizen Tribune, 205 W Buck, Caldwell TX 77836.........713-567-3286
Burleson Star, 319 N Burleson Blvd, Burleson TX 76028.............................817-295-0486
Burnet Bulletin, 101E Jackson, Burnet TX 78611 512-756-6136
Caller-Times*+, 820 N Broadway, Corpus Christi TX 78401.....................512-884-2011
Cameron Herald, 108 E 1st St, Cameron TX 76520.....................................817-697-6671

Carrollton Times Chronicle, 1712 Beltline, Carrollton TX 75006 214-446-0303
Carthage Panola Watchman, 109 W Panola St, Carthage TX 75633 214-693-6631
Cedar Creek Pilot, Rt 5 Box 184 Hwy 85, Kemp TX 75143 214-432-3132
Cedar Hill Journal, 104-A4 Chowning St, Besoto TX 75115.....................214-223-8308
Center Champion, Box 351, Center TX 75935......................................409-598-3838
Childress Index, 226 Main St, Childress TX 79201 817-937-2525
The Citizen*, 17511 El Camino Real, Houston TX 77058.........................713-488-1108
Cleburne Times-Review*, 108 S Anglin, Cleburne TX 76031 817-645-2441
Cleveland Advocate, 101 E Houston, Cleveland TX 77237 713-592-2626
Clute Brazosport Facts*, 720 S Main, Clute TX 77531............................713-265-7411
Coleman County Chronicle, 210 W Pecan, Coleman TX 76834...............915-625-4128
Commerce Journal, 2548 Mangum St, Commerce TX 75428.....................214-886-3196
Conroe Courier*, 100 Ave A, Conroe TX 77301....................................409-756-6671
Copperas Cove Press, 115 E Ave E, Copperas Cove TX 76522.................817-547-4207
Corsicana Daily Sun*, 405 E Collin, Corsicana TX 75110........................214-872-3931
Courier Times*+, 410 W Erwin, Tyler TX 75702...................................214-597-8111
Courier Times-Morning Telegraph*, 410 W Erwin, Tyler TX 75710.........214-597-8111
Cuero Record, 119 E Main St, Cuero TX 77954......................................512-275-3131
Dalhart Daily Texan*, 410 Denrock, Dalhart TX 79002 806-249-4511
Dallas Morning News*+, Communications Center, Dallas TX 75265.......214-977-8222
Dallas Observer+, PO Box 190289, Dallas TX 75219 214-637-2072
Dallas Suburban Tribune, 8011 Lake June Rd, Dallas TX 75217 214-398-1456
Dallas Times Herald*+, 1101 Pacific, Dallas TX 75202...........................214-720-6111
De Soto News-Advertiser, 249 N Hampton, Desoto TX 75115..................214-223-3655
Deer Park Progress-Broadcaster, 1609 Center St, Deer Park TX 77536...713-479-2760
Del Rio News-Herald*, 321 S Main St, Del Rio TX 78840........................512-775-1551
Denison Herald*, 331 W Woodard, Denison TX 75020 214-465-7171
Denton Record-Chronicle*, 314 E Hickory St, Denton TX 76201............817-387-3811
Duncanville Journal, 249 N Hampton, Desoto TX 75115..........................214-223-3655
Eagle Lake Headlight, 220 E Main St, Eagle Lake TX 77434 713-234-2783
Eagle Pass News Guide, 1342 Main St, Eagle Pass TX 78852 512-773-2309
Edinburg Daily Review*, 215 E University Ave, Edinburg TX 78539 512-383-2705
Edna Herald, Drawer B, Edna TX 77957..512-782-3547
El Campo Leader-News, 203 E Jackson, El Campo TX 77437.....................409-543-3363
El Paso Herald-Post*, 401 Mills Ave, El Paso TX 79999...........................915-546-6365
El Paso Times*+, 401 Mills Ave, El Paso TX 79999 915-546-6100
Farmers Branch Times, 1712 Beltline, Carrollton TX 75006 214-446-0303
Fayette County Record, 127 S Washington, La Grange TX 78945..............409-968-3155
Floresville Chronicle-Journal, 1433 3rd, Floresville TX 78114....................512-393-2111
Floyd County Hesperian, 111 E Missouri, Floydada TX 79235...................806-983-3737
Ft Bend Advocate, 6812 Banaway, Houston TX 77072.............................713-498-7680
Ft Stockton Pioneer, 210 N Nelson St, Ft Stockton TX 79735...................915-336-2281
Ft Worth Eastside News, 6538 Meadowbrook, Ft Worth TX 76112...........817-451-6870
Ft Worth La Vida News, 1621 Miller Ave, Ft Worth TX 76101 817-531-3879
Ft Worth News-Tribune, 212 S Main St, Ft Worth TX 76104....................817-338-1055
Ft Worth Star-Telegram*+, 400 West 7th St, Ft Worth TX 76102 817-390-7400
Gainesville Daily Register*, 306 E California, Gainesville TX 76240.........817-665-5511
Galveston Daily News*, 8522 Teichman, Galveston TX 77553....................409-744-3611
Garland Daily News*, 613 State St, Garland TX 75040.............................214-272-6591
Gatesville Messenger, 116 S 6th St, Gatesville TX 76528...........................817-865-5212
Giddings Times & News, 170 N Knox Ave, Giddings TX 78942 512-542-2222
Gilmer Mirror, 214 E Marshall St, Gilmer TX 75644 214-843-2503
Gladewater Mirror, 201 S Dean St, Gladewater TX 75647..........................214-845-2235

Glen Rose Reporter, Box 888, Glen Rose TX 76043.................817-897-2282
Grand Prairie Daily News*, 109 E Main, Grand Prairie TX 75050...........214-263-2707
Greenville Herald Banner*, 2305 King St, Greenville TX 75401 214-455-4220
Groesbeck Journal, Box 440, Groesbeck TX 76642.....................817-729-5103
Hallettsville Tribune-Herald, 108 S Texana, Hallettsville TX 77964.........512-798-2481
Hamilton Herald-News, 112 E Main, Hamilton TX 76531 817-386-3145
Henderson Daily News*, 1711 Hwy 79S, Henderson TX 75652 214-657-2501
Hereford Brand, 130 W 4th, Hereford TX 79045.....................806-364-2030
Hondo Anvil Herald, Box 400, Hondo TX 78861 512-426-3346
Hood County News, 111 E Bridge, Granbury TX 76048.................817-573-1177
Houston Chronicle*+, 801 Texas Ave, Houston TX 77002.................713-220-7171
Houston County Courier, Box 551, Crockett TX 75835 713-544-2238
Houston Forward Times, PO Box 2962, Houston TX 77001.............713-526-4727
Houston Informer, PO Box 3086, Houston TX 77001.....................713-527-8261
Houston Post*+, 4747 Southwest Fwy, Houston TX 77027.............713-840-5600
Houston Teens+, 6939 Bellaire Blvd, Houston TX 77074 713-337-3233
Humble Echo, Drawer E, Humble TX 77338.....................713-446-9610
Herald & Zeitung, 186 S Castell, New Braunfels TX 78130.............512-625-7813
Hockley County News-Press, 711 Anstin St, Levelland TX 79336.........806-894-3121
Huntsville Item*, 1409 10th St, Huntsville TX 77340.................413-295-5407
InBetween Magazine, 520 Tremont St, Galveston TX 77550 409-763-2020
Irving Daily News*, 1622 W Irving Blvd, Irving TX 75061 214-254-6161
Jacksonville Daily Progress*, 201 Austin, Jacksonville TX 75766 214-586-2236
Jasper News-Boy, 302 N Wheeler, Jasper TX 75951.....................409-384-3441
Johnson County News, 206 E Chambers, Cleburne TX 76031 817-645-0266
Karnes Citation, 110 S Market St, Karnes TX 78118 512-780-3924
Kaufman Herald, 202 W Grove St, Kaufman TX 75142 214-932-2171
Kermit Winkler County News, 109 S Poplar, Kermit TX 79745.........915-586-2561
Kerrville Daily Times*, 429 Jefferson St, Kerrville TX 78028 512-896-7000
Kerrville Mountain Sun, 208 Rodriguez St, Kerrville TX 78028.........512-257-3300
Kilgore News Herald*, 610 E Main St, Kilgore TX 75662 214-984-2593
Killeen Daily Herald*, 100 East Ave A, Killeen TX 76540 817-634-2125
Kingsville Record, Box 951, Kingsville TX 78363.....................512-592-4304
La Marque Times, Box 158, La Marque TX 77568 409-935-2431
La Porte Bayshore Sun, 911 Broadway, La Porte TX 77571.............713-471-1234
Lamb County Leader-News, 313 W 4th, Littlefield TX 79339 806-385-4481
Lamesa Press-Reporter, 523 N 1st St, Lamesa TX 79331.............806-872-2177
Lancaster Journal, 249 N Hampton, Desoto TX 75115 214-223-3655
Laredo Citizen, 1206 Santa Maria Ave, Laredo TX 78040.............512-722-7556
Laredo Morning Times*, 111 Esperanza Dr, Laredo TX 78041 512-723-2901
Laredo News*, 2920 Saunders Ave, Laredo TX 78041.................512-724-8386
League City News*, 202 Reynolds, League City TX 77573.............713-332-6567
Lewisville Leader*, 591 W Main St, Lewisville TX 75067 214-436-3566
Light & Champion, 137 San Augustine St, Center TX 75935.............409-598-3377
Llano News, 813 Berry St, Llano TX 78643 915-247-4433
Lockhart Post Register, Box 360, Lockhart TX 78644.................512-398-5209
Longview Daily News*, 314 E Methvin, Longview TX 75606.............214-757-3311
Longview Morning Journal*, 314 E Methvin, Longview TX 75601.............214-757-3311
Lubbock Avalanche-Journal*+, 710 Avenue J, Lubbock TX 79408.........806-762-8844
Lufkin Daily News*, 300 Ellis, Lufkin TX 75901 409-632-6631
Luling Newsboy & Signal, 415 E Davis, Luling TX 78648.............512-875-2116
Marble Falls Highlander, 206 Main, Marble Falls TX 78654.............512-693-4367
Marlin Daily Democrat*, 211 Fortune St, Marlin TX 76661 817-883-2554

McAllen Monitor*, 1100 Ash St, McAllen TX 78501.................................512-686-4343
McAllen Valley Town Crier+, 1811 N 23rd St, McAllen TX 78501 512-682-2423
McKinney Courier Gazette*, 4005 W University, McKinney TX 75069.....214-542-2631
Medical Gazette, 122 E Byrd, Universal City TX 78148.............................512-658-7424
Mesquite Daily News*, 303 N Galloway, Mesquite TX 75149 214-285-6301
Metrocrest News, 2567 Valley View, Farmers Branch TX 75234................214-243-0194
Mexia Daily News*, 214 Railroad St, Mexia TX 76667...............................817-562-2868
Mid-Cities Daily News*, 728 Brown Trail, Hurst TX 76053 817-282-2571
Midcountry Chronicle, 2112 Nederland Ave, Nederland TX 77627............713-722-0479
Midland Reporter-Telegram*, 201 E Illinois, Midland TX 79702 915-682-5311
Mineral Wells Index*, 300 SE 1st St, Mineral Wells TX 76067..................817-325-4466
Monahans News, 107 W 2nd, Monahans TX 79756 915-943-4312
Moore County News-Press, 7th & Meredith, Dumas TX 79029................806-935-4111
Mt Pleasant Daily Tribune*, 1705 Industrial, Mt Pleasant TX 75455........214-572-1705
Nacogdoches Daily Sentinel*, 4920 Colonial, Nacogdoches TX 75963 409-564-8361
Navasota Examiner Review, 115 Railroad St, Navasota TX 77868 409-825-6484
North San Antonio Times, Box 6819, Alamo Heights TX 78209 512-828-3321
Oak Cliff Advertiser+, 4575 S Westmoreland, Dallas TX 75224.................214-339-3111
Oak Cliff Tribune, Westcliff Mall, Dallas TX 75224...................................214-339-3111
Odessa American*, 222 E 4th St, Odessa TX 79760 915-337-4661
Orange Leader*, 200 Front Ave, Orange TX 77630....................................713-883-3571
Palestine Herald-Press*, 519 Elm St, Palestine TX 75801.........................214-729-0281
Pampa News*, Box 2198, Pampa TX 79065...806-669-2525
Paris News*, 138 Lamar Ave, Paris TX 75460 214-785-8744
Park Cities News, 6060 N Central Expy, Dallas TX 75206.........................214-369-7570
Pasadena Citizen*, 102 S Shaver, Pasadena TX 77506..............................713-477-0221
Pecos Enterprise*, 324 S Cedar, Pecos TX 79772.....................................915-445-5475
Pittsburg Gazette, 112 Quitman St, Pittsburg TX 75686 214-856-3388
Plainview Herald*, 820 Broadway, Plainview TX 79072............................806-293-1343
Plano Daily Star-Courier*, 1301 19th St, Plano TX 75074.........................214-424-6565
Pleasanton Express, 114 Goodwin, Pleasanton TX 78064 512-569-2341
Polk County Enterprise, Box 221, Livingston TX 77351 713-327-4357
Port Arthur News*, 549 4th St, Port Arthur TX 77640..............................409-963-0533
Port Isabel-South Padre Press, Box 308, Port Isabel TX 78578................512-943-5545
Port Lavaca Wave*, 301 S Colorado St, Port Lavaca TX 77979.................512-552-9788
The Progress, 209 Willcox St, Anahuac TX 77514.....................................409-267-6131
Randolph AFB Wingspread, 122 E Byrd, Universal City TX 78148...........512-658-7424
Richardson Daily News*, Box 630, Richardson TX 75080 214-234-1131
River Oaks News, 7820 Wyatt Dr, Ft Worth TX 76108 817-246-2473
Robstown Record, 104 N 5th St, Robstown TX 78380...............................512-387-4511
Rockdale Reporter, 221 E Cameron, Rockdale TX 76567...........................512-446-5838
Round Rock Leader, 105 S Blair, Round Rock TX 78664............................512-255-5827
San Angelo Standard Times*, 34 W Harris, San Angelo TX 76903 915-653-1221
San Antonio Current+, 110 Broadway #25, San Antonio TX 78205.........512-225-0945
San Antonio Express-News*+, Ave E & 3rd St, San Antonio TX 78297...512-225-7411
San Antonio Light*+, 420 Broadway, San Antonio TX 78291 512-271-2700
San Augustine Rambler, 114 N Harrison St, San Augustine TX 75972 713-275-2753
San Augustine Tribune, 315 W Columbia St, San Augustine TX 75972....409-275-2181
San Benito News, Box 1791, San Benito TX 78586.....................................512-399-2436
San Marcos Daily Record*, I H 35 S 1910, San Marcos TX 78666............512-392-2458
Sealy News, 111 Main St, Sealy TX 77474..713-885-3562
Seguin Gazette-Enterprise, 1100 N Camp St, Seguin TX 78155................512-379-5402
Silsbee Bee, 410 Hwy 96 S, Silsbee TX 77656..409-385-5278

Snyder News*, Box 949, Snyder TX 79549...............................915-573-5486
Southwest Advocate, 6812 Banaway, Houston TX 77072..............................713-498-7680
Southwest Suburban Journal, 6939 Bellaire, Houston TX 77074...............713-337-3233
Spring North Harris County News, Box 430, Spring TX 77373....................713-353-2476
Stafford Ft Bend Mirror, Box 640, Stafford TX 77477............................713-499-1684
Standard-Radio Post, 108 E Main, Fredericksburg TX 78624.....................512-997-2156
Stephenville Empire-Tribune*, 110 S Columbia, Stephenville TX 76401..817-965-3124
Sulphur Springs News-Telegram*, Box 598, Sulphur Springs TX 75482...214-885-8663
Sweetwater Reporter*, 112 W 3rd St, Sweetwater TX 79556.....................915-236-6677
Taylor Press*, 211 W 3rd St, Taylor TX 76574.....................................512-252-3621
Temple Daily Telegram*, 10 S 3rd St, Temple TX 76501........................817-778-4444
Terrell Tribune*, 1125 S Virginia, Terrell TX 75106.............................214-563-6476
Texan Newspaper, 4562 Bissonnet Ste 203, Bellaire TX 77401...............713-660-7112
Texarkana Gazette*, 313 Pine St, Texarkana TX 75501.........................214-794-3311
Texas City Sun*, 624 4th Ave N, Texas City TX 77590.........................713-945-3441
Texas Observer, 600 W 7th, Austin TX 78701....................................512-477-0746
Times & Record News*+, 1301 Lamar, Wichita Falls TX 76307.............817-767-8341
Tyler Morning Telegraph*+, 410 W Erwin, Tyler TX 75702.................214-597-8111
Uvalde Leader-News, 110 N East, Uvalde TX 78801..........................512-278-3337
Valley Morning Star*, 1310 S Commerce, Harlingen TX 78550...........512-423-5511
Vernon Daily Record*, 1531 Cumberland, Vernon TX 76384...............817-552-5454
Victoria Advocate*, 311 E Constitution, Victoria TX 77901.................512-575-1451
Waco Citizen, 1020 N 25th St, Waco TX 76707...............................817-754-3511
Waco Tribune Herald*+, 900 Franklin Ave, Waco TX 76703.............817-753-1511
Waxahachie Daily Light*, 200 W Marvin, Waxahachie TX 75165.........214-937-3310
Weatherford Democrat*, 512 Palo Pinto St, Weatherford TX 76086.......817-594-7447
Weimar Mercury, 200 W Main, Weimar TX 78962............................713-725-8444
Wharton Journal-Spectator, 115 W Burleson St, Wharton TX 77488.......713-532-8840
White Rocker News, 10809 Garland Rd, Dallas TX 75218......................214-327-9335
White Settlement News, 7820 Wyatt Dr, Ft Worth TX 76108.................817-246-2473
Williamson County Sun, 709 Main St, Georgetown TX 78627...............512-863-6555
Winnsboro News, 105 E Locust St, Winnsboro TX 75494......................214-342-5247
Wise County Messenger, 115 S Trinity, Decatur TX 76234..................817-627-5987
Yoakum Herald-Times, 312 Lott St, Yoakum TX 77995.....................512-293-2335

UTAH

Ben Lomond Beacon, Box 207, Roy UT 84067.................................801-825-1666
Box Elder News & Journal, PO Box 370, Brigham City UT 84302..............801-723-3471
Clearfield Courier, Box 207, Roy UT 84067...................................801-825-1666
Daily Spectrum*, 155 N 400 W, St George UT 84770.........................801-673-3511
Daily Spectrum-Iron County, 415 S Main, Cedar City UT 84720..............801-586-7646
Davis County Clipper, 76 S Main, Bountiful UT 84010.......................801-295-2251
Logan Herald Journal*, 75 W 3rd N, Logan UT 84321........................801-752-2121
Murray Eagle, 155 E 4905 S, Salt Lake City UT 84107......................801-262-6682
News Advertiser, 155 E 4905 S, Salt Lake City UT 84107...................801-262-6682
Ogden Standard-Journal*+, 455 23rd St, Ogden UT 84401..................801-394-7711
Provo Daily Herald*+, 1555 N 200 West, Provo UT 84601..................801-373-5050
Richfield Reaper, 43 S Main, Richfield UT 84701............................801-896-4431
Salt Lake City Deseret News*+, 30 E 1st S, Salt Lake City UT 84110.......801-237-2100
Salt Lake Tribune*+, 143 S Main St, Salt Lake City UT 84111...............801-237-2011
Sun Advocate, 76 W Main, Price UT 84501..................................801-637-0732
Sun Times, Box 207, Roy UT 84067...801-825-1666

Tooele Bulletin, 58 N Main, Tooele UT 84074................................801-882-0050
Tooele Transcript, 58 N Main, Tooele UT 84074.............................801-882-0050
Uintah Basin Standard, 268 S 200 E, Roosevelt UT 84066......................801-722-5131
Vernal Express, 54 N Vernal Ave PO Box 1000, Vernal UT 84078............801-789-3511
Washington County News, 23 E St George, St George UT 84770..............801-673-6116
West Valley View, 155 E 4905 S, Salt Lake City UT 84107............................801-262-6682

VERMONT

Addison County Independent, Box 31, Middlebury VT 05753.....................802-388-4944
Bennington Banner*, 425 Main St, Bennington VT 05201.......................802-447-7567
Bennington Pennysaver Press, 107 South St, Bennington VT 05201..........802-442-5449
Brattleboro Reformer*, Black Mountain Rd, Brattleboro VT 05301.........802-254-2311
Burlington Free Press*+, 191 Vollege St, Burlington VT 05401..................802-863-3441
County Weekly, Box 109, Essex Junction VT 05452............................802-878-5444
Franklin County Courier, 54 Orchard St, Enosburg Falls VT 05450.........802-933-4375
Hardwick Gazette, Box 367, Hardwick VT 05843...............................802-472-6521
Journal Opinion, Main St, Bradford VT 05033................................802-222-5281
Morrisville Transcript, Brooklyn St, Morrisville VT 05661.....................802-888-2212
Newport Daily Express*, Hill St, Newport VT 05855.........................802-334-6568
Rutland Herald*, 27 Wales, Rutland VT 05701.............................802-775-5511
St Albans Messenger*, 281 N Main, St Albans VT 05478...................802-524-9771
St Johnsbury Caledonian-Record*, 25 Federal, St Johnsbury VT 05819...802-748-8121
Stowe Reporter, School St, Stowe VT 05672................................802-253-4889
Times Argus*, 540 N Main St, Barre VT 05641.............................802-479-0191
Vanguard Press, 87 College St, Burlington VT 05401.........................802-864-0506
White River Valley Herald, 30 Pleasant St, Randolph VT 05060.................802-728-3232

VIRGINIA

Abingdon Virginian, 170 E Main St, Abingdon VA 24210............................703-628-2962
Alexandria Gazette*, 717 N St Asaph, Alexandria VA 22314.....................703-549-0004
Alexandria Journal*, 6885 Commercial Dr, Springfield VA 22159.............703-750-2000
Altavista Journal, 503 3rd St, Altavista VA 24517................................804-369-6633
Appomattox Times-Virginian, 507 Court St, Appomattox VA 24522.........804-352-8215
Arlington Journal*, 6885 Commercial Dr, Springfield VA 22159................703-750-2000
Arlington Northern Virginia Sun*, 1227 N Ivy St, Arlington VA 22201....703-524-3000
Bedford Bulletin Democrat, 202 E Main St, Bedford VA 24523....................703-586-8612
The Bee*, 700 Monument St, Danville VA 24541.................................804-793-2311
Blacksburg Sun, Drawer B, Blacksburg VA 24060................................703-552-3411
Blackstone Courier-Record, 207 S Main St, Blackstone VA 23824..............804-292-3019
Bland Messenger, 460 W Main St, Wytheville VA 24382.........................703-288-6611
Bristol Herald Courier*, 320 Morrison Blvd, Bristol VA 24201..................703-669-2181
Bristol Virginia-Tennessean*, 320 Morrison Blvd, Bristol VA 24201........703-669-2181
Brunswick Times-Gazette, Box 250, Lawrenceville VA 23868...................804-848-2114
Burke Herald, 717 N St Asaph St, Alexandria VA 22314.........................703-549-0004
Caroline Progress, Box 69, Bowling Green VA 22427............................804-633-5005
Carroll News, 302 Main St, Hillsville VA 24343.................................703-728-7311
Central Virginian, 2 Elm Ave, Louisa VA 23093................................703-967-0368
Charlotte Gazette, 100 Main St, Drakes Branch VA 23937.......................804-568-3341
Chesapeake Post, 1024 Battlefield Blvd, Chesapeake VA 23320.................804-547-4571
Chesterfield Journal, 1601 Pinebark Rd, Chester VA 23831....................804-748-6341
Christiansburg Blacksburg News, Box 419, Christiansburg VA 24073......703-382-6171

Clinch Valley News, Main St, Tazewell VA 24651.................................703-988-4770
Covington Virginian*, 343 Monroe Ave, Covington VA 24426................703-962-2121
Crewe-Burkville Journal, 133 W Carolina Ave, Crewe VA 23930............804-645-7534
Culpeper News, 605 S Main St, Culpeper VA 22701.............................703-825-3232
Daily Advance*, Wyndale Dr, Lynchburg VA 24502.............................804-237-2941
Daily News Leader*, 11 N Central Ave, Staunton VA 24401...................703-885-7281
Daily News-Record*, 231 S Liberty St, Harrisonburg VA 22801.............703-433-2702
Daily Progress*, 413 E Market, Charlottesville VA 22902.....................804-295-0866
Danville Commercial Appeal, 500 Arnett Blvd, Danville VA 24543..........804-792-1372
Emporia Independent-Messenger, Box 786, Emporia VA 23847..............804-634-4153
Emporia Southside Sun, 410 S Main St, Emporia VA 23847...................804-634-5128
The Enterprise, 22 E Main St, Stuart VA 24171..................................703-694-3101
Fairfax Journal*+, 6885 Commercial Dr, Springfield VA 22159..............703-750-2000
Farmville Herald, 114 North St, Farmville VA 23901............................804-392-4151
Fauquier Democrat, 39 Culpepper St, Warrenton VA 22186...................703-347-4222
Fincastle Herald, Roanoke & Herndon Sts, Fincastle VA 24090..............703-473-2741
Floyd Press, Box 155, Floyd VA 24091..703-745-2127
Fort Belvoir Castle, Bldg 216, Ft Belvoir VA 22060............................703-664-2838
Franklin County Times, 732 N Main, Rocky Mt VA 24151......................703-483-5203
Franklin News-Post, Box 250, Rocky Mt VA 24151.............................703-483-5113
Free Lance-Star*, 616 Amelia St, Fredericksburg VA 22401..................703-373-5000
Galax Gazette, 108 W Stuart Dr, Galax VA 24333...............................703-236-5178
Gazette-Goochland, PO Box 290, Manakin-Sabot VA 23103..................804-784-3315
Gloucester Mathews Gazette Journal, Main St, Gloucester VA 23061......804-693-3101
Gretna Gazette, Box 938, Gretna VA 24557.......................................804-565-6291
Hanover Herald-Progress, 114 Thompson St, Ashland VA 23005.............804-798-9031
Henry County Journal, Box 150, Accomac VA 23301............................804-787-1200
Hopewell News*, 560 E Randolph Rd, Hopewell VA 23860....................804-458-8511
Kenbridge-Victoria Dispatch, Box 40, Victoria VA 23974.....................804-696-5550
Lebanon News, Main St, Lebanon VA 24266......................................703-889-2112
Ledger-Star*+, 150 W Brambleton Ave, Norfold VA 23510....................804-446-2000
Lexington News Gazette, 20 W Nelson St, Lexington VA 24450..............703-463-3113
Loudoun Times-Morror, 9 E Market St, Leesburg VA 22075...................703-777-1111
Luray Page News & Courier, 17 S Broad St, Luray VA 22835.................703-743-5123
Lynchburg News*, Wyndale Dr, Lynchburg VA 24502..........................804-237-2941
Madison County Eagle, Main St, Madison VA 22727............................703-948-5121
Manassas Journal Messenger*, 9009 Church St, Manassas VA 22110......703-368-3101
Martinsville Bulletin*, 204 Broad St, Martinsburg VA 24112.................703-638-8801
Newport News Daily Press*+, 7505 Warwick, Newpt News VA 23607......804-244-8421
Newport News Times-Herald*, 7505 Warwick, Newpt News VA 23607.....804-247-4600
News & County Press, PO Box 791, Buena Vista VA 24416....................703-463-6549
News Journal*, 1st & Grove St, Radford VA 24141..............................703-639-2436
Norfolk Journal & Guide, Box 209, Norfolk VA 23501..........................804-625-3686
North Virginia Daily*, 120 N Holliday St, Strasburg VA 22657...............703-465-5137
Northumberland Echo, Box 198, Heathsville VA 22473.........................804-787-1200
Norton Coalfield Progress, 725 Park Ave, Norton VA 24273..................703-679-1101
Orange County Review, Box 589, Orange VA 22960.............................703-672-1266
Petersburg Progress-Index*, 15 Franklin St, Petersburg VA 23803..........804-732-3456
The Post, Wood Ave, Big Stone Gap VA 24219..................................703-523-1141
Potomac News*, 14010 Smoketown Rd, Woodbridge VA 22192..............703-670-8151
Powell Valley News, K St, Pennington Gap VA 24227..........................703-546-1210
Radford Messenger, Box 772, Radford VA 24141................................703-639-2436
The Recorder, Box 10, Monterey VA 24465.......................................703-468-2147

Reston Times, 11401 North Shore Dr, Reston VA 22090................................703-437-5400
Richlands News Press, 1221 E Front St, Richlands VA 24641.....................703-963-1081
Richmond News Leader*+, 333 E Grace St, Richmond VA 23219............804-649-6000
Richmond Times-Dispatch*+, 333 E Grace St, Richmond VA 23219.......804-649-6000
Roanoke Tribune, Box 6021, Roanoke VA 24017......................................703-343-0326
Rockridge Weekly, PO Box 791, Buena Vista VA 24416............................703-463-6549
Salem Times-Register, 1633 W Main St, Salem VA 24153 703-389-9355
Shenandoah Valley-Herald, Box 507, Woodstock VA 22664.....................703-459-4078
Silver Spg-Wheaton Advertiser+, 3827 Pickett, Fairfax VA 22031 702-323-1010
Smyth County News, Box 640, Marion VA 24354.....................................703-783-5121
South Boston Gazette-Virginian, 3201 Halifax, S Boston VA 24592..........804-572-3945
South Boston News & Record, 202 S Main St, South Boston VA 24592....804-572-2928
South Hill Enterprise, 914 W Danville St, South Hill VA 23970 804-447-3178
Southside Sun, Box 488, Emporia VA 23847...804-634-5128
Southwest Times*, 227 N Washington Ave, Pulaski VA 24301 703-980-5220
Star-Tribune, Box 111, Chatham VA 24531..804-432-2791
Suffolk News-Herald*, 130 S Saratoga St, Suffolk VA 23434 804-539-3437
Sussex-Surry Dispatch, Fleetwood St, Wakefield VA 23888......................804-899-6397
Tidewater Review, PO Box 271, West Point VA 23181...............................804-843-2282
Times & World-News*+, 201 W Campbell, Roanoke VA 24010................703-981-3100
Urbanna Southside Sentinel, Box 549, Urbanna VA 23175 804-758-2328
USA Today*+, 1000 Wilson Blvd, Arlington VA 22209 703-276-3400
Valley Banner, 143 W Spotswood Trail, Elkton VA 22827.........................703-298-9444
Vinton Messenger, 118 Lee Ave, Vinton VA 24179 703-343-0720
Virginia Beach Beacon+, Box 62244, Virginia Beach VA 23462 804-490-2330
Virginia Beach Sun, 138 Rosemont Rd, Virginia Beach VA 23452...........804-486-3430
Virginia Gazette, 173 2nd St, Williamsburg VA 23185...............................804-220-1736
Virginia Mountaineer, 105 Main St, Grundy VA 24614 703-935-2123
Virginia-Tennessean*, 320 Morrison, Bristol VA 24201 703-669-2181
Virginian-Leader, 511 Mountain Lake Ave, Pearisburg VA 24134.............703-921-3434
Virginian-Pilot*+, 150 W Brambleton Ave, Norfolk VA 23510.................804-446-2000
Washington County News, 152 E Main St, Abingdon VA 24210 703-628-7101
Waynesboro News-Virginian*, 544 W Main St, Waynesboro VA 22980....703-949-8213
Westmoreland News, Box 698, Montross VA 22520 804-493-8096
Winchester Star*, 2 N Kent St, Winchester VA 22601................................703-667-3200

WASHINGTON

Anacortes American, PO Box 39, Anacortes WA 98221 206-293-3122
Bainbridge Review, 382 Madison N, Bainbridge Is WA 98110 206-842-6613
Battle Ground Reflector, 21914 N 112th Ave, Battle Ground WA 98604..206-687-5151
Bellingham Herald*, PO Box 1277, Bellingham WA 98227.......................206-676-2600
Bremerton Sun*, 545 5th St, Bremerton WA 98301...................................206-377-3711
Burien Highline Times, 207 SW 150th, Seattle WA 98166.........................206-242-0100
Camas-Washougal Post Record, 425 NE 4th Ave, Camas WA 98607 206-892-2000
Central Area Times, 2921 E Madison St, Seattle WA 98112 206-322-1431
Chinook Observer, 212 S Oregon St, Long Beach WA 98631 206-642-3131
Colfax Gazette, 211 N Main, Colfax WA 99111 509-397-4333
Columbia Basin Daily Herald*, 813 W 3rd, Moses Lake WA 98837 509-775-4561
Columbia River Viewpoint, 425 NE 4th Ave, Camas WA 98607.................206-892-2000
The Columbian*+, 701 W 8th, Vancouver WA 98666................................206-694-3391
Colville Statesman-Examiner, 220 S Main St, Colville WA 99114.............509-684-4567
Daily Chronicle*, 321 N Pearl St, Centralia WA 98531.............................206-736-3311

Daily Journal of Commerce*, 83 Columbia, Seattle WA 98104...................206-622-8272
Daily World*, 315 S Michigan, Aberdeen WA 98520 206-532-4000
Deer Park Tribune, W 114 1st, Deer Park WA 99006 509-276-5043
Des Moines News, 207 SW 150th, Seattle WA 98166...............................206-242-0100
Ellensburg Daily Record*, 4th & Main, Ellensburg WA 98926 509-925-1414
Federal Way News, 1634 S 312th St, Auburn WA 98003 206-839-9799
Fort Lewis Ranger, Box 1521, Tacoma WA 98401...................................206-584-1212
Goldendale Sentinel, Box 246, Goldendale WA 98620 509-773-3777
Grant County Journal, 29 Alder SW, Ephrata WA 98823...........................509-754-4636
The Herald*+, Grand & California, Everett WA 98201 206-339-3000
Issaquah Press, 45 Front St S, Issaquah WA 98027.................................206-392-6434
Journal of the San Juans, 301 Tucker Ave, Friday Harbor WA 98250......206-378-4191
Journal-American*, 1705 132nd NE, Bellevue WA 98005 206-455-2222
Kitsap County Herald, 134 1st Ave, Poulsbo WA 98370.............................206-779-4464
Lacey Leader, PO Box 3526, Olympia WA 98503......................................206-491-8000
Lewis River News, 435 Davidson, Woodland WA 98674 206-225-8287
Longview Daily News*, 770 11th Ave, Longview WA 98632.........................206-577-2500
Lynden Tribune, 113 N 6th St, Lynden WA 98624 206-354-4444
Lynnwood Enterprise, 7300A 196th SW, Lynnwood WA 98036....................206-775-7521
Mercer Island Reporter, 3006 78th Ave SE, Mercer Island WA 98040 206-232-1215
Newport Miner & Gem State Miner, 317 S Union, Newport WA 99156...509-447-2433
News Review, 1007 Main St, Sumner WA 98390.......................................206-863-8171
Northshore Citizen, 10200 NE Citizen Plz, Bothell WA 98011 206-486-1231
Oak Harbor Whidbey News Times, Box 10, Oak Harbor WA 98277.........206-675-6611
The Olympian*, 1268 E 4th Ave, Olympia WA 98507 206-754-5400
Omak-Okanogan County Chronicle, 109 N Main, Omak WA 98841.........509-826-1110
Peninsula Daily News*, 305 W 1st St, Port Angeles WA 98362 206-452-2345
Peninsula Gateway, 7521 Pioneer Way, Gig Harbor WA 98335 206-851-9921
Pierce County Herald, Box 517, Puyallup WA 98371................................206-845-7511
Port Orchard Independent, 791 Bethel Ave, Port Orchard WA 98366......206-876-4414
Port Townsend Leader, 226 Adams St, Port Townsend WA 98368.............206-385-2900
Pullman Herald, S 410 Grand Ave PO Box 609, Pullman WA 99163 509-334-4500
Seattle Argus Magazine, 2312 3rd Ave, Seattle WA 98121 206-682-1212
Seattle Capitol Hill Times, 1605 12th Ave, Seattle WA 98122 206-323-5777
Seattle Facts, 2765 E Cherry, Seattle WA 98122....................................206-324-0552
Seattle Post-Intelligencer*+, 101 Elliott Ave W, Seattle WA 98121..........206-448-8000
Seattle Times*+, Fairview Ave N & John St, Seattle WA 98111................206-464-2111
Seattle Weekly, 1931 2nd Ave, Seattle WA 98101...................................206-441-5555
Sequim Press, 337 W Washington Ave, Sequim WA 98382........................206-683-4113
Shelton-Mason County Journal, 3rd & Cota, Shelton WA 98584 206-426-4412
Silverdale Kitsap Journal, Box 986, Silverdale WA 98383 206-692-5411
Skagit Farmer, Box 153, Lynden WA 98624 206-354-4444
Skagit Valley Herald*, 1000 E College Way, Mt Vernon WA 98273..........206-424-3273
Snohomish County Tribune, 127 Ave C, Snohomish WA 98290..................206-684-1210
Spokane Chronicle*+, PO Box 2160, Spokane WA 99210 509-459-5000
Spokane Community Press+, PO Box 19037, Spokane WA 99219 509-244-5581
Spokane Spokesman-Review*+, W 999 Riverside, Spokane WA 99201....509-459-5000
Spokane Valley Herald, E 9618 1st Ave, Spokane WA 99206.....................509-924-2440
Sun Press, 228 S 2nd St, Yakima WA 98901 509-575-5600
Sunnyside Sun, 528 E Edison Ave, Sunnyside WA 98944..........................509-837-3701
Tacoma News Tribune*+, 1950 S State, Tacoma WA 98411......................206-597-8511
Tacoma Suburban Times, PO Box 99669, Tacoma WA 98499 206-473-2500
Toppenish Review, 11 E Toppenish Ave, Toppenish WA 98948...................509-865-4055

Tri-City Herald*, 107 N Cascade St, Kennewick WA 99336.........................509-586-2121
The Weekly, 1931 2nd Ave, Seattle WA 98101 206-441-5555
Wenatchee World*, Box 1511, Wenatchee WA 98801 509-663-5161
West Seattle Herald, 3237 California Ave SW, Seattle WA 98116...............206-932-0300
Westside Record-Journal, Box 38, Ferndale WA 98248................................206-384-1411
Whatcom County Shopping News, Box 153, Lynden WA 98624 206-354-4444
White Center News, 10033 13th Ave SW, Seattle WA 98146 206-767-3350
Willapa Harbor Herald, Box 627, Raymond WA 98577................................206-942-3466
Yakima Herald-Republic*, 114 N 4th St, Yakima WA 98909......................509-248-1251

WEST VIRGINIA

The Advertiser*, 946 5th Ave, Huntington WV 25720 304-696-5678
Barbour Democrat, 113 Church St, Philippi WV 26416 304-457-2222
Baxton Democrat, 109 E Main St, Glenville WV 26351 304-462-7309
Bluefield Daily Telegraph*, 412 Bland St, Bluefield WV 24701 304-327-6171
Braxton Democrat, 109 2nd St, Sutton WV 26601.......................................304-765-5555
Buckhannon Record-Delta, 7 N Locust St, Buckhannon WV 26201...........304-472-2800
Cabell Bulletin, 2085 Rt 60, Culloden WV 25510..304-562-6214
Cabell Record, 1030 Smith St, Milton WV 25541.......................................304-743-9231
Calhoun Chronicle, 353 Main St, Grantsville WV 26147 304-354-6917
Charleston Daily Mail*+, 1001 Virginia St, Charleston WV 25301...........304-348-5140
Charleston Gazette*+, 1001 Virginia St, Charleston WV 25301 304-348-5100
Evening Journal*, 207 W King St, Martinsburg WV 25401 304-263-8931
Franklin Pendleton Times, Box 428, Franklin WV 26807 304-358-2304
Glenville Democrat, 207 E Main St, Glenville WV 26351 304-462-7309
Grant County Press, 47 S Main, Petersburg WV 26847 304-257-1844
The Green Tab, 518 7th St, Moundsville WV 26041....................................304-845-4050
Hampshire Review, 25 S Grafton St, Romney WV 26757 304-822-3871
Herald Record, 202 E Main St, West Union WV 26456...............................304-873-1600
Hinton News*, 210 2nd Ave, Hinton WV 25951 304-466-0005
Huntington Herald-Dispatch*, 946 5th Ave, Huntington WV 25701 304-526-4000
Independent Herald, Rt 10, Pineville WV 24874..304-732-6060
The Intelligencer*, 1500 Main St, Wheeling WV 26003...............................304-233-0100
The Inter-Mountain*, 520 Railroad Ave, Elkins WV 26241 304-636-2121
Jackson Herald, Court St, Ripley WV 25271..304-372-2421
Keyser Daily News Tribune*, 24 Armstrong, Keyser WV 26726.................304-788-3333
Logan Banner*, 437 Stratton St, Logan WV 25601......................................304-752-6950
Madison Coal Valley News, Smoot Ave, Danville WV 25053......................304-369-1165
Meadow River Post, Box 747, Rainelle WV 25962..304-438-8893
Montgomery Herald, 406 Lee St, Montgomery WV 25136...........................304-442-4156
Moorefield Examiner, 132 S Main St, Moorefield WV 26836 304-538-2342
Moundsville Daily Echo*, 715 Lafayette, Moundsville WV 26041...............304-845-2660
Panhandle Press, 180 Carolina Ave, Chester WV 26034...............................304-387-1835
Parkersburg News*, 519 Juliana St, Parkersburg WV 26101.......................304-485-1891
Parsons Advocate Inc, 212 Main St, Parsons WV 26287 304-478-3533
Piedmont Herald, 34 Railroad St, Piedmont WV 26705...............................304-355-2381
Pocahontas Times, 810 2nd Ave, Marlington WV 24954..............................304-799-4973
Point Pleasant Register*, 200 Main St, Pt Pleasant WV 25550....................304-675-1333
Preston County News, Box 10, Terra Alta WV 26764..................................304-789-2462
Ravenswood News, 410 Race St, Ravenswood WV 26164 304-273-9333
Register Herald*, 801 N Kanawha St, Beckley WV 25801 304-255-4400
Ritchie Gazette, 112 E Main St PO Box 215, Harrisville WV 26362...........304-643-2221

The Sentinel*, 519 Juliana St, Parkersburg WV 26101 304-485-1891
Spencer Times-Record, 341 Main St, Spencer WV 25276 304-927-2360
Spirit of Jefferson-Advocate, 210 N George, Charles Town WV 25414.....304-725-2046
Times-West Virginian*, Quincy-Ogden St, Fairmont WV 26554.................304-363-5000
Tri-State Shoppers Guide News+, 310 Central, Wayne WV 25570 304-272-3433
Wayne County News, 310 Central Ave, Wayne WV 25570...........................304-272-3433
Weirton Daily Times*, 114 Lee Ave, Weirton WV 26062 304-748-0606
Welch Daily News*, 125 Wyoming St, Welch WV 24801.............................304-436-3144
West Virginia Hillbilly, 1277 S Broad St, Summersville WV 26651...........304-872-6456
Wetzel Chronicle, 1100 3rd St, New Martinsville WV 26155 304-455-3300
Williamson Daily News*, 100 E 3rd Ave, Williamson WV 25661 304-235-4242

WISCONSIN

Amery Free Press, 215 S Keller, Amery WI 54001 715-268-8101
Banner Journal, 119 Fillmore, Black River Falls WI 54615.......................715-284-4304
Baraboo News-Republic*, 219 1st St, Baraboo WI 53913............................608-356-4808
Barron County News Shield, 219 E La Salle, Barron WI 54812...................715-537-3117
Beaver Dam Daily Citizen*, 805 Park Ave, Beaver Dam WI 53916............414-887-0321
The Bee, 115 N Lake, Phillips WI 54555...715-339-3036
Beloit Daily News*, 149 State St, Beloit WI 53511......................................608-365-8811
Berlin Journal, 301 June, Berlin WI 54923...414-361-1515
Bloomer Advance, 1202 15th Ave, Bloomer WI 54724................................715-568-3100
Boscobel Dial, 805 Wisconsin Ave, Boscobel WI 53805..............................608-375-4458
Brookfield Elm Grove Post, 3117 S 108th St, Milwaukee WI 53227 414-321-9400
Burlington Standard Press, 140 Commerce St, Burlington WI 53105.......414-763-3511
Capital Times*, 1901 Fish Hatchery Rd, Madison WI 53713 608-252-6400
Chetek Alert, 117 Knapp St, Chetek WI 54728 715-924-4118
Chilton Times Journal, 19 E Main St, Chilton WI 53014.............................414-849-4651
Chippewa Herald Telegram*, 321 Frenette, Chippewa Falls WI 54729 715-723-5515
Clintonville Tribune-Gazette, 13 11th St, Clintonville WI 54929................715-823-3151
County Ledger Press, 105 Main, Balsam Lake WI 54810.............................715-485-3121
Courier Press, 132 S Beaumont Rd, Prairie Du Chien WI 53821 608-326-2441
Crawford County Independent, 805 Wisconsin Ave, Boscobel WI 53805..608-375-4458
Cumberland Advocate, 1375 2nd Ave, Cumberland WI 54829.....................715-822-4469
Daily Register*, 309 Dewitt, Portage WI 53901..608-742-2111
Darlington Republican Journal, 316 S Main St, Darlington WI 53530......608-776-4425
De Pere Journal, 126 S Broadway, De Pere WI 54115.................................414-336-4221
Delavan Enterprise, 1436 Mound Rd, Delavan WI 53115............................414-728-3411
Dodge County Independent News, 350 E Oak St, Juneau WI 53039 414-386-5568
Dodgeville Chronicle, 106 W Merrimac St, Dodgeville WI 53533................608-935-2331
Door County Advocate, 233 N 3rd Ave, Sturgeon Bay WI 54235.................414-743-3321
Dunn County News, Box 40, Menomonie WI 54751 715-235-3411
Durand Courier-Wedge, 103 W Main St, Durand WI 54736 715-672-4252
Edgerton Reporter, 21 N Henry St, Edgerton WI 53534.............................608-884-3367
Elkhorn Independent, Box 211, Elkhorn WI 53121......................................414-723-2250
Evansville Leader, 116 E Main, Evansville WI 53536 608-882-4850
Fond Du Lac Reporter*, 33 W 2nd St, Fond Du Lac WI 54935 414-922-4600
Fort Atkinson Daily*, 28 W Milwaukee Ave, Ft Atkinson WI 53538 414-563-5551
Germantown Banner Press, PO Box 13155, Milwaukee WI 53213.............414-476-8788
Grant County Herald Independent, 208 W Cherry, Lancaster WI 53813..608-723-2151
Green Bay News-Chronicle*, 133 S Monroe, Green Bay WI 54301............414-432-2941
Green Bay Press-Gazette*+, 435 E Walnut St, Green Bay WI 54307........414-435-4411

Hartford Times Press, 26 N Main St, Hartford WI 53027 414-673-3500
Herald-Times-Reporter*, 902 Franklin, Manitowoc WI 54220..................414-684-4433
Hudson Star-Observer, 226 Locust St Box 147, Hudson WI 54016............715-386-9333
Inter-County Leader, 303 N Wisconsin, Frederic WI 54837 715-327-4236
The Isthmus, 14 W Mifflin St, Madison WI 53703......................................308-251-5627
Janesville Gazette*, 1 S Parker Dr, Janesville WI 53545............................608-754-3311
Juneau County Chronicle, 500 La Crosse, Mauston WI 53948 608-843-7711
Kaukauna Times, 103 E 3rd St, Kaukauna WI 54130.................................414-766-4651
Kenosha News*, 715 58th St, Kenosha WI 53141 414-657-1000
LaCrosse Tribune*, 401 N 3rd St, La Crosse WI 54601.............................608-782-9710
Ladysmith News, 120 W 3rd St, Ladysmith WI 54848...............................715-532-5591
Lake Geneva Regional News, 315 Broad St, Lake Geneva WI 53147........414-248-4444
Lakeland Times, Box 790, Minocquae WI 54548..715-356-5236
Leader Telegram*, 701 S Farwell, Eau Claire WI 54701 715-833-9208
Loyal Tribune Record Gleaner, 318 N Main, Loyal WI 54446 715-255-8531
Marshfield News Herald*, 111 W 3rd St, Marshfield WI 54449..................715-384-3131
Mauston Star, 500 La Crosse, Mauston WI 53948......................................608-843-7711
Mayville News, 126 Bridge St, Mayville WI 53050 414-387-2211
Medford Star News, 116 S Wisconsin Ave, Medford WI 54451 715-748-2626
Menomonee Falls News, 11063 W Blue Mound, Milwaukee WI 53226......414-476-8788
Menomonee Falls Post, 3117 S 108th St, Milwaukee WI 53227.................414-321-9400
Milwaukee County News, 4124 S Austin St, Milwaukee WI 53207............414-744-1769
Milwaukee Courier, 2431 W Hopkins St, Milwaukee WI 53206.................414-445-2031
Milwaukee Journal*+, 333 W State St, Milwaukee WI 53201 414-224-2000
Milwaukee Sentinel*+, 918 N 4th St, Milwaukee WI 53201......................414-224-2000
Milwaukee Star, 2431 W Hopkins St, Milwaukee WI 53206......................414-445-2031
Monroe County Democrat, 114 W Oak St, Sparta WI 54656.......................608-269-3186
Monroe Evening Times*, 1065 4th Ave W, Monroe WI 53566....................608-328-4202
Mukwonago Chief, 110 Main St, Mukwonago WI 53149 414-363-4045
New London Press Star, 416 N Water St, New London WI 54961 414-982-4321
New Richmond News, 145 W 2nd St, New Richmond WI 54017..................715-246-6881
North Berlin This Week, 3117 S 108th St, Milwaukee WI 53227................414-321-9400
Northwest Trader-Advocate, 515 Front St, Spooner WI 54801 715-635-2181
Oconto County Times Herald, 107 S Main St, Oconto Falls WI 54154......414-846-3427
Oshlosh Northwestern*, 224 State St, Oshlosh WI 54901 414-235-7700
Park Falls Herald, 500 Court, Park Falls WI 54552....................................715-762-3261
Peshtigo Times, Box 187, Peshtigo WI 54157...715-582-4541
Platteville Journal, 115 W Main, Platteville WI 53818 608-348-3006
Port Washington Ozaukee Press, 125 E Main, Pt Wash WI 53074 414-284-2626
Post-Crescent*+, 306 W Washington St, Appleton WI 54912....................414-733-4411
Racine Journal Times*, 212 4th St, Racine WI 53403 414-634-3322
Racine Shoreline Leader, 214 State St, Racine WI 53403 414-637-8211
Reedsburg Times Press, 117 S Walnut St, Reedsburg WI 53959 608-524-4336
Rhinelander Daily News*, 314 S Courtney, Rhinelander WI 54501...........715-362-6397
Rice Lake Chronotype, 28 S Main St, Rice Lake WI 54868 715-234-2121
Richland Center Observer, 172 E Court St, Richland Center WI 53581 ...608-647-6141
Sawyer County Record, 120 Iowa Ave, Hayward WI 54843 715-634-4881
Seymour Times Press, 227 S Main St, Seymour WI 54165..........................414-833-6800
Shawano Evening Leader*, 1464 E Green Bay St, Shawano WI 54166......715-526-2121
Sheboygan Press*, 632 Center Ave, Sheboygan WI 53081..........................414-457-7711
South Side Bay Viewer, 723 Milwaukee Ave, S Milwaukee WI 53172........414-762-2520
Star Countryman, 112 Market St, Sun Prairie WI 53590 608-837-5161
Stevens Point Daily Journal*, 1200 3rd St, Stevens Point WI 54481 715-344-6100

Superior Evening Telegram*, 1226 Ogden Ave, Superior WI 54880.........715-394-4411
Thorp Courier, 402 N Washington, Thorp WI 54771..............................715-669-5525
The Times, 630 Kenosha St, Walworth WI 53184................................414-275-2166
Tomah Journal, 1108 Superior Ave, Tomah WI 54660..........................608-372-4123
Tomah Monitor Herald, 1108 Superior Ave, Tomah WI 54660..................608-372-4123
Tri-County Press, 301 S Main, Cuba City WI 53807.............................608-744-2107
Vernon County Broadcaster, 122 W Jefferson St, Viroqua WI 54665........608-637-3137
Vilas County News Review, 330 W Division St, Eagle River WI 54521......715-479-4421
Watertown Daily Times*, Box 140, Watertown WI 53094......................414-261-4949
Waukesha Freeman*, 200 Park Pl, Waukesha WI 53187.......................414-542-2501
Waukesha Post, 3117 S 108th St, Milwaukee WI 53227........................414-321-9400
Waupun Leader News, 520 E Main St, Waupun WI 53963.....................414-324-5555
Wausau Daily Herald*, 800 Scott St, Wausau WI 54401........................715-842-2101
Wautoma Waushara Argus, Box 838, Wautoma WI 54982.....................414-787-3334
Wauwatosa Post, 3117 S 108th St, Milwaukee WI 53227.......................414-321-9400
West Bend News*, 100 S Sixth Ave, West Bend WI 53095......................414-338-0622
Westline Report, 1113 Main St, Union Grove WI 53182.........................414-878-1300
Westosha Report, 140 Main St, Twin Lakes WI 53181...........................414-877-2813
Wisconsin Rapids Tribune*, 220 1st Ave S, Wisc Rpds WI 54494..............715-423-7200
Wisconsin State Farmer, 717 10th St, Waupaca WI 54981.....................715-258-5546
Wisconsin State Journal*+, 1901 Fish Hatchery, Madison WI 53713........608-252-6100

WYOMING

Buffalo Bulletin, Box 730, Buffalo WY 82834......................................307-684-2223
Casper Star Tribune*, 170 Star Ln, Casper WY 82602...........................307-266-0500
Cody Enterprise, 1549 Sheridan, Cody WY 82414................................307-587-2231
Jackson Hole Guide, 185 N Glenwood, Jackson WY 83001.....................307-733-2430
Jackson Hole News, 215 S Scott Ln, Jackson WY 83001..........................307-733-3070
Lander Wyoming State Journal, 267 Main St, Lander WY 82520................307-332-2323
News-Record*, 1201 W Second St, Gillette WY 82716.............................307-682-9306
Northern Wyoming Daily News*, 723 Robertson, Worland WY 82401.....307-347-3241
Rawlins Daily Times*, 6th & Buffalo, Rawlins WY 82301........................307-324-3411
Riverton Ranger*, 421 E Main, Riverton WY 82501...............................307-856-2244
Rock Springs Daily Rocket-Miner*, 215 D St, Rock Springs WY 82902...307-362-3637
Sunday Tribune Eagle*, 110 E 17th St, Cheyenne WY 82001..................307-634-3361
Uinta County Herald, 926 Main St, Evanston WY 82930.........................307-789-2170
Wyoming Eagle*, 110 E 17th St, Cheyenne WY 82001............................307-634-3361
Wyoming State Tribune*, 110 E 17th St, Cheyenne WY 82001.................307-634-3361

NEWSPAPER MAGAZINE SUPPLEMENTS

Acadiana Profile Magazine, PO Box 52247, Lafayette LA 70505................318-981-0859
Arts & Books, 750 Ridder Park Dr, San Jose CA 95190...........................408-920-5000
Atlanta Weekly, 72 Marietta St NW, Atlanta GA 30302..........................404-526-5415
Baltimore Business Journal, 811 S Broadway, Baltimore MD 21231........301-522-4000
Beacon Magazine, 44 E Exchange St, Akron OH 44328..........................216-375-8269
Boston Globe Magazine, 135 Morrissey Blvd, Boston MA 02107..............617-929-2000
California Living Magazine, 110 5th St, San Francisco CA 94103.............415-777-7905
Chicago Tribune Magazine, 435 N Michigan Ave, Chicago IL 60611........312-222-3232
Columbus Dispatch Magazine, 34 S 3rd St, Columbus OH 43216.............614-461-5250
Dallas Life Magazine, Communications Center, Dallas TX 75265.............214-745-8432

Dawn, 628 N Eutaw St, Baltimore MD 21203 301-728-8200
Detroit Magazine, 321 W Lafayette, Detroit MI 48231 313-222-6477
Dixie, 3800 Howard Ave, New Orleans LA 70140 504-586-3620
Enquirer Magazine, 617 Vine St, Cincinnati OH 45201 513-721-2700
Family Weekly, 1515 Broadway, New York NY 10036 212-719-6900
The Inquirer Magazine, 400 N Broad St, Philadelphia PA 19101 215-854-2000
Insight Magazine, Box 661, Milwaukee WI 53201 414-224-2344
Life in the Times, Times Journal Bldg, Springfield VA 22159 703-750-8672
Los Angeles Times Magazine, Times Mirror Sq, Los Angeles CA 90053..213-972-5000
Magazine of the Midlands, Omaha World-Herald, Omaha NE 68102......402-444-1000
The Magazine, 4th & Ludlow Sts, Dayton OH 45401 513-225-2360
Magazine of the Midlands, World Herald Sq, Omaha NE 68102...............402-444-1000
Michiana Magazine, Colfax at Lafayette, S Bend IN 46626.........................219-233-6161
Michigan Magazine, 615 Lafayette Blvd, Detroit MI 48231 313-222-2620
Mid-South Magazine, 495 Union Ave, Memphis TN 38103 901-529-2794
Natl Black Monitor, 410 Central Park W, New York NY 10025................212-222-3555
The Nevadan, PO Box 70, Las Vegas NV 89101..702-385-4241
New York Daily News Magazine, 220 E 42nd St, New York NY 10017......212-210-2100
New York Times Magazine, 229 W 43rd St, New York NY 10036...............212-556-1234
The Newsday Magazine, Newsday Inc, Long Island NY 11747....................516-454-2020
Northeast Magazine, 285 Broad St, Hartford CT 06115 203-241-3700
Northwest Magazine, 1320 SW Broadway, Portland OR 97201 503-221-8327
Pacific, 1120 John St, Seattle WA 98111 206-464-2283
Parade, 750 3rd Ave, New York NY 10017 212-573-7000
PD, 900 N Tucker Blvd, St Louis MO 63101 314-622-7000
Pennywhistle Press, 1000 Wilson Blvd, Arlington VA 22209 703-276-3780
Pittsburgh Press Magazine, 34 Blvd of the Allies, Pittsburgh PA 15230 ...412-263-1510
Plain Dealer Magazine, 1801 Superior Ave, Cleveland OH 44120.............216-344-4546
Scene Magazine, 22 E 41 St, New York NY 10017..212-689-3526
Show/Book Week, 401 N Wabash Ave, Chicago IL 60611 312-321-2131
Style Magazine, 434 N Michigan Ave, Chicago IL 60011 312-222-4176
Sun Magazine, 501 N Calvert St, Baltimore MD 21278...............................301-332-6600
Sunday Advocate Magazine, PO Box 588, Baton Rouge LA 70821............504-383-1111
Sunday Magazine, 425 Portland Ave, Minneapolis MN 55488...................612-372-4141
Sunday Morning Magazine, 20 Franklin St, Worcester MA 01613 617-793-9100
Sunday Plain Dealer Magazine, 1801 Superior, Cleveland OH 44114 216-344-4500
Sunday Woman Plus, 235 E 45th St, New York NY 10017...........................212-682-5600
Texas, 801 Texas Ave, Houston TX 77002...713-220-7171
Texas Weekly, 102 S Shaver St, Pasadena TX 77506....................................713-477-0221
The Times Magazine, Times Journal Bldg, Springfield VA 22159...............703-750-2000
Toledo Magazine, 541 Superior St, Toledo OH 43660................................419-245-6121
TriState Magazine, 617 Vine St, Cincinnati OH 45201 513-369-1938
Tropic Magazine, 1 Herald Plaza, Miami FL 33132....................................305-376-3432
Upstate Magazine, 55 Exchange St, Rochester NY 14614 716-232-7100
USA Weekend, 1000 Wilson Blvd, Arlington VA 22209...............................703-276-3400
Vista Focus on Hispanic Amer, 2355 Salzedo, Coral Gables FL 33314 305-442-2462
Washington Post Magazine, 1150 15th St NW, Washington DC 20071.....202-334-7585
We Alaskans Magazine, PO Box 6616, Anchorage AK 99502.....................907-786-4318
West Magazine, 750 Ridder Park Dr, San Jose CA 95190 408-920-5747
Wisconsin, PO Box 661, Milwaukee WI 53201 414-224-2341
Young American, PO Box 12409, Portland OR 97212 503-230-1895

NEWS SERVICES & FEATURE SYNDICATES

Adventure Feature Syndicate, 329 Harvey Dr, Glendale CA 91206 818-247-1721
The Alburn Bureau, PO Box 5745, Tucson AZ 85703 602-624-0721
Allied Feature Syndicate, 520 Citizens Bldg, Cleveland OH 44114 216-228-6725
Altamont Advertising, PO Box 8995, Ashville NC 28814 704-258-9049
Amer Baptist News Service, PO Box 851, Valley Forge PA 19482 215-768-2247
American Features Syndicate, 964 3rd Ave, New York NY 10155 212-371-6488
American Intl Syndicate, 1324 N 3rd St, St Joseph MO 64501.....................816-279-9315
American Newspaper Syndicate, PO Box 19, Brooklyn NY 11234 212-444-7427
American Newspaper Syndicate, 9 Woodrush Dr, Irvine CA 92714..........714-559-8047
American Way Features, 128 Lighthouse Dr, Jupiter FL 33458...................305-746-7815
Amusement Features Syndicate, 218 W 47th St, New York NY 10036......212-221-2627
Antiques & Auction News, Rt 230 W Box 500, Mt Joy PA 17552.................717-653-9797
AP Newsfeatures, 50 Rockefeller Plaza, New York NY 10020 212-621-1821
Arcadia Feature Syndicate, PO Box 5263, Chicago IL 60680 312-276-0715
Arkin Magazine Syndicate, 761 NE 180th St, N Miami Beach FL 33162 ..305-651-5696
Arthur's Intl, PO Box 10599, Honolulu HI 96816 808-955-4969
Artists & Writers Syndicate, 1034 Natl Press Bldg, Wash DC 20045.........202-882-8882
Sydney Ascher Syndicate, 214 Boston Ave, Mays Landing NJ 08330 609-927-1842
Associated Church Press, 321 James St, Geneva IL 60134............................312-232-1055
Associated Press, 50 Rockefeller Plaza, New York NY 10020 212-262-1500
Australian Information Service, 636 5th Ave, New York NY 10020..........212-245-4000
Auto News Syndicate, 1524 S Ocean Shore, Flagler Beach FL 32036.........904-439-2747
Buddy Basch Feature Syndicate, 771 West End, New York NY 10025 212-666-2300
The Bascome Syndicate, 62 Cobbets Ln, Shelter Island NY 11964.............516-749-0111
Bernard Retail Mktg Report, 25 Sutton Pl S 19D, New York NY 10022...212-753-1862
Berry Publishing, 300 N State St, Chicago IL 60610 312-222-9245
Bips-Bernsen's Intl Press Service, 50 Fryer Ct, San Ramon CA 94583 415-829-4807
Black Conscience Syndication, 1 Hediger Dr, Wheatley Hts NY 11798....516-491-7774
Black Press Service, 166 Madison Ave, New York NY 10016 212-686-6850
Joe E Buresch, 6142 Carlton Ave, Sarasota FL 33581 813-922-8833
Business Features Syndicate, PO Box 9844, Ft Lauderdale FL 33310.......305-485-0795
Business Wire, 44 Montgomery St Ste 2150, San Francisco CA 94104 415-986-4422
C-K Special Features, 8000 E Girard Ave Ste 502, Denver CO 80231.......303-671-0369
Calif Town Meeting News, 523 N Fairfax, Los Angeles CA 90036.............213-651-1931
Capitol News Service, PO Box 38607, Los Angeles CA 90038.....................213-462-6371
Harriet Carlson Newspaper Syndicate, 1943 Lake, Wilmette IL 60091.....312-251-2653
The Caruba Organization, PO Box 40, Maplewood NJ 07040 201-763-6392
Century Features, PO Box 597, Pittsburgh PA 15230.................................412-471-6533
Chronicle Features, 870 Market St, San Francisco CA 94102 415-777-7212
City News Bureau of Chicago, 135 E Wacker Dr, Chicago IL 60601..........312-782-8100
Nonnee Coan, 6200 N Braeswood, Houston TX 77024................................713-776-9639
College Press Service, 2505 W 2nd Ave, Denver CO 80219..........................303-936-9930
Collegiate Baseball, 2717 N Euclid, Tucson AZ 85719...............................602-623-7495
Comedy Center Reports Publ, 700 Orange St, Wilmington DE 19801.......302-656-2209
Commodity News Service, 2100 W 89th St, Shawnee Mission KS 66206....913-642-7373
Community & Suburban Press, PO Box 639, Frankfort KY 40602............502-223-1736
Community Club Awards, PO Box 151, Westport CT 06881.......................203-226-3377
Conley Feature Syndicate, PO Box 3707, Santa Barbara CA 93105 805-687-2311

Consumer News Inc, Natl Press Bldg, Washington DC 20045.....................202-737-1190
Copley News Service, PO Box 190, San Diego CA 92112 619-293-1818
DANY News Service, 22 Lesley Dr, Syosset NY 11791.................................516-265-2016
Dear Publication & Radio, 1093 Natl Press Bldg, Wash DC 20045............203-393-0979
Salvatore Didato PhD, 175 Seton Rochelle, New Rochelle NY 10804.......212-697-0900
Fred Dodge, 1702 St Mary's St, Raleigh NC 27608.....................................919-829-0587
Doubleday Syndicate, 245 Park Ave, New York NY 10017............................212-953-4451
The Dow Jones News Service, 200 Liberty St, New York NY 10281...........212-416-2000
Dunkel Sports Research, PO Box 2167, Ormond Beach FL 32074 904-677-6100
Economic & Research FNS, 410 Park Ave 14th fl, New York NY 10022 ..212-752-4545
Economic News Agency, PO Box 174, Princeton NJ 08542 609-921-6594
EditAide/Lethbridge Group, 16 Ramblewood Dr, Rochester IL 62563 217-789-2782
Editor's Copy Syndicate, PO Box 532, Orangeburg SC 29115....................803-534-1110
Editor's Digest, 4510 Regent St, Madison WI 53705..................................608-233-6099
Editorial Consultant Service, PO Box 524, W Hempstead NY 11552 516-481-5487
Editorial Research Reports, 1414 22nd St NW, Washington DC 20037 202-296-6800
The Edman Co, 390 Woodstock Ave, Putnam CT 06260...............................203-928-3500
The Eighties, PO Box 15, Delhi NY 13753 607-746-3186
The Elegant Touch, 2230 Hilside Ct, Walnut Creek CA 94596 415-934-5646
Entertainment News, 310 E 44th St, New York NY 10017...........................212-682-4030
Hiawatha Estes & Assoc, 8766 Amigo, Northridge CA 91324......................213-885-6588
Exclusive Features Press, 400 Paradise Rd, Swampscott MA 01907..........617-599-4990
Exclusive News Service, PO Box 872, Santa Monica CA 90406...................213-451-4312
Fairchild Syndicate, 7 E 12th St, New York NY 10003 212-741-5814
Fashion 'N Figure, PO Box 255, Bath OH 44210...216-659-6231
Feature News Service, 2330 S Brentwood Blvd, St Louis MO 63144..........314-961-2300
Fiction Network, PO Box 5651, San Francisco CA 94101...........................415-391-6610
Field News Service, 401 N Wabash, Chicago IL 60611 312-321-3000
Fillers for Publications, 1220 Maple Ave, Los Angeles CA 90015 213-747-6542
Freelance Syndicate Inc, Box 1626, Orem UT 84057.................................801-785-1300
Gannett News Service, 1000 Wilson Blvd, Arlington VA 22209 703-276-5800
Garden State Media News Service, PO Box 104, Oradell NJ 07649 201-385-2000
Gelman Feature Syndicate, 826 E 14th St, Brooklyn NY 11230..................718-434-6050
General News Syndicate, 147 W 42nd St, New York NY 10036 212-221-0043
Generation News Inc, 345 W 85th St Ste 46, New York NY 10024..............212-713-5165
Glasserfield Dir of Features, 10240 Camarillo, N Hollywood CA 91602...818-769-4774
Global Press, 1307 4th St NE, Washington DC 20002.................................202-543-9428
Globe Press Intl, 422 W Market St, York PA 17405 717-854-9745
Dave Goodwin & Assoc, PO Box 54-6661, Miami FL 33154 305-531-0071
Luther A Gotwald Jr, PO Box 404, Davidsville PA 15928............................814-479-4434
Graphic News Bureau, PO Box 38, New York NY 10010 212-254-8863
The Green Thumb, Naples NY 14512..716-374-5400
Arthur S Green, 485 S Robertson Blvd Ste 5, Beverly Hills CA 90211 213-274-1283
Harris & Assoc Publ Div, 5353 La Jolla Blvd #34, La Jolla CA 92037......619-488-3851
Hearst Metrotone News, 235 E 45th St, New York NY 10017.......................212-682-7690
Hearst Special News & Features, 235 E 45th St, New York NY 10017......212-687-8807
Henrikson Illinois Cartoon Svc, 27 N Meyer Ct, Des Plaines IL 60016 312-296-1309
Heritage Features Syndicate, 214 Mass Ave NE, Wash DC 20002.............202-542-0440
Highway Safety Features, Kennebunkport ME 04046 207-967-4412
Hispanic Link News Service, 1420 N St NW, Washington DC 20005.........202-234-0280
Hollywood Inside Syndicate, PO Box 49957, Los Angeles CA 90049.........714-678-6237
Home Town Flavor, 1504 S Marengo, Pasadena CA 91106 818-799-0467
Hopkins Syndicate, Hopkins Bldg, Mellott IN 47958 317-295-2253

Hyde Park Media, 7158 Lee St, Chicago IL 60648 312-967-7666
Ideas Unlimited, 1545 New York Ave NE, Washington DC 20002 202-529-5700
Inter-American Features, PO Box 680002, Miami FL 33168.....................305-685-3211
Inter-Presse de France, 100 Beekman St, New York NY 10038 212-285-1872
Intermedia News & Feature Svc, 799 Broadway, New York NY 10003.....212-777-8383
Interpress of London & NY, 400 Madison Ave, New York NY 10017.......212-832-2839
Intl Labor Press Assn, 815 16th St NW, Washington DC 20006.................202-637-5068
Intl Medical Tribune Syndicate, 600 New Hampshire, Wash DC 20037...202-338-8866
Island Wide News Service, 79-14 Parson Blvd, Flushing NY 11366...........212-526-9069
Januz Newsfeatures, 49-C Sherwood Ter, Lake Bluff IL 60044 312-295-6550
Jericho News Service, 152 11th St SE, Washington DC 20003....................202-547-1707
Jewish Telegraphic Agency, 165 W 46th St #511, New York NY 10036....212-575-9370
Keister-Williams News Svcs, 1807 Emmet, Charlottesville VA 22906......804-293-4709
Keystone Press Inc, 156 5th Ave, New York NY 10010..............................212-924-8123
King Features Syndicate, 235 E 45th St, New York NY 10017 212-682-5600
The Kirk Syndicate, 14 Bayfield Rd, Wayland MA 01778..........................617-653-7241
Knight-Ridder Financial Info, 55 Broadway, New York NY 10006............212-269-1110
Knowledge News & Features, PO Box 100, Kenilworth IL 60043 312-234-0081
Law Education Inst, 50 N Terrace Pl, Valley Stream NY 11580..................516-561-1483
Jeffrey Lee Syndicate, 2 Holly Dr, New Rochelle NY 10801......................914-235-2347
Guy Livingston News Assn, 80 Boylston St Ste 306, Boston MA 02116.....617-482-0716
Los Angeles Times Syndicate, 218 S Spring St, Los Angeles CA 90012.....213-237-7987
LUI Assoc, 19490 Birwood Ave, Detroit MI 48221 313-341-3056
Fred Luks, 40 E Birch St, Mt Vernon NY 10552..914-669-2247
Mel Martin Enterprises, PO Box 22505, Houston TX 77227......................713-664-0503
Ed Marzula & Assoc, 8831 Sunset Blvd Ste 408, Los Angeles CA 90069 ..213-652-7481
Master's Agency, PO Box 427, Capitola CA 95010.....................................408-688-8396
Marie Mattson, 1250 Vallejo St, San Francisco CA 94109.........................415-885-5064
The McNaught Syndicate, 537 Steamboat Rd, Greenwich CT 06830...........203-661-4990
Merrell Enterprises, 1500 Massachusettes Ave NW, Wash DC 20005......202-659-8280
Midland Features, PO Box 2578, Sarasota FL 33578 813-371-8544
Miller News Agency, 376 Sunrise Cir, Glencoe IL 66022...........................312-835-5063
Minority Features Syndicate, PO Box 421, Farrell PA 16146 412-342-5300
Mark Morgan Inc, PO Box 995, Newman GA 30264 404-253-5355
MSC Inc, PO Box 40457, Tucson AZ 85717..602-299-9615
Munsey News Service, 502 Gardens Dr, Pompano Bch FL 33069 305-972-0057
Natl Catholic News Service, 1312 Mass Ave NW, Wash DC 20005...........202-659-6722
Natl Education Program, 2501 E Memorial, Oklahoma City OK 73111...405-478-5190
Natl News Bureau, 2019 Chancellor St, Philadelphia PA 19103.................215-569-0700
New York Times Syndicate, 130 5th Ave, New York NY 10011 212-645-3000
New York Today Inc, 78-11 Kew Forest Ln, Forest Hills NY 11375...........718-544-1254
News Flash Intl Inc, 2262 Centre Ave, Bellmore NY 11710........................516-679-9888
Newspaper Enterprise Assn Inc, 200 Park Ave, New York NY 10166.......212-557-5870
Newspix, 92 S Lansdowne Ave, Lansdowne PA 19050................................215-622-2200
NMD Features, 1263 W Pratt Blvd, Chicago IL 60626...............................312-973-1060
The North America Syndicate, 1703 Kaiser Ave, Irvine CA 92714.............714-250-4000
Numismatic Info Service, Rossway Rd, Pleasant Valley NY 12569............914-635-2361
Bernard O'Brien, PO Box 824, Hollywood FL 33022.................................305-922-3609
Oceanic Press Service, 4717 Laurel Canyon, N Hollywood CA 91607.......213-980-6600
Mort Olshan Sport Features, 9255 Sunset Blvd, Los Angeles CA 90069 ..213-274-1913
Joan Orth Syndicates, 401 E 65th St Ste 14J, New York NY 10021...........212-734-9497
Paul Assoc, 2617 Lynn St, Bakersfield CA 93305 805-871-8569
Gloria Pitzer Secret Recipe Publ, PO Box 152, St Clair MI 48079 313-329-7696

PR Newswire, 900 Wilshire Blvd, Los Angeles CA 90017..............................213-626-5501
Press Assoc Inc, 806 15th St NW, Washington DC 20005...........................202-638-0444
Press News Syndicate, 1780 Broadway, New York NY 10019 212-265-7330
Pulse News Service, 9009 Manchester, St Louis MO 63144 314-962-6563
Quiz Features, 4007 Connecticut Ave NW, Washington DC 20008............202-966-0025
Randall-Pedroza Syndicate, 523 N Fairfax Ave, Los Angeles CA 90036 ...213-651-1931
Religious News Service, 104 W 56th St, New York NY 10019 212-688-7094
Reuters Information Services, 1700 Broadway, New York NY 10019 212-603-3300
Elinor K Rose, 5517 Navajo Tr, Pinkney MI 48169................................313-231-1011
Science News, 1719 N St NW, Washington DC 20036................................202-785-2255
Scripps-Howard News Svc, 1110 Vermont Ave NW, Wash DC 20005.......202-833-9520
SCW Editorial Services, 20433 Nordhoff St, Chatsworth CA 91311 818-882-7200
John Shropshire & Assoc, 2204 Milltown Rd, Wilmington DE 19808.......302-995-7071
Singer Media Corp, 3164 Tyler Ave, Anaheim CA 92801..........................714-550-3164
SIPA News Service, 59 E 54th St, New York NY 10022 212-759-5571
The Skies Today, PO Box 188, West Burke VT 05871................................802-467-3134
Al Smith Feature Service, Drake Rd, Bomoseen VT 05732 802-468-5736
Southern Baptist Convention, 901 Commerce St, Nashville TN 37203......615-244-2355
Sovfoto/Eastfoto, 225 W 34th St, New York NY 10122 212-564-5485
The Space Press, 645 West End Ave, New York NY 10025..........................212-724-5919
Spades Syndicate Inc, 2 Bridge St, Milford NJ 08848................................201-995-2201
Stafford Graphology Features, 3100 NE 28th St, Ft Ldrdale FL 33308.....305-564-1182
Stamp News Bureau, PO Box 1, S Richmond Hill NY 11419......................718-843-4242
Standard Press Assn, 172 Lincoln Ave, Hastings-Hudson NY 10706........914-478-0324
Star Service Syndicate, 613 Sea Turtle Way, Ft Lauderdale FL 33324 305-472-8774
Syndicated Writers & Artists, 2901 Tacoma, Indianapolis IN 46218 317-924-4311
Tass News Agency, 50 Rockefeller Plaza, New York NY 10020.................212-245-4250
Robert Thornton Features, 3110 NE 86th Ave, Portland OR 97220..........503-252-6369
Trans World Communications, 166 Madison Ave, New York NY 10016 .212-686-6850
Transworld Feature Syndicate, 2 Lexington Ave, New York NY 10010....212-997-1880
Triangle News Service Inc, Natl Press Bldg, Washington DC 20045..........301-622-5677
Tribune Media Services, 64 E Concord St, Orlando FL 32801 305-422-8181
United Cartoonist Syndicate, PO Box 7081, Corpus Christi TX 78415......512-855-2480
United Feature Syndicate, 200 Park Ave, New York NY 10166...................212-557-2333
United Media, 200 Park Ave, New York NY 10166 212-692-3700
United Press Intl, 220 E 42nd St, New York NY 10017 212-850-8600
Universal Press Syndicate, 4900 Main St, Kansas City MO 64112 816-932-6600
Views & People In The News, 1212 5th Ave #13B, New York NY 10029 ..212-876-6503
Washington Banktrends, 910 16th St NW, Washington DC 20006..............202-466-7490
Washington Post Writers Group, 1150 15th St NW, Wash DC 20071.......202-334-6377
Weiss Philatelic-Numismatic, 16000 Terrace, Cleveland OH 44112 216-451-3331
Wide World Info Services, 360 1st Ave, New York NY 10010....................212-677-7839
Wideworld News Service, PO Box 20056, St Louis MO 63144....................314-361-1552
World Media Syndicate, 1299 E Laguna Ave, Las Vegas NV 89109 702-735-0924
World News Syndicate Ltd, 6223 Selma Ave, Los Angeles CA 90078........213-469-2333
World Press, 1811 Monroe, Dearborn MI 48124 313-563-0360
World Press, 5742 Aldingbrooke Cir S, West Bloomfield MI 48033 313-563-0360
Worldwide News Service, Gardensides Ave, Lexington KY 40544..............606-858-4240
Youth Research Inst, 404 E 55th St, New York NY 10022 212-752-3489

PERMISSIONS

These firms will assist authors in obtaining permission to use material from copyrighted works. See also Bibliographers and Researchers.

Amer Books Intl, 220 E 67th St, New York NY 10021 212-988-3808
Author Consultation Services, 226 W Pensacola, Tallahassee FL 32301...904-681-0019
Rae Barlow, 55 W 74th St, New York NY 10023 212-580-0443
Barbara Blitzer Inc, 11 Dickinson Ct, Red Bank NJ 07701 201-530-0662
Books Alive Inc, PO Box 791, Montclair NJ 07042....................................201-783-3988
The Bookworks Inc, PO Box 1189, Chicago IL 60690................................312-236-8472
Jean-Louis Brindamour, 2594 15th Ave, San Francisco CA 94127............415-664-8112
Business Media Resources, 150 Shoreline Hwy, Mill Valley CA 94941.....415-331-6021
BZ/Rights & Permissions Inc, 145 W 86th St, New York NY 10024........212-580-0615
Carlisle Graphics, 2530 Kerper Blvd, Dubuque IA 52001 319-557-1500
Chestnut House Group Inc, 540 N Lake Shore Dr, Chicago IL 60611.......312-222-9090
Herbert J Cohen, 161 Locust Ave, Rye NY 10580.....................................914-967-5316
E R Cole, PO Box 91277, Cleveland OH 44101..216-234-1775
Cunningham & Walsh, 260 Madison Ave, New York NY 10016.................212-683-4900
Curtis Clark & Rigan, 1416 Laguna St Ste 4, Santa Barbara CA 93101....805-965-3590
Nancy L Daniels, Box 68, Lemont PA 16851..814-237-7711
Valerie Eads Et Al, PO Box 1459, New York NY 10016 212-228-0900
Editcetera, 2490 Channing Way Rm 507, Berkeley CA 94704.....................415-849-1110
Editmasters/Mizelle, 4545 Connecticut Ave NW, Wash DC 20008............202-686-7252
Editorial & Graphic Services, Martinsville NJ 08836..................................201-469-2195
Educational Challenges Inc, 1009 Duke St, Alexandria VA 22314.............703-683-1500
Effective Learning, 7 N MacQuesten Pkwy, Mt Vernon NY 10550............914-664-7944
The K S Giniger Co Inc, 235 Park Ave S, New York NY 10003.................212-533-5080
The Guilford Group, 124 Jerry Ln, Davisville RI 02854.............................401-884-3101
Harkavy Publishing Service, 33 W 17th St, New York NY 10011.................212-929-1339
Heidelberg Graphics, 1116 Wendy Way, Chico CA 95926...........................916-342-6582
Susan Herner Rights Agency, 666 3rd Ave 10th fl, New York NY 10017..212-983-5232
Jean Highland, 12 E 97th St, New York NY 10029.....................................212-289-5318
Mildred Hird, 180 Riverside Dr, New York NY 10024 212-874-6742
Intl Book Marketing Ltd, 210 5th Ave, New York NY 10010 212-683-3411
Malcom C Johnson Assoc, Box 154, West Long Branch NJ 07764.............201-222-3608
KPL & Assoc, 1090 Generals Hwy, Crownsville MD 21032........................301-923-6611
L/A House Editorial, 5822 Uplander Way, Culver City CA 90230.............213-216-5812
Lazy Brown Assoc, 2800 Quebec St NW Ste 618, Wash DC 20008............202-686-0975
Linick Mktg Research, 7 Putter Bldg, Middle Island NY 11953 516-924-3888
E Trina Lipton, 60 E 8th St Box 310, New York NY 10003........................212-533-3148
Kathye Pettebone Long, 1090 Generals Hwy, Crownsville MD 21032........301-923-6611
J T Mandeville Publishing Assocs, 11 Walden Rd, Ossining NY 10562....914-762-5350
McCartan Publishing Consulting, 325 E 57th St, New York NY 10022....212-421-2641
MDZ Communications, 1136 E Stuart #220, Ft Collins CO 80525.............303-493-5532
Barbara Mele, 9525 Holland Ave, Bronx NY 10467 212-654-8047
Tom Mellers, 849 E 12th St, New York NY 10003 212-254-4958
MS/Smiths Editorial Consult, RR 1 Box 447, Bridgewater CT 06752......203-354-0866
Publishers Marketing Assoc, 257 W 29th St, New York NY 10001.............212-563-9035
Publishing Resources Inc, Box 41307, San Juan PR 00940........................809-724-0318

Marian Reiner, 71 Disbrow Ln, New Rochelle NY 10804 914-235-7808
Rights Unlimited, 156 5th Ave Ste 408, New York NY 10010 212-741-0404
Sylvia J Rosenstein, 82 Green Bay Rd, Highland Park IL 60035 312-432-5840
Richard Selman, 14 Washington Pl, New York NY 10003............................212-473-1874
Bobbe Siegel Rights Rep, 41 W 83rd St, New York NY 10024 212-877-4985
Special Press, Box 2524, Columbus OH 43216..614-297-1281
Tannenbaum Services ltd, 27 E 61st St, New York NY 10021 212-371-4120
Turner & Winston, 5306 38th St NW, Washington DC 20015......................202-363-6459
Toby Wertheim, 240 E 76th St, New York NY 10021 212-472-8587
Western Reserve Publ Services, 1640 Franklin Ave, Kent OH 44240.........216-673-2577
Wordsworth Assoc, 9 Tappan Rd, Wellesley MA 02181 617-237-4761

PHOTOGRAPHERS & STOCK PHOTOS

An asterisk (*) indicates a firm which maintains a stock photo library. See Researchers for firms providing photo research services.

Adams/Johansson Photography, 264 Barrow St, Jersey City NJ 07302.....201-332-0066
Peter Adelberg Euro Art Color*, 120 W 70th St, New York NY 10023 212-877-9654
Walter R Aguiar*, PO Box 328, New York NY 10011................................212-929-9045
Laurance Aiuppy, Box 26, Livingston MT 59047 406-222-7308
Alaskaphoto*, 1530 Westlake Ave N, Seattle WA 98109 206-282-8116
Rodelinde Albrecht, 250 Columbus Ste 203, San Francisco CA 94133.......415-362-5949
Alinari*, 65 Bleecker St 9th Fl, New York NY 10012..................................212-505-8700
Amer Heritage Library*, 60 5th Ave, New York NY 10011.........................212-206-5500
George Ancona Inc, Crickettown Rd, Stony Point NY 10980 914-786-3043
Gordon Anderson, 2846 Merry Ln, Colo Spgs CO 80909............................303-597-9953
Jim Anderson, 188-190 Grand St, Brooklyn NY 11211................................718-388-1083
Animals Animals Enterprises*, 203 W 81st St, New York NY 10024.........212-580-9595
Anthro Photo File*, 33 Hurlbut St, Cambridge MA 02138 617-868-4784
Aperture PhotoBank Inc*, 1530 Westlake Ave N, Seattle WA 98109 206-282-8116
Peter Arnold Inc*, 1466 Broadway 14th fl, New York NY 10036................212-840-6928
Art Resource Inc*, 65 Bleecker St, New York NY 10012.............................212-505-8700
Artichoke Publications, 5809 Harvest Hill, Dallas TX 75230......................214-233-2486
Atoz Images*, 213 W Institute Pl Ste 503, Chicago IL 60610......................312-664-8400
Miriam Austerman, 6805 Parkside Ave, San Diegon CA 92139 619-475-6629
Authenticated News Intl*, 29 Katonah Ave, Katonah NY 10536 914-232-7726
Awani Press Inc, PO Box 881, Fredericksburg TX 78624............................512-997-5514
B D Picture Service*, 15 Hamilton Ave, Bronxville NY 10708....................914-337-0396
Baja Bush Pilots, PO Drawer 27310, Escondido CA 92027..........................619-489-0590
Barksdale Agri-Comm, PO Box 17726, Memphis TN 38117 901-767-9540
Billy Barnes Photography, 313 Severin St, Chapel Hill NC 27514...............919-942-6350
William C Baughman, 1190 Yellowstone Rd, Cleveland OH 44121............216-382-7192
Tom Bean Bean Photographer, Box 1567, Flagstaff AZ 86002 602-779-4381
Beanie Enterprises, 7443 Stanford, St Louis MO 63130..............................314-725-5012
James Bell, 18 Fairview Pl, Ossining NY 10562..914-941-7475
Berg & Assoc*, 8334 Clairemont Mesa Blvd #203, Diego CA 92111........619-292-8257
Lester V Bergman*, RD 2 E Mountain Rd S, Cold Spring NY 10516........914-265-3656
Miriam Berkley, 353 W 51st St, New York NY 10019..................................212-246-7979
Marion Bernstein, 110 W 96th St, New York NY 10025..............................212-663-6674
Bettmann Archive*, 136 E 57th St, New York NY 10022.............................212-758-0362

Biological Photo Service*, Box 490, Moss Beach CA 94038 415-726-6244
Black Star Publishing Co*, 450 Park Ave S, New York NY 10016 212-679-3288
Raimondo & Roberto Borea, 245 W 104th St, New York NY 10025...........212-663-4463
Steven Borns, PO Box 311, New York NY 10113...212-606-2081
Len Bouche, PO Box 5188, Santa Fe NM 87502..505-471-2044
Gary Braasch, PO Box 1465, Portland OR 97207 206-695-3844
Matt Bradley, 15 Butterfield Lane, Little Rock AR 72212...........................501-224-0692
Phil Brodatz, 100 Edgewater Dr, Coral Gables FL 33133.............................305-661-5771
Dennis Brokaw Photography*, Box 273, Carmel CA 93921 408-624-6133
Edward A Brozyna, Box 401, Bloomsbury NJ 08804....................................201-479-6113
Cecile Brunswick, 127 W 96th St, New York NY 10025 212-222-2088
D Donne Bryant*, PO Box 80155, Baton Rouge LA 70898..........................504-387-1602
Fred Burrell, 54 W 21st St, New York NY 10010..212-691-0808
Ed Buryn Photography, PO Box 31123, San Francisco CA 94131 415-824-8938
Cactus Clyde Productions, PO Box 14876, Baton Rouge LA 70898 504-387-3704
Calif Historical Society*, 6300 Wilshire Blvd, Los Angeles CA 90048.......213-651-5655
Camera Clix*, 275 7th Ave, New York NY 10001...212-689-1340
Camerique*, 1701 Skippack Pike, Blue Bell PA 19422.................................215-272-4000
Tim Celenza, 2705 Houston Rd, Cincinnati OH 45247.................................513-742-0526
Walter Chandoha Photography, Box 287 Rt 1, Annandale NJ 08801 201-782-3666
Paul Chesley Photographer, Box 94, Aspen CO 81612.................................303-925-2317
James Chotas, 265 E 78th St, New York NY 10021.......................................212-288-2188
Click/Chicago Ltd*, 213 W Institute Pl Ste 503, Chicago IL 60610............312-787-7880
Commercial Photographic Illustrator, 2460 Eliot St, Denver CO 80211 ..303-458-0288
Comstock Inc*, 32 E 31st St, New York NY 10016.......................................212-889-9700
Tom Conroy Potography, 75 Ontario St, Honeoye Falls NY 14472.............716-624-4861
Creative Services, Box 5162, Carmel CA 93921..408-624-7573
Criterion Photocraft Co, 151 W 46th St, New York NY 10036 212-221-3940
Culver Pictures Inc*, 660 1st Ave, New York NY 10016...............................212-687-5054
Cumberland Valley Photographic, 3726 Central, Nashville TN 37205 615-269-6494
Scott Cunningham Sports Photo*, 100 Peachtree St, Atlanta GA 30303..404-525-7777
Cyr Color Photo Agency*, Box 2148, Norwalk CT 06852.............................203-838-8230
Dandelet Interlinks*, 126 Redwood Rd, San Anselmo CA 94960 415-456-1260
Kent & Donna Dannen, 851 Peak View, Estes Park CO 80517.....................303-586-5794
Nicholas De Vore III, 1280 Ute Ave, Aspen CO 81611 303-925-2317
Leo De Wys Inc*, 1170 Broadway, New York NY 10001...............................212-689-5580
Design Conceptions*, 112 4th Ave, New York NY 10003 212-254-1688
Devaney Stock Photos*, 7 High St Ste 308, Huntington NY 11743.............516-673-4477
Larry Dorn Assoc Inc*, 5550 Wilshire Blvd, Los Angeles CA 90036 213-935-6266
Double D Assoc, N 85 W 16282 May Ave, Menomonee Falls WI 53051....414-255-5879
DRK Photo*, 743 Wheelock Ave, Hartford WI 53027 414-673-6496
Valerie Eads Et Al, PO Box 1459, New York NY 10163 212-228-0900
Earth Scenes*, 203 W 81st St, New York NY 10024......................................212-580-9595
Eastern Photo Service*, 15 Columbus Cir #906, New York NY 10023.....212-586-7710
Eastfoto Agency*, 225 W 34th St, New York NY 10122................................212-564-5485
Robert V Eckert Jr, Box 430, Carlton OR 97111...503-852-7417
EKM Nepenthe*, Box 430, Carlton OR 97111..503-852-7417
Elich & Assoc George, PO Box 255016, Sacramento CA 95825...................916-481-5021
Steve Elmore Photography, 61-35 98th St #15E, Rego Park NY 11734 212-472-2463
Elysium Growth Press, 5436 Fernwood Ave, Los Angeles CA 90027........213-455-1000
Rohn Engh, Pine Lake Farm, Osceola WI 54020 715-248-3800
ENTHEOS, Green Mountain Rd, Seabeck WA 98380 206-830-4758
Esto Photographics Inc*, 222 Valley Pl, Mamaroneck NY 10543...............914-698-4060

F&S Ltd Inc, PO Box 2509, Daytona Beach FL 32015 904-252-8087
Jerry L Ferrara Photographer, General Del, Palomar Mtn CA 92060......619-742-3421
Focus West*, 4112 Adams Ave, San Diego CA 92116 619-280-3595
Paul Fortin, 318 W Washington St, Hanson MA 02341 617-447-2614
Four By Five Inc*, 485 Madison Ave, New York NY 10022 212-355-2323
FPG International Corp*, 251 Park Ave S, New York NY 10010 212-777-4210
David R Frazier Photolibrary*, 1921 Cataldo Dr, Boise ID 83705............208-342-9250
Gerard Fritz*, PO Box 9141, Charlotte NC 28299 704-523-1832
Larry & Helen Fritz, 217 Spring House Lane, Merion PA 19066 215-664-7129
Frost Publishing Group Ltd*, 117 E 24th St, New York NY 10010...........212-598-4280
Fundamental Photographs*, 210 Forsyth St, New York NY 10002.............212-473-5770
Ron Galella Ltd, 17 Glover Ave, Yonkers NY 10704......................................914-237-2988
Ewing Galloway*, 1466 Broadway, New York NY 10036 212-719-4720
Douglas C Gamage, 26 Glen St, Riverside RI 02915.......................................401-433-2874
Gamma-Liaison Photo News*, 150 E 58th St, New York NY 10155 212-888-7272
Elizabeth Gee, 280 Madison Ave, New York NY 10016 212-683-6924
Bonnie S Geller, 57 W 93rd St, New York NY 10025 212-864-5922
John H Gerard, 628 E 20th St, Alton IL 62002..618-465-4101
John Gerlach Photography, 1674 Madeline Dr, Lapeer MI 48446 313-664-3529
Globe Photos Inc*, 275 7th Ave, New York NY 10001...................................212-689-1340
Jeff Gnass Photography, Box 2196, Orville CA 95965....................................916-533-6788
Joel Gordon Photography, 112 4th Ave, New York NY 10003......................212-254-1688
Geoffrey Gove, 117 Waverly Pl, New York NY 10011...................................212-260-6051
Diane Graham-Henry Photo, 1717 W Flectcher, Chicago IL 60657 312-327-4493
The Granger Collection*, 1841 Broadway, New York NY 10023................212-586-0971
Martus Granirer, 390 Broadway, New York NY 10013..................................212-431-8383
Berne Greene*, Box 14084, Portland OR 97214...503-232-5964
Arthur Griffin*, 22 Euclid Ave, Winchester MA 01890 617-729-2690
Stuart M Gross Photography, 32 Union Sq E, New York NY 10003 212-674-6513
Jeffrey Grosscup, 4801 Portland Ave S, Minneapolis MN 55417................612-825-3587
Henry Grossman, 37 Riverside Dr, New York NY 10023................................212-580-7751
Al Grotell Underwater Photo, 170 Park Row, New York NY 10038 212-349-3165
Ken Haas Inc, 15 Sheridan Sq, New York NY 10014..212-255-0707
Gabriel D Hackett*, 130 W 57th St, New York NY 10019 212-265-6842
Wally Hapton Photo*, 4190 Rockaway Bch, Bainbridge Is WA 98110.......206-842-9900
Harmony House Publ*, 1008 Kent Rd, Goshen KY 40026 502-228-4446
Harper Horticultural Slides*, 219 Robanna Shrs, Seaford VA 23696 804-898-6453
Havestman Assoc, PO Box 271, Menlo Park CA 94026 916-771-0353
Grant Heilman Photography*, 506 W Lincoln Ave, Lititz PA 17543 717-626-0296
J M Heninger Photographer, 1937 Euclid Ave, Bristol VA 24201...............703-669-8804
Diana Mara Henry Photography, 1160 5th Ave, New York NY 10029......212-722-8803
Michal Heron, 28 W 71st St, New York NY 10023 212-787-1272
Historical Pictures Service*, 921 W Van Buren, Chicago IL 60607...........312-346-0599
Cliff Hollenbeck Photography, Box 4247 Pioneer Sq, Seattle WA 98104 ..206-682-6300
Tom Hollyman, 300 E 40th St, New York NY 10016 212-867-2383
David K Horowitz Studio, 920-22 Chestnut St, Philadelphia PA 19107 215-925-3600
George H Huey Photography, Box 2561, Prescott AZ 86302 602-778-0715
Image Photos*, Main St, Stockbridge MA 01262 413-298-5500
The Image Works Inc*, Box 443, Woodstock NY 12498 914-679-7172
Index/Stock International Inc*, 126 5th Ave, New York NY 10011...........212-929-4644
Intl Stock Photography Ltd*, 113 E 31st St, New York NY 10016.............212-696-4666
Reggie Jackson, 135 Sheldon Ter, New Haven CT 06511 203-787-5191
Jeroboam Inc*, 120-D 27th St, San Francisco CA 94110................................415-824-8085

Rodney C Jones Inc*, 1602 Front St, San Diego CA 92101 619-236-0477
Wolfgang Kaehler Photo*, 13641 NE 42nd St, Bellevue WA 98005 206-881-6581
Clemens Kalischer, Main St, Stockbridge MA 01262 416-298-5500
William Keochling, 339 E Madison Ave, Wheaton IL 60187........................312-665-4379
Keystone Press Agency*, PO Box 2136, New York NY 10163....................212-924-8123
W Scott Knoke, 178 N Bridge St, Somerville NJ 08876...........................201-526-4682
Jill Krementz, 228 E 48th St, New York NY 10017....................................212-688-0480
George E Landis Photography, 16 Prospect Hill, Cromwell CT 06416......203-635-4720
Frans Lanting, 714-A Riverside Ave, Santa Cruz CA 95060 408-429-9490
Robert Lee II Photography, 1512 Northlin Dr, St Louis MO 63122...........314-965-5832
Jess Lee Photography, 6799 Derek Ln, Idaho Falls ID 83401 208-529-4535
Tom & Pat Leeson, PO Box 2498, Vancouver WA 98668 206-256-0436
Freda Leinwand, 463 West St, New York NY 10014...................................212-691-0997
Max Lent Productions, 24 Wellington Ave, Rochester NY 14611 716-328-5126
Frederic Lewis Inc*, 134 W 29th St, New York NY 10001..........................212-594-8816
Lewis Sloan Publishing Co*, 2546 Etiwan Ave, Charleston SC 29407.......803-766-4735
Library of Congress*, Prints & Photographs Div, Wash DC 20540 202-287-6394
Life Picture Service*, Time-Life Bldg, New York NY 10020......................212-841-4800
Harry Liles Productions, 1060 N Lillian Way, Los Angeles CA 90038......213-466-1614
Tony Linck, 2100 Linwood Ave, Fort Lee NJ 07024....................................201-944-5454
Lincoln Farm Camp*, 140 Heatherdell Rd, Ardsley NY 10502...................914-693-4222
Lincoln Picture Studio*, 225 Lookout Dr, Dayton OH 45419....................513-293-9234
E Trina Lipton*, 60 E 8th St Box 310, New York NY 10003.......................212-533-3148
Marty Loken, 1530 Westlake Ave N, Seattle WA 98109..............................206-282-8116
Rafael Macia, 55 W 82nd St, New York NY 10024......................................212-799-4441
Magnum Photos Inc*, 251 Park Ave S, New York NY 10010 212-475-7600
Michael Philip Manheim*, PO Box 35, Marblehead MA 01945...................617-631-3560
Marine Mammal Fund*, Ft Mason Ctr Bldg E, San Fransico CA 94123..415-775-4636
Jim Markham, 2739 SE Loop 410, San Antonio TX 78222 512-648-0403
Alec Marshall, 308 E 73rd St, New York NY 10021 212-772-8523
Lynn McAfee, 11159 Acama St, N Hollywood CA 91602..............................213-761-1317
Fred W McDarrah, 505 La Guardia Pl, New York NY 10012.......................212-777-1236
Jack McDowell, 2120 Santa Cruz Ave, Menlo Park CA 94025 415-854-0408
Lynn Mclaren, Box 297, 104 Charles St, Boston MA 02114.......................617-227-7448
Bruce A McMillan, Box 85, Shapleigh ME 04076..207-324-9453
Robert Mentken Concept & Design, 51 E 97th St, New York NY 10029...212-534-5101
Louis Mercier*, 15 Long Lots Rd, Westport CT 06880................................203-227-1620
Michael Ochs Archives*, 45 Breeze Ave, Venice CA 90291.......................213-396-0202
Benn Mitchell, 103 5th Ave, New York NY 10003 212-255-8686
Christopher Morrow Photo, 163 Pleasant St, Arlington MA 02174 617-648-6770
B Morse Inc/Computer Slide Co, 16 Aberdeen St, Boston MA 02215......617-262-1550
The Museums at Stony Brook*, 1208 Rt 25A, Stony Brook NY 11790......516-751-0066
Natl Baseball Library*, Main St, Cooperstown NY 13326 607-547-9988
Naturegraphs, 224 Flora Way, Golden CO 80401.......................................303-279-8097
Natures Image Design*, PO Box 255, Davenport CA 95017 408-426-8205
New West Agency*, PO Box 19039, Denver CO 80219................................303-935-0277
Marvin E Newman*, 227 Central Park W, New York NY 10024 212-362-2044
Newspix, 92 S Lansdowne Ave, Lansdowne PA 19050................................215-622-2200
Dianora Niccolini Creations, 356 E 78th St, New York NY 10021............212-288-1698
Nick Nicholson Photography, 1503 Brooks Ave, Raleigh NC 27607.........919-787-6076
Boyd Norton Photoghrapher, Box 2605, Evergreen CO 80439...................303-674-3009
Jack Novak, 505 W Windsor Ave, Alexandria VA 22302............................703-836-4439
NYT Pictures*, 229 W 43rd St, New York NY 10036 212-556-1243

Robert O'Connor, 1556 E New York Dr, Altadena CA 91001 818-791-9478
John Okladek, 1226 16th St, Fort Lee NJ 07024.....................................201-224-3309
Arleen Olson, 57 Glen Lane, Novato CA 94947.....................................415-892-4161
Omni Photo Comm*, 521 Madison Ave, New York NY 10022 212-751-6530
Nadine Orabona, 3008 Petite Ct, Los Angeles CA 90039 213-660-0473
Outreach Press, 198 Yerba Buena Ave, San Francisco CA 94127 415-661-5969
Pacific West Photographics*, Box 1844, Corvallis OR 97339.....................503-757-8761
Nancy Palmer*, Box 329, Bantam CT 06750 203-567-5543
Tom Pantages, 7 Linden Ave, Gloucester MA 01930 617-525-3678
Pell Studio, 300 E 40th St, New York NY 10016 212-490-2845
Pensacola Historical Society*, 405 S Adams St, Pensacola FL 32501 904-433-1559
People Weekly Syndication*, Time & Life Bldg, New York NY 10020.....212-841-4145
Robert Perron Photographer, 119 Chestnut St, Branford CT 06405 203-481-2004
Allan A Philiba*, 3408 Bertha Dr, Baldwin NY 11510.............................212-286-0948
Phillips Photo Illustrators*, 4 New St, Colts Neck NJ 07722.....................201-462-6404
Photo Communications Co, 488 Madison Ave, New York NY 10022.......212-688-1930
Photo Researchers Inc*, 60 E 56th St, New York NY 10022.......................212-758-3420
Photo Trends*, PO Box 650, Freeport NY 11520.................................516-379-1440
Photofile Intl Ltd*, 32 E 31st St, New York NY 10016 212-889-9700
Photographers Aspen*, 1280 Ute Ave, Aspen CO 81611.........................303-925-2317
Photographix, PO Box 8213, Ann Arbor MI 48107.................................313-769-6756
Photography for Industry*, 1697 Broadway, New York NY 10019 212-757-9255
Photophile*, 2311 Kettner Blvd, San Diego CA 92101 619-234-4431
Photoreporters Inc, 875 Ave of the Americas, New York NY 10001 212-736-7602
Photos By Arthur Matula, 6444 Cleo St, Diego CA 92115 619-582-8286
PhotoSource Intl, Pine Lake Farm, Osceola WI 54020 715-248-3800
Phototake*, 4523 Broadway, New York NY 10040.................................212-942-8185
Photri Photo Research*, PO Box 26428, Alexandria VA 22313.....................703-836-4439
Pictorial Parade Inc*, 130 W 42nd St, New York NY 10036 212-840-2026
Picturemakers Inc, One Paul Dr, Succasunna NJ 07876...........................201-584-3000
Ted Polumbaum Photography, 326 Harvard St, Cambridge MA 02139 617-491-4947
Press Photo Service, 79-14 Parsons Blvd, Flushing NY 11366.....................212-526-9069
Norman Prince Photographer, 3245 25th St, San Francisco CA 94110......415-821-6595
Gordon A Reims, Box 250, Cashtown PA 17310.....................................717-334-2949
Reynolds Photography*, 3630 W 183rd St, Homewood IL 60430 312-799-6851
H Armstrong Roberts Inc*, 4203 Locust St, Philadelphia PA 19104.........215-386-6300
Rosenthal Art Slides*, 5456 S Ridgewood Ct, Chicago IL 60615.................312-324-3367
Jeffrey L Rotman, 14 Cottage Ave, Somerville MA 02144 617-666-0874
Shelly Rusten, 225 1st Ave, New York NY 10003.................................212-982-7063
Nick Samardge Inc, 568 Broadway, New York NY 10012 212-226-6770
Scala Fine Arts Transparencies*, 65 Bleecker St, New York NY 10012...212-673-4988
Carl Schreier, Box 193, Moose WY 83012 406-538-8960
Schroeder Eastwood Photo, 627 Kentucky Ave SE, Wash DC 20003.........202-543-2929
Science Photo Library Intl*, 118 E 28th St, New York NY 10016.............212-683-4028
Mark Sexton, 32 Mason St, Salem MA 01970.....................................617-745-7653
J L Shaffer Photo Services, 2015 Lombard St, Dubuque IA 52001 319-582-0843
Shashinka Photo Inc*, 501 5th Ave Ste 2102, New York NY 10017...........212-490-2180
Ray Shaw, 255 W 90 St, New York NY 10024.....................................212-873-0808
Shelburne Museum Inc*, Shelburne VT 05482.....................................802-985-3346
Shellphoto Bob Shell, 202 3rd Ave, Radford VA 24141 703-639-6577
Bradley Shostal Assoc Inc*, 164 Madison Ave, New York NY 10016 212-686-8850
Sickles Photo Reporting Service, Box 98, Maplewood NJ 07040 201-763-6355
Layle Silbert, 505 La Guardia Pl #16C, New York NY 10012 212-677-0947

Dick Smith Photography, Box X, N Conway NH 03860................................603-356-2814
Elliott Varner Smith, Box 5268, Berkeley CA 94705 415-654-9235
Chris Sorensen, PO Box 1760 Murray Hill Sta, New York NY 10156.......212-684-0551
Southern Stock Photos*, 3601 W Commercial, Ft Lauderdale FL 33309..305-949-5191
Specil Assignments, PO Box 27025, Honolulu HI 96827.............................808-524-7750
Sports Action Photography, Box 1545, Princeton NJ 08542......................609-924-9002
Sports Illustrated Pictures*, 19th Fl, New York NY 10020......................212-841-3663
Tom Stack & Assoc*, 3645 Jeannie Dr #212, Colorado Spgs CO 80907...303-570-1000
David C Stambaugh, 1508 S 37th St, Fort Smith AR 72903.......................501-783-4354
Starwood Assoc*, PO Box 40503, Washington DC 20016 202-362-7404
Larry Stein, 568 Broadway Rm 706, New York NY 10012 212-219-9077
Lucille Stewart, 4925 Edgerton Ave, Encino CA 91436.............................818-789-4595
Sticht Martin, 217 Dean St, Brooklyn NY 11217 718-643-0857
Stock Imagery*, 711 Kalamath St, Denver CO 80204................................303-592-1091
The Stock Market*, 1181 Broadway, New York NY 10001 212-684-7878
David M Stone, 7 Granston Way, Buzzards Bay MA 02532 617-759-9666
Erika Stone, 327 E 82nd St, New York NY 10028.......................................212-737-6435
Fred Swartz, 135 S La Brea, Los Angeles CA 90036...................................213-939-2789
Arthur Swoger, 63 Savoy St, Providence RI 02906 401-331-0440
Sygma*, 225 W 57th St, Ste 700, New York NY 10019................................212-765-1820
Taurus Photos Inc*, 118 E 28th St, New York NY 10016............................212-683-4025
Max Tharpe Photos*, 520 NE 7th Ave #3, Ft Lauderdale FL 33301 305-763-5449
Three Lions Inc*, 145 E 32nd St, New York NY 10016................................212-725-2242
Time Pix Syndication*, Time & Life Bldg, New York NY 10020 212-841-3866
Tom Tuttle, Box 91529 Victoria Sta, Santa Barbara CA 93190 805-683-2812
Uniphoto Picture Agency*, 1071 Wisconsin Ave NW, Wash DC 20007.....202-333-0500
United States Naval Institute*, Annapolis MD 21402...............................301-268-6110
Don & Pat Valenti Photo, 2784 Mavor Ln, Highland Park IL 60035..........312-432-7653
Mary Van de Ven*, PO Box 27025, Honolulu HI 96827 808-538-7665
Visualworld*, Box 804, Oak Park IL 60303 312-366-5084
Mike L Wannemacher, 10555 Washington Blvd, Indianapolis IN 46280....317-844-6190
Joseph Flack Weiler, 288 Lexington St, Watertown MA 02172.................617-926-5160
Weinrauch & Assoc, Box 13251, St Paul MN 55113....................................612-341-8243
Jerome Wexler Nature Photo*, 13 Langshire Dr, Madison CT 06443........203-245-2396
White Eyes Design, 24514 TR 167, Fresno OH 43824 614-545-6881
Wide World Photos Inc*, 50 Rockefeller Plaza, New York NY 10020.......212-621-1930
W G Williams Assoc, 1100 17th St NW #1000, Washington DC 20036.....202-463-8017
Mike Wilson Studio, 441 Park Ave S, New York NY 10016.........................212-683-3557
Words & Photographs/S Trimble, Box 8828, Salt Lake City UT 84108....801-364-3031
Joan Yarfitz Photo Env*, 2021 Vista del Mar, Los Angeles CA 90068......213-465-9947
Katherine Young Agency*, 140 E 40 St, New York NY 10016....................212-684-0999
Donald Young, 166 E St Apt 3C, New York NY 10021 212-593-0010

PLAY PUBLISHERS

This section includes firms that publish plays. See also Theatres, Theatrical Workshops, and Contests & Awards for other playwriting programs.

Anchorage Press Inc, PO Box 8067, New Orleans LA 70182 504-283-8868
Aran Press, 1320 S 3rd St, Louisville KY 40208..502-636-0115
Art Craft Publishing Co, PO Box 1058, Cedar Rapids IA 52406 319-364-6311
Arte Publico Press, Univ of Houston 4800 Calhoun, Houston TX 77004..713-749-4768
Walter H Baker Co, 100 Chauncy St, Boston MA 02111................................617-482-1280
Ball State Univ Forum, English Dept, Muncie IN 47306 317-285-8456
Box 749: Printable Arts Soc, PO Box 749, New York NY 10011 212-980-0519
Broadway Play Publishing, 357 W 20th St, New York NY 10011 212-563-3820
Callaloo, Univ of Kentucky, Lexington KY 40503 606-257-6784
Calyx, PO Box B, Corvallis OR 97339...503-753-9384
Carroll College, Helena MT 59625..406-442-3450
CCLM, 2 Park Ave, New York NY 10016 212-481-5245
Center For Puppetry Arts, 1404 Spring St NW, Atlanta GA 30309............404-873-3089
Charles River Creative Arts Press, 56 Centre St, Dover MA 02030 617-785-1260
Children's Playmate, 1100 Waterway Blvd, Indianapolis IN 46202............317-636-8881
I E Clark Inc, St Johns Rd PO Box 246, Schulenburg TX 78956 409-743-3232
Coach House Press Inc, Box 458, Morton Grove IL 60053............................312-967-1777
Confrontation, CW Post College LIU, Greenville NY 11548.........................516-299-2391
Contemporary Drama Service, 885 Elkton Dr, Colo Spgs CO 80907 303-630-8940
Dimension, PO Box 26673, Austin TX 78755...512-345-0622
Drama Book Publishers, PO Box 816 Gracie Sta, New York NY 10028 ...212-517-4455
Dramatic Publishing Co, 4150 N Milwaukee, Chicago IL 60641 312-545-2062
Dramatics Magazine, 3368 Central Pkwy, Cincinnati OH 45225 513-559-1996
Dramatists Play Service, 440 Park Ave S, New York NY 10016..................212-683-8960
Eldridge Publishing Co, Drawer 216, Franklin OH 45005............................513-746-6531
Feedback Theatrebooks, PO Box 5187, Bloomington IN 47402...................812-334-0325
Samuel French Inc, 45 W 25th St, New York NY 10010 212-206-8990
Golden Rod Puppets, 218 Northeast Ave, Swannoano NC 28778 704-686-5386
Hawaii Review, Univ of Hawaii English Dept, Honolulu HI 96822 808-948-8548
Helicon Nine, PO Box 22412, Kansas City MO 64113....................................913-345-0802
Heuer Publ Co, Box 248, Cedar Rapids IA 52406 319-364-6311
Instructor, 545 5th Ave, New York NY 10017 212-503-2888
JH Press, PO Box 294 Village Sta, New York NY 10014 212-255-4713
Lation Plawrights Co, 466 Grand St, New York NY 10002 212-598-0400
Lillenas Publishing Co, PO Box 419527, Kansas City MO 64141 816-931-1900
Massachusetts Review, Univ of Mass, Amherst MA 01003 413-545-2689
Midwest Play Lab Prog, 2301 Franklin E, Minneapolis MN 55406 612-332-7481
Modern Intl Drama, Theatre Dept SUNY, Binghamton NY 13901............607-777-2704
Modern Liturgy, 160 E Virginia St #290, San Jose CA 95112 408-285-8505
Nederlander Organization Inc, 1564 Broadway, New York NY 10036......212-730-8200
New Plays Inc, Box 273, Rowyaton CT 06853 203-866-4520
New Southern Lit Messenger, 400 S Laurel, Richmond VA 23220.............804-780-1244
North Amer Mentor, 1745 Madison St, Fennimore WI 53809......................608-822-6237
Oracle Press Ltd, 5323 Heatherstone Dr, Baton Rouge LA 70820 504-766-5577
Joseph Papp Producer, 425 Layfayette St, New York NY 10003.................212-598-7129

Performing Arts Jour Publ, 325 Spring St #318, New York NY 10013 212-243-3885
Pioneer Drama Service, 2171 S Colorado Blvd, Denver CO 80222 303-759-4297
Players Press Inc, PO Box 1132, Studio City CA 91604 818-789-4980
Plays Inc, 120 Boylston St, Boston MA 02116...617-423-3157
Read Magazine, 245 Long Hill Rd, Middletown CT 06457........................203-347-7251
Scholastic Scope, 730 Broadway, New York NY 10003................................212-505-3000
Geo Spelvin's Theatre Book, Box 361, Newark DE 19715.........................302-737-5803
Tejas Art Press, 207 Terrell Rd, San Antonio TX 78209...........................512-826-7803
Theater, 222 York St, New Haven CT 06520..203-432-1568
Touchstone Magazine, Kansas State Univ, Manhattan KS 66502...............913-532-6716
TSL Press, 139 W 22nd St, New York NY 10011 212-741-1032
West Coast Plays, PO Box 7206, Berkeley CA 94707.................................415-841-3096

PRINTERS

This section includes printers that specialize in book printing. Some provide complete
book manufacturing services, including typesetting, paste-up, printing and binding.
See also Typesetters, Illustrators & Designers, Book Producers and Subsidy Book
Publishers for other firms providing book production services.

AC Publications, PO Box 238, Homer NY 13077..607-749-4040
Academy Books, 10-12 Cleveland Ave Box 757, Rutland VT 05701............802-773-9194
Access Composition Services, 110 S 41st Ave, Phoenix AZ 85009..............602-272-7778
Ad Infintum Press, 7 N MacQuesten Pkwy, Mount Vernon NY 10551 914-664-5930
Adams & Abbott, 46 Summer St, Boston MA 02110....................................617-542-1621
The Adams Group Inc, 225 Varick St, New York NY 10014.......................212-255-4900
Adams Press, 30 W Washington St, Chicago IL 60602 312-676-3426
Algen Press Corp, 18-06 130th St, College Point NY 11356........................718-463-4605
Amer Offset Printers Inc, 3600 S Hill St, Los Angeles CA 90007...............213-231-4133
Amer Pizzi Offset Corp, 141 E 44th St, New York NY 10017 212-986-1658
Amko Color Graphics, 1133 Broadway Ste 404, New York NY 10010.......212-929-2326
Anthoesen Press, 37 Exchange St, Portland ME 04112 207-774-3301
Apollo Books, 263 W 5th St, Winona MN 55987...507-454-7372
Arcata Graphics, 101 Merritt 7 Box 6030, Norwalk CT 06856 203-846-6000
Arcata Graphics/Fairfield, 100 N Miller St, Fairfield PA 17320 717-642-5871
Arcata Graphics/Halliday, Cicuit St, West Hanover MA 02339 617-826-8385
Arcata Graphics/Kingsport, PO Box 711, Kingsport TN 37662..................615-378-1000
D Armstrong Co Inc, 2000-M Govenors Circle, Houston TX 77092..........713-688-1441
Athol Press, 225 Exchange St PO Box A, Athol MA 01331 617-249-3535
Autopage Book Composition, 2463 Long Beach, Oceanside NY 11572.....516-766-6355
Banta Co, Curtis Reed Plaza, Menasha WI 54952 414-722-7771
Bay Port Press Inc, 100 W 35th St, Natl City CA 92050 619-420-6296
Harold Berliner, 224 Main St, Nevada city CA 95959.................................916-273-2278
Bireline Publishing Co, 220 S Fulton, Newell IA 50568 712-272-4417
Bojalad Color Corp, PO Box 107, Beaver Springs PA 17812 212-819-0045
The Book Press Inc, Putney Rd, Brattleboro VT 05301 802-257-7701
Book Promotions Unlimited, Box 122, Flushing MI 48433 313-659-6683
Book-Mart Press Inc, 2001 423rd St, N Bergen NJ 07047..........................201-864-1887
Bookbuilders Ltd, 1170 Broadway Rm 1004, New York NY 10001............212-686-3533
BookCrafters Inc, 140 Buchanan St, Chelsea MI 48118 313-475-9145
BookMasters, 830 Claremont Ave PO Box 159, Ashland OH 44805.........419-289-6051

BookWrights, 220 Main St Box 49, Neshkoro WI 54960 414-293-8355
Braceland Brothers Inc, 7625 Suffolk Ave, Philadelphia PA 19153............215-492-0200
Braun-Brumfield Inc, 100 N Staebler Rd, Ann Arbor MI 48106 313-662-3291
Brennan Printing, 100 Main St, Deep River IA 52222 515-595-2000
The R L Bryan Co, Box 368 Greystone Exec Park, Columbia SC 29202....803-779-3560
C&M Press, 850 E 73rd Ave #12, Thornton CO 80229 303-289-4757
Capital City Press Inc, PO Box 546, Montpelier VT 05602.........................802-223-5207
Carnes Publication Services, 23811 Chagrin, Beachwood OH 44122 216-292-7959
Carqueville Printing Co, 2200 Estes Ave, Elk Grove Vilg IL 60007..........312-439-8700
Chanticleer Co Inc, 424 Madison Ave, New York NY 10017 212-486-3900
The Chaucer Press Inc, 201 Clark Rd, Duryea PA 18642.............................717-655-2905
Clarkwood Corp, 690 Union Blvd, Totowa NJ 07512 201-256-2456
Colortone Press, 2400 17th St NW, Washington DC 20009 202-387-6800
Coneco Laser Graphics, 58 Dix Ave, Glen Falls NY 12801 518-793-3823
Connecticut Printers Inc, 55 Granby St, Bloomfield CT 06002...................203-242-0711
Conservatory of Amer Letters, PO Box 123, S Thomaston ME 04858.......207-354-6550
Contemporary Lithographers Inc, 1501 Blount St, Raleigh NC 27603......919-821-2211
Cookbook Publishers Inc, 2101 Kansas City Rd, Olathe KS 66061 913-764-5900
Corley Printing Co, 9804 Page Blvd, St Louis MO 63132..............................314-426-3900
The Country Press Inc, PO Box 489, Middleborough MA 02346 617-947-4485
Courier Graphics, 4325 Old Shepherdsville Rd, Louisville KY 40218 502-458-5303
Crane Duplicating Service Inc, PO Box 487, Barnstable MA 02630.........617-362-3441
Creative Press & Mfg, 1133 Broadway Ste 404, New York NY 10010 212-929-2326
Crest Litho Inc, PO Box 12125, Albany NY 12212..518-456-2296
Cushing Malloy Inc, 1350 N Main St, Ann Arbor MI 48107 313-663-8554
Custom Color Communication, 77 Main St, Tappan NY 10983.................914-365-0414
Daamen Inc Publishing Co, Industrial Park, West Rutland VT 05777 802-438-5472
Dalee Bookbinding Co Inc, 267 Douglass St, Brooklyn NY 11217.............718-852-6969
Danner Press Corp, 1250 Camden Ave SW, Canton OH 44706 216-454-5692
Davis Printing Corp, 35 Green St, Hackensack NJ 07601 201-343-5100
John H Dekker & Sons, 2941 Clydon St SW, Grand Rapids MI 49509......616-538-5160
The Delmar Co, 9601 Monroe Rd, Charlotte NC 28222................................704-847-9801
Delta Lithograph, 28210 N Ave Stanford, Valencia CA 91355...................805-257-0584
Dharama Press, 1241 21st St, Oakland CA 94607 415-839-3931
Dickinson Press Inc, 630 Myrtle St NW, Grand Rapids MI 49504............616-451-2957
Dinner & Klein, 600 S Spokane St PO Box 3814, Seattle WA 98124.........206-682-2494
Diversified Printing & Publishing, 2632 Saturn St, Brea CA 92621 714-993-4541
DNP America Inc, 1633 Broadway 15th fl, New York NY 10019 212-397-1880
R R Donnelley & Sons Co, 2223 S M L King Dr, Chicago IL 60616...........312-326-8000
W J Doran Inc, Willows Ave, Collingdale PA 19023.....................................215-583-5741
Dunn & Co Inc, Miles Bldg Orchard St, S Lancaster MA 01561 617-368-8505
Eastern Lithographing Corp, 28-15 N 17th St, Philadelphia PA 19132 215-225-1150
Eastwood Printing Co, 2901 Blake St, Denver CO 80205 303-296-1905
EBS Inc Book Services, 290 Broadway, Lynbrook NY 11563 516-593-1199
Economy Bookcraft, 681 Market St #531, San Francisco CA 94105 415-777-9509
Edison Lithographing & Printing, 418 W 25th St, New York NY 10001 ..212-741-2212
Edwards Brothers Inc, 2500 S State St, Ann Arbor MI 48106 313-769-1000
Eerdmans Printing Co, 231 Jefferson Ave SE, Grand Rapids MI 49503...616-451-0763
Fairfield Graphics, N Miller Rd, Fairfield PA 17320 717-642-5871
Fairview Litho, 72 Fairview Ave, Poughkeepsie NY 12601 914-473-4747
FDC Publishing, PO Box 206, Stewartsville NJ 08886 201-479-6191
Federated Lithographers-Printers, 369 Prairie, Providence RI 02901.......401-781-8100
Fleetwood Litho Corp, 304 Hudson St, New York NY 10013......................212-924-4422

Foote & Davis/Lincoln, PO Box 81608, Lincoln NE 68501 402-474-5825
Fort Orange Press Inc, 31 Sand Creek Rd, Albany NY 12201 518-489-3233
Four Winds Press, 401 Lincoln, Coulee Dam WA 99116.........................509-633-2060
Franklin Press, 210 S Des Plaines, Chicago IL 60060.............................312-648-1512
Ray Freiman & Co, 184 Brookdale Rd, Stamford CT 06903 203-322-2474
Futura Printing, 517 E Ocean Ave, Boynton Beach FL 33425....................305-734-0825
G & H/Soho Ltd, 39 W 14th St, New York NY 10011................................212-645-5444
Gaylord Ltd, 633 N La Peer Dr, Los Angeles CA 90069.........................213-274-5407
Geiger Brothers, Box 1609 Mount Hope Ave, Lewiston ME 04240 207-783-2001
General Offset Co Inc, 234 16th St, Jersey City NJ 07310 201-420-0500
John M Gettler Bookbinder, 225 Varick St, New York NY 10014 212-675-2110
Goshen Litho Inc, Rt 17M, Chester NY 10918 914-469-2102
Graphic Publishing Co, Box 158, Lake Mills IA 50450 515-492-2000
Great Northern/Design Printing Co, 5401 Fargo Ave, Skokie IL 60077 ...312-674-4740
Griffin Printing & Lithograph, 544 W Colorado St, Glendale CA 91204.213-245-3671
Griffon Graphics/Litho Prestige, 747 3rd Ave, New York NY 10017 212-223-4603
GRT Book Printing, 3960 E 14th St, Oakland CA 94601 415-534-5032
Haddon Craftsmen Inc, Ash St & Wyoming Ave, Scranton PA 18509 717-348-9211
W F Hall Inc, 1 Pierce Pl, Itasca IL 60143 312-941-5600
Halliday Lithograph, Circuit St, West Hanover MA 02339 617-826-8385
Hamilton Printing Co, PO Box 232, Renselaer NY 12144........................518-477-9345
Harlo Printing Co, 50 Victor, Detroit MI 48203 313-883-3600
David Haworth Assoc, 2550 M St NW #525, Washington DC 20037.........202-293-9065
Haymarket Press, 3451 Cedar Ave S, Minneapolis MN 55407....................612-721-4401
Heffernan Press Inc, 35 New St, Worcester MA 01605.............................800-922-8229
Heritage Printers Inc, 510 W 4th St, Charlotte NC 28202 704-372-5784
The D B Hess Co, 1150 McConnell Rd, Woodstock IL 60098.....................815-338-6900
Hooven-Dayton Corp, 430 Leo St, Dayton OH 45404..............................513-224-1108
Carl Hungness Publishing, PO Box 24308, Speedway IN 46224................317-244-4792
Inter-Collegiate Press, 6015 Travis Ln, Shawnee Mission KS 66201 913-432-8100
Interactive Composition, 3333 Vincent Rd, Pleasant Hill CA 94523 415-935-4810
Interstate Book Mfrs Inc, PO Box 594, Danville IL 61832 217-446-0500
Interstate Book Mfg Inc, 2115 E Kansas City Rd, Olathe KS 66061 913-764-5600
Interstate Printers & Publishers, 19 N Jackson St, Danville IL 61832 217-446-0500
Interstate Printing Co, 2002-22 N 16th St, Omaha NE 68103 402-341-8028
Jersey Printing Co, 111 Linnet St, Bayonne NJ 07002.............................201-436-4200
The Job Shop, PO Box 305, Woods Hole MA 02543 617-548-9600
The Johnson & Harden Co, 3600 Red Bank Rd, Cincinnati OH 45227.....513-271-8834
Johnson Graphics, 120 Frentree Lake Rd, East Dubuque IL 61025...........815-747-6511
Johnson Publishing Co, 1880 57th Ct, Boulder CO 80301.......................303-443-1576
Jostens Printing & Publ, 5501 Norman Ctr Dr, Minneapolis MN 55437 ..612-830-8415
Kaumagraph Corp, 14th & Poplar Sts, Wilmington DE 19899...................302-575-1500
Kent Associates Inc, 480 Canal St, New York NY 10013..........................212-226-8080
Kimberly Press Inc, PO Box 399, Goleta CA 93116.................................805-964-7079
KNI Inc Book Mfg, 1061 S St College Pkwy, Anaheim CA 92806...........714-956-7300
C J Krehbiel Co, 3962 Virginia Ave, Cincinnati OH 45227......................513-271-6035
W A Krueger Co, 16555 W Rogers Dr, New Berlin WI 53151....................414-784-2000
Lake Book/John F Cuneo, 2085 N Cornell Ave, Melrose Park IL 60160 ..312-345-7000
The Lane Press Inc, 305 St Paul St, Burlington VT 05401 802-863-5555
Latham Process Corp, 200 Hudson St, New York NY 10013.....................212-966-4500
Hal Leighton Printing, PO Box 3952, N Hollywood CA 91605..................213-983-1105
Little King Publishing & Novelty, 6126 Broadway, Cleveland OH 44120..216-641-2119
Lorell Press, Bodwell St Avon Industrial Park, Avon MA 02322.................617-471-7750

Lorrah & Hitchcock, 301 S 15th St, Murray KY 42071................................502-753-3759
John D Lucas Printing Co, 1820 Portal St, Baltimore MD 21224................301-633-4200
Mack Printing Co, 20th & Northampton Sts, Easton PA 18042 215-258-9111
Madadori-AME Publishing Ltd, 740 Broadway, New York NY 10003......212-758-6050
Major Press Inc, 448 W 16th St, New York NY 10011................................212-947-5100
Malloy Lithographing Inc, 5411 Jackson Rd, Ann Arbor MI 48106 313-665-6113
Mandarin Offset Inc, 1501 3rd Ave, New York NY 10028 212-772-1030
Maple-Vail Book Mfg Group, Willow Springs Ln, York PA 17405 717-764-5911
Marbridge Printing Co Inc, 225 Varick St, New York NY 10014................212-255-4900
Mariposa Press, 447 E Channel Rd, Benicia CA 94510................................707-746-0800
Maverick Publications, Drawer 5007, Bend OR 97708 503-382-6978
The Mazer Corp, 2501 Neff Rd, Dayton OH 45414....................................513-276-6181
McClain Printing Co, 212 Main St, Parsons WV 26287..............................304-478-2881
McGill/Jensen Inc, 655 Fairview Ave N, St Paul MN 55104 612-645-0751
McGregor & Werner/St Mary's, 6411 Chillum Pl NW, Wash DC 20012..202-722-2200
McNaughton & Gunn Inc, PO Box M-2060, Ann Arbor MI 48106............313-429-5411
Memex Books Inc, 200 Pond Ave, Middesex NJ 08846................................201-752-7220
Meriden-Stinehour Press, 47 Billard St, Meriden CT 06450 203-235-7929
Merit Engraving Co, 307 W 38th St, New York NY 10018..........................212-279-8252
Messenger Graphics, 1207 E Washington St, Phoenix AZ 85030 602-254-7231
Micro Book Manufacturing Co, 723 S Wells St, Chicago IL 60607 312-922-2083
Modern World Publishing Co, PO Box 65766, Los Angeles CA 90065 213-221-8044
Moran Colorgraphic Inc, PO Box 66538, Baton Rouge LA 70896..............504-923-2550
Morgan Press, 145 Palisade St, Dobbs Ferry NY 10522............................914-693-0023
Morgan Printing, 900 Old Koenig Lane #135, Austin TX 78756 512-459-5194
Morningrise Printing, 1525 W MacArthur #1, Costa Mesa CA 92626 714-957-8494
Multi Business Press, 135 N Main, Hillsboro KS 67063 316-947-3966
Multiprint Inc, Stonehouse Rd, Jay NY 12941 212-488-9797
Murray Printing Co, Pleasant St, Westford MA 01886 617-692-6321
Muscle Bound Bindery Inc, 701 Plymouth Ave, Minneapolis MN 55411 ..612-522-4406
Museum Press Inc, 1500 Eckington Pl NE, Washington DC 20002 202-832-4886
Natl Publishing Co, 24th & Locust Sts, Philadelphia PA 19101................215-732-1863
Natl Reproductions Corp, 433 E Larned, Detroit MI 48226......................313-961-5252
Naturegraph Publishers, 3543 Indian Creek, Happy Camp CA 96039......916-493-5353
William S Nein & Co Inc, 1285 Main St, Buffalo NY 14209......................716-882-2600
Newsfoto Publishing Co, 2027 Industrial Blvd, San Angelo TX 76902......915-949-3776
Nexus Press, 608 Ralph McGill Blvd, Atlanta GA 30312 404-544-3579
North Plains Books and Art, PO Box 1830, Aberdeen SD 57402................605-226-3548
Offset Paperback Manufactures Inc, Box N Rt 309 N, Dallas PA 18612..717-675-5261
Olivestone Publishing Services, 6 W 18th St, New York NY 10011 212-691-8420
The Ovid Bell Press Inc, 1201-05 Bluff St, Fulton MO 65251....................314-642-4117
Oxford Group, PO Box 269, Norway ME 04268..207-743-8958
Oxford Group, 151 Main St, Berlin OH 03570 603-752-2339
Packrat Press, 4366 N Diana Ln, Oak Arbor WA 98277 206-675-6016
Pantagraph Printing, 217 W Jefferson St, Bloomington IL 61701............309-829-1071
Paperback Press, 300 Fairfield Rd, Fairfield NJ 07006............................201-575-7070
Paraclete Press, Box 1568 Hilltop Plz Rt 6A, Orleans MA 02653 617-255-4685
Parthenon Press, 201 8th Ave S, Nashville TN 37202 615-749-6464
Patterson Printing, 1550 Territorial Rd, Benton Harbor MI 49022............616-925-2177
H Paul Publishing Co, 4883 Ronson Ct #L, San Diego CA 92111..............619-277-4850
Pearl Pressman Liberty Printing, 5th & Poplar Sts, Phila PA 19123........215-925-4900
Phillips Brothers Printers, 1555 W Jefferson, Springfield IL 62705............217-787-3014
Photo Data Inc, 419 7th St NW Ste 500, Washington DC 20004................202-783-1010

Pine Hill Press, 700 East 6th St, Freeman SD 57029 605-925-4228
Port City Press Inc, 1323 Greenwood Rd, Baltimore MD 21208................301-486-3000
Preferred Press, 1151 E Broadway, Winona MN 55987 507-452-8581
The Press In Tuscany Alley, 1 Tuscany Alley, San Francisco CA 94133....415-986-0641
Prinit Press, PO Box 65, Dublin IN 47335 317-478-4885
The Print Center, 68 Jay St, Brooklyn NY 11202................................212-875-4482
Providence Lithograph Co, 369 Prarie Ave, Providence RI 02901 401-781-8100
Publishers Choice Book Mfg, Box 848 Mars Indus Pk, Mars PA 16046....412-625-3555
Publishers Press, 1900 W 2300 South, Salt Lake City UT 84119 801-972-6600
Publishers Press Inc, 1 4th Ave, Sheperdsville KY 40165....................502-543-2251
Quad/Graphics Inc, Du Plainville Rd, Pewaukee WI 53072....................414-691-9200
Quinn-Woodbine Inc, Oceanview Rd, Woodbine NJ 08270....................609-861-5352
Quixott Press, 3291 Church School Rd, Doylestown PA 18901..................215-794-7107
Rae Publishing Co Inc, 282 Grove Ave, Cedar Grove NJ 07009................201-239-1600
Rand McNally & Co, PO Box 7600, Chicago IL 60680..........................312-267-6868
Rapport Printing Corp, 195 Hudson St, New York NY 10013................212-226-5501
Recorder Sunset Press, 99 S Van Ness Ave, San Francisco CA 94103.......415-621-5400
Regensteiner Press, 1224 W Van Buren St, Chicago IL 60607..................312-666-4200
Rich Printing Co Inc, 7131 Centennial Blvd, Nashville TN 37209 615-385-3500
Rollins Press Inc, 1624 Forsyth Rd, Orlando FL 32807 305-677-5533
Rose Printing Co Inc, 2503 Jackson Bluff Rd, Tallahassee FL 32314 904-576-4151
Sauls Lithograph Co Inc, 2424 Evarts St NE, Washington DC 20018.......202-529-9100
The Saybrook Press Inc, 146 Elm St, Old Saybrook CT 06475 203-388-5737
G Schirmer Inc, 866 3rd Ave, New York NY 10022................................212-702-5500
Science Press, 300 W Chestnut St, Ephrata PA 17522............................717-733-7981
Seaboard Lithograph Corp, 37 E 18th St, New York NY 10003................212-475-3481
Semline Inc, 180 Wood Rd, Braintree MA 02184................................617-843-8100
Serif Press Inc, 1331 H St NW, Washington DC 20005..........................202-737-4650
Service Webb Offset Corp, 2500 S Dearborn St, Chicago IL 60616............312-567-7000
Sheridan Press, Fame Ave, Hanover PA 17331 717-632-3535
Singapore Trade Dev Board, 350 S Figueroa, Los Angeles CA 90071.......213-617-7358
Smith Edwards Dunlap Co, 2867 E Allegheny, Phila PA 19134................215-425-8800
Southeastern FRONT, 565 17th St NW, Cleveland TN 37311..................615-479-3244
Southeastern Printing Co, 3601 SE Dixie Hwy, Stuart FL 33494 305-287-2141
Spilman Printing Co, 1801 9th St, Sacramento CA 95814 916-448-3511
Spiritual Healing Ministry, 2020 9th St SW, Canton OH 44706................216-454-1598
Staked Plains Press Inc, PO Box 816, Canyon TX 79015 806-655-1061
Standard Printing Service, 162 N State St, Chicago IL 60601....................312-346-0499
Stevens Graphics Inc, 100 W Oxmoor Rd, Birmingham AL 35201............205-942-0511
The Stinehour Press, Lunenburg VT 05906 802-328-2507
Sultana Press/Premier Printing, 124 W Wilshire, Fullerton CA 92632....714-871-3121
Sutherland Publishing, 169566 McGregor Blvd, Ft Myers FL 33908........813-466-1626
Sweet Printing Co, PO Box 49390, Austin TX 78765 512-255-1055
John S Swift Co Inc, 1248 Research Blvd, St Louis MO 63132..................314-991-4300
Taylor Publishing Co, 1550 W Mockingbird Ln, Dallas TX 75235............214-637-2800
Telegraph Press, Cameron & Keller Sts, Harrisburg PA 17105................717-234-5091
Thomson-Shore Inc, 7300 W Joy Rd, Dexter MI 48130 313-426-3939
Toppan Printing Co Inc, 680 5th Ave, New York NY 10019......................212-975-9060
Torch Publications, 5353 Mission Ctr #124, San Diego CA 92108............619-299-2111
Town House Press Inc, 28 Midway Rd, Spring Valley NY 10977................914-425-2232
Tracor Publications, 6500 Tracor Ln, Austin TX 78721..........................512-929-2222
Univ Press, E 28 Sharp Ave, Spokane WA 99202................................509-326-2133
Univ Press, 21 East St, Winchester MA 01890....................................617-729-8000

Universal Lithographers, 10626 York Rd, Corkeyville MD 21030 301-666-2600
Universal Printing Co, 1701 Mackind Ave, St Louis MO 63110 314-771-6900
USA Inc, 50 West 34th St Ste 8A7, New York NY 10001 212-947-0618
VA Graphics Corp, 225 Varick St, New York NY 10014.............................212-255-4900
Van Volumes, 15 Railroad Ave, Wilbraham MA 01095..............................413-596-2113
Vicks Lithograph & Printing, Commercial Dr, Yorkville NY 13495 315-736-9346
Von Hoffman Pres Inc, 1000 Camera Ave, St Louis MO 63126 314-966-0909
Waldon Press Inc, 216 W 18th St, New York NY 10011 212-691-9220
Walker Prismatic Engraving, 141 E 25th St, New York NY 10010 212-689-5353
Wallace Press, 4600 W Rosevelt Rd, Hillside IL 60162.............................312-626-2000
Walsworth Publishing Co, 306 N Kansas Ave, Marceline MO 64658 816-376-3543
Warrin Graphics, 102 Swinick Dr, Dunmore PA 18512.............................717-961-5410
Webb & Sons Inc, 370 Lexington Ave, New York NY 10017......................212-889-5392
The Webb Co, 1999 Shepard Rd, St Paul MN 55116.................................612-690-7200
Webcrafters Inc, 2211 Fordem Ave, Madison WI 53707 608-244-3561
Weidner Associates Inc, Box C-50, Cinnaminson NJ 08077.......................609-486-1755
Western Publishing Co Inc, 850 3rd Ave, New York NY 10022 212-753-8500
Whitehall Co, 1200 S Willis, Wheeling IL 60090......................................312-541-9290
Whittet & Shepperson, 3rd & Canal Sts, Richmond VA 23204 804-649-9047
Wickersham Printing Co Inc, 2959 Old Tree Dr, Lancaster PA 17603 717-299-5731
Wilcox Press, Box 9, Ithaca NY 14850 607-272-1212
Wimmer Brothers Inc, 4210 B F Goodrich Blvd, Memphis TN 38181.......901-362-8900
Worzalla Publishing Co, 3535 Jefferson St, Stevens Point WI 54481 715-344-9600
Writers Publishing Service Co, 1512 Western Ave, Seattle WA 98101......206-284-9954
Henry Wurst Inc, 1331 Saline St, N Kansas City MO 64116.......................816-842-3113
Xerographic Reproduction Ctr, 400 S Dean, Englewood Clfs NJ 07631 ...201-871-4011
Yarrow Inc, PO Box 442, Summit NJ 07901 201-273-8390
Yorktown Graphics, 2305 Garry Rd, Cinnaminson NJ 08077.....................609-829-0559

PUBLICISTS

These firms provide public relations services and publicity for books and authors. An asterisk (*) indicates a firm providing escort service for authors on tour.

About Books Inc, PO Box 538, Saguache CO 81149 303-589-8223
Accent on Broadcasting, 165 W 66th St, New York NY 10023....................212-362-3616
Alice B Acheson, 136 E 36th St, New York NY 10016 212-532-2282
Ad Infinitum Advertising, 7 N MacQueston, Mt Vernon NY 10550..........914-664-7944
The Alexander Co, 239 E 32nd St, New York NY 10016 212-684-0340
All Bright Promotions, 7744 31 Ave NE, Seattle WA 98115.......................206-524-2818
Amer Media Escorts*, 501 Knickerbocker Pl, Kansas City MO 64111 816-931-8916
Carolyn Anthony PR, 213 St Johns Pl, Brooklyn NY 11217.......................718-638-1822
Author's Roundtable, 20 W 37th St 8th fl, New York NY 10018.................212-239-2000
Ted Barkus Co Inc, 225 S 15th St, Philadelphia PA 19102.........................215-545-0616
Micheal D Beinner Assoc, 342 Madison Ave, New York NY 10017...........212-986-5758
Aleon Bennett*, 13455 Ventura Blvd Ste 212, Sherman Oaks CA 91423 ...818-990-8070
The Blaine Group, 7465 Beverly Blvd, Los Angeles CA 90036....................213-938-2577
Blitz Media Direct, Communication Twrs, Middle Island NY 11953 516-924-3888
The Booker, 200 W 51st St, New York NY 10019.......................................212-247-2159
Rosalie Brody, 360 E 72nd St, New York NY 10021...................................212-988-8951
Anita Helen Brooks Assoc, 155 E 55th St, New York NY 10022.................212-755-4498

Anthony Broy, 85-17 57th Rd, Elmhurst NY 11373......................................718-779-2259
Broyles Garamella Kavanaugh, 8226 Sunset, Los Angeles CA 90046........213-650-9888
Lisl Cade, 172 W 79th St, New York NY 10024..212-595-6225
Canaan Communications, 310 E 44th St #1408, New York NY 10017.....212-682-4030
Liane Kupferberg Carter, One Garrett Pl, Bronxville NY 10708 914-793-3442
Catalyst Publications, 143 Dolores St, San Francisco CA 94103.................415-552-5045
Catalysts Unlimited, 145 W 58th St, New York NY 10019 212-265-5612
Celebrity Guide of Calif*, 2568 Albatross 3F, San Diego CA 92101 619-233-1054
Joyce K Cole Literary Agency*, 797 San Diego Rd, Berkeley CA 94707 ...415-526-5165
The Hal Copeland Co Inc, 5924 Royal Lane, Dallas TX 75230...................214-361-8788
Cunningham & Walsh PR, 260 Madison Ave, New York NY 10016 212-683-4900
Alison Davis Public Relations, 426 Hudson St, Hackensack NJ 07601......201-641-4910
Steve Davis Publishing*, PO Box 190831, Dallas TX 75219 214-823-8660
Steve Davis Publishing*, 2626 Cole Ave, Dallas TX 75204 214-954-4469
Carol Dechant & Assoc, 2930 N Commonwealth, Chicago IL 60657.........312-935-7116
Wendy Doremus PR & Publicity, 876 Broadway, New York NT 10003.....212-673-3809
Dorf & Stenton Communications, 111 5th Ave, New York NY 10003.......212-420-8100
Dougherty & Assoc PR, 139 S Beverly Dr, Beverly Hills CA 90212..............213-273-8177
Michael B Druxman Public Relations, Box 8086, Calabasas CA 91302.....818-992-0633
Eisenman-Todd Inc, 222 Cedar Lane, Teaneck NJ 07666...........................201-836-5900
Eldrich Assoc, 189 23rd St, Brooklyn NY 11232..718-499-1465
Embassy Images, PO Box 11531, Denver CO 80211...................................303-595-7037
Escortguide*, 535 Cordova Rd Suite 125, Santa Fe NM 87501 505-988-7099
Richard Falk Assoc, 1472 Broadway, New York NY 10036..........................212-221-0043
Elane Feldman & Assoc, 101-A Clark St Apt 17B, Brooklyn NY 11201 718-875-3383
Russ Fons Public Relations, 15920 Haynes St, Van Nuys CA 91406..........818-994-4332
Ford & Ford Public Relations, PO Box 1426, La Canada CA 91011 818-352-5353
Frank Promotion Corp, 60 E 42nd St Ste 2119, New York NY 10017.......212-687-3383
V M Frantz & Co, 155 E 38th St, New York NY 10016................................212-697-4288
Susan M Friedman PR, 107-19 70th Ave, Forest Hills NY 11375 718-544-8210
GBM Books, 4850 Whitsett Ave #4, North Hollywood CA 91607.............818-763-0942
John Gile Communications, 1710 N Main St, Rockford IL 61103...............815-968-6601
Diane Glynn Publicity & PR, 200 Madison Ave, New York NY 10016......212-686-6950
Lynn Goldberg, 41 5th Ave Ste 8B, New York NY 10003 212-674-6878
Donna Gould Assoc, 250 5th Ave, New York NY 10001 212-725-0190
Graphic Comm Services, 7 N MacQueston, Mt Vernon NY 10550 914-664-7944
Tania Grossinger, 1 Christopher St, New York NY 10014 212-243-5063
Haddon Lynch & Baughman PR, 875 N Michigan, Chicago IL 60611.......312-649-0371
Benn Hall Assoc Inc, 420 Lexington Ave #3102, New York NY 10017.....212-687-6350
Havestman Assoc, PO Box 271, Menlo Park CA 94026 916-771-0353
Barbara J Hendra Assoc, 350 5th Ave Ste 1101, New York NY 10118......212-947-9898
Image Marketing/PR, 2695 Villa Creek Dr Ste 100, Dallas TX 75234......214-243-6302
Images International, 6624 Newcastle Ave, Reseda CA 91335 818-344-5279
Jacobson Altman Assoc, 369 Lexington Ave, New York NY 10017.............212-697-2620
Johanses Bookworks Ltd, PO Box 143, Big Sur CA 93920 408-667-2222
Kaufman Inc, 12 E 86th St Ste 831, New York NY 10028...........................212-988-0506
The Kelly Co, 14618 Tyler Foote Blvd, Nevada CA 95959 916-292-3096
Keynote Division, 24 W 40th St, New York NY 10018................................212-398-9970
Joyce Megginson Kircher, 545 Patrick Ave, Merritt Island FL 32953........305-452-4894
Janet Laib PR/Publicity, 169 E 69th St, New York NY 10021....................212-772-7226
M Lande Promotions Inc, 200 Madison Ave, New York NY 10016...........212-689-0930
Levinson Assoc, 650 N Bronson Ave Ste 250, Los Angeles CA 90004........213-460-4545
Norma Liebert, 521 5th Ave, New York NY 10175 212-751-4955

Literary Promotions Network, 6515 Lipmann St, San Diego CA 92122 619-455-5435
Chris Casson Madden Assoc PR, Holly Lane, Rye NY 10580.................914-967-9114
Manning Selvage & Lee, 233 Michigan, Chicago IL 60601 312-565-0927
Media Distribution Co-op, 1745 Louisiana St, Lawrence KS 66044...........913-842-3176
Bruce Merrin PR, 6320 Canoga Ave #220, Woodland Hills CA 91367.....213-887-5066
Janice Morgan Comm, 301 W 53rd St 13B, New York NY 10019 212-581-7068
Morton D Wax & Assoc Inc, 1560 Broadway, New York NY 10036 212-302-5360
The Betsy Nolan Group, 50 W 29th St 9W, New York NY 10001................212-420-6000
Alice Norton Public Relations, PO Box 516, Ridgefield CT 06877.............203-438-4064
The T R Nugent Agency, 1058 Main St Ste 10, Malden MA 02148 617-322-7273
On-Line Publicity, 200 Madison Ave, New York NY 10016 212-686-6959
Parkhurst Communications, 461 Park Ave, New York NY 10016...............212-683-0506
David Parry & Assoc, 5900 Wilshire Blvd, Los Angeles CA 90036............213-938-7138
Lawrence Penzell & Assoc, 239 E 52nd St, New York NY 10022................212-759-7411
Pesce/BP&R Advertising, 150 E 35th St, New York NY 10016.................212-807-0048
Photos By Merilu Div of IBP, PO Box 248, Hurst TX 76053.....................817-232-9347
Planned Television Arts Ltd, 25 W 43rd St, New York NY 10036...............212-921-5111
Eileen Prescott Co Inc, 733 3rd Ave, New York NY 10017 212-922-1270
Pro Video News Service, 303 S Crescent Hts, Los Angeles CA 90048........213-655-4774
Promotion Finders, 200 Park Ave Ste 230, New York NY 10166 212-972-1212
Public Relations Aids Inc, 330-W 34th St, New York NY 10001.................212-947-7733
Public Relations of Cape Cod, PO Box 61, Yarmouth Port MA 02675 617-394-7369
Public Relations Services Inc, 21 Middle St, Gloucester MA 01930 617-281-3102
Publishers Mktg Services, 11661 San Vicente, Los Angeles CA 90049 213-820-8672
Publishers Media, 5507 Morella Ave, North Hollywood CA 91607 818-980-2666
The Raleigh Group Ltd, 250 W 57th St Ste 2507, New York NY 10019.....212-265-4160
Peggy Raub Public Relations, 350 E 50th St, New York NY 10022............212-371-3629
Gail Rentsch Public Relations, 175 W 72nd St, New York NY 10023........212-595-9800
Thomas L Richmond Inc, 888 7th Ave Ste 2600, New York NY 10106 212-581-4200
Rivendell Marketing Co, 666 Ave of Americas, New York NY 10010.......212-242-6863
Rockwell & Newell Inc, 439 E 51st St, New York NY 10022....................212-421-5220
Richard Roffman Assoc, 697 West End Ave 6A, New York NY 10025 212-749-3647
Howard Ronan Assoc, 11 Buena Vista Ave, Spring Valley NY 10977........914-356-6668
Pat Rose Public Relations, 1207 Solano Ave Apt B, Albany CA 94706.....415-524-1165
Fred Rosen Assoc Inc, 660 Madison Ave, New York NY 10021 212-751-2970
Ruder Finn & Rotman, 110 E 59th St, New York NY 10022....................212-593-6400
Carl Ruff Assoc, 280 Mdison Ave, New York NY 10016 212-889-3761
Ruskin Assoc Public Relations, 305 E 24th St, New York NY 10010........212-679-6761
Savvy Management Inc, 80 4th Ave, New York NY 10003 212-477-1717
Blanche Schlessinger*, 12 S 12th St, Philadelphia PA 19107....................215-627-4665
Selma Shapiro PR, 501 5th Ave Ste 500, New York NY 10017................212-867-7038
Sensible Solutions Inc, 6 E 39th St, New York NY 10016 212-532-5280
Shapian & Assoc, 5900 Wilshire Blvd #1400, Los Angeles CA 90036.......213-937-3611
R L Silver Assoc Inc, 384 Park Ave S, New York NY 10016 212-684-0560
Solters/Roskin/Friedman, 5455 Wilshire Blvd, Los Angeles CA 90036 ...213-936-7900
Sotres Link Ltd, 244 Madison Ave, New York NY 10016.........................212-532-4164
Sourdough Enterprises, 16401 3rd Ave SW, Seattle WA 98166..................206-244-8115
Charles M Stern Assoc, 319 Coronet, San Antonio TX 78216 512-349-6141
Stutman Assoc Inc, 22 Chatam Rd, Chappaqua NY 10514 914-238-9613
Annette Swanberg PR, 7424 W 81st St, Los Angeles CA 90045 213-215-9059
Peggy Tagliarino Public Relations, 105 5th Ave, New York NY 10003 212-741-0079
Harriette Waterman, 1000 Park Ave, New York NY 10028 212-988-6171
Watermark Communications, 624-A Laurel St, Petaluma CA 94953........707-763-0252

Richard Weiner Inc, 888 7th Ave, New York NY 10106 212-315-8000
Jane Wesman PR, 928 Broadway #903, New York NY 10010 212-598-4440
Whitney & Whitney Inc, 220 White Plains Rd, Tarrytown NY 10591.........914-332-4930
W G Williams Assoc, 1100 17th St NW #1000, Washington DC 20036 202-463-8017
Writers Free Lance Inc, 12 Cavalier Dr, Ambler PA 19002 215-646-7550
Gloria Zigner & Assoc, 328 N Newport Blvd, Newport Bch CA 92663......714-645-6300
Irwin Zucker, 6430 Sunset Blvd, Hollywood CA 90028 213-461-3921

RESEARCHERS

This section includes firms providing research services for writers. See also Data
Bases & Electronic Mail and Libraries

AA's & PE's, 428 Lafayette St, New York NY 10003.....................................212-228-8707
Abisch-Kaplan, 166 W Waukena Ave, Oceanside NY 11572.....................516-764-9828
About Books Inc, PO Box 538, Saguache CO 81149 303-589-8223
Action Research Assoc, 2111 Edinburg Ave, Cardiff-by-Sea CA 92007.....619-944-0752
ADR Typing Service, PO Box 184 Bath Beach Sta, Brooklyn NY 11214....718-837-3484
AEIOU Inc, 74 Memorial Plaza, Pleasantville NY 10570 914-769-1135
Alternative Research, PO Box 432, New York NY 10015 212-683-3478
Amer Family Records Assn, 311 E 12th St, Kansas City MO 64106..........816-376-6570
The Antique Doorknob, 3900 Latimer Rd N, Tillamook OR 97141............503-842-2244
Appalachian Trail Conference, PO Box 807, Harpers Ferry WV 25425....304-535-6331
Associated Editors, 49 Hazelwood Ln, Stamford CT 06905 203-322-3836
Astro Psychology Inst, 2640 Greenwich #403, San Francisco CA 94123...415-921-1192
Faren Bachelis, 1628 Chorro St, San Luis Obispo CA 93401......................805-543-8297
Baldwin Literary Services, 935 Hayes St, Baldwin NY 11510....................516-546-8338
Bernice & Leo Balfour, 1219 Ralston St, Anaheim CA 92801 714-774-4944
Kathleen Barnes, 238 W 4th St #3C, New York NY 10014........................212-924-8084
Barbara M Beyda, Box 222763, Carmel CA 93922....................................408-624-6636
Carol Billman, Box 114, Landenburg PA 19350 215-274-2145
Susan N Bjorner, 10 Cannongate, Tyngsborough MA 01879 617-649-9746
Gilbert J Black, 399 West St, Harrison NY 10528......................................914-835-3160
Barbara J Bloch, 21 Dupont Ave, White Plains NY 10605 914-946-7715
Blue Pencil Group, PO Box 3392, Reston VA 22090..................................202-471-1998
Rhoda Blumberg, 1 Rockefeller Plaza, New York NY 10020....................212-246-6950
Hazel Blumberg-McKee, 136 S Oxford, St Paul MN 55105.......................612-292-1680
The Bookmill, 234 12th St, Santa Monica CA 90402.................................213-393-3843
The Bookworks Inc, PO Box 1189, Chicago IL 60690.................................312-236-8472
Linda Bradford, 222 E 10th St, New York NY 10003..................................212-473-1578
Elsa Branden, 222 W 77th St Ste 1218, New York NY 10024.....................212-362-1100
Robert Brightman, 5 Sussex Rd, Great Neck NY 11020 516-482-2074
Agnes Brite, 242 Beacon St Apt 10, Boston MA 02116...............................617-267-0369
Norman Brown & Assoc, 21 Luzon Ave, Providence RI 02906...................401-751-2641
Business Media Resources, 150 Shoreline Hwy, Mill Valley CA 94941.....415-331-6021
Luis R Caceres Jr, 8711 SW 20th Ter, Miami FL 33165 305-552-8433
Robert M Cammarota, 215 W 92nd St 12E, New York NY 10025.............212-724-3775
Richard Carlin, 25 Oleander Ct, Lawrenceville NJ 08648 609-896-4465
Carlisle Graphics, 2530 Kerper Blvd, Dubuque IA 52001 319-557-1500
Diane Carlson, 1215 Hull Terrace, Evanston IL 60202 312-869-7642
Anne Carson Assoc, 3323 Nebraska Ave, Washington DC 20016.............202-244-6679

Claudia Caruana, PO Box 20077, Elmont NY 10017 516-488-5815
Curtis Casewit, PO Box 19039, Denver CO 80219.....................................303-935-0277
Ctr for Economic Mgmt Research, Univ of Okla, Norman OK 73019.......405-325-2931
Ctr for Migration Studies, 209 Flagg Pl, Staten Island NY 10304..............718-351-8800
John Charnay, 19961 Stratern St, Canoga Park CA 91306.....................818-998-2652
James Chotas, 265 E 78th St, New York NY 10021.....................................212-243-0035
Civil War Veterans Service Records, 1725 Farmers, Tempe AZ 85281.....602-967-5405
Tina Clark, 318 Harvard St Ste 10, Brookline MA 02146 617-734-0807
E R Cole, PO Box 91277, Cleveland OH 44101..216-234-1775
Frances G Conn Assoc, 8320 Woodhaven Blvd, Bethesda MD 20817........301-365-5080
Cooper Heller Research, 801 Arch St, Philadelphia PA 19107....................215-625-4719
Nancy L Daniels, Box 68, Lemont PA 16851...814-237-7711
Data Research, 9 Prairie Ave, Suffern NY 10901 914-357-8215
Steve Davis Publishing, PO Box 190831, Dallas TX 75219 214-823-8660
Steve Davis Publishing, 2626 Cole Ave, Dallas TX 75204 214-954-4469
Randall De Leeuw, 21 Prince St, New York NY 10012..................................212-226-7086
John G Deaton, Box 26559, Austin TX 78755 512-345-1465
Dell-Naatz Publication Arts, 106 Pinion Ln, Manitou Spgs CO 80829.......303-685-9719
May Dikeman, 70 Irving Pl, New York NY 10003 212-475-4533
Valerie Eads Et Al, PO Box 1459, New York NY 10016 212-228-0900
Editing Unlimited, 196 Wykagyl Ter, New Rochelle NY 10804 914-636-2637
The Editor's Bureau Ltd, PO Box 68, Westport CT 06881 203-227-9275
Editorial & Graphic Services, Martinsville NJ 08836................................201-469-2195
Editorial Consultants Inc, 1605 12th Ave Ste #7, Seattle WA 98122........206-323-6475
Editorial Consultants Inc, 3221 Pierce St, San Francisco CA 94123..........415-931-7239
Educational Challenges Inc, 1009 Duke St, Alexandria VA 22314.............703-683-1500
J M B Edwards Writer-Editor, 2432 California, Berkeley CA 94703........415-644-8287
Effective Learning, 7 N MacQuesten Pkwy, Mt Vernon NY 10550 914-664-7944
Henry W Engel, 441 E 20th St, New York NY 10010....................................212-477-2597
Ensemble Productions Inc, 175 W 93rd St #5-J, New York NY 10025 212-866-2016
Pearl Eppy, 201 E 79th St, New York NY 10021 212-737-0354
Eros Publishing Co, PO Box 355 Parkchester Station, Bronx NY 10462...212-328-5569
Herta Erville, 320 West End Ave, New York NY 10023 212-874-3988
Evergreen Editors, Box 763, Laurel MD 20707 301-953-1861
Family History Services, 5760 Clement Court, Toledo OH 43613...............419-472-9538
Karen Feinberg, 5755 Nahant Ave, Cincinnati OH 45224............................513-542-8328
Jerry Felsen, 84-13 168th St, Jamaica NY 11432...718-739-4242
Free Lance Exchange Inc, 111 E 85th St, New York NY 10028 212-722-5816
Yvonne R Freund, 67 Riverside Dr, New York NY 10024 212-724-7550
Norma R Fryatt, 227 Granite St, Rockport MA 01966.................................617-546-6490
Gabriel House Inc, 5045 W Oakton St, Skokie IL 60077.............................312-675-1146
Givat Haviva Educ Foundation, 150 5th Ave, New York NY 10011 212-255-2992
Martha & Dennis Gleason, Box 540, Boothbay Harbor ME 04538.............207-633-2336
Genevieve S Gray, 8932 E Calle Norlo, Tucson AZ 85710...........................602-886-7829
Isabel S Grossner, 61 Tuxedo Rd, Montclair NJ 07042................................201-746-5371
Michael Haldeman, 2066 S Milwaukee, Denver CO 80210...........................303-758-8549
Hallberg Hallmundsson, 30 5th Ave, New York NY 10011..........................212-982-0407
Linda Hardcastle, 13707 FM 149 Ste 218, Houston TX 77086....................713-440-8876
Harkavy Publishing Service, 33 W 17th St, New York NY 10011................212-929-1339
Harriett, 135 54th St, New York NY 10022 212-688-0094
Hendershot Individ Instruct, 4114 Ridgewood, Bay City MI 48706...........517-684-3148
Mary L Hey, 1919 Grove St, Boulder CO 80302 303-442-3638
Jean Highland, 12 E 97th St, New York NY 10029..212-289-5318

Daniel W Hill, 3023 Honeysuckle Way N E, Salem OR 97303 503-364-9210
Historic Baltimore Soc, 4 Willow Brook, Randallstown MD 21133 301-922-3649
Diane Hodges, 220 E 87 St, New York NY 10128.....................................212-722-0856
Hoffman Research Services, Box 342, Rillton PA 15678...............................412-446-3374
Marcia Holly PhD, 214 Maple St, New Haven CT 06511...............................203-787-9699
Information on Demand Inc, PO Box 9550, Berkeley CA 94709 415-644-4500
Thomas Jackrell, 12 Campbell Ave, Belleville NJ 07109................................201-759-5318
Jewish Genealogical Soc, 1025 Antique Ln, Northbrook IL 60062 312-564-1025
Cliff Johnson & Assoc, 10867 Fruitland Dr, Studio City CA 91604...........818-761-5665
Juvenescent Research Corp, 807 Riverside Dr, New York NY 10032........212-795-8765
Betty Keim, 26 W 17th St 8th Fl, New York NY 10011..............................212-206-1442
Deborah Kopka, 3208 S Barrington Ste G, Los Angeles CA 90066...........213-391-4300
KPL & Assoc, 1090 Generals Hwy, Crownsville MD 21032.......................301-923-6611
Kraft & Kraft, 43 Market St, Newburyport MA 01950..............................617-546-2460
John Kremitske, 111 8th Ave Ste 1507, New York NY 10011 212-989-4783
L/A House Editorial, 5822 Uplander Way, Culver City CA 90230...........213-216-5812
Lazy Brown Assoc, 2800 Quebec St NW Ste 618, Wash DC 20008............202-686-0975
Judith Lechner, 1314 Ocean Pwy, Brooklyn NY 11230 718-336-5649
S Lenninger, Box 292, Geneseo IL 61254 309-944-2274
Ligature Inc, 165 N Canal St, Chicago IL 60606..312-648-1233
Linick Marketing Research, 7 Putter Bldg, Middle Island NY 11953........516-924-3888
E Trina Lipton, 60 E 8th St Box 310, New York NY 10003.........................212-533-3148
Literary Business Assocs, PO Box 2415, Hollywood CA 90078..................213-465-2630
Theotes Logos Research, 4318 York Ave S, Minneapolis MN 55410..........612-922-3202
Lombardi Indexing & Info Svcs, 2900 Sandy Ln, Santa Cruz CA 95062....408-476-1131
Marsha Luevane, PO Box 36326, Denver CO 80236 303-989-1036
William Lurie, 1005 145th Pl SE, Bellevue WA 98007................................206-747-2022
Dick Luxner, 145-B Park Ave, Park Ridge NJ 07656..................................201-391-5935
Makeready Inc, 233 W 77 St, New York NY 10024......................................212-595-5083
Malamud Rose, 38 Stonywood Rd, Commack NY 11725..............................516-543-7121
Daniel Marcus Editorial Services, 125 Boyd St, Watertown MA 02172....617-926-1697
Frank H Marks, 4940 East End Ave, Chicago IL 60615 312-684-3124
Frances Martin, 2154 W 73rd St, New York NY 10023 212-877-8160
Maryland Historical Soc, 201 W Monument St, Baltimore MD 21201 301-685-3700
The Master Teacher, PO Box 1207, Manhattan KS 66502 913-539-0555
MDZ Communications, 1136 E Stuart, Ft Collins CO 80525 303-493-5532
Media Distribution Co-op, 1745 Louisiana St, Lawrence KS 66044...........913-842-3176
Tom Mellers, 849 E 12th St, New York NY 10003 212-254-4958
Metropolitan Research Co, 100 Haven Ave, New York NY 10032 212-781-0264
Robert J Milch, 9 Millbrook Dr, Stony Brook NY 11790.............................516-689-8546
Sondra Mochson, 18 Overlook Dr, Port Washington NY 11050...................516-883-0984
Mount Ida Press, Box 87, Troy NY 12181..518-272-4597
Natl Assn Educ of Young Children, 1834 Connecticut, Wash DC 20009....202-232-8777
Natl Conf of State Legislatures, 1050 17th St #2100, Denver CO 80265...303-623-7800
Natl Ctr Urban Ethnic Affairs, PO Box 33279, Washington DC 20033.....202-232-3600
Natl Evaluation Systems, 30 Gatehouse Rd, Amherst MA 01004 413-256-0444
The Natl Tombstone Epitaph, PO Box 1880, Tombstone AZ 85638..........602-457-2211
Lois Newman, 6545 Hollywood Blvd #201, Hollywood CA 90028..............213-464-8382
Osborne Enterprises, Box 28312, Tempe AZ 85282.....................................602-437-3461
Parapsychology Press, Box 6847 College Station, Durham NC 27708.......919-688-8241
Patriotic Publishers, 159 Woodland Ave, Verona NJ 07044 201-239-7299
Dick Pawelek, 57-12 66 St, Maspeth NY 11378...718-446-2189
J Michael Pearson, PO Box 402844, Miami Beach FL 33140......................305-538-0346

Carol Penne, 10625 Greenacres Dr, Silver Spring MD 20903.....................301-434-7415
Pensacola Historical Society, 405 S Adams St, Pensacola FL 32501..........904-433-1559
Perry Roe & Assoc, 111 Acorn St, Millis MA 02154.....................................617-376-8459
Picture Research, 6307 Bannockburn Dr, Bethesda MD 20817..................301-229-6722
Wm Pitt, PO Box 356, Riverdale MD 20737...301-454-6003
Primary Sources, 124 E 79th St, New York NY 10021..................................212-472-0419
Deborah Pritzker, 2676 Grand Concourse, Bronx NY 10458......................212-364-3832
Professional Editing & Typing, 410 E 20th St 3A, New York NY 10009...212-477-0615
Generosa Gina Protano, 16 N Chatsworth #104, Larchmont NY 10538...914-834-8896
PS Assoc Inc, PO Box 959, Brookline MA 02146..617-277-9158
Publishers Editorial Services, 23 McQueen St, Katonah NY 10536..........914-232-7816
Publishing Resources Inc, Box 41307, San Juan PR 00940.........................809-724-0318
The Questor Group, 16215 9th NE, Seattle WA 98155.................................206-364-4672
Mary H Raitt, 3024 Tilden St N W, Washington DC 20008...........................202-966-1154
C Frederic Raker, 60 E 42 St Ste 1701, New York NY 10165.......................212-370-1706
Reitt Editing Services, 3505 Hampton Hall Way, Atlanta GA 30319.........404-255-5790
Research Findings in Print, 26 W Jefferson Rd, Pittsford NY 14534.......716-248-3947
Rocky Mountain Research Center, PO Box 4694, Missoula MT 59806.....406-549-6330
Linda E Rogers, 1350 County Road 83, Boulder CO 80302...........................303-444-8150
Sylvia J Rosenstein, 82 Green Bay Rd, Highland Park IL 60035.................312-432-5840
Carol Z Rothkopf, 16 Rotary Ln, Summit NJ 07901.....................................201-273-1255
Royal Literary Publications, PO Box 6794, Laguna Niguel CA 92677.......714-495-5049
C J Scheiner Books, 275 Linden Blvd Apt B2, Brooklyn NY 11226............718-469-1089
Keith Schiffman, 117 Bank St Apt 1C, New York NY 10014.......................212-989-5582
Schroeder Editorial Svcs, 2606 Old Mill, Rolling Meadows IL 60008.......312-303-0989
Michael Scofield, 3323 Bryant, Palo Alto CA 94306.....................................415-856-1478
Scripts For All Reasons, 15222 Baughman Dr, Silver Spring MD 20906...301-622-3520
Richard Selman, 14 Washington Pl, New York NY 10003..............................212-473-1874
Sherwin Assoc, 2616 N Dayton, Chicago IL 60614.......................................312-935-1581
Jean M Shirhall, 2700 N Norwood St, Arlington VA 22207.........................703-528-2617
Monica Shoffman-Graves, 101600 Overseas Hwy, Key Largo FL 33037...305-451-1462
Roger W Smith, 33-45 90 St Apt 5H, Jackson Heights NY 11372.................718-565-2855
SMS Publishing Corp, PO Box 2276, Glenview IL 60025.............................312-724-1427
Snyder Inst of Research, 508 Pac Coast Hwy, Redondo Bch CA 90277....213-372-4469
Sons of Sherman's March to the Sea, 1725 Farmers, Tempe AZ 85281....602-967-5405
Soyfoods Center, PO Box 234, Lafayette CA 94549..415-282-2991
Maxwell Sproge Publications, 731 N Cascade, Colo Spgs CO 80903.........303-633-5556
Sri Shirdi Sai Publications, 251 Wilbur Ave, Pittsburgh PA 15145............412-823-1296
Autumn Stanley, 241 Bonita los Trancos Wds, Portola Vly CA 94025.......415-851-1847
Paul Stimler, 1546 Dolores St, San Francisco CA 94104..............................415-285-6279
Elizabeth Peirce Swift, Pleasant Point Rd, Cushing ME 04563..................207-354-2467
I N Thut World Educ Ctr, Box U-32 School of Educ, Storrs CT 06268.....203-486-3321
M A Timmons Comm Svcs, 555 Evening St, Worthington OH 43085........614-846-2887
Turner & Winston, 5306 38 St NW, Washington DC 20015.........................202-363-6459
Walking Bird Publication Services, PO Box 19499, Seattle WA 98109.....206-285-1575
Warner-Cotter Co, 49 Water St, San Francisco CA 94133.............................415-441-4011
Washington Research Inc, 2103 N Lincoln St, Arlington VA 22207...........703-276-8260
Washington Researchers Ltd, 2612 P St NW, Washington DC 20007.......202-333-3533
A Cynthia Weber, 195 Sunny Hill Rd, Northampton PA 18067....................215-837-9615
Lehman Weichselbaum, 83 Harrison Ave, Brooklyn NY 11206................718-388-6486
Toby Wertheim, 240 E 76 St, New York NY 10021.......................................212-472-8587
Western Reserve Publ Services, 1640 Franklin Ave, Kent OH 44240.........216-673-2577
Western World Press, Box 366, Sun City CA 92381......................................714-652-8288

Eleanor B Widdoes, 417 W 120 St, New York NY 10027..............................212-686-1100
Bayla Winters, 2700 Scott Rd, Burbank CA 91504.....................................818-846-1879
The Wordsmith, 106 Mason Rd, Durham NC 27712.....................................919-477-8430
Wordsworth Communication, Box 9781, Alexandria VA 22304 703-642-8775
Betty Wright & Assoc, PO Box 1069, Moore Haven FL 33471...................813-946-0293
The Write Way, 2512 Orchard, Toledo OH 43606.......................................419-531-2944
Writers Alliance Ltd, 104 E 40th St, New York NY 10016 212-986-2830
The Writing Service, 315 W 102 St Ste 7B, New York NY 10025 212-866-5930
Barbara Wurf/Indexpert Svcs, 3122 Cardiff, Los Angeles CA 90034........213-837-1654
Joan Yarfitz Photo Env, 2021 Vista del Mar, Los Angeles CA 90068........213-465-9947

SCHOOLS

These institutions offer programs in creative writing or journalism or other special programs for writers. See also Conferences & Workshops and Theatrical Workshops for other educational programs for writers.

Agnes Scott College, Decatur GA 30030..404-373-2571
Alderson-Broaddus College, Philippi WV 26416..304-457-1700
American University, Washington DC 20016...202-686-2000
Antioch Univ, Yellow Springs OH 45387..513-767-7331
Arizona State University, Tempe AZ 85287 602-965-9011
Arkansas Tech University, Russellville AR 72801...501-968-0389
Auburn University, Auburn AL 36849 205-279-9110
Austin Peay State Univ, College St, Clarkville TN 37040.............................615-648-7011
Baylor University, Waco TX 76798 817-755-1011
Behrend College Penn State Univ, Station Rd, Erie PA 16563 814-898-1511
Bemidji State University, 2815 Bemidji Ave N, Bemidji MN 56601 218-755-2000
Bennington College, Bennington VT 05201..802-442-5401
Bethel College, 3900 Bethel Dr, St Paul MN 55112.....................................612-638-6400
Blue Ridge Christian Writers' Conf, PO Box 188, Black Mtn NC 28711...704-669-8421
Boston University, Boston MA 02215 617-353-2000
Bowling Green State Univ, Bowling Green OH 43403 419-372-2531
Brandeis University, 415 South St, Waltham MA 02254..............................617-647-2000
Brigham Young University, Provo UT 84602..801-378-1211
Brooklyn College, City University of New York, New York NY 11210......718-780-5485
Broward Community College, 3501 SW Davie, Ft Lauderdale FL 33314..305-475-6500
Brown University, Providence RI 02912 401-863-1000
Bucknell Univ, Lewisburg PA 17837...717-523-1271
Calif Lutheran College, 60 W Olsen Rd, Thousand Oaks CA 91360 805-492-2411
Calif State Univ, 18111 Nordhoff St, Northridge CA 91330.......................818-885-1200
Calif State Univ, 6000 J St, Sacramento CA 95819......................................916-454-6011
Calif State Univ Dominguez Hills, 1000 E Victoria, Carson CA 90747 213-516-3300
Calif State Univ, 1250 Belleflower Blvd, Long Beach CA 90840................213-498-4111
Calif State Univ Chico, Chico CA 95929 916-895-6116
Calif State Univ Fresno, Fresno CA 93740 209-294-4240
Calif State Univ Hayward, Hayward CA 94542 415-881-3000
Camden College of Rutgers Univ, 406 Penn, Camden NJ 08102................609-757-1766
Carnegie-Mellon Univ, 5000 Forbes Ave, Pittsburgh PA 15213 412-578-2000
Case Western Reserve Univ, 1 Adelbert Hall, Cleveland OH 44106.........216-368-4440
Catholic Univ of Amer, Dept of English, Washington DC 20064................202-635-5488

Central Connecticut State Univ, 1615 Stanley St, New Britain CT 06053..203-827-7000
Central Michigan University, Mt Pleasant MI 48859 517-774-4000
Central State University, 100 N University Dr, Edmond OK 73034...........405-341-2980
Central Washington University, Ellensburg WA 98926 509-963-1111
Chapman College, 333 N Glassell St, Orange CA 92666 714-997-6815
City College of NY, 138th St & Convent Ave, New York NY 10031 212-690-6741
Clarion State College, Clarion PA 16214..814-226-2000
Colby College, Waterville ME 04901 207-873-1131
Colgate University, Hamilton NY 13346...315-824-1000
College of St Catherine, 2004 Randolph Ave, St Paul MN 55105 612-690-6000
College of William & Mary, Williamsburg VA 23185.................................804-253-4000
College of Wooster, Wooster OH 44691 216-264-1234
Colorado State University, Ft Collins CO 80523..303-491-1101
Columbia College, 600 S Michigan Ave, Chicago IL 60605.......................312-663-1600
Columbia College, Columbia SC 29203..803-786-3012
Columbia University, School of General Studies, New York NY 10027....212-280-4710
Conservatory of Amer Letters, PO Box 123, S Thomaston ME 04858.......207-354-6550
Cornell Univ, Ithaca NY 14853 607-256-1000
Cosumnes River College, 8401 Center Pkwy, Sacramento CA 95823.........916-686-7300
Dartmouth College, Hanover NH 03755...603-646-1110
Denison University, Granville OH 43023...614-587-0810
DePauw University, Greencastle IN 46135...317-658-4800
Dowling College, 150 Idle Hi Blvd, Oakdale NY 11769 516-589-6100
Drake University, 2501 Univeristy Ave, Des Moines IA 50311 515-271-2011
Duquesne University, 600 Forbes Ave, Pittsburgh PA 15219......................412-434-6000
Dutchess Community College, 53 Pendell Rd, Poughkeepsie NY 12601 ...914-471-4500
East Carolina University, Greenville NC 27834...919-276-3652
Eastern Arizona University, Thatcher AZ 85552..602-428-1133
Eastern Oregon State College, La Grande OR 97850 503-963-2171
Eastern Washington University, Cheney WA 99004 509-359-2371
Eckerd College, St Petersburg FL 33733..813-867-1166
Elon College, PO Box 398, Elon College NC 27244 919-584-5571
Emerson College, 100 Beacon St, Boston MA 02116 617-578-8600
Emory & Henry College, Emory VA 24327...703-944-3121
Emporia State Univ, 2100 Commercial St, Emporia KS 66801 316-343-1200
Fairleigh Dickinson Univ, 285 Madison Ave, Madison NJ 07940 201-593-8500
Florida Inst of Technology, Univ Blvd, Melbourne FL 32901 305-723-3701
Florida Intl Univ, 11200 SW 8th St, Miami FL 33190.................................305-554-2000
Florida State Univ, 600 W College Ave, Tallahassee FL 32306 904-488-4234
Fordham Univ, E Fordham Rd, Bronx NY 10458...212-933-2233
George Mason Univ, 4400 University Dr, Fairfax VA 22030 703-323-2000
George Washington Univ, Journalism Dept, Washington DC 20052...........202-676-6225
Georgia State Univ, Writing Center, Atlanta GA 30303..............................404-658-2906
Hamilton College, Clinton NY 13323 315-859-4011
Hardin-Simmons Univ, 2200 Hickory St, Abilene TX 79698......................915-677-7281
Harvard Univ, Cambridge MA 02138 617-495-1000
Haverford College, Haverford PA 19041 215-896-1000
Hiram College, Hiram OH 44234 216-569-3211
Hofstra University, Hempstead NY 11550...516-560-6600
Hollins College, Hollins College VA 24020...703-362-6000
Idaho State University, 741 S 7th Ave, Pocatello ID 83209 208-236-0211
Illinois Benedictine College, 5700 College Rd, Lisle IL 60532 312-960-1500
Illinois State Univ, Normal IL 61761 309-483-2111

Indiana State Univ, 217 N 6th St, Terre Haute IN 47809..............................812-237-2121
Indiana Univ, Bloomington IN 47405...812-332-0211
Indiana Univ South Bend, 1825 North Side Blvd, South Bend IN 46615...219-237-4111
Johns Hopkins Univ, Charles & 34th St, Baltimore MD 21218.................301-338-8000
Johnson State College, Johnson VT 05656...802-635-2356
Juniata College, 1700 Moore St, Huntingdon PA 16652 814-643-4310
Kansas State University, Manhattan KS 66506..913-532-6011
Kent State Univ, Kent OH 44242...216-672-2121
Keuka College, Keuka Park NY 14478..315-536-4411
King's College, Wilkes-Barre PA 18711...717-826-5900
Knox College, Galesburg IL 61401...309-343-0112
Lake Forest College, Lake Forest IL 60045..312-234-3100
LaSalle University, 20th St & Olney Ave, Philadelphia PA 19141...........215-951-1000
Lawrence University, Appleton WI 54911 414-739-3681
Herbert H Lehman College, Bedford Park Blvd W, Bronx NY 10468........212-960-8000
Lesley College, 29 Everett St, Cambridge MA 02238..............................617-868-9600
Linfield College, McMinnville OR 97128..503-472-4121
Lock Haven State College, Lock Haven PA 17745...................................717-893-2011
Loras College, Dubuque IA 52001..319-588-7100
Louisiana State Univ, 99 Univ Lakeshore Dr, Baton Rouge LA 70803.....504-388-6935
Macalester College, St Paul MN 55105..612-696-6000
Mankato State University, Mankato MN 56001.......................................507-389-2463
Mary Washington College, Fredericksburg VA 22401..............................703-899-4100
Mass Inst of Technology, 77 Massachusetts Ave, Cambridge MA 02139 ..617-253-1000
McMurry College, Abilene TX 79697 915-692-4130
McNeese State University, Lake Charles LA 70609..................................318-477-2520
Memphis State University, Memphis TN 38152..901-454-2040
Mercer Univ, 1400 Coleman Ave, Macon GA 31207 912-745-2700
Metropolitan State College, 1006 11th St, Denver CO 80204....................303-629-2400
Miami Univ, Oxford OH 45056...513-529-2161
Michigan Romance Studies, Univ of Mich, Ann Arbor MI 48109..............313-747-2361
Michigan State Univ, East Lansing MI 48824...517-355-1855
Middlebury College, Middlebury VT 05753 802-388-3711
Missouri Southern State College, Joplin MO 64801.................................417-624-8100
Moorhead State University, 11th St South, Moorhead MN 56560...............218-236-2011
Morehead State Univ, 100 University Blvd E, Morehead KY 40351 601-783-2221
Morningside College, 1501 Moringside Ave, Sioux City IA 51106..............712-274-5000
Murray State University, Univ Station, Murray KY 42071........................502-762-3011
Museum of Art, Pennsylvania State Univ, University Park PA 16802 814-865-7672
Natl Poetry Foundation, 302 Neville Univ of Maine, Orano ME 04469 207-581-3814
The Natl Writers School, 1450 S Havana Ste 638, Aurora CO 80012.........303-751-7844
New College of Calif, 777 Valencia St, San Francisco CA 94110.................415-626-1694
New Mexico State Univ, PO Box 30001, Las Cruces NM 88003.................505-646-3121
New York Univ, Washington Sq, New York NY 10003..............................212-598-1212
North Carolina State Univ, Raleigh NC 27650.......................................919-737-2011
Northwestern University, Evanston IL 60201..312-492-3741
Oberlin College, Oberlin OH 44074 216-775-8285
Ohio State Univ, Columbus OH 43210 614-422-6446
Ohio Univ, Athens OH 45701...614-594-5511
Ohio Wesleyan Univ, Writing Resource Ctr, Delaware OH 43015............614-369-4431
Oklahoma State University, Stillwater OK 74078 405-624-5000
Old Dominion University, 5215 Hampton Blvd, Norfolk VA 23508..........804-440-3000
Otterbein College, Westerville OH 43081...614-890-3000

Pasadena City College, 1570 E Colorado Blvd, Pasadena CA 91106..........818-578-7073
Pennsylvania State Univ, University Park PA 16802 814-865-4700
Pomona College, Claremont CA 91711...714-621-8000
Princeton Univ, Princeton NJ 08544...609-452-3000
Queens College CUNY, 65-30 Kissena Blvd, Flushing NY 11367 718-520-7000
Radford University, Radford VA 24142 703-731-5000
Randolph-Macon Woman's College, Lynchburg VA 24503 804-846-7392
Rice University, PO Box 1892, Houston TX 77005 713-527-8101
Rockland Community College SUNY, 145 College, Suffern NY 10901......914-356-4650
Rocky Mountain College, 1511 Poly Dr, Billings MT 59102 406-657-1000
Roger Williams College, Old Ferry Rd, Bristol RI 02809.............................401-253-1040
Rollins College, Winter Park FL 32789..305-646-2000
Rosary College, River Forest IL 60305...312-366-2490
Rutgers Univ, New Brunswick NJ 08903...201-932-1766
St Andrews Presbyterian College, Laurinburg NC 28352...........................919-276-3652
St Cloud State University, St Cloud MN 56301..612-255-0121
St Edward's University, 3001 S Congress Ave, Austin TX 78704................512-444-2621
St Lawrence University, Rt 340, Canton NY 13617...914-359-9500
St Mary College, 4100 S 4th St Trafficway, Leavenworth KS 66048...........913-682-5151
St Mary's College, Notre Dame IN 46556..219-232-3031
Salisbury State College, Salisbury MD 21801 301-546-3261
San Diego State University, San Diego CA 92182..619-265-5200
San Francisco State Univ, 1600 Holloway, San Francisco CA 94132 415-469-2141
San Jose State Univ, 129 S 10th St, San Jose CA 95192 408-277-2000
Sarah Lawrence College, Bronxville NY 10708...914-337-0700
Skidmore College, Saratoga Springs NY 12866...518-584-5000
Smart Communications, PO Box 963, New York NY 10750.........................212-486-1894
Sonoma State Univ, 1801 E Cotati Ave, Rohnert Park CA 94928 707-664-2880
Southampton College, Southampton NY 11968 516-283-4000
Southern Connecticut State Univ, 501 Crescent, New Haven CT 06515 ...203-397-4234
Southern Illinois Univ, Edwardsville IL 62026...618-692-2000
Southern Illinois Univ, Carbondale IL 62901 618-453-2683
Southern Methodist Univ, Dallas TX 75275 214-692-2000
Southwest Missouri State Univ, 901 S National, Springfield MO 65804....417-836-5000
Southwest Texas State Univ, San Marcos TX 78666.......................................512-245-2111
Stanford Univ, Stanford CA 94305 415-497-2300
State Univ of NY, College at Oswego, Oswego NY 13126...............................315-341-2500
State Univ of NY, College at Brockport, Brockport NY 14420.....................716-395-2211
State Univ of NY, Vestal Pkwy E, Binghampton NY 13901 607-798-2000
State Univ of NY Albany, English Dept, Albany NY 12222 518-442-4055
Stephens College, Columbia MO 65201..314-442-2211
Sweet Briar College, Sweet Briar VA 24595...................................... 804-381-6100
Syracuse Univ, Syracuse NY 13210..315-423-1870
Tarkio College, Tarkio MO 64491 816-736-4131
Temple University, Philadelphia PA 19122..215-787-7700
Texas Tech University, Lubbock TX 79409 806-742-2011
Trinity College, Hartford CT 06106..203-527-3151
Trinity University, 715 Stadium Dr, San Antonio TX 78284 512-736-7011
Tufts University, Medford MA 02155...617-628-5000
Tulane University, New Orleans LA 70118...504-865-5000
Univ of Alabama, School of Communications, University AL 35486..........205-348-5520
Univ of Alaska, Fairbanks AK 99701..907-474-7211
Univ of Arizona, Tucson AZ 85721..602-626-0111

Univ of Arkansas, Little Rock AR 72204...501-569-3000
Univ of Arkansas, Fayetteville AR 72701 501-575-2000
Univ of Baltimore, 1420 N Charles St, Baltimore MD 21201 301-659-3161
Univ of Bridgeport, Bridgeport CT 06602 203-576-4000
Univ of Calif Davis, Davis CA 95616...916-752-1011
Univ of Calif Irvine, Irvine CA 92717..714-833-5011
Univ of Calif Los Angeles, 405 Hilgard Ave, Los Angeles CA 90024 213-825-4321
Univ of Calif San Diego, San Diego CA 92093 619-452-2230
Univ of Calif Santa Cruz, Santa Cruz CA 95064....................................408-429-0111
Univ of Central Florida, Alfaya Trail, Orlando FL 32816...........................305-275-9101
Univ of Chicago, 5835 S Kimbark, Chicago IL 60637...............................312-702-1722
Univ of Cincinnati, Cincinnati OH 45221 513-475-8000
Univ of Colorado, Austin Bluff Parkway, Colorado Springs CO 80907......303-596-3737
Univ of Colorado, Boulder CO 80309 303-492-0111
Univ of Colorado Denver, 1100 14th St, Denver CO 80202.........................303-629-2800
Univ of Connecticut, Storrs CT 06268..203-486-2000
Univ of Denver, University Park, Denver CO 80210 303-753-2036
Univ of Evansville, 1800 Lincoln Ave, Evansville IN 47702.......................812-477-6241
Univ of Florida, Gainesville FL 32611..904-392-3261
Univ of Georgia, Athens GA 30602...404-542-2112
Univ of Houston, Houston TX 77004 713-749-1011
Univ of Idaho, Moscow ID 83843...208-885-6111
Univ of Illinois, Urbana IL 61801...217-333-1000
Univ of Illinois at Chicago, Circle Box 4348, Chicago IL 60680................312-996-3000
Univ of Iowa, Iowa City IA 52242...319-353-2121
Univ of Kansas, Lawrence KS 66045..913-864-2700
Univ of Louisville, 2301 S 3rd St, Louisville KY 40292 502-588-5555
Univ of Maryland, 5401 Wilkens Ave, Catonsville MD 21228.....................301-455-1000
Univ of Maryland, College Park MD 20742...301-454-3011
Univ of Massachusetts, Amherst MA 01003...413-545-5111
Univ of Massachusetts Boston, Boston MA 02125 617-929-7000
Univ of Miami, Coral Gables FL 33124 305-284-2211
Univ of Michigan, Ann Arbor MI 48109...313-764-1817
Univ of Missouri Columbia, Columbia MO 65211 314-882-2121
Univ of Missouri Kansas City, 5100 Rockhill, Kansas City MO 64110......816-276-1000
Univ of Montana, Missoula MT 59812...406-243-0211
Univ of Nebraska Lincoln, Lincoln NE 68588 402-472-7211
Univ of Nebraska Omaha, 60th & Dodge St, Omaha NE 68182.................402-554-2800
Univ of New Hampshire, Durham NH 03824.......................................603-862-1234
Univ of New Mexico, Albuquerque NM 87131....................................505-277-0111
Univ of North Carolina, PO Box 2688, Chapel Hill NC 27514.................919-962-6981
Univ of North Carolina, 1000 Spring Garden St, Greensboro NC 27412 ..919-379-5000
Univ of North Dakota, Grand Forks ND 58202....................................701-777-2011
Univ of Oklahoma, Norman OK 73019..405-325-0311
Univ of Oregon, Eugene OR 97403 503-686-3111
Univ of Pennsylvania, 34th & Spruce Sts, Philadelphia PA 19104 215-243-5000
Univ of Pittsburgh, Pittsburgh PA 15260..412-624-4141
Univ of Pittsburgh Johnstown, Johnstown PA 15904 814-266-9661
Univ of Redlands, 1200 E Colton, Redlands CA 92373 714-793-2121
Univ of Richmond, Richmond VA 23173...804-285-6000
Univ of Santa Clara, Santa Clara CA 95053 408-984-4256
Univ of South Alabama, Mobile AL 36688...205-460-7021
Univ of South Dakota, Vermillion SD 57069 605-677-5011

Univ of Southern Calif, Los Angeles CA 90089.................................213-743-2311
Univ of Southern Mississippi, Southern Sta, Hattiesburg MS 39406.........601-266-7011
Univ of SW Louisiana, E University Ave, Lafayette LA 70504 318-231-6000
Univ of Tampa, 401 J F Kennedy Blvd W, Tampa FL 33606 813-253-8861
Univ of Tennessee, 615 McCallie Ave, Chattanooga TN 37403 615-755-4510
Univ of Tennessee, Knoxville TN 37916...615-974-0111
Univ of Texas Austin, Austin TX 78712...512-471-3434
Univ of Texas Dallas, Richardson TX 75080...214-690-2111
Univ of Texas El Paso, El Paso TX 79968 915-747-5684
Univ of Tulsa, 600 S College Ave, Tulsa OK 74104..................................918-592-6000
Univ of Utah, Salt Lake City UT 84112..801-581-7200
Univ of Virginia, Charlottesville VA 22903 804-924-0311
Univ of Washington, Seattle WA 98195...206-543-1766
Univ of Wisconsin, 610 Langdon St, Madison WI 53703 608-262-2368
Univ of Wisconsin Green Bay, Green Bay WI 54302................................414-465-2000
Univ of Wisconsin Milwaukee, Milwaukee WI 53201 414-963-4835
Univ of Wyoming, Box 3434 Univ Sta, Laramie WY 82071........................307-766-4121
Upsala College, Prospect St, East Orange NJ 07019.................................201-266-7000
Vanderbilt University, Nashville TN 37240 615-322-3311
Vermont College of Norwich Univ, Montpelier VT 05602 802-828-2401
Virginia Commonwealth Univ, 910 W Franklin, Richmond VA 23284......804-257-1000
Virginia Polytechnic Institute, Blacksburg VA 24061..............................703-961-6000
Warren Wilson College, MFA Prog for Writers, Swannanoa NC 28778....704-298-3325
Washburn University of Topeka, Topeka KS 66621 913-295-6300
Washington College, Chestertown MD 21620..301-778-2800
Washington University, Lindell & Skinner, St Louis MO 63130.................314-889-5100
Wayne State University, Detroit MI 48202...313-577-2424
Wells College, Aurora NY 13026 315-364-3264
Wesleyan University, 110 Mt Vernon St, Middletown CT 06457 203-344-7918
West Chester University, West Chester PA 19383 215-436-1000
West Georgia College, Carrollton GA 30118...404-834-1211
West Virginia Univ, Morgantown WV 26506...304-293-0111
Western Kentucky Univ, Bowling Green KY 42101..................................502-745-4295
Western Maryland College, Westminster MD 21157.................................301-848-7000
Western Michigan University, Kalamazoo MI 49008 616-383-1600
Western Washington Univ, Journalism Dept, Bellingham WA 98225 206-676-3252
Westminster College, New Wilmington PA 16142 412-946-8761
Westminster College, Fulton MO 65251...314-642-3361
Wichita State University, Wichita KS 67208 316-689-3456
Williams College, Williamstown MA 01267 413-597-3131
Wright State Univ, 3640 Colonel Glenn Hwy, Dayton OH 45435...............513-873-3333
Writer's Digest School, 1507 Dana Ave, Cincinnati OH 45207 513-531-5222

SUBSIDY BOOK PUBLISHERS

The publishers in this section produce books on a subsidy basis, meaning that the author pays all or part of the production cost. See also Book Printers.

Adventure Publications, 102 N 6th St, Staples MN 56479............................218-894-3592
Aegina Press, 4937 Humphrey Rd, Huntington WV 25704..........................304-429-7204
Amereon Ltd, Box 1200, Mattituck NY 11952..516-298-5100
M Arman Publishing Inc, PO Box 785, Ormond Beach FL 32074.............904-673-5576
ASC II, 14715 Terrace Ln, Eagle River AK 99577 907-696-0022
Book Promotions Unlimited, Box 122, Flushing MI 48433 313-659-6683
BookWrights, 220 Main St Box 49, Neshkoro WI 54960 414-293-8355
Don Bosco Publications, 475 North Ave, New Rochelle NY 10802............914-576-0122
Brooklyn Publishing Co, PO Box 340328, Brooklyn NY 11234..................718-251-3690
Brunswick Publishing Co, Rt 1 Box 1A1, Lawrenceville VA 23868 804-848-3865
Cambric Press, 912 Strowbridge Dr, Huron OH 44839 419-433-6266
Carlton Press Inc, 11 W 32nd St, New York NY 10001 212-714-0300
Columbia Publishing Co Inc, 234 E 25th St, Baltimore MD 21218............301-366-7070
Dorrance & Co, 828 Lancaster Ave, Bryn Mawr PA 19010 215-527-7880
Dow Jones-Irwin, 1818 Ridge Rd, Homewood IL 60430.............................312-798-6000
Exposition Press, 1701 Blount Rd Ste C, Pompano Beach FL 33069.........305-979-3200
Fairway Press, 628 S Main, Lima OH 45804...419-229-2665
The Golden Quill Press, Avery Rd, Francestown NH 03043.......................603-547-6622
The Gutenberg Press, PO Box 9875, Berkeley CA 94709............................415-548-3776
Helix Press, 4410 Hickey, Corpus Christi TX 78413 512-852-8834
Kendall Hunt Publishing Co, 2460 Kerper Blvd, Dubuque IA 52001 319-588-1451
Little Red Hen Press, Rt 2 Box 28, Mankato MN 56001...............................507-947-3614
Mho & Mho Works, PO Box 33135, San Diego CA 92103 619-488-4991
Moss Publications, PO Box 729, Orange VA 22960 703-672-5921
New Forums Press Inc, PO Box 876, Stillwater OK 74076...........................405-372-6158
Or Publishing, 1481 Lafayette Rd, Claremont CA 91711.............................714-624-1792
QED Press, 155 Cypress St, Ft Bragg CA 95437...707-964-9520
R & E Publishers, PO Box 2008, Saratoga CA 95070 408-866-6303
Peter Randall Publisher, 500 Market, Portsmouth NH 03801 603-431-5667
Ronin Publishing Inc, PO Box 1035, Berkeley CA 94701............................415-540-6278
Howard W Sams & Co Inc, 4300 W 62nd St, Indianapolis IN 46268..........317-298-5400
Sky River Press, 236 E Main, Ashland OR 97520 503-488-0645
Source Productions, 2635 Griffith Pk Bwd, Los Angeles CA 90039............213-660-5976
Summa Publications, PO Box 20725, Birmingham AL 35216......................205-822-0463
Univ of Alaska Press, Signers' Hall, Fairbanks AK 99701..........................907-474-6389
Vantage Press, 516 W 34th St, New York NY 10001.....................................212-736-1767
Bess Wallace Assoc, 1502 N Mitchell, Payson AZ 85541............................602-474-2983
Wash State Historical Soc, 315 N Stadium Way, Tacoma WA 98403........206-593-2830
Weidner Associates Inc, Box C-50, Cinnaminson NJ 08077.........................609-486-1755
Westburg Assoc Publishers, 1745 Madison St, Fennimore WI 53809 608-822-6237
Wheat Forders Press, PO Box 6317, Washington DC 20015 202-362-1588
Wimmer Brothers Inc, 4210 B F Goodrich Blvd, Memphis TN 38181........901-362-8900
Writers Publishing Service Co, 1512 Western Ave, Seattle WA 98101......206-284-9954
Ye Galleon Press, PO Box 287, Fairfield WA 99012.....................................509-283-2422

THEATRES

This section lists theatres and theatrical companies. See also Theatrical Workshops and Contests & Awards for other playwriting programs.

AART, 527 30th St, San Francisco CA 94131...415-776-0995
Abbeville Opera House, Box 247, Abbeville SC 29620.................................803-429-2157
Acacia Theatre, PO Box 11952, Milwaukee WI 53211................................414-962-2380
Acad of Media & Theatre Arts, Ft Mason Ctr, San Francisco CA 94123..415-776-4720
The Acting Group Inc, PO Box 1252, New York NY 10113 212-645-1459
Actors Alley Repertory, 4334 Van Nuys, Sherman Oaks CA 91403...........818-986-2278
Actors Alliance Theatre, 30800 Evergreen Rd, Southfield MI 48075 313-642-1326
Actors Co-op, 505 4th St, Brooklyn NY 11215 212-499-0594
Actors for Themselves, 7657 Melrose Ave, Los Angeles CA 90046.............213-653-3279
Actors Forum, 3365 Cahuenga Blvd, Los Angeles CA 90068 213-850-9016
Actors Inscape, 100 Memorial Pkwy #1-F, New Breunswick NJ 08901.....201-846-8525
Actors Lab Theatre, 11901 Wornall Rd, Kansas City MO 64145.................816-942-8400
Actors Outlet Theatre Ctr, 120 W 28th St, New York NY 10001.................212-807-1590
Actors Repertory, 308 S Dixie Hwy, W Palm Beach FL 33407.....................305-655-2122
Actors Repertory Theatre, 1211 4th St, Santa Monica CA 90401................213-394-9779
Actors Space, 104 Franklin St, New York NY 10013 212-783-3043
Actors Theatre of Louisville, 316 W Main St, Louisville KY 40202.............502-584-1265
Actors Theatre of Sonoma Cty, 813 Humboldt, Santa Rosa CA 95404......707-523-4185
Actors Theatre of St Paul, 28 W 7th Pl, St Paul MN 55102 612-297-6868
Actors Theatre of Tulsa, Box 2116, Tulsa OK 74101 918-749-7488
Actors Workshop, PO Box 741, Ashland OR 97520 503-482-5501
AD Players, 2710 W Alabama, Houston TX 77098 713-526-2721
Advanced Theatre Arts Players, 120 S St Joseph, S Bend IN 46601...........219-282-4185
Alaska Repertory Theatre, 705 W 6th Ave, Anchorage AK 99501 907-276-2327
Alaska Theatre of Youth, PO Box 104036, Anchorage AK 99510...............907-248-6033
Alhambra Dinner Theatre, 12000 Beach Blvd, Jacksonville FL 32216.......904-641-1212
Allegheny College, N Main St, Meadville PA 16335..................................814-724-2370
Allen Ctr for Culture & Art, 171 W 85th St, New York NY 10024..............212-496-0120
Alley Theatre, 615 Texas Ave, Houston TX 77002 713-228-9341
Alliance Theatre, 1280 Peachtree St, Atlanta GA 30309 404-898-1132
Alonzo Players, 317 Clermont Ave, Brooklyn NY 11205............................718-622-5062
AMAS Repertory Theatre Inc, 1 E 104th St, New York NY 10029................212-369-8000
Amer Conservatory Theatre, 450 Geary St, San Francisco CA 94102........415-771-3880
Amer Jewish Theatre, 1395 Lexington Ave, New York NY 10128................212-427-6000
Amer Legion Theatre Ctr, 2035 N Highland, Hollywood CA 90068............213-851-3030
The Amer Line, 810 W 183rd St #5C, New York NY 10033........................212-795-3104
Amer Living History Theatre, Box 2677, Hollywood CA 90078..................213-876-2202
Amer Music Theatre Festival, 1617 JFK Blvd #905, Phila PA 19103........215-988-9050
Amer Playhouse, 1776 Broadway, New York NY 10019.............................212-757-4300
Amer Renaissance Theatre, 112 Charlton St, New York NY 10014............212-929-4718
Amer Repertory Theatre, 64 Brattle St, Cambridge MA 02138....................617-495-2668
Amer Stage Co, 1000 River Rd, Teaneck NJ 07666....................................201-692-7720
Amer Stage Co, PO Box 1560, St Petersburg FL 33731 813-823-1600
Amer Stage Festival, PO Box 225, Milford NH 03055...............................603-673-7515
Amer Stage, 2320 Dana St, Berkeley CA 94704 415-849-1675

Amer Stanislavski Theatre, 485 Park Ave #6A, New York NY 10022......212-755-5120
Amer Theatre Arts, 11114 Weddington, N Hollywood CA 91061................213-466-2462
Amer Theatre Co, PO Box 1265, Tulsa OK 74101..918-747-9494
Amer Writers Theatre Foundation, PO Box 810, New York NY 10108....212-777-7005
The Amer Place Theatre, 111 W 46th St, New York NY 10036....................212-246-3730
Maxwell Anderson Playwrights Series, 1 Rogers, Stamford CT 06902......203-348-2787
Judith Anderson Theatre, 422 W 42nd St, New York NY 10036.................212-736-7930
Anniston Community Theatre, Box 1454, Anniston AL 36201....................205-236-8347
Apple Corps Theatre, 336 W 20th St, New York NY 10011 212-929-2955
Arena Players Rep Co of LI, 296 Rt 109, E Farmingdale NY 11735 516-293-0674
Arena Stage, 6th & Maine Ave SW, Washington DC 20024 202-554-9066
Arizona Theatre Co, 53 W Congress PO Box 1631, Tucson AZ 85702......602-884-8210
Arkansas Arts Ctr, PO Box 2137, Little Rock AR 72203.............................501-372-4000
Arkansas Repertory Theatre, 712 E 11th St, Little Rock AR 72202...........501-378-0405
Arte Unido, 484 W 43rd St #12-0, New York NY 10036..............................212-695-7397
Artists Unlimited, 225 W 28th St, New York NY 10001...............................212-736-7253
ArtReach Touring Theatre, 3074 Madison Rd, Cincinnati OH 45209......513-871-2300
Artsangle, 25 5th Ave #10-H, New York NY 10003 212-226-4090
Asian Amer Theatre Co, Ft Mason Ctr, San Francisco CA 94123 415-928-8922
Asolo Touring Theatre Commissions, Drawer E, Sarasota FL 33578........813-355-7115
Aspen Community Theatre, Box 743, Aspen CO 81612 303-923-3327
Assoc Children's Theatre, 4949 E Shaw Butte, Scottsdale AZ 85254.........602-996-3333
Attic Theatre, PO Box 02457, Detroit MI 48202...313-875-8284
Auburn Civic Theatre, Box 506, Auburn NY 13021......................................315-255-1305
Avante Theatre Co, 106 W Logan St, Philadelphia PA 19144......................215-844-6854
Avila College Actors Lab, 11901 Wornall, Kansas City MO 64145...........816-942-8400
Back Alley Theatre, 15231 Burbank Blvd, Van Nuys CA 91411 818-780-2240
Backdoor Theatre, Box 896, Wichita Falls TX 76307..................................817-322-5000
Backstage Theatre, Box 297, Brekenridge CO 80424.................................303-453-0199
Baldwin Theatre, 160 W 74th St, New York NY 10023 212-799-8190
Ball State Univ, Dept of Theatre, Muncie IN 47308....................................317-285-8740
Barter Theatre, PO Box 867, Abingdon VA 24210 703-628-2281
Basement Workshop Inc, 22 Catherine St 3rd fl, New York NY 10038.....212-732-0770
Bathhouse Theatre, 7312 W Greenlake Dr N, Seattle WA 98103.................206-524-3608
Bay Theatre Co, Box 4489, Berkeley CA 94704 415-842-1801
Bedford Theatre Co, 16 W 16th St #11, New York NY 10011 212-255-0054
Bedini Theatre Project, 3368 Jackson St, San Francisco CA 94118 415-221-0070
Belrose Performing Arts Ctr, 1415 5th Ave, San Rafael CA 94901...........415-454-6422
Benicia Old Town Theatre, Box 602, Benicia CA 94510.............................707-745-2270
Berea College Dramatics Lab, CPO 591, Berea KY 40404...........................606-986-9341
Berekley Jewish Theatre, 1414 Walnut St, Berkeley CA 94709 415-849-0498
Berkeley Repertory Theatre, 2025 Addison St, Berkeley CA 94704............415-841-6108
Berkeley Shakespeare Festival, Box 969, Berkeley CA 94701 415-548-3422
Berkshire Public Theatre, Box 860, Pittsfield MA 01202............................413-445-4631
Berkshire Theatre Festival, E Main St, Stockbridge MA 01262 413-298-5536
Bes Children's Educ Theatre, 2431 Spaulding, Berkeley CA 94703............415-486-1591
Beverly Hills Playhouse, 254 S Robertson Blvd, Beverly Hills CA 90212..213-652-6483
Big Small Theatre, 3601 Locust Walk, Philidelphia PA 19104 215-386-1551
Bigfork Playhouse, Box 456, Bigfork MT 59911 406-837-4886
Bilingual Foundation of Arts, 421 North Ave, Los Angeles CA 90031......213-225-4044
Black Repertory Group, 1719 Alcatraz Ave, Berkeley CA 94703 415-652-2120
Black Spectrum Theatre, 205-21 Linden Blvd, Queens NY 11412.............212-527-0836
Blue Masque, Catawba College, Salisbury NC 28144...................................704-637-4417

BoarsHead Mich Public Theatre, 425 S Grand, Lansing MI 48933............517-484-7800
Body Politic Theatre, 2261 N Lincoln Ave, Chicago IL 60614.....................312-348-7901
Bond Street Theatre Coalition, 2 Bond St, New York NY 10012.............212-206-7564
Bonfils Theatre, E Colfax Ave & Elizabeth St, Denver CO 80206.............303-399-5418
Boston Shakespeare Co, 52 St Botolph St, Boston MA 02116.....................617-267-5606
Bridge Theatre Co, 40-44 24th St, Long Island City NY 11101....................718-392-9786
Bridge Theatre Prod Co, 107 W 70th St 5R, New York NY 10023.............212-724-2751
Broadway Tomorrow, 191 Claremont #53, New York NY 10027.............212-864-4736
Broken Arrow Playhouse, PO Box 452, Broken Arrow OK 74013.............918-258-0077
Brooklyn Playworks, 674 4th Ave, Brooklyn NY 11232.......................718-499-2293
Browadway Playhouse, 550 W Broadway, San Gabriel CA 91776.............213-282-9487
The Clarence Brown Co, UT Box 8450, Knoxville TN 37996.....................615-974-3447
Brown Grand Theatre, Concordia KS 66901..913-243-2553
Bubbles Players, Box 4162, Long Island City NY 11104............................718-784-0143
Burbage Theatre Ensemble, 2330 Sawtelle Blvd, Los Angeles CA 90064..213-478-0897
Cal Arts Theatre Co, Calif Inst of Arts, Valencia CA 91355 805-255-1050
Calif Conservatory Theatre, Box 894, San Leandro CA 94577 415-632-8850
Calif State Univ, Theatre Dept, Fresno CA 93740.....................................209-294-2465
Calif Theatre Ctr, Box 2007, Sunnyvale CA 94087.....................................408-245-2979
Calif Young People's Theatre, 6840 Chiala Ln, San Jose CA 95129 408-245-2979
Cameron Univ, 2800 W Gore, Lawton OK 73505.....................................405-581-2346
Candlewood Playhouse, Box 8209, New Fairfield CT 06812.....................203-746-6557
Capital Repertory Co, PO Box 399, Albany NY 12202.............................518-462-4531
Capuchino Community Theatre, Box 714, Millbrae CA 94030 415-588-3358
Carroll College Little Theatre, Dept of Fine Arts, Helena MO 59625 406-442-3450
Casa Manana Playhouse, 3103 W Lancaster, Ft Worth TX 76107 817-332-9319
Celebration Theatre, 1765 N Highland Ave #536, Hollywood CA 90028..213-876-4257
Center for Puppetry Arts, 1404 Spring St NW, Atlanta GA 30309 404-873-3089
Center Stage, 700 N Calvert St, Baltimore MD 21202................................301-685-3200
Center Theatre Group, 135 N Grand Ave, Los Angeles CA 90012 213-972-7353
Chagrin Valley Little Theatre, 40 River St, Chagrin Falls OH 44022.........216-247-8955
Chamber Theatre, 3727 Buchanan St. #203, San Francisco CA 94123......415-346-4558
Changing Scene Theatre, 1527 Champa St, Denver CO 80202 303-893-5775
Chelsea Theatre Ctr, 645 W 46th St 3rd fl, New York NY 10036.............212-765-6559
Chicago Theatre Co, 500 E 67th St, Chicago IL 60637 312-493-1305
Children's Classics Theatre, 1708 S 16th St, Philadelphia PA 19145 215-389-5646
Children's Radio Theatre, PO Box 53057, Washington DC 20009 202-234-4136
Children's Repertory Co, 3707 Garrett Rd, Drexel Hill PA 19026.............215-284-1319
Childsplay, Box 517, Tempe AZ 85281...602-966-7980
Chimera Theatre Co, 30 E 10th St, St Paul MN 55101 612-293-0355
Chocolate Bayou Theatre Co, PO Box 270363, Houston TX 77277...........713-528-0070
Cincinnati Playhouse In The Park, PO Box 6537, Cincinnati OH 45206...513-421-5440
Circle In The Square Theatre, 1633 Braodway, New York NY 10019 212-307-2700
Circle Repertory Co, 161 Ave of the Americas, New York NY 10013 212-691-3210
Circuit Playhouse, 51 S Cooper, Memphis TN 38104................................901-725-0776
City Players of St Louis, 212 N Kingshighway Blvd, St Louis MO 63108 ..314-367-0060
City Stage Co, 136 E 13th, New York NY 10003 212-677-4210
City Theatre Co, B-39 Univ of Pittsburgh, Pittsburgh PA 15260................412-624-4101
City Theatre Festival, 62 E 4th St, New York NY 10009............................212-724-7400
Civic Arts Repertory Co, 1641 Locust St, Walnut Creek CA 94596...........415-943-5865
Civic Little Theatre, 527 N 19th St, Allentown PA 18104.........................215-432-8943
Clear Eyes Project, 323 Frederick St, San Francisco CA 94117 415-665-1617
The Cleveland Play House, 8500 Euclid Ave, Cleveland OH 44106 216-795-7010

Club Chandalier, 120 Ave C, New York NY 10009 718-384-7351
Coconut Grove Playhouse, 3500 Main Hwy, Miami FL 33133 305-442-2662
Cocteau Repertory, 333 Bowery, New York NY 10012 212-677-0060
Coldwater Community Theatre, 895 Division St, Coldwater MI 49036......517-278-2389
Coleman Puppet Theatre, 1516 S 2nd Ave, Maywood IL 60153..................312-344-2920
Colony/Studio Theatre, 1944 Riverside, Los Angeles CA 90039................213-665-0280
Comm Children's Theatre, 8021 E 129th Ter, Grandview MO 64030........816-761-5775
Company Theatre, 1768 Dryden Rd, Freeville NY 13068 607-347-4411
Contemporary Arts Ctr, 900 Camp St, New Orleans LA 70130................504-523-1216
A Contemporary Theatre, 100 W Roy St, Seattle WA 98109....................206-285-3220
Contra Costa Civic Theatre, 6636 Cutting Blvd, El Cerrito CA 94530......415-235-0785
Contract Players Theatre, 1 Beaufort Pl E3, New Rochelle NY 10801 914-636-1676
Coterie, 2450 Grand Ave, Kansas City MO 64108................................816-474-6785
Counterstage, 34 8th Ave #2-C, New York NY 10014.............................212-279-9321
Creation Production Co, 127 Greene St, New York NY 10012.................212-674-5593
Creative Theatre Unlimited, 33 Mercer St, Princeton NJ 08540.............609-924-3489
Creede Repertory Theatre, Box 269, Creede CO 81130.........................303-658-2541
Cresson Lake Playhouse, 201 1st United Fedl, Ebensburg PA 15931........814-472-4333
The Cricket Theatre, 528 Hennepin Ave, Minneapolis MN 55403 612-333-5241
Crossroads Theatre Co, 320 Memorial Pkwy, New Brunswick NJ 08901..201-249-5625
Cucaracha Theatre Club, 213 Henry St, New York NY 10022 212-513-0472
Cumberland County Playhouse, PO Box 484, Crossville TN 38557 615-484-2300
D'Verse Theatre Co, 846 Ainslie #1, Chicago IL 60657.........................312-477-0389
Dakota Theatre Caravan, Box 1014, Spearfish SD 57783 605-642-8120
Dallas Repertory Theatre, 150 NorthPark Ctr, Dallas TX 75225.............214-692-5611
Dallas Theatre Ctr, 3636 Turtle Creek Blvd, Dallas TX 75219 214-526-8210
Daytona Playhouse, 100 Jessamine Blvd, Daytona Beach FL 32018..........904-255-2431
Deja Vu Coffeehouse, 1705 N Kenmore, Los Angeles CA 90027...............213-666-0434
Delaware Theatre Co, PO Box 516, Wilmington DE 19899.....................302-658-6448
Dell'Arte Players Co, PO Box 816, Blue Lake CA 95525........................707-668-5411
Delray Beach Playhouse, 950 NE 9th St, Delray Beach FL 33444............305-272-1281
Denver Ctr Theatre Co, 1050 13th St, Denver CO 80204......................303-893-4200
Detroit Repertory Theatre, 13103 Woodrow Wilson, Detroit MI 48238....313-868-1347
Direct Theatre, 115 W 77th St, New York NY 10024.............................212-362-0657
Dobama Theatre, 1846 Coventry Rd, Cleveland Hts OH 44118.................216-932-6838
Steve Dobbins Productions, 25 Van Ness Ave, San Francisco CA 94102..415-861-6655
Dolphins Theatre Co, 1449 Bob White Pl, San Jose CA 95131 408-926-8207
Don Quijote Exp Theatre, PO Box 112, New York NY 10108 212-244-5372
Dordt College, Theatre Arts Dept, Sioux Ctr IA 51250 712-722-3771
Dorset Theatre Festival, PO Box 519, Dorset VT 05251........................806-867-2223
Downtown Caberet Theatre, 263 Golden Hill St, Bridgeport CT 06604.....203-576-1634
Drama Committee Repertory, 118 W 79th St, New York NY 10024..........212-595-1733
John Drew Theatre Of Guild Hall, 158 Main St, E Hampton NY 11937...516-324-4051
Driftwood Showboat, Box 1032, Kingston NY 12401.............................914-331-0400
East West Players, 4424 Santa Monica Blvd, Los Angeles CA 90029.........213-660-0366
Eastern Montana College Theatre, 1500 N 30th St, Billings MT 59101.....406-657-2178
Eccentric Circles Theatre, 400 W 43rd St # 4N, New York NY 10036......212-564-3798
Eckerd College Theatre, St Petersburg FL 33733................................813-867-1166
El Teatro Campesino, Box 1240, San Juan Bautist CA 95045 408-623-2444
Empire State Inst for Perf Art, Empire State Plz, Albany NY 12223.........518-474-1199
The Empty Space, 95 S Jackson St, Seattle WA 98104...........................206-587-3737
Ensemble Studio Theatre, 549 W 52nd St, New York NY 10019.................212-581-9603
Ensemble Studio Theatre, 839 S Grand Ave, Los Angeles CA 90017.........213-763-9723

Equinox Theatre Co, 355 W 39th St #B, New York NY 10018....................212-947-9116
Etre Ensemble, 83 St Marks Pl #1, Staten Island NY 10301 212-273-0099
Eureka Theatre Co, 2730 16th St, San Francisco CA 94103.......................415-558-9811
Exit Theatre, 2141 Powell #C, San Francisco CA 94133.............................415-956-4530
Facets Performance Ensemble, 1517 W Fullerton, Chicago IL 60614........312-281-9075
Fairbanks Drama Assn Inc, PO Box 81327, College AK 99708....................907-456-2643
Fairbanks Light Opera Theatre, PO Box 2787, Fairbanks AK 99707........907-456-5631
Fairfield Civic Theatre, Box 887, Suisun CA 94585 707-864-8556
Fairmont Theatre of the Deaf, 11206 Euclid Ave, Clevland OH 44106......216-231-8787
Fallon House Theatre, Box 543, Columbia CA 95310..............................209-532-4644
Fargo-Moorehead Community Theatre, Box 644, Fargo ND 58107............701-235-1901
Fig Tree Theatre, 1110 N Hudson Ave, Hollywood CA 90038 213-463-6893
The Firehouse Theatre, 514 S 11th St, Omaha NE 68102 402-346-6009
Firelite Dinner Theatre, 4350 Transport St #104, Ventura CA 93003.......805-642-8515
First All Children's Theatre, 37 W 65th St, New York NY 10023 212-873-6400
First City Players, 338 Main St, Ketchikan AK 99901 907-225-4792
Florida Studio Theatre, 1241 N Palm Ave, Sarasota FL 34236.................813-366-9017
Folger Theatre, 201 E Capitol St SE, Washington DC 20003.....................202-547-3230
Foothills Civic Theatre, Box 9077, Ft Collins CO 80525 303-493-7556
Ford's Theatre Society, 511 10th St NW, Washington DC 20004.................202-638-2941
Forum Italian Amer Playrights, 358 W 44th St, New York NY 10036......212-245-5792
Foundation Theatre, 7048 Earl NW, Seattle WA 98117.............................206-789-3241
Fountain Theatre, 5060 Fountain Ave, Los Angeles CA 90029...................213-663-1525
Frohman Acad New Wharf Theatre, Box I, Carmel CA 93921 408-625-9900
Front Room Theatre Guild, 9757 Evanston N, Seattle WA 98103...............206-789-1527
Front Row Theatre Co, 1370 Euclid Ave, Berkeley CA 94708....................415-843-9717
Fulton Opera House, PO Box 1865, Lancaster PA 17603 717-394-7133
Gallery Players of Park Slope, 93 6th Ave, Brooklyn NY 11217 718-783-4596
Galveston Performance Co, 400 W 43rd St 29H, New York NY 10036 212-564-1597
Gaslamp Quarter Theatre, 547 4th Ave, San Diego CA 92101 619-232-9608
Will Geer Theatricum Botanicum, Box 1222, Topanga CA 90280...........213-455-2322
George St Playhouse, 391 George St, New Brunswick NJ 08901.................201-846-2895
Germantown Theatre Guild, 4821 Germantown, Phila PA 19144..............215-843-8596
Geva Theatre, 75 Woodbury Blvd, Rochester NY 14607.............................716-232-1366
Emmy Gifford Children's Theatre, 3504 Center St, Omaha NE 68105......402-345-4852
The Glines, 240 W 44th St, New York NY 10036 212-354-8899
Globe of the Great Southwest, 2308 Shakespeare, Odessa TX 79761.........915-332-1586
The Gloucester Stage Co, 90 Prospect St, Gloucester MA 01930 617-281-4099
Golden Gate Actors Ensemble, 580 Constanzo St, Stanford CA 94305......415-326-0337
Golden Rod Puppets, 218 Northeast Ave, Swannanoa NC 28778 704-686-5386
Goodman Theatre, 200 S Columbus Dr, Chicago IL 60603 312-443-3811
Goodspeed Opera House, East Haddam CT 06423 203-873-8664
Grambling State Univ Theatre, Box 417, Grambling LA 71245..................318-274-2732
Great Amer Theatre Co, Box 92123, Milwaukee WI 53202.......................414-276-4230
Great Grand Forks Comm Theatre, Box 895, Grand Forks ND 58206 701-746-0847
Great Lakes Theatre Festival, 1501 Euclid Ave, Cleveland OH 44115......216-241-5490
Great N Amer History Theatre, 75 W 5th St, St Paul MN 55102.................612-227-1416
The Group Theatre Co, 3940 Brooklyn Ave NE, Seattle WA 98105...........206-545-4969
Grove Shakespeare Festival, 12852 Main St, Garden Grove CA 92640.....714-636-7213
The Guthrie Theatre, 725 Vineland Pl, Minneapolis MN 55403.................612-347-1100
Haight Ashbury Repertory, 1703 Page, San Francisco CA 94117..............415-552-5514
Harrisburg Community Theatre, 513 Hurlock St, Harrisburg PA 17110..717-238-7382
Hartford Stage Co, 50 Church St, Hartford CT 06103 203-525-5601

Hartman Theatre, PO Box 521, Stamford CT 06904 203-324-6781
Hedgerow Theatre, Rose Valley Rd, Wallingford PA 19086........................215-565-4211
Heights Showcase, 711 W 168th St, New York NY 10003............................212-927-5009
Highlight Theatre, Suny, Stony Brook NY 11794..516-246-7698
The Hippodrome State Theatre, 25 SE 2nd Pl, Gainsville FL 32601........904-373-5968
Billie Holiday Actors' Theatre, 1368 Fulton St, Brooklyn NY 11216..........718-857-6363
Hollywood Actors Theatre Inc, PO Box 5618, Santa Rosa CA 95402.........707-528-7631
Hollywood Theatre Co, 12838 Lling St, Studio City CA 91604 213-984-1867
Home Theatre for New Columbia, PO Box 75356, Wash DC 20013...........202-265-0407
Honolulu Community Theatre, 520 Makapuu Ave, Honolulu HI 96816 ...808-734-8763
Honolulu Theatre for Youth, PO Box 3257, Honolulu HI 96801 808-521-3487
Horizon Theatre Co, PO Box 5376 Station E, Atlanta GA 30307................404-584-7450
Nat Horne Musical Theatre, 440 W 42nd St, New York NY 10036............212-633-4591
Horse Cave Theatre, PO Box 215, Horse Cave KY 42749 502-786-1200
Hudson Guild Theatre, 441 W 26th St, New York NY 10001......................212-760-9839
Huntington Playhouse, 28601 Lake Rd, Bay Village OH 44140..................216-871-8333
Huntington Theatre Co, 264 Huntington Ave, Boston MA 02115 617-353-3320
Idaho Shakespeare Festival, Box 9365, Boise ID 84707...............................208-336-9798
Illinois Repertory Theatre, 500 Goodwin, Urbanart Ctr IL 61801 217-333-2371
Illinois Theatre Ctr, 400 A Lakewood Blvd, Park Forest IL 60466 312-481-3510
Illusion Theatre, 528 Hennepin Ave #704, Minneapolis MN 55401 612-339-4944
Illustrated Stage Co, Box 640063, San Francisco CA 94164 415-495-6566
The Independent Eye Ltd, 208 E King St, Lancaster PA 17602.....................717-393-9088
Indiana Repertory Theatre, 140 W Washington, Indianapolis IN 46204....317-635-5277
Indiana River Players, Box 1534, Melbourne FL 32902 305-723-6935
Instituto De Arte Teatral Intl, 9 E 16th St, New York NY 10003.................212-242-9861
Interart Theatre, 549 W 52nd St, New York NY 10019..................................212-246-1050
Intiman Theatre Co, PO Box 2763, Seattle WA 98111 206-624-4541
Invisible Theatre, 1400 N First Ave, Tucson AZ 85719.................................602-882-9721
Jackson Recr Childrens Theatre, 400 S Highland, Jackson TN 38301.......901-423-0075
Jackson State Univ, Drama Dept Danby Hall, Jackson MS 39042...............601-968-2428
Janus Theatre Co, PO Box 65, Phoenix AZ 85001.......................................605-258-9773
Jewish Community Ctr, 3505 Mayfield Rd, Cleveland Hts Oh 44118 216-382-4000
Jewish Repertory Theatre, 344 E 14th St, New York NY 10003 212-674-7200
Joe Johnson, 9418 Alondra Blvd, Bellflower CA 90706................................213-925-0441
The Julian Theatre, 953 De Haro St, San Francisco CA 94107....................415-647-5525
Kalamazoo Civic Players, 329 S Park St, Kalamazoo MI 49007..................616-343-1313
Kilgore College Theatre, 1100 Broadway, Kilgore TX 75662........................214-983-8117
Kline Theatre, Box 428, Gettysburg PA 17325...717-334-3131
Kopia Theatre, 4942 Parkside Ave, Philadelphia PA 19131..........................215-877-4426
La Mama, 74 E 4th St, New York NY 10003 212-254-6468
LA Theatre Works, 681 Venice Blvd, Venice CA 90291................................213-827-0808
Lake George Dinner Theatre, Box 266, Lake George NY 12845 518-668-2198
Lakeland Arts Ctr, 4121 Mosby Ave, Littleton NC 27850.............................919-586-3124
Lakewood Little Theatre, 17801 Detroit Ave, Lakewood OH 44107..........216-521-2540
Lamb's Players Theatre, 500 Plaza Blvd Box 26, Natl City CA 92050........619-474-3385
Las Cruces Community Theatre, Box 1281, Las Cruces NM 88001 505-523-1200
Latin Amer Theatre Ensemble, PO Box 1259, New York NY 10101..........212-246-7478
Le Petit Theatre Du Vieux Carre, 616 St Peter, New Orleans LA 70116...594-522-9958
Lehigh Univ, Chandler Hall, Bethlehem PA 18015.......................................215-861-3640
Lesbian & Gay Men's Community Ctr, Box 1124, San Diego CA 92112...619-692-2077
Lilliput Players, 1347 Divisadero St #5, San Francisco CA 94115 415-562-5204
Lion Theatre Company, 422 W 42nd St, New York NY 10036....................212-736-7930

Little Oscar Theatre, 8244 Louise Ave, Northridge CA 91406....................818-343-3423
Long Beach Comm Players, 5021 E Anaheim, Long Bch CA 90804 213-494-1014
Long Island Stage, PO Box 190, Hempstead NY 11550...............................516-546-4600
Long Wharf Theatre, 222 Sargent Dr, New Haven CT 06511 203-787-4284
Looking Glass Theatre, 175 Mathewson St, Providence RI 02903..............401-331-9080
Los Altos Conservatory Theatre, PO Box 151, Los Altos CA 94023..........415-941-5228
Los Angeles Children's Theatre, 310 Main St, Los Angeles CA 90012......213-687-8801
Los Angeles Designers' Theatre, PO Box 1883, Studio City CA 91604.......818-769-9000
Los Angeles Public Theatre, 8105 W 3rd St, Los Angeles CA 90048..........213-651-0491
Los Angeles Theatre Ctr, 514 S Spring St, Los Angeles CA 90013.............213-627-6500
Los Angeles Theatre Unit, 839 S Grand Ave, Los Angeles CA 90017........213-614-9209
Lotus Productions, 6777 Hollywood Blvd #401, Los Angeles CA 90036 ..213-461-8225
Mabou Mimes, 150 First Ave, New York NY 10009......................................212-473-0559
Mac-Haydn Theatre, PO Box 204, Chatham NY 12037 518-392-2262
Madison Repertory Theatre, 211 State St, Madison WI 53703....................608-256-0029
Magic Circle Theatre, 615 W Wellington Ave, Chicago IL 60657.............312-929-0542
Magic Theatre, Ft Mason Ctr Bldg D, San Francisco CA 94123.................415-441-8001
Main Street Theatre, Box 232 Roosevelt Island, New York NY 10044......212-371-6140
Manhattan Punch Line, 410 W 42nd St 3rd fl, New York NY 10036.........212-239-0827
Manhattan Theatre Club, 453 W 16th St, New York NY 10011..................212-645-5590
Marin Theatre Co, PO Box 1439, Mill Valley CA 94942............................415-388-5200
Mark Taper Forum, 135 N Grand Ave, Los Angeles CA 90012.................213-972-7353
Market House Theatre, 141 Kentucky Ave, Paducah KY 42001.................502-444-6828
Marquis Public Theatre, 3717 India St, San Diego CA 92103....................619-298-8111
Mary Baldwin College Theatre, Staunton VA 24401 703-887-7189
Masquers Playhouse, 105 Park Place, Pt Richmond CA 94801...................415-232-3888
McCarter Theatre, 91 University Pl, Princeton NJ 08540 609-683-9100
Meat and Potatoes Co, 306 W 38th St 4th Floor, New York NY 10018.....212-564-3292
Medicine Show Theatre Emsemble, 6 W 18th St, New York NY 10011.....212-255-4991
Megaw Theatre, 17601 Saticoy St, Northridge CA 91325 213-881-8167
Melrose Theatre, 733 N Seward St, Los Angeles CA 90038........................213-465-1885
Mendocino Preforming Arts Co, Box 800, Mendocino CA 95460 707-937-4477
Mercyhurst College, 501 E 38th St, Erie PA 16546....................................814-825-0020
Meridian Gay Theatre, PO Box 294 Village Sta, New York NY 10014 212-279-4200
Merrimack Repertory Theatre, PO Box 228, Lowell MA 01853.................617-454-6324
Merry Go Round Playhouse, Box 506, Auburn NY 13021 315-255-1305
Met Theatre, Box 93458, Los Angeles CA 90093..213-932-8614
Mettawee River Theatre Co, RD2 Salem, New York NY 12865 518-854-9357
Mill Mountain Theatre, 1 Market Sq, Roanoke VA 24011.........................703-342-5730
Millbrook Playhouse, 305 W 45th St #3-M, New York NY 10036.............212-541-7600
Milwaukee Repertory Theatre, 108 E Wells St, Milwaukee WI 53202.......414-224-9490
Mirror Repertory Co, 352 E 50th St, New York NY 10022 212-888-6087
Montford Park Players, Box 2663, Asheville NC 28802 704-254-4540
Morning Glory Theatre, Box 723, San Anselmo CA 94960.........................415-456-8787
Robt Morris Colonial Theatre, Narrows Run, Corapolis PA 15108...........412-262-8336
Morristown Theatre Guild, Box 1502, Morristown TN 37814....................615-586-9260
Mother's Theatre, 423 1st St, Ithaca NY 14850..607-273-4226
Mountain View Cabaret, 201 S Rengstorff, Mtn View CA 94040 415-961-6288
Music Hall Theatre, 931 Larkin, San Francisco CA 94109 415-585-8405
Music-Theatre Group, 735 Washington St, New York NY 10014...............212-924-3108
Musical Theatre Group, 5343 Denny Ave, N Hollywood CA 91605 818-762-3538
Musical Theatre North, Box 526, Potsdam NY 13676.................................315-265-3070
Nantahala Players, Box 482 President, Franklin NC 28734 704-369-8653

Nashville Acad Theatre, 724 2nd Ave S, Nashville TN 37210 615-254-6020
Natl Black Theatre, 2033 5th Ave, Harlem NY 10035 212-427-5615
Natl Radio Theatre, 600 N McClug CT #502-A, Chicago IL 60611 312-751-1625
Natl Theatre of the Deaf, 305 Great Neck Rd, Waterford CT 06385...........203-443-5378
Nebraska Theatre Caravan, 6915 Cass St, Omaha NE 68132 402-553-4890
Negro Ensemble Co, 1560 Broadway Ste 409, New York NY 10036...........212-575-5860
New Amer Theatre, 118 S Main St, Rockford IL 61101 815-963-9454
New Arts Theatre, 702 Ross Ave, Dallas TX 75202.....................................214-761-9064
New Arts Theatre Co, 561 Broadway #12-C, New York NY 10012.............212-925-1630
New Castle Playhouse, Box 241, New Castle PA 16103 412-946-2656
New Conserv Children's Theatre, 1537 Franklin, San Fran CA 94109 415-441-0565
New Federal Theatre, 466 Grand St, New York NY 10002............................212-598-0400
New Jersey Shakespeare Festival, Rt 24 Drew Univ, Madison NJ 07940..201-377-5330
New Playwrights Foundation, 1705 N Kenmore, Los Angeles CA 90027..213-666-0434
New Playwrights Theatre, 1742 Church St NW, Washington DC 20036 202-232-4527
New Playwrights Theatre, 31 Water St, Ashland OR 97520.......................503-482-9236
The New Rose Theatre, 904 SW Main St, Portland OR 97205.....................503-222-2495
New Shakespeare Co, Box 590458, San Francisco CA 94159 415-668-7633
New Stage Theatre, PO Box 4792, Jackson MS 39216 601-948-3531
New Tuners Theatre, 1225 W Belmont Ave, Chicago IL 60657...................312-929-7367
New Voices, 551 Tremont St, Boston MA 02116.......................................617-357-5667
New York Shakespeare Festival, 425 Lafayette St, New York NY 10003 ..212-598-7100
New York Theatre Strategy, 1 Sheridan Sq, New York NY 10014..............212-741-0590
New York Theatre Studio, 130 W 8th St, New York NY 10024....................212-239-9068
Newberry College Theatre, Dept of Theatre, Newberry SC 29108..............803-276-5010
Newport Harbor Actors Theatre, Box 2417, Newport Beach CA 92663....714-631-5110
The Next Theatre Co, 927 Noyes St, Evanston IL 60201..............................312-475-6763
Nine O'Clock Players, 1370 N St Andrews Pl, Los Angeles CA 90028.......213-469-1973
Noh Oratorio Society, 1384 Masonic Ave, San Francisco CA 94117 415-861-7644
North Carolina Black Repertory, Box 2793, Winston-Salem NC 27102 919-723-7907
North Florida Jr College, 1000 Turner Davis Dr, Madison FL 32340..........904-973-2288
Northlight Theatre, 2300 Green Bay Rd, Evanston IL 60201 312-869-7732
Northside Theatre Co, 848 E William St, San Jose CA 95116......................408-288-7820
Oakland Civic Theatre, 1520 Lakeside, Oakland CA 94612 415-452-2909
Oakland Ensemble Theatre, 1428 Alice St #289, Oakland CA 94612........415-763-7774
Odyssey Theatre Ensemble, 12111 Ohio Ave, Los Angeles CA 90025 213-826-1626
Off Center Theatre, 436 W 18th St, New York NY 10011.............................212-929-8299
The Old Creamery Theatre Co, PO Box 160, Garrison IA 52229 319-477-3925
Old Globe Theatre, PO Box 2171, San Diego CA 92112 619-231-1941
Old Log Theatre, PO Box 250, Excelsior MN 55331...................................612-474-5951
Oldcastle Theatre Co, Box 1555, Bennington VT 05201 802-447-0564
Omaha Magic Theatre, 1417 Farnam St, Omaha NE 68102.......................402-342-2821
On Stage Production, 50 W 97th St #8H, New York NY 10025...................212-666-1716
One Act Theatre Co, 430 Mason St, San Francisco CA 94102.....................415-421-5359
Open Air Theatre, Box 68, Titusville NJ 08560 609-446-0301
The Open Eye New Stagings, 270 W 89th St, New York NY 10024.............212-769-4143
Open Stage Theatre & Co, 127 N College Ave, Ft Collins CO 80524.........303-221-5805
Opera Variety Theatre, 3944 Balboa St, San Francisco CA 94121..............415-566-8805
Oregon Shakespearean Festival, PO Box 158, Ashland OR 98520 503-482-2111
Organic Theatre Co, 3319 N Clark, Chicago IL 60657 312-327-5588
Ottawa Civic Theatre, 703 S Main, Ottawa KS 66067..............................913-242-1827
Our Theatre Project, 512 7th Ave 44th fl, New York NY 10018 718-783-4194
Pacifica Spindrift Players, Box 1176, Pacifica CA 94004 415-355-9167

Pan Asian Repertory Theatre, 74 A E 4th St, New York NY 10003...........212-505-5655
Paper Mill Playhouse, Milburn NJ 07041...201-379-3636
Payson Community Theatre, 317 E 100 S, Payson UT 85651.......................801-465-3317
PCPA Theaterfest, PO Box 1700, Santa Maria CA 93456.........................805-928-7731
The Pearl Theatre Co, PO Box 29, New York NY 10108............................212-246-6538
Penguin Repertory Co, PO Box 91, Stony Point NY 10980.......................914-947-3741
Penobscot Theatre Co, Box 1188, Bangor ME 04401................................207-942-3333
People Speaking Theatre, 237 Crescent Rd, San Anselmo CA 94960........415-459-4457
The People's Light & Theatre Co, 39 Conestoga Rd, Malvern PA 19355..215-647-1900
The Performers Ensemble Inc, PO Box 562, New York NY 10185.............212-242-4266
Performing Arts Theatre, 339 11th St, Richmond CA 94801....................415-234-5624
Permian Playhouse of Odessa, PO Box 6713, Odessa TX 79767.................915-362-2329
Perseverance Theatre, 914 3rd St, Douglas AK 99824..............................907-364-2421
Peterborough Players, PO Box 1, Peterborough NH 03458......................603-924-7585
The Philadelphia Co, 21 S 5th St Ste 735, Philadelphia PA 19106.............215-592-8333
Philadelphia Festival Theatre, 3900 Chestnut St, Phila PA 19104............215-222-5000
Philadelphia Theatre Caravan, 3680 Walnut St, Phila PA 19104..............215-898-6068
Phoenix Little Theatre, 25 E Coronado Rd, Phoenix AZ 85004.................602-258-1974
Phoenix Theatre, 301 8th St #201-A, San Francisco CA 94123.................415-759-7696
Phoenix Theatre, 37 E 9th St, Indianpolis IN 46204................................317-635-7529
Pier One Theatre, Box 894, Homer AK 99603...907-235-7333
Pilgrim Project, 311 W 43rd St #902-A, New York NY 10036 212-333-2471
Pioneer Playhouse, R R 2 Box 12, Danville KY 40422.............................606-236-2747
Pioneer Repertory Players, Box 2882, Sitka AK 99835...........................907-747-6234
Pioneer Square Theatre, 512 2nd Ave, Seattle WA 98104.......................206-622-2016
Pioneer Theatre Co, 300 South & University, Salt Lake City UT 84112 801-581-6356
Piper Productions, 963 Corona St, Denver CO 80218..............................303-832-4638
Pittsburgh Playhouse Theatre Ctr, 222 Craft Ave, Pittsburge PA 15213...412-621-4445
Pittsburgh Public Theatre, 1 Allegheny Sq G100, Pittsburgh PA 15212....412-323-8200
Play Group, 803 S Gay St, Knoxville TN 37902.......................................615-523-7641
The Play Works Co, PO Box 25152, Philadelphia PA 19147.....................215-236-8488
Players Co, 2811 W Magnolia Blvd, Burbank CA 91505 213-842-4755
Players Guild of Canton, 1001 Market Ave N, Canton OH 44702.............216-453-7619
Players Theatre, Box 306, Eunice LA 70535 318-457-2616
Playhouse 51, 51 W 19th St, New York NY 10011...................................212-989-4574
Playhouse on the Square, 51 S Cooper, Memphis TN 38104......................901-725-0776
Playmakers Repertory, 203 Graham Memorial, Chapel Hill NC 27514 919-962-1122
The Playmakers, PO Box 5745, Tampa FL 33675.....................................813-248-693'
Playworks, Ft Mason Ctr Blvd, San Francisco CA 94123 ....415-885-276'
Playwright's Alliance, 8 Thompkins Ave, Babylon NY 11702...................516-587-894:
Playwright's Fund Of NC, PO Box 646, Greenville NC 27835...................919-758-3628
Playwrights Horizons, 416 W 42nd St, New York NY 10036....................212-564-1235
Plutonium Players, 1600 Woolsey #7, Berkeley CA 94307.......................415-841-6500
Ponca Playhouse, PO Box 1414, Ponca City OK 74602 405-765-7786
Poplar Pike Playhouse, 7653 Old Poplar Pike, Germantown TN 38138 901-755-7775
Portland Stage Co, PO Box 1458, Portland ME 04104.............................207-774-1043
The Possible Theatre, 733 Amsterdam 14J, New York NY 10025..............212-982-2458
Post Theatre Co, CW Post Campus, Greenvale NY 11542.........................516-299-2353
Powerhouse, 3116 2nd St, Santa Monica CA 90405.................................213-392-6529
Pregones Puerto Rican Theatre, 965 Longwood, Bronx NY 10459 212-542-7853
Primary Stages Co, 584-86 9th Ave, New York NY 10036.........................212-333-7471
Princeton Rep Co, 13 Witherspoon St, Princeton NJ 08542......................609-921-3682
Process Studio Theatre, 4113 Foster Ave, Brooklyn NY 11203 212-226-1124

The Production Co, 303 Park Ave S #406A, New York NY 10010 212-533-7570
Promised Valley Playhouse, 132 S State St, Salt Lake City UT 84111.......801-364-5696
Quaigh Theatre, 205 W 89th St, New York NY 10024...................................212-595-6185
The Quartz Theatre, PO Box 465, Ashland OR 97520 503-482-8119
Queens Theatre in the Park, 100-08 Queens, Forest Hls NY 11375...........212-592-5700
Raft Theatre, 432 W 42nd St, New York NY 10036 212-947-8389
Rainbow Co Children's Theatre, 821 Las Vegas, Las Vegas NV 89101.....702-386-6553
Rainbow Theatre Co, 248 Anza St, San Francisco CA 94118......................415-751-4864
Repertorio Espanol, 138 E 27th St, New York NY 10016............................212-889-2850
Repertory Theatre Bucks County, Box 104, Newtown PA 18940.................215-968-6701
The Repertory Theatre of St Louis, PO Box 28030, St Louis MO 63119...304-968-7340
Rhode Island Feminist Theatre, Box 9083, Providence RI 02940...............401-273-8654
Rise Repertory Theatre, 238 W 71st St, New York NY 10023......................212-496-9378
Rites and Reason, Box 1148 Brown Univ, Providence RI 02912..................401-863-3558
Riverside Shakespeare Co, 165 W 86th St, New York NY 10024 212-877-6810
The Road Co, PO Box 5278, Johnson City TN 37603.................................615-926-7726
Roadside Theatre, Box 743, Whitesburg KY 41858.....................................606-633-0108
Forest Roberts Theatre, Northern Mich Univ, Marquette MI 49855.........906-227-2553
Rochester Civic Theatre, Mayo Park, Rochester NY 55904 507-282-7633
Rooftop Repertory Co, 425 W 57th St #2-J, New York NY 10019 212-265-6284
Round House Theatre, 12210 Bushey Dr, Silver Spring MD 20902............301-468-4233
Roundabout Theatre Co, 100 E 17th St, New York NY 10003.....................212-420-1360
Ryan Repertory Co, 2445 Bath Ave, Brooklyn NY 11214............................718-373-5208
Sacramento Theatre Co, 1419 H St, Sacramento CA 95814........................916-446-7501
Saint Bart's Playhouse, 109 E 50th St, New York NY 10022.......................212-833-8782
Salt & Pepper Mime Co, 320 E 90th St, New York NY 10128 212-262-4989
Salt Lake Acting Co, 168 W 500 N, Salt Lake City UT 84103.....................801-363-0526
San Diego Repertory Theatre, 1620 6th Ave, San Diego CA 92101............619-231-3586
San Francisco Actors Theatre, 808 Post #306, San Francisco CA 94109..415-524-1306
San Francisco Intl Theatre Festival, 500 4th St, San Fran CA 94107 415-543-8820
San Francisco Mime Troupe, 855 Treat St, San Francisco CA 94110........415-285-1717
San Francisco Playwrights Ctr, 1001 Pine #803, San Fran CA 94109.......415-931-2392
San Francisco Repertory, 4147 19th St, San Francisco CA 94114...............415-864-3305
San Jose Repertory Co, PO Box 2399, San Jose CA 95109.........................408-294-7572
San Jose State Univ Theatre, 1 Washington Sq, San Jose CA 95192 408-277-2763
Santa Clara Univ Theatre, Santa Clara CA 95053......................................408-554-4989
Santa Cruz Theatre Co, 146 Rose Valley Rd, Moylan PA 19086.................215-565-4211
Santa Fe Festival Theatre, PO Box DD, Santa Fe NM 87502.....................505-983-9495
Schenectady Civic Players, 12 S Church St, Schenectady NY 12305...........518-382-2081
Zachary Scott Theatre, PO Box 244, Austin TX 78767 512-476-0594
Seattle Children's Theatre, 4649 Sunnyside Ave N, Seattle WA 98103......206-633-4591
Seattle Repertory Theatre, 155 Mercer St, Seattle WA 98109....................206-447-2210
Second Story Ensemble, 325 Bleecker St #17, New York NY 10014.........212-242-7909
Sheboygan Community Players, 607 S Water St, Sheboygan WI 53081.....414-459-3779
Shepard Theatre Studios, 6468 Santa Monica, Hollywood CA 90038........213-462-9399
Shipping Dock Theatre, 3690 East Ave, Rochester NY 14618 716-385-8400
Shur-Gold Productions, PO Box 621, New York NY 10011........................212-477-6659
Smith College, Theatre Dept, Northampton MA 01063..............................413-584-2700
Society Hill Playhouse, 507 S 8th St, Philadelphia PA 19147.....................215-923-0210
Soho Repertory Theatre, 80 Varick St, New York NY 10013.......................212-925-2588
Solano Arts Theatre, Box 4404, Vallejo CA 94590......................................707-552-2787
Solomon/Tyler Productions, 1 Lincoln Plz 33U, New York NY 10023.....212-724-1911
Sonoma Vintage Theatre, Box 312, Sonoma CA 95476 707-938-9182

South Coast Repertory, PO Box 2197, Costa Mesa CA 92628 714-957-2602
South Park Conservatory Theatre, Box 253, Bethel Park PA 15102..........412-831-8552
Southern Appalachian Theatre, Box 53, Mars Hill NC 28754....................704-689-1203
Southern Calif Arts Ctr, 6753 Selma Ave #5, Los Angeles CA 90028 213-655-3054
Southern Conn State Univ, Dept of Theatre, New Haven CT 06515 203-397-4432
Southern Univ, Theatre Dept, Baton Rouge LA 70813................................504-771-3190
Spectrum Theatre, 1 E 104th St #B-9, New York NY 10029 212-860-5535
Spokane Civic Theatre, PO Box 5222, Spokane WA 99205 509-325-1413
Spokane Interplayers Ensemble, PO Box 1961, Spokane WA 99210 509-624-5902
Springside Inn, 41 W Lake Rd Box 327, Auburn NY 13021.......................315-252-7247
Stage #1, PO Box 31607, Dallas TX 75231 214-559-3754
Stage Left, Box 3251, New York NY 10185..212-989-4682
Stage Left Theatre, 3244 N Clark, Chicago IL 60657.................................312-883-8830
Stage One Children's Theatre, 425 W Market St, Louisville KY 40202.....502-589-5946
Stage Three, 600 West End Ave #4-A, New York NY 10024.......................212-663-3685
Stage West, 821 W Vickery, Ft Worth TX 76113..817-332-6265
Stage West, 1 Columbus Ctr, Springfield MA 01103..................................413-781-4470
Stages Repertory Theatre, 3201 Allen Pkwy #101, Houston TX 77019.....713-527-0240
Staret Directors Co, 311 W 43rd St #603, New York NY 10036 212-246-5877
Staten Island Shakespearean Theatre, 163 Malone, Staten Is NY 10306..718-667-6479
Steppenwolf Theatre Co, 2851 N Halsted St, Chicago IL 60657...................312-472-4515
Stokes County Art Council, Box 66, Danbury NC 27016 919-593-8159
Stonewall Repertory Theatre, PO Box 94, New York NY 10113 212-677-4904
Stop-Gap, PO Box 484, Laguna Beach CA 92652 714-722-7727
Strand Street Theatre, 2317 Mechanic St, Galveston TX 77550 409-763-4591
Lee Strasberg Theatre Inst, 7936 Santa Monica, Los Angeles CA 90046..213-650-7777
The Street Theatre, 228 Fisher Ave Rm 226, White Plains NY 10606.........914-761-3307
Studio 8, Rt 2 Box 273-A, Sterling VA 22170..703-430-2905
Studio Arena Theatre, 710 Main St, Buffalo NY 14202.............................716-856-8025
Studio Theatre, 141 S Wellwood Ave, Lindenhurst NY 11757 515-226-1838
The Studio Theatre, 1401 Church St NW, Washington DC 20005...............202-232-7267
Summer Music Theatre, Box 1310, Daytona Beach FL 32105 904-252-3395
Sunset Playhouse, PO Box 2, Elm Grove WI 53122 414-782-4430
Synthaxis Theatre Co, Box 15036, N Hollywood CA 91606........................213-877-4726
Syracuse Stage, 820 Genesee St, Syracuse NY 13210 315-423-4008
Tacoma Actors Guild, 1323 S Yakima Ave, Tacoma WA 98405.................206-272-3107
Tale Spinners Theatre, Ft Mason Ctr Bldg C, San Francisco CA 94123 ...415-776-8477
Tarradiddle Players, 436 E Pape Ave, Charlotte NC 28203 704-375-5449
Teatro Duo, Box 1363 Grand Cnt Sta, New York NY 10017 212-598-4320
Thalia Spanish Theatre, PO Box 4368, Sunnyside NY 11104......................718-729-3880
Theater Ludicrum Inc, 64 Charlesgate St, Boston MA 02215 617-424-6831
Theatre 40, Box 5401, Beverly Hills CA 90210...213-277-4221
Theatre Artists of Marin, Box 473, San Rafeal CA 94915 415-454-2380
Theatre AUM, Auburn Univ at Montgomery, Montgomery AL 36117......205-272-9632
Theatre by the Sea, 125 Bow St PO Box 927, Portsmouth NH 03801.........603-431-5846
Theatre Exchange, 11855 Hart St, N Hollywood CA 91605 213-765-9005
Theatre for a New Audience, 26 Grove St Ste 6G, New York NY 10014 ...212-505-8345
Theatre for the New City, 155 1st Ave, New York NY 10003 212-254-1109
Theatre for Young People, Univ of NC, Greensboro NC 27412...................919-379-5562
Theatre Guild of San Francisco, 2961 16th St, San Francisco CA 94103...415-863-7576
Theatre in the Park, PO Box 12151, Raleigh NC 27605 919-755-6936
Theatre in the Park, Box 1336, Flushing NY 11352 212-592-5700
Theatre in the Round Players, 245 Cedar Ave, Minneapolis MN 55454....612-333-3010

Theatre in the Works, PO Box 532016, Orlando FL 32853............................305-678-5002
Theatre IV, 114 Broad St, Richmond VA 23220 804-353-1048
Theatre of the Blue Rose, 2525 8th St, Berkeley CA 94710.......................415-540-5037
Theatre of Youth Co, 681 Main St, Buffalo NY 14203.............................716-856-4401
Theatre on the Square, 450 Post St, San Francisco CA 94105.....................415-775-1634
Theatre Project Co, 4219 Laclede, St Louis MO 63108..............................314-531-1301
Theatre Rapport, 8128 Gould Ave, Hollywood CA 90046..........................213-464-2662
Theatre Rhinoceros, 2926 16th St, San Francisco CA 94103.......................415-522-4100
Theatre Southwest, 3767 Harper St, Houston TX 77005.............................713-667-8480
Theatre Three, 2800 Routh St, Dallas TX 75201 214-651-7225
Theatre Three Productions, Box 512, Port Jefferson NY 11777 516-928-9202
Theatre Three Repertory Co, 15644 Fulton St, Fresno CA 93721.................209-486-3381
Theatre West Virginia, PO Box 1205, Beckley WV 25801 304-253-8317
Theatre X, PO Box 92206, Milwaukee WI 53202......................................414-278-0555
Theatre-Studio, 750 8th Ave #200, New York NY 10036............................212-730-0235
TheatreVirginia, Boulevard & Grove Ave, Richmond VA 23221.................804-257-0840
Theatrevisions, 255-09 West End Dr, Great Neck NY 11020.......................516-466-9464
Theatreworks, 1305 Middlefield Rd, Palo Alto CA 94301............................415-328-0600
Theatreworks Univ of Colo, PO Box 7150, Colo Spgs CO 80933.................303-593-3232
Theatreworks/USA, 131 W 86th St, New York NY 10024 212-595-7500
Theatrical Outfit, PO Box 7098, Atlanta GA 30357...................................404-872-0665
13th St Repertory Co, 50 W 13th St, New York NY 10011..........................212-675-6677
Threshold Theatre Co, 251 W 87th St #416, New York NY 10024.............212-724-9129
Tour de Force, 2850 Sneath Ln #8, San Bruno CA 94066 415-695-7846
Transart Productions, 1501 Broadway #2001, New York NY 10036............212-869-9669
Tri-Crown Family Theatre, Box 175, Sterling KS 67579.............................316-278-3248
Triangle Theatre Co, 104 Charles St Box 127, Boston MA 02114...............617-497-9516
Trinity Sq Repertory Co, 201 Washington St, Providencre RI 02903.........401-521-1100
Trinity Theatre, 22840 Sheridan Rd, Evanston IL 60201.............................312-328-0330
Trinity Theatre Productions, Trinity College, Burlington VT 05401..........802-658-0337
The Triplex, 199 Chambers St, New York NY 10007...................................212-618-1900
24th St Experiment, 411 SW 24th St, San Antonio TX 78285.....................512-435-2103
Typical Theatre of Brooklyn, 112 Wyckoff Ave, Brooklyn NY 11207.........718-366-1390
United Theatre of the Americas, 55 Audubon, New Haven CT 06501.......212-468-1645
Univ of Calif, Theatre Dept, Riverside CA 90251.....................................714-787-3221
Univ of Calif LA, 10995 Leconte Ave, Los Angeles CA 90024.....................213-825-9415
Univ of Cincinnati, Festival of New Works, Cincinnati OH 45221..............513-475-5803
Univ of Houston, Dept of Drama, Houston TX 77004................................713-749-1427
Univ of Judaism, 15600 Mulholland Dr, Bel Air CA 90077.........................213-558-3752
Univ of Minn Duluth Theatre, 10 University Dr, Duluth MN 55812..........218-726-8562
Univ of Nevada, 4505 Maryland Pkwy, Las Vegas NV 89154.....................702-739-3666
Univ of New Orleans, Performing Arts Ctr, New Orleans LA 70148 504-286-6345
Univ of North Carolina, Dept of Creative Arts, Charlotte NC 28223........704-597-4471
Univ of Oklahoma, School of Drama, Norman OK 73019............................405-325-4021
Univ of Texas at Austin, Dept of Drama, Austin TX 78712 512-471-5793
Univ of Utah, 306 Pioneer Memorial Theatre, Salt Lake City UT 84112...801-581-6356
Univ of West Florida, 1000 University Pky, Pensacola FL 32514.................904-474-2146
Univ of Wisconsin, 821 University Ave, Madison WI 53706.........................608-263-2329
University Theatre, 129 Fine Arts, Columbia MO 65211.............................314-882-2021
USC Amer Mystery Theatre, Student Union, Los Angeles CA 90089........213-743-6296
Veterans Ens Theatre, 1100 Ave of Amer 13-10, New York NY 10019.....212-664-0023
Veterans Ensemble Theatre Co, 314 W 54th St, New York NY 10019.......212-664-0023
Victorian Theatre, 4201 Hooker, Denver CO 80211...................................303-433-5050

Victory Gardens Theatre, 2257 N Lincoln Ave, Chicago IL 60614 312-549-5788
Victory Theatre, 3326 W Victory Blvd, Burbank CA 91505 818-843-9253
Village Performers Theatre, 98-A 3rd Ave, New York NY 10003 212-473-8835
Virginia Stage Co, PO Box 3770, Norfolk VA 23514 804-627-6988
Vortex Theatre Co, 164 11th Ave, New York NY 10011................................212-206-1764
Walnut Street Theatre Co, 9th & Walnut Sts, Philadelphia PA 19107.......215-574-3550
Waterloo Community Playhouse, Box 433, Waterloo IA 50704.................319-235-0367
The Wayside Theatre, PO Box 260, Middletown VA 22645.......................703-869-1782
West Coast Ensemble Theatre, PO Box 38728, Los Angeles CA 90038 213-871-8673
Western Carolina Univ, Dept of Theatre Arts, Cullowhee NC 28723........704-227-7491
Western Public Radio, Ft Mason Ctr, San Francisco CA 94123 415-771-1160
Western Washington Univ Theatre, Bellingham WA 98225......................206-676-3876
Westport country Playhouse, Box 629, Westport CT 06881 203-227-5137
Whole Theatre, 544 Bloomfield Ave, Montclair NJ 07042 201-744-2996
Williams County Playhouse, Lawrence Ave, Montpelier OH 43543 419-485-3861
Williamstown Theatre Festival, PO Box 448, New York NY 10013............212-608-8811
Wilma Theatre, 2030 Sansom St, Philadelphia PA 19103..........................215-963-0249
Windward Theatre Guild, Box 624, Kailua HI 96734 808-261-4885
Winter Haven Community Theatre, Box 1615, Winter Haven FL 33882...813-299-9428
Wisdom Bridge Theatre, 1559 W Howard St, Chicago IL 60626 312-743-0486
Women in Theatre, 1129 E 6th St, Houston TX 77009...............................713-868-2419
Women in Theatre, Box 1147 FDR Station, New York NY 10150.............212-570-9058
Women's Theatre, 6757 Palatine Ave N, Seattle WA 98103........................206-789-6001
Women's Theatre Project, 203 N Howell, St Paul MN 55104 612-647-1953
Woodstock Playhouse, PO Box 396, Woodstock NY 12498........................914-679-6000
Woodward Community Theatre, Box 1441, Woodard OK 73802.................405-256-7120
Woolly Mammoth Theatre Co, PO Box 32229, Washington DC 20007 202-393-3939
Wooster Group, 33 Wooster St, New York NY 10013.................................212-966-9796
Worcester Foothills Theatre Co, PO Box 236, Worcester MA 01602........617-754-4018
Working Theatre, 402 W 45th St #2-B, New York NY 10036......................212-582-1488
WPA Theatre, 519 W 23rd St, New York NY 10010 212-691-2274
Writers' Theatre, Box 810 Times Square Station, New York NY 10016....212-226-1991
Yale Repertory Theatre, 222 York St, New Haven CT 06520 203-436-1589
York Community High School, 355 W St Charles, Elmhurst IL 60126......312-530-1240
York Little Theatre, 27 S Belmont St, York PA 17403 717-854-3894
The York Theatre Co, 2 E 90th St, New York NY 10128 212-534-5366
Yucaipa Little Theatre, 11837 Peach Tree Cir, Yucaipa CA 92399 714-797-9677
Zephyr Theatre, 7456 Melrose Ave, Los Angeles CA 90046.......................213-653-4667

THEATRICAL WORKSHOPS

This section lists playwriting workshops and other special theatrical programs. See also Theatres and Contests & Awards for other playwriting programs.

Academy Playwrights Lab, PO Box 77070, Atlanta GA 30357 404-873-2518
Alabama New Playwrights Prog, Box 6386 UA, University AL 35486 205-348-5283
Amer Minority Playwrights, 3940 Brooklyn Ave NE, Seattle WA 98105...206-545-4969
Amer Indian Community House, 942 Broadway, New York NY 10003.....212-598-0100
Amer Theatre of Actors, 314 W 54th St, New York NY 10019....................212-581-3044
ASCAP Musical Theatre Wkshp, 1 Lincoln Plz, New York NY 10023 212-870-7545
At the Foot of the Mountain, 2000 S 5th St, Minneapolis MN 55454 612-375-9487

Atlanta New Play Project Festival, PO Box 14252, Atlanta GA 30324.......404-233-6516
Bay Area Playwrights Festival, PO Box 1191, Mill Valley CA 94942.........415-381-3311
BMI-Lehman Engel Workshop, 320 W 57th St, New York NY 10019 212-586-2000
The Cast Theatre, 804 N El Centro Ave, Hollywood CA 90038....................213-462-9872
Celtic Arts Center, 5651 Hollywood Blvd, Hollywood CA 90028.................213-462-6844
Chicago Dramatists Workshop, 3315 N Clark St, Chicago IL 60657 312-472-7832
Children's Theatre Workshop, 519 Kittinger Dr, Pleasanton CA 94566....415-846-5400
Douglass Creative Arts Ctr, 168 W 46th St, New York NY 10036 212-944-9870
Lehman Engel Workshop, 508 Grace Ave, Los Angeles CA 90301.............213-672-3698
Florida Keys Community College, Fine Arts Ctr, Key West FL 33040 305-296-9081
Hispanic Drama Studio, 1337 Gates Ave, Brooklyn NY 11221 718-453-5322
Hispanic Playwrights Lab, Box 788, New York NY 10108 212-695-6134
INTAR, 420 W 42nd St, New York NY 10108...212-695-6134
ISD Theatre Center, PO Box 1310, Miami FL 33153....................................305-756-8313
Preston Jones New Play Symposium, Box 270363, Houston TX 77277......713-528-0070
Missouri Repertory Theatre, 4949 Cherry St, Kansas City MO 64110.......816-276-1576
Musical Theatre Lab, Radcliffe College, Cambridge MA 02138 617-495-8676
Musical Theatre Works, 133 2nd Ave, New York NY 10003 212-677-0040
Natl Inst for Music Theatre, Kennedy Ctr, Washington DC 20566.............202-965-2800
Natl Music Theater Network, 1457 Broadway, New York NY 10036.........212-382-0984
Natl Oper/Music Theater Conf, 305 Great Neck, Waterford CT 06385 ...203-443-5378
Natl Playwrights Conf, 234 W 44th St Ste 901, New York NY 10036.........212-382-2790
New Dramatists, 424 W 44th St, New York NY 10036 212-757-6960
New Theatre, PO Box 650696, Miami FL 33265 305-595-4260
Northwest Playwrights Conf, 95 S Jackson St, Seattle WA 98104...............206-587-3737
Northwest Playwrights Forum, 605 1st Ave S #315, Seattle WA 98104 206-343-9654
Padua Hills Playwrights Wkshp, 681 Venice Blvd, Venice CA 90291 213-827-0808
Pennsylvania Stage Co, 837 Linden St, Allentown PA 18101 215-434-6110
Philadelphia Drama Guild, 112 S 16th St #802, Philadelphia PA 19102...215-563-7530
Play Lab, 4649 Sunnyside Ave N, Seattle WA 98103..................................206-633-4591
Playwrights Platform, 43 Charles St, Boston MA 02114 617-720-3770
The Playwrights' Center, 2301 E Franklin Ave, Minneapolis MN 55406 ...612-332-7481
Primafacie, 1050 13th St, Denver CO 80204..303-893-4200
Puerto Rican Theatre Playwrights, 304 W 47th St, New York NY 10036..212-354-1293
Readers Theatre Inst, PO Box 17193, San Diego CA 92117.........................619-276-1948
River Arts Repretory, 361 W 36th St, New York NY 10018 212-736-2012
Shenandoah Playwrights Retreat, Box 167 F Rt 5, Staunton VA 24401 703-248-1868
Frank Silvera Writers Wkshp, 317 W 125th St, New York NY 10027 212-662-8463
Summer Solstice Theatre Conf, PO Box 1859, E Hampton NY 11937......718-237-9303
Sundance Ctr Playwrights Lab, 19 Exchange Pl, Salt Lk City UT 84111 ..801-521-9330
Theatre East, 12655 Ventura Blvd, Studio City CA 91604 213-760-4760
Theatre in the Works, 112 Fine Arts Ctr, Amherst MA 01003....................413-545-3490
Theatre West, 3333 Cahuenga Blvd West, Hollywood CA 90068.................213-851-4839
Westbeth Theare Ctr, 151 Bank St, New York NY 10014.............................212-242-7103
The Women's Project, 111 W 46th St, New York NY 10036 212-246-3730
Works In Progress, 528 Hennepin Ave, Minneapolis MN 55403.................612-333-5241
The Yard, 325 Spring St, New York NY 10013 212-206-7885

TV & RADIO NETWORKS

ABC Radio, 3321 S La Cienega, Los Angeles CA 90016 213-557-7777
ABC TV, 2040 Ave of the Stars, Los Angeles CA 90067 213-557-7777
ABC TV & Radio, 1330 Ave of the Americas, New York NY 10019 212-887-7777
Amer Business Network, 1615 H St NW, Washington DC 20062 202-463-5690
AP Radio, 1825 K St NW #615, Washington DC 20006 202-955-7200
Arts & Entertainment, 555 5th Ave, New York NY 10017 212-661-4500
Black Entertainment TV, 1232 31st St NW, Washington DC 20077 202-337-5260
Black Radio Network, 166 Madison Ave, New York NY 10016 212-686-6850
C-SPAN, 400 N Capitol St NW #412, Washington DC 20001 202-737-3220
Cable News Network, 1 CNN Center, Atlanta GA 30348 404-827-1500
CBN, CBN Center, Virginia Beach VA 23463 804-424-7777
CBS Radio, 6121 Sunset Blvd, Los Angeles CA 90028 213-460-3000
CBS TV, 7800 Beverly Blvd, Los Angeles CA 90036 213-852-2345
CBS TV & Radio, 51 W 52nd St, New York NY 10019 212-975-4321
Continuum Broadcasting, 345 W 85th St, New York NY 10024 212-713-5208
Discovery Channel, 8201 Corporate Dr #1260, Landover MD 20785........301-577-1999
Disney Channel, 4111 W Alameda, Burbank CA 91505 818-569-7500
ESPN, ESPN Plaza, Bristol CT 06010 203-584-8477
Financial News Network, 2525 Ocean Park, Santa Monica CA 90405 213-450-2412
Fox TV, 5746 Sunset Blvd, Los Angeles CA 90028 213-856-1720
Galavision Inc, 5358 Melrose Ave, Los Angeles CA 90038 213-463-4168
Group W Productions, 5842 Sunset Blvd, Los Angeles CA 90028..............213-960-2407
Group W Radio, 6230 Yucca St, Los Angeles CA 90028.............................213-462-5392
Home Box Office, 1100 Ave of Americas #13-10, New York NY 10019....212-664-0023
Home Sports Ent, 5251 Gulfton, Houston TX 77081..................................713-661-0078
Hughes TV, 4 Penn Plaza, New York NY 10001...212-563-8900
Learning Channel, 1414 22nd St NW, Washington DC 20037......................202-331-8100
Lifetime Cable Network, 1211 Ave of Americas, New York NY 10036......212-719-7230
Lifetime Cable Network, 3575 Cahuenga W, Los Angeles CA 90068.........213-850-0373
Madison Sq Garden Network, 1 Penn Plaza, New York NY 10001.............212-563-8000
McGraw-Hill Inc, 1221 Ave of the Americas, New York NY 10020...........212-512-2000
MTV Networks/VH1, 1775 Broadway, New York NY 10019.....................212-713-6400
Mutual Broadcasting Sys, 1755 S Davis Hwy, Arlington VA 22202...........703-685-2000
Mutual Broadcasting Sys, 2029 Century Pk E, Los Angeles CA 90067.....213-277-7700
Nashville Network, 2806 Opryland Dr, Nashville TN 37214 615-889-6840
National Christian Network, 1150 W King St, Cocoa FL 32922 305-632-1000
Nationality Broadcasting, 11906 Madison, Lakewood OH 44107................216-221-0330
Natl Public Radio, 2025 M St NW, Washington DC 20036..........................202-822-2000
NBC TV & Radio, 30 Rockefeller Plaza, New York NY 10020 212-664-4444
NBC TV & Radio, 3000 W Alameda, Burbank CA 91523 818-840-4444
Nickelodeon, 1775 Broadway, New York NY 10019...................................212-713-6400
Pro Video News Service, 303 S Crescent Hts, Los Angeles CA 90048........213-655-4740
Public Broadcasting Service, 1320 Braddock Pl, Alexandria VA 22314 703-739-5000
Public Broadcasting Service, 4401 Sunset Blvd, Los Angeles CA 90027 ...213-667-9289
Public Broadcasting Service, 609 5th Ave, New York NY 10017.................212-753-7373
Radio for Peace, 35 SE 60th, Portland OR 97215......................................503-231-3771
Reuters Information Service, 1700 Broadway, New York NY 10019 212-603-3285
Sheridan Broadcast Network, 411 7th Ave, Pittsburgh PA 15219...............412-281-6751

Showtime/Movie Channel, 10900 Wilshire Blvd, Los Angeles CA 90024..213-208-2340
Sportsvision, 820 W Madison, Oak Park IL 60302..312-524-9444
Tempo Network, PO Box 702160, Tulsa OK 74170 918-481-0881
Turner Broadcasting, 1 CNN Center, Atlanta GA 30348 404-827-1500
United Stations Radio Networks, 1440 Broadway, New York NY 10018..212-576-6100
Univision, 460 W 42nd St, New York NY 10036..212-826-5200
UPI Cable News, 220 E 42nd St, New York NY 10017 212-850-8639
UPI Radio, 1400 I St, Washington DC 20005 202-898-8120
USA Network, 1230 Ave of the Americas, New York NY 10020..................212-408-9100
Weather Channel, 2840 Mt Wilkinson, Atlanta GA 30339...........................404-434-6800

TYPESETTERS

These firms typeset books and other publications. See also Book Printers and Book
Producers.

Adroit Graphic Composition, 537 Greenwich St, New York NY 10013 212-243-1929
Alexander Typesetting, 125 N East St, Indianapolis IN 46204......................317-634-2206
All In Graphic Arts, 10550 NW 77th Ct #303, Hialeah Gdns FL 33016....305-558-3454
All Languages Graphics, 116 Bishop Allen Dr, Cambridge MA 02139 617-864-3900
Allen-Wayne Communication, 44 Cooper Sq, New York NY 10003 212-674-2900
Allservice Phototypesetting, 10844 N 23rd Ave #1, Phoenix AZ 85029.....602-997-7347
Alpine Press, 100 Alpine Cir, Stoughton MA 02072......................................617-341-1800
Amer Graphics Corp, 959 NE 45th St, Ft Lauderdale FL 33334.................305-771-6777
Amer Lazertype, Rancho Conejo Blvd #501, Newbury Park CA 91320 805-498-2215
Amer-Stratford Graphic Services, PO Box 810, Brattleboro VT 05301 802-254-6073
Anco/Boston, 441 Sturat St, Boston MA 02116 617-267-9700
Any Photo Type, 350 W 31st St, New York NY 10001 212-244-1130
M Arman Publishing, PO Box 785, Ormond Beach FL 32074 904-673-5576
The Artwerks Group, 6116 N Central Expy Ste 305, Dallas TX 75206.......214-361-7750
Auromere, 1291 Weber St, Pomona CA 91768 714-629-8255
Austex Printing & Mailing, 118 Neches, Austin TX 78701 512-476-7581
Auto Graphics Inc, 751 Monterey Pass Rd, Monterey Park CA 91754......213-269-9451
Automatech Graphics Corp, 770 Broadway, New York NY 10003 212-674-3022
Automated Composition Svc, 122 E St, New York NY 10168.....................212-867-0340
Barsch Co Inc, 17 S 19th St, Camp Hill PA 17011 717-761-3260
Bask Press Inc, 351 E 84th St, New York NY 10028 212-535-9384
Beech Hill Publishing, Box 136 Forest Ave, SW Harbor ME 04679 207-244-3931
Beljan Ltd, 2870 Baker Rd, Dexter MI 48130...313-426-2415
Better Music Type, PO Box 101245 S Sta, Nashville TN 37210 615-360-3361
Birmy Graphics of America, 2244 NW 21 Terr, Miami FL 33142 305-633-5241
Black Ink Typographers, 165 W 46th St Ste 1306, New York NY 10036...212-819-0045
Books Inc, 3635 McCord St, Montgomery AL 36109....................................205-272-5924
The William Boyd Printing Co, 49 Sheridan Ave, Albany NY 12210.........518-436-9686
Browne Book Composition Inc, PO Box 6065, Lawrenceville NJ 08648 609-737-8779
Burmar Technical Corp, 175 I U Wilets Rd, Albertson NY 11507 516-484-6000
Wm Byrd Press, 2901 Byrdhill Rd, Richmond VA 23261.............................804-264-2711
Canterbury Press, 301 Mill St, Rome NY 13440...315-337-5900
Caravan Publishing Group, 303 5th Ave Ste 208, New York NY 10016....615-584-0168
Carlisle Graphics, 2530 Kerper Blvd, Dubuque IA 52001 319-557-1500
Case-Hoyt Corp, 800 St Paul St, Rochester NY 14601 716-232-6840

Central Publishing Co, 401 N College, Indianapolis IN 46206....................317-636-4504
Christian Publishing & Services, 2600 S Nova, Daytona Bch FL 32019....904-761-2100
The Clarinda Co, 220 N 1st St, Clarinda IA 51632...712-542-5131
Coghill Composition Co, 1627 Elmdale Ave, Richmond VA 23224..........804-231-0224
A Colish Inc, 40 Hartford Ave, Mount Vernon NY 10550..............................914-667-1000
Columbia Publishing Co, 234 E 25th St, Baltimore MD 08825....................301-366-7070
Comp-Type Inc, 155 Cypress St, Ft Bragg CA 95437.....................................707-964-9520
Composing Room, 2303 Kalamazoo Ave SE, Grand Rapids MI 49507.....616-452-2171
Composing Room, 131 Beverly St, Boston MA 02114.....................................617-742-4866
Composition House Ltd, 456 Sicomac Ave, Wyckoff NJ 07481....................201-891-8553
Composition Services, 81-08 160 Ave, Howard Beach NY 11414................718-835-4200
Computer Composition, 1401 Girard Ave, Madison Hts MI 48071...........313-545-4330
Computer Typesetting Svcs, 407 W Chevy Chase, Glendale CA 91204.....213-245-9000
Computype Inc, 2285 W County Rd C, St Paul MN 55113.........................612-633-0633
Concepts Unlimited Inc, PO Box 111, Acton MA 01720................................617-263-6777
Conch Typesetting, 102 Normal Ave, Buffalo NY 14213................................716-885-3686
CPC Typographers, 200 Turnpike Rd, Southborough MA 01772................617-480-0205
Crosby Typographers, 130 Crosby St, New York NY 10012..........................212-966-5750
Cybertext Corp, 702 Jefferson, Ashland OR 97520.......................................503-482-0733
DataServ Inc, 925 Chestnut St, Philadelphia PA 19107..............................212-840-1177
Delmas, 209 S 4th Ave Ste 9A, Ann Arbor MI 48104....................................313-662-2799
Desktop Composition Systems, PO Box 5279161, Reno NV 89513..........702-322-1884
Dix Type Inc, One Commerce Blvd, Syracuse NY 13220...............................315-437-9925
Eastern Press Inc, Box 1650 654 Orchard St, New Haven CT 06507.........203-777-2353
Eastern Typesetting Co, 515 John Fitch Blvd, S Windsor CT 06074.........203-528-9631
Ecocenters, 21111 Chagrin Blvd, Beachwood OH 44122.............................216-991-9000
Expertype Inc, 44 W 28th St, New York NY 10001..212-532-6222
EYE Type, 611 Broadway Ste 609, New York NY 10012................................212-674-0911
Faculty Press Inc, 1449 37th St, Brooklyn NY 11218...................................718-851-6666
Finn Typographic Service, PO Box 1261, Stamford CT 06904.....................203-325-3896
Fisher Composition Inc, 118 E 25th St 3rd fl, New York NY 10010..........212-598-0200
Fjord Press Typography, PO Box 16501, Seattle WA 98116.......................206-625-9363
Fleetwood Graphics, 588 Grand Canyon, Madison WI 53719......................608-829-3536
The Four Corner Press, 2056 College SE, Grand Rapids MI 49507..........616-243-2015
Freedmen's Organization, 3311 Beverly Blvd, Los Angeles CA 90004.......213-384-6642
Friedrich Typography, 636 N Milpas St, Santa Barbara CA 93103............805-966-6319
Pam Frye Typesetting, 834 E Rand Rd, Mt Prospect IL 60056....................312-394-4820
G & S Typesetters Inc, 410 Baylor, Austin TX 78703....................................512-478-5341
G S Lithographers, One Kero Rd, Carlstadt NJ 07072.................................201-933-8585
Ralph Garner Assoc, 460 Park Ave S, New York NY 10016..........................212-686-0311
General Graphic Services, 700 Linden Ave, York PA 17404........................717-845-1551
Genesis Typograph Ltd, 2269 W Country Rd C, St Paul MN 55113..........612-631-3267
Graphic Composition Inc, 240 Hawthorne Ave, Athens GA 30606...........404-546-8688
Graphic Litho Corp, 130 Shepard St, Lawrence MA 01843..........................617-683-2766
A Graphic Method Inc, 3285 Long Beach Rd, Oceanside NY 11572..........516-764-1144
Graphic Technique Inc, 122 E 42nd St, New York NY 10168.......................212-867-0340
Graphic World, 2272 Grissom Dr, St Louis MO 63146.................................314-567-9854
Graphics International, 555 Madison Ave, New York NY 10022....................212-688-0564
Graphics Service Co, 1640 Mahoning, Youngstown OH 44509......................216-793-4063
Graphics West, 2935 N Prospect Ste 101, Colorado Springs CO 80907.....303-633-4446
Guinn Printing Co Inc, 70 Hudson St, Hoboken NJ 07030...........................201-659-9000
Hawkes Publishing, 3775 S 5th W, Salt Lake City UT 84115.......................801-262-5555
Heidelberg Graphics, 1116 Wendy Way, Chico CA 95926.............................916-342-6582

Heminway Corp, 155 S Leonard St, Waterbury CT 06720 203-753-3620
Holladay Tyler Printing, 1900 Chapman Ave, Rockville MD 20852............301-881-8050
Huron Valley Graphics, 704 Airport Blvd Ste 1, Ann Arbor MI 48104......313-769-5795
Independent Printing Co, 141 E 25th St, New York NY 10010.....................212-689-5100
Intl Computaprint Corp, 475 Virginia Dr, Ft Washington PA 19034 215-641-6000
J & L Graphics Inc, 2200 Carlson Dr, Northbrook IL 60062 312-272-8560
Kexis Press, 3220 Sacramento St, San Francisco CA 94115.....................415-567-5454
Keyboard Communications, 10 Forbes Rd, Braintree MA 02184 617-848-3900
Gearld M Konecky Co Inc, PO Box 1226, Sag Harbor NY 11963 516-883-3873
Landmann Associates Inc, 341 State St, Madison WI 53703 608-255-5262
The Language Center Inc, 71 Valley St, S Orange NJ 07079 201-762-4455
LC Typesetting Co Inc, 326 W La Salle, S Bend IN 46601.........................219-232-4700
Leonardo Literary Services, PO Box 5688, Santa Monica CA 90405.........213-392-2395
Letter Graphics/CPC Inc, 1907 Wyandotte, Kansas City MO 64108........816-471-2585
Lettick Typografic Inc, 227 Wheeler Ave, Bridgeport CT 06606 203-367-6491
Oscar Leventhal Typographers, 75 Varick St, New York NY 10013...........212-925-3338
The Lexington Press Inc, 7 Oakland St, Lexington MA 02173 617-862-8900
Mackintosh Typography, 319 Anacapa, Santa Barbara CA 93101 805-962-9915
Peter F Mallon Inc, 45-29 Courty Sq, Long Island City NY 11101 718-786-2000
Maryland Composition Co, 6711 Dover Rd, Glen Burnie MD 21061 301-760-7900
Master Typographers, 7227 Devonshire, St Louis MO 63119 314-645-2878
The McFarland Co, Crescent & Mulberry Sts, Harrisburg PA 17105........717-234-6235
Merrill Corp, 1731 University Ave, St Paul MN 55104.............................612-646-4501
Metricomp Inc, PO Box 1, Grundy Center IA 50638.................................319-824-6689
John C Meyer & Son, 432 N 6th St, Philadelphia PA 19123 215-627-4320
Modern Graphics Inc, 5 Federal St, Weymouth MA 02188 617-331-5000
Monotype Composition Co, 2050 Rockrose Ave, Baltimore MD 21211....301-467-3300
Murphy-Parker Inc, 6808 Greenway Ave, Philadelphia PA 19141 215-724-0610
Music Book Assoc Inc, 711 Amsterdam Ave, New York NY 10025...........212-222-1611
Natl Photocomposition Svc Inc, 40 Underhill Blvd, Syosset NY 11791 516-921-8620
New England Typographic Service, 14 Tobey Rd, Bloomfield CT 06002..203-242-2251
The News Circle, 1250 W Glenoaks, Glendale CA 91201............................818-545-0333
Nimrod Press, 170 Brookline Ave, Boston MA 02215.............................617-437-7900
Noble Book Press Corp, 900 Broadway, New York NY 10003.....................212-777-1300
Nova Typesetting Co Inc, PO Box 6215, Bellevue WA 98008......................206-747-5880
Offset Composition Svcs, 419 7th St NW #505, Washington DC 20034....202-783-1010
Phoenix Typography, 100 Massachusetts Ave, Boston MA 02115 617-536-5390
Pioneer Graphics, 426-A 1st St, Eureka CA 95501 707-443-9735
Polebridge Press, SR 68, Bonner MT 59823 406-258-6407
The Polyglot Press, 224 W 20th St, New York NY 10011...........................212-675-5714
J M Post Graphics Inc, 12 Church St Box 338, Leansburg NJ 07734.........201-787-1400
Prof Advancement Ent, 126 Manchester SW, Grand Rpds MI 49508........616-243-0544
Professional Composition, 317 MAC Ave, East Lansing MI 48823............517-332-8447
Progressive Typographers, PO Box 278, Emigsville PA 17318 717-764-5908
Publications Arts, 683 Lafayette Ave, Hawthrone NJ 07506 201-652-9393
Publications Illus Presentations, 149 W Merrick, Freeport NY 11520....516-546-6996
Publications West, 5544 Cahuenga Blvd, N Hollywood CA 91601 818-769-6632
Publishers Phototype Intl, 463 Barell Ave, Carlstadt NJ 07072 201-935-3200
Publishing Resources, 1795 Pearl, Boulder CO 80302 303-442-1100
Publishing Resources, Box 41307, San Juan PR 00940.............................809-724-0318
Rainsford Type, 900 Ethan Allen Hwy, Ridgefield CT 06877......................203-438-2622
Rembrandt Graphics Div, 222 E 46th St, New York NY 10017...................212-687-9425
Repro Art Service, 102 Swinick Dr, Dunmore PA 18512.............................717-961-5410

Ridge Type Service, 521 Lafayette Ave, Hawthorne NJ 07506.....................201-652-5412
S Rosenthal & Co, 9933 Alliance Rd, Cincinnati OH 45242........................513-984-0710
Roxbury Publishing Co, PO Box 491044, Los Angeles CA 90049.............213-458-3493
Ruttle Shaw & Wetherill, 270 Commerce Dr, Ft Washington PA 19034...215-628-4620
Sans Serif Inc, 2378 E Stadium Blvd, Ann Arbor MI 48104.......................313-971-1050
Scarlett Letters Inc, 75 Spring St, New York NY 10012.............................212-966-3560
Science Typographers, 15 Industrial Blvd, Medford NY 11763.................516-924-4747
Second Generation Type, 1970 Washington, Birmingham MI 48009.........313-644-4365
Sedgwick Printout Systems, 1020 US Rt 1 S, Princeton NJ 08540.............609-452-1660
David E Seham Associates, 14 Charles St, Metuchem NJ 08840................201-548-6160
Service Typesetting & Printing, 505 Thompson Lane, Austin TX 78742...512-385-7060
ShareGraphics Services, 1931 N Market Ctr #105, Dallas TX 75207 214-651-1025
Skillcraft Group, 480 Canal St, New York NY 10013................................212-925-6400
Solaris Press, PO Box 1009, Rochester MI 48063....................................313-656-9667
Southern New England Typographic, 2115 Dixwell, Hamden CT 06514...203-288-1611
The Studley Press, 151 E Housatonic St, Dalton MA 01226.....................413-684-0441
Sugden & Co, 1117 8th St, La Salle IL 61301 815-223-1231
Superior Type, 1303 N Harris, Champaign IL 61820 217-352-4226
Techna Type Inc, 2500 W Market St, York PA 17404..............................717-792-3581
TechType Graphics, 307 Burlington Ave, Delanco NJ 08075 609-461-8200
Tek Translation & Intl Print, 1133 Ave Ste 3122, New York NY 10036 ...212-254-4851
Text & Type, 601 Bergen Mall, Paramus NJ 07652 201-368-1772
Text Processing Ltd, 50 W 34th St Ste 8A7, New York NY 10001............212-947-0618
TG & IF, 9 Commerce Rd, Fairfield NJ 07006 201-882-0942
Top Notch Typesetting, PO Box 526, Sicklerville NJ 08081 609-228-4948
Total Typography Inc, 901 W Monroe St, Chicago IL 60607...................312-421-4313
Type for U, 4 Brattle St, Cambridge MA 02138 617-661-1225
The Type House Inc, 7412 Manchester Ave, St Louis MO 63143.............314-644-1404
Typographic Innovations, 246 W 38th St, New York NY 10018 212-764-6464
Typographic Insight Ltd, 6111 Jackson Rd, Ann Arbor MI 48103............313-994-3904
Typographic Sales Inc, 1035 Hanley Industrial Ct, St Louis MO 63144 314-968-6800
Typoservice Corp, 1233 W 18th St, Indianapolis IN 46202......................317-634-1234
Unitron Graphics Inc, 4710 32nd Pl, Long Island City NY 11101 718-784-9292
Univ Graphics, West & Lincoln Aves, Atlantic NJ 07716 201-872-0800
US Lithograph Inc, 853 Broadway, New York NY 10003.........................212-673-3210
Volt Information Sciences, 711 Stewart Ave, Garden City NY 11530........516-222-8844
Volt/Alphanumeric Publ Sys, 6315 Arizona Pl, Los Angeles CA 90045....213-641-3870
W R Bean & Son Inc, 4800 Frederick Dr SW, Atlanta GA 30378...............404-691-5020
Vance Weaver Composition, 3 Cedar Lane, Sherman CT 06784 203-354-6570
F A Weber & Sons Inc, 175 S 5th Ave, Park Falls WI 54552......................715-762-3707
Fred Weidner & Son Printers, 111 8th Ave, New York NY 10011.............212-989-1070
Westernlore Typographics, 609 N 4th Ave, Tucson AZ 85795...................602-297-5491
Whitehall Composition, 632 5th St, Whitehall PA 18052.........................215-264-3521
Williams Press Inc, PO Box 4025 Patroon Sta, Albany NY 12204.............518-434-1141
The Word Shop, 3719 6th Ave, San Diego CA 92103 619-291-9126
Wrightson Typographers, 86 Rosedale Rd, Watertown MA 02172............617-926-9600
York Graphic Services Inc, 3600 W Market St, York PA 17404..................717-792-3551
Zadock Typesetting, 516 N Sweetzer Ave, Los Angeles CA 90048.............213-651-2657

TYPISTS & WORD PROCESSING SERVICES

A&W Typing Service, Box 149, Flushing NY 11352 718-780-0199
A+ Word Proc Service, 4323 Rosedale Ave, Bethesda MD 20814 301-951-0926
A-1 Typing Service, 1722 S Mission, Mt Pleasant MI 48858....................517-773-0664
A-Z Secretarial Services, 2995 LBJ Fwy #200, Dallas TX 75234....................214-484-2823
Aardvark Typing, 526 W 112th St, New York NY 10025 212-662-0354
The Ability Group, 1511 K St NW, Washington DC 20005 202-659-7676
Academic & Literary MS, 825 West End Ave, New York NY 10025 212-663-5791
Accu Data Proc, 107 Pennsylvania SE, Albuquerque NM 87108....................505-255-1671
Accu-Word Proc Service, PO Box 817, New York NY 10274 718-951-9250
Accu-Write, 503 E St Julian, Savannah GA 31401 912-233-4481
Accuracy Plus Typing Service, 2201 Sweetbriar, Cincinnati OH 45239......513-541-7534
Ad Infinitum Copy Service, 7 N MacQuesten, Mt Vernon NY 10551........914-664-5930
ADR Typing Service, PO Box 184 Bath Beach Sta, Brooklyn NY 11214....718-837-3484
Advantage Typing Service, 53 Clements Pl, Hartsdale NY 10530.............914-949-6482
Alpha Typing Service, 807 27th St, Rockford IL 61108.....................815-399-9530
Amer Intl Manuscript Services, 14824 Oakvine Dr, Lutz FL 33549...........813-977-9050
Ann's Typing & Etc, 4514 Cole Ave Ste 110, Dallas TX 75205.....................214-526-6400
Carol Zane Atkinson, 148 Tinker St, Woodstock NY 12498....................914-679-9707
The Author's Friend, 160 W 71st St Apt 11E, New York NY 10023............212-877-1510
AVRA, PO Box 2619, Hendersonville NC 28739 704-697-0546
Grace Loney Baldwin, 112-31 Dillon St, Jamaica NY 11433....................718-526-6677
Gerald W Barrett, 411 W 48th St, New York NY 10036 212-247-4318
Adele Baylinson, 65 W 90th St, New York NY 10024 212-840-1234
Beehive Prof Typing Service, 5265 S 2500 W, Roy UT 84067 801-776-2249
Helen R Berger, 186 Bowers St, Jersey City NJ 07307 201-659-8498
Estelle Billing, 4050 E Cactus Rd. Apt 207, Phoenix AZ 85032 602-996-1031
Susan N Bjorner, 10 Cannongate, Tyngsborough MA 01879 617-649-9746
Fay L Brett, Box 307 RD4, Greensburg PA 15601 412-668-2800
Bretz Inc, 22 E Washington #316, Indianapolis IN 46204.....................317-634-1545
Alice Bruno, 27 Lillian Ln, Plainview NY 11803 516-433-5293
Frances Burns, 3302 Canongate Ct, San Jose CA 95121.....................408-270-3630
Capital Secretarial, 5307 E Mockingbird Ln Ste 401, Dallas TX 75206 214-823-7950
Carefree Script Service, PO Box 2027, Carefree AZ 85377.....................602-488-2410
Carlsbad Publications, 3242 McKinley St, Carlsbad CA 92008 619-729-9543
Agnes E Carlson, 22301 Englehardt H21, St Clair Shr MI 48080.....................313-779-5355
Harla J Cassol, 3109 Osceola Dr, Plano TX 75074.....................214-424-2439
Nina W Cavlier, 26 Ridge Rd, High Bridge NJ 08829 201-638-6333
Executives Choice, 5 Lantern Ln, Lynnfield MA 01940.....................617-334-4402
Codate, PO Box 12509, La Crescenta CA 91214.....................818-249-7915
College Secretarial Service, 4584 68th St, La Mesa CA 92041 619-466-0616
Communications Plus, 360 Park Ave S, New York NY 10010 212-686-9570
Complete Computer service, 190 Oak Hill Dr, Latrobe PA 15650 412-423-6970
Compu-Type Prof Word Proc, 1025 S Santa Fe #D, Vista CA 92083........619-724-0977
Computrail Inc, 900 Rahway Ave 52B, Avenel NJ 07001.....................201-634-5775
Connexions, 14011 Brookgreen Dr, Dallas TX 75240.....................214-234-4519
Conservatory of Amer Letters, PO Box 123, S Thomaston ME 04858.......207-354-6550
A Creative Secretary, 2930B W Greenbrier Ln, Peoria IL 61614.....................309-693-3983
The Creative Secretary, Box 817, Forest Hills NY 11375.....................718-459-1441

Creative Typing Services, 4602 Louisiana Ave N, Crystal MN 55428.........612-537-7564
Creative Writer's Service, 1028 McKeen, Terre Haute IN 47802................812-235-5910
Sally Dalton, 40 Joni Ave Abbott Commons, Hamilton Sq NJ 08690 210-821-9758
Data Group Mgmt, 501 Westbrook, Raleigh NC 27615 919-848-3237
Datarray, 247 W Peterson, Libertyville IL 60048.....................................312-680-3699
Dataword Office Systems, 126 Carleton Ave, Islit Terrace NY 11752........516-665-5538
Del-Ray Word Proc, 70 W 95th St Apt 4C, New York NY 10025 212-662-0750
Dell-Naatz Publication Arts, 106 Pinion Ln, Manitou Springs CO 80829..303-685-9719
Sarah Deming, 210 Willow Oaks Ct Rt 5, Eufaula AL 36027.....................205-687-2194
Dial-A-Secretary, 521 5th Ave, New York NY 10028.................................212-348-9575
Dianne F Davidson, 4809 Overland Trail, Grand Prairie TX 75052...........214-660-4007
Diversified Office Services, 17949 Archwood, Reseda CA 91335 818-342-2221
DLG Secretarial Services, 514 Shockley, DeSoto TX 75115.......................214-224-2209
DLM Assoc, PO Box 394, Bronxville NY 10708.......................................914-668-7738
D Duncan, 11543 Sylvan St Apt 5, North Hollywood CA 91606 818-763-5644
Editcetera, 2140 Syattuck Ave Ste 405, Berkely CA 94704........................415-849-1110
Electronic Fingers, 7444 Lake St, Morton Grove IL 60053.........................312-967-0739
Electronic Keyboarding, 140 Weldon Pkwy, Maryland Hts MO 63043.....314-567-1780
Encore Office Services, 1705 Metro Dr #229, Carrollton TX 75006...........214-446-1347
Enterprise Word Proc, 3106 Alexander Ave, Santa Clara CA 95051 408-839-6081
Etcetera Enterprises, 269 Lake Rd, Congers NY 10920.............................914-268-9323
Executive Business Assistance, 5217 Ross Ave #804, Dallas TX 75206....214-826-4657
Executive Office Services, Box 4033, Yakima WA 98901 509-575-6969
Executive Secretarial Svc, 1451 SW 6th Way, Deerfield Bch FL 33441 305-421-5329
Executive Typing Service, 1600 Williams Way, Norristown PA 19403........215-631-1420
Expert Typing Service, 18 Stuyvesant Oval, New York NY 10009 212-254-7349
Expert Typing Service, 7808 SW 7th St, N Lauderdale FL 33068...............305-721-9160
EZ Word Proc, 4930 Havelok St, Fair Oaks CA 95628...............................916-961-1015
First Word Computers, PO Box 38245, Dallas TX 75238............................214-348-3200
Fletcher Business Sevice, 11863 207th St, Lakewood CA 90715 213-860-3629
Betty Foley, 855 W Eight Mile #8, Whitmore Lake MI 48189 313-449-4023
Debbie Fultz, 467 Southington Blvd, Painesville OH 44077 216-352-9286
Goehringer & Sons Assoc, PO Box 9626, Pittsburgh PA 15226 412-531-9549
Hadassah Gold, 222 W 83rd St, New York NY 10024................................212-787-5668
Marilyn Gomrick, 109 Jane Ln, Uniontown NJ 15401...............................412-438-0748
Elaine Goodman, 454 W 46th St, New York NY 10036..............................212-581-5178
Glenna Goulet, PO Box 647, Alamo CA 94507...415-829-1360
Greater Data, 646 10th St, Brooklyn NY 11215 718-499-2522
Greaves Typing Service, 200 W 18th St, New York NY 10011 212-741-1658
Diane G Green, 44 Winfield Ave, Mount Vernon NY 10552........................914-667-0768
Donna J Harrel, 11901 Patricia Box 607, Boron CA 93516.........................619-762-5580
Helping Hands Word Proc, PO Box 152, Little Chute WI 54140...............414-738-7064
Eva Henderson Word Proc, 5535 Edlen St, Dallas TX 75220.....................214-369-4298
Dianne J Herrera, 17 Stony Rd, Edison NJ 08817......................................201-572-9570
M Hollander, 135-30 Grand Central Pkwy, Kew Gardens NY 11435..........718-263-0046
Laura Hollitt Typing Service, Box F, Cumberland KY 40823 606-589-2958
Humanics Assoc, 1776 Peachtree NW #505 N, Atlanta GA 30309 404-873-3947
Hyper-Typers, 21 Harrison St #3, New York NY 10013...............................212-925-4130
Information Compiling Systems, 225 S 15th St #1507, Phila PA 19102....215-545-4506
JFK Typing Service, 150 Augusta Ave, Staten Island NY 10312.................718-356-0832
JL Works, PO Box 8111, Newport Beach CA 92658.....................................714-649-2110
Diane L Johnstone, 1306 Zora, Houston TX 77055 713-683-1047
Suzanne Jones Prof MS Prep, 614 Pressler, Austin TX 78703.....................512-477-2890

Freda Jones Secretarial Services, Box 879, Pampa TX 79065......................806-665-4609
Just Your Type, 1783 Sespe Dr, Ventura CA 93004...805-659-2680
S L Kenney Type Extraordinaire, 12610 Central #263, Chino CA 91710..714-591-2443
Kepler & Assoc, 100 Saw Mill, Lafayette IN 47905 317-474-3993
Keyboard Communications Inc, 10 Forbes Rd, Braintree MA 02184.......617-848-3900
Joan Klang, 18595 Woodbank Way, Saratoga CA 95070 408-741-5880
Gail Klotz, 7836 Miller Fall Rd, Rockville MD 20855 301-977-2105
Kopy Katz Kwik Typing Svc, 3950 Atlantic, Long Beach CA 90807...........213-595-4329
Helen Krinke, PO Box 158, Twisp WA 98856 509-997-7402
Susan La Fountaine, 1772 Cambridge Park E, Maumee OH 43537............419-893-4186
Becky Laman-Hynes, 688 N E 1st St, Dania FL 33004....................................305-920-2738
Barbara Laskowski Word Proc, 18228 Rockwood Ct, Yelm WA 98597....206-894-2989
Letter Perfect, PO Box 234, Belton MO 64012 816-331-9181
Letter Perfect, 1990 SW 17 Dr, Deerfield Beach FL 33442............................305-427-9663
Linda Logsdon, PO Box 3427, Tulsa OK 74101..918-588-4137
Linda Lund & Assoc, Box 618 Rt 117, Coventry RI 02816............................401-861-4407
The Magic Typewriter, 224 Atlantic Ave, Brooklyn NY 11201.....................718-625-2470
Manchester Executive Secy, 57 S River Rd, Bedford NH 03102..................603-624-8641
Manuscript Services, PO Box 112310, Carrollton TX 75011........................214-418-9148
Manuscripts Unltd, 3344 Commercial Ave, Northbrook IL 60062...............312-564-4005
Margo's Typing Service, 10610 Mountana St, Melrose Park IL 60164........312-451-9339
Marie Marrammao, 100-15 Co-op City Blvd, Bronx NY 10475 212-671-6246
Michele McCarren, 1040 Village Mill, Birmingham AL 35215 205-853-2614
Mechanical Secretary Inc, 1220 Broadway, New York NY 10001 212-695-6110
Barbara A Mele, 2525 Holland Ave, Bronx NY 10467....................................212-654-8047
Barbara Mary Merson, 14 Heathrow Ln, Old Bridge NJ 08857 201-591-0882
Metrocrest Bookkeeping, 1721 Big Canyon Tr, Carrollton TX 75007........214-323-5069
Metroplex Data Service, 2853 Live Oak, Mesquite TX 75150.......................214-686-9683
Ingeborg Michalak, 6461 Rosemont, Detroit MI 48228.................................313-271-5049
A J Miescke Prof Typing Service, 305 Ellison, Horicon WI 53032................414-485-2626
Marjorie L Miller, 170 West End Ave Apt 12L, New York NY 10023 212-873-2206
Mills Office Services, 105-10 221st St, Queens Village NY 11429................718-217-1487
Miriam's Word Proc Svc, 5941 Alta Mesa Way, San Diego CA 92115......619-583-3268
James Mitchell Professional Processing, 1532 McCoy, Dallas TX 75204.214-821-8821
MPC Clerical Services, 1050 Louisville Rd, Frankfort KY 40601.................502-875-1614
Muri's Typing Service, Box 3548, Clearlake CA 95422.................................707-995-0128
Peter F Muro, 3 Via Maria Dr, Scotia NY 12302 518-399-3106
Carol Naab, 6211A Bandera, Dallas TX 75225..214-363-5141
Sara Nicoll MS Typing Svc, 444 Central Park W, New York NY 10025 ...212-866-3410
Noteworthy Typing Svc, 95 E Wayne Ave #412, Silver Spg MD 20901 301-585-3096
Judy Nuss, 4157 Lawnview, Dallas TX 75227 214-381-6156
O'Brien Literary Service, 15016 Des Moines Way S, Seattle WA 98148....206-242-5000
Oak Cliff Word Proc & Typing, 1881 Sylvan #200, Dallas TX 75208........214-744-2944
The Office Annex, 126 21st Ave N, St Petersburg FL 33704...........................813-823-5552
Paheel's Personalized Word Proc, 1363 E 12th St, Brooklyn NY 11230 718-998-2435
Patricia's Secretarial Svc, 13772 Golden West, Westminster CA 92683....714-891-5161
Georgia M Payne, 201 S Maple, Wyanet IL 61379 815-699-2212
PC Services, PO Box 66374, Portland OR 97266..503-658-5163
The Perfect Page, 1220 Alameda #8, Belmont CA 94002.............................415-593-1511
Perfect Touch Typing, 3684 Ionia St, Seaford NY 11783.............................516-783-7901
Perfect Typing, 21 Harrison St Ste 3, New York NY 10013 212-925-4130
Pieper Word Proc Services, 1230 Acton Ave, Duncanville TX 75137 214-298-6081
Marion Pines, 107 Warner Ave, Roslyn Heights NY 11577...........................516-484-6218

Melva Pointer, 1795 S Dawson Way, Aurora CO 80012..............................303-696-7530
Private Lines, 801 Noragate Rd, Knoxville TN 37919..............................615-693-8598
Processing Unlimited, 13210 N 50 St, Scottsdale AZ 85254......................602-996-2516
Professional Editing & Typing, 410 E 20th St 3A, New York NY 10009...212-477-0615
Professional Typing Sevice, 1275 E Morgan Ave, Evansville IN 47711......812-423-0388
Quik-Type Service, 63 Mason St, Greenwich CT 06830 203-629-3884
Shirley Radl, 220 Miramonte Ave, Palo Alto CA 94306.............................415-327-3070
REA Holt Word Proc, 1246 Lake Summerset, Davis IL 61019 815-248-4100
Reina's Secretarial Service, 152355 E Carnell St, Whittier CA 90603........213-695-5529
Shields Remine, Box 13 Village Sta, New York NY 10014 212-989-2398
Riehl Typing Service, 41 Wm Penn Dr, Stony Brook NY 11790...................516-689-9668
Right Advice Office Svcs, 12983 Ridgedale, Minnetonka MN 55343...........612-593-1980
Dottie Ritt, 29122 Kensington Dr, Laguna Niguel CA 92677.......................714-495-5705
Rush Typing Service, 301 E 64th St Apt 6K, New York NY 10021................212-249-5494
Marcia Seale, 6828 Deloache, Dallas TX 75225 214-824-5663
Secretarial Service of Sarasota, 240 N Washington, Sarasota FL 33577 ...813-366-0036
Secretarial Services Unltd, 909 Leonard Ct, La Porte IN 46350..................219-326-5365
Secretarial Word Proc, 10534 N Park Ave, Seattle WA 98133.....................206-367-6858
Secretariette Service, PO Box 907, St Marys PA 15857...............................814-781-7747
Select Typing Service, Box 1125, Pigeon Forge TN 37863..........................615-428-1664
Sharon's Type, PO Box 1374, Mt Vernon WA 98273...................................206-336-2342
Doris Silverstein, 3461 Amboy Rd, Staten Island NY 10306 718-979-3247
Marilynn Simones, 8904 Capri Dr, Dallas TX 75238...................................214-340-5968
Sisters Typing Service, 61 Forest Ave, West Babylon NY 11704.................516-587-0280
Joyce Slater Word Proc, 9656 Lynbrook, Dallas TX 75238..........................214-341-3803
Smith Secretarial Services, 10708 Ash Ct, Thornton CO 80233 303-452-7204
Patricia A Smith, 4 Warren St, Ipswich MA 01938.....................................617-356-4537
Soft-Words, 9319 LBJ Fwy #115, Dallas TX 75243......................................214-231-6678
Somerville & Assoc, 2035 Western, Topeka KS 66604.................................913-233-3816
Specialty Services Ltd, 1034 Rambling Rd, Simi Valley CA 93065..............805-527-6465
Shirley M Stabin, 1308 SW 9th Ave, Ft Lauderdale FL 33315......................303-525-1209
Star Data Systems, 2222 W Vickery Blvd #1, Ft Worth TX 76102.............718-877-3898
Jan Stenberg, 377 Lake St, Fruitport MI 49415..616-865-6754
Studio Typing Pool Inc, 8555 Sunset Blvd, Los Angeles CA 90049...........213-652-0325
Substitute Secretary Typing Svc, 4477 Emerald C130, Boise ID 83706.....208-344-8973
Susan's Typing-Word Proc, 914 Beach Park #84, Foster City CA 94404..415-349-8545
Susie's Typing Service, PO Box 612, Van Nuys CA 91408 818-780-7555
Sweda Business Services, 500 Carbon St, Syracuse NY 13208 315-424-0271
TAC Productions, 29 Clinton #2B, New York NY 10002.............................212-868-1121
Talented Fingers, 5531 Dyer Ste 101, Dallas TX 75206...............................214-691-2009
Tampa Assn of Business Services, 9310 N 16th St, Tampa FL 33612........813-989-0514
Technical Services, 42 Broadway Rm 1524, New York NY 10004 212-425-5540
Term Computer Services, PO Box 725, New Providence NJ 07974.............201-665-0923
Timpy Press, PO Box 65541, St Paul MN 55165...612-735-6193
Tina's Typing & Word Proc, 24666 Conley Ct, Moreno Vly CA 92388......714-242-8183
TMI Desktop Publishing, 12083 Regal Ct W, W Palm Bch FL 33414 305-793-6413
Touchtype, 1118 High Mesa, Garland TX 75041..214-278-5776
Kathryn E Trego, 524 Twin Oaks Dr, Wynnewood PA 19096......................215-649-3315
Type 'N Store, 1 Reservoir Rd, Parsippany NJ 07054...................................201-334-4322
Typing By Chris, 215 St Paul #219, Denver CO 80206 303-355-2700
Typing Etc, 89 Stephen Dr, Plainview NY 11803...516-681-7328
Typing Etc, Box 234, Belton MO 64012 816-331-9181
Typing Plus, 3301 15th St, Menominee MI 49858 906-863-3820

Typing Unlimited, 160 E 89th St, New York NY 10128.................................212-410-4788
Village Typing & Steno Service, 68 Bedford St, New York NY 10014........212-675-2070
Word Broker, Box 1133, Wenatchee WA 98801...509-884-5242
Word Magic, Box 384B Rt 4, Fayetteville AR 72701.....................................501-442-6160
Word Mill, N 916 Ella Rd #1, Spokane WA 99212..509-928-2719
Word Processing, 225 E 8th Ave Apt 2B, Homestead PA 15120..................412-461-3019
Word Proc/Secr Svcs, 5327 Meadow Wood Pl, Concord CA 94521...........415-687-6737
The Word Processor, 7124 Rutgers Dr, Dallas TX 75214............................214-343-3047
Word Wrangler, 6134 W Garfield, Phoenix AZ 85043..................................602-272-9215
Wordmill, Box 948, Middletown CT 06457..203-344-0440
Words Etc, 1217 Linden Ave, Baltimore MD 21227.....................................301-247-1443
Words Etc, Box 308, Galveston TX 77551..409-744-2078
Words Etc, 3907 Calle Olivo NE, Albuquerque NM 87111..........................505-294-4515
Words Unlimited, 601 Ewing St Ste B-7, Princeton NJ 08540.....................609-921-0096
Wordsmith, 35 Sagamore Rd, Weymouth MA 02191...................................617-337-2619
Wordsmith, 20235 Foix Pl, Chatsworth CA 91311.......................................818-700-0260
Wordsmith Services, 26911 Westwood Ln, Cleveland OH 44138.................216-235-8231
Wordtuners, PO Box 884581, San Francisco CA 94188................................415-648-2321
Wordwrights Typing Service, Box 1131, Darien GA 31305..........................912-832-5441
Writer's Asst, PO Box 47, Millbrae CA 94030...415-692-1364
Writer's Desktop Toolbox, 1121 W George St, Chicago IL 60657.................312-525-6969
Writers' Resource, PO Box 40310, St Paul MN 55104.................................612-644-5455
Wyndon's Writers Service, 20120 W Coral Rd, Marengo IL 60152................815-568-6371
Your Executive Secy, 1417 Gables Ct #102, Plano TX 75075........................214-867-0667

WORD PROCESSING EQUIPMENT & SUPPLIES

This section includes manufacturers and distributors of typewriters, personal computers, printers, ribbons and other word processing equipment and supplies. See also Computer Software Publishers.

ACR Systems, 8016 Atlantic Blvd, Jacksonville FL 32211.............................904-721-8211
Addressograph Farrington, Randolph Indus Pk, Randolph MA 02368.....617-963-8500
Adler-Royal Business Machines, 1600 Rt 22, Union NJ 07083....................201-964-3200
Allied Computer Service, 255 W 98th St, New York NY 10025.....................212-222-5665
Alphacom, 2108 Bering Dr, San Jose CA 95131...408-436-0801
ALPS America, 3553 N 1st St, San Jose CA 95134.......................................408-432-6000
Amstrad Computers, 1915 Westridge, Irving TX 75038...............................214-518-0668
Andcx Inc, 1001 Flynn Rd, Camarillo CA 93010..805-987-9660
Antech Inc, 788 Myrtle St, Roswell GA 30075...404-993-7270
Apple Computer, 20525 Mariani Ave, Cupertino CA 95014..........................408-973-2222
Armor America, 4151 E Tennessee St, Tuscon AZ 85714.............................602-747-2991
Arvey Paper & Supplies, 3351 W Addison St, Chicago IL 60618..................312-463-0030
Asmann USA Ltd, 333 5th Ave, New York NY 10016....................................212-679-1037
Aspen Ribbons Inc, 555 Aspen Ridge Dr, Lafayette CO 80026.....................303-666-5750
AT&T, 5 Wood Hollow Rd, Parsippany NJ 07054..201-581-7382
Beckner Vision/Computer, Box 1541, Lumberton NC 28359........................919-739-1135
Beta Business Systems Inc, 9174 Chesapeake Dr, San Diego CA 92123...619-565-4505
Bob Bianco Sales Inc, 2405 Church Ln, San Pablo CA 94806........................415-232-1556
Blue Chip Electronics, 2 W Alameda Dr, Tempe AZ 85282............................602-829-7217
Brother Intl Corp, 8 Corporate Pl, Piscataway NJ 08854..............................201-981-0300

Burroughs Corp, 300 Cross Keys Office Pk, Fairport NY 14450 716-425-1800
Business Development Intl, Box 329, Pembina ND 58271 204-837-8509
Cado Systems Corp, 2055 W 190th St, Torrance CA 90510....................213-323-8170
Cal-Abco, 6041 Variel Ave, Woodland Hills CA 91367 818-704-9100
Canon USA Inc, One Canon Plaza, Lake Success NY 11042....................516-488-6700
Cascade Graphics Systems, 16842 Von Karman Ave, Irvine CA 92714 714-474-6200
Case Duplicating Supplies, 42 W 48th St, New York NY 10036..................212-869-5900
CBM America Corp, 2999 Overland Ave, Los Angeles CA 90064.............703-558-0961
Centronics Data Computer Corp, 1 Wall St, Hudson NH 03051.................603-883-0111
Certron Corp, 1651 S State College Blvd, Anaheim CA 92806 714-634-4280
Check-Mate Interior Systems, 433 Liberty St, Little Ferry NJ 07643.........201-321-6000
CIE Systems Inc, 2515 McCabe Way, Irvine CA 92713.............................714-660-1800
Citadel Data Group Inc, 30 Jefryn Blvd, Deer Park NY 11729..................516-243-0190
Citizen America Corp, 2425 Colorado Ave, Santa Monica CA 90404........213-453-0614
City News Service, PO Box 39, Willow Spgs MO 65793 417-469-2423
The Coated Film Co, 500 State St, Chicago IL 60411 312-758-0500
Codo Manufacturing Corp, Ave B, Leetsdale PA 15056 412-741-2010
Compal Inc, 8500 Wilshire Blvd, Beverly Hills CA 90211.......................213-652-2263
Complete Electronics, 23501 Ridge Rte Dr, Laguna Hills CA 92653.........714-458-0130
Comprint, 1421 Old Country Rd, Belmont CA 94002 415-592-5700
Compu-Rite Corp, 6010 Yolanda Ave, Tarzana CA 91356......................213-708-2000
Compucorp, 2211 Michigan Ave, Santa Monica CA 90404......................213-829-7453
Computech Group Inc, 23028 Commerce, Farmington Hills MI 48024.....313-471-5880
Computer Preferred Inc, 9500 Ainslie St, Schiller Park IL 60176.............312-671-7281
Computer Systems, 26401 Harper Ave, St Clair Shores MI 48081 313-779-8700
Computer Transceiver Systems, E 66 Midland Ave, Paramus NJ 07652...201-261-6800
Computers Intl Inc, 3540 Wilshire Blvd, Los Angeles CA 90010................213-386-3111
Contitronix Inc, 3848 Marquis Dr, Garland TX 75042............................214-276-0555
Copal USA Inc, 2291 205th St, Torrance CA 90501 213-618-0225
CPT Corp, 8100 Mitchell Rd, Minneapolis MN 55440 612-937-8000
Crown Computer Supplies, 17630 Davenport, Dallas TX 75252 214-733-1000
CRS Inc, 2909 Anthony Ln NE, Minneapolis MN 55418 612-781-3474
Crystal Computers Inc, 11555 W 83rd Ter, Lenexa KS 66214 913-541-3030
Curtis-Young Corp, 2550 Haddonfield Rd, Pennsauken NJ 08110............609-665-6650
Cyber/Source, 24000 Telegraph Rd, Southfield MI 48034........................313-353-8660
Daily Business Products Inc, 110 Parkway Dr S, Hauppauge NY 11788...516-543-6100
Daisy Systems Holland BV, 3731 Northcrest, Atlanta GA 30340.................404-451-0257
Daisywriter, 3540 Wilshire Blvd, Los Angeles CA 90010 213-286-3111
Data General Corp, 4400 Computer Dr, Westboro MA 01581 617-366-8911
Data Technology Industries, 431 McCormick, San Leandro CA 94541.....415-638-1206
Data Terminals & Communication, 590 Division, Campbell CA 95008....408-378-1112
Datapoint Corp, 9725 Datapoint Dr, San Antonio TX 78284......................512-699-7000
Dataproducts Corp, 6200 Canoga Ave, Woodland Hills CA 91365............818-887-8000
Datasouth Computer Corp, 4216 Stuart Andrew, Charlotte NC 28210.....704-523-8500
Datatel Minicomputer Co, 3700 Mt Vernon Ave, Alexandria VA 22305 ..703-549-4300
Dataworld Distributing, 8705 Unicorn Dr, Knoxville TN 37923..................615-691-2011
DBS Intl Inc, Welsh Rd & Park Dr, Montgomeryville PA 18936 215-628-4810
DBS Intl Inc, 525 Main St, Reading MA 01867 617-942-0220
Dealer Supplies, 228 Byers Rd Ste 201 C, Miamisburg OH 45342 513-865-0947
Delete Products, 201 O'Brien Hwy, Cambridge MA 02141.......................617-491-4529
Dennison Carter's, 275 Wyman St, Waltham MA 02254............................617-890-6350
Design Enterprises of SF, PO Box 14695, San Francisco CA 94114...........415-282-8813
Diablo Supplies, 910 Page Ave, Fremont CA 94537...............................415-498-7000

A B Dick Co, 5700 Touhy Ave, Chicago IL 60648.................................321-647-8800
Dictation Systems, 333 5th Ave, New York NY 10016 212-683-7800
Digital Equipment Corp, 146 Main St, Maynard MA 01754....................617-897-5111
Distinguished Brands, 108 Newtown Rd, Plainview NY 11803.................516-694-6268
Durango Systems Inc, 3003 N 1st St, San Jose CA 95134 408-946-5000
Echodata Corp, 5985 Financial Dr, Norcross GA 30071.........................404-447-4766
Eclectic Solutions Corp, PO Box 4162, Cleveland TN 37311 615-336-3658
800-Software Inc, 940 Dwight Way Ste 14, Berkeley CA 94710................415-644-3611
En-Pak Inc, 840 E Lewiston, Ferndale MI 48220 313-399-2433
Epson America Inc, 2780 Lomita Blvd, Torrance CA 90505 213-539-9140
Facit Inc, 9 Executive Park Dr Box 334, Merrimack NH 03054 603-424-8000
Feith Systems & Software, 1 Bala Plaza, Bala Cynwyd PA 19004............215-667-5575
Finotti & Assoc, PO Box 18178, Pittsburgh PA 15236 412-881-0330
Florida Data Corp, 600 D John Rodes Blvd, Melbourne FL 32935 305-259-4700
Frankel Manufacturing Co, 5125 Race Ct, Denver CO 80216.................303-297-9900
Franklin Ribbon & Carbon Co, 485 W John St, Hicksville NY 11802.......516-433-3010
Frye Copysystems Inc, 2205 Bell Ave, Des Moines IA 50321.................515-246-2300
Fujitsu America Inc, 3055 Orchard Dr, San Jose CA 95134....................408-946-8777
Gateway Business Forms, 5101 Firestone Blvd, South Gate CA 90290 213-567-8874
General Electric, Consumer Electronics, Portsmouth VA 23705................804-483-5000
General Ribbon Corp, 20650 Prairie St, Chatsworth CA 91313................818-709-1234
Great Lakes Ribbon Co, PO Box 292512, Kettering OH 45429 513-294-4946
Head Cleaning Products Inc, 20545 Plummer St, Chatsworth CA 91311..818-341-2000
Hecon Corp, 15 Meridian Rd, Eatontown NJ 07724................................201-542-9200
Hermes Products Inc, 1900 Lower Rd, Linden NJ 07036........................201-574-0300
Hewlett-Packard Co, 3000 Hanover St, Palo Alto CA 94304 415-857-1501
Honeywell Inc, 200 Smith St, Waltham MA 02154 617-895-6000
IBM Corp, Box 10, Princeton NJ 08540 201-329-7000
ImageTek Corp, 1431 Greenway Ste 200, Irving TX 75038....................214-256-1110
Infoscribe, 2720 S Croddy Way, Santa Ana CA 92704...........................800-222-8595
Insurance Sales Systems, 8001 W 63rd Ste 1, Merriam KS 66202............913-722-0065
C Itoh Electronics, 301 Beethoven St, Los Angeles CA 90066..................213-327-9100
ITT Qume Corp, 2350 Qume Dr, San Jose CA 95131 408-942-4000
Jacom, 21900 Plummer St, Chatsworth CA 91311.................................818-882-8009
Jade Computer Products, Box 5046, Hawthorne CA 90251 213-973-7707
Juki Office Machine Corp, 20437 S Western Ave, Torrance CA 90501.....213-320-4860
Kaypro Corp, 533 Stevens Ave, Solano Beach CA 92075........................619-481-4300
Kentek Information Systems Inc, 6 Pearl Ct, Allendale NJ 07401 301-825-8500
Kinball Systems Inc, 151 Cortlandt St, Belleville NJ 07109 201-759-6500
Kleen-Strike Inc, 9167 Red Branch Rd, Columbia MD 21045 301-997-5868
Ko-Rec-Type, 67 Kent Ave, Brooklyn NY 11211...................................718-782-2601
Kores Nordic, 2745 W 5th North St, Summerville SC 29483 803-871-6084
Leedall Products Mfg Co, 130 Van Liew Ave, Milltown NJ 08850............201-828-1045
Lextel Inc, 3307 Edward Ave, Santa Clara CA 95054 408-986-8280
Lobo Systems Inc, 318 E Gutierrez St, Santa Barbara CA 93140................805-564-3356
Magic Computer Co, 333 Rte 46 W, Fairfield NJ 07006 201-227-8833
Magnavox, 1111 Northshore Dr, Knoxville TN 37919.............................615-558-5211
Majestic Ribbon Corp, 15804 W 6th Ave, Golden CO 80401....................303-279-8676
Marlborough, 87 34th St, Brooklyn NY 11232......................................718-768-2000
Mayday Software, Rock Creek Rd Box 66, Phillips WI 54555...................715-339-3966
John A & Geraldine Mead, 545 E 14th St 3C, New York NY 10009 212-674-3278
Louis Melind Co, 3524 N Clark St, Chicago IL 60657 312-880-6680
Mimeo Manufacturing Co Inc, 43 Werman Ct, Plainview Ln NY 11803...516-249-4092

Minolta Corp, 101 Williams Dr, Ramsey NJ 07446 201-288-6900
MMBA, 5670 Randolph Blvd, San Antonio TX 78233 512-654-8574
Modular Computer Systems, 1650 W McNab, Ft Lauderdale FL 33310...305-974-1380
Molecudyne Inc, 201 Msgr O'Brien Hwy, Cambridge MA 02141...............617-491-4529
Molty Stryk Corp, 49 Sylvester St, Westbury NY 11590.........................516-997-7051
Morse Typewriter Co, 4005 Crescent St, Long Island City NY 11101 718-361-8222
Nason Trading Co Inc, 230 5th Ave, New York NY 10001........................212-686-3307
NBI Inc, 13800 E 39th Ave, Aurora CO 80011.......................................303-373-2800
NEC Information Systems, 1414 Mass Ave, Boxborough MA 01719.........617-264-8000
Norcom Electronics Corp, 18 Lois St, Norwalk CT 06851 203-849-1999
Northern Lights Computers Inc, 1331 8th St, Berkeley CA 94710.............415-527-4448
Okidata, 532 Fellowship Rd, Mt Laurel NJ 08054...................................609-235-2600
Olivetti USA, 765 US Hwy 202, Somerville NJ 08876 201-526-8200
Olympia USA Inc, PO Box 22, Somerville NJ 08876.................................201-722-7000
Optimum Tested Products Inc, 30 Jefryn Blvd W, Deer Park NY 11729..516-586-8300
OSM Computer Corp, 665 Clyde Ave, Mountain View CA 94043 408-961-8680
Pacific Wholesale Ofc Equip, 643 S San Pedro, Los Angeles CA 90014....213-627-2434
Packard Bell Electronics, 6045 Variel Ave, Woodland Hills CA 91367.....818-704-3905
PC's Ltd/Dell Computer,9505 Arboretum, Austin TX 78759.....................800-426-5150
Pelikan Inc, 200 Beasley Dr, Franklin TN 37064 615-790-6171
Peregrine Software, 1160 Appleseed Ln, St Louis MO 63132...................314-997-2369
Peridata Intl, 13700 Gramercy Pl, Gardena CA 90249.............................213-217-9155
Personal Micro Computers, 275 Santa Ana Ct, Sunnyvale CA 94086........408-737-8444
Pfanstiehl, 3300 Washington St, Waukegan IL 60085 312-623-1360
Philips Information Systems, 15301 Dallas Pkwy, Dallas TX 75248 214-980-2000
Phillips Process Co Inc, 192 Mill St, Rochester NY 14614......................716-232-1825
Pilot Corp, 60 Commerce Dr, Trumbull CT 06611 203-377-8800
Plexus Computers Inc, 3833 N 1st St, Santa Fe CA 95134........................408-943-9433
Primages Inc, 151 Trade Zone Dr, Ronkonkoma NY 11779.......................516-585-8200
Printek Inc, 1517 Townline Rd, Benton Harbor MI 49022 616-925-3200
Productive Computer Systems, 111 E Wacker Dr, Chicago IL 60601........312-546-3494
QDP Computer Systems, 10220 Brecksville Rd, Cleveland OH 44141 216-526-0838
QSR Service Corp, 1029 Teaneck Rd, Teaneck NJ 07666...........................201-837-3977
Raymond Packer Co, 51 Doty Cir, West Springfield MA 01089 413-733-4129
RCA Service Co, Rt 38, Cherry Hill NJ 08358 609-338-4375
Reliable Ribbons, 305 Coney Island Ave, Brooklyn NY 11218...................718-972-7744
Remtronic Typewriter Corp, 19405 Wlek Dr, Sun City AZ 85373.............602-974-4607
Rena Systems Inc, 290 Hansen Access Rd, King of Prussia PA 19406.......215-265-8420
Repeat-O-Type Mfg Corp, 665 State Hwy 23 S, Wayne NJ 07470.............201-696-3330
Responsive Computer Systems Inc, 1601 Capital Ave, Plano TX 75074 ...214-423-5944
Ribbon House, 354 26th St, Fair Lawn NJ 07410......................................201-791-6972
Ricoh Corp, 5 Dedrick Pl, W Caldwell NJ 07006......................................201-882-2000
Rittenhouse Paper Co, 250 S Northwest Hwy, Park Ridge IL 60068..........312-692-9130
Royal Consumer Business Products, 500 Day Hill, Windsor CT 06095 203-683-2222
Sanyo Business Systems Corp, 51 Joseph St, Noonachie NJ 07074...........201-440-9300
Search, 106 Sterling Ave, Mt Sterling KY 40353 606-498-0661
Sears, Sears Tower, Chicago IL 60684..312-875-1400
Seattle Platen Co, 1510 7th Ave, Seattle WA 98101.................................201-682-7780
Seicom Inc, 1305 W Belt Line Rd, Carrolton TX 75006............................214-446-9055
Selectone Corp, 28301 Industrial Blvd, Hayward CA 94545.......................415-887-1950
Sercomp Corp, 20721 Superior St, Chatsworth CA 91311 818-341-1680
Sharp Electronics Corp, 10 Sharp Plaza, Paramus NJ 07652 201-265-5600
Sheaffer Eaton, 75 S Church St, Pittsfield MA 01201 413-499-2210

Silver-Reed America Inc, 19600 S Vermont Ave, Torrance CA 90502.......213-516-7008
SK Merchandising Corp, Box 408, Scranton PA 18501................................717-347-2742
Smith Corona, 65 Locust Ave, New Canaan CT 06840 203-972-1471
Star Micronics, 200 Park Ave, New York NY 10166................................212-986-6770
The Storms Co, 1100 Lousons Rd, Union NJ 07083 201-851-9400
Stow Davis Furniture, 25 Summer Ave NW, Grand Rapids MI 49502......616-456-9681
Sumicom Inc, 17862 E 17th St, Tustin CA 92680 714-730-6061
Swintec Corp, 320 W Commercial Ave, Moonachie NJ 07074 201-935-0115
Syntrex Inc, 246 Industrial Way W, Eatontown NJ 07724..........................201-524-1500
Systems & Solutions, 700 Main St, E Greenwich RI 02818.......................401-884-7971
Tab Products Co, 1400 Page Mill Rd, Palo Alto CA 94304........................415-852-2400
The Talor-Merchant Corp, 212 W 35th St, New York NY 10001 212-757-7700
Tandy/Radio Shack, Two Tandy Ctr, Ft Worth TX 76102........................817-390-3919
Teal Industries Inc, 1741 Lomita Blvd, Lomita CA 90717........................213-539-7244
TEC America, 2160 W 190th St, Torrance CA 90504................................213-320-8900
Telecom Products Inc, 1058 N Allen Ave, Pasadena CA 91104 312-228-5444
Texas Instruments Inc, PO Box 2909, Austin TX 78769..........................512-250-7111
Texas Liftoff Correction Ribbon, 11220 Grader St, Dallas TX 75238........214-348-1500
Text Sure, 20 Plaza St, Brooklyn NY 11238...212-673-2419
Tiffany Business Products Corp, Box 420, Long Beach NY 11561 212-219-0119
Toshiba America Inc, 2441 Michelle Dr, Tustin CA 92680.......................714-730-5000
Towa Corp of Amer, 1313 S Pennsylvania Ave, Morrisville PA 19067........215-295-8103
Trebilco Intl, Box 02370, Cleveland OH 44102.....................................216-941-1200
TTX Group, 366 Paseo Sonrisa, Walnut CA 91789 714-595-6146
TYP-E-CO, 21-55 44th Rd, Long Island City NY 11101............................718-706-6666
Typerite Ribbon Mfr, 3804 48th St, Long Island City NY 11104 718-784-3535
Vision Electronics, 3419 East Commerce, San Antonio TX 78220...........512-224-5801
VITEK Inc, 930 G Boardwalk Ave, San Marcos CA 92069.......................619-744-8305
W G Computer Supply Group, Box 69, Naselle WA 98638........................206-465-2345
Wang Laboratories Inc, 1 Industrial Ave, Lowell MA 01851 617-459-5000
West Coast Platen Co, 643 S San Pedro St, Los Angeles CA 90014..........213-627-2431
Wholesale Data Products, 1019 Arch St, Philadelphia PA 19107................215-627-6040
Wilson Jones Co, 6150 Touhy Ave, Chicago IL 60648 312-774-7700
Wordex Corp, 14400 Catalina St, San Leandro CA 94577..........................415-351-8777
WordPerfect Corp, 288 W Center St, Orem UT 84057 801-227-4000
Wordplex Corp, 141 Triunfo Canyon Rd, Westlake Village CA 91361......818-889-4455
WordStar Hotline, 174 Maple Hill Rd, Huntington NY 11743 516-549-3748
The Writing Consultant, 65 W 96th St, New York NY 10025 212-864-6415
Xerox Corp, Xerox Sq 100 Clinton Rd, Rochester NY 14644....................716-423-5078
Zenith Data Systems, 1000 Milwaukee Ave, Glenview IL 60025................312-391-8860
Ziyad Inc, 100 Ford Rd, Denville NJ 07834...201-627-7600

INDEX